STREET ATLAS

Cardiff, Swansea and the Valleys

First published in 1995 as
Cardiff, Swansea and Glamorgan by

Philip's, a division of
Octopus Publishing Group Ltd
2–4 Heron Quays, London E14 4JP

First colour edition 2001
Second impression with revisions 2002

ISBN 0-540-07973-1
© Philip's 2002

Ordnance Survey®

This product includes mapping data licensed
from Ordnance Survey® with the permission of
the Controller of Her Majesty's Stationery Office.
© Crown copyright 2001. All rights reserved.
Licence number 100011710

Printed and bound in Spain
by Cayfosa-Quebecor

Contents

Inside front cover:
Administrative and Postcode boundaries

II Key to map symbols

IV Key to map pages

VI Route planning

1 Street maps at 3½ inches to 1 mile

218 Street maps at 1¾ inches to 1 mile

232 Town maps of Abergavenny, Carmarthen,
Chepstow and Caldicot

234 Index of towns and villages

235 Index of streets, hospitals, industrial estates, railway
stations, schools, shopping centres and universities

Digital Data

The exceptionally high-quality mapping found in this atlas is available as digital data in TIFF
format, which is easily convertible to other bit mapped (raster) image formats.

The index is also available in digital form as a standard database table. It contains all the details
found in the printed index together with the National Grid reference for the map square in which
each entry is named.

For further information and to discuss your requirements, please contact Philip's on
020 7531 8439 or george.philip@philips-maps.co.uk

(22a)	**Traffordd** gyda rhif y gyffordd
	Prif dramwyfeydd – ffordd ddeuol/un lôn
	Ffordd A – ffordd ddeuol/un lôn
	Ffordd B – ffordd ddeuol/un lôn
	Ffyrdd bychan – ffordd ddeuol/un lôn
	Ffyrdd bychan eraill – ffordd ddeuol/un lôn
	Ffordd yn cael ei hadeilau
	Mân cerddwyr
DY7	**Ffiniau codau-post**
	Ffiniau Sir ac awdurdod unedol
	Rheilffordd
	Tramffordd
	Rheilffordd ar raddfa fychan
	Trac gwledig, ffordd breifat, neu ffordd mewn ardal ddinesig
	Llidiart neu rhwystr i draffig (gall fod cyfyngiadau ddim yn ddilys ar gyfer bob amser neu i bob drafnidiaeth)
	Llwybr, llwybr march, cilffordd yn agored i bob trafnidiaeth, ffordd a ddefnyddir yn lwybr cyhoeddus
	Nid yw ymddangosiad unrhyw ffordd arall neu drac neu lwybr ar yr atlas hwn yn tystio fod hawl tramwy ar hyd-ddynt
219 84	**Dangosydd dalennau gyffiniol** (Mae lliw yr arwydd yn dangos graddfa y tudalen gyffiniol - gweler y graddfeudd isod)
25 49	**Dangosydd y tudalen cyffiniol yn dangos y tudalennau sy'n gyffiniol a phen a gwaelod y dudalen**
1	**Dangosir ardal y map tu mewn i'r band glâs mewn graddfa mawr ar y tudalen a ddangosir gan y bloc glâs â'r arwydd**

Allot Gdns	**Gerddi ar osod**	Meml	**Coffa**
Acad	**Academi**	Mon	**Cofgolofn**
Cemy	**Mynwent**	Mus	**Amgueddfa**
C Ctr	**Canolfan ddinesig**	Obsy	**Arsyllfa**
CH	**Tŷ Clwb**	Pal	**Palas brenhinol**
Coll	**Coleg**	PH	**Tŷ tafarn**
Crem	**Amlosgfa**	Recn Gd	**Maes chwaraeon**
Ent	**Menter**	Resr	**Cronfa ddŵr**
Ex H	**Neuadd Arddangos**	Ret Pk	**Parc adwerthu**
Ind Est	**Ystad ddiwydiannol**	Sch	**Ysgol**
Inst	**Institiwt**	Sh Ctr	**Canolfan Siopa**
Ct	**Llys cyfraith**	TH	**Neuadd y dref**
L Ctr	**Canolfan hamdden**	Trad Est	**Ystad Fasnachol**
LC	**Croesfan wastad**	Univ	**Prifysgol**
Liby	**Llyfrgell**	Wks	**Gwaith**
Mkt	**Marchnad**	YH	**Hostel ieuenctid**

Walsall	**Gorsaf rheilffordd**
	Gorsaf rheilffordd breifat
	Gorsaf fysiau
	Gorsaf ambiwlans
	Gorsaf gwylwyr y glannau
	Gorsaf Dân
	Swyddfa'r heddlu
	Mynedfa damwain ac argyfwng i'r ysbyty
H	**Ysbyty**
	Lle o addoliad
i	**Canolfan gwybodaeth** (a'r agor drwy'r flwyddyn)
P	**Parcio**
P&R	**Parcio a chludo**
PO	**Swyddfa'r post**
	Safle gwersylla
	Safle carafan
	Cwrs golff
	Safle picnic
Prim Sch	**Adeiladau pwysig, ysgolion, colegau, prifysgolion ac ysbytai**
River Medway	**Enw dŵr**
	Nant
	Afon neu gamlas – bach a mawr
	Dŵr
	Dŵr llanw
	Coed
	Tai
House	**Hynafiaeth anrhufeinig**
VILLA	**Hynafiaeth rhufeinig**

■ Y mae'r rhifau bach o gwmpas ochrau'r mapiau yn dynodi llinelli grid cenedlaethol 1 cilomedr

■ Mae'r ffin llwyd tywyll ar ochr fewn rhai tudalennau yn dynodi nad yw'r mapio yn canlyn ymlaen i'r tudalen gyffiniol

Graddfa y mapiau yw 5.52 cm i 1km, 3½ modfedd i'r filltir 1: 18103

0	¼	½	¾	1 milltir
0	250m 500m 750m	1 km		

Graddfa y mapiau ar y tudalennau wedi ei rhifo mewn gwyrdd yw 2.76 cm i 1km, 1¾ modfedd i'r filltir 1:36206

0	¼	½	¾	1 milltir
0	250m 500m 750m 1 km			

Motorway with junction number	
Primary route – dual/single carriageway	
A road – dual/single carriageway	
B road – dual/single carriageway	
Minor road – dual/single carriageway	
Other minor road – dual/single carriageway	
Road under construction	
Pedestrianised area	
DY7 Postcode boundaries	
County and unitary authority boundaries	
Railway	
Tramway	
Miniature railway	
Rural track, private road or narrow road in urban area	
Gate or obstruction to traffic (restrictions may not apply at all times or to all vehicles)	
Path, bridleway, byway open to all traffic, road used as a public path	
The representation in this atlas of a road, track or is no evidence of the existence of a of a right of way	
219 84 Adjoining page indicators (The colour of the arrow indicates the scale of the adjoining page - see scales below)	
25 49 Adjoining page indicator showing the pages adjoining the top and bottom halves of the current page	
1 The map area within the blue band is shown at a larger scale on the page indicated by the blue block and arrow	

Allot Gdns	**Allotments**	Meml	**Memorial**
Acad	**Academy**	Mon	**Monument**
Cemy	**Cemetery**	Mus	**Museum**
C Ctr	**Civic Centre**	Obsy	**Observatory**
CH	**Club House**	Pal	**Royal Palace**
Coll	**College**	PH	**Public House**
Crem	**Crematorium**	Recn Gd	**Recreation Ground**
Ent	**Enterprise**	Resr	**Reservoir**
Ex H	**Exhibition Hall**	Ret Pk	**Retail Park**
Ind Est	**Industrial Estate**	Sch	**School**
Inst	**Institute**	Sh Ctr	**Shopping Centre**
Ct	**Law Court**	TH	**Town Hall/House**
L Ctr	**Leisure Centre**	Trad Est	**Trading Estate**
LC	**Level Crossing**	Univ	**University**
Liby	**Library**	Wks	**Works**
Mkt	**Market**	YH	**Youth Hostel**

Walsall	Railway station
	Private railway station
	Bus, coach station
	Ambulance station
	Coastguard station
	Fire station
	Police station
	Accident and Emergency entrance to hospital
H	Hospital
	Place of worship
i	Information Centre (open all year)
P	Parking
P&R	Park and Ride
PO	Post Office
	Camping site
	Caravan site
	Golf course
	Picnic site
Prim Sch	Important buildings, schools, colleges, universities and hospitals
River Medway	Water name
	Stream
	River or canal – minor and major
	Water
	Tidal water
	Woods
	Houses
House	Non-Roman antiquity
VILLA	Roman antiquity

■ The small numbers around the edges of the maps identify the 1 kilometre National Grid lines

■ The dark grey border on the inside edge of some pages indicates that the mapping does not continue onto the adjacent page

The scale of the maps is 5.52 cm to 1 km 3½ inches to 1 mile 1: 18103

0		¼		½		¾		1 mile

0	250m	500m	750m	1 kilometre

The scale of the maps on pages numbered in green is 2.76 cm to 1 km 1¾ inches to 1 mile 1: 36206

0	¼	½	¾	1 mile

0	250m	500m	750m	1 kilometre

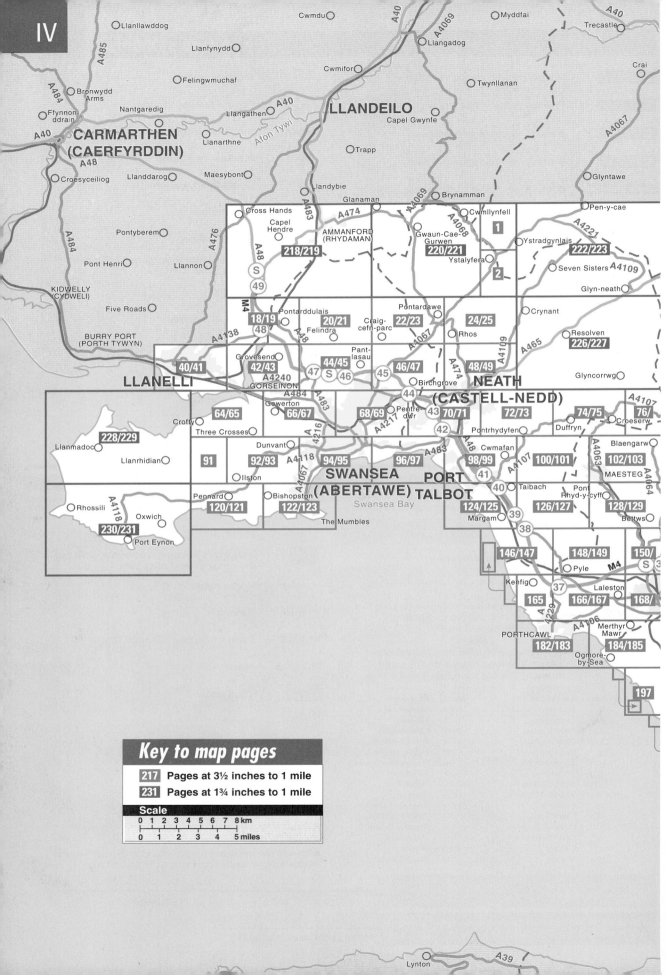

IV

Cwmdu
Myddfai
Trecastle
A40
A4069
Llanllawddog
A485
Llanfynydd
Cwmifor
Llangadog
Crai
Felingwmuchaf
Bronwydd Arms
Twynllanan
A484
Nantgaredig
Llangathen
A40
Ffynnon-ddrain
CARMARTHEN
(CAERFYRDDIN)
Llanarthne
Afon Tywi
LLANDEILO
Capel Gwynfe
Glyntawe
A4067
A48
Trapp
Croesyceiliog
Llanddarog
Maesybont
Llandybie
Pen-y-cae
Pontyberem
A476
Cross Hands
Capel Hendre
Glanaman
A4069
Brynamman
A4068
Cwmllynfell
A4221

1

Pont Henri
Llannon
A483
A474
AMMANFORD
(RHYDAMAN)
Gwaun-Cae-Gurwen
Ystradgynlais
A4221
Ystalyfera
Seven Sisters
A4109
KIDWELLY
(CYDWELI)
A48
218/219
220/221

2
Glyn-neath

Five Roads
M4
Pontarddulais
Pontardawe
Crynant
BURRY PORT
(PORTH TYWYN)
A4138
18/19
A48
20/21
Felindra
Craig-cefn-parc
22/23
A4067
Rhos
24/25
Resolven
226/227
Grovesend
Pant-lasau
A465
A4109
Glyncorrwg
40/41
42/43
44/45
46/47
48/49
A4240
47
S
46
45
Birchgrove
NEATH
A4107
LLANELLI
GORSEINON
A484
A483
44
(CASTELL-NEDD)
A4107
Gowerton
A216
Pentre-dwr
43
70/71
72/73
74/75
76
228/229
64/65
66/67
A4217
68/69
42
Pontrhydyfen
Croeserw
Crofty
Three Crosses
Cwmafan
Duffryn
Blaengarw
A4063
91
92/93
A4118
94/95
96/97
A483
98/99
100/101
102/103
Llanmadoc
Dunvant
A4067
A48
41
A4107
MAESTEG
A4064
Llanrhidian
Ilston
SWANSEA
PORT
40
Taibach
Rhossili
A4118
Pennard
Bishopston
(ABERTAWE)
TALBOT
124/125
Pont Rhyd-y-cyff
128/129
Oxwich
120/121
122/123
Swansea Bay
Margam
39
126/127
Bettws
230/231
Port Eynon
The Mumbles
38
146/147
148/149
150/
S
Kenfig
M4
A229
37
Laleston
165
166/167
168/
PORTHCAWL
A4106
Merthyr Mawr
182/183
184/185
Ogmore-by-Sea
A39
197
Lynton

Key to map pages

217 Pages at 3½ inches to 1 mile
231 Pages at 1¾ inches to 1 mile

Scale
0 1 2 3 4 5 6 7 8 km
0 1 2 3 4 5 miles

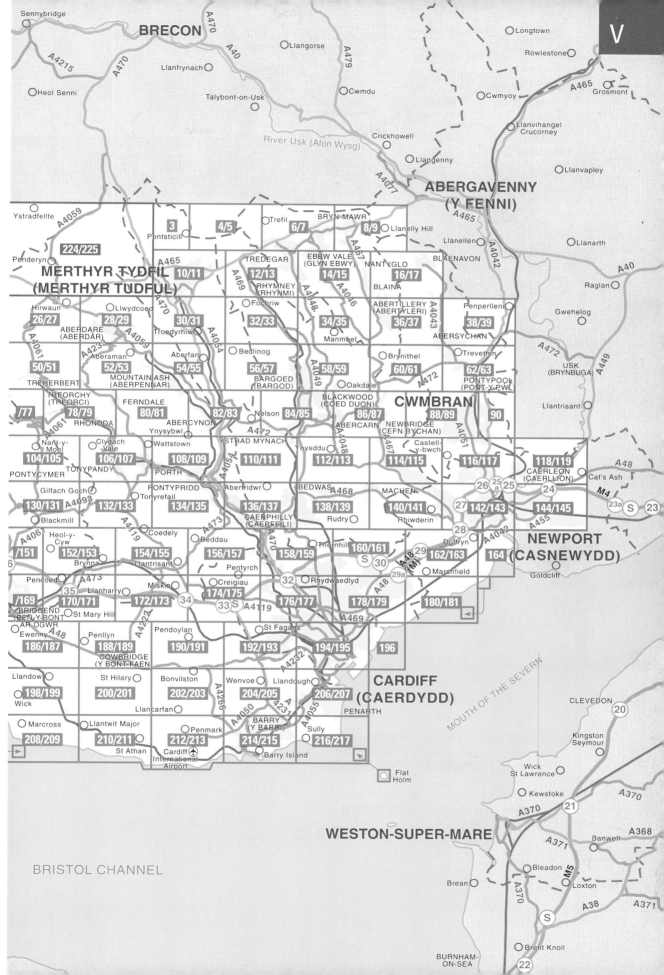

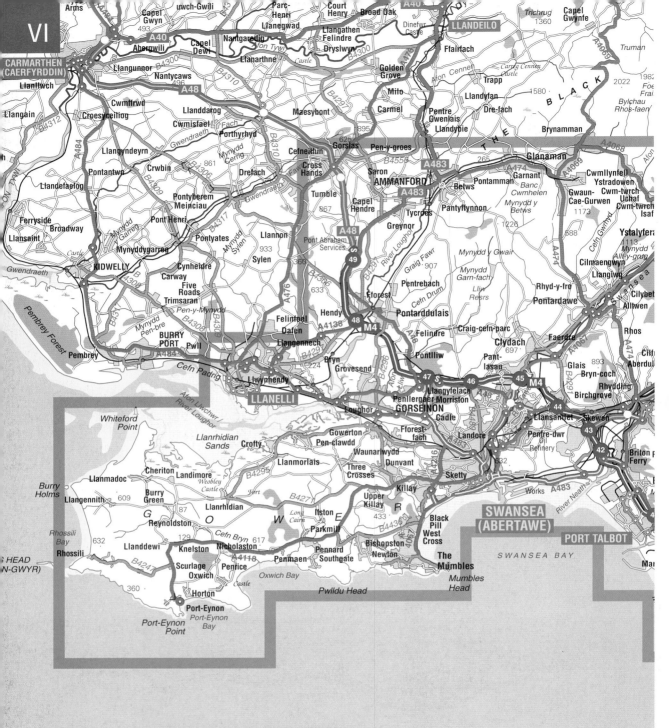

Route planning

Scale

| 0 | 1 | 2 | 3 | 4 | 5 | 6 | 7 | 8 km |

| 0 | 1 | 2 | 3 | 4 | 5 miles |

BRISTOL CHANNEL

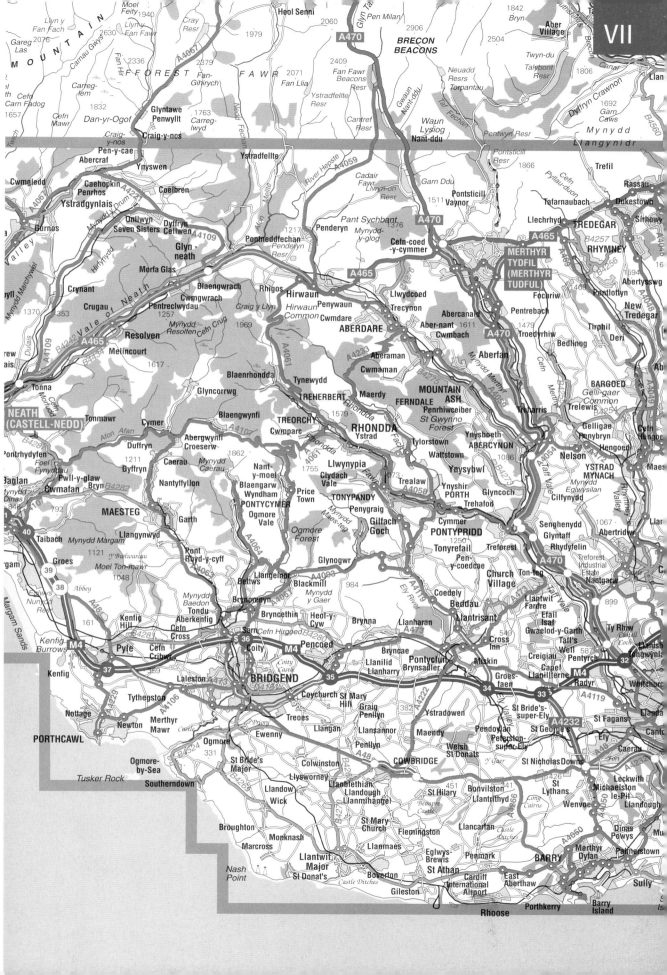

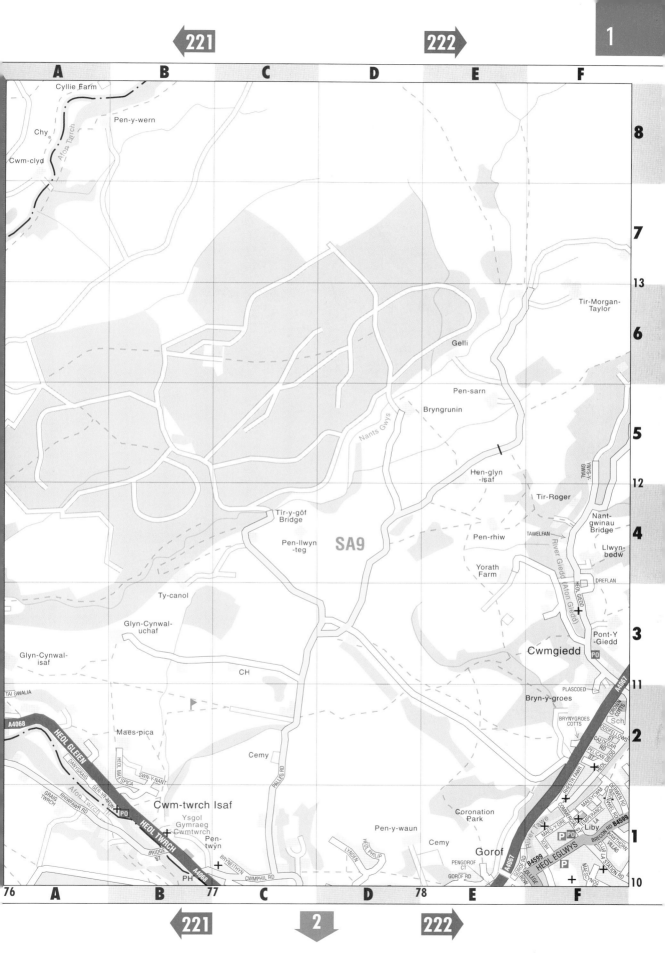

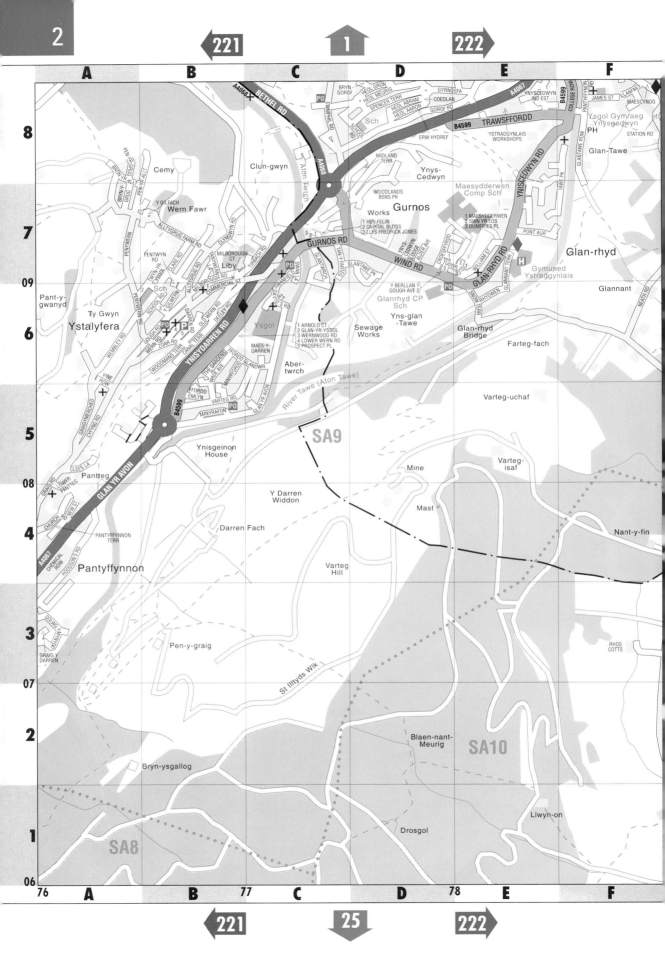

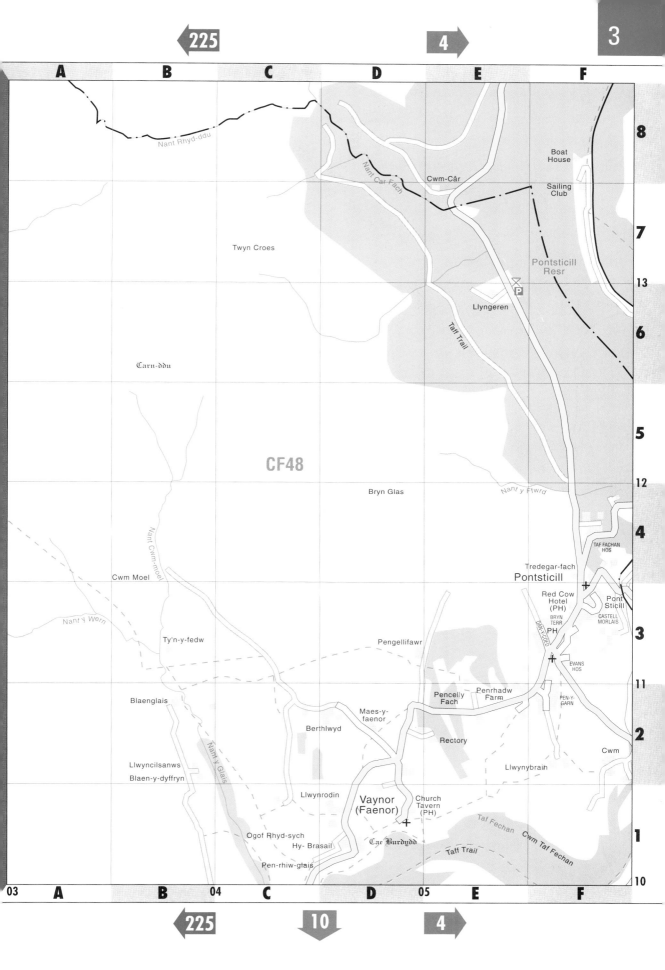

NP8

NP22

Trefil Ddu

Pine Tree
House

Quarrymen's Arms
(PH)

Sports
Field

Twyn Ceilog

Odyn-fach

Nant y Llechau

Sirhowy River (Afon Sirhywi)

Carn yr Helyg

Rhyd y Milwyr

Pyllau-
duon

Rhymney River (Afon Rhymni)

Nant Pitwellt

Traed y Milwyr

Pitwellt

Blaen-Rhymney

Waun-lâs

Blaen Rhymney
(Blaen Rhymni)

TAFARNAUBACH
IND EST

BREDON TERR

Pencoedcae
Farm

Old Prince
Farm

MERTHYR RD

HEADS OF THE VALLEYS RD

A465

Nant Trefil

09 A   B   10   C   D   11   E   F   10

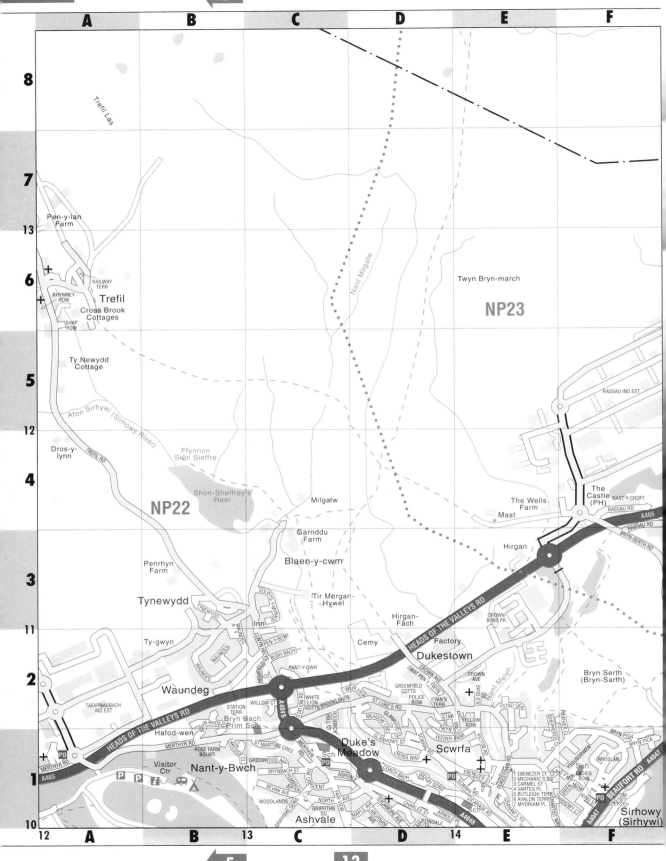

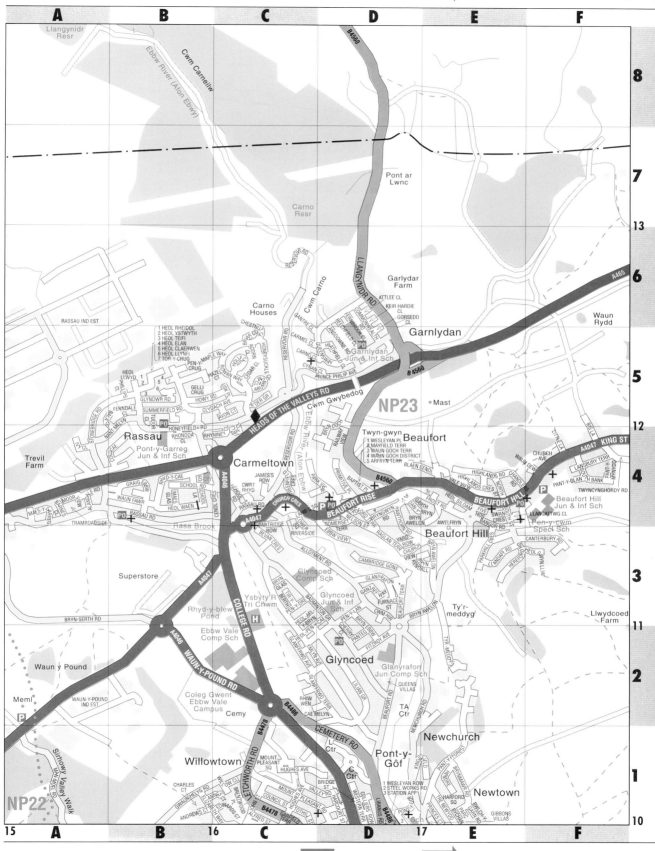

A B C D E F

8

Pant Mawr

Gwaun y Ffa

Resr

7

13

Clydach Terrace

Coedcae-mawr

Hafod

6

A465

River Clydach

Cwm Nantmelyn

Cwm yr Hafod

Clydach Dingle

Pont Gam

Brynmawr Comp Sch

Sports Gd

Rhydw

Sewage Works

A465

5

ANEURIN PL

BRONHAFOD

St Mary's Jun & Inf Sch

HEDDFAN

Cwm Nant-gam

Cemy

BRYNAWEL

INTERMEDIATE RD

RHYD CLYDACH

KING EDWARD

Mynydd Rheinallt

NP7

HEOL DERW

GURNOS EST

HILL

CHURCH LA

THORNHILL CL

12

HEOL ONEN

HARCE

PLEASANT VIEW

DUMFRIES PL

QUEEN ST

ALMA TERR

DAREN FELEN

1 KING ST
2 PONTYGOF

HEOL HELIG

HEOL ISAF

HILL CREST

SCHS

WELL ST

WORCESTER ST

POUND RD

CLOS GOLWG

A461

A4047

HEADS OF THE VALLEYS RD

4

CROFT CT

TWYNCYNGHORDY RD

BATH LA

BROOK ST

GEORGE ST

BAILEY ST

Liby

FACTORY ST

GREENLAND RD

OLD BLAC

HAFOD

KING ST

B4248

WINDSOR RD

TWYNCYNGHORDY PL

PARK CRES

MARKET SQ

CATHOLIC RD

SERVICE ST

CLOS LLWYN Y PWLL

NOBEL SQUARE IND EST

BRYNMAWR

WESTERN AVE

LANSBURY RD

PARK VIEW

Sch

Twyn-blaen-nant

HENDERSON RD

COBURNE RD

WARWICK RD

BLAEN-AFON RD

B4248

Twyn Cynhordy

Factories

BLAINA RD

Blaenycwm Jun & Inf Sch

Cwm Crachen

Twyn-Blaen-nant

3

NP23

POND RD

BAILEY FIELD RD

BLAENANT IND EST

WAUNHEULOG

11

L Ctr

SCHOOL VIEW

Nantyglo Comp Sch

LIMESTONE RD

CHAPEL RD

BLAEN NANT RD

2

BRYNAWELON

WAEN-FAWR

GOLF VIEW

PORTERS RD

BANNA BGLWS

1 WESLEY BLDGS
2 CWM CRACHEN
3 TY-HAULWEN

NP7

Winchestown

WAUN-EBBW BGLWS

WAUN-EBBW RD

GLEN VIEW BGLWS

MARKET RD

NEW RD

TWYNDERWYN FLATS

NANTYGLO

Mulfran

Twyn Garncanddo

Pen-y-waun

CH

FAIR VIEW TERR

BRYN VIEW

BEACON RD

VINCENT AVE

Blaen Cwm-celyn

1

ROUNDHOUSE RD

PRINCE ST

MILFRAEN AVE

GWENT TERR

Garn Fach

NP13

Nant-y-glo Round Towers

WOODLAND TERR

FARM RD

KING ST

GARN RD

Garnfach Inf Sch

FFOSMAEN

Blaen-yr-Ystruth

10

18 A B 19 C D 20 E F

B4
1 CEMETREY RD
2 COSY PL
3 FFYNNON CT
4 HATTER ST
5 MOUNTAIN VIEW
6 QUEEN SQ
7 TUDOR CRES

C4
1 SOMERSET ST
2 FIREMANS CT
3 TRAFALGAR CL
4 LOWER BAILEY ST
5 DAVIES ST
6 WESLEY HO
7 OLD BLAEN-AFON RD
8 ALEXANDRIA TERR
9 CURZON ST

10 GLADSTONE ST
11 STATION ST

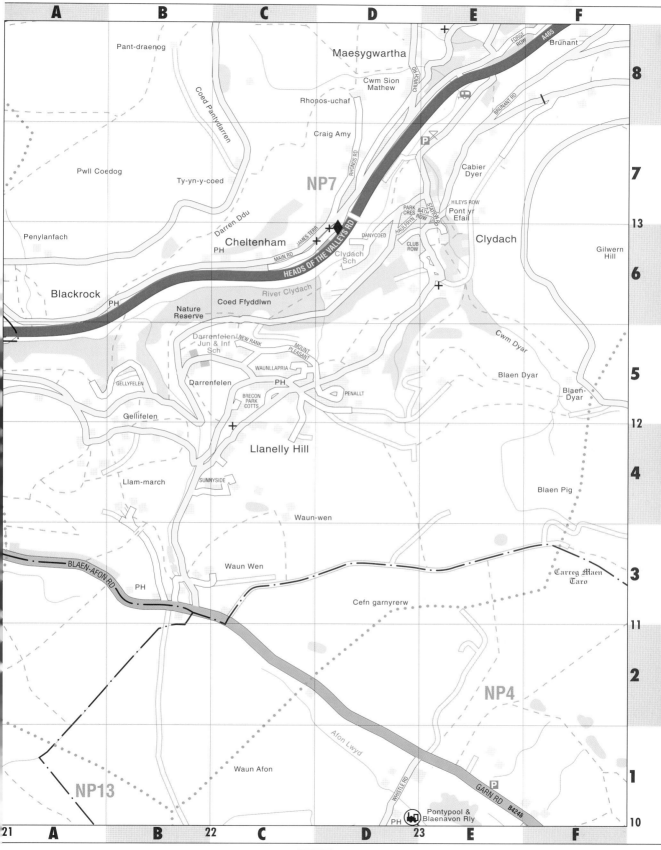

Pant-draenog

Coed Pantydarren

Maesygwartha

Cwm Sion Mathew

Rhonos-uchaf

Craig Amy

Brunant

FORGE ROW

A465

BRUNANT RD

CHURCH RD

RHONOS RD

NP7

Cabier Dyer

Pwll Coedog

Ty-yn-y-coed

Darren Ddu

HILEYS ROW

Pont yr Efail

Clydach

STATION RD

BATH ROW

PARK CRES

HAULFRYN

Penylanfach

Cheltenham

JAMES TERR

MAIN RD

DANYCOED

Clydach Sch

DANYCOED

CLUB ROW

Gilwern Hill

HEADS OF THE VALLEYS RD

PH

Blackrock

PH

River Clydach

Coed Ffyddlwn

Cwm Dyar

Nature Reserve

Darrenfelen Jun & Inf Sch

NEW BANK

MOUNT PLEASANT

WAUNLLAPRIA

Blaen Dyar

Blaen-Dyar

GELLYFELEN

Darrenfelen

PH

PENALLT

BRECON PARK COTTS

Gellifelen

Llanelly Hill

Blaen Pig

Llam-march

SUNNYSIDE

Waun-wen

BLAEN-AFON RD

Waun Wen

Carreg Maen Taro

PH

Cefn garnyrerw

Afon Lwyd

NP4

NP13

Waun Afon

WHISTLE RD

GARN RD

B4248

PH

Pontypool & Blaenavon Rly

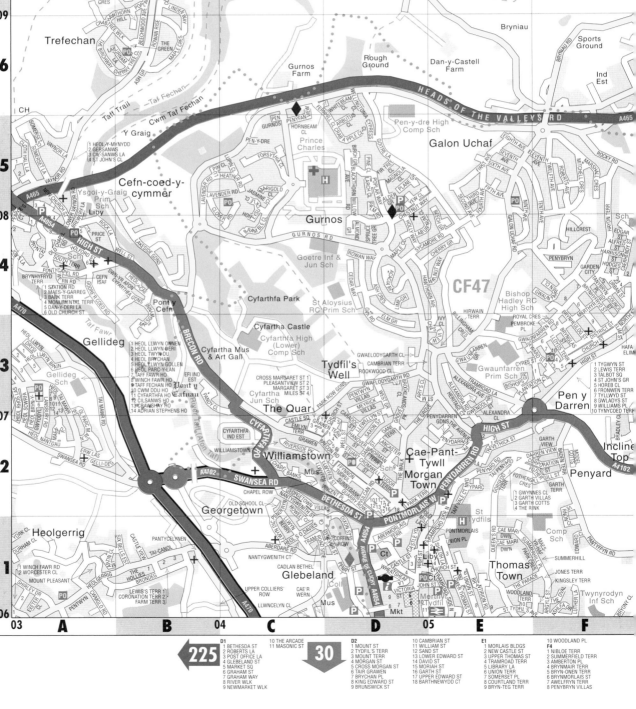

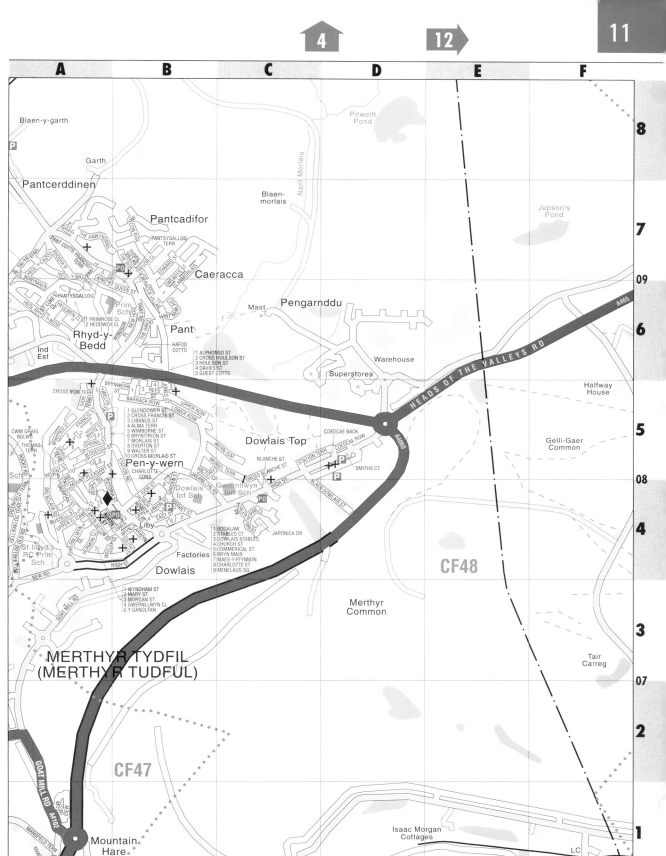

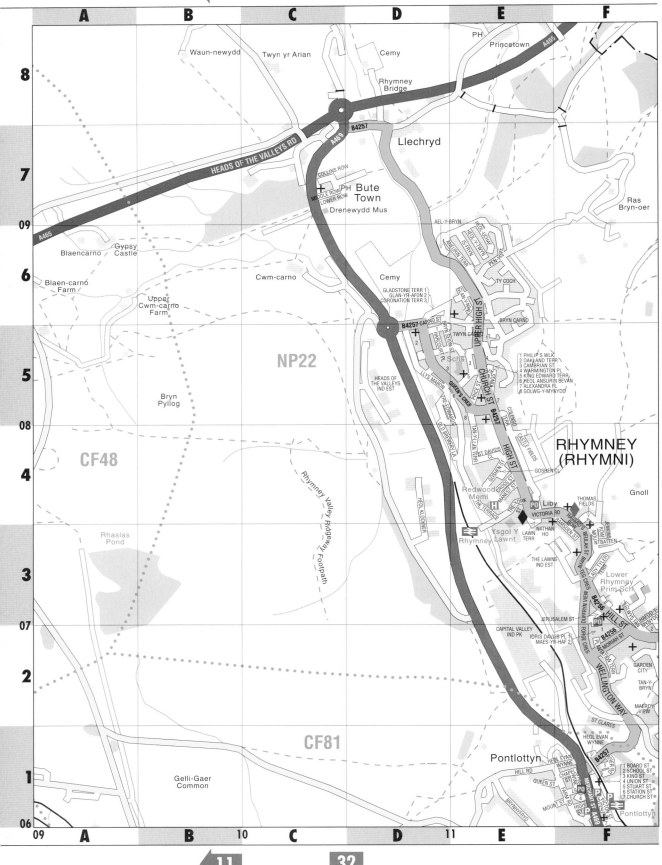

A B C D E F

Waun-newydd

Twyn yr Arian

Cemy

PH

Princetown

A465

Rhymney Bridge

A463

B4257

Llechryd

HEADS OF THE VALLEYS RD

A465

COLLINS ROW

MIDDLE ROW
LOWER ROW

PH

Bute Town

Drenewydd Mus

Blaencarno

Gypsy Castle

Blaen-carno Farm

Upper Cwm-carno Farm

Cwm-carno

Cemy

AEL-Y-BRYN

HEOL IORIE

HEOL-Y-TWYN

PEN-Y-RE

ANEURIN TERR

BRYN CARNO

TY COCH

GLADSTONE TERR 1
GLAN-YR-AFON 2
CORONATION TERR 3

B4257 CARNO ST

UPPER HIGH ST

NP22

Bryn Pyllog

HEADS OF THE VALLEYS IND EST

TWYN CAE

BRYN SEION ST

HARCOURT ST

PL SCHS

BLAEN-Y-CWM

QUEENS CRES

PRICE ST

CHURCH ST

1 PHILIP'S WLK
2 OAKLAND TERR
3 CAMBRIAN ST
4 WARMINGTON PL
5 KING EDWARD TERR
6 HEOL ANSURIN BEVAN
7 ALEXANDRA PL
8 GOLWG-Y-MYNYDD

Rhymney Valley Ridgeway Footpath

LLYS MABON

TY-R-EDWARDS

OLD BRENHEN LA

TAN-Y-LLAN TERR

ST DAVIDS CL

COLENSO TERR

CASTLE FIELDS

HIGH ST

RHYMNEY (RHYMNI)

CF48

HEOL KLOCHMER

GOSHEN ST

CROSS ST

MANEST ST

THE TERRACE

TRE YORK

GOSHEN CL

Redwood Meml

Liby

PO

VICTORIA RD

HAVARD ST

RAMSDEL ST

THOMAS FIELDS

Gnoll

Rhaslas Pond

Rhymney Lawnt

Ysgol Y Lawnt

NATHAN HO

LAWN TERR

JENKINS ROW

BEULAH ST

BRYN TEG CRES

MAESYFFYNC FORGE CRES

MOUNTBATTEN

THE LAWNS IND EST

LADY TYLER TERR

B4256

HILL ST

Lower Rhymney Prim Sch

JERUSALEM ST

PO

B4256

HAFODYRYNYS

JENKINS

GARDEN CITY

TAN-Y-BRYN

CAPITAL VALLEY IND PK

IDRIS DAVIES PL 1
MAES-YR-HAF 2

MORIAH ST

PL ANN TERR

WELLINGTON WAY

MAERDY VIEW

ST CLARES

CF81

HEOL EVAN WYNNE

B4257

Gelli-Gaer Common

Pontlottyn

HILL RD

QUEEN ST

HEOL EVAN WYNNE

CHAPEL ST

PO

MERCHANT ST

MOUNT ST

BRYNHYFRYD

HIGH ST

1 BOARD ST
2 SCHOOL ST
3 KING ST
4 UNION ST
5 STUART ST
6 STATION ST
7 CHURCH ST

A469

Pontlottyn

09 A B 10 C D 11 E F

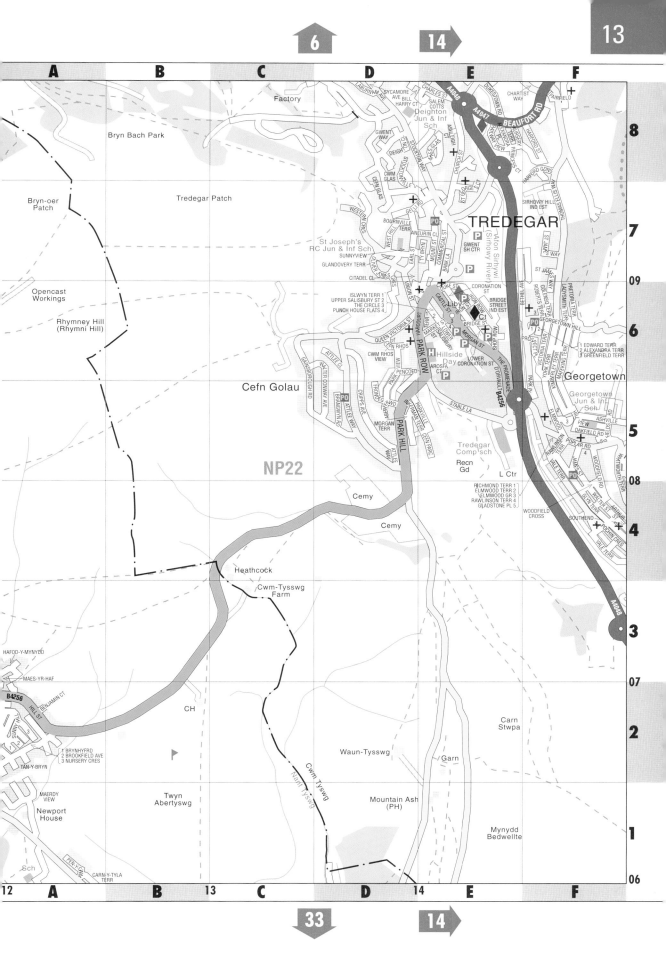

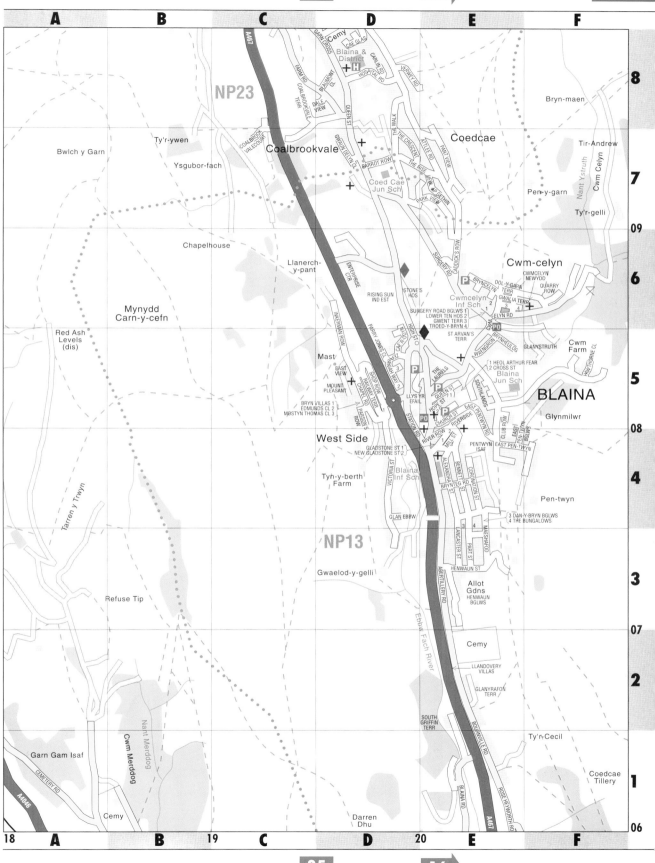

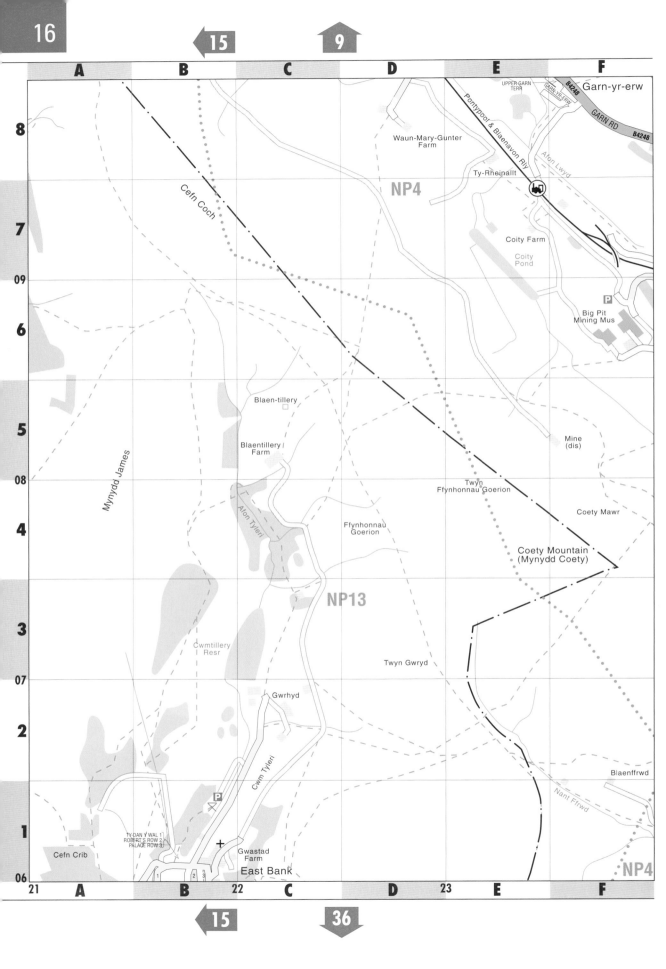

15
9

Garn-yr-erw

UPPER GARN TERR

GARN-YR-ERW

B4248

GARN RD

B4248

Waun-Mary-Gunter Farm

Pontypool & Blaenavon Rly

Aton Lwyd

Ty-Rheinallt

NP4

Cefn Coch

Coity Farm

Coity Pond

P

Big Pit Mining Mus

Blaen-tillery

Mine (dis)

Blaentillery Farm

Mynydd James

Afon Tyleri

Twyn Ffynhonnau Goerion

Coety Mawr

Ffynhonnau Goerion

Coety Mountain (Mynydd Coety)

NP13

Cwmtillery Resr

Twyn Gwryd

Gwrhyd

Cwm Tyleri

Blaenffrwd

Nant Ffrwd

P

TY-DAN Y WAL 1
ROBERT S ROW 2
PALACE ROW 3

Cefn Crib

Gwastad Farm

East Bank

NP4

15
36

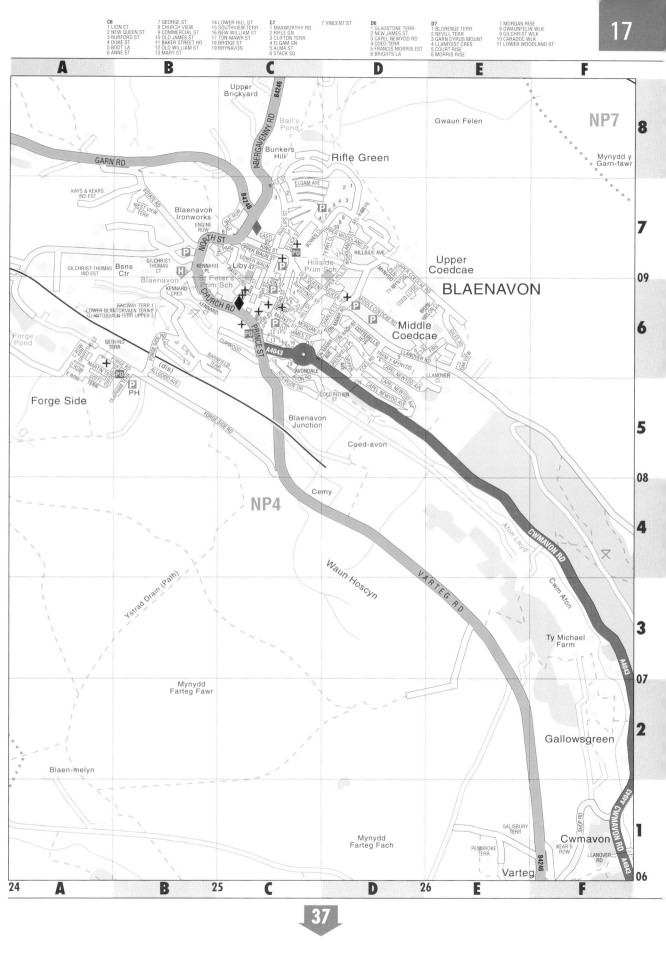

C6
1 LION CT
2 NEW QUEEN ST
3 BURFORD ST
4 DUKE ST
5 BOOT LA
6 ANNE ST

7 GEORGE ST
8 CHURCH VIEW
9 COMMERCIAL ST
10 OLD JAMES ST
11 BAKER STREET HO
12 OLD WILLIAM ST
13 MARY ST

14 LOWER HILL ST
15 SOUTHVIEW TERR
16 NEW WILLIAM ST
17 TON-MAWR ST
18 BRIDGE ST
19 BRYNAVON

C7
1 MAXWORTHY RD
2 RIFLE GN
3 CLIFTON TERR
4 ELGAM GN
5 ALMA ST
6 STACK SQ

7 VINCENT ST

D6
1 GLADSTONE TERR
2 NEW JAMES ST
3 CAPEL NEWYDD RD
4 COED TERR
5 FRANCIS MORRIS EST
6 BRIGHTS LA

D7
1 BLORENGE TERR
2 NEVILL TERR
3 GARN DYRUS MOUNT
4 LLANFOIST CRES
5 COURT RISE
6 MORRIS RISE

7 MORGAN RISE
8 GWAUNFELIN WLK
9 GILCHRIST WLK
10 CARADOC WLK
11 LOWER WOODLAND ST

Upper
Brickyard

Gwaun Felen

NP7

Mynydd y
Garn-fawr

GARN RD

Bunkers
Hill

Rifle Green

Ball's
Pond

KAYS & KEARS
IND EST

Blaenavon
Ironworks

Blaenavon

ESTATE RD

WEST VIEW
TERR

ENGINE
ROW

Upper
Coedcae

BLAENAVON

GILCHRIST-THOMAS
IND EST

Bsns
Ctr

GILCHRIST
THOMAS
CT

KENNARD
PL

St Peter's
Prim Sch

Liby St

Hillside
Prim Sch

Hillside Ave

Middle
Coedcae

KENNARD
CRES

RAILWAY TERR 1
LOWER GLANTORVAEN TERR 2
GLANTORVAEN TERR UPPER 3

Forge
Pond

GETHING
TERR

MARTIN TERR

FORGE RD

Barnfield
Terr

CURWOOD

Avondale

AVON RD

Blaenavon
Junction

Coed-avon

Forge Side

FORGE SIDE RD

Cemy

NP4

Waun Hoscyn

VARTEG RD

Afon Lwyd

CWMAVON RD

Cwm Afon

Ty Michael
Farm

Ystrad Drain (Path)

Mynydd
Farteg Fawr

Gallowsgreen

Blaen-melyn

Mynydd
Farteg Fach

SALISBURY
TERR

SHOP RD

Cwmavon

KEAR'S
ROW

PEMBROKE
TERR

LLANOVER
RD

Varteg

B4246

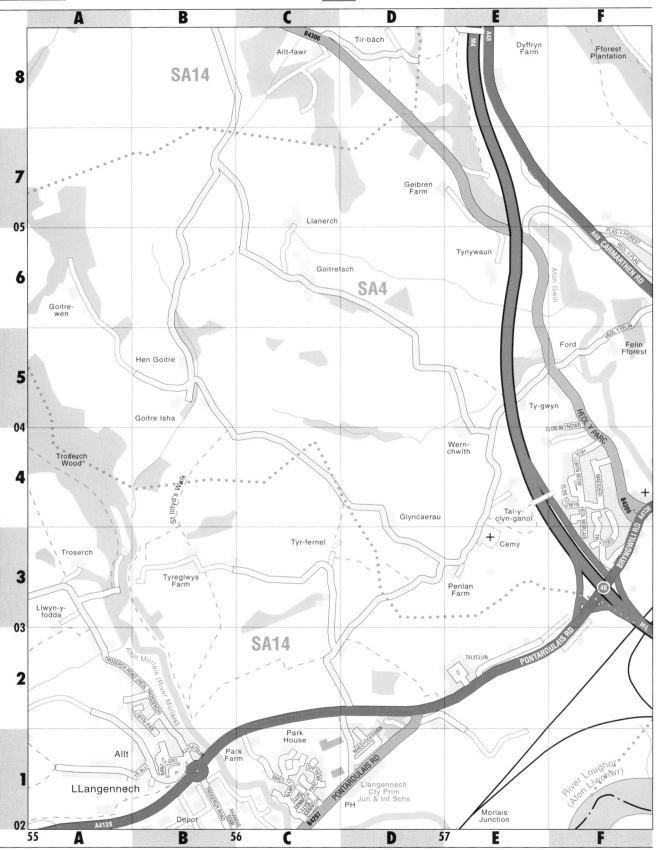

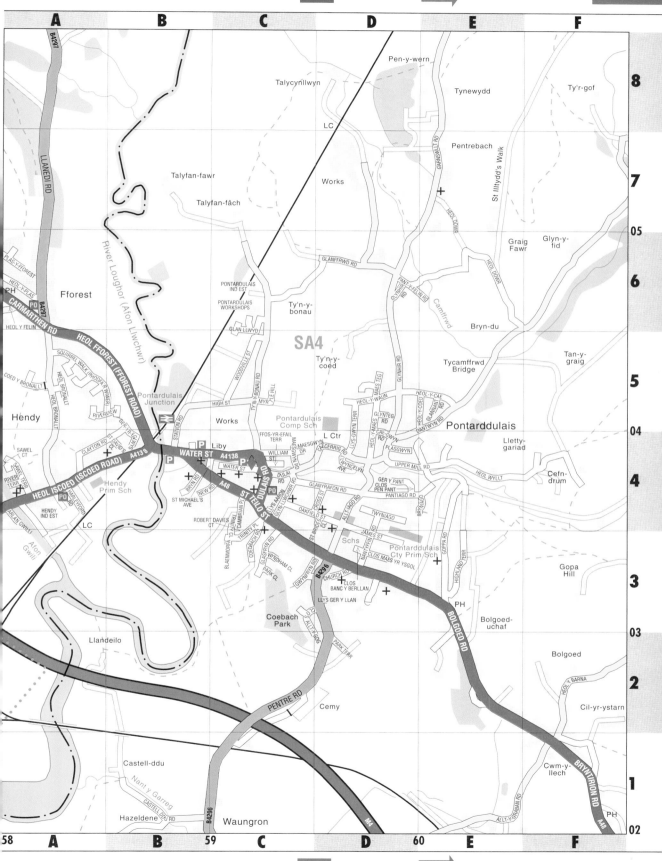

19
219

A **B** **C** **D** **E** **F**

8

Twŷn tyle

Twyn
Tyle

Llandremor
ganol

Gelli-gwm-
isaf

Blaen-nant-
ddu

Llandremor-
fawr

7

Gelli-gwm-
uchaf

Cwm-
Dulais

Camffrwd

05

Tir-
bâch

Cwm Dulais

Penlle'r
Bebyll

6

Twr
Maggie

Mynydd
Pysgodlyn

Cefn
Drum

Hafod
las

Palé-mawr

Ffynnon-
Sant

Palé-bâch

Craig y Bedw

5

SA4

Hen-
glawd

Dulais

04

Nature
Reserve

4

Ysgïach-
uchaf

Ysgïach

SA5

Llwyngwenno

Cwm
Dulais

Cwrt-
mawr

HEOL GLYN-DYFAL

Cwm Ysgïach

3

Bryn-bach-
Common

Ffynnon-
fedw

Careg-
lwyd

HEOL Y BARNA

03

Bryn-
Bâch

Twŷn

BWLCH Y GWYN

Ysgol Gynradd Gymraeg
Felindre

2

Pant-y-ffin

Sewage
Works

PH

BRYN BÂCH RD

Tyn-y-cwm

Felindre

Brynawel

Tynrheol

Gelli-wern
Ganol

Cîl faen

1

Ty-llwyd

Crwca

Gelli-wern-
isaf

Gelli-wern-
fawr

02

61 **A** **B** 62 **C** **D** 63 **E** **F**

19
44

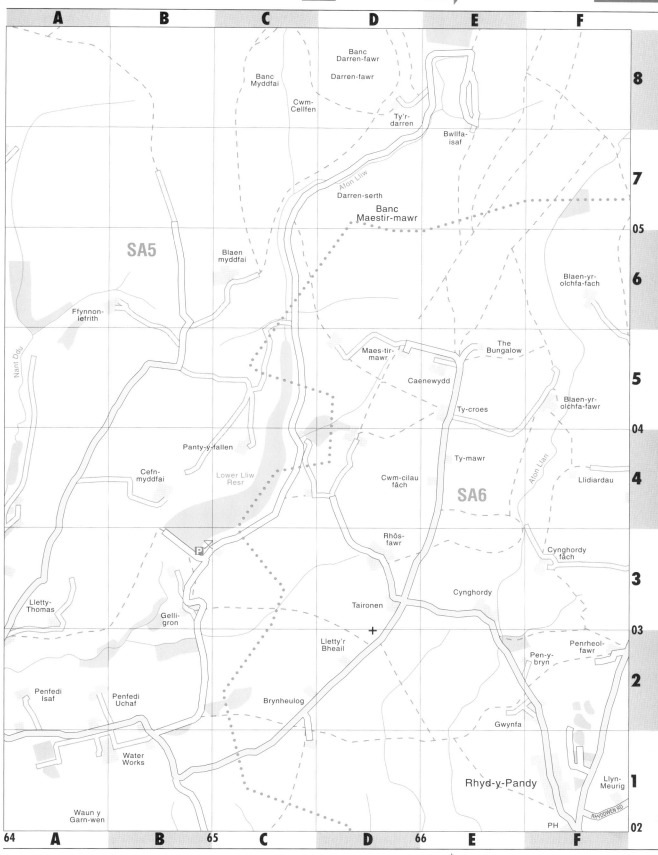

219

22

8

Banc
Darren-fawr
Banc
Myddfai   Darren-fawr

Cwm-
Cellfen

Ty'r-
darren

Bwllfa-
isaf

7

Afon Lliw

Darren-serth

Banc
Maestir-mawr

05

SA5

Blaen
myddfai

Blaen-yr-
olchfa-fach

6

Ffynnon-
lefrith

Maes-tir-
mawr

The
Bungalow

5

Caenewydd

Ty-croes

Blaen-yr-
olchfa-fawr

Panty-y-fallen

04

Nant Ddu

Cefn-
myddfai

Lower Lliw
Resr

Cwm-cilau
fâch

Ty-mawr

SA6

Afon Llan

Llidiardau

4

Rhôs-
fawr

Cynghordy
fâch

Lletty-
Thomas

Gelli-
gron

Taironen

Cynghordy

3

Lletty'r
Bheail

03

Penrheol-
fawr

Pen-y-
bryn

2

Penfedi
Isaf

Penfedi
Uchaf

Brynheulog

Gwynfa

Water
Works

Rhyd-y-Pandy

Llyn-
Meurig

1

Waun y
Garn-wen

PH

RHYDDWEN RD

02

45

22

21
220

	A	B	C	D	E	F

SA8

Cwm-bryn

8

Glyneithrym-uchaf

Pen y banc
Cottage

SA5

7

Tan-y-
Graig

Tor Clawdd

Ty-Uchaf-
Cwm

05

Llechart-
fâch

Llechart-
fawr

6

Tyn-y-
berllan

Pont
Llechart

Nant Llwydyn

Lluast
Treharne

Glyn-
côch

Gwern-
llwyn

5

Ty-
llwydyn

Lluast
Lewis

Cwm Clydach

Maes-y-
mynydd

Lower Clydach River

04

SA8

Allt-y-
fanog

4

Rhyd-y-
gwin

Cathelyd-
uchaf

Craig yr-
Allt

Spite

Craig-cefn-parc
CtyiPrim Sch

SA6

Cathelyd-
ganol

3

Bwlchy
Gwynt

Cefn-
parc

Nant y Capel

03

Penrheol-
fach

Cathelyd-
isaf

Cefn-eithrim-
isaf

PH

2

Craig-cefn-
parc

HEOL RHYD

CLYDACH RD

FAGWR RD

CADWGAN RD

FAGWR ISAF

LON HEOLYCH

PH

PO

Gelli-onnen-
isaf

Fagwyr

FFORDD CLYN

CLOS
CHENDRA

Coniston

Penydre

Llwyn-y-
domen

RHYDOWEN PL

RHYDOWEN RD

GOLWG Y MYNYDD

MOUNTAIN RD

Nant y Milwr

Graig Felin

LONE RD

MINYRAFON RD

TANYRALLT

TAN-Y-LON

EDISON CRES

DYSON RD

NEWTON RD

SHORT ST

GROVE RD

KELVIN RD

FARADAY RD

RAMSAY RD

BRUNNER DR

CARLTON RD

LANGER WAY

LLWYNON

GELLIONEN RD

BRYNAMLWG

PENYDRE RD

TANYCOED RD

HEOL-Y-FAGWR

1

Pant-y-
baban

TY FLORENCE ASHER

Craig
Ty-gwyn

02

Nant-y-
milwr

Pant-yr-
eithin

WALINGRON

67	A		B	68	C		D	69	E		F

21
46

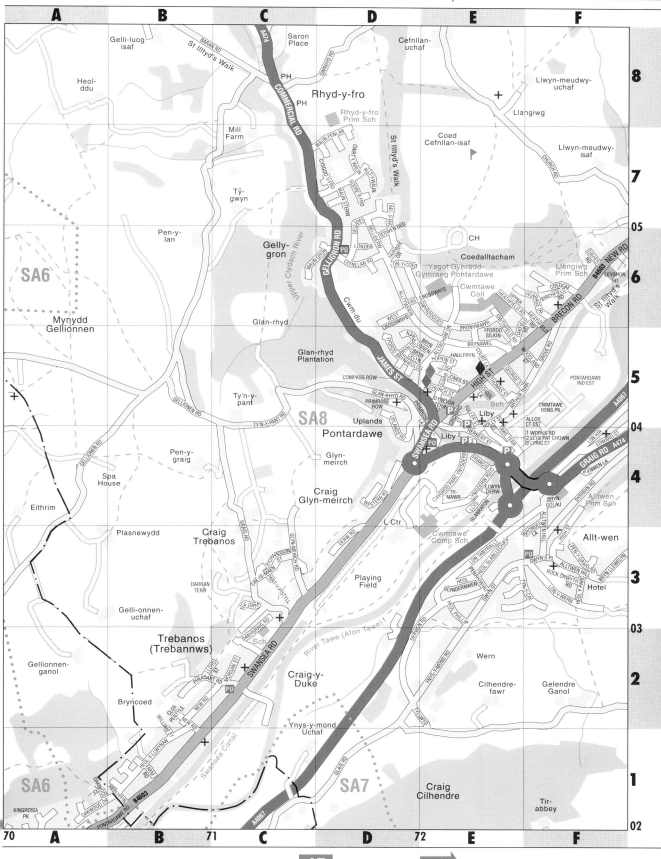

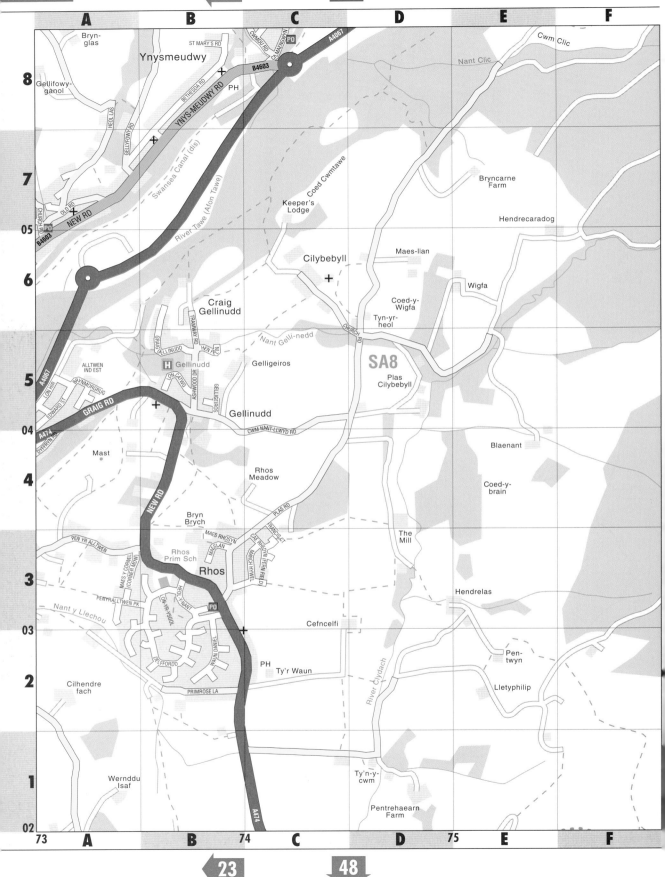

A B C D E F

8

Nant Clic

Crynant Forest

Graig
Gelligaled

7

05

SA8

Gelli-galed

Nant Ddu

BRON ALLT

MAES-MAWR RD

6

Graig Boeth

Graig Fach

Hendregynnen

Ty'n-y-graig
Farm

5

Coed-y-
glyn

04

Mynydd Marchywel

4

A4109

SA10

Nant Ysgubo

Glyn-y-bedd

Cefn Coed
Colliery Mus

Dulais

P

Cefn-coed
Cottages

3

Nant Cwmyrysbryd

Abernant
Farm

03

Cefn-coed
Sidings

2

Tirlan

Craig yr Hendy

Llwynffelish

Ty-wern

1

Glynrhigos

Ty-wern

Llwyn-
coed

A4109

02

76 A B 77 C D 78 E F

227 224

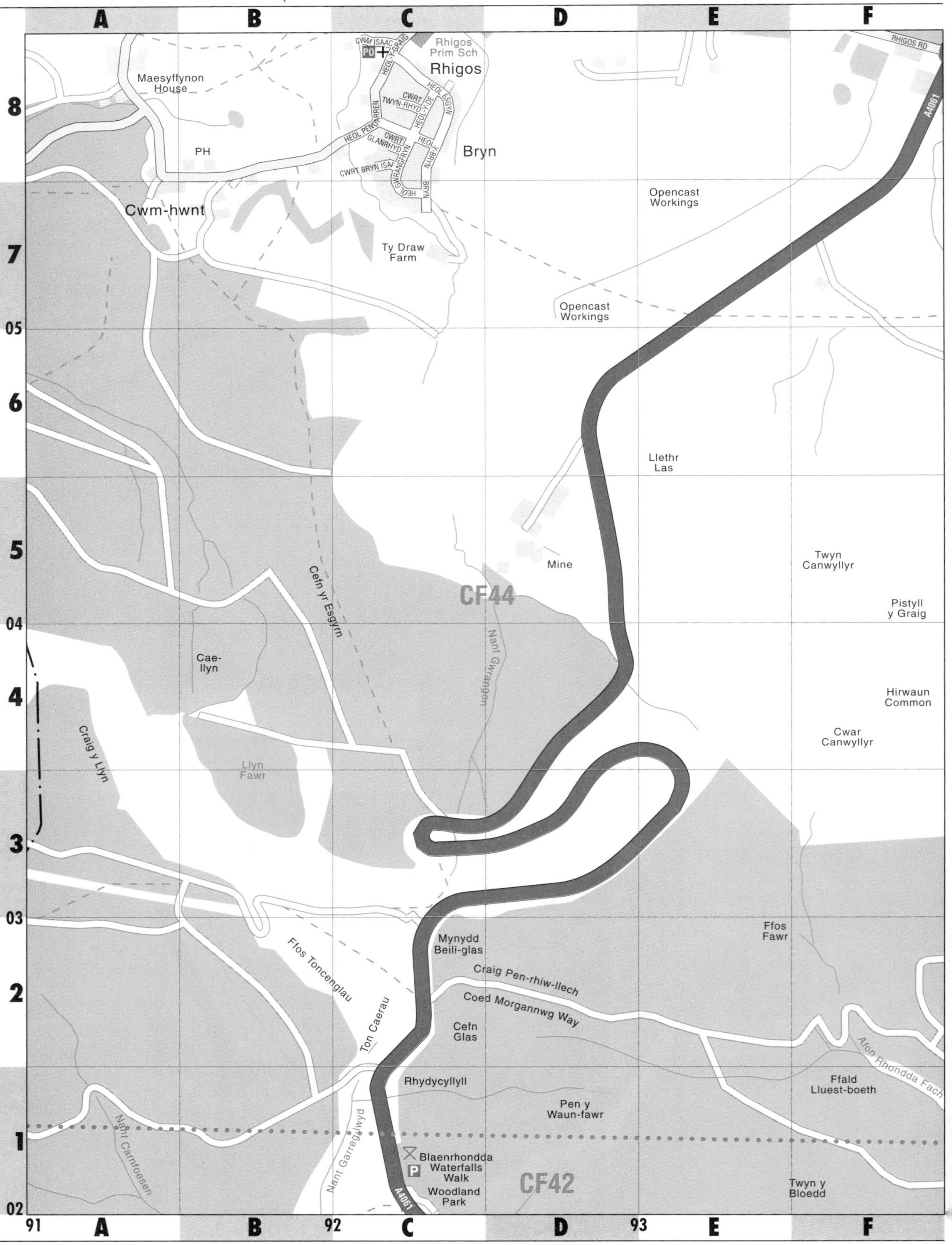

A
B
C
D
E
F
CWM ISAAC
HEOL-Y-GRAIG
PO
Rhigos Prim Sch
Rhigos
Maesyffynon House
RHIGOS RD
A4061
HEOL ESGYN
CWRT TWYN-RHYD
HEOL-Y-DE
HEOL PENDARREN
CWRT GLANRHYD
HEOL-Y-BRYN
CWRT BRYN ISAF
HEOL GWRANGRYN
BRYN
PH
Bryn
Cwm-hwnt
Opencast Workings
Ty Draw Farm
Opencast Workings
05
Llethr Las
Mine
Twyn Canwyllyr
Cefn yr Esgyrn
CF44
Pistyll y Graig
04
Nant Gwrangon
Cae-llyn
Hirwaun Common
Craig y Llyn
Cwar Canwyllyr
Llyn Fawr
03
Ffos Fawr
Mynydd Beili-glas
Ffos Toncenglau
Craig Pen-rhiw-llech
Coed Morgannwg Way
Ton Caerau
Cefn Glas
Afon Rhondda Fach
Rhydycyllyll
Ffald Lluest-boeth
Pen y Waun-fawr
Nant Carnfoesen
Nant Garreg-lwyd
Blaenrhondda Waterfalls Walk
P
Woodland Park
CF42
Twyn y Bloedd
A4061
8
7
6
5
4
3
2
1
02
91
92
93

227 50

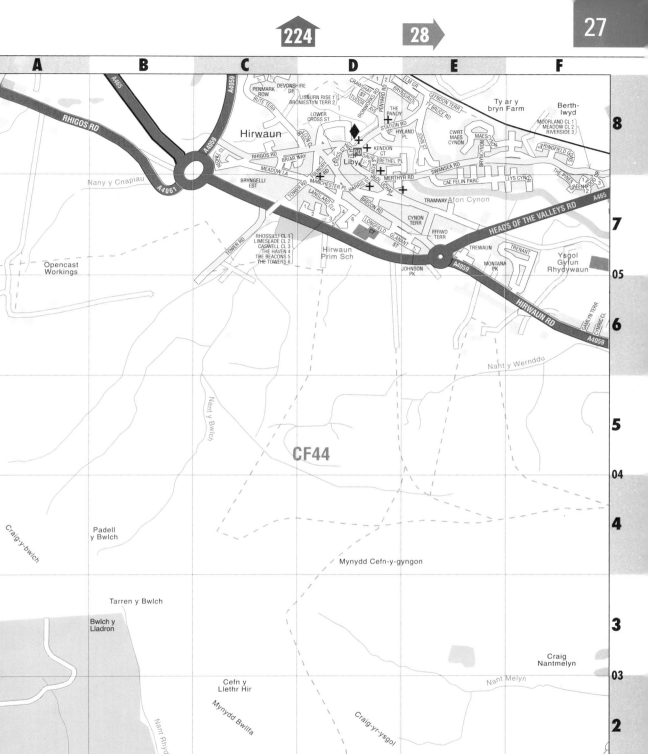

A B C D E F

8

Court Farm

Nant Hir

Cwm Cae 'rodyn

Nant y Gwyddel

Tre-Ifor

Plâs-Newydd

PH

HEADS OF THE VALLEYS RD

Gelli-tarw

Cwm Ynysmintan

A465

Tir-Mawr

Pencoed Cottages

Tre'r

HOREB TERR PH

MERTHYR RD

GREY'S PL

B4276

Gelli-uchaf Farm

7

PO

EXHIBITION ROW

CORNER HOUSE ST

Tre-Gibbon

Penybryn

05

PENTWYN CL

BRYN GWYN CL

HEOL BRYN GWYN

DAN-YR-HEOL

PEN-YR-HEOL

BRODAWG

LON LAS

CHURCHFIELD

PLASNEWYDD

MAES-YR-HAF

KINGSBURY PL

KINGSBURY

BRYN MORGAN RD

Llwydcoed Prim Sch

MORIAH PL

DELFRYN

Llwydcoed

6

LAWRENCE AVE

GARWELLT

DERLWYN

PERTHLWYD

A4059

MANGOED

ARFRYN

AR HEOL

GELYNEN

GER-Y-BOM

BRYN PENGOED

LLWYNDERI

HAULFRYN

COEDGLAS

AELFRYN

BRONLLYS

GWLAD-Y-LLYSWEN

Penywaun Inf Sch

Penywaun Jun Sch

HEOL SIWN

DYFED RD

HEOL CARADOC

Gamlyn Isaf Farm

Aton Cynon

Cwm Nant-yr-hwch

MELLTE VILLAS

DOLCOED

SCALES HOS

LLWYDCOED RD

MAES YR HAF

HAFANDEG

FOUNDERS ROW

SHOP HOS

A6
1 SHOPPING CTR
2 WAUN LWYD
3 HEOL UCHAF

Penywaun

HEOL KEIR HARDIE

HIRWAUN RD

B4275

GELLI-ISAF

5

Ty-Rhos

Cemy

Works

04

CF44 Aberdare Coll

Maesgwyn Specl Sch

LLEWELYN CT

PETERS FIELD

PETELIN

CHURCH ROW

HARRIET ST

CLIVE PL

F4
1 CYNON ST
2 ST JOHN ST
3 GADLYS UCHAF

4

Nant Melyn Farm

MAESGWYN

HEOL-Y-TWYN

HEOL-Y-GARTH

THE CRES

Maesgwyn Rd

Graigwaud

Aberdare Boys Comp Sch

PEN LLEW CT

AEL-Y-BRYN

LLEWELLYN ST

WINDSOR ST

EDWARD ST

PRIMROSE HILL

CEMETERY RD

CLEVLYN TERR

MILL ST

MOUNT ST

FREDERICK ST

BRELE

MONK ST

JONES CT

MERTON ST

Lby

Schs

WATERLOO PL

PLAS DAFYDD

HIRWAUN RD

LC

WELLINGTON ST

A4059

3

Graig Lwyd

KING ST

QUEEN ST

Cwmdare PH

PO

JAMES ST

DAVID ST

CRAIG Y DARREN

BWLLFA RD

DARE RD

LAKESIDE

City Prim Sch

BRYN TERR

YCOED

BRYN BRYNAU

MAES BRYNAU

HEOL NANT

HEOL WATKINS

HEOL-Y-DDERWEN

PEN-Y-DRE

CLOS BYCHAN

GELLI AUR

THE RISE

BRONCYNON TERR

HILLSIDE

HAULFRYN

PARC GLAS

LAUREL CL

GLASFRYN

BRYN EITHIN

REDWOOD

HAWTHORNE

LABURNUM DR

CHERRY DR

Park Farm

Park Lane Specl Sch

Trecynon

Aberdare Park

BRONIESTYN TERR

GROVE

TUDOR TERR

Railway ST

PO

WAYNE ST

OXFORD ST

NEVILLE

GADLYS ST

DAN LAS

GADLYS RD

B4275

Gadlys

03

THE RIDINGS

THE RIDINGS

LINDEN CL

HAZEL DR

BIRCH CL

OAK CRES

OAKWOOD

BEECHWOOD AVE

SYCAMORE CT

ALDER RD

ASH RD

MAPLE CL

ELM GROVE

GLAN RD

ELMWOOD AVE

PRICE'S PL

MAELGWYN TERR

MORGAN ST

EAST AVE

LAMBERT TERR

SOUTH AVE 1
DARE VILLAS 2

CLIFTON CT

CLIFTON

BRYNAWEL

BRONDEG TERR

PENDARREN ST

UNITY ST

2

Dare Valley Ctry Pk

Coed Pen-rhiw llêch

Cwm Dâr

Dare River (Aton Dar)

Dare Valley Ctr Visitor Ctr

Craig Pen-Rhiw-llêch

Coed Morgannwg Way

St John Baptist CW Comp Sch

St Margaret's RC Sch

TY FRY

HEOL-Y-MYNYDD

ARNOTT'S

HARLECH PL 1
GRAIG ISAF 2

OAKLAND

GRAIG PL A4233

1

Nant Troedrhiw-llêch

Greenmeadow Riding Ctr

Llwyn-helyg

ABERDARE
(ABERDAR)

02

97 A 98 B C 98 D 99 E F

C3
1 HOWELLS ROW
2 GOBAITH ROW
3 HOLFORD TERR
4 MAESMELYN

E4
1 MAES-RHYDWEN FLATS
2 EBENEZER ST

A B C D E F

8 7 05 6 5 04 4 3 03 2 1 02

00 A B 01 C D 02 E F

A1
1 GRIFFITH ST
2 PRICE ST
3 RACHEL ST
4 JENKIN ST
5 CATHERINE ST
6 MARY ST
7 JOHN ST
8 GLAN-NANT ST
9 LITTLE WIND ST
10 UPPER REGENT ST
11 DAVID PRICE ST
12 HAWTHORNE TERR
13 NITH ST
14 CROSS ST
15 MERCHANT ST
16 NANT ROW

A2
1 GADLYS GDNS
2 BANKES ST
3 WHITCOMBE ST
4 WEATHERAL ST
5 CHURCH ST
6 COMMERCIAL ST
7 MARKET ST
8 STATION ST
9 CHAPEL ROW

Bryn-defaid Patch
Dyllas Farm
Opencast Workings
MERTHYR RD
B4276
Dyllas Cottage
Twyn Ddisgwylfa
Mynydd Aberdâr
Waun y Gwair
Cain Pentyle-bir
Mast
Mast
Mast
CF48
Bryn Pica
Pen Llwynmelyn
Cefn Ffordd
Tir-ergyd
Bryn Mawr
Nant y Wenallt
Twyn Blaen-nant
Blean-nant
Blaencanaid
CF44
Coedcae Farm
 Owersyll
Coed Morgannwg Way
Garn Las
Ysgubor-wen House
Gwrhyd
Ysgubor-wen Farm
PH
Twyn y Werfa
Robertstown
Moss Rd
Werfa Cl
Nant-yr-eos
Heol-y-parc
Greenway
Werfa La
Werfa La
Werfa House
Aber-nant Cty Prim Sch
Richmond Terr
Aberdare General H
Abernant Rd
Hurst Gr
Forge Pl
Fothergill St
Windsor Terr
Agent's Row
Abernant
Maes-y-dre
Mus
Park View Terr
The Walk
Wenallt Rd
Wenallt Ct
Alltwen
CH
A4059
Phillip St
Thomas St
Bridge St
Wellington St
College St
Alexandra Terr
Crichton Farm
Craig-Llyn Cres
Cenarth Dr
A4233
Hall St
Gloucester St
Pembroke St
Seymour St
Dean St
Plasdraw Av
Plasdraw Rd
Ty-draw Av
Ty-draw Rd
Aberdare Sch
Glanynys Ho
Plasdraw Rd
Superstore
Gower Rd
Gower Rd
Claerwen Cl
Elan Cl
Clwyd Av
Conway Dr
Mus
A4233
High St
Canon St
Victoria Sq
Ct
Gordon Villas
Cwmbach Rd
Kendal Cl
Finecroft Ave
Rheidol Cl
Derwent Dr
Libby
Cardiff St
Monk St
A4233
A4059
Clifton St
Alon Cynon
Bethuel St
Sports Ctr
Heath Cl
Larkfield Ave
Panfield Cl
Bracken Rise
Windermere Cl
Nynscynon Terr
1 Brookbank Cl
2 Meadowbank Cl
Well Pl
Fairfield
Conway Dr
Conway Dr
Coniston Rise
Grasmere Rd
Langorse Rd
Cwmbach Jun Sch
Incline Rd
Daniel St
Waterloo St
Blaenanty-groes Rd
Blaenanty-groes Rd
Nant y Groes
Blaen-nant-y-groes
B4275
Ysgol Synradd Cymraeg Aberdar
B4275
A4059
Cwmbach Rd
Cwmbach
FoundryTown

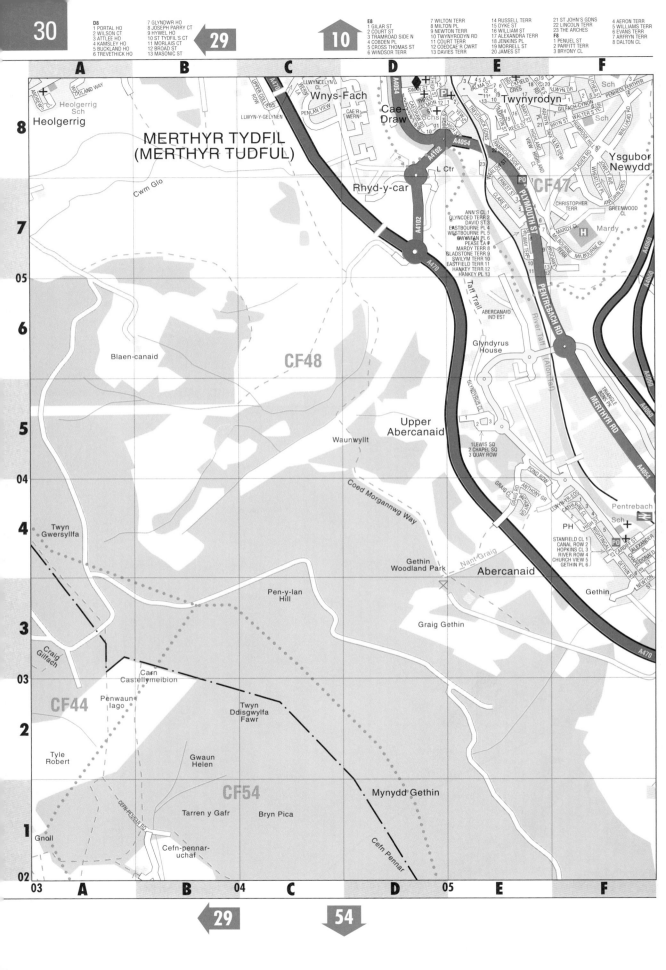

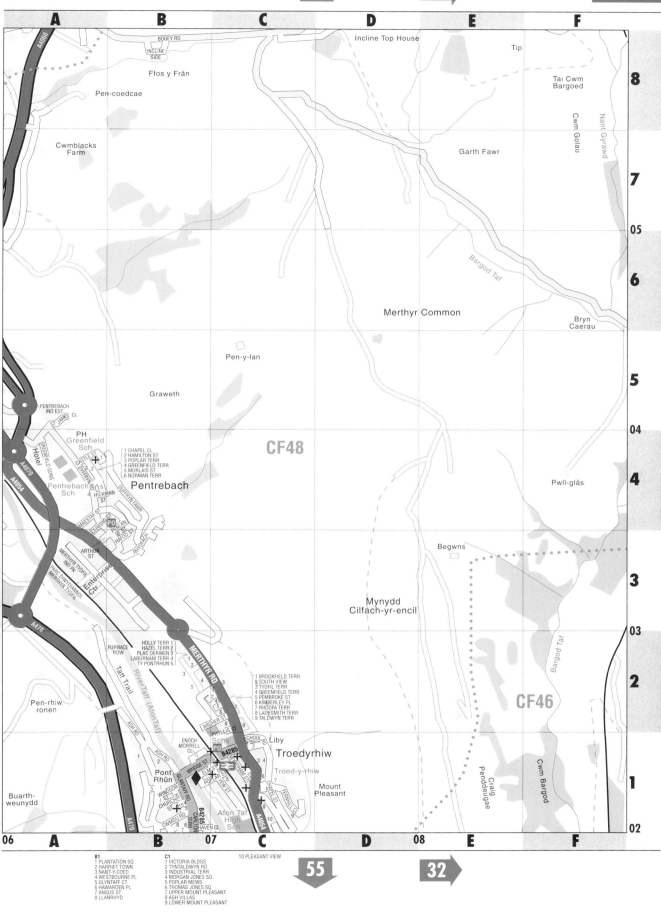

A   B   C   D   E   F

BOGEY RD
INCLINE SIDE
Incline Top House
Tip
8
Ffos y Frân
Tai Cwm Bargoed
Pen-coedcae
Cwm Golau
Nant Gyrawd
Cwmblacks Farm
Garth Fawr
7
05
Bargod Taf
6
Merthyr Common
Bryn Caerau
Pen-y-lan
5
Graweth
04
CF48
Pwll-glâs
4
PENTREBACH IND EST
ST JAMES CL
PH
Greenfield Sch
Hotel
Greenfield GDNS
CASTLE ST
DYFFRYN
1 CHAPEL CL
2 HAMILTON ST
3 POPLAR TERR
4 GREENFIELD TERR
5 MORLAIS ST
6 NORMAN TERR
A4070
A4054
Pentrebach Sch
HICKMAN ST
Pentrebach
DYFFRYN FAWR
MAESTAF ST
CREDENHILL ST
PO
HAFOD ST
RHYD FAGOR
Begwns
ARTHUR ST
MERTHYR TYDFIL IND PK
PARC CWMDUUMOL MERTHYR TYDFIL
Enterprise Ct
Mynydd Cilfach-yr-encil
3
A470
03
FURNACE ROW
HOLLY TERR 1
HAZEL TERR 2
PLAS DERWEN 3
LABURNAM TERR 4
TY PONTRHUN 5
MERTHYR RD
Bargod Taf
2
Taff Trail
River Taff (Afon Taf)
1 BROOKFIELD TERR
2 SOUTH VIEW
3 TYDFIL TERR
4 GREENFIELD TERR
5 PEMBROKE ST
6 KIMBERLEY PL
7 RHODFA TERR
8 LADYSMITH TERR
9 TALDWYN TERR
CF46
Pen-rhiw ronen
ASH RD
ARCHER ST
PHYLLIS ST
SCHOOL ST
Liby
CARLTON TERR
1
ENOCH MORRELL CL
PO
B4285
Troedyrhiw
Troed-y-rhiw
Craig Penddeugae
Cwm Bargod
Buarth-weunydd
WINDSOR RD
GLANTAF RD
BRIDGE ST
CHURCH ST
ELM ST
Pont Rhûn
CHAPEL ST
FERNHILL CL
Mount Pleasant
CWMDU RD
B4285
CARLTON TERR
HAVEN CL
Afon Taf High Sch
A4054
02

06   A   B   07   C   D   08   E   F

B1
1 PLANTATION SQ
2 HARRIET TOWN
3 NANT-Y-COED
4 WESTBOURNE PL
5 GLYNTAFF CT
6 HAWARDEN PL
7 ANGUS ST
8 LLANRHYD

C1
1 VICTORIA BLDGS
2 TYNTALDWYN RD
3 INDUSTRIAL TERR
4 MORGAN JONES SQ
5 POPLAR MEWS
6 THOMAS JONES SQ
7 UPPER MOUNT PLEASANT
8 ASH VILLAS
9 LOWER MOUNT PLEASANT

10 PLEASANT VIEW

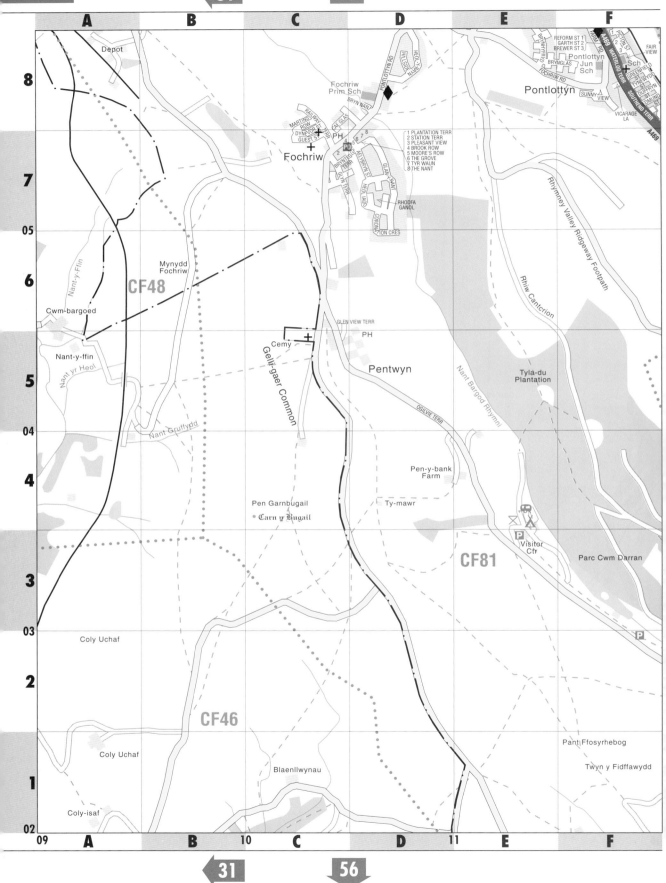

A B C D E F

8

7

05

6

04

5

04

4

03

3

03

2

1

02

09 A B 10 C D 11 E F

Depot

Fochriw Prim Sch

BRYN MAWR

1 PLANTATION TERR
2 STATION TERR
3 PLEASANT VIEW
4 BROOK ROW
5 MOORE'S ROW
6 THE GROVE
7 TYR WAUN
8 THE NANT

REFORM ST 1
GARTH ST 2
BREWER ST 3.

Pontlottyn Jun Sch

Pontlottyn

FAIR VIEW

SUNNY VIEW

VICARAGE LA

MARTINS ROW
DYNEVOR
GUEST ST
RAILWAY TERR
KAE GLAS
PH
PO
BRYNTEG TERR
GLYN TERR
ACLYBRYN ST
HEOL AGG
GLAN Y NANT
RHODFA GANOL
CORONATION CRES

Fochriw

Mynydd Fochriw

CF48

Cwm-bargoed

Nant-y-ffin

Nant-y-Ffin

Nant yr Heol

Nant Gruffydd

Gelli-gaer Common

Cemy

GLEN VIEW TERR

PH

Pentwyn

OGILVIE TERR

Nant Bargod Rhymni

Rhiw Cantcrion

Rhymney Valley Ridgeway Footpath

Tyla-du Plantation

Pen-y-bank Farm

Ty-mawr

Pen Garnbugail

Carn y Bugail

Visitor Ctr

CF81

Parc Cwm Darran

P

Coly Uchaf

CF46

Coly Uchaf

Blaenllwynau

Coly-isaf

Pant Ffosyrhebog

Twyn y Fidffawydd

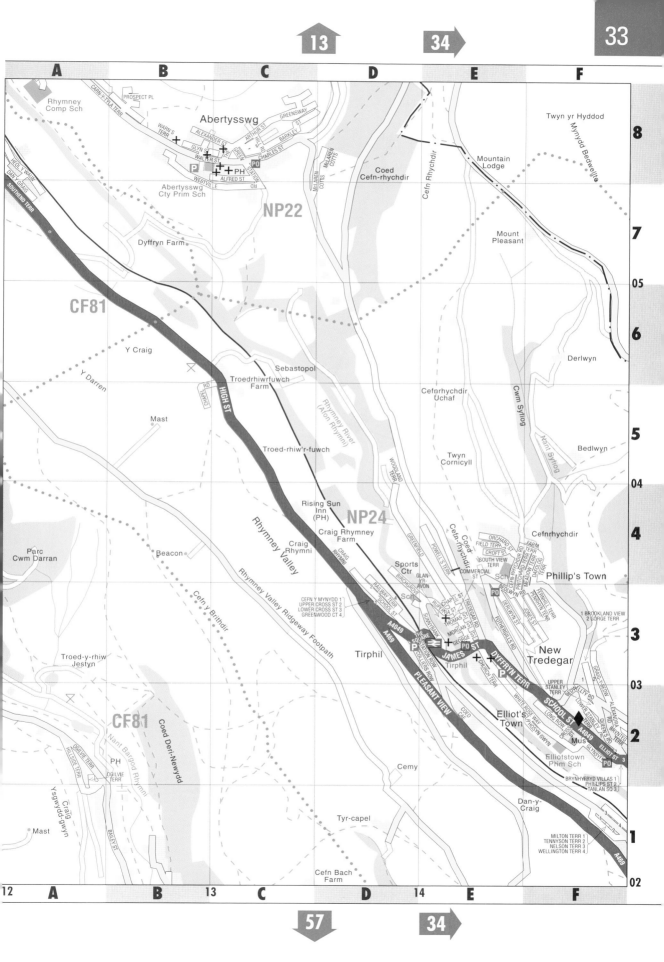

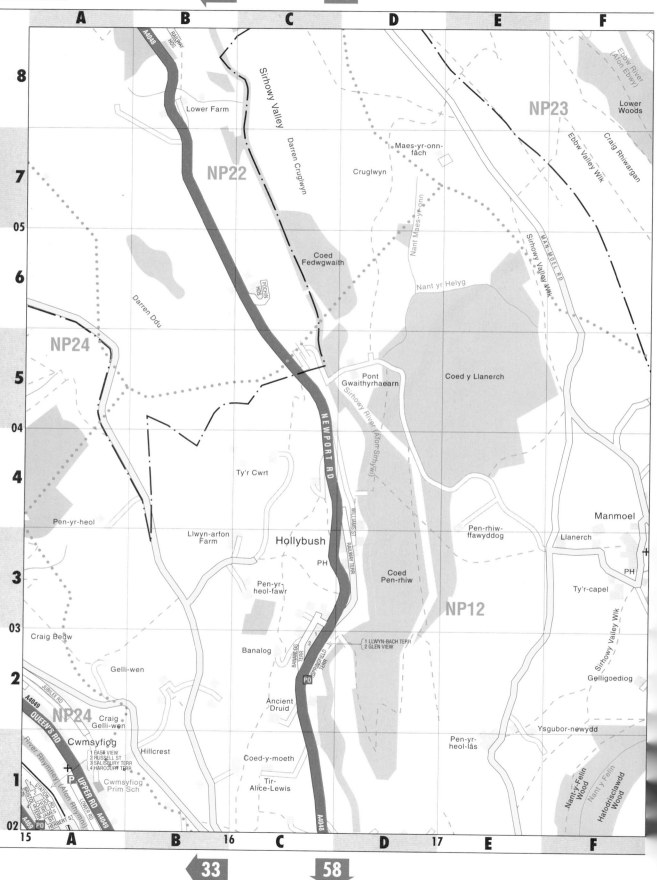

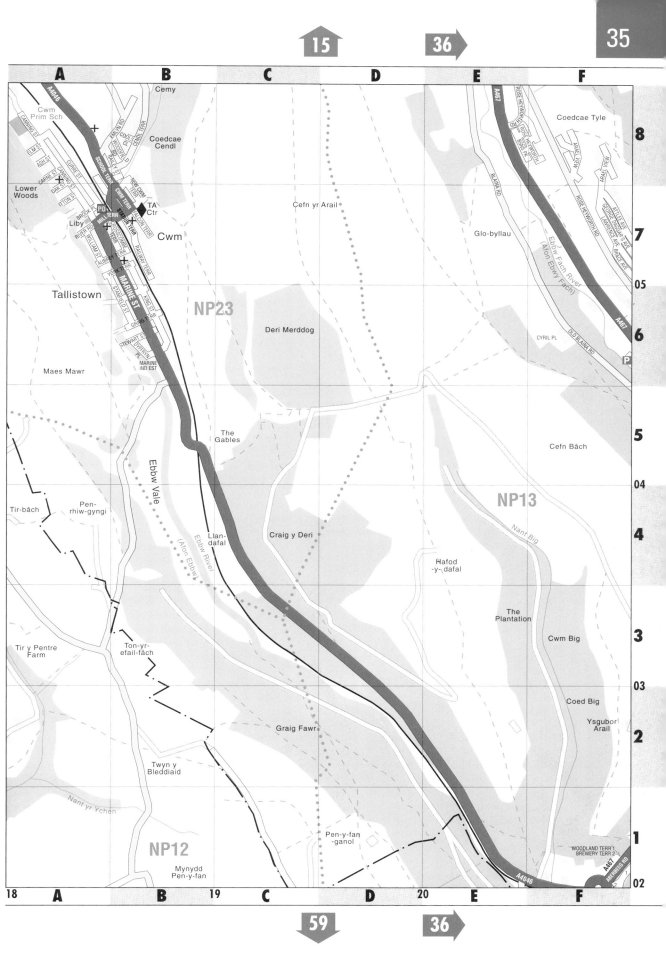

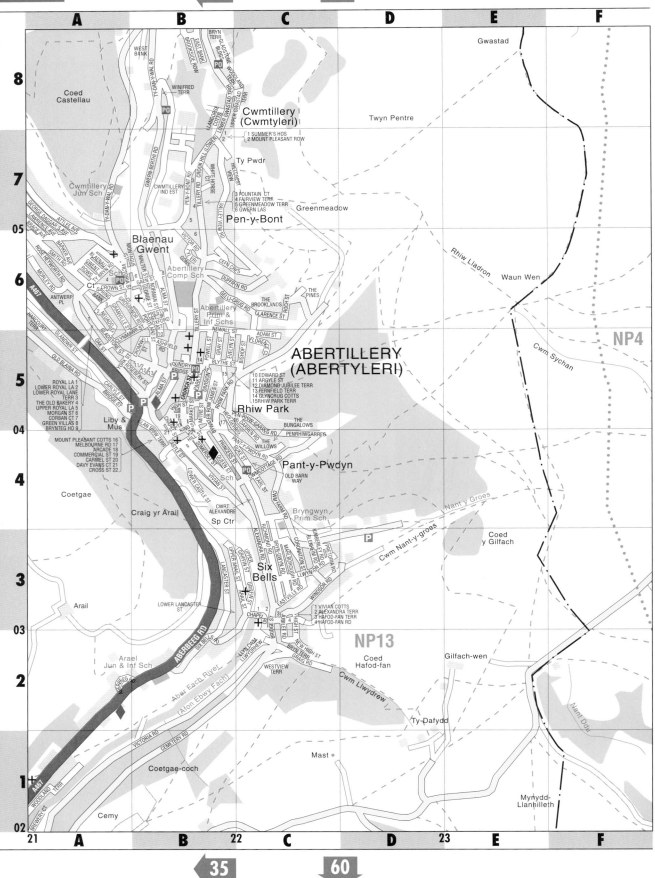

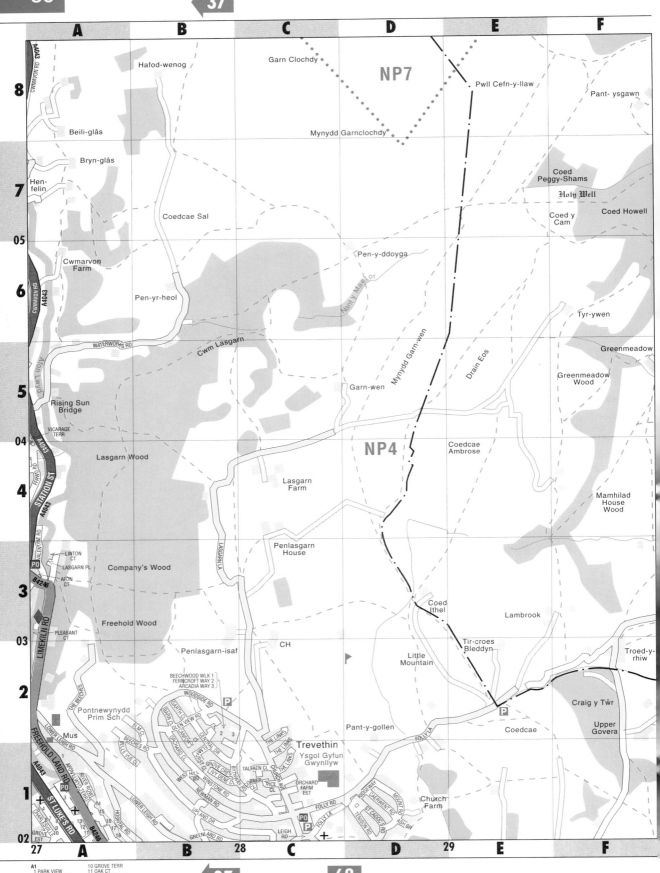

A1
1 PARK VIEW
2 TORFAEN TERR
3 MACHINE MDW
4 MITCHELL TERR
5 ROCHDALE TERR
6 PARK TERR
7 CHURCH TERR
8 GROVESIDE VILLAS
9 COLLEGE TERR
10 GROVE TERR
11 OAK CT
12 NEWLANDS CT
13 BELLE VIEW CT
14 BELGRAVE CT
15 CAPEL CT
16 WEST BANK CT
17 HARDY CT
18 PARKSIDE CT

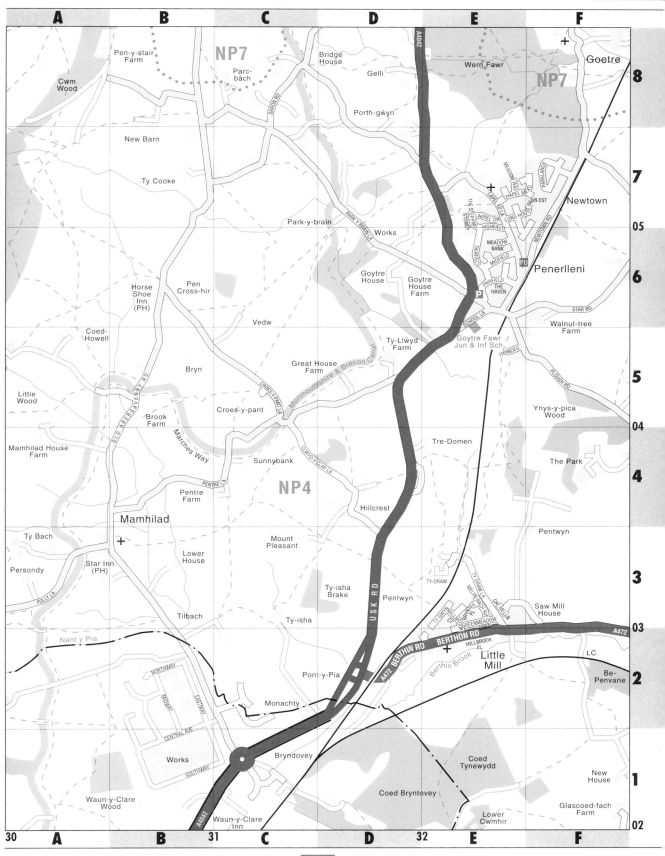

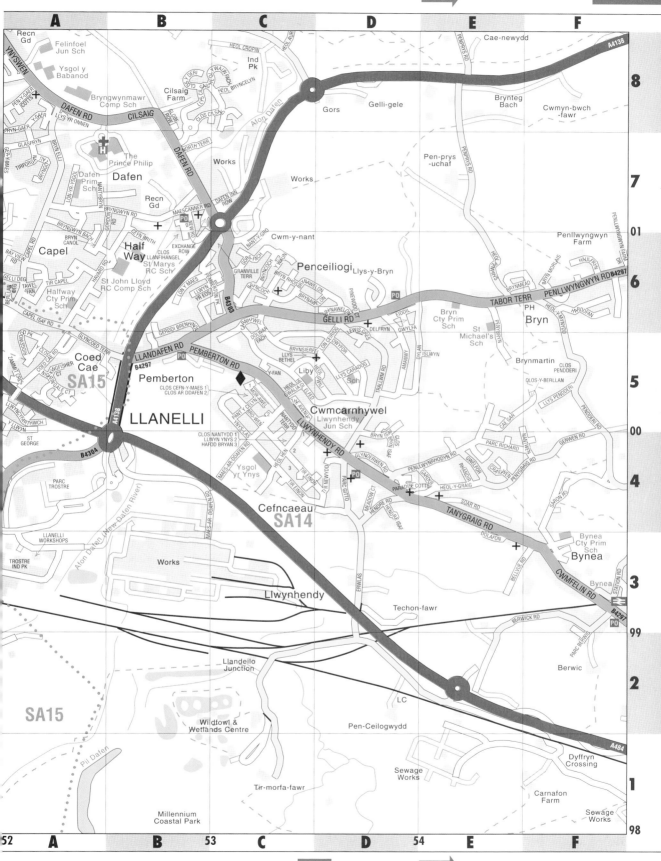

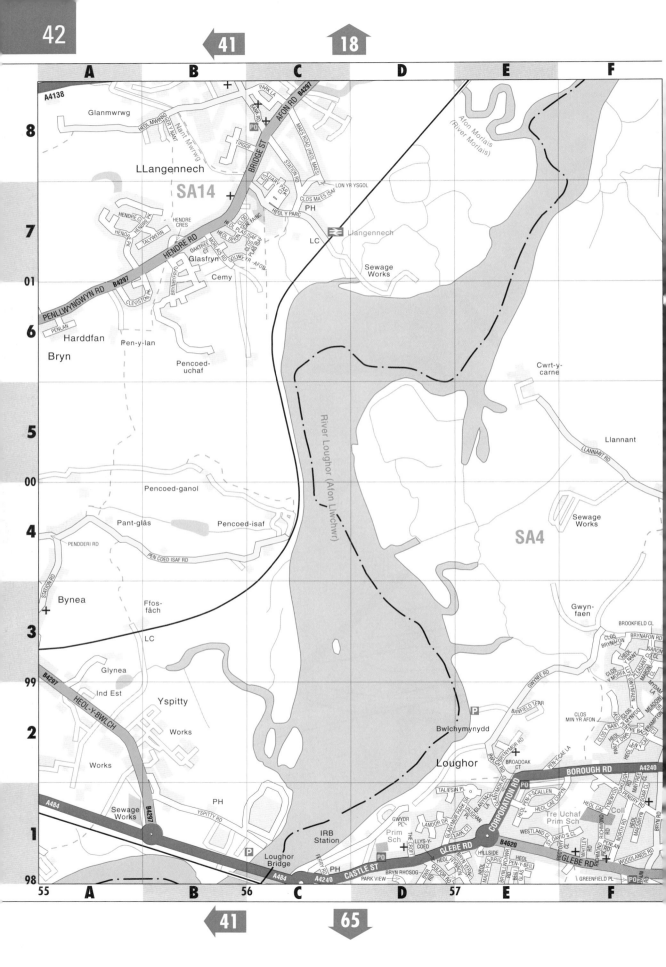

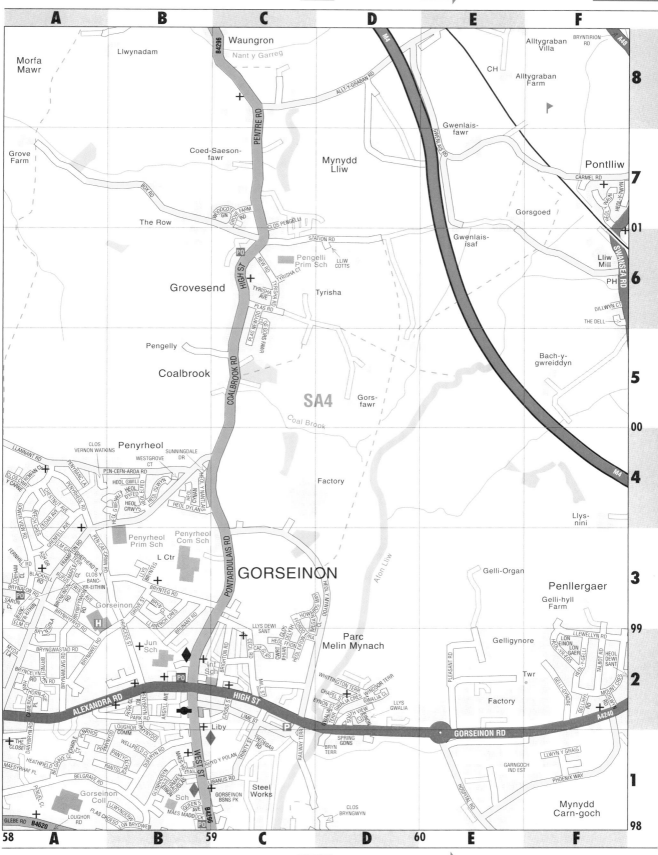

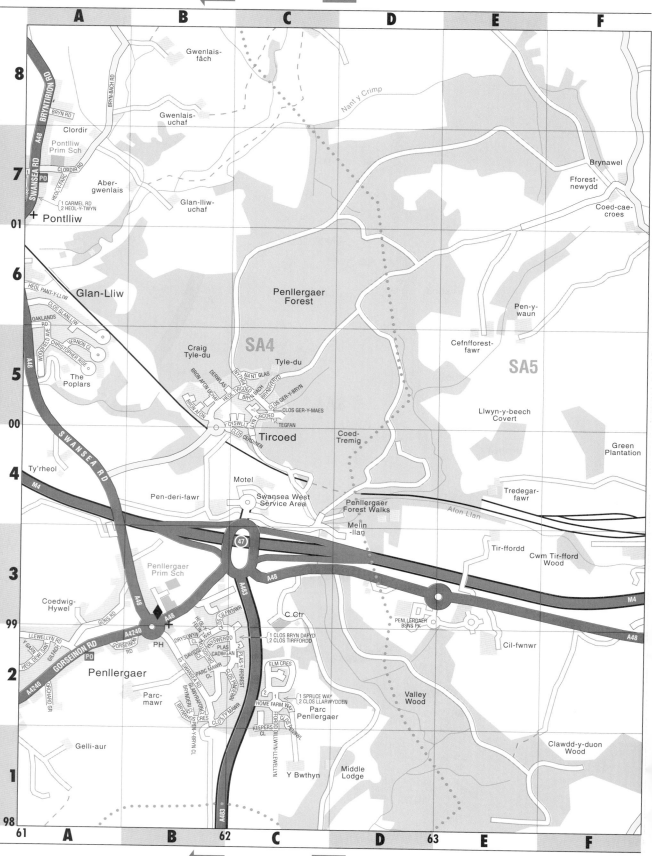

43
20

A B C D E F

8

Gwenlais-fâch

Nant y Crimp

7

BRYNTIRION RD
BRYN RD
BRYN-BACH RD
Clordir
Gwenlais-uchaf
Pontlliw
Prim Sch
A48
Brynawel
Fforest-newydd
SWANSEA RD
PO
CLORDIR RD
HEOL-Y-FRAC
Aber-gwenlais
Glan-lliw-uchaf
Coed-cae-croes
01
1 CARMEL RD
2 HEOL-Y-TWYN
Pontlliw

6

HEOL PANT-Y-LLIW
CLOS GLANLLIW
Glan-Lliw
Penllergaer
Forest
Pen-y-waun

OAKLANDS RD
WOODFIELD AVE
VERNON CL
CHRISTOPHER RISE
A48
SA4
Cefnforest-fawr
SA5

5
The Poplars
Craig
Tyle-du
Tyle-du
BRON AFON UCHAF
DERWLAS
NANT GLAS
YN THRA BACH
HEOL TIRCOED
BRYN
BRYNTYRYD
CLOS GER-Y-BRYN
Llwyn-y-beech
Covert

00
BRON AFON
Y CYSWLLT
LLWYN TIRCOED
CLOS GER-Y-MAES
TEGFAN
Coed-Tremig
CLOS CERDINEN
Tircoed

Green
Plantation

4
Ty'rheol
M4
SWANSEA RD
Motel
Pen-deri-fawr
Swansea West
Service Area
Penllergaer
Forest Walks
Afon Llan
Tredegar-fawr

Melin-llan
Tir-ffordd
Cwm Tir-ffordd
Wood

3
Coedwig-Hywel
Penllergaer
Prim Sch
A48
47
A48
A483
PENLLERGAER
BSNS PK
M4
A48

99
LLEWELLYN RD
Y GAEN
HEOL DEWI SANT
GIL PLACE
PORSEINON RD
GORSEINON RD
A4240
PH
A48
PO
HEOL FELIN
SALEM
DRYSLWYN
CIL NE WAY
ST DAVIDS
TY SWERDD
GALFWNWR
PLAS-Y-FFOREST
C Ctr
1 CLOS BRYN DAFYD
2 CLOS TIRFFORDD
Cil-fwnwr

2
Penllergaer
Parc-mawr
SWANSEA RD
PARC MAWR CL
PLAS
CADWGAN
CLOS PFNTERNI
ELM CRES
Valley
Wood

A4240
ORCHARD GR
GLANYMARNEL
BRYNDERW CL
BRYNRHOS CRES
PEN-Y-BRYN CL
CLOS TY MAWR
HOME FARM WAY
FFORDD DILLWYN-LLEWELLYN
1 SPRUCE WAY
2 CLOS LLARWYDDEN
CLOS RONDWL
Parc
Penllergaer
KEEPERS CL

1
Gelli-aur
Y Bwthyn
Middle
Lodge
Clawdd-y-duon
Wood

98
A483

61 A B C D 63 E F

43
67

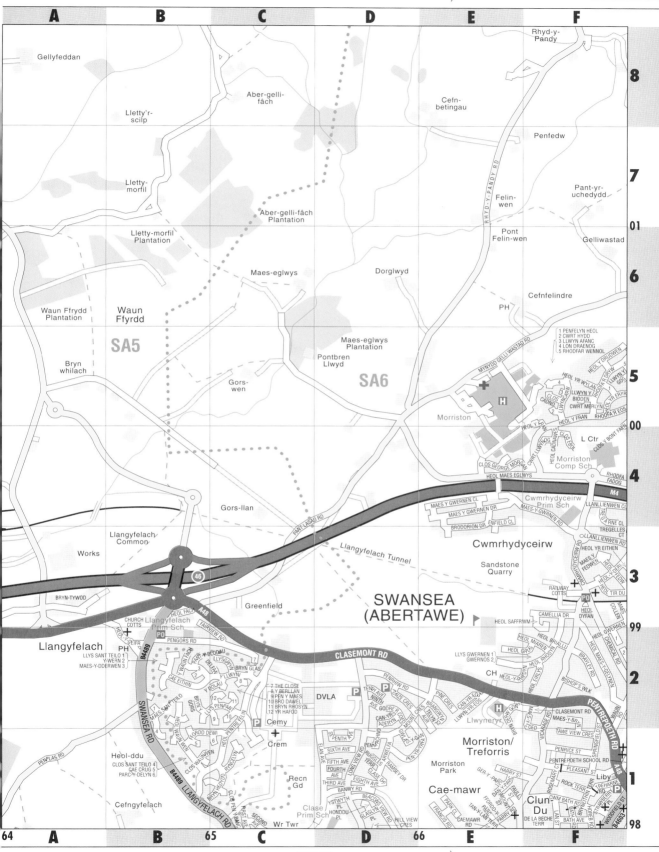

8

7

01

6

5

00

4

3

99

2

1

98

Pant-y-coedcae

Ty-côch

Mynydd Gelliwastad

Graigfelen

Upper Forge

Faerdre

Trebannwg Prim Sch

Woodlands Ave

Waverly Pk

Waverly Cl

Llys Perl

Kingcrosia Pk

Pearl Cl

Ty-gwyn

Penrheol-las

Graigfelen Co Prim Sch

Clydach Jun Sch

Pontardawe Rd   B4603

Cae Pant-y-dugoed

Quarr-Clydach

Clydach

Inf Sch

High St

Liby

Ynys-Penllwch Rd   B4291

Banwen

Pen-y-rhedyn

Cae-mawr

Cwm-dwr

Hebron Rd

Mount Pleasant

Aber Clydach

Clydach

Chy

Works

A4067

Y Gwernydd Station Rd

Cefn Rd

Garth Rd

Mynydd Gelli Wastad Rd

Ynystawe

Pen-rhiw-gwysfa

Ffordd Cwm Tawe

Pentwyn

Rhodfa'r Dryw

Llwyn yr Iar

Llwyn y Gog

Clydach Rd

PH

Gwern-Fadog Plantation

Ynystawe Prim Sch

Woodland Pk

SA6

SA7

Glyncollen Prim Sch

Ynystanglws Farm

Ynys-tanglws Bridge

M4

Ynysforgan

River Tawe (Afon Tawe)

Ynys-allan Farm

Coed Glyn-y-gors

45

Ynys-Forgan Farm

Cwm-felin-Fâch

Llys Gwernen

Ynysallan Rd

Heol-las

Heol-las Farm

Neath Rd

Clydach Rd

1 Waun Rd
2 Cwrt Ivor Sims
3 Llys Yr Ardd

Heol-las Cl

Tircanol

1 Woodfield St
2 The Cross
3 New Cross Bldgs
4 Glantawe St

Recn Gd

Mast

Sway Rd

Dyffryn Sch

Camffrwd Way

Tre-gof Farm

Cwrt Y Fedwen

Felin Fran

Cwrt Emily

Tirpenry

Clase Rd

A48

Works

Morriston North Ind Est

Ashmount Bsns Parc

St Johns Cl

Clarion Cl

Acorn Cl

Upper Forest Way

Pant-y-Blawd

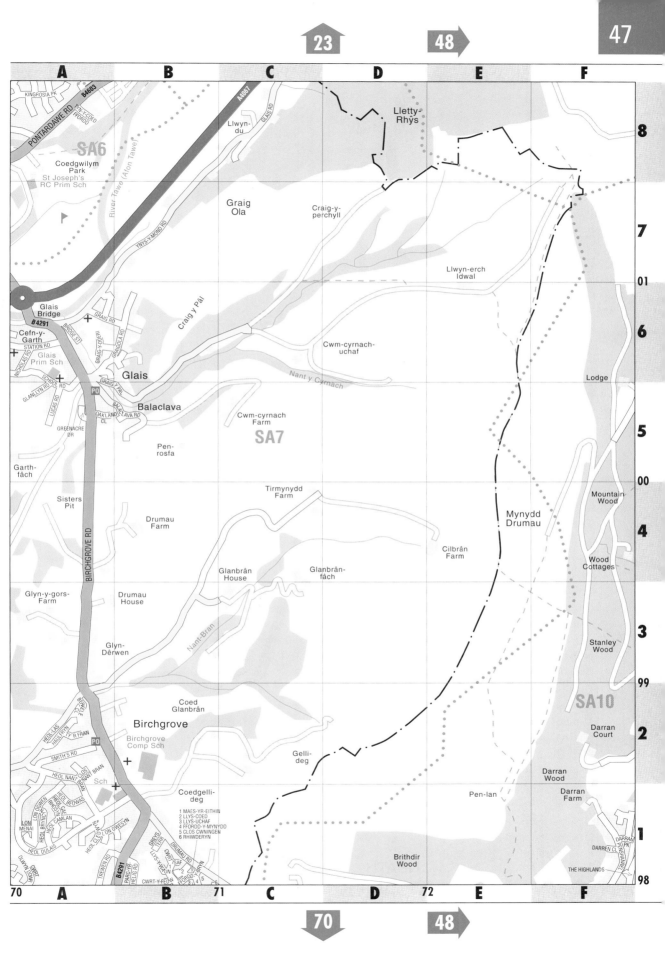

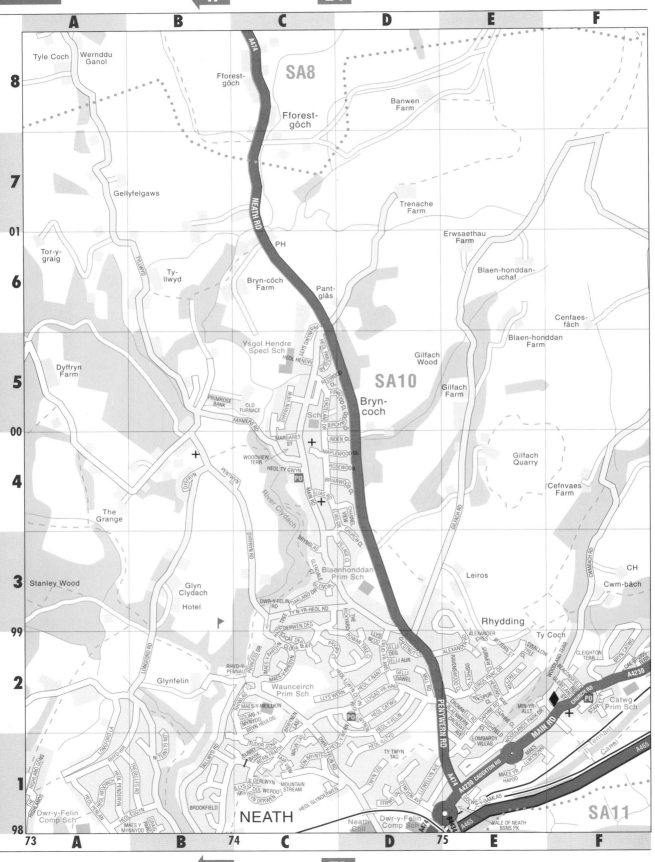

47
24

A   B   C   D   E   F

8

Tyle Coch   Wernddu Ganol
Fforest-gôch
SA8
Fforest-gôch
Banwen Farm

7
NEATH RD
A474
Gellyfelgaws

01
Tor-y-graig
PH
Trenache Farm
Erwsaethau Farm

6
Ty-llwyd
Bryn-côch Farm
Pant-glâs
Blaen-honddan-uchaf
Cenfaes-fâch
Blaen-honddan Farm

5
Dyffryn Farm
Ysgol Hendre Specl Sch
HEOL HENDRE
LLYS GWYNN
HEOL PANTYCELYN
REDWOOD
FIRWOOD CL
FURZELAND DR
BIRCH
Gilfach Wood
SA10
Bryn-coch
Gilfach Farm

00
PRIMROSE BANK
OLD FURNACE
FARMERS RD
DYFFRYN VIEW
Sch
MARGARET ST
MAPLEWOOD CL
LINDEN CL
OAK CL
ROSEWOOD
Gilfach Quarry

4
DYFFRYN
PENTWYN CL
WOODVIEW TERR
HEOL TY GWYN
PO
BRIARWOOD CL
ELIAS RD
MAIN RD
River Clydach
ELIAS DR
CHANNEL VIEW
CHURCH CL
VILLAGE CL
Cefnvaes Farm
GILFACH RD

3
Stanley Wood
The Grange
DYFFRYN RD
BRYNGLAS
GLENDALE DR
GLENDALE
Blaenhonddan Prim Sch
Leiros
Cwm-bâch
CH
CWMBACH RD

99
Glyn Clydach Hotel
DWR-Y-FELIN RD
TY-N-YR-HEOL RD
HEOL TREE
DERWEN DEG
CAE DEG
CLODA AVE
THE ROWAL
TREE CL
PRIVA CL
LLYS NEDD
CHIDO-YR-HEOL
GELLI DEG
GELLI AUR
Rhydding
ALEXANDER CRES
ALEXANDR
PITTERN CL
TREL CL
SWALLOW
Ty Coch
WOODLAND TERR
CLEIGHTON TERR
BRYN CATWG
CAE BROSS TERR

2
Glynfelin
LONGFORD RD
RHYD-Y-PENNAU
PRINCESS DR
MAES-Y-RHEDYN
MAES-Y-RHEDYN
RHIWAS
Waunceirch Prim Sch
MAES-Y-MEILLION
GOLWG-Y-MYNYDD
BRYN HEULOG
BRYNDEN
LLYS WERN
HEOL LLWYN
HEOL-Y-NANT
HEOL CATWG
LLYGAD-YR-HAUL
HEOL-Y-FELIN
PO
GELLI DAWEL
MILL RD
CROMWELL RD
BLAENWERN
CROMWELL
DAPHNE RD
DAPHNE CL
PENTWERN RD
A474
A4230 CADOXTON RD
WOODLANDS PARK DR
LOMBARDY VILLAS
MIN-YR-ALLT
MAIN RD
BEACONSFIELD
GLEBELAND
Catwg Prim Sch
A4230
CHURCH RD
STANLEY
PO

1
THE HIGHLANDS
LONGFORD LA
RHYD-YR
TREGELLES RD
LON GLANRHYD
HEOL PENDERYN
HEOL HEDDWCH
TALLWYD RD
SUNNY BANK
WERN FRAITH
FAIR VIEW
GN BRYNTEG
Mountain Stream
DWR-Y-FELIN
TWYN TEG
HEOL-Y-FELIN
HEOL LLTYD
TY TWYN TAG
VALE RD
DYNEVOR AVE
LLEWELLYN AVE
MAES YR HAFOD
GOLWG-Y-GAMLAS
Tennant Canal
MAES
LLWYNONN
SA11

98
THE HIGHLAND COINS
Dwr-y-Felin Comp Sch
HEOL ESGYN
CRAIG PARC
MAES Y MYNYDD
BROOKFIELD
HEOL GLYNDERWEN
NEATH
Neath Coll
Dwr-y-Felin Comp Sch
A474
B4434
A465
VALE OF NEATH BSNS PK
A465

73   A   B   74   C   D   75   E   F

47
71

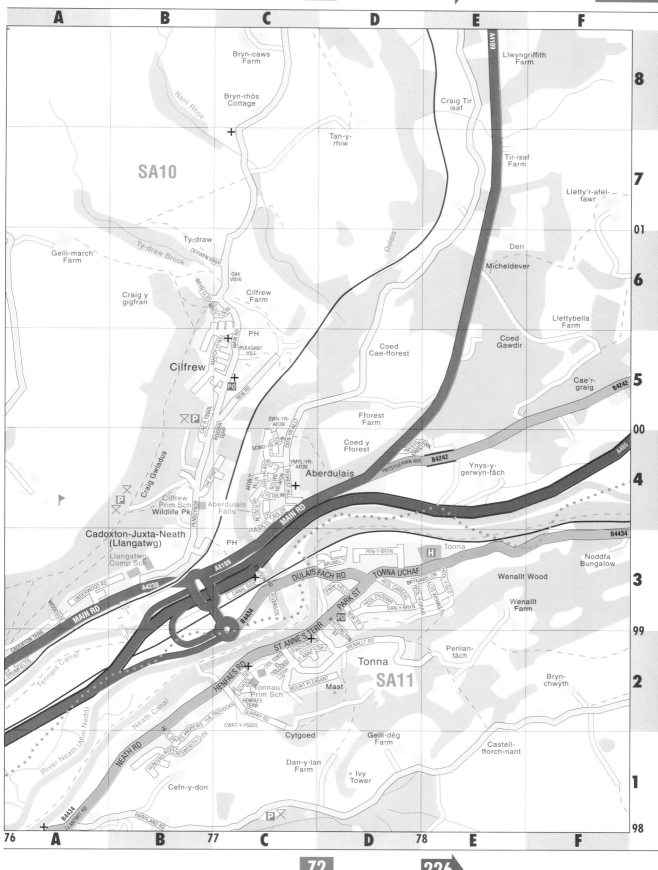

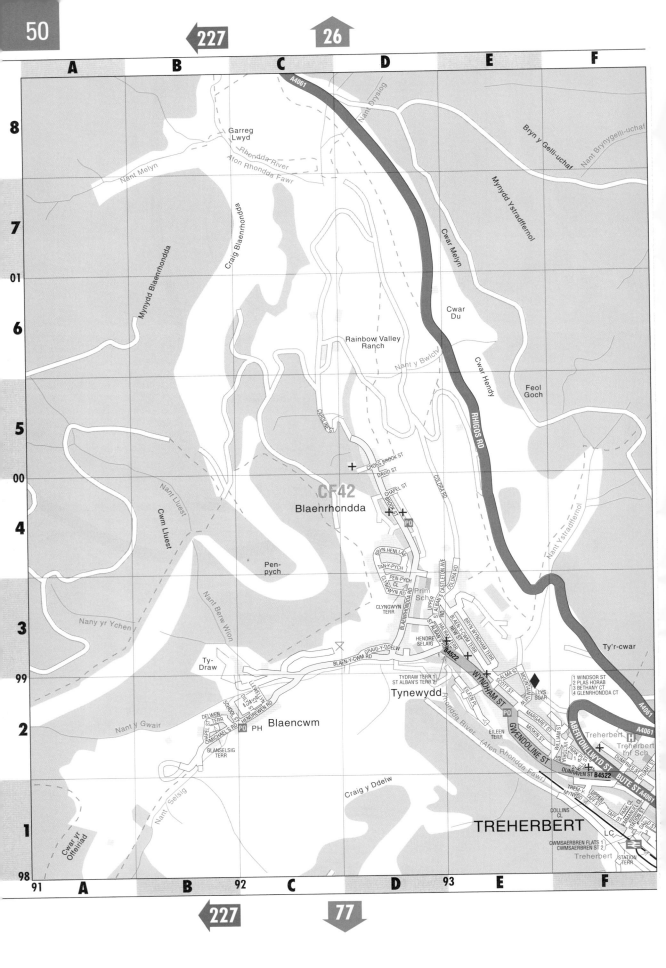

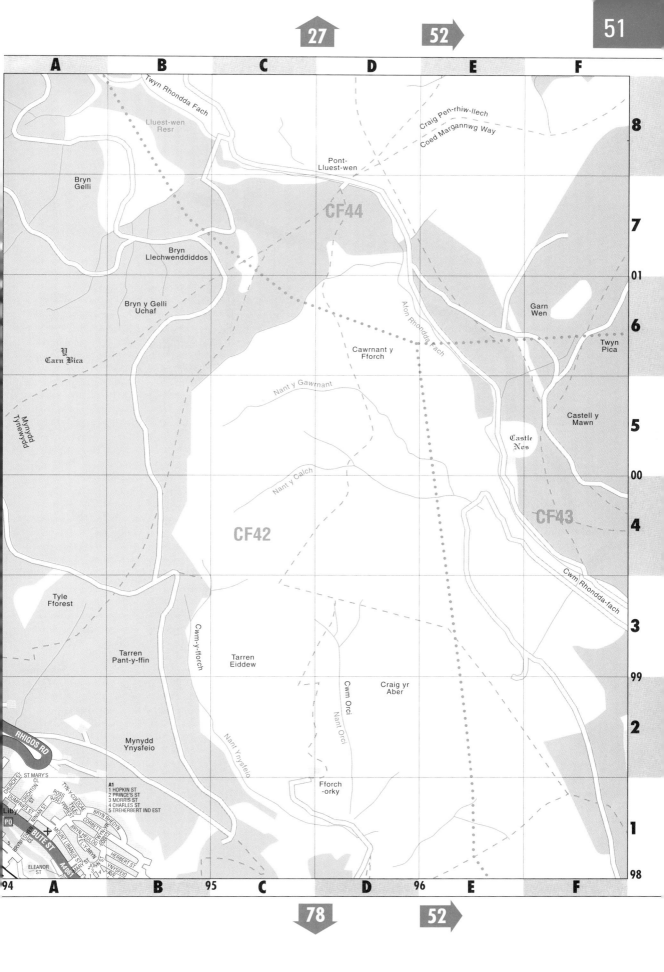

A   B   C   D   E   F

Twyn Rhondda Fach

Lluest-wen Resr

Craig Pen-rhiw-llech

Coed Margannwg Way

8

Pont-Lluest-wen

CF44

7

Bryn Gelli

01

Bryn Llechwenddiddos

Garn Wen

6

Bryn y Gelli Uchaf

Twyn Pica

Cawrnant y Fforch

Aфon Rhondda Fach

Y Carn Bica

Nant y Gawrnant

Castell y Mawn

5

Castle Nos

Mynydd Tynewydd

Nant y Calch

00

CF43

4

CF42

Cwm Rhondda-fach

Tyle Fforest

3

Cwm-y-fforch

Tarren Pant-y-ffin

Tarren Eiddew

99

Craig yr Aber

Cwm Orci

Nant Orci

2

Mynydd Ynysfeio

Nant Ynysfeio

RHIGOS RD

Fforch -orky

ST MARY'S CL

TYN-Y-CHEDCAE

A1
1 HOPKIN ST
2 PRINCE'S ST
3 MORRIS ST
4 CHARLES ST
5 TREHERBERT IND EST

1

Lib

PO

BUTE ST

A4061

ELEANOR ST

98

94   A   B   95   C   D   96   E   F

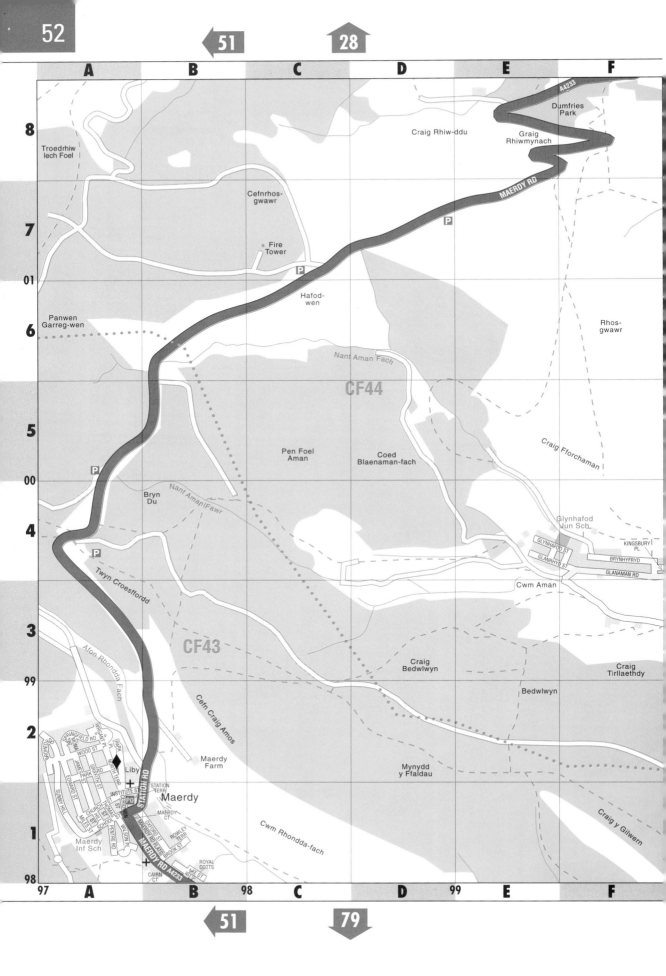

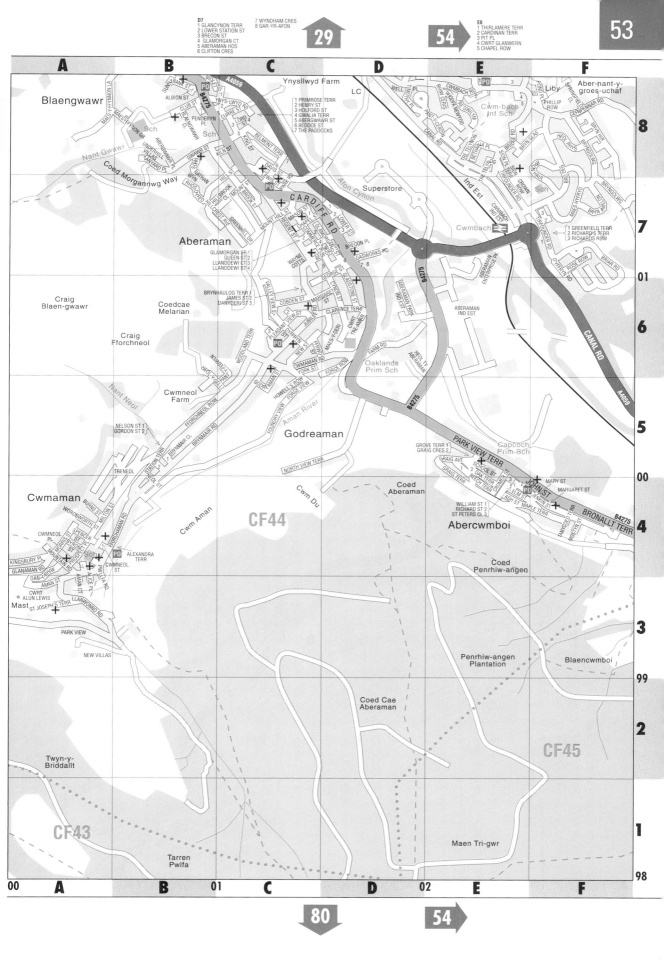

D7
1 GLANCYNON TERR
2 LOWER STATION ST
3 BRECON ST
4 GLAMORGAN CT
5 ABERAMAN HOS
6 CLIFTON CRES
7 WYNDHAM CRES
8 GAR-YR-AFON

E8
1 THIRLAMERE TERR
2 CARDINAN TERR
3 PIT PL
4 CWRT GLANWERN
5 CHAPEL ROW

Blaengwawr

Ynysllwyd Farm

LC

Aber-nant-y-groes-uchaf

Cwm-bach Inf Sch

Liby

Cwmbach

1 PRIMROSE TERR
2 HENRY ST
3 HOLFORD ST
4 GWALIA TERR
5 ABERGWAWR ST
6 BEDDOE ST
7 THE PADDOCKS

Aberaman

Superstore

CARDIFF RD

Aberaman Park

Ind Est

1 GREENFIELD TERR
2 RICHARD'S TERR
3 RICHARDS ROW

GLAMORGAN ST 1
QUEEN ST 2
LLANDDEWI CT 3
LLANDDEWI ST 4

Craig Blaen-gwawr

Coedcae Melarian

BRYNHAULOG TERR 1
JAMES ST 2
DANYDERI ST 3

Craig Fforchneol

Aberaman IND EST

Oaklands Prim Sch

Cwmneol Farm

Nant Neol

Godreaman

NELSON ST 1
GORDON ST 2

PARK VIEW TERR

Capcoch Prim Sch

GROVE TERR 1
GRAIG CRES 2

GRAIG AVE

TRENEOL

NORTH VIEW TERR

Coed Aberaman

MARY ST

MARGARET ST

Cwmaman

Cwm Du

CF44

JOHN ST

Abercwmboi

WILLIAM ST 1
RICHARD ST 2
ST PETERS CL 3

BRONALLT TERR

Cwm Aman

Coed Penrhiw-angen

Mast

St JOSEPH'S TERR

PARK VIEW

NEW VILLAS

Penrhiw-angen Plantation

Blaencwmboi

Coed Cae Aberaman

CF45

Twyn-y-Briddallt

CF43

Tarren Pwlfa

Maen Tri-gwr

A B C D E F

CF44

Ffyñnon-y-gôg

Mast

CEFNPENNAR RD

CEFN-PENNAR RD

Nant Pennar

Coed Tir Estyll

Cefn-pennar Farm

PH

Cefnpennar

Resr

GREENFIELD TERR

FFORDD-Y-DERWEN

1 LLWYN BEDW
2 BLACKBERRY PL

TŶ-CROCHENDY TERR

Panwaun Pwll-gwellt

Mynydd Merthyr

Twyn Sych

CF48

CF45

Rhyd y Ceubren

Pen Rhiwporthmon

THE AVENUE

Cràig y Dyffryn

CH

Gelli-ddu-fawr Plantation

Gelli-ddu-fâch

Gelli-ddu-fâch Plantation

Cwmpennar

Cwar y Wningen

LON-Y-FELIN

HEOL PENRHIW

MIDDLE ROW

HIGH ROW

LOW ROW

MILL RD

Mountain Ash General

H

Cwm Boi

B4275

Fernhill

FERNHILL

GLENBOI

Mountain Ash Comp Sch Ysgol Gyfun Aberpennar

Mountain Ash Flats

LADY ABARDARE FLATS

Liby

BECKETT ST

THE TRIANGLE

Cemy

ABER-FERNIG RD

Caegarw

MOUNTAIN ASH (ABERPENNAR)

ABERDARE RD

PDI CL

Cemy

GLENBOI

GLEN CL

ABERDARE ROW-ISAF RD

CWM ALARCH CL

CWM ALARCH

Glenboi Prim Sch

PO

Fernhill

FOREST VIEW

SIERRA PINES

MEADOW CL

HARCOURT RD

CADWALADR ST

WOODLAND ST

COMMERCIAL ST

NEW RD

Alun Cynon

OXFORD ST

CRESSELLY VILLAS

ALLEN ST

AUSTIN ST

FOX ST

PHILLIP ST

LONDON

ARNOLD ST

Sch

FFOREST TERR

1 ALEXANDRA TERR
2 DAN-Y-COED
3 THE POPLARS
4 ROWAN CL
5 CRESSELLY VILLAS
6 NAVIGATION YD
7 CLAS -Y- DDERWEN

Fforest-uchaf

Glenboi

Graig Isaf

Graig-Hwnt Plantation

Pen Rhiw-fer

Craig Abercwmboi

Darranlas

Craig Darren-las

GORSEDD ST

ROCK ST

ABERPENNAR ST

KINGCRAFT ST

CERIDWEN ST

COPLESTONE ST

GWERNIFOR ST

CWRT LLANWONNO

GILHAUL TERR

GILHAUL RD

TH

Cts

WOODLAND RD

HAMILTON ST

LYTE ST

PARK HILL

VICTOR ST

PAMELA ST

CLIFF ST

STREAM ST

PRYCE ST

BEADON ST

DARRAN RD

1 CARADOC RD
2 CARADOC RD

MISKIN RD

Sch

BROOK ST

BAILEY ST

CONSORT ST

ALBERT ST

VICTORIA ST

CARDIFF RD

BRYN-Y-TERR

FOREST LEVEL

UPPER FOREST LEVEL

LOWER FOREST LEVEL

DWR FFOREST

Fforest

Newtown

JOHN ST

STRAND ST

1 CLAS GWERNIFOR
2 MISKIN TERR

Miskin

PENRHIWCEIBER RD

B4275

A4059

PWM CYNON IRNS PK

Bryn Ifor

MOUNT PLEASANT

CLARENCE ST

OAKLAND

YORK ST

ALBANY ST

THOMAS ST

ARTHUR ST

WINDSOR RD

GWENNYTH ST

GLANDYION ST

Sch

Sch

D3
1 NAVIGATION ST
2 THE POPLARS
3 FOUNTAIN ST
4 GRAIG ST
5 UNION ST
6 TY SEION
7 CHANCERY LA
8 KNIGHT ST
9 BRUCE ST

10 QUARRY RD
11 QUARRY COTTS
E1
1 MOUNT PLEASANT COTTS
2 NAVIGATION VILLAS
3 JONES ST
4 HUGHES ST
5 JAMES ST
6 MOUNT PLEASANT PL
7 EDWARDS ST

8 PROSSER ST
9 MORGAN ST
10 HILL HO
11 PARK HILL
12 WOODFIELD TERR
13 PARK ST
14 TY RFELIN ST
15 GLADSTONE ST
16 GLADSTONE TERR

03 A 04 B C 05 D E F

8 7 01 6 00 5 4 3 99 2 1 98

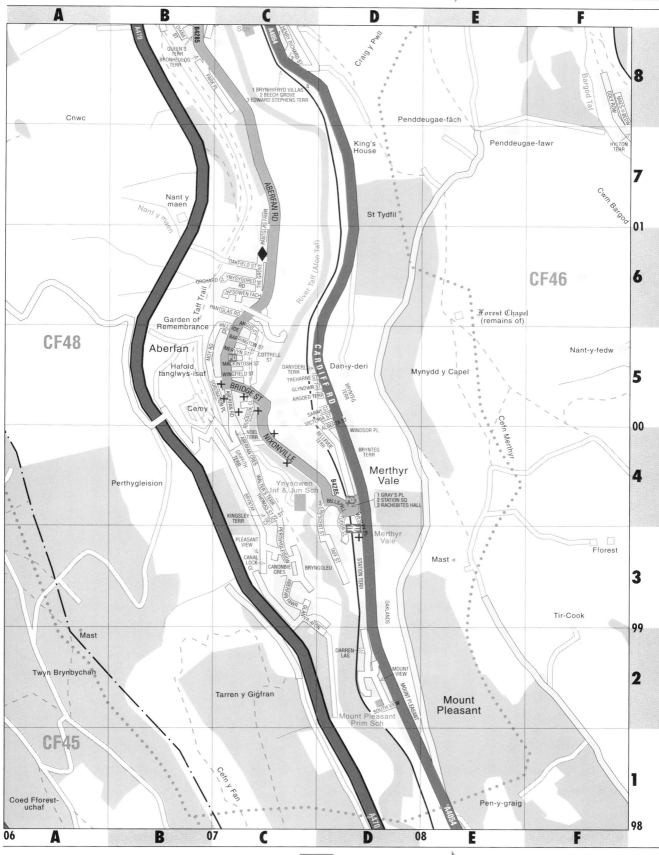

A **B** **C** **D** **E** **F**

8

Bedlinog Farm

y Graig

Coed yr Hendre

Bryn-rhe

Cefn Gelligaer

CF81

Mount Pleasant

Bedlinog

Tylaglas

Blaen-Nant-wen

Garth-gynydd

Llan Uchaf

7

Bedlinog Cty Jun Sch

Cwmfelin Farm

Bedlinog Cty Inf Sch

MORIAH ST

B4255

PO

EDWARDS PLACE

STATION TERR

CHAPEL ST

HIGH ST

MURIEL TERR

1 WOODLAND PL

1 ASHGROVE VILLAS
2 WOODLAND COTTS

BEDLINOG TERR

GROVE TERR

HYLTON TERR

BEDW RD

HIGH ST

UPPER

GRAIG TERR

LEWIS ST

PLEASANT ST

GEORGE ST

MARY ST

DRAIG-Y-HENDRE

COMMERCIAL ST

01

Bryn-rhedyn

PH

GARTH TERR

OAKLAND ST

Cwmfelin

6

Mast

Twyn-giden Farm

Pen-mount

Clawdd-trawscae

5

Nant y Fedw

Ty'r-ywen

LC

CF46

Cemy

Craig-fargoed

Cware Mawr

00

Cefn Gelligaer

4

Coed Cae

Cwm Bargod

Bargod Taf

Craig Fargod

Taff Bargoed Ctr

Gilfach-maen Uchaf

3

Tirlan Farm

Nant Ddu

99

Tynewydd

Pen-craig-fargoed

2

Cwm Cothi

Penrhiw

CF82

1

Cefn-fforest

Coed Cefn-fforest

AEL-Y-BRYN

Coed Cwm-cothi

Taff Merthyr Garden Village

B4255

BRON-DEG

MAEN GILFACH

MAEN CANOL

98

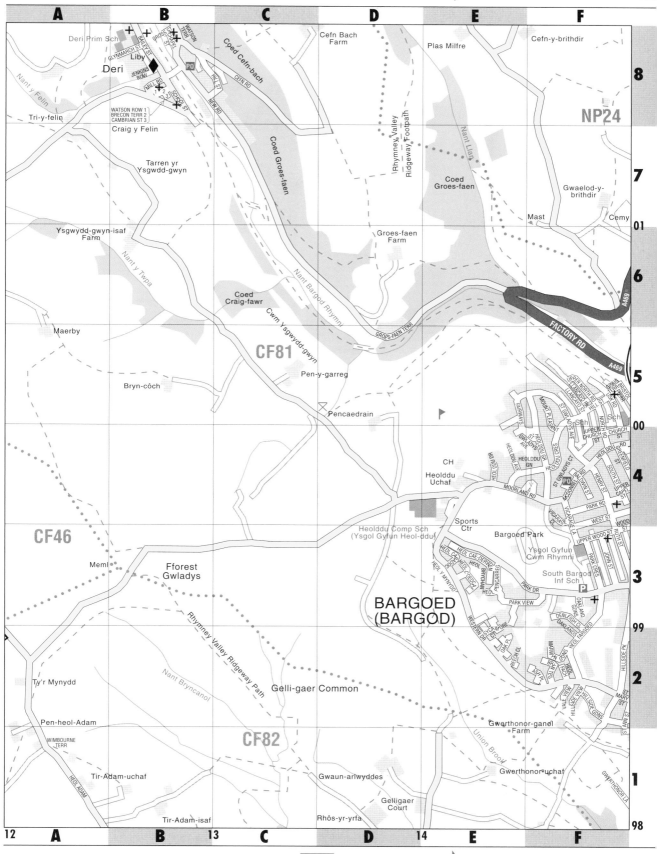

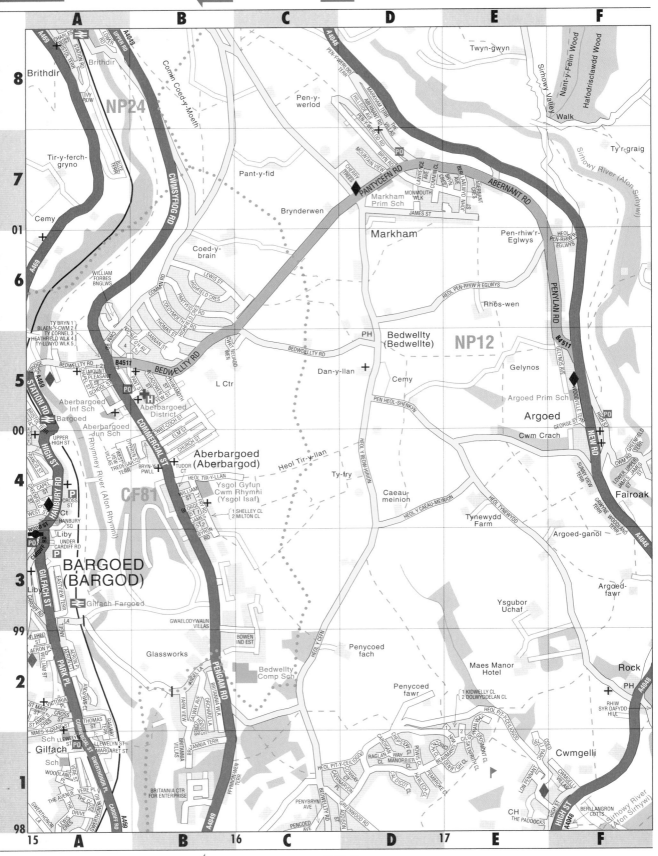

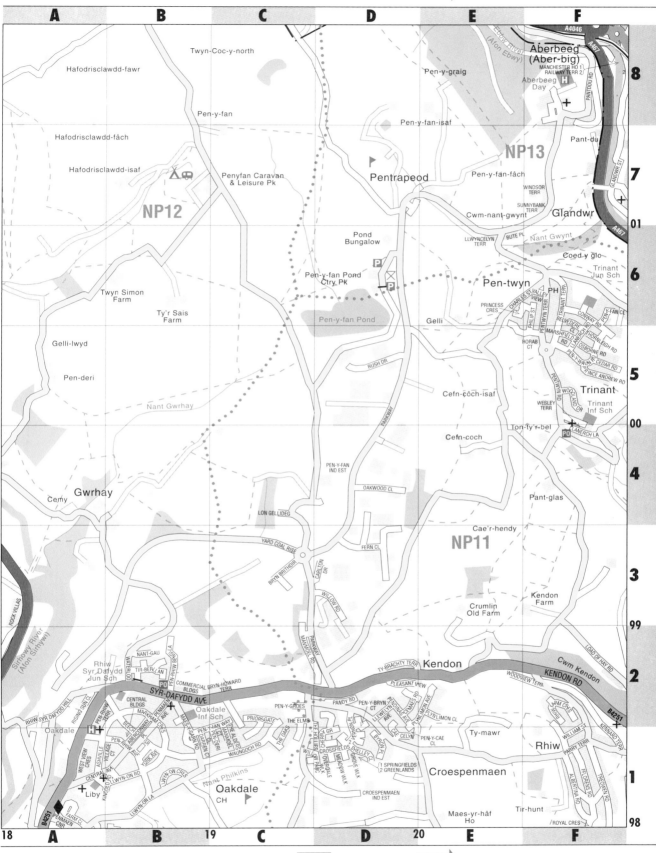

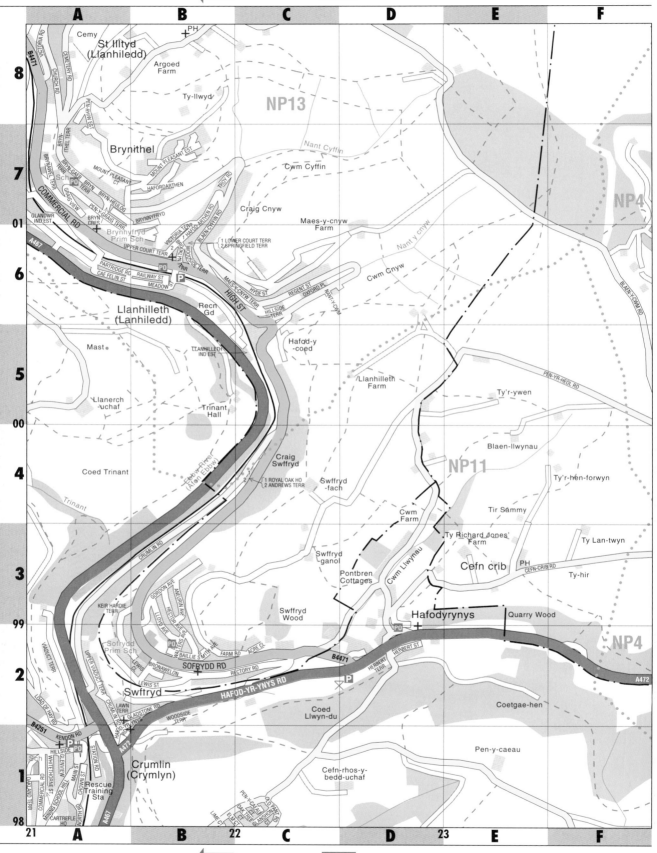

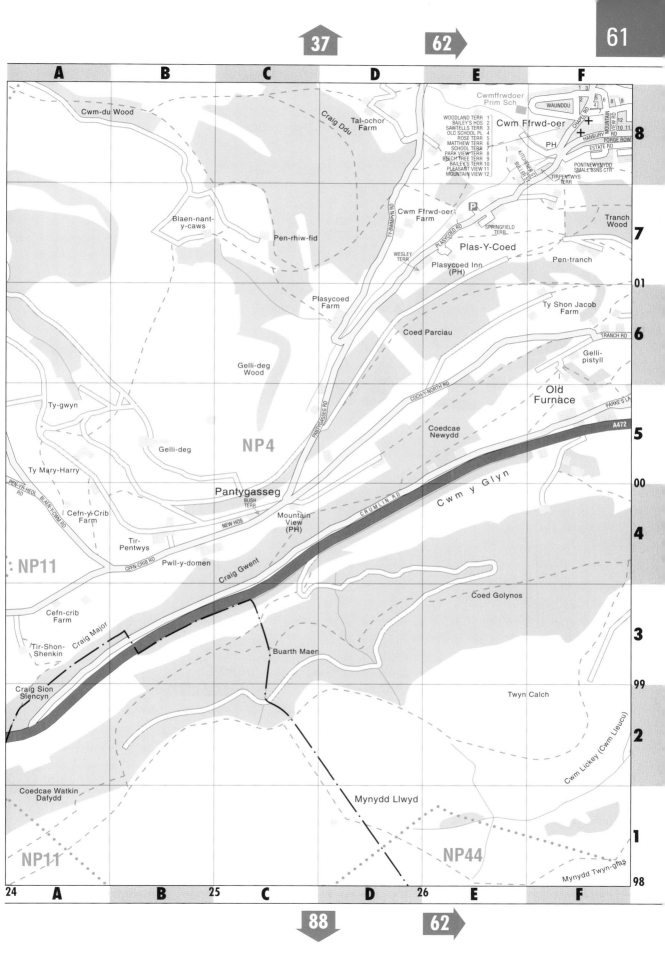

A B C D E F

8

WOODLAND TERR 1
BAILEY'S HOS 2
SAWTELLS TERR 3
OLD SCHOOL PL 4
ROSE TERR 5
MATTHEW TERR 6
SCHOOL TERR 7
PARK VIEW TERR 8
BEECH TREE TERR 9
BAILEY'S TERR 10
PLEASANT VIEW 11
MOUNTAIN VIEW 12

Cwmffrwdoer Prim Sch
WAUNDDU
Cwm Ffrwd-oer
PH
FORGE ROW
PONTNEWYNYDD SMALL BSNS CTR
TIRPENTWYS TERR

Cwm Ffrwd-oer Farm
SPRINGFIELD TERR
Tranch Wood
7

Plas-Y-Coed
Plasycoed Inn (PH)
Pen-tranch
01

WESLEY TERR

Cwm-du Wood
Craig Ddu
Tal-ochor Farm

Blaen-nant-y-caws
Pen-rhiw-fid

Plasycoed Farm
Coed Parciau
Ty Shon Jacob Farm
6
TRANCH RD
Gelli-pistyll

Gelli-deg Wood
Old Furnace
PARKE'S LA

Ty-gwyn
COCH-Y-NORTH RD
Coedcae Newydd
A472
5

NP4
Gelli-deg
Cwm y Glyn
00

Ty Mary-Harry
Pantygasseg
PEN-YR-HEOL RD   BLAEN-CWM RD
Cefn-y-Crib Farm
BUSH TERR
NEW HOS
Mountain View (PH)
CRUMLIN RD
4

Tir-Pentwys
Pwll-y-domen
Craig Gwent
Coed Golynos

: NP11
CEFN-CRIB RD
Cefn-crib Farm
Buarth Maen
3

Craig Major
Tir-Shon-Shenkin
Twyn Calch
99

Craig Sion Slencyn
2

Cwm Lickey (Cwm Lleucu)

Coedcae Watkin Dafydd
Mynydd Llwyd
1

NP11
NP44
Mynydd Twyn-glas
98

24 A   B   25 C   D   26 E   F

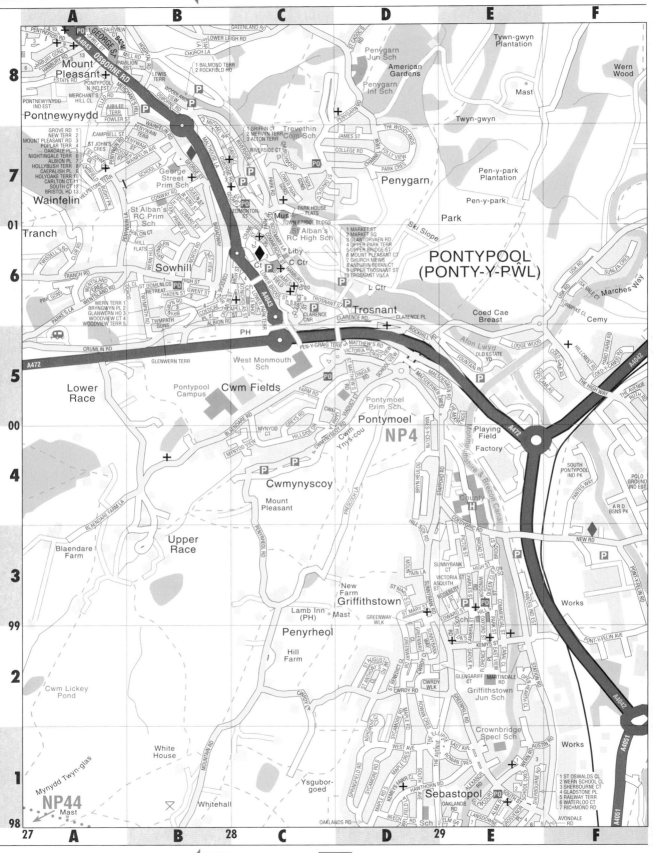

A B C D E F

8

Mount Pleasant

Pontnewynydd

7

Wainfelin

01

Tranch

Sowhill

6

PONTYPOOL
(PONTY-Y-PWL)

Penygarn

Park

Trosnant

5

Lower Race

Cwm Fields

Pontymoel

NP4

00

4

Cwmynyscoy

Mount Pleasant

Griffithstown

Upper Race

3

Blaendare Farm

New Farm

99

Penyrheol

Lamb Inn (PH)

Hill Farm

2

Cwm Lickey Pond

1

Mynydd Twyn-glas

NP44
Mast

White House

Ysgubor-goed

Sebastopol

Whitehall

Works

98

27 A 28 B C 28 D 29 E F

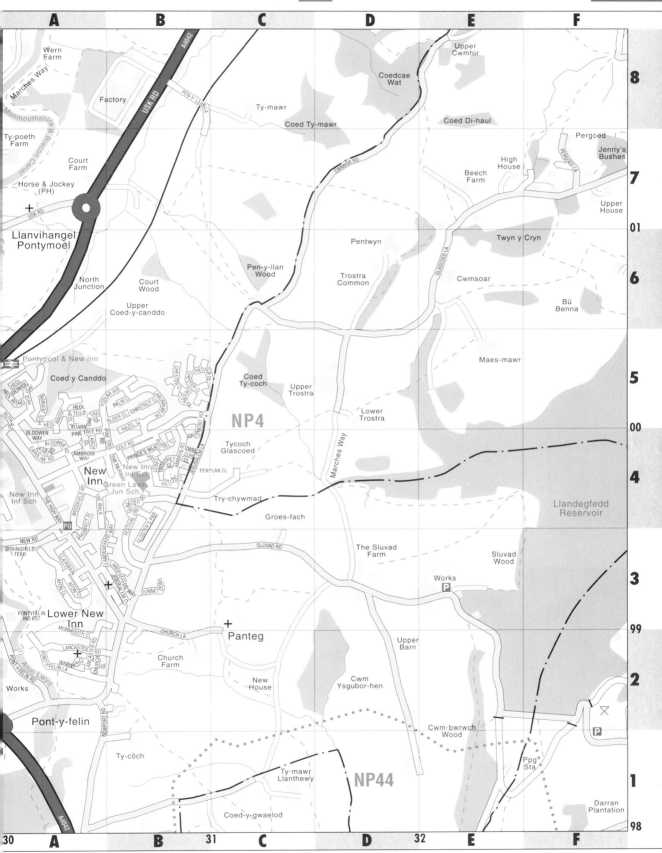

Wern Farm
Marches Way
Monmouthshire & Brecon Canal
Ty-poeth Farm
Court Farm
Horse & Jockey (PH)
Llanvihangel Pontymoel
North Junction
Factory
USK RD
PEN-Y-LLAN LA
USK RD
A4042

Ty-mawr
Coed Ty-mawr
CWMHIR RD
Pen-y-llan Wood
Court Wood
Upper Coed-y-canddo

Upper Cwmhir
Coedcae Wat
Coed Di-haul
High House
Beech Farm
GLASCOED LA
Pentwyn
Trostra Common
Twyn y Cryn
Cwmsoar
Bû Benna

Pergoed
Jenny's Bushes
PERGOED LA
Upper House

Pontypool & New Inn
Coed y Canddo
NP4
Coed Ty-coch
Upper Trostra
Lower Trostra
Maes-mawr

New Inn
New Inn Inf Sch
Green Lawn
New Inn Jun Sch
New Inn Inf Sch
Tycoch Glascoed
PENYLAN CL
Try-chywmad
Groes-fach
Marches Way
00

Llandegfedd Reservoir

New Rd
Springfield Terr
PO
Pontyfelin Ind Est
Lower New Inn
Pont-y-felin
Works
MONMOUTH CL
CHURCH LA
LANCASTER RD
Panteg
Church Farm
New House
SLUVAD RD
The Sluvad Farm
Works
P
Sluvad Wood
Upper Barn
Cwm Ysgubor-hen

Ty-côch
Ty-mawr Llanthewy
NP44
Coed-y-gwaelod
Cwm-bwrwch Wood
Ppg Sta
Darran Plantation

A B C D E F

8

7

97

6

5

96

4

3

95

2

1

94

52 A B 53 C D 54 E F

SA14

Morfa-Bacas

Millennium Coastal Park

River Loughor
(Afon Llwchwr)

Dalton's Point

Sewage Farm

WEST END   BEACH RD
GLANMOR TERR   PH
SEA VIEW
1 BELLE VUE
2 BLODWEN TERR
STATION TERR
STATION RD
B4295
THE PROMENADE
HALL LA
GREENACRES
CRAIG-Y-COED
CAE FOLLAND
BENSON ST
PO
BENSON RD
TAN-Y-BRYN TERR
NURSES CAR
MILL ST
GOWER TERR
PENCHENDY RD
Pen-y-Lan
Parc-hendy
TRINITY LA
PARK RD
Sch
BANC BACH
BETHEL RD
MAES-YR-HAF
DUNRAVEN CL
1
2
3
VICTORIA RD
AEL-Y-BRYN
PEN-Y-LAN
PARC HENDY CRES
Pen y Gaer
MYRTLE
BENSON TERR 1
BRYNFA TERR 2
VICTORIA ROW 3
Pen-clawdd
Llottrog
Cemy
BLAENCEDI
BLUE ANCHOR RD
CHURCH LA
CABAN ISAAC RD
LLWYNEWYDD
Cefn-bychan

Sewage Works

Salthouse Point

Salthouse Pill

Crofty
CROFTY IND EST
PENCAERFENNI PK
SALTHOUSE CL
RHYD Y FENNI
FORGE RD
PO
PH
CHAPEL RD
HAZELTREE COPSE
PENCAERFENNI LA
NEW RD
Pen-caer-fenny

Gelli-orllwyn

SA4

RIVERSIDE
Llanmorlais
TRE M Y MOR
STATION RD
WERN RD
Wern Fabian Farm

Morlais River

Pwll-y-froga

Llanmorlais Prim Sch

Cwm-cynnar

Llwyndyris Farm

B4295

Cerrig Màn

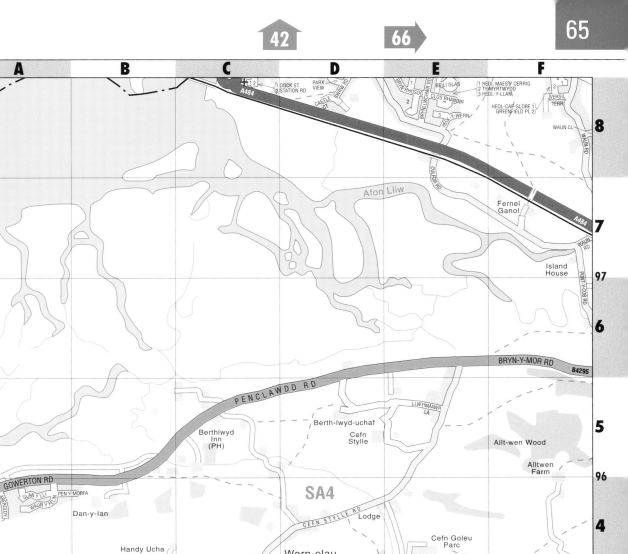

A B C D E F

8 7 97 6 5 96 4 3 95 2 1 94

55 A B 56 C D 57 E F

1 DOCK ST
2 STATION RD

PARK VIEW

CASTLE CT
BWLW RD

1 HEOL MAES Y CERRIG
2 TY MYRTWYDD
3 HEOL-Y-LLAN

BRYNLWYCHWR RD
BEILI GLAS
CLOS RHANDIR
HEOL-Y-WERN
BRYN RHOSOG

HEOL-CAE-GLOBE 1
GREENFIELD PL 2

VERSIL TERR

A484

WAUN CL
WAUN RD

CULFON RD

Afon Lliw

Fernel Ganol

WAUN RD

PONT-Y-COB RD

Island House

A484

BRYN-Y-MOR RD

B4295

PENCLAWDD RD

LLWYNMAWR LA

Berth-lwyd-uchaf
Cefn Stylle

Allt-wen Wood

Alltwen Farm

Berthlwyd Inn (PH)

GOWERTON RD

ABERGEDY
GLAN Y LLI
WAUN Y PEN
PEN Y MORFA

LLINEL RD

SA4

Dan-y-lan

CEFN STYLLE RD
Lodge

Cefn Goleu Parc

Craig Cefngolau

Handy Ucha

Wern-olau

Heol-las

Rhean-fawr

CH

Cefngoleu Farm

CAE MANSEL RD

Tir-cethin

Blue Anchor

BLUE ANCHOR RD

PH

Cwm-mawr -isaf

Gron-gaer

Wernbwll

Pant-glas

Pen-y-wern Wood

GOWERTON RD

Bryn-hir Farm

Penyrheol

Poundffald

PENTWYN

Wr Twr

MISTY HILLS CL

PH

JOINERS RD

DUNVANT RD

Cefn-draw

CEFN-Y-DRAW
TRAMWYDOL RD
CILONEN RD

BRYN-Y-MOR
COED LAN
PANT Y DWR
WYNDERW

PO

CHAPEL RD

Three Crosses

Cwm-nant- uchaf

MAES Y CEFN
ORCHARD DR

Crwys Prim Sch

Prior's Wood

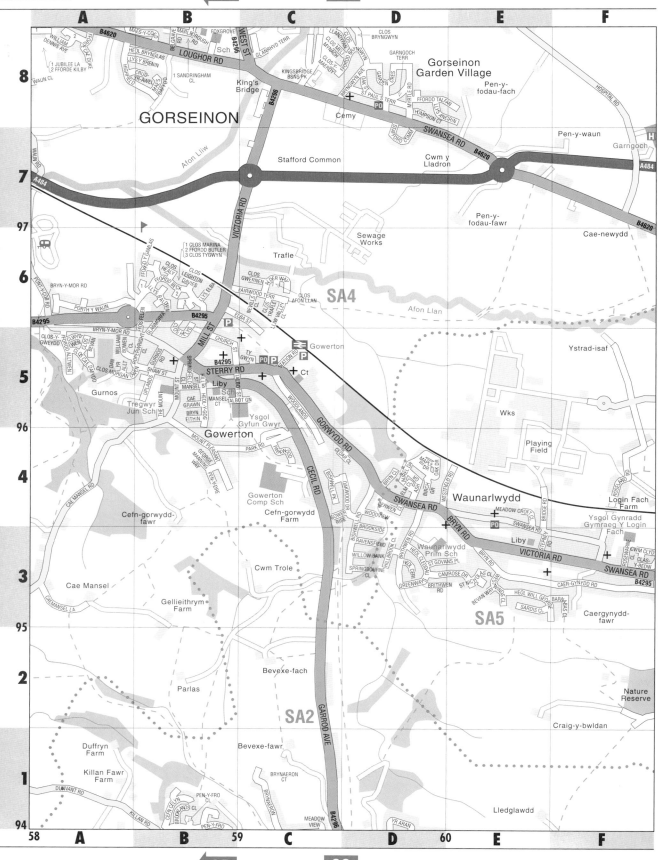

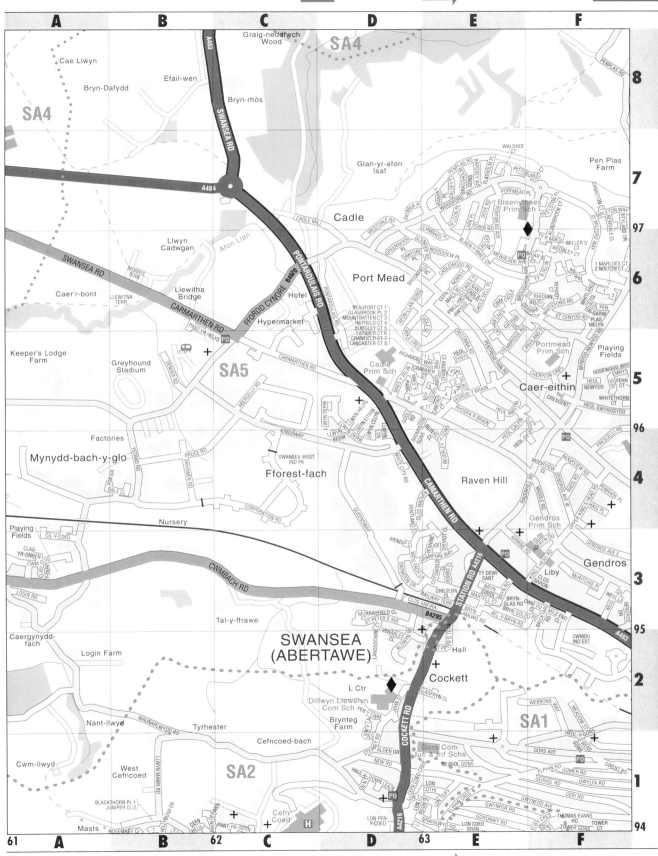

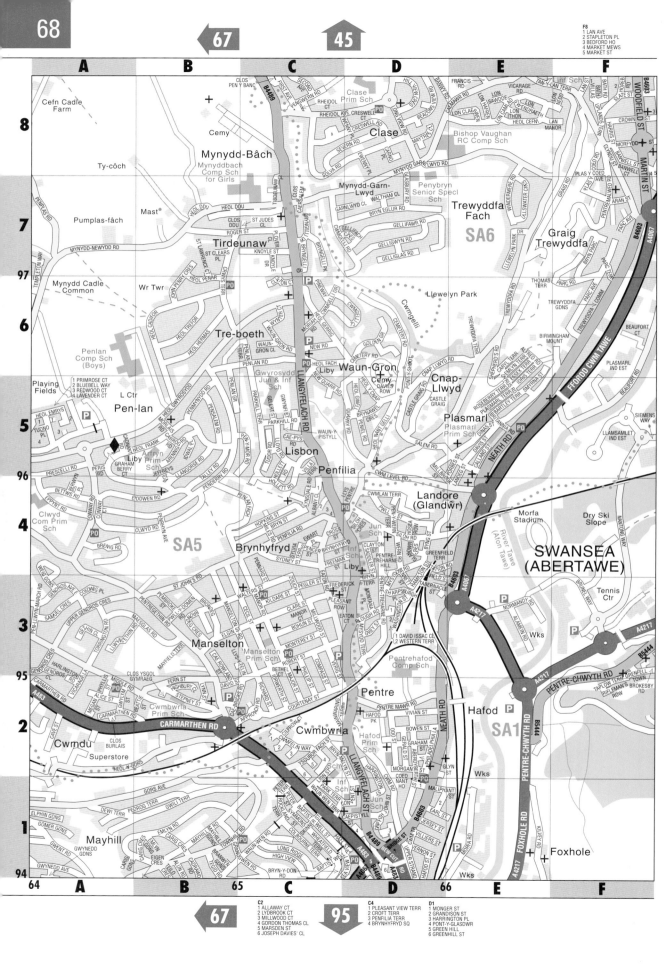

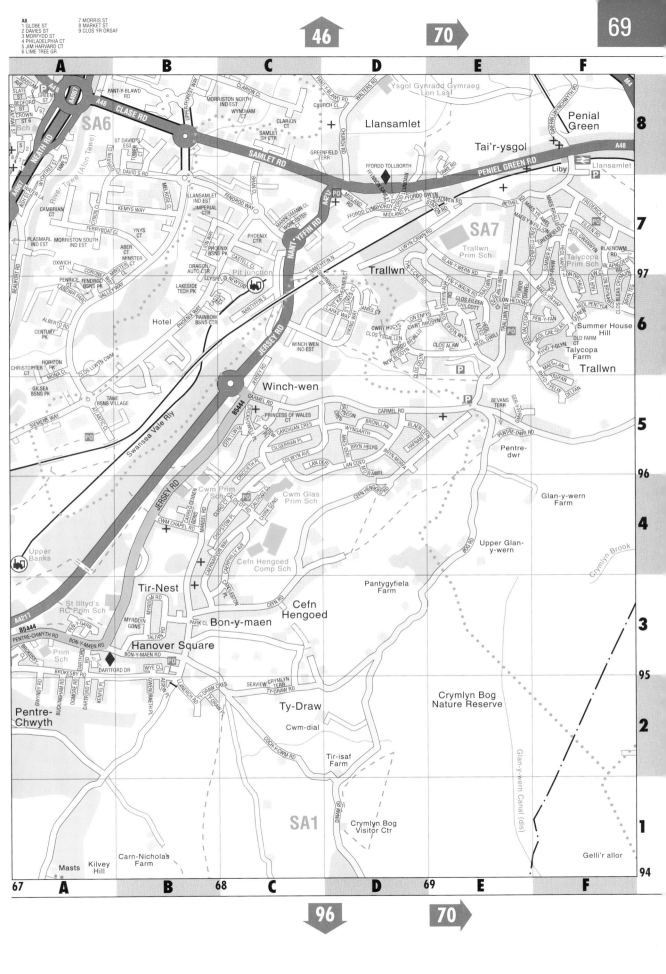

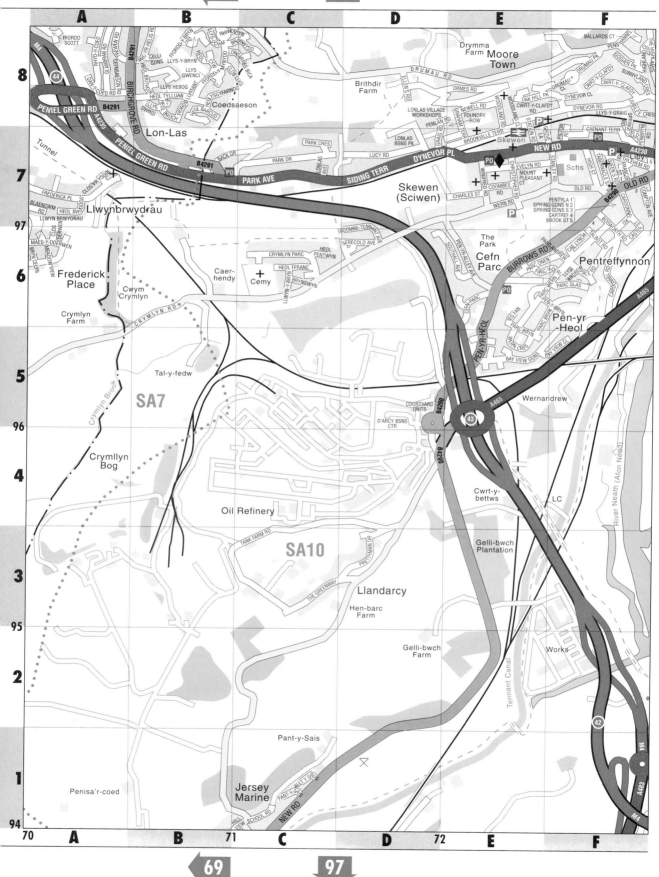

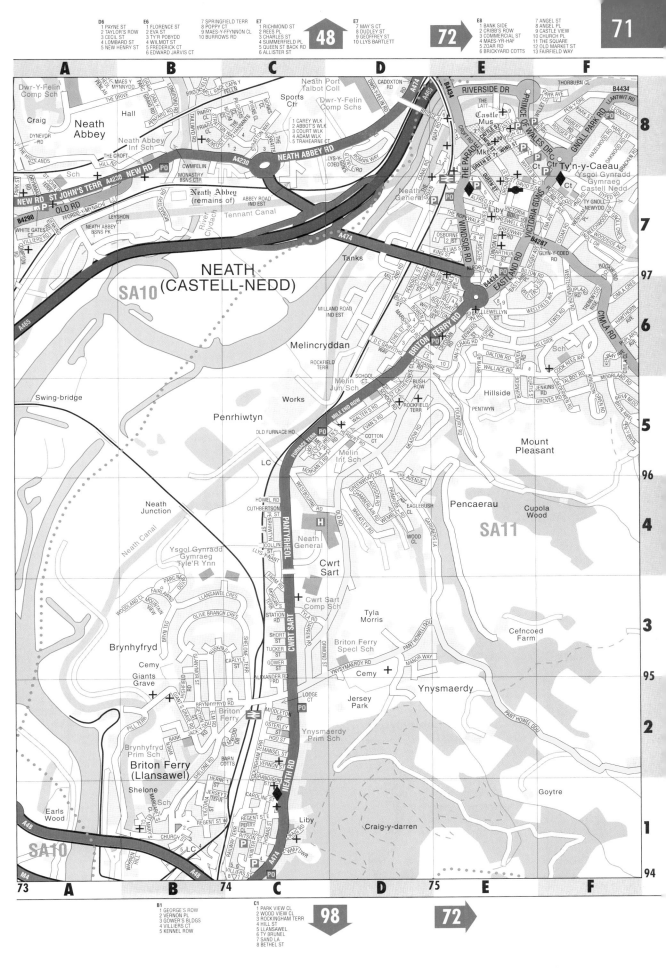

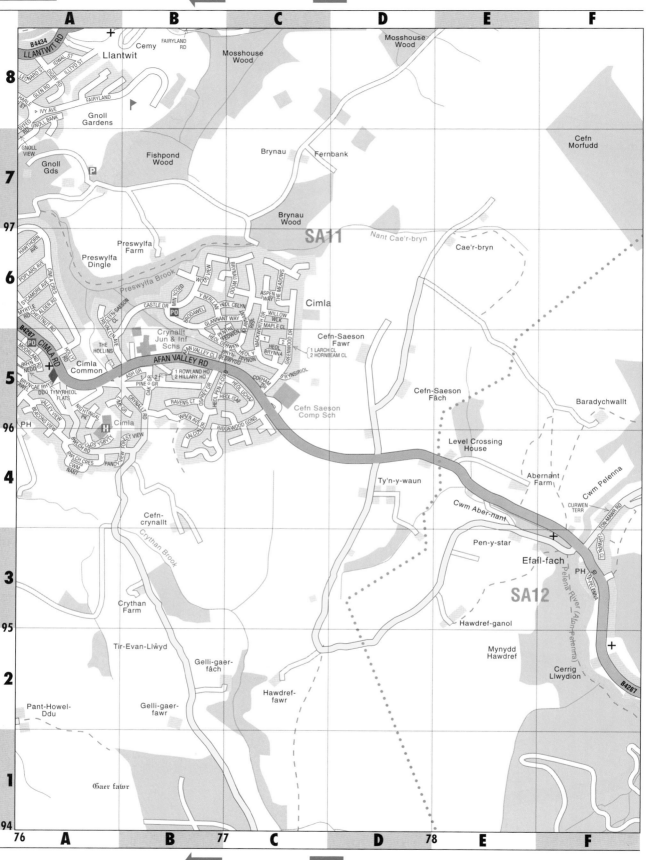

A **B** **C** **D** **E** **F**

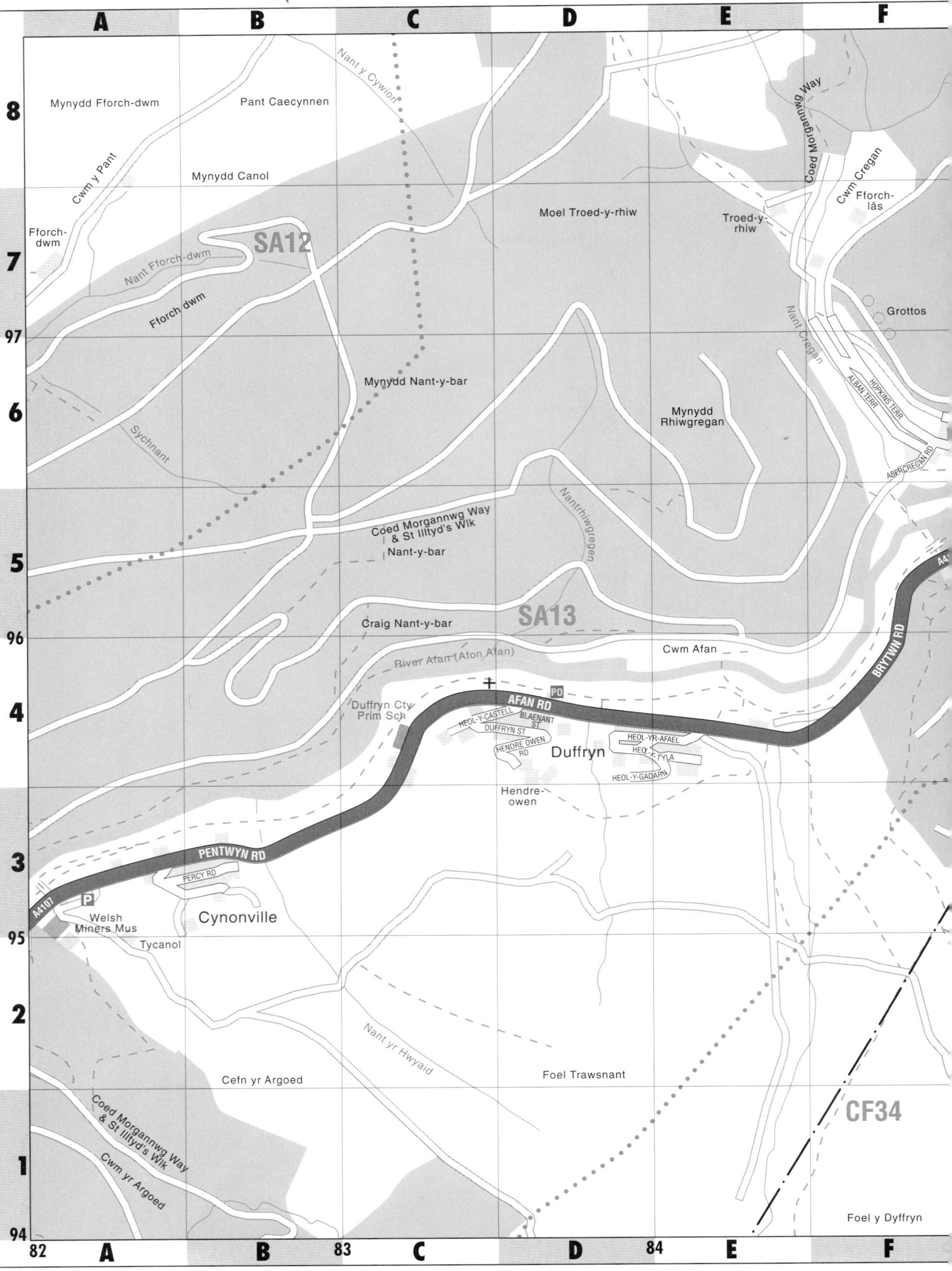

8

Mynydd Fforch-dwm

Pant Caecynnen

Cwm y Pant

Mynydd Canol

Coed Morgannwg Way

Cwm Cregan

Fforch-
dwm

Fforch-
lâs

7

Nant Fforch-dwm

SA12

Moel Troed-y-rhiw

Troed-y-
rhiw

97

Fforch dwm

Grottos

Sychnant

Mynydd Nant-y-bar

HOPKINS TERR

ALBAN TERR

6

Mynydd
Rhiwgregan

Nant Cregan

ABERCREGAN RD

5

Coed Morgannwg Way
& St Illtyd's Wlk

Nant-y-bar

Nantrhiwgregan

SA13

BRYTWN RD

A4

96

Craig Nant-y-bar

River Afan (Afon Afan)

Cwm Afan

4

Duffryn Cty
Prim Sch

HEOL-Y-CASTELL

DUFFRYN ST

BLAENANT
ST

PO

AFAN RD

HEOL-YR-AFAEL

HEOL-Y-TYLA

HENDRE OWEN
RD

Duffryn

HEOL-Y-GADARN

Hendre-
owen

3

PENTWYN RD

PERCY RD

A4107

95

P

Welsh
Miners Mus

Cynonville

Tycanol

2

Nant yr Hwyaid

1

Coed Morgannwg Way
& St Illtyd's Wlk

Cwm yr Argoed

Cefn yr Argoed

Foel Trawsnant

CF34

94

Foel y Dyffryn

82 **A** **B** **83** **C** **D** **84** **E** **F**

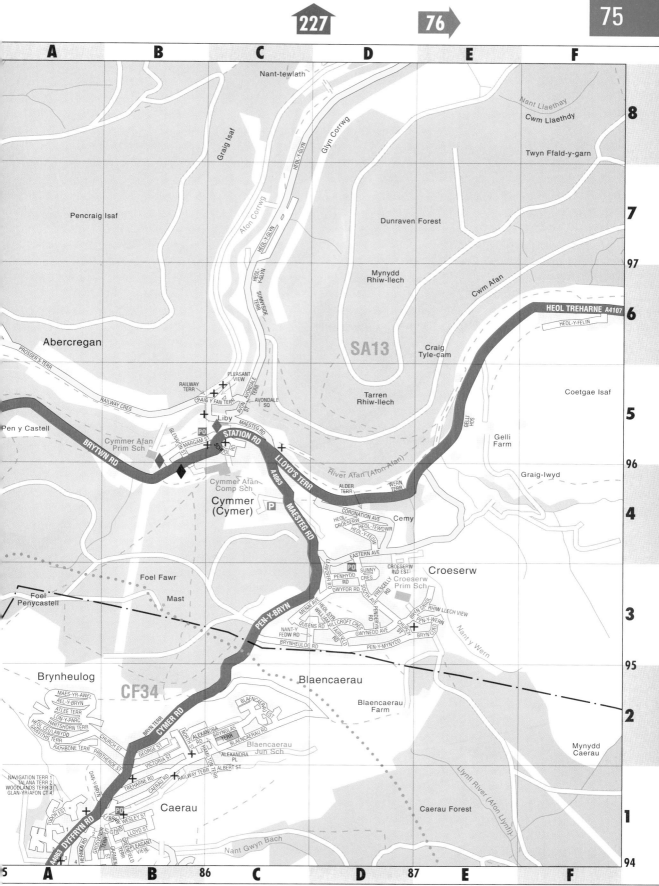

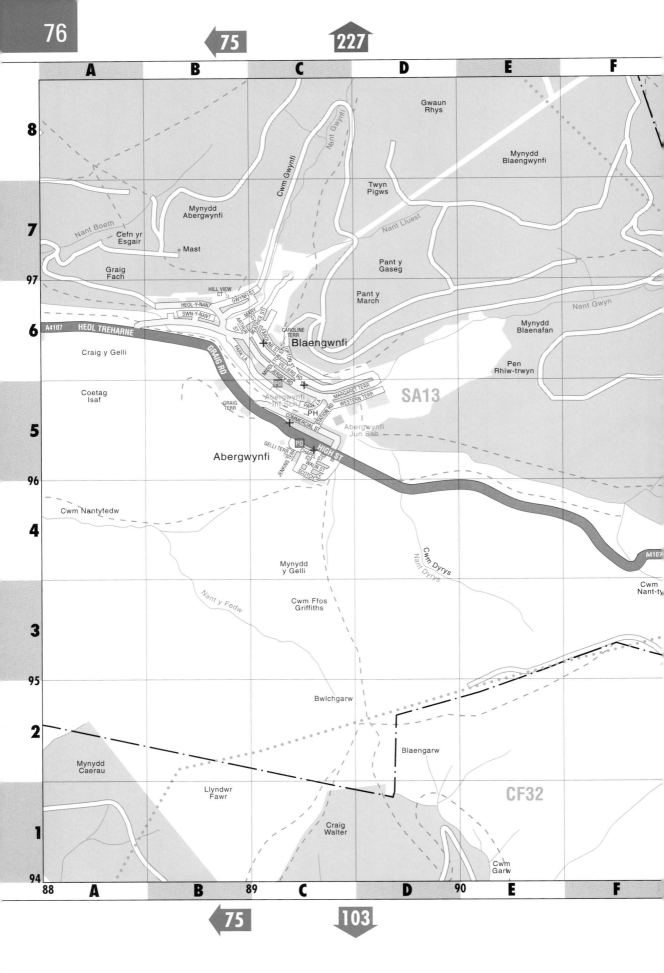

A **B** **C** **D** **E** **F**

8

Gwaun
Rhys

Mynydd
Blaengwynfi

Nant Gwynfi

Cwm Gwynfi

Twyn
Pigws

7

Mynydd
Abergwynfi

Nant Boeth

Cefn yr
Esgair

Mast

Nant Lluest

Pant y
Gaseg

Nant Gwyn

97

Graig
Fach

HILL VIEW
CT

GWYNFI ST

Pant y
March

Mynydd
Blaenafan

HEOL-Y-NANT

SWN-Y-NANT

MARY ST

ARTHUR ST

BEATRICE ST

CAROLINE
TERR

Blaengwnfi

Pen
Rhiw-trwyn

6

A4107 HEOL TREHARNE

GRAIG RD

PARK LA

MIDDLETON ST

SKIPTON ST

VILLIERS RD

JERSEY RD

Craig y Gelli

SA13

Coetag
Isaf

GRAIG
TERR

Abergwynfi
Int Sch

PARK LA

STATION RD

MARGARET TERR

WESTERN TERR

PO

PH

5

COMMERCIAL ST

Abergwynfi
Jun Sch

Abergwynfi

GELLI TERR

JENKINS TERR

PO

HIGH ST

CHAPEL ST

WAUN ST

SCOTCH ST

96

Cwm Nantyfedw

4

Mynydd
y Gelli

Cwm Dyrys

Nant Dyrys

A4107

Cwm
Nant-ty

Nant y Fedw

Cwm Ffos
Griffiths

3

95

Bwlchgarw

2

Blaengarw

CF32

Mynydd
Caerau

Llyndwr
Fawr

1

Craig
Walter

Cwm
Garw

94

88 **A** **B** 89 **C** **D** 90 **E** **F**

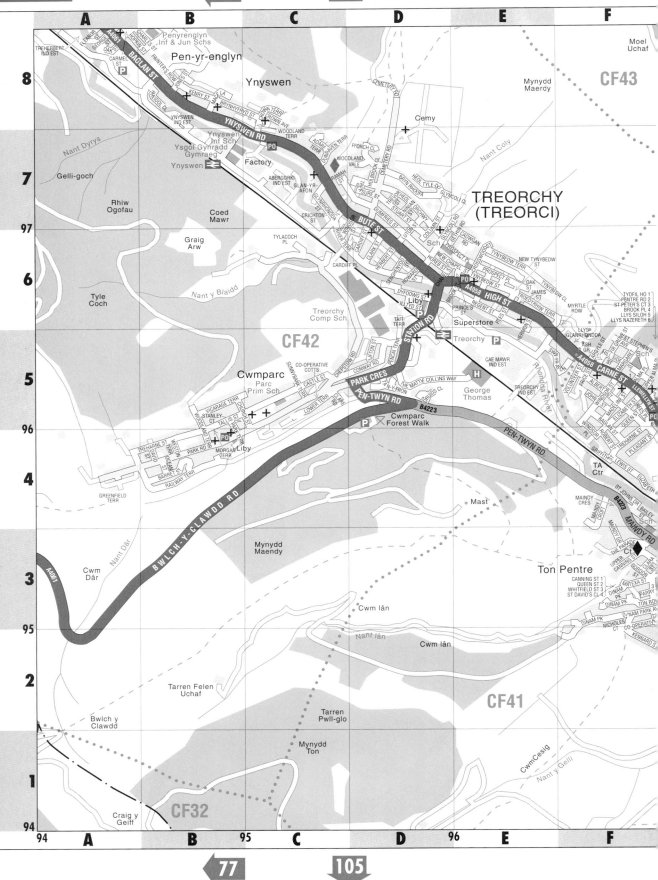

77
51

A B C D E F

8

7

97

6

5

96

4

3

95

2

1

94

94 95 96

A B C D E F

77
105

TREHERBERT IND EST

Penyrenglyn Inf & Jun Schs
Pen-yr-englyn
Ynyswen

Moel Uchaf

CF43

Mynydd Maerdy

ELENNOR RD
GEORGE ST
CHARLES ST
HOPKIN ST
OAK ST
CARMEL ST
TREDDOL CL
KENRY ST
BRYNHYFRYD ST
ST ALBANS
CROWN AVE
JOHN TERR
LA
Ynyswen IND EST
Ynyswen Inf Sch
Ysgol Gynradd Gymraeg
Ynyswen
Factory
PO
WOODLAND TERR
ADARE TERR
DINASWEN TERR
FFORCH CL
WOODLAND VALE
CEMETERY RD

Cemy

BAGLAN ST
YNYSWEN RD

Gelli-goch

Nant Dyrys

Rhiw Ogofau

Tyle Coch

Coed Mawr

Graig Arw

Nant y Blaidd

Nant Coly

Cwm Dâr

A4061

Nant Dâr

CF42

Treorchy Comp Sch

TYLACOCH PL
CRICHTON ST
GLYNRHONDDA ST
GLAN-YR-AFON
ABERGORKI IND EST

Cardiff PL

BUTE ST
STATION RD

RAMAH ST
CSURE ST
DUMFRIES ST
CLARK ST
HERBERT ST
HOWARD ST
CROSS ST
CLIFTON ST
BENCLA TERR
CHEPSTON RD
CONWAY RD
CASTLE ST
SUNNYBANK
LOWER TERR
N-Y-FRON
CHURCH ST
TALLIS ST
VICARAGE RD
STANLEY ST
WOODLAND TERR
TREHARNE ST
WESTON TERR
POBLAN
DAVID ST
BARNET TERR
RAILWAY TERR
MORGAN TERR
PARK RD
Liby
PO
GREENFIELD TERR

Cwmparc
Parc Prim Sch
Co-OPERATIVE COTTS

PARK CRES
PEN-TWYN RD
The MATTIE COLLINS WAY
BRIGGS CL
B4223
Cwmparc Forest Walk
P

BWLCH-Y-CLAWDD RD

Mynydd Maendy

Tarren Felen Uchaf

Bwlch y Clawdd

CF32

Craig y Geiff

TREORCHY (TREORCI)

HEOL TYLE-DU
GLYNCOLI CL
BRYN RHODFA
BERW ST
SCHOOL ST
STUART ST
COLLINS ST
PROSPECT PL
HEOL CADWGAN
Sch
NEW CHAPEL PL
HOREB ST
CHAPEL ST
PRINCE'S ST
REGENT ST
REES ST
HERMON ST
DYFODWG ST
ILLTYD ST
TAFF TERR
PENGELLI TERR
TYNYBEDW TERR
NEW TYNYBEDW ST
PROSPECT PL
OAK ST
JAMES ST
TYNYBEDW CL
TROEDYRHIW TERR
MYRTLE ROW
LLYS GLANRHONDDA

PO
A4058 HIGH ST
Liby
Superstore
A
Treorchy
P
CAE MAWR IND EST
George Thomas
H

Rhondda River

STATION RD

TYDFIL HO 1
PENTRE RD 2
ST PETER'S CT 3
BROOK PL 4
LLYS SILOH 5
LLYS NAZERETH 6

ASH GR
FIR ST
ST STEPHEN'S Sch
BRYNET ST
EAGLE ST
VOLUNTEER ST
PRICE ALBERT ST
MOHR ST
ELIZABETH ST
BAGLAN ST
WINDSOR ST
QUEEN ST
PLEASANT ST
LEWIS ST
ELIZABETH ST
TRE HARNE ST

CARNE ST
A4058
LLEWELYN ST
PRICE

TREORCHY IND EST

SWN-YR-AFON
GRIFFITH ST

CF41

Mast

TA Ctr

ST JOHN'S DR
BAILEY
Sch

MAINDY CRES
MAINDY CR
MAINDY GR
B4223
MAINDY RD
The PARADE
UPPER CANNING ST
GORDON ST
CANNING ST 1
QUEEN ST 2
WHITFIELD ST 3
ST DAVID'S CL 4
Ton Pentre
DINAM PK
MATEXA ST
PARRY ST
TON RD
D/NAM PARK AV
NICHOLES
CO-OPERATIVE
KENNARD ST
DINAM PK

Cwm lân
Nant lân
Cwm lân

CwmCesig
Nant y Gelli

Tarren Pwll-glo

Mynydd Ton

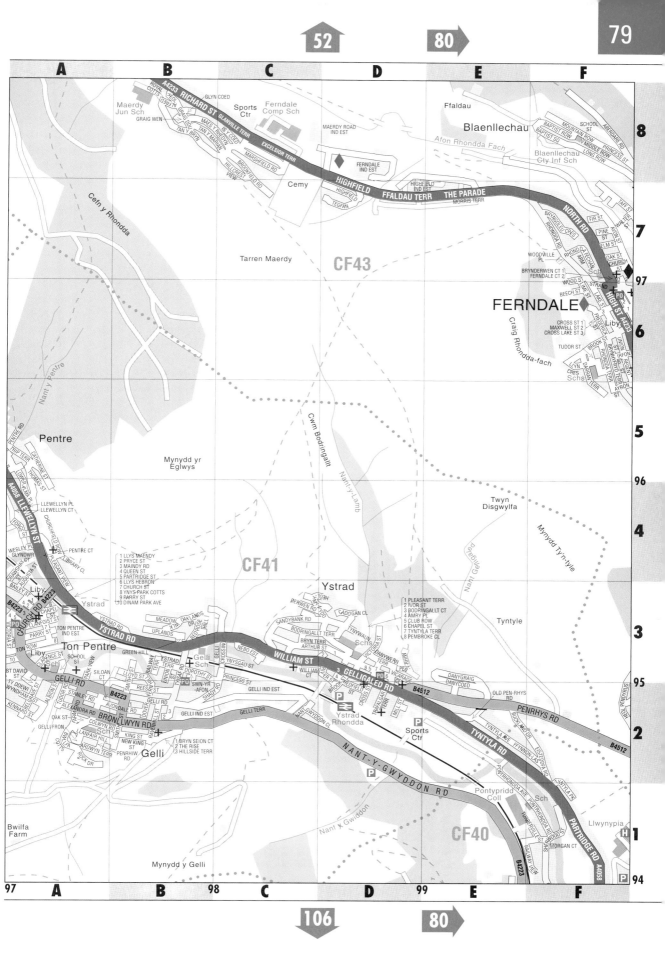

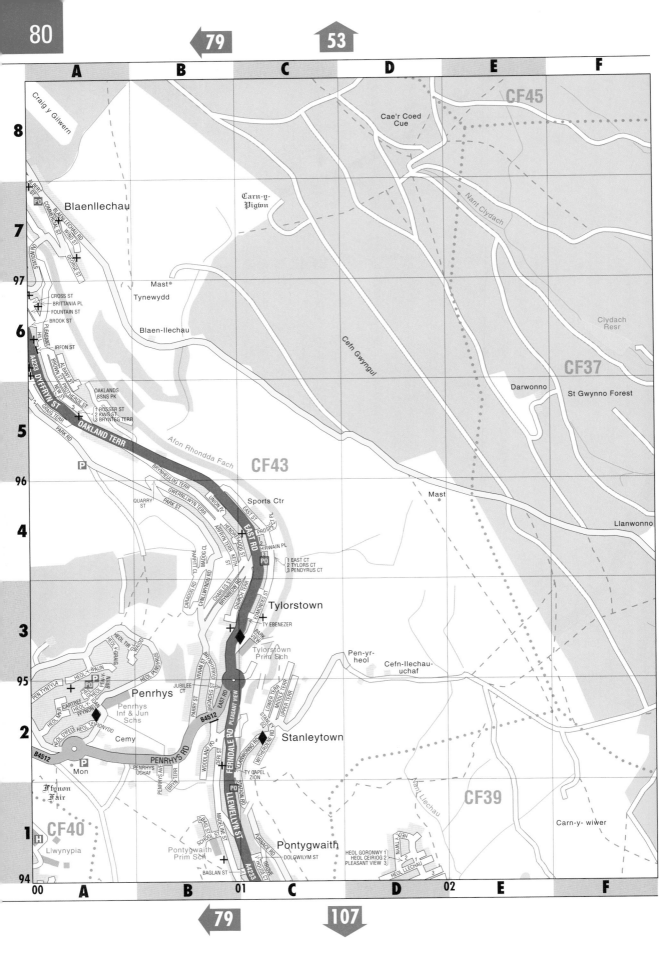

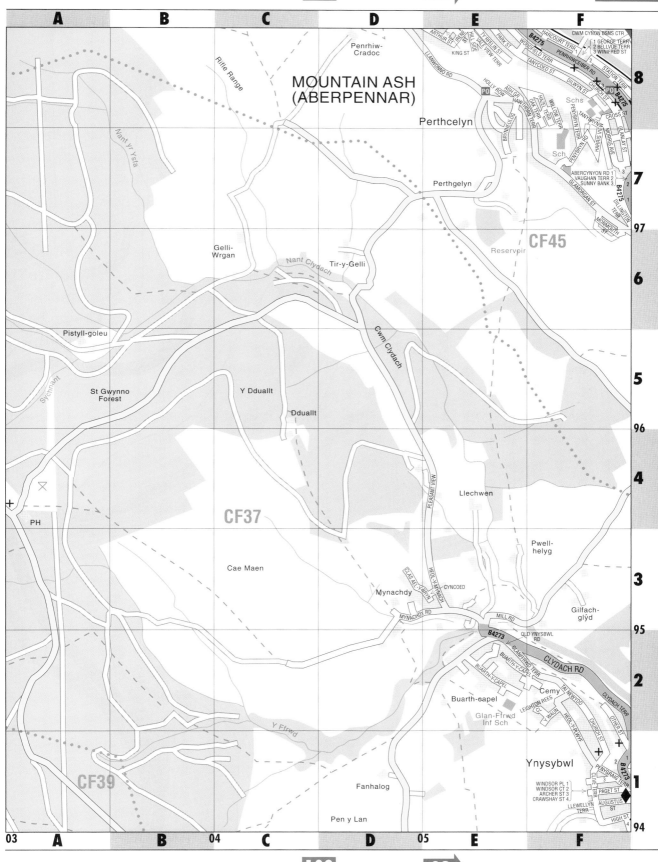

Penrhiw-Cradoc

Rifle Range

MOUNTAIN ASH (ABERPENNAR)

Perthcelyn

Perthgelyn

Nant yr Ysfa

Gelli-Wrgan

Tir-y-Gelli

Nant Clydach

CF45

Reservoir

Cwm Clydach

Pistyll-goleu

St Gwynno Forest

Y Dduallt

Dduallt

Pleasant View

Llechwen

Pwell-helyg

PH

CF37

Cae Maen

Mynachdy

Cyncoed

Heol-y-Mynach

Clas Ael-y-Bryn

Mynachdy Rd

Gilfach-glŷd

Mill Rd

B4273

Old Ynysybwl Rd

Clydach Rd

Glanfrwd Terr

Buarth-y-Capel

Buarth-y-Capel

Buarth-capel

Tal Newydd

Cemy

Glanfrwd Terr

Leighton Rees

Clydach Terr

Y Waun

Heol-y-Lawnt

Church St

Glan-Ffrwd Inf Sch

Y Ffrwd

Ynysybwl

Penygraig Terr

Clive Terr

Paget St

Augustus St

B4273

Other St

CF39

Fanhalog

Pen y Lan

Llewellyn Terr

High St

WINDSOR PL 1
WINDSOR CT 2
ARCHER ST 3
CRAWSHAY ST 4.

Sychnant

CWM CYNON BSNS CTR

1 GEORGE TERR
2 BELLVUE TERR
3 WINIFRED ST

B4275

Harcourt Terr

Penrhiwceiber Rd

Station Terr

Woodfield Terr

Arthur St

Irene St

King St

Park St

Hill Side

Tyreefin St

Vale View Terr

Llanwonno Rd

Holly Row

Ash Gr

Hazel Terr

Hawthorn Terr

Oak Terr

Willow Terr

Bryngoleu

Schs

Sch

Tanybryn

Pentwyn Terr

Harris St

Morris Ave

Glamorgan St

Cross St

Galway St

Church St

Dilwyn St

B4275

ABERCYNYON RD 1
VAUGHAN TERR 2
SUNNY BANK 3

Dilwnstn Terr

B4275

Monmouth St

PO

PO

8

7

97

6

5

96

4

3

95

2

1

94

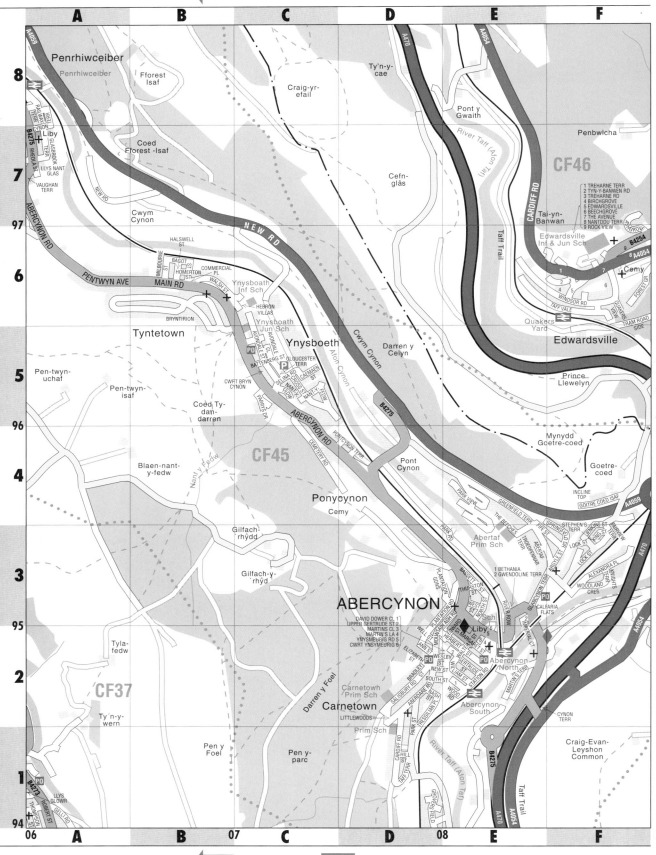

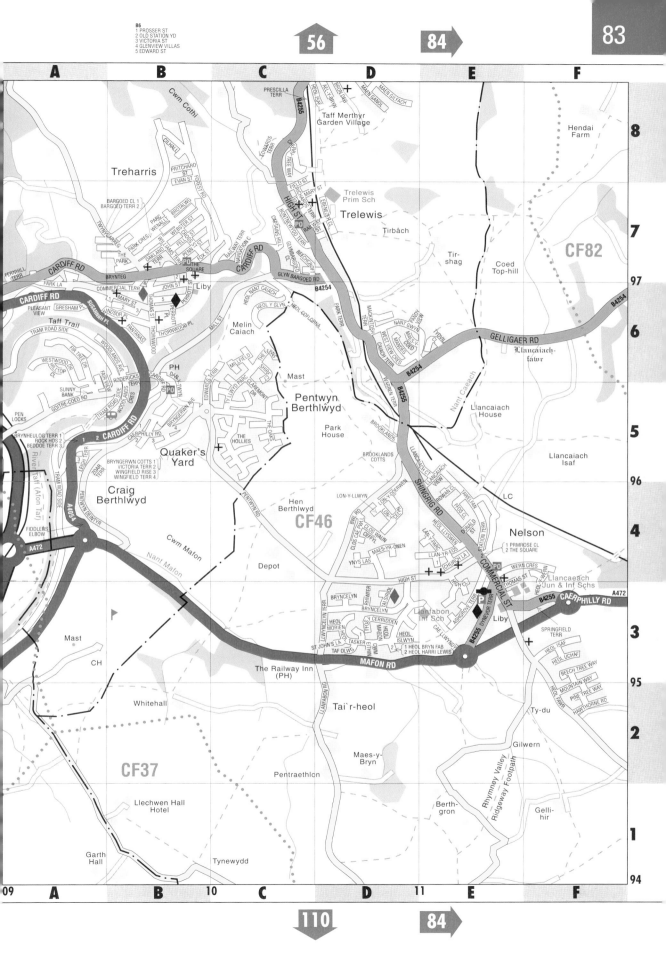

A B C D E F

8

7

97

6

5

96

4

3

95

2

1

94

12 A 13 B C 13 D 14 E F

CF81
Cascade House

Pen-pedair-heol

PENGAM RD   B4254
Berllan-lwyd   NP12

Mount Pleasant

Tir Jack Farm

Churchfield Terr

Tir-y-berth

Tophill
Green Acres
B4254

GELLIGAER RD

Llwyn-goleu
Tir-y-rhen

Maen Cattwg

PH
HADRIAN'S CL
ROMAN RIDGE

LEGION'S WAY
Greenhill Prim Sch

CHURCH RD

Cemy

CHURCH MDW

Castle Hill
Rhymney Valley Ridgeway

Gelligaer Village Prim Sch

Gelliargwellt Uchaf Farm

Gelligaer
Castle Cotts
MAEN RHYDD
HEOL CATTWG
Foot Path

Glyn Gaer
Cefn Hengoed

CF82

Penybryn

Waun Rydd

Rhymney Valley Ridgeway Foot Path

PENALLTA IND EST

Gelliargwellt
GELLIARGWELLT RD
Cefn-llwynau

Waun Rydd

Hengoed Prim Sch

CF46

PH
A472 CAERPHILLY RD
Wern-ganol

Pont y Saeson

Wern-isaf

Tredomen

Tredomen
Tir Twyn Farm

Penalltau-isaf
PENALLTA VILLAS
PENALLTA RD

Tredomen Ind Pk

Ton-teilwr
Penywaun

YSTRAD MYNACH

Ystrad Mynach

Sports Ctr
Cherry Grove Spec Sch
Lewis Girls' Comp Sch

Trinity Fields Sch

A469   A472

F2
1 THE BUNGALOW
1 THE BUNGALOW
2 SHEEN CT

85
59

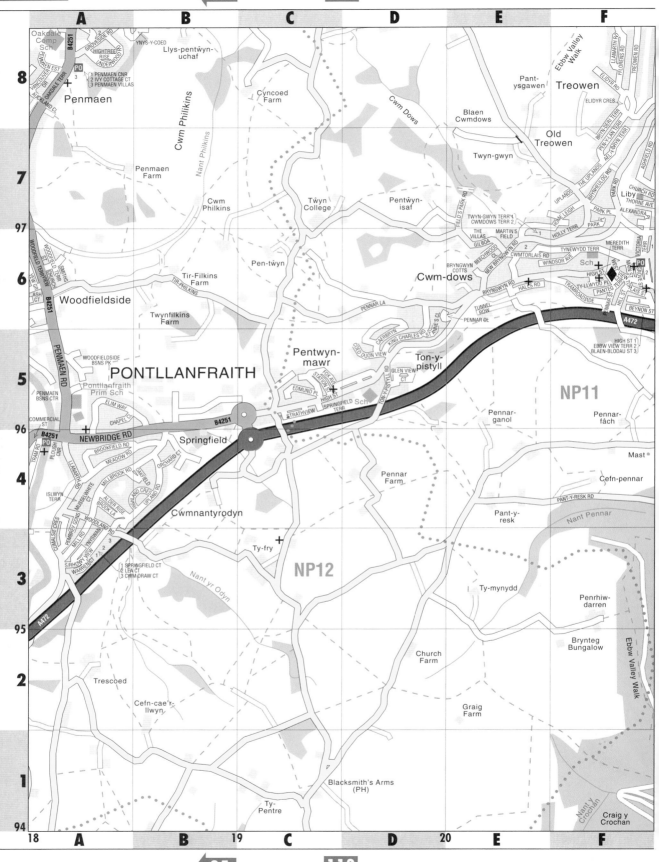

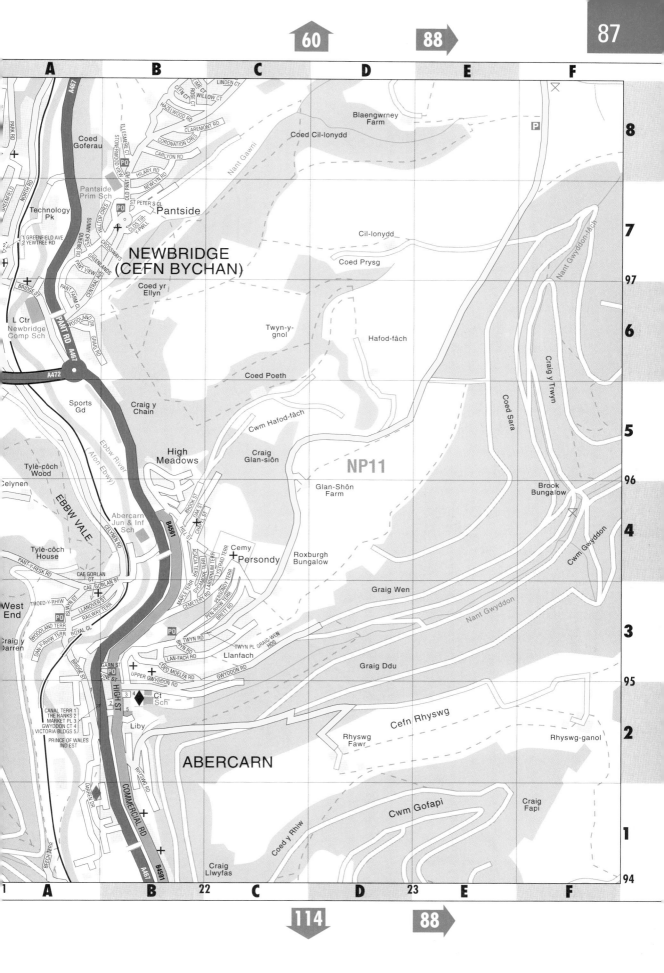

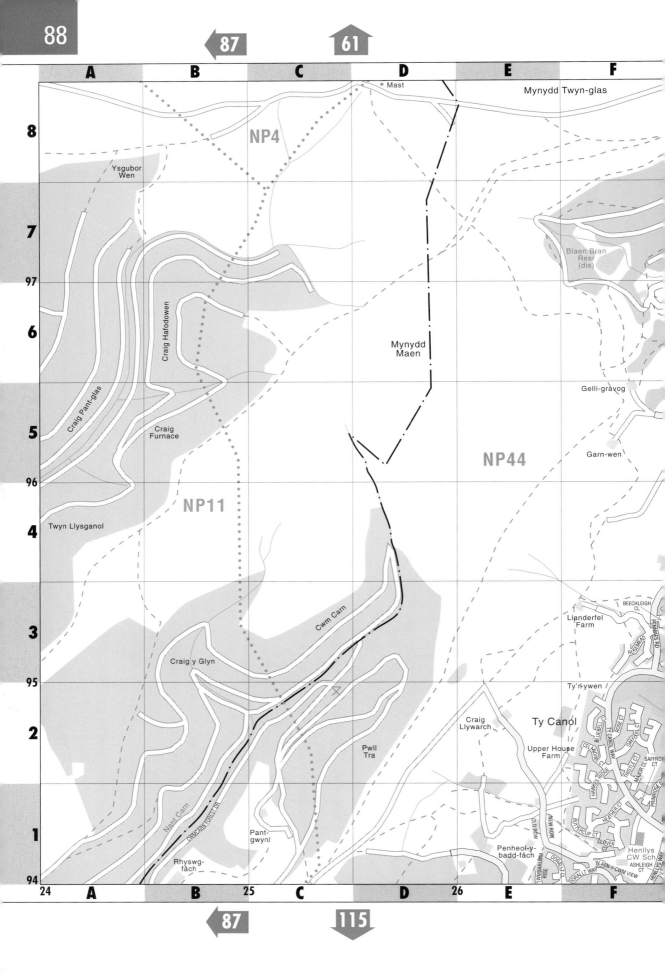

A B C D E F

8

Mynydd Twyn-glas

Mast

NP4

Ysgubor
Wen

7

Blaen Bran
Resr
(dis)

97

Craig Hafodowen

6

Mynydd
Maen

Gelli-gravog

Craig Pant-glas

5

Craig
Furnace

NP44

Garn-wen

96

NP11

4

Twyn Llysganol

Cwm Carn

3

Craig y Glyn

Llanderfel
Farm

BEECHLEIGH
CL

ROSEMEAD
PENNAES HO

95

Ty'n-ywen

Craig
Llywarch

Ty Canol

2

Pwll
Tra

Upper House
Farm

Nant Carn

CWMCARN FOREST DR

Pant-gwyn

1

Penheol-y-
badd-fâch

Rhyswg-
fâch

Henllys
CW Sch

94

24 A B 25 C D 26 E F

A B C D E F

8

Aïon Llwyd

Craig-y-felin Wood

NP4

Pentwyn Farm

Sor Brook Pichic Site
P

Brook House

NP18

Llanddewi Ct

7

PONTRHYDYRUN HO

Race Farm

CH

Greenmeadow Farm

Marches Way

Sor Brook

Crem

97

GROSMONT PL
BRYN GOMER PL
CHAPEL LA
PLAS
SPRINGFIELD
NEWPORT RD

Coed Tre-Herbert

Croeswen

Pen-topyn

6

CHEPSTOW CL
BRYN GOMER RD
GOYER CL
GOYER GARW
CARWEN RD
HARLECH
CARDIGAN CRES
GLAW CT
CEFN

WOOD PATH
COED CARW
STEEPLE

SOR CL
HOLLY
CEFN
PENTINGALE RD
LLANGATTOCK

1 HOLLYLODGE CL
2 HOLLY LODGE GN
3 LLANTHEWY CL

THE HERBERT RD

Granary

Glebe Farm

PO

EDLOGAN SQ
GREENCOURT

Coed Llwyd Farm

Croesyceiliog

FIVE OAKS LA
EDLOGAN WAY
SWITHDOG CT
YNYS LA
YEW TREE TERR
BRYNHYFRYD
CLARE DREW WAY

HOLLY LODGE GDNS

Irongate Farm

5

THE WILLOWS
BRYN EGLWYS CL
COLDSTREAM CL
NORTH RD
WHITE CL
MEADOW LA
THE GARW
THE GARW ROW
THE HIGHWAY
WELDON CL
N CLO GROMSBY
CROESYCEILIOG BY-PASS

Church Farm

TEWDRIC CT

Cwm-heron Wood

NP44

Perthellic Farm

The Old Rectory

96

1 HAWTHORN CT
2 ST MARY'S RD
3 BRONLLYS PL

CHURCH LA
BRYN GARW
SPRING
POPLAR LA
FAIRCAK
CHERRY
PO
THE OAKS
ASHFORD CL
OAK FREDDY

ROSE GDNS

Celynen

Cefn-tilla

WOODLAND RD
WOODLAND CT
HANBRO

PLAS DERWEN
PLANTATION DR

CWM

Cwm-heron Farm

Cefn-tilla-bâch

4

Recn Gd

ROYAL OAK GN 1
BRAN-Y-GARTH 2
ALLEYN HO 3
BAMBER HO 4
CALCOT HO 5
DANTON HO 6
EBURY HO 7
FOLEY HO 8

Candwr Brook

White House

NP18

Croesyceiliog Comp Sch

1 MISKIN HO
2 WORCESTER PATH
3 ROATH CT
4 MILLERS RIDE

Cty H

Mast

Waun-y-pwll Farm

Gwern Dywyll

3

Aïon Llwyd
MISKIN PATH
MISKIN HO
WORCESTER CL
THE PASTURES
TURNPIKE RD
GLOUCESTER CL

Gwent Police HQ

1 DYNEVOR CL
2 CILGERRAM CT
3 RUMNEY WLK
4 TRETOWER CT

Ysgubornewydd Farm

GREY WATERS
AVON PL
CAERLEON
GWEN DR
KEWIG
AVON CRES
DORSTONE WLK
NARBETH CRES
PEMBROKE
LLANYRAFON WAY
LISWERRY RD

Llanyrafon

95

RIVERSMEAD
Recn Gd

Sch

KIDWELLY
DUNRAVEN RD
KIDWELLY RD
B4236

Ty-llwyd

Berth-llwyd

2

ST BRIDES CL 1
LLAN-YR-AVON SQ 2
LLANGORSE RD 3
LLANGORSE PATH 4
P

PO
P
THE WOODS
MILL LA
TWM BARLWM VIEW
WEST BANK
BATH GN
CROWN RISE
WHITE MILL LA

PO
CAERLEON RD

H

Llanfrechfa Grange

Llanyrafon Farm Mus
P

LLYSWEN WLK 1
PADDOCK RISE 2

OLWG
LLWYD OWEN CT
BEAUMARIS GN
THE PADDOCKS
HIGH CL
MITCHELL CL

1

Ind Est

COURT RD
PENARTH CT
FRIARS GDN
THE ALDERS
TURNPIKE RD
A4042
EDGEHILL
WOOD CL
SOUTH CL
NANTWCH CL
B4236

Glansirhowy Farm

Creigydd Farm

THE COLD STORE

94

30 A B 31 C D 32 E F

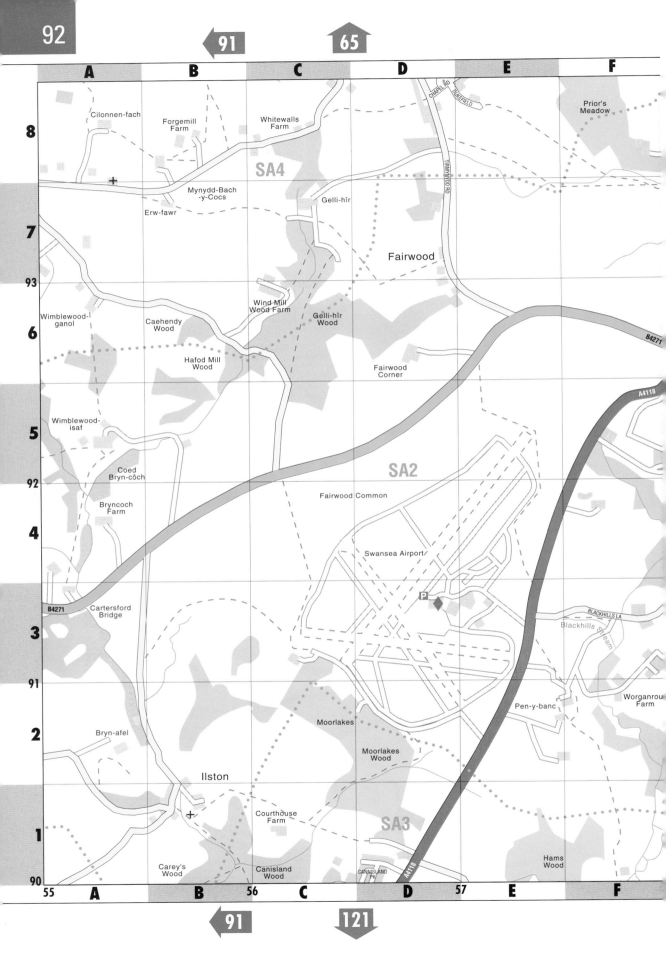

A B C D E F

8
Cilonnen-fach
Forgemill Farm
Whitewalls Farm
CHAPEL RD
FOLKEFIELD
Prior's Meadow
SA4
TRAMWOOD RD
Mynydd-Bach -y-Cocs
Erw-fawr
Gelli-hîr

7
Fairwood

93
Wimblewood- ganol
Caehendy Wood
Wind Mill Wood Farm
Gelli-hîr Wood
B4271

6
Hafod Mill Wood
Fairwood Corner
A4118

5
Wimblewood- isaf

92
Coed Bryn-côch
SA2
Fairwood Common

4
Bryncoch Farm
Swansea Airport
P

3
B4271
Cartersford Bridge
BLACKHILLS LA
Blackhills
Blackhills Stream

91
Pen-y-banc
Worganrou Farm

2
Bryn-afel
Moorlakes
Moorlakes Wood

Ilston
Courthouse Farm
SA3

1
Carey's Wood
Canisland Wood
CANISLAND PK
A4118
Hams Wood

90
55 A B 56 C D 57 E F

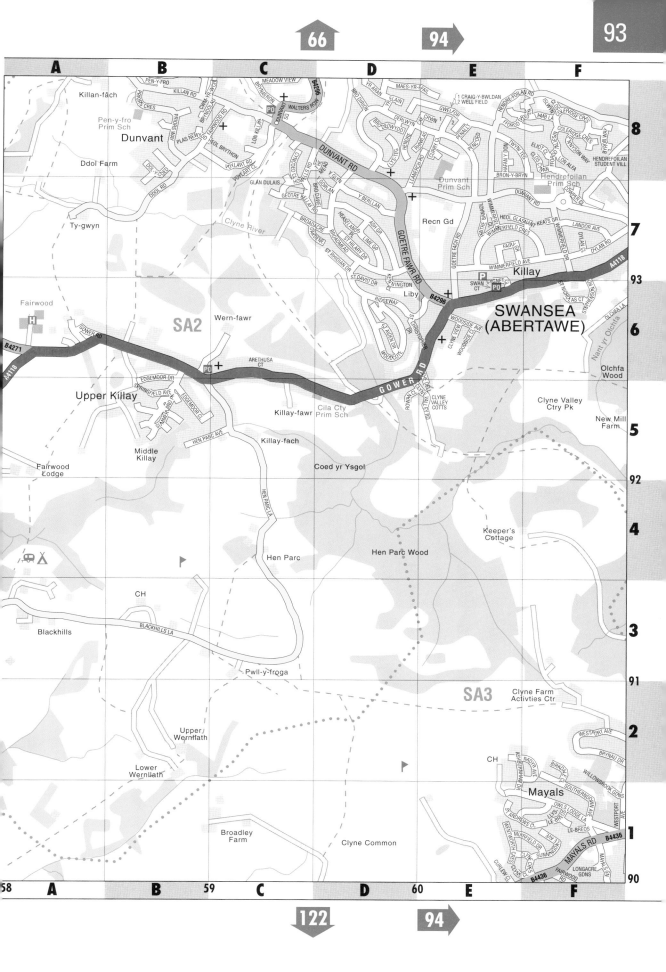

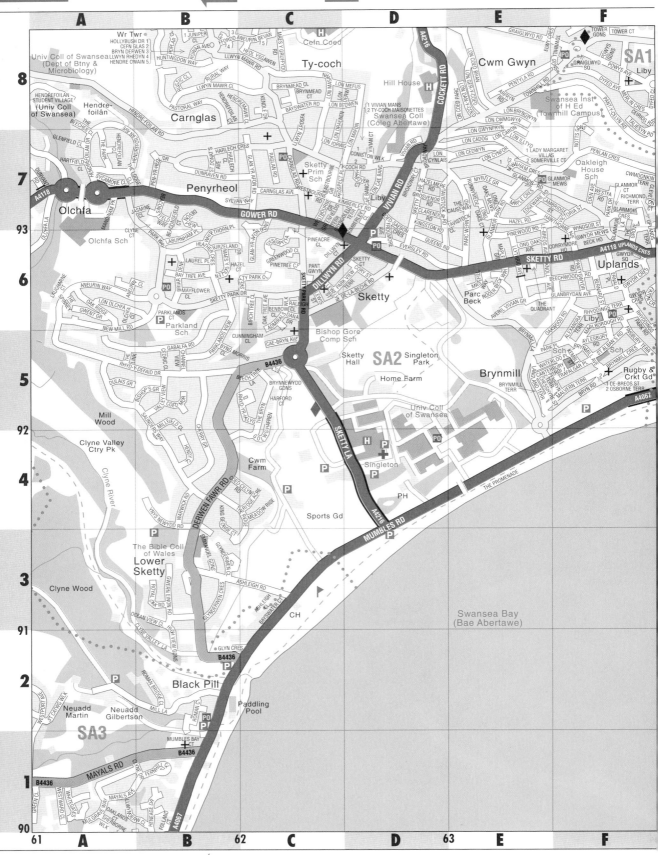

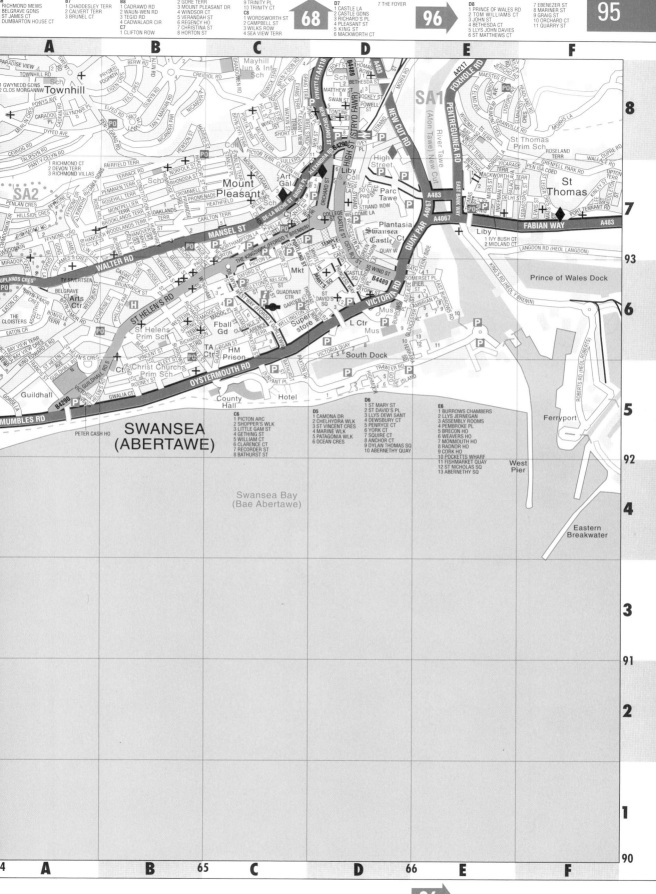

A6
1 RICHMOND MEWS
2 BELGRAVE GDNS
3 ST JAMES CT
4 DUMBARTON HOUSE CT

B7
1 CHADDESLEY TERR
2 CALVERT TERR
3 BRUNEL CT

B8
1 CADRAWD RD
2 WAUN-WEN RD
3 TEGID RD
4 CADWALADR CIR

C7
1 CLIFTON ROW

C8
1 WORDSWORTH ST
2 CAMPBELL ST
3 WILKS ROW
4 SEA VIEW TERR

2 GORE TERR
3 MOUNT PLEASANT DR
4 WINDSOR CT
5 VERANDAH ST
6 REGENCY HO
7 CHRISTINA ST
8 HORTON ST

9 TRINITY PL
10 TRINITY CT

D7
1 CASTLE LA
2 CASTLE GDNS
3 RICHARD'S PL
4 PLEASANT ST
5 KING ST
6 MACKWORTH CT

7 THE FOYER

D8
1 PRINCE OF WALES RD
2 TOM WILLIAMS CT
3 JOHN ST
4 BETHESDA CT
5 LLYS JOHN DAVIES
6 ST MATTHEWS CT

7 EBENEZER ST
8 MARINER ST
9 GRAIG ST
10 ORCHARD CT
11 QUARRY ST

68

96

Townhill

Mount Pleasant

SA2

SA1

SA1

St Thomas

St Thomas
Prim Sch

Prince of Wales Dock

Ferryport

West
Pier

Eastern
Breakwater

Guildhall

**SWANSEA
(ABERTAWE)**

Swansea Bay
(Bae Abertawe)

C6
1 PICTON ARC
2 SHOPPER'S WLK
3 LITTLE GAM ST
4 GETHING ST
5 WILLIAM CT
6 CLARENCE CT
7 RECORDER ST
8 BATHURST ST

D5
1 CAMONA DR
2 CHELHYDRA WLK
3 ST VINCENT CRES
4 MARINE WLK
5 PATAGONIA WLK
6 OCEAN CRES

D6
1 ST MARY ST
2 ST DAVID'S PL
3 LLYS DEWI SANT
4 DEWSBURY CT
5 PENRYCE CT
6 YORK CT
7 SQUIRE CT
8 ANCHOR CT
9 DYLAN THOMAS SQ
10 ABERNETHY QUAY

E6
1 BURROWS CHAMBERS
2 LLYS JERNEGAN
3 ASSEMBLY ROOMS
4 PEMBROKE PL
5 BRECON HO
6 WEAVERS HO
7 MONMOUTH HO
8 RADNOR HO
9 CORK HO
10 POCKETTS WHARF
11 FISHMARKET QUAY
12 ST NICHOLAS SQ
13 ABERNETHY SQ

A B C D E F

HILL VIEW
ST MARGARET'S AVE
SCHOOL RD
LOCAL VIEW
Crymlyn Bridge
ASHLEIGH TERR
MARINE HO
PO
Hotel
Tower
Tennant Canal (dis)
B4290
CH
SA10
Works
Works
FABIAN WAY
ELBA CRES
Crymlym Burrows
SA1
A483

Swansea Bay
(Bae Abertawe)

SA10
Witford Point
Flares
Baglan Burrows
SA12
Tanks
Tanks

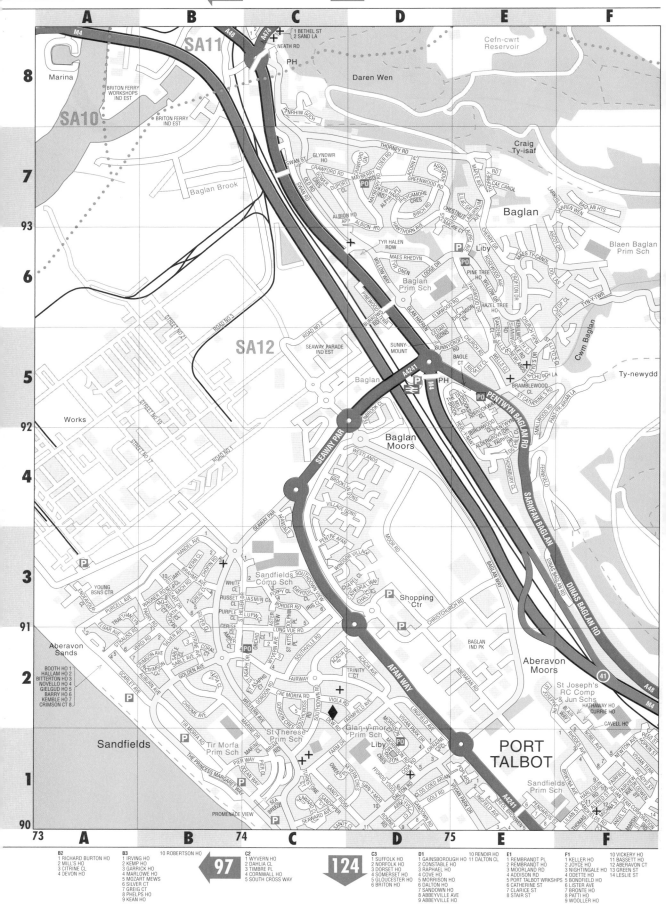

PORT
TALBOT

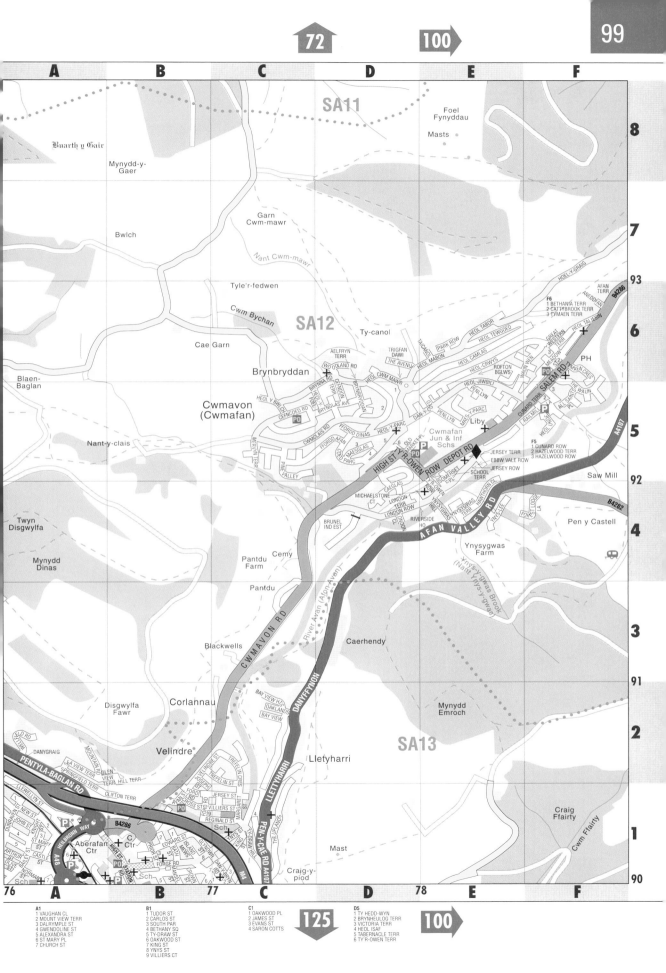

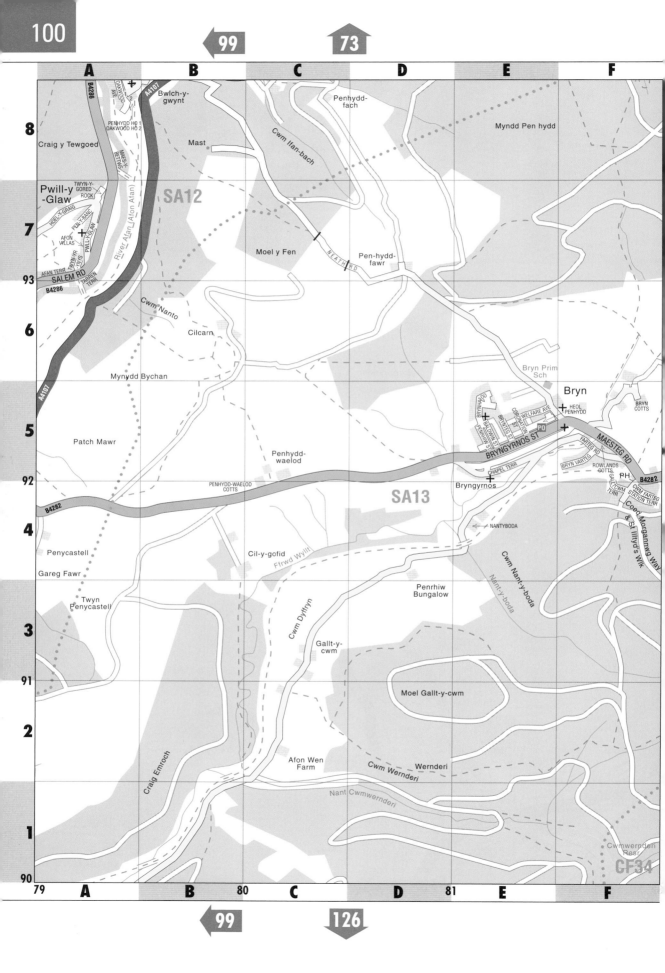

A   B   C   D   E   F

8
7
93
6
5
92
4
92
3
91
2
1
90

Ffynnon y Dafarn

Nant Cynon

Foel y Dyffryn

Tonnau Dafaid

Pen Disgwylfa

Parc y Bryn

Pen-y-lan

Cae'r Mynydd

Rhiw Tor Cymry

Garn Wen

SA13

Coed Morgannwg Way & St Illtyd's Wlk

Nantyffyllon Prim Sch

Cwm Ton-hir

Nant Drysiog

BROWN ST 1
DUFFRYNMADOG 2
JOHN ST
UNION ST
DYFFRYN

CF34

Cefn Cethin

MAESTEG RD

Ty Gwyn

Cwm Farteg

Nant Cwmfarteg

Nant y Crynwydd

HEOL TY GWYN IND EST

FORGE FACTORY EST

Coed Morgannwg Way & St Illtyd's Wlk

CH

TAIR WAUN PL

NEATH RD

General

Sports Ctr

SMITH ST

Mast

EXCHANGE ST

Mynydd Bach

HEOL Y MOCH

Brynmawr

SALISBURY RD

VICARAGE TERR

PRIORY TERR

B4282

BRYNMAWR PL

Stone

MAESTEG

Cwmcerwyn

Cwm y Goblyn

Nant Cwmcerwyn

Nant y Goblyn

Llynfi

Blaen-cwmcerwyn

Rhiwlas

HEOL PENTRE
HEOL CEFN YDFA
HEOL GELLI LENOR
BRYNLLYWARCH
LANSBURY CL
CRES
AER HARDIE RD
BRYNTEG

Nant Sychbant

Nant y Glo Fach

Cwm Sychbant

Moel Sychbant

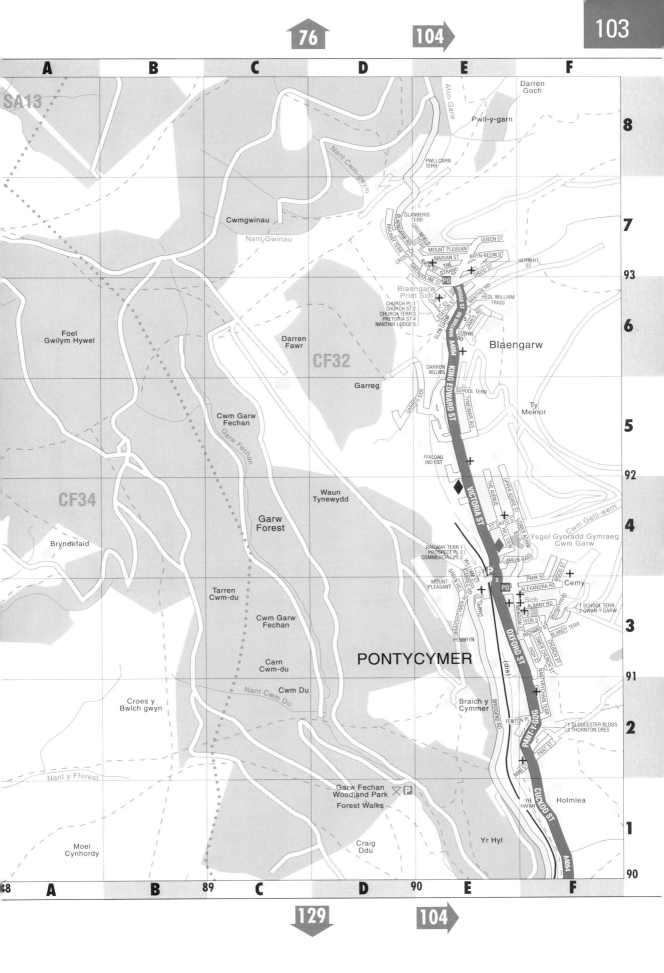

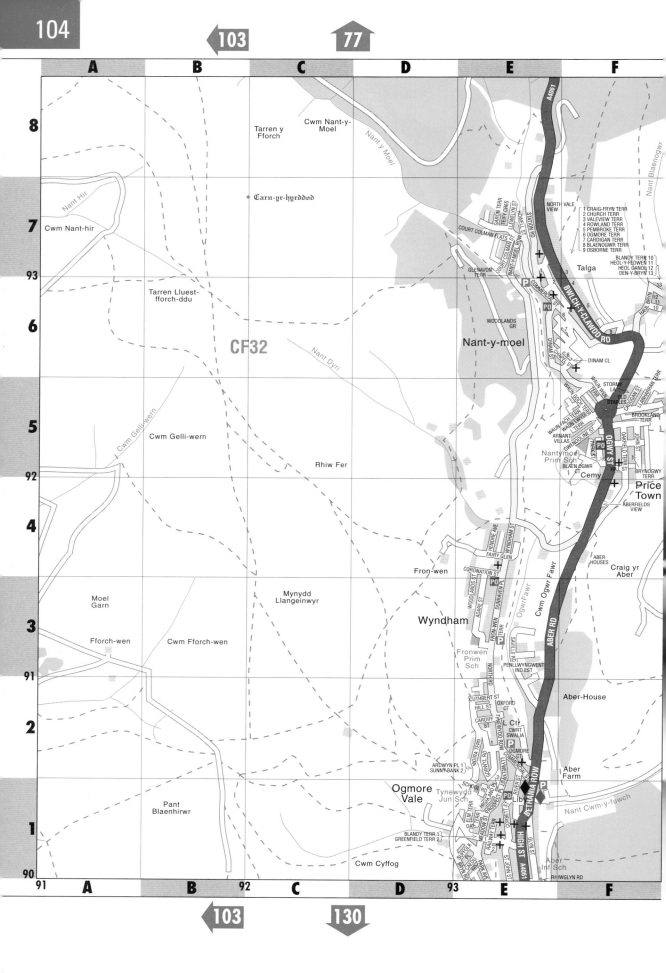

A B C D E F

8 Tarren y Fforch Cwm Nant-y-Moel Nant y Moel NORTH VALE VIEW Nant Blaenogwr

Carn-yr-hyrddod 1 CRAIG-FRYN TERR
2 CHURCH TERR
3 VALEVIEW TERR
4 ROWLAND TERR
5 PEMBROKE TERR
6 OGMORE TERR
7 CARDIGAN TERR
8 BLAENOGWR TERR
9 OSBORNE TERR

7 Cwm Nant-hir BLANDY TERR 10
HEOL-Y-FEDWEN 11
HEOL GANOL 12
DEN-Y-BRYN 13

93 Talga

Tarren Lluest-fforch-ddu WOODLANDS GR

6 CF32 Nant Dyri Nant-y-moel DINAM CL

STORMY LA
OLD STABLES

5 Cwm Gelli-wern BROOKLAND TERR
BLAEN OGWR
Ct BRYNOGWY TERR

92 Rhiw Fer Cemy Price Town

4 Moel Garn Fron-wen FAIRY GLEN ABER HOUSES Craig yr Aber

Mynydd Llangeinwyr CORONATION ST

3 Fforch-wen Cwm Fforch-wen Wyndham Cwm Ogwr Fawr Aber-House

Fronwen Prim Sch PENLLWYNGWENT IND EST

91 Aber Farm

2 CUTHBERT ST
HILL ST OXFORD CT
CARDIFF ST L Ctr
CWRT SWALIA Aber Farm

ARDWYN PL 1
SUNNY BANK 2

Ogmore Vale Tynewydd Jun Sch Library

1 Pant Blaenhirwr BLANDY TERR 1
GREENFIELD TERR 2 Aber Inf Sch

90 Cwm Cyffog RHIWGLYN RD

91 A B 92 C D 93 E F

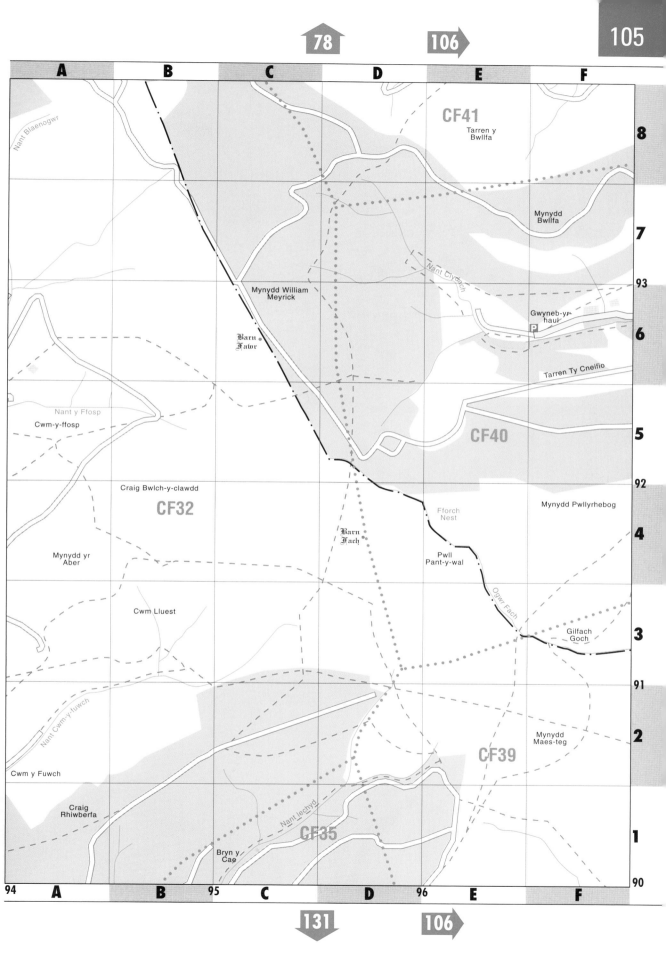

A B C D E F

CF41

Tarren y
Bwllfa

8

Mynydd
Bwllfa

7

Nant Clydach

93

Mynydd William
Meyrick

Gwyneb-yr-
haul
P

6

Tarren Ty Cneifio

Barn
Fawr

Nant y Ffosp

CF40

Cwm-y-ffosp

5

Craig Bwlch-y-clawdd

92

CF32

Fforch
Nest

Mynydd Pwllyrhebog

4

Barn
Fach

Mynydd yr
Aber

Pwll
Pant-y-wal

Ogwr Fach

Cwm Lluest

Gilfach
Goch

3

91

Nant Cwm-y-tuwch

Mynydd
Maes-teg

2

Cwm y Fuwch

CF39

Craig
Rhiwberfa

Nant Iechyd

CF35

1

Bryn y
Cae

90

94 A B 95 C D 96 E F

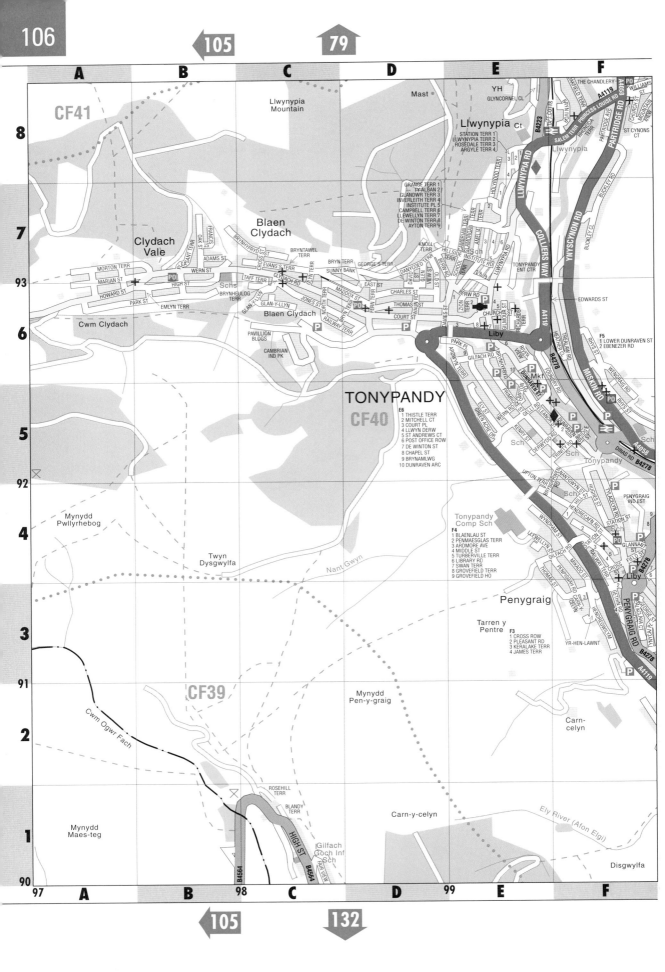

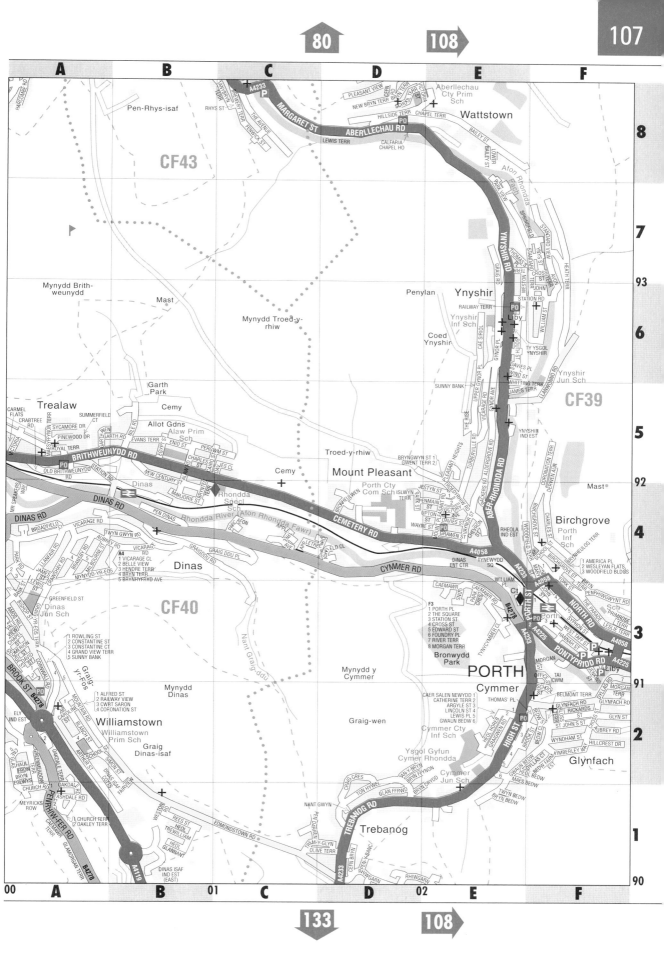

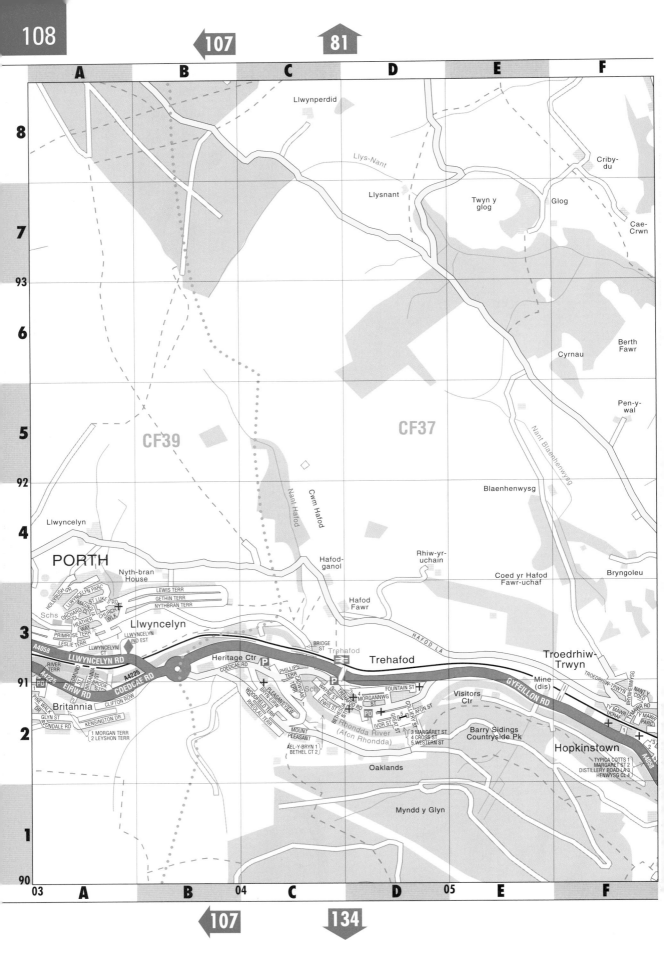

Map

A B C D E F

8
Sch
B4273
GELLI RD
ROBERT ST
GWYN MYNACH ST
CRAWSHAY ST
THOMPSON VILLAS
CWRT GLYN
1 GROVE TERR
2 CRIBYN-DU ST
3 GLYN ST

Coed Pen-y-parc

Craig-Evan-Leyshon Common

CF45

Parc-newydd

Pen-y-parc

7
NEW RD
DAN Y BRYN
OLD PARISH ROAD IND EST
OLD PARISH RD
BROOKFIELD

Works

93
GOWER DAVIES CT 1
FFORDD GOWER DAVIES 2
LLYS TREROBANT

GROVERS FIELD
A470
A4054
GER Y AFON
ABERNYNION RD

Coed y Cwm
HEOL CELYNEN
HAFAN HEULOG
NANT-Y-MYNYDD
PLAS-Y-FEDWEN
BRYN HIR
LON HELYGEN 1
LLYS DERWEN 2
PEN-Y-MYNYDD 3
MAES GLAS
HEOL FER-Y-FAEL
BRYN RHEDYN
BRYN AWEL
MAES COCH
HEOL FEN-Y-PARC
LLYS COED

ALBION IND EST
The Coedylan Comp Sch
PANT-DU RD
PARK PL

6
Nant Clydach
TAI'R HEOL

Mill Farm
River Taff (Afon Taf)

Cilfynydd
CWRT BETHEL 1
ALBION FLATS 2

Jones St

5
The Cefn
Cefn Prim Sch
PINEWOOD VIEW
FOREST VIEW
CEFN CL
CEFN LA
WESTFIELD
ASHFORD CL
GREENFIELD
ELMGROVE CL
CLAYTON CRES
CONWAY CL
ORCHARD DR
YNYSYBWL RD
ASHGROVE
THE GROVE
GROVERS CL
HEULOG
CLYDACH CL
DERWENDEG AVE
GREENMEADOW CL
PORCHER AVE
HIGH VIEW WAY
PEARSON CRES
COED-Y-LAN RD
GARTH AVE
GARDNER CL
PEN CL
BRYN
Fan Craig-yr-Hesg Prim Sch
CEFN LA
DARREN CT
Glyncoch
GLYNCOCH TERR

CILFYNYDD RD
RICHARD ST
CROSS ST
WILLIAM ST
MARY ST
JONATHANS TERR
Sch
BOWENARTH RD
BERW RD
HOWELL ST
TAL ANN
ANN ST
WOOD ST
OAKLAND CRES
HEOL CRIWLA

92
Glyncoch
BERWEDD-DY COTTS

BRYNDERWEN CL
OAKLAND RD

4
Gelli-lwch
Di-goed
Quarries
Coed Craig-yr-hesg
ROGART TERR
DAERI-DDU RD

Taff Trail
PONTSHONNORTON RD
LLANFABON CT
Sch
FFORDD TALIESIN
FFORDD CATRAETH
FFORDD TRYWERYN
HEOL NANT
HEOL MYNYDD
BROOKSIDE CL
CYNON VIEW
HILLTOP AVE
ALBION CT

CF37

3
Lan
Lan Wood
PRIORY CL
PEN-Y-DARREN CL
LLANWOOD RD
GRAIGYRHESG RD
GRAIGYRHESG PL
DARRAN PK
LEWIS TERR
LOWER TAFF VIEW
DEWI ST
FRAM-Y-TERR
Bodwenarth
Pont-Siôn-Norton
Ysgol Gynradd Gymraeg Pont-Sion-Norton
1 EVANS SQ
2 BELGRAVE TERR
3 CORONATION TERR

91
Penygraigwen
UNDERWOOD TERR 1
TYMAWR TERR 2
LLANWONNO CL
GRAIGWEN PARC
MAES-Y-DERI
HEOL-Y-DERI
IVY TERR
ROCK COTTS
WHITEROCK RD
WHITEROCK AVE
FRONHEULOG
WHITEROCK DR
BERW RD
BONVILSTON RD
THURSTON RD
PARADE
Sch
BASSETT ST
ALPHA ST
CLOS PANTGLAS
PLEASANT VIEW
BRYN DLWG
Ely Brook
BROOKFIELD
CORDDENARTH RD
HEATHERVIEW RD
PENHEOL ELY RD

2
Pantygraig-Wen
TELELKEIBIG RD
CROCKETT PL
PANTYGRAIGWEN RD
GRAIGWEN RD
SUNNY SIDE
MAYFIELD RD
RIDGWAY DR
HILLSIDE VIEW
BLANCHE ST 1
HILLSIDE TERR 2
YNYS-GYFEILLON RD 8
Coed-y-lan Comp Sch
Prim Sch
LANPARK RD
GRAIG ST
WEST ST
MIDDLE ST
EAST ST
NORTH ST
SOUTH ST
LLANVER RD
THE AVENUE
MACKINTOSH RD
WINGFIELD RD
YSGWL TY DU
HILL TOP CRES
COMMON RD
Coed-Pen-Maen
CH
Mast
PONTYPRIDD
PENGOED AVE
HOSPITAL RD
PENTREBACH RD

1
Trehopcyn Prim Sch
AELYBRYN
CHARLES ST
SHEPPARD ST
BARRY RD
JENKINS
Graigwen
RHONDDA RD
HOPKINSTOWN RD
Rhondda River / Afon Rhondda
Pwllgwaun
LLANDRAW WOODS
LLANDRAW RD
LLANDRAW
QUARRY RD 1
CLOS BRON IESTYN 2
ST MARK'S VILLAS 3
DANYLAN RD
BOLGAFAR EGLWYS
LANELA CRES
RHONDDA RD A4223
MILL ST
A4054
Sch
GELLIWASTAD RD
CHAPEL ST
LIBRARY RD
THOMAS ST
PENCERRIG ST
LLYNFICA CRES
LLYN
B4273
Mus
Bridge
BRIDGE ST A4223
CROSSBROOK ST
MARKET ST
CHURCH ST
TAFF ST
Library
TEMPERANCE PL
NEWBRIDGE CT
PARK SIDE LA
LLANOVER RD
YNYSANGHARAD RD
LOCK CT
Pen-coed
Pontypridd & District H
Ynysangharad Park

06 A 07 B C D 08 E F 90

B1
1 BRYNHYFRYD TERR
2 HIGHFIELD TERR
3 LLANBRADACH ST
4 HEATH TERR
5 ROSE COTTS
6 VAUGHAN ST
7 UPPER VAUGHAN ST
8 MERLIN CL

C1
1 TAFF VALE PREC
2 FRATERNAL PAR
3 UPPER CHURCH ST
4 CHURCH ST
5 CATHERINE ST
6 MILL ST

D2
1 CROSSWAYS ST
2 BONVILSTON TERR
3 CROSS ST
4 CENTRAL SQ
5 PLAS YR EGLWYS
6 CHANDLERS CT
7 NEWBRIDGE CT
8 BAKERS WHARF

E2
1 CHURCH RD
2 DODDINGTON PL
3 JONES PL
4 FRON TERR
5 SCARBOROUGH RD
6 LLYS TY GWYN

109
83

	A	B	C	D	E	F

Garth-Fawr

Bryntaldwyn

Bryn-du

Greyhound Inn (PH)

Pengelli

CF46

Llanfabon

Cwm bâch

Nant Ddu

Tai'r-waun-uchaf

Ty-draw

Nant Cae-dudwg

Trefychan Farm

Fid-gelyn

Ffos yr Haidal

Coed Pant-du Isaf

Tirmynydd

Pant-du

CF37

PANT-DU RD

Rhymney Valley Ridgeway Footpath

Coed Pant-du Uchaf

Cwmeldeg

Mynydd Eglwysilan

Cilfynydd

Carneddi Llwydion

HEOL NANT

HEOL MWYD

Cilfynydd Farm

Glawnant

Cilfynydd

Craig-yr-Hufen

Glan Nant

Coed Bodwenarth

Caer-moel

Nant Cae'r-moel

Twyn-y-gwynt

GENYDD TERR

GRAIG TERR

PHILLIPS TERR

WOODLAND TERR

CF83

Parc-mawr

Saw Mill

CORONATION TERR

ALEXANDRA TERR

Masts

Twyn Hywel

Nant y parc Prim Sch

UPPER BRYNHYFRYD TERR

Ysgol Ifor Bach

SCHOOL ST

BRYNHYFRYD TERR

LOWER

PENHEOL ELY RD

PARC TERR

GROVE TERR

PARC CWM

STANLEY ST

CROSS ST

HIGH ST

B4263

PARRISH PL

CLIVE ST

Pant Waungorrwg

Foel-ddu

STATION TERR

GWERN AVE

WIMPOLE PL

GLYN-Y-COED

COMMERCIAL ST

Penheol Ely

Cefn Eglwysilan

EGLWYSILAN RD

WESTSIDE RD

RIVERSIDE CT

Parc-newydd

Senghenydd

CAERPHILLY RD

TAN-Y-BRYN

B4263

Garnedd Llwyd

109
136

	A	10	C		D	11	E	F

09

90

91

92

93

1

2

3

4

5

6

7

8

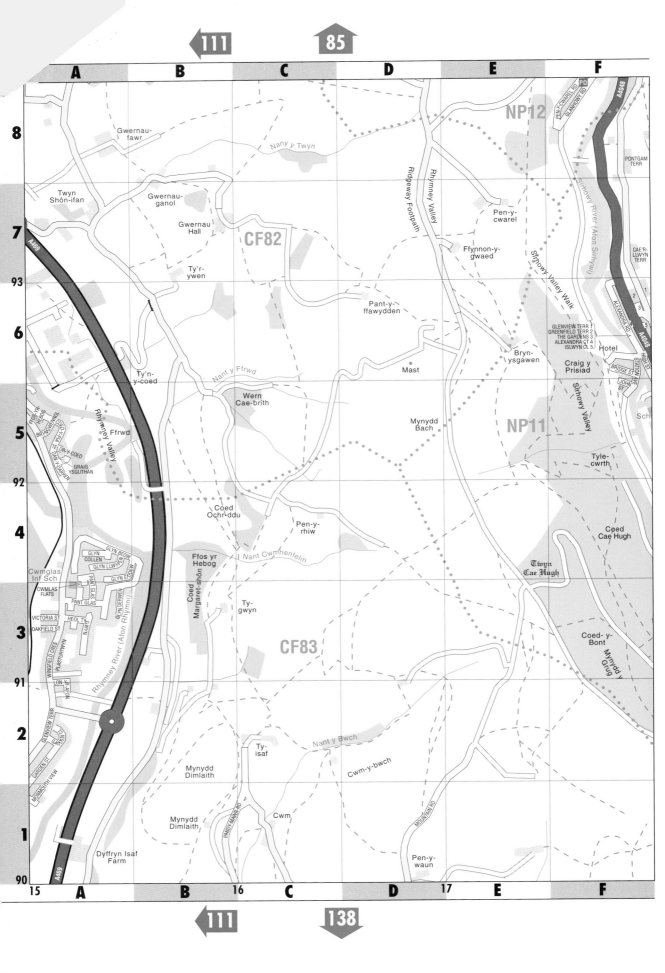

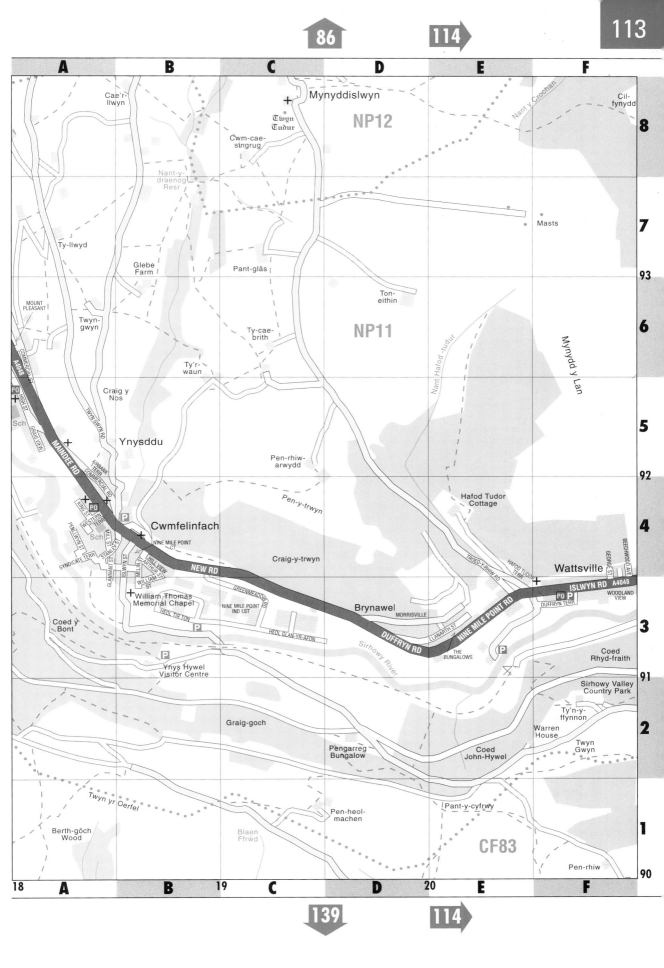

113
87

A B C D E F

8

Cwmcarn High Sch
B4591
A467
BRYN-ROSVILLE
JAMESVILLE
PRIORY CT
Cwmcarn
FOREST VEIW
Tir-Shams-yr-helwr
MARNE ST
CHAPEL FARM TERR
UPPER TRIBUTE AVE
RAMPING RD
GEORGE ST
REECE'S TERR
NEWPORT RD
TRIBUTE AVE
ABERCARN FACH
NANTCARN RD
Visitor Centre
Cwm Carn
BRIERLY PL
Llay
EDWARD ST
CWMCARN FOREST DR
CWMCARN FOREST DR
IVOR ST

7

Craig Carnau
Pen Ifynydd
FEEDER TOWN
BERNARD ST
P
P
TWYN CARN TERR
CORONATION PL
1 CASTLE LA
2 CASTLE GL
Coed Medart
Raven Wlk
BROOK LANDS TERR
THE MEWS
SILVER ST
NORTH RD
TWYNCARN RD
Pegwn-y-bwlch
P

93

Medart
ARCH HILL
HILLARY RISE
GREEN BRIARS
NP11

6

Cwm Llwch
Ebbw Valley Walk
PO
GELLI-UNIG RD
TRINITY HILL
Gelli-unig Farm
Pontywaun
MOUNT PLEASANT TERR
GELLI-UNIG RD
Gelli-unig Terr
Cwm Byr
Hansons Lodge

5

Craig y Pandy
FIELDS PARK TERR 1
WESTERN TERR 2
OLD SCHOOL CT 3
HIGH ST
PARK VIEW
PARK PL
HALL'S RD
HALL'S ROAD
PANDY VIEW
BEECHER TERR
OAK TERR
CARLTON PL
Darren
Coed y Darren
CWMCARN FOREST DR

92

Pandy Park
B4591
CAR LION TERR
Coed Mam-gu
Crosskeys

4

NORTH BLACKVEIN IND EST
SOUTH BLACKVEIN IND EST
Pont y Cymmer
WOODWARD RD
PO
BRIGHT ST
COBDEN ST
SALISBURY ST
WALNUT ST
WAUNFAWR TERR
RISCA RD
Monmouthshire & Brecon Canal
GREENMEADOW DR
CROMWELL STREET BNGLWS
MEDART ST
Coed y Garn
F3
1 CWRT YR YSGOL
2 EXCHANGE RD
3 EXCHANGE CT
4 RIFLEMAN ST
5 YORK PL
6 BELVEDERE TERR
7 SARN PL
8 TEMPERANCE HILL
A467
A4048
ISLWYN RD
NEWTOWN IND EST
GLADSTONE ST
ST CATHERINE'S ST
CORBEN ST
Waunfawr Jun Sch
Crosskeys Coll
MEDART PL
Fernlea
FERNLEA
TAYLOR ST
TREDEGAR ST
TREDEGAR TERR
TREDEGAR CT
Ebbw River (Afon Ebwy)
WAUNFAWR PARK RD
THE MEADOWS
NEW PARK RD
1 MEADOW CL
2 THE POPLARS
CROMWELL RD
LC
RAGLAN ST
Ty Darran
ST MARY'S ST
CHURCH RD
GROVE RD
CRESCENT RD
TANGTON RD
PO
1
3
5
LEYDENE CL
PISHFIELD CL
FERNLEA
CARSTOM CT

3

A467
Full Moon Visitor Centre
Newtown
BLACKVEIN RD
Coed Waun-fawr
Black Vein
Glenside Bungalow
RAILWAY ST
BRYN-HYFRYD TERR
TRINITY PL
BRIDGE ST
PHILLIP ST
EBBW ST
MACHEN ST
CLARENCE PL
P
DAN Y GRAIG
DAN Y GRAIG RD
STATION RD
PARK RD
TREDEGAR ST

91

Mast
Gelli-ffiniog
Raven Wlk
Buck Farm
Danygraig
GWENDOLINE RD
GWENDOLINE PL
TIR-Y-CWM RD
TIR-Y-CWM LA
TREDEGAR TERR
WESLEY PL
Cemy

2

Rhymney Valley Ridgeway Footpath
Sirhowy Valley Walk
Waun Pen-y-gam
DANYGRAIG BGLWS

1

CF83
Pen-rhiw-Warren
Mynydd Machen
Mast
A467
Pontymister

90

21 A B 22 C D 23 E F

113
140

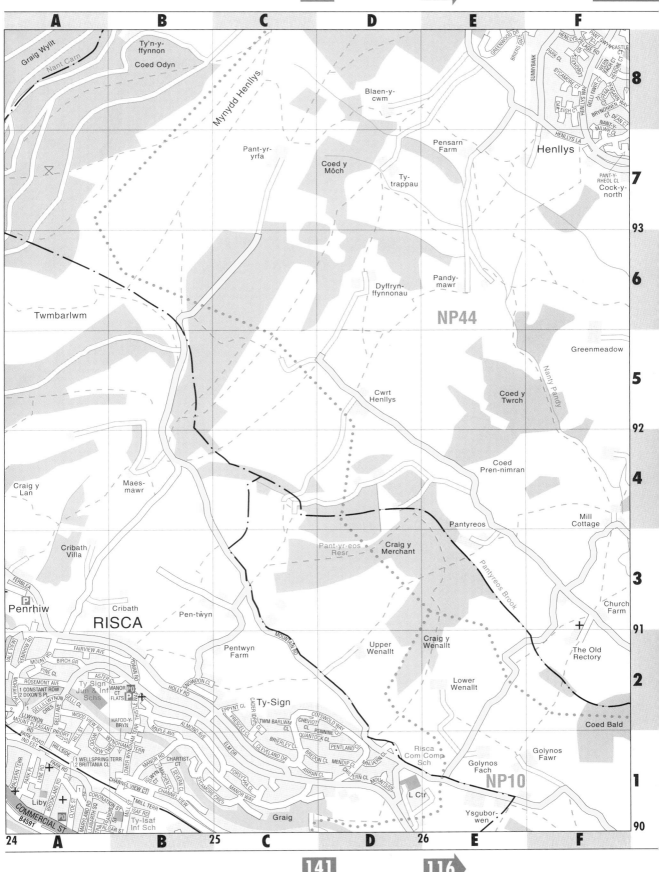

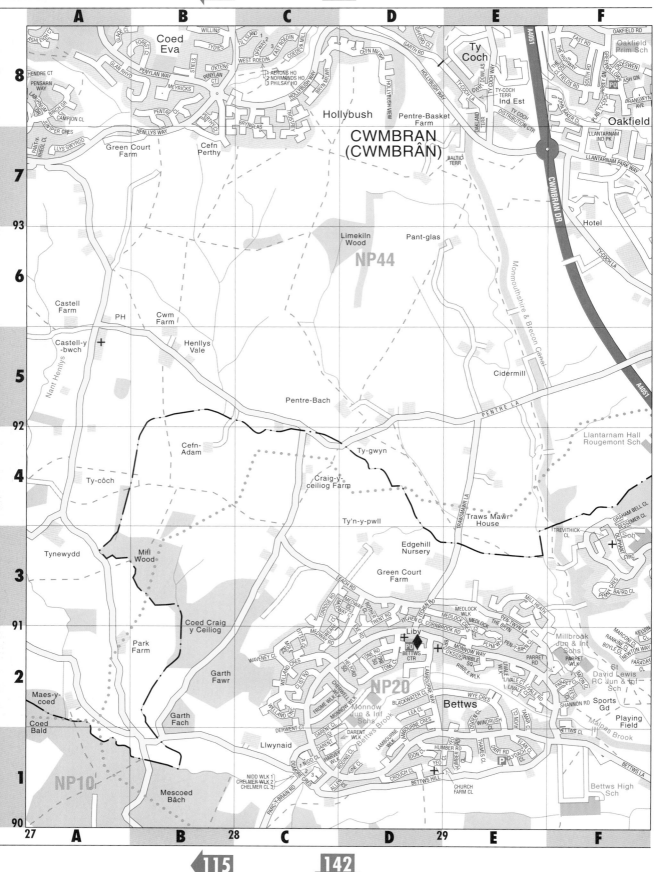

115
89
115
142

CWMBRAN (CWMBRÂN)

NP44

NP20

NP10

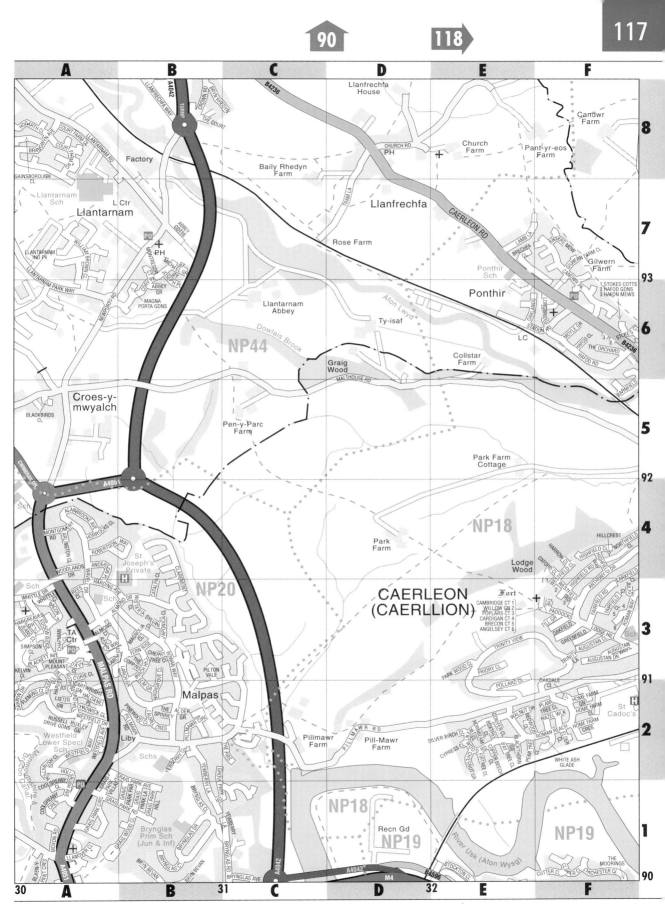

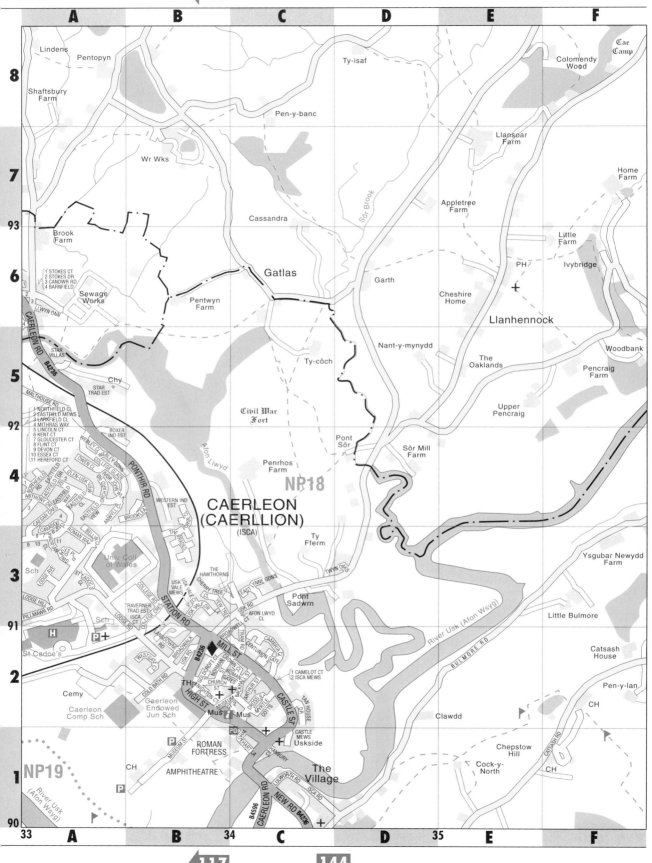

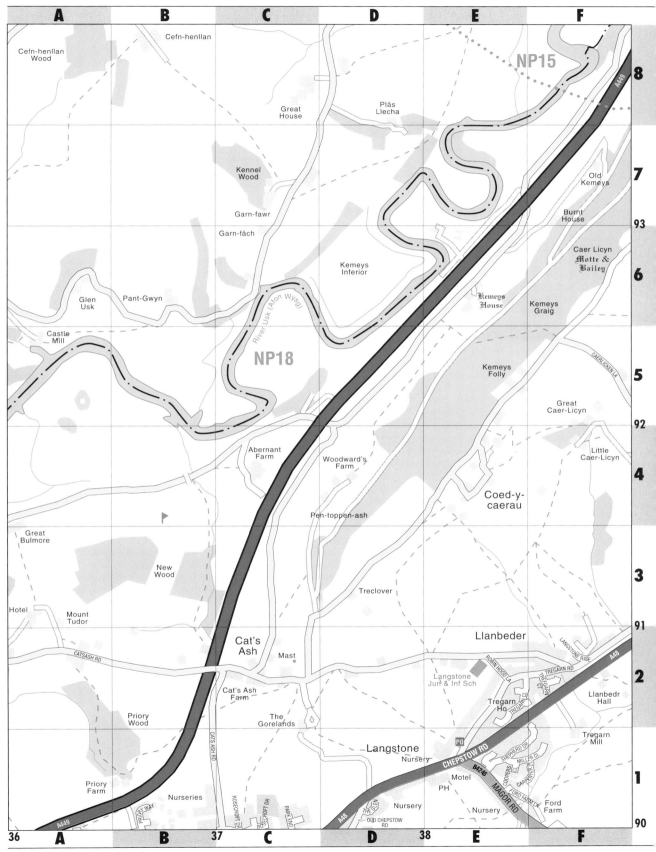

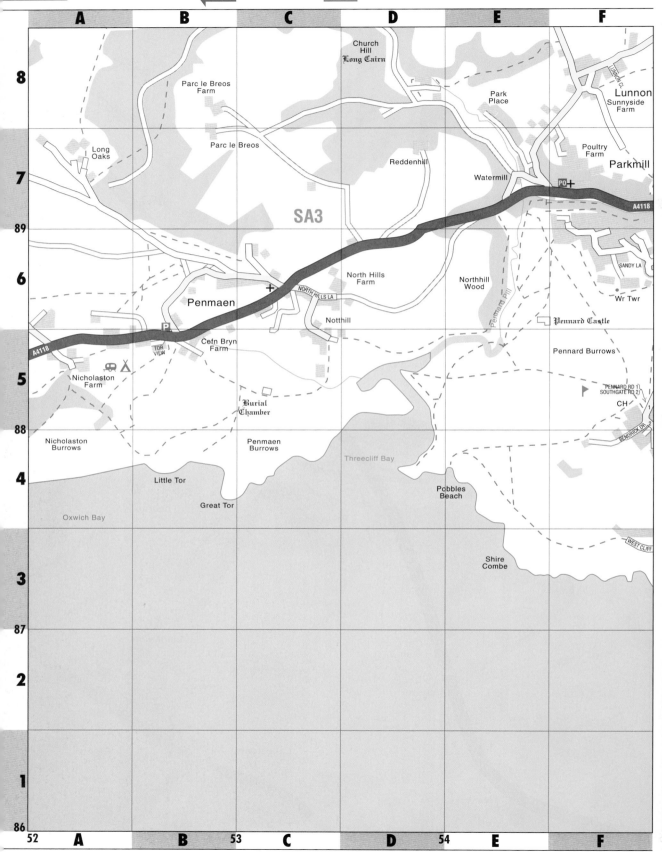

A B C D E F

8

Church Hill
Long Cairn

Parc le Breos Farm

Park Place

Lunnon

Sunnyside Farm

Long Oaks

Parc le Breos

Poultry Farm

Parkmill

7

Reddenhill

Watermill

PO

SA3

SANDY LA

89

North Hills Farm

Northhill Wood

Pennard Pill

Wr Twr

6

Penmaen

NORTH HILLS LA

Notthill

Pennard Castle

Pennard Burrows

P

Cefn Bryn Farm

A4118

TOR VIEW

Nicholaston Farm

PENNARD RD 1
SOUTHGATE RD 2

CH

5

Burial Chamber

BENDRICK DR

88

Nicholaston Burrows

Penmaen Burrows

Threecliff Bay

WEST CLIFF

4

Little Tor

Pobbles Beach

Great Tor

Oxwich Bay

Shire Combe

3

87

2

1

86

52 A B 53 C D 54 E F

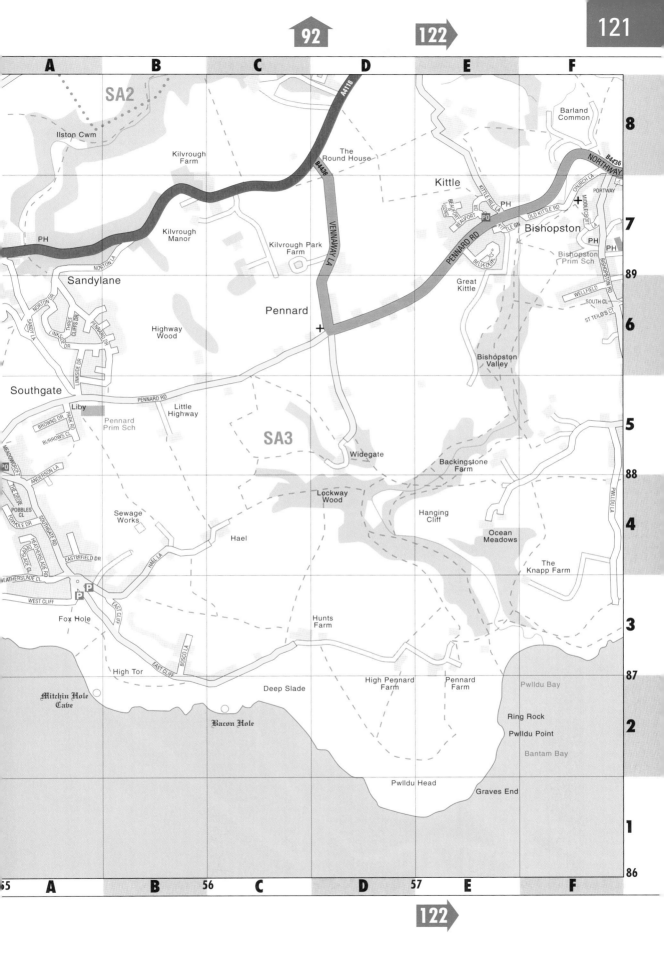

Swansea Bay

West Cross

Norton

Oystermouth
Oystermouth
Castle
Oystermouth
Prim Sch

THE DUNNS

1 ALBERT PL
2 WINDSOR PL
3 WESTBOURNE PL
4 UPPER CHURCH PK
5 BROADVIEW LA
6 IRVINE CT
7 HALLBANK
8 HALLBANK TERR
9 ROCKHILL
10 TICHBOURNE ST

SA3

The
Mumbles

MUMBLES RD

1 HILL ST
2 DICKSLADE
3 SOUTHEND
4 CHANDLERS REACH

GEORGE
BANK

CLIFTON
TERR

The Knab

IRB Sta

LB Sta

Pier

Mumbles Hill

Thistleboon

Hotel

Middle
Head

Mumbles
Head

Bracelet Bay

Limeslade

Mast

Limeslade
Bay

Rams Tor

1 WESTCLIFF MEWS
2 AEL-Y-BRYN
3 LIMESLADE CT

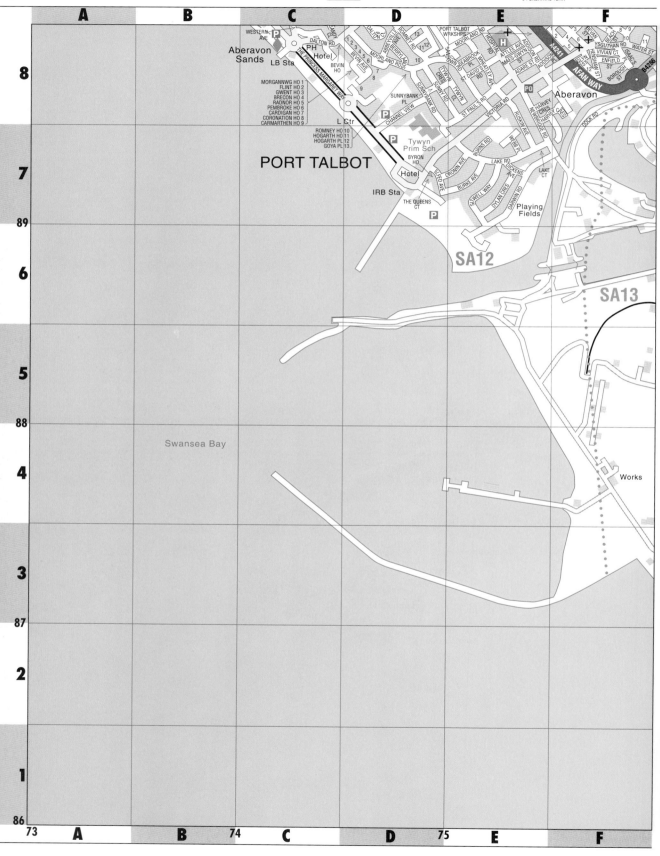

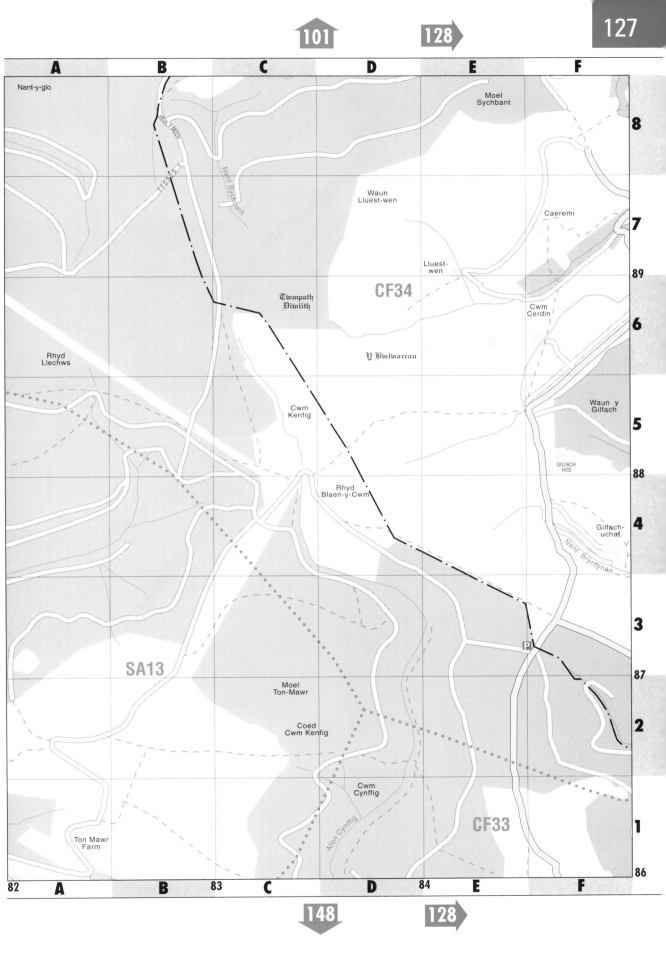

127
102

A B C D E F

8

Gellilenor-fach

Pentre

LLWYN RD
BRYN CELYN
GARTH RD
GWENDOLINE TERR
PARK VIEW
MAIDEN ST
JENKINS TERR
Garth
PH
A4063
MILL ST B4282
FAIRMEAD
RHODFA'R COED
HAFAN DEG
RHOS HELYG
HEOL WILLIAM
DYMIS
GWELAN DYMIS
HEOL GERDIN
GLAN-YR-AFON
MILL VIEW
LLETYR BUGAIL
MAESTEG RD

Ty-maen

Craigtycanol

Cwm Du

Nant Cwm-du

Gelliheblyg

Cwmfelin Prim Sch
Cwmfelin

7

Moel Troed-y-Rhiw

Drysity'n-y-waun

Pont Rhyd-y-cyff

Y DDERWEN
DARREN VIEW

PH

89

WHITE HART COTTS
LLAN RD
PH
Llangynwyd

Llangynwyd Prim Sch
HEOL-YR-YSGOL
HEOL LLWYNDERW
HEOL MIL HODCYN
HEOL-Y-BRYN
CORONATION RD
HEOL CYNWYD
HEOL CADRAWD
PROSPECT PL
HEOL TYN-Y-WAUN
PARC-TYN-Y-WAUN
STATION RD
PO
PH
GREENFIELD TERR
BRIDGEND RD

Llety Brongu

GELLI-SIRIOL COTTS
Llynfi River / Afon Llynfi

6

Waun y Gilfach

CF34

Ty'n-y-waun

Maesteg Comp (Upper) Sch

Cae-mab-Ifor

Sewage Works

5

Foel Fâch

Gadlys

Nant y Gadlys

Gelli-siriol

88

Ty'nton

Nant Bryncynan

Bryn-Cynan

Brynllywarch-fawr

4

Maescadlawr

Bryn-y-fro

Mill

3

87

A4063

2

Craig yr Aber
Nant Craigyrafon
CF33

Mynydd Ty-talwyn

Cwm Nant-gwyn

Cefn Ydfa

CF32

1

Cwm Cefnydfa

86

85 A 86 B C 87 D E F

129
104

A B C D E F

8

Nant Llwyncria

Craig Cae-du

VALE VIEW
PARK AVE
ST JOHN ST
HIGH ST
BRIDGE ST
RHIWGLYN RD
Aber Inf Sch
FERN ST
THE BUNGALOWS
BRYN RD
WALTERS RD
A4061
RIVERSIDE FLATS
PH
WATER ST
ALMA TERR
SUNNYSIDE
RHIWGLYN RD

Pen y Foel

Mast

Craig Llyscwmllorwg

Ogmore Forest

7

Ffawyddog

Nant y Ci

Cwm Nant-y-ci

CEMETERY RD

Cemy

Llyscwmllorwg

89

The Bungalows

A4064

Graig Wen

CF32

Cwm Ogwr Fawr

6

Tylagwyn

Cwm Garw

Ffynnon-dwym

MOUNT PLEASANT COTTS

Lewistown

LLANGEINOR TERR
PENTREBELL
PENTREBELL TERR
BLACKMILL RD
Ogwr Fawr

1 MIN-Y COED
2 DANYGRAIG

5

88

Cefngelli

Aon Garw
(dis)

1 CAE FORGAN COTTS
2 ROSE COTTS
3 OLD TAVERN
4 CWM COTTS
5 THE CROFT

Cae Abbot

LYN DAVIES AVE
HILLSIDE TERR
HEOL AEL BRYN
DAN YR HEOL

PO

4

LC

GREEN MEADOW TERR

2
3
4

A4093

The Llangeinor Arms (PH)

WOODLAND TERR
HILLSIDE
HEOL PANT-YR-AWEL

Pant-yr-awel

A4093

HEOL TY NANT

Tynyrheol Prim Sch

Glyn-y-glowr

Dolau-Ifan-ddu

EBENEZER TERR

GRAIG TERR
A4093

3

HEOL LLANGEINOR
HEOL LLWYNYFFYNNON
HEOL GELLIORA
A4064
HEOL PANDY

Llangeinor

Llwynffynnon

IFOR TERR

OAK RIDGE

DOLAU IFAN DDU TERR
ISFRYN IND EST
EBENEZER CT

87

GRAIGLAS
CAE FACH

Bryn y Wrach

A4093
PH
Blackmill

PO

MEADOW VIEW
OLD PARISH RD

Cwm Ogwr Fach

2

Cefnmachen-uchaf

Mast

DAN Y COED

Cwm Dwr

86

Blaenclydwyn

Nant Clydwyn

CF35

Tal-y-fan Farm

Craig Tal-y-fan

Coedtal-y-fan

Ogmore Valley (Cwm Ogwr)

Ogmore River (Afon Ogmore)

A4061

Nant Cwm-dwr

Lan Farm

1

Cefnmachen-isaf

91 A 92 B C 93 D E F

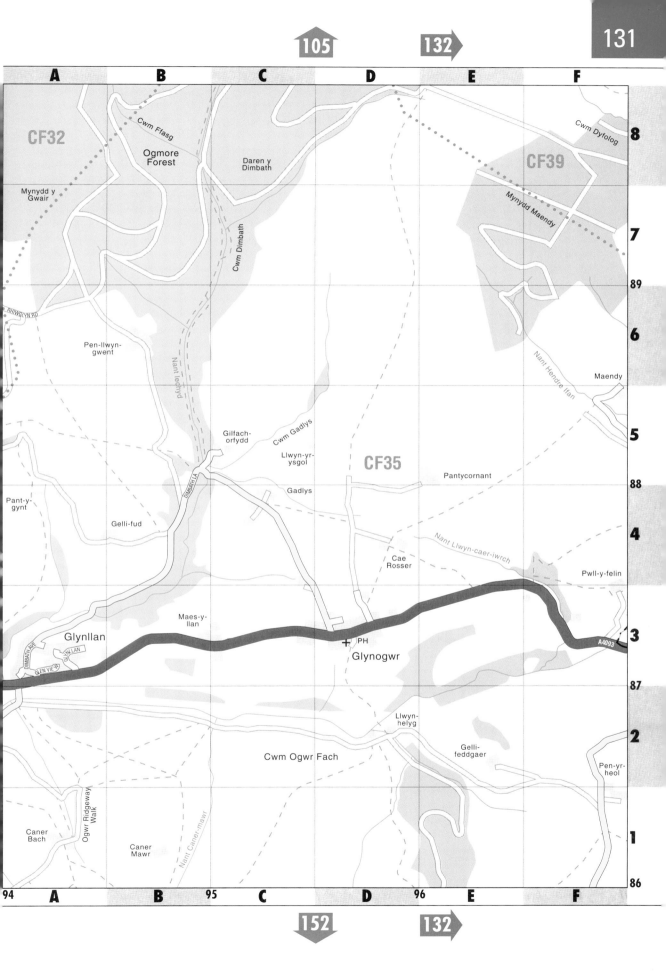

105
132

A B C D E F

8

CF32

Cwm Ffasg

Ogmore Forest

Daren y Dimbath

Cwm Dyfolog

CF39

Mynydd y Gwair

Mynydd Maendy

7

89

Cwm Dimbath

RHIWGLYN RD

6

Pen-llwyn-gwent

Nant Iechyd

Nant Hendre Ifan

Maendy

Gilfach-orfydd

Cwm Gadlys

5

Llwyn-yr-ysgol

CF35

88

Pant-y-gynt

Gadlys

Pantycornant

DIMBATH LA

4

Gelli-fud

Nant Llwyn-caer-iwrch

Cae Rosser

Pwll-y-felin

Maes-y-llan

Glynllan

DIMBATH AVE

GLEN LAN

GLEN VIEW

+ PH

Glynogwr

A4093

3

87

Llwyn-helyg

2

Cwm Ogwr Fach

Gelli-feddgaer

Pen-yr-heol

Ogwr Ridgeway Walk

Nant Caner-mawr

1

Caner Bach

Caner Mawr

86

94 A B 95 C D 96 E F

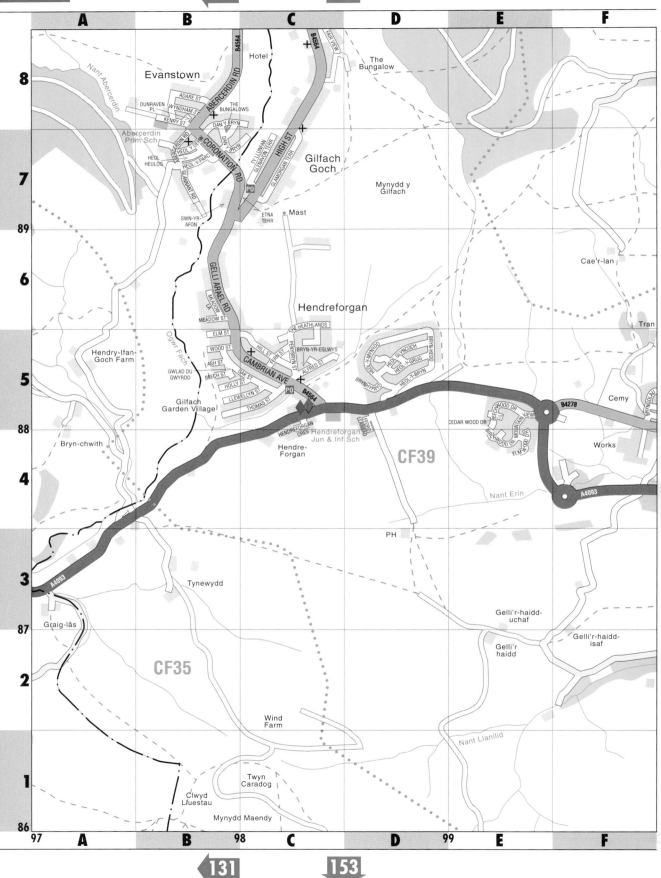

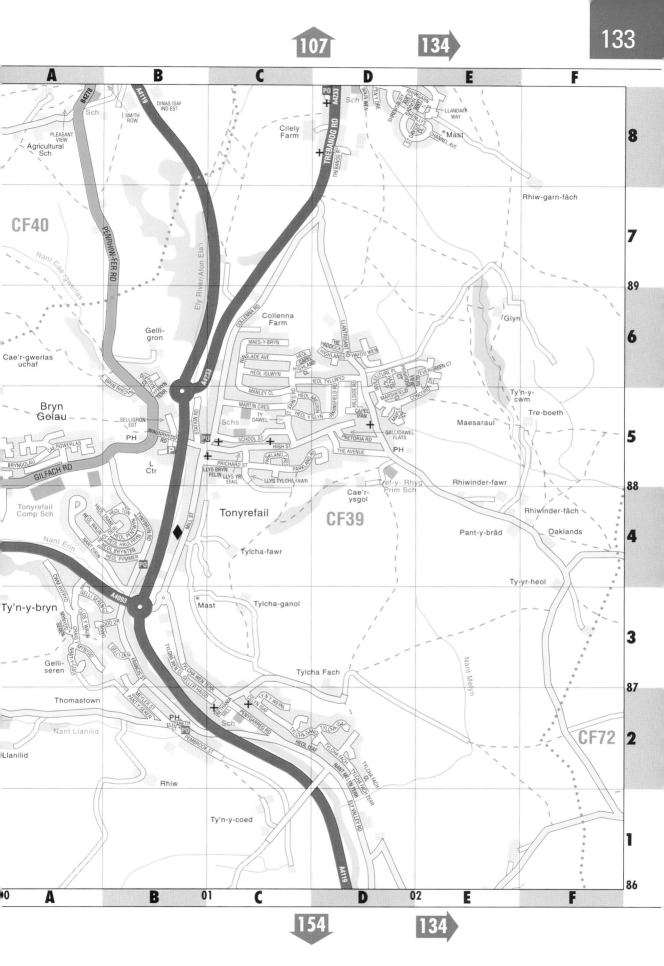

133
108

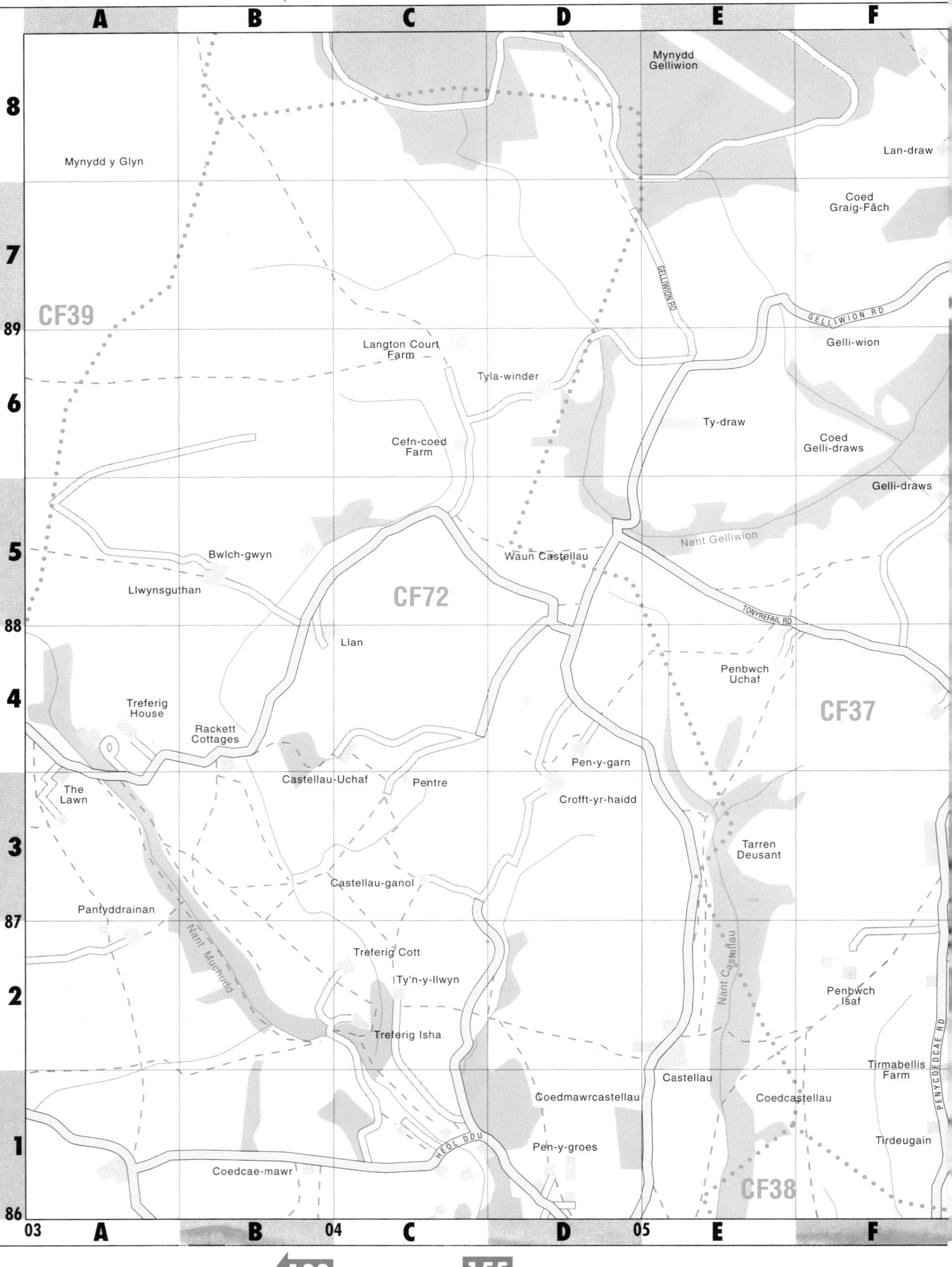

A **B** **C** **D** **E** **F**

8

Mynydd y Glyn

Mynydd
Gelliwion

Lan-draw

Coed
Graig-Fâch

7

CF39

GELLIWION RD

GELLIWION RD

89

Gelli-wion

Langton Court
Farm

Tyla-winder

Ty-draw

Coed
Gelli-draws

6

Cefn-coed
Farm

Gelli-draws

Nant Gelliwion

Bwlch-gwyn

Waun Castellau

TONYREFAIL RD

5

Llwynsguthan

CF72

88

Llan

Penbwch
Uchaf

4

Treferig
House

CF37

Rackett
Cottages

Castellau-Uchaf

Pentre

Pen-y-garn

The
Lawn

Crofft-yr-haidd

Tarren
Deusant

3

Nant Muchudd

Nant Castellau

Castellau-ganol

87

Pantyddrainan

Treferig Cott

Penbwch
Isaf

2

Ty'n-y-llwyn

PENYCOEDCAE RD

Treferig Isha

Castellau

Tirmabellis
Farm

Coedmawrcastellau

Coedcastellau

HEOL DDU

1

Pen-y-groes

Tirdeugain

Coedcae-mawr

CF38

86

03 **A** 04 **B** **C** 04 **D** 05 **E** **F**

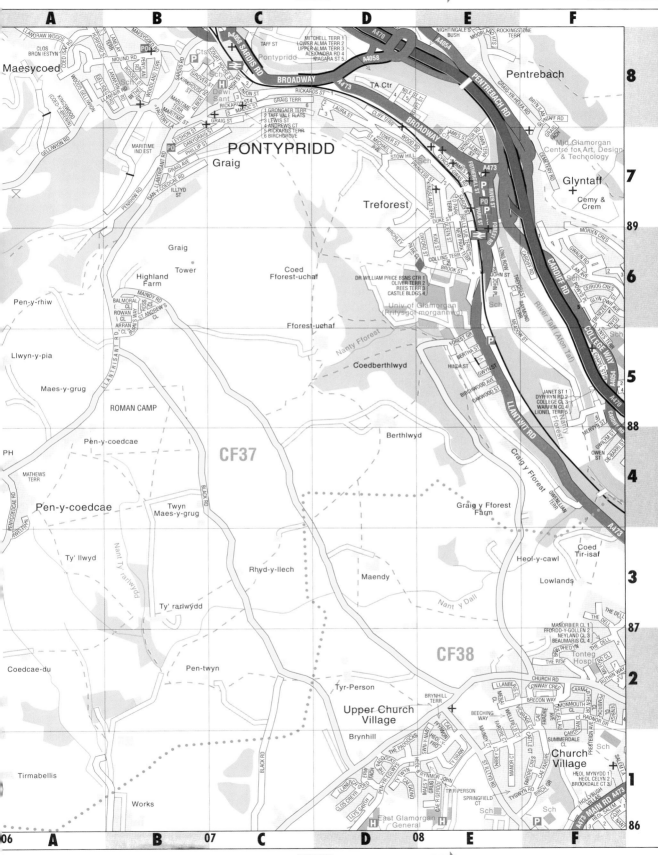

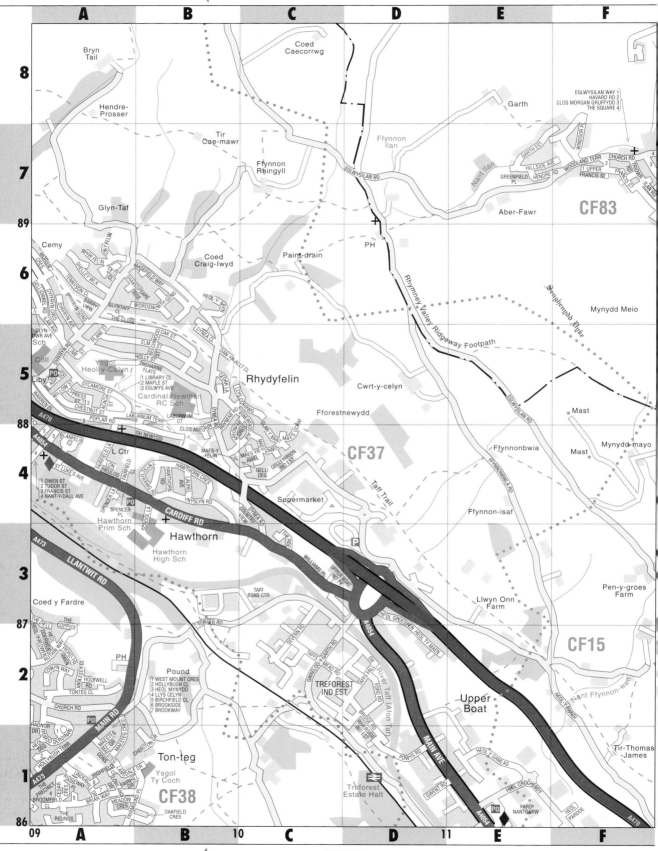

A   B   C   D   E   F

8

Bryn Tail

Coed Caecorrwg

Garth

EGLWYSILAN WAY 1
HAVARD RD 2
CLOS MORGAN GRUFFYDD 3
THE SQUARE 4

7

Hendre-Prosser

Tir Cae-mawr

Ffynnon Rhingyll

Ffynnon Ilan

CF83

Aber-Fawr

89

Glyn-Taf

Cemy

Coed Craig-lwyd

Paint-drain

PH

6

Masefield Way

Heol-y-Bryn

Mynydd Meio

5

Ysgol Heol-y-Celyn J

1 LIBRARY CL
2 MAPLE ST
3 EGLWYS AVE

Rhydyfelin

Cwrt-y-celyn

Mynydd Meio

Mast

88

A470

Cardinal Newman RC Sch

Fforestnewydd

CF37

Ffynnonbwia

Mast

Mynydd-mayo

Mast

A4054

L Ctr

Maes-y-Felin

Taff Trail

Ffynnon-isaf

4

1 OWEN ST
2 TUDOR ST
3 FRANCIS ST
4 NANT-Y-DALL AVE

St LUKE'S AVE

Hawthorn Cres

Supermarket

Hawthorn Prim Sch

CARDIFF RD

Hawthorn

Hawthorn High Sch

Upper Boat

Llwyn Onn Farm

Pen-y-groes Farm

3

A473

LLANTWIT RD

TAFF BSNS CTR

P
UPPER BOAT IND PK

HEOL GROESNEWYDD HEOL TY MAEN

CF15

87

Coed y Fardre

THE DELL
THE COPPICE

TONTEG RD

Pound

1 WEST MOUNT CRES
2 HOLLYBUSH CL
3 HEOL MYNYDD
4 LLYS CELYN
5 BIRCHFIELD CL
6 BROOKSIDE
7 BROOKWAY

TREFOREST IND EST

River Taff (Afon Taf)

Upper Boat

Tir-Thomas-James

2

PH

HOLYWELL RD

CHURCH RD

MAIN RD

PO

Ton-teg

Ysgol Ty Coch

CF38

Treforest Estate Halt

MAIN AVE

PARC NANTGARW

1

A473

PO

86

09   A   B   10   C   D   11   E   F

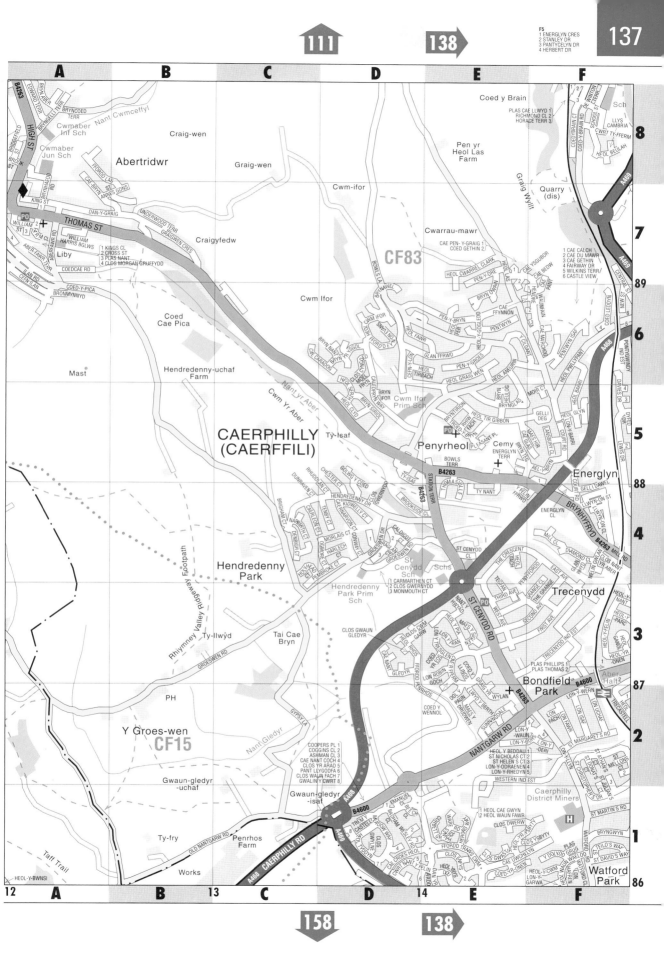

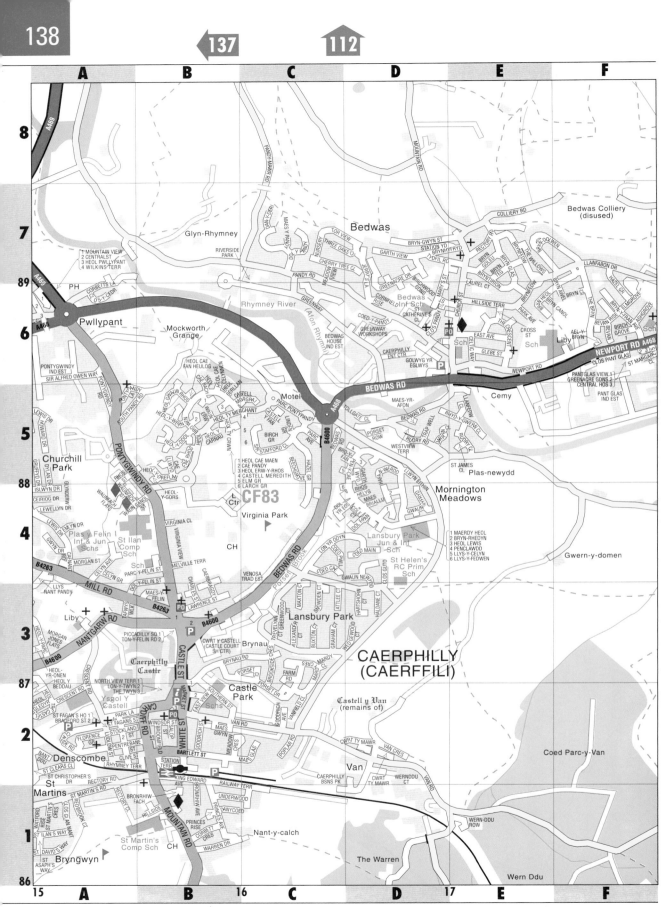

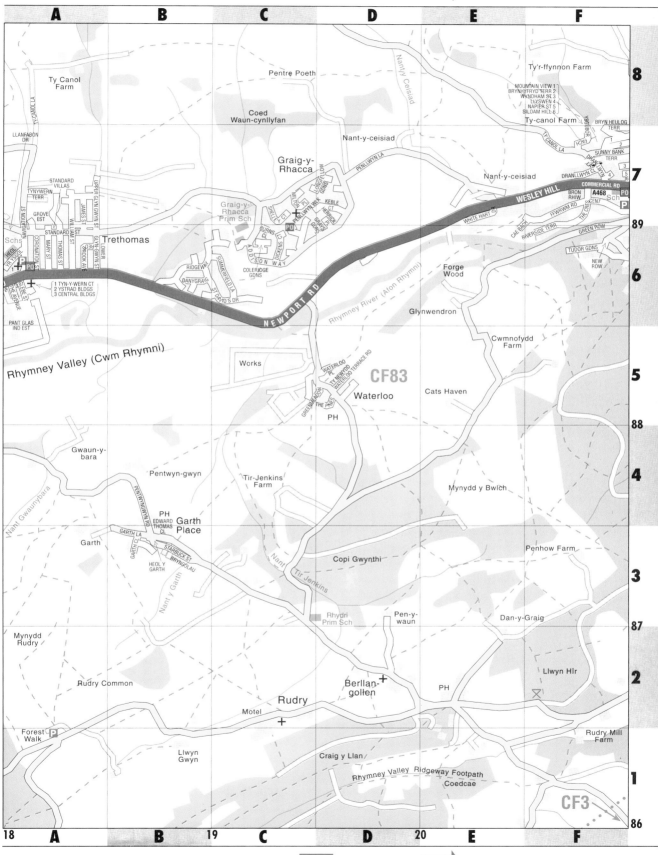

139
114

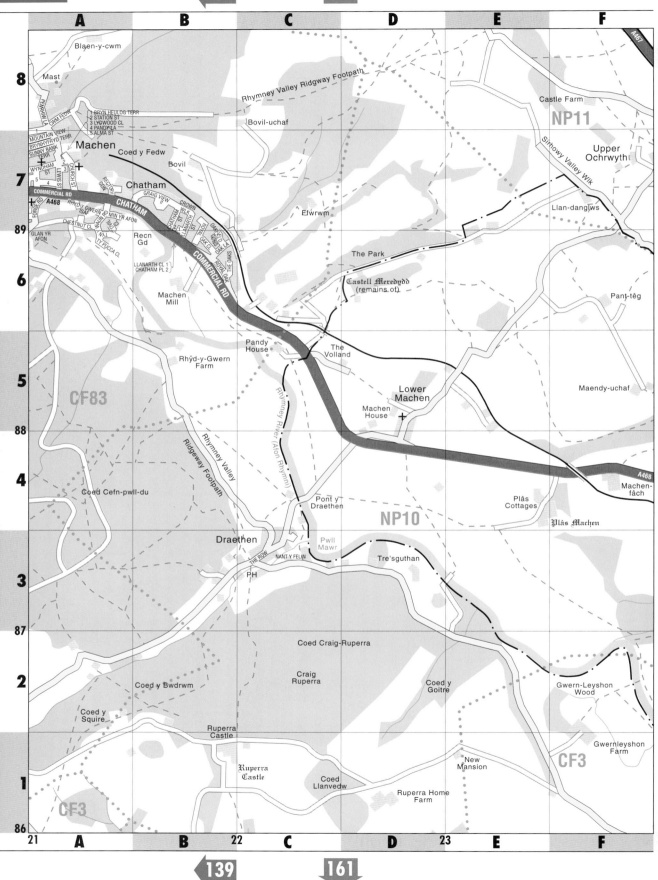

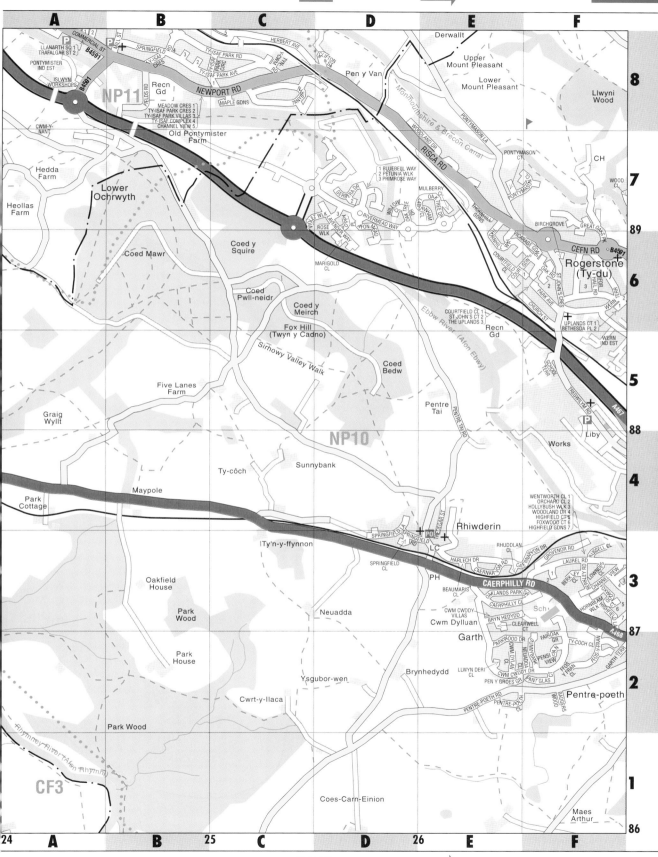

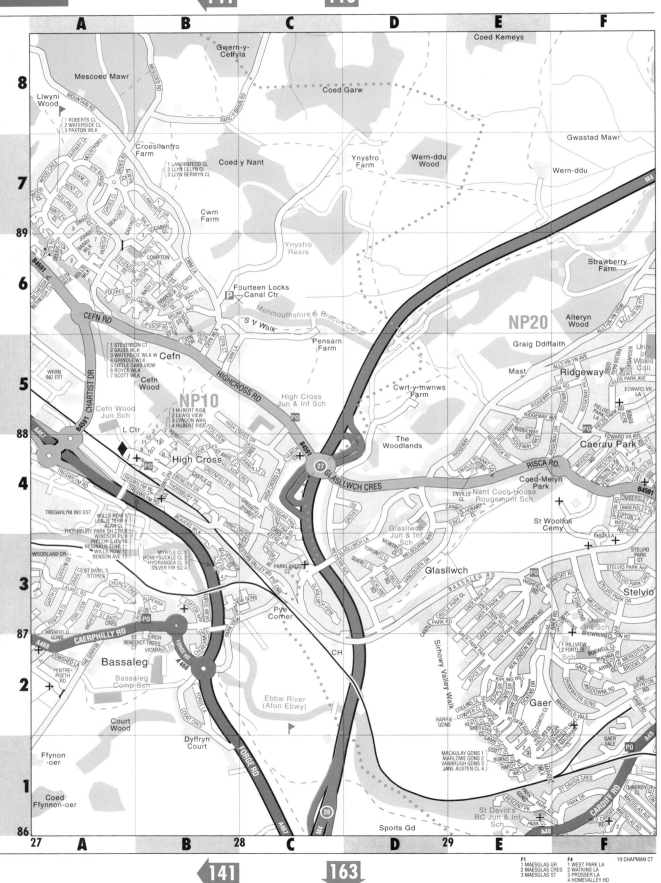

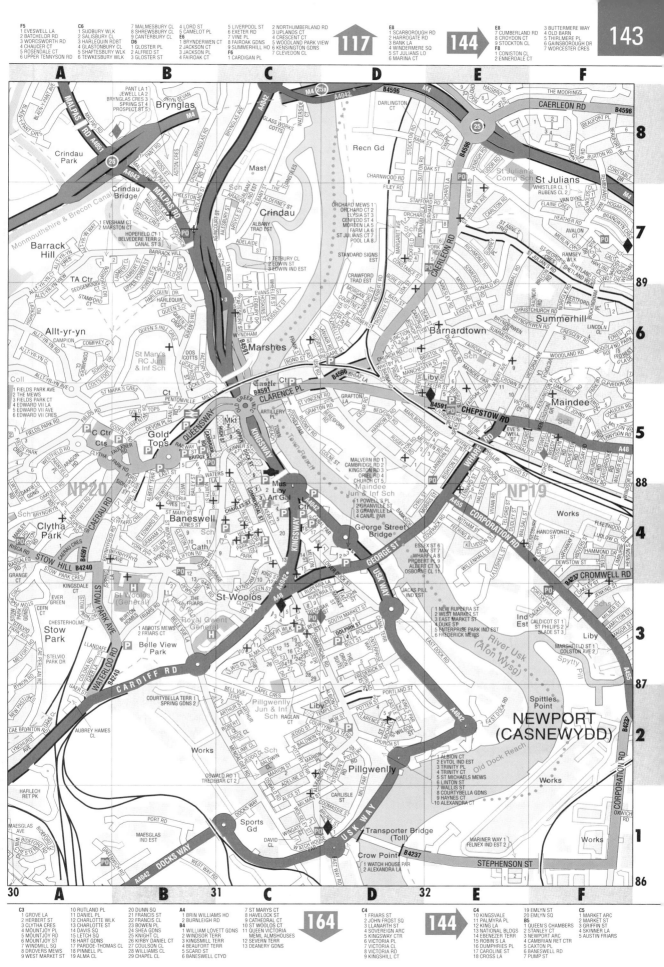

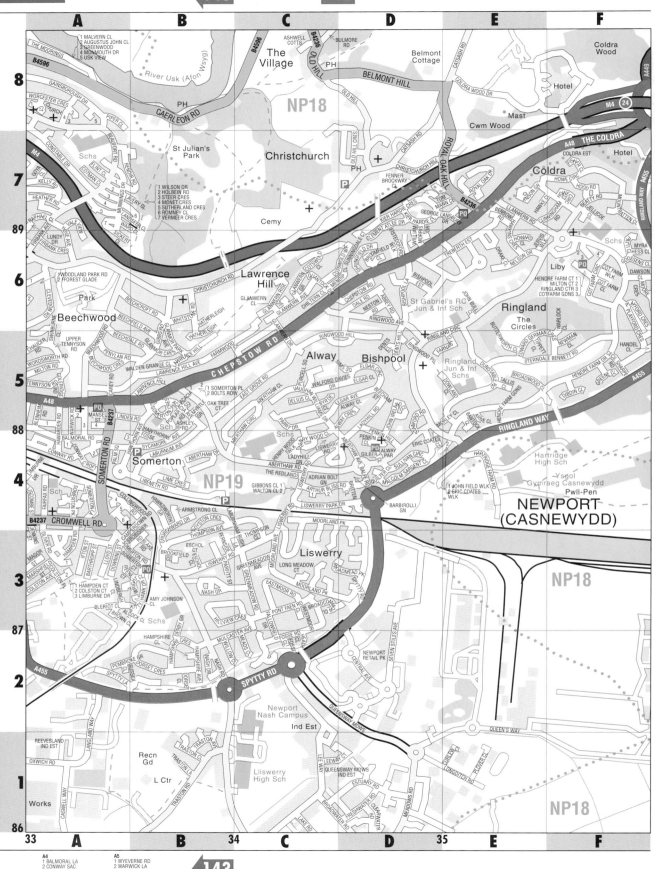

143
118

A4
1 BALMORAL LA
2 CONWAY SAC
3 HAWTHORNE SQ
4 COLLINGWOOD CRES
5 COLLINGWOOD RD
6 COLLINGWOOD CL
7 CROMWELL CT

A5
1 WYEVERNE RD
2 WARWICK LA
3 KENILWORTH RD
4 LLEWELLIN ST

143

125

A
B
C
D
E
F
8
7
85
6
5
84
4
3
83
2
1
82
76
77
78
Works
GRANGE RD
Upper Mother Ditch
LC
HEOL CAER BONT
Margam Sands
Margam Moors
SA13
Margam Burrows
Dunes
Afon Cynffig
Swansea Bay
Kenfig Burrows
Kenfig Sands
CF33
G
H
82
81
80
78
79
Kenfig Burrows
CF33
Kenfig Sands
CF36
Sker Point

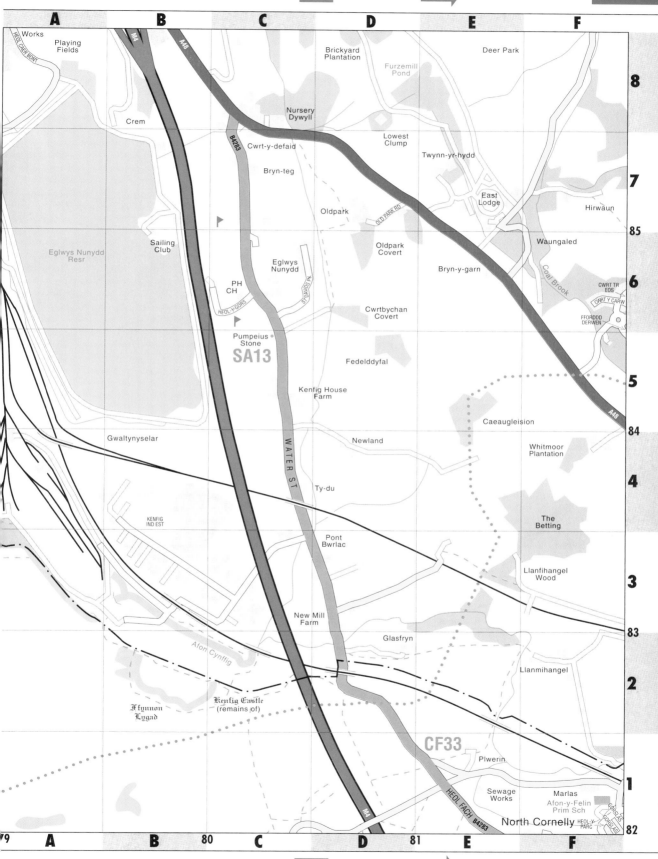

126
148
165
148

Works

Playing Fields

Crem

M4

A48

B4283

Sailing Club

Eglwys Nunydd Resr

Brickyard Plantation

Furzemill Pond

Nursery Dywyll

Cwrt-y-defaid

Bryn-teg

Oldpark

OLD PARK RD

Lowest Clump

Deer Park

Twynn-yr-hydd

East Lodge

Hirwaun

Waungaled

Coal Brook

CWRT TR EOS

CWRT Y CARW

FFORDDD DERWEN

PH CH

HEOL-Y-GORS

ST DAVIDS PK

Pumpeius Stone

SA13

Eglwys Nunydd

Oldpark Covert

Bryn-y-garn

Cwrtbychan Covert

Fedelddyfal

Kenfig House Farm

Caeaugleision

Whitmoor Plantation

A48

Gwaltynyselar

Newland

Ty-du

Pont Bwrlac

KENFIG IND EST

The Betting

Llanfihangel Wood

New Mill Farm

Afon Cynffig

Glasfryn

Llanmihangel

WATER ST

Ffynnon Lygad

Kenfig Castle (remains of)

CF33

Plwerin

HEOL FACH

B4283

M4

Sewage Works

Marlas

Afon-y-Felin Prim Sch

North Cornelly

HEOL-Y-PARC

GORSLAS

GORSLAS

8 7 85 6 5 84 4 3 83 2 1 82

79 80 81

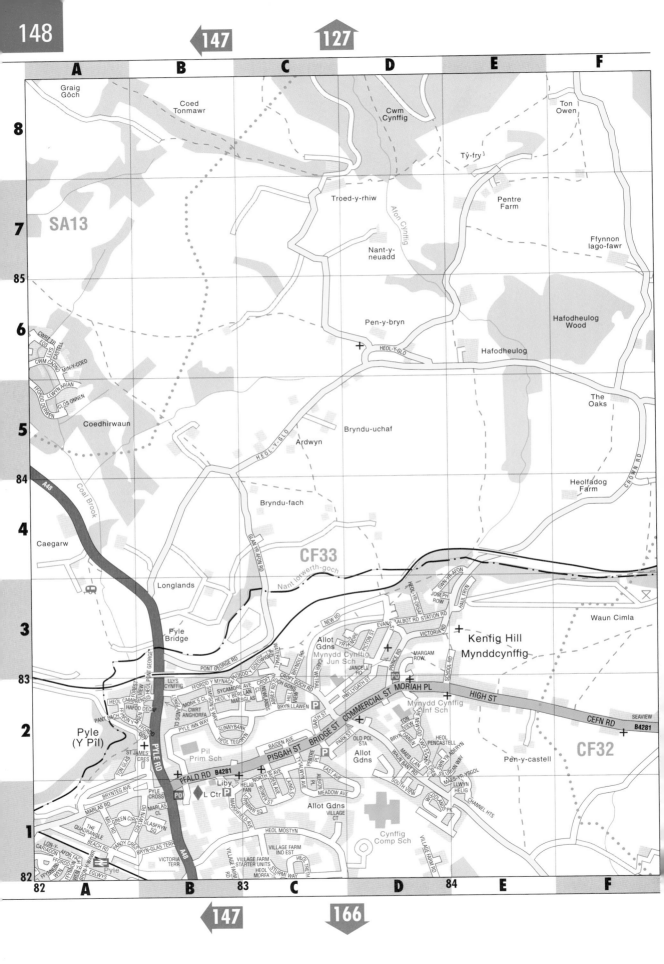

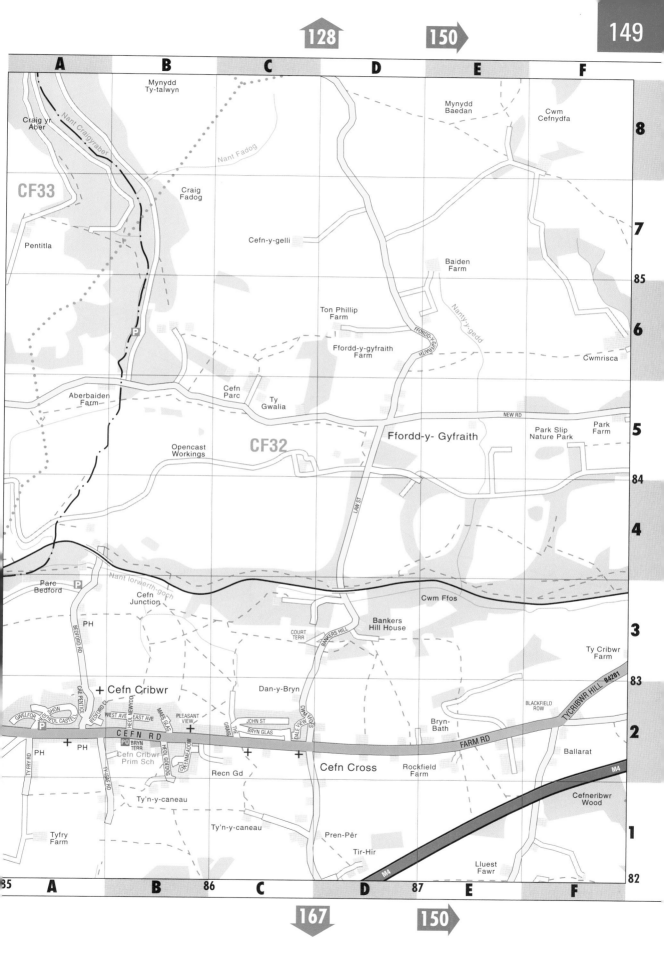

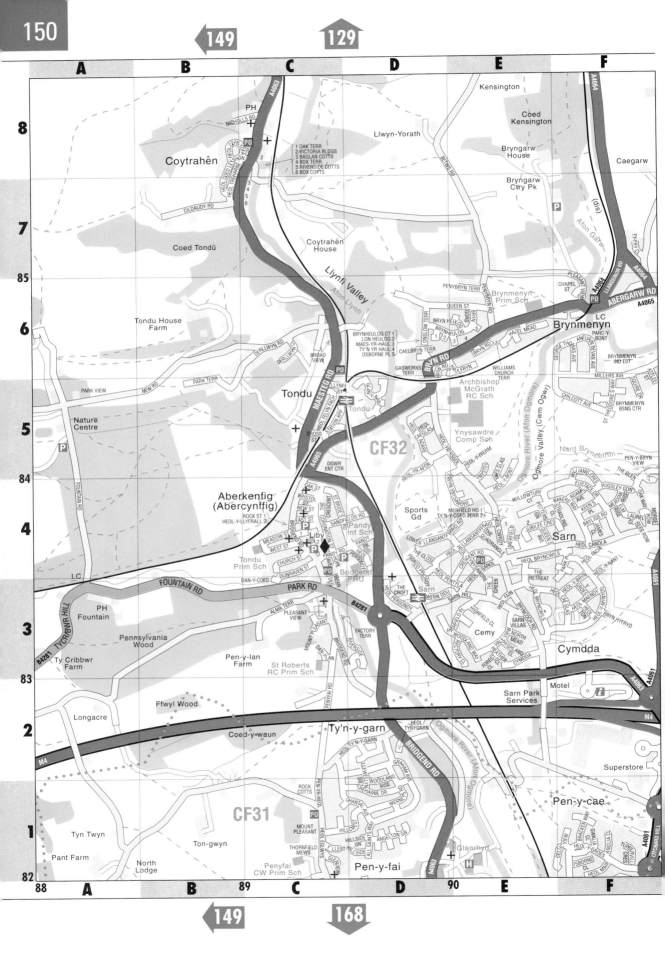

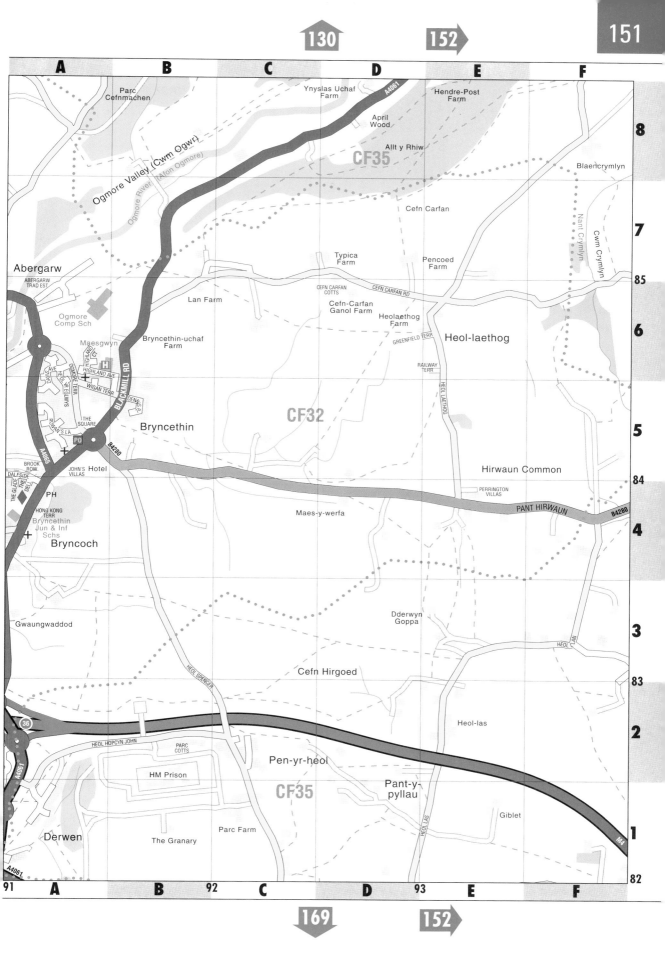

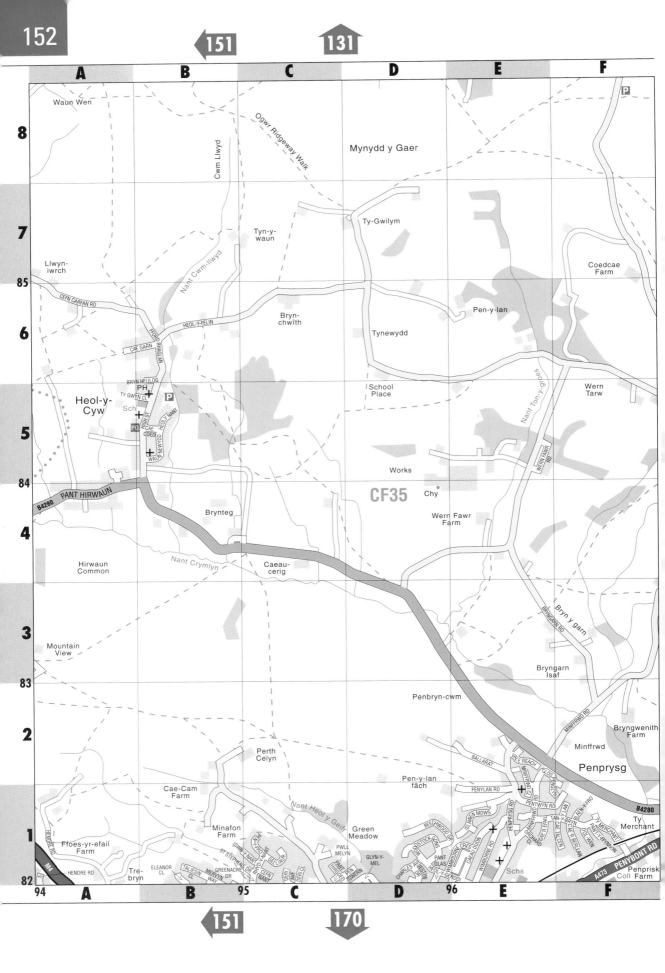

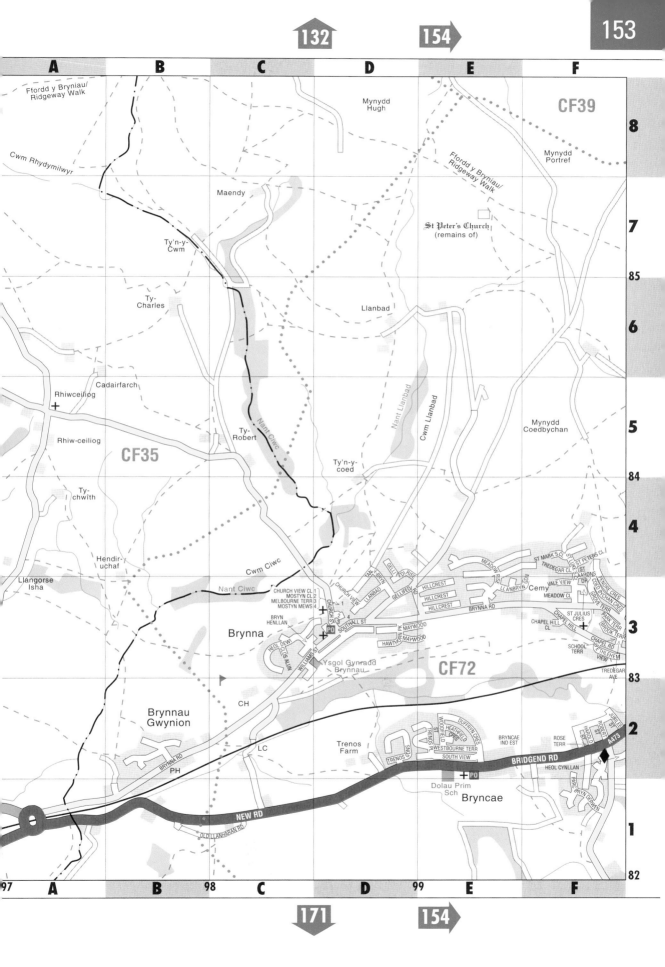

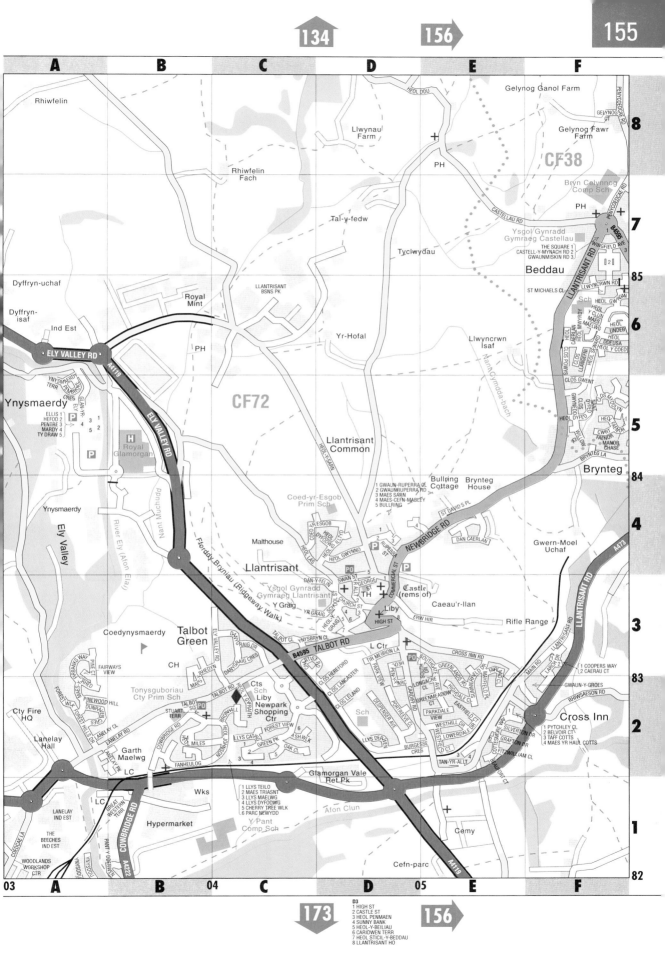

Rhiwfelin

Gelynog Ganol Farm

Llwynau
Farm

Gelynog Fawr
Farm

PH

CF38

8

Rhiwfelin
Fach

Bryn Celynnog
Comp Sch

Castellau Rd

PH

Tal-y-fedw

7

Ysgol Gynradd
Gymraeg Castellau

Tyclwydau

THE SQUARE 1
CASTELL-Y-MYNACH RD 2
GWAUNMISKIN RD 3.

Dyffryn-uchaf

LLANTRISANT
BSNS PK

Royal Mint

Beddau

St MICHAELS CL

85

Dyffryn-
isaf

Ind Est

PH

Yr-Hofal

Llwyncrwn
Isaf

HEOL Y COED

6

ELY VALLEY RD

Ynysmaerdy

CF72

Llantrisant
Common

Brynteg

84

ELLIS 1
HEFOD 2
PENTRE 3
MARDY 4
TY DRAW 5

Royal
Glamorgan

MANOR
CHASE

5

Ynysmaerdy

Coed-yr-Esgob
Prim Sch

Bulling
Cottage

Brynteg
House

1 GWAUN-RUPERRA CL
2 GWAUNRUPERRA RD
3 MAES SARN
4 MAES-CEFN-MABLEY
5 BULLING

St DAVID S PL

84

River Ely (Afon Elai)

Ely Valley

Ffordd Bryniau (Ridgeway Walk)

Malthouse

NEWBRIDGE RD

Dan Caerlan

Gwern-Moel
Uchaf

A473

4

Ysgol Gynradd
Gymraeg Llantrisant

Llantrisant

Y Graig

Caeau'r-Ilan

LLANTRISANT RD

Castle
(rems of)

TH

Rifle Range

3

Coedynysmaerdy

Talbot
Green

Liby
HIGH ST

L Ctr

CROSS INN RD

83

Fairways
View

CH

TALBOT RD

1 COOPERS WAY
2 CAERAU CT

Tonysguboriau
Cty Prim Sch

Cts
Sch
Liby
Newpark
Shopping
Ctr

Sch

Cross Inn

1 PYTCHLEY CL
2 BELVOIR CT
3 TAFF COTTS
4 MAES YR HAUL COTTS

2

Cty Fire
HQ

Lanelay
Hall

Garth
Maelwg

LC

Glamorgan Vale
Ret Pk

LANELAY
IND EST

LC

Wks

1 LLYS TEILO
2 MAES TRIASNT
3 LLYS MAELWG
4 LLYS DYFODWG
5 CHERRY TREE WLK
6 PARC NEWYDD

Afon Clun

Cemy

1

THE BEECHES
IND EST

COWBRIDGE RD

A222

Hypermarket

Y Pant
Comp Sch

WOODLANDS
WORKSHOP
CTR

A4119

Cefn-parc

82

D3
1 HIGH ST
2 CASTLE ST
3 HEOL PENMAEN
4 SUNNY BANK
5 HEOL-Y-BEILIAU
6 CARIDWEN TERR
7 HEOL STICIL-Y-BEDDAU
8 LLANTRISANT HO

A | B | C | D | E | F

8

Works

Penycoedcae Rd

Foel

Croesged

Croesged House

Llest Farm

Llys Coed Derw
Peny-Yr-Eglwys
Clos-Yr-Maedd
The Oaks
Nelyn

THE PARADE
PO
Liby PH
MAIN RD
1 LEWIS ST
2 GARTH VIEW
3 DUFFRYN TERR
4 ALMA TERR

Church Village

Dyffryn Dowlais

Dyffryn Bach Farm

Dyffryn Bach Terr

Heol Bryn Heulog 1
Parc-Y-Bryn 2

Ty Crwyn

Clos Y Coed

Tynant

Cwrt Pentwyn

Cwrt-Y-Goedwig

Green Wood Dr

WOODLANDS

Codgers Cnr

Alexandra Terr

B4595

Gwynfryn Terr

Llantwit Fardre
(Llanilltud Faerdref)

Maes-y-Byrn
Prim Sch

Station Terr

Bryn Terr

Newtown Ind Est

Nant Dowlais

Nant Celyn

7

85

Tynant

Parish Rd

Tynant Rd

Liby

Garth View

Zion Ct

PO

Heol Gwrgan

Heol Cawrdaf

Heol Ap Pryce

Schs

Gwaun Meisgyn
Gwaun Miskin

Beddau

Ystradbarwig Terr

Kingsacre

St Andrews Cl

Church Cl

Queens Dr

Marlborough Dr

PO

Heol-Y-Ffynnon

Heol Tir Coch

Heol
Ffordd-Y-Capel

PH

Efail Isaf

6

Maes Trane

Colbourne Cl

Magnolia Way

CF38

Heol Dowlais

Nant Y Felin

Heol Iscoed

5

Hotel

1 Hibiscus Ct
2 Birch Cres

Ystrad Barwig Isaf

Ty Mawr

84

Nant Mydydyn

Brynteg La

Brynteg Ct

Brook Farm

Nant y Felin

Ty Mawr

4

A473

Rhiwbrwdwal Farm

Disgwylfa

Coed Hendre-Isguthan

Hendrescythan

3

CF72

Coedcaerau-bach

Tyuchaf

Ty Mawr Farm

Heol Creigiau

Craig Gwilym

Nant y Cesair

83

Rhiwsaeson Rd

Rhiwsaeson

Fforddy Bryniau (Ridgeway Walk)

Tŷ'n-y-coed

2

Tor-y-coed

Sewage Works

PH

Ty'n-y-coed Rd

CF15

Afon Clun

Llwyn-y-brain

1

Llwynmilwas

Y Graig

Coed y Creigiau

82

06 | A | B | 07 | C | D | 08 | E | F

A5
1 DYLAN AVE
2 MANOR CHASE
3 CWRT Y WAUN
4 CLOS CADWGAN
5 CWRT Y GARTH
6 CALDICOTT CL
7 CAMPERLY CL
8 CARSHALTON RD

A6
1 COMMON APP
2 GWAUNRHYDD
3 TREM-Y-CWM
4 HEOL GELYNOG

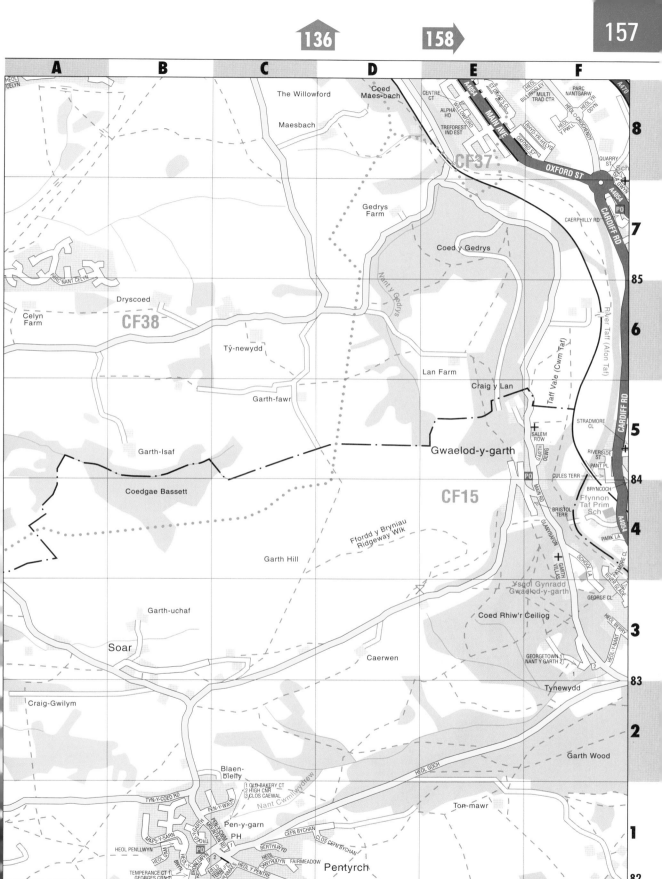

A   B   C   D   E   F

8

7

85

6

5

84

4

3

83

2

1

82

The Willowford
Coed Maes-bach
Maesbach
CENTRE CT
CF37
OXFORD ST
QUARRY ST
CAERPHILLY RD
CARDIFF RD
Gedrys Farm
Coed y Gedrys
Nant y Gedrys
CF38
Dryscoed
Celyn Farm
PARC NANT CELYN
Tý-newydd
Lan Farm
River Taff (Afon Taf)
Taff Vale (Cwm Taf)
Garth-fawr
Craig y Lan
CARDIFF RD
Garth-Isaf
Gwaelod-y-garth
SALEM ROW
STRADMORE CL
RIVERSIDE ST
PANT PL
CULES TERR
BRYNCOCH
Coedgae Bassett
CF15
Ffynnon Taf Prim Sch
BRISTOL TERR
MAIN RD
PARK LA
Ffordd y Bryniau
Ridgeway Wlk
GLANYRAFON
Garth Hill
GARTH VILLAS
SCHOOL LA
Ysgol Gynradd
Gwaelod-y-garth
GEORGE CL
Garth-uchaf
Coed Rhiw'r Ceiliog
HEOL BERRY
HEOL-Y-NANT
Soar
Caerwen
GEORGETOWN 1
NANT Y GARTH 2
Tynewydd
Craig-Gwilym
Garth Wood
HEOL GOCH
Ton-mawr
Blaen-blelty
1 OLD BAKERY CT
2 HIGH CNR
3 CLOS CAEWAL
Nant Cwmllwydrew
TYN-Y-COED RD
PEN-Y-WAUN
PEN-Y-GARN
MOUNTAIN RD
Pen-y-garn
PH
CEFN BYCHAN
CLOS CEFN BYCHAN
HEOL PENLLWYN
BERTHLWYD
FAIRMEADOW
TEMPERANCE CT
GEORGES CRN
Pentyrch

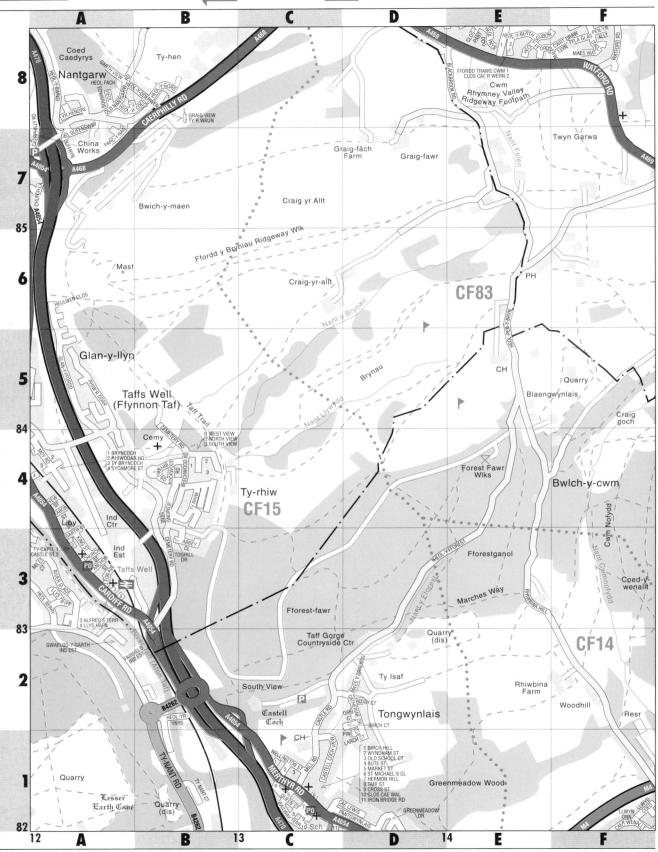

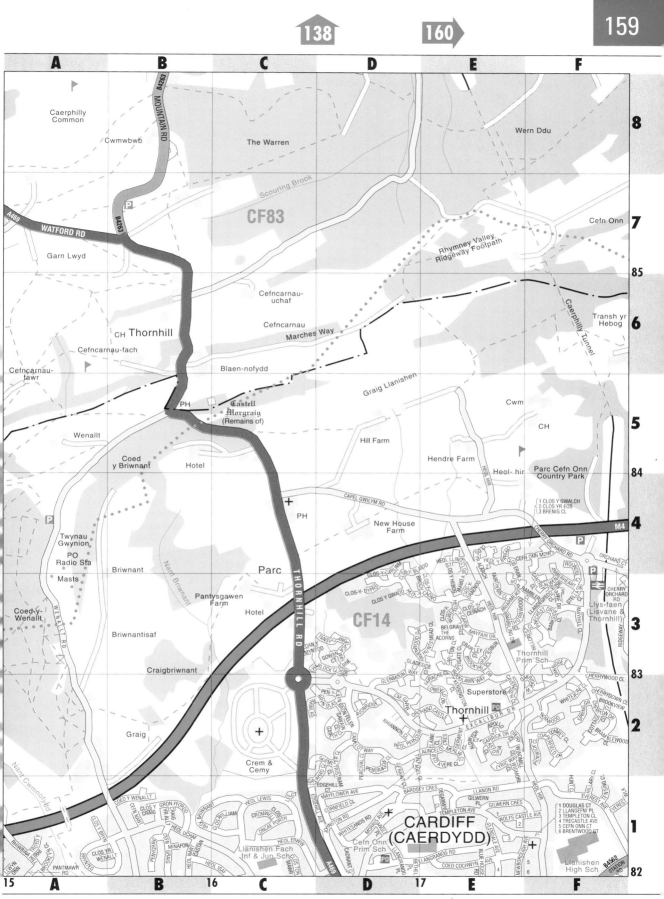

138
160

A B C D E F

8

Caerphilly
Common

Cwmbwb

The Warren

Wern Ddu

Scouring Brook

CF83 7

A469

WATFORD RD

B4253

MOUNTAIN RD

P

B4253

85

Garn Lwyd

Cefncarnau-
uchaf

Rhymney Valley
Ridgeway Footpath

Cefn Onn

6

CH Thornhill

Cefncarnau

Cefncarnau-fach

Marches Way

Caerphilly Tunnel

Transh yr
Hebog

Cefncarnau-
fawr

Blaen-nofydd

Graig Llanishen

Cwm

5

PH

Wenallt

Castell
Morgraig
(Remains of)

Hill Farm

CH

Coed
y Briwnant

Hotel

Hendre Farm

Heol-hir

Parc Cefn Onn
Country Park

84

Capel Gwilym Rd

1 CLOS Y GWALCH
2 CLOS YR EOS
3 BRENIG CL

4

P

PH

New House
Farm

M4

Twynau
Gwynion

PO
Radio Sta

Masts

Briwnant

CHERRY ORCHARD RD

P

CHERRY
ORCHARD
RD

Llys-faen
(Lisvane &
Thornhill)

Parc

CF14

Coed-y-
Wenallt

Pantysgawen
Farm

Nant Briwnant

WENALLT RD

Hotel

Thornhill
Prim Sch

3

Briwnantisaf

Superstore

83

CHERRYWOOD CL

BROOKVIEW

Craigbriwnant

Thornhill

PO

EXCALIBUR DR

BRAMBLEWOOD
CL

2

Graig

Crem &
Cemy

LLANON RD

GILWERN
PL

GILWERN CRES

WOLFS CASTLE AVE

1 DOUGLAS CT
2 LLANGEFNI PL
3 TEMPLETON CL
4 TRECASTLE AVE
5 CEFN ONN CT
6 BRENTWOOD CT

1

Nant Cwmnofydd

CARDIFF
(CAERDYDD)

Llanishen Fach
Inf & Jun Sch

Cefn Onn
Prim Sch

PO

Llanishen
High Sch

B4562

STATION RD

82

15 A B 16 C D 17 E F

159
139

A B C D E F

8

7

85

6

5

84

4

3

83

2

1

82

Rhymney Valley Ridgeway Footpath
Marches Way
Coed Cefn-Onn
Nant y Cwm
Ty'n-y-graig
Coed Coesau-whips
Crynant Farm
Coed Llwyn-celyn
Llwyncelyn
Llwyncelyn
Nant Cwmcrynant
Forest Walk
CF83
Pant Glas
Coed y Graig
Pentwyn
Coed Gwineu
CF3
Craig Llysfaen
Tai-mawr
The Mount
Coed y Coedcae
CEFN PORTH RD
Springmeadow
Coed-bach
Cefn Porth
Brynhill Farm
Rudry Rd
Nant Fawr
PH
Graig Rd
Pant Teg Farm
The Hollies
Fair Oak Farm
Graig-llwyn
Nant Ty-draw-fach
GRAIG-LLWYN RD
Wern Fawr
GRAIG LLWYN RD
CEFN MABLY RD
Coed-y-Ilan
M4
CF14
Yellow-wells
Nant Ty-draw
Llan Farm
M4
Church House Farm
Ty-yn-y-Berllan
Malthouse Wood
CEFN MABLY RD
Liby
Llysfaen Prim Sch
PO
Maes y Felin
Malthouse
CHURCH RD
PH
Mill Farm
ST MELLONS RD
Lisvane (Llys Faen)
CLOS COED-Y-DARAN
MAERDY LA
Nant Glandulas
Maerdy
B4562
LISVANE RD
Christ the King RC Prim Sch
P Llanishen
CF23
Llangattock
Bryngolau
Corpus Christi RC High Sch
CARDIFF (CAERDYDD)
STATION RD B4562
Sch
NEWLANDS CT
THE GLADE
GWERN RHUDDI RD
ALDERBROOK
PENTWYN RD
BLACK OAK RD
FOREST OAK CL
HAMPTON CRES W
THE FAIRWAY
CLOS NANT COSLECH   1
OAKLEAFE DR   2
AMBERGATE DR   3
AMBER CL   4
AMBLECOTE CL   5
AVENUE INDUSTL   6
HUNTINGDON DR   7
FELSTED CL   8
CLOS ALYN   9
SINDERCOMBE CL   10
DUNGARVAN DR   11

159
178

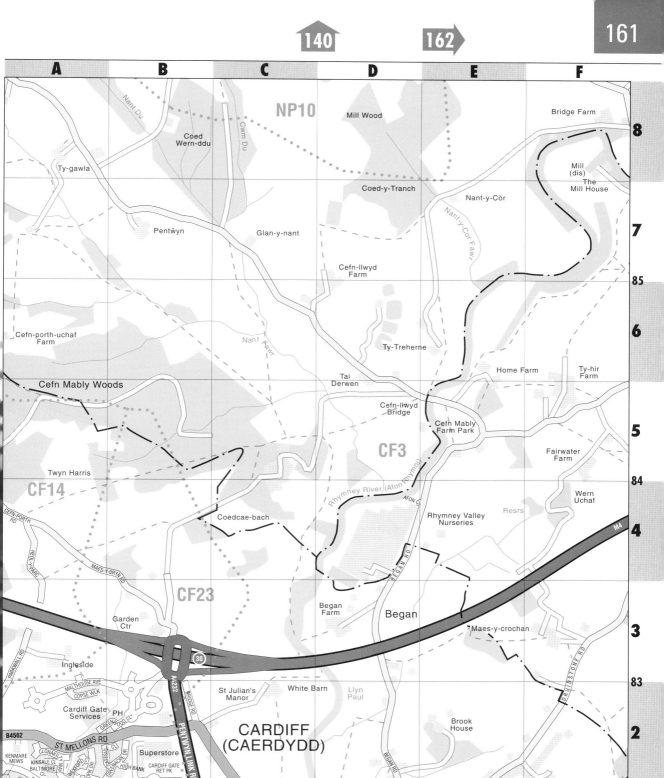

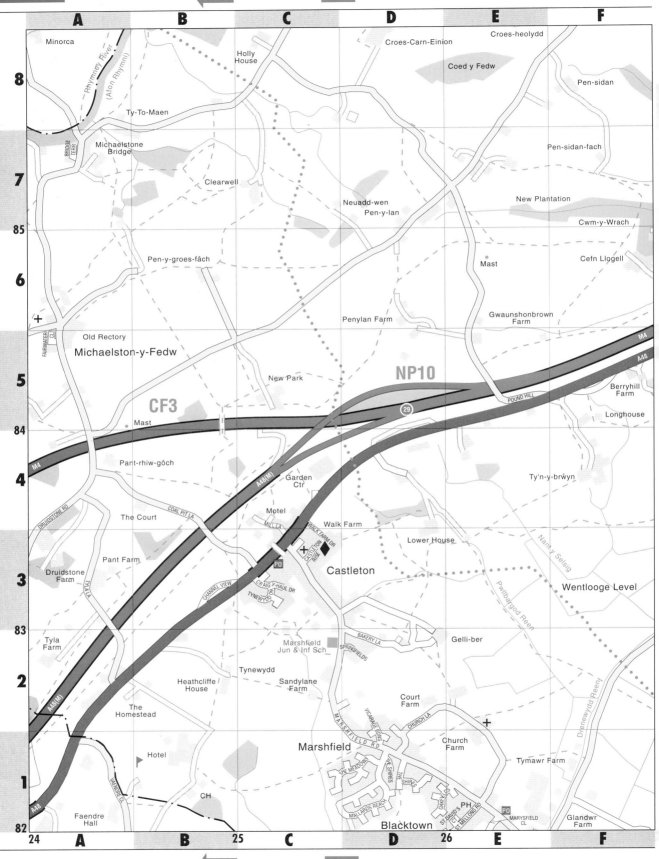

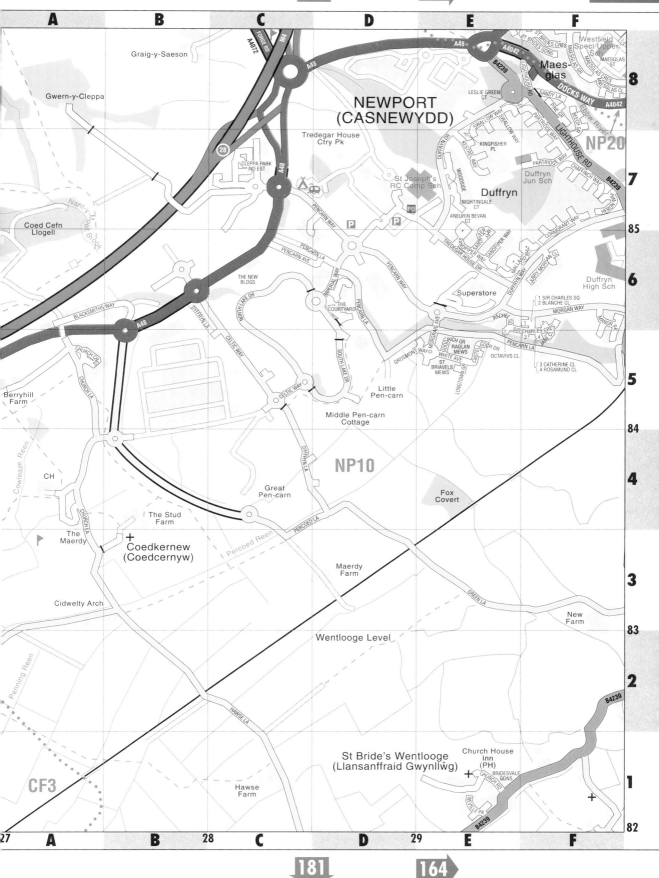

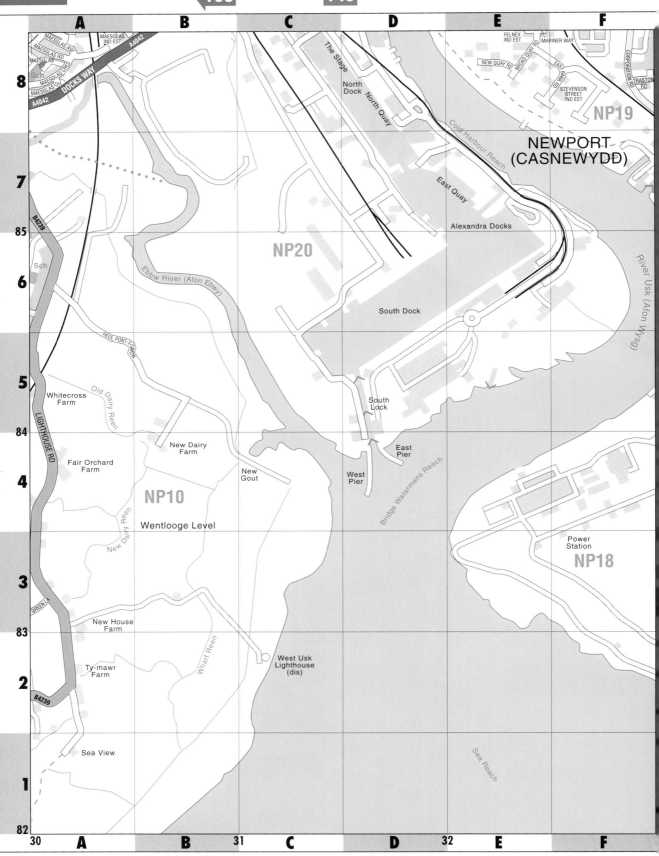

163
143

A **B** **C** **D** **E** **F**

8

MAESGLAS AVE
MAESGLAS IND EST
A4042
DOCKS WAY
MAESGLAS RD
MAESGLAS ST
MAESGLAS CRES
Sch
MAESGLAS CL
A4042

The Stage
North Dock
North Quay

FELNEX IND EST
MARINER WAY
NEW QUAY RD
BROAD QUAY RD
EAST BANK RD
CORPORATION RD
STEVENSON STREET IND EST
TRASTON RD

NP19

7

B4239

Cold Harbour Reach

East Quay

NEWPORT
(CASNEWYDD)

85

Sch

Alexandra Docks

NP20

6

Ebbw River (Afon Ebwy)

South Dock

River Usk (Afon Wysg)

HEOL PONT-Y-CWCW

5

Whitecross Farm
Old Dairy Reen

South Lock

84

LIGHTHOUSE RD

Fair Orchard Farm
New Dairy Farm

East Pier

4

NP10

New Gout

West Pier

Bridge Watermans Reach

Wentlooge Level

New Dairy Reen

Power Station

NP18

3

GREEN LA

New House Farm

Wharf Reen

83

Ty-mawr Farm

2

B4239

West Usk Lighthouse (dis)

Sea Reach

1

Sea View

82

30 **A** **B** 31 **C** **D** 32 **E** **F**

165 148

A B C D E F

8

7

81

6

5

80

4

3

79

2

1

78

CAE'R CYNFFIG
GIBBONS WAY
PIL-Y-CYNFFIG
BRON-Y-WAWR
AEL-Y-BRYN
BRYN-YR-ORSAF
HEOL TYDRAW
TYDRAW CRES
PYLE RD
A48
A4229
Factory
Afon Fach
Stormy

TIR NEWYDD
PLAS MOR-AEL
PLAS HEDDWCH
HEOL-Y-PARC
BIRNAM
FFORDD YR BRWYS
Cemy
School Terr
Fairfield
Hall Dr
PH
HEOL NEUADD
HEOL JULIAN'S WAY
WOODLAND WAY
BALLAS WAY
GLAN-Y-LLYN
MOUNTAIN VIEW
LLWYN TAE GLAS
HEOL FAWR
FFORDD-Y-FRON
HEOL-Y-SHEET
PEN-Y-FRON
PEN-Y-FRON
THOMAS CRES

M4 37 M4
A4229
A48

HEOL-Y-SHEET
Ty Tanglwyst Farm
Old Ballas
Ballas Cottage
Ballas Farm
Stormy Down
CF33

LAMB ROW
PH
RAILWAY TERR
Pant Mawr Quarries (dis)
HEOL-Y-SPLOT
Cornelly Quarry
Stormy Down Quarry
A48

SOUTH CORNELLY IND EST
Cornelly Quarry
Grove Quarry
CF32

A4229
The Grove
CH
Tyllau Gro
Ty Coch Farm
MOUNT PLEASANT RD
Mount Pleasant Farm
Newton Down

Jubilee Farm
Pant yr Hyl
Ty'n-y-caeau
The Beacons

Orchard Farm
JUBILEE GDNS
ZIG-ZAG LA
TIN-Y-CAEAU LA
Tir Hapus
Pant yr lards

St David's Well
PYLE RD
Cemy
CF36
MOOR LA
Manor Farm
Coedargraig
A4106
BRIDGEND RD

MARLPIT LA
A4229
A4106
The Bungalow
ELDER DR
Dan-y-graig
Wig-fach Farm

Nottage Court
NEWTON NOTTAGE RD
A4106

82 A 83 B C 84 D E F

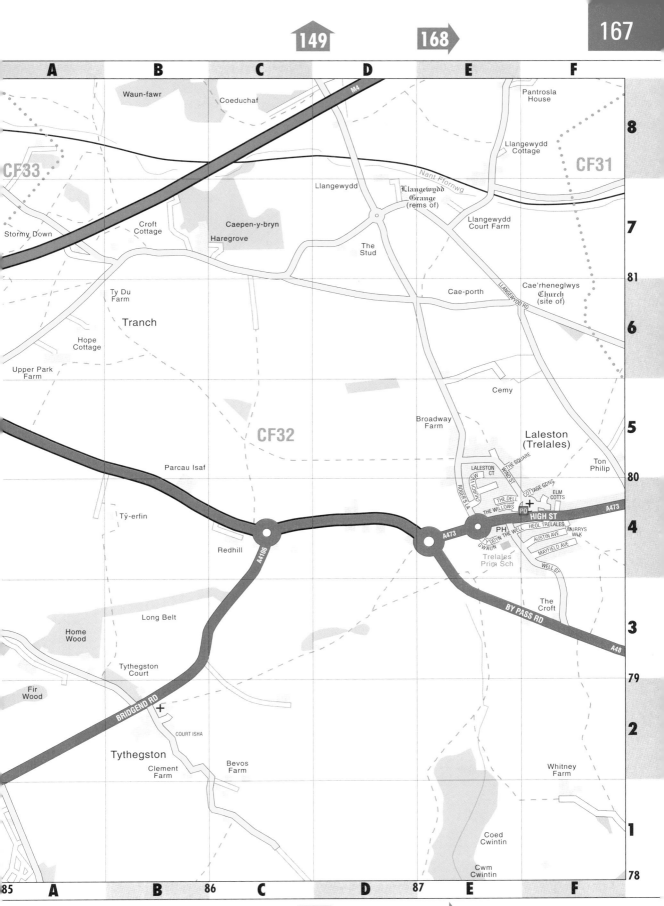

149
168

A   B   C   D   E   F

8

7

81

6

5

80

4

3

79

2

1

78

Waun-fawr

Coeduchaf

M4

Pantrosla House

CF33

Llangewydd Cottage

CF31

Stormy Down

Croft Cottage

Caepen-y-bryn

Haregrove

Llangewydd

Nant Ffornwg

Llangewydd Grange (rems of)

Llangewydd Court Farm

Ty Du Farm

The Stud

Cae-porth

LLANGEWYDD RD

Cae'rheneglwys Church (site of)

Tranch

Hope Cottage

Upper Park Farm

Cemy

Broadway Farm

Laleston (Trelales)

Ton Philip

Parcau Isaf

CF32

THE SQUARE

LALESTON CT

WIND ST

COTTAGE GDNS

ELM COTTS

Tŷ-erfin

Redhill

A4106

CHURCH VIEW

ROGER'S LA

THE DELL

THE WILLOWS

PO

HIGH ST

A473

A473

PH

HEOL TRELALES

MURRYS WLK

AUSTIN AVE

MAYFIELD AVE

WELL ST

Trelales Prim Sch

GWAUN

Y DDYN THE WELL

Long Belt

Home Wood

The Croft

BY PASS RD

A48

Tythegston Court

Fir Wood

79

BRIDGEND RD

Tythegston

COURT ISHA

Clement Farm

Bevos Farm

Whitney Farm

Coed Cwintin

Cwm Cwintin

184
168

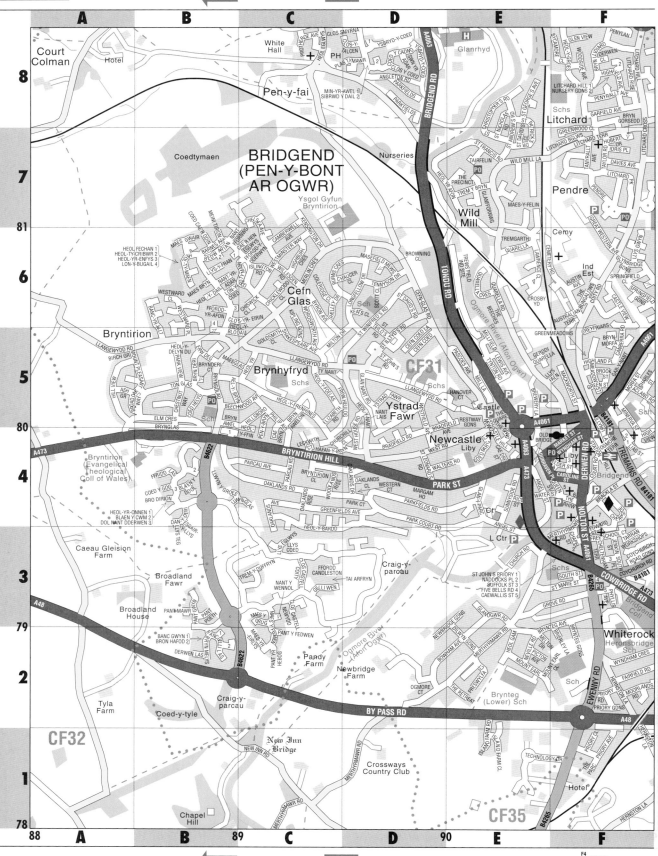

F4
1 LLYNFI ST
2 ODDFELLOWS' ST
3 ADARE ST
4 CROSS ST
5 THE RHIW CTR
6 NOLTON ARC
7 BRACKLA STREET CTR

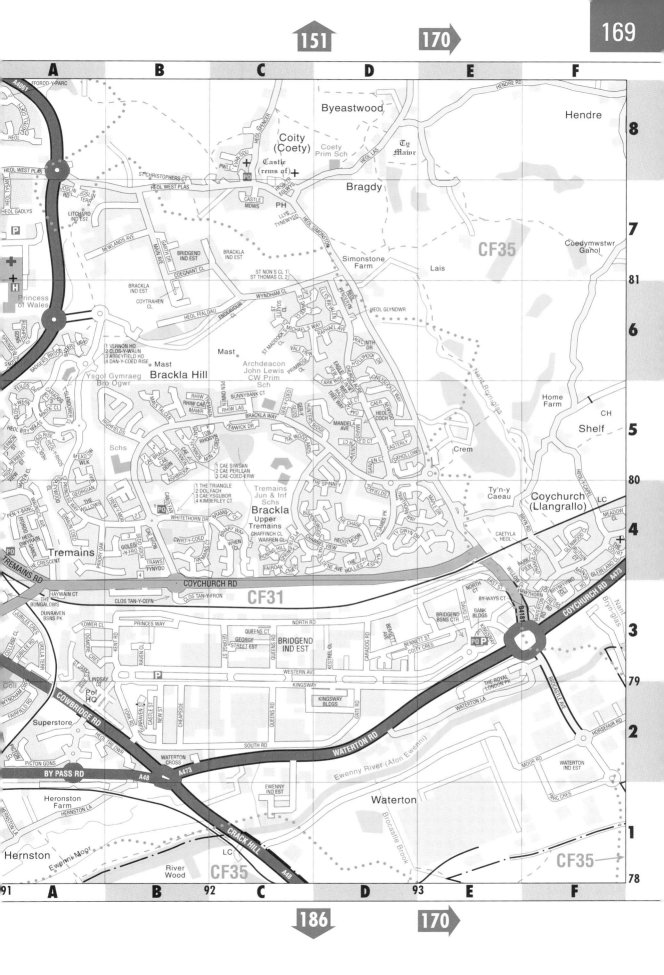

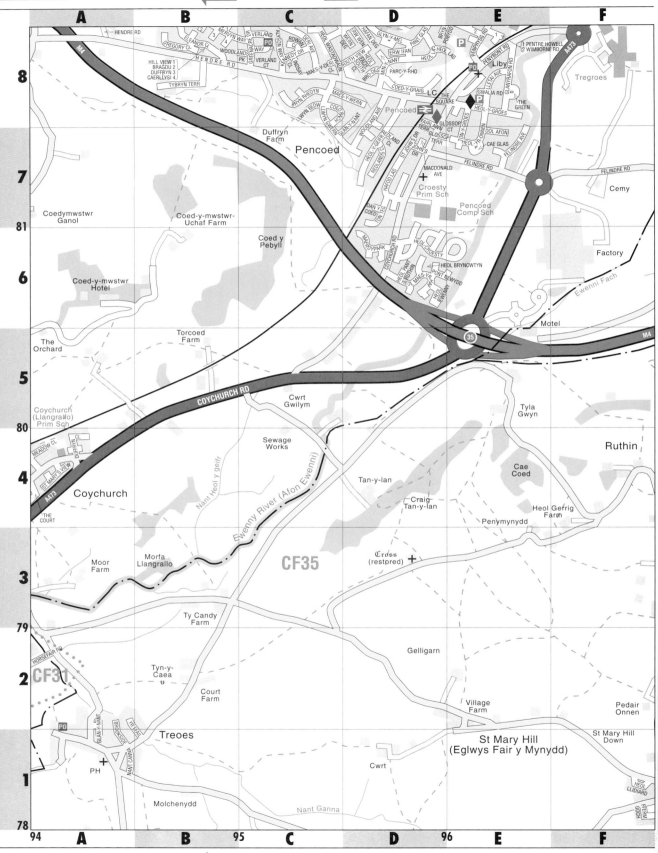

A   B   C   D   E   F

8

7

81

6

5

80

4

3

79

2

1

78

HENDRE RD
M4
HILL VIEW 1
BRAGDU 2
DUFFRYN 3
CAERLLYSI 4
TYBRYN TERR
HENDRE RD
GREGORY CL
ELEANOR CT
MERVYN WAY
WOODLANDS
PK
GREENACRE
VERLAND
VERLAND
CT
ANSON WAY
KENNEDY DR
LINDSAY
SOUTH VIEW
MAES-Y-DERI
ROWAN AVE
DERI AVE
HEOL WASTADWEN
HAZAN DEG
WERN
GLYN-Y-MEL
PANT GLAS
ERW IFAN
BRYN
PENPRYSG
P
P
11 PENTRE HOWELL
12 WIMBORNE RD
PENYBONT RD
PENPRYSG RD
PO
Liby
Tregroes

Duffryn
Farm
BRYN RHEDYN
LLWYN BEDW
LLWYN ONNEN
LLWYN-Y-NANT
COED-Y-GRAIG
MAES-Y-WERN
WOODLAND AVE
BRO-DEG
MIN-Y-NANT
PARC-Y-RHO
COED-Y-GRAIG
LC
THE
SQUARE
GWALIA RD
GLANYRAFON RD
LLETAI AVE
PO
P
THE
GREEN
Pencoed
FAIRLAWN
TERR
GLOSSOP
CT
GLOSSOP
TERR
HEOL-Y-GROES
DOL AFON
CAE GLAS
HEOL-Y-CYNHON
FELINDRE AVE
Pencoed

REDLAND
REDLANDS CL
HEOL-Y-GEFN
HAGOEL LAS
ST JOHN'S
CT
ST JOHN'S
DR
MACDONALD
AVE
Croesty
Prim Sch
FELINDRE RD
Felindre RD
Cemy

Coedymwstwr
Ganol
Coed-y-mwstwr-
Uchaf Farm
Coed y
Pebyll
DAN-Y-
COED
TON TEG
Pencoed
Compl Sch
Factory

Coed-y-mwstwr
Hotel
Torcoed
Farm
MAPYPARK
COYCHURCH RD
HEOL PANT
HEOL
RHUTHIN
MAES-YR-
EGLWYS
HEOL-CROESTY
HEOL BRYNCWTYN
PONT NEWYDD
HEOL
EWENNI
Ewenni Fach
Motel
35
M4

The
Orchard
COYCHURCH RD
Cwrt
Gwilym
Tyla
Gwyn
Ruthin

Coychurch
(Llangrallo)
Prim Sch
MEADOW CL
DUFFRYN CL
ST MARY'S VIEW
Sewage
Works
Nant Heol y gelfr
Tan-y-lan
Cae
Coed

THE
COURT
Coychurch
A473
Ewenny River (Afon Ewenni)
Craig
Tan-y-lan
Penymynydd
Heol Gefrig
Farm

Moor
Farm
Morfa
Llangrallo
CF35
Cross
(restored)

Ty Candy
Farm
Gelligarn

CF31
HORSEFAIR RD
Tyn-y-
Caea
Court
Farm
Village
Farm
Pedair
Onnen

PO
GLAN-Y-NANT
PYE HALL
BROOKSIDE
NANT CAMNA
Treoes
St Mary Hill
(Eglwys Fair y Mynydd)
St Mary Hill
Down
HEOL
LLIDIARD

PH
Cwrt
FFERM
GOCH
Molchenydd
Nant Ganna

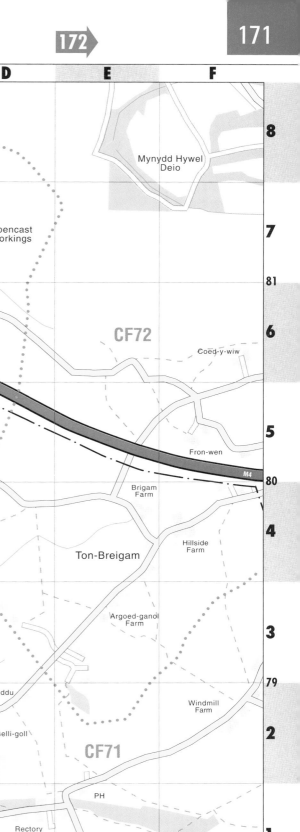

A B C D E F

8

Tir-eithin

Llanilid

Mynydd Hywel
Deio

Motel

Felindre

Celynog
Fâch

7

PH

FELINDRE RD

Velindre
Farm

Opencast
Workings

81

Tre-Frân

CF72

6

Coed-y-wiw

Coed y
Brynau

Craig-y-Ruthin

CH

CF35

Fron-wen

5

Ruthyn
Fawr

Brigam
Farm

M4

80

Mynydd
Ruthin

Garwa
Quarry

Ton-Breigam

Hillside
Farm

4

Coed
Breigam

Pant-y-lliwydd
Farm

Argoed-ganol
Farm

3

Ruthin
Quarry

River Thaw (Afon Ddawan)

Cae-Rhys-ddu

79

Windmill
Farm

Coed
Pant-llywydd

Gelli-goll

2

CF71

Pont y
Rhyd

City

Isycoed
Farm

PH

Graig

1

Rectory
Farm

FFERM
GOCH

78

97 A B 98 C D 99 E F

173
156

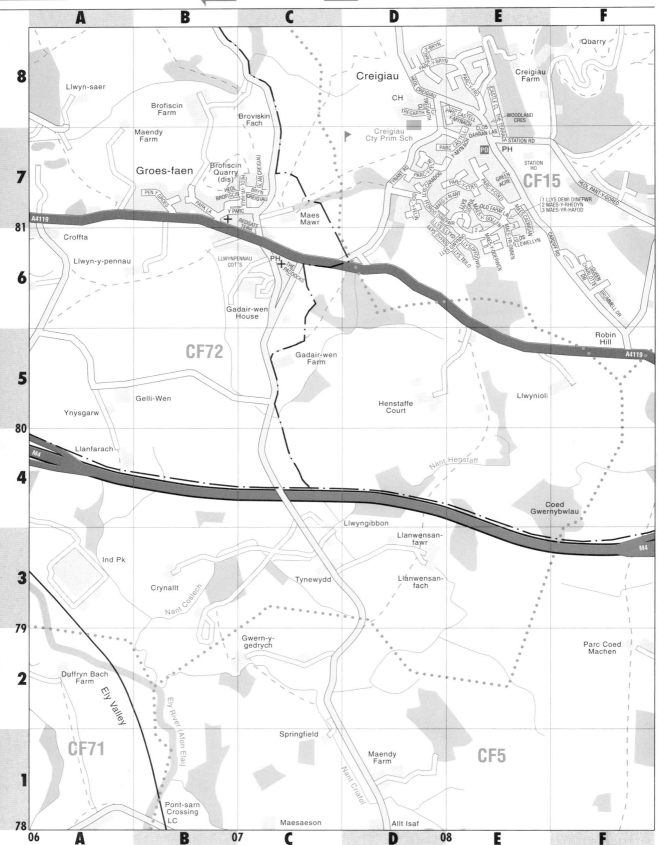

173
191

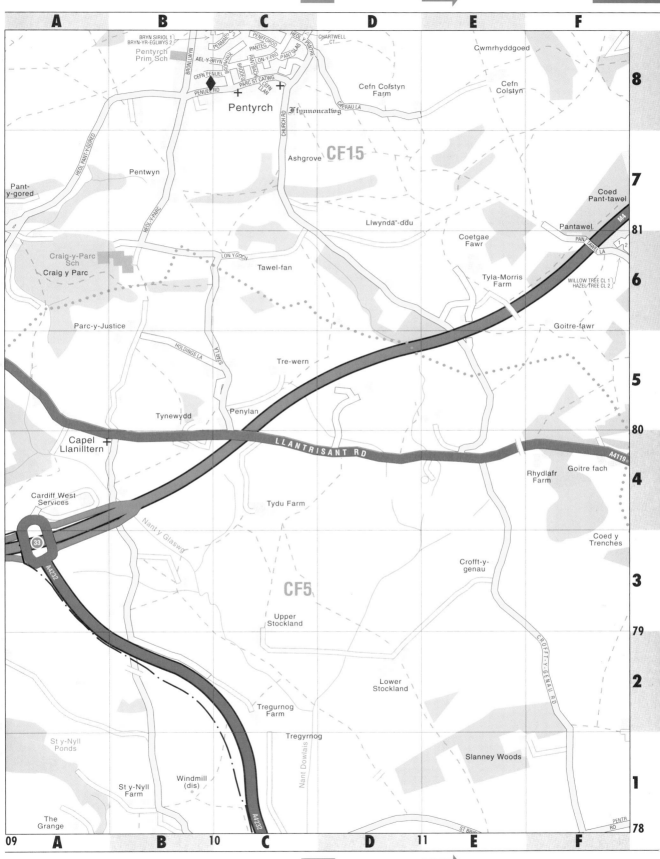

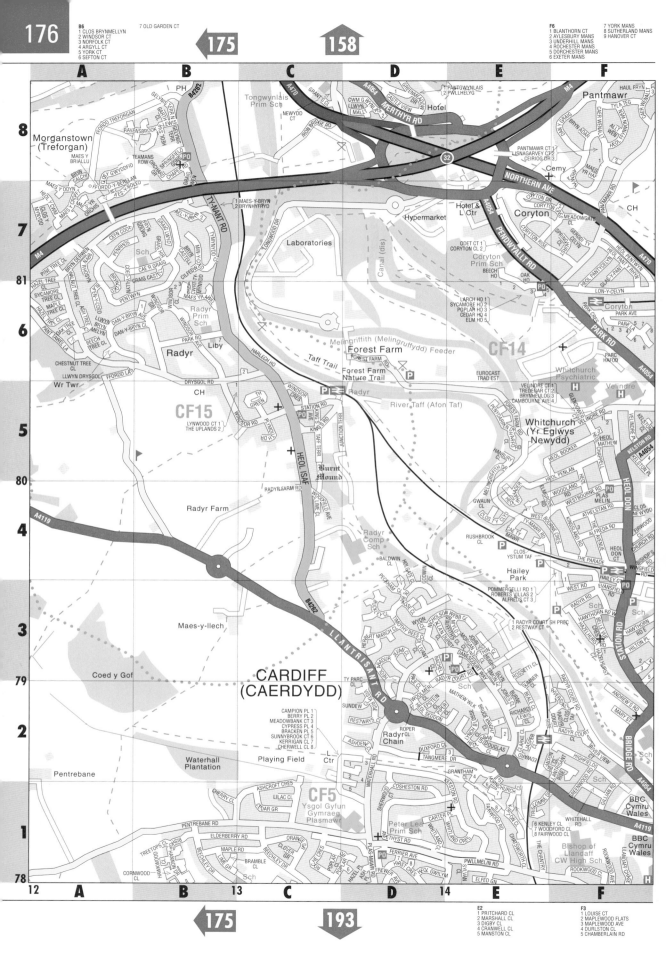

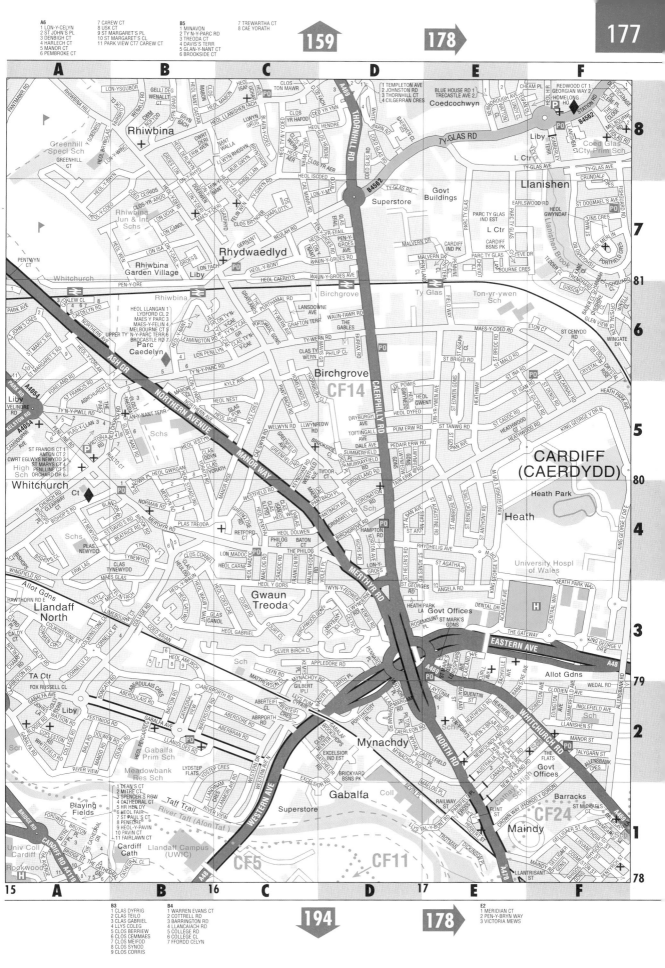

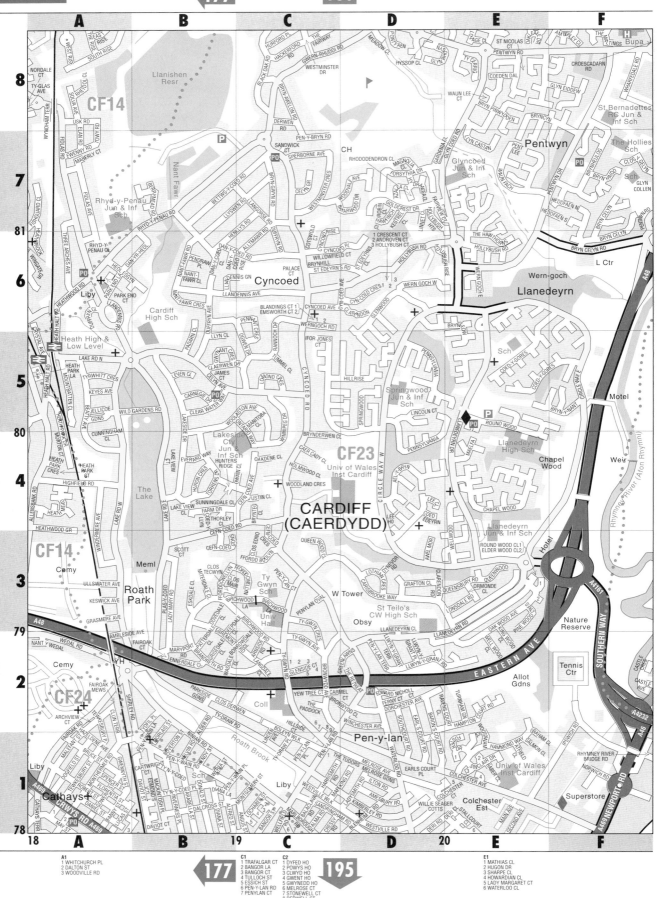

A1
1 WHITCHURCH PL
2 DALTON ST
3 WOODVILLE RD

C1
1 TRAFALGAR CT
2 BANGOR LA
3 BANGOR CT
4 TULLOCH ST
5 ESSICH ST
6 PEN-Y-LAN RD
7 PENYLAN CT

C2
1 DYFED HO
2 POWYS HO
3 CLWYD HO
4 GWENT HO
5 GWYNEDD HO
6 MELROSE CT
7 STONEWELL CT
8 REDWELL CT
9 OLDWELL CT

E1
1 MATHIAS CL
2 HUGON DR
3 SHARPE CL
4 HOWARDIAN CL
5 LADY MARGARET CT
6 WATERLOO CL

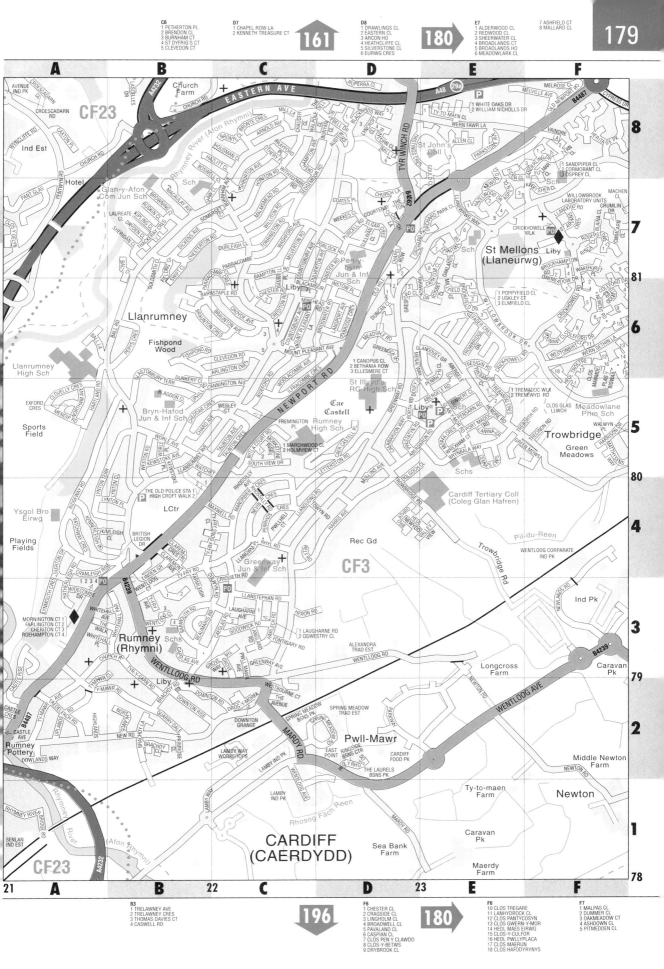

A6
1 THRUSH CL
2 STONECHAT CL
3 WINDHOVER CL
4 CLOS Y BERLLAN
5 GLOS-Y-GORNANT
6 CLOS HAFREN

7 CLOS CAS-BACH
8 CLOS DYFNAINT
9 CLOS GLANABER
10 CLOS GWLAD-YR-HAF
11 CLOS MAES-Y-MOR
12 LOCKE GR

A7
1 CARADOC CL
2 BASSALEG CL
3 BLAENAVON CL
4 BEDWAS CL
5 HORNBEAM CL
6 ASTER CL

7 WINDFLOWER CL
8 WHINCHAT CL
9 CHARTLEY CL
10 ABERNETHY CL

A8
1 LYTHAM GR
2 ST PIERRE CL
3 BIRKDALE CL
4 WENTWORTH CL
5 VAINDRE CL
6 VAINDRE DR

7 CWRT PENTRE BACH
8 FAIRHAVEN CL
9 FAIRVIEW CL
10 FENNEL CL
11 COMFREY CL
12 CHERVIL CL
13 EUGENE CL

14 CARAWAY CL
15 OREGANO CL

179
162

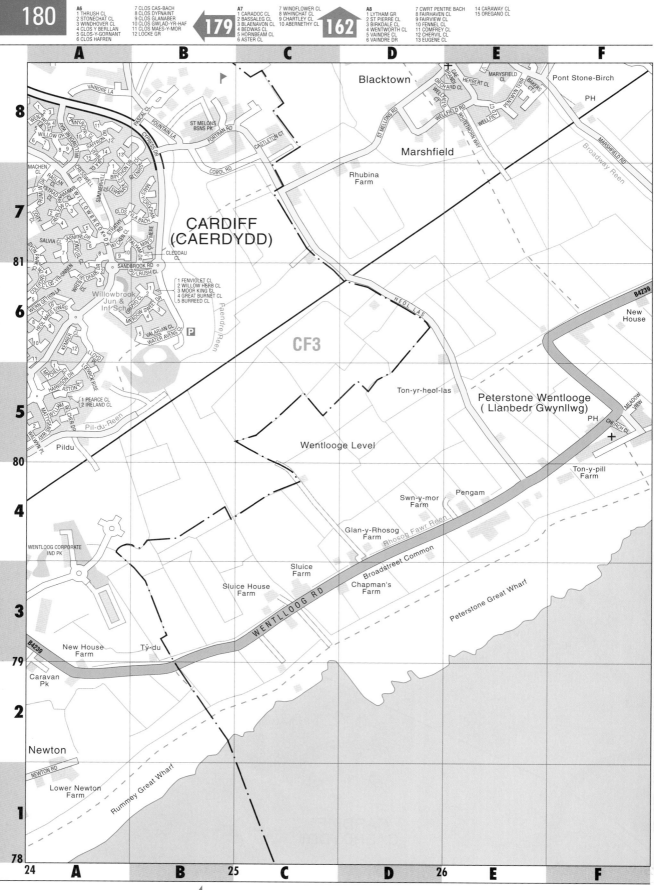

179

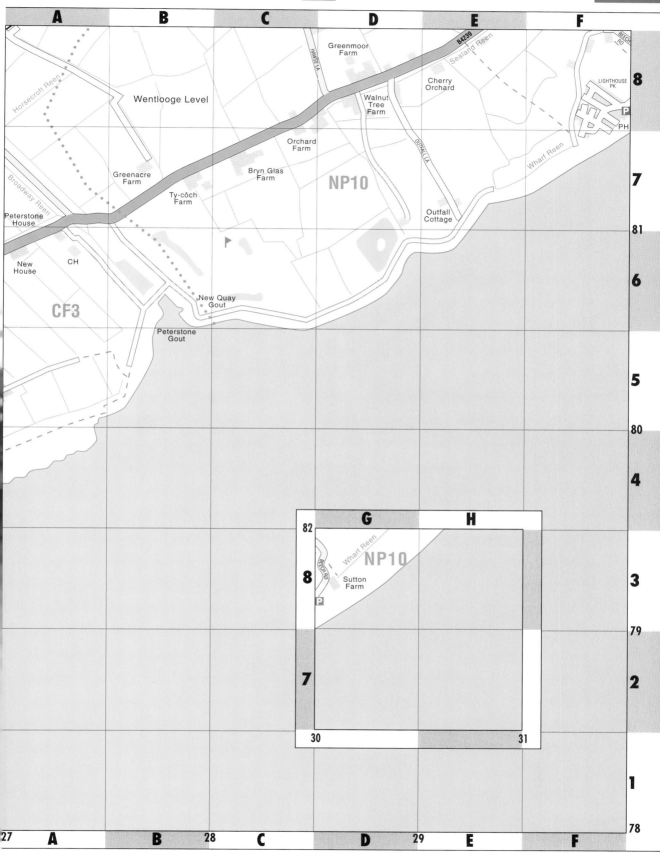

A **B** **C** **D** **E** **F**

Horsecroft Reen

Wentlooge Level

Greenmoor
Farm

HANSE LA

B4239

Sealand Reen

Cherry
Orchard

LIGHTHOUSE
PK

8

P

PH

Walnut
Tree
Farm

Orchard
Farm

OUTFALL LA

Broadway Reen

Greenacre
Farm

Bryn Glas
Farm

NP10

Wharf Reen

7

81

Ty-côch
Farm

Peterstone
House

Outfall
Cottage

New
House

CH

CF3

New Quay
Gout

6

Peterstone
Gout

5

80

4

G **H**

82

Wharf Reen

NP10

BEECH RD

8

Sutton
Farm

3

P

79

7

2

30 31

1

27 **A** **B** 28 **C** **D** 29 **E** **F** 78

BEECH RD

PORTHCAWL

CF36

Rest Bay

Lock's Common

Nottage
Prim Sch

Porthcawl
Comp Sch

Hutchwns
Point

Irongate Point

Porthcawl
Point

East
Pier

Lifeboat Rd 1
Marine Terr 2

A B C D E F

DE BREOS DR
A4106
NEWTON NOTTAGE RD
1 MARLPIT LA
2 YNYSLAS
TYN-Y-CAEAU LA
A4106

The Wilderness

ST DAVID'S WAY
WAUNLON
ELDER DR
HAZEL CL
CHESTNUT DR
Y Graig
Wig Fach

HEOL-Y-GOEWIG
CIL PARC
MEADOW LA
Porthcawl Prim Sch
PWLL-Y-WAUN
THE MERCIES
AUSTIN AVE
AUSTIN CL
CHERRY TREE AVE
WENGATES
ORCHARD DR
WILLOW CL
DANYGRAIG AVE
CEDAR GDNS

8

HEOL-PAIR GEORGIANI C
GREENWAYS
PANT MORFA
WOODLAND AVE
HOOKLAND RD
ALISON CT
ST MICHAEL'S CT
ST CHRISTOPHER'S RD
ALDENHAM RD
HEOL-Y-GRAIG
CLEVISTON CT
GREYFRIARS CT
1 SYCAMORE AVE
2 MANOR GR
ASH GR
BIRCH WLK
LABURNUM DR
HOLLY WLK
ROWAN DR
MAPLE WLK
LINDEN WAY
Gorwelion
Caeaullaprau

KING'S AVE
POPLAR AVE
NICHOLLS AVE
POPLAR AVE
ST ANNE'S CRES
NEW RD
ST MARY ST
PINE CL
BRICKYARD
THE BRICKYARD
CHURCH ST
Schs
LARCH CL
THE FIRS
BEECH GR
LIME TREE WAY
CYPRESS GDNS
Newton Burrows
CF32

7

BRIAN CRES
POPLAR CRES
VINTIN TERR
VINTIN LA
QUEEN'S AVE
Newton Prim Sch
PARC-Y-BERLLAN
BRYCH AVE
CF36
Newton
THE MEADOWS
ST JOHN'S DR
MAYFIELD AVE
BEACH RD
BAY VIEW RD
BRYNEGLWYS AVE
BRYNEGLWYS GDNS
ACACIA AVE
OAK TREE DR
JUNIPER CL
Newton Burrows
Rifle Range (dis)

GRIFFIN PARK CT
1 WELLFIELD CRES
2 POPLAR CRES
MAESTEG
BUNGALOW AVE
MACKWORTH CT
SANDY LA
P
Coney Beach Amusement Park
P
P

77

EASTERN PROM
WELLFIELD AVE

Sandy Bay
Rhych Point
Trecco Bay
Newton Point
Black Rocks

6

5

76

4

3

75

2

1

74

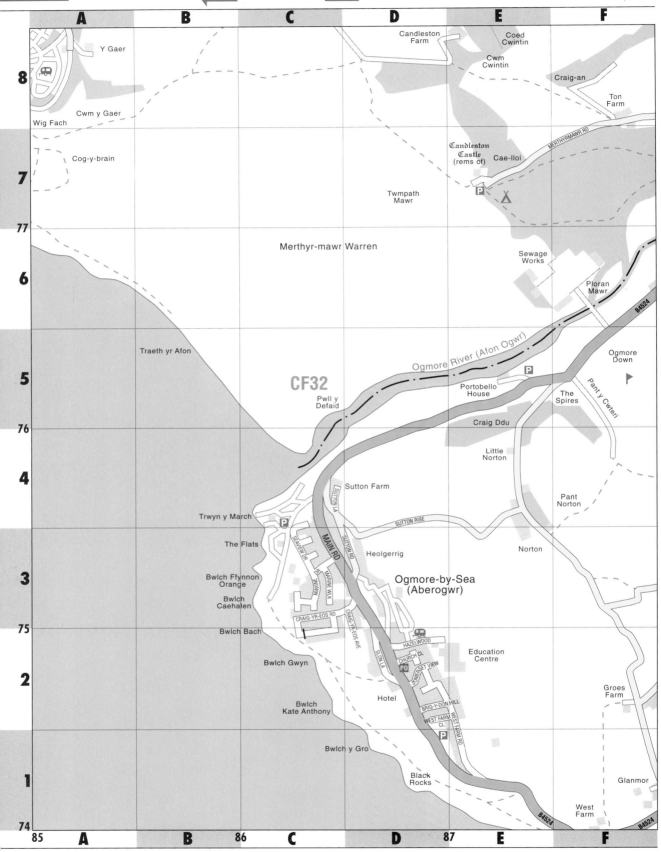

A B C D E F

8

Y Gaer

Candleston
Farm

Coed
Cwintin

Cwm
Cwintin

Craig-an

Ton
Farm

Cwm y Gaer

Wig Fach

Cog-y-brain

Candleston
Castle
(rems of)

Cae-lloi

MERTHYRMAWR RD

7

Twmpath
Mawr

P

77

Merthyr-mawr Warren

Sewage
Works

Ploran
Mawr

B4524

6

Traeth yr Afon

Ogmore River (Afon Ogwr)

Ogmore
Down

5

CF32

Pwll y
Defaid

P

Portobello
House

The
Spires

Pant y Cwteri

76

Craig Ddu

Little
Norton

4

Sutton Farm

Pant
Norton

Trwyn y March

SUTTON LA

SUTTON RISE

Norton

The Flats

P

SEAVIEW DR

MAIN RD

SUTTON RD

Heolgerrig

Ogmore-by-Sea
(Aberogwr)

3

Bwlch Ffynnon
Orange

MARINE DR

MARINE WLK

Bwlch
Caehalen

CRAIG-YR-EOS RD

75

Bwlch Bach

CRAIG-YR-EOS AVE

HAZELWOOD

Education
Centre

Bwlch Gwyn

SLON LA

CHURCH CL

PO

SOMERSET VIEW

2

Hotel

BRIG-Y-DON HILL

WEST FARM RD

Groes
Farm

Bwlch
Kate Anthony

WEST FARM
CL

P

1

Bwlch y Gro

Black
Rocks

Glanmor

West
Farm

B4524

B4524

74

85 A B 86 C D 87 E F

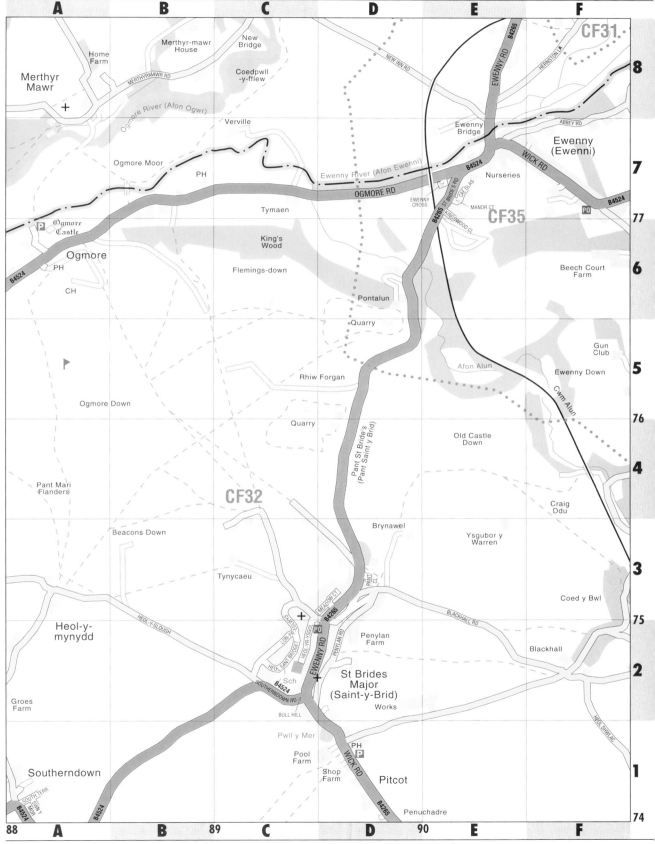

A B C D E F

CF31

8

Home
Farm

Merthyr-mawr
House

New
Bridge

Merthyr
Mawr

Coedpwll
-y-fflew

MERTHYRMAWR RD

Ogmore River (Afon Ogwr)

Verville

Ewenny RD

HERNSTON LA

Ewenny
Bridge

ABBEY RD

Ewenny
(Ewenni)

7

Ogmore Moor

PH

Ewenny River (Afon Ewenni)

OGMORE RD

B4524

WICK RD

Nurseries

B4524

Tymaen

EWENNY
CROSS

ST BRIDE'S RD

CAE GLAS

MANOR CT

CF35

PO

77

P

Ogmore
Castle

King's
Wood

B4265

KINGSWOOD CL

Beech Court
Farm

6

B4524

PH

Flemings-down

Gun
Club

CH

Ogmore

Pontalun

Quarry

Afon Alun

Ewenny Down

5

Rhiw Forgan

Cwm Alun

Ogmore Down

76

Quarry

Old Castle
Down

Pant St Bride's
(Pant Saint y Brid)

4

Craig
Ddu

Pant Mari
Flanders

CF32

Brynawel

Ysgubor y
Warren

3

Beacons Down

Coed y Bwl

PANT
CL

Tynycaeu

HEOL-Y-SLOUGH

MEADOW CT

B4265

BLACKHALL RD

75

Heol-y-
mynydd

LON-YR-YSGOL

PO

Penylan
Farm

Blackhall

HEOL-Y-SAINT BRIDGET

EWENNY RD

PENYLAN RD

2

Groes
Farm

Sch

SOUTHERNDOWN RD

B4524

St Brides
Major
(Saint-y-Brid)

Works

HEOL SIMLAC

BULL HILL

Pwll y Mer

PH

P

Southerndown

Pool
Farm

Shop
Farm

WICK RD

Pitcot

1

SOUTH TERR

SWN Y MOR

B4524

B4265

Penuchadre

74

88 A B 89 C D 90 E F

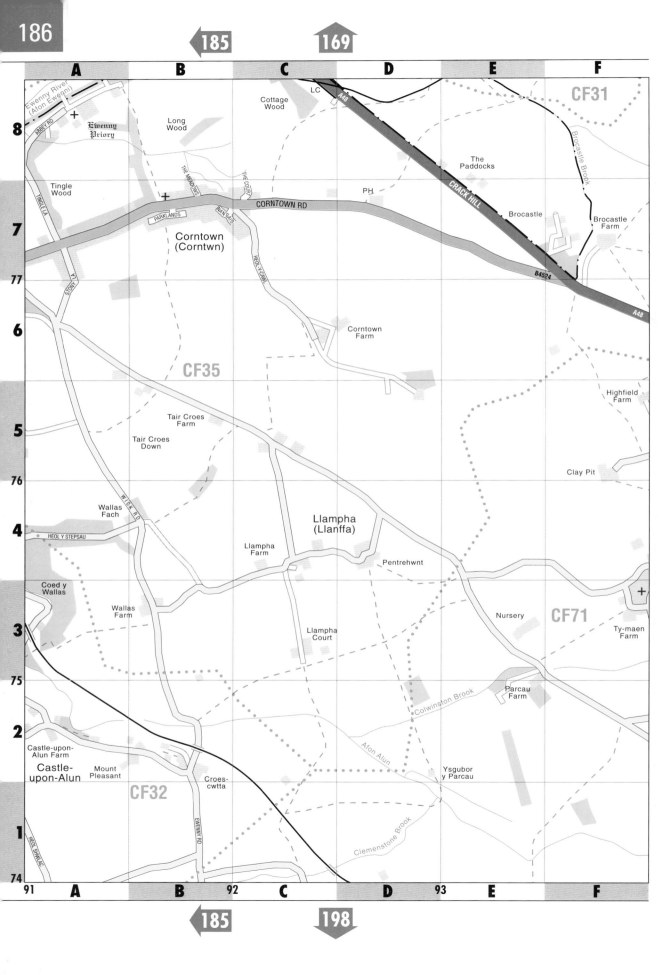

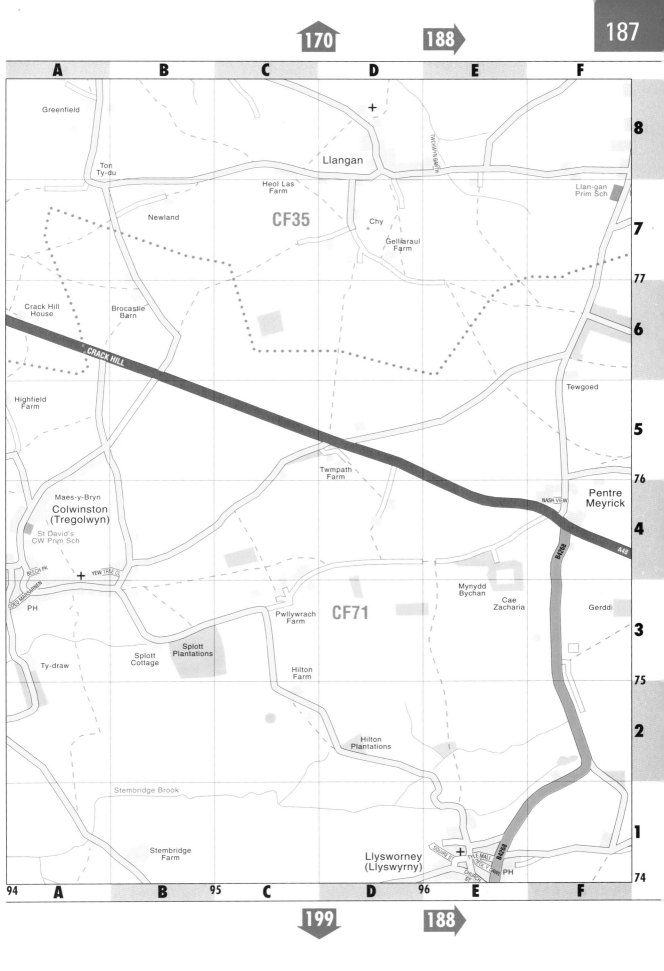

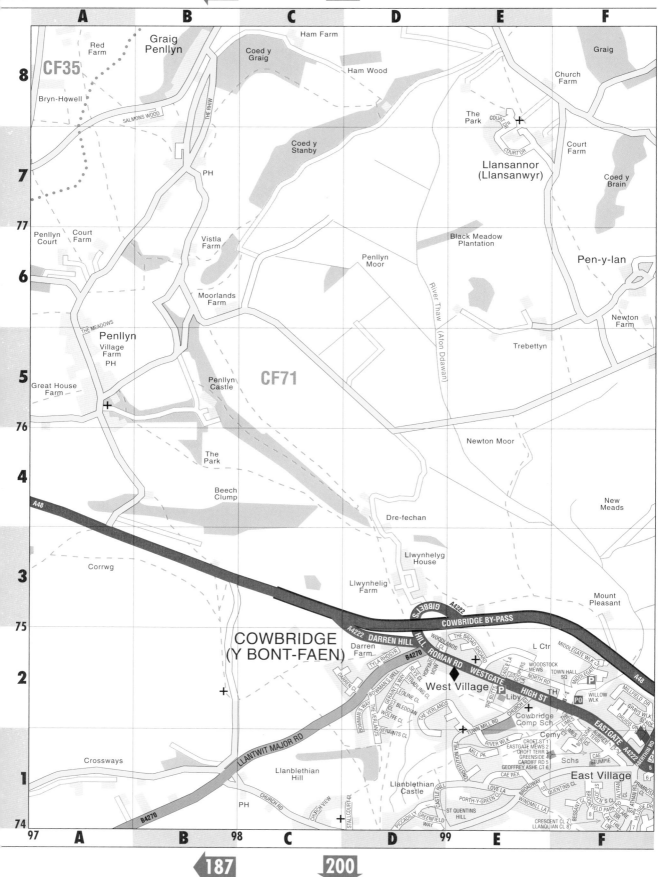

187
171

A B C D E F

8

CF35

Red Farm

Graig Penllyn

Coed y Graig

Ham Farm

Ham Wood

Graig

Church Farm

Bryn-Howell

SALMONS WOOD

The Park

COURT DR

7

THE RHIW

PH

Coed y Stanby

COURT DR

Llansannor
(Llansanwyr)

Court Farm

Coed y Brain

77

Penllyn Court

Court Farm

Vistla Farm

Black Meadow Plantation

Pen-y-lan

6

THE MEADOWS

Penllyn Moor

River Thaw (Afon Ddawan)

Newton Farm

Moorlands Farm

Trebettyn

Penllyn

Village Farm PH

CF71

5

Great House Farm

Penllyn Castle

Newton Moor

76

The Park

4

A48

Beech Clump

Dre-fechan

New Meads

3

Corrwg

Llwynhelyg House

Llwynhelig Farm

Mount Pleasant

A4222

GIBBET'S

COWBRIDGE BY-PASS

75

COWBRIDGE
(Y BONT-FAEN)

A4222

DARREN HILL

B4270

Darren Farm

ROMAN RD

HILL

THE BROAD SHOARD

WOODLANDS CL

L Ctr

MIDDLEGATE WLK

A48

2

TYLA RHOSYR

BOWMAN'S WELL

STRADLING CL

EDOLINE CL

HOPYARD

WESTGATE

WOODSTOCK MEWS

NORTH RD

TOWN HALL SQ

MIDDLEGATE

West Village

HIGH ST

P

Liby

TH

PO

WILLOW WLK

P

MILLFIELD DR

GRAYS WLK

DRUIDS GRN

DARREN CL

GERAINTS WAY

SCKS CL

ST BLEDDIAN CL

WOLFFE CL

THE VERLANDS

GERAINTS CL

THE BUTTS

COOPERS

EAGLE LA

CHURCH ST

Cowbridge Comp Sch

THE LIMES

LIMES CT

BROADWAY TERR

Cemy

EASTGATE

AUBREY LA

BERTHIN RD

A4222

1

Crossways

LLANTWIT MAJOR RD

Llanblethian Hill

Town Mill Rd

RIVER WLK

MILL PK

CAE REX

Llanblethian Castle

LOVE LA

PORTH-Y-GREEN CL

WINDMILL LA

Schs

CAE STUMPIE

CROFT ST 1
EASTGATE MEWS 2
CROFT TERR 3
GREENSIDE 4
CARDIFF RD 5
GEOFFREY ASHE CT 6

East Village

QUENTINS CL

BESSANT CL

BROADFIELD PARK RD

ST JOHN'S CL

CLARE CT

TALYFAN CL

ST ATHAN RD

TAKE HILL

HILLSIDE DR

PRIMROSE

74

B4270

CHURCH RD

PH

CHURCH VIEW

STALLCOURT CL

ST QUENTINS HILL

St Quentins Hill

PICCADILLY

GREENFIELD WAY

CRESCENT CL 7
LLANQUIAN CL 8

97 A 98 B C 98 D 99 E F

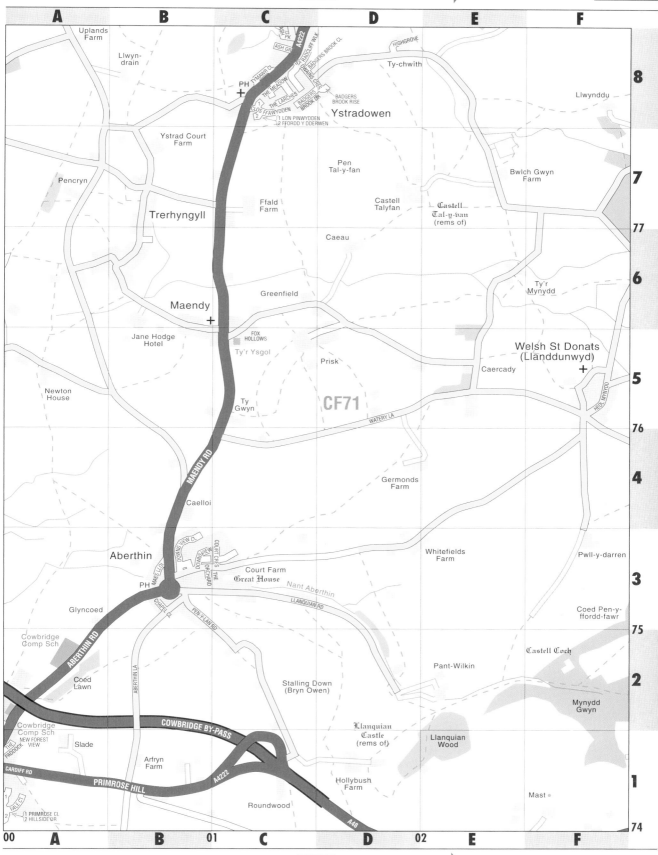

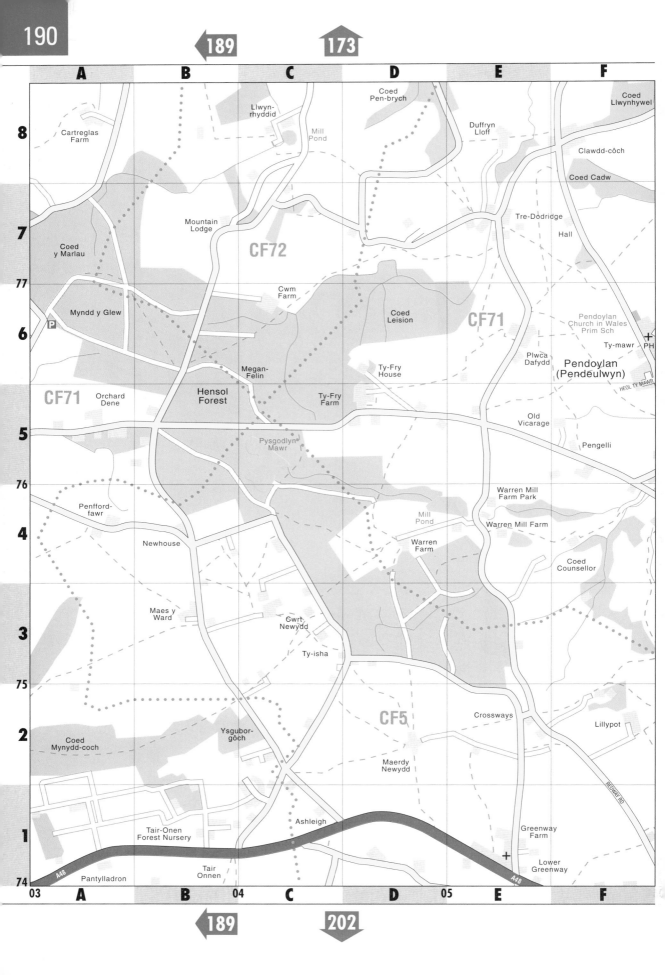

A B C D E F

8 Cartreglas Farm | Llwyn-rhyddid | Mill Pond | Coed Pen-brych | Duffryn Lloff | Coed Llwynhywel | Clawdd-côch | Coed Cadw

7 Coed y Marlau | Mountain Lodge | CF72 | Tre-Dodridge | Hall

77 Myndd y Glew | Cwm Farm | Coed Leision | CF71 | Pendoylan Church in Wales Prim Sch

6 P | Megan-Felin | Ty-Fry House | Plwca Dafydd | Ty-mawr | PH | Pendoylan (Pendeulwyn) | HEOL TY MAWR

CF71 | Orchard Dene | Hensol Forest | Ty-Fry Farm | Old Vicarage

5 Pysgodlyn Mawr | Pengelli

76 Penfford-fawr | Warren Mill Farm Park

4 Newhouse | Mill Pond | Warren Mill Farm | Warren Farm | Coed Counsellor

3 Maes y Ward | Cwrt Newydd | Ty-isha

75 Crossways | Lillypot

2 Coed Mynydd-coch | Ysgubor-gôch | CF5 | Maerdy Newydd | Greenway Farm

1 Tair-Onen Forest Nursery | Ashleigh | Lower Greenway

74 Pantylladron | Tair Onnen | A48 | A48

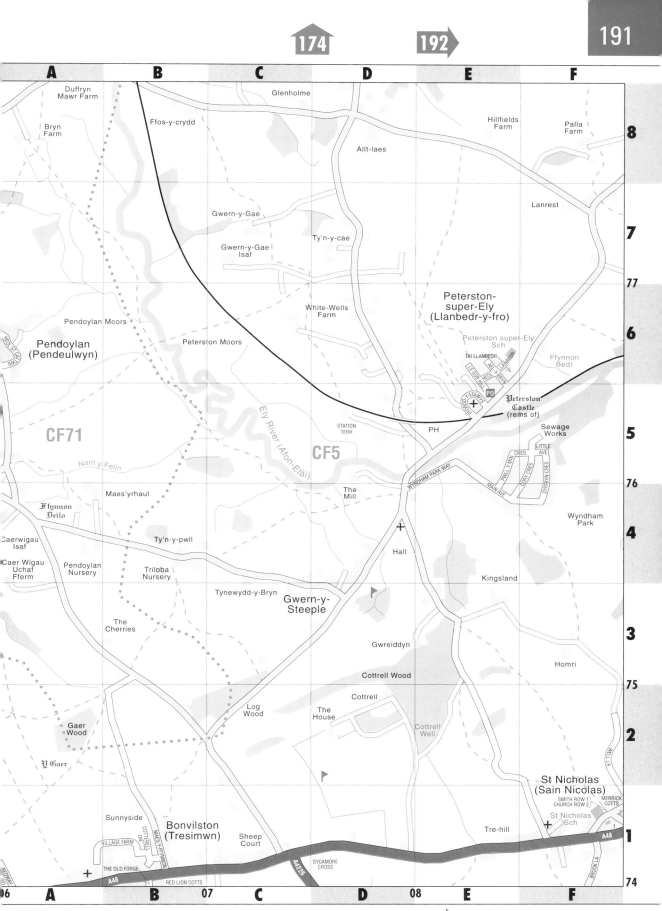

A B C D E F

8
7
77
6
5
76
4
3
75
2
1
74

Duffryn Mawr Farm
Bryn Farm
Ffos-y-crydd
Glenholme
Allt-laes
Hillfields Farm
Palla Farm
Lanrest
Gwern-y-Gae
Ty'n-y-cae
Gwern-y-Gae Isaf
Peterston- super-Ely (Llanbedr-y-fro)
Pendoylan Moors
White-Wells Farm
Peterston super-Ely Sch
Pendoylan (Pendeulwyn)
Peterston Moors
TAI LLANBEDR
Ffynnon Bedr
CF71
Ely River (Afon-Elái)
CF5
FFORDD-Y-EGLWYS
HEOL LLANBEDR
LE SGR HEOL
HEOL-Y-BRYN
PO
Peterston Castle (rems of)
Nant y Felin
STATION TERR
PH
Sewage Works
CF5
CRES
LITTLE AVE
Maes'yrhaul
The Mill
WYNDHAM PARK WAY
PWLL Y MIN
CORY CRES
DYFFRYN CRES
MAIN AVE
Ffynnon Deilo
Hall
Wyndham Park
Caerwigau Isaf
Ty'n-y-pwll
Caer Wigau Uchaf Fferm
Pendoylan Nursery
Triloba Nursery
Tynewydd-y-Bryn
Gwern-y-Steeple
Kingsland
The Cherries
Gwreiddyn
Homri
Cottrell Wood
Log Wood
Cottrell
The House
Cottrell Well
Gaer Wood
Y Gaer
St Nicholas (Sain Nicolas)
SMITH ROW 1
CHURCH ROW 2
MERRICK COTTS
St Nicholas Sch
Sunnyside
Bonvilston (Tresimwn)
Sheep Court
Tre-hill
WELL LA
A48
VILLAGE FARM
COTTRELL DR
MAES-Y-FFYNNON
THE OLD FORGE
A48
RED LION COTTS
A4226
SYCAMORE CROSS
BROOK LA
BEDWAY

06 A B 07 C D 08 E F

A B C D E F

8

Willows Farm
St BRIDE'S RD
A4232
Tregochas
Tynewydd
Pwll Arthur

Forty Farm
St BRIDES PL
St Bride's-super-Ely
(Llansanffraid-ar-Elai)
Nant Rhych

7

Welsh Folk Mus
Castle
CASTLE HILL
Llwyn-yr-eos

77

Morlanga
Gwern Rhyd
LC

6

LC
Ely River
Ely Valley
(Afon Elái)
St Georges
PH

Ty-fry

PERSONDY LA

5

CLOS-Y-CWARRA
NANT Y DOWLAIS 1
NANT-YR-ELY 2
NANT YR ARTHUR 3
SWALLOWHURST CL 4
LONGREACH CL 5
DEEPDENE CL

76

Ffordd Cottages
CF5
Drope
Drope Farm
Nant y Plac
NANT Y PEPRA
NANT Y PLAC

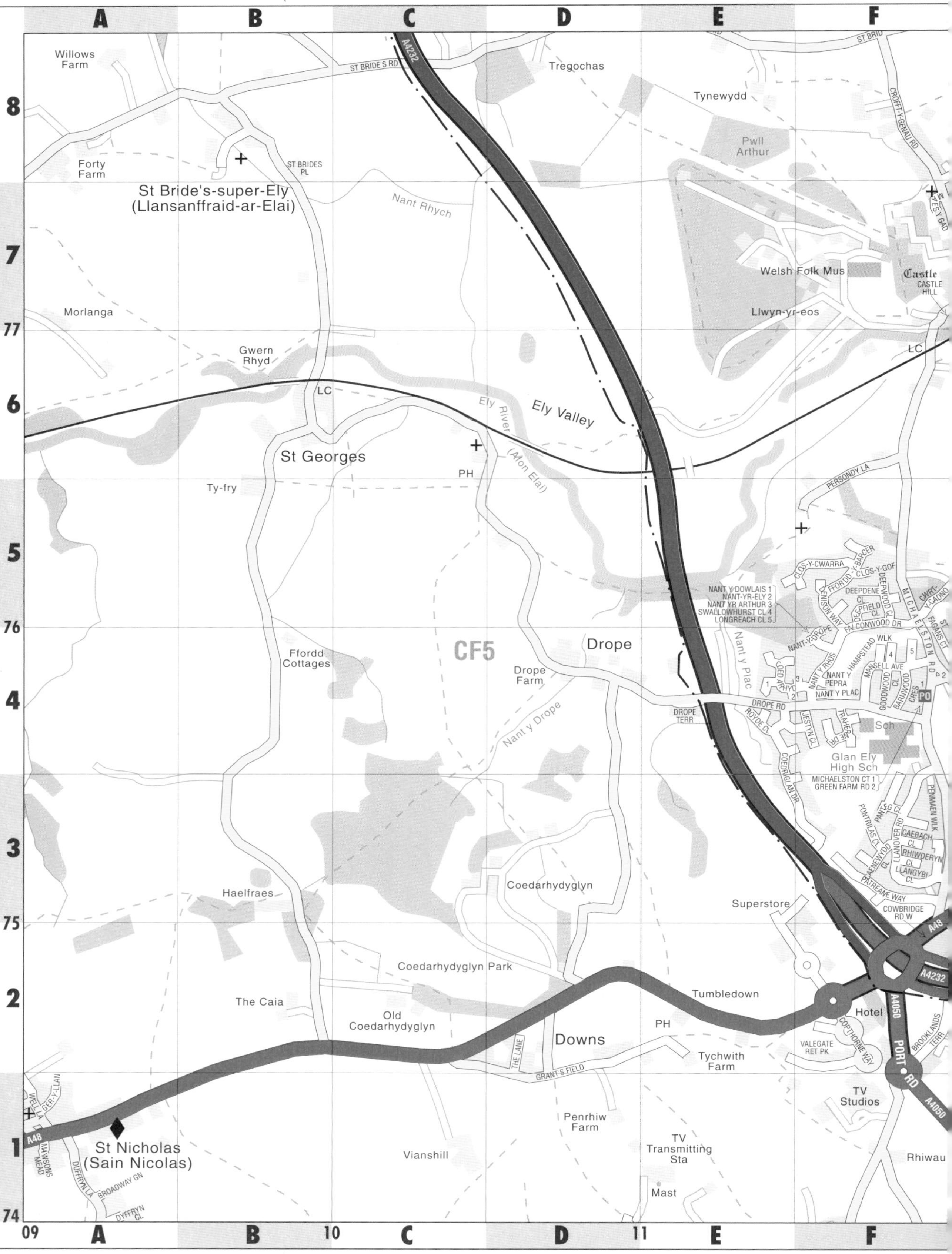

4

Nant y Drope
DROPE TERR
DROPE RD
Sch
Glan Ely High Sch
MICHAELSTON CT 1
GREEN FARM RD 2

3

Haelfraes
Coedarhydyglyn
Superstore
COWBRIDGE RD W
A48

75

Coedarhydyglyn Park
Tumbledown

2

The Caia
Old Coedarhydyglyn
THE LANE
Downs
PH
Tychwith Farm
Hotel
VALEGATE RET PK
PORT RD
A4050

GRANT'S FIELD
TV Studios

1

A48
St Nicholas
(Sain Nicolas)
DUFFRYN LA
Vianshill
Penrhiw Farm
TV Transmitting Sta
Mast
Rhiwau

BROADWAY GN
DYFFRYN CL

74

09 A B 10 C D 11 E F

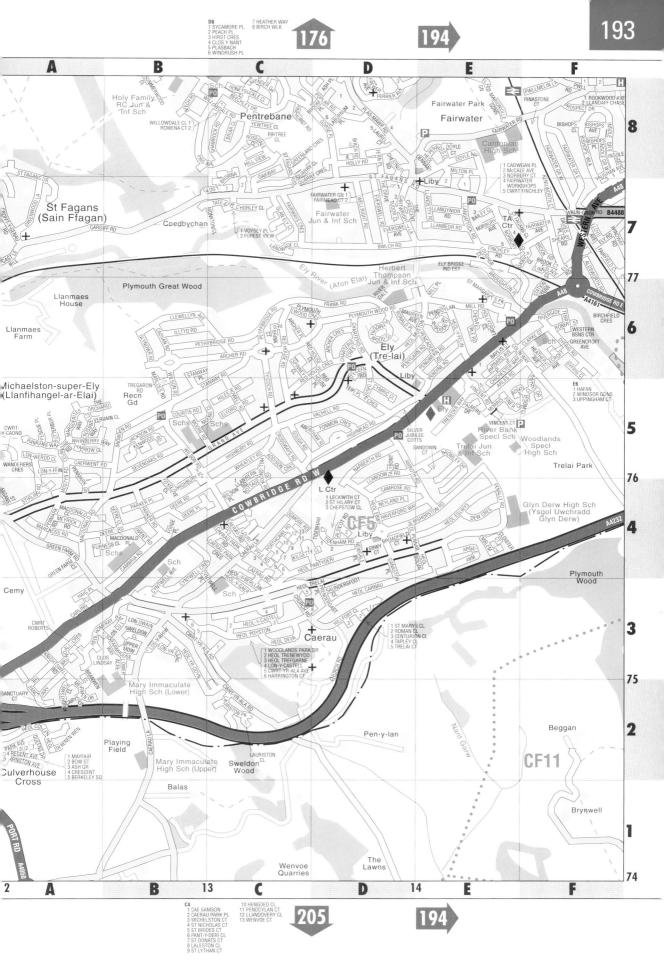

193
177

CF14

Pontcanna Fields

Llandaff (Llandâf)

Llandaff Fields

Pontcanna

WESTERN AVE

CARDIFF RD

MILL LA

PENCISELY RD

PEN-HILL RD

B4488

B4267

Taff Trail

River Taff (Afon Taf)

Taff Trail

CF24

Sports Gd

Blackweir

NORTH RD

A470

Univ of Wales

CF10

Welsh Off

Nat Cricket Ctr (Canolfan Criced Genedlaethol)

Welsh Inst of Sport (Athrofa Chwaraeon Cymru)

Welsh Coll of Music & Drama (Coleg Cerdd a Drama Cymru)

Victoria Park

Canton

CF5

Bute Park

COWBRIDGE RD

A4161

LANSDOWNE RD

WELLINGTON ST

COWBRIDGE RD E

A416

CASTLE ST (Heol Y Castell)

Cardiff Arms Park

Millennium Stad

Riverside

CLARE ST

Works

Playing Fields

Lansdowne

Fitzalan Com High Sch

LECKWITH RD

ATLAS RD

Ninian Park

Saltmead

CLARE RD

Ysgol Gymraeg Pwll Coch

CF11

Ninian Park (Cardiff City AFC)

CF5

Leckwith Woods

Playing Field

Ely River (Afon Elái)

Athletics Stad

Cardiff City Farm (Ffarm Dinas Caerdydd)

Leckwith

Allot Gdns

Ninian Park Jun & Inf Sch

Recn Gd

Liby

Grangetown

PENARTH RD

A4119 CORPORATION

A4160

Leckwith Bridge House

Mast

Leckwith Hill Farm

Woodlands

Cock Hill

Factory Wood

Ynyston Farmhouse

LECKWITH RD

GRANGETOWN LINK

HPO

Grangetown

Gas Works

The Marl

Leckwith (Lecwydd)

West Hill Wood

The Gower

THE GREEN

Nant Cydfin

CF64

A2232

B4267

Cardiff Bay Ret Pk (Parc Manwertnu Bae Caerdydd)

193
206

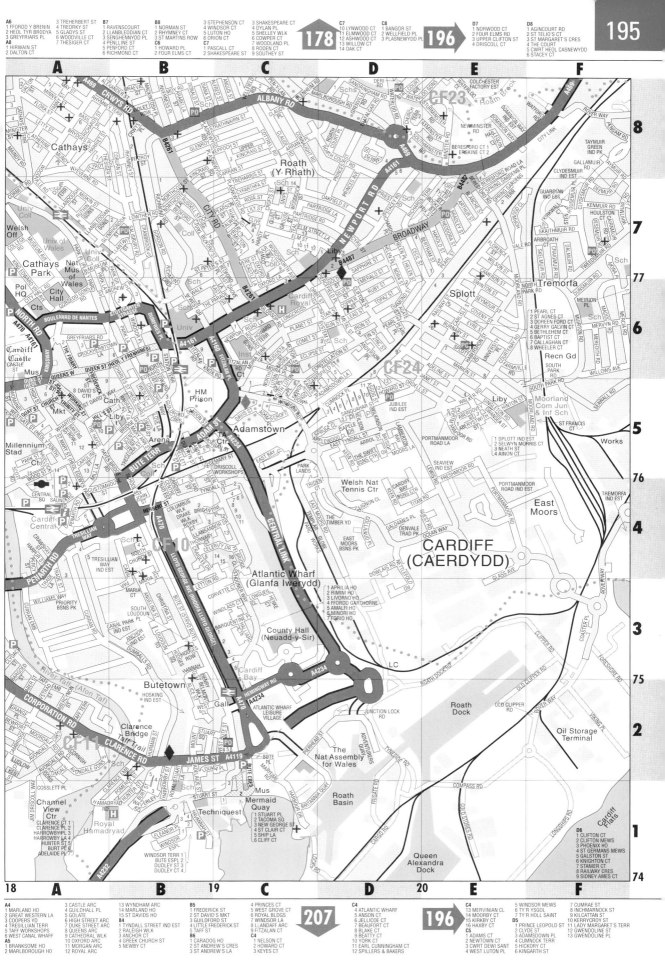

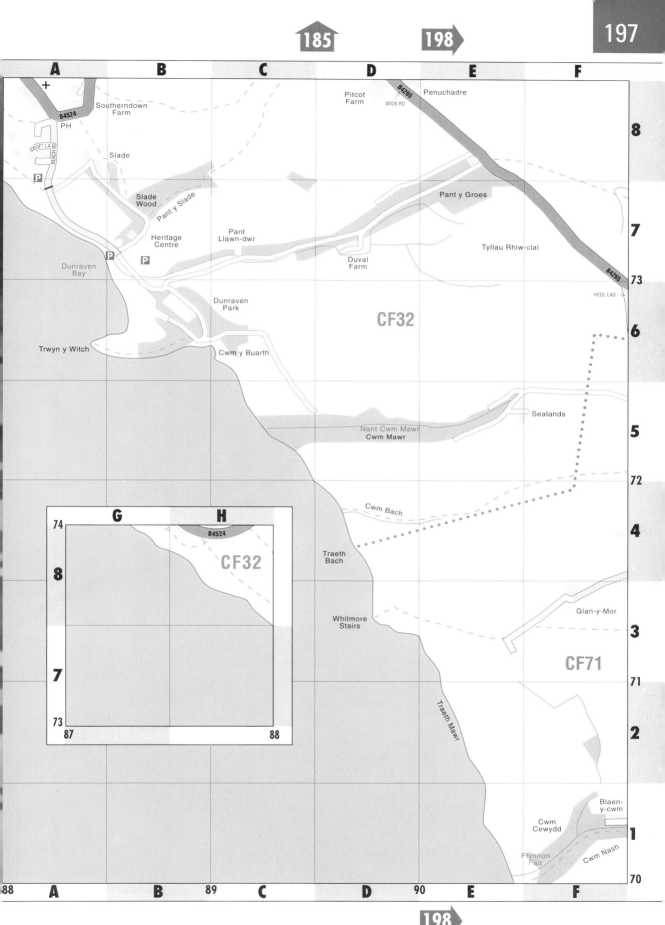

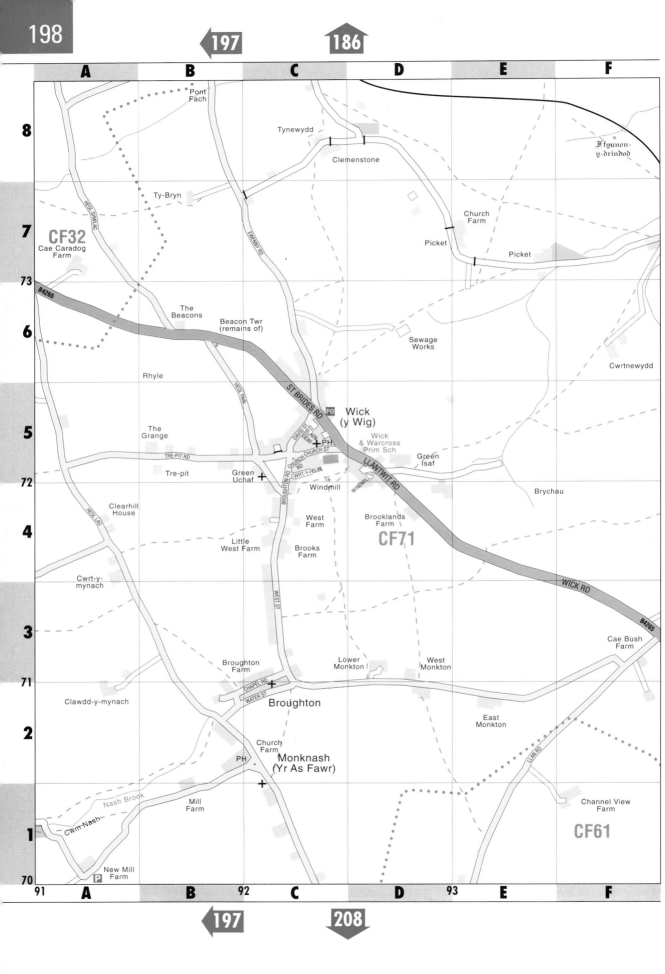

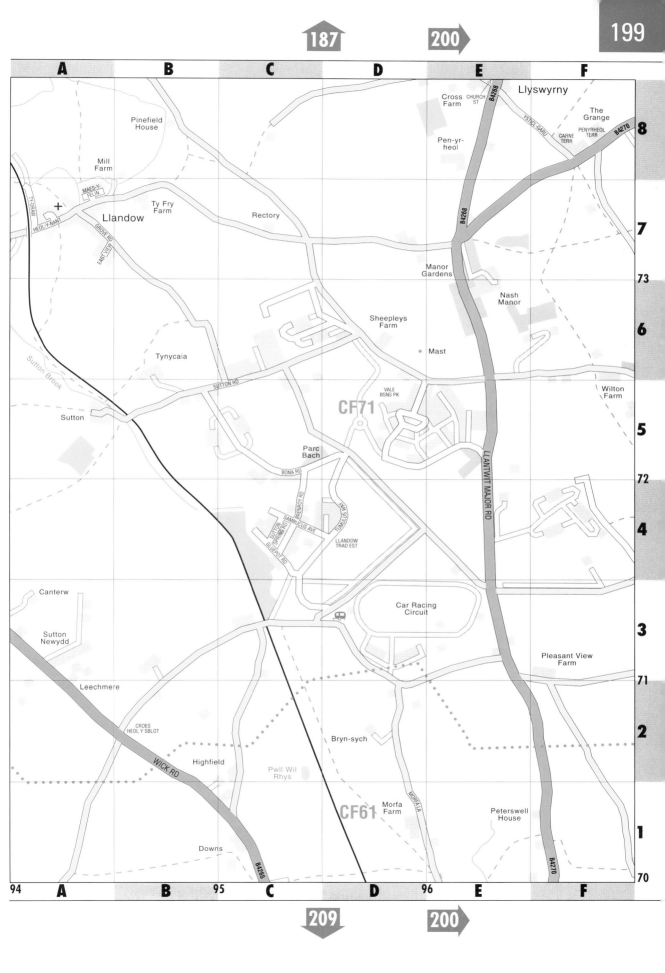

A   B   C   D   E   F

8

7

73

6

5

72

4

3

71

2

1

70

Llyswyrny

Cross Farm
CHURCH ST
The Grange
Pen-yr-heol
YSTRCL GARU
PENYRHEOL TERR
CARNE TERR
B4270
B4268

Mill Farm
Pinefield House
MAES-Y-FELIN
TY-DRAW
HEOL-Y-NANT
Llandow
Ty Fry Farm
GROVE RD
EAST VIEW
Rectory
Manor Gardens
Nash Manor
B4268

Sheepleys Farm

Sutton Brook

Tynycaia
Mast
SUTTON RD
Wilton Farm

Sutton
CF71
VALE BSNS PK

Parc Bach
BONA RD
BRENROY RD
SAMBUCUS AVE
SUTTON SPRING RD
GLUEPOT RD
SYNWMLI
Llandow Trad Est
LLANTWIT MAJOR RD

Canterw
Sutton Newydd

Car Racing Circuit

Pleasant View Farm

Leechmere
CROES HEOL Y SBLOT
Bryn-sych
Pwll Wil Rhys
WICK RD
Highfield
CF61
Morfa Farm
MORFA LA
Peterswell House
B4270
Downs
B4265

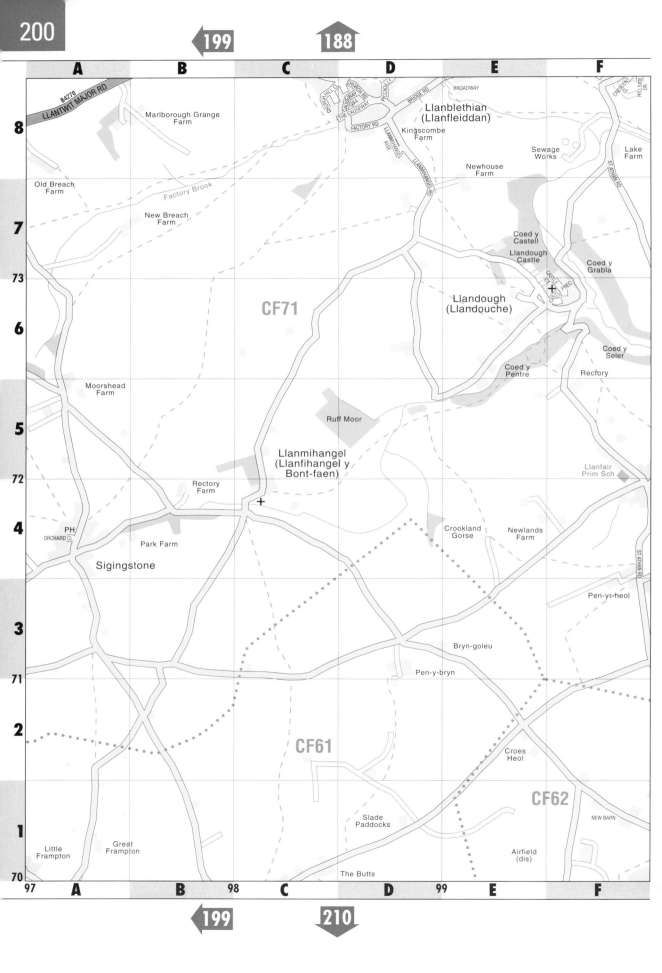

199
188

A B C D E F

8

Llanblethian
(Llanfleiddan)

B4270
LLANTWIT MAJOR RD

Marlborough Grange
Farm

CHURCH CL
THE CAUSEWAY
CHURCH RD
PICCADILLY
BROADWAY

FACTORY RD

Kingscombe
Farm

LLANMIHANGEL RISE

LLANMIHANGEL RD

CRESCENT CL
HILLSIDE DR

ST ATHAN RD

Lake
Farm

Sewage
Works

7

Old Breach
Farm

Factory Brook

New Breach
Farm

Newhouse
Farm

Coed y
Castell

Llandough
Castle

Coed y
Grabla

73

CF71

Llandough
(Llandouche)

CASTLE CT
CASTLE PREC

Coed y
Seler

6

Moorshead
Farm

Coed y
Pentre

Rectory

5

Ruff Moor

Llanmihangel
(Llanfihangel y
Bont-faen)

Llanfair
Prim Sch

72

Rectory
Farm

4

PH
ORCHARD CL

Park Farm

Sigingstone

Crookland
Gorse

Newlands
Farm

Pen-yr-heol

ST ATHAN RD

3

Bryn-goleu

71

Pen-y-bryn

2

CF61

Croes
Heol

CF62

1

Little
Frampton

Great
Frampton

Slade
Paddocks

NEW BARN

Airfield
(dis)

70

The Butts

97 A B 98 C D 99 E F

189
202

A   B   C   D   E   F

A48

Masts

Pant y
Lladron

Ty'n-y-caeau

St Hilary
Down

Pant y Moch

8

East Down

Coed y
Seler

The
Garn

New
Beaupre

PH
CHURCH
TERR

7

Long
Grove

St Hilary
(Saint Hilari)

LLANTRITHYD RD

Morawelon

New Beaupre
Farm

73

The Old
Vicarage

Coed Hills

6

Spring
Hill

Coed y
Grabla

Coed y
Ffynnon

ST ATHAN RD

Cross Barn

Coed Hills

Howe Mill
Farm

5

Beaupre
Castle

CF71

72

The Herberts

Old Beaupre
Farm

River Thaw (Afon Ddawan)

4

Coed yr
Arglwydd

Kingsland

Cross
Inn

TALBOT
TERR

MILLCROFT
CT

Gigman
Mill

Treguff
Cottage

St Mary Church
(Llan Fair)

URCH
RR

Gigman
Bridge

Green

Church
Farm

3

71

Maesybryn
Farm

Fishweir

Nant Tre-gof

ST ATHAN RD

2

Tre-gof
Moor

Nant y Creek

CF62

Tydraw
Farm

1

The Old
Rectory

Flemingston
Moor

NEW BARN

CWRT-YR-
LOLO

Flemingston
(Trefflemin)

70

A   B   01   C   D   02   E   F

211
202

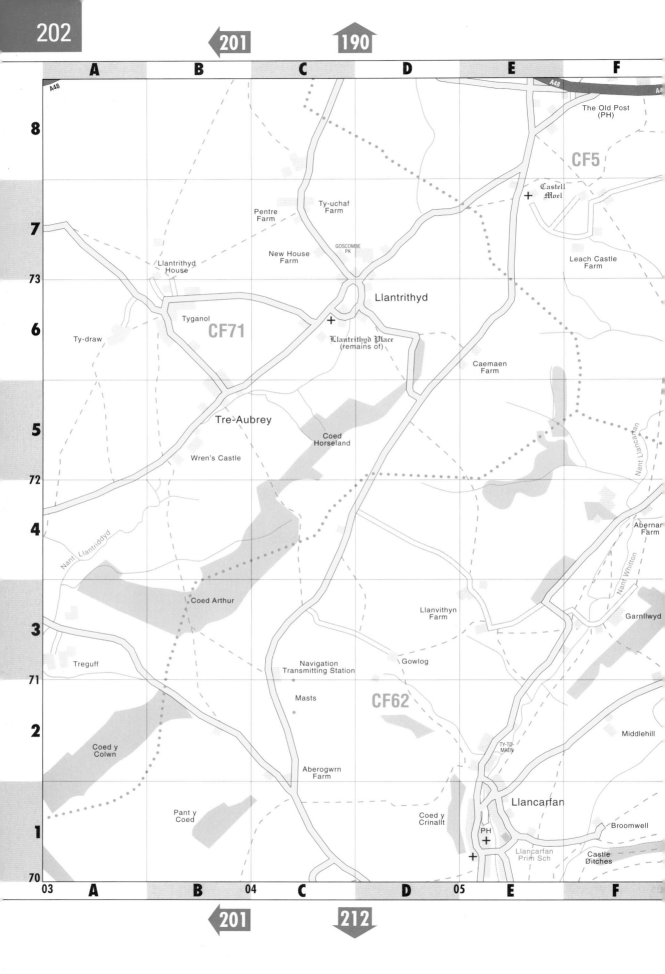

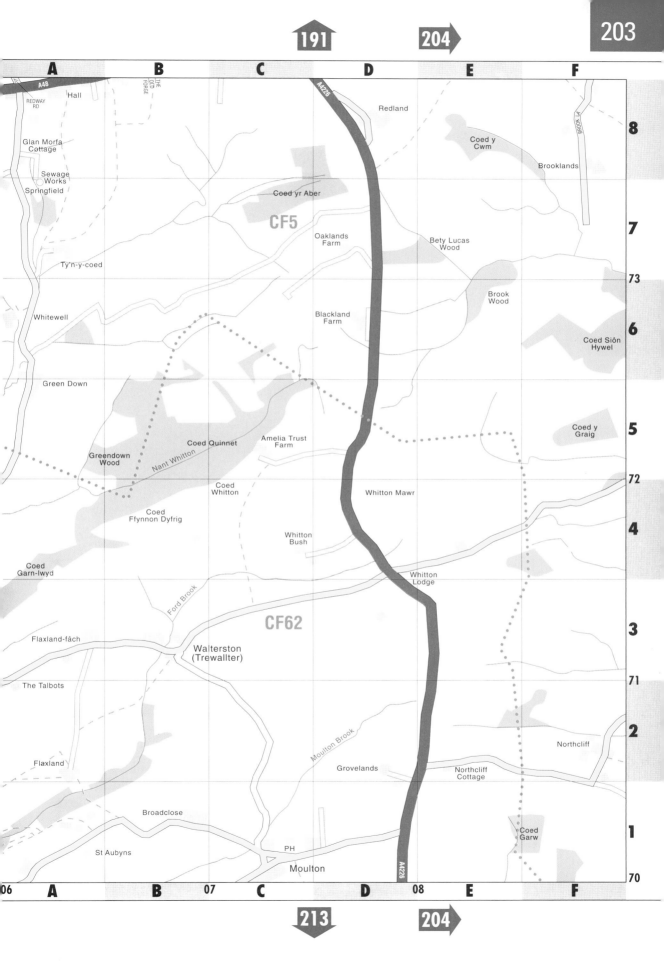

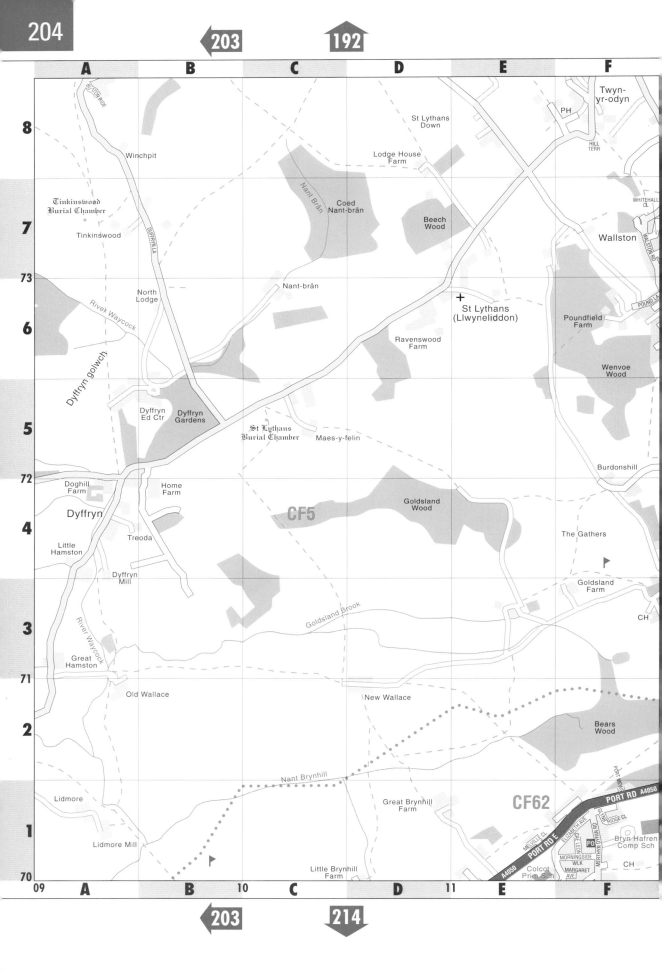

203
192

A **B** **C** **D** **E** **F**

Twyn-yr-odyn

PH

HILL TERR

8

St Lythans Down

WHITEHALL CL

Winchpit

Lodge House Farm

WALSTON RD

Wallston

Tinkinswood Burial Chamber

Nant Brân

Coed Nant-brân

Beech Wood

7

Tinkinswood

DUFFRYN LA

73

North Lodge

Nant-brân

St Lythans (Llwyneliddon)

POUND LA

River Waycock

Poundfield Farm

6

Ravenswood Farm

Wenvoe Wood

Dyffryn golwch

Dyffryn Ed Ctr

Dyffryn Gardens

St Lythans Burial Chamber

Maes-y-felin

Burdonshill

5

72

Doghill Farm

Home Farm

Goldsland Wood

CF5

The Gathers

Dyffryn

4

Little Hamston

Treoda

Goldsland Farm

CH

Dyffryn Mill

Goldsland Brook

River Waycock

3

Great Hamston

71

Old Wallace

New Wallace

Bears Wood

2

Nant Brynhill

Lidmore

Great Brynhill Farm

CF62

PORT RD A4050

MELVILLE CL

PORT RD E

ELIZABETH AVE

GLYND

RIDGE CL

PORT MEAD

1

Lidmore Mill

MORNINGSIDE

WLK

MARGARET AVE

GLYNDWR DYFAN

CAE LEON

MERTHYR DYFAN RD

Bryn Hafren Comp Sch

A4050

Colcot Prim Sch

CH

Little Brynhill Farm

70

A **B** 10 **C** **D** 11 **E** **F**

203
214

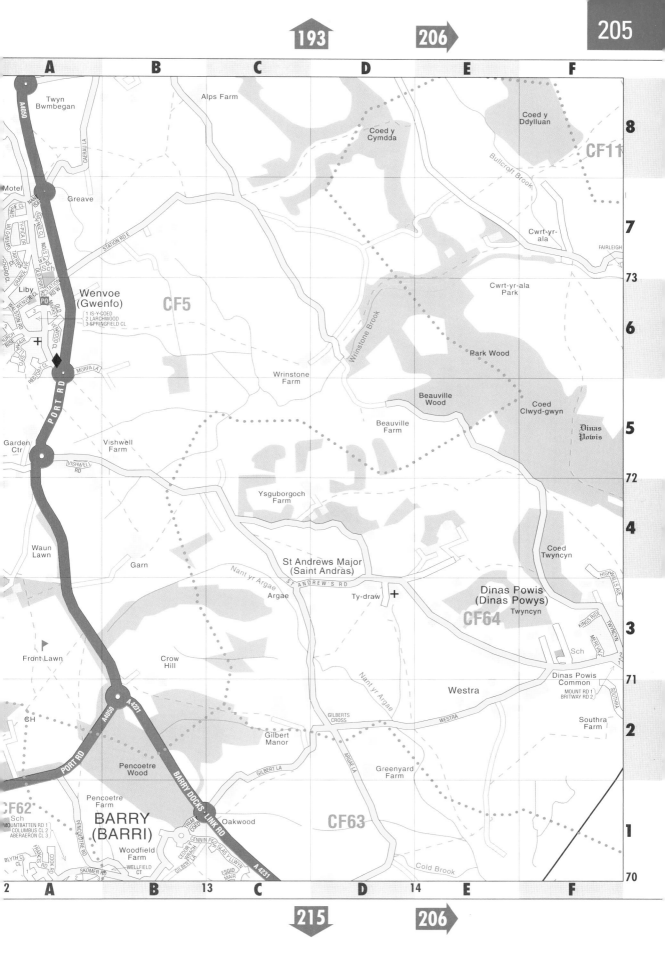

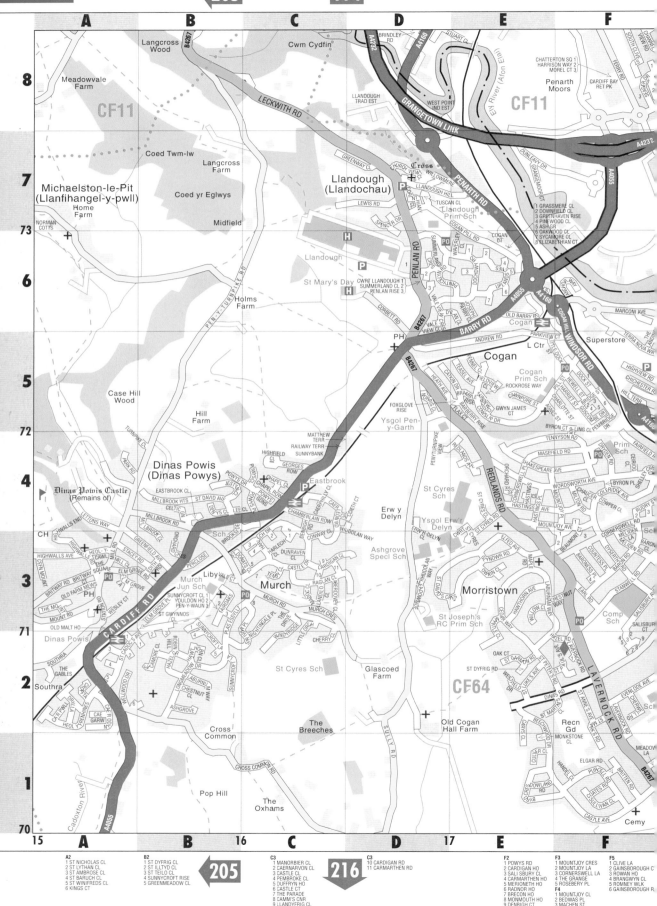

A2	B2	C3	C3	F2	F3	F5
1 ST NICHOLAS CL	1 ST DYFRIG CL	1 MANORBIER CL	10 CARDIGAN RD	1 POWYS RD	1 MOUNTJOY CRES	1 CLIVE LA
2 ST LYTHAN CL	2 ST ILLTYD CL	2 CAERNARVON CL	11 CARMARTHEN RD	2 CARDIGAN HO	2 MOUNTJOY LA	2 GAINSBOROUGH C
3 ST AMBROSE CL	3 ST TEILO CL	3 CASTLE CL		3 SALI SBURY CL	3 CORNERSWELL LA	3 ROWAN HO
4 ST BARUCH CL	4 SUNNYCROFT RISE	4 PEMBROKE CL		4 CARMARTHEN HO	4 THE GRANGE	4 BRANGWYN CL
5 ST WINIFREDS CL	5 GREENMEADOW CL	5 DUFFRYN HO		5 MERIONETH HO	5 ROSEBERY PL	5 ROMNEY WLK
6 KINGS CT		6 CASTLE CT		6 RADNOR HO		6 GAINSBOROUGH R
		7 THE PARADE		7 BRECON HO	F4	
		8 CAMM'S CNR		8 MONMOUTH HO	1 MOUNTJOY CL	
		9 LLANDYFRIG CL		9 DENBIGH CT	2 BEDWAS PL	
					3 MACHEN ST	

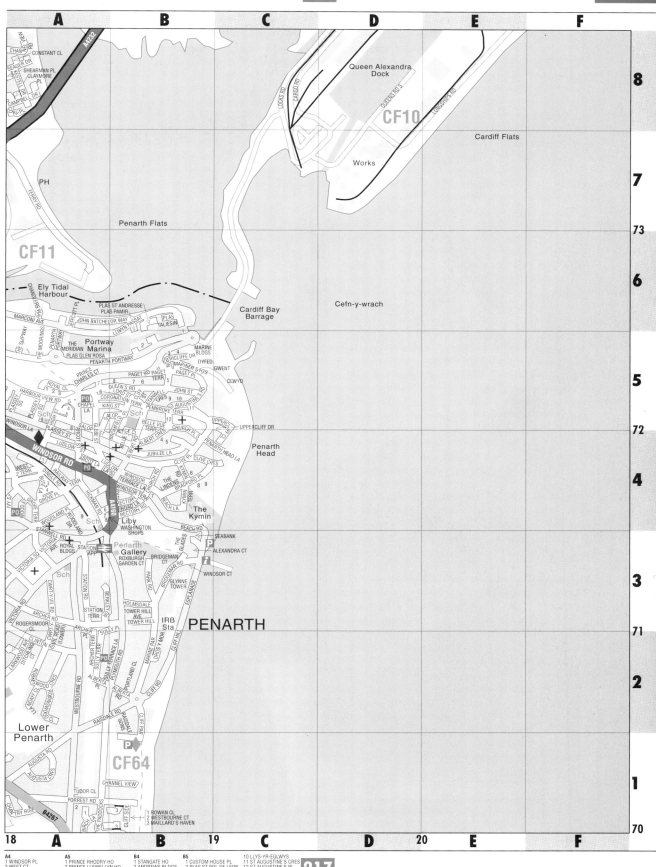

8

7

73

6

5

72

4

3

71

2

1

70

CF10

CF11

CF64

Queen Alexandra Dock

Cardiff Flats

Works

Penarth Flats

Ely Tidal Harbour

Cefn-y-wrach

Cardiff Bay Barrage

Portway Marina

Penarth Head

The Kymin

PENARTH

Lower Penarth

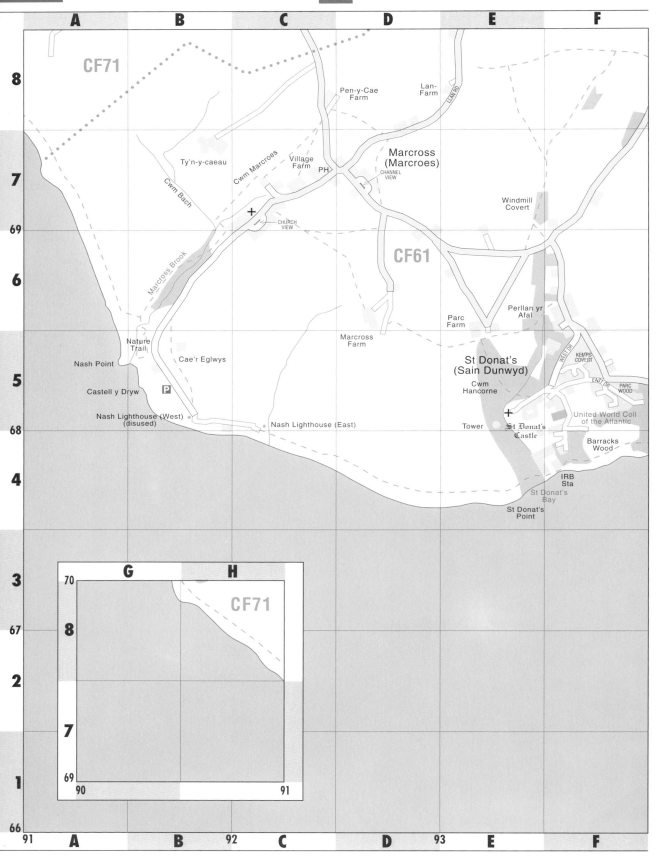

A B C D E F

8

CF71

Pen-y-Cae Farm

Lan-Farm

LLAN RD

7

Ty'n-y-caeau

Cwm Marcroes

Village Farm

PH

Marcross (Marcroes)

CHANNEL VIEW

Windmill Covert

Cwm Bach

69

CHURCH VIEW

CF61

6

Marcross Brook

Parc Farm

Perllan yr Afal

Marcross Farm

St Donat's (Sain Dunwyd)

WEST DR

KEMPS COVERT

Nature Trail

Nash Point

Cae'r Eglwys

EAST DR

PARC WOOD

5

Castell y Dryw

P

Cwm Hancorne

Nash Lighthouse (West) (disused)

Nash Lighthouse (East)

Tower

St Donat's Castle

United World Coll of the Atlantic

68

Barracks Wood

4

IRB Sta

St Donat's Bay

St Donat's Point

3

G H

70

CF71

67

8

2

7

69

1

90 91

66

91 A B 92 C D 93 E F

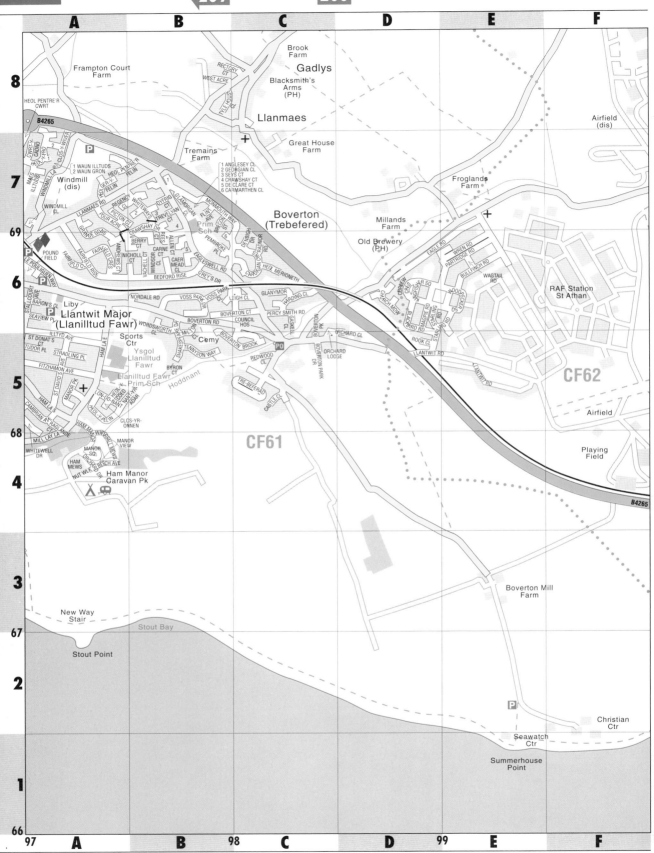

A   B   C   D   E   F

8

Ty Newydd Farm
NEW BARN

Flemingstone Court Farm

Greenfield

Llanbydderi Moor

Picketston

Eglwys-Brewis

Mast

Nant y Stepsau

ST ATHAN RD

CEDAR RD

ELM GR
PINEWOOD SQ
CHESTNUT AVE
PICKETSTON CL
LIME GR
OAK GR

ASH

SYCAMORE AVE

MARGAM CL 1
CRYNANT CL 2
TALYBONT CL 3

EBBW CL

TINTERN CL

CELYN CL

CWOOD CRES

FLEMINGSTON RD

BURLEY CT
BURLEY PL

Sports Gd

7

Mast

WALNUT GR 1
YEWTREE GR 2
ROWAN GR 3

MALLORY CL

SCOTT CL

LIVINGSTONE WAY

SHACKLETON
CLIVE RD

DRAKE CL

69

RAF Station St Athan

CWRIBRIDGE RD

6

Airfield

Beggars Pound

Pant-yn-Awel Farm

Castleton

Oxmoor Wood

BINGLE LA

St John's Valley

CF62

ST DAVIDS CRES

JOHN'S HILL

CASTLETON RD

Rills Valley

Castleton Wood

5

West Farm

Higher End

JOHN'S VIEW

ROBERTS CL
TATHAN CRES
ST MICHAEL'S CL

RECTORY DR

Rock Farm

River Thaw (Afon Ddawan)

LLANTWIT RD

LLANTWIT GARDENS CL

RECTORY RD

Liby
PH

CLWYCH LA

68

Briarbank

WARLOW CL
GLYNDWR AVE
GLEBELAND ST

PANT-Y-CELYN RD
LOUGHER PL

1 2
3

St Athan Prim Sch

East Orchard Wood

Batslays

1 OWAIN CT
2 THE WILLOWS
3 FFEAM-Y-GRAIG

St Athan (Sain Tathan)

B4265

4

GILESTON RD

Baronswell

Seaview

West Lodge

3

Gileston Farm

Gileston Manor

Cemy

ORCHARD WAY

St Athan Boys Village

67

Gileston (Silstwn)

CF61

West Aberthaw Farm

West Aberthaw

2

Walls Pool

The Walls

Limpert

P
SEA PL

NORTH RD

PUMP HOUSE RD

132KV SWITCH HOUSE RD

MAIN ACCESS RD

Penry Bay

Limpert Bay

Power Station

BOILER HOUSE RD

PRECIPITATION RD

CHIMNEY RD

Chy

B STA ACCESS RD

COAL PLANT

1

ASH PLANT RD

SOUTH RD

TOWER RD

132KV SWITCH HOUSE RD

CONTROL RD

OCEAN HOUSE RD

The Leys

66

ADMINISTRATION RD

212 →

NORTH WALL RD

DIAGONAL RD

TURBINE ANNEXE RD

AUXILLARY BOILER RD

GARAGE CIRCUS

Breaksea Point

Leys Beach

0   A   B   01   C   D   02

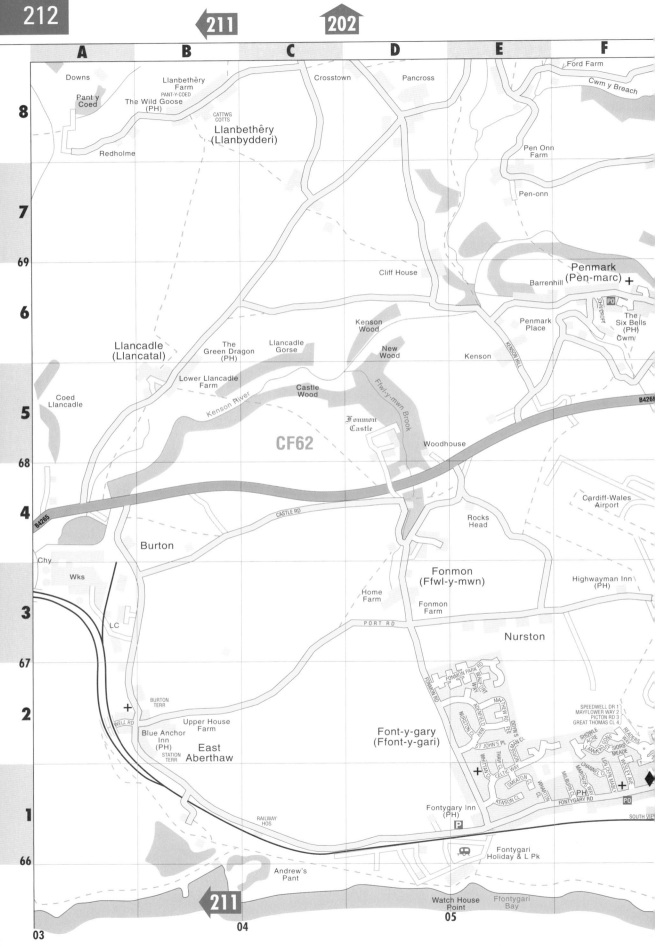

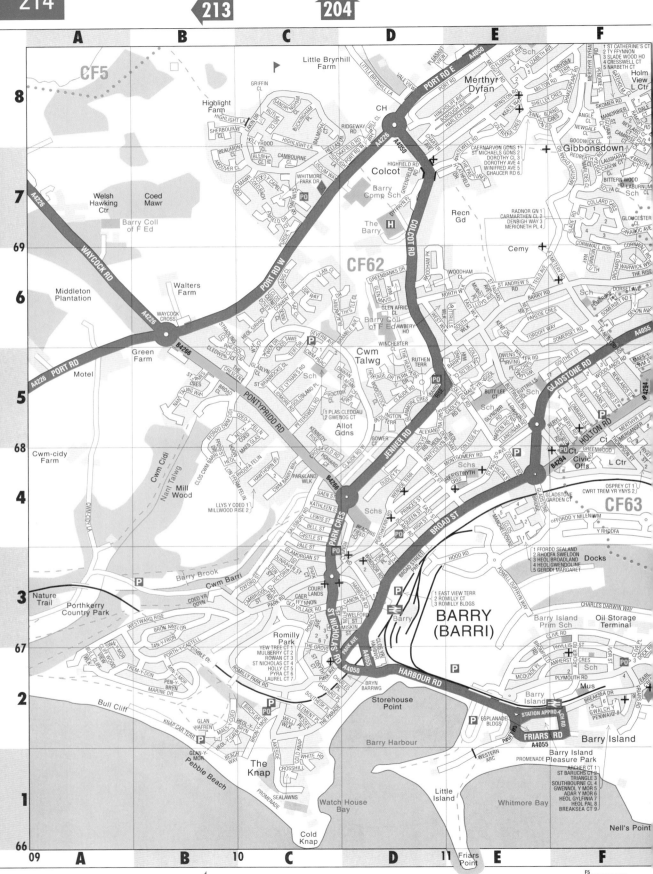
A B C D E F

8

CF5

Little Brynhill
Farm

Highlight
Farm

Griffin
CL

Merthyr
Dyfan

Holm
View
L Ctr

Port Rd E

A4050

1 ST CATHERINE S CT
2 TY FFYNNON
3 SLADE WOOD HO
4 CRESSWELL CT
5 NARBETH CT

HIGHLIGHT LA

Gibbonsdown

Colcot

CH

7

Welsh
Hawking
Ctr

Coed
Mawr

WAYCOCK RD

Barry Coll
of F Ed

Whitmore Park Dr

Barry
Comp Sch

Highfield Rd

The
Barry

H

Colcot Rd

Recn
Gd

RADNOR GN 1
CARMARTHEN CL 2
DENBIGH WAY 3
MERIONETH PL 4

Cemy

69

A4226

Port Rd W

CF62

St Andrew's
Rd

6

Middleton
Plantation

A4226

Walters
Farm

Waycock
Cross

Green
Farm

Pontypridd Rd

Woodham

Barry Coll
of F Ed
Awbery
Ho

Cwm
Talwg

Winchester

Sch

Woodham
CL

Glen Afric
CL

Barry Rd

A4055

B4294

5

A4226 Port Rd

Motel

B4266

Sch

1 PLAS CLEDDAU
2 GWENOG CT

Allot
Gdns

Jenner Rd

Gladstone Rd

Holton Rd

68

Cwm-cidy
Farm

Cwm Cidi

Nant Talwg

Mill
Wood

LLYS Y COED 1
MILLWOOD RISE 2

Sch

B4266

Montgomery Rd

Schs

Civic
Offs

L Ctr

Greenwood

CF63

OSPREY CT 1
CWRT TREM YR YNYS 2

4

Park Cres

Schs

Broad St

Gladstone
Garden Ct

OFFORDD Y MILENIWM

Y Rhodfa

Docks

1 FFORDD SEALAND
2 RHODFA SWELDON
3 HEOL BROADLAND
4 HEOL GWENDOLINE
5 GERDDI MARGARET

3

Nature
Trail

Porthkerry
Country Park

Barry Brook

Cwm Barri

Romilly
Park

YEW TREE CT 1
MULBERRY CT 2
ROWAN CT 3
ST NICHOLAS CT 4
HOLLY CT 5
PYRA CT 6
LAUREL CT 7

St Nicholas Rd

1 EAST VIEW TERR
2 ROMILLY CT
3 ROMILLY BLDGS

Barry

BARRY
(BARRI)

Barry Island
Prim Sch

67

A4050

Harbour Rd

Mus

Barry Island

2

Bull Cliff

GLAN-Y-MOR

The
Knap

Storehouse
Point

A4055

Barry
Island

ESPLANADE
BLDGS

STATION APPRO

FRIARS RD
A4055

Barry Island

1

Pebble Beach

SEALAWNS

Watch House
Bay

Barry Harbour

Little
Island

Whitmore Bay

Barry Island
Pleasure Park

ARCHER CT 1
ST BARUCHS CT 2
TRIANGLE 3
SOUTHBOURNE CL 4
GWENNOL Y MOR 5
ADAR Y MOR 6
HEOL GYLFINA 7
HEOL PAL 8
BREAKSEA CT 9

Nell's Point

66

Cold
Knap

Friars
Point

09 A B 10 C D 11 E F

F5
1 COPPERFIELD CT
2 HANOVER ST
3 BYRON ST
4 WOODLANDS CT
5 GLADSTONE CT
6 SPENCER ST
7 THE MEWS
8 BELVEDERE CRES
9 DUNLIN CT

A8
1 MOUNTBATTEN RD
2 BEATTY CL
3 CWRT PENCOEDTRE
4 BROUGHTON PL
5 GIBBONSDOWN CL
6 GWILYM PL

B6
1 BLACKWELL CL
2 LLANOVER ST
3 COURT NEWTON
4 COURT MEWS
5 DAVNIC CL
6 FOSTER ST

7 WESTON ST
8 RECTORY RD
9 COURTENAY RD
10 WESTERN ST
11 TENSING TERR
12 HUNT PL
13 HILLARY MEWS

B7
1 PADDOCK PL
2 JENKIN ST
3 COWBRIDGE ST
4 NEW HOUSE CT
5 TY CERRIG

C8
1 FFORDD GWYNETH
2 PARC CLWYD
3 EASTBOURNE CT
4 HATHAWAY PL
5 STRATFORD GN

A **B** **C** **D** **E** **F**

8

Downs

Oakdene

Downs Wood

Downs Farm

CF63

Cosmeston Lakes Country Park

Cog Moors

Cogan Plantation

7

Sully Brook

Cog Bridge

CF64

Visitor Ctr

69

Sully Moors

Cog Farm

Cosmeston Medieval Village

Lower Cosmeston Farm

6

Cog

Home Farm

ASHBY RD

DONIFORD CL

SOUTHGLADE

COG RD

UPHILL CL

SLADE CL

LAVERNOCK RD

Ty-r-Orsaf

MEADOW VIEW CT

SOUTHGLADE

COMBE RD

1 WESTMINSTER DR
2 CANNINGTON CL
3 LYNTON CL
4 GRIMSON CL

De Sully Grange

RODNEY CL

BASSETT RD

KINGSLEY CL

DESPENSER RD

GLASTONBURY RD

DULVER

The Vineyard

5

B4267

ELWORTHY CL

SWANBRIDGE RD

Sully

DUNSTER DR

HOLMS CT

SOUTH RD

WIMBORNE CRS

ARLINGTON

BRACE CT

BREAKSEA CL

WINSFORD RD

SWANBRIDGE GR

68

MINEHEAD AVE

BURNHAM AVE

WESTON RD

ELM CL

HIGHBRIDGE CL

SWAN

LYNMOUTH

SMITHIES AVE

PO

Swanbridge

Sully Cty Prim Sch

CLEVEDON AVE

4

DYS

BEND

SIMS VIEW

RSET

BEACH RD

SWANBRIDGE FARM

St Mary's Well Bay

Sully Bay

Sports Gd

PH

St Hilary

Ball Bay

ST MARY'S WELL BAY RD

Swanbridge Bay

3

Sully Sound

67

West Point

Sully Island

Fort

East Point

2

1

66

15 **A** **B** 16 **C** **D** 17 **E** **F**

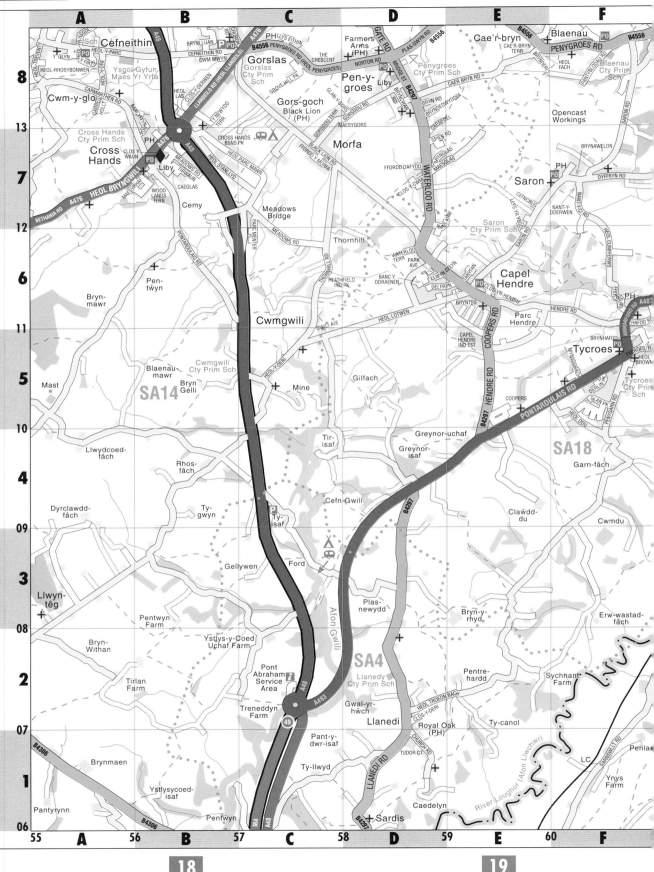

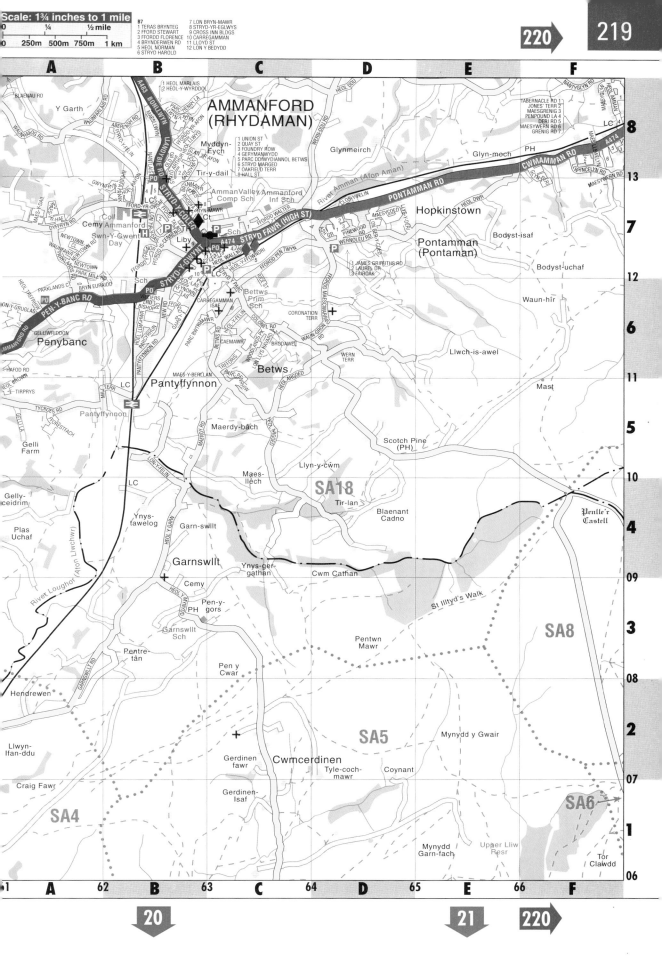

Scale: 1¾ inches to 1 mile

0 ¼ ½ mile
0 250m 500m 750m 1 km

A B C D E F

GLANAMMAN WORKSHOPS
TABERNACLE
TRYCOED RD
GER YR AFON
LC's
SATURN RD
LON LLWYD
FOLLAND RD
CLOS FELEN
HEOL FELEN
MAES-YR-HENDRE
HENDRE RD
HIGHFIELD RD
LLANDEILO RD
Cwm Aman
NANT GWINI RD
GREENFIELD RD
BRYN BACH RD
MAES Y CERI
Sch
A4069
PH
Gorsto

8 A474
SCETI LLO RD
PO
HEOL CWMAMMAN (CWMAMMAN RD)
RHODFA BRYN RHOS
BRYN RHOS
BRO RYAN
Glanaman
NEW SCHOOL
NEW CWERN RD
Sch
PO
VICTORIA RD
LC
JOLLY RD
NEUADD RD
LON BRYNNENADD
Lower Brynamman
HEOL GODDEU
CANNON ST
PARK ST
PO
BANWEN
Sch
AMMAN RD
PH Brynamman

Cemy
Garnant
Cty Prim Sch
PO
Garnant
Liby
POWELL RD
STEPNEY
TYLE GLAS
DYNEVOR RD
BRO NANT FER
LLYS NANT FER
BRYNAMMAN RD
Gwaun-Leision
WAUNLEISION
ST DAVIDS RD
CWMNANTHIR TERR

13

7
B8
1 MAES Y FRON
2 PARC GLANFFRWD
3 ARCADE TERR
4 LOWER STATION RD
5 UPPER STATION RD
6 CHURCH ROW
7 BISHOP RD
8 CORONATION RD
PENYRALLT
BRYNCETHIN RD
BRYNSIRIOL
GRAIG RD
Gwaun Cae Gurwen Prim Sch
LC
LAUGHARNE RD
HALF CT
KING EDWARD RD
Tairgwaith

12
Nant Garenig
Ty'n-domen
WATER ST
PO
DURIN RD
CRESCENT
GRON RD
HEOL CAE GURWEN
UPPER COL
COLBREN RD
NEW RD
GORSTO RD
LC's
PH
MORRISTON RD
GARTH RD
LLWYNCELYN RD
Tairgwaith Prim Sch

6
Foel
Banc Cwmhelen
SA18
LOWER COLBREN RD
CHURCH LA
CWMGORS IND EST
DERWYDD AVE
LON BELLI GLAS
HEOL HIR
Gwaun-Cae-Gurwen
Cemy
Penlle'rfedwen

11
Mynydd y Betws
St Illtyd's Walk
GORS LA
PANT Y FEDWEN Baily Glas Uchaf
PO
LLWYN HIR
ABERNANT RD
Mynydd Uchaf

5
Bancbryn
Gelli-fawr
Nantricket
HEOL-Y-GORS
BOLWG-Y-CWN
Ysgol Cwmgors
UPLANDS
Cwmgors
Mynydd Uchaf

10
Henrhyd
Nant-melyn
LLWYN-NANT
LLWYN-hên
Blaen-egel-fawr
Graig Ddu

4
Hafod Wennol Farm
Penlanau
Tresgyrch Fawr
Nant-melyn
PH
Cwm-nant Hopkin
Cwrt-y-bariwns

09
Bryn Mawr
Pwllwatkin Farm
PONTARDAWE RD
Nant-y-gaseg-uchaf

3
Lygos
SA9

08
Llwyn-Ifan
River Egel
SA8
Garth

2
Nant-Moel-uchaf
St Illtyd's Walk
Myrydd Carnlechart
Upper Clydach River
Gelilwca Fawr
Carn Llwyd

07

1
SA6
BARAN RD
Gelli-luog-uchaf
HEOL LAS

06
Ty-melin-uchaf
Carn Llechart
A474

67 A 68 B 69 C 70 D 71 E 72 F

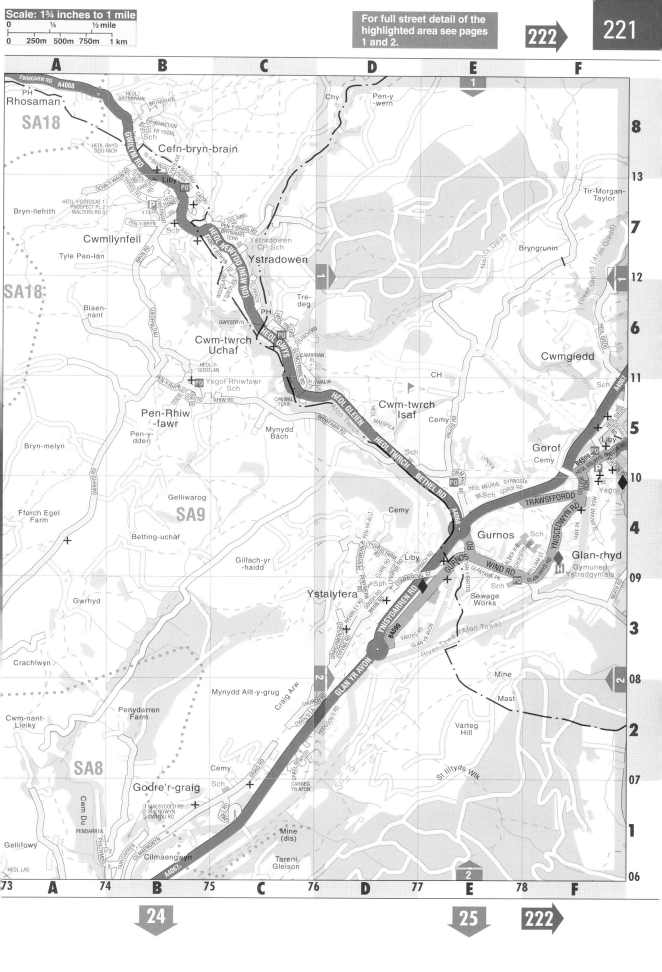

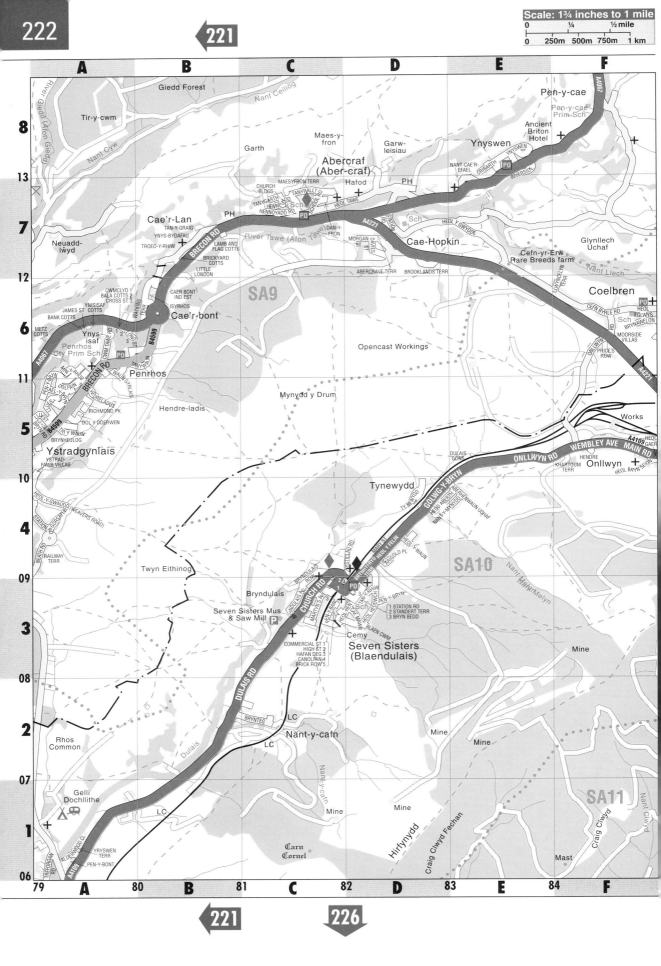

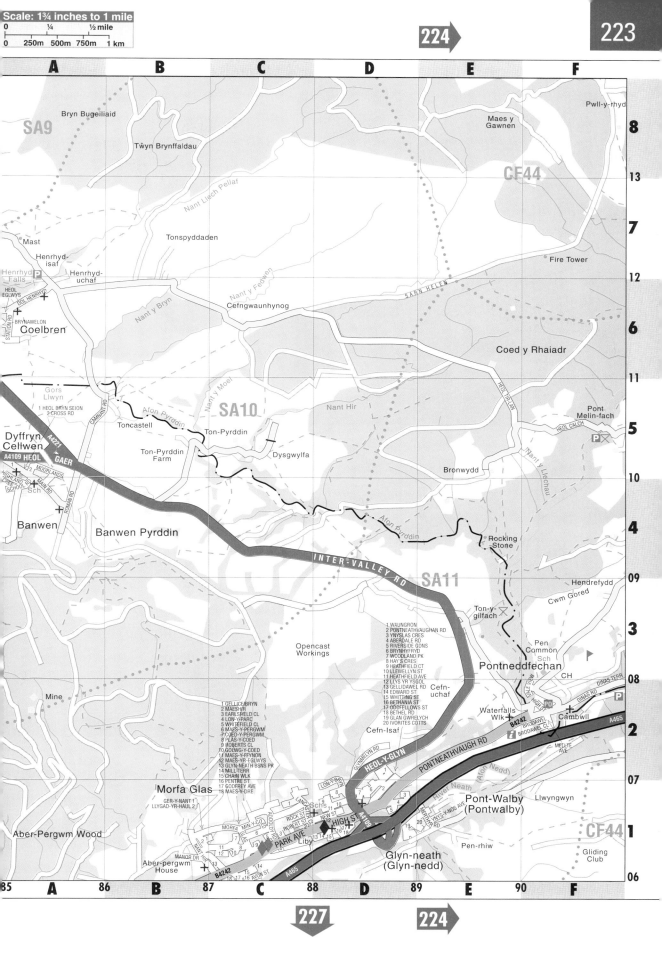

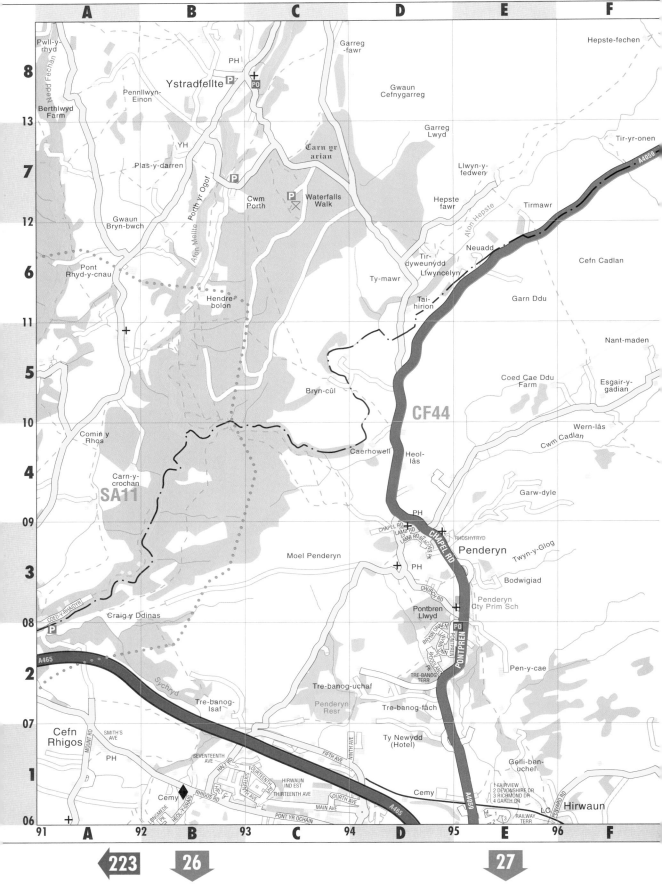

A   B   C   D   E   F

8

13

7

12

6

11

5

10

4

09

3

08

2

07

1

06

91   A   92   B   93   C   94   D   95   E   96   F

Pwll-y-rhyd

Nedd Fechan

Berthlwyd Farm

Pennllwyn-Einon

Ystradfellte

PH

P

PO

Garreg-fawr

Hepste-fechen

Gwaun Cefnygarreg

Garreg Lwyd

Tir-yr-onen

A4059

YH

Plas-y-darren

Carn yr arian

Llwyn-y-fedwen

Hepste fawr

Tirmawr

P

Afon Melite

Porth yr Ogot

Cwm Porth

P

Waterfalls Walk

Afon Hepste

Neuadd

Cefn Cadlan

Gwaun Bryn-bwch

Tir-dyweunydd
Llwyncelyn

Pont Rhyd-y-cnau

Hendre-bolon

Ty-mawr

Tai-hirion

Garn Ddu

Nant-maden

Bryn-cûl

Coed Cae Ddu Farm

Esgair-y-gadian

Comin y Rhos

CF44

Caerhowell

Heol-lâs

Wern-lâs

Cwm Cadlan

Carn-y-crochan

SA11

Moel Penderyn

Garw-dyle

COED-Y-RHAIDYR

P

Craig y Ddinas

Chapel Rd

LAMB RD

LAMB RD

BEACONS PK

CHAPEL RD

RHOSHYFRYD

Penderyn

Twyn-y-Glog

Bodwigiad

PH

PH

CHURCH RD

Pontbren Llwyd

Penderyn Cty Prim Sch

A465

Sychryd

Tre-banog-Isaf

BRYN ONNEN

NANT ONNEN

MADOG LANE

PONTPREN

PO

PONTPREN

Pen-y-cae

Tre-banog-uchaf

Tre-bandg TERR

Tre-banog-fâch

Ty Newydd (Hotel)

Gelli-ben-uchel

Cefn Rhigos

MOUNT RD

SMITH'S AVE

PH

Penderyn Resr

A465

Cemy

A4059

PENYARD RD

Hirwaun

Cemy

SEVENTEENTH AVE

HALT RD

RHIGOS RD

SIXTEENTH AVE

FOURTEENTH AVE

HIRWAUN IND EST

THIRTEENTH AVE

FIFTH AVE

NINTH AVE

DURTH AVE

MAIN AVE

PONT YR OCHAIN

LONGSMEDE PK

HEOL-Y-BRAG

Cemy

1 FAIRVIEW
2 DEVONSHIRE DR
3 RICHMOND DR
4 GARTH DR

1
2 3

RAILWAY TERR

LO

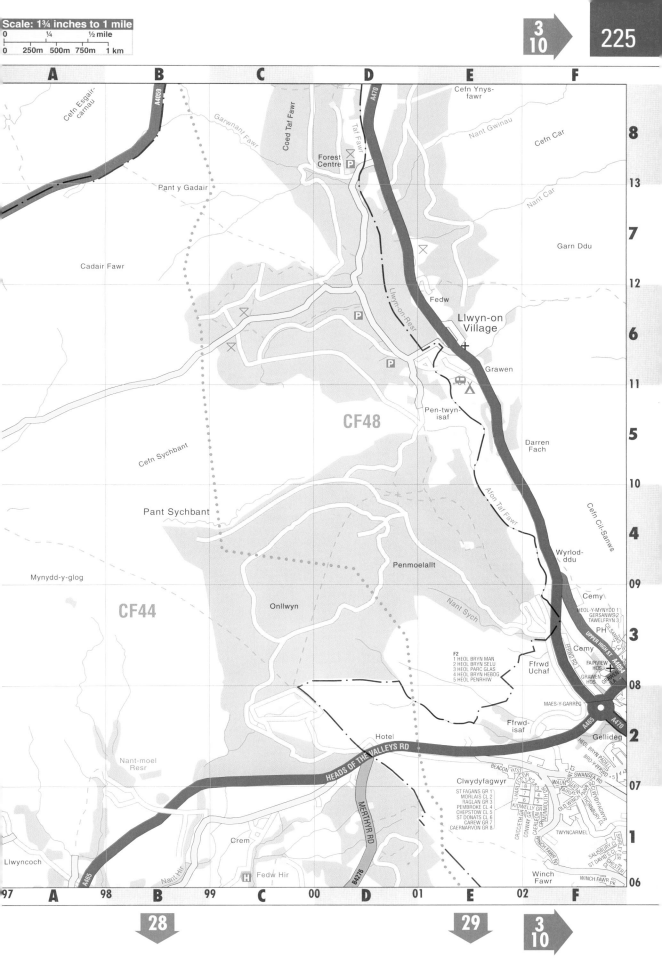

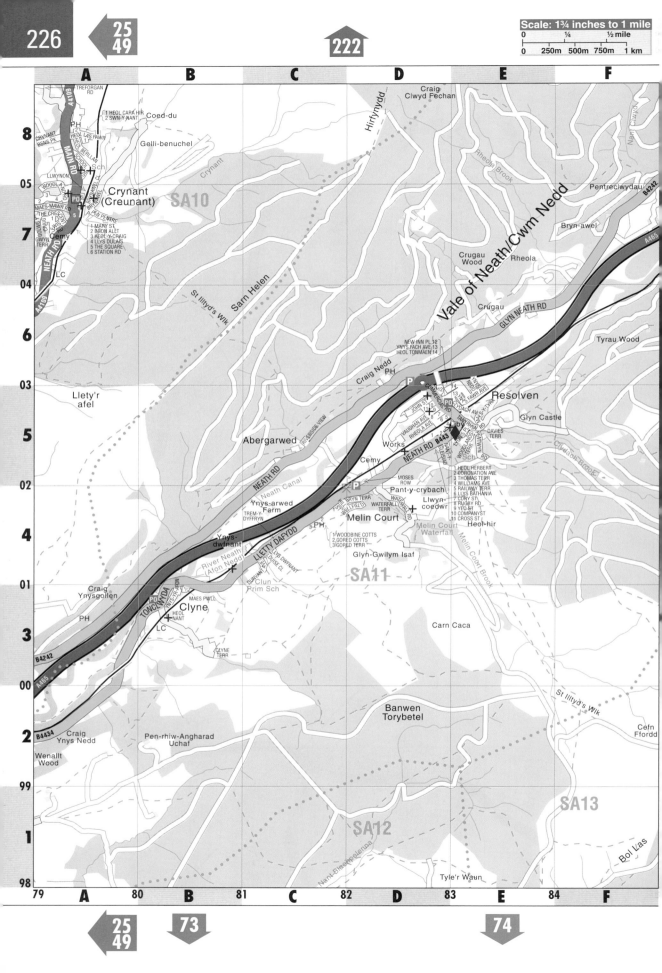

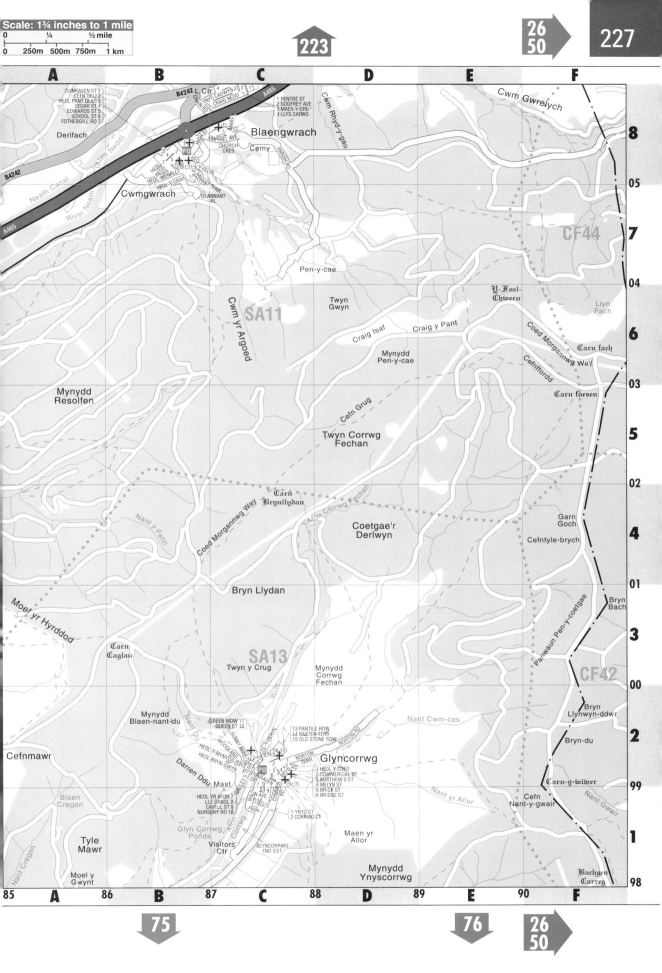

Map labels:

DUNRAVEN ST 1
CEFN GELI 2
HEOL PANT GLAS 3
CEDAR ST 4
EDWARDS ST 5
SCHOOL ST 6
FOTHERGILL RD 7

1 PENTRE ST
2 GODFREY AVE
3 MAES-Y-DRE
4 LLYS CATWG

Derifach

B4242 L. Ctr

Blaengwrach

Cemy

CHURCH CRES

EMPIRE AVE

Cwmgwrach

GLANNANT PL

Neath Canal

River Neath

B4242

A465

Cwm Rhyd-y-gau

Cwm Gwrelych

CF44

Pen-y-cae

Twyn Gwyn

Cwm yr Argoed

SA11

Y-Foel-Chwern

Craig Isaf

Craig y Pant

Llyn Fach

Mynydd Resolfen

Mynydd Pen-y-cae

Coed Morgannwg Way

Cefnffordd

Carn fach

Carn foesen

Cefn Grug

Twyn Corrwg Fechan

Carn Brynllydan

Coed Morgannwg Way

Nant y Felin

Afon Corrwg Fechan

Coetgae'r Derlwyn

Garn Goch

Cefntyle-brych

Moel yr Hyrddod

Bryn Llydan

Bryn Bach

Carn Caglau

SA13

Panwaun Pen-y-coetgae

CF42

Twyn y Crug

Mynydd Corrwg Fechan

Nant Cwm-cas

Bryn Llynwyn-ddwr

Cefnmawr

Mynydd Blaen-nant-du

Nant Du

GREEN MDW 11
QUEEN ST 12

WOODLAND
HEOL-Y-MYNYDD
HEOL BRYN GWYN

13 PANTILE ROW
14 BAXTER TERR
15 OLD STONE ROW

NORTON RD

Bryn-du

Darren Ddu Mast

Glyncorrwg

Carn-y-twitwer

1 HEOL Y COED
2 COMMERCIAL ST
3 MATTHEW S ST
4 MELYN ST
5 BRICK ST
6 BRIDGE ST

Nant yr Allor

Cefn Nant-y-gwair

Nant Gwair

Blaen Cregen

HEOL YR AFON 7
LLE CANOL 8
CAVELL ST 9
NURSERY RD 10

1 YNYS CT
2 CORRWG CT

Glyn Corrwg Ponds

Maen yr Allor

Tyle Mawr

Visitors Ctr

GLYNCORRWG IND EST

Moel y Gwynt

Nant Cregan

Mynydd Ynyscorrwg

Bachgen Carreg

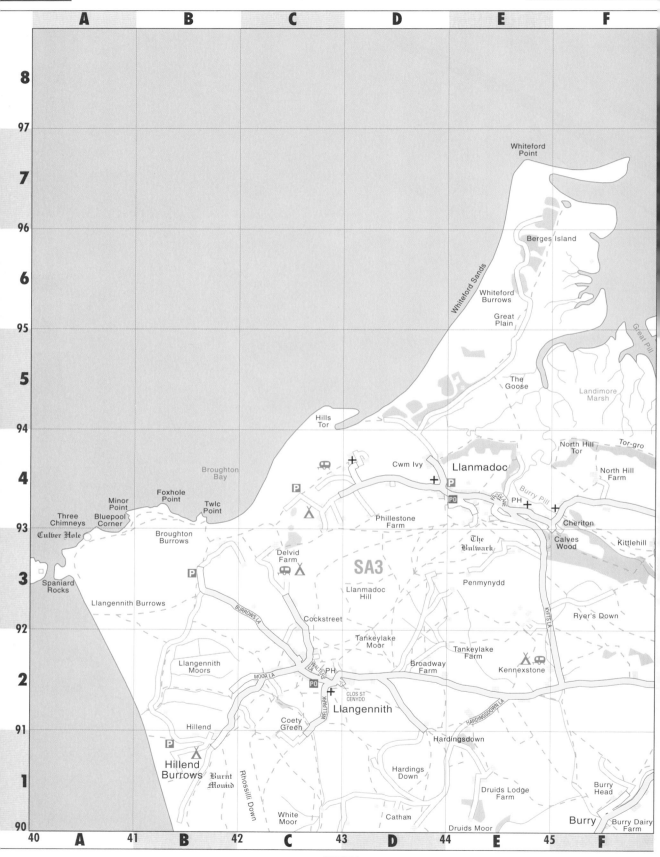

A   B   C   D   E   F

8

97

7

96

6

95

5

94

4

93

3

92

2

91

1

90

40   A   41   B   42   C   43   D   44   E   45   F

Whiteford Point
Berges Island
Whiteford Sands
Whiteford Burrows
Great Plain
Great Pill
The Goose
Landimore Marsh
North Hill Tor
Tor-gro
North Hill Farm
Hills Tor
Cwm Ivy
Llanmadoc
Burry Pill
PH
Cheriton
Kittlehill
Phillestone Farm
The Bulwark
Calves Wood
Broughton Bay
Foxhole Point
Twlc Point
Minor Point
Bluepool Corner
Three Chimneys
Culver Hole
Broughton Burrows
Delvid Farm
SA3
Llanmadoc Hill
Penmynydd
Ryer's Down
Spaniard Rocks
Llangennith Burrows
BURROWS LA
Cockstreet
Tankeylake Moor
Tankeylake Farm
Kennexstone
KYFTS LA
Llangennith Moors
MOOR LA
WELLPARK
WALTERS
PH
PO
CLOS ST CENYDD
Llangennith
Broadway Farm
Hardingsdown
HARDINGSDOWN LA
Hillend
Coety Green
Hardings Down
Druids Lodge Farm
Burry Head
Hillend Burrows
Burnt Mound
Rhossili Down
White Moor
Cathan
Druids Moor
Burry
Burry Dairy Farm

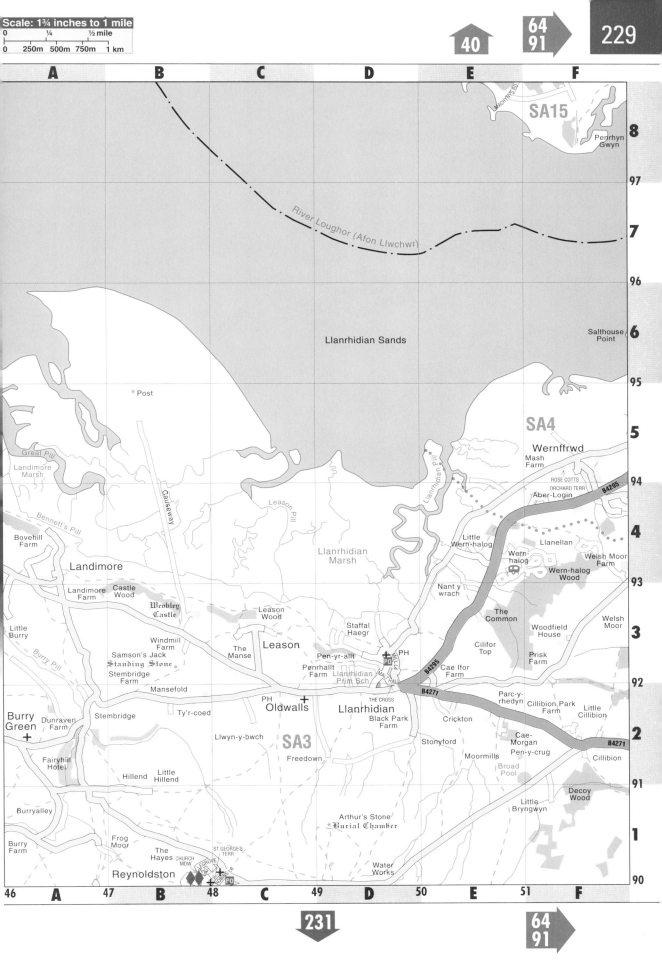

228

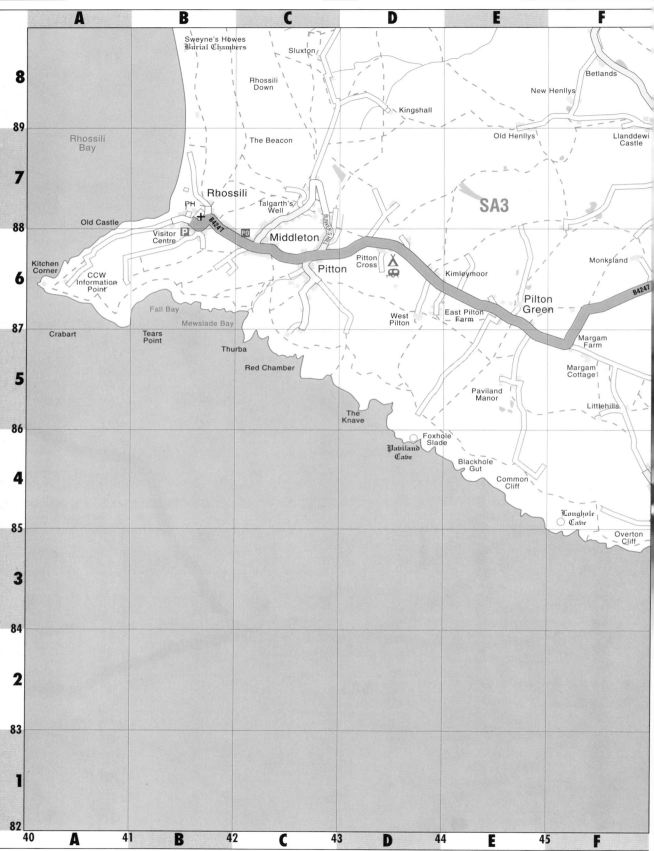

Scale: 1¾ inches to 1 mile

Rhossili Bay

Sweyne's Howes Burial Chambers

Sluxton

Rhossili Down

The Beacon

Kingshall

Betlands

New Henllys

Old Henllys

Llanddewi Castle

SA3

Rhossili

PH

Talgarth's Well

Old Castle

Visitor Centre

P

B4247

PO

Middleton

BUNKERS HILL

Kitchen Corner

CCW Information Point

Pitton

Pitton Cross

Kimleymoor

Pilton Green

Monksland

B4247

Fall Bay

West Pilton

East Pilton Farm

Mewslade Bay

Crabart

Tears Point

Margam Farm

Thurba

Margam Cottage

Red Chamber

Paviland Manor

Littlehills

The Knave

Foxhole Slade

Paviland Cave

Blackhole Gut

Common Cliff

Longhole Cave

Overton Cliff

229

120

Scale: 1¾ inches to 1 mile

| 0 | ¼ | ½ mile |
| 0 | 250m | 500m | 750m | 1 km |

A B C D E F

Reynoldston

King Arthur Hotel (PH)

Lake Farm

Llanddewi

Knelston Prim Sch

Stout Hall

Ty Bryn

The Cross

Little Reynoldston

Great Walterston

Little Walterston

Cefn Bryn

Home Farm

Perriswood

Nicholaston

Knelston

Kittle Top

Penrice Castle

A4118

Forest Walks

Nicholaston Woods

Penrice

Scurlage

Berry

Sanctuary Farmhouse

SA3

Pitt

Oxwich Burrows

SALISBURY
MONKSLAND
B4247

PH

Gower Holiday Village

Moor Corner Farm

HANGMAN'S CROSS

Oxwich

Nature Reserve

Oxwich Bay

Norton

Oxwich Leisure Pk

Oxwich Castle

Oxwich Green

Port-Eynon

Horton

ROCK LA

UNDERHILL LA

Slade

The Cove

The Sands

NEW PARK HOLIDAY PK

ORCHARD CL

HIGHFIELDS HOLIDAY PK

SPRINGFIELD

PH

THE BOARLANDS
A4118

Overton

Port-Eynon YH

The Salt House (rems of)

Port-Eynon Bay

Holy's Wash

Oxwich Point

Overton Mere

Culver Hole

Port-Eynon Point

46 A 47 B 48 C 49 D 50 E 51 F

8 89 7 88 6 87 5 86 4 85 3 84 2 83 1 82

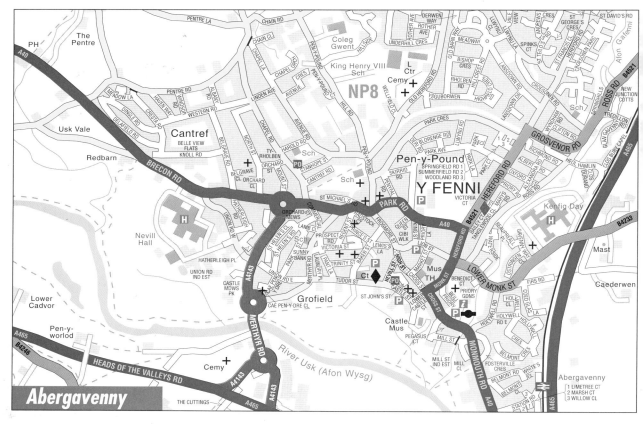

Abergavenny

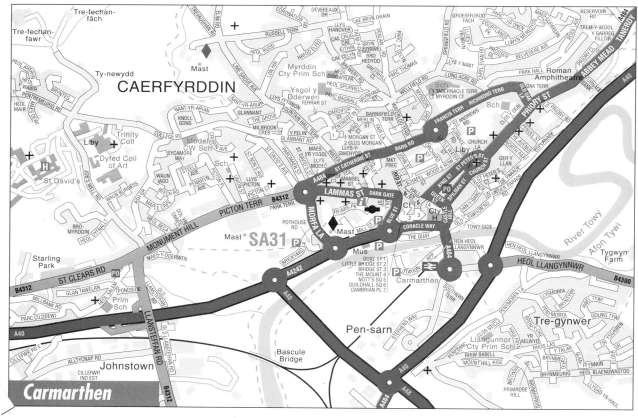

Carmarthen

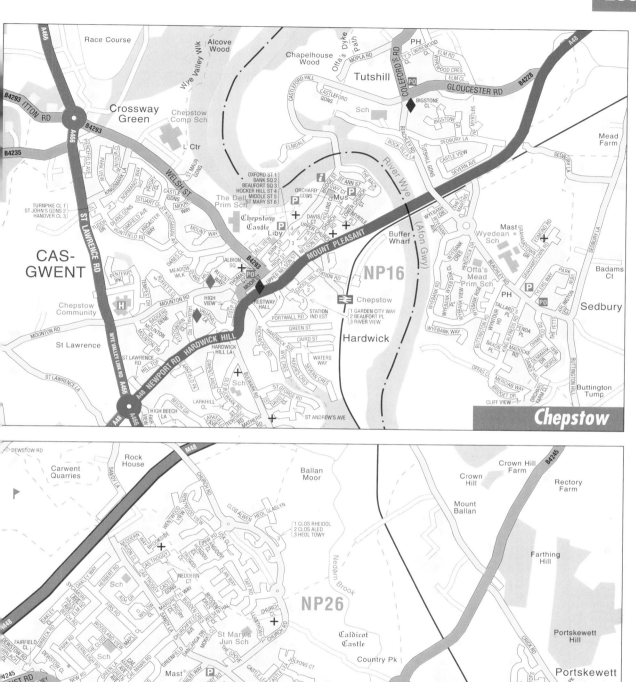

Chepstow

Caldicot

Index

Street names are listed alphabetically and show the locality, the Postcode District, the page number and a reference to the square in which the name falls on the map page

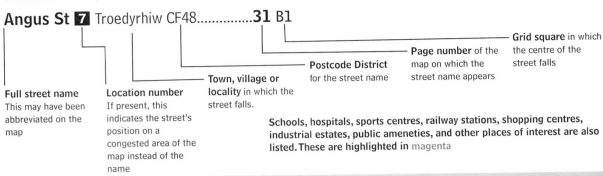

Angus St 7 Troedyrhiw CF48..............31 B1

- **Grid square** in which the centre of the street falls
- **Page number** of the map on which the street name appears
- **Postcode District** for the street name
- **Town, village or locality** in which the street falls.
- **Location number** If present, this indicates the street's position on a congested area of a map instead of the name
- **Full street name** This may have been abbreviated on the map

Schools, hospitals, sports centres, railway stations, shopping centres, industrial estates, public amenities, and other places of interest are also listed. These are highlighted in magenta

Abbreviations used in the index

App **Approach**	Cl **Close**	Espl **Esplanade**	N **North**	S **South**
Arc **Arcade**	Comm **Common**	Est **Estate**	Orch **Orchard**	Sq **Square**
Ave **Avenue**	Cnr **Corner**	Gdns **Gardens**	Par **Parade**	Strs **Stairs**
Bvd **Boulevard**	Cotts **Cottages**	Gn **Green**	Pk **Park**	Stps **Steps**
Bldgs **Buildings**	Ct **Court**	Gr **Grove**	Pas **Passage**	St **Street, Saint**
Bsns Pk **Business Park**	Ctyd **Courtyard**	Hts **Heights**	Pl **Place**	Terr **Terrace**
Bsns Ctr **Business Centre**	Cres **Crescent**	Ind Est **Industrial**	Prec **Precinct**	Trad **Trading Est**
Bglws **Bungalows**	Dr **Drive**	**Estate**	Prom **Promenade**	Wlk **Walk**
Cswy **Causeway**	Dro **Drove**	Intc **Interchange**	Ret Pk **Retail Park**	W **West**
Ctr **Centre**	E **East**	Junc **Junction**	Rd **Road**	Yd **Yard**
Cir **Circus**	Emb **Embankment**	La **Lane**	Rdbt **Roundabout**	

Town and village index

Aberavon 124 F8
Aberbargoed 58 B4
Abercanaid 30 E4
Abercarn 87 B2
Abercraf 222 C8
Abercwmboi 53 E4
Abercynon 82 D3
Aberdare 29 C2
Aberdulais 49 C4
Aberfan 55 B5
Abergarw 151 A7
Abergwynfi 76 C5
Aberkenfig 150 C4
Aberthin 189 B3
Abertillery 36 C5
Abertridwr 137 B8
Abertysswg 33 C8
Ammanford 219 C8
Argoed 58 F5
Baglan 98 E7
Banwen 223 A4
Bargoed 58 A3
Barry 214 E3
Bassaleg 142 A2
Beddau 156 B6
Bedlinog 56 B7
Bedwas 138 D7
Bettws(Bridgend) 129 E2
Bettws(Newport) 116 B2
Birchgrove 47 B2
Bishopston 121 F7
Bishton 145 F3
Blackmill 130 E2
Blackwood 85 D8
Blaenavon 17 E6
Blaencwm 50 C2
Blaengarw 103 E6
Blaengwrach 227 C8
Blaengwynfi 76 C6
Blaenrhondda 50 D4
Blaina 15 F5
Bonvilston 191 B1
Boverton 210 C7
Bridgend 168 C7
Briton Ferry 71 B2
Bryn(Caerphilly) 85 D4
Bryn(Llanelli) 41 F6
Bryn(Maesteg) 100 F5
Brynamman 220 E8
Bryncae 153 E1
Bryncethin 151 B5
Brynmawr 8 D4
Brynmenyn 150 F6
Brynna 153 C3
Bynea 41 F3
Caerleon 118 C4
Caerphilly 138 D3
Capel Hendre 218 E6
Cardiff 195 E4
Castle-upon-Alun 186 A2
Castleton 162 C3
Cefn Cribwr 149 A4
Cefn Hengoed 84 E4
Cefn-bryn-brain 221 B8
Cefneithin 218 A8
Cheltenham 9 C1
Church Village 135 F2
Cilfrew 49 B5

Cilfynydd 109 E5
Cimla 72 C6
Clydach(Bryn-mawr) ...9 E6
Clydach(Swansea) 46 D7
Clyne 226 B3
Coedely 154 E8
Coedkernew 163 B3
Coelbren 222 F6
Coity 169 C8
Colwinston 187 A4
Corntown 186 B7
Cowbridge 188 C2
Coytrahen 150 B8
Craig-Cefn-Parc 22 A2
Creigiau 174 D8
Croesyceiliog 90 B5
Crofty 64 B3
Cross Hands 218 A7
Crynant 226 A7
Cwm 35 B7
Cwm-twrch Isaf 1 B1
Cwm-twrch Uchaf 221 C6
Cwmaman 53 A4
Cwmavon(Blaenavon) ...17 F1
Cwmavon(Neath) 99 C5
Cwmbran 89 D3
Cwmdare 28 C3
Cwmfelin 128 C8
Cwmfelinfach 113 B4
Cwmllynfell 221 B7
Cwmparc 78 C5
Cymmer 75 C4
Cynonville 74 B3
Deri 57 B8
Dinas Powys 206 B4
Dowlais 11 B4
Duffryn 74 D4
Dunvant 93 B8
Dyffryn Cellwen 223 A5
East Aberthaw 212 B2
Ebbw Vale 14 F8
Efail Isaf 156 F5
Evanstown 132 B8
Ewenny 185 F7
Fairwood 92 D7
Felindre 20 F2
Ferndale 79 F6
Fforest 19 A6
Fleur De Lis 85 B6
Fochriw 32 C7
Forge Side 17 A5
Garnswllt 219 B4
Gelligaer 84 D6
Gelligroes 85 E2
Georgetown 13 F6
Gileston 211 E3
Gilfach Goch 132 C7
Glais 47 B6
Glan y Nant 85 A7
Glanaman 220 A8
Glyncorrwg 227 D2
Glynneath 223 D1
Godrergraig 221 B1
Gorseinon 43 C3
Gorslas 218 C8
Gowerton 66 B4
Goytre 125 F7
Graig Penllyn 188 B8
Groesfaen 174 B7
Grovesend 43 C6

Gwaun-Cae-Gurwen 220 E6
Hawthorn 136 B3
Hendreforgan 132 C6
Hendy 19 A5
Hengoed 85 A3
Heol-y-Cyw 152 A5
Heolgerrig 10 A1
Hirwaun 27 C8
Hollybush 34 C3
Horton 231 B4
Killay 93 E7
Knelston 231 A7
Laleston 167 F5
Langstone 119 D1
Lavernock 217 A5
Leckwith 194 B1
Lewistown 130 E5
Llanbethêry 212 B8
Llanblethian 200 D8
Llanbradach 111 F1
Llancarfan 202 E1
Llandough 200 E6
Llandow 199 A7
Llanedi 218 D2
Llanelli 41 B5
Llanelly Hill 9 C4
Llanfrechfa 117 D7
Llangan 187 D8
Llangeinor 130 B3
Llangennech 42 B8
Llangennith 228 C2
Llangynwyd 128 B6
Llanharan 154 A3
Llanharry 172 A5
Llanmadoc 228 E4
Llanmaes 210 C8
Llanmorlais 64 C2
Llanrhidian 229 D2
Llansamlet 69 D8
Llansannor 188 E7
Llantarnam 117 A4
Llantrisant 155 C4
Llantrithyd 202 D6
Llantwit Fardre 156 E7
Llantwit Major 209 E5
Llanwern 145 B5
Llwydcoed 28 F6
Llysworney 187 D1
Loughor 42 E2
Machen 140 A7
Maerdy 52 B1
Maesteg 102 B1
Maesycwmmer 85 B1
Maesygwartha 9 D8
Marcross 208 D7
Margam 125 E4
Markham 58 D6
Marshfield 162 D1
Merthyr Mawr 185 A8
Merthyr Tydfil 11 A3
Merthyr Vale 55 D4
Michaelston-y-Fedw ...162 A5
Miskin 173 E6
Monknash 198 C2
Morganstown 176 A8
Mountain Ash 54 F3
Mumbles 123 B4
Nant-y-Moel 104 A6
Nantgarw 158 A8
Nantyglo 8 D2

Neath 71 B7
Neath Abbey 71 A8
Nelson 83 E4
New Tredegar 33 F3
Newbridge 87 B7
Newport 143 F2
North Cornelly 165 E7
Ogmore 185 A6
Ogmore Vale 104 D1
Ogmore-By-Sea 184 D3
Oxwich 231 D5
Pantyrawel 130 E4
Parkmill 120 F7
Pen-clawdd 64 E3
Pen-Rhiw-fawr 221 B5
Pen-y-fai 150 D1
Penarth 207 B3
Pencoed 170 C7
Penderyn 224 E3
Pendoylan 190 F6
Pengam 85 B7
Penllergaer 44 A2
Penllyn 188 A5
Penmaen 120 B6
Penpedairheol 84 D8
Penperlleni 39 F6
Penrhiwtyn 71 C5
Penrhys 80 B2
Pentre 78 A5
Pentre Meyrick 187 F4
Pentrebach 31 B4
Pentyrch 175 A7
Penybryn 84 C5
Penycoedcae 135 A4
Penygroes 218 D8
Penywaun 28 A5
Peterston-Super-Ely ..191 E6
Peterstone Wentlooge ..180 E5
Pitton 230 C6
Pont Rhyd-y-cyff 128 C7
Pontardawe 23 D4
Pontarddulais 19 E5
Ponthir 117 E6
Pontllanfraith 86 B5
Pontlliw 44 A7
Pontlottyn 12 E1
Pontneddfechan 223 E3
Pontrhydyfen 73 B1
Pontsticill 3 F4
Pontwalby 223 E1
Pontyclun 173 B6
Pontycymer 103 E3
Pontypool 62 E6
Pontypridd 135 C7
Pontyrhyl 129 F8
Port Talbot 98 E1
Porteynon 231 A4
Porth 107 E3
Porthcawl 182 D6
Pyle 148 A2
Quakers Yard 83 B5
Radyr 176 B6
Rassau 7 B4
Resolven 226 E5
Reynoldston 229 B1
Rhigos 26 C8
Rhoose 213 B1
Rhydyfelin 136 C5
Rhydyfro 23 D8
Rhymney 12 F4

Risca 115 A3
Rogerstone 141 F6
Rudry 139 C2
St Athan 211 D4
St Brides Major 185 D2
St Brides Wentlooge ..163 E1
St Donat's 208 E5
St Fagans 193 A7
St Hilary 201 C7
St Mary Church 201 A4
St Nicholas 192 A1
Sarn 150 F4
Scurlage 231 A6
Senghenydd 110 E2
Seven Sisters 222 D3
Sigingstone 200 A4
Sirhowy 6 F1
Skewen 70 D7
South Cornelly 165 F8
Southerndown 185 A1
Southgate 121 A5
Sully 216 B5
Swansea 95 B5
Taffs Well 158 A5
Talbot Green 155 B3
Thomastown 133 A2
Three Crosses 65 E1
Tir-y-Berth 84 F6
Tondu 150 C5
Ton Pentre 79 A3
Tonna 49 D2
Tonypandy 106 D5
Tonyrefail 133 C4
Tredegar 13 E7
Tredomen 84 D1
Trefechan 10 A6
Trehafod 108 D3
Treharris 83 B8
Treherbert 50 E1
Trelewis 83 D7
Treoes 170 B1
Treorchy 78 E7
Troedyrhiw 31 C1
Tycroes 218 F5
Tylorstown 80 C3
Tylorstown 80 C3
Upper Boat 136 E2
Upper Killay 93 B5
Varteg 17 E1
Wattstown 107 E8
Waunarlwydd 66 E4
Wenvoe 205 A6
Wern-olau 65 D4
Wick 198 D5
Wyllie 85 E1
Ynysddu 113 B8
Ynysforgan 46 C4
Ynysmaerdy 155 A5
Ynysmeudwy 24 B8
Ynystawe 46 C6
Ynysybwl 81 F1
Ystalyfera 2 A6
Ystrad 79 D3
Ystrad Mynach 84 F1
Ystradgynlais 222 A5
Ystradowen 189 D8
Ystradowen 221 C7

A R D Bsns Pk NP4 . . . . . .62 F4
Abbey Cl CF15 . . . . .158 B3
Abbey Cotts NP44 . . . . . .117 B7
Abbey Ct CF38 . . . . .135 E1
Abbey Gn NP44 . . . . .116 F8
Abbey Gr NP44 . . . . .117 A6
Abbey Rd
  Cwmbran NP44 . . . . .89 E2
  Ewenny CF35 . . . . .185 E8
  Newport NP19 . . . . . . .144 D6
  Port Talbot SA13 . . . . .125 C7
  Pyle CF33 . . . . .148 C2
Abbey Road Ind Est
  SA10 . . . . .71 C7
Abbeyfield Ho CF31 . .169 A5
Abbeyville Ave
  Port Talbot SA12 . . . . .124 D8
  8 Port Talbot SA12 . . .98 D1
Abbeyville Ct SA12 . . . .98 D1
Abbeyville Ho **9** SA12 98 D1
Abbot's Wlk SA10 . . . . . .71 C8
Abbots Mews NP20 . . . . .143 B3
Abbott's Cl SA13 . . . . . .125 F3
Abbott's Mews SA13 . . . .125 F3
Aber Ct SA6 . . . . .69 B7
Aber Halt CF83 . . . . . . .137 F2
Aber Houses CF32 . . . . . .104 F4
Aber Inf Sch CF32 . . . . .130 E8
Aber Rd CF32 . . . . .104 E3
Aber St CF11 . . . . .195 A2
Aber-Fawr Terr CF83 . . . .137 A7
Aber-Ffrwd Rd CF45 . . . . .54 D4
Aber-nant Cty Prim Sch
  CF44 . . . . .29 C3
Aber-Rhondda Rd
  CF39 . . . . .107 D8
Aberaeron Cl CF62 . . .215 A8
Aberafan Rd SA12 . . . . . .98 C2
Aberaman Enterprise Pk
  CF44 . . . . .53 E7
Aberaman Hos **5**
  CF44 . . . . .53 E6
Aberaman Ind Est
  CF44 . . . . .53 E6
Aberaman Park Ind Est
  CF44 . . . . .53 D6
Aberbargoed & District
  Hospl CF81 . . . . .58 B5
Aberbargoed District
  Hospl CF81 . . . . .58 B5
Aberbargoed Inf Sch
  CF81 . . . . .58 A5
Aberbargoed Jun Sch
  (Ysgol Iau Aberbargoed)
  CF81 . . . . .58 A5
Aberbeeg Day Hospl
  NP13 . . . . .59 F8
Aberbeeg Rd NP13 . . . . . .36 B2
Aberbran Rd CF14 . . .177 C2
Abercanaid Ind Est
  CF48 . . . . .30 E6
Abercanaid Prim Sch
  CF48 . . . . .30 F4
Abercarn Fach NP11 . . . .114 C8
Abercarn Jun & Inf Sch
  NP11 . . . . .87 B4
Abercedy SA4 . . . . .65 A4
Abercerdin Prim Sch
  CF39 . . . . .132 B7
Abercerdin Rd CF39 . .132 B8
Aberclydach Pl SA6 . . .46 D7
Aberconway CF Pty NP12 .59 B1
Abercrave Cty Prim Sch
  SA9 . . . . .222 C3
Abercrave Terr SA9 . .222 D7
Abercregan Rd SA13 . . .74 F6
Abercwmboi-Isaf Rd
  CF45 . . . . .54 B3
Abercynon Inf Sch
  CF45 . . . . .82 E3
Abercynon North Sta
  CF45 . . . . .82 E2
Abercynon Rd
  Abercynon CF45 . . . . . .82 C5
  Mountain Ash CF45 . . . . .82 A6
  Pontypridd CF37 . . . . .109 D7
Abercynon South Sta
  CF45 . . . . .82 E2
Abercynon St CF11 . . .195 A2
Aberdale Rd SA11 . . .223 D1
Aberdare Boys Comp Sch
  CF44 . . . . .28 D4
Aberdare Coll CF44 . . . .28 D4
Aberdare General Hospl
  CF44 . . . . .29 B3
Aberdare Girls Comp Sch
  (Upper) CF44 . . . . .29 B2
Aberdare Girls Lower
  Comp Sch CF44 . . . . . .28 F2
Aberdare Rd
  Abercynon CF45 . . . . . .82 D2
  Ferndale CF43 . . . . . . .79 F8

Aberdare Rd *continued*
  Glynneath SA11 . . . . . .223 D1
  Merthyr Tydfil CF48 . . . . .10 C1
  Mountain Ash CF45 . . . . .54 B3
Aberdare Sta CF44 . . . . .29 A2
Aberdare Town CW Prim
  Sch CF44 . . . . .29 B1
Aberdaron Rd CF3 . . .179 E5
Aberdore Rd CF14 . . .177 C2
Aberdovey Cl CF64 . . . .206 C3
Aberdovey St CF24 . . . .195 E5
Aberdulais Cres CF14 177 B2
Aberdulais Falls SA10 . .49 C4
Aberdulais Rd CF14 . . .177 B2
Aberdyberthi St SA1 . .68 D2
Aberfan Cres CF48 . . . . .55 C4
Aberfan Fawr CF48 . . . . .55 C3
Aberfan Rd CF48 . . . . . .55 C7
Aberfawr Rd CF83 . . .137 A7
Aberffrwd NP22 . . . . . . .13 D5
Aberfields View CF14 .104 F4
Abergarw Rd CF32 . . .150 F6
Abergarw Trad Est
  CF32 . . . . .151 A6
Abergavenny Rd NP4 . .17 C8
Abergele Cl CF3 . . . . .179 E6
Abergele Ct CF3 . . . . .179 E5
Abergelly Rd SA5 . . . . .67 C5
Abergorki Ind Est
  CF42 . . . . .78 C7
Abergwawr Pl CF44 . . . .53 B8
Abergwawr St CF44 . . . .53 C8
Abergwernffrwd Row
  SA12 . . . . .73 C5
Abergwynfi Inf Sch
  SA13 . . . . .76 C5
Abergwynfi Jun Sch
  SA13 . . . . .76 C5
Aberhenwaun Uchaf
  SA10 . . . . .222 E4
Aberlash Rd SA18 . . .219 B8
Aberllechau Cty Prim Sch
  CF39 . . . . .107 D8
Aberllechau Rd CF39 107 D8
Abermorlais Terr
  CF48 . . . . .10 D1
Abernant Cres NP12 . . .58 E7
Abernant Rd
  Aberdare CF44 . . . . . . .29 B3
  Gwaun-Cae-Gurwen
  SA18 . . . . .220 D5
  Markham NP12 . . . . .58 F7
Abernethy Cl **10** CF3 . .180 A7
Abernethy Quay **10**
  SA1 . . . . .95 D6
Abernethy Sq **13** SA1 . .95 E6
Aberpennar St CF45 . . .54 D2
Aberporth Rd CF14 . . .177 B2
Abersychan Comp Sch
  NP4 . . . . .37 F4
Abertaf CF45 . . . . .37 F4
Abertaf Prim Sch CF45 82 E3
Aberteifi Cl CF14 . . . .177 C2
Aberteifi Cres CF14 . . .177 C2
Aberthaw Ave NP19 . . .144 D4
Aberthaw Circ NP19 . . .144 C5
Aberthaw Cl NP19 . . . .144 C5
Aberthaw Dr NP19 . . . .144 B4
Aberthaw Rd
  Cardiff CF5 . . . . .193 D5
  Newport NP19 . . . . . . .144 C4
Aberthin La CF71 . . . .189 B2
Aberthin Rd CF71 . . . .189 A2
Abertillery Comp Sch
  NP13 . . . . .36 B6
Abertillery Prim & Inf Schs
  NP13 . . . . .36 B6
Abertillery Rd NP3 . . . .15 E3
Abertonllwyd St CF42 . .50 F2
Abertysswg Cty Prim Sch
  NP22 . . . . .33 B8
Aberystwith St CF24 . .195 E5
Aberystwyth Cres
  CF62 . . . . .214 E4
Abingdon St CF63 . . .215 B4
Acacia Ave
  Hengoed CF82 . . . . .84 F3
  Merthyr Tydfil CF47 . . . . .10 D4
  Newport NP19 . . . . . . .144 B5
  Port Talbot SA12 . . . . . .98 D2
  Porthcawl CF36 . . . . . .183 D7
Acacia Cl SA12 . . . . . . .98 C2
Acacia Rd SA3 . . . . . .123 A8
Acacia Sq NP19 . . . . . .144 B5
Acacia St CF37 . . . . . .136 A5
Acacia Terr NP11 . . . . . .87 B4
Academic Avenue
  (Coedlan y Coleg)
  CF14 . . . . .177 E3
Acer Ave CF38 . . . . . .156 C6
Acer Ct CF72 . . . . . . .172 C6
Acland Rd CF31 . . . . .168 F5
Acorn Cl
  Abersychan NP4 . . . . . .37 F3
  Ebbw Vale NP23 . . . . . . .7 C1
Acorn Ct SA6 . . . . .46 B8
Acorn Gr Cardiff CF23 .161 A1
  Llantwit Fardre CF38 . . .156 E8
Acorn Pl SA12 . . . . . . .98 D7
Acorns The
  Cardiff CF14 . . . . .159 E3
  Llanmartin NP18 . . . . . .145 E7
Acre Cl NP11 . . . . .60 C2
Adam St
  Abertillery NP13 . . . . . .36 C5
  Cardiff CF24 . . . . .195 B5
Adam Wlk SA10 . . . . . . .71 C8
Adams Ave CF32 . . . . .150 F4

Adams Ct **1** CF24 . . . .195 C5
Adams Sq NP23 . . . . . . .14 E8
Adams St CF40 . . . . . . .106 B7
Adamscroft Pl CF10 . . .195 C5
Adamsdown La CF24 . . .195 D5
Adamsdown Pl **3**
  CF24 . . . . .195 D5
Adamsdown Sq CF24 . .195 C5
Adamstown Com Jun & Inf
  Sch CF24 . . . . .195 D6
Adare St
  3 Bridgend CF31 . . . .168 F4
  Evanstown CF32 . . . . . .132 B8
  Ogmore Vale CF32 . . . .104 E3
  Port Talbot SA12 . . . . .124 E8
Adare Terr CF42 . . . . . .78 C7
Addison Ave CF72 . . . .172 A5
Addison Cres CF5 . . . .193 C5
Addison Pl SA12 . . . . .124 E8
Addison Rd Neath SA11 71 D4
  Port Talbot SA12 . . . . .124 E8
Addison St NP12 . . . . . .85 D8
Addoldy Rd SA11 . . . . .223 C1
Adelaide Cl NP12 . . . . . .85 D6
Adelaide Pl CF10 . . . . .195 B2
Adelaide St
  Cardiff CF10 . . . . .195 B2
  Newport NP20 . . . . . . .143 C7
  Swansea SA1 . . . . .95 D6
Adeline St
  Cardiff CF24 . . . . .195 E6
  Newport NP20 . . . . . . .143 C7
Adenfield Way CF62 . .212 D2
Ader y Mor CF62 . . . . .214 F2
Adit Wlk NP44 . . . . .89 C5
Administration Rd
  CF62 . . . . .211 E1
Admirals Wlk SA2 . . . . .94 C6
Adrian Bolt Gn NP19 . .144 C4
Adrian Cl CF36 . . . . . .182 E8
Adrian Stephens Ho
  CF48 . . . . .10 A3
Adventurers Quay
  CF10 . . . . .195 D2
Ael y Bryn CF82 . . . . . .85 A2
Ael-y-Bryn CF31 . . . . .168 B5
Ael-y-Bryn
  Beddau CF38 . . . . .156 A7
  Bedwas CF83 . . . . .138 F6
  Blaenavon NP4 . . . . . . .17 D7
  Caerphilly CF83 . . . . . .137 F5
  Cardiff CF23 . . . . .178 D4
  Cwmdare CF44 . . . . . . .28 D3
  Maesteg CF34 . . . . .75 A2
  Mumbles SA3 . . . . .123 C3
  North Cornelly CF33 . . .166 A8
  Pen-clawdd SA4 . . . . . . .64 F4
  Pentyrch CF15 . . . . . . .175 C8
  Peterston-Super-Ely
  CF5 . . . . .191 E6
  Radyr CF15 . . . . .176 B7
  Rhymney NP22 . . . . .12 D6
  Trehafod CF37 . . . . . . .108 C2
  Trelewis CF46 . . . . .83 D8
  Ystradgynlais SA9 . . . .222 A5
Ael-y-Bryn Rd SA5 . . . .67 E3
Ael-y-Bryn Terr NP11 . .86 F7
Ael-y-Coed CF62 . . . . .214 C5
Ael-y-dor SA3 . . . . . . .122 F3
Ael-y-Fro SA8 . . . . .23 D7
Aelfryn CF72 . . . . .172 B5
Aelfryn Terr SA12 . . . . .99 D6
Aelybryn Cl SA15 . . . . . .40 E8
Aelybryn Dr SA15 . . . . . .40 E8
Aelybryn St CF81 . . . . . .32 C7
Aeron Cl CF62 . . . . . . .214 D5
Aeron Ct CF81 . . . . .58 A2
Aeron Pl Bargoed CF81 .58 A2
  Swansea SA6 . . . . .69 B2
Aeron Terr **4** CF47 . . . .30 F8
Aerons Ho NP44 . . . . . .116 C8
Afan Argoed Ctry Prk
  SA13 . . . . .73 F1
Afan Cl CF62 . . . . .214 D5
Afan Coll SA13 . . . . . .125 F3
Afan Rd SA13 . . . . .74 D4
Afan Terr SA12 . . . . . . .99 F6
Afan Valley Cl SA11 . . . .72 B5
Afan Valley Rd
  Cimla SA11 . . . . .72 B5
  Cwmavon SA12 . . . . . . .99 E4
  Pontrhydyfen SA12,SA13 73 C2
Afan Way
  Aberavon SA12 . . . . . . .124 F8
  Port Talbot SA12 . . . . . .98 D2
Afandale SA12 . . . . .98 C4
Afon Cl
  Michaelston-y-Fedw
  CF3 . . . . .161 D4
  Pontypool NP4 . . . . .63 A3
Afon Ct NP4 . . . . .38 A3
Afon Fach CF33 . . . . . .148 A1
Afon Llwyd Terr NP4 . . .38 A1
Afon Lwyd CF NP18 . . .118 C3
Afon Mead NP10 . . . . . .141 D7
Afon Rd SA14 . . . . .42 C8
Afon St CF37 . . . . .108 D2
Afon Terr NP44 . . . . . . .89 F5
Afon Villas SA12 . . . . .100 A7
Afon-Llan Gdns SA5 . . .67 D6
Afon-y-Felin Cl SA10 . .49 C4
Afon-y-Felin Prim Sch
  CF33 . . . . .147 F1

Africa Gdns CF14 . . . .177 E2
Agate St CF24 . . . . . . .195 D6
Agent's Row CF44 . . . . . .29 C3
Agincourt Cl **1**
  CF23 . . . . .195 D8
Agincourt St NP20 . . . . .7 A4
Agnes St CF24 . . . . . . .206 E5
Ailesbury St NP20 . . . .143 C7
Ainon Ct CF24 . . . . . . .195 E5
Aintree Dr CF5 . . . . . .193 F5
Airport Bsns Pk CF62 213 C4
Alamein Rd SA1 . . . . . . .68 E3
Alan Cl NP10 . . . . .142 B4
Alan Terr CF38 . . . . . .156 F8
Alanbrooke Ave
  NP20 . . . . .117 A4
Alandale Rd CF62 . . . . . .7 A4
Alaw Prim Sch CF40 . . .107 A5
Alaw Rd CF40 . . . . . . .107 B5
Alban Ct SA15 . . . . .40 E6
Alban Terr SA13 . . . . . .74 F6
Albany Cl SA5 . . . . .68 C4
Albany Com Jun & Inf Sch
  CF24 . . . . .195 B8
Albany Ct **7** CF64 . . . .207 B4
Albany Ind Est NP20 . .143 C7
Albany Rd
  Caerphilly NP12 . . . . . . .85 E6
  Cardiff CF24 . . . . .195 C8
  Pontycymer CF32 . . . . .103 F3
Albany St
  Ferndale CF43 . . . . .80 A6
  Mountain Ash CF45 . . . . .54 D1
  Newport NP20 . . . . . . .143 C7
Albany Trad Est
  NP20 . . . . .143 C7
Albert Ave NP19 . . . . . .143 E6
Albert Cres CF64 . . . . .207 B4
Albert Ct
  Newport NP19 . . . . . . .143 E5
  4 Penarth CF64 . . . . .207 B4
Albert Cty Prim Sch
  CF64 . . . . .207 B4
Albert Pl SA3 . . . . . . .123 A5
Albert Rd
  Abersychan NP4 . . . . . .37 D5
  Penarth CF64 . . . . .207 B4
  Pontypridd CF37 . . . . .135 B8
Albert Row SA1 . . . . . . .95 D6
Albert St Aberdare CF44 29 A1
  Barry CF63 . . . . .215 D6
  Cardiff CF11 . . . . .194 D5
  Ferndale CF43 . . . . .80 A7
  Llanelli SA15 . . . . .40 C4
  Maesteg CF34 . . . . .75 C1
  Mountain Ash CF45 . . . . .54 D1
  Newport NP20 . . . . . . .143 C3
  Pentre CF41 . . . . .78 F5
Albert Terr
  Maesteg CF34 . . . . . . .101 F3
  Newport NP20 . . . . . . .143 B4
Albert Wlk **9** CF11 . . .194 D5
Alberta Pl CF64 . . . . . .207 A2
Alberta Rd CF64 . . . . . .207 B2
Alberta St CF48 . . . . . .55 C5
Albertina Rd NP11 . . . . .59 F1
Alberto Rd SA6 . . . . . . .69 A6
Albion Cl NP20 . . . . . . .143 D2
Albion Ct
  Newport NP20 . . . . . . .143 D2
  Pontypridd CF37 . . . . .109 F5
Albion Flats CF37 . . . .109 F5
Albion Ind Est CF37 . . .109 F5
Albion Pl Pontypool NP4 62 A8
  Pontypool NP4 . . . . . . .62 B6
Albion Rd App SA12 . . .98 C7
Albion St
  Aberdare CF44 . . . . . . .53 B8
  Newport NP20 . . . . . . .143 C2
  Ton Pentre CF41 . . . . . .79 A2
Albion Terr NP12 . . . . . .85 F6
Alcock Cl NP19 . . . . . .144 B3
Alden Dr SA2 . . . . .67 D1
Aldenham Rd CF36 . . . .183 C7
Alder Ave SA9 . . . . .2 D7
Alder Cl NP4 . . . . .63 B5
Alder Dr CF44 . . . . .28 C2
Alder Gr Ebbw Vale NP23 .7 C5
  Llantwit Fardre CF38 . . .156 C5
Alder Rd Cardiff CF23 .178 B2
  Llanharry CF72 . . . . . .172 B5
  Neath SA11 . . . . .72 A1
Alder Rise NP12 . . . . . .86 A4
Alder Terr SA13 . . . . . .75 D4
Alder Way
  Gowerton SA4 . . . . .66 C6
  Mumbles SA3 . . . . .122 F7
Alderbrook CF23 . . . . .160 D1
Alderbrook Cl SA5 . . . . .67 F6
Aldergrove Cl SA12 . . . .98 E4
Aldergrove Rd CF39 . . .107 C5
Alderman Cl NP12 . . . . .85 D7
Alderman Davies Prim Sch
  SA11 . . . . .71 E7
Alderney St NP20 . . . . .143 C7
Alders The
  Blackwood NP12 . . . . . . .59 C1
  Llanvaravon NP44 . . . . . .90 B1
Alderwood Cl
  1 Cardiff CF3 . . . . . .179 E7
  Crynant SA10 . . . . . . .222 A1
Alderwood Rd SA3 . . . .123 A4
Aldsworth Rd CF5 . . . .193 F7
Aldwych Cl CF14 . . . . .159 E2

Alltacham Dr SA8 . . . . . .23 E5
Alltmawr Rd CF23 . . . .178 C6
Alltwen CF44 . . . . .29 C3
Alltwen Hill SA8 . . . . . .23 F3
Alltwen Ind Est SA8 . . . .24 A5
Alltwen Prim Sch SA8 . .23 F4
Alltygrug Farm Rd SA9 . .2 B7
Alltygrug Rd SA9 . . . . . .2 B7
Alltywerin SA8 . . . . .23 D6
Alma Cl **19** NP11 . . . . .143 C3
Alma Pl Pentre CF41 . . . .78 F5
  Pontypool NP4 . . . . .62 E1
Alma Rd Cardiff CF23 . .178 C5
  Maesteg CF34 . . . . .102 B2
Alma St Aberdare CF44 . .28 F4
  Abertillery NP13 . . . . . .36 B6
  5 Blaenavon NP4 . . . .17 C7
  Brynmawr NP23 . . . . . . .8 C4
  Dowlais CF48 . . . . .11 A5
  Machen CF83 . . . . .140 A7
  Merthyr Tydfil CF47 . . . . .30 E8
  Newport NP20 . . . . . . .143 C3
  Treherbert CF42 . . . . . .50 E2
Alma Terr
  Aberkenfig CF32 . . . . . .150 C3
  Brynmawr NP23 . . . . . . .8 D5
  Dowlais CF48 . . . . .11 A5
  Maesteg CF34 . . . . .102 B2
  Ogmore Vale CF32 . . . .130 E8
  Port Talbot SA13 . . . . .125 D6
Almond Ave NP11 . . . . .115 B2
Almond Cl CF38 . . . . . .156 C6
Almond Ct NP20 . . . . . .117 A3
Almond Dr
  Cardiff CF23 . . . . .160 F1
  Newport NP20 . . . . . . .117 B3
Almond Gr CF47 . . . . . . .10 D4
Alpha Ho CF15 . . . . . . .157 E8
Alpha Pl Baglan SA12 . . .98 D7
  Pontypridd CF37 . . . . .109 D2
Alpha St CF37 . . . . . . .109 D2
Alphonso St CF48 . . . . .11 B5
Als St SA15 . . . . .40 E5
Althorp Dr CF64 . . . . . .217 A8
Alton Terr NP4 . . . . .62 B7
Alun Rd SA1 . . . . .68 B1
Alway Cl NP19 . . . . . . .144 D5
Alway Cres NP19 . . . . .144 D5
Alway Inf Sch NP19 . . .144 C4
Alway Jun Sch NP19 . . .144 C4
Alway Par NP19 . . . . . .144 D4
Alwen Dr Barry CF62 . .214 C6
  Cardiff CF14 . . . . .159 F3
Alwyn Cl NP10 . . . . . . .142 A7
Alyson Way CF35 . . . . .170 C8
Amalfi Ho CF10 . . . . . .195 C3
Aman Ct CF44 . . . . .53 A3
Aman St CF44 . . . . .53 A3
Amanwy SA14 . . . . .41 D5
Amber Cl Cardiff CF23 .160 F1
  Port Talbot SA12 . . . . . .98 B2
Ambergate Dr CF23 . . .160 F1
Amberheart Dr CF14 . .159 F3
Amberley Cl CF23 . . . .178 F8
Amberley Dr SA3 . . . . .123 A4
Amberton Pl **4** CF47 . .10 F4
Amberwood Cl CF23 . .160 F1
Amblecote Cl CF23 . . .160 F1
Ambleside Ave CF23 . .178 A2
Ambleside Cl CF82 . . . .84 E8
Ambleside Pl SA3 . . . .123 A8
Ambrooke CF23 . . . . . .160 F1
Ambrose Way NP4 . . . . .63 A4
Ambryn Rd NP4 . . . . . . .63 B4
Amelia Terr CF40 . . . . .106 E4
Amelia Trust Farm
  CF62 . . . . .203 C5
America Pl CF39 . . . . . .107 F4
Amesbury Rd CF23 . . . .178 D1
Amethyst Rd CF5 . . . . .176 D1
Amherst Cres CF62 . . .214 F2
Amherst St CF11 . . . . .194 F2
Amman Rd SA18 . . . . . .220 E8
Amman Valley Comp Sch
  SA18 . . . . .219 C7
Amman Valley Hospl
  SA18 . . . . .220 A6
Ammanford Cty Prim Sch
  SA18 . . . . .219 C7
Ammanford Inf Sch
  SA18 . . . . .219 C7
Ammanford Rd
  Ammanford SA18 . . . . .219 A6
  Tycroes SA18 . . . . . . .218 F6
Ammanford Sta SA18 219 B7
Amos Hill CF40 . . . . . .107 A3
Amos St SA15 . . . . .40 C4
Amroth Ct CF62 . . . . . .214 F7
Amroth Rd CF5 . . . . . .193 D5
Amroth Wlk NP44 . . . . . .89 C2
Amry Pl CF41 . . . . .79 D3
Amy Johnson Cl
  NP19 . . . . .144 B3
Amyas Cl CF11 . . . . . . .194 E3
Anchor Ct
  3 Cardiff CF10 . . . . .195 B4
  8 Swansea SA1 . . . . . .95 D6
Anchor Ind Est CF10 . .195 B3
Anchor St CF15 . . . . . .158 A3
Anchor Way CF64 . . . . .206 F6
Anderson La SA3 . . . . .121 A5
Anderson Pl
  Cardiff CF24 . . . . .195 D6
  Newport NP20 . . . . . . .117 A4

Andover Cl CF62 .....214 B7
Andrew Cres SA6 ......46 B4
Andrew Rd CF64 ....206 E5
Andrew St SA15 ......40 E6
Andrew's Rd CF14 ...176 F2
Andrews Bldgs **2**
CF64 ....207 B4
Andrews Cl
Bargoed CF81 ....58 A2
Merthyr Tydfil CF48 ...30 A8
Andrews Ct
Boverton CF61 ....210 A6
Ebbw Vale NP23 ....7 B1
Pontypridd CF37 .....135 C8
Andrews Terr NP11 ...60 C4
Androven Ct CF23 ....178 D6
Aneddfan SA12 ....99 F6
Aneurin Ave
Newbridge NP11 ......60 B3
Pengam NP12 ....85 B6
Aneurin Bevan Ave
Brynmenyn CF32 .....150 F6
Gelligaer CF82 ....84 C6
Aneurin Bevan Ct
Newport NP10 ....163 E7
Pontypool NP4 ....62 C6
Aneurin Bevan's Way
CF34 ....102 D2
Aneurin Cl
Swansea SA2 ....94 A6
Tredegar NP22 ....13 E7
Aneurin Cres CF47 ...30 F7
Aneurin Pl NP23 ......8 C5
Aneurin Rd CF63 ....215 A6
Aneurin Terr NP22 ...12 E6
Aneurin Way SA2 .....94 A6
Angel La Bargoed CF81 .58 A3
Blackwood NP12 ......58 B2
Angel Pl SA11 ....71 E8
Angel Sq NP23 ....14 D6
Angel St Aberavon SA12 .98 F1
Bridgend CF31 ......168 E4
Neath SA11 ....71 E8
Angelica Way CF14 ..159 D3
Angelina St CF10 ....195 B3
Angelsey Ct NP18 ...117 F3
Angleton Gn CF31 ...150 D1
Angleton Rd CF31 ...168 D8
Angle Cl CF62 ......214 F8
Angle Pl CF14 ....159 F1
Anglesey Cl
Boverton CF61 ....210 B7
Church Village CF38 .136 A2
Anglesey St **10** CF5 ..194 C6
Anglesey Way CF36 ..165 E1
Angleton Rd CF31 ...168 D8
Anglia Cl CF31 ......150 F1
Angus St Aberfan CF48 ..55 C5
Cardiff CF24 ....178 C1
7 Troedyrhiw CF48 ..31 B1
Ann St Abercynon CF45 ..82 D2
Aberdare CF44 ....28 F3
Cardiff CF11 ....194 D5
Llanelli SA15 ....40 D4
Pontypridd CF37 ....109 F5
Ann's Cl CF47 ....30 E7
Anne St **6** NP4 ....17 C6
Annes Ct NP23 ....7 C1
Annesley Rd NP19 ..143 E6
Annesley St SA15 ....40 C5
Anson Ct **5** CF10 .195 C4
Anson Gn NP19 ......144 E7
Anstee Ct **7** CF5 ..194 D5
Anthony Dr NP18 ....117 F4
Anthony Gr CF48 .....30 E4
Anton Ct CF14 ......177 A5
Antwerp Pl NP13 .....36 A6
Anwyll Cl NP18 .....118 A4
Apollo Cl CF14 ......159 E2
Apollo Way NP12 .....85 D7
Appledore Pl SA3 ...122 E6
Appledore Rd CF14 .177 D3
Applegrove SA3 .....229 B1
Appletree Ave CF40 .107 C4
Appletree Rd CF40 ...40 D4
Applewood Cl CF24 .195 D5
Approach Rd SA5 .....68 C2
Aprilia Ho CF10 .....195 C3
Aqueduct Terr SA12 ..73 B1
Ar y Nant CF63 ......215 A7
Arabella St CF24 ....178 B1
Arael Jun & Inf Sch
NP13 ....36 B2
Arael View NP13 .....35 F8
Aragon Ho NP20 ....143 B6
Aragon St NP20 .....143 C7
Arail St NP13 ....36 C3
Aran Ct NP44 ....89 B5
Aran St SA6 ....68 F7
Arbroath Ct CF24 ...195 F7
Arbutus Cl CF47 .....10 D5
Arcade Abertillery NP13 ..36 B5
1 Llanelli SA15 ...40 D5
Arcade Terr **3** SA18 .220 B8
Arcade The
Cwmbran NP44 ....89 D4
10 Merthyr Tydfil CF47 .10 D1
Arcadia Way NP4 .....38 B2
Arch Hill NP11 .....114 C6
Archbishop Mcgrath RC
Sch CF32 ....150 E5
Archdeacon John Lewis
CW Prim Sch CF32 ..169 C5
Archer Cres CF5 ....193 D6
Archer Ct CF62 .....214 F2

Archer Pl Cardiff CF5 ..193 C6
Penarth CF64 ....207 A3
Archer Rd Barry CF62 .214 F2
Cardiff CF5 ....193 C6
Cwmbran NP44 ....89 B3
Penarth CF64 ....207 A3
Archer St
Troedyrhiw CF48 .....31 C2
Ynysybwl CF37 ....81 F1
Archer Terr CF64 ...207 A2
Arches The **22** CF47 ...30 E8
Archibald St NP19 ..143 E5
Archiview Ct CF24 ..178 A2
Arcon Ho **3** CF3 ..179 C8
Arcot La CF64 ......207 A4
Arcot Lane N **4** CF64 207 A5
Arcot St CF64 ......207 A4
Arden Way CF63 ....215 C7
Ardmore Ave **3** CF40 106 F4
Ardwyn CF14 ....176 F8
Ardwyn Pl CF32 ....104 E2
Ardwyn Terr
Ton Pentre CF41 .....79 A2
Tonypandy CF40 ....106 E6
Arennig Rd SA5 ......68 B5
Arethusa Ct SA2 .....93 C6
Arfonfab Cres CF37 .136 B4
Arfryn CF44 ....28 A6
Arfryn Ave SA15 .....40 E7
Arfryn Pl CF47 ....30 E8
Arfryn Prim Sch SA5 .68 B5
Arfryn Rd SA2 ....94 E8
Arfryn Terr
Ebbw Vale NP23 ......7 D4
7 Merthyr Tydfil CF47 .30 F8
Tylorstown CF43 .....80 B4
Argae La CF63 ......205 D2
Argoed Ave CF72 ...154 A3
Argoed Prim Sch NP12 58 F5
Argoed Terr CF48 ....55 D5
Argyle St
Abercynon CF45 ......82 A5
Abertillery NP13 .....36 B5
Merthyr Tydfil CF47 ...10 F1
Newport NP20 ......143 C7
Pentre CF41 ....78 F5
Porth CF39 ....107 E2
Swansea SA1 ....95 B6
Argyle Terr CF40 ...106 E8
Argyle Way CF5 ....193 E4
Argyll Ave SA4 ....43 B2
Argyll Ct **4** CF15 ..176 B6
Arlan Gwilli SA4 .....19 A4
Arles Rd CF5 ....193 E5
Arlington Cl NP20 ..117 A4
Arlington Cres CF3 .179 C6
Arlington Pl CF36 ..182 F7
Arlington Rd
Porthcawl CF36 .....182 F7
Sully CF64 ....216 B5
Armine Rd SA5 ....67 E3
Armoury Terr NP23 ..14 D7
Armstrong Cl NP19 .144 B4
Arnant Villas CF32 ..104 F5
Arne Cl NP19 ......144 E5
Arno Rd CF63 ......215 C7
Arnold Ave CF3 ....179 C8
Arnold Cl NP20 ....142 F2
Arnold Ct SA9 ....2 B6
Arnold Pl **5** CF5 ..54 E3
Arnside Rd CF23 ...178 C2
Arnott's Pl CF44 ....28 F1
Arosfa Ave CF36 ...183 D8
Arosfa Ct NP22 .....13 E6
Arran Cl
Penycoedcae CF37 ..135 B6
Risca NP11 ....115 C1
Arran Ct CF24 .....195 C8
Arran St CF24 .....195 C8
Arrol St CF24 ......195 D5
Arthur Bliss Rd NP19 144 C4
Arthur Cl NP20 ....143 C2
Arthur St
Aberavon SA12 ......99 A1
Abertysswg NP22 ....33 C8
Barry CF63 ....215 B6
Blaengwynfi SA13 ....76 B6
Caerleon NP18 ......118 C2
Cardiff CF24 ....195 E7
Cwmfelinfach NP11 ..113 B4
Llanelli SA15 ....40 D5
Mountain Ash CF45 ...54 D1
Neath SA11 ....71 F4
Newport NP20 ......143 C2
Pentrebach CF48 .....31 A3
Tonypandy CF40 ....107 A2
Ystrad CF41 ....79 C3
Arthur Terr SA8 .....23 E5
Artillery Pl NP19 ..143 C5
Arundel Cl NP44 .....89 A3
Arundel Pl CF11 ...194 D2
Arundel Rd NP19 ..143 F5
Arvonia Terr NP12 ...85 B6
Arwelfa SA6 ....45 D1
Ascot Cl CF5 ....193 F5
Ascot Dr SA12 ......98 E6
Asgog St CF24 .....195 D5
Ash Cl Caerphilly NP12 ..85 F6
Pontllanfraith NP12 ..86 A6
Ash Gn NP44 ....116 F8
Ash Gr
Ammanford SA18 ...219 D7
Barry CF63 ....215 C2
Bridgend CF31 .....168 A5
Cardiff CF14 ....177 B6
Cardiff CF5 ....193 A2

Ash Gr continued
Cimla SA11 ....72 B5
Ebbw Vale NP23 .....14 E6
Gorseinon SA4 ....43 A3
Killay SA2 ....93 D7
Llandough CF64 ....206 E6
Llanharry CF72 .....172 B5
Llanmartin NP18 ...145 E6
Mountain Ash CF45 ..81 E8
Pentre CF41 ....78 F5
Pontyclun CF72 ....172 F8
Pontypool NP4 ....38 D1
Trefechan CF48 .....10 B6
Waunarlwydd SA5 ...66 D4
Ystradowen CF71 ...189 C8
Ash La CF62 ....211 B7
Ash Pk CF71 ....189 C8
Ash Pl Bargoed CF81 ..57 F2
Cardiff CF5 ....176 D1
Ash Plant Rd CF62 .211 E1
Ash Rd CF48 ....31 B1
Ash Sq CF37 ....136 A5
Ash St Abercwmboi CF44 53 E4
Cwm NP23 ....35 A8
Gilfach Goch CF39 ..132 B5
Swansea SA6 ....69 A7
Ash Tree Cl CF15 ..176 A6
Ash Villas **8** CF48 ...31 C1
Ash Wlk CF72 ......155 C2
Ashbourne Ct CF48 ..28 D2
Ashbrook CF31 .....169 B5
Ashburnham Dr SA3 ..93 E2
Ashburton Ave CF3 .179 C7
Ashby Rd CF64 .....216 A6
Ashchurch Cl CF14 .177 A5
Ashcroft Cres CF5 .176 C1
Ashdale Cl CF40 ...107 A1
Ashdene Cl CF5 ....176 D2
Ashdown Cl **4** CF3 .179 F7
Ashfield Cl **7** CF3 ..179 E7
Ashfield Rd
Abertillery NP13 .....36 B5
Newbridge NP11 .....86 F7
Ashford CF14 ......160 A2
Ashford Cl
Croesyceiliog NP44 ..90 B5
Pontypridd CF37 ....109 C5
Ashford Cl N NP44 ..90 B5
Ashford Cl S NP44 ..90 B4
Ashgrove
Aberdare CF44 ....28 F3
Baglan SA12 ....98 D7
Bedwas CF83 ......138 F6
Bryn NP12 ....85 E5
Dinas Powys CF64 ..206 B2
Llantwit Major CF61 .209 F6
Pontypridd CF37 ....109 D6
Treharris CF46 ......82 F6
Ystrad Mynach CF82 ..84 F2
Ashgrove Cl N NP44 ..62 D1
Ashgrove Specl Sch
CF64 ....206 D3
Ashgrove Terr CF46 ..83 B4
Ashgrove Villas CF46 ..56 A4
Ashlea Dr CF47 ......10 F1
Ashleigh Cl SA2 .....94 C3
Ashleigh Ct
Cwmbran NP44 ....89 A1
Tredegar NP22 ....13 E8
Ashleigh Rd SA2 ....94 C3
Ashleigh Terr SA10 ..97 E8
Ashley Rd NP19 ....144 B5
Ashman Cl CF83 ....137 D1
Ashmount Bsns Parc
SA6 ....46 B1
Ashton Ho NP44 .....89 D2
Ashvale NP22 ....6 C1
Ashville
Blackwood NP12 .....59 A1
Tredegar NP22 ....13 F5
Ashwell Cotts NP18 .144 C8
Ashwood Cl NP12 ...85 E5
Ashwood Cl **12** CF24 195 C5
Ashwood Dr SA8 .....24 B5
Aspen Ave NP12 .....85 E5
Aspen Cl CF3 ......179 D3
Aspen Way Cimla SA11 ..72 C6
Llantwit Fardre CF38 156 C6
Newport NP20 ......117 A3
Asquith Ct SA1 .....95 A6
Asquith St
Pontypool NP4 ....62 E3
Tir-y-Berth CF82 .....85 A4
Assembly Rooms **3**
SA1 ....95 E6
Aster Cl **6** Cardiff CF3 180 A7
Risca NP11 ....115 A2
Aster View SA12 .....98 C3
Aston Cres NP20 ...143 B8
Aston Pl CF3 ......180 A5
Astoria Cl CF14 ....159 E2
Atfield Cl CF23 ....178 E1
Athelstan Rd CF14 .176 F4
Atlantic Cl SA7 ......69 A5
Atlantic Cres CF63 .215 C3
Atlantic Pl CF63 ...215 C7
Atlantic Trad Est
CF63 ....215 C3
Atlantic Way CF63 .215 B3
Atlantic Wharf **4**
CF10 ....195 C4
Atlantic Wharf Leisure
Village CF10 .....195 C2
Atlas Pl **5** CF5 ...194 D5
Atlas Rd CF5 ......194 D5
Atlee Terr CF34 .....75 A2

Attlee Ave
Abertillery NP13 .....36 A7
Port Talbot SA12 ...124 E8
Attlee Cl Ebbw Vale NP23 7 D6
Tredegar NP22 ....13 D6
Attlee Ct CF83 .....138 C3
Attlee Ho **3** CF47 ...30 D8
Attlee Rd
Blackwood NP12 .....85 E7
Nantyglo NP23 ....15 E7
Attlee St CF32 .....150 F5
Attlee Way NP22 ....13 D5
Aubrey Ave CF5 ....194 A7
Aubrey Hames Cl
NP20 ....143 A2
Aubrey Rd Porth CF39 ..107 F2
Tonypandy CF40 ....107 A4
Aubrey Terr
Cowbridge CF71 ....188 F1
Cwm NP23 ....35 B7
Auburn Ave CF23 ....98 B2
Auckland Cl NP12 ...86 A4
Auckland Rd NP20 ..142 D3
Augusta Cres CF64 .207 A1
Augusta Pk NP23 ...14 F2
Augusta Rd CF64 ..207 A1
Augusta St
Cardiff CF24 ....195 C6
Ebbw Vale NP23 .....14 A3
Treorchy CF41 ....79 A3
Augustan Cl NP18 ..117 F3
Augustan Dr NP18 ..117 F3
Augustan Way NP18 .117 F3
Augustus John Cl
NP19 ....144 A8
Augustus St CF37 ...81 F1
Austen Cl CF3 .....179 D8
Austin Ave
Bridgend CF31 .....168 F6
Laleston CF32 ......167 F4
Porthcawl CF36 ....183 C8
Austin Cl CF36 ....183 D8
Austin Friars **5**
NP20 ....143 C5
Austin Rd NP4 ......62 F1
Austin St CF45 ......54 D3
Australia Rd CF14 .177 E2
Australian Terr CF43 .168 F6
Auxiliary Boiler House Rd
CF62 ....211 E1
Avalon Ct
Newport NP19 .....143 F7
Pontypool NP4 ....62 B6
Avalon Dr NP19 ....143 F7
Avalon Terr NP22 ....6 E1
Avan St SA13 ....99 B1
Avenue Cilfig The
SA15 ....40 D6
Avenue Cl CF82 .....84 F2
Avenue De Clichy
CF47 ....10 D1
Avenue Ind Est CF23 .160 F1
Avenue Ind Pk CF23 .179 A8
Avenue The
Abersychan NP4 .....37 E6
Bargoed CF81 ....58 A1
Bedwas CF83 ......139 A6
Cardiff CF14 ....176 F4
Cardiff CF3 ....179 C2
Cardiff CF5 ....177 A1
Cwmavon SA12 ......99 D6
Llanbradach CF83 ..111 F1
Llanelli SA14 ....41 C5
Llanelli SA15 ....40 E2
Merthyr Tydfil CF47 ...10 E2
Mountain Ash CF45 ..54 D3
Neath SA11 ....71 D4
Pontycymer CF32 ...103 E5
Pontypool NP4 ......62 D1
Pontypool NP4 ....62 F5
Pontypridd CF37 ....109 D2
Tonyrefail CF39 ....133 D5
Treharris CF46 ......82 F6
Tylorstown CF43 ...107 C8
Wyllie NP12 ....85 F1
Ystrad Mynach CF82 ..85 A2
Averil Vivian Gr SA2 .94 E6
Avis Terr SA15 ......40 E5
Avoca Pl CF11 .....194 E3
Avocet Ct CF63 ....215 A5
Avon Cl Barry CF62 .215 C7
Bettws NP20 ......116 E2
Bryn NP12 ....85 D3
Avon Cl NP23 ....7 C5
Avon Pl NP44 ....90 A3
Avon Rd NP4 ....17 C5
Avon St Cymmer SA13 ..75 C5
Ferndale CF43 ....79 F7
Glynneath SA11 ....223 C1
Avon Terr CF39 ....107 F7
Avondale NP4 ....17 C6
Avondale Cl
Abercynon CF45 .....82 C5
Cwmbran NP44 ......89 F6
Avondale Cres
Cardiff CF11 ....195 A2
Cwmbran NP44 ......89 F7
Avondale Dr NP44 ..89 F7
Avondale Gdns CF11 .195 A2
Avondale Gdns S
CF11 ....195 A2
Avondale Ind Est NP44 89 F6
Avondale Rd
Cardiff CF11 ....195 A2
Cwmbran NP44 ......89 F7
Pontypool NP4 ......62 D1
Porth CF39 ....108 A2
Ton Pentre CF41 .....79 B2

Avondale Sq SA13 ...75 C5
Avondale St CF45 ....82 C5
Avondale Terr SA13 ..75 C5
Avondale Way NP44 ..89 F6
Avonmuir Rd CF24 .196 A8
Avonridge CF14 ....159 D2
Awel Mor CF23 ....178 D3
Awelfryn
Penycoedcae CF37 ..135 A3
Penywaun CF44 ......28 B6
Awelfryn Cl NP23 ....7 E4
Awelfryn Terr **7** CF47 .10 F4
Axbridge Cres CF3 .179 D6
Axminster Rd CF23 .195 E8
Aylesbury Mans **2**
CF14 ....176 F6
Aylesbury Rd SA2 ...94 C5
Aynho Pl NP23 .....14 D8
Ayron St CF43 ....79 F5
Ayton Terr CF40 ...106 E7
Azalea Cl CF23 ....178 D7
Azalea Pk CF48 .....11 C4

B

B Sta Access Rd
CF62 ....211 E1
Baber Cl CF23 .....178 E1
Bach Cl SA12 ....98 B3
Backhall St NP18 ...118 C2
Bacon Pl CF23 ....117 A3
Bacton Rd CF14 ...196 A8
Baden Powell Com Jun &
Inf Sch CF24 .....195 F6
Baden Rd CF24 ....196 A6
Baden Terr CF47 ....10 F2
Bader Cl CF14 .....177 F6
Badgers Brook CF31 .169 A6
Badgers Brook Cl
CF71 ....189 C8
Badgers Brook Dr
CF71 ....189 C8
Badgers Brook Rise
CF71 ....189 C8
Badgers Mdw CF71 ..117 F2
Badgers Mead CF31 .169 A6
Badgers Mede **4**
NP44 ....89 B3
Badgers Wood NP10 .141 F2
Badham Cl CF83 ...137 D1
Badminton Gdns SA5 .67 E5
Badminton Gr CF23 .178 C1
Badminton Rd NP19 .143 F6
Baglan Cotts CF32 ..150 C7
Baglan Hts SA12 ....98 F4
Baglan Ind Pk SA12 ..98 E5
Baglan Prim Sch SA12 98 D6
Baglan Sta CF23 ....98 D5
Baglan St Pentre CF41 ..78 F5
Swansea SA1 ....96 A7
Treherbert CF42 .....78 A8
Tylorstown CF43 .....80 C1
Baglan Way SA12 ...98 E3
Bagle Ct SA12 ......98 E5
Bagley Ct NP44 .....89 B5
Bagot St CF45 ......82 B6
Baiden Ave CF33 ...148 C2
Bailey Cl CF5 ......193 E7
Bailey Cres NP4 .....37 E6
Bailey St
Aberavon SA12 ......99 A1
Abersychan NP4 .....37 E6
Brynmawr NP23 ......8 C2
Deri CF81 ....33 B1
Mountain Ash CF45 ..54 D2
Newport NP20 ......143 B4
Ton Pentre CF41 .....78 F4
Treorchy CF41 ....79 A3
Wattstown CF39 ....107 E8
Bailey's Hos CF41 ...61 F8
Bailey's Terr NP4 ....61 F8
Baillie Smith Ave
NP11 ....60 B2
Baird Cl NP20 .....116 F3
Baird Rise CF62 ...214 D5
Baker Street Ho **11**
NP4 ....17 C6
Baker's La CF61 ...209 E7
Bakers Ct
5 Cardiff CF5 ....194 B7
Marshfield CF3 ....180 E8
Bakers Row CF10 ..195 A5
Bakers Way CF32 ..150 F4
Bakers Wharf **8**
CF37 ....109 D2
Bakery La CF3 .....162 D2
Bala Cl NP23 ....7 F5
Bala Dr NP10 ......142 F2
Bala Rd CF14 ......177 A2
Balaclava Ct CF40 .106 F3
Balaclava Rd
Cardiff CF23 ....178 C1
Dowlais CF48 ....11 A4
Glais SA7 ....47 B5
Balaclava St SA1 ....95 E7
Balance Mdws CF37 ..37 C2
Balance Rd NP4 .....37 C7
Baldwin Cl
Cardiff CF5 ....176 D3
Newport NP20 .....143 C2
Baldwin St
Bargoed CF81 ....57 F4
Bryn SA13 ....100 E5

Baldwin St continued
Newport NP20 .....143 C2
Baldwin's Cres SA1 ..96 E7
Balfe Rd NP19 .....144 D4
Ball Cl CF3 ....179 B7
Ball La CF3 ....179 A6
Ball Rd CF3 ....179 B6
Ballarat CF35 ......152 E2
Ballards SA10 ....70 F8
Ballas Cl CF33 .....166 A7
Balmond Terr NP4 ...62 B8
Balmoral
Cardiff CF14 ....160 B2
Penycoedcae CF37 ..135 B6
Balmoral Cl CF62 ..214 C8
Balmoral La **1** NP19 .144 A4
Balmoral Rd NP19 .144 A4
Baltic Terr NP44 ...116 E7
Baltimore Ct CF23 ..161 A2
Bamber Ho NP44 ....90 B4
Bampton Rd CF3 ...179 F7
Bananlog Terr NP12 ..34 C2
Banastre Ave CF14 .177 E2
Banc Bach SA4 .....64 E4
Banc Gelli Las CF31 .168 B2
Banc Gwyn CF31 ...168 B2
Banc y Ddraenen
SA18 ....218 D6
Banc-yr-Allt CF31 ..168 B6
Banc-Yr-eithin SA4 ..43 A3
Bancyffynnon SA14 .218 B7
Baneswell Ctyd **6**
NP20 ....143 B4
Baneswell Rd **6**
NP20 ....143 B5
Banfield Terr SA4 ...42 E2
Bangor Ct **3** CF24 ..178 C1
Bangor Ct **2** CF24 .178 C1
Bangor Rd NP23 .....7 E4
Bangor St
Cardiff CF24 ....178 C1
Maesteg CF34 .....102 A6
Bangor Terr CF34 ..102 A6
Bank Bldgs CF83 ...169 E3
Bank Cotts SA9 ....222 A6
Bank La
3 Newport NP19 .143 E8
Tredegar NP22 ......13 E7
Bank Rd SA14 ....42 C8
Bank Side SA11 .....71 E8
Bank St Maesteg CF34 102 B3
Newport NP19 .....143 D8
Tonypandy CF40 ...107 A3
Bank Terr CF48 ......10 A4
Bankers Hill CF32 ..149 D3
Bankes St **2** CF44 ..29 A2
Bankside NP19 .....143 D4
Bankside Cl CF14 ..159 F3
Bannau Bglws NP23 ..8 C2
Bantock Cl NP19 ...144 E5
Banwell Ct
Cwmbran NP44 ......89 B5
Swansea SA6 ....68 F8
Banwell Pl CF3 ....179 C6
Banwell St SA6 ......68 F8
Banwen La SA8 .....23 F4
Banwen Pl SA18 ...220 D8
Banwy Rd SA6 ......45 D1
Baptist Ct CF24 ...195 E6
Baptist Pl NP23 .....7 D4
Baptist Row CF43 ...79 F4
Baptist Sq CF43 ....79 F8
Baptist Well Pl SA1 ..68 C1
Baptist Well St SA1 ..68 C1
Baran Rd
Pontardawe SA8 ...220 D1
Rhydyfro SA8 ......220 D1
Barberry Rise CF64 .206 E5
Barbirolli Gn NP19 ..144 E4
Barbrook Cl CF14 ..160 A2
Bardsey Ave SA5 ....67 E7
Bardsey Cl CF36 ...165 E1
Bardsey Cres CF14 .159 E1
Bardsi Cl NP19 ....143 F7
Bargoed Cl CF46 ....83 B7
Bargoed Inf Sch CF81 .57 F5
Bargoed Sta CF81 ...58 A5
Bargoed Terr CF46 ..83 B7
Barker Ave NP13 ....36 A6
Barkley St NP22 .....33 C8
Barley Field Rd NP23 ..8 C3
Barmouth Rd CF3 ..179 B3
Barn Cl NP4 ....38 B2
Barn Cotts SA11 ....71 C2
Barnabas Cl SA5 ....66 F3
Barnard Ave CF5 ..193 E6
Barnard St NP19 ...143 D6
Barnardo St CF34 ..102 A6
Barnes Ave CF31 ...168 B6
Barnes NP44 ....7 A4
Barnets NP44 ....89 B3
Barnfield
Caerleon NP18 .....117 F5
Ponthir NP18 ......117 F5
Barnfield Cl CF23 ..161 B1
Barnfield Pl NP44 ...89 C5
Barnfield Terr NP4 ..17 B6
Barnstaple Rd CF3 .179 C6
Barnwood CF14 ....160 A2
Barnwood Cres CF5 .192 F4
Baron Cl CF64 ......206 F3
Baron's Cl CF61 ...210 A6
Baron's Court Rd
CF23 ....178 D1
Baroness Pl CF64 ..206 F3
Barquentine Pl CF10 .195 C3

Barrack Hill NP20 ....143 B7
Barrack La CF10 ....195 B5
Barrack Row CF48 ....11 B5
Barrett St CF42 ......78 B4
Barrians Way CF62 ..214 E5
Barrie Gdns NP20 ....142 E2
Barrington Rd **3**
  CF14 ....177 B4
Barrington St CF48 ...55 C5
Barry Cl CF82 ....84 E7
Barry Coll (Annexe)
  CF62 ....213 C4
Barry Coll of F Ed
  CF62 ....214 A7
  Barry CF62 ....214 D6
Barry Comp Sch
  CF62 ....214 D7
Barry Docks Link Rd
  CF63 ....215 D8
Barry Docks Sta
  CF63 ....215 A4
Barry Ho SA12 ....98 A2
Barry Hospl The
  CF62 ....214 D7
Barry Island Pleasure Pk
  CF62 ....214 E2
Barry Island Prim Sch
  CF62 ....214 F3
Barry Island Prim Sch
  Annexe CF62 ....214 F2
Barry Island Sta CF62 214 F2
Barry Rd Barry CF63 ..215 A6
  Gwaun-Cae-Gurwen
  SA18 ....220 D7
  Penarth CF64 ....206 E6
  Pontypridd CF37 ......109 A1
Barry Sidings Countryside
  Pk CF37 ....108 A2
Barry Sta CF62 ....214 D3
Barry View CF37 ......136 A6
Barry Wlk NP10 ....142 A6
Barthnewydd Ct **18**
  CF47 ....10 A2
Barthropp St NP19 ...144 A3
Bartlett St CF83 ......138 B2
Bartley Terr SA6 ......68 E5
Basil Pl CF24 ....195 A8
Bassaleg Sch **3** CF3 ..180 A7
Bassaleg Comp Sch
  NP10 ....142 A2
Bassaleg Rd NP20 ....142 E2
Bassett Ho **11** SA12 ...98 F1
Bassett Rd CF64 ......216 A5
Bassett St
  Abercynon CF45 ....82 E3
  Barry CF63 ....215 B6
  Cardiff CF5 ....194 C5
  Pontypridd CF37 ......109 C2
Bastian Cl CF63 ......215 C7
Batchelor Rd
  Cardiff CF14 ....177 D2
  2 Newport NP19 ......143 F5
Bath Ave SA6 ....45 F1
Bath Gn NP44 ....90 B2
Bath La Brynmawr NP23 ..8 A4
  Swansea SA1 ....95 D6
Bath Rd SA6 ....45 F1
Bath Row NP7 ....9 E7
Bath St Newport NP19 143 D6
  Port Talbot SA13 ......99 B1
Bath Villas SA6 ....68 F8
Bathurst St
  Swansea SA1 ....95 C5
  8 Swansea SA1 ......95 C6
Baton Ct CF14 ....177 C4
Batten Way CF37 .....109 F4
Battenberg St CF45 ..82 C5
Baxter Terr SA13 .....227 C2
Bay St SA1 ....96 A7
Bay Tree Ave SA2 .....94 B6
Bay Tree Cl NP18 .....117 E2
Bay View
  Port Talbot SA13 ......99 C2
  Swansea SA1 ....95 E8
Bay View Cl SA10 .....70 F5
Bay View Cres SA1 ....95 A6
Bay View Gdns SA10 ..70 E5
Bay View Hts SA13 ...99 C3
Bay View Rd
  Llanelli SA14 ....41 A6
  Porthcawl CF36 ....183 D6
Bay View Terr SA1 ....95 A6
Baylis Ct CF5 ....193 E6
Bayliss Rd CF32 ......150 F4
Baynton Cl CF5 ....176 E2
Bayside Rd CF24 .....195 D5
Bayswater St SA3 ....94 C3
Bayswater Rd SA2 ....94 C8
Baywood Ave SA3 ....123 A8
BBC Cymru Wales
  CF5 ....176 F1
Beach La CF64 ....207 B4
Beach Rd Llanelli SA15 40 A6
  Pen-clawdd SA4 ....64 E4
  Penarth CF64 ....207 B4
  Porthcawl CF36 ....183 D7
  Pyle CF33 ....148 A1
  Southerndown CF32 ..197 A8
  Sully CF64 ....216 D4
Beach St
  Aberavon SA12 ....124 F8
  Swansea SA1 ....95 B5
Beachway CF62 ....214 B1
Beacon Hts CF48 .....225 E4
Beacon St CF11 ......194 C7
Beacon View NP23 ....8 D1
Beacons Cl NP10 .....142 A7
Beacons Pk CF44 ....224 D3

Beacons The CF44 ....27 D7
Beacons View SA11 ...72 A5
Beacons View Rd SA6 .68 D8
Beaconsfield Ct SA2 ..94 B7
Beaconsfield Ho
  CF62 ....214 D4
Beaconsfield Rd SA10 .48 F1
Beaconsfield Way SA2 94 B7
Beadon St CF45 ......54 D2
Beale Cl CF5 ....176 E2
Beatrice Rd
  Barry CF63 ....215 B6
  Cardiff CF14 ....177 B4
Beattie St SA5 ....68 B2
Beatty Ave CF23 .....178 A5
Beatty Cl **2** CF62 ....215 A8
Beatty Ct **9** CF10 ....195 C4
Beatty Rd NP19 ......144 F2
Beatty St CF82 ....85 A6
Beauchamp St CF11 ..194 F5
Beaufort Ave SA3 ....123 A3
Beaufort Cl
  Cwmbran NP44 ....89 C1
  Mumbles SA3 ....123 A3
  Tredegar NP22 ....6 F1
Beaufort Ct
  7 Cardiff CF10 ......195 C4
  Llantrisant CF72 .....155 E2
  Swansea SA5 ....67 E5
  Swansea SA6 ....68 F6
Beaufort Dr SA3 .....121 E7
Beaufort Gdns SA3 ..121 E7
Beaufort Hill NP23 ...7 E4
Beaufort Hill Jun & Inf Sch
  NP23 ....7 F4
Beaufort Pl NP19 ....143 F8
Beaufort Rd
  Ebbw Vale NP23 ......7 D2
  Newport NP19 ....144 A3
  Swansea SA6 ....68 F5
  Tredegar NP22 ....6 F1
Beaufort Rise NP23 ..7 D4
Beaufort St SA13 .....8 C4
Beaufort Terr
  Ebbw Vale NP23 ......7 D3
  4 Newport NP20 .....143 B4
Beaufort Way CF62 ..212 E2
Beaumaris Cl
  Bassaleg NP10 ....141 E3
  Church Village CF38 ..135 F2
Beaumaris Dr NP44 ..90 B1
Beaumaris Ho **10** NP44 90 B2
Beaumaris Rd SA3 ...179 B3
Beaumaris Way NP12 58 E1
Beaumont Cl
  Barry CF62 ....214 D2
  Nantyglo NP23 ....15 D8
Beaumont Cres SA1 ..95 B8
Beaumont Ct CF64 ...206 F3
Beaupre Castle CF71 201 B5
Beavers Wlk NP10 ....142 B4
Beck Ho SA2 ....94 F6
Beckett St CF45 ......54 D4
Beckgrove Cl CF24 ..196 A7
Beda Rd CF5 ....194 C5
Bedavere Cl CF14 ....159 E2
Beddick NP44 ....89 A3
Beddoe St CF44 ......53 C8
Beddoe Terr CF46 ....83 A5
Bedford Cl
  Cefn Cribwr CF32 ....149 A2
  Cwmbran NP44 ....89 A3
Bedford Ho **3** SA6 ...68 E8
Bedford Pl CF24 .....195 C7
Bedford Rd
  Cefn Cribwr CF32 ....149 A3
  Newport NP19 ....143 D5
Bedford Rise CF61 ...210 B6
Bedford St
  Aberdare CF44 ....53 D7
  Cardiff CF24 ....195 B7
  Swansea SA6 ....69 A8
Bedlington Terr
  CF62 ....214 D7
Bedlinog Cty Inf Sch
  CF46 ....56 A7
Bedlinog Cty Jun Sch
  CF46 ....56 A7
Bedlinog Terr CF46 ..56 A7
Bedwas Cl **4** CF3 ....180 A7
Bedwas Comp Sch
  CF83 ....138 E6
Bedwas House Ind Est
  CF83 ....138 C6
Bedwas Inf Sch CF83 138 D6
Bedwas Jun Sch
  CF83 ....138 E6
Bedwas Pl **2** CF64 ...206 F4
Bedwas Rd
  Caerphilly CF83 ......138 C4
  Caerphilly CF83 ......138 D5
Bedwas St CF11 .....194 E3
Bedwellty Rd CF81,
  NP12 ....58 C5
Bedwellty Comp Sch
  NP12 ....58 C2
Bedwellty Pits NP22 ..14 B1

Bedwellty Rd
  Aberbargoed CF81 ....58 B5
  Blackwood NP12 ......85 C8
  New Tredegar NP24 ..33 F2
Bedwlwyn Cl CF82 ...84 F2
Bedwlwyn Rd CF82 ..84 F2
Bedwlwyn St CF82 ...84 F2
Beech Ave Bryn NP12 ..85 E4
  Llantwit Major CF61 ..210 A4
Beech Cl Bargoed CF81 57 E2
  Caerphilly CF83 ......137 D1
  Cwmbran NP44 ....89 D6
  Llanmartin NP18 .....145 E6
Beech Cres SA4 ......43 A4
Beech Ct CF15 ....158 D2
Beech Dr CF82 ....84 F3
Beech Emb CF82 .....84 F2
Beech Gr
  Blackwood NP12 ......59 B1
  Ebbw Vale NP23 ......14 E2
  Merthyr Tydfil CF47 ..10 C4
  Newport NP19 ....163 F8
  Porthcawl CF36 ....183 D8
  Troedyrhiw CF48 .....55 C8
Beech Ho CF14 ....176 E2
Beech Pk CF71 ....187 A4
Beech Pk Cardiff CF5 .193 B8
  Llanharry CF72 ....172 B5
  Pontypool NP4 ....62 D1
  Pontyrhyl CF32 ....129 F8
Beech St Ferndale CF43 79 F6
  Gilfach Goch CF39 ...132 B5
Beech Terr
  Abercarn NP11 ....87 A1
  Abercwmboi CF44 ....53 E4
Beech Tree Cl CF15 ..176 A6
Beech Tree La SA2 ...94 C5
Beech Tree Terr NP4 .61 F8
Beech Tree Way CF46 83 F3
Beecham St NP19 ....144 D5
Beechcroft Bryn NP12 85 E3
Beechcroft NP19 .....144 B6
Beechdale Rd NP19 ..144 A5
Beecher Ave CF11 ...194 F1
Beecher Terr NP11 ..114 C5
Beeches Ind Est The
  CF72 ....155 A1
Beeches Rd NP4 .....38 B1
Beeches The
  Abercynon CF45 ......82 E3
  Bridgend CF31 ....168 E6
  Cwmbran NP44 ....89 D2
  Pontypool NP4 ....38 A2
Beechfield Ave
  Hengoed CF82 ....85 A3
  Newport NP19 ....144 B6
Beechfield Cl NP23 ..7 D6
Beechgrove
  Caerphilly CF83 ......138 C5
  Treharris CF46 ....82 F6
Beeching Way CF38 ..135 E2
Beechlee Cl CF72 ....173 D7
Beechleigh Cl NP44 ..88 F3
Beechley Dr CF5 .....193 C8
Beechwood Ave
  Aberdare CF44 ....28 E2
  Bridgend CF31 ....168 C5
  Cwmfelinfach NP11 ..113 F4
  Neath SA11 ....71 F7
  Trefechan CF48 ....10 B6
Beechwood Cl NP11 ..86 E6
Beechwood Cres
  NP19 ....144 A5
Beechwood Dr
  Llantwit Fardre CF38 156 C6
  Merthyr Tydfil CF48 ..29 F8
  Penarth CF64 ....206 E2
  Tonyrefail CF39 ......132 E5
Beechwood Gr CF35 .152 D1
Beechwood Rd
  Margam SA13 ....125 F3
  Newport NP19 ....144 A5
  Swansea SA2 ....94 F6
  Taffs Well CF15 ......158 B4
Beechwood St CF37 .136 B5
Beechwood Wlk NP4 .38 B2
Began Rd CF3 ....161 D4
Beignon Cl CF24 .....195 D4
Beili Glas SA4 ....42 E1
Beili Glas Rd NP12 ..85 B5
Bela Ho **2** NP44 .....89 C2
Belgrave Cl
  1 Cardiff CF11 ......194 F5
  14 Pontypool NP4 ...79 A2
  Swansea SA1 ....95 A6
Belgrave Ct
  Barry CF62 ....214 D4
  Gorseinon SA4 ......43 A1
Belgrave Gdns **2** SA1 95 A6
Belgrave La SA1 .....95 A6
Belgrave Rd SA4 .....43 A1
Belgrave St SA1 .....79 A2
Belgrave Terr CF37 ..109 E3
Bell La NP4 ....79 A2
Bell St Aberdare CF44 28 F4
  Barry CF62 ....214 D4
Bell Vue Terr NP20 ..143 C2
Belle View **2** CF40 ...107 A4
Belle Vue
  Aberdare CF44 ....82 E3
  Ebbw Vale NP23 ......14 D4
  Pen-clawdd SA4 .....64 F4
Belle Vue Cl
  Penarth CF64 ....207 B4
  Pontypool NP4 ....38 A1

Belle Vue Cres CF14 .176 F3
Belle Vue La NP20 ...143 B3
Belle Vue Terr
  Barry CF64 ....215 C7
  Penarth CF64 ....207 B5
  Pontypridd CF37 .....135 C6
Belle Vue Way SA1 ..95 C7
Bellevue Gdns NP44 .89 E2
Bellevue Rd
  Cwmbran NP44 ....89 D2
  Mumbles SA3 ....122 F6
Bellevue Terr
  Merthyr Vale CF48 ...55 C4
  Mountain Ash CF45 ..81 D4
Bellin Cl NP18 ....118 A3
Bells Hill CF48 ....55 C4
Bellvue Cl NP44 .....89 E2
Bellvue Rd SA14 .....41 E3
Belmont Cl CF34 ....102 B3
Belmont Hill NP18 ...144 D8
Belmont St CF63 ....215 A6
Belmont Terr
  Aberdare CF44 ....53 C8
  Porth CF39 ....107 F2
Belmont Wlk CF10 ..195 B2
Belvedere Cl
  Abertillery NP11 .....59 F6
  Bishopston SA3 .....121 E7
Belvedere Cres **8** SA15 40 C6
Belvedere Rd SA15 ..40 C6
Belvedere Terr
  Newport NP20 ....143 B7
  6 Risca NP11 ....114 F3
Belvoir Ct CF72 .....155 E2
Ben Jonson Way
  NP20 ....142 E2
Benbow Cl SA2 ......94 C6
Benbow Rd NP19 ....144 E7
Bendrick Dr SA3 .....120 F5
Bendrick Rd CF63 ...215 C4
Benecrofte CF62 .....213 C4
Benedict Cl SA10 ....71 B8
Benjamin St NP22 ...13 A2
Bennett Ave CF31 ...169 D3
Bennett St Blaina NP13 15 E4
  Bridgend CF31 ....169 D3
  Swansea SA1 ....68 D3
Benson Ave NP10 ....142 B4
Benson Rd SA4 ......64 F4
Benson St SA4 ......64 F4
Benson Terr SA4 ....64 E4
Benthall Pl SA1 .....95 E7
Bentley Cl NP10 .....142 A7
Beresford Cl NP19 ..143 D5
Beresford Rd
  Cardiff CF24 ....195 C7
  Newport NP19 ....143 D5
Beresford Road La
  CF24 ....195 E7
Berkeley Cl SA7 .....47 A2
Berkeley Cres NP4 ..89 E8
Berkeley Ct NP44 ...89 B5
Berkeley Sq CF5 ....193 A6
Berkley Cl NP10 .....141 F3
Berkley Dr CF64 .....207 A3
Berkley Rd NP10 ....141 F3
Berkrolles Ave CF62 211 D4
Berllan Deg SA15 ...40 E2
Berllangron Cotts
  NP12 ....58 F1
Berllanlwyd Ave NP12 58 E7
Berllanlwyd St CF82 .84 E8
Berma Cl SA3 ....123 C3
Bernard Ave CF5 ....194 A4
Bernard St
  Abercarn NP11 ....114 C7
  Swansea SA2 ....94 F6
Berry Ct CF61 ....210 B6
Berry Pl CF5 ....176 D2
Berry Sq CF48 ....11 A4
Berrylands SA12 ....124 D4
Berrymead Rd CF23 .178 B7
Bertha Pl SA13 ......125 E3
Bertha Rd SA13 .....125 F3
Bertha St CF37 ......135 E5
Berthin NP44 ....89 B3
Berthin Rd NP4 .....39 D2
Berthlwyd CF15 .....157 C1
Berthon Rd NP4 ....39 E2
Berthwin St CF11 ...194 D7
Bertram St CF24 ....195 E7
Berw Rd
  Pontypridd CF37 .....109 D2
  Swansea SA1 ....95 B8
  Tonypandy CF40 .....106 C6
Berwedd-dy Cotts
  CF37 ....109 E4
Berwick Cl SA14 .....41 F5
Berwick Terr SA1 ...95 C8
Berwyn Pl SA5 ......68 A4
Beryl Pl CF62 ....214 E5
Beryl Rd Barry CF62 .214 F5
  Clydach SA6 ....46 F8
Bessant Cl CF71 ....188 F1
Bessborough Dr
  CF11 ....194 E3
Bessemer Cl
  Cardiff CF11 ....194 D2
  Newport NP20 ....116 F4
Bessemer Close
  Workshops CF11 ....194 C2
Bessemer Rd CF11 ..194 D3
Bethania CF45 ....82 E3
Bethania CF34 ....102 B2
Bethania Hill CF39 ..133 C2
Bethania Pl CF44 ....53 E4
Bethania Rd
  Clydach SA6 ....46 D7
  Pontypool NP4 ....38 A1

Bethania Rd continued
  Cross Hands SA14 ...218 A7
Bethania Row
  Cardiff CF3 ....179 D7
  Ogmore Vale CF32 ..104 C1
Bethania St
  Glynneath SA11 .....223 D1
  Maesteg CF34 ....102 B2
Bethania Terr
  1 Cwmavon SA12 ...99 F6
  Llanelli SA15 ....40 E2
Bethany Cl CF82 ....84 E1
Bethany Ct CF42 ....50 F2
Bethany La SA3 .....123 A3
Bethany Sq **4** SA13 .99 B1
Bethcar St NP23 ....14 D7
Bethel Ave NP22 ....13 E6
Bethel Cl
  Abersychan NP4 .....37 E6
  Swansea SA5 ....68 E8
  Trehafod CF37 ....108 C2
Bethel La NP44 ......89 B6
Bethel Pl Cardiff CF14 159 D1
  Hirwaun CF44 ....27 D8
Bethel Rd
  Glynneath SA11 .....223 D1
  Pen-clawdd SA4 .....64 E4
  Swansea SA7 ....69 E7
  Ystradgynlais SA9 ..2 C5
Bethel St
  Briton Ferry SA11 ...98 C8
  Merthyr Tydfil CF47 ..10 D1
  Swansea SA1 ....95 D8
  Trehafod CF37 ....108 C2
Bethlehem Ct CF44 .195 E6
Bethlehem Rd SA10 .70 F7
Bethlehem View
  CF72 ....153 F2
Bethuel St CF44 .....29 B1
Bettsland SA3 ....122 F8
Bettws Cl NP20 .....116 F1
Bettws Ctr NP20 ....116 D1
Bettws Cty Prim Sch
  SA18 ....219 C6
Bettws High Sch
  NP20 ....116 F1
Bettws Hill NP20 ....116 D1
Bettws La NP20 .....116 E1
Bettws Rd SA5 ......68 A4
Bettws-y-Coed Rd
  CF23 ....178 B7
Betws Prim Sch CF32 129 E2
Betws Rd CF32 ......129 D1
Betwyns **9** NP44 ....89 B1
Beulah Rd CF14 .....177 C2
Beulah St NP22 .....12 F3
Bevan Ave NP22 ....6 C1
Bevan Cl CF83 ......138 C6
Bevan Cres
  Blackwood NP12 .....85 D8
  Ebbw Vale NP23 .....7 C3
Bevan Rise CF83 ....138 F6
Bevan St SA12 ......124 F8
Bevan Way SA5 .....66 E3
Bevan's La NP4,NP44 89 C8
Bevan's Terr SA12 ..73 A2
Bevans Row SA1 ....96 B7
Bevans Terr SA7 ....69 E5
Beverley Cl SA5 .....67 E4
Beverley Gdns SA5 .67 E4
Beverley St
  Barry CF63 ....215 B7
  Port Talbot SA13 ....125 B8
Bevin Ave SA12 .....124 D8
Bevin Rd SA12 ......124 C8
Bevin Pl CF14 ......177 C8
Beynon St NP11 ....86 F6
Bible Coll of Wales The
  SA2 ....94 B3
Bicester Ct CF64 ...215 E6
Biddulph SA15 .....40 E2
Bideford Cl NP20 ...143 A1
Bideford Rd
  Cardiff CF3 ....179 C5
  Newport NP20 ....143 A1
Big La NP23 ....7 F4
Big Pit Mining Mus
  NP4 ....16 F6
Bigyn Cty Prim Sch
  SA15 ....40 E4
Bigyn La SA15 ......40 E4
Bigyn Park Terr SA15 40 E4
Bigyn Rd SA15 .....40 E4
Bill Harry Ct NP22 ..13 D8
Billingham Cres CF47 10 E3
Bilston St NP19 .....143 E6
Bilton Rd SA11 .....71 C7
Bingle La CF62 .....211 D6
Birch Cres
  Cefn Hengoed CF82 ..84 F4
  Llantwit Fardre CF38 156 C5
Birch Ct CF15 ....158 D2
Birch Gr Barry CF62 .214 C2
  Bridgend CF31 ......168 A5
  Brynmawr NP23 .....8 A5
  Caerphilly CF83 .....138 C3

Birch Gr continued
  Cwmbran NP44 ....116 A8
  Llanharry CF72 ......172 B5
  Merthyr Tydfil CF47 ..10 D5
  Risca NP11 ....115 A2
  Waunarlwydd SA5 ...66 D4
Birch La CF64 ....207 A1
Birch Rd Baglan SA12 98 D7
  Cardiff CF5 ....193 D8
  Llanmartin NP18 ....145 F7
Birch Tree Cl SA2 ...94 C6
Birch Trees NP10 ...142 B2
Birch Wlk
  8 Cardiff CF5 ....193 D8
  Porthcawl CF36 .....183 D8
Birches The NP44 ...89 C5
Birchfield CF38 ......136 A1
Birchfield Cres CF5 ..193 F7
Birchfield Rd
  Mumbles SA3 ....122 F8
  Pontardawe SA8 ....23 F6
Birchgrove
  Aberdare CF44 ....28 E2
  Bedwas CF83 ....138 F6
  New Tredegar NP24 ..33 D3
  Pontypridd CF37 .....135 C8
  Rogerstone NP10 ...141 F6
  Treharris CF46 ......82 F6
Birchgrove Cl NP20 ..117 B2
Birchgrove Comp Sch
  SA7 ....47 B2
Birchgrove Jun & Inf Sch
  Birchgrove SA7 ......47 A1
  Cardiff CF14 ....177 D4
Birchgrove Rd
  Cardiff CF14 ....177 D4
  Glais SA7 ....47 A4
  Swansea SA7 ....70 A8
Birchgrove St CF39 ..107 F4
Birchgrove Sta CF14 177 D6
Birchley CF37 ....135 D6
Birchway The CF46 ..10 A6
Birchwood Ave CF37 135 E5
Birchwood Cl
  Baglan SA12 ....98 E5
  Bryn SA12 ....85 E5
  Bryn-côch SA10 .....48 C5
Birchwood Dr CF23 ..132 E2
Birchwood Gdns
  Bedwas CF83 ....138 C6
  Cardiff CF14 ....177 C3
Birchwood La CF23 ..178 C3
Birchwood Rd CF23 ..178 C3
Birkdale Cl
  3 Cardiff CF3 ....180 A8
  Mumbles SA3 ....93 F2
Bishop Childs CW Jun &
  Inf Sch CF3 ....179 F7
Bishop Gore Comp Sch
  SA2 ....94 C6
Bishop Hadley RC High
  Sch CF47 ....10 E3
Bishop Hannon Dr
  CF5 ....176 B1
Bishop of Llandaff CW
  High Sch CF5 ....176 F1
Bishop Rd
  Ammanford SA18 ...219 B6
  7 Glanaman SA18 ..220 B8
Bishop St
  Abertillery NP13 .....36 C5
  Cardiff CF11 ....194 E3
  Newport NP19 ......143 D6
  Tonypandy CF40 ....107 A3
Bishop Vaughan RC Comp
  Sch SA6 ....68 E8
Bishop's Gr SA2 ....94 B5
Bishop's Pl NP23 ...14 D8
Bishop's Rd CF14 ..177 A4
Bishop's Wlk SA6 ..45 F2
Bishop's Wood Nature
  Reserve SA3 ....122 C4
Bishops Cl CF14 ....177 A4
Bishops Ct CF14 ....177 A4
Bishops Gr CF47 ...10 E3
Bishops Pl CF14 ....177 A4
Bishops' Ave CF5 ...193 E6
Bishops' Cl CF5 ....193 E6
Bishops' Gr CF5 ....193 E6
Bishops' Wlk CF5 ..193 E6
Bishopston Comp Sch
  SA3 ....122 A7
Bishopston Prim Sch
  SA3 ....122 A7
Bishopston Rd
  Bishopston SA3 .....121 F6
  Cardiff CF5 ....193 E4
Bishopswood CF31 ..169 D4
Bishpool Est NP19 ..144 D6
Bishpool La NP19 ...144 D6
Bishton Rd NP18 ...145 B5
Bishton St NP19 ....143 E5
Bisley Cl CF24 ......196 B7
Bittern Cl SA10 .....48 E2
Bittern Way CF64 ...217 A8
Bitterton Ho SA12 ..98 A2
Black Lion St SA14 .218 C7
Black Oak Rd CF23 .178 C8
Black Rd
  Church Village CF38 135 C1
  Pontypridd CF37 .....135 B4

Blackberry Dr CF62 . . . . . 214 C6
Blackberry Pl CF45 . . . . . . 54 B6
Blackbird Cl NP10 . . . . . 142 C3
Blackbird Rd CF62 . . . . . 210 D6
Blackbirds Cl NP44 . . . . . 117 A5
Blackbirds Way CF3 . . . . 179 D8
Blackbrook Rd CF83 . . . . 158 E8
Blackett Ave NP20 . . . . . . 117 A4
Blackfield Row CF32 . . . . 149 F2
Blackhall Rd CF32 . . . . . 185 E3
Blackhill Rd SA4 . . . . 43 A3
Blackhills La
Fairwood SA2 . . . . 92 F3
Upper Killay SA2 . . . . . . 93 B3
Blackmill Rd
Bryncethin CF32 . . . . . . 151 B5
Lewistown CF32 . . . . . . 130 E5
Blackmoor Pl CF3 . . . . . 179 C6
Blacksmiths Way
NP10 . . . . 163 A6
Blackstone St **9**
CF11 . . . . 194 E5
Blackthorn Ave CF47 . . . . 10 D5
Blackthorn Gr NP18 . . . . 117 E2
Blackthorn Pl SA2 . . . . . . 67 B1
Blackvein Rd NP11 . . . . . 114 C3
Blackweir Terr CF10 . . . . 194 F4
Blackwell Cl **1** CF63 . . . . 215 B6
Blackwood Comp Sch
NP12 . . . . 85 D8
Blackwood Inf Sch
NP12 . . . . 85 D7
Blackwood Jun Sch
NP12 . . . . 85 E8
Blackwood Rd NP12 . . . . . 85 F4
Blaen Baglan Prim Sch
SA12 . . . . 98 F6
Blaen Cefn SA12 . . . . 69 D5
Blaen Cendl NP23 . . . . 7 E4
Blaen Cwm SA12 . . . . . 222 D3
Blaen Dewi CF71 . . . . . . 198 C5
Blaen Dowlais St CF48 . . 11 D4
Blaen Ogwr Ct CF32 . . . 104 F5
Blaen Wern
Cwmdare CF44 . . . . 28 D3
Ebbw Vale NP23 . . . . . . 14 B8
Blaen y Cwm CF31 . . . . 168 B4
Blaen y Ddol CF31 . . . . 168 B4
Blaen-Afon Rd NP7,
NP23 . . . . 8 F3
Blaen-Blodau St NP13 . . . 60 B6
Blaen-Cyffin Rd NP13 . . . 60 B6
Blaen-gwawr Prim Sch
CF44 . . . . 53 B8
Blaen-Nant Rd NP23 . . . . .8 C2
Blaen-y-Coed
Cardiff CF14 . . . . 177 C8
Radyr CF15 . . . . 179 A6
Blaen-y-Cwm CF81 . . . . . 58 A5
Blaen-y-Cwm Rd
Abertillery NP11 . . . . 60 F6
Pontypool NP4 . . . . 61 A4
Treherbert CF42 . . . . 50 D3
Blaen-y-Cwm Terr
CF42 . . . . 50 E3
Blaen-y-Cwm View
NP44 . . . . 88 F1
Blaen-y-Fro CF35 . . . . . 152 F1
Blaen-y-Maes Dr SA5 . . . 67 E6
Blaen-y-Morfa SA15 . . . . 40 F2
Blaen-y-Pant Ave
NP20 . . . . 143 A8
Blaen-y-Pant Cres
NP20 . . . . 143 A8
Blaen-y-Pant Pl
NP20 . . . . 143 A8
Blaenant St SA13 . . . . 74 D4
Blaenau Cty Prim Sch
SA18 . . . . 218 F8
Blaenau Gwent Inf Sch
NP13 . . . . 36 A6
Blaenau Gwent Rows
NP13 . . . . 36 A6
Blaenau Rd SA13 . . . . . . 74 D4
Blaenavon Cl **3** CF3 . . . 180 A7
Blaenavon Hospl NP4 . . 17 B7
Blaenavon Ironworks
NP4 . . . . 17 B7
Blaenavon Terr SA12 . . . . 73 C6
Blaencaerau Est CF34 . . . 75 C2
Blaencaerau Jun Sch
CF34 . . . . 75 C2
Blaencaerau Rd CF34 . . . 75 C2
Blaencedi SA4 . . . . 64 F3
Blaenclydach Pl **3**
CF11 . . . . 194 F3
Blaenclydach St CF11 . . 194 F3
Blaencoed Rd SA7 . . . . . . 69 F7
Blaencwm Rd SA7 . . . . . . 70 A7
Blaendare Farm La
NP4 . . . . 62 A4
Blaendare Rd NP4 . . . . . . 62 C5
Blaendulais Prim Sch
SA10 . . . . 222 D3
Blaengarw Prim Sch
CF32 . . . . 103 E6
Blaengarw Rd CF32 . . . . 103 D7
Blaengwawr Cl CF44 . . . . 53 B8
Blaengwawr Comp Sch
CF44 . . . . 53 B8
Blaengwrach Prim Sch
SA11 . . . . 227 B8
Blaenhonddan Prim Sch
SA10 . . . . 48 D3

Blaenlau St **1** CF40 . . 106 F4
Blaenllechau Cty Inf Sch
CF43 . . . . 79 F8
Blaenllechau Rd CF43 . . 80 A7
Blaenmorfa SA4 . . . . 19 C3
Blaennantygroes Rd
CF44 . . . . 29 E1
Blaenogwr Terr CF32 . . 104 F6
Blaenrhondda Rd
CF42 . . . . 50 D3
Blaenrhondda Waterfalls
Wlk CF42 . . . . 26 C1
Blaenwern
Cwmbran NP44 . . . . 89 F6
Neath SA10 . . . . 48 E2
Blaenycwm Jun & Inf Sch
NP23 . . . . 8 C3
Blaenymaes Prim Sch
SA5 . . . . 67 E7
Blagdon Cl CF3 . . . . 179 B5
Blaina & District Hospl
NP23 . . . . 15 D8
Blaina Cl CF3 . . . . 179 F7
Blaina Inf Sch NP13 . . . . 15 E4
Blaina Jun Sch NP13 . . . 15 E1
Blair Way SA12 . . . . 98 F2
Blaise Pl CF11 . . . . 194 E2
Blake Ct **8** CF10 . . . . . 195 C4
Blake Rd NP19 . . . . 144 B3
Blake St CF43 . . . . 52 B1
Blanch St CF40 . . . . 107 A2
Blanche Cl NP10 . . . . . . 163 F6
Blanche St
Cardiff CF24 . . . . 195 E7
Dowlais CF48 . . . . 11 C4
Pontypridd CF37 . . . . . . 109 C2
Blandings Ct CF23 . . . . . 178 C6
Blandon Way CF14 . . . . 177 B4
Blandy Terr
Gilfach Goch CF39 . . . . 106 C1
Nant-y-Moel CF32 . . . . 104 F6
Ogmore Vale CF32 . . . . 104 E1
Pontycymer CF32 . . . . . 103 F3
Blanthorn Ct **1** CF14 . 176 F6
Blenheim Cl CF62 . . . . . 214 C7
Blenheim Cl NP44 . . . . . . 89 C2
Blenheim Rd
Abertillery NP13 . . . . . . 36 C3
Cardiff CF23 . . . . 178 D1
Cwmbran NP44 . . . . 89 C2
Newport NP19 . . . . 144 A5
Blenheim Sq NP44 . . . . . 89 C2
Bleriot Cl NP19 . . . . 144 A3
Blewitt St NP20 . . . . 143 B4
Blodwen Rd NP4 . . . . 63 A4
Blodwen St SA12 . . . . 98 F1
Blodwen Terr SA4 . . . . . . 64 F4
Blodwen Way NP4 . . . . . . 63 A4
Bloom St CF11 . . . . 194 C4
Bloomfield Rd NP12 . . . . . 85 D7
Blorenge Terr **1** NP4 . . . 17 C7
Bloss Terr CF39 . . . . 107 F2
Blosse Rd CF14 . . . . 177 A2
Blosse St CF34 . . . . 102 A6
Blossom Cl NP18 . . . . . . 145 B8
Blossom Dr CF44 . . . . . . 160 A4
Blue Anchor Rd SA4 . . . . 64 F3
Blue House Rd CF14 . . . 177 E8
Bluebell Cl NP44 . . . . 88 F2
Bluebell Dr CF3 . . . . 179 D8
Bluebell Way
Rogerstone NP10 . . . . . 141 D7
Swansea SA5 . . . . 68 A5
Bluett's Rd CF5 . . . . 37 C5
Blundell Ave CF36 . . . . . 182 F6
Blyth Cl CF62 . . . . 205 A1
Blythe St NP13 . . . . 36 B5
Board St CF81 . . . . 12 F1
Boarlands The SA3 . . . . . 231 A4
Bodalaw CF48 . . . . 11 B4
Bodnant Cl CF3 . . . . 179 F6
Bodringallt Ct CF41 . . . . . 79 D3
Bodringallt Prim Sch
CF41 . . . . 79 D3
Bodringallt Terr CF41 . . . 79 C3
Bodwenarth Rd CF37 . . . 109 F4
Bog Rd SA7,SA10 . . . . . . 69 E4
Bogey Rd CF48 . . . . 31 B8
Bohun St SA5 . . . . 68 C3
Boi Cl CF45 . . . . 54 B3
Boiler House Rd
CF62 . . . . 211 E1
Boleyn Wlk CF23 . . . . . . 178 C1
Bolgoed Rd SA4 . . . . 19 C2
Bolt Cl NP20 . . . . 143 D3
Bolt St NP20 . . . . 143 D3
Bolton Rd NP20 . . . . 143 A4
Bolts Row NP19 . . . . 144 B5
Bon-y-Maen Rd SA1 . . . . 69 A3
Bona Rd CF71 . . . . 199 C5
Boncath Rd CF14 . . . . . . 177 A2
Bond Ave SA15 . . . . 40 E4
Bond St Aberdare CF44 . . 29 A1
Newport NP19 . . . . 143 C6
Swansea SA1 . . . . 68 A5
Bondfield Ho **5** SA12 . . 98 F1
Bonllwyn SA18 . . . . 219 B8
Bont Cl NP12 . . . . 85 D7
Bontnewydd Terr
CF46 . . . . 83 C7
Bonville Terr SA1 . . . . . . 95 A6
Bonvilston Rd CF37 . . . . 109 D2

Bonvilston Terr **2**
CF37 . . . . 109 D2
Booker St CF24 . . . . 195 E7
Boon Cl CF63 . . . . 215 A7
Boot La **5** NP4 . . . . 17 C6
Boot The CF82 . . . . 85 A1
Booth Ho SA12 . . . . 98 A3
Borage Cl CF23 . . . . 160 E1
Border Rd SA12 . . . . 98 C3
Borfa Pl NP12 . . . . 85 C7
Borough Ave CF62 . . . . . 214 E8
Borough Cl CF71 . . . . . . 188 F1
Borough Rd SA4 . . . . 42 F2
Borough St SA12 . . . . . . 124 F8
Borrowdale Cl CF23 . . . . 178 C2
Borth Rd CF3 . . . . 179 D5
Bosco La SA3 . . . . 121 B3
Bosham Dr NP20 . . . . . . 142 F2
Bosworth Dr NP20 . . . . . 143 A7
Bosworth Rd SA10 . . . . . . 70 F7
Boulevard De Nantes
CF10 . . . . 195 A6
Boulevard The NP20 . . . . 14 E3
Boundary St NP23 . . . . . . 8 B4
Bournville Rd NP13 . . . . 15 E1
Bournville Terr NP22 . . . . 13 C7
Boverton Brook CF61 . . . 210 C5
Boverton Ct CF61 . . . . . 210 C6
Boverton Park Dr
CF61 . . . . 210 C5
Boverton Pk CF61 . . . . . 210 B7
Boverton Rd CF61 . . . . . 209 F6
Boverton St CF23 . . . . . 178 B1
Bovil Cl CF83 . . . . 140 A7
Bow St CF5 . . . . 193 A2
Bowden Rd SA11 . . . . 71 E6
Bowen Cl NP4 . . . . 17 C6
Bowen Ind Est NP12 . . . . 58 C2
Bowen Pl **2** NP20 . . . . 143 C3
Bowen St Neath SA11 . . . 71 D6
Swansea SA1 . . . . 68 D2
Bowen Terr SA15 . . . . . . 40 F3
Bower St CF33 . . . . 148 C1
Bowham Ave CF31 . . . . . 168 E2
Bowleaze NP44 . . . . 89 B3
Bowls La CF83 . . . . 137 D7
Bowls Terr CF83 . . . . 137 E5
Bowman's Way CF71 . . . 188 D2
Bowman's Well CF71 . . . 188 D2
Box Cotts CF32 . . . . 150 C7
Box Rd SA4 . . . . 43 B7
Box Terr
Coytrahen CF32 . . . . . . 150 C4
3 Llanelli SA15 . . . . . 40 F6
Boxer Ind Est NP18 . . . . 118 A4
Boxtree Cl NP18 . . . . . . 117 E2
Boyle Ct NP20 . . . . 116 F2
Brachdy Cl CF3 . . . . 179 B2
Brachdy La CF3 . . . . 179 B2
Brachdy Rd CF3 . . . . 179 B2
Bracken Pl CF5 . . . . 176 D1
Bracken Rd
Margam SA13 . . . . 125 E4
Neath SA11 . . . . 71 F8
Bracken Rise CF44 . . . . . 29 D1
Bracken Way CF31 . . . . . 150 F1
Brackla Ind Est CF31 . . . 169 C7
Brackla Inf Sch CF31 . . . 169 B5
Brackla Jun Sch
CF31 . . . . 169 B5
Brackla St CF31 . . . . 168 F4
Brackla Street Ctr **7**
CF31 . . . . 168 F4
Brackla Way CF31 . . . . . 169 C5
Bradenham Pl **5**
CF64 . . . . 207 A4
Brades The NP18 . . . . . . 118 B3
Bradfield Ave CF36 . . . . 168 D5
Bradfield Rd CF31 . . . . . 168 D4
Bradford Pl CF64 . . . . . . 207 B4
Bradford St
Caerphilly CF83 . . . . . . 138 A2
Cardiff CF11 . . . . 195 A2
1 Llanelli SA15 . . . . . 40 F6
Bradley Cl CF47 . . . . 10 F2
Bradley St
Abercynon CF45 . . . . . . 82 D2
Cardiff CF24 . . . . 195 E7
Braeval St CF24 . . . . 195 B8
Bragdu CF35 . . . . 170 B8
Brahms Ave SA12 . . . . . . 98 B3
Braichycymer Rd
CF32 . . . . 103 E3
Brain Cl NP19 . . . . 145 A6
Bramble Ave CF62 . . . . . 214 D6
Bramble Cl
Bridgend CF31 . . . . 169 C4
Cardiff CF5 . . . . 176 B1
Merthyr Tydfil CF47 . . . . 10 C4
Bramble Rise CF64 . . . . 206 E5
Bramblewood Cl
Baglan SA12 . . . . 98 E5
Cardiff CF14 . . . . 159 C4
Brambling Dr CF14 . . . . 159 C4
Bramley Cl NP18 . . . . . . 145 C8
Bramley Dr SA3 . . . . 122 F6
Bramshill Dr CF23 . . . . . 161 B1
Bran Cl SA7 . . . . 69 C7
Bran-y-Garth NP44 . . . . . 90 B2
Brandon Cres SA4 . . . . . 69 D5
Brandreth Rd CF23 . . . . 178 B2
Brandy Cove Rd SA3 . . . 123 B4
Brandy Cove Rd SA3 . . . 123 B4
Brangwyn Ave NP44 . . . 117 A8
Brangwyn Cl
4 Penarth CF64 . . . . 206 F5

Brangwyn Cl continued
Swansea SA6 . . . . 45 E2
Brangwyn Cres NP19 . . 143 F7
Brangwyn Rd NP22 . . . . 13 D5
Branksome Ho **1**
CF10 . . . . 195 A5
Bransby Rd CF40 . . . . . . 107 A5
Branwen Cl CF5 . . . . 193 A2
Branwen Gdns SA1 . . . . . 68 B1
Braunton Ave CF3 . . . . . 179 D6
Braunton Cres CF3 . . . . 179 B6
Brayford Pl CF3 . . . . 179 C8
Brayley Rd SA6 . . . . 45 F2
Breaksea Cl CF64 . . . . . 216 B4
Breaksea Ct CF62 . . . . . 214 F2
Breaksea Dr CF62 . . . . . 214 F2
Brean Cl CF64 . . . . 216 C5
Brechfa Cl NP18 . . . . 117 E7
Brecon Cl CF64 . . . . 216 C5
Brecon Ct Barry CF62 . . 215 A6
8 Cardiff CF5 . . . . . . 194 C6
Brecon Ho
7 Penarth CF64 . . . . 206 F2
Port Talbot SA12 . . . . . . 124 D8
Brecon Hts NP23 . . . . . . 14 E2
Brecon Park Cotts NP7 . .9 C5
Brecon Pl CF47 . . . . 53 D7
Brecon Rd
Abercraf SA9 . . . . 222 B7
Hirwaun CF44 . . . . 27 D7
Merthyr Tydfil CF47 . . . . 10 B3
Merthyr Tydfil CF47 . . . . 10 D3
Newport NP19 . . . . 143 F7
Pontardawe SA8 . . . . . . 23 F6
Ystradgynlais SA9 . . . . . 1 F1
Ystradgynlais SA9 . . . . 222 A6
Brecon Terr Deri CF81 . . 57 B8
Tredegar NP22 . . . . .5 F1
Brecon Way CF38 . . . . . 135 F2
Brecon Wlk NP44 . . . . . . 89 D3
Bredenbury Gdns
CF36 . . . . 165 E1
Bredon Cl NP11 . . . . 115 C1
Brendon Cl **2** CF3 . . . 179 C6
Brendon View Cl
CF62 . . . . 213 A2
Brenig Cl Barry CF62 . . 214 C6
Cardiff CF14 . . . . 159 F3
Brenig Rd SA5 . . . . 68 A4
Brenroy Rd CF71 . . . . . . 199 C4
Brentwood Ct CF14 . . . . 159 F1
Brentwood Pl NP23 . . . . . 7 C1
Breon Rd CF64 . . . . 215 E6
Bres Rd SA15 . . . . 40 D5
Brett Rd NP11 . . . . 87 C3
Brettenham St SA15 . . . . 40 C6
Brewer St CF81 . . . . 32 F8
Brewery Ct NP13 . . . . 36 A1
Brewery La
Bridgend CF31 . . . . 168 E5
Cefn Coed CF48 . . . . 10 A4
Brewery Terr
Abertillery NP13 . . . . . . 35 F1
Tylorstown CF43 . . . . . . 107 C8
Brian Cres CF36 . . . . . . 182 F7
Brianne Dr CF14 . . . . . . 159 F3
Briar Cl Cardiff CF5 . . . . 193 C4
Ebbw Vale NP23 . . . . 7 C5
Briar Dene SA2 . . . . 94 B6
Briar Rd Aberdare CF44 . 53 F7
Port Talbot SA12 . . . . . . 98 C1
Briar Way
Church Village CF38 . . . 136 A1
Hirwaun CF44 . . . . 27 C8
Briar's Ct SA5 . . . . 67 F6
Briarmeadow Dr
CF14 . . . . 159 E3
Briarwood Cl SA10 . . . . . 48 D4
Briarwood Dr CF23 . . . . 178 D7
Briarwood Gdns SA3 . . 122 D5
Briary Way CF31 . . . . . . 169 C4
Brick Row
Maesteg CF34 . . . . 102 C1
Seven Sisters SA10 . . . 222 C3
Brick St SA13 . . . . 227 C2
Brickfield Cres CF47 . . . 30 E8
Brickyard Bsns Pk
CF14 . . . . 177 D2
Brickyard Cotts
Abercraf SA9 . . . . 222 B7
Neath SA11 . . . . 71 E8
Brickyard Rd SA5 . . . . . . 67 F3
Brickyard The CF36 . . . . 183 C7
Bridesvale Gdns
NP10 . . . . 163 E1
Bridge Rd
Aberdare CF44 . . . . 53 E8
Cardiff CF3 . . . . 161 C1
Cardiff CF5,CF14 . . . . . 176 F2
Llanbleddian CF71 . . . . 200 D8
Upper Boat CF37 . . . . . 136 D2
Waunarlwydd SA5 . . . . . 66 E4
Bridge St
Abercarn NP11 . . . . 87 A3
Aberdare CF44 . . . . 29 A3
Aberfan CF48 . . . . 55 C5
Abertillery NP13 . . . . . . 36 A5
Abertillery NP13 . . . . . . 36 C2
Bargoed CF81 . . . . 58 A5

Bridge St continued
Barry CF63 . . . . 215 B7
18 Blaenavon NP4 . . . . 17 C6
Blaengarw CF32 . . . . . . 103 E6
Caerphilly NP12 . . . . 85 F6
Cardiff CF10 . . . . 195 B5
Cardiff CF5 . . . . 177 A1
Cwm-twrch Isaf SA9 . . . . 1 B1
Ebbw Vale NP23 . . . . .7 D1
Glais SA7 . . . . 47 A6
Glyncorrwg SA13 . . . . . 227 C2
Llanelli SA15 . . . . 40 D6
Llangennech SA14 . . . . . 42 C8
Maesteg CF34 . . . . 102 B3
Neath SA11 . . . . 71 E8
Newbridge NP11 . . . . . . 87 A6
Newport NP20 . . . . 143 B5
Ogmore Vale CF32 . . . . 130 E8
Penarth CF64 . . . . 206 F5
Penygroes SA14 . . . . . . 218 D8
Pontypool NP4 . . . . 62 C3
Pontypridd CF37 . . . . . 109 C1
3 Pontypridd CF37 . . 135 C7
3 Port Talbot SA13 . . 125 C8
Pyle CF33 . . . . 148 C2
Risca NP11 . . . . 114 F2
Swansea SA1 . . . . 68 C1
Tonypandy CF40 . . . . . 106 F5
Tredegar NP22 . . . . 13 C6
Trehafod CF37 . . . . 108 C3
Troedyrhiw CF48 . . . . . . 31 C1
Ynysddu NP11 . . . . 112 F6
Bridge Street Ind Est
NP22 . . . . 13 C6
Bridge Terr
Michaelston-y-Fedw
CF3 . . . . 162 A7
2 Port Talbot SA13 . . 125 C8
Bridgefield St CF37 . . . . 137 A8
Bridgeman Ct CF64 . . . . 207 B3
Bridgeman Rd CF64 . . . 207 B3
Bridgend Bsns Ctr
CF31 . . . . 169 E3
Bridgend Coll CF31 . . . . 168 F3
Bridgend Ind Est
Bridgend CF31 . . . . 169 E3
Bridgend CF31 . . . . 169 C3
Bridgend PRU CF32 . . . 150 D4
Bridgend Rd
Aberkenfig CF32 . . . . . 150 C4
Bryncae CF72 . . . . 153 F2
Laleston CF32,CF36 . . 167 B2
Maesteg CF34 . . . . 102 C2
Pen-y-fai CF32 . . . . 150 D2
Pont Rhyd-y-cyff CF34 . 128 D6
Pontycymer CF32 . . . . . 103 E2
Porthcawl CF36 . . . . . . 183 D8
Bridgend Sta CF31 . . . . 168 F4
Bridgewater Rd CF3 . . . 179 C6
Bridle Mews SA3 . . . . . . 123 C3
Bridle Rd CF3 . . . . 179 B6
Brierley Cl NP11 . . . . 115 C1
Brierley La CF31 . . . . . . 168 F2
Brierly Pl NP11 . . . . 114 B8
Briers Gate NP44 . . . . . . 115 E8
Briery Ct NP23 . . . . .14 D6
Briery Hill Jun & Inf Sch
NP23 . . . . 14 D6
Brig-y-Don Hill SA4 . . . . 184 D2
Brigantine Pl CF10 . . . . 195 C4
Brigham Ct CF83 . . . . . . 137 C4
Bright St NP11 . . . . 114 C4
Brighton Rd SA4 . . . . 43 C2
Brights La **6** NP4 . . . . . 17 D6
Brin Williams Ho **1**
NP20 . . . . 143 A4
Brindley Rd CF11 . . . . . . 194 D1
Brisbane Ct NP12 . . . . . . 85 C6
Bristol Ho NP4 . . . . 62 A8
Bristol Terr
Bargoed CF81 . . . . 58 A5
New Tredegar NP24 . . . . 58 A8
Taffs Well CF15 . . . . 157 F4
Bristol View Cl NP44 . . . . 89 A4
Britannia Ctr for
Enterprise NP12 . . . . . 58 C1
Britannia Quay CF10 . . 195 C2
Britannia Rd SA6 . . . . . . 68 E5
Britannia St CF39 . . . . . 108 A2
Britannia Terr NP12 . . . . 58 B1
Britannia Villas NP12 . . . 58 B1
Britannia Wlk NP12 . . . . 58 B2
Brithdir St CF24 . . . . 177 F1
Brithdir Sta NP24 . . . . . . 58 A8
Brithwen Rd SA5 . . . . . . 66 D3
Brithweunydd Rd
CF40 . . . . 107 A5
British Legion Dr
CF3 . . . . 179 B4
British Rd NP4 . . . . 37 C4
British School Cl NP4 . . . 37 C4
Briton Ferry Ind Est
SA12 . . . . 98 B8
Briton Ferry Rd SA11 . . . 71 E6
Briton Ferry Specl Sch
SA11 . . . . 71 D3
Briton Ferry Sta SA11 . . 71 C2
Briton Ferry Workshops
Ind Est SA11 . . . . 98 A8
Briton Ho **6** SA12 . . . . . 98 C3
Brittania Cl NP11 . . . . . . 115 A1
Brittania Pl CF43 . . . . . . 80 A5
Britten Cl NP19 . . . . 144 D4
Britten Rd CF64 . . . . 206 F1

Britway Rd CF64 . . . . . . 206 A3
Brixham CF33 . . . . 166 A8
Bro Athro CF3 . . . . 179 D4
Bro Dawel Dunvant SA2 . 93 D7
Pontyclun CF72 . . . . 173 A6
Swansea SA6 . . . . 45 C2
Bro Dedwydd SA2 . . . . . 93 D8
Bro Deg CF44 . . . . 53 F8
Bro Dirion
Bridgend CF31 . . . . 168 B4
Dunvant SA2 . . . . 93 D8
Bro Nant Fer SA18 . . . . 220 D7
Bro Ryan SA18 . . . . 220 A8
Bro-Deg CF35 . . . . 170 D8
Bro-Wen SA14 . . . . 41 C5
Bro-y-Fan CF83 . . . . 138 D5
Bro-y-Ffrwd CF48 . . . . . 225 F2
Broad Cl CF62 . . . . 214 B5
Broad Oak Way CF31 . . 168 B5
Broad Pl CF11 . . . . 194 C5
Broad Quay Rd NP19 . . 164 C6
Broad Shoard The
CF71 . . . . 188 C2
Broad St
Abersychan NP4 . . . . . . 37 F3
Barry CF62 . . . . 214 D4
Blaenavon NP4 . . . . 17 C6
Cardiff CF11 . . . . 194 C5
Dowlais CF48 . . . . 11 A4
12 Merthyr Tydfil CF47 . 30 D7
Newport NP20 . . . . 143 D3
Pontypool NP4 . . . . 62 E3
Port Talbot SA13 . . . . . 125 C8
Broad Street Par
CF62 . . . . 214 D3
Broad View
Cwmbran NP44 . . . . 89 C5
Tondu CF32 . . . . 150 C6
Broadacre CF44 . . . . 93 C2
Broadacres CF11 . . . . . . 194 C5
Broadcommon Cl
NP19 . . . . 144 C3
Broadfield Cl CF40 . . . . 107 A4
Broadfield Ct CF5 . . . . . 193 D4
Broadhaven CF11 . . . . . 194 C4
Broadlands Ct **4** CF3 . 179 E7
Broadlands Ho **5**
CF3 . . . . 179 E7
Broadmead Bryn NP12 . . 85 D4
Killay SA2 . . . . 93 D4
Broadmead Cres SA3 . . 122 B6
Broadmead Pk NP19 . . 144 D3
Broadoak Ct SA4 . . . . . . 42 E1
Broadparks SA3 . . . . . . 122 F8
Broadstairs Rd CF11 . . . 194 C5
Broadview Cl SA3 . . . . . 123 B4
Broadview La SA3 . . . . . 123 B4
Broadwalk NP18 . . . . . . 118 B2
Broadwater Rd NP19 . . 144 C1
Broadway
Cardiff CF24 . . . . 195 D2
Llanbleddian CF71 . . . . 188 E1
Pontypool NP4 . . . . 62 B6
Pontypridd CF37 . . . . . 135 D8
Swansea SA2 . . . . 94 D7
Broadway Ct SA2 . . . . . . 94 D7
Broadway Gn CF5 . . . . . 192 A1
Broadweir Rd NP44 . . . . 89 F2
Broadwell Cl **4** CF3 . . 179 F6
Broadwood Cl NP18 . . . 118 B2
Broadwood Cl NP19 . . . 144 E5
Brocastle Ave CF31 . . . . 169 F2
Brocastle Rd CF14 . . . . . 177 B6
Brock St CF63 . . . . 215 B4
Brockhampton Rd
CF3 . . . . 179 F7
Brockhill Rise CF64 . . . . 217 A8
Brockhill Way CF64 . . . . 217 A8
Brodawel
Ammanford SA18 . . . . . 219 C6
Cimla SA11 . . . . 72 B6
Maesteg CF34 . . . . 102 B3
Merthyr Tydfil CF47 . . . . 30 F7
Penywaun CF44 . . . . . . 223 F2
Brodawel Cl SA11 . . . . . 223 F2
Brodeg CF15 . . . . 175 C8
Brodorion Dr SA6 . . . . . . 45 E3
Brokesby Cl SA1 . . . . 69 A3
Brokesby Rd SA1 . . . . . . 69 A3
Brombil SA13 . . . . 125 F4
Brombil Ct SA13 . . . . . . 125 F4
Brombil Gdns SA13 . . . . 125 F4
Brombil St SA13 . . . . . . 125 D5
Bromfield Pl CF64 . . . . . 207 B5
Bromfield Rd CF62 . . . . 214 E4
Bromfield St CF11 . . . . . 194 C2
Bromley Dr CF5 . . . . 193 E6
Brompton Pl NP22 . . . . . 14 A3
Bromsgrove St CF11 . . . 194 F2
Bron Afon SA4 . . . . 44 B5
Bron Afon Uchaf SA4 . . . 44 B5
Bron Allt SA10 . . . . 226 A7
Bron Awelon CF62 . . . . . 214 B3
Bron Deg CF66 . . . . 56 D1
Bron Felen CF14 . . . . . . 159 D2
Bron Hafod CF31 . . . . . . 168 B2
Bron Las CF82 . . . . 84 F6
Bron Rhiw CF83 . . . . 139 F7
Bron Yr Allt SA9 . . . . .2 A8
Bron-y-Bryn SA2 . . . . 93 C4
Bron-y-De NP23 . . . . 14 C7
Bron-y-Deri CF45 . . . . . . 54 E3
Bron-y-Garth CF82 . . . . . 84 E7
Bron-y-Mor CF62 . . . . . . 214 C2
Bron-y-Waun CF34 . . . . 102 D2

Bron-y-Wawr CF33 ..148 A1
Bronallt Terr CF44 ...53 F4
Bronawelon NP11 ......60 B2
Broncynon Terr CF44 ..28 D3
Brondeg
 Heolgerrig CF48 ......10 B1
 Swansea SA5 ....68 B3
Brondeg Cres SA5 ...68 B3
Brondeg La SA8 ......23 F3
Brondeg St SF43 ......80 B2
Brondeg Terr CF44 ....28 F1
Bronhafod NP23 ......8 C5
Bronhall CF72 ......155 C2
Bronhaul CF15 .....175 C8
Bronheulwen CF39 ....107 D4
Broniestyn Terr
 Aberdare CF44 ....28 F1
 Hirwaun CF44 ....27 D8
Bronllan SA1 ....69 D5
Bronllwyn CF15 ....175 B8
Bronllwyn Rd CF41 ...79 B2
Bronllys CF44 ....28 B6
Bronllys Pl NP44 .....90 A5
Bronmynnyd CF83 ...137 A6
Bronrhiw Ave CF83 ..138 B1
Bronrhiw Fach CF83 .138 B1
Bronte Cl CF3 ......179 C8
Bronte Cres CF3 ....179 C8
Bronte Gr NP20 ......142 E2
Bronte Ho 7 SA12 ..98 F1
Bronwydd SA7 ....70 C8
Bronwydd Ave CF23 ..178 D2
Bronwydd Cl CF23 ...178 D2
Bronwydd Rd CF24 ..196 A8
Bronynawr SA8 ......23 E5
Brook Ct CF5 ......193 F7
Brook La
 Pontllanfraith NP12 ...86 A4
 St Nicholas CF5 ....203 F8
 Treorchy CF41 ....79 B2
Brook Pl Cwm NP23 ...35 A7
Brook Rd Cardiff CF14 .177 B4
 Cardiff CF5 ....193 F7
Brook Row
 Bryncethin CF32 .....151 A5
 Fochriw CF81 ....32 C7
Brook St Abercarn NP11 87 B4
 Aberdare CF44 ....53 C7
 Abertridwr CF83 ....137 A8
 Barry CF63 ....215 A5
 Blaenrhondda CF42 ...50 D4
 Bridgend CF31 ......168 F5
 Brynmawr NP23 ......8 B4
 Cardiff CF11 ....194 F5
 Cwmbran NP44 ....89 E7
 Ferndale CF43 ....79 F6
 Maerdy CF43 ....52 B1
 Mountain Ash CF45 ...54 D2
 Neath SA10 ....70 F7
 Pontypridd CF37 ....135 E6
 Port Talbot SA13 ...125 C2
 Porth CF39 ....107 A3
 Treorchy CF42 ....78 E6
 Ystrad CF41 ....79 D2
Brook Terr
 Gwaun-Cae-Gurwen
  SA18 ....220 E7
 Llanharan CF72 .....220 E7
Brookbank Cl CF44 ...29 D1
Brookdale St CF38 ...156 F8
Brookdale St SA11 ...71 E6
Brookfield Neath SA10 .48 B1
 Neath Abbey SA10 ...71 B8
 Ynysybwl CF37 .....109 A6
Brookfield Ave
 Barry CF63 ....215 A4
 Rhymney NP22 ....13 A2
Brookfield Cl
 Gorseinon SA4 ....42 F3
 Newport NP19 ......144 B3
Brookfield Ct CF3 ...179 E6
Brookfield La CF37 ..109 E3
Brookfield Park Rd
 CF71 ....188 F1
Brookfield Pl SA5 ...67 E6
Brookfield Prim Sch
 NP44 ....89 E3
Brookfield Rd
 Maerdy CF43 ....79 C8
 Maesteg CF34 ......102 D2
 Pontllanfraith NP12 ..86 A4
Brookfield Terr CF48 .31 C2
Brookland Ho 2 NP44 89 E5
Brookland Rd NP11 ..115 A1
Brookland Terr
 Cwmbran NP44 ....89 E6
 Nant-y-Moel CF32 ...104 F5
Brookland View NP24 .33 F3
Brooklands
 Nelson CF46 ....83 D5
 Tredegar NP22 ....6 C2
Brooklands Cl
 Dunvant SA2 ....66 B1
 Maesycwmmer CF82 ..85 B2
 Merthyr Tydfil CF47 ..10 D3
Brooklands Cotts
 CF46 ....83 D5
Brooklands Terr
 Abercarn NP11 ......114 C7
 Abercraf SA9 ....222 D7
 Cardiff CF5 ....192 F2
 Swansea SA1 ....95 B7
Brooklands The NP13 .36 C6
Brooklea NP18 ......118 B4
Brooklyn Cl CF14 ....159 A1

Brooklyn Gdns
 Baglan SA12 ....98 C4
 Mumbles SA3 ....123 A6
Brooklyn Terr
 Abertillery NP13 .....60 B6
 Mumbles SA3 ....122 F5
Brookside
 Bettws NP20 ....116 E2
 Church Village CF38 .136 A1
 Cwmbran NP44 ....89 C2
 Dinas Powys CF64 ..206 B4
 Gowerton SA4 ....66 D3
 Treoes CF35 ....170 A1
Brookside Cl
 Baglan SA12 ....98 E5
 Caerphilly CF83 ....137 B6
 Cardiff CF14 ....177 D5
 Pontypridd CF37 ....109 F4
Brookside Cres CF14 .177 D5
Brookside Ct 6 CF14 177 B5
Brookside Row NP13 ..36 B8
Brookvale Dr CF14 ..159 E3
Brookvale Rd SA3 ...122 F7
Brookview CF14 .....159 F2
Brookville Terr SA10 .70 E7
Brookway CF38 .....136 A1
Brookway Cl SA12 ...98 E5
Broom Pl CF5 ......193 D8
Broome Path NP44 ...89 C2
Broomfield Cl
 Church Village CF38 .136 A1
 Newport NP19 ......144 B3
Broomfield St CF83 .138 B2
Broomhill SA13 .....125 D6
Brotalwg CF46 ....83 B7
Broughton Ave SA5 ..67 E6
Broughton Pl 4
 CF63 ....215 A8
Broughton Rd CF71 ..198 C4
Brown Ave SA15 .....40 F2
Brown Cl NP19 ......144 A3
Brown St Ferndale CF43 80 A6
 Maesteg CF34 ......101 F5
Browning Cl
 Bridgend CF31 ......168 D6
 Cardiff CF3 ....179 B7
 Newport NP20 ......142 F2
Browns Dr SA3 .....121 A5
Bruce Knight Cl CF5 .176 E2
Bruce Rd SA5 ....67 B4
Bruce St Cardiff CF24 .178 A1
 9 Mountain Ash CF45 ..54 D3
Brummell Dr CF15 ..174 F6
Brunant Rd Clydach NP7 .9 E4
Brundall Cres CF5 ..193 A3
Brunel Ave CF14 ....142 B6
Brunel Cl Barry CF63 .215 D8
 Penpedairheol CF82 ..84 E7
 Tonna SA11 ....49 D3
Brunel Ct 3 SA1 .....95 B7
Brunel Ind Est SA12 ..99 D4
Brunel St Cardiff CF11 194 F5
 Newport NP20 ......143 D1
Brunel Way SA1 ......68 F3
Brunner Dr SA6 ......22 E1
Brunswick Mews CF5 194 C5
Brunswick St
 Cardiff CF5 ....194 C6
 9 Merthyr Tydfil CF47 ..10 D3
 Swansea SA1 ....95 B6
Bruton Pl CF5 ......177 A1
Brwyna Ave SA12 ....98 F1
Brwynen Las SA10 ...48 C2
Bryanston Rd CF64 ..215 E6
Brychan 1 SA5 ......40 F4
Brychan Pl 7 CF47 ...10 D2
Brydges Pl CF24 ....195 A8
Brymbo Ave SA13 ...125 D5
Bryn CF44 ....26 C7
Bryn Aber CF83 .....137 A8
Bryn Adar CF14 ....176 F8
Bryn Amlwg
 Hengoed CF82 ....84 F3
 North Cornelly CF33 .165 F8
Bryn Aur CF37 .....109 C6
Bryn Awel
 Bedwas CF83 ....138 F6
 Bettws CF32 ....129 E3
 Bridgend CF31 .....168 B5
 Hengoed CF82 ....85 A4
 Neath SA11 ....71 F5
 Pontypridd CF37 ....109 D6
Bryn Awelon
 Aberdare CF44 ....53 F7
 Bridgend CF31 .....168 C5
 Ebbw Vale NP23 ......7 D4
 Penpedairheol CF82 ..84 E7
Bryn Bach
 Cardiff CF14 ....177 B8
 Pontlliw SA4 ....44 C5
Bryn Bach Cotts
 CF32 ....129 D2
Bryn Bach Rd
 Brynamman SA18 ....220 D8
 Pontlliw SA4 ....44 C5
Bryn Barrwg CF62 ..214 D2
Bryn Bedd SA15 ....40 F4
Bryn Bedw CF39 ....107 E1
Bryn Bevan NP20 ...143 B8
Bryn Brithdir NP11 ...59 C3
Bryn Calch CF15 ...176 A8
Bryn Canol
 Bedwas CF83 ....138 E6
 Cefn Hengoed CF82 ..84 F5

Bryn Carno NP22 .....12 E8
Bryn Carwyn CF48 ...11 B4
Bryn Castell CF15 ...176 B7
Bryn Catwg SA10 ....48 F2
Bryn Celyn
 Cardiff CF23 ....178 F7
 Maesteg CF34 ......102 A1
 Pontardawe SA8 .....23 D5
 Swansea SA7 ....70 A6
Bryn Celyn Jun & Inf Sch
 CF23 ....178 F7
Bryn Celyn Pl NP44 ..89 D5
Bryn Celyn Rd
 Cardiff CF23 ....178 F6
 Cwmbran NP44 ....89 C5
Bryn Cl Bedwas CF83 .138 F6
 Gorseinon SA4 ....43 B3
 Gowerton SA4 ....66 D4
Bryn Coch NP23 ......7 D4
Bryn Coed SA13 .....75 E3
Bryn Cotts Bryn SA13 .100 F5
 Pontyrhyl CF32 .....129 F7
Bryn Creigiau CF72 .174 C7
Bryn Cres
 Abertillery NP13 .....60 A7
 Markham NP12 ....58 E2
Bryn Crydd CF39 ...107 D1
Bryn Cty Prim Sch
 SA14 ....41 E6
Bryn Deri
 Bridgend CF31 .....168 B5
 Ebbw Vale NP23 .....14 C7
Bryn Deri Cty Prim Sch
 CF15 ....176 B7
Bryn Derw
 Beddau CF38 ....156 A7
 Caerphilly NP12 .....58 E2
Bryn Derw Gdns SA6 .45 E2
Bryn Derwen
 Cwmdare CF44 ....28 C3
 Pontardawe SA8 .....23 D5
 Radyr CF15 ....176 A7
 Swansea SA2 ....67 B1
Bryn Ebbw NP23 ......7 D3
Bryn Eglur Rd SA6 ..68 D7
Bryn Eglwys
 Croesyceiliog NP44 ..90 A5
 Llanharan CF72 ....154 A3
 Tonypandy CF40 ....107 A2
Bryn Eglwys Ct NP23 .14 D6
Bryn Eithin
 Cwmdare CF44 ....28 C3
 Gowerton SA4 ....66 B5
Bryn Elli SA14 ......41 A7
Bryn Euraidd SA18 .219 A6
Bryn Ffynon CF39 ..107 D2
Bryn Garw NP44 .....90 A5
Bryn Glas
 Aberdare CF44 ....53 E8
 Bedwas CF83 ....138 E7
 Cardiff CF14 ....159 D2
 Cefn Cribwr CF32 ..149 C2
 Ebbw Vale NP23 ......7 C3
 Swansea SA6 ....45 C2
 Ystrad Mynach CF82 ..84 F2
Bryn Golau
 Hengoed CF82 ....85 A4
 Pontardawe SA8 .....23 F4
Bryn Goleu CF83 ...138 E7
Bryn Goleu Rd SA5 ..67 F3
Bryn Golwg CF15 ...176 B7
Bryn Gomer NP44 ...90 A5
Bryn Gorof SA9 ......2 D8
Bryn Gors CF32 ....150 E6
Bryn Gorsedd CF31 .168 F7
Bryn Gwyn Cl CF44 ..28 A6
Bryn Hafren Comp Sch
 CF62 ....204 F3
Bryn Haidd CF23 ...178 F7
Bryn Hawddgar SA6 ..46 E8
Bryn Hedydd
 Bassaleg NP10 .....141 B3
 Swansea SA6 ....45 C1
Bryn Helyg SA1 ......69 D5
Bryn Henllan
 Brynna CF72 ....153 C3
 Treherbert CF42 .....50 D4
Bryn Heol CF83 .....138 E6
Bryn Heulog
 Brynmenyn CF32 ....150 E6
 Caerphilly CF83 ....137 E5
 Heol-y-Cyw CF35 ...152 B6
 Neath SA10 ....48 C1
 Pontypool NP4 ....62 D4
 Treherbert CF42 .....51 A1
Bryn Heulog Terr
 CF83 ....139 F7
Bryn Hir CF44 ....53 F8
Bryn Hyfryd CF32 ..150 F3
Bryn Ifor
 Caerphilly CF83 ....137 D5
 Mountain Ash CF45 ..54 D2
Bryn Ilan CF37 .....135 F4
Bryn Isaf SA14 ......41 D4
Bryn Ivor CF40 .....106 F8
Bryn Kendall NP23 ...7 C3
Bryn La NP12 ....85 D3
Bryn Llawen CF33 ..148 C2
Bryn Llewelyn SA8 ..23 F3
Bryn Llidiard CF31 ..168 F4
Bryn Mair CF48 ......11 B4
Bryn Melys CF31 ...168 B2
Bryn Milwr NP44 ...116 C8
Bryn Moreia CF44 ...28 E6
Bryn Morfa
 Bridgend CF31 .....168 F5

Bryn Morfa continued
 Swansea SA1 ....69 D5
Bryn Morlais SA14 ...41 F6
Bryn Nant
 Caerphilly CF83 ....137 D6
 Fochriw CF81 ....32 D8
Bryn Nedd SA11 .....71 F5
Bryn Olwg CF37 ....109 E2
Bryn Onnen
 Penderyn CF44 .....224 D2
 Pontardawe SA8 .....23 D5
 Pyle CF33 ....148 D2
Bryn Owain CF83 ...137 E6
Bryn Parc SA6 ....68 F7
Bryn Pica NP22 ......6 F1
Bryn Pinwydden
 CF23 ....178 E8
Bryn Pl 6 SA15 .....40 C4
Bryn Pobydd CF35 ..170 D8
Bryn Prim Sch
 Bryn NP12 ....85 D3
 Bryn SA13 ....100 E5
Bryn Rd Abercarn NP11 .87 B3
 Blackwood NP12 .....85 D7
 Bridgend CF35 .....169 F4
 Bryn NP12 ....85 D3
 Bryn NP12 ....85 E3
 Brynmenyn CF32 ....150 D6
 Caerphilly NP12 .....85 D6
 Clydach SA6 ....46 D8
 Cwmllynfell SA9 ...221 B7
 Glyncorrwg SA13 ..227 C2
 Llanelli SA15 ....40 C4
 Loughor SA4 ....42 F1
 Markham NP12 ....58 D7
 Neath SA11 ....71 E6
 Ogmore Vale CF32 ..130 E8
 Penygraes SA14 ....218 D8
 Pontarddulais SA4 ...19 B4
 Pontlliw SA4 ....44 A8
 Swansea SA2 ....94 F5
 Swansea SA5 ....67 E3
 Waunarlwydd SA5 ...66 E3
 Ystradgynlais SA9 ..222 A5
Bryn Rhedyn
 Church Village CF38 .135 F2
 Llanyravon NP44 ...117 B8
 Pencoed CF35 ......170 C8
 Pontypridd CF37 ....109 D6
 Tonyrefail CF39 ....133 B5
 Treherbert CF42 .....51 B1
Bryn Rhodfa CF42 ...78 D7
Bryn Rhos
 Glanaman SA18 ....220 A8
 Llanelli SA14 ....41 C6
 Penywaun CF44 .....28 A6
Bryn Rhosog SA4 ....65 E8
Bryn Rhosyn
 Radyr CF15 ....176 A7
 Swansea SA6 ....45 C2
 Tredegar NP22 ......6 B2
Bryn Seion Ct CF41 ..79 B2
Bryn Seion St NP22 ..12 D5
Bryn Siriol
 Bettws CF32 ....129 D1
 Caerphilly CF83 ....137 D5
 Cymmer SA13 ....75 E3
 Penpedairheol CF82 ..84 F7
 Pentyrch CF15 .....175 C8
 Swansea SA6 ....67 E3
Bryn St
 Merthyr Tydfil CF47 ..30 F8
 Swansea SA5 ....67 E3
Bryn Teg Bargoed CF81 .57 F2
 Bedwas CF83 ....138 E7
 Briton Ferry SA11 ...71 B3
 Caerphilly CF83 ....137 E5
 Hengoed CF82 ....85 A3
 Swansea SA7 ....70 A4
Bryn Terr
 Abertillery NP13 .....36 B8
 Abertillery NP13 .....36 C2
 Abertillery NP13 .....60 A7
 Cefn Cribwr CF32 ..149 B2
 Clyne SA11 ....226 C4
 Cwmdare CF44 ....28 C4
 Ebbw Vale NP23 .....14 F3
 Gorseinon SA4 ....43 D1
 Hengoed CF82 ....85 A3
 1 Llanelli SA15 ....40 C4
 Llangynwyd CF34 ..129 A6
 Llantwit Fardre CF38 .156 D7
 Maesteg CF34 ....75 B2
 Merthyr Tydfil CF47 ..11 A1
 Mumbles SA3 ....123 B4
 Pontsticill CF48 ......3 F3
 Pontyclun CF72 ....172 F6
 Porth CF39 ....107 F3
 Swansea SA1 ....68 D3
 Tonypandy CF40 ....106 D6
 4 Tonypandy CF40 ..107 A4
 Treorchy CF43 ....80 B2
 Wattstown CF39 ...107 D8
 Ystrad CF41 ....79 C3
Bryn The Bedwas CF83 138 F6
 Bettws NP20 ....116 E6
 Swansea SA2 ....94 C5
Bryn Tirion SA6 .....46 E8
Bryn Varteg SA13 ..100 F5
Bryn Vernel SA14 ....42 E1
Bryn View NP23 ......8 D1
Bryn View Cl SA3 ...123 A4
Bryn Villas Blaina NP13 .15 D5
 Pontyrhyl CF32 .....129 F7
Bryn Wyndham Terr
 CF42 ....50 E3
Bryn y Gors SA6 ....45 B2

Bryn Yr Ysgol CF83 .137 D6
Bryn-Amlwg Rd SA5 ..67 E3
Bryn-Awelon Rd
 CF23 ....178 C8
Bryn-Bach Rd SA4 ...44 A8
Bryn-Bedw St CF32 .103 E7
Bryn-Dedwydd SA11 ..72 C5
Bryn-Deri Terr NP11 ..86 F8
Bryn-Dolwen CF83 ..138 E7
Bryn-Eirw CF37 .....108 C2
Bryn-Gaer SA14 .....41 A7
Bryn-Gaer Terr NP13 ..60 A7
Bryn-Garreg NP4 .....37 F5
Bryn-Glas Rd SA5 ...67 E3
Bryn-Glas Terr CF33 .148 B1
Bryn-Gwyn Rd
 Abertillery NP13 .....36 C3
 Cardiff CF23 ....178 C8
Bryn-Gwyn St CF83 .138 D7
Bryn-Hafod Jun & Inf Sch
 CF3 ....179 B8
Bryn-Hedd CF39 ....132 D5
Bryn-Heulog NP13 ...60 A7
Bryn-Howard Terr
 NP12 ....59 C2
Bryn-Hyfryd Terr
 NP11 ....114 F2
Bryn-Ithel Terr SA13 ..60 A7
Bryn-Lloi Rd SA18 ..220 A8
Bryn-Melyn St SA1 ...68 D2
Bryn-Mor Rd SA15 ...40 C4
Bryn-onen Terr 5
 CF47 ....10 E1
Bryn-Rhedyn
 Caerphilly CF83 ....138 D4
 Caerphilly NP12 .....85 D6
Bryn-Serth Rd NP23 ..7 A3
Bryn-Seton St CF48 ..11 A4
Bryn-Syfi Terr SA1 ...95 C8
Bryn-Teg Cres NP12 ..12 F3
Bryn-teg Terr 9 CF47 .10 E1
Bryn-tywod SA4 .....45 A3
Bryn-Welon Cl NP4 ..17 C6
Bryn-y-Don Rd SA1 ..95 C8
Bryn-y-Fran Ave
 CF83 ....138 F6
Bryn-y-Grug SA9 .....2 A7
Bryn-y-Gwynt NP23 ..14 B8
Bryn-y-Mor SA4 .....65 D1
Bryn-y-Mor Rd
 Gowerton SA4 ....65 F6
 Gowerton SA4 ....66 A5
 Swansea SA4 ....95 A6
Bryn-y-Nant CF23 ..178 F5
Bryn-y-Neill CF41 ...58 B4
Bryn-yr-eglwys
 Hendreforgan CF39 .132 C5
 Pentyrch CF15 .....175 C8
Bryn-yr-Orsaf CF33 .166 A8
Brynaeron CF42 .....66 C1
Brynaeron Ct SA2 ...66 C1
Brynafon Rd SA4 ....43 A3
Brynallt Terr SA15 ...40 F5
Brynamlwg Clydach SA6 22 F1
 Llanelli SA15 ....40 F6
 Pontyclun CF72 ....173 C8
 9 Tonypandy CF40 ..106 E6
Brynamlwg Rd SA4 ..43 A2
Brynamman Rd SA18 220 D7
Brynau Dr SA3 ......93 F2
Brynau Rd
 Caerphilly CF83 ....138 B3
 Taffs Well CF15 ....158 A4
Brynau Wood SA11 ..72 C6
Brynavon 19 NP4 ....17 C6
Brynavon Terr CF83 ..85 A3
Brynawel
 Aberdare CF44 ....28 F1
 Brynmawr NP23 ......8 B5
 Caerphilly CF83 ....137 D6
 Crynant SA10 ......226 A7
 Pontardawe SA8 .....23 E5
 Swansea SA7 ....70 A4
Brynawel Cl SA10 ..226 A7
Brynawel Cres SA5 ..68 D5
Brynawel Rd
 Gorseinon SA4 ....43 A2
 Ystradgynlais SA9 ....1 C1
Brynawel Terr
 Abertillery NP13 .....60 A7
 Ystradowen SA9 ...221 C7
Brynawelon
 Ammanford SA18 ...218 F8
 Cefn-bryn-brain SA9 .221 B8
 Coelbren SA10 .....222 F6
 Llanelli SA14 ....41 C6
 Nantyglo NP23 ......8 B2
 Tonna SA11 ....49 E3
Brynbach St NP22 ....6 C1
Brynbala Way CF3 ..179 C5
Brynbedw Rd CF43 ..80 B3
Brynbrain SA9 .....221 B8
Brynbryddan SA12 ...99 D5
Bryncae Ind Est CF72 153 E2
Bryncelyn Blaina NP13 .15 E6
 Nelson CF46 ....83 D3
 Swansea SA6 ....45 C1
Bryncelyn Rd SA4 ....43 A2
Bryncerdin Rd SA3 .122 E5
Bryncethin Jun & Inf Sch
 CF32 ....151 A4
Bryncethin Rd SA18 .220 C7
Bryncoch Llanelli SA14 .41 C6
 Taffs Well CF15 ....158 A4
Bryncoch CW Prim Sch
 SA10 ....48 C5
Bryncoch Rd CF32 ..150 E3
Bryncoed
 Penywaun CF44 .....28 A6

Bryncoed continued
 Radyr CF15 ....176 A6
Bryncoed Terr
 Abertridwr CF83 ...137 A8
 Penpedairheol CF82 ..84 E8
Bryncwar Rd SA14 ..218 D8
Bryncyn CF23 ......178 E8
Bryncynon CF44 .....27 E8
Bryndedwyddfa SA14 218 D8
Brynderi SA18 ......218 E8
Brynderi Cl SA4 .....44 B2
Brynderi Clos CF14 .177 C7
Brynderi Ct CF31 ...168 B5
Brynderwen CF37 ..109 F5
Brynderwen Cl CF23 .178 C4
Brynderwen Ct
 Ferndale CF43 ....79 F7
 1 Newport NP19 ...143 E6
Brynderwen Gr NP19 143 E6
Brynderwen Rd
 4 Ammanford SA18 .219 F7
 Newport NP19 ......143 E6
 Pontypridd CF37 ....109 F5
 Tonypandy CF40 ...106 F4
Bryndolau SA2 ....93 B8
Bryndu Rd CF33 ....148 C3
Bryndulais Ave
 Llanelli SA14 ....40 F7
 Seven Sisters SA10 .222 C4
Bryndulais Row SA14 222 C4
Bryneglwys Ave CF36 183 D7
Bryneglwys Gdns
 CF36 ....183 D7
Bryneinon Rd SA4 ...43 A3
Bryneithin Rd SA4 ...43 A2
Bryneithin Terr SA6 ..45 F1
Bryneithyn SA9 ......1 C1
Brynfa Terr 64 C4
Brynfab Rd CF37 ...136 B5
Brynfedw
 Bedwas CF83 ....138 C6
 Cardiff CF23 ....178 E6
Brynfedwen Cl CF42 ..51 A1
Brynffrwd Cl CF35 ..169 F3
Brynffynnon Rd SA4 ..43 A3
Brynffynon Cl CF44 ..29 A1
Brynfield Ct SA3 ....122 F4
Brynfield Rd SA3 ...122 E4
Bryngarn Rd CF35 ..152 E3
Bryngarw Ctry Pk
 CF32 ....150 E7
Bryngelli Dr SA5 ....68 C7
Bryngelli Est CF42 ...27 C7
Bryngelli Pk SA5 ....68 C7
Bryngelli Rd SA5 ....68 C7
Bryngelli Terr CF43 ..68 C7
Bryngerwn Ave CF46 .83 B5
Bryngerwn Cotts CF46 83 B5
Brynglas
 Bridgend CF31 .....168 B4
 Bryn-côch SA10 .....48 C3
 Caerphilly CF83 ....137 E5
 Cwmbran NP44 .....116 C8
 Penygroes SA14 ....218 D7
 Pontlottyn CF81 .....32 E8
Brynglas Ave
 Cwmavon SA12 ......99 D5
 Newport NP20 ......143 C8
 Pontllanfraith NP12 ..85 F4
Brynglas Cl NP20 ...117 B1
Brynglas Cres NP20 .143 B8
Brynglas Ct NP20 ...117 B1
Brynglas Dr NP20 ..117 B1
Brynglas Prim Sch (Jun &
 Inf) NP20 ....117 B1
Brynglas Rd NP20 ..143 B8
Brynglas St CF47 ....10 F3
Brynglas Terr CF34 ..75 C2
Brynglau
 Bridgend CF31 .....168 B5
 Gorseinon SA4 ....43 A2
 Llanelli SA14 ....41 A7
 Rudry CF83 ....139 B3
 Tonyrefail CF39 ....133 A5
Bryngoleu CF48 .....11 B4
Bryngoleu Cres CF43 .79 F7
Bryngoleu St NP12 ..85 C7
Bryngoleu Terr
 2 Pontllanfraith NP12 .85 F4
 Swansea SA2 ....94 D7
Bryngolwg CF44 .....53 F8
Bryngwastad Rd SA4 .43 A2
Bryngwennol CF83 .112 A5
Bryngwili Rd SA4 ....18 F3
Bryngwyn
 Caerphilly CF83 ....137 F1
 Neath SA10 ....70 C6
Bryngwyn Ave SA4 ..66 D8
Bryngwyn Bach SA14 .66 D8
Bryngwyn Cotts NP11 86 E6
Bryngwyn Pl NP4 ....62 B6
Bryngwyn Prim Sch
 NP13 ....36 C4
Bryngwyn Rd
 Ebbw Vale NP23 ......7 D4
 Llanelli SA14 ....41 A7
 Newbridge NP11 .....86 E6
 Newport NP20 ......143 A4
 Pontypool NP4 ....62 B6
Bryngwyn St
 Fleur De Lis NP12 ...85 B5
 Fleur De Lis NP12 ...85 B6
 Porth CF39 ....107 E4
Bryngwynmawr Comp Sch
 SA14 ....41 A8

Bryngyrnos St SA13 . . . .100 E5
Brynhafod Bryn SA13 . .100 E5
Tycroes SA18 . . . . .218 F5
Brynhafod Rd CF83 . . .137 A7
Brynhaulog Terr CF44 . .53 C6
Brynhenwysg CF37 . . . .108 F2
Brynheulog
Blaina NP13 . . . . .15 E5
Brynmenyn CF32 . . . . .150 D6
Cardiff CF14 . . . . .176 F5
Cardiff CF23 . . . . .178 F7
Llanelli SA14 . . . . .40 F8
Mountain Ash CF45 . . . .81 E8
Ystradgynlais SA9 . . . .222 A5
Brynheulog Ct CF32 . .150 D6
Brynheulog Pl [6]
SA13 . . . . .125 C8
Brynheulog Rd
Cymmer SA13 . . . . .75 C3
Newbridge NP11 . . . . . . .86 F7
Brynheulog Terr
Ebbw Vale NP23 . . . . . .14 C8
Merthyr Tydfil CF47 . . . .10 F3
Penybryn CF82 . . . . .84 D5
[5] Port Talbot SA13 . . .125 C8
Brynheulog Terr
[2] Cwmavon SA12 . . . . .99 D5
Porth CF39 . . . . .107 F4
Tonypandy CF40 . . . . .106 C6
Treharris CF46 . . . . .83 A5
Tylorstown CF43 . . . . . .80 B5
Brynhill CF23 . . . . . . .178 C6
Brynhill Cl CF62 . . . . .214 D6
Brynhill Terr CF35 . . . .135 E2
Brynhy Fryd CF39 . . . .132 D5
Brynhyfryd NP22 . . . . . .13 A2
Brynhyfryd
Aberdare CF44 . . . . .52 F4
Beddau CF38 . . . . .156 A7
Bedwas CF83 . . . . .138 D7
Bettws CF32 . . . . .129 D3
Caerphilly CF83 . . . . . .137 F4
Croesyceiliog NP44 . . . .90 A5
Glynneath SA11 . . . . . .223 D1
Llangennech SA14 . . . . .42 B6
Pontlliw SA4 . . . . .44 C5
Pontlottyn CF81 . . . . . . .12 E1
Pontycymer CF32 . . . . .103 F3
Radyr CF15 . . . . .176 B7
Tonypandy CF40 . . . . .106 C6
Tylorstown CF43 . . . . . .80 B4
Brynhyfryd Ave
Nantyglo NP23 . . . . .8 D1
Newport NP20 . . . . . . .143 B4
[5] Tonypandy CF40 . . .107 A4
Brynhyfryd Inf Sch
SA5 . . . . .68 C4
Brynhyfryd Jun Sch
SA1 . . . . .68 C4
Brynhyfryd Prim Sch
Abertillery NP13 . . . . . .60 B6
Briton Ferry SA11 . . . . .71 B2
Brynhyfryd Rd
Briton Ferry SA11 . . . . .71 B2
Gorseinon SA4 . . . . .43 A3
Llanelli SA15 . . . . .40 D6
Margam SA13 . . . . . . .125 E3
Newport NP20 . . . . . . .143 A4
Brynhyfryd Sq [4] SA5 .68 C4
Brynhyfryd St
Merthyr Tydfil CF47 . . . .10 F4
Pontllanfraith NP12 . . . .85 F4
Swansea SA5 . . . . .68 C4
Tonypandy CF40 . . . . .106 C7
Treorchy CF42 . . . . .78 B8
Brynhyfryd Terr
Cefn Coed CF48 . . . . . .10 A4
Ebbw Vale NP23 . . . . . .14 F2
Ferndale CF43 . . . . .79 F6
Machen CF83 . . . . .140 A7
Penpedairheol CF82 . . . .84 E8
[1] Pontypridd CF37 . .109 B1
Seven Sisters SA10 . . . .222 D4
Brynhyfryd Villas
New Tredegar NP24 . . . .33 F2
Troedyrhiw CF48 . . . . . .55 C8
Bryniago SA4 . . . . .19 E4
Bryniau Rd CF48 . . . . . .10 F6
Brynlluan SA14 . . . . . .218 B8
Brynllwchwr Rd SA4 . . .65 E8
Brynllywarch CF34 . . . .101 F1
Brynmair Cl CF44 . . . . .53 B5
Brynmair Rd CF44 . . . . .53 B5
Brynmair Terr [5] CF47 .10 F4
Brynmawr CF32 . . . . . .129 D3
Brynmawr Cl CF32 . . . .180 A7
Brynmawr Comp Sch
NP23 . . . . .8 C4
Brynmawr Cres SA18 .219 B7
Brynmawr Pl CF34 . .102 A3
Brynmawr RC Jun & Inf
Sch NP23 . . . . .8 C4
Brynmawr Rd NP23 . . . .7 F2
Brynmead SA14 . . . . . . .41 E6
Brynmead Cl SA2 . . . . . .94 C8
Brynmead Ct SA2 . . . . . .94 C8
Brynmelyn Ave SA15 . . .40 E6
Brynmenyn Bsns Ctr
CF32 . . . . .150 F5
Brynmenyn Ind Est
CF32 . . . . .150 F6
Brynmenyn Prim Sch
CF32 . . . . .150 E6
Brynmill Ave SA2 . . . . . .94 F5
Brynmill Cres SA2 . . . . .94 F5

Brynmill La SA2 . . . . . . .94 E5
Brynmill Primary Sch
SA2 . . . . .94 F5
Brynmill Terr SA2 . . . . . .94 E5
Brynmor Rd SA15 . . . . . .40 C4
Brynmorgrug SA8 . . . . . .24 A5
Brynmorlais St [1]
CF47 . . . . .10 F4
Brynmynach Ave CF82 .84 E1
Brynna Rd
Brynna CF32 . . . . .153 A3
Cwmavon SA12 . . . . . . .99 D5
Pencoed CF35 . . . . . . .153 B2
Brynnewydd Gdns SA2 94 C5
Brynnyfryd NP13 . . . . . .60 B7
Brynogwy Terr CF32 . . .104 F5
Brynonnen Ct NP44 . . .115 F8
Brynrhos Cres SA4 . . . . .44 B2
Brynsierfel SA14 . . . . . . .41 D5
Brynsierfel Sch SA14 . . .41 D5
Brynsiriol Cimla SA11 . . .72 C5
Gwaun-Cae-Gurwen
SA18 . . . . .220 D7
Hirwaun HF44 . . . . .27 E8
Llanelli SA14 . . . . .40 F7
Pontrhydyfen SA12 . . . . .73 B5
Bryntaf Aberfan CF48 . . .55 C4
Cefn Coed CF48 . . . . . .10 A4
Bryntawe Hall Cl SA6 . .46 B5
Bryntawe Rd SA6 . . . . . .46 B5
Bryntawel Terr CF40 . . .106 C7
Brynteg Abersychan NP4 37 F3
Capel Hendre SA18 . . . .218 E6
Cardiff CF14 . . . . .159 A1
Clydach SA6 . . . . .46 D7
Maesteg CF34 . . . . . . .101 F3
Seven Sisters SA10 . . . .222 C2
Treharris CF46 . . . . .83 B7
Brynteg (Lower) Sch
CF31 . . . . .168 E2
Brynteg (Upper) Sch
CF31 . . . . .168 F2
Brynteg Ave
Bridgend CF31 . . . . . . .168 F3
Pontllanfraith NP12 . . . .85 F4
Pyle CF33 . . . . .148 A1
Brynteg Cl CF23 . . . . . .178 C4
Brynteg Ct CF38 . . . . . .156 A5
Brynteg Gdns CF31 . . . .168 F2
Brynteg Ho NP23 . . . . . .36 B6
Brynteg La CF38 . . . . . .156 A5
Brynteg Pl NP4 . . . . .39 E3
Brynteg Rd Blaina NP13 15 E4
Gorseinon SA4 . . . . .43 B3
Brynteg St SA13 . . . . . .100 E5
Brynteg Terr
Ebbw Vale NP23 . . . . . .14 C8
Ferndale CF43 . . . . .80 A4
Fochriw CF81 . . . . .32 C7
New Tredegar NP24 . . . .33 F2
Tonypandy CF40 . . . . .107 B4
Bryntirion
Bedwas CF83 . . . . .138 E7
Caerphilly CF83 . . . . . .137 E5
Cardiff CF14 . . . . .177 C8
Mountain Ash CF45 . . . .82 B6
Bryntirion (Evangelical
Theological Coll of
Wales) CF31 . . . . . . .168 B4
Bryntirion Cl CF31 . . . .168 C4
Bryntirion Hill CF31 . . .168 C4
Bryntirion Hospl SA15 .40 E6
Bryntirion Inf Sch
CF31 . . . . .168 B5
Bryntirion Jun Sch
CF31 . . . . .168 C5
Bryntirion Rd
Merthyr Tydfil CF47 . . . .10 E1
Pontarddulais SA4 . . . . .19 F1
Pontlliw SA4 . . . . .44 A8
Bryntirion St CF48 . . . . .11 A5
Bryntirion Terr SA15 . . . .40 F6
Brynview Ave CF82 . . . . .84 E1
Brynwern NP4 . . . . .62 B6
Brynwern St CF48 . . . . . .11 B5
Brynygroes Cotts SA9 . . .1 F2
Brynymor Rd SA4 . . . . . .42 E2
Bryony Cl [3] CF47 . . . . .30 F8
Brython Dr CF3 . . . . . .180 A7
Brytwn Rd SA13 . . . . . . .75 A5
Buarth y Capel CF37 . . . .81 E2
Buchan NP20 . . . . .142 F2
Buckingham Cl CF14 . . .160 B2
Buckingham Cres
NP19 . . . . .143 F6
Buckingham Pl
Barry CF62 . . . . .214 C8
Newport NP19 . . . . . . .143 F6
Buckingham Rd SA1 . . . .69 A2
Buckland Dr CF41 . . . . . .79 E2
Buckland Ho [5] CF47 . . .30 D8
Buckley Cl Cardiff CF5 .176 D3
Tonypandy CF40 . . . . .106 F7
Buckley Rd CF40 . . . . . .106 F7
Bude Haven Terr
SA3 . . . . .123 A6
Bude Terr NP12 . . . . . . .85 B6
Bull Cliff Wlk CF62 . . . .214 A2
Bull Hill CF32 . . . . .185 C2
Buller St NP4 . . . . .61 E8
Bullfinch Rd CF42 . . . . .210 E6
Bullin's La SA1 . . . . .95 A7
Bullmore Rd NP18 . . . .118 E2
Bulrush Cl CF3 . . . . . . .180 B6
Bungalow Ave CF36 . . .183 A7

Bungalows The
Abersychan NP4 . . . . . .37 C7
Abertillery NP13 . . . . . .36 C4
Blaina NP13 . . . . .15 E4
Bridgend CF31 . . . . . . .168 F6
Bridgend CF31 . . . . . . .169 A3
Cwmfelinfach NP11 . . . .113 A5
Evanstown CF32 . . . . . .132 B8
Ogmore Vale CF32 . . . .130 D8
Pontyrhyl CF32 . . . . . . .130 A6
[1] Ystrad Mynach CF82 .84 F2
Bunker's Hill SA3 . . . . .230 C6
Bunyan Cl CF3 . . . . . . .179 D8
BUPA Hospl Cardiff
CF23 . . . . .178 B8
Burford St [3] NP4 . . . . . .17 C6
Burgess Pl CF11 . . . . . .194 E3
Burgesse Cres CF72 . . .155 D2
Burgley St SA5 . . . . .67 E5
Burial La CF61 . . . . . . .209 F6
Burke Ave SA12 . . . . . .124 E7
Burleigh Rd [2] NP20 . . .143 A4
Burley Pl CF62 . . . . . . .211 D7
Burlington Rd CF63 . . . .215 B5
Burlington Terr CF5 . . . .194 B7
Burman St SA1 . . . . .95 B7
Burn's Way CF37 . . . . . .135 B6
Burnaby St CF24 . . . . . .195 E6
Burne Jones Cl CF5 . . . .176 E2
Burnet Dr CF32 . . . . . . .84 E6
Burnfort Rd NP20 . . . . .142 F3
Burnham Ave
Cardiff CF3 . . . . .179 C7
Sully CF64 . . . . .216 B5
Burnham Ct [3] CF3 . . . .179 C6
Burnham Dr SA3 . . . . . .122 E6
Burns Cl Machen CF83 . .139 C6
Newport NP20 . . . . . . .142 F1
Burns Cres Barry CF62 214 F8
Bridgend CF31 . . . . . . .168 C6
Burns La NP44 . . . . .89 D2
Burns Rd SA12 . . . . . . .124 E7
Burns St CF44 . . . . .53 A4
Burnside SA11 . . . . .71 E5
Burreed Cl CF3 . . . . . . .180 B6
Burrows Chambers [1]
SA1 . . . . .95 E6
Burrows Cl SA3 . . . . . . .121 A5
Burrows La SA3 . . . . . . .228 C3
Burrows Pl SA1 . . . . .95 D6
Burrows Rd
Baglan SA12 . . . . .98 D6
Neath SA10 . . . . .70 E6
Swansea SA1 . . . . .95 B5
Burrows The CF36 . . . . .183 E7
Burry Rd SA15 . . . . .40 E1
Burry St SA15 . . . . .40 C3
Burt Pl CF10 . . . . .195 B2
Burt St CF10 . . . . .195 B1
Burton Homes NP20 . . .143 B3
Burton Rd NP19 . . . . . . .143 F8
Burton Terr CF62 . . . . . .212 B2
Burwell Cl CF23 . . . . . . .161 B1
Bush Bach NP22 . . . . . . .6 C2
Bush Rd Morriston SA6 . .46 A1
Mountain Ash CF45 . . . .54 E1
Bush Row SA11 . . . . . . .71 D5
Bush Terr NP4 . . . . .61 C4
Bushy Pk NP4 . . . . .62 A7
Bute Cres CF10 . . . . . . .195 C2
Bute Espl CF10 . . . . . . .195 B1
Bute La CF64 . . . . .207 E4
Bute Pl Abertillery NP13 59 E6
Cardiff CF10 . . . . .195 C2
Bute St Aberdare CF44 . .29 A1
Cardiff CF10 . . . . .195 B2
Cardiff CF15 . . . . .158 C1
Treherbert CF42 . . . . . . .78 D7
Bute St (Stryd Bute)
CF10 . . . . .195 B3
Bute Terr Cardiff CF10 .195 B5
Hirwaun CF44 . . . . .27 C8
New Tredegar NP24 . . . .58 A7
Butleigh Ave CF5 . . . . . .194 A7
Butleigh Terr NP22 . . . . . .6 E1
Butler's St NP4 . . . . .37 E6
Butt Lee Ct CF62 . . . . . .214 E5
Butterbur Pl CF5 . . . . . .193 A5
Buttercup Cl NP44 . . . . . .88 F1
Butterfield Dr CF23 . . . .160 E1
Buttermere Way [3]
NP19 . . . . .143 F8
Butterslade Gr SA6 . . . . .46 A4
Butterworth Cl NP19 . . .144 E5
Button Ride CF5 . . . . . .204 A8
Buttrills Cl CF62 . . . . . .214 E5
Buttrills Rd CF62 . . . . . .214 E6
Buttrills Wlk CF62 . . . . .214 E6
Buttry Terr NP12 . . . . . . .85 B5
Butts The CF71 . . . . . . .188 E2
Buxton Cl NP20 . . . . . . .142 F1
Buxton Ct CF83 . . . . . . .138 C3
Bwl Rd CF46 . . . . .83 D4
Bwlch Cres SA11 . . . . . . .72 A4
Bwlch Rd Cardiff CF5 . .193 D7
Loughor SA4 . . . . .42 E2
Neath SA11 . . . . .72 A4
Bwlch y Gwyn SA5 . . . . .20 C2
Bwlch-y-Clawdd Rd
CF32,CF42 . . . . .77 F2
Bwlch-y-Garn Rd NP23 .7 F1
Bwlffa Cotts CF41 . . . . . .79 A2
Bwlffa Rd
Cwmdare CF44 . . . . . . .28 B3
Ynystawe SA6 . . . . .46 C5
Bwrw Rd SA4 . . . . .65 D8

By Pass Rd CF31,
CF32 . . . . .168 D2
By-Ways Ct CF35 . . . . . .169 F3
Byass St SA13 . . . . .125 E4
Bynea Cty Prim Sch
SA14 . . . . .41 F3
Bynea Sta SA14 . . . . . . .41 F3
Byng Morris Cl SA2 . . . .94 B5
Byng St SA1 . . . . .68 D4
Byrd Cres CF64 . . . . . . .206 E1
Byrde Cl NP19 . . . . .144 C5
Byron Ave
Beddau CF38 . . . . .156 A5
Bridgend CF31 . . . . . . .168 C2
Byron Cl
Llantwit Major CF61 . . .210 B5
Penarth CF64 . . . . .206 F5
Byron Ho SA12 . . . . . . .124 D7
Byron Pl
Blackwood NP11 . . . . . .59 C3
Cwmbran NP44 . . . . .89 D2
Penarth CF64 . . . . .206 F5
Byron Rd
Aberbargoed CF81 . . . . .58 B3
Newport NP20 . . . . . . .142 F2
Byron St
[3] Barry CF63 . . . . . . .214 F5
Cardiff CF24 . . . . .195 C7
Cwmaman CF44 . . . . . . .53 A4
Byron Way SA2 . . . . .93 F8
Bythway Rd NP4 . . . . . . .38 B4
Bywater Row NP13 . . . . .36 B5
Byways NP44 . . . . .89 B3

C

C Row NP4 . . . . .17 A6
Ca'r Pwll CF44 . . . . . . .206 A2
Caban Cl NP10 . . . . . . .142 B7
Caban Isaac Rd SA4 . . . .64 F3
Caddick's Row NP13 . . . .15 E6
Cader Idris Cl NP11 . . . .115 C2
Cadfan Rd SA1 . . . . .95 A8
Cadlan Bethel CF48 . . . . .10 C1
Cadle Cl SA5 . . . . .67 E6
Cadle Cres SA5 . . . . . . .67 D5
Cadle Dell Pl SA5 . . . . . .67 E6
Cadle Mill SA5 . . . . .67 C7
Cadle Pl SA5 . . . . .67 E6
Cadle Prim Sch SA5 . . . .67 D5
Cadlewood Rd SA5 . . . . .67 E6
Cadman Cl CF24 . . . . . .196 A7
Cadnant Cl CF14 . . . . . .159 D1
Cadnant Rd SA5 . . . . . . .68 A5
Cadoc Cres CF63 . . . . . .215 D6
Cadoc Rd [5] NP44 . . . . .89 C6
Cadogan Cl CF24 . . . . . .196 A7
Cadogan St CF32 . . . . . .104 F5
Cadoxton Rd SA10 . . . . .71 D8
Cadoxton Sta CF63 . . . .215 C6
Cadoxton Terr SA10 . . . .49 A2
Cadrawd Rd SA1 . . . . . . .68 B1
Cadvan Rd CF5 . . . . . . .193 B6
Cadwaladr Cir [4] SA1 . .95 B8
Cadwaladr St CF45 . . . . .54 C3
Cadwgan Pl CF5 . . . . . .193 E7
Cadwgan Rd
Craig-Cefn-Parc SA6 . . . .22 B2
Treorchy CF42 . . . . .78 E6
Cadwgan Terr CF32 . . . .108 C2
Cae Bach
Llangeinor CF32 . . . . . .130 A3
Machen CF83 . . . . .139 E7
Cae Banc SA2 . . . . .94 D7
Cae Bedw CF83 . . . . . . .137 F7
Cae Bracla CF31 . . . . . .169 B5
Cae Brandi CF3 . . . . . . .180 E8
Cae Bron CF31 . . . . . . .169 B4
Cae Bryn CF31 . . . . . . .168 C4
Cae Brynton Rd NP20 143 A2
Cae Cadno CF38 . . . . . .135 D1
Cae Calch CF83 . . . . . . .137 F6
Cae Canol SA12 . . . . . . .98 E7
Cae Caradog CF83 . . . . .137 D6
Cae Celyn NP11 . . . . . . .59 D1
Cae Coed CF35 . . . . . . .152 B5
Cae Collen NP12 . . . . . . .85 D6
Cae Cotton SA14 . . . . . . .40 F6
Cae Croes Heol CF83 . .137 D1
Cae Crug SA6 . . . . .45 B1
Cae Crwn SA2 . . . . .93 E8
Cae Delyn Cl SA15 . . . . .40 B7
Cae Derw SA10 . . . . .48 C2
Cae Derwen NP44 . . . . . .89 D1
Cae Dre St CF31 . . . . . .168 E4
Cae Du Mawr CF83 . . . .137 F6
Cae Eithin SA6 . . . . .45 B2
Cae Fardre CF38 . . . . . .135 F1
Cae Felin St NP13 . . . . . .60 A6
Cae Ffynnon
Bridgend CF31 . . . . . . .169 B5
Caerphilly CF83 . . . . . .137 E6
Church Village CF38 . . .135 E2
Penybryn CF82 . . . . .84 D5
Cae Folland SA4 . . . . . . .64 C4
Cae Forgan Cotts
CF32 . . . . .130 B4
Cae Ganol CF36 . . . . . . .165 E2
Cae Gar SA14 . . . . .41 E5
Cae Garn CF35 . . . . . . .152 B6
Cae Garw Cardiff CF5 . .159 D2
Cae Gethin CF83 . . . . . .137 F6
Cae Glas Barry CF63 . . .215 B7
Caerphilly CF83 . . . . . .137 E6
Ewenny CF35 . . . . .185 E7

Cae Glas continued
Fochriw CF81 . . . . .32 C8
Gorseinon SA4 . . . . .43 C2
Nantyglo NP23 . . . . .15 D8
Pencoed CF35 . . . . . . .170 E7
Tonypandy CF40 . . . . . .107 A2
Cae Gorlan Ct NP11 . . . .87 A3
Cae Gorlan St NP11 . . . .87 B3
Cae Grawn SA4 . . . . .66 B5
Cae Gwyn Rd CF14 . . . .177 C5
Cae Leon CF62 . . . . . . .204 F1
Cae Lewis CF15 . . . . . . .158 C1
Cae Llwyd CF83 . . . . . . .138 B5
Cae Llwydy CF46 . . . . . . .83 E3
Cae Lynch SA10 . . . . . . .70 F6
Cae Maen CF14 . . . . . . .177 D4
Cae Maen Lloyd CF82 . .84 E5
Cae Mansel Rd
Gowerton SA4 . . . . .64 A4
Three Crosses SA4 . . . . .65 F3
Cae Marchog CF83 . . . . .137 F6
Cae Mawr SA10 . . . . . . .222 D3
Cae Mawr Ind Est
CF42 . . . . .78 E5
Cae Mawr Rd CF14 . . . .177 C7
Cae Mellin NP4 . . . . .39 E3
Cae Melyn NP23 . . . . .7 C2
Cae Morfa Rd SA12 . . . . .98 C2
Cae Nant Coch CF83 . . .137 D1
Cae Nant Gledyr
CF83 . . . . .137 D3
Cae Odin CF31 . . . . . . .169 B5
Cae Pandy CF83 . . . . . .138 B5
Cae Pant CF83 . . . . . . .137 F6
Cae Pen-y-Graig
CF83 . . . . .137 E7
Cae Pentice CF32 . . . . .149 A2
Cae Perllan CF31 . . . . . .169 B5
Cae Perllan Rd NP20 . . .143 A4
Cae Rex CF71 . . . . .188 C1
Cae Rhedyn
Croesyceiliog NP44 . . . . .90 B4
Pontardawe SA8 . . . . . . .24 C3
Cae Rhos CF83 . . . . . . .138 B5
Cae Rhys Ddu SA15 . . . .72 A5
Cae Rowland St SA5 . . . .68 B3
Cae Samson [1] CF5 . . .193 C4
Cae Siriol CF39 . . . . . . .107 E6
Cae Siwsan CF31 . . . . . .169 B5
Cae Stumpie CF71 . . . . .188 F1
Cae Syr Dafydd CF11 . .194 C7
Cae Talcen CF35 . . . . . .152 F1
Cae Terr SA15 . . . . .40 F5
Cae Ty Mawr CF14 . . . .176 E4
Cae Uwchllyn CF83 . . . .137 E1
Cae Yorath [8] CF14 . . .177 B5
Cae Ysgubor
Bridgend CF31 . . . . . . .169 B4
Caerphilly CF83 . . . . . .137 F6
Cefn Hengoed CF82 . . . .84 E5
Cae'r Berllan CF35 . . . . .152 F1
Cae'r Cynffig CF33 . . . .166 A8
Cae'r Efail CF35 . . . . . .152 E1
Cae'r Fferm CF83 . . . . . .137 A7
Cae'r Gerddi CF38 . . . . .135 E4
Cae'r Graig CF15 . . . . . .176 B7
Cae'r Hen Eglwys
CF31 . . . . .168 C6
Cae'r Odyn CF64 . . . . . .206 A2
Cae'r Wern CF48 . . . . . . .30 D8
Cae'r Ysgol SA10 . . . . . .49 B4
Cae'r- Llwyn Terr
NP11 . . . . .112 F7
Cae'r-bryn Terr
SA18 . . . . .218 E8
Cae'r-Odyn NP13 . . . . . .15 D5
Cae'rgwerlas CF39 . . . .133 A5
Cae-Bricks Rd SA5 . . . . .68 B2
Cae-Bryn CF83 . . . . . . .137 A7
Cae-Bryn Ave SA2 . . . . .94 C5
Cae-Coed-Erw CF31 . . .169 B6
Cae-Du-Bach [1] SA15 . .40 E6
Cae-Is-Maen SA8 . . . . . .23 C3
Cae-Nan SA6 . . . . .46 B3
Cae-Pys Rd SA5 . . . . . . .68 C5
Cae-Yr-Ebol NP44 . . . . . .89 C5
Caeau Duon CF35 . . . . .152 E1
Caebach Cl CF5 . . . . . . .192 F3
Caecerrig Rd SA4 . . . . . .19 D4
Caeconna Rd SA5 . . . . . .67 E5
Caedegar Rd SA9 . . . . . . .1 F2
Caedelyn Rd CF14 . . . . .177 A6
Caederwen Rd SA11 . . . .71 F5
Caedraw Prim Sch
CF47 . . . . .30 D8
Caedraw Rd CF47 . . . . . .30 D8
Caedu Rd
Cwmllynfell SA9 . . . . . .221 B2
Ogmore Vale CF32 . . . .104 E1
Caegarw Cty Prim Sch
CF45 . . . . .54 D3
Caeglas
Cross Hands SA14 . . . .218 B7
Cwmavon SA12 . . . . . . .99 D4
Llanelli SA14 . . . . .40 F8
Caeglas Ave CF3 . . . . . .179 B3
Caeglas Rd CF3 . . . . . . .179 C3
Caegwenith Clos SA11 49 B1
Caehopkin Cty Prim Sch
SA9 . . . . .222 A7
Caelbryn Terr CF32 . . . .150 D6
Caemaen St CF45 . . . . . .82 C5
Caemansel La SA4 . . . . . .66 A3
Caemawr SA18 . . . . .219 C6
Caemawr Gdns CF39 . . .107 E3

Caemawr Rd
Porth CF39 . . . . .107 E3
Swansea SA6 . . . . .68 E8
Caemawr Terr CF40 . . . .107 A1
Caenant [1] CF37 . . . . . .135 F6
Caenant Rd CF83 . . . . . .138 A4
Caenant Terr SA10 . . . . .70 F7
Caenewydd Cl CF5 . . . .192 F3
Caepalish Pl NP4 . . . . . . .62 A8
Caepistyll St SA1 . . . . . . .68 D1
Caer Bont Ind Est
SA9 . . . . .222 B6
Caer Bryn Rd SA14,
SA18 . . . . .218 E8
Caer Cady Cl CF23 . . . . .178 C4
Caer Castell Pl CF3 . . . .179 D5
Caer Ffynnon CF62 . . . .214 C3
Caer Gymrig CF34 . . . . .102 C3
Caer Mead Cl CF71 . . . .210 B6
Caer Newydd CF31 . . . .169 D5
Caer Salem Newydd
CF39 . . . . .107 E2
Caer St SA1 . . . . .95 D7
Caer Ty Clwyd CF61 . . .209 F7
Caer Wenallt CF14 . . . . .158 F1
Caer Wetral CF33 . . . . . .148 C2
Caer Worgan CF61 . . . . .209 F7
Caer-Gynydd Rd SA5 . . .66 F3
Caeracca Villas CF48 . . . .11 B6
Caerau Com Inf Sch
CF5 . . . . .193 C3
Caerau Court Rd CF5 193 C4
Caerau Cres NP20 . . . . .143 A4
Caerau Ct CF72 . . . . . . .155 F3
Caerau La Cardiff CF5 . .193 B2
Cardiff CF5 . . . . .193 C4
Pentyrch CF15 . . . . . . .175 D8
Wenvoe CF5 . . . . .205 A8
Caerau Park Cres
CF5 . . . . .193 C4
Caerau Park Pl [2]
CF5 . . . . .193 C4
Caerau Park Rd CF5 .193 C4
Caerau Rd Cardiff CF5 193 C4
Maesteg CF34 . . . . .75 B1
Newport NP20 . . . . . . .143 A4
Caerbragdy CF83 . . . . . .138 B3
Caerbryn NP11 . . . . .86 D5
Caerhendy St CF47 . . . . .10 F4
Caerleon (Lodge Hill) Inf
Sch NP18 . . . . .118 A3
Caerleon (Lodge Hill) Jun
Sch NP18 . . . . .117 F3
Caerleon Cl CF3 . . . . . .180 A7
Caerleon Comp Sch
NP18 . . . . .118 A4
Caerleon Ct CF83 . . . . .137 C4
Caerleon Endowed Jun
Sch NP18 . . . . .118 A2
Caerleon Gr CF48 . . . . .225 F1
Caerleon Rd
Caerleon NP18 . . . . . . .118 A5
Cardiff CF14 . . . . .177 D2
Dinas Powys CF64 . . . .206 A4
Newport NP19 . . . . . . .143 F8
Ponthir NP18,NP44 . . . .117 F2
Caerlicken La NP18 . . . .119 F5
Caerllysi CF35 . . . . .170 B8
Caernarvon Cl [1]
CF64 . . . . .206 C3
Caernarvon Cres NP44 90 A3
Caernarvon Ct CF83 . . .137 D4
Caernarvon Dr NP10 . . .141 F3
Caernarvon Gdns
CF62 . . . . .214 C8
Caernarvon Gr CF48 . . .225 F1
Caernarvon Pl NP12 . . . .58 C7
Caernarvon Rd NP10 . . .141 F3
Caernarvon Way
Cardiff CF3 . . . . .179 D5
Swansea SA1 . . . . .69 B4
Caerphilly Ave SA1 . . . . .69 C4
Caerphilly Bsns Pk
CF83 . . . . .138 C2
Caerphilly Castle
CF83 . . . . .138 B3
Caerphilly Cl
Bassaleg NP10 . . . . . . .141 E8
Dinas Powys CF64 . . . .206 C4
Caerphilly District Miners
Hospl CF83 . . . . .137 F1
Caerphilly Ent Ctr
CF83 . . . . .138 C2
Caerphilly Rd
Bassaleg NP10 . . . . . . .141 E8
Cardiff CF14 . . . . .177 C6
Nantgarw CF15 . . . . . .158 B8
Nelson CF46 . . . . .83 F3
Senghenydd CF83 . . . .110 F1
Tredomen CF46 . . . . . . .84 A3
Treharris CF46 . . . . .83 B5
Ystrad Mynach CF82 . . .111 F8
Caerphilly Sta CF83 . . . .138 B2
Caersalem Terr [2]
SA15 . . . . .40 D3
Caerwent Rd
Cardiff CF5 . . . . .193 A5
Croesyceiliog NP44 . . . . .90 A6
Pontypool NP4 . . . . .38 D1
Caesar Cres SA18 . . . . .118 A4
Caetyla Heol CF35 . . . . .169 F4
Caewal Rd CF5 . . . . . . .194 A8
Caewallis St CF31 . . . . .168 F3
Caiach Terr CF46 . . . . . .83 D6
Cairn Ct CF43 . . . . .52 B1
Cairnmuir Rd CF24 . . . .195 F7
Cairo St CF40 . . . . .107 B5
Calcot Ho NP44 . . . . . . .90 B4

Calderton Rd CF38 ....156 A6
Caldey Pl SA5 ....67 E7
Caldicot Cl
 Blackwood NP12 ......58 D1
 Swansea SA1 ....69 C4
Caldicot Ct CF83 ....137 C4
Caldicot Rd
 Cardiff CF5 ....193 D4
 Swansea SA1 ....69 C4
Caldicot Way NP44 ....89 F6
Caldwell Ct CF38 ....156 A5
Caldicott Cl **6** CF38 ..156 A5
Caldy Cl Barry CF62 ..214 E8
 Newport NP19 ....143 F7
 Porthcawl CF36 .....165 E1
Caldy Ct CF14 ......177 A3
Caldy Rd CF14 ......177 A3
Caledfryn Way CF83 ..137 D5
Calfaria Chapel Ho
 CF39 ....107 D8
Calfaria Flats CF45 ..82 E3
Callaghan Ct CF24 ...195 E6
Calland St SA6 ......68 E5
Calvert Terr **2** SA1 ...95 B7
Calyn Ct **4** NP44 .....89 A5
Cam Ct NP44 ....89 A5
Camarthen Rd SA5 ....67 E4
Cambell Ct CF63 ....215 A4
Camberwell Ave
 CF31 ....168 C6
Cambourne Ave CF14 .176 F5
Cambourne Cl CF62 ..214 C2
Cambray Cl CF36 ....182 E8
Cambria Cl NP18 ....118 C2
Cambria Rd CF5 .....193 B4
Cambria St NP4 ......62 C2
Cambrian Ave
 Hendreforgan CF39 ..132 C5
 Llantwit Major CF61 .210 A5
Cambrian Ct
 Barry CF63 ....215 A5
 Swansea SA6 ....69 A7
Cambrian Ind Est
 CF72 ....173 A8
Cambrian Ind Pk
 CF40 ....106 C6
Cambrian Pl
 Cwm-twrch Uchaf SA9 .221 C6
 5 Llanelli SA15 ....40 C4
 Pontarddulais SA4 ...19 C4
 1 Pontypridd CF37 ..135 E7
 Port Talbot SA13 ...125 C7
 Swansea SA1 ....95 E6
Cambrian Ret Ctr 4
 NP20 ....143 B5
Cambrian St Deri CF81 .57 B8
 Llanelli SA15 ....40 C4
 10 Merthyr Tydfil CF47 .10 D2
 Rhymney NP22 ....12 E5
Cambrian Terr
 Merthyr Tydfil CF47 ..10 D3
 Tonypandy CF40 .....106 E7
Cambridge Cl SA3 ....123 A3
Cambridge Ct NP18 ..117 F3
Cambridge Gdns
 Ebbw Vale NP23 ......7 D3
 Mumbles SA3 ....123 B4
Cambridge Rd
 Mumbles SA3 ....123 A4
 Newport NP19 ....143 D5
Cambridge St
 Barry CF62 ....214 C3
 Cardiff CF11 ....195 A2
 Swansea SA2 ....94 F7
Camellia Cl CF44 .....28 D3
Camellia Dr SA6 ......45 F3
Camelot Ct NP11 .....35 A8
Camelot Pl **5** NP19 ..143 D6
Camelot Way CF14 ...159 D2
Cameron Pl SA4 ......43 A2
Cameron St CF24 ....195 D6
Camffrwd Way SA6 ...46 C1
Camm's Cnr **8** CF64 .206 C3
Camnant CF82 ......111 E7
Camnant Rd SA10 ...223 A5
Camona Dr **1** SA1 ....95 D5
Campbell Dr CF11 ...207 A8
Campbell St
 Llanelli SA15 ....40 E2
 Pontypool NP4 ....62 A2
 2 Swansea SA1 ......95 C8
Campbell Terr
 Mountain Ash CF45 ...54 D3
 Tonypandy CF40 .....106 E7
Camperdown Rd
 NP19 ....144 B3
Camperly Cl **7** CF38 .156 A5
Campion Cl
 Cwmbran NP44 ......116 A8
 Newport NP19 ....143 A6
Campion Pl CF5 .....193 D4
Campton Pl CF38 ....156 B5
Camrose Ct CF62 ....214 F8
Camrose Dr SA5 ......66 E4
Camrose Rd CF5 .....193 D4
Camrose Wlk NP44 ....89 D2
Can-Yr-Aderyn SA6 ...45 D3
Can-Yr-Eos SA6 ......45 C2
Canada Rd CF14 ....177 C6
Canal Cl NP4 ....38 C2
Canal Lock Cl CF48 ...55 C3
Canal Par Cardiff CF10 195 B3
 Newport NP20 ....143 B6
Canal Park Ind Est
 CF10 ....195 A4
Canal Rd Aberdare CF44 53 E8
 Aberdare CF44 ....53 F6

Canal Rd continued
 Neath SA11 ....71 D8
Canal Row CF48 ......30 F4
Canal Side SA10 .....49 C3
Canal St NP20 ......143 B7
Canal Terr
 Abercarn NP11 ....87 A2
 Newport NP20 ....143 D3
 Ystalyfera SA9 ....2 B6
Canaston Ct SA5 .....67 F7
Canaston Pl CF5 ....193 D4
Canberra Cl
 Blackwood NP12 ......85 F8
 Cwmbran NP44 ....89 D7
Canberra Cres NP20 .142 E4
Canberra Rd CF31 ...168 F5
**Candleston Castle (rems
 of)** CF32 ....184 E7
Candleston Cl CF36 ..165 E4
Candleston Pl SA1 ....69 C3
Candwr Pk NP18 ....117 F7
Candwr Rd NP18 ....118 A6
Canford Cl NP4 ......38 B2
Canning St Cwm NP23 .35 A8
 Ton Pentre CF41 .....78 F3
Cannington Ave CF5 .179 C5
Cannington Cl CF64 .216 B5
Cannisland Pk SA3 ...92 D1
Cannon St SA18 ....220 D8
Canolfan
 Bridgend CF31 ......169 B4
 Seven Sisters SA10 ..222 C3
Canon St
 Aberdare CF44 ....29 A2
 Barry CF62 ....214 D4
 Newport NP20 ....143 D6
Canonbie Cres CF48 ..55 C3
Canopus Cl CF3 .....179 D6
Canterbury Cl 9
 NP20 ....143 C6
Canterbury Rd
 Ebbw Vale NP23 ......7 F3
 Swansea SA2 ....94 E5
Canton Ct **12** CF11 ..194 D5
Cantonian High Sch
 CF5 ....193 E8
Cantref Cl
 Cardiff CF14 ....159 F3
 Rogerstone NP10 ....142 B7
Cantref Cs SA5 ......67 E5
Capcoch Prim Sch
 CF44 ....53 E6
Capel Cres NP20 ....143 C2
Capel Ct **15** NP44 ....38 A1
Capel Ed La NP4 .....39 E7
Capel Gwilym Rd
 CF14 ....159 D4
Capel Hendre Ind Est
 SA18 ....218 A5
Capel Ifan CF31 ....133 D5
Capel Isaf Rd SA15 ...41 A6
Capel Newydd Ave
 NP4 ....17 D5
Capel Newydd Rd 3
 NP4 ....17 D6
Capel Rd Clydach SA6 .46 F8
 Llanelli SA14 ....41 A6
Capel St Bargoed CF81 .58 A4
 Pontypool NP4 ....62 C6
Capel Terr SA15 .....40 F6
Capel-Newydd La
 SA15 ....40 D6
Capital Bldgs SA9 .....2 C1
Capital Valley Ind Pk
 NP22 ....12 E2
Caple Rd CF62 ......214 C3
Captains Hill CF46 ...83 C7
Caradoc Ave CF62,
 CF63 ....215 A7
Caradoc Cl **1** CF3 ...180 A7
Caradoc Ho
 Cwmbran NP44 ....89 E4
 Mountain Ash CF45 ...54 D2
Caradoc St
 Abercarn NP11 ......114 C7
 Abersychan NP4 ......37 F3
 Merthyr Tydfil CF47 ..10 D2
 Mountain Ash CF45 ...54 D2
Caradoc Wlk **10** NP4 ..17 D7
Caradog Cl
 Bridgend CF31 ......169 A5
 Caerleon NP18 .....118 A3
Caradog Cty Prim Sch
 CF44 ....29 A1
Caradog Ho **1** CF10 .195 A6
Caradog Pl SA1 ......95 A8
Caradog Rd
 Bridgend CF31 ......169 D3
 Tylorstown CF43 .....80 B3
Caradog St SA13 ....125 D7
Caraway Cl **14** CF3 ..180 A8
Cardiff Arms Pk CF10 194 F5
Cardiff Bay Bsns Ctr
 CF24 ....195 D4
Cardiff Bay Ret Pk
 CF11 ....206 F8
**Cardiff Bay Ret Pk (Parc
 Manwertnu Bae
 Caerdydd)** CF11 ....194 F1
Cardiff Bay Sta CF10 .195 C2
Cardiff Bsns Pk CF14 177 E2
Cardiff Castle CF10 .195 A6
Cardiff Central Sta
 CF10 ....195 A4
Cardiff Centre Trad Est
 CF10 ....195 B4

**Cardiff City Farm (Ffarm
 Dinas Caerddyd)**
 CF11 ....194 C3
Cardiff Food Pk CF3 .179 D2
Cardiff Gate Ret Pk
 CF23 ....161 B2
Cardiff Gate Services
 CF23 ....161 A2
Cardiff High Sch
 CF23 ....178 B6
Cardiff Ind Pk CF14 .177 E7
Cardiff International Arena
 CF10 ....195 B5
Cardiff Pl CF42 ......78 D6
Cardiff Queen Street Sta
 CF10 ....195 B6
Cardiff Rd
 Abercynon CF45 ......82 D1
 Aberdare CF44 ....53 C7
 Bargoed CF81 ....58 A3
 Barry CF63 ....215 E6
 Caerphilly CF83 ....138 B2
 Cardiff CF5 ....194 B8
 Cowbridge CF71 ....189 A1
 Creigiau CF15 ......174 F6
 Dinas Powys CF64 ..206 A3
 Glan y Nant NP12 ....85 A7
 Llantrisant CF72 ...155 D2
 Merthyr Vale CF48 ...55 D5
 Mountain Ash CF45 ...54 E2
 Newport NP20 ....143 B3
 Pontypridd CF37 ....135 F6
 Quakers Yard CF46 ...83 B5
 Rhydyfelin CF37 ....136 B4
 St Fagans CF5 ......193 A7
 Taffs Well CF15 ....157 F5
 Treharris CF46 ......83 A6
 Treharris CF46 ......83 A7
 Trelewis CF46 ......83 C7
Cardiff Royal Infmy
 CF24 ....195 C6
Cardiff St
 Abercanaid CF48 .....30 F4
 Aberdare CF44 ....29 A2
 Ogmore Vale CF32 ..104 E2
 Treorchy CF42 ....78 D6
**Cardiff Tertiary Coll (Coleg
 Glan Hafren)** CF5 ..179 E4
**Cardiff-Wales Airport
 (Maes Awyr
 Caerdydd-Cymru)**
 CF62 ....213 B3
Cardigan Cl
 Church Village CF38 .135 F1
 Croesyceiliog NP44 ..89 F4
 Dinas Powys CF64 ..206 C3
 Porthcawl CF36 .....165 C3
Cardigan Cres
 Boverton CF61 ......210 C6
 Croesyceiliog NP44 ..89 F6
 Swansea SA1 ....69 C5
Cardigan Ct
 Caerleon NP18 .....117 F3
 6 Cardiff CF5 ......194 C6
Cardigan Ho
 2 Penarth CF64 ....206 F2
 Port Talbot SA12 ...124 D8
Cardigan Pl **1** NP19 .143 F6
Cardigan St CF5 ....194 C6
Cardigan Terr CF32 ..104 F6
Cardigan Way NP12 ...58 D1
Cardinal Dr CF14 ....160 A4
Cardinal Newman RC Sch
 CF37 ....136 B5
Cardinan Terr **2** CF44 .53 E8
Cardonnel Rd SA10 ...70 F6
Carew Cl CF62 ......214 F7
Carew Ct **7** CF14 ....177 A6
Carew Gr CF48 ......225 F1
Carew Pl SA1 ....69 C5
Carey Rd NP19 ......144 A5
Carey Wlk SA10 ......71 C8
Carfax Path NP44 ....89 B1
Cargill Cl CF38 .....156 B5
Cargo Rd CF10 ......195 D1
Caridwen Terr
 6 Llantrisant CF72 .155 D3
 Llantrisant CF72 ...155 D3
Carig Cres SA1 ......68 E1
Carig Gdns SA1 .....68 E1
Carisbrooke Rd NP19 143 F5
Carisbrooke Way
 CF23 ....178 D3
Carlin Rd NP23 ......15 D8
Carling Ct CF5 .....193 A3
Carlisle St
 Cardiff CF24 ....195 E6
 Newport NP20 ....143 D2
Carlos St **2** SA13 ...99 M8
Carlton Cl CF14 .....159 E3
Carlton Cres CF38 ..156 A5
Carlton Ct NP4 ......62 A8
Carlton Dr NP11 .....59 D3
Carlton Pl
 Abercarn NP11 ......114 C5
 Porthcawl CF36 .....182 E7
Carlton Rd Clydach SA6 22 E1
 Newport NP19 ....143 F7
Carlton Terr
 Abercarn NP11 ......114 C5
 Swansea SA1 ....95 C7
 Troedyrhiw CF48 .....31 B1
Carlyle St
 Abertillery NP13 .....36 A5
 Briton Ferry SA11 ...71 C3
Carlyon Rd NP11 .....87 B8

Carmarthen Cl
 Barry CF62 ....214 F7
 Boverton CF61 ......210 B6
Carmarthen Ct
 Caerphilly CF83 ....137 C4
 7 Cardiff CF5 ......194 C6
Carmarthen Ct CF38 .135 F2
Carmarthen Ho
 4 Cardiff CF64 ....206 F2
 6 Dinas Powys CF64 206 C3
 Port Talbot SA12 ...124 D8
Carmarthen Rd
 Cross Hands SA14 ..218 A8
 Dinas Powys CF64 ..206 C3
 Fforest SA4 ....18 F6
 Swansea SA1,SA5 ....68 B2
Carmarthen St CF5 ..194 C6
**Carmathenshire Coll of
 Tech & Art** SA18 ...219 B7
Carmel Cl **9** CF5 ......7 C5
Carmel Ct CF24 .....178 C1
Carmel Flats CF40 ..107 A5
Carmel Rd Pontlliw SA4 .43 F7
 Swansea SA1 ....69 D5
Carmel St
 Abertillery NP13 .....36 B5
 Tredegar NP22 ....6 C1
 Treherbert CF42 .....78 A8
Carmen CF34 ......102 B8
Carn Celyn CF38 ...156 A5
Carn-y-Celyn CF40 ..106 F3
Carn-y-Tyla Terr
 Abertysswg NP22 ....33 A8
 Rhymney NP22 ....13 A1
Carne Ct CF61 ......210 B6
Carne St Cwm NP23 ...35 A8
 Pentre CF41 ....78 F3
Carne Terr CF71 ....199 F8
Carnegie Dr CF23 ..178 B5
Carnetown Jun Sch
 CF45 ....82 D2
Carnglas Ave SA2 ....94 C7
Carnglas Rd SA2 ....94 C7
Carnhywel SA14 .....41 C6
Carno Ct NP23 ....7 C5
Carno Pl SA6 ....68 D8
Carno St SA6 ....12 D6
Caroline Ave CF33 ..165 F8
Caroline Ct NP4 .....63 A4
Caroline St
 Blaengwynfi SA13 ...76 C6
 Blaenrhondda CF42 ..50 C5
 Bridgend CF31 ......168 F4
 Cardiff CF10 ....195 A5
 3 Llanelli SA15 ....40 C3
 17 Newport NP20 ...143 C4
 Tonypandy CF40 ....107 A2
Caroline Terr SA13 ...76 C6
Carpenter Cl NP18 ..119 F1
Carreg Arwyn CF72 ..172 A5
Carreg Cennen Gdns
 SA1 ....69 B4
Carreg Yr Afon SA9 .221 C2
Carregamman 10
 SA18 ....219 B7
Carregamman Isaf
 SA18 ....219 B7
Carrick Ave SA15 ....40 D7
Carrog Rd SA5 ....68 B5
Carshalton Rd 8
 CF38 ....156 A5
Carswell Cl CF38 ...156 B6
Carter Pl CF5 ......176 D1
Cartersford Pl SA3 ..123 A4
Cartref SA10 ....70 F7
Cartrefle Ho NP11 ...60 A1
Cartwright Ct CF24 ..178 B1
Cartwright Gn NP20 .117 A2
Cartwright La CF5 ..193 D7
Caryl Terr SA6 ......68 E6
Carys Cl Cardiff CF5 193 A2
 Penarth CF64 ......206 E2
Cascade View CF44 ..28 C3
Casllwchwr Cty Prim Sch
 SA4 ....122 E4
Caspian Cl **6** CF3 ...179 F6
Castan Rd CF72 .....173 B7
Castell Arc SA7 .....69 C7
Castell Coch CF15 ..158 C2
Castell Coch View
 CF15 ....158 C1
Castell Ddu Rd SA4 ...19 B1
Castell Llwyd CF82 ..111 F7
Castell Meredith
 CF83 ....138 C5
Castell Morgraig
 CF83 ....138 C5
Castell Morlais CF48 ...3 C1
Castell Tal-y-van
 CF71 ....189 E7
Castell y Fan CF83 ..138 C5
Castellau Rd CF38,
 CF72 ....155 E2
Castle Acre SA3 ....123 A6
Castle Arc **3** CF10 ..195 A5
Castle Ave CF3 .....178 F2
Castle Bailey St SA1 .95 D7
Castle Bldgs CF37 ..135 E6
Castle Cl
 Abercarn NP11 ......114 C6
 Boverton CF61 ......210 C5
 Creigiau CF15 ......174 F8
 3 Dinas Powys CF64 206 C3
 Rogerstone NP10 ....142 B4

Castle Coch CF71 ...189 F2
Castle Cotts CF82 ....84 D6
Castle Cres
 Cardiff CF3 ....178 F2
 Mumbles SA3 ....123 A5
Castle Ct
 Church Village CF38 .135 F1
 Cwmbran NP44 ....115 F8
 Dinas Powys CF64 ..206 C3
 Llandough CF71 ....200 F6
 Llantwit Major CF61 .209 F6
 Loughor SA4 ....65 D8
 Maesteg CF34 ......102 A4
 Swansea SA7 ....69 B8
Castle Dr Cimla SA11 ..72 B6
 Dinas Powys CF64 ..206 C3
Castle Fields NP22 ...12 C4
Castle Gdns **2** SA1 ...95 D7
Castle Graig SA6 ....68 D5
Castle Graig Rd SA6 ..68 D5
Castle Hill
 Llanblethian CF71 ..188 C1
 Penpedairheol CF82 ..84 D6
 St Fagans CF5 ......193 A7
Castle Ivor St CF37 ..109 A1
Castle La
 Abercarn NP11 ......114 C6
 Cardiff CF24 ....195 D7
 1 Swansea SA1 .....95 D7
Castle Mdws CF35 ..169 C7
Castle Mews NP18 ..118 C1
Castle Park Cl NP20 .142 D3
Castle Park Rd NP20 142 D3
Castle Prec CF71 ...200 F6
Castle Rd Cardiff CF15 158 C2
 East Aberthaw CF62 .212 C4
 Mumbles SA3 ....123 A5
 Rhoose CF62 ....213 A1
Castle Rise CF3 ....179 A2
Castle Sq
 Merthyr Tydfil CF47 ..10 C2
 Mumbles SA3 ....123 A5
Castle St
 Aberavon SA12 ......99 A1
 Abertillery NP13 .....36 B4
 Barry CF62 ....214 C4
 Blaenavon NP4 ......17 C7
 Bridgend CF31 ......169 B2
 Caerleon NP18 .....118 C2
 Caerphilly CF83 ....138 B3
 Fleur De Lis NP12 ...85 B5
 Glyncorrwg SA13 ...222 C2
 2 Llantrisant CF72 .155 D3
 Llantwit Major CF61 .209 F7
 Loughor SA4 ....42 D1
 Maesteg CF34 ......102 B3
 Merthyr Tydfil CF47 ..10 C1
 Mumbles SA3 ....123 A5
 Neath SA10 ....70 F7
 Neath SA11 ....71 E8
 Newport NP20 ....143 C4
 Pentrebach CF48 ....31 A4
 5 Pontypridd CF37 .135 E7
 Swansea SA1 ....95 D7
 Taffs Well CF15 ....158 A3
 Tredegar NP22 ....13 E6
 Treorchy CF42 ....78 C5
Castle View
 Bridgend CF31 ......168 F6
 Caerphilly CF83 ....137 F6
 Heolgerrig CF48 .....10 B1
 Neath SA11 ....71 E8
 Tongwynlais CF15 ..176 B8
Castle Wood NP4 .....37 D5
Castle Yd CF10 ......10 D1
Castlefield Pl CF14 .177 E2
Castleford CF38 ....156 A6
Castleland St CF63 .215 A5
Castleton Ave CF42 ..50 D4
Castleton Ct CF3 ...180 C8
Castleton Rd CF3 ...211 D5
Castleton Rise CF3 .162 C3
Caswell Ave SA3 ....122 E4
Caswell Bay Rd SA3 122 A3
Caswell Cl CF44 .....27 D7
Caswell Dr SA3 .....122 D4
Caswell Rd
 Bishopston SA3 ....122 E4
 4 Cardiff CF3 ......179 B3
 Mumbles SA3 ....122 E4
Caswell St Llanelli SA15 40 E3
 Swansea SA1 ....95 B6
Caswell Way NP19 ..144 C4
Catalpa Cl NP20 ....117 B3
Cath Cob Cl CF3 ....179 E7
Cathan Cl SA5 ....67 E6
Cathan Cres SA5 ....67 E6
Cathays High Sch
 CF14 ....177 C1
Cathays Sta CF10 ...195 A7
Cathays Terr CF24 ..195 A7
**Cathedral Church of SS
 Peter & Paul with SS
 Dyfrif, Teild & Euddogwy**
 CF14 ....177 B1
Cathedral Cl CF5 ...177 B1
Cathedral Ct
 Cardiff CF5 ....177 A1
 9 Newport NP20 ...143 B4
Cathedral Gn The
 CF5 ....177 A1
Cathedral Rd
 Cardiff CF11 ....194 D7
 Cardiff CF11 ....194 E7
Cathedral Sch The
 CF5 ....194 B8

Cathedral View CF14 .177 B2
Cathedral Way CF14 ..98 D3
Cathedral Wlk 9
 CF10 ....195 A5
Catherine Cl
 Abercanaid CF48 .....30 F4
 Newport NP10 ......163 F5
Catherine Dr
 Cardiff CF15 ....158 E2
 Marshfield CF3 .....180 E8
Catherine Meazey Flats 6
 CF64 ....207 A6
Catherine St
 6 Aberavon SA12 ....98 E1
 5 Aberdare CF24 ....29 A1
 Cardiff CF24 ....195 A6
 Llanelli SA15 ....40 C3
 5 Pontypridd CF37 .109 C1
 Swansea SA1 ....95 B6
Catherine Terr CF39 .107 A2
Catholic Rd NP23 .....8 C4
Catkin Dr CF64 .....206 F6
Catsash Rd NP18 ...118 F1
Cattle St SA11 ......71 E8
Cattwg Cl CF61 .....209 F7
Cattwg Cotts CF62 ..212 B8
Cattybrook Terr 2
 SA12 ....99 F8
Catwg Prim Sch SA10 .48 F2
Causeway Hill CF71 .200 D8
Causeway The
 Llanblethian CF71 ..200 D8
 Swansea SA2 ....94 E1
Cavan Row CF34 ....102 A4
Cave St SA5 ....68 A2
Cavell Ho SA12 ......98 F2
Cavell St SA13 .....227 C1
Cavendish Cl CF14 ..159 C2
Cavendish Pl CF38 ..156 B6
Cawdor Pl SA15 .....40 D6
Cawley Pl CF63 .....215 B7
Cawnpore St CF64 ..206 F6
Caxton Pl CF23 ....179 A8
 5 Newport NP20 ...143 B5
Caynham Ave CF64 .217 A8
Cecil Rd Gorseinon SA4 .43 C2
 Gowerton SA4 ....66 C4
Cecil Sharp Rd NP19 143 C6
Cecil St Cardiff CF24 195 D7
 Neath SA11 ....71 D6
 Swansea SA5 ....68 C3
Cedar Ave SA4 ......44 A4
Cedar Cl Aberdare CF44 28 E2
 Bryn NP12 ....212 E5
 Ebbw Vale NP23 ......7 C5
 Gowerton SA4 ....66 D4
Cedar Cres
 Church Village CF38 .136 A1
 Mumbles SA3 ....122 F8
Cedar Gdns
 Baglan SA12 ....98 D5
 Porthcawl CF36 ....183 E8
Cedar Gr CF5 ....176 C1
Cedar Ho CF14 .....176 E6
Cedar La CF37 ......136 B5
Cedar Rd
 Abertillery NP11 .....59 F5
 Neath SA11 ....71 F7
 Newport NP19 ....143 D5
 St Athan CF62 .....211 B7
Cedar St SA11 ......227 B8
Cedar Way
 Merthyr Tydfil CF47 ..10 D4
 Penarth CF64 ......206 E2
 Ystrad Mynach CF82 ..84 E1
Cedar Wlk NP19 .....89 B5
Cedar Wood Dr CF39 132 E5
Cedars The NP18 ...145 F7
Cedor y Wrach CF63 205 B1
Cedric Cl SA2 ....94 B5
Cedric St SA15 ......40 E5
Cefn Brith SA14 .....41 B6
Cefn Bryn CF39 ....107 D1
Cefn Bychan CF15 ..157 C1
Cefn Byrle Rd SA10 .222 F6
Cefn Carfan Cotts
 CF32 ....151 D6
Cefn Carfan Rd CF32 151 D6
Cefn Carnau Rd CF14 177 F5
Cefn Celyn SA2 ......66 B1
Cefn Cl
 Croesyceiliog NP44 ..90 B6
 Pontypridd CF37 ....109 C6
 Rogerstone NP10 ...142 B5
Cefn Coch CF15 ....176 A7
Cefn Coed Ave CF23 178 C4
Cefn Coed Colliery Mus
 SA10 ....25 E3
Cefn Coed Cres SA2 ..67 D1
Cefn Coed Hospl SA2 67 D1
Cefn Coed La CF31 ..168 D5
Cefn Cres SN13 ......35 B6
Cefn Cribwr Prim Sch
 CF32 ....149 B2
Cefn Ct Blackwood NP12 85 E7
 Newbridge NP11 .....87 B8
 Newport NP20 ....143 A3
 Rogerstone NP10 ...142 B5
Cefn Dr NP10 ......142 B5
Cefn Fforest Inf Sch
 NP12 ....85 C8
Cefn Fforest Jun Sch
 NP12 ....85 C8

Cefn Ffynon SA13 ....125 F3
Cefn Gelli SA11 ....227 B8
Cefn Glas Swansea SA2 ..94 B8
Tredegar NP22 ....13 D7
Ynysforgan SA6 ....46 A3
Cefn Glas Inf Sch
CF31 ....168 D6
Cefn Graig CF14 ....177 B8
Cefn Gwrgan Rd
SA13 ....125 C3
Cefn Helyg SA2 ......67 B1
Cefn Hengoed Comp Sch
SA1 ....69 C4
Cefn Hengoed Rd SA1 69 D4
Cefn Ilan CF83 ....137 A6
Cefn Isaf CF48 ....10 A4
Cefn La CF37 ....109 C5
Cefn Llan CF15 ......175 C8
Cefn Llwyn SA1 ......69 C4
Cefn Llwyn St CF82 ..84 C4
Cefn Mably Farm Pk
CF3 ....161 E5
Cefn Mably Rd CF14 ..160 C3
Cefn Milwr NP44 ....116 D8
Cefn Mount CF64 ....206 A3
Cefn Nant
Cardiff CF14 ....159 F1
Pencoed CF35 ....152 C1
Cefn Onn Ct CF14 ....159 F1
Cefn Onn Mdws CF14 159 F4
Cefn Onn Prim Sch
CF14 ....159 E1
Cefn Parc NP22 ....13 E5
Cefn Penuel CF15 ....175 C8
Cefn Prim Sch CF37 ..109 C5
Cefn Rd
Blackwood NP12 ......85 E8
Cardiff CF14 ....177 C3
Cefn Cribwr CF32 ....149 B2
Deri CF81 ....57 C8
Glais SA7 ....46 F6
Gwaun-Cae-Gurwen
SA18 ....220 D6
Hengoed CF82 ....85 A3
Rogerstone NP10 ....142 A6
Swansea SA1 ....69 C3
Wattstown CF39 ......107 D8
Cefn Rhos NP22 ......13 D6
Cefn Rise NP10 ......142 A6
Cefn Saeson Comp Sch
SA11 ....72 C5
Cefn Wlk NP10 ....142 B5
Cefn Wood Jun Sch
NP10 ....142 A5
Cefn y Mynydd NP24 ..33 D3
Cefn-Coed Cres
CF23 ....178 C3
Cefn-Coed Gdns
CF23 ....178 B3
Cefn-Coed Rd CF23 ..178 B4
Cefn-Crib Rd
Newbridge NP11 ......60 E3
Pontypool NP4 ....61 B4
Cefn-Draw SA4 ....65 D1
Cefn-Fforest Ave
Blackwood NP12 ......85 C4
Blackwood NP12 ......85 C8
Cefn-Glas Rd CF31 ..168 D6
Cefn-Parc CF37 ......85 C8
Cefn-Pennar Rd CF45 ..54 B8
Cefn-Porth Rd CF14 ..160 F6
Cefn-Rhychdir Rd
NP24 ....33 E4
Cefn-Saeson Rd SA11 72 A6
Cefn-y-Lon CF83 ....137 D6
Cefn-y-Maes SA5 .....67 E6
Cefn-yr-Allt SA10 ....49 C4
Cefn-yr-Erw Rare Breeds
farm SA4 ....222 E7
Cefnbrynbrain Cty Prim
Sch SA9 ....221 B8
Cefncoed Rd SA12 ....99 C5
Cefncrug SA18 ....218 E7
Cefndon Terr
Cwmavon SA12 ......99 D5
Hirwaun CF44 ....27 E8
Cefneithin Cty Prim Sch
SA14 ....218 A8
Cefneithin Rd SA14 ..218 A8
Cefnllan Rd SA8 .....23 D6
Cefnpennar Rd
Aberdare CF44 ....53 F8
Mountain Ash CF45 ..54 B7
Cefnsaeson Rd SA7 ..70 A8
Ceidrim Rd SA18 ....220 B8
Ceiriog Cl Barry CF63 215 A8
Penarth CF64 ....206 F4
Ceiriog Cres CF37 ..135 F6
Ceiriog Dr
Caerphilly CF83 ......138 A4
Cardiff CF14 ....176 F8
Ceiriog Rd SA1 ....95 A8
Celandine Ct NP44 ..182 B7
Celandine CF5 ......193 A5
Celerity Dr CF10 ....195 C4
Celtic Gn CF64 ......206 B4
Celtic Rd Cardiff CF14 177 D3
Maesteg CF34 ....102 D1
Celtic View CF31 ....150 F1
Celtic Way
Bedwas CF83 ....138 E6
Newport NP10 ....163 C5
Rhoose CF62 ....212 E1

Celyn Ave
Caerphilly CF83 ......138 A4
Cardiff CF23 ....178 B5
Celyn Cl CF62 ....211 C7
Celyn Gr
Caerphilly CF83 ......138 A4
Cardiff CF23 ....178 C2
Celyn Isaf CF39 .....133 C2
Celynen Rd NP11 .....87 B4
Cemaes Cres CF3 ....179 E5
Cemaes Rd NP11 .....59 D2
Cemetery Rd
Abercarn NP11 ....87 B3
Abercynon CF45 ......82 C4
Aberdare CF44 ....28 E4
Abertillery NP13 ......36 B1
Barry CF62 ....214 F6
Bridgend CF31 ....168 E6
Ebbw Vale NP23 ......15 A1
Ebbw Vale NP23 ......7 D1
Gwaun-Cae-Gurwen
SA18 ....220 D6
Maesteg CF34 ....102 C3
Ogmore Vale CF32 ..130 E2
Pontypridd CF37 ....135 F7
Porth CF39 ....107 D4
Swansea SA5 ....68 D6
Taffs Well CF15 ......158 B3
Taffs Well CF15 ......158 B4
Treorchy CF42 ....78 D7
Cemetry Rd ❶ NP23 ..8 B4
Cenarth Dr CF44 .....29 C2
Cendl Cres NP23 ......7 C4
Cendl Terr NP23 .....35 B8
Cenfedd St NP19 ....143 D7
Cennin Pedr CF63 ..205 B1
Centenary Ct CF38 ..156 B6
Central Ave
Blackwood NP12 ......59 A1
Blackwood NP12 ......85 C8
Newbridge NP11 ......87 A6
Newport NP19 ....144 D2
Pontypool NP4 ....39 B1
Central Bldgs
Bedwas CF83 ....139 A6
Blackwood NP12 ......59 B1
Central Dr NP4 ....38 B1
Central Hos CF83 ....138 F6
Central Inf Sch SA13 125 C7
Central Jun Sch
SA13 ....125 B8
Central Link CF10 ..195 C4
Central Rd SA13 ....125 D3
Central Sq
Cardiff CF10 ....195 A4
❷ Pontypridd CF37 ..109 D2
Central St
Caerphilly CF83 ......137 F6
Ystrad Mynach CF82 ..84 E1
Central Way
Barry CF64 ....215 E6
Cwmbran NP44 ....89 C5
Central Way (Ffordd
Ganolog) CF14 .....177 E5
Centre Ct CF15 .....157 E8
Centurion Cl CF5 ..193 D3
Centurion Gate NP18 118 C2
Cenydd Terr CF83 ..110 F4
Cerdin Ave CF72 ....173 B7
Ceredig Cl ❻ NP44 ..90 B2
Ceredig St CF48 .....31 A4
Ceri Ave CF62 ....213 B2
Ceri Rd Rhoose CF62 213 B2
Swansea SA1 ....67 F1
Ceridwen St
Maerdy CF43 ....52 A1
Mountain Ash CF45 ..54 C2
Cerise Cl SA12 ....98 B3
Chaddesley Terr ❶
SA1 ....95 B7
Chadwick Cl NP20 ..117 A2
Chaffinch Cl CF31 ..169 C4
Chaffinch Way NP10 163 F7
Chain Rd SA11 ......227 B8
Chain Wlk SA11 ....223 C1
Chalfont Cl CF38 ....156 B6
Chalice Ct SA12 ......98 D3
Challacombe Pl SA3 102 E6
Chalvington Ct CF38 156 B6
Chamberlain Rd
Cardiff CF14 ....177 A3
Neath SA11 ....71 D4
Chamberlain Row
CF64 ....206 C4
Chancery La
Cardiff CF11 ....194 D5
❼ Mountain Ash CF45 ..54 D3
Chandlers Ct ❻ CF37 109 D2
Chandlers Rd NP23 ..7 C4
Chandlers Reach
Llantwit Fardre CF38 156 C5
Mumbles SA3 ....123 C4
Chandlers Way CF64 207 A6
Chandlery The CF40 107 A7
Channel Ave CF39 ..133 E8
Channel Cl CF62 ....212 F1
Channel Hts CF33 ..148 E1
Channel View
Bassaleg NP10 ......141 F3
Bridgend CF31 ....169 D4
Bryn-côch SA10 ......48 D4
Castleton CF3 ......162 B3
Cwmbran NP44 ....89 C5
Marcross CF61 ......208 D2
Penarth CF64 ....207 B1
Pontypool NP4 ....62 D7
Port Talbot SA12 ....124 D8

Channel View continued
Risca NP11 ....115 B1
Swansea SA2 ....94 B1
Channel View Ct
NP11 ....115 B1
Channel View Ctr
CF11 ....195 A1
Channel View Rd
CF11 ....194 F1
Chantal Ave CF31 ...150 D1
Chantry Ct SA5 ......67 E5
Chantry Rise CF64 ..207 A1
Chantry The CF5 ....176 E1
Chapel Banks CF48 ..10 C2
Chapel Cl
Abersychan NP4 ......37 E6
Aberthin CF71 ....189 D3
Baglan SA12 ....98 D3
Dinas Powys CF64 ..206 C4
❷ Newport NP20 ....143 C3
Pentrebach CF48 .....31 A4
Pontllanfraith NP12 ..86 A5
Chapel Farm Terr
NP11 ....114 B8
Chapel Hill CF72 ....153 F3
Chapel Hill Cl CF72 153 F3
Chapel La
Croesyceiliog NP44 ..90 A7
Penarth CF64 ....207 A5
Chapel Mead NP4 ...39 E7
Chapel Rd
Abertillery NP13 ......36 C3
Blaina NP13 ....15 D5
Crofty SA4 ....64 B2
Llanharan CF72 .....154 A3
Monknash CF71 .....198 C2
Morganstown CF15 ..176 B8
Nantyglo NP23 ....8 C2
New Tredegar NP24 ..33 B5
Penderyn CF44 ......224 D3
Pontypool NP4 ....61 B8
Three Crosses SA4 ..65 E1
Chapel Row
❾ Aberdare CF44 ....29 A2
Cardiff CF3 ....179 D7
Dinas Powys CF64 ..206 C4
Merthyr Tydfil CF47 ..10 C2
❺ Aberdare CF44 ....53 E8
Chapel Row La ❶
CF3 ....179 D7
Chapel Sq CF48 .....30 E5
Chapel St
Aberbargoed CF81 ....58 A5
Abercanaid CF48 .....30 F4
Abercarn NP11 ....87 B4
Aberdare CF44 ....53 C7
Abergwynfi SA13 .....76 C5
Abertillery NP13 ......36 B5
Bedlinog CF46 ....56 A7
Blaencwm CF42 ......50 B2
Blaenrhondda CF42 ..50 D4
Bridgend CF31 ....168 F3
Brynmawr NP23 ....8 A3
Brynmenyn CF32 ....150 F6
Cardiff CF5 ....194 B8
Cwmbran NP44 ....89 C5
Deri CF81 ....57 B8
Gorseinon SA4 ....43 D2
Mumbles SA3 ....123 A5
Nant-y-Moel CF32 ..104 F6
New Tredegar NP24 ..33 E3
Pontlottyn CF81 ......12 F1
Pontycymer CF32 ...103 E3
Pontypridd CF37 ....109 C1
Pontypridd CF37 ....135 F5
Ton Pentre CF41 .....79 A3
❽ Tonypandy CF40 ..106 C6
Tonypandy CF40 ....107 A3
Treorchy CF42 ....78 D6
Troedyrhiw CF48 .....31 C1
Ystrad CF41 ....79 D3
Chapel Terr
Bryn SA13 ....100 E5
Hengoed CF82 ....84 F3
❷ Port Talbot SA13 ..125 C6
Wattstown CF39 .....107 E8
Chapel Wood CF23 ..178 E4
Chapman Cl NP20 ..117 A3
Chapman Ct ❿ CF63 109 D2
Chapman St SA15 ....40 C6
Chard Ave CF3 ......179 B5
Chargot Rd CF5 ....194 B7
Charles Ave CF35 ...152 D1
Charles Ct
Ebbw Vale NP23 ......7 B1
Gorseinon SA4 ....43 A1
Charles Darwin Way
CF62 ....214 F3
Charles Pl CF62 ....214 E2
Charles Row CF34 ..102 A4
Charles St
Abertillery NP11 ......59 E6
Abertysswg NP22 ....33 C8
Blaenavon NP4 ......17 D6
Bridgend CF31 ....168 F5
Caerphilly CF83 ......138 B3
Cwmbran NP44 ....89 C6
Llanelli SA15 ....40 F5
Neath SA11 ....70 E7
Neath SA11 ....71 E4
New Tredegar NP24 ..58 A8
Newport NP20 ......143 C4
Pontypool NP4 ....62 E3
Pontypridd CF37 ....109 A1
Porth CF39 ....107 F4
Tonypandy CF40 ....107 B5
Tredegar NP22 ....6 D1

Charles St continued
Treherbert CF42 ......78 A8
Tylorstown CF43 .....80 B3
Charles St (Heol Siarl)
CF10 ....195 B2
Charles Terr SA15 ....40 C4
Charlesville NP4 ......38 A1
Charlock Cl CF14 ...159 D3
Charlotte Dr NP20 ...14 A3
Charlotte Gdns CF48 ..11 B3
Charlotte Pl CF63 ..215 B6
Charlotte Sq CF14 ..177 C7
Charlotte St
Dowlais CF48 ....11 B4
❻ Newport NP20 ....143 C3
Penarth CF64 ....206 F5
Charlotte Wlk ❿
NP20 ....143 C3
Charnwood Ct SA1 ..69 D6
Charnwood Dr CF23 261 A1
Charnwood Rd NP19 143 D5
Charston NP44 ......89 C3
Charter Ave CF62 ..214 D8
Charteris Cl CF44 ..217 A8
Charteris Cres CF5 193 D6
Charteris Rd CF5 ..193 D6
Chartist Ct NP11 ...115 B1
Chartist Dr NP10 ...142 A5
Chartist Rd CF72 ...155 D3
Chartist Way
Blackwood NP12 ......85 D7
Tredegar NP22 ....6 E1
Chartley Cl ❾ CF3 ..180 A7
Chartwell Ct CF15 ..175 C8
Chartwell Dr CF14 ..175 A1
Charwood Ho ❹ NP44 89 C2
Chase The CF31 ....169 A6
Chase View CF47 ....10 E3
Chatham CF83 ......140 A7
Chatham Pl CF83 ...140 B7
Chatham St CF83 ...140 B7
Chatsworth Cl CF5 ..176 C1
Chatterton Sq CF11 206 F8
Chaucer Cl
Bridgend CF31 ....168 C6
Cardiff CF3 ....179 C8
Penarth CF64 ....206 F4
Chaucer Ct ❹ NP19 143 F5
Chaucer Rd
Barry CF62 ....214 F6
Newport NP19 ......143 F5
Chave Terr CF82 .....85 B2
Cheam Pl CF14 .....177 F8
Cheapside
Bridgend CF31 ....168 F4
Bridgend CF31 ....169 B2
Cheddar Cres CF3 ..179 B5
Chelhydra Wlk ❷ SA1 95 D5
Chelmer Cl NP20 ...116 C1
Chelmer Wlk NP20 ..116 C1
Chelsea Ave CF31 ..168 C7
Chelston Pl NP20 ..116 B3
Cheltenham Rd CF36 182 E8
Cheltenham Terr
CF31 ....168 F3
Chemical Rd
Morriston SA6 ....46 A2
Swansea SA6 ....45 F2
Chemical Row SA9 ..2 A4
Chepstow Cl
Blackwood NP12 ......58 D1
Cardiff CF5 ....193 D4
Croesyceiliog NP44 ..90 A6
Merthyr Tydfil CF48 ..225 F1
Chepstow Ct CF83 ..137 D4
Chepstow Pl SA1 ....69 C4
Chepstow Rd
Langstone NP18 .....145 B8
Newport NP19 ......144 C5
Treorchy CF42 ....78 D7
Chepstow Rise NP44 90 A6
Cheriton Ave CF82 ..84 F5
Cheriton Cres SA5 ..67 F5
Cheriton Ct CF3 ....179 A3
Cheriton Dr CF14 ..159 F2
Cheriton Gr CF38 ..136 B1
Cheriton Path NP44 89 B2
Cherry Cl Cardiff CF5 176 B1
Croesyceiliog NP44 ..90 B5
Ebbw Vale NP23 ......7 D2
Penarth CF64 ....217 A8
Cherry Dr CF44 ......28 D3
Cherry Gr Baglan SA12 98 E6
Blackwood NP11 .....59 D1
Merthyr Tydfil CF47 ..10 E4
Swansea SA2 ....94 B4
Cherry Grove Specl Sch
CF82 ....84 C7
Cherry Orchard Rd
CF14 ....159 F4
Cherry Tree Ave
CF36 ....183 E8
Cherry Tree Cl
Bedwas CF83 ....138 C7
Caerleon NP18 ......118 B3
Croesyceiliog NP44 ..90 B5
Langstone NP18 .....145 B8
Newport NP20 ......117 B3
Trefechan CF48 ......10 B6
Cherry Tree Rd NP12 59 E8
Cherry Tree Way NP46 83 C8
Cherry Tree Wlk
CF72 ....155 C2
Cherry Trees NP12 ..58 D7
Cherrydale Rd CF5 193 E6
Cherrydown Cl CF14 159 F2
Cherrywood CF14 ..159 F2

Chervil ❿ CF3 ......180 A8
Cherwell Cl CF5 ....176 D1
Cherwell Rd CF64 ..206 F2
Cherwell Wlk NP20 116 C1
Cheshire Cl CF14 ..177 F6
Chesnut Gr NP18 ...117 C2
Chesshyre St SA2 ...94 E5
Chester Cl
❶ Cardiff CF3 ....179 F6
Merthyr Tydfil CF48 ..225 F1
Pontypool NP4 ....63 B5
Chester Ct CF83 ....137 D4
Chester Pl CF11 ....194 F3
Chester St CF11 ....194 F3
Chesterfield St CF63 215 B7
Chesterholme NP20 143 A3
Chesterton Rd CF3 179 B7
Chestnut Ave
Gorseinon SA4 ....43 A4
Mumbles SA3 ....122 E8
St Athan CF62 ......211 B7
Chestnut Cl
Aberdare CF44 ....28 E2
Dinas Powys CF64 ..206 B2
Ebbw Vale NP23 ......7 C5
Machen CF83 ....140 A7
Neath SA10 ....48 D2
Pontypool NP4 ....63 B5
Chestnut Dr CF36 ..183 E8
Chestnut Gn NP44 ..89 B6
Chestnut Gr Bryn NP12 85 E3
Maesteg CF34 ....102 C3
Chestnut Rd
Baglan SA12 ....98 E7
Cardiff CF5 ....193 D8
Neath SA11 ....72 A6
Chestnut St CF37 ..136 A5
Chestnut Tree Cl
CF15 ....176 A6
Chestnut Way
Bridgend CF31 ....168 B5
Merthyr Tydfil CF47 ..10 D5
Penarth CF64 ....206 F3
Chestnuts The CF72 173 D6
Cheviot Cl
Cardiff CF14 ....177 E7
Risca NP11 ....115 C2
Swansea SA5 ....67 E3
Chevron St CF37 ....109 E4
Chichester Cl NP19 117 F1
Chichester Rd CF64 206 F5
Chichester Way CF5 193 E6
Chick La NP20 ......142 F4
Chilcote St CF63 ...215 B6
Chilcott Ave CF32 ..150 F5
Childrens Orthopaedic
Hospl SA1 ....95 B6
Chiltern Cl
Cardiff CF14 ....177 E7
Newport NP19 ......144 C6
Risca NP11 ....115 C1
Swansea SA5 ....67 E3
Chimney Rd CF62 ..211 C1
Chirk Gdns SA1 .....69 C4
Chiswick Cl CF31 ..168 C6
Chopin Rd SA12 .....98 B3
Chorley Cl CF5 ....193 C7
Chorleywood Cl CF31 169 A4
Christ Church Prim Sch
SA1 ....95 B5
Christ The King RC Prim
Sch CF14 ....160 A1
Christchurch Hill
NP18 ....144 D7
Christchurch Rd
Baglan SA12 ....98 D3
Blackwood NP12 ......85 F8
Newport NP19 ......144 B6
Christina Cres NP10 142 C4
Christina St
Cardiff CF10 ....195 B3
❼ Swansea SA1 ....95 C7
Christopher Ct SA6 ..69 A6
Christopher Rd
Maesteg CF34 ....102 C3
Neath SA10 ....70 E7
Ynysforgan SA6 ......46 B4
Christopher Rise SA4 44 A5
Christopher St SA15 40 E4
Christopher Terr CF47 30 F7
Chrome Ave SA12 ...98 B2
Chumleigh Cl CF3 ..179 A4
Church Acre CF31 ..169 D6
Church Ave
Ebbw Vale NP23 ......7 F4
Llwydcoed CF44 .....28 E6
❺ Penarth CF64 .....207 B4
Pontypool NP4 ....38 C1
Church Bldgs SA9 ..222 C7
Church Cl
Bryn-côch SA10 ......48 D3
Cardiff CF14 ....160 C3
Croesyceiliog NP44 ..90 A5
Llantwit Fardre CF38 156 D6
Ogmore-By-Sea CF32 184 D2
Peterstone Wentlooge
CF3 ....180 F5
Pontypool NP4 ....63 A2
Rogerstone NP10 ...142 C4
Swansea SA7 ....69 D8
Church Cotts SA5 ...45 B2
Church Cres
Bassaleg NP10 ......142 A3
Blaengwrach SA11 ..227 D3
Coedkernew NP10 ..163 A5
Ebbw Vale NP23 ......14 D6
Ebbw Vale NP23 ......7 C3

Church Ct
Newport NP19 ......143 F6
Newport NP19 ......144 B3
Church Farm Cl NP16 116 E1
Church Hill Cl CF71 200 D8
Church La Baglan SA12 98 E5
Bishopston SA3 .....121 F7
Brynmawr NP23 ....8 C5
Cardiff CF3 ....179 D7
Coedkernew NP10 ..163 A4
Gwaun-Cae-Gurwen
SA18 ....220 D6
Llantwit Major CF61 ..209 F6
Marshfield CF3 ......162 D2
Nantgarw CF15 .....158 A7
Nelson CF46 ....83 E4
Pen-clawdd SA4 ....64 F2
Pontypool NP4 ....62 B8
Pontypool NP4 ....63 B5
St Athan CF62 ......211 D4
Church Mdw
Boverton CF61 ......210 D6
Gelligaer CF82 ......84 D7
Reynoldston SA3 ...229 B1
Church Mews NP4 ..62 C6
Church Park La SA3 123 B4
Church Pk 123 B4
Church Pl
Bargoed CF81 ....58 A4
Blaengarw CF32 ....103 E6
Maesteg CF34 ....102 A3
Neath SA11 ....71 E8
Porthcawl CF36 .....182 F6
Church Pl S CF64 ..207 B5
Church Rd
Abersychan NP4 ......37 E4
Abertillery NP13 ......60 A8
Abertridwr CF83 .....136 F7
Baglan SA12 ....98 E5
Barry CF63 ....215 B7
Blaenavon NP4 ......17 C6
Bridgend CF31 ....168 E3
Cardiff CF14 ....160 C3
Cardiff CF14 ....177 A4
Cardiff CF3 ....161 C1
Cardiff CF5 ....179 B3
Cardiff CF5 ....193 C3
Cardiff CF5 ....194 D5
Church Village CF38 135 F2
Cwmbran NP44 ....89 D7
Gelligaer CF82 ......84 C7
Gorslas SA14 ......218 B8
Llanbethian CF71 ...188 C1
Llanelli SA4 ....218 D1
Llanfrechfa NP44 ...117 D8
Maesygwartha NP7 ..9 D8
Neath SA10 ....48 F2
Newbridge NP11 .....86 F7
Newport NP19 ......143 D6
Penarth CF64 ....207 B4
Penderyn CF44 .....224 D3
Pentyrch CF15 .....175 C8
Pontardawe SA8 .....24 A7
Pontardawe SA8 .....24 D5
Pontarddulais SA4 ..19 D3
❶ Pontypridd CF37 ..109 E2
Rhoose CF62 ....213 A1
Risca NP11 ....114 F3
Seven Sisters SA10 222 C3
St Brides Wentlooge
NP10 ....163 E1
Swansea SA7 ....69 D8
Ton Pentre CF41 .....79 A3
Tonypandy CF40 ...107 A1
Wick CF71 ....198 C5
Ynysmeudwy SA8 ...23 F7
Church Rise CF5 ...205 B4
Church Row
Aberdare CF44 ....28 E4
Dowlais CF48 ....11 B4
❻ Glanaman SA18 ...220 B8
St Nicholas CF5 ....191 F1
Church St
❼ Aberavan SA12 ...99 A1
Aberbargoed CF81 ..58 B4
❺ Aberdare CF44 ....29 A2
Aberkenfig CF32 ...150 C4
Abertillery NP13 ......36 B5
Bargoed CF81 ....57 F4
Bedwas CF83 ....138 E6
Blaengarw CF32 ....103 E6
Blaina NP13 ....15 E5
Briton Ferry SA11 ...71 B4
Brynna CF72 ....153 D3
Caerleon NP18 ......118 B2
Cardiff CF10 ....195 A5
Cowbridge CF71 ....188 C2
Cymmer SA13 ....75 D3
Dowlais CF48 ....11 B4
Ebbw Vale NP23 ......14 D6
Ferndale CF43 ....79 F7
Gowerton SA4 ......66 B5
Llanbradach CF83 ..111 F1
Llanelli SA15 ....40 C5
Llantrisant CF72 ....155 D3
Llantwit Major CF61 ..209 F6
Llysworney CF71 ...187 E1
Machen CF83 ....140 A7
Maerdy CF43 ....52 A1
Maesteg CF34 ....102 A3
Maesteg CF34 ....75 B2
Merthyr Tydfil CF47 ..10 D2
Merthyr Tydfil CF47 ..10 E1
Mountain Ash CF45 ..81 F8
Newport NP20 ......143 D2
Pontardawe SA8 .....23 E5

Church St continued
Pontlottyn CF81 . . . . .12 F1
Pontycymer CF32 . . . . . .103 F3
🏠4 Pontypridd CF37 . .109 C1
Porthcawl CF36 . . . . . . .183 D8
Rhymney NP22 . . . . .12 E5
Rogerstone NP10 . . . . .141 F6
Taffs Well CF15 . . . . . .158 A3
Ton Pentre CF41 . . . . . .79 A3
Tonypandy CF40 . . . . . .106 E6
Tonypandy CF40 . . . . . .106 F8
Tredegar NP22 . . . . .13 E8
Treherbert CF42 . . . . . . .51 A1
Treorchy CF42 . . . . .78 B5
Troedyrhiw CF48 . . . . . .31 B1
Wick CF71 . . . . .198 C5
Ynysybwl CF37 . . . . . . .81 F1
Ystrad Mynach CF82 . . .84 E1
Church Terr
Blaengarw CF32 . . . . . . .103 E6
Cardiff CF23 . . . . .195 D8
Llanharan CF72 . . . . . .154 A3
Nant-y-Moel CF32 . . . .104 E6
New Tredegar NP24 . . . .33 E3
🏠7 Pontypool NP4 . . . . .38 A1
St Hilary CF71 . . . . . . .201 D7
St Mary Church CF71 . .201 A4
Tonypandy CF40 . . . . . .107 A1
Tylorstown CF43 . . . . . . .80 C3
Church View
Baglan SA12 . . . . .98 E5
🏠8 Blaenavon NP4 . . . . .17 C1
Brynna CF72 . . . . .153 D3
Ebbw Vale NP23 . . . . . . .7 D3
Laleston CF32 . . . . . . .167 E4
Llanblethian CF71 . . . .188 C1
Marcross CF61 . . . . . . .208 C7
Pontllanfraith NP12 . . . .86 A6
Abercanaid CF48 . . . . . .30 F4
Church View Cl
Brynna CF72 . . . . .153 D3
Llandough CF64 . . . . . .206 D7
Church Wlk CF39 . . . .108 A3
Church Wood Rd
NP44 . . . . .89 D5
Churchfield Cl CF82 . . .84 F6
Churchfield Row CF41 .79 A4
Churchfields CF63 . . .215 B8
Churchill Cl
Bridgend CF31 . . . . . . .168 D4
Cardiff CF14 . . . . .160 A4
Churchill Terr CF63 . .215 C6
Churchill Way CF10 . .195 B5
Churchmead NP10 . . .142 B2
Churchward Dr NP19 144 B4
Churchwood Cl NP4 . . .62 C7
Cil Heol Hendy CF72 .173 C7
Cil-Hendy CF72 . . . . .173 C7
Cil-Sanws La CF48 . . . .10 A5
Cil-y-Coed SA5 . . . . . . .67 A3
Cila Cty Prim Sch SA2 93 D5
Cilduady Rd CF32 . . . .150 B7
Cilfedw CF15 . . . . . . .176 B7
Cilfrew Prim Sch SA10 49 B4
Cilfrew Ct SA1 . . . . . . .68 C2
Cilfynydd Prim Sch
CF37 . . . . .109 F5
Cilfynydd Rd CF37 . . .109 F5
Cilgerran Cl NP44 . . . . .90 B3
Cilgerran Cres CF14 . .177 D8
Cilgerran Pl SA1 . . . . . .71 F6
Cilgerran Way NP12 . . .58 E1
Cilhall CF46 . . . . .83 B8
Cilhaul Terr CF45 . . . . .54 C1
Cilmaengwyn
Godregraig SA8 . . . . . .221 B1
Pontardawe SA8 . . . . . . .24 C8
Cilonen Rd SA4 . . . . . . .65 D1
Cilparc CF36 . . . . .183 A8
Cilsaig Rd SA14 . . . . . . .41 B8
Cilsanws Ho CF48 . . . . .10 A3
Cilsanws La CF48 . . . .225 F3
Cimla Cl SA11 . . . . .71 F6
Cimla Cres SA11 . . . . . .72 A6
Cimla Hospl SA11 . . . . .72 A5
Cimla Rd SA11 . . . . . . .71 F6
Cinema Bldgs 🏠3 SA15 40 D3
Circle The Bryn NP12 . . .85 E3
Cwmbran NP44 . . . . . . .89 D1
Tredegar NP22 . . . . .13 E6
Circle Way E CF23 . . . . .78 F3
Circle Way W CF23 . . .178 D4
Citadel CF NP22 . . . . . .13 D7
Citrine Ave SA12 . . . . . .98 E3
Citrine Cl 🏠3 SA12 . . . .98 B2
City Hall CF10 . . . . . . .195 A6
City Hall Rd CF10 . . . .195 A6
City Link CF24 . . . . . . .195 F8
City Rd Bettws CF32 . .129 D1
Cardiff CF24 . . . . .195 B7
Claerwen CF82 . . . . . . .84 B4
Claerwen Cl CF44 . . . . .29 E2
Claerwen Dr CF23 . . . .178 E5
Clairwain NP4 . . . . .63 A3
Clan-yr-Afon CF72 . . .173 B7
Clapham Terr NP4 . . . . .17 B5
Clara St CF41 . . . . .78 F3
Clarbeston Rd CF14 . . .177 A3
Clare Ct SA4 . . . . .42 E1
Clare Dr CF71 . . . . . . .188 F1
Clare Drew Way NP44 190 A5
Clare Gdns 🏠9 CF11 . .194 F5
Clare Pl 🏠10 CF11 . . . .194 F4
Clare Rd CF11 . . . . . . .194 F4
Treorchy CF42 . . . . .78 C5
Ystalyfera SA9 . . . . .2 B7
Clare St Cardiff CF11 .194 F5
Merthyr Tydfil CF47 . . . . .30 E7

Clare St continued
Swansea SA5 . . . . .68 C3
Claremont NP20 . . . . .117 B4
Claremont Ave CF3 . . .179 B4
Claremont Cres CF3 . .179 B4
Claremont Dr CF46 . . . .83 C5
Claremont Rd NP11 . . . .87 B8
Clarence Cnr NP4 . . . . .62 C6
Clarence Ct
Cardiff CF10 . . . . .195 B1
Maesteg CF34 . . . . .102 A3
Swansea SA1 . . . . .95 C6
Clarence Emb CF10 . .195 B2
Clarence Pl
Cardiff CF10 . . . . .195 B1
Newport NP19 . . . . . . .143 C5
Risca NP11 . . . . .114 F2
Clarence Rd
Cardiff CF10 . . . . .195 B2
Pontypool NP4 . . . . .62 D6
Clarence St
Abertillery NP13 . . . . . . .36 C6
Brynmawr NP23 . . . . .8 C4
Mountain Ash CF45 . . . . .54 D1
Newport NP20 . . . . .143 D2
Pontypool NP4 . . . . .62 C6
Swansea SA1 . . . . .95 C6
Ton Pentre CF41 . . . . . . .79 A3
Clarence Terr
Aberdare CF44 . . . . .53 D6
Swansea SA1 . . . . .95 C6
Clarendon CF23 . . . . . .178 D6
Clarendon Rd
Cardiff CF23 . . . . .178 D3
Swansea SA2 . . . . .94 D7
Clarice St 🏠7 SA12 . . . .98 E1
Clarion Cl Swansea SA6 46 B1
Swansea SA6 . . . . .69 C8
Clarion Ct SA6 . . . . . . .69 C8
Clark Ave NP44 . . . . . . .89 E6
Clark St CF42 . . . . .78 D6
Clarke St CF5 . . . . .193 F6
Clarke Way SA1 . . . . . . .69 A6
Clas -y-Dderwen CF45 54 E3
Clas Ael-y-Bryn CF37 . .81 D3
Clas Cwm CF37 . . . . . .109 D6
Clas Dyfrig 🏠1 CF14 . .177 B3
Clas Gabriel 🏠3 CF41 .177 B3
Clas Gwernifor CF45 . . .54 E2
Clas Heulog CF14 . . . .177 B4
Clas Illtyd CF14 . . . . . .177 C4
Clas Isan CF14 . . . . . . .177 B5
Clas Odyn CF14 . . . . . .177 B5
Clas Teilo 🏠2 CF14 . . . .177 B4
Clas Ty Wern CF14 . . .177 C6
Clas Ty'n-y-Cae
CF14 . . . . .177 C6
Clas Tynewydd CF14 . .177 B4
Clas Yorath CF14 . . . . .177 B5
Clas-Ty-Gelli CF37 . . .109 D6
Clas-y-Bedw SA5 . . . . . .66 F3
Clas-y-Deri SA5 . . . . . . .67 A3
Clas-yr-Onnen SA5 . . . .67 A3
Clase Dr SA6 . . . . .45 D1
Clase Prim Sch SA6 . . .68 D8
Clase Rd Morriston SA6 .46 A1
Swansea SA6 . . . . .69 B8
Clasemont Rd SA6 . . . . .45 D2
Claude Pl CF24 . . . . . .195 C8
Claude Rd Barry CF62 214 D5
Caerphilly CF83 . . . . . . .138 A2
Cardiff CF24 . . . . .195 C8
Claude Rd W CF62 . . . .214 D4
Claverton Cl CF38 . . . .156 B6
Claymore Pl CF11 . . . .207 A8
Clayton Cres CF37 . . . .109 C5
Clayton Rd SA4 . . . . . . .19 A4
Clayton St
Newport NP19 . . . . . . .143 D6
Swansea SA1 . . . . .68 D4
Clear Water CF3 . . . . . . .19 D3
Clearwater Rd NP19 . .144 D1
Clearway Ct CF14 . . . .177 A4
Clearwell Ct NP10 . . . .141 E3
Cleddau Cl CF3 . . . . . .180 B7
Cledwen Cl CF62 . . . . .214 B5
Cledwyn Terr CF44 . . . .28 E4
Clees La SA9 . . . . .2 A5
Cleeve Dr CF14 . . . . . .177 E2
Cleeves Terr NP4 . . . . . .61 E1
Cleighton Terr SA10 . . .48 F2
Clement Atlee Dr
NP19 . . . . .144 D7
Clement Pl CF62 . . . . .214 C2
Cleppa Park Ind Est
NP10 . . . . .163 C7
Clevedon Ave CF64 . . .216 B4
Clevedon Ct 🏠7 NP19 .143 F6
Clevedon Ct
🏠5 Cardiff CF3 . . . . . .179 C6
Swansea SA2 . . . . .94 F7
Clevedon Rd
Cardiff CF3 . . . . .179 C6
Newport NP19 . . . . . . .144 A6
Cleveland Ave SA3 . . . .123 C3
Cleveland Dr NP11 . . . .115 C1
Clevis Cres CF36 . . . . .183 D8
Clevis Ct CF33 . . . . . . .165 F6
Clevis Hill CF36 . . . . . .183 D8
Clevis La CF36 . . . . . . .183 D8
Clevisfield Ave CF36 . .183 D8
Cleviston Gdns CF36 . .183 C8
Cleviston Pk SA14 . . . . .42 A6
Clewer Court Mews 🏠7
NP20 . . . . .142 F4
Clewer Ct 🏠6 NP20 . . .142 F4
Cliff Ct CF10 . . . . .195 C2

Cliff Hill CF64 . . . . . . .207 B2
Cliff Par CF64 . . . . . . .207 B2
Cliff Pl CF5 . . . . .194 B6
Cliff Rd Blackwood NP12 85 F7
Penarth CF64 . . . . .207 B2
Cliff Side CF64 . . . . . . .207 B1
Cliff St
Mountain Ash CF45 . . . . .54 D2
Penarth CF64 . . . . .207 B5
Cliff Terr CF37 . . . . . . .135 D8
Cliff Wood View
CF62 . . . . .214 A2
Clifflands Cl SA3 . . . . .122 F4
Clifford St SA11 . . . . . . .71 D6
Clifton Cres 🏠6 CF44 . . .53 D7
Clifton Ct
Aberdare CF44 . . . . .28 F2
🏠1 Cardiff CF24 . . . . .195 D6
Swansea SA5 . . . . .68 C6
Clifton Hill SA1 . . . . . . .95 C4
Clifton Mews 🏠2
CF24 . . . . .195 D6
Clifton Pl NP20 . . . . . .143 B4
Clifton Rd NP20 . . . . . .143 B4
Clifton Row
Porth CF39 . . . . .108 A2
🏠1 Swansea SA1 . . . . . .95 C4
Clifton Sq NP4 . . . . .62 E3
Clifton St
Aberdare CF44 . . . . .28 F1
Barry CF62 . . . . .214 D3
Cardiff CF24 . . . . .195 D6
Risca NP11 . . . . .141 D8
Treorchy CF42 . . . . .78 D5
Clifton Terr
Aberavon SA12 . . . . .99 B1
🏠3 Blaenavon NP4 . . . .17 C1
🏠2 Llanelli SA15 . . . . . .40 F6
Mumbles SA3 . . . . .123 C4
Clinton Rd CF64 . . . . . .207 A2
Clipper Cl NP19 . . . . . .117 F1
Clipper Rd CF10 . . . . . .195 F3
Clist Rd NP20 . . . . .116 C2
Clive Cres CF64 . . . . . .207 B4
Clive Ct CF5 . . . . .194 B6
Clive La Cardiff CF11 . .194 F2
🏠1 Penarth CF64 . . . . .206 F5
Clive Mews CF5 . . . . . .194 B6
Clive Pl Aberdare CF44 . .28 F1
Barry CF62 . . . . .214 F2
Cardiff CF24 . . . . .195 C7
Penarth CF64 . . . . .207 B1
Clive Rd Barry CF62 . . .214 F3
Cardiff CF5 . . . . .194 B6
St Athan CF62 . . . . . . .211 D6
Clive St Aberdare CF44 . .28 E4
Caerphilly CF83 . . . . . . .138 A2
Cardiff CF11 . . . . .194 F2
Senghenydd CF83 . . . . .110 F2
Clive Terr CF37 . . . . . . .81 F1
Cloda Ave SA10 . . . . . . .48 C1
Clodien Ave CF14 . . . .177 F2
Cloister Ct CF5 . . . . . . .193 E4
Cloisters The SA1 . . . . .95 A6
Clomendy Rd NP44 . . . .89 E2
Clonakilty Way CF23 . .161 A2
Clordir Rd SA4 . . . . . . .44 A7
Clos Aderyn Du SA5 . . .67 F3
Clos Afon Llan SA4 . . . .66 C6
Clos Afon Tywi NP12 . . .85 C6
Clos Alaw SA7 . . . . .69 C6
Clos Allt-y-Gog SA4 . . . .19 C3
Clos Alun CF72 . . . . . . .153 C3
Clos Alyn CF23 . . . . . . .160 F1
Clos Aneira SA5 . . . . . . .67 D3
Clos Ar Ddafen SA14 . . .41 C5
Clos Avro CF24 . . . . . . .196 B7
Clos Banc y Berllan
SA4 . . . . .19 D3
Clos Berriew 🏠5 CF14 177 B3
Clos Bevan SA4 . . . . . . .66 A5
Clos Blean Crymlyn
SA7 . . . . .69 E6
Clos Bron Iestyn
CF37 . . . . .109 A1
Clos Bryn Celyn CF37 . .84 E3
Clos Bryn Dafyd SA4 . . .44 C2
Clos Bryn Isaf SA14 . . . .41 D4
Clos Brynafon SA4 . . . . .42 F3
Clos Bryngwyn
Garden Village SA4 . . . . .43 D1
Gorseinon SA4 . . . . .66 D8
Clos Brynmellyn 🏠1
CF15 . . . . .176 B6
Clos Burlais SA5 . . . . . . .68 A2
Clos Bychan CF44 . . . . .28 C3
Clos Cadno SA6 . . . . . . .45 F5
Clos Cadwgan 🏠4
CF38 . . . . .156 A5
Clos Cae Dafydd SA4 . .66 A5
Clos Cae Fainc SA14 . . .42 B7
Clos Cae Mawr CF82 . . .84 F7
Clos Cae Pwll CF64 . . . .83 D4
Clos Cae Wal CF15 . . . .158 C1
Clos Cae'r Wern
CF83 . . . . .158 E8
Clos Caer Elms SA15 . . .40 B6
Clos Caersalem SA6 . . . .68 F7
Clos Caewal CF15 . . . . .157 C1
Clos Camlas CF37 . . . . .109 D2
Clos Caradog CF38 . . . .156 D8
Clos Carolyn NP12 . . . .85 C6
Clos Cas-Bach CF3 . . . .180 A6
Clos Castell Coity
CF31 . . . . .168 C3

Clos Castell Newydd
CF31 . . . . .168 C3
Clos Cefn Bychan
CF15 . . . . .157 D1
Clos Cefn-y-Maes
SA1 . . . . .41 C5
Clos Cefni CF62 . . . . . .214 C6
Clos Ceirw NP12 . . . . . .85 C6
Clos Celyn SA7 . . . . . . .69 D6
Clos Cemmaes 🏠6
CF14 . . . . .177 B3
Clos Cenawon SA6 . . . . .46 A3
Clos Cerdinen SA4 . . . . .44 C4
Clos Cilfwnwr SA4 . . . . .44 B3
Clos Claerwen NP12 . . .85 C6
Clos Coed Arian SA12 . .98 D1
Clos Coed Duon NP12 . .85 D6
Clos Coedydafarn
CF14 . . . . .160 C2
Clos Cornel CF14 . . . . .177 B4
Clos Corris 🏠9 CF14 . .177 B3
Clos Creyr CF38 . . . . . .135 C1
Clos Cromwell CF14 . . .159 C1
Clos Crucywel SA6 . . . . .46 A4
Clos Cwm Creunant
CF14 . . . . .160 F1
Clos Cwm Du CF23 . . . .160 F1
Clos Cwm Garw CF83 137 D3
Clos Cwningen SA7 . . . .47 B1
Clos Cwrt y Carne SA4 43 A4
Clos Cynan SA2 . . . . . . .93 F8
Clos Cyncoed CF83 . . . .137 D6
Clos Darran Las CF15 174 E7
Clos Ddu SA5 . . . . .68 B7
Clos Delyth SA4 . . . . . . .43 C2
Clos Derwen
Cardiff CF23 . . . . .178 B2
Swansea SA7 . . . . .70 A6
Clos Dewi Medi SA15 . . .40 E2
Clos Dwerw CF83 . . . . .137 C1
Clos Dyfnaint 🏠8 CF3 .180 A6
Clos Ebol SA6 . . . . .45 F4
Clos Edno CF23 . . . . . .178 C3
Clos Eileen Chilcott
SA7 . . . . .69 E6
Clos Enfys CF83 . . . . . .137 E1
Clos Eran CF14 . . . . . . .159 E4
Clos Fach CF14 . . . . . . .177 C8
Clos Felen SA18 . . . . . .220 B8
Clos Ffawydden CF71 189 C8
Clos Gathen SA15 . . . . .40 C4
Clos George Morgan
SA6 . . . . .45 E4
Clos Ger-y-Bryn SA4 . . .44 C5
Clos Ger-y-Maes SA4 . . .44 C5
Clos Glan Nant CF83 . .138 A1
Clos Glan-y-Wern
SA7 . . . . .69 E6
Clos Glanaber 🏠9 CF3 180 A6
Clos Glanlliw SA4 . . . . . .44 A6
Clos Glanmor SA15 . . . .40 C4
Clos Glas Llwch CF3 . .179 F5
Clos Glyndwr SA4 . . . . .18 F5
Clos Golwyg Yr Hafod
NP23 . . . . .8 D4
Clos Gors Fawr SA4 . . . .43 C6
Clos Graddfa CF62 . . . .111 F7
Clos Granby SA15 . . . . .40 E2
Clos Gronw NP12 . . . . . .85 C6
Clos Guto CF83 . . . . . . .138 D4
Clos Gwastir CF83 . . . . .137 E1
Clos Gwaun Gledyr
CF83 . . . . .137 D3
Clos Gwendraeth
NP12 . . . . .85 C6
Clos Gwent CF38 . . . . .155 F5
Clos Gwern-y-Mor 🏠13
CF3 . . . . .179 F6
Clos Gwernen SA4 . . . . .66 C6
Clos Gwernydd CF83 . . .137 D4
Clos Gwlad-Yr-Haf 🏠10
CF3 . . . . .180 A6
Clos Gwy CF23 . . . . . . .160 F1
Clos Gwylne CF83 . . . . .137 D1
Clos Gwynedd CF38 . . .155 F5
Clos Hafodyrynys 🏠18
CF3 . . . . .179 F6
Clos Hafren 🏠6 CF3 . . .180 A6
Clos Healy SA4 . . . . .66 B6
Clos Hector CF24 . . . . .196 B7
Clos Helyg SA4 . . . . .66 B5
Clos Hendra SA6 . . . . . . .22 B2
Clos Hendre CF14 . . . . .177 D8
Clos Henfaes CF33 . . . .165 E8
Clos Hereford CF72 . . .155 D2
Clos Islwyn SA2 . . . . . . .93 E8
Clos Lancaster CF72 . . .155 D2
Clos Leighton Davies
SA4 . . . . .66 B6
Clos Leland CF72 . . . . .155 D2
Clos Lindsay CF5 . . . . .193 A3
Clos Llandyfan SA4 . . . .66 D8
Clos Llanfair CF5 . . . . .205 A6
Clos Llanfihangel
SA14 . . . . .41 B6
Clos Llangefni CF38 . . .155 F6
Clos Llarwydden SA4 . .44 C2
Clos Llawhaden CF62 215 A8
Clos Llewellyn CF15 . . .174 E6
Clos Llwyn Cwm SA6 . . .69 A6
Clos Llwyn y Pwll NP23 .8 D4
Clos Llyg SA7 . . . . .70 B8
Clos Madlen SA5 . . . . . . .67 D3
Clos Maerun 🏠17 CF3 .179 F6
Clos Maes Isaf SA14 . . .42 C7

Clos Maes Yr Ysgol
SA4 . . . . .19 D3
Clos Maes-y-mor 🏠11
CF3 . . . . .180 A6
Clos Mair CF23 . . . . . . .178 B3
Clos Mancheldowne
CF62 . . . . .214 E4
Clos Manmoel CF3 . . . .179 F6
Clos Marina SA4 . . . . . . .66 B6
Clos Meifod 🏠7 CF14 . .177 B3
Clos Melin Ddwr
CF14 . . . . .160 A2
Clos Melin Mynach
SA4 . . . . .66 C8
Clos Menter CF14 . . . . .177 D1
Clos Min Yr Afon SA4 . .42 F2
Clos Morgan Gruffydd
CF83 . . . . .136 F7
Clos Morgan Owen
SA4 . . . . .66 A5
Clos Morgannwg SA1 . .95 A8
Clos Myddlyn CF83 . . . .155 F5
Clos Nant Bran SA7 . . . .47 A2
Clos Nant Coslech
CF23 . . . . .160 C2
Clos Nant Ddu CF23 . . .160 F1
Clos Nant Glaswg
CF23 . . . . .160 E1
Clos Nant Mwlan
CF23 . . . . .160 F1
Clos Nant y Cor CF23 160 F1
Clos Nant y Cwm
CF23 . . . . .160 C2
Clos Nant Yr Aber
CF83 . . . . .137 F4
Clos Nantydd SA14 . . . . .41 C4
Clos Newydd CF14 . . . .176 F4
Clos Ogney CF61 . . . . . .209 F7
Clos Onnen SA13 . . . . .148 A5
Clos Pandy CF83 . . . . . .138 D6
Clos Pant Glas CF83 . . .138 F6
Clos Pantycosyn 🏠12
CF3 . . . . .179 F6
Clos Pen Pant SA4 . . . . .19 D3
Clos Pen y Banc SA4 . . .68 C8
Clos Pen y Clawdd 🏠7
CF3 . . . . .179 F6
Clos Penbwl SA4 . . . . . .44 C2
Clos Pendderi SA14 . . . .41 F5
Clos Penderri SA4 . . . . .44 C2
Clos Pengelli SA4 . . . . .43 C7
Clos Penglyn CF35 . . . .152 E2
Clos Pentyle SA8 . . . . . .23 B2
Clos Penyfai SA15 . . . . .40 F7
Clos Plas Isaf SA14 . . . .42 C7
Clos Powys CF38 . . . . . .155 F6
Clos Rhandir SA4 . . . . . .65 E8
Clos Rhedyn SA4 . . . . . .46 A4
Clos Rhymni SA6 . . . . . .46 A4
Clos San Pedr 🏠5 SA15 40 D4
Clos Sant Paul SA14 . . . .40 D4
Clos Sant Teilo SA5 . . . .41 B1
Clos Saron SA5 . . . . .67 F3
Clos Smyrna CF31 . . . . .168 D8
Clos St Cenydd SA3 . . .228 C2
Clos Synod 🏠8 CF14 . . .177 B3
Clos Taf CF5 . . . . .176 F2
Clos Tan-y-cefn
CF31 . . . . .169 B3
Clos Tan-y-fron
CF31 . . . . .169 B3
Clos Tawe CF62 . . . . . . .214 C6
Clos Tecwyn CF23 . . . . .178 B3
Clos Tir Rwyn CF82 . . . .111 F7
Clos Tir-y-Pwll NP11 . . .87 B7
Clos Tirffordd SA4 . . . . .44 C2
Clos Ton Mawr CF14 . . .159 C1
Clos Trafle SA14 . . . . . . .66 C6
Clos Trefin NP12 . . . . . .85 F3
Clos Tregare 🏠10 CF3 . .179 F6
Clos Ty Bronna CF5 . . .193 C2
Clos Ty Clyd CF14 . . . . .176 E4
Clos Ty Mawr SA4 . . . . .44 B2
Clos Ty-Gwyn SA4 . . . . .18 F4
Clos Tygwyn
Clydach SA6 . . . . .46 E8
Gowerton SA4 . . . . .66 B6
Clos Tyla Bach CF3 . . . .180 B7
Clos Vernon Watkins
SA4 . . . . .43 A4
Clos Waun Ceffyl
CF46 . . . . .83 C4
Clos Waun Fach
CF83 . . . . .137 D1
Clos Waun Wen SA6 . . .45 B1
Clos William CF14 . . . . .159 C1
Clos y Banc-yr-Eithin
SA4 . . . . .43 A3
Clos y Berllan 🏠4 CF3 180 A6
Clos y Bont Faen
Cwmrhydyceirw SA6 . . . .46 A5
Swansea SA6 . . . . .45 F5
Clos y Bryn CF14 . . . . .159 A1
Clos y Coed
Llantwit Fardre CF38 . . .156 E4
Pen-y-Fai CF31 . . . . . . .168 D8
Clos y Craig CF14 . . . . .159 B1
Clos y Crydd NP23 . . . . . .8 C1
Clos y Deri SA14 . . . . . . .41 B8
Clos y Dolydd CF38 . . . .156 A5
Clos y Dryw CF14 . . . . .159 E4
Clos y Ffynnon CF23 . . .160 F1
Clos y Gelyn CF23 . . . . .179 A7
Clos y Gwadd CF14 . . . .159 E4
Clos y Gwalch CF14 . . .159 E4
Clos y Gwyddfid
CF15 . . . . .176 A8
Clos y Hebog CF14 . . . .159 E4

Clos y Morfa SA4 . . . . . .42 F3
Clos y Mynydd
Gorseinon SA4 . . . . .42 F2
Morganstown CF15 . . . .176 A7
Clos y Nant
🏠4 Cardiff CF5 . . . . . .193 D8
Gorseinon SA4 . . . . .42 F2
Clos y Waun
Cross Hands SA14 . . . . .218 B7
Thomastown CF39 . . . . .133 A3
Clos y Wern CF14 . . . . .177 C8
Clos Yr Aer CF14 . . . . . .177 C8
Clos Yr Alarch CF14 . . .159 E4
Clos Yr Arad CF83 . . . . .137 D1
Clos Yr Eos CF14 . . . . . .159 E4
Clos Yr Hafod CF14 . . . .177 C8
Clos yr Harbwr CF62 . .214 D2
Clos Yr Onnen SA4 . . . . .46 D1
Clos Yr Orsaf SA6 . . . . . .69 A8
Clos Yr Wenallt CF14 . .159 B1
Clos Yr Ysgol SA7 . . . . . .70 A7
Clos Ysbyty
Caerphilly CF83 . . . . . . .137 F1
Neath SA11 . . . . .72 A4
Clos Ysgallen SA7 . . . . . .69 D6
Clos Ysgol Gymraeg
SA5 . . . . .68 B2
Clos Ystum Taf CF14 . . .176 E4
Clos-Mabon CF14 . . . . .177 B8
Clos-y- Dyfrisi CF14 . . .159 D3
Clos-y- Felin SA18 . . . . .219 D7
Clos-y-Berllan 🏠8 CF3 .179 F6
Clos-y-Blaidd CF14 . . . .159 D4
Clos-y-Broch CF14 . . . .159 E3
Clos-y-Carlwm CF14 159 D4
Clos-y-Cedr CF83 . . . . . .138 A4
Clos-y-Ceinach CF14 159 E4
Clos-y-Culfor 🏠15 CF3 179 F6
Clos-y-Cwarra CF5 . . . . .92 D4
Clos-y-Cwm SA14 . . . . .218 D7
Clos-y-Deri
Llanedi SA4 . . . . .218 D2
Porthcawl CF36 . . . . . . .182 F8
Clos-y-Derwen SA14 218 B8
Clos-y-Draenog
CF14 . . . . .159 E3
Clos-y-Felin SA18 . . . . .219 D7
Clos-y-Gof CF5 . . . . . . .192 F5
Clos-y-Grug CF36 . . . . .182 F8
Clos-y-Gweydd SA4 . . . .66 C8
Clos-y-Maerdy SA4 . . . . .66 C8
Clos-y-pant CF83 . . . . .158 E8
Clos-y-Rhiw CF5 . . . . . .193 B3
Clos-y-Talcen CF31 . . . .168 D8
Clos-y-Waun CF31 . . . . .169 A5
Clos-y-Wern CF31 . . . . .169 A5
Clos-y-Wiver CF61 . . . . .210 A2
Clos-y-Wiwer CF14 . . . .159 E3
Clos-yr- Eirin CF31 . . . .168 B6
Clos-yr-Ardd CF14 . . . .177 D1
Clos-yr-Eos CF33 . . . . . .165 F6
Clos-yr-Gornant 🏠5
CF3 . . . . .180 A6
Clos-yr-Hendre SA18 218 E6
Clos-yr-Onnen
Cardiff CF3 . . . . .180 A6
Llantwit Major CF61 . . .210 A5
Close The
Aberdare CF44 . . . . .29 A1
Bargoed CF81 . . . . .58 A1
Cardiff CF14 . . . . .177 F8
Cefn Hengoed CF82 . . . .84 F4
Cwmbran NP44 . . . . . . .116 F4
Gorseinon SA4 . . . . .43 A1
Rhydyfelin CF37 . . . . . .136 A6
Sarn CF32 . . . . .150 D4
Swansea SA5 . . . . .45 C2
Clost Reoda CF14 . . . . .177 B5
Cloth Hall La CF48 . . . . .10 A5
Clovelly Ave NP23 . . . . .14 E5
Clovelly Cres CF3 . . . . .179 A5
Clovelly Pl SA3 . . . . . . .122 E6
Clover Ct NP44 . . . . .88 F1
Clover Gr CF5 . . . . .176 C1
Clover Rd CF47 . . . . .10 C4
Club La SA9 . . . . .1 F1
Club Rd NP4 . . . . .62 A6
Club Row Blaina NP13 . . .15 E5
Clydach NP7 . . . . .9 D6
Ystrad CF42 . . . . .79 D3
Club St CF44 . . . . .53 B8
Clun Ave CF72 . . . . . . .173 B8
Clun Cres CF72 . . . . . . .173 B8
Clun Prim Sch SA11 . .226 C4
Clun Terr CF24 . . . . . . .178 A2
Clwyd CF64 . . . . .207 C5
Clwyd -Wen SA4 . . . . . . .66 A5
Clwyd Ave CF44 . . . . . . .29 E2
Clwyd Com Prim Sch
SA5 . . . . .68 B2
Clwyd Ho 🏠3 CF23 . . . .178 C2
Clwyd Rd
Gwaun-Cae-Gurwen
SA18 . . . . .220 D6
Swansea SA5 . . . . .68 B4
Clwyd Way CF62 . . . . . .211 D7
Clwyd-y-Clap La NP4 . . .39 C7
Clwydyfagwyr CF48 . . .225 F1
Clydach Ave
Ebbw Vale NP23 . . . . .7 C5
Resolven SA11 . . . . .226 E1
Clydach Cl
Bettws NP20 . . . . .116 E1
Pontypridd CF37 . . . . . .109 D5
Clydach Inf Sch SA6 . . .46 D7

Clydach Jun Sch SA6 ....46 D8
Clydach Rd
 Craig-Cefn-Parc SA6 ....22 B2
 Tonypandy CF40 ......106 C7
 Ynysforgan SA6 ....46 A2
 Ynystawe SA6 ....46 C5
 Ynysybwl CF37 ....81 F2
Clydach Sch NP7 ....9 D6
Clydach St
 Brynmawr NP23 ....8 C5
 Cardiff CF11 ....195 A3
Clydach Terr CF37 ......81 F2
Clydach War Meml Hospl
 SA6 ....46 D7
Clyde Cl NP12 ....85 D4
Clyde St
 [2] Cardiff CF24 ......195 D5
 Risca NP11 ....115 A1
Clydesmuir Ind Est
 CF24 ....195 F8
Clydesmuir Rd CF24 ....195 F7
Clyffard Cres NP20 ....143 B4
Clyffes NP44 ....89 D3
Clyndu St SA6 ....68 F8
Clyne Cl SA3 ....93 F1
Clyne Cres SA3 ....93 F1
Clyne Dr SA2 ....94 B1
Clyne Farm Activities Ctr
 SA3 ....93 F2
Clyne Rd CF82 ....84 F5
Clyne Terr SA11 ....226 F1
Clyne Valley Cotts SA2 93 F1
Clyne Valley Ctry Pk
 SA2 ....94 A4
Clyne Valley La SA2 ...94 B2
Clyne Valley Rd SA2 ...93 F1
Clyne View SA2 ....93 E6
Clyngwyn Rd
 Treherbert CF42 ....50 D3
 Ystalyfera SA9 ....2 B7
Clyngwyn Terr CF42 ....50 D3
Clynmaes Pl SA5 ....67 E6
Clynmawr St NP13 .....36 A5
Clyro Ct SA1 ....69 C4
Clyro Pl CF14 ....177 A3
Clytha Cres [3] NP20 ..143 C3
Clytha Inf & Jun Sch
 NP20 ....142 F4
Clytha Park Rd NP20 ..143 A4
Clytha Sq NP20 ....143 C3
Cnap Llwyd Rd SA6 ....68 D6
Co-operative Cotts
 CF42 ....78 C5
Co-operative St CF41 ..78 F3
Coach Rd NP22 ....6 D1
Coal Pit La CF3 ......162 B4
Coal Plant Control Rd
 CF62 ....211 F1
Coalbrook Rd SA4 .....43 C5
Coalbrook Valecourt
 NP23 ....15 C7
Coalbrookvale Terr
 NP23 ....15 C8
Coaster Pl CF10 ......195 F3
Coates Pl CF3 ....179 D7
Coates Rd CF64 ....206 F1
Cobblers Ct [1] SA15 ..40 C7
Cobden Pl
 Abercarn NP11 ....114 C4
 [4] Merthyr Tydfil CF47 ..30 E8
Cobden St
 Abercarn NP11 ....114 C4
 Aberdare CF44 ....53 C6
Cobham Cl SA4 ....43 A3
Cobham Dr SA11 ....72 C5
Cobner Cl NP4 ....38 C1
Cobol Rd CF3 ....180 B7
Coburn St CF24 ....195 B8
Coch-y-Cwm Rd SA1 ...69 C2
Coch-y-North NP4 .....61 C5
Cocker Ave NP44 ......89 D1
Cockett Rd SA2 ....67 C4
Codgers Cnr CF38 .....156 B7
Coed Arhyd CF5 ....192 E4
Coed Arian CF14 ......177 B3
Coed Bach Barry CF62 214 C7
 Pencoed CF35 ....170 C8
Coed Bychan Cres
 CF72 ....153 F3
Coed Cae
 Caerphilly CF83 ......138 C4
 Cwmbran NP44 ....89 C5
 New Tredegar NP24 ...33 E2
Coed Cae Jun Sch
 NP13 ....15 D7
Coed Cae Rd
 Llanelli SA15 ....40 F5
 Llanelli SA15 ....41 F5
Coed Cae Uchaf SA15 ..40 F5
Coed Cae'r Odin
 CF31 ....168 B6
Coed Camlas NP4 ......62 F5
Coed Ceirios
 Cardiff CF14 ....177 B7
 Llansamlet SA7 ....46 D1
Coed Celyn Rd SA2 ....94 B4
Coed Cochwyn Ave
 CF14 ....177 B7
Coed Duon View NP11 86 D5
Coed Edeyrn CF23 ....178 E8
Coed Eithen St NP4 ...17 D6
 NP44 ....89 B1
Coed Garw NP44 ......90 A6
Coed Gelli Parc NP12 ..58 E1

Coed Gethin CF83 .....137 E7
Coed Glas NP44 ....89 D1
Coed Glas Cty Prim Sch
 CF14 ....177 F8
Coed Glas Rd CF14 ...177 D8
Coed Helyg CF31 .....168 B5
Coed Isaf Rd CF37 ...135 A8
Coed Lan SA4 ....65 D1
Coed Leddyn CF83 ....137 F6
Coed Lee NP44 ....89 C1
Coed Lee Ct NP44 ....89 C1
Coed Llydd NP4 ......17 D6
Coed Main CF83 ......138 D4
Coed Marsarnen
 CF71 ....187 A3
Coed Mawr
 Barry CF62 ....214 C7
 Ystrad Mynach CF82 ..111 E7
Coed Moelfa Rd NP11 .87 B3
Coed Mor SA2 ....94 B5
Coed Nant Ho SA1 ....68 C2
Coed Parc SA12 ......99 D5
Coed Parc Ct CF31 ...168 E4
Coed Pwll CF83 ......138 C4
Coed Rd NP4 ....17 D6
Coed Terr
 Abersychan NP4 ......37 E4
 [4] Blaenavon NP4 ....17 D6
Coed Tymaen CF31 ...168 C6
Coed y Bronallt SA4 ..19 A5
Coed y Bryn NP12 ....85 D6
Coed y Cadno CF31 ...168 B8
Coed y Capel CF62 ...214 C2
Coed y Gog CF31 .....168 B4
Coed y Llinos CF83 ..137 E3
Coed y Wenallt CF14 .159 B1
Coed y Wennol CF83 ..137 E3
Coed Yr Eos CF83 ....137 E3
Coed Yr Esgob CF72 ..155 C4
Coed yr Odyn CF42 ...214 B3
Coed Yr Ynn CF14 ....177 D8
Coed-Cae-Ddu Rd
 NP4 ....85 F4
Coed-pen-Maen Sch
 CF37 ....109 D2
Coed-Saeson Cres
 SA2 ....94 D7
Coed-y-Brain Prim Sch
 CF83 ....137 F8
Coed-y-Brain Rd
 CF83 ....137 F8
Coed-y-Cando Rd
 NP4 ....62 F5
Coed-y-Felln CF62 ...214 C5
Coed-y-Garn NP23 ...14 F2
Coed-y-Gores CF23 ..178 E5
Coed-y-Graig CF35 ..170 D8
Coed-y-Ian Comp Sch
 CF37 ....109 C2
Coed-y-Ian Prim Sch
 CF37 ....109 C2
Coed-y-Lan Rd CF37 109 D5
Coed-y-Llyn
 Cardiff CF23 ....178 A4
 Radyr CF15 ....176 A7
Coed-y-Pandy CF83 ..138 D6
Coed-y-Pergwm
 SA11 ....223 C1
Coed-y-Pia CF83 .....112 A5
Coed-y-pica CF83 ....137 A6
Coed-y-Rhaidyr
 SA11 ....224 A3
Coed-yr-Esgob Prim Sch
 CF72 ....155 C4
Coed-yr-Haf CF82 ....84 D1
Coed-yr-Onen CF83 ..137 E1
Coedbach SA4 ....19 C3
Coedcae Ebbw Vale NP23 7 B4
 Pontardawe SA8 ......23 F6
 Ystrad Mynach CF82 ..111 E8
Coedcae Back CF48 ...11 D5
Coedcae Comp Sch
 SA15 ....40 F5
Coedcae Ind Est
 CF72 ....154 F1
Coedcae La
 Pontyclun CF72 ......172 F8
 Talbot Green CF72 ...155 A1
Coedcae Pl NP4 ......62 B6
Coedcae Rd
 Abertridwr CF83 ......137 A7
 Porth CF39 ....108 A2
 Trehafod CF37 ....108 B3
Coedcae Row CF48 ...11 D5
Coedcae St CF11 .....194 F3
Coedcae Terr NP4 ....62 B6
Coedcae Wlk NP12 ..85 D7
Coedcae'r Cwrt [12]
 CF47 ....30 E8
Coeden Dal CF23 .....178 E8
Coedeva Mill NP44 ...116 C3
Coedffaldau SA9 .....221 B6
Coedglas SA4 ....28 B6
Coedlan SA9 ....2 D1
Coedpenmaen Rd
 Pontypridd CF37 .....109 D1
 Pontypridd CF37 .....109 E2
Coedriglan Dr CF5 ...192 E3
Coedwig Pl SA1 ......68 A3
Coedybrain Ct CF83 ..137 E8
Coedygric Rd NP4 ....62 E3
Coedylan Comp Sch The
 CF37 ....109 F6

Coegnant Cl CF31 ....169 B7
Coegnant Cotts CF34 102 A7
Coegnant Rd
 Maesteg CF34 ....102 A6
 Maesteg CF34 ....102 A7
Coelbren Cty Prim Sch
 SA10 ....222 F6
Coety Prim Sch CF35 169 D8
Coffins Row CF48 ....10 D1
Cog Rd CF64 ....216 B6
Cogan Ct CF64 ....206 E6
Cogan Hill CF64 .....206 F6
Cogan Pill Rd CF64 ..206 E6
Cogan Prim Sch
 CF64 ....206 E5
Cogan Sta CF64 ......206 E6
Cogan Terr CF24 .....195 A7
Coggins Cl CF83 .....137 D1
Coigne Terr CF63 ....215 B5
Coity Cl CF3 ....180 A7
Coity Cres CF31 .....169 E3
Coity Rd CF31 ....168 F6
Coity Terr NP4 ....17 A5
Colbourne Rd CF38 ..156 A6
Colbourne Terr SA1 ..68 C1
Colbourne Wlk [8]
 CF11 ....194 D5
Colbren Sq SA18 ....220 D5
Colchester Ave CF23 178 E1
Colchester Ct CF23 ..178 D1
Colchester Factory Est
 CF23 ....195 E8
Colcot Prim Sch
 CF62 ....204 E1
Colcot Rd CF62 ......214 D7
Cold Bath Rd NP18 ..118 B2
Cold Knap Way CF62 214 C1
Cold Store The NP44 ..90 A1
Cold Stores Rd CF10 195 E1
Coldbrook Rd E CF63 215 C8
Coldbrook Rd W
 CF63 ....215 B7
Coldra Est NP18 .....144 F7
Coldra Rd
 Blaenrhondda CF42 ..50 D4
 Newport NP20 ....143 A3
 Treherbert CF42 .....50 E3
Coldra The NP18 .....144 F7
Coldra Wood Dr
 NP18 ....144 B8
Coldstream Cl NP44 ..90 A5
Coldstream St SA15 ..40 C6
Coldstream Terr
 CF11 ....194 F5
Cole Ct CF83 ....138 D4
Coleford Dr CF3 .....180 A6
Colenso Terr
 Rhymney NP22 ....12 C5
 Tredegar NP22 ....13 F6
Coleridge Ave CF64 ..206 F4
Coleridge Cl CF31 ...168 C5
Coleridge Cres
 Barry CF62 ....214 E8
 Swansea SA2 ....93 F8
Coleridge Gdns CF83 139 C6
Coleridge Gn NP44 ..89 C2
Coleridge Rd
 Cardiff CF11 ....194 D1
 Newport NP19 ....144 A5
Coleshill Terr SA15 ..40 C5
Colhugh Cl CF61 .....209 F6
Colhugh Pk CF61 ....209 F5
Colhugh St CF61 .....209 F5
Colin Way CF5 ....193 E6
Collard Cres CF62 ...214 F7
College Cl
 Bridgend CF31 ....169 A3
 [6] Cardiff CF14 ....177 B4
 Pontypridd CF37 ....135 F5
College Cres NP11 ..118 B3
College Fields Cl
 CF62 ....214 E5
College Gdns CF61 ..209 F6
College Glade NP18 .118 A4
College Gn SA13 ....125 F3
College Hill SA15 ...40 E5
College Pl CF62 .....214 E5
College Rd Barry CF62 214 E5
 Caerleon NP18 ......118 B3
 Cardiff CF14 ....177 B3
 Ebbw Vale NP23 .....7 C3
 Pontypool NP4 ......62 D7
College Row SA9 ....2 F8
College Sq SA15 .....40 E5
College St
 Aberdare CF44 ......29 B2
 Llanwit Major CF61 209 F6
 Swansea SA1 ....95 D7
College Terr [9] NP4 ..38 A1
College Way Cardiff Rd
 CF37 ....135 F5
Collenna Rd CF39 ...133 C6
Collier St NP19 ......143 D6
Colliers Row NP24 ..33 D3
Colliers Way (Ffordd y
 Glowyr) CF40 ......106 E7
Colliers' Row NP23 ..7 D1
Colliery Rd
 Bedwas CF83 ....138 E7
 Llanbradach CF83 ..111 F4
Colliery St CF37 ....108 D2
Collingwood Ave [1]
 NP19 ....144 B4
Collingwood Cl [4]
 NP19 ....144 A4
Collingwood Cres [3]
 NP19 ....144 A4

Collingwood Rd [5]
 NP19 ....144 A4
Collins Cl
 Newport NP20 ....142 E2
 Treherbert CF42 .....50 F1
Collins Row NP22 ....12 C7
Collins St SA11 ....71 C4
Collins Terr CF37 ....135 E6
Collivaud Pl CF24 ...195 D6
Collwyn Rd CF33 ....148 B1
Collwyn St CF39 .....154 D8
Colne St NP19 ....143 D5
Colonel Road SA18 ..219 C6
Colston Ave NP19 ...144 A3
Colston Ct NP19 .....144 A3
Colston Ho CF11 ....194 E6
Colston Rd NP19 ....195 C8
Colts Foot Cl NP20 ..143 A6
Coltshill Dr SA3 ....122 F5
Colum Dr CF10 ....194 B4
Colum Pl CF10 ....194 B4
Colum Rd CF10 ......194 B4
Colum Terr CF10 ....194 F7
Columbia Row [12]
 SA15 ....40 D5
Columbus Cl CF62 ..215 A8
Columbus Wlk CF10 195 B4
Column St Barry CF64 215 E6
 Treorchy CF42 ......78 D6
Colwill Rd CF14 .....177 B2
Colwinston Cl CF14 .177 A3
Colwinston St CF14 177 A3
Colwyn Ave SA1 .....69 C5
Colwyn Rd Cardiff CF3 179 C3
 Ton Pentre CF41 ....79 A2
Coly Row CF46 ......55 F8
Comet St CF24 ......195 C6
Comfrey Cl
 [11] Cardiff CF3 ....180 A8
 Newport NP20 ......143 A6
Comin Cty Jun Mix Sch
 CF44 ....28 F3
Comin Inf Sch CF44 .28 F3
Commerce Pl CF44 ..53 C7
Commercial Bldgs
 Blackwood NP12 ....59 B2
 Port Talbot SA13 ...125 B7
Commercial Cl NP4 ..37 C5
Commercial Pl
 [5] Cwmbran NP44 ..89 E5
 Mountain Ash CF45 .82 B6
 Pontycymer CF32 ..103 E3
Commercial Rd
 Abercarn NP11 ....87 B1
 Abersychan NP4 ....37 E5
 Barry CF63 ....215 A4
 Cwmfelinfach NP11 ..113 A4
 Machen CF83 ....140 B6
 Newbridge NP11 ....60 A1
 Newport NP20 ......143 C3
 Port Talbot SA13 ...125 C6
 Resolven SA11 ......226 D5
 Rhydfro SA8 ....23 C8
Commercial St
 Aberbargoed CF81 ..58 B4
 [6] Aberdare CF44 ..29 A2
 Abergwynfi SA13 ...76 F5
 Abertillery NP13 ....36 B5
 Bargoed CF81 ....58 A1
 Beddau CF38 ....156 A7
 Bedlinog CF46 ......54 A7
 [9] Blaenavon NP4 ..17 C6
 Cwmbran NP44 .....89 E2
 Cwmbran NP44 .....89 E2
 Cwmfelinfach NP11 ..113 A6
 Ebbw Vale NP23 ....14 D6
 Ferndale CF43 ......80 A7
 Gelligaer CF82 ......84 D7
 Glyncorrwg SA13 ...227 C2
 Llantrisant CF72 ....155 D3
 Llantwit Major CF61 209 F6
 Maesteg CF34 ......102 A3
 Mountain Ash CF45 .54 D3
 Nant-y-Moel CF32 ..104 E6
 Neath SA11 ....71 E8
 Nelson CF46 ....83 E3
 New Tredegar NP24 .33 E2
 Newport NP20 ......143 C4
 Ogmore Vale CF32 ..104 E4
 Pengam NP12 ....85 B7
 Pontllanfraith NP12 .85 F4
 Pontypool NP4 ......62 C6
 Pontypool NP4 ......62 D7
 Pyle CF33 ....148 D2
 Risca NP11 ....115 A1
 Senghenydd CF83 ..110 F2
 Seven Sisters SA10 222 C3
 Tredegar NP22 ......13 E7
 Ystalyfera SA9 .....2 B6
 Ystrad Mynach CF82 84 F1
 Ystradgynlais SA9 ..1 F1
Commercial Terr CF46 83 B6
Commerical St CF48 ..11 B4
Commin Cl NP12 .....58 D7
Commin Rd CF37 ....109 D1
Commonwealth Rd
 NP23 ....7 D6
Company St SA11 ...226 D5
Compass Rd CF10 ...195 E1
Compass Row SA8 ..23 D7
Compass St SA5 ....68 C3
Compton Ave SA10 ..70 F7
Compton Cl NP10 ...142 E6
Compton Rd
 Skewen SA10 ....71 A7

Compton Rd continued
 Tonypandy CF40 .....106 C5
Compton St CF11 ....194 F4
Concorde Dr CF39 ...133 E5
Conduit Pl SA13 .....125 D7
Conduit St SA13 .....125 D7
Coney Beach Amusement
 Pk CF36 ....183 A6
Conifer Cl NP18 .....117 E2
Coniston Cl [1] NP19 143 F8
Coniston Ho NP44 ..89 B3
Coniston Rise CF44 .29 E1
Coniston Wlk SA2 ...94 D7
Connaught Cl CF36 ..165 F2
Connaught Ho CF11 194 E6
Connaught Rd CF24 195 C8
Connaught St SA13 .125 C8
Consort St CF45 ....54 L1
Constable Dr NP19 .144 A8
Constable Ho [2] SA12 98 D1
Constance St NP19 ..143 D7
Constant Cl CF11 ...207 A8
Constant Rd SA13 ..125 D6
Constant Row NP11 115 A2
Constantine Ct CF40 107 A3
Constantine St CF40 107 A3
Constellation St
 CF24 ....195 D6
Constitution Hill
 Cowbridge CF71 ....188 E1
 Swansea SA1 ....95 B7
Convent St SA1 .....68 D1
Conville Rd CF32 ...103 E6
Conway Cl
 Cwmbran NP44 .....89 E4
 Dinas Powys CF64 .206 C3
 Pontypridd CF37 ...109 C5
Conway Cres CF38 ..135 F2
Conway Croft NP19 144 A4
Conway Ct
 Blackwood NP12 ...58 D7
 Caerphilly CF83 ....137 D4
 Swansea SA5 ....68 A4
Conway Dr
 Aberdare CF44 .....29 E1
 Barry CF62 ....214 C6
Conway Gr CF48 ....225 F1
Conway Rd
 Abertillery NP11 ....59 F6
 Cardiff CF11 ....194 D1
 Newport NP19 .....144 A4
 Pontypool NP4 .....62 B7
Conway Sac [2] NP19 144 A4
Conway Terr NP44 ..89 F5
Conybeare Rd
 Cardiff CF5 ....194 B2
 Sully CF64 ....216 B5
Conybeare St CF45 ..54 D2
Cook Rd CF62 ....205 A1
Cook Rees Ave SA11 .71 F6
Coolgreany Cl NP20 .117 A1
Coolgreany Cres
 NP20 ....117 A1
Cools Cl NP23 ....35 B8
Coomassie St SA10 .143 D1
Coombe-Tennant Ave
 SA10 ....70 D7
Coombes Rd SA10 ..70 F7
Coopers SA18 ....218 E5
Coopers Ct NP18 ...119 E1
Coopers La CF71 ....188 E2
Coopers Pl CF83 ....137 D1
Coopers Rd SA18 ..218 E5
Coopers Terr CF82 ..111 E7
Coopers Way CF72 ..155 F3
Coopers Yd [3] CF10 195 A4
Copleston Rd CF14 ..177 A2
Copleston St CF45 ..54 D2
Copley Cl SA3 ....122 X4
Copley Lodge SA3 ..122 B7
Copley St SA3 ....54 C4
Copper Beech Cl
 NP18 ....117 E2
Copper St CF24 .....195 D6
Copperfield Ct [1]
 CF62 ....214 F4
Copperfield Dr CF14 159 F2
Copperworks Prim Sch
 SA15 ....40 D5
Copperworks Rd SA15 40 D5
Coppice The CF38 ...136 A2
Coppins The
 Cardiff CF14 ....160 B3
 Newport NP20 .....117 B3
Copse The CF48 ....10 B7
Copse Wlk CF23 ....161 A2
Copthorne Way CF5 192 F2
Cora St CF63 ....215 A5
Corban Ct CF14 .....13 B6
Corbett Cres CF83 .138 B1
Corbett Gr CF83 ....137 E1
Corbett Rd
 Cardiff CF10 ....194 F7
 Llandough CF64 ....206 D6
Corbett St
 Ogmore Vale CF32 .104 E1
 Treherbert CF42 ....51 A1
Corbetts La CF83 ...138 A6
Corelli St NP19 .....143 D6
Coriander Cl NP20 ..143 A6
Corinthian Cl CF64 .206 D7
Cork Dr CF23 ....161 A2
Cork Ho [3] SA1 ....95 E6
Cormorant Cl
 Cardiff CF3 ....179 F8

Cormorant Cl continued
 Llanelli SA15 ....40 B6
Cormorant Way
 Mumbles SA3 ....122 E6
 Newport NP10 ....163 F7
Corn St NP20 ....143 C5
Cornbrook Rd NP20 .116 E2
Corneli Jun Sch CF33 165 F8
Cornelly Cl CF14 ....177 A3
Cornelly St CF14 ....177 A3
Corner House St CF44 28 E7
Cornerswell La [3]
 CF64 ....206 F3
Cornerswell Pl CF64 206 F4
Cornerswell Rd CF64 206 F4
Cornfield Cl CF14 ...159 D1
Cornfield Rise CF83 138 D6
Cornflower Cl CF14 .160 A4
Cornish Cl CF11 ....195 A2
Cornish Pl SA15 ....40 E2
Corntown Rd CF35 .186 C7
Cornwall Cl CF11 ...194 E3
Cornwall Ho [4] SA12 98 C2
Cornwall Pl SA3 ....123 B5
Cornwall Rd
 Barry CF62 ....214 F6
 Newport NP19 .....143 E7
 Tonypandy CF40 ...107 A3
Cornwall Rise CF62 214 F6
Cornwall St CF11 ...194 F4
Cornwood Cl CF5 ...176 B1
Coronation Ave
 Cymmer SA13 ......75 C4
 Resolven SA11 .....226 D5
Coronation Cres
 Fochriw CF81 ....32 D6
 Newbridge NP11 ...87 B8
Coronation Pl
 Abercarn NP11 .....114 C7
 Aberfan CF48 ......55 C5
Coronation Rd
 Caerphilly NP12 ....85 E6
 Cardiff CF14 ....177 D4
 Evanstown CF39 ...132 B7
 [8] Glanaman SA18 220 B8
 Llanelli SA15 ......219 F5
 Pont Rhyd-y-cyff CF34 128 D6
Coronation St
 Aberkenfig CF32 ...150 C4
 Abertillery NP13 ..36 C3
 Barry CF63 ....215 A4
 Bedwas CF83 ......139 A6
 Blaina NP13 ....15 E4
 Bryn SA13 ....100 E5
 Ogmore Vale CF32 104 E4
 Risca NP11 ....115 A1
 Tonypandy CF40 ...107 A2
 Tredegar NP22 ....13 E6
Coronation Terr
 Abersychan NP4 ...37 F4
 Ammanford SA18 ..219 D6
 Heolgerrig CF48 ...10 B1
 Maesteg CF34 .....102 A5
 Penarth CF64 ......207 B5
 Pontypridd CF37 ..109 E3
 Porth CF39 ....107 F5
 Rhymney NP22 ....12 D5
 Senghenydd CF83 .110 F3
Coronet Way SA6 ...69 A7
Corporation Ave SA15 40 E7
Corporation Cl SA15 40 E6
Corporation Rd
 Aberavon SA12 ....98 F1
 Cardiff CF11 ....195 A2
 Loughor SA4 ....42 E1
 Newport NP19 .....143 C4
 Newport NP19 .....164 F8
 Swansea SA5 ......67 C4
Corporation St CF47 10 F2
Corpus Christi RC High
 Sch CF23 ....160 D1
Corris NP44 ....89 D1
Corrwg Ct SA13 ....227 C1
Corrymore Ho SA2 ..94 F6
Corvette Ct CF10 ..195 C3
Corwen Cres CF14 ..177 A3
Cory Cres CF5 ......191 F5
Cory Pk NP44 ......117 B6
Cory Pl CF11 ....207 A8
Cory St Resolven SA11 226 D5
 Swansea SA2 ......94 C6
Cory Way CF63 .....215 A3
Coryton Cl CF14 ...176 F7
Coryton Cres CF14 .176 F7
Coryton Dr CF14 ...176 F7
Coryton Halt CF14 .176 F6
Coryton Prim Sch
 CF14 ....176 F7
Coryton Rise CF14 .176 F7
Cosheston Rd CF5 ..176 D1
Cosmeston Dr CF64 217 E8
Cosmeston Lakes Ctry Pk
 CF64 ....216 F6
Cosmeston Medieval
 Village CF64 ....216 F6
Cosmeston St CF24 177 F3
Cosslett Pl CF11 ...195 A2
Cosy Pl [2] SA8 ....8 B4
Cot Farm Circ NP19 144 F6
Cot Farm Cl NP19 ..144 F6
Cot Farm Wlk NP19 144 F6
Cot Hill NP18 ......145 A6
Cotfarm Gdns NP19 144 F6
Cotman Cl NP19 ...144 F5
Cotswold Ave CF14 .160 B3
Cotswold Cl
 Newport NP19 .....144 C6

Cotswold Cl continued
Swansea SA5 ....67 E3
Cotswold Ct CF23 ...178 C6
Cotswold Rise CF63 .215 B6
Cotswold Way
Newport NP19 .....144 C6
Risca NP11 ....115 D2
Cottage Cl CF14 ....159 F2
Cottage Gdns CF32 ..167 F4
Cottesmore Way
CF72 ....155 E2
Cotton St SA11 .....71 D5
Cottrell Rd
2 Cardiff CF14 ....177 B4
Cardiff CF24 ......195 C8
Cottrell Sq CF63 ...215 A8
Cottrell St CF48 ....55 C5
Coulson Cl 27 NP20 .143 C3
Council Hos
Boverton CF61 .....210 C6
Cwmbran NP44 .....89 E2
Council St
Ebbw Vale NP23 .....7 C1
Merthyr Tydfil CF47 ...10 F4
Cound Terr 4 SA13 ..125 C7
Coundley Cl NP12 ....85 B5
Countess Pl CF64 ..206 F3
Countisbury Ave CF3 .176 C4
Country View CF3 ...136 C4
County Hospl NP4 ....62 E4
Court Cl Cardiff CF14 .177 C3
Llantwit Major CF61 .209 F7
Court Colman Flats
CF32 ....104 E7
Court Colman St
CF32 ....104 E7
Court Cres
Aberthin CF71 .....189 C3
Bassaleg NP10 .....142 B2
Court Dr CF71 .....188 E2
Court Farm Cl NP44 .117 A8
Court Farm Rd NP44 .117 A8
Court Gdns NP10 ....141 F6
Court House St CF37 .135 C4
Court Isha CF32 ....167 B2
Court La CF32 .....167 B2
Court Mdw NP18 ....145 C8
Court Mews 4 CF63 .215 B6
Court Newton 3
CF63 ....215 B6
Court Pl 3 CF40 ...106 E6
Court Rd Barry CF63 .215 A5
Barry CF63 ....215 B6
Bridgend CF31 .....168 F4
Caerphilly CF83 ....137 F4
Caerphilly CF83 ....137 F5
Cardiff CF11 ......194 F4
Cardiff CF14 ......177 C3
Cwmbran NP44 .....90 A1
Court Rise 5 NP4 ...17 D7
Court Sch The CF14 .160 A1
Court St Maesteg CF34 101 F3
2 Merthyr Tydfil CF47 .30 E8
Tonypandy CF40 ....106 D6
Court Terr
Cefn Cribwr CF32 ...149 C3
11 Merthyr Tydfil CF47 .30 E8
Court The
Bridgend CF35 .....169 F4
Cardiff CF14 ......160 B4
4 Cardiff CF24 ....195 D8
Corntown CF35 ....186 C7
Llanravon NP44 ....117 B8
Court View NP18 ...145 C8
Court Wlk SA10 ....71 C8
Courtenay Cl CF3 ...179 D7
Courtenay Rd
9 Barry CF63 .....215 B6
Cardiff CF24 ......195 E6
Llanelli SA15 .....40 C6
Courtenay St SA5 ...68 C2
Courtis Rd CF5 ....193 B5
Courtland Bldgs
SA13 ....125 B8
Courtland Pl SA13 ..125 B8
Courtland Terr 8
CF47 ....10 E1
Courtlands CF62 ...214 C3
Courtlands The 7
NP44 ....89 B3
Courtlands Way SA5 .67 E3
Courtney St NP19 ...143 D6
Courtyard The
Newport NP10 .....163 D6
Porthcawl CF36 ....165 D3
Courtyard Units SA10 .70 D5
Courtybella Gdns
NP20 ....143 D2
Courtybella Terr
Newport NP20 .....143 D2
Newport NP20 .....143 D2
Cove Ho 4 SA12 ....98 C1
Cove Rd SA12 .....98 D1
Coveny St 4 CF24 ..195 E6
Coverack Rd NP19 ..143 C4
Covert Wlk NP44 ....89 B1
Cowbridge By-Pass
CF71 ....188 E3
Cowbridge Comp Sch
Cowbridge CF71 ....188 E2
Cowbridge CF71 ....189 A2
Cowbridge Rd
Bridgend CF31 .....169 A2
Pontyclun CF72 ....172 E4
St Athan CF62 .....211 D7
Talbot Green CF72 ..155 B1

Cowbridge Rd continued
Talbot Green CF72 ..155 B2
Cowbridge Rd E
Cardiff CF11 ......194 F5
Cardiff CF5 ....194 A6
Cardiff CF5 ....194 C6
Cowbridge Rd W CF5 193 C4
Cowbridge St 3
CF63 ....215 B2
Cowell Prec 8 SA15 .40 D5
Cowell Rd SA18 ....220 C7
Cowell St SA15 ....40 D5
Cowper Cl
Newport NP20 .....142 B2
Penarth CF64 .....206 F4
Swansea SA2 ......93 F7
Cowper Ct 6 CF24 ..195 C7
Cowper Pl CF24 ....195 C7
Cowshed La NP10 ..142 A2
Cowslip Cl CF23 ...161 A1
Cowslip Dr CF64 ...206 E5
Coychurch Rd
Bridgend CF31 .....169 B3
Pencoed CF35 .....170 B5
Coychurch Rise CF63 215 A8
Coychurch Road Gdns
CF31 ....168 F3
Coytrahen Cl CF31 ..169 B6
Crabapple Cl CF47 ...10 D5
Crabtree Cl CF40 ...107 A5
Crabtree Wlk CF44 ..10 A6
Crack Hill CF31, CF35 .186 E7
Craddock St CF11 ..194 E5
Cradoc Rd CF14 ....177 C4
Cradock St
Llanelli SA15 .....40 D4
Swansea SA1 ......95 C7
Cragside Cl 2 CF3 ..179 F6
Craig Castell CF15 ..176 B7
Craig Cres CF39 ....107 D2
Craig Nedd SA11 ...227 C8
Craig Rd
Briton Ferry SA11 ...71 C1
Cwmbran NP44 .....89 A3
Craig Rhymni SA12 ..33 D4
Craig View Terr NP4 .37 D6
Craig y Darren CF44 .28 C3
Craig y Fan Terr SA13 .75 C5
Craig y Mynydd CF39 133 A3
Craig y Nos NP22 ....6 F1
Craig Yr Allt CF14 ..159 B1
Craig-cefn-parc Cty Prim
Sch SA6 ....22 B4
Craig-fryn Terr CF32 .104 E7
Craig-y-Bwldan SA2 .93 E8
Craig-y-Haul Dr CF3 162 C3
Craig-y-Hendre CF46 .56 B7
Craig-y-Llyn Cres
CF44 ....29 E2
Craig-y-Parc Sch
CF15 ....175 B6
Craig-yr-Eos Ave
CF32 ....184 D3
Craig-yr-Eos Rd
CF37 ....184 C2
Craig-yr-Hesg Prim Sch
CF37 ....109 D5
Craigddu View NP44 .37 E7
Craiglas Cres NP12 ..85 C8
Craiglee Dr CF10 ...195 B4
Craigmuir Rd CF24 .195 F7
Craigwen SA14 .....41 E4
Cramic Way SA13 ..125 B8
Cranbourne Way
CF23 ....160 E1
Cranbrook St CF24 .195 B7
Crane St NP4 ......62 C6
Cranfield Ct SA5 ...67 E5
Cranham Ho NP44 ...89 C2
Cranleigh Rise CF3 .179 A4
Cranmer Ct
Cardiff CF5 ....194 A8
Swansea SA5 ......67 E5
Cranwell Cl 4 CF5 ..194 A8
Craven Wlk CF64 ...217 B8
Crawford Cl CF38 ..156 B6
Crawford Dr CF23 ..161 A1
Crawford Gn SA12 ..98 D7
Crawford Rd SA12 ..98 C7
Crawford St NP19 ..143 D6
Crawford Trad Est
NP19 ....143 D7
Crawley Cl CF14 ...159 E3
Crawshay Ct
Llantwit Major CF61 .210 B7
Mumbles SA3 .....122 F3
Crawshay Dr CF61 ..210 B7
Crawshay Ho CF48 ..10 A3
Crawshay Rd CF40 ..107 A4
Crawshay St
Cardiff CF10 ......195 A4
Hirwaun CF44 .....27 D8
Treorchy CF42 .....79 A4
Ynysybwl CF37 ....109 A8
Crediton Rd CF3 ...179 C6
Creidiol Rd SA1 ....95 C8
Creigiau Prim Sch
CF15 ....174 D8
Cres The CF44 .....28 C4
Crescent Cl CF71 ..189 A2
Crescent Ct
Cardiff CF23 ......178 D6
4 Newport NP19 ..143 F6
Crescent Pk NP20 ..142 E1
Crescent Rd
Caerphilly CF83 ....138 A3

Crescent Rd continued
Gwaun-Cae-Gurwen
SA18 ....220 D6
Newport NP19 .....143 F6
Risca NP11 ....114 E3
Sarn CF32 ....150 E4
Crescent St CF48 ....55 D4
Crescent The
Aberkenfig CF32 ...150 C4
Barry CF62 ....214 B5
Bedwas CF83 .....138 E6
Bridgend CF31 .....169 A4
Caerphilly CF83 ....137 E4
Cardiff CF5 ....193 D7
Cardiff CF5 ....194 B8
Crynant SA10 .....226 A7
Cwmbran NP44 .....89 D1
Ebbw Vale NP23 ....14 D8
Gorslas SA14 .....218 C8
Machen CF83 .....139 F7
Maesycwmmer CF82 .85 B1
Nantyglo NP23 .....15 D7
Swansea SA5 ......67 F5
Tredegar NP22 .....6 D1
Cresselly Villas CF45 .54 E3
Cressfield Dr CF23 .161 B1
Cresswell Cl CF3 ...180 A7
Cresswell Ct CF62 ..214 F8
Cressy Rd CF23 ....178 C1
Crest Acre Cl SA3 ..122 E5
Creswell Ct SA6 ....68 D8
Creswell Rd
Neath SA11 ....71 E7
Swansea SA6 .....68 D8
Creunant Prim Sch
SA10 ....226 A8
Cribarth SA9 ......222 E8
Cribb's Row SA11 ...71 E8
Cribbwr Sq CF33 ...148 C1
Cribyn-Du St CF37 ..109 A8
Criccieth Cl NP12 ...58 D1
Criccieth Ct CF4 ...206 C4
Criccieth Gr CF48 ..225 E1
Criccieth Pl SA1 ....69 C5
Criccieth Rd CF3 ...179 C3
Crichton St
Treherbert CF42 ....51 A1
Treorchy CF42 .....78 C7
Crickhowell Pl SA1 ..69 C5
Crickhowell Rd CF3 .179 F6
Crickhowell Wlk CF3 .179 F6
Cricklewood Cl CF31 .168 C6
Crimson Ave SA12 ..98 C8
Crimson Cl SA12 ...98 B2
Crimson Ct SA12 ...98 B2
Crindau Jun & Inf Sch
NP20 ....143 C7
Crindau Rd NP20 ..143 B8
Cripps Ave NP22 ...13 D8
Crockett St NP20 ...10 C2
Crockherbtown La
CF10 ....195 A6
Croes-y-Pant La NP4 .39 C5
Croescadarn Cl CF23 161 A1
Croescadarn Rd CF23 160 F1
Croescade Rd CF38 .156 B8
Croeserw Ind Est
SA13 ....75 D3
Croeserw Prim Sch
SA13 ....75 D3
Croesffyrdd SA9 .....2 D7
Croespenmaen Ind Est
NP11 ....59 D4
Croesty Prim Sch
CF35 ....170 D7
Croeswen NP44 ....116 F8
Croesyceiliog By-Pass
NP44 ....90 B5
Croesyceiliog Comp Sch
NP44 ....90 A4
Croesyceiliog Jun Sch
NP44 ....90 A5
Croesyceiliog North Road
Inf Sch NP44 ....90 A5
Crofft-y-Genau Rd
CF5 ....175 F2
Croffta CF64 ......206 A4
Croft Ct NP23 ......8 A4
Croft Gdns CF64 ...216 A5
Croft Goch Gdns
CF33 ....148 C2
Croft Goch Rd CF33 .148 C2
Croft La CF32 .....197 A8
Croft Rd SA11 .....71 E8
Croft St
Cowbridge CF71 ...188 F1
New Tredegar NP24 .33 E4
Swansea SA5 .....95 D8
Croft Terr
Cowbridge CF71 ...188 F1
2 Swansea SA5 ...68 C4
Croft The Bettws CF32 129 D3
Llangeinor CF32 ...130 B4
Loughor SA4 ......42 D1
Neath Abbey SA10 ..71 B8
Crofta CF14 ......160 B1
Croften Mede NP44 .89 B1
Croftfield Cres SA3 .122 C6
Crofton Dr SA12 ...98 E6
Crofts Cnr 3 NP44 ..89 B3
Crofts St CF24 ....195 C7
Crofty Ind Est SA4 ..64 B3
Crole St SA1 ......95 B7
Cromer St CF44 ....53 C4
Cromwell Ave SA10 ..48 E2
Cromwell Ct 6 NP19 144 A4
Cromwell Pl 9 NP44 .89 E5

Cromwell Rd
Cardiff CF14 ......177 D4
Neath SA10 ......48 E2
Newport NP19 .....143 F4
Risca NP11 ....114 E3
Cromwell St
Abertillery NP13 ....36 B5
Merthyr Tydfil CF47 ..10 D4
Swansea SA1 ......95 B7
Cromwell Street Bnglws
NP11 ....114 E3
Cronin Ave SA12 ...124 E7
Crook Hill (lower)
NP13 ....36 B7
Crosby Yd CF31 ....168 E6
Cross Acre SA3 ....122 E7
Cross Blanche St CF48 11 C5
Cross Brook St CF37 ..50 D5
Cross Common Rd
CF64 ....206 C1
Cross Francis St CF48 .11 A5
Cross Hands Bsns Pk
SA14 ....218 A8
Cross Hands Cty Prim Sch
SA14 ....218 A8
Cross Houlson St CF48 11 B5
Cross Ifor Terr CF48 ..11 A5
Cross Inn Bldgs 9
SA18 ....219 B7
Cross Inn Rd CF72 ..155 E3
Cross King St CF48 ..11 A7
Cross La 18 NP20 ...143 C4
Cross Lake St CF48 ..79 F6
Cross Mardy St CF47 ..11 A1
Cross Margaret St
CF47 ....10 C2
Cross Morgan St 5
CF47 ....10 D2
Cross Morlais St CF48 .11 A5
Cross Pl CF14 .....177 E1
Cross Rd
Dyffryn Cellwen SA10 .223 A5
Llanelli SA15 .....40 D6
Cross Row 1 CF40 ..106 F3
Cross St
Abercynon CF45 ....82 C5
14 Aberdare CF44 ..29 A1
Aberfan CF48 .....55 C4
Abersychan NP4 ....37 E6
Abertillery NP13 ....36 B5
Abertridwr CF83 ...137 A7
Bargoed CF81 .....58 A2
Bargoed CF81 .....58 A4
Barry CF63 ....215 A5
Bedwas CF83 .....138 E6
Blaenavon NP4 ....17 C6
Blaengarw CF32 ...103 D7
Blaina NP13 ......15 E5
4 Bridgend CF31 ..168 F4
Caerleon NP18 ....118 C2
Cardiff CF15 ......158 C1
Cilfynydd CF37 ....109 F5
Deri CF81 ....57 B8
Ferndale CF43 .....79 F6
Gorseinon SA4 ....43 C2
Hirwaun CF44 .....27 D8
Maesteg CF34 ....102 B3
Mountain Ash CF45 ..81 F8
New Tredegar NP24 .33 F2
Pontarddulais SA4 ..19 D4
Port Talbot SA13 ...99 B1
Porth CF39 ....107 F2
2 Porth CF39 .....107 F2
Resolven SA11 ....226 D5
Rhymney NP22 .....12 E4
Senghenydd CF83 ..110 F2
Swansea SA5 .....68 C4
Tondu CF32 ......150 C5
Tonypandy CF40 ...106 C7
Tonypandy CF40 ...106 C7
3 Trallwn CF37 ...109 D2
Trehafod CF37 ....108 D2
Treharris CF46 .....83 B7
Ystrad CF41 ......79 D2
Ystradgynlais SA9 ..222 A6
Cross The
Llanrhidian SA3 ...229 D2
2 Morriston SA6 ...46 A1
Cross Thomas St 5
CF47 ....10 E8
Cross Way NP22 .....6 D1
Crossbrook St CF37 .109 C1
Crosscombe Terr
NP23 ....35 B7
Crossfield Ave CF36 .182 E7
Crossfield Rd CF62 .214 C4
Crossfields NP15 ...59 D1
Crosshill CF62 ....214 C1
Crosskeys Coll NP11 .114 A4
Crossways NP11 ....87 B7
Crossways Rd CF5 ..193 C5
Crossways St
Barry CF63 ....215 A5
1 Pontypridd CF37 .109 D2
Crosswells Way CF5 .193 A5
Crosswood St CF42 ..78 E6
Crouch Cl NP20 ...116 D1
Crown Ave
Tredegar NP22 .....6 D2
Treorchy CF42 .....78 C8
Crown Bsns Pk NP22 .6 E3
Crown Cl
Caerleon NP18 ....118 C2
Cwmbran NP44 .....89 D6
Crown Cotts SA9 ....1 F2
Crown Est NP12 ....85 D3
Crown Hill CF38 ...156 C6

Crown Hill Dr CF38 .156 C6
Crown La NP12 .....85 D3
Crown Rd
Llanravon NP44 ....90 B1
Maesteg CF34 ....102 C3
Pyle CF33 ....148 F5
Crown Rise
Llanravon NP44 ....90 B1
Maesteg CF34 ....102 C3
Crown Row
Aberdare CF44 .....53 E7
Maesteg CF34 ....102 B3
Crown St
Abertillery NP13 ....36 A6
Newbridge NP11 ...60 A1
Newport NP19 .....143 E6
Port Talbot SA13 ...99 B1
Swansea SA6 .....68 F8
Crown Terr CF42 ....78 C8
Crown Way (Ffordd y
Goron) CF14 .....177 C1
Crown Wlk CF47 ...140 B7
Crownbridge Specl Sch
NP4 ....62 E1
Croyde Ave CF3 ...179 C6
Croydon Cl NP19 ..143 E8
Croydon Ct 8 NP19 .143 E8
Crud-yr-Awel
Gorseinon SA4 ....66 B8
Neath SA10 ......48 D2
Crumlin Dr CF3 ....180 A7
Crumlin High Level Jun
Sch NP11 ......60 A1
Crumlin Rd
Newbridge NP11 ...60 A2
Newbridge NP11 ...60 B3
Pontypool NP4 ....61 C9
Crumlin St NP4 ....62 B6
Crundale Cres CF14 .177 F8
Crwys La CF63 ....215 B8
Crwys Pl CF24 ....195 B8
Crwys Prim Sch (Ysgol
Gynradd y Crwys)
SA4 ....65 E1
Crwys Rd CF24 ....195 B8
Crwys Terr SA5 ....68 B6
Cryddan Rd SA11 ...71 E6
Crymlyn Bog Visitor Ctr
SA1 ....69 D1
Crymlyn Parc SA10 ..70 A6
Crymlyn Rd SA7,SA10 .70 B6
Crymlyn St SA1 ....96 F1
Crymlyn Terr SA1 ...69 C2
Crynallt Inf Sch SA11 .72 B5
Crynallt Jun Sch SA11 .72 B5
Crynallt Rd SA11 ...72 B5
Crynant Bsns Pk
SA10 ....226 A8
Crynant Cl CF62 ...211 D2
Crystal Ave CF23 ..178 A5
Crystal Glen CF14 ..177 F6
Crystal Rise CF14 ..177 F6
Crystal Wood Rd
CF14 ....177 F6
Cty Fire Hq CF72 ..155 A2
Cty H CF10 ....195 A6
Cty H (Neuadd-y-Sir)
CF10 ....195 C3
Cty Prim Sch SA18 .220 D6
Cuckoo St CF32 ...103 F1
Cules Terr CF15 ...157 F5
Culfor Rd SA4 .....65 E8
Culver Cl CF64 ....206 E1
Cumalsie Cres NP12 .86 A3
Cumberland Rd 7
NP19 ....143 E9
Cumberland St CF5 .194 C5
Cumnock Pl CF24 ..195 D5
Cumnock Terr 4
CF24 ....195 D5
Cumrae St 7 CF24 .195 D5
Cunard Row 1 SA12 .99 F5
Cunard Terr SA12 ..99 F5
Cunningham Cl
Cardiff CF23 ......178 C3
Swansea SA2 .....94 C6
Cunningham Rd
NP19 ....144 F7
Curie Cl NP20 .....117 A3
Curlew Cl Cardiff CF14 177 A6
Llanelli SA15 .....40 A6
Mumbles SA3 .....93 E1
Neath SA10 ......48 E2
Newport NP19 .....144 F7
Porthcawl CF36 ....165 D1
Curlew Cres CF62 ..210 D6
Curlew Rd CF36 ...165 D1
Curll Ave CF14 ....177 E3
Curran Emb CF10 ..195 A3
Curran Rd CF10 ...195 A3
Curre St Aberdare CF44 53 C8
Cwm NP23 ....35 A8
Currie Ho SA12 ...98 F2
Curry Cl SA2 ......93 E8
Curtis St SA11 ....71 E5
Curwen Cl SA12 ...72 F3
Curwen Terr
North Cornelly CF33 .165 F7
Pontrhydyfen SA12 ..74 F4
Curwood NP4 .....17 C6
Curzon St NP23 .....8 C4
Custom House Pl 1
CF64 ....207 B5
Customhouse St
CF10 ....195 A4
Cuthbert St CF44 ...10 D4
Cuthbert St 3 CF14 .104 E2
Cuthbertson St SA11 .71 C4
Cutter Cl NP19 ....117 F1

Cwat Pen y Twyn NP22 ..6 D2
Cwm Alarch CF45 ...54 B3
Cwm Alarch Cl CF45 .54 B3
Cwm Arian SA6 ....46 A2
Cwm Barry Way CF62 214 A4
Cwm Bath Rd SA6 ...45 F1
Cwm Cadle SA5 ....67 E6
Cwm Cadno SA13 ..45 E5
Cwm Chapel Rd SA1 .69 B4
Cwm Clyd SA5 ....67 A3
Cwm Cotts CF32 ...130 B4
Cwm Crachen NP23 ..8 C3
Cwm Cwddy Dr NP10 141 E2
Cwm Cynon Bsns Ctr
CF45 ....81 F8
Cwm Cynon Bsns Pk
CF45 ....54 F1
Cwm Ddu Ho CF48 ..10 A1
Cwm Draw Ct NP12 ..86 A3
Cwm Draw Ind Est
NP23 ....14 E8
Cwm Du Cl SA5 ....67 B3
Cwm Dylan Cl NP10 .141 E2
Cwm Eithin CF46 ...83 D3
Cwm Farm La NP4 ..62 D5
Cwm Farm Rd NP13 .36 A6
Cwm Farteg SA13 ..100 F4
Cwm Fedw CF83 ...140 A8
Cwm Ffoes CF32 ..149 C2
Cwm Glas NP22 ....13 D8
Cwm Glas Prim Sch
SA1 ....69 C4
Cwm Graig Bglws
CF47 ....11 A4
Cwm Gwynlais CF15 .176 D8
Cwm Hir NP23 ......7 D3
Cwm Hyfryd CF39 ..133 A3
Cwm Ifor Prim Sch
CF83 ....137 D5
Cwm Isaac CF44 ...26 C8
Cwm La NP10 .....142 B6
Cwm Level Rd SA6 ..68 D1
Cwm Mwyn SA14 ..218 B8
Cwm Nant SA11 ...72 A4
Cwm Nant-Llwyd Rd
SA8 ....24 C5
Cwm Nedd Prim Sch
SA11 ....223 D1
Cwm Nofydd CF14 .177 B8
Cwm Parc CF62 ...214 C5
Cwm Prim Sch SA1 .69 B4
Cwm Rd
Abergarbuoed CF81 .58 A5
Argoed NP12 .....58 F4
Ebbw Vale NP23 ...14 F2
Swansea SA1 ......68 D1
Cwm Rhos View NP22 13 D6
Cwm Sor SA14 .....63 B4
Cwm Tawe Rd SA9 ..222 A6
Cwm Terr Cwm NP23 .35 B7
2 Llanelli SA15 ....40 C7
Swansea SA1 ......68 D1
Cwm y Dwr SA11 ...71 C1
Cwm-bach Inf Sch
CF44 ....53 E8
Cwm-Celyn Rd NP13 .15 E6
Cwm-Cidy La CF62 ..214 A4
Cwm-lai Jun & Inf Schs
CF39 ....133 C2
Cwm-y-Nant NP11 ..141 A7
Cwm-y-Nant Fields
NP44 ....89 D2
Cwm-Yr-Wch SA2 ...93 B8
Cwmaber Inf Sch
CF83 ....137 A8
Cwmaber Jun Sch
CF83 ....137 A8
Cwmafan Inf Sch SA12 99 E5
Cwmafan Jun Sch
SA12 ....99 E5
Cwmaman Inf Sch
CF44 ....53 A4
Cwmaman Rd CF44 ..53 C6
Cwmamman Rd SA18 219 F8
Cwmavon Rd
Abersychan NP4 ...37 F7
Blaenavon NP4 ....17 F4
Cwmavon SA12 ....99 C3
Cwmbach CW Prim Sch
CF44 ....53 F7
Cwmbach Ind Est
CF44 ....53 E7
Cwmbach Jun Sch
CF44 ....29 E1
Cwmbach Rd
Aberdare CF44 .....29 C2
Aberdare CF44 .....29 D1
Llanelli SA15 .....40 A8
Neath SA10 ......48 F3
Swansea SA5 .....67 C3
Cwmbran Sta CF44 ..53 E3
Cwmbran Sta NP44 ..89 E4
Cwmbran Sta NP44 ..89 E4
Cwmbwrla Prim Sch
SA5 ....68 B2
CwMCarn Cl CF3 ...179 F7
Cwmcarn Forest Dr
NP11 ....114 B8
Cwmcarn High Sch
NP11 ....114 B8
Cwmcarn Jun & Inf Sch
NP11 ....114 C7
Cwmcelyn Inf Sch
NP13 ....15 E6

Cwmcelyn Newydd NP13 15 F6
Cwmclais Rd SA12 99 D5
Cwmclyd SA9 222 A6
Cwmclydach Inf & Jun Mix Schs CF44 106 B7
CwMCottage Rd NP13 36 C4
Cwmdar Cty Prim Sch CF44 28 C3
Cwmdare Rd CF44 28 C4
Cwmdare St CF24 177 F1
Cwmdonkin Dr SA2 95 A7
Cwmdonkin Terr SA2 94 F7
Cwmdows Terr NP11 86 E6
Cwmdu Ind Est SA5 67 F2
Cwmdu Rd
Godrergraig SA8 221 B1
Maesteg CF34 102 D3
Pontardawe SA8 24 C8
Troedyrhiw CF48 31 B1
Cwmdu St CF34 102 B3
Cwmfelin SA10 71 B8
Cwmfelin Prim Sch CF34 128 C8
Cwmfelin Rd SA14 41 F3
Cwmfelin Way SA1 68 C2
Cwmfelinfach Jun & Inf Sch NP11 113 A4
Cwmffrwdoer Prim Sch NP4 61 E8
Cwmgarw Rd SA18 221 A8
Cwmgelli Cl SA5 68 D6
Cwmgelli Dr SA5 68 C6
Cwmgelli Rd SA6 68 C7
Cwmgelli Villas NP12 58 F1
Cwmglas Inf Sch CF83 112 A3
Cwmglo Rd CF48 10 A1
Cwmgors Ind Est SA18 220 D6
Cwmgwili Cty Prim Sch SA14 218 C5
Cwmhir Rd NP4 63 D7
Cwmlan Terr SA1 68 D4
Cwmlas Flats CF83 112 A3
Cwmllynfell Prim Sch SA9 221 B7
Cwmnanthir Terr SA18 220 E7
Cwmneol Pl CF44 53 A4
Cwmneol St CF44 53 A4
Cwmparc Forest Wlk CF42 78 D5
Cwmphil Rd SA9 1 C1
Cwmrhydyceirw Prim Sch SA6 45 F4
Cwmrhydyceirw Rd SA6 45 F3
Cwmsaerbren Flats CF42 50 F1
Cwmsaerbren St CF42 50 F1
Cwmsyfiog Prim Sch NP24 34 A1
Cwmsyfiog Rd CF81 58 B7
Cwmtawe Bsns Pk SA8 23 F5
Cwmtawe Comp Sch (Ysgol Gyfun Cwmtawe) SA8 23 E3
Cwmtawe Cty Comp (upper) Sch SA8 23 E6
Cwmtillery Ind Est NP13 36 B7
Cwmtillery Jun Sch NP13 36 A7
Cwmtorlais Rd NP11 86 E6
Cwmynyscoy Rd NP4 62 C4
Cwmynysmintan Rd CF44 28 D7
Cwndonkin Cl SA2 95 A7
Cwrdy La NP4 62 C2
Cwrdy Rd NP4 62 D2
Cwrdy Wlk NP4 62 D2
Cwrt Alexander CF36 36 C4
Cwrt Alun Lewis CF44 53 A3
Cwrt Anghorfa CF33 148 B2
Cwrt Bethel CF37 109 F5
Cwrt Bethell CF72 173 B8
Cwrt Bleddyn NP44 89 D1
Cwrt Bryn Cynon CF45 82 C5
Cwrt Bryn Isaf CF44 26 C8
Cwrt Cefn CF14 160 B2
Cwrt Ceri CF14 177 B8
Cwrt Cilmeri SA6 46 A2
Cwrt Coed Parc CF34 102 B2
Cwrt Deri CF14 177 F8
Cwrt Dewi Sant [3] CF24 195 C5
Cwrt Dowlais NP44 116 E8
Cwrt Draw Llyn CF83 158 F8
Cwrt Eglwys Newydd CF14 177 A5
Cwrt Elusendy [4] SA15 40 E5
Cwrt Emily SA7 46 F1
Cwrt Faenor CF38 155 F5
Cwrt Fforest CF45 54 E2
Cwrt Finchley CF5 193 E7
Cwrt Glanhowy NP12 85 E8
Cwrt Glanrhyd CF44 26 C8
Cwrt Glanwern [4] CF44 53 E8
Cwrt Glyn CF37 109 A8
Cwrt Hendre NP12 85 C7
Cwrt Heol Casnewydd [5] CF24 195 D8
Cwrt Hocys SA7 69 D6

Cwrt Hydd SA6 45 F5
Cwrt Isaf SA7 47 B1
Cwrt Ivor Sims SA6 46 A2
Cwrt Llandough CF64 206 D6
Cwrt Llanwonno CF45 54 D1
Cwrt Llechau CF72 172 D6
Cwrt Llwyn Fedwen SA6 46 A1
Cwrt Llwynog SA6 45 F4
Cwrt Maes Cynon CF44 27 E8
Cwrt Merlyn SA6 45 F5
Cwrt Nant y Felin CF83 137 D1
Cwrt Neuadd Wen CF81 58 C5
Cwrt Neville [2] SA15 40 D4
Cwrt Olwyn Ddwr SA7 47 A1
Cwrt Pencoedtre [3] CF62 215 A8
Cwrt Pentre Bach [7] CF3 180 A8
Cwrt Pentwyn CF38 156 B7
Cwrt Rhian SA4 43 C2
Cwrt Rhosyn SA7 69 D6
Cwrt Rhyd NP23 7 C4
Cwrt Roberts CF5 193 A3
Cwrt Saron CF40 107 A2
Cwrt Sart SA11 71 C3
Cwrt Sart Comp Sch SA11 71 C3
Cwrt St Cyres CF64 206 E4
Cwrt Swalia CF32 104 E2
Cwrt Syr Dafydd CF81 209 F7
Cwrt Tr Eos SA13 148 A6
Cwrt Tre-aman CF44 53 D6
Cwrt Trem yr Ynys CF83 214 F4
Cwrt Twyn-Rhyd CF44 26 C8
Cwrt Ty Mawr CF83 138 D2
Cwrt Ty-Fferm CF83 137 F8
Cwrt Waddl [3] SA15 40 D4
Cwrt y Carw SA13 147 F6
Cwrt y Castell (Castle Court Sh Ctr) CF83 138 B3
Cwrt y Coed NP12 85 D6
Cwrt y Fedwen SA7 46 D1
Cwrt y Garth [5] CF38 156 A5
Cwrt y Mwnws CF34 102 A4
Cwrt y Waun
[3] Beddau CF38 156 A5
Caerphilly NP12 85 C7
Rhydyfro SA8 23 D7
Cwrt Ynysmeurig CF45 82 E2
Cwrt Yr Aeron SA6 46 A4
Cwrt Yr Gollen NP23 14 D6
Cwrt Yr Ysgol [1] NP11 114 F3
Cwrt-Coch St CF81 58 B4
Cwrt-Ty-Mynydd CF15 176 B6
Cwrt-Ucha Terr [7] SA13 125 C7
Cwrt-y- Goedwig CF38 156 B7
Cwrt-y-Cadno
Cardiff CF5 192 F5
Llantwit Major CF61 210 A7
Cwrt-y-Clafdy SA10 70 F8
Cwrt-y-Clafdy Rd SA10 70 F8
Cwrt-y-Coed CF31 169 B4
Cwrt-y-Farchnad [1] CF5 194 D6
Cwrt-y-Felin CF71 198 C5
Cwrt-y-Vil Rd CF64 207 A3
Cwrt-y-Vil Road (Lower) CF64 207 A2
Cwrt-y-Ysgol SA11 49 C2
Cwrt-yr-Ala Ave CF5 193 B3
Cwrt-yr-Ala Com Jun Sch CF5 193 B4
Cwrt-yr-Ala Rd CF5 193 C2
Cwrt-yr-Lolo CF62 201 C1
Cwrt-yy-Fedw SA7 47 B1
Cwrtglas NP44 90 A4
Cyfarthfa Jun Sch CF47 10 C3
Cyfartha Mus & Art Gall CF47 10 C3
Cyfarthfa Gdns CF48 10 A4
Cyfarthfa High (Lower) Comp Sch CF47 10 C3
Cyfarthfa High (Upper) Comp Sch CF47 10 F1
Cyfarthfa Ho CF48 10 C2
Cyfarthfa Ind Est CF47 10 C2
Cyfarthfa Rd CF24 195 C7
Cyfyng Rd SA9 2 A5
Cygnet Cl SA2 3 G6
Cylla St CF82 84 D5
Cymdda CF32 150 E3
Cymer Rd CF34 75 B2
Cymmer Afan Comp Sch SA13 75 C4
Cymmer Afan Prim Sch SA13 75 B5
Cymmer Cty Inf Sch CF39 107 E2
Cymmer Jun Sch CF39 107 E2
Cymmer Rd
Glyncorrwg SA13 227 C1
Porth CF39 107 D4
Cymmer St CF11 194 F3

Cymric Cl Cardiff CF5 193 D5
Hirwaun CF44 27 F6
Cymtawe Coll SA8 23 E6
Cyn-Coed Ave CF23 178 D6
Cyn-Coed Cres CF23 178 D6
Cynan Cl Barry CF63 215 B8
Beddau CF38 156 A5
Ebbw Vale NP23 7 D5
Cyncoed CF37 81 E3
Cyncoed Ave CF23 178 C6
Cyncoed Cl SA2 93 C8
Cyncoed Pl CF23 178 C6
Cyncoed Rd
Cardiff CF23 178 C5
Margam SA13 125 E3
Cyncoed Rise CF23 178 C6
Cynffig Comp Sch CF33 148 B1
Cynlais Cty Prim Jun & Inf Sch SA9 1 F2
Cynllwyndu Rd CF43 80 B3
Cynon Cl SA6 69 A7
Cynon Inf Sch CF45 54 C3
Cynon St
[1] Aberdare CF44 28 F4
Aberdare CF44 53 D6
Cynon Terr
Abercynon CF45 82 C6
Hirwaun CF44 27 E7
Mountain Ash CF45 82 A7
Cynon Valley Mus CF44 29 A3
Cynon View CF37 109 F3
Cyntwell Ave CF5 193 B3
Cyntwell Cres CF5 193 B4
Cyntwell Pl CF5 193 B4
Cynwal Terr SA9 221 C5
Cypress Ave SA3 122 F8
Cypress Cl
Caerleon NP18 117 E2
Merthyr Tydfil CF47 10 D5
Cypress Ct CF44 28 E2
Cypress Dr CF3 180 B8
Cypress Gdns CF36 183 E7
Cypress Pl CF5 176 D2
Cypress St CF37 136 A5
Cyrch-y-Gwas Rd CF37 135 E7
Cyres St CF47 10 F3
Cyril Pl NP13 35 F6
Cyril St Barry CF63 215 B5
Cardiff CF24 195 D7
Newport NP19 143 D4
Cysgod-y-Fro SA8 23 D7

D

D C Griffiths Way SA11 71 D6
D Row NP4 17 A6
D'arcy Bsns Ctr SA10 70 D5
Dafen Inn Row SA14 41 C7
Dafen Rd Llanelli SA14 41 A8
Llanelli SA15 41 B7
Dafen Row SA15 40 E2
Daffodil Cl SA12 98 C3
Daffodil Cl NP44 88 F2
Daffyn St NP4 37 E6
Dafolog Terr NP24 33 F4
Dafydd Pl CF63 215 A8
Dahlia Cl [2] SA12 98 C2
Daisy St CF5 194 B6
Daisy View NP5 62 D5
Dalcross St CF24 178 B1
Dale Ave CF14 177 D5
Dale Cl SA5 67 B4
Dale Ct CF62 214 F8
Dale Path NP44 89 B2
Dale Rd NP19 144 D6
Dale View
Cefn Cribwr CF32 149 C2
Nantyglo NP23 15 D8
Daleside CF32 151 A5
Dalmuir Rd CF24 195 F7
Dalrymple St [3] SA12 99 A1
Dalton Cl
[8] Merthyr Tydfil CF47 30 F8
Port Talbot SA12 124 D8
Dalton Ct [2] CF24 195 A8
Dalton Ho [6] SA12 98 D1
Dalton Rd Neath SA11 71 C6
Port Talbot SA12 98 D1
Dalton St CF24 195 A8
Dan Caerlan CF72 155 E3
Dan y Bryn CF39 132 B7
Dan y Coed CF35 170 D7
Dan y Cribyn CF37 109 A7
Dan y Graig
Cardiff CF14 176 F8
Pontlottyn CF81 33 A7
Risca NP11 114 F2
Dan y Graig Rd NP11 114 F2
Dan y Mynydd CF14 159 C3
Dan Yr Allt SA4 66 A5
Dan Yr Ardd CF83 137 E1
Dan Yr Heol CF32 130 E4
Dan-y-Bryn
Maesteg CF34 75 A1
Tonna SA11 49 D3
Dan-y-Bryn Ave CF15 176 A6
Dan-y-bryn Bglws NP13 15 E4
Dan-y-Bryn Cl CF15 176 B6
Dan-y-Bryn Rd SA13 125 C6
Dan-y-Coed
Aberkenfig CF32 150 C3

Dan-y-Coed continued
Blackmill CF35 130 E1
Cefn Hengoed CF82 84 F4
Cwmavon SA12 99 E5
Mountain Ash CF45 54 E3
Pontrhydyfen SA12 73 B5
Pontsticill CF48 3 F3
Dan-y-Coed Cl CF23 178 B6
Dan-y-Coed Rd
Cardiff CF23 178 B6
Swansea SA7 70 A8
Dan-y-Coed Rise
Bridgend CF31 169 A5
Cardiff CF23 178 B6
Dan-y-Coedcae Rd CF37 135 B7
Dan-y-Craig Rd SA11 71 E6
Dan-y-darren CF83 112 A5
Dan-y-Deri
Bedwas CF83 138 C7
Bridgend CF31 168 B4
Dan-y-Deri La CF48 10 A4
Dan-y-Felin CF72 155 D3
Dan-y-fron SA9 222 C2
Dan-y-Gaer Rd CF83 84 C6
Dan-y-Graig CF83 137 A7
Dan-y-Graig Rd SA10 71 B8
Dan-y-Lan CF32 150 C3
Dan-y-Parc SA6 45 E1
Dan-y-Rhiw CF44 53 A3
Dan-y-Rhiw Terr NP11 87 A3
Dan-y-twyn CF46 85 B5
Dan-yr-Allt Cl CF37 136 B5
Dan-Yr-Heol
Cardiff CF23 178 B6
Penywaun CF44 28 B6
Dana Dr SA2 94 C6
Dane Ct SA7 10 D2
Dane Terr CF41 10 D2
Danescourt Halt CF5 176 E2
Danescourt Jun & Inf Sch CF5 176 E2
Danescourt Way CF5 176 E3
Daniel Hopkin Cl CF61 209 F5
Daniel Pl [1] NP20 143 C3
Daniel St
Aberdare CF44 29 F1
Barry CF63 215 B7
Cardiff CF24 178 A1
Swansea SA5 68 B2
Tonypandy CF40 106 D7
Tonypandy CF40 107 A3
Treherbert CF42 50 F1
Treorchy CF42 78 B4
Wick CF71 198 C5
Danton Ho NP44 90 B4
Dantwyn Rd SA4 19 E5
Danybanc SA15 40 E8
Danybryn CF72 172 F6
Danybryn Rd SA4 43 A1
Danycoed
Caerphilly CF83 138 B1
Clydach NP7 9 D6
Tonypandy CF41 79 E2
Danycwm SA14 40 F7
Danyderi St SA14 53 C6
Danyderi Terr CF48 55 C5
Danyffynon SA13 99 C2
Dangraig
Aberavon SA12 99 A2
Abercanaid CF48 30 C8
Croesyceiliog NP44 90 A7
Cwm-twrch Isaf SA9 1 A2
Lewistown CF32 130 E5
Machen CF83 139 B6
Ystrad CF41 79 E3
Danygraig Ave CF36 183 E8
Danygraig Bglws NP11 114 E1
Danygraig Cres CF72 155 C3
Danygraig Dr CF72 155 C3
Danygraig Prim Sch SA1 96 A7
Danygraig Rd
Llanharan CF72 154 A3
Pontardawe SA8 23 C2
Swansea SA1 96 B7
Danygraig Terr CF72 154 A3
Danylan Rd CF37 109 A1
Danyparc CF10 72 D3
Danyrallt SA14 40 F8
Danywern Terr CF41 79 D3
Daphne Cl SA10 48 E2
Daphne Rd SA10 48 E2
Darby Cres NP23 14 B8
Darby Rd CF24 196 A4
Dare Ct CF44 28 C2
Dare Rd CF44 28 C2
Dare Valley Ctry Pk CF44 28 B2
Dare Valley Visitor Ctr CF44 28 C2
Dare Villas CF44 28 F2
Daren Ct CF34 102 D2
Daren Ddu Rd CF37 109 C4
Daren-Felen Rd NP23 8 C4
Darent Cl NP20 116 C1
Darent Rd NP20 116 C1
Darent Wlk NP20 116 D1
Darlington Ct NP19 143 D8
Darran Park Prim Sch CF43 79 F6
Darran Pk
Neath Abbey SA10 47 F8
Pontypridd CF37 109 D3
Darran Rd
Mountain Ash CF45 54 D2
Risca NP11 114 E4
Darran St CF24 194 F8

Darran Terr
Ferndale CF43 79 F6
Pontardawe SA8 23 B3
Darran Bglws CF32 103 E6
Darren Cl
Caerphilly CF83 138 D5
Cowbridge CF71 188 D2
Neath Abbey SA10 47 F1
Darren Ct
Blackwood NP12 59 B1
Pontypridd CF37 109 D5
Darren Dr NP11 87 A1
Darren Hill CF71 188 D2
Darren Las CF48 55 D2
Darren Rd
Abertillery NP13 36 C5
Briton Ferry SA11 71 C3
Ystalyfera SA9 2 B6
Darren View
Merthyr Tydfil CF47 10 F2
Pont Rhyd-y-cyff CF34 128 D7
Darren Wen SA12 98 F7
Darrenfelen Jun & Inf Sch NP7 9 B5
Darrenlas Prim Sch CF45 54 D2
Dart Rd NP20 116 E1
Dartford Dr SA1 69 A3
Dartford Pl SA1 69 A3
Dartford Rd SA1 69 A3
Dartington Dr CF23 160 E1
Darwin Dr NP20 117 A2
Darwin Rd SA12 124 E7
David Cl NP20 143 C1
David Davies Rd CF63 215 B4
David Dower Cl CF45 82 E2
David Issac Cl SA1 68 D3
David Price St [11] CF44 29 A1
David St Aberdare CF44 28 E3
Barry CF63 215 A5
Blaengarw CF32 103 E7
Blaenrhondda CF42 50 D4
Caerphilly NP12 85 F6
Cardiff CF10 195 B5
Cwmdare CF44 28 C3
Ebbw Vale NP23 14 C8
[14] Merthyr Tydfil CF47 10 D2
Merthyr Tydfil CF47 30 E7
Swansea SA5 68 B2
Tonypandy CF40 106 D7
Tonypandy CF40 107 A3
David Williams Terr SA1 96 C7
David's Ct CF72 173 B8
Davies Andrews Heol SA11 49 B1
Davies Andrews Rd SA11 49 B1
Davies Ave
Bridgend CF31 168 F7
Porthcawl CF36 165 F1
Davies Cl CF40 107 C5
Davies Dr CF83 137 F5
Davies Pl Cardiff CF5 193 F7
Porth CF39 107 E6
Davies Rd Neath SA11 71 E7
Ynysmaerdy SA8 23 F6
Davies Row
Hirwaun CF44 27 D8
Swansea SA5 68 A1
Davies Sq [3] SA15 40 E5
Davies St
Abercrraf SA9 222 D7
Barry CF63 215 A6
Blackwood NP12 85 C7
[5] Brynmawr NP23 8 C4
Dowlais CF48 11 B5
Porth CF39 107 E4
Davies Terr CF34 101 F6
Daviot Ct CF24 178 B1
Daviot St CF24 178 B1
Davis Ave CF32 151 A6
Davis Cl NP4 62 C7
Davis Sq [14] NP20 143 C3
Davis St Aberdare CF44 53 C8
Cardiff CF24 195 C5
Swansea SA6 68 E5
Davis's Terr [4] CF14 177 B5
Davnic Cl [5] CF63 215 B6
Davy Cl NP20 117 A3
Davy Evans Ct NP13 36 B4
Dawan Cl CF62 214 D5
Dawlish Cl SA3 122 C6
Dawson Cl NP19 144 F6
Dderi Rd SA9 221 B5
Ddol Rd SA2 93 B2
De Berclos CF36 182 F8
De Braose Cl CF5 176 D3
De Breos Dr CF5 183 A8
De Burgh Pl [8] CF11 194 E5
De Burgh St CF11 194 E5
De Clare Cl CF36 182 F8
De Clare Dr CF64 210 B6
De Croche Pl CF11 194 E5
De Granville Cl CF36 182 F8
De Haviland Rd CF24 196 A4
De La Beche St SA1 45 F1
De Londres Cl CF36 182 F8
De Turberville Cl CF36 182 F8

De Winton St [7] CF40 106 E6
De Winton Terr
Caerphilly CF83 137 F8
Tonypandy CF40 106 C7
De-Barri St CF37 135 F4
De-Breos St SA2 94 F5
De-La Beche St SA1 95 C7
De-La-Beche Rd SA2 94 D6
Dean Ct NP44 115 F4
Dean St Aberdare CF44 29 A1
Newport NP19 143 E6
Dean's Ct CF5 177 A1
Deanery Gdns [13] NP20 143 B4
Deans Cl CF5 194 B8
Deans Ct CF62 213 A2
Dee Pl SA6 46 A4
Deeley Rd SA9 2 B6
Deemuir Rd CF24 195 F7
Deepdale Cl CF23 178 B3
Deepdene Cl CF5 192 F5
Deepfield Cl CF5 192 F5
Deepslade Cl SA3 121 A4
Deepwood Cl CF5 192 F5
Deerbrook NP44 89 B2
Deere Cl CF5 193 B4
Deere Pl CF5 193 B4
Deere Rd CF5 193 B4
Llantwit Fardre CF38 156 C6
Deganwy Cl CF14 159 E1
Dehewydd Isaf CF38 156 D8
Dehewydd La CF38 156 D7
Deighton Cl NP22 13 D8
Delabeche St SA15 40 D4
Delfan Swansea SA6 45 C2
Swansea SA9 69 F5
Delffordd SA8 24 B2
Delfryn
Capel Hendre SA18 218 D6
Llanelli SA14 41 D6
Llwydcoed CF44 28 F6
Delhi St SA1 95 E7
Delius Cl
Newport NP19 144 C5
Rogerstone NP10 142 A6
Dell The Baglan SA12 98 E5
Bryncethin CF32 151 A4
Cardiff CF3 179 D8
Church Village CF38 135 F4
Laleston CF32 167 E4
Llanelli SA15 40 C8
Pontlliw SA4 43 F6
Swansea SA2 93 E6
Delta St [3] CF11 194 D5
Delwen Terr CF42 50 B2
Den-y-bryn CF32 104 E4
Denbigh Cl
Blackwood NP12 58 E1
Church Village CF38 135 F2
Denbigh Cres SA6 46 B5
Denbigh Ct
Caerphilly CF83 137 C4
[3] Cardiff CF14 177 A6
[9] Penarth CF64 206 F2
Denbigh Dr CF61 210 D6
Denbigh Rd
Dinas Powys CF64 206 C4
Newport NP19 143 E8
Denbigh St CF11 194 D7
Denbigh Way CF62 214 F7
Denham Ave SA15 40 A7
Denison Way CF5 192 F5
Denleigh Cl CF81 57 F3
Dennis Pl CF32 151 B5
Dennithorne Cl CF48 11 C4
Dental Drive (Rhodfa'r Deintyddion) CF14 177 E3
Denton Rd CF5 194 D5
Dents Cl NP19 144 D5
Dents Hill NP19 144 D5
Denvale Trad Pk CF24 195 D4
Denver Rd SA5 67 B5
Denys Cl CF64 206 B4
Depot Rd
Aberdare CF44 28 F2
Cwmavon SA12 99 E5
Derby Gr NP19 144 B2
Deri Ave CF35 170 C6
Deri Cl Cardiff CF23 178 E1
Pencoed CF35 152 C1
Deri Prim Sch CF81 57 D8
Deri Rd Cardiff CF23 178 D6
Glanaman SA18 219 F8
Deri St CF43 80 B2
Dering Rd CF23 161 B1
Derlin Pk SA18 218 F5
Derllwyn Cl CF32 150 C6
Derllwyn Rd CF32 150 C6
Derlwyn Dunvant SA2 93 D8
Neath SA10 48 C1
Penywaun CF44 28 A6
Derlwyn St NP24 33 E3
Derw SA8 23 D3
Derwen Aur CF39 107 F6
Derwen
Blackwood NP12 85 E8
Bridgend CF31 168 F8
Tredomen CF82 84 D1
Waunarlwydd SA5 66 D4
Derwen Deg
Neath SA10 48 C3
Pontardawe SA8 23 D6
Derwen Fawr SA1 94 B4
Derwen Fawr Rd SA2 94 B4
Derwen Las CF31 168 B2

Derwen Rd
Bridgend CF31 ....168 F4
Cardiff CF23 ....178 C8
Pontardawe SA8 .....23 D2
Pontyclun CF72 ......173 B7
Ystrad CF41 ....79 C3
Ystradgynlais SA9 ....1 F1
Derwendeg Ave
Blackwood NP12 ......85 C8
Cefn Hengoed CF82 ...84 F4
Pontypridd CF37 .....109 D5
Derwendeg Prim Sch
CF82 ....84 F5
Derwent Cl CF14 ...159 E2
Derwent Ct NP20 ...116 C1
Derwent Dr CF44 ....29 E1
Derwent Ho 3 NP44 ..89 C2
Derwent St SA15 ....40 D6
Derwlas SA4 ....44 B5
Derwydd Ave SA18 ..220 D6
Derwydd Rd CF40 ...106 C5
Despenser Ave CF72 .155 D2
Despenser Gdns 11
CF11 ....194 F5
Despenser Pl 12
CF11 ....194 F5
Despenser Rd CF64 ..216 A5
Despenser St CF11 ..194 F5
Dessmuir Rd CF24 ...195 F7
Devon Ave CF63 ....214 D6
Devon Cl NP18 ......118 C4
Devon Ho 4 SA12 ....98 B2
Devon Pl Cardiff CF11 .194 F3
Mumbles SA3 ....123 B4
Newport NP20 ....143 B5
Devon St CF11 ......194 E3
Devon Terr SA1 ......95 A7
Devon View SA2 ......94 B7
Devonshire Dr CF44 .224 C4
Devonshire Pl SA13 .125 C2
Dew Cres CF5 ....193 E4
Dew Rd SA12 ....98 C2
Dewi Cl CF5 ....194 A8
Dewi Sant Hospl
CF37 ....135 C8
Dewi St CF37 ....109 E3
Dewi Terr SA1 ....68 A1
Dewsbury Ct 4 SA1 ..95 D6
Dewsland Park Rd
NP20 ....143 B3
Dewstow St NP19 ....143 F4
Diagonal Rd CF62 ...211 E1
Diamond Cl CF83 ....137 F4
Diamond Jubilee Terr
NP13 ....36 B5
Diamond St CF24 ....195 D6
Diana La CF24 ....178 B1
Diana St Cardiff CF24 .178 B1
Troedyrhiw CF48 ......55 B8
Dibdin Cl NP19 ......144 F5
Dickens Ave
Cardiff CF3 ....179 B7
Port Talbot SA12 .....124 E7
Dickens Cl CF83 ....139 C6
Dickens Dr NP20 ....142 E6
Dickinson Cl SA12 ...98 E6
Dickslade SA3 ......123 C4
Digby Cl 3 CF5 .....176 E2
Digby Rd SA11 ....72 A8
Digby St CF63 ......215 A5
Dillington Terr CF45 ..81 F7
Dillwyn Ct Pontlliw SA4 .43 F6
Swansea SA2 ....94 C6
Dillwyn Llewelyn Com Sch
SA2 ....67 D2
Dillwyn Rd SA2 ......94 C4
Dillwyn St Llanelli SA15 .40 D4
Swansea SA1 ....95 C6
Dilwyn Ave CF82 .....84 F2
Dilwyn Gdns CF31 ...168 E2
Dilwyn Rd SA4 ....43 F2
Dilwyn St CF45 ......81 F8
Dilys St CF42 ....50 C2
Dimbath Ave CF35 ..131 A3
Dimbath La CF35 ....131 B5
Dimlands Rd CF61 ...209 D5
Dimpath Terr SA15 ...40 E7
Dinam Cl CF32 ......104 F6
Dinam Park Ave CF41 .78 F3
Dinam Pk CF41 ....78 F3
Dinam Rd SA1 ....69 D1
Dinam St CF32 ......104 F6
Dinas Baglan Rd SA12 .98 D1
Dinas Ent Ctr CF39 ..107 E4
Dinas Isaf Cotts CF40 107 A1
Dinas Isaf Ind Est
CF40 ....133 B8
Dinas Isaf Ind Est (east)
CF40 ....107 B1
Dinas Jun Sch CF40 107 B2
Dinas Path NP44 .....89 B2
Dinas Pl CF11 ....194 F3
Dinas Powis Inf Sch
CF64 ....206 B3
Dinas Powis Sta
CF64 ....206 A2
Dinas Rd Penarth CF64 206 F2
Pontneddfechan SA11 .223 D3
Tonypandy CF40 ......107 A4
Dinas Sta CF40 ....107 B4
Dinas Terr SA11 .....223 F2
Dingle Cl CF62 ......214 B2
Dingle La
2 Cwmbran NP44 ....89 C6
3 Penarth CF64 .....207 A4

Dingle Rd
Penarth CF64 ....207 A4
Pontypool NP4 ....62 D5
Dingle The NP23 .....14 D8
Distillery Road La
CF37 ....108 F2
District St CF47 ......10 F3
Ditchling Ct CF64 ...207 A2
Division St NP13 ......36 B5
Dixon St CF47 ....10 E1
Dixon's Pl NP11 .....115 A2
Dobbins Rd CF63 ....215 D2
Dochdwy Rd CF64 ...206 E6
Dock Rd Barry CF62 ..214 D4
Port Talbot SA13 .....125 A7
Dock St Loughor SA4 ..65 C8
Penarth CF64 ....206 F5
Porthcawl CF36 ......182 F6
Dock View Rd CF63 ..215 A4
Docks Way NP20 ....164 A8
Dockwell Terr NP18 .145 B4
Doddridge Way CF36 .182 E6
Dodington Pl 2
CF37 ....109 E2
Dogfield St CF24 ....178 A1
Dogo St CF11 ....194 D7
Dol Afon CF35 ....170 E7
Dol Coed Pl SA11 .....49 C2
Dol Fach CF31 ......169 B4
Dol Fran CF83 ....138 D4
Dol Henryd SA10 ....223 A6
Dol Las SA12 ....98 E6
Dol Nant Dderwen
CF31 ....168 B4
Dol Werdd SA10 ......48 C1
Dol y Dderwen SA9 ..222 A5
Dol y Pandy CF83 ...138 C2
Dol y Paun CF83 ....137 E2
Dol yr Eos CF83 ....138 C4
Dol-Wen CF35 ....152 F1
Dol-y-Coed SA2 ......93 B8
Dol-y-Felin CF15 ....174 D7
Dol-y-Felin St CF83 .138 B4
Dol-y-Garn Terr NP13 .15 E6
Dol-y-Llan CF72 .....173 D8
Dolafon SA14 ....41 E3
Dolau Cl SA15 ....40 E2
Dolau Fach SA15 .....40 E3
Dolau Fawr SA15 .....40 E3
Dolau Ifan Ddu Terr
CF35 ....130 F2
Dolau Prim Sch CF72 153 E2
Dolau Rd SA15 ....40 E3
Dolawel SA9 ....221 C2
Dolcoed CF44 ....28 E6
Dolcoed Terr SA11 ...49 C2
Dolfain SA9 ....222 A5
Dolgellau Ave CF38 ..135 F2
Dolgoch CF3 ....179 D5
Dolgoy Cl SA3 ....123 A7
Dolgwilym St CF43 ...80 C1
Dolphin Pl SA12 .....98 C3
Dolphin St NP20 ....143 D3
Dolwar Fach SA14 ....41 C5
Dolwen Rd CF14 .....177 A2
Dolwerdd SA14 ....40 F8
Dolwyddelan Cl NP12 .58 E1
Dombey Cl CF14 .....159 F2
Domen Ct NP23 ......14 D6
Dominion Way Ind Est
CF24 ....195 E8
Don Cl NP20 ....116 D1
Donald St
Abercanaid CF48 ......30 F4
Cardiff CF24 ....178 B1
Nelson CF46 ....83 E4
Doniford Cl CF64 ....216 B6
Donnen St SA13 .....125 D5
Donnington Rd CF64 .215 E6
Dorallt Cl NP44 ......88 E1
Dorallt Way NP44 ....88 F1
Dorchester Ave CF23 178 D2
Dorchester Mans 5
CF14 ....176 F6
Dorleigh Ct NP44 ....89 B5
Dorothy Ave CF62 ...214 E8
Dorothy Cl CF62 ....214 E8
Dorothy St
Pontypridd CF37 .....109 D2
Ton Pentre CF41 ......79 B3
Dorset Ave CF63 ....214 F6
Dorset Cl NP19 .....144 B2
Dorset Cres NP19 ...144 B2
Dorset Ho 3 SA12 ...98 C3
Dorset St CF11 ......194 F3
Dorstone Wlk NP44 ..90 A3
Dos Cotts NP20 .....143 B6
Dos Rd NP20 ....143 B7
Douglas Cl CF5 .....176 E2
Douglas Ct
Bishopston SA3 ......122 A5
Cardiff CF14 ....159 A1
Dove Rd SA5 ....67 E2
Dovedale Cl CF23 ...178 B3
Dovedale St CF63 ...215 B6
Dover Pte
Mountain Ash CF45 ...54 D2
Ton Pentre CF41 ......79 B2
Dovey Cl Barry CF62 .214 C6
Cardiff CF3 ....179 D5
Dowlais Inf Sch CF48 .11 B4
Dowlais Rd CF24 ....195 D4
Dowlais St SA4 ......28 C7
Dowlais Stables CF48 .11 B4
Dowland Cl NP19 ....144 E5
Dowland Rd CF3 .....206 E1
Dowlands Way CF3 ..179 A2

Down Leaze SA2 .....67 D1
Down St SA6 ....46 E7
Downey Gr CF82 ......84 E6
Downfield Cl CF64 ...206 E6
Downing St
Llanelli SA15 ....40 C4
Newport NP19 ....144 A3
Downs Cl SA5 ....67 E3
Downs The SA3 .....231 C8
Downs View CF71 ...189 B3
Downs View Cl CF71 .189 B3
Downton Grange
CF3 ....179 C2
Downton Rd CF3 ....179 B3
Downton Rise CF3 ..179 B2
Doyle Ave CF5 ......193 E8
Doyle Ct CF5 ....193 E8
Dr William Price Bsns Ctr
CF37 ....135 C8
Dragon Auto Ctr SA7 ..69 B7
Dragonfly Dr CF62 ..213 A5
Drake Cl
Newport NP19 ....144 B4
St Athan CF62 ....211 D7
Drake Wlk CF10 .....195 B4
Drangway CF61 ......209 F6
Dranllwyn Cl CF83 ...139 F7
Dranllwyn La CF83 ..139 F7
Drawlings Cl 1 CF3 .179 D8
Drayton Ct NP44 .....89 C3
Dreflan CF37 ....74 A8
Dring St SA1 ....95 E8
Drenewydd Mus NP22 .12 C7
Drinkwater Gdns
NP20 ....142 F2
Driscoll Ct 4 CF24 ..195 D7
Driscoll Workshops
CF10 ....195 C5
Drive The Bargoed CF81 58 A1
Cardiff CF5 ....193 D7
Dinas Powys CF64 ...206 C3
Miskin CF72 ....173 D6
Neath Abbey SA10 ...71 D4
Southgate SA3 ....121 A4
Drope Rd CF5 ....192 C4
Drope Terr CF5 .....192 E4
Dros Col CF72 ....172 B5
Dros y Mor CF64 ....207 B2
Dros-y-Morfa CF3 ...179 C2
Drovers Mews 8
NP20 ....143 C3
Druce St SA15 ....40 C3
Druids Cl
Mumbles SA3 ....123 A6
Treorchy CF42 ....78 D5
Druids Gn CF71 .....188 F2
Druidstone Rd CF3 ..161 F3
Druidstone Way SA4 ..44 B2
Drumau Cl SA10 .....70 F8
Drumau Pk SA10 ....70 F8
Drumau Rd
Birchgrove SA7 ....47 B1
Neath SA7,SA10 ......70 D8
Drumfields SA10 .....49 A2
Drury Cl CF14 ....159 E2
Druslyn Rd SA3 .....122 F7
Drybrook Cl
9 Cardiff CF3 ....179 F6
Cwmbran NP44 ......89 F3
Dryburgh Ave CF14 .177 D5
Dryden Cl CF3 ......179 B7
Dryden Rd CF64 ....206 F4
Dryden Terr CF62 ...214 F8
Drylla CF64 ....206 A2
Drymmau Rd SA11 ...71 A7
Drysgol Rd CF15 ....176 B5
Drysiog Ct NP23 .....14 D6
Drysiog St NP23 .....14 D6
Dryslwyn Cl SA4 .....44 B2
Duckpool Rd NP19 ..143 E6
Dudley Cl CF10 .....195 B1
Dudley Pl CF62 .....214 D4
Dudley St Cardiff CF10 195 B1
Neath SA11 ....71 E7
Newport NP19 ....143 E4
Duffryn CF35 ....170 B8
Duffryn Ave CF23 ...178 B6
Duffryn Bsns Pk CF82 111 F6
Duffryn Cl
Bassaleg NP10 ....142 A3
Bridgend CF35 ....170 A4
Cardiff CF23 ....178 A6
Penpedairheol CF82 ..84 D8
Tonyrefail CF39 ......133 B6
Duffryn Cres CF72 ..153 E2
Duffryn Cty Prim Sch
SA13 ....74 C4
Duffryn Dr NP10 ....163 C4
Duffryn Fawr CF48 ...31 B4
Duffryn High Sch
NP10 ....163 F6
Duffryn Ho 5 CF64 .206 C3
Duffryn Jun Sch
NP10 ....163 F7
Duffryn La CF5 ......204 B7
Duffryn Rd
Abertillery NP13 ......36 B6
Cardiff CF23 ....178 C6
Cwmfelinfach NP11 ..113 D3
Gorseinon SA4 ....43 B1
Duffryn St
Cardiff CF24 ....195 B5
Duffryn SA13 ....74 A4
Pontlottyn CF81 ......32 F8
Tir-y-Berth CF82 ......85 A6
Ystrad Mynach CF82 ..84 F3

Duffryn Terr
Church Village CF38 ..156 F8
Cwmfelinfach NP11 ..113 F3
Duffryn View NP22 ...12 F3
Duffryn Way NP10 ..163 E6
Dugdale Wlk 14 CF11 194 D5
Duke St Aberdare CF44 .29 A2
Abertillery NP13 ......36 C4
4 Blaenavon NP4 .....17 C6
Maesteg CF34 ....102 C2
Newport NP20 ....143 D3
Pontypridd CF37 .....135 C2
Port Talbot SA13 .....125 D5
Swansea SA1 ....95 B6
Tredegar NP22 ....13 E6
Duke St (Heol y Dug)
CF10 ....195 A5
Duke Street Arc 7
CF10 ....195 A5
Dukefield SA4 ....92 E8
Dukestown Rd NP22 ..6 E1
Dulais Cl SA10 ....49 C4
Dulais Dr SA10 ....49 C4
Dulais Fach Rd SA10,
SA11 ....49 C3
Dulais Gdns SA10 ...222 E5
Dulais Gr SA2 ....94 A5
Dulais Rd
Pontarddulais SA4 ....19 C4
Seven Sisters SA10 ...222 C2
Dulverton Ave CF3 ..179 F7
Dulverton Dr CF64 ..216 B5
Dulwich Gdns CF5 ..194 C7
Dulwich Ho CF5 .....194 C7
Dumballs Rd CF10 ..195 B3
Dumbarton House Ct 1
SA1 ....95 A6
Dumfries Pl
Brynmawr NP23 ....8 C5
Cardiff CF10 ....195 B6
16 Newport NP20 ...143 C4
Ystradgynlais SA9 .....2 E7
Dumfries St
Aberdare CF44 ....29 A1
Treherbert CF42 ......50 F2
Treorchy CF42 ....78 D7
Dummer Cl 2 CF3 ...179 F7
Dunbar Cl CF23 .....161 A1
Duncan Cl CF3 ......179 D6
Dungarvan Dr CF23 .161 A1
Dunkery Cl CF3 .....179 B5
Dunleavy Dr CF11 ..206 E7
Dunlin Cl CF36 .....182 D8
Dunlin Ct 9 CF63 ..214 F5
Dunn Sq 20 NP20 ..143 C3
Dunnet Gdns NP4 ...63 B3
Dunns Cl SA3 ....123 B5
Dunns La SA3 ....123 B5
Dunns The SA3 .....123 B5
Dunraven Arc 10
CF40 ....106 E6
Dunraven Bsns Pk
CF31 ....169 A3
Dunraven Cl
Dinas Powys CF64 ...206 C3
Pen-clawdd SA4 ......64 E4
Dunraven Cres CF72 .155 A2
Dunraven Ct CF83 ..137 C4
Dunraven Ho 5 CF10 194 F5
Dunraven Pl
Bridgend CF31 ....168 E4
Evanstown CF39 .....132 B8
Ogmore Vale CF32 ...104 E3
Dunraven Rd
Cardiff CF11 ....194 D4
Llanyravon NP44 ......90 B2
Swansea SA2 ....94 B7
Dunraven St
Aberavon SA12 ....99 A1
Aberkenfig CF32 .....150 C4
Barry CF62 ....214 C3
Blaengwrach SA11 ...227 B8
Bridgend CF31 ....169 B2
Glyncorrwg SA13 ....227 C2
Tonypandy CF40 .....106 E5
Treherbert CF42 ......50 F1
Dunraven Terr CF42 ..78 C7
Dunsmuir Rd CF24 ..195 F6
Dunstable Rd NP19 .144 E5
Dunster Cl SA3 ......122 C6
Dunster Dr CF64 ....216 B5
Dunster Rd CF3 .....179 D7
Dunvant Ave SA11 ..226 C4
Dunvant Pl SA1 ......95 C5
Dunvant Prim Sch SA2 93 E8
Dunvant Rd
Dunvant SA2 ....93 D8
Three Crosses SA4 ....65 F1
Dunvant Sq SA2 ......93 C8
Duport Cl SA12 ......98 C2
Dupre Rd SA1 ....95 F8
Durell St CF61 ......209 F6
Durham La NP19 ....143 D7
Durham Rd NP19 ....143 D7
Durham Road Jun & Inf
Sch NP19 ....143 D7
Durham St CF11 ....194 F3
Durleigh Cl CF3 .....179 D7
Durlston Cl 4 CF14 .176 F7
Duxford Cl CF5 .....176 D2
Dwr-y-Felin Comp Sch
Neath SA10 ....48 A1
Neath SA10 ....48 D1
Neath Abbey SA10 ...71 A8

Dwr-y-Felin Comp Schs
SA10 ....71 D8
Dwr-y-Felin Rd
Neath SA10 ....48 C1
Neath SA10 ....48 C3
Dwyfor SA14 ....41 D5
Dwyfor Rd SA13 ......75 D3
Dyfan Rd CF63 ......215 A7
Dyfatty St SA1 ......95 D8
Dyfed CF64 ....207 B5
Dyfed Ave SA1 ....95 A8
Dyfed Cl SA1 ....94 F8
Dyfed Dr CF83 ......137 F5
Dyfed Ho 1 CF23 ...178 C2
Dyfed St SA11 ....71 F7
Dyffryn Bryn-côch SA10 .48 B4
Penpedairheol CF82 ..84 D7
Dyffryn Ave CF37 ...136 A6
Dyffryn Bach Terr
CF38 ....156 F7
Dyffryn Cl
St Nicholas CF5 .....192 A1
Swansea SA6 ....69 A8
Dyffryn Comp Sch
SA13 ....125 F3
Dyffryn Cres
Peterston-Super-Ely
CF5 ....191 F5
Rhydyfelin CF37 .....136 A6
Dyffryn Gdns
Rhydyfelin CF37 .....136 A6
Wenvoe CF5 ....204 B5
Dyffryn La
Coedkernew NP10 ...163 C4
Newport NP10 ....163 B6
Dyffryn Lower Comp Sch
SA13 ....125 F4
Dyffryn Lower Comp Sch
Dyffryn Row CF34 ...101 F5
Dyffryn Rd
Aberdare CF44 ....53 F7
Ammanford SA18 ....219 A4
Bryn-côch SA10 ......48 C3
Ebbw Vale NP23 ......14 F3
Maesteg CF34 ....75 D4
Mountain Ash CF45 ...54 D4
Pentrebach CF48 ......31 A4
Pontardawe SA8 ......23 F4
Pontypridd CF37 ....136 A5
Port Talbot SA13 .....125 D7
Rhydyfelin CF37 .....136 A5
Dyffryn Terr
Morriston SA6 ....46 A1
New Tredegar NP24 ..33 D4
Tonyrefail CF39 ......133 B5
Dyffryn View SA10 ...48 C5
Dyffryn-Aur Rd SA7 ..69 E6
Dyfnallt Rd CF63 ....215 A8
Dyfodwg St CF42 .....78 D6
Dyfrig Cl SA11 ......49 C6
Dyfrig Ct CF61 ......210 B7
Dyfrig Rd CF5 ....193 F6
Dyfrig St Barry CF62 .215 A4
Cardiff CF11 ....194 E7
Dyke St 15 CF47 .....30 E8
Dylan SA14 ....41 D5
Dylan Ave
1 Beddau CF38 ......156 A5
Blackwood NP12 ......85 C7
Dylan Cl
Llandough CF64 .....206 E6
Swansea SA2 ....93 F7
Dylan Cres Barry CF63 215 B8
Port Talbot SA12 .....124 E7
Dylan Dr CF83 ......138 A5
Dylan Pl 4 CF24 ....195 C7
Dylan Rd SA2 ....93 F7
Dylan Thomas Sq 3
SA1 ....95 D6
Dyllas Ct CF39 ......107 F2
Dyllas Rd CF39 .....107 F3
Dynea Cl CF37 ......136 B5
Dynea Rd CF37 .....136 B5
Dynevor Ave SA10 ...48 D1
Dynevor Cl
Llanyravon NP44 ......90 B3
Neath SA10 ....70 F8
Dynevor Comp Sch
SA1 ....95 C7
Dynevor Pl Neath SA10 70 D7
Swansea SA10 ....95 C7
Dynevor Rd
Cardiff CF23 ....178 D3
Glanaman SA18 ......220 B7
Neath SA10 ....70 F8
Dynevor St
Fochriw CF81 ....32 C7
Merthyr Tydfil CF48 ..10 D1
Dynevor Terr
Nelson CF46 ....83 E3
Pontardawe SA8 ......23 C5
Dyrus Rd SA6 ....68 C5
Dyserth Rd CF64 ....206 F3
Dysgwylfa SA2 ......94 C6
Dyson Cl SA6 ....22 D1

E

E Row NP4 ....17 A6
Eagle La CF71 ....188 E2

Eagle Mews SA13 ...125 B8
Eagle Rd CF62 ......210 D6
Eagle St SA13 ......125 B8
Eagle View CF31 ....169 D6
Eaglebush Ave SA11 ..71 D4
Eagles Pl SA15 ......67 E6
Eagleswell Prim Sch
CF61 ....210 B7
Eagleswell Rd CF61 .210 B6
Earl Cl NP4 ....37 E6
Earl Cres CF62 ......214 F2
Earl Cunningham Ct 11
CF10 ....195 C4
Earl La CF11 ....194 F1
Earl Rd Margam SA13 .125 F1
Penarth CF64 ....206 F3
Earl St Abersychan NP4 .37 F3
Abertillery NP13 ......36 C4
Cardiff CF11 ....194 F1
Swansea SA1 ....68 D1
Tredegar NP22 ....13 D7
Earl's Court Rd CF23 .178 D2
Earle Pl CF5 ....194 D5
Earls Court Pl CF23 ..178 D1
Earlsfield Cl SA11 ...223 C1
Earlsmede 5 NP44 ..89 B3
Earlswood Rd CF14 .177 E7
East Ave Aberdare CF44 .29 A2
Bedwas CF83 ....138 E6
Caerphilly CF83 .....137 F4
Cefn Cribwr CF32 ...149 B2
Pontypool NP4 ....62 E1
Pyle CF33 ....148 C2
East Bank NP13 ......36 B8
East Bank Way NP18 .164 F8
East Bank Way (Ffordd
Glan y Dwyrain) SA1 .95 E7
East Bay Cl CF10 ....195 C5
East Burrows Rd SA1 .95 E6
East Cliff SA3 ....122 E1
East Crossways SA8 ..23 D6
East Ct CF43 ....80 C4
East Dock Rd
Newport NP20 ....143 E2
Newport NP20 ....143 E3
East Dr CF61 ....208 F5
East Gr CF24 ....195 C6
East Grove La CF24 ..195 C6
East Grove Rd NP19 .144 C5
East Lynne Gdns
NP18 ....118 C3
East Market St NP20 143 D3
East Moors Bsns Pk
CF24 ....195 D4
East Moors Rd CF24 .195 D3
East Pen-Twyn NP13 .15 E4
East Pen-Twyn Bglws
NP13 ....15 E4
East Pentwyn Rd NP13 15 E5
East Point CF3 ......179 D2
East Rd Barry CF64 ..215 F6
Cefn Hengoed CF82 ..84 E5
Cwmbran NP44 ......116 A4
Port Talbot SA13 .....125 D3
Treorchy CF43 ....80 B2
Tylorstown CF43 ......80 C4
East Rise CF14 ......178 A8
East Roedin NP44 ...116 C8
East St
Aberkenfig CF32 .....150 C4
Barry CF62 ....214 D4
Bridgend CF31 ....169 E3
Dowlais CF48 ....11 B4
Goytre SA13 ....125 F8
Llantwit Major CF61 .209 F6
Newport NP20 ....143 B5
Pontypridd CF37 .....109 D2
Tonypandy CF40 .....106 D6
Tylorstown CF43 ......80 C4
East Tyndall St CF24 195 D5
East Usk Rd NP19 ..143 C6
East View Blaina NP13 .15 D5
Caerphilly CF83 .....138 B2
Llandow CF71 ....199 A7
New Tredegar NP24 ..34 A1
Pontypool NP4 ....62 B6
Pontypool NP4 ....62 E2
East View Terr CF24 .214 D3
East Way Rd NP20 ..143 D1
East Wlk CF62 ......214 E6
Eastbourne Ct 8
CF63 ....215 C8
Eastbourne Gr SA2 ..94 C7
Eastbourne Pl CF47 ..30 E7
Eastbrook Cl CF64 ..206 B4
Eastbrook Sta CF64 .206 C4
Easterfield Dr SA3 ..121 A4
Easterly Cl CF31 ....169 D5
Eastern Ave
Cardiff CF23 ....178 E2
Cymmer SA13 ....75 D4
Eastern Cl 2 CF3 ...179 D8
Eastern Prim Sch
SA13 ....125 D6
Eastern Prom CF36 .183 A6
Eastfield Cl NP18 ...118 A4
Eastfield Cl CF72 ...155 C2
Eastfield Dr NP18 ...118 A4
Eastfield Mews NP18 118 A4
Eastfield Rd NP18 ...118 A4
Eastfield Terr CF47 ..30 E7
Eastfield View NP18 .118 A4
Eastfield Way NP18 .118 A4
Eastgate CF71 ......188 F1
Eastgate Mews CF71 .188 F1

Eastland Cl SA3 .....**122** E7
Eastland Pl SA11 .....**71** E6
Eastland Rd SA11 .....**71** E7
Eastlands Pk SA3 .....**122** A7
Eastmoor Park Cres
SA3 .....**122** E7
Eastmoor Rd NP19 .....**144** C3
Eastview Terr CF81 .....**58** A3
Eastville Rd
Abertillery NP13 ....**36** C3
Ebbw Vale NP23 ......**14** F5
Eastway NP4 ....**39** E2
Eaton Cres SA1 .....**95** A6
Eaton Cl SA5 ....**68** D3
Eaton Rd SA5 ....**68** C3
Ebbw Cl CF62 ....**211** C7
Ebbw St NP11 .....**114** F2
Ebbw Vale Coll of F Ed
NP23 ....**7** C2
Ebbw Vale Comp Sch
NP23 ....**7** C2
Ebbw Vale Row SA12 ...**99** E5
Ebbw View NP23 ......**7** D3
Ebbw View Terr NP11 ...**86** F6
Ebenezer Cl CF46 .....**83** D7
Ebenezer Ct
Blackmill CF35 ....**130** F2
Tredegar NP22 ....**6** E1
Ebenezer Dr NP10 .....**142** B4
Ebenezer Rd CF40 .....**106** F5
Ebenezer St
2 Aberdare CF44 .....**28** E4
Pontypridd CF37 .....**135** F6
7 Swansea SA1 ....**95** D8
Tredegar NP22 ....**6** E1
Ebenezer Terr
Blackmill CF35 ....**130** F3
14 Newport NP20 .....**143** C4
Ebury Ho NP44 ....**90** B4
Ebwy Ct CF5 ....**193** D4
Eckley Rd CF64 .....**216** A5
Eclipse St CF24 .....**195** C6
Eddystone Cl CF11 ....**194** E3
Eden Ave SA2 ....**94** F7
Edgar St CF47 ....**10** F4
Edgcort NP44 ....**89** B1
Edgehill Bryn NP12 .....**85** D5
Llanyravon NP44 ......**90** B1
Edgehill Ave CF14 ....**159** C1
Edgehill SA12 ....**98** E4
Edgehill Cl CF14 .....**159** D1
Edgemoor Cl SA2 .....**93** B5
Edgemoor Dr SA2 .....**93** B6
Edgeware Rd SA2 .....**94** E7
Edinburgh Cl NP44 .....**89** A3
Edinburgh Ct 10
CF11 ....**194** E5
Edington Ave CF14 ...**177** F2
Edison Cres SA6 ......**22** D1
Edison Ridge NP20 ...**117** A3
Edith Rd CF5 ....**206** B3
Edlogan Sq NP44 .....**90** A6
Edlogan Way NP44 ....**90** A5
Edmond's Ct CF24 ....**178** B1
Edmondes St CF43 ....**80** C3
Edmondstown Rd
CF40 ....**107** C4
Edmonton Ct NP4 .....**62** C7
Edmund Pl
Barry CF63 ....**215** D6
Newbridge NP11 ......**86** C5
Edmund St
Pontlottyn CF81 ....**32** F8
Porth CF39 ....**108** A3
Edmunds Cl NP13 .....**15** D5
Edward Cl CF47 ....**10** F1
Edward Clarke Cl
CF5 ....**176** E2
Edward German Cres
NP19 ....**144** E5
Edward Ho 13 CF11 ...**194** E5
Edward Jarvis Cl SA11 ..**71** E6
Edward Nicholl Ct
CF23 ....**178** D2
Edward St
Abercarn NP11 ......**114** C8
Abercynon CF45 ......**82** D2
Aberdare CF44 ....**28** E4
Abertillery NP13 ......**36** B6
Barry CF63 ....**215** B7
Bridgend CF31 ......**168** F3
Cardiff CF10 ....**195** B6
Glynneath SA11 .....**223** D1
Maerdy CF43 ....**52** A1
Neath SA11 ....**71** E6
Pant CF48 ....**11** B7
Pengam NP12 ....**85** B6
Pontardawe SA8 ......**23** F4
Pontypool NP4 ....**62** B7
Pontypool NP4 ....**62** E3
Port Talbot SA13 .....**99** B1
5 Porth SA39 ....**107** F3
5 Treharris CF46 .....**83** B6
Ystrad Mynach CF82 ..**111** E7
Edward Stephens Terr
CF48 ....**55** C8
Edward Terr
Abertridwr CF83 .....**137** A8
Tredegar NP22 ....**13** F6
Edward Thomas Cl
CF83 ....**137** A8
Edward Vii Ave NP20 ..**142** F4
Edward VII Cres
NP20 ....**143** A5
Edward VII La NP20 ...**143** A5

Edwardian Way CF72 .**173** D7
Edwards Ct NP23 ....**7** C1
Edwards St
Blaengwrach SA11 ....**227** B8
7 Mountain Ash CF45 ..**54** E1
Tonypandy CF40 .....**106** F6
Edwards Terr
Bedlinog CF46 ....**56** A7
Treharris CF46 ....**83** B5
Trelewis CF46 ....**83** C8
Edwardsville
Abercarn NP11 ......**114** B8
Treharris CF46 ....**82** F6
Edwin Ind Est NP20 ...**143** C7
Edwin St NP20 ....**143** C7
EFI Ind Est CF47 ......**10** B3
Egerton St CF5 ....**194** C6
Egham St CF5 ....**194** C6
Eglwys Ave CF37 .....**136** A5
Eglwys Newydd Jun & Inf
Sch CF14 ....**177** B5
Eglwysilan Rd
Abertridwr CF83, CF83 .**136** D7
Rhydyfelin CF37 .....**136** E5
Eglwysilan Way CF83 ..**136** F7
Egremont Rd CF23 ....**178** B2
Egypt St
Pontypridd CF37 .....**135** E8
Tonypandy CF40 .....**107** B5
Eiddil SA14 ....**41** D6
Eiddwen Rd SA5 ......**68** B4
Eider Cl CF3 ....**179** E8
Eifion Cl CF63 ......**215** A8
Eigen Cres SA1 ......**95** B8
Eighth Ave
Merthyr Tydfil CF47 ...**10** A2
Swansea SA6 ....**45** D1
Eileen Pl CF42 ....**50** B2
Eileen Rd SA7 ....**69** F7
Eileen Terr CF42 .....**50** B2
Einon Ct SA4 ....**43** D2
Eirw Rd CF39 ....**108** A2
Eisteddfa Rd CF40 .....**79** F2
Eisteddford Wlk
NP19 ....**144** D6
Eithen Pl CF36 ......**182** E6
Elaine Cl CF14 ......**159** E2
Elaine Cres NP19 .....**143** F7
Elan Ave SA6 ....**45** D1
Elan Cl Aberdare CF44 ..**29** E2
Barry CF62 ....**214** C6
Bettws NP20 ....**116** E1
Elan Rd CF14 ....**178** A7
Elan Wlk NP44 ....**89** C2
Elba Ave SA13 ......**125** D5
Elba Cres SA1 ....**97** A7
Elba St SA4 ....**66** C6
Elder Cl NP18 ......**117** F2
Elder Dr CF36 ......**166** D1
Elder Rd SA12 ....**98** D7
Elder St CF31 ......**168** F4
Elder Wood Cl CF23 ..**178** E3
Elderberry Rd CF5 ...**176** B1
Eldon Ct 12 CF11 ....**194** E5
Eleanor Cl CF35 .....**170** B8
Eleanor Pl CF10 .....**195** B1
Eleanor St
Tonypandy CF40 .....**106** E5
Treherbert CF42 ......**78** A4
Eleven St CF64 ......**215** E6
Eleventh Ave CF47 ....**10** F5
Elfed Ave
Penarth CF64 ....**206** E3
Port Talbot SA12 ....**124** D7
Elfed Gn CF5 ....**176** E1
Elfed Rd SA1 ....**95** B8
Elfed Way CF63 .....**215** B7
Elford Rd CF5 ......**193** C5
Elgam Gn 4 NP4 ......**17** C7
Elgar Ave
Newport NP19 ......**144** D5
Port Talbot SA12 .....**98** A2
Elgar Circ NP19 .....**144** D5
Elgar Cl Caerphilly NP12 **85** C7
Newport NP19 ......**144** D5
Elgar Cres CF3 ......**179** D7
Elgar Rd CF64 ......**206** F1
Elgin St SA5 ....**68** B3
Elias Dr SA10 ....**48** D4
Elias Rd SA10 ....**48** C4
Elias St SA11 ....**71** E7
Elidyr Cres NP11 .....**86** F8
Elidyr Rd NP11 .....**86** F8
Elim St CF47 ....**10** F3
Elim Way NP12 ......**86** A5
Eliot Cl SA2 ....**93** F8
Elizabeth Ave CF62 ..**204** F1
Elizabeth Cl
Pentre CF41 ....**78** F4
Ynysforgan SA6 ......**46** A4
Elizabeth Maisonettes
CF11 ....**194** E4
Elizabeth Rd CF31 ...**168** C5
Elizabeth Row NP4 ....**37** C3
Elizabeth St
Abercynon CF45 ......**82** D2
Aberdare CF44 ....**29** A1
Llanelli SA15 ....**40** D5
Pentre CF41 ....**78** F5
Thomastown CF39 ....**133** B2
Elizabeth Way NP23 ....**7** C1
Elizabethian Ct CF64 .**206** E6
Elled Rd NP4 ....**62** A8
Ellen St CF10 ......**195** B5
Ellen's Rd SA10 ......**70** D8
Ellesmere Ct
Cardiff CF5 ....**179** D6
Newbridge NP11 ......**87** B8

Ellick St NP4 ....**17** C7
Elliot St NP24 ....**33** E7
Elliot's Colliery Winding
House Mus NP24 .....**33** F2
Elliotstown Prim Sch
NP24 ....**33** F2
Ellipse The NP4 ......**62** D1
Ellis CF72 ....**155** A5
Ellwood Cl CF3 .....**179** F6
Ellwood Path NP44 ....**89** B2
Elm Cl
Llanmartin NP18 ....**145** E6
Pontypool NP4 ....**38** B2
Sully CF64 ....**216** C4
Waunarlwydd SA5 .....**66** D4
Elm Cotts CF32 .....**167** F4
Elm Cres
Bridgend CF31 ......**168** B5
Penllergaer SA4 ......**44** C2
Elm Ct Caerphilly NP12 ..**85** F6
Gorseinon SA4 ....**43** A3
Newbridge NP11 ......**60** C1
Elm Dr NP11 ....**115** C1
Elm Gr Aberdare CF44 ...**28** F2
Barry CF63 ....**215** C8
Caerphilly CF83 .....**138** C5
Gorseinon SA4 ....**43** A3
Hirwaun CF44 ....**27** D4
Merthyr Tydfil CF47 ...**10** D3
Newport NP20 ......**117** B2
Pontypool NP4 ....**62** E1
St Athan CF62 ....**211** B7
Elm Grove La CF64 ...**206** A3
Elm Grove Pl CF64 ...**206** B3
Elm Grove Rd CF64 ...**206** A3
Elm Ho CF14 ....**176** E6
Elm Rd
Briton Ferry SA11 .....**71** B2
Llanharry CF72 .....**172** B5
Porthcawl CF36 .....**183** D8
Elm Rise CF32 ......**150** F4
Elm St
Aberbargoed CF81 .....**58** B4
Abercwmboi CF44 .....**53** E4
Cwm NP23 ....**35** A8
Ferndale CF43 ....**79** F7
Gilfach Goch CF39 ...**132** B5
Rhydyfelin CF37 .....**136** B5
Troedyrhiw CF48 ......**31** B1
Elm Street La CF24 ...**195** C7
Elm Terr CF32 ......**104** E1
Elm Tree House Sch
CF5 ....**194** B7
Elmfield Cl CF3 .....**179** E6
Elmgrove CF83 .....**138** F6
Elmgrove Cl CF37 ....**109** C5
Elmgrove Rd
Cardiff CF14 ....**176** E4
Mumbles SA3 ......**122** F8
Elmhurst Cl NP4 ......**38** B1
Elmhurst Cres SA1 ....**95** E8
Elms Pk CF72 ......**173** D6
Elms The NP12 ......**59** C2
Elmwood Sq NP22 ....**13** F5
Elmwood Cl 11 CF24 .**195** C7
Elmwood Dr
Briton Ferry SA11 .....**71** C2
Tonyrefail CF39 .....**132** E4
Elmwood Gr NP22 ....**13** F5
Elmwood Rd SA12 ....**98** D6
Elmwood Terr NP22 ...**13** F5
Elphin Cres SA1 ......**67** E1
Elphin Gdns SA1 .....**68** A1
Elphin Rd SA1 ....**67** F1
Elworthy Cl CF64 ....**216** B5
Elwy Cres SA2 ....**67** F1
Elwy Gdns SA2 ......**67** F1
Elwyn Dr CF47 ....**30** F8
Elwyn St CF39 ......**154** D8
Ely Bridge Ind Est
CF5 ....**193** E7
Ely Hospl CF5 ......**193** E5
Ely Ind Est CF40 ....**107** A2
Ely Rd CF5 ....**194** A8
Ely St Pontyclun CF72 ..**173** B8
Tonypandy CF40 .....**106** E5
Ely Valley Ind Est
CF72 ....**173** A8
Ely Valley Rd
Coedely CF39 ......**133** D1
Llantrisant CF72 ....**155** B5
Talbot Green CF72 ...**155** C3
Ynysmaerdy CF72 ....**154** F7
Elysia St NP19 ......**143** D7
Emanuel Cl CF83 .....**137** E4
Embankment Rd SA15 .**40** E2
Emblem Cl CF5 ......**193** E4
Emerald St CF24 .....**195** D7
Emlyn Ave NP23 ....**7** C2
Emlyn Dr CF83 ......**138** A4
Emlyn Gdns SA1 ......**68** B1
Emlyn Rd
Abersychan NP4 ......**37** E5
Cwm NP23 ....**35** B8
Swansea SA1 ....**68** B1
Emlyn Sq 20 NP20 ...**143** C4
Emlyn St 19 NP20 ...**143** C4
Emlyn Terr
Merthyr Tydfil CF47 ...**10** C2
Swansea SA6 ....**68** E6
Tonypandy CF40 .....**106** B6
Emma St SA15 ....**40** D4
Emmanuel Ct CF47 ....**50** F1
Emmanuel Gdns SA2 ..**94** B3
Empire Ave SA11 ....**227** C8
Empire Terr NP4 ......**37** E6
Emroch St SA13 .....**125** E8

Emsworth Ct CF23 ...**178** C6
Ena Ave SA11 ....**71** F7
Endeavour Cl
Bridgend CF31 ......**169** C6
Port Talbot SA12 .....**98** A3
Endyngs NP44 ....**89** B1
Energlyn Cl CF83 ....**137** F4
Energlyn Cres 1
CF83 ....**137** F5
Energlyn Terr CF83 ...**137** F5
Enfield Cl SA6 ....**45** E4
Enfield Dr CF62 .....**214** C7
Enfield St SA12 .....**107** B5
Engine Row NP4 ......**17** B7
Enid Rd SA6 ....**46** F8
Enid St CF40 ....**107** B5
Ennerdale Cl CF23 ...**178** B2
Ennerdale Cl 2 NP19 .**143** F5
Enoch Morrell Cl CF48 .**31** B1
Enterprise Ctr NP13 ...**15** D6
Enterprise Park Ind Est
NP20 ....**143** D3
Enterprise Way NP20 .**143** D3
Enville Cl NP20 .....**142** E4
Enville Rd NP20 .....**142** E4
Eppynt Cl NP11 .....**115** C2
Eppynt Rd SA5 ......**68** A4
Epsom Cl CF5 ......**193** F5
Epstein Cl CF5 ......**176** D2
Erasmus Terr CF82 ....**85** B2
Eric Coates Cl NP19 ..**144** D4
Eric Coates Wlk
NP19 ....**144** E4
Eridge Rd NP4 ....**37** F5
Ernald Pl SA2 ....**94** F6
Ernest St CF47 ....**30** E7
Erskine Ct CF24 .....**195** E7
Erw Deg CF31 ......**168** B5
Erw Fach CF38 ......**135** D1
Erw Hir CF72 ....**155** E3
Erw Hydref SA9 ....**2** D8
Erw Ifan CF35 ......**170** D8
Erw Las Cardiff CF14 ...**177** A4
Merthyr Tydfil CF48 ...**10** A2
Penywaun CF44 ......**28** C6
Erw Rd SA15 ....**40** C5
Erw Wen Cardiff CF14 .**177** B8
North Cornelly CF33 ..**165** F7
Pencoed CF35 ......**163** D6
Erw'r-Delyn Cl CF64 ..**206** D4
Erwlas SA14 ....**41** D3
Erwlon Rd SA15 ......**40** C5
Eschol Cl NP19 .....**144** B3
Eschol Ct NP19 .....**144** B3
Esgair-y-llys CF31 ...**168** B4
Esgid Mair CF63 .....**205** C1
Eskdale Cl CF23 .....**178** B3
Espalone SA3 ....**122** C6
Esplanade
Penarth CF64 ....**207** B3
Porthcawl CF36 .....**182** F6
Esplanade Ave CF36 ..**182** F6
Esplanade Bldgs
CF62 ....**214** E2
Essex Ct NP18 ......**118** A3
Essex St NP19 ......**143** E4
Essex Terr SA6 ......**68** E6
Essich St 5 CF24 ....**178** C1
Estate Rd
Blaenavon NP4 ....**17** B7
Pontypool NP4 ....**62** A8
Esterling Dr SA10 ...**182** F8
Estuary Pk SA14 .....**42** C7
Estuary Rd NP19 ....**144** D1
Ethel St Cardiff CF5 ..**194** B6
Neath SA11 ....**71** D6
Etna Terr CF39 ......**132** C7
Eton Ct CF14 ....**177** F4
Eton Pl 1 CF5 ......**194** D5
Eton Rd NP19 ......**143** D5
Eton St CF62 ....**214** C3
Eugene Cl 18 CF3 ...**180** A8
Eureka NP23 ....**14** D7
Eurgan Cl CF61 .....**209** F5
Eurocast Trad Est
CF14 ....**176** E6
Eurwg Cres 6 CF3 ...**179** D8
Eustace Dr CF32 ....**150** F4
Eva St
Mountain Ash CF45 ...**54** D2
Neath SA11 ....**71** E6
Evan St CF46 ....**83** B8
Evan's Rd SA11 ......**71** D5
Evan's Terr NP22 ......**6** D2
Evans Hos CF48 ....**3** F3
Evans Sq CF37 .....**109** E3
Evans St Barry CF62 ..**214** F5
Newport NP20 ......**143** C6
3 Port Talbot SA13 ...**99** C1
Pyle CF33 ....**148** D3
Evans Terr
Maesteg CF34 ......**102** B8
6 Merthyr Tydfil CF47 .**30** F8
North Cornelly CF33 ..**165** F7
Swansea SA1 ....**95** C8
Tonypandy CF40 .....**107** B5
Evans' Terr CF40 ....**106** F7
Evans's Terr CF40 ...**106** F7
Evansfield Rd CF14 ..**176** F3
Eve's Well Ct NP19 ..**143** E5
Eveline Terr SA13 ...**125** B8
Evelyn Rd SA10 ......**70** D7
Evelyn St
Abertillery NP13 ......**36** B5
Cardiff CF10 ....**195** C2
Evenlode Ave CF64 ..**206** A5
Evenlode Prim Sch
CF64 ....**206** E2
Evenwood Cl CF23 ...**160** F1

Everard St CF63 .....**215** B6
Everard Way CF23 ...**178** B6
Everest Ave CF14 ....**159** F1
Everest Wlk CF14 ....**159** F1
Evergreen NP20 .....**143** A3
Evergreen Cotts
CF33 ....**165** D8
Evergreen Ct CF39 ...**133** E6
Eversley Rd SA2 .....**94** D6
Everswell Ave CF5 ...**193** D7
Everswell Rd CF5 ...**193** D7
Evesham Ct NP20 ...**143** A7
Eveswell Jun & Inf Sch
NP19 ....**143** F5
Eveswell La 1 NP19 .**143** F5
Eveswell Park Rd
NP19 ....**143** F5
Eveswell St NP19 ...**143** F5
Evtol Ind Est NP20 ..**143** D2
Ewanni Fach CF72 ...**154** A3
Ewart Pl SA5 ....**68** C4
Ewbank Cl CF3 .....**215** C8
Ewenny Cl Barry CF63 .**215** A8
Porthcawl CF36 .....**165** E2
Ewenny Cross CF35 ..**185** E7
Ewenny Ind Est CF31 .**169** C1
Ewenny Pl SA6 ......**68** D8
Ewenny Priory CF35 ..**186** A8
Ewenny Rd
Bridgend CF31,CF35 ..**168** F2
Cardiff CF24 ....**178** A7
Castle-upon-Alun CF32 **198** C7
Maesteg CF34 ......**102** B2
St Brides Major CF32 .**185** D2
Wick CF71 ....**198** C7
Ewenny Road Sta
CF34 ....**102** B2
Excalibur Dr CF14 ...**159** E2
Excelsior Ind Est
CF14 ....**177** D2
Excelsior Rd CF14 ...**177** C2
Excelsior St SA12 ....**14** F2
Excelsior Terr CF43 ...**79** C8
Exchange Ct 3 NP11 .**114** F3
Exchange Rd
Neath SA11 ....**71** D6
2 Risca NP11 ....**114** F3
Exchange Row SA14 ..**41** C7
Exchange St CF34 ...**101** F3
Exe Rd NP20 ......**116** D2
Exeter Cl
Cwmbran NP44 ....**89** A3
Heolgerrig CF48 ......**10** A1
Exeter Pl NP4 ....**37** F5
Exeter Rd 8 NP19 ...**143** E6
Exeter St NP19 .....**143** E5
Exford Cres CF3 .....**179** A5
Exhibition Row CF44 ..**28** E2
Eynon St SA4 ....**43** D2
Eyre St CF24 ....**195** E6

F

Faber Way CF11 ....**194** D3
Fabian Way SA1,SA10 ..**96** C7
Factory La
Abersychan NP4 ......**37** F4
Pontypridd CF37 .....**135** B8
Factory Rd
Bargoed CF81 ....**57** F5
Brynmawr NP23 ....**8** C4
Clydach SA6 ....**46** D7
Llanblethian CF71 ...**200** D8
Newport NP20 ......**143** B6
Factory Terr CF32 ...**150** C3
Fagwr Isaf SA6 ......**22** B2
Fagwr Pl SA6 ....**46** A1
Fagwr Rd SA6 ....**22** B2
Fair View
Gilfach Goch CF39 ...**106** C1
Neath SA10 ....**48** C1
Pengam NP12 ....**85** C7
Pontlottyn CF81 ......**32** F8
Tredegar NP22 ....**6** C1
Treharris CF46 ....**83** B5
Fair View Cl
Pontyclun CF72 .....**173** B7
Swansea SA7 ....**69** F6
Fair View Terr NP23 ...**8** C1
Fairacre Cl CF14 ....**159** E2
Fairbrook Cl CF14 ...**177** B8
Fairfax Cres CF36 ...**182** E7
Fairfax Rd
Cardiff CF14 ....**177** D6
Newport NP19 ......**144** A4
Fairfield Aberavon SA12 **98** F1
Abersychan NP4 ......**37** F4
North Cornelly CF33 ..**166** A8
Penperlleni NP4 ......**39** E6
Pontypool NP4 ....**62** A7
Tredegar NP22 ....**13** F8
Fairfield Ave
Cardiff CF14 ....**194** A6
Maesteg CF34 ......**102** A2
Fairfield Cl
Aberdare CF44 ....**29** D1
Caerleon NP18 ......**117** F3
Caerphilly NP12 ......**85** E6
Cardiff CF5 ....**193** F7
Hawthorn CF37 .....**136** A4
Llantwit Major CF61 ..**210** A6
Fairfield Cres CF61 ..**210** A6
Fairfield Ind Est
CF15 ....**158** A2
Fairfield La CF37 ....**136** A4

Fairfield Prim Sch
CF64 ....**206** A2
Fairfield Rd
Bridgend CF31 ......**169** A2
Caerleon NP18 ......**117** F3
Cymmer SA13 ....**75** D3
Penarth CF64 ......**206** F4
Fairfield Rise CF61 ...**210** A6
Fairfield Terr SA1 .....**95** B7
Fairfield Way SA11 ...**71** E8
Fairford St CF63 .....**215** B8
Fairhaven Cl 8 CF3 ..**180** A8
Fairhaven Ct SA3 ...**123** A3
Fairhill NP44 ....**89** B2
Fairhill Dr Baglan SA12 ..**98** E4
Church Village CF38 ..**136** B1
Fairhill Wlk NP44 ....**89** B2
Fairland Cl CF72 ....**155** E3
Fairlawn Ct CF5 ....**177** A1
Fairlawn Terr CF35 ..**170** D8
Fairlawns SA11 ......**71** B3
Fairleigh CF5 ....**205** F7
Fairleigh Cl CF11 ...**194** D8
Fairleigh Rd CF11 ...**194** D7
Fairmead CF5 ......**193** D7
Fairmeadows CF34 ..**128** C8
Fairmound Pl CF38 ..**136** B1
Fairoak SA18 ....**219** D7
Fairoak Ave NP19 ...**143** E6
Fairoak Chase CF31 .**169** C4
Fairoak Cres CF44 ...**28** E2
Fairoak Ct
Cardiff CF23 ....**178** A2
4 Newport NP19 ...**143** E6
Fairoak Gdns 8
NP19 ....**143** E6
Fairoak Gr NP10 ....**141** F2
Fairoak La NP44 .....**90** B4
Fairoak Mews CF7 ...**178** A2
Fairoak Rd CF24 ....**178** A1
Fairoak Terr NP19 ...**143** E5
Fairoaks CF64 ......**206** B3
Fairthorn Cl CF14 ...**159** E3
Fairview Beddau CF38 .**156** B7
Ebbw Vale NP23 .....**14** C8
Hirwaun CF44 ......**224** E1
Tonypandy CF40 .....**107** B3
Fairview Ave
Aberavon SA12 ......**98** F1
Risca NP11 ....**115** A2
Fairview Ct 9 CF3 ...**180** A8
Fairview Ct
Cardiff CF23 ....**178** E7
Pontypool NP4 ....**62** A8
Fairview Est CF48 ...**225** F1
Fairview Hos CF48 ..**225** F3
Fairview Rd SA5 .....**45** C2
Fairview Terr
Abercynon CF45 ......**82** F3
Abersychan NP4 ......**37** E5
Abertillery NP13 ......**36** B7
Merthyr Tydfil CF47 ...**30** E8
Fairwater (Tyllgoed) Halt
CF5 ....**193** E8
Fairwater Ave CF5 ..**193** D7
Fairwater Cl
Cwmbran NP44 ....**89** B2
Michaelston-y-Fedw
CF3 ....**162** A5
Fairwater Gn CF5 ...**193** D7
Fairwater Gr E CF5 .**193** F8
Fairwater Gr W CF5 .**193** F8
Fairwater Jun & Inf Sch
CF5 ....**193** D7
Fairwater Jun & Inf Schs
NP44 ....**89** C2
Fairwater Rd CF5 ...**193** F8
Fairwater Square Shops
NP44 ....**89** C2
Fairwater Way NP44 ..**89** B1
Fairwater Workshops
CF5 ....**193** E7
Fairway SA12 ....**98** C2
Fairway Cl NP10 ....**142** A7
Fairway Dr
Caerphilly CF83 .....**137** F6
Pontardawe SA8 ......**23** D6
Fairway The
Cardiff CF23 ....**160** C1
Pontypool NP4 ....**63** B4
Fairways Bargoed CF81 .**57** E5
North Cornelly CF33 ..**165** E8
Fairways Cres CF5 ...**193** C7
Fairways The NP12 ...**85** E8
Fairways View CF72 .**155** A3
Fairwood Cl CF5 ....**176** E1
Fairwood Dr SA12 ..**198** E8
Fairwood Hospl SA2 ..**93** A6
Fairwood Rd
Cardiff CF5 ....**176** E1
Dunvant SA2 ....**93** C8
Mumbles SA3 ......**123** A8
Fairwood Terr SA4 ...**66** C6
Fairy Glen CF32 ....**104** E4
Fairy Gr SA2 ....**93** E7
Fairyland SA11 ......**72** A8
Fairyland Rd SA11 ...**49** B1
Falcon Chambers 4
SA15 ....**40** D6
Falcon Dr SA11 ......**72** B4
Falcon Gr CF64 .....**217** A7
Falcon Pl SA5 ....**67** E7
Falcon Rd CF63 .....**215** D7
Falcon Terr NP23 ....**35** B7
Falconwood Dr CF5 ..**192** F5
Falfield Cl CF14 ....**160** A2
Fallowfield 11 NP44 ..**89** B1

Fal – Fre **249**

Fallowfield Dr NP19 .144 C3
Fan Heulog CF37 ...109 D6
Fanheulog CF72 ....155 B2
Fanny St Cardiff CF24 .178 A1
Cardiff CF24 ....195 A8
Faraday Cl NP20 ...116 F2
Faraday Rd SA6 ......22 E1
Fardre Cres CF38 ....135 F1
Fardre Ct CF38 ......135 E1
Farlays NP44 ....89 A1
Farlington Ct CF3 ...179 A4
Farlow Wlk NP44 ......89 D2
Farm Cl
Abertridwr CF83 ....137 A7
Blackwood NP12 .....59 E4
Farm Dr Cardiff CF23 .178 B4
Port Talbot SA12 .....98 C1
Farm Fields Rd NP23 ..14 D6
Newport NP19 ....143 F4
Farm La Cwmbran NP44 89 F4
Farm Rd Aberdare CF44 53 D6
Abersychan NP4 ......37 D5
Briton Ferry SA11 ....71 C3
Caerphilly CF83 .....138 C3
Cefn Cribwr CF32 ...149 E2
Ebbw Vale NP23 ......14 D5
Nantyglo NP23 ....15 C8
Newbridge NP11 .....60 B2
Pontardawe SA8 ......23 B1
Pontlottyn CF81 ......12 F1
Pontypool NP4 ....62 C5
Ton Pentre CF41 .....79 C2
Farm Terr NP44 ......33 F4
Farm View NP12 ......58 B3
Farmers Rd SA10 .....48 C5
Farmfield Ave SA12 ...98 C4
Farmhouse Way CF5 .193 B3
Farmleigh CF3 ....179 B7
Farmville Rd CF24 ...195 E6
Farmwood Cl NP19 ..144 B5
Farnaby Cl NP19 ....144 B5
Farraday Dr CF82 .....84 E7
Farteg Rd SA13 .....100 F5
Farthings The CF23 .160 F1
Faulkner Rd NP20 ...143 B3
Faull St SA6 ....45 E1
Fedw Hir Hospl CF44 225 C1
Feeder Bank NP22 .....6 D1
Feeder Row NP11 ....114 C2
Feering St NP19 .....143 E4
Felbridge Cl CF10 ...195 C4
Felbrigg Cres CF23 .160 E1
Felin Fach CF14 .....177 B3
Felin Fran SA7 ....46 C2
Felin Wen CF14 .....177 C2
Felindre Ave CF35 ...170 E7
Felindre Rd CF35 ....170 F7
Felinfach SA9 ....221 C6
Felinfoel Jun Sch
SA14 ....41 A8
Felinfoel Rd SA15 ...40 C1
Fell St CF46 ....83 B7
Felnex Ind Est NP19 .164 E8
Felsted Cl CF23 .....160 F1
Fenbrook Cl SA12 ....98 D5
Fendrod Bsns Pk SA6 .69 A6
Fendrod Way SA7 ....69 C7
Fennel Cl
10 Cardiff CF3 .....180 A8
Penarth CF64 ....206 E5
Fenner Brockway Cl **1**
NP19 ....144 D7
Fenton Pl
Pontycymer CF32 ....103 F2
Porthcawl CF36 .....182 F7
Fenviolet Cl CF3 .....180 B6
Fenwick Dr CF31 ....169 C5
Fenwick St CF43 ....107 C8
Fermoy Ct SA5 ....67 F6
Fern Cl NP11 ....59 D3
Fern Cres CF44 ......28 D2
Fern Ct SA5 ....67 F5
Fern Dr CF62 ....214 D5
Fern Hill CF41 ....79 B2
Fern Pl CF5 ....193 D8
Fern Rise NP20 .....117 B3
Fern St Cardiff CF5 ..194 B6
Hendreforgan CF39 ..132 C5
Ogmore Vale CF32 ...130 E8
Swansea SA5 ....68 E2
Fern Terr NP40 ......106 D6
Fernbank NP44 ......89 B2
Fernbrook Cl NP23 ....7 D6
Ferncroft Way NP4 ...38 E2
Ferndale Cl CF3 ......7 B5
Ferndale Comp Sch
CF43 ....79 C8
Ferndale Ct CF43 ....79 F7
Ferndale Ind Est CF43 79 D8
Ferndale Inf Sch CF43 79 F7
Ferndale Rd CF43 ....80 B2
Ferndale St CF11 ....194 F3
Fernfield SA12 ....98 E4
Fernfield Terr NP13 ...36 B5
Fernhill CF45 ....54 A3
Fernhill Cl
Merthyr Tydfil CF47 ...10 D5
Mumbles SA2 ....94 B1
Troedyrhiw CF48 .....31 C1
Fernhill Rd SA4 ......43 A3
Fernhill Sta CF45 ....54 B4
Fernhill Terr
New Tredegar NP24 ...33 F3
Treharris CF46 ....83 A7
Fernlea NP11 ....114 F3
Ferns The
4 Penarth CF64 ...207 B5
Quakers Yard CF46 ...83 C6

Fernside NP19 ......144 B3
Ferntree Dr CF3 .....179 E7
Ferny Ct CF23 ....178 D2
Ferrara St SA1 ....95 D5
Ferrier Ave CF5 .....176 D1
Ferrier's Row CF34 .102 B3
Ferry La **7** CF64 ...207 B5
Ferry Rd Cardiff CF11 .206 F8
Loughor SA4 ....42 C1
Ferry Side SA1 ....95 E6
Ferryboat Cl SA6 .....69 A7
Fescue Pl CF5 ......193 A5
Festiniog Rd CF14 ..177 A2
Festival Cres NP4 ....63 B4
Festival Dr NP23 ....14 E4
Festival Pk NP23 .....14 F1
Fetty Pl NP44 ....89 D1
Ffald Rd CF3 ....148 B2
Ffaldau Terr CF43 ...79 D7
Ffaldau Ind Est CF32 .103 F3
Ffaldau Prim Sch
CF32 ....103 F3
Ffeam-y-Graig CF62 .211 D4
Fferm Goch CF35 ...170 F1
Fferm-y-Bryn CF82 ...84 F1
Fferws Rd SA18 ....218 F6
Fflorens Rd NP11 ....59 F1
Fforch Cl CF42 ......78 D7
Fforch-Dwm Rd SA12 .73 E6
Fforchaman Rd CF44 .53 B4
Fforchneol Row CF44 .53 B5
Fford Llanbad CF39 .132 C5
Fford Rhaglan CF35 .152 B6
Fford-yr-Orsaf SA18 .219 B7
Fford-yr-Ywen CF38 .136 A2
Ffordd -yr-Afon
CF31 ....168 B6
Ffordd Abiah SA6 .....46 E8
Ffordd Afan SA12 ....99 D5
Ffordd Alltwen SA4 ...66 A5
Ffordd Aneurin Bevan
SA2 ....94 C8
Ffordd Beck SA4 .....66 B6
Ffordd Bodlyn CF23 .178 C3
Ffordd Briallu SA7 ...69 D6
Ffordd Bryngwyn SA4 .66 D8
Ffordd Brynheulog
SA8 ....23 D5
Ffordd Butler SA4 ...66 B6
Ffordd Candleston
CF31 ....168 C3
Ffordd Catraeth CF37 109 F3
Ffordd Celyn **7** CF14 177 B4
Ffordd Cwell Yn
CF23 ....178 C3
Ffordd Cwellyn CF23 .178 B3
Ffordd Cwm Cidi
CF62 ....214 B5
Ffordd Cwm Tawe
Swansea SA6 ....68 F6
Ynysforgan SA6,SA7 ..46 D5
Ffordd Cynghordy
SA7 ....69 D7
Ffordd Cynore SA15 ...67 C6
Ffordd Dafydd SA14 .218 D7
Ffordd Dawel SA7 ....69 E6
Ffordd Ddu CF3 .....148 B2
Ffordd Derwen SA13 .148 A6
Ffordd Dewi SA6 ....45 B1
Ffordd Dillwyn-Llewellyn
SA4 ....66 D8
Ffordd Dinas SA12 ...99 D5
Ffordd Dinefwr CF15 .174 D7
Ffordd Draenen Ddu
SA3 ....122 E6
Ffordd Dryden SA2 ...93 E8
Ffordd Eira SA4 ......43 C2
Ffordd Elin CF63 ....215 D7
Ffordd Ellen SA6 ....22 B2
Ffordd Emlyn SA9 .....2 B5
Ffordd Erw CF83 ....158 E8
Ffordd Eynon Evans
CF83 ....137 D6
Ffordd Florence **3**
SA18 ....219 B7
Ffordd Ganol CF31 ...169 A4
Ffordd Garthorne
CF10 ....195 C3
Ffordd Gerdinan
CF38 ....136 A1
Ffordd Glandwr SA2 ..2 B6
Ffordd Gower Davies
CF37 ....109 A7
Ffordd Gwyn SA7 ....69 D7
Ffordd Gwyneth **1**
CF63 ....215 C8
Ffordd Is-Cennen
SA18 ....219 B7
Ffordd Las
Abertridwr CF83 .....137 A8
Radyr CF15 ....176 A6
Ffordd Llundain SA7 ..69 D7
Ffordd Llyffant SA7 ...70 B8
Ffordd Maescwarrau
SA18 ....219 D6
Ffordd Newydd CF33 .166 A8
Ffordd Parc Ynysderw
SA8 ....23 E4
Ffordd Pen Twyn
SA18 ....219 C7
Ffordd Pengam CF24 196 A8
Ffordd Penrhos CF83 137 D3
Ffordd Priordy CF32 .150 D4
Ffordd Scott
Birchgrove SA7 ......46 F1
Swansea SA7 ....70 A8
Ffordd Sealand CF62 .214 A4
Ffordd Silkin SA8 ....23 E5

Ffordd Stewart **2**
SA18 ....219 B7
Ffordd Talbot SA18 .219 B7
Ffordd Talfan SA4 ....66 D8
Ffordd Taliesin
Pontypridd CF37 ....109 F4
Swansea SA2 ....93 F8
Ffordd Talygarn
CF72 ....173 A7
Ffordd Tollborth SA7 .69 D7
Ffordd Traws Cwm
CF83 ....137 E1
Ffordd Trecastell
CF72 ....172 D6
Ffordd Treforgan
CF15 ....176 A8
Ffordd Tryweryn
CF37 ....109 F3
Ffordd Walter SA18 .219 C7
Ffordd y Bedol CF37 .109 D6
Ffordd y Brain SA5 ...67 C5
Ffordd y Brenin **1**
CF10 ....195 A6
Ffordd y Dderwen
CF71 ....189 C8
Ffordd y Faenor
SA18 ....219 B7
Ffordd y Frenhines
CF34,SA13 ....126 E6
Ffordd y Gamlas SA4 .66 B6
Ffordd y Goedwig
CF33 ....148 C3
Ffordd y Mileniwm
CF62,CF63 ....214 F4
Ffordd y Morfa SA14 .218 C7
Ffordd y Mynach
CF33 ....148 B2
Ffordd y Rhyd SA18 .219 B6
Ffordd yr Eglwys
CF33 ....166 A8
Ffordd Ysgol SA12 ...98 D1
Ffordd-y-Barcer CF5 .192 F5
Ffordd-y-Berllan
CF15 ....176 A7
Ffordd-y-Bryn
Birchgrove SA7 ......47 B1
Swansea SA7 ....70 B8
Ffordd-y-Capel CF38 156 F6
Ffordd-y-Dderwyn
CF31 ....168 C6
Ffordd-y-Derwen
CF45 ....54 B6
Ffordd-y-Eglwys CF5 191 E5
Ffordd-y-Gollen
CF38 ....135 F2
Ffordd-y-Gyfraith
CF32 ....149 E6
Ffordd-y-Mynach
SA10 ....71 A7
Ffordd-y-Mynydd
Birchgrove SA7 ......47 B1
Swansea SA7 ....70 B8
Ffordd-y-Parc
Bridgend CF31 ......169 A8
Swansea SA6 ....45 A1
Fforde Cae Duke SA4 .66 A8
Fforde Kilby SA4 .....66 A8
Fforest Dr CF42 .....214 B4
Fforest Glade NP19 .143 F6
Fforest Hill SA10 ....49 C4
Fforest Rd
Llanharry CF72 .....172 C4
Mountain Ash CF45 ...54 C4
Fforestfach SA18 ....219 A5
Ffos Cl SA4 ....83 E4
Ffos Felen SA4 ......66 B5
Ffos y Cerridden CF82 83 D3
Ffos y Fran NP10 ...141 F2
Ffos-y-Fran **1** CF14 .141 F2
Ffos-yr-Efail Terr
SA4 ....177 C3
Ffos-yr-Hebog CF83 .112 A5
Ffosmaen Rd NP23 ...8 B7
Ffridd Las CF31 .....168 B4
Ffrwd Cres CF45 .....54 D3
Ffrwd Rd
Abersychan NP4 ......38 A4
Merthyr Tydfil CF48 .225 F3
Ffrwd St CF41 ....53 C6
Ffrwd Terr
Hirwaun CF44 ....27 E7
Llanbradach CF83 ...111 F2
Ffrwd Vale SA10 .....48 D1
Ffrwd-Wyllt St SA13 .125 C6
Ffrwd-y-Felin SA18 .219 B8
Ffrwdwyllt Cotts **4**
SA13 ....125 C6
Ffwrwm Rd CF83 ...139 F7
Ffynnon Ct **3** NP23 ...8 B7
Ffynnon Deilo CF71 .191 A4
Ffynnon Samlet SA7 ..69 D7
Ffynnon Tudful CF47 ..10 D7
Ffynnon Wen
Clydach SA6 ....46 C7
North Cornelly CF33 .148 A1
Ffynnon-Las CF14 ...79 F2
Ffynnon-wen Terr
NP12 ....58 B1
Ffynnonbwla Rd
CF37 ....136 C4
Ffynon y Maen CF33 .148 A2
Ffynone Cl SA1 ......95 A7
Ffynone Dr SA1 ......95 A7
Ffynone Rd SA1 .....95 A7
Ffynonn Las SA18 ...219 B5

Fiddlers Elbow CF46 ..83 A4
Fidlas Ave CF14 .....178 A7
Fidlas Rd CF14 .....178 A7
Field Cl SA6 ....46 A2
Field St Swansea SA1 ..68 D3
Tonypandy CF40 ....106 F4
Trelewis CF46 ....83 C7
Field Terr
New Tredegar NP24 ...33 F4
Pentyrch CF15 ......157 C1
Port Talbot SA12 ...125 D8
Field View NP44 .....90 A5
Field View Rd CF63 .215 A7
Field Way CF14 .....177 E6
Field's Park Rd NP11 .86 E7
Fieldfare Dr CF3 ....180 A6
Fielding Cl CF3 .....179 B7
Fieldings **7** NP44 ...89 B1
Fields Ave NP44 .....89 D6
Fields Ct CF11 ......194 C7
Fields Park Ave NP20 142 F5
Fields Park Cres
NP20 ....143 A5
Fields Park Ct NP20 .143 A5
Fields Park Gdns
NP20 ....142 F5
Fields Park La NP20 .142 F5
Fields Park Rd
Cardiff CF11 ....194 D8
Newport NP20 ......142 F5
Fields Park Terr
NP11 ....114 B5
Fields Rd
Cwmbran NP44 .....116 F8
Newport NP20 ......143 A5
Risca NP11 ....141 B8
Tredegar NP22 ....13 F5
Fieldview Cl CF64 ...206 E5
Fife St CF45 ....82 E6
Fifth Ave
Hirwaun CF44 ......224 C1
Merthyr Tydfil CF47 ...10 E5
Swansea SA6 ....45 D1
Filey Rd NP19 ......143 D7
Finchley Rd CF5 ....193 E7
Finchway Ct NP4 ....37 E7
Finsbury Terr SA2 ...94 F5
Fir Grove St CF41 ....78 F5
Fir St CF43 ....79 F7
Fir Tree Cl CF47 ......10 D5
Fir Tree Cotts CF33 ..146 B8
Fir Tree Dr CF46 .....83 A6
Firbank Ave NP19 ...144 A7
Firbank Cres NP19 .144 A6
Firbank Terr NP11 ..113 A5
Firbanks Way CF72 .155 A3
Firemans Ct **2** NP23 ...8 C4
Firm St SA1 ....95 C8
Firs Ave CF5 ....193 B8
Firs The Blaenavon NP4 .17 E6
Newport NP20 ......117 C2
Porthcawl CF36 .....183 E7
First Ave
Caerphilly CF83 .....137 E5
Merthyr Tydfil CF47 ...10 E5
Swansea SA6 ....68 C3
Firth Rd
Ebbw Vale NP23 .....14 B8
Llanelli SA15 ....40 E4
Firtree Cl
Caerleon NP18 ......117 E2
Cardiff CF5 ....193 C8
Firwood Cl
Bryn-côch SA10 .....48 C5
Cardiff CF14 ....176 F4
Fisher Cl NP19 ......144 F7
Fishguard Cl CF14 ..178 A7
Fishguard Rd CF14 .177 F7
Fishmarket Quay **11**
SA1 ....95 E6
Fishpond Rd CF3 ...179 B6
Fitzalan Com High Sch
CF11 ....194 B5
Fitzalan St **9** CF24 .195 B6
Fitzalan Pl CF24 ....195 C6
Fitzalan Rd
Cardiff CF24 ....195 B6
Cardiff CF24 ....195 C6
Fitzhamon Ave CF61 .127 C4
Fitzhamon Emb CF11 194 F5
Fitzhamon La CF11 .194 F5
Fitzhamon Rd CF36 .182 F8
Fitzroy Ave NP23 .....7 D2
Fitzroy Lodge NP12 ..85 C7
Fitzroy St
Brynmawr NP23 ......8 B5
Cardiff CF24 ....195 A8
Fitzwilliam Cl CF72 .155 E2
Five Bells Rd CF31 ..168 F3
Five Hos NP23 ....7 F4
Five Locks Cl NP44 ..89 D7
Five Locks Rd NP44 ..89 D6
Five Oaks La NP44 ...90 A6
Flanders Mdw CF61 .209 F5
Flanders Rd CF61 ...209 F5
Flatholm Pl SA5 .....67 E7
Flatholm Way CF36 .165 E1
Flats The CF14 .....177 E2
Flax Ct CF64 ....206 E5
Flaxland Ave CF14 .177 E3
Fleet St SA1 ....95 B5
Fleet Way CF11 ....194 E2
Fleetwood Cl NP19 ..143 E4
Fleming Cl NP20 ....117 A2
Flemingston Rd CF62 211 D7
Fleur-de-lis Prim Sch
NP12 ....85 B5

Fleur-De-Lys Ave
NP12 ....85 E4
Flint Ave CF61 .....210 B7
Flint Cl NP19 ....144 B3
Flint Ct NP18 ....118 A3
Flint Ho SA12 ......124 D8
Flint St CF14 ....177 E1
Flora St CF24 ......195 A8
Floral Ave NP12 .....85 B7
Florence Ave CF62 .214 E8
Florence Cl NP13 ...36 C5
Florence Gr CF83 ...138 A2
Florence Pl NP4 .....62 E2
Florence St
Cardiff CF24 ....195 E7
Llanelli SA15 ....40 E3
Neath SA11 ....71 C4
Porthcawl CF36 .....165 F1
Florentia St CF24 ..178 A1
Fochriw Prim Sch
CF81 ....32 D8
Fochriw Rd CF81 ....32 E8
Foel View Cl CF38 ..156 F7
Foley Ho NP44 ....90 B4
Folland Cl SA2 ......94 B1
Folland Rd SA18 ....220 B8
Folly La Penperlleni NP4 39 A3
Pontypool NP4 ......38 C1
Folly Rd NP4 ....38 C1
Folly View NP4 ......62 D7
Fonmon Cres CF5 ...193 D5
Fonmon Park Rd
CF62 ....212 E2
Fonmon Rd CF62 ...212 D6
Fontigary Rd CF3 ...179 C3
Fontygari Holiday & L Pk
CF62 ....212 E1
Fontygary Rd CF62 .212 F1
Forbes St CF24 ......68 E5
Ford Farm La NP18 .119 E1
Ford Rd
Fleur De Lis NP12 ...85 B4
Pontypridd CF37 ....109 A1
Port Talbot SA13 .....99 B1
Upper Boat CF37 ....136 D2
Ford St NP20 ....143 B5
Fordwell CF5 ....177 A1
Foreland Rd CF14 ..177 A5
Foreshore Rd CF10 .195 F2
Forest Ave CF82 .....84 F5
Forest Cl
Cwmbran NP44 .....116 B8
Newport NP19 ......143 F6
Forest Farm Nature Trail
CF14 ....176 D6
Forest Farm Rd
Cardiff CF14 ....176 E5
Radyr CF14 ....176 D6
Forest Fawr Wlks
CF83 ....158 E4
Forest Gr
Pontypridd CF37 ....135 E5
Treharris CF46 ......82 F6
Forest Hill NP12 .....85 E3
Forest Hills Dr CF72 155 A2
Forest Level CF45 ...54 E2
Forest Lodge La SA12 .99 F4
Forest Oak Cl CF23 .160 C1
Forest Rd
Beddau CF38 ....156 A6
Pontypridd CF37 ....135 E6
Treharris CF46 ......83 B7
Forest Veiw NP11 ...114 D8
Forest View
Cardiff CF5 ....193 C7
Mountain Ash CF45 ...54 A3
Neath SA11 ....72 B4
Pontypridd CF37 ....109 C6
Pyle CF33 ....148 A2
Talbot Green CF72 ..155 C2
Forest Wlk CF72 ....155 A2
Forge Cl NP18 ......118 B4
Forge Cres NP22 ....12 F2
Forge Fach SA6 .....46 D7
Forge Factory Est
CF34 ....101 F4
Forge Hammer Ind Est
NP44 ....89 D4
Forge La NP10 .....142 B2
Forge Mews NP10 ..142 B3
Forge Pl Aberdare CF44 29 B3
Cardiff CF5 ....193 B4
Forge Rd
Blaenavon NP4 ......17 B6
Crofty SA4 ....64 B2
Machen CF83 ....140 A7
Newport NP10 ......142 C1
Port Talbot SA13 .....99 B1
Forge Row
Aberdare CF44 ......53 D6
Maesygwartha NP7 ....9 E8
Pontypool NP4 ....61 F8
Forge Side Rd NP4 ..17 B5
Forge St CF41 ....79 A4
Forge Trip CF44 .....29 B3
Forge Way CF36 ....182 F8
Forgeside NP44 ......89 E4
Forio Ho CF10 .....195 C2
Forrest Rd Cardiff CF5 194 B6
Penarth CF64 ....207 A1
Forrest St CF11 ....194 F7
Forster Rd SA11 ....71 F7
Forsythia Cl
Merthyr Tydfil CF47 ...10 C5
Risca NP11 ....115 C1

Forsythia Dr CF23 ..178 D7
Fort Rd CF64 ......217 A5
Fort St CF24 ....195 E7
Fort View NP10 .....142 A3
Fortlee NP20 ....142 E3
Fortran Rd CF3 .....180 B8
Fosse Cl NP19 .....144 C2
Fosse Rd NP19 ....144 C2
Foster Dr CF23 .....178 E1
Foster St **6** CF63 ..215 B6
Fothergill Cl CF47 ...59 B2
Fothergill Rd SA11 .227 B8
Fothergill St
Aberdare CF44 ......29 B3
Merthyr Tydfil CF47 ...10 E7
Pontypridd CF37 ....135 E7
Fothergills Rd NP24 ..33 E3
Founders Row CF44 ..28 E5
Foundry Bridge NP13 .36 B5
Foundry Pl
Pontypridd CF37 ....109 D2
6 Porth CF39 .....107 F3
Foundry Rd
Abersychan NP4 ......37 E3
Hirwaun CF44 ....27 D8
Morriston SA6 ....46 A1
Neath SA11 ....71 E5
Pontypridd CF37 ....109 A1
Tonypandy CF40 ....106 F6
Foundry Row
Ammanford SA18 ...219 C7
Neath SA10 ....70 E8
Foundry View CF44 ..53 E5
Fountain Ct NP13 ....36 B7
Fountain La CF3 ....180 B8
Fountain Rd
Aberkenfig CF32 ....150 B3
Pontypridd NP4 ......62 E5
Fountain St
Ferndale CF43 ....80 A6
3 Mountain Ash CF45 .54 D3
Trehafod CF37 ......108 D2
Fountain Terr CF32 .129 D2
Four Acre CF61 .....210 A7
Four Elms Ct **2** CF24 195 C6
Four Elms Rd **2**
CF24 ....195 D7
Fouracres Cl CF63 ..215 C7
Fourteen Locks Canal Ctr
NP10 ....142 B6
Fourteenth Ave CF44 224 C1
Fourth Ave
Hirwaun CF44 ......224 C1
Merthyr Tydfil CF47 ...10 E5
Swansea SA6 ....45 D1
Fowler St NP4 ....62 A8
Fowler's Pl CF34 ...102 A8
Fox Ave NP11 ....86 C5
Fox Gr SA5 ....67 A4
Fox Hollows CF71 ..189 C5
Fox Russell Cl CF14 .177 A2
Fox St Cardiff CF24 .195 E7
Treharris CF46 ......83 B7
Foxberry Cl CF23 ...161 B1
Foxfields CF31 .....169 D4
Foxglove Cl CF5 ....193 B4
Foxglove Rise CF64 .206 E5
Foxgrove SA4 ....66 B8
Foxhole Dr SA3 .....121 A4
Foxhole Rd SA1 .....68 E1
Foxhollows CF31 ...169 D5
Foxwood Cl NP10 ..141 F3
Foxwood Rd NP10 ..141 F3
Foyer The **7** SA1 ...95 D7
Frampton Ct SA4 ....42 F2
Frampton Rd SA4 ...43 A3
Francis Cl **22** NP20 .143 C3
Francis Ct SA8 ......24 C4
Francis Dr NP20 ...143 C3
Francis Morris Est **5**
NP4 ....17 D6
Francis Rd Barry CF62 205 A1
Swansea SA6 ....45 E1
Francis St
Abertridwr CF83 ....136 F7
Bargoed CF81 ....58 A4
Dowlais CF48 ....11 A5
Fleur De Lis NP12 ...85 B6
Hawthorn CF37 .....136 A4
Neath SA10 ....70 F7
21 Newport NP20 ...143 C3
Pontardawe SA8 .....23 E4
Risca NP11 ....115 A1
Swansea SA1 ....95 A5
Thomastown CF39 ..133 B3
Tonypandy CF40 ....106 F6
Francis Terr Pant CF48 .11 A7
Pontypridd CF37 ....109 E3
Frank Rd CF5 ......193 D6
Frank St NP19 .....143 C6
Franklen Rd CF14 ..177 C4
Franklen St **4** CF11 .194 F3
Fransham St **3** SA15 .40 E6
Fraternal Par **2**
CF37 ....109 C2
Frederick Ct SA11 ...71 E6
Frederick Mews
NP20 ....143 C3
Frederick Rd SA7 ...69 C7
Frederick St
Aberdare CF44 ......28 E4
Cardiff CF24 ....195 A6
1 Cardiff CF10 ....195 B5
Ferndale CF43 ....79 F6

Frederick St continued
2 Llanelli SA15 . . . .**40** D5
Newport NP20 . . . .**143** D3
1 Port Talbot SA12 . . **124** F8
Swansea SA5 . . . .**68** C3
Free School Ct CF31 .**168** F3
Freehold Land Rd NP4 **38** A1
Freeman St SA5 . . . .**68** C4
Fremington PI CF3 .**179** C5
Freshmoor Rd CF24 .**195** E5
Freshwater Rd NP19 .**144** D1
Frewer Ave CF5 . . . . . .**176** D1
Friars CI SA10 . . . .**71** B8
Friars Ct NP20 . . . .**143** B3
Friars Field NP20 . . . .**143** B3
Friars Gdn NP44 . . . . . .**90** B1
Friars Rd Barry CF62 . .**214** F2
Barry CF62 . . . .**214** F2
Newport NP20 . . . .**143** B3
Friars St 1 NP20 . . . .**143** C4
Friars The NP20 . . . . . .**143** B3
Friary The CF10 . . . . . .**195** A6
Frigate Rd CF10 . . . . . .**195** D1
Frobisher Rd NP19 . .**144** B3
Froglane SA3 . . . .**228** E4
Frogmore Ave SA2 . . . .**94** D6
Frome Wlk NP20 . . . . .**116** C2
Fron Heulog CF31 . . . .**168** D5
Fron Terr Llanelli SA15 . . .**40** E3
4 Pontypridd CF37 . .**109** E2
Fron Wen NP12 . . . . . .**85** C6
Fron-Wen Terr CF32 . .**104** E3
Frondeg
Penperlleni NP4 . . . . . .**39** E5
Tredegar NP22 . . . .**13** D5
Frondeg Terr SA15 . . . .**40** F6
Fronheulog CF37 . . . .**109** A2
Fronwen Prim Sch
CF32 . . . .**104** E3
Fronwen Terr CF47 . . . .**10** F3
Frost PI NP12 . . . .**85** D7
Frost Rd NP23 . . . .**7** E4
Fryatt St CF63 . . . .**215** A4
Full Moon Visitor Ctr
NP11 . . . .**114** A3
Fuller St SA8 . . . .**23** E5
Fullers Row SA1 . . . . . .**95** C7
Fulmar CI Cardiff CF3 .**179** F8
Mumbles SA3 . . . .**122** E4
Penarth CF64 . . . .**217** A7
Fulmar Rd CF36 . . . . .**182** E8
Furnace Prim Sch
SA15 . . . .**40** B7
Furnace Rd CF43 . . . . .**80** C1
Furnace Row CF48 . . . .**31** B2
Furnace St Barry CF64 **215** E6
Ebbw Vale NP23 . . . .**7** D3
Furnace Terr SA11 . . . .**71** C5
Furness CI CF5 . . . . . .**193** B4
Furze Cres SA6 . . . .**45** D2
Furzeland Dr
Bryn-côch SA10 . . . . . .**48** C4
Swansea SA2 . . . .**94** B6
Fynnon Caeconna SA5 **67** E6

G

Gabalaf Wookshops
CF14 . . . .**177** D2
Gabalfa Ave CF14 . . . .**177** A2
Gabalfa Prim Sch
CF14 . . . .**177** D2
Gabalfa Rd
Cardiff CF14 . . . .**177** A2
Swansea SA2 . . . .**94** B5
Gables The
Cardiff CF14 . . . .**177** D2
Dinas Powys CF64 . . . .**206** A2
Gadley's Terr SA13 . . .**227** C2
Gadlys Gdns 1 CF44 . .**29** A2
Gadlys Rd CF44 . . . . . .**28** F2
Gadlys Rd E CF62 . . . .**214** D5
Gadlys Rd W CF62 . . . .**214** D5
Gadlys St CF44 . . . .**28** F2
Gadlys Terr CF44 . . . . .**28** F2
Gadlys Uchaf 3 CF44 .**28** F4
Gaen St
Abertillery NP13 . . . . . .**36** B6
Barry CF62 . . . .**214** C4
Gaer Inf Sch NP20 . . .**142** F3
Gaer Jun Sch NP20 . .**142** F2
Gaer La NP20 . . . .**143** A3
Gaer Park Ave NP20 . .**142** E3
Gaer Park Dr NP20 . . .**142** E3
Gaer Park Hill NP20 . .**142** E3
Gaer Park La NP20 . . .**142** E2
Gaer Park Par NP20 . .**142** E2
Gaer Park Rd NP20 . . .**142** E3
Gaer PI CF82 . . . .**84** C6
Gaer Rd Newport NP20 **142** F2
Newport NP20 . . . .**142** F3
Gaer St NP20 . . . .**143** A2
Gaer Vale NP20 . . . . . .**142** F1
Gaerwen CI CF14 . . . .**177** D8
Gainsborough CI
NP44 . . . .**117** A8
Gainsborough Ct 2
CF64 . . . .**206** F5
Gainsborough Dr
NP19 . . . .**144** A8
Gainsborough Ho 1
SA12 . . . .**98** D1
Gainsborough Rd
6 Penarth CF64 . . . .**206** F5

Gainsborough Rd continued
Tredegar NP22 . . . .**13** C6
Galahad CI CF14 . . . .**159** D2
Galdames PI CF24 . . .**195** D4
Gallamuir Rd CF24 . . .**195** F7
Gallidawel Flats
CF39 . . . .**133** D5
Gallipoli Row SA13 . .**125** D5
Galltcwm Terr SA13 . .**100** F4
Galon Uchaf Rd CF47 . . .**10** E4
Galston St 5 CF24 . . .**195** D6
Gamlyn Terr CF44 . . . .**27** F6
Gantre CI NP23 . . . .**7** C5
Gantref Way NP21 . . . . .**7** D3
Gar-y-nant CF31 . . . .**168** F5
Gar-yr-afon 8 CF44 . .**53** D7
Garage Circular Rd
CF62 . . . .**211** E1
Gardd Jolyon NP12 . . .**85** C6
Gardde SA14 . . . .**41** E4
Garden City
Merthyr Tydfil CF47 . . . .**10** F4
Rhymney NP22 . . . .**12** F2
Garden CI CF83 . . . . . .**112** A2
Garden Cres SA4 . . . . . .**66** D8
Garden Ct CF31 . . . . . .**169** D5
Garden St Dowlais CF48 **11** B4
Ebbw Vale NP23 . . . .**14** D8
Llanbradach CF83 . . . . .**112** A2
Swansea SA1 . . . .**95** C6
Garden Suburbs
NP11 . . . .**114** C6
Gardenia CI CF23 . . . .**178** D7
Gardens The
Ynysddu NP11 . . . .**112** F6
Ystalyfera SA9 . . . .**2** B6
Gardner CI CF37 . . . . .**109** D5
Gardners La SA11 . . . .**71** D4
Garesfield St SF24 . . .**195** D6
Gareth CI CF14 . . . . . .**159** D2
Garfield Ave SA13 . . .**168** F8
Garfield St NP12 . . . . .**85** E6
Garfield Terr NP23 . . . .**7** C1
Garn Cross NP23 . . . . .**15** D8
Garn Dyrus Mount 3
NP4 . . . .**17** D7
Garn Rd Blaenavon NP4 .**16** F8
Maesteg CF34 . . . .**102** B2
Nantyglo NP23 . . . .**8** C1
Garn St NP11 . . . .**87** B3
Garn Terr NP23 . . . .**14** F3
Garn-yr-erw NP4 . . . . .**16** F8
Garnant Cty Prim Sch
SA18 . . . .**220** B8
Garnfoel SA14 . . . .**218** D7
Garnfach Inf Sch NP23 . .**8** D1
Garngoch Hospl SA4 . .**66** F7
Garngoch Ind Est SA4 .**43** E1
Garngoch Terr SA4 . . . .**66** D8
Garnlwyd CI SA4 . . . . .**68** C7
Garnlydan Jun & Inf Sch
NP23 . . . .**7** D5
Garnswllt Rd SA4 . . . .**218** F1
Garnswllt Sch SA4 . . .**219** B3
Garnteg Prim Sch NP4 **37** F6
Garnwen Rd CF34 . . . .**101** F6
Garnwen Terr CF34 . . .**101** F6
Garon Terr CF32 . . . . .**104** E7
Garreg Hollt SA14 . . . .**218** A8
Garreg Rd CF32 . . . . . .**103** E3
Garreg Side CF32 . . . .**103** E5
Garreg-Wen CF82 . . . . .**84** D8
Garrick Dr CF14 . . . . .**159** E2
Garrick Ho 3 SA12 . . . .**98** B3
Garrod Ave SA2 . . . . . .**66** C2
Garth Ave
Maesteg CF34 . . . .**102** D2
Pontypridd CF37 . . . . .**109** D5
Garth CI
Bassaleg NP10 . . . .**142** A3
Morganstown CF15 . . . .**176** B8
Pontypool NP4 . . . .**38** B2
Rudry CF83 . . . .**139** B3
Garth Cotts CF47 . . . . .**10** C2
Garth Dan-y-Bryn
NP23 . . . .**7** D4
Garth Dr CF31 . . . .**169** B7
Garth Est CF83 . . . . . .**136** C7
Garth Gr CF44 . . . .**224** E1
Garth La CF31 . . . .**139** B3
Garth Lwyd CF83 . . . . .**138** D5
Garth Olwg CF15 . . . .**157** F5
Garth PI CF14 . . . .**177** D6
Garth Prim Sch CF34 .**102** D1
Garth Rd
Cwmbran NP44 . . . . . .**116** D8
Glais SA7 . . . .**46** F6
Gwaun-Cae-Gurwen
SA18 . . . .**220** E6
Tonypandy CF40 . . . . .**107** B5
Ynystawe SA6 . . . .**46** D4
Garth St Cardiff CF24 . .**195** B8
Coedely CF39 . . . .**154** D8
Pontlottyn CF81 . . . .**32** F8
Pyle CF33 . . . .**148** C2
Taffs Well CF15 . . . .**158** A3
Garth Sta CF34 . . . . . .**128** C8
Garth Terr
Bassaleg NP10 . . . .**141** F2
Bedlinog CF46 . . . .**56** A6
Merthyr Tydfil CF47 . . . .**10** F2
Garth View
Beddau CF38 . . . .**156** A6
Bedwas CF83 . . . .**138** D7
Merthyr Tydfil CF47 . . . .**10** F2
Nantgarw CF15 . . . .**158** A8
Ynysforgan SA6 . . . .**46** B4

Garth View continued
Church Village CF38 . . .**156** F8
Garth Villas
Merthyr Tydfil CF47 . . . . .**10** E2
Taffs Well CF15 . . . . . .**157** F4
Garth Wen CF40 . . . . .**107** A5
Garw Fechan (Woodland
Park) Forest Walks
CF32 . . . .**103** D1
Garw Row NP44 . . . . . .**90** B5
Garw The NP44 . . . .**90** B5
Garw Wood Dr NP44 . . .**90** A6
Garwellt CF44 . . . .**28** A6
Garwfechan Rd CF32 .**129** E8
Gas Rd CF37 . . . .**109** C1
Gaskell CI CF61 . . . . . .**210** C6
Gaskell St NP19 . . . . .**143** F3
Gaspard PI CF24 . . . . .**214** C2
Gasworks Rd CF44 . . . .**53** D7
Gasworks Terr CF32 . .**150** D6
Gate Rd
Bridgend CF31 . . . .**169** D2
Penygroes SA14 . . . . . .**218** D8
Gateholm CI CF62 . . . .**214** F8
Gateside CI CF23 . . . .**161** A2
Gateway (Y Porth) The
CF14 . . . .**177** E3
Gathen Terr 11 SA15 . .**40** E4
Gaudi Wlk NP10 . . . . .**142** A6
Gaulden Gr CF23 . . . . .**160** E1
Gawain CI CF14 . . . . . .**159** D2
Gaynors NP44 . . . .**89** B1
Geifr Rd SA13 . . . .**125** E5
Geiriol Gdns SA1 . . . . .**67** E1
Geiriol Rd SA1 . . . .**67** E1
Gelert St SA5 . . . .**68** C5
Gelli Arael Rd CF39 . .**132** B6
Gelli Aur
Cwmdare CF44 . . . .**28** C3
Neath SA10 . . . .**48** D2
Gelli Ave NP11 . . . .**115** A2
Gelli CI NP11 . . . .**115** A2
Gelli Crossing CF41 . . .**79** C3
Gelli Crug NP23 . . . .**7** B5
Gelli Dawel
Caerphilly CF83 . . . . . .**137** F5
Neath SA10 . . . .**48** D2
Gelli Deg
Caerphilly CF83 . . . . . .**137** F5
Cardiff CF14 . . . .**177** B8
Llanelli SA14 . . . .**41** A6
Neath SA10 . . . .**48** D2
Rhydyfelin CF37 . . . . . .**136** C4
Gelli Fawr Ct NP44 . . .**115** F8
Gelli Fedi Rise CF72 . .**153** D4
Gelli Fron CF41 . . . .**79** A2
Gelli Gdns SA7 . . . .**70** B8
Gelli Hirion Ind Est
CF37 . . . .**136** C4
Gelli Hos SA13 . . . .**75** E5
Gelli Ind Est CF41 . . . .**79** C2
Gelli La
Ammanford SA18 . . . . .**219** A5
Pontllanfraith NP12 . . . .**85** F3
Gelli Llwynon Cres
NP11 . . . .**115** A2
Gelli Prim Sch CF41 . . .**79** B3
Gelli Rd Llanelli SA14 . . .**41** D6
Llanharry CF72 . . . .**172** C5
Ton Pentre CF41 . . . . . .**79** A3
Tonypandy CF40 . . . . . .**106** E5
Tredegar NP22 . . . .**13** D3
Ynysybwl CF37 . . . .**82** A1
Gelli Rhwy Rd NP4 . . . .**37** C6
Gelli Seren CI CF39 . . .**133** A3
Gelli St Maesteg CF34 . .**102** A8
Swansea SA1 . . . .**96** B7
Gelli Terr
Abergwynfi SA13 . . . . . .**76** C5
Ton Pentre CF41 . . . .**79** C2
Gelli Wen CF31 . . . . . .**168** C3
Gelli'r Haidd CF39 . . . .**133** B3
Gelli- Isaf CF44 . . . .**28** E5
Gelli-Crug Rd NP13 . . .**36** C6
Gelli-deg
Merthyr Tydfil CF48 . . . .**10** A2
Thomastown CF39 . . . .**133** B3
Gelli-Deg St CF82 . . . . .**85** B2
Gelli-Groes Rd NP12 . .**85** F3
Gelli-Gynore SA4 . . . . .**43** F2
Gelli-Onn SA15 . . . .**40** D6
Gelli-Ron CF82 . . . .**84** D8
Gelli-siriol Cotts
CF34 . . . .**128** C6
Gelli-Unig PI NP11 . . .**114** C6
Gelli-unig Rd NP11 . . .**114** C5
Gelli-unig Terr NP11 . .**114** C6
Gelliargwellt Rd CF82 .**84** D5
Gelliau CF35 . . . .**152** C1
Gelliceibryn SA11 . . . .**223** C1
Gellidawel Rd
Glynneath SA11 . . . . . .**223** D1
3 Pontypridd CF37 . .**135** F4
Rhydyfelin CF37 . . . . . .**136** A6
Gellidderw SA8 . . . .**23** D6
Gellideg SA8 . . . .**23** D6
Gellideg CI CF82 . . . . . .**85** C2
Gellideg Hts CF82 . . . . .**85** C2
Gellideg Inf & Jun Sch
CF48 . . . .**10** A3
Gellideg Rd CF37 . . . .**135** B8
Gellifach Cres SA6 . . . .**68** C5
Gellifaelog Old Rd
CF47 . . . .**11** A4
Gellifaelog Prim Sch
CF47 . . . .**11** A4
Gellifaelog Terr CF47 .**11** A4
Gellifawr Rd SA6 . . . . .**68** D7

Gellifedi Rd CF72 . . . .**153** D3
Gelligaer Gdns CF24 .**177** F1
Gelligaer La CF24 . . . .**177** F1
Gelligaer Rd
Cefn Hengoed CF82 . . . .**84** F4
Gelligaer CF82 . . . .**84** F4
Trelewis CF46 . . . .**83** E6
Gelligaer St CF24 . . . .**177** F1
Gelligaer Village Prim Sch
CF82 . . . .**84** D6
Gelligaled Rd CF41 . . . .**79** D3
Gelligeiros SA8 . . . .**24** B5
Gelliglas Rd SA6 . . . . . .**68** D7
Gelligron Est CF39 . . .**133** B5
Gelligron Rd SA8 . . . . .**23** D6
Gelligwyn Rd SA6 . . . . .**68** D7
Gellihaf Rd NP12 . . . . .**85** B5
Gellihyll Rd SA4 . . . . . .**43** F3
Gellinudd Hospl SA8 . .**24** B5
Gellionen Rd
Clydach SA6,SA8 . . . . . .**22** C7
Pontardawe SA8 . . . . . .**23** B5
Gellionnen CI SA6 . . . . .**46** E8
Gelliwastad Gr SF37 .**109** C1
Gelliwastad Rd CF37 .**109** C1
Gelliwen St CF82 . . . . . .**84** D5
Gelliwion Rd CF37 . . . .**134** F7
Gelliwriddon SA18 . . .**219** A4
Gellyfelen NP7 . . . .**9** B5
Gellyfowy Rd SA8 . . . . .**24** A7
Gelynis Terr CF15 . . . .**176** B8
Gelynis Terr N CF15 . .**176** B8
Gelynog Ct CF38 . . . . .**155** F8
Gelynos Ave NP12 . . . . .**58** F5
Gendros Ave E SA5 . . .**68** A3
Gendros Ave W SA5 . . .**67** F3
Gendros CI SA5 . . . .**68** A3
Gendros Cres SA5 . . . . .**68** A3
Gendros Dr SA5 . . . .**68** A3
Gendros Prim Sch SA5 **67** F3
General Hospl CF34 . .**101** D4
General Rees Sq 5
NP44 . . . .**89** E4
Genwen Rd SA14 . . . . .**41** F4
Geoffrey Ashe Ct
CF71 . . . .**188** F1
Geoffrey St SA11 . . . . .**71** E7
George Bank SA13 . . .**123** C4
George CI CF15 . . . . . .**157** F7
George Daggar's Ave
NP13 . . . .**35** F7
George Lansbury Dr 2
NP19 . . . .**144** D6
George Manning Way
SA4 . . . .**86** B4
George St
Abergbargoed CF81 . . . .**58** B4
Abercarn NP11 . . . .**114** C8
Aberdare CF44 . . . .**53** D7
Abertillery NP13 . . . .**36** B6
Argoed NP12 . . . .**58** F5
Barry CF63 . . . .**215** A5
Bedlinog CF46 . . . .**56** A7
Blackwood NP12 . . . .**86** A5
7 Blaenavon NP4 . . . .**17** C6
Bridgend CF31 . . . .**169** C3
Brynmawr NP23 . . . .**8** B4
Cwmbran NP44 . . . .**89** E4
Cwmfelinfach NP11 . . . .**113** F4
Ferndale CF43 . . . .**80** A7
Llanelli SA15 . . . .**40** D3
Llantrisant CF72 . . . . . .**155** D3
Maesteg CF34 . . . .**75** B2
Neath SA11 . . . .**71** E6
New Tredegar NP24 . . . .**33** E3
Newport NP19,NP20 . . .**143** D4
Pontardawe SA8 . . . . . .**23** E5
Pontypool NP4 . . . .**62** A8
Pontypool NP4 . . . .**62** B7
Port Talbot SA13 . . . . . .**125** C7
Porthcawl CF36 . . . . . .**182** F7
Swansea SA1 . . . .**95** B6
Tonypandy CF40 . . . . . .**106** F3
Treherbert CF42 . . . .**78** A8
Ystrad Mynach CF82 . . . .**84** E2
George Street Bridge
NP19 . . . .**143** E5
George Street Est
CF31 . . . .**169** C3
George Street Prim Sch
NP4 . . . .**62** B7
George Terr CF45 . . . . .**81** F8
George Thomas Ave
CF32 . . . .**150** F6
George Thomas CI
CF36 . . . .**182** F7
George Thomas Hosp
CF42 . . . .**78** E5
George's Row SA11 . . .**71** B1
George's Terr CF40 . . .**106** F4
Georges Row CF64 . . .**206** C4
Georgetown CF15 . . . .**157** F7
Georgetown Hill NP22 .**13** F6
Georgetown Jun & Inf Sch
NP22 . . . .**13** F6
Georgetown Villas
CF48 . . . .**10** C2
Georgian CI
Llantwit Major CF61 . . .**210** B7
Porthcawl CF36 . . . . . .**183** A8
Georgian Way
Bridgend CF31 . . . .**169** A4
Cardiff CF14 . . . .**177** F8
Miskin CF72 . . . .**173** D7
Geotre Bellaf Rd SA2 .**93** C7
Ger Nant CF32 . . . .**111** E2
Ger y Afon CF37 . . . . .**109** D6

Ger y Llan SA15 . . . . . .**40** D4
Ger y Nant SA14 . . . . . .**42** B8
Ger y Nant SA18 . . . . . .**19** D4
Ger Yr Afon SA18 . . . .**220** A8
Ger-y-Bont CF44 . . . . .**28** A6
Ger-y-Coed CF31 . . . .**169** C5
Ger-y-Ffrwd SA7 . . . . .**69** E5
Ger-y-Llan CF5 . . . . . .**192** A1
Ger-y-Llyn CF36 . . . . .**183** A8
Ger-y-Maes SA14 . . . . .**41** A7
Ger-y-Nant SA11 . . . . .**223** B1
Ger-y-Parc SA6 . . . .**45** C1
Ger-y-Sedd CF31 . . . .**169** C5
Ger-yr-Afon
Aberdulais SA10 . . . . . .**49** C4
Cwm-twrch Isaf SA9 . . . . .**1** A1
Gwaun-Cae-Gurwen
SA18 . . . .**220** D6
Geraint CI CF14 . . . . .**159** D2
Geraint Ho SA13 . . . . .**125** E3
Geraint PI CF63 . . . . .**215** A7
Geraint's Way CF71 . .**188** D2
Geraints CI CF71 . . . .**188** D1
Gerald St
5 Aberavon SA12 . . .**124** F8
Swansea SA1 . . . .**68** D2
Gerbera Dr NP10 . . . .**141** D7
Gerddi Brenhinol
SA14 . . . .**41** B6
Gerddi Margaret
CF62 . . . .**214** F4
Gerddi Quarella CF31 **168** E5
Gerddi Ty Celyn CF14 **176** F7
Gernant CF14 . . . .**177** C7
Gernant La CF48 . . . . . .**29** F8
Gerrard St 4 CF11 . . .**194** E5
Gerretts CI SA3 . . . . . .**122** A5
Gerry Galvin Ct CF24 .**195** E6
Gersanws
Cefn Coed CF48 . . . .**10** A5
Merthyr Tydfil CF48 . . . .**225** F3
Gertrude St CF45 . . . . .**82** E2
Gerymanwydd SA18 . .**219** C7
Gethin CI SA5 . . . .**68** A3
Gethin PI CF48 . . . .**30** F4
Gethin Rd
Tonypandy CF40 . . . . . .**106** F3
Treorchy CF42 . . . .**78** E6
Gethin St
Abercanaid CF48 . . . . . .**30** F4
Briton Ferry SA11 . . . . . .**71** B2
Gethin Terr CF39 . . . .**108** B3
Gethin Woodland Pk
CF48 . . . .**30** D4
Gething St 4 SA11 . . . .**95** C6
Gething Terr NP4 . . . . .**17** A6
Giant's Grave Rd SA11 .**71** B2
Gibbet's Hill CF71 . . . .**188** D3
Gibbons CI NP19 . . . . .**144** C4
Gibbons Villas NP23 . . . .**7** E1
Gibbons Way CF83 . . .**166** B8
Gibbsdown CI 5
CF63 . . . .**215** A8
Gibbonsdown Prim Sch
CF62 . . . .**214** F7
Gibbonsdown Rise
CF63 . . . .**215** A7
Gibbs CI NP12 . . . .**85** D7
Gibbs Rd NP19 . . . . . .**144** B5
Gibson CI CF14 . . . . . .**177** F6
Gielgud Ho SA12 . . . . . .**98** A2
Gifford CI NP44 . . . .**89** D1
Gilar St 1 CF47 . . . . . .**30** E8
Gilbert CI NP19 . . . . . .**144** D4
Gilbert Cres SA15 . . . . .**40** D6
Gilbert La CF63 . . . . . .**205** C2
Gilbert PI CF14 . . . . . .**177** C2
Gilbert Rd SA15 . . . . . .**40** D6
Gilbert St CF63 . . . . . .**215** A7
Gilberts Cross CF63 . .**205** D2
Gilbertscliffe SA3 . . . .**122** F4
Gilboa NP11 . . . .**86** E6
Gilchrist Thomas Ct
NP4 . . . .**17** B7
Gilchrist Wlk 9 NP4 . . .**17** D7
Gilchrist-Thomas Ind Est
NP4 . . . .**17** A7
Gildas CI CF61 . . . .**209** F7
Giles Rd NP4 . . . .**17** E6
Gileston Rd
Cardiff CF11 . . . .**194** D7
St Athan CF62 . . . .**211** D3
Gileston Wlk 6 NP44 . .**89** C2
Gilfach SA4 . . . .**44** A2
Gilfach Fargod Prim Sch
CF81 . . . .**58** A1
Gilfach Fargoed Sta
CF81 . . . .**58** A3
Gilfach Goch Inf Sch
CF39 . . . .**106** C1
Gilfach Hos CF34 . . . .**127** F5
Gilfach Rd
Cwm-twrch Uchaf SA9 .**221** C6
Neath SA10 . . . .**48** E4
Tonypandy CF40 . . . . . .**106** C4
Tonyrefail CF39 . . . . . .**133** A5
Gilfach St SA11 . . . .**58** A3
Gilfach-Cynon CF47 . . .**30** F4
Gillian Rd CF5 . . . .**176** F1
Gilmour St CF40 . . . . .**106** E6
Gilsea Bsns Pk SA6 . . .**69** A5
Gilwern Cres CF14 . . .**159** E1
Gilwern Farm CI
NP18 . . . .**117** F7
Gilwern PI
Cardiff CF14 . . . .**159** E1

Gilwern PI continued
Cwmbran NP44 . . . .**89** D5
Glade CI NP44 . . . .**116** A8
Glade The
Bryncethin CF32 . . . . . .**151** A4
Cardiff CF14 . . . .**160** A1
Mumbles SA3 . . . .**122** F8
Porthcawl CF36 . . . . . .**165** F1
Glades The CF64 . . . . .**207** B3
Gladeside CI CF14 . . . .**159** E3
Gladstone Bldgs NP13 .**36** B8
Gladstone Bridge
CF62 . . . .**214** F2
Gladstone Ct 5 CF62 .**214** F5
Gladstone Garden Ct
CF62 . . . .**214** F2
Gladstone Jun & Inf Sch
CF24 . . . .**177** F1
Gladstone PI
Pontypool NP4 . . . .**62** E1
Tredegar NP22 . . . .**13** F5
Gladstone Prim Sch
CF62 . . . .**214** F5
Gladstone Rd
Barry CF62 . . . .**215** A6
Newbridge NP11 . . . . . .**60** D2
Gladstone St
Abercarn NP11 . . . .**114** C4
Aberdare CF44 . . . .**53** D6
Abertillery NP13 . . . .**36** A5
Blaina NP13 . . . .**15** E4
10 Brynmawr NP23 . . . . .**8** C4
Maesteg CF34 . . . .**102** A3
15 Mountain Ash CF45 . .**54** E1
Gladstone Terr
Abersychan NP4 . . . .**37** E8
1 Blaenavon NP4 . . . .**17** C6
Merthyr Tydfil CF47 . . . .**30** F7
16 Mountain Ash CF45 . .**54** E1
Rhymney NP22 . . . .**12** D5
Gladys St
Abervavon SA12 . . . .**98** F1
5 Cardiff CF24 . . . . .**195** A4
Coedely CF39 . . . .**154** D8
Glais Prim Sch SA7 . . .**47** A6
Glais Rd SA7 . . . .**23** D1
Glamorgan CI 4 CF44 **53** D7
Glamorgan St
Aberdare CF44 . . . .**53** D7
Aberdare CF44 . . . .**53** D7
Barry CF62 . . . .**214** C3
Brynmawr NP23 . . . .**8** B4
Cardiff CF5 . . . .**194** C6
Mountain Ash CF45 . . . .**81** F7
Swansea SA1 . . . .**95** D6
Glamorgan Street Mews 11
CF5 . . . .**194** C6
Glamorgan Terr
Gilfach Goch CF39 . . . .**132** C2
Tonypandy CF40 . . . . . .**106** F2
Tonypandy CF40 . . . . . .**107** A1
Glamorgan Vale Ret Pk
CF72 . . . .**155** D3
Glan Creigiau CF72 . . .**174** C7
Glan Dulais SA2 . . . . . .**93** C7
Glan Ebbw NP13 . . . . . .**15** D4
Glan Ebbw Terr
Abertillery NP13 . . . .**36** B5
Ebbw Vale NP23 . . . .**14** E3
Glan Ely CI CF5 . . . . . .**193** C7
Glan Ely High Sch
CF5 . . . .**192** F4
Glan Ffrwd
Caerphilly CF83 . . . . . .**137** E6
Porth CF39 . . . .**107** D1
Glan Gwrelych SA11 . .**223** D1
Glan Hafren
Baglan SA12 . . . .**98** D4
Barry CF62 . . . .**214** B2
Glan Islwyn NP12 . . . . .**85** E4
Glan Llwyd SA4 . . . .**19** C6
Glan Nant Rd CF31 . . .**168** D3
Glan Rd Aberdare CF44 . .**28** E2
Porthcawl CF36 . . . . . .**183** A7
Glan Rhyd
Caerphilly CF83 . . . . . .**137** F4
Cwmbran NP44 . . . .**116** A8
Glan y Lli SA4 . . . .**65** A4
Glan y Nant CF37 . . . .**136** C4
Glan yr Afon
Ammanford SA18 . . . . .**219** B8
Llanelli SA15 . . . .**40** F8
Machen CF83 . . . .**140** A8
Glan Yr Afon Rd
Pyle CF33 . . . .**148** C3
Swansea SA2 . . . .**94** D3
Glan Yr Avon St 4 . . . .**2** C5
Glan-Ddu Rd NP12 . . . .**85** D3
Glan-Ddu Terr CF82 . . .**85** A6
Glan-Ffrwd Inf Sch
CF37 . . . .**81** E2
Glan-nant Row CF32 . .**129** D2
Glan-Nant St 8 CF44 . .**29** A1
Glan-Pelenna SA12 . . .**72** F3
Glan-Rhyd Rd
Pontardawe SA8 . . . . . .**23** D5
Ystradgynlais SA9 . . . . . .**2** E1
Glan-taf Cty Inf Sch
CF37 . . . .**135** F4
Glan-y-Afon Com Jun Sch
CF3 . . . .**179** D2
Glan-y-Fforiid CF15 . . .**158** A5
Glan-y-Gors SA14 . . . .**218** D3
Glan-y-Llyn
North Cornelly CF33 . . .**166** A7
Tonypandy CF40 . . . . . .**106** C6
Glan-y-Mor CF62 . . . . .**214** B2

Glan-y-Mor Ave SA13 ...125 E4
Glan-y-mor Prim Sch SA12 ...98 D1
Glan-y-Mor Rd CF3 ...179 E5
Glan-y-Nant
  Fochriw CF81 ...32 D7
  Pencoed CF35 ...170 D7
  Rhymney NP22 ...12 E8
  Tondu CF32 ...150 D5
  Treoes CF35 ...170 A2
Glan-y-Nant Cl NP44 ...89 D1
Glan-y-nant Ct 5 CF14 ...177 B5
Glan-y-nant Inf Sch NP12 ...85 A7
Glan-Y-Nant Rd CF14 177 B5
Glan-y-Nant Terr CF14 ...177 B5
Glan-y-Parc CF31 ...168 E4
Glan-y-Wern Rd SA7 ...69 E7
Glan-yr- Afon CF42 ...78 C7
Glan-Yr-Afon
  Aberfan CF48 ...55 C3
  Cwmfelin CF34 ...128 C8
  Rhymney NP22 ...12 D5
Glan-Yr-Afon Ct CF34 75 A1
Glan-yr-Afon Gdns SA2 ...94 C6
Glan-y-avon NP24 ...33 C3
Glan-Yr-Ely CF72 ...155 A5
Glan-Yr-Ysgol SA9 ...2 B6
Glanafan Comp (Lower) Sch SA13 ...99 C1
Glanafan Comp Sch SA13 ...125 B8
Glanafon Terr CF34 ...102 A8
Glanaman Cty Prim Sch SA18 ...220 A8
Glanaman Rd
  Aberdare CF44 ...52 F4
  Cwmaman CF44 ...53 A4
Glanaman Workshops SA18 ...220 A8
Glanberis Terr CF32 ...103 D7
Glanbran Rd SA7 ...70 A8
Glanbrydan Ave SA2 ...94 F6
Glancynon St CF45 ...54 E1
Glancynon Terr
  Abercynon CF45 ...82 E3
  1 Abercynon CF44 ...53 D7
Glandafen Rd SA15 ...40 F2
Glandovey Gr CF3 ...179 E6
Glandwr Cres SA1 ...68 D4
Glandwr Ind Est NP13 ...60 A7
Glandwr Pl CF14 ...177 B4
Glandwr St
  Abertillery NP13 ...36 A5
  Abertillery NP13 ...59 F7
Glandwr Terr CF40 ...106 E7
Glandyffryni Cl SA13 ...125 D7
Glanfelin CF37 ...136 A4
Glanffornwg Cl SA13 ...168 E2
Glanffrrwd Ave NP23 ...7 C2
Glanffrrwd Rd SA4 ...19 D6
Glanffrrwd Terr
  Ebbw Vale NP23 ...7 D2
  Ynysybwl CF37 ...81 F2
Glanheulog NP23 ...8 B5
Glanhowy Jun & Inf Sch NP22 ...6 E1
Glanhowy Rd NP12 ...112 F8
Glanhowy St NP22 ...6 D1
Glanlay St CF45 ...81 F7
Glanllyn Rd SA7 ...47 A5
Glanmor Cres
  Newport NP19 ...144 B5
  Swansea SA2 ...94 F7
Glanmor Ct SA2 ...94 F7
Glanmor La SA2 ...94 F7
Glanmor Mews SA2 ...94 E7
Glanmor Park Ave NP19 ...144 B5
Glanmor Park Rd SA2 ...94 E7
Glanmor Pl 3 SA15 ...40 C4
Glanmor Rd
  Llanelli SA15 ...40 D4
  Swansea SA2 ...94 E7
Glanmor Terr
  2 Llanelli SA15 ...40 C4
  Pen-clawdd SA4 ...64 E4
Glanmore Cres CF214 ...215 D2
Glanmorfa SA4 ...66 B5
Glanmorlais CF48 ...11 B7
Glanmuir Rd CF24 ...196 A8
Glannant Pl SA11 ...227 B8
Glannant Rd
  Evanstown CF39 ...132 B4
  Pontarddulais SA4 ...19 E5
Glannant Rise SA11 ...72 C6
Glannant St
  Cwmfelinfach NP11 ...113 A4
  Tonypandy CF40 ...106 F4
Glannant Terr
  Blaengwrach SA11 ...227 B8
  Ystradgynlais SA9 ...2 E7
Glannant Way SA11 ...72 B6
Glanogwr Rd CF31 ...168 E3
Glanrhyd CF14 ...177 C7
Glanrhyd Cl NP22 ...6 D1
Glanrhyd CP Sch SA9 ...2 B1
Glanrhyd Hospl CF31 168 E8
Glanrhyd St SA4 ...52 E4
Glanrhyd Terr SA4 ...66 C4
Glanselsig Terr CF42 ...50 B2
Glanshon Ct NP11 ...60 C1
Glansychan Hos NP4 ...37 F4

Glantaff Rd CF48 ...31 B1
Glantawe Pk SA9 ...2 D7
Glantawe Row SA9 ...2 F8
Glantawe St
  4 Morriston SA6 ...46 A1
  Swansea SA6 ...69 A8
Glantorvaen Rd NP4 ...62 C6
Glantorvaen Terr Upper NP4 ...17 B6
Glantwrch SA9 ...2 C7
Glanville Terr CF43 ...79 C8
Glanwern Ave NP19 ...144 C6
Glanwern Cl NP19 ...144 C6
Glanwern Ct CF14 ...176 F5
Glanwern Ho NP4 ...62 B6
Glanwern Rise NP19 ...144 C6
Glanymor Cl SA4 ...44 B2
Glanymor La SA2 ...94 C6
Glanymor Park Dr SA4 42 D1
Glanymor Rd SA4 ...42 D1
Glanymor St SA11 ...71 B3
Glanynys Ho CF44 ...29 B2
Glanyrafon
  Ebbw Vale NP23 ...7 D3
  Taffs Well CF15 ...210 A3
Glanyrafon Cl SA4 ...44 B2
Glanyrafon Jun Comp Sch NP23 ...7 D2
Glanyrafon Rd
  Pencoed CF35 ...170 E8
  Pontarddulais SA4 ...19 D4
Glanyrafon Terr NP13 ...15 C3
Glanystruth NP13 ...15 F5
Glas Canol CF14 ...177 B3
Glas Fryn CF82 ...84 E7
Glas Ifor CF14 ...177 C5
Glas y Llwyn CF63 ...205 C1
Glas-y-Pant CF14 ...176 F7
Glasbrook Pl SA5 ...67 E5
Glasbrook Terr CF45 ...82 A7
Glasbury Rd SA6 ...68 D7
Glascoed La NP4 ...63 E6
Glascoed Rd NP4 ...63 B4
Glasfryn
  Bridgend CF31 ...169 D4
  Caerphilly NP12 ...85 D6
  Cwmdare CF44 ...28 D3
  Llanelli SA14 ...41 A7
Glasfryn Cl SA2 ...67 E2
Glasfryn Rd SA4 ...19 C3
Glasfryn Sq CF33 ...148 B1
Glasfryn Terr SA15 ...40 E7
Glasier Rd CF47 ...30 F8
Glasllwch Cres CF10, NP20 ...142 C4
Glasllwch Jun & Inf Sch NP20 ...142 D4
Glasllwch La NP20 ...142 D3
Glasllwch View NP20 ...142 C3
Glaslyn Cl CF62 ...214 C5
Glaslyn Ct NP44 ...90 A6
Glaslyn Dr SA4 ...29 C2
Glaslyn Pl SA6 ...45 D1
Glass Ave CF24 ...195 E4
Glass Works Cotts NP20 ...143 C6
Glastonbury Cl 4 NP20 ...143 C6
Glastonbury Rd CF64 ...216 B5
Glastonbury Terr CF3 179 B6
Glebe Pl CF14 ...177 E8
Glebe Rd SA4 ...42 F1
Glebe St Barry CF63 ...215 B1
  Bedwas CF83 ...138 E6
  Newport NP19 ...143 E5
  Penarth CF64 ...207 A4
Glebe The SA3 ...122 A7
Glebeland Cl CF35 ...169 F4
Glebeland Pl CF62 ...211 D4
Glebeland St
  4 Merthyr Tydfil CF47 ...10 D1
  Neath SA10 ...48 F2
Glen Afric Cl CF62 ...214 D6
Glen Cl CF45 ...54 B3
Glen Coed CF82 ...85 A1
Glen Garw CF82 ...103 E6
Glen Mavis Way CF62 ...
Glen Rd Mumbles SA3 ...122 F6
  Neath SA11 ...72 A8
Glen The
  Langstone NP18 ...119 D1
  Sarn CF32 ...150 F4
Glen View
  Blackmill CF35 ...131 A3
  Bridgend CF31 ...168 F8
  Cardiff CF14 ...177 F6
  Cwmbran NP44 ...89 D4
  Hollybush NP12 ...34 C2
  Maesycwmmer CF82 ...85 A1
  Ystrad Mynach CF82 ...84 E2
Glen View Bglws NP23 ...8 B2
Glen View Ct NP11 ...86 D5
Glen View Rd NP44 ...89 D4
Glen View St CF40 ...106 D7
Glen View Terr
  Aberavon SA12 ...99 A2
  Fochriw CF81 ...32 C6
Glen-Usk View NP18 ...118 A4
Glenalla Rd SA15 ...40 E5
Glenavon Cres CF36 ...182 D7
Glenavon St
  12 Aberavon SA12 ...124 F8
  Cymmer SA13 ...75 B5
Glenavon Terr
  Gilfach Goch CF39 ...132 C7
  Nant-y-Moel CF32 ...104 E7

Glenboi CF45 ...54 B3
Glenboi Prim Sch CF45 ...54 B3
Glenbrook CF45 ...54 B3
Glenbrook Dr CF63 ...215 D8
Glencoe St CF63 ...215 A6
Glencourt NP4 ...62 C1
Glendale SA10 ...48 C3
Glendale Ave CF14 ...159 E1
Glendale Ct SA10 ...48 C3
Glendale Gdns NP22 ...85 A5
Glendower Cl CF31 ...169 A5
Glendower Ct CF14 ...176 F5
Glendower St SA4 ...11 A5
Glenfield Cl SA2 ...94 A7
Glengariff Ct NP4 ...62 E2
Glengower Cl SA3 ...123 A5
Glenmount Way CF14 ...159 D2
Glenrhondda Ct CF42 ...50 F2
Glenrise St CF3 ...180 B7
Glenroy Ave SA1 ...95 E8
Glenroy St CF24 ...195 C8
Glenside NP44 ...89 D6
Glenside Ct CF24 ...178 C1
Glenside Rd SA5 ...67 E6
Glenview
  Newbridge NP11 ...60 A1
  Pen-y-fai CF31 ...150 C1
Glenview Terr
  Llanbradach CF83 ...112 A4
  Ynysddu NP11 ...112 F6
Glenview Villas 4 CF46 ...83 B6
Glenville Rd SA3 ...123 A6
Glenwern Terr NP4 ...62 B5
Glenwood CF23 ...178 D6
Glenwood Cl CF35 ...169 F4
Glevering St SA15 ...40 E5
Globe Hill NP13 ...14 D6
Globe Row SA14 ...41 B8
Globe St 1 SA6 ...69 A8
Globe Works CF24 ...195 D4
Glossop Ct CF35 ...170 E7
Glossop Rd CF24 ...195 C6
Glossop Terr CF35 ...170 D7
Gloster Pl 1 NP19 ...143 D6
Gloster St 3 NP19 ...143 D6
Gloster's Par NP4 ...63 B3
Gloucester Bldgs CF32 ...103 F2
Gloucester Cl
  Barry CF62 ...214 F6
  Llanyravon NP44 ...90 B3
Gloucester Ct NP18 ...118 A3
Gloucester Ho 5 SA12 ...98 C3
Gloucester Pl
  Mumbles SA3 ...123 B4
  Swansea SA1 ...95 E6
Gloucester St
  Aberdare CF44 ...29 A2
  Cardiff CF11 ...194 F5
Gloucester Terr CF45 ...82 C5
Gluepot Rd CF71 ...199 C4
Glyn Bargoed Rd CF46 83 C7
Glyn Bedw CF83 ...112 A4
Glyn Coed CF43 ...79 B8
Glyn Coed Rd CF23 ...178 E7
Glyn Collen CF83 ...112 A4
Glyn Cres SA3 ...94 C2
Glyn Derwen CF83 ...112 A3
Glyn Eiddew
  Cardiff CF23 ...178 F8
  Llanbradach CF83 ...112 A4
Glyn Hirnant SA6 ...46 A3
Glyn Llwyfen CF83 ...112 A4
Glyn Neath Rd SA11 ...226 E6
Glyn Rd SA18 ...220 D8
Glyn Rhosyn CF23 ...178 E8
Glyn Simon Cl CF5 ...176 E2
Glyn St Aberavon SA12 124 F8
  Abertysswg NP22 ...33 B8
  Ogmore Vale CF32 ...104 E1
  Porth CF39 ...107 F2
  Swansea SA1 ...68 D2
  Ynysybwl CF37 ...109 A8
Glyn Teg CF32 ...129 D1
Glyn Terr Fochriw CF81 ...32 C7
  Tonypandy CF40 ...106 C7
  Tredegar NP22 ...13 F4
Glyn View CF39 ...133 G6
Glyn-Deri SA18 ...219 F8
Glyn-Gaer Rd CF82 ...84 E7
Glyn-Llwchwr Rd SA4 ...11 A3
Glyn-Meirch Rd SA8 ...23 C3
Glyn-Mynach St CF37 ...109 A8
Glyn-neath Bsns Pk SA11 ...223 C1
Glyn-y-Coed Rd SA11 ...71 F7
Glyn-y-Mel CF35 ...170 D8
Glynbargoed Cl CF46 ...83 C7
Glynbridge Cl CF62 ...204 F1
Glynbridge Gdns CF31 ...168 F6
Glyncoch Terr CF37 ...109 C5
Glyncoed Comp Sch NP23 ...7 C3
Glyncoed Jun & Inf Sch
  Cardiff CF23 ...178 E7
  Ebbw Vale NP23 ...7 D3
Glyncoed Terr
  Llanelli SA15 ...41 A5
  Merthyr Tydfil CF47 ...30 E7
Glyncoli Cl CF42 ...78 D7
Glyncoli Rd CF42 ...78 D6

Glyncollen Cres SA6 ...46 A3
Glyncollen Dr SA6 ...46 A3
Glyncollen Prim Sch SA6 ...46 A4
Glyncornel Cl CF40 ...106 E8
Glyncorrwg Ind Est SA13 ...227 C1
Glyncorrwg Prim Sch SA13 ...227 C2
Glyncrug Cotts NP13 ...36 B5
Glyncynwal Rd SA9 ...221 C6
Glynderw CF83 ...138 C2
Glynderwen Cl SA2 ...94 B3
Glynderwen Cres SA2 ...94 B3
Glynderwen Rd SA14 ...41 D4
Glyndwr Ave CF21 ...211 D4
Glyndwr Ct CF41 ...79 A4
Glyndwr Ho
  Baglan SA12 ...98 C7
  Cwmbran NP44 ...89 F3
  7 Merthyr Tydfil CF47 ...30 D8
Glyndwr Pl SA1 ...95 A8
Glyndwr St
  Merthyr Vale CF48 ...55 D5
  Port Talbot SA13 ...99 B1
Glyndyrus Cl CF48 ...30 C5
Glynfach Rd CF39 ...107 F2
Glyngwyn St CF45 ...54 E1
Glynhafod Jun Sch CF44 ...52 F4
Glynhafod St CF44 ...52 E4
Glynhir Rd SA14 ...50 D6
Glynleiros Gdns SA10 ...71 D8
Glynmarch St CF81 ...52 B8
Glynmelyn Rd SA11 ...223 D2
Glynn Vivian Art Gal SA1 ...95 C7
Glynne St CF11 ...194 D6
Glynne Twr CF64 ...207 B3
Glynrhondda St
  Cardiff CF24 ...195 B7
  Treorchy CF42 ...78 C2
Glynrhosyn SA4 ...43 B1
Glynstell Cl CF11 ...194 D4
Glynstell Rd CF36 ...165 F1
Glynsyfi NP24 ...33 F2
Glyntaf Ct 5 CF48 ...31 B1
Glyntaff CF37 ...136 A4
Glyntaff Rd CF37 ...135 F8
Glynteg Rd SA4 ...19 D5
Glyntirion NP44 ...89 D1
Gnoll Ave SA11 ...71 F7
Gnoll Bank SA11 ...72 A7
Gnoll Cres SA11 ...71 F7
Gnoll Dr SA11 ...71 F8
Gnoll Gdns SA11 ...72 A8
Gnoll Park Rd SA11 ...71 F8
Gnoll Rd SA9 ...221 C1
Gnoll View SA11 ...72 A7
Goat Mill Rd
  Dowlais CF48 ...11 A3
  Merthyr Tydfil CF47 ...11 A1
Gobaith Row 2 CF44 ...28 C3
Godre'r Coed SA6 ...45 D2
Godre'r Coed Rd CF48 ...10 A4
Godre'r Fro SA8 ...23 D7
Godre'Rgraig CP Sch SA9 ...221 C1
Godreaman St CF44 ...53 C5
Godrer Coed CF82 ...84 F7
Godwin Cl CF15 ...176 D4
Goetre Bellaf Rd SA2 ...93 C7
Goetre Fach Rd SA2 ...93 D7
Goetre Fawr Rd SA2 ...93 D7
Goetre Inf & Jun Sch CF47 ...10 C4
Goitre Coed Isaf CF45 ...82 F4
Goitre La CF47 ...10 D5
Goitre-Coed Rd CF46 ...83 A5
Golate 5 CF10 ...195 D6
Gold St CF24 ...195 D6
Gold Tops NP20 ...143 B5
Goldcliff Ct NP4 ...89 F3
Goldcliff Ho NP44 ...89 F3
Goldcrest Dr CF23 ...178 D7
Goldcroft Ct NP18 ...118 B2
Golden Ave SA12 ...98 B2
Golden Cl SA3 ...122 F7
Golden Gr SA5 ...68 D6
Golden Terr CF34 ...102 B3
Goldsland Pl CF62 ...214 C5
Goldsmith Cl
  Bridgend CF31 ...168 C5
  Cardiff CF3 ...179 B7
  Newport NP20 ...142 E2
Goleg-y-Fro CF31 ...169 B4
Golf Rd Pontypool NP4 ...63 B4
  Port Talbot SA12 ...98 D1
Golf View NP23 ...8 C2
Golwg Hafren SA2 ...94 C4
Golwg y Coed CF83 ...137 D5
Golwg y Craig SA10 ...226 C5
Golwg y Mynydd
  Craig-Cefn-Parc SA6 ...22 B1
  Godrergraig SA9 ...2 A3
Golwg-y-Bryn SA2 ...2 D6
Golwg-y-coed SA11 ...223 C1
Golwg-y-Cwm SA18 ...220 D5

Golwg-y-Gamlas SA10 48 E1
Golwg-y-Mynydd
  Neath SA10 ...48 C2
  Rhymney NP22 ...12 E5
Golwg-Yr-Afon SA10 ...49 C4
Golwg yr Eglwys CF83 ...138 D6
Golwyg-y-mynydd NP22 ...6 C3
Golygafar Eglwys CF37 ...109 A1
Golygfor SA15 ...40 F4
Gomer Gdns SA1 ...68 A1
Gomer Rd SA1 ...67 F1
Gonhill SA3 ...122 E8
Goodrich Cl CF83 ...138 C2
Goodrich Cres NP20 ...143 B7
Goodrich Gr NP10 ...163 E5
Goodrich Rd NP20 ...143 B7
Goodrich St CF83 ...138 B2
Goodwick Cl CF62 ...214 F8
Goodwick Rd CF3 ...179 C3
Goodwin St SA14 ...102 E8
Goodwood Cl CF5 ...192 F4
Goole Rd SA5 ...66 F7
Goose Island SA1 ...95 D5
Goossens Cl NP19 ...144 F6
Goppa SA4 ...19 C3
Gordings NP44 ...89 B3
Gordon Ave NP4 ...37 C4
Gordon Cl NP12 ...85 D6
Gordon Cres SA2 ...98 C2
Gordon Rd
  Abersychan NP4 ...37 C4
  Caerphilly NP12 ...85 E6
  Cardiff CF24 ...195 B7
  Llanelli SA14 ...41 B7
  Port Talbot SA12 ...98 C2
  Porthcawl CF36 ...182 F6
Gordon St
  Aberdare CF44 ...53 B5
  Newport NP19 ...143 E5
  Ton Pentre CF41 ...78 F3
Gordon Thomas Cl 4 SA1 ...68 C2
Gordon Villas CF44 ...29 B2
Gore St NP19 ...143 D7
Gore Terr 2 SA1 ...95 C7
Gored Cotts SA11 ...226 C4
Gored Terr SA11 ...226 C4
Gorge Terr NP24 ...33 F3
Goring Rd SA15 ...40 D6
Gorof Rd SA9 ...2 D8
Goronwy Rd SA1 ...67 E1
Gors Ave SA1 ...68 B1
Gors Com Jun & Inf Schs SA1 ...67 E1
Gors Goch Rd SA18 ...220 D8
Gors La SA14 ...220 D8
Gors Rd SA4 ...44 A3
Gors-Fach SA14 ...41 C6
Gorsafle SA9 ...222 A4
Gorsddu Rd SA18 ...218 D8
Gorsddu Terr SA14 ...218 C8
Gorse La SA1 ...95 A5
Gorse Pl CF5 ...193 D8
Gorsedd SA15 ...40 F4
Gorsedd Cl NP23 ...7 D5
Gorsedd Gardens Rd CF10 ...195 A6
Gorsedd St CF45 ...54 D2
Gorsedd Terr CF47 ...10 E2
Gorseinon Bsns Pk SA4 ...43 C1
Gorseinon Coll
  Gorseinon SA4 ...43 A1
  Loughor SA4 ...42 F1
Gorseinon Inf Sch SA4 43 C2
Gorseinon Jun Sch SA4 ...43 B2
Gorseinon Rd SA4 ...43 E1
Gorslas CF33 ...147 F3
Gorslas Cty Prim Sch SA14 ...218 B8
Gorslwyn Terr SA18 ...220 D5
Gorsto Rd
  Gwaun-Cae-Gurwen SA18 ...220 D7
  Pen-Rhiw-fawr SA9 ...221 B5
Gorwydd Rd SA4 ...66 C4
Gorwyl Rd CF32 ...104 E2
Goscombe Dr CF64 ...206 F5
Goscombe Pk CF71 ...202 C7
Goshen Cl NP22 ...12 E4
Goshen Pk SA10 ...70 F8
Goshen St NP22 ...12 E4
Gospel Hall Terr CF4 ...28 F3
Gough Ave SA9 ...2 D7
Gough Rd Cardiff CF5 ...193 C5
  Ystalyfera SA9 ...2 B6
Gould Cl CF3 ...179 C8
Govilion Pl NP44 ...89 F3
Gowan Ct CF14 ...159 D3
Gower Cres SA12 ...98 C7
Gower Ct CF62 ...214 D5
Gower Davies Ct CF37 ...109 A7
Gower Gn NP44 ...90 A6
Gower Holiday Village SA3 ...231 A6
Gower Pl SA3 ...123 A5
Gower Rd
  Aberdare CF44 ...29 E1
  Killay SA2 ...93 D5
  Swansea SA2 ...94 C7
Gower Rise SA4 ...66 C4

Gower St
  Briton Ferry SA11 ...71 C3
  Cardiff CF24 ...178 A1
  Port Talbot SA13 ...125 C7
Gower Terr SA4 ...64 F4
Gower View SA15 ...40 E8
Gower View Rd SA4 ...43 A4
Gower's Bldgs SA11 ...71 B1
Gowerton SA4 ...66 C8
Gowerton Comp Sch SA4 ...66 C4
Gowerton Rd
  Pen-clawdd SA4 ...65 A4
  Three Crosses SA4 ...65 F2
Gowerton Sta SA4 ...66 C5
Goya Cl NP19 ...144 A7
Goya Pl SA12 ...124 D8
Goytre Cl SA13 ...125 C5
Goytre Cres SA13 ...125 E8
Goytre Fawr Jun & Inf Sch NP4 ...39 E5
Goytre Rd SA13 ...125 F8
Graddfa Ind Est CF83 ...111 F2
Gradon Cl CF63 ...215 C6
Grafog St SA1 ...96 B7
Grafton Cl CF23 ...178 D3
Grafton Dr CF72 ...155 E2
Grafton La NP19 ...143 D5
Grafton Rd NP19 ...143 C5
Grafton Terr CF14 ...177 C6
Graham Ave CF31 ...150 D2
Graham Bell Cl NP20 ...116 F4
Graham Berry Ct SA5 ...68 A5
Graham Cl CF23 ...178 C2
Graham Ct CF83 ...138 C3
Graham St
  6 Merthyr Tydfil CF47 ...10 D1
  Newport NP20 ...143 B4
  Swansea SA2 ...68 D2
Graham Terr SA10 ...70 E7
Graham Way 7 CF47 ...10 D1
Graham Wlk 10 CF11 ...194 D5
Graham's Yd NP22 ...6 E1
Graig Ave
  Abercwmboi CF44 ...53 E5
  Llanelli SA15 ...40 E4
  3 Margam SA13 ...125 E4
  Pontypridd CF37 ...135 B7
Graig
  Abercanaid CF48 ...30 E4
  Bassaleg NP10 ...142 A3
Graig Cotts CF72 ...173 D6
Graig Cres SA4 ...53 E5
Graig Ddu CF43 ...79 B8
Graig Ddu Pl CF40 ...107 C4
Graig Ebbw NP23 ...7 B4
Graig Fach CF37 ...135 F7
Graig Gellinudd SA8 ...24 B5
Graig Hir CF15 ...176 B7
Graig Inf Sch SA6 ...68 F8
Graig Jun Sch The (Ysgol Iav y Graig) CF81 ...57 F4
Graig Llwyn Rd CF14 160 D4
Graig Lwyd CF15 ...176 B7
Graig Newydd SA9 ...221 C2
Graig Parc Neath SA10 ...48 B1
  Neath Abbey SA10 ...71 B8
Graig Park Ave NP20 ...117 A1
Graig Park Circ NP20 ...117 A1
Graig Park Hill NP20 ...117 A1
Graig Park La NP20 ...117 A1
Graig Park Par NP20 ...117 A1
Graig Park Rd NP20 ...117 A1
Graig Park Villas NP20 ...117 A1
Graig Pl Aberdare CF44 ...28 F1
  Swansea SA1 ...95 D8
Graig Rd
  Abercanaid CF48 ...30 E4
  Abergwynfi SA13 ...76 B6
  Abertillery NP13 ...36 C2
  Cardiff CF14 ...160 A5
  Cwmbran NP44 ...89 A5
  Glais SA7 ...47 A6
  Glanaman SA18 ...220 C7
  Godrergraig SA9 ...221 C2
  Neath SA10 ...70 D7
  Newbridge NP11 ...87 A6
  Pontardawe SA8 ...23 C3
  Pontardawe SA8 ...24 A5
  Porth CF39 ...107 E7
  Swansea SA6 ...68 F7
  Ystrad Mynach CF82 ...84 F2
Graig St Aberdare CF44 ...28 F1
  4 Mountain Ash CF45 ...54 D3
  Pontypridd CF37 ...135 C8
  9 Swansea SA1 ...95 D8
  Tylorstown CF40 ...80 B1
Graig Terr
  Abercwmboi CF44 ...53 E5
  Abergwynfi SA13 ...76 B5
  Bargoed CF81 ...57 F5
  Bedlinog CF46 ...56 A7
  Blackmill CF35 ...130 F2
  Cwm NP23 ...35 B6
  Dowlais CF48 ...11 A5
  Ferndale CF43 ...80 A5
  Pontypridd CF37 ...135 C8
  Senghenydd CF83 ...110 F4
  Swansea SA1 ...95 C8
Graig The
  Bridgend CF31 ...168 E4
  Cefn Cribwr CF32 ...149 C2
Graig Twrch SA9 ...1 A1

Graig View
Abertillery NP13 . . . . .60 A7
Cardiff CF14 . . . . .160 B3
Cwmfelinfach NP11 . . . .113 A5
Machen CF83 . . . . .140 B7
Nantgarw CF15 . . . . . .158 B8
Risca NP11 . . . . .114 F1
Graig Wen
Maerdy CF43 . . . . .79 B8
Morganstown CF15 . . . .176 B8
Graig Wood Cl NP20 . .117 B1
Graig y Darren SA9 . . . .2 A3
Graig y Pal SA7 . . . . . . .47 A5
Graig Yr Wylan CF83 .137 E2
Graig Ysguthan CF83 .112 A5
Graig-Llwyn Rd CF14 160 E4
Graig-Wen Hos NP11 .187 C3
Graig-y-Bedw NP24 . . .33 F3
Graig-y-Ddelw CF42 . .50 D3
Graig-y-Dderi SA7 . . .47 A6
Graig-y-Rhacca Prim Sch
CF83 . . . . .139 C6
Graig-y-Wion Cty Prim
Sch CF37 . . . . .135 C8
Graig-Yr-Eos Terr
CF40 . . . . .107 A3
Graig-Yr-Helfa Rd
CF37 . . . . .135 E8
Graigddu Rd CF40 . . .107 B4
Graigfelen Co Prim Sch
SA6 . . . . .46 C8
Graiglas CF32 . . . . . . .130 A2
Graiglwyd CF44 . . . . . .28 C4
Graiglwyd Rd SA2 . . . .94 E8
Graiglwyd Sq SA1 . . . .94 F8
Graigola Rd SA7 . . . . .47 B4
Graigwen Cres CF83 .137 B7
Graigwen Parc CF37 .109 A3
Graigwen Pl CF37 . . . .109 B1
Graigwen Rd
Pontypridd CF37 . . . . . .109 B2
Porth CF39 . . . . .107 E2
Graigyrhesg Pl CF37 .109 D3
Graigyrhesg Rd CF37 109 D3
Grampian Way SA5 . . .67 E3
Grand Ave CF5 . . . . . .193 C5
Grand View Terr
CF40 . . . . .107 A3
Grandison St
Briton Ferry SA11 . . . . . .71 C2
2 Swansea SA1 . . . . . .68 D1
Grange Ave CF5 . . . . .205 A7
Grange Cl
Caerphilly CF83 . . . . . .137 F3
Wenvoe CF5 . . . . .205 A7
Grange Cres
Bridgend CF35 . . . . . . .169 F4
Mumbles SA3 . . . . .123 A7
Grange Ct Barry CF63 215 D6
Newport NP20 . . . . . . .143 A4
Grange Gdns
Cardiff CF11 . . . . .194 F2
Llantwit Major CF61 . .210 A4
Grange Hill NP12 . . . . .85 C6
Grange Ind Site SA4 . .89 F2
Grange La
4 Cwmbran NP44 . . . . .89 C4
Mumbles SA3 . . . . .123 A8
Grange Prim Sch
SA3 . . . . .123 A7
Grange Rd
Cwmbran NP44 . . . . .89 C3
Mumbles SA3 . . . . .123 A7
Grange St SA13 . . . . .125 C8
Grange Terr CF40 . . . .106 F2
Grange The
Caerphilly CF83 . . . . . .137 F3
Cardiff CF5 . . . . .194 A8
Miskin CF72 . . . . .173 D7
4 Penarth CF64 . . . . .206 F3
Grangemoor Ct CF11 .206 F7
Grangetown Jun & Inf Sch
CF11 . . . . .194 F2
Grangetown Link
Cardiff CF11 . . . . .194 C2
Penarth CF11 . . . . . . .206 D8
Grangetown Sta
CF11 . . . . .194 E2
Grangewood Cl CF23 161 B1
Granogwen Rd SA1 . . .68 C1
Granston Ho NP44 . . . .89 B2
Granston Sq NP44 . . . .89 B2
Grant St SA15 . . . . . . .40 E4
Grant's Cl CF15 . . . . . .176 C8
Grant's Field CF5 . . . .192 D2
Grantham Cl CF5 . . . . .176 E2
Granville Ave CF5 . . . .194 A7
Granville Cl NP10 . . . .142 C4
Granville La NP20 . . . .143 D4
Granville Rd SA1 . . . . .95 E3
Granville St
Abertillery NP13 . . . . . . .36 A6
Newport NP20 . . . . . . .143 D4
Granville Terr
Llanelli SA14 . . . . .41 C6
Mountain Ash CF45 . . . .54 D4
Grasmere Ave CF23 . .178 A3
Grasmere Dr CF44 . . . .29 E1
Grassholm Gdns SA5 . .67 E4
Grassholm Way CF36 165 D1
Grassmere Cl CF64 . . .206 E6
Grawen CF47 . . . . .10 C2

Grawen Hos CF48 . . . .225 F3
Grawen La CF48 . . . . .225 F3
Grawen St CF39 . . . . .107 E4
Grawen Terr CF47 . . . .10 D2
Gray La CF11 . . . . . . .194 D6
Gray St Abertillery NP13 36 B5
Cardiff CF11 . . . . .194 D6
Gray's Pl CF48 . . . . . . .55 D4
Graylands The CF14 .177 C6
Grays Gdns CF83 . . . .139 D6
Grays Wlk CF71 . . . . .188 F2
Great Burnet Cl CF3 .180 B6
Great House Mdws
CF61 . . . . .209 F7
Great Oaks Pk NP10 .141 F7
Great St CF37 . . . . . . .108 C2
Great Thomas Cl
CF62 . . . . .212 F2
Great Western Ave
CF31 . . . . .168 F6
Great Western Cres
SA15 . . . . .40 D3
Great Western Ct
CF5 . . . . .194 C5
Great Western La 2
CF10 . . . . .195 A4
Great Western Terr
Cwmavon SA12 . . . . .99 F6
1 Llanelli SA15 . . . . . .40 D3
Talbot Green CF72 . . . .155 B1
Greave Cl CF5 . . . . . .205 A7
Greek Church St 4
CF10 . . . . .195 B4
Green Acre
Creigiau CF15 . . . . .174 E7
Cwmbran NP44 . . . . .89 D1
Green Acre Dr CF40 . .106 E5
Green Ave The CF36 .182 E6
Green Bank Rd SA3 . . .122 F7
Green Circ CF35 . . . . .148 A1
Green Cl SA2 . . . . .94 A1
Green Dragon La SA1 . .95 D6
Green Farm Cl CF5 . . .193 A4
Green Farm Rd CF5 . .193 A4
Green Field Terr
CF32 . . . . .129 C2
Green Hill
Pontycymer CF32 . . . . .103 E3
5 Swansea SA1 . . . . . .68 D1
Ton Pentre CF41 . . . . . .79 B3
Green La Barry CF63 . .215 C8
Llantwit Major CF61 . .209 D6
St Brides Wentlooge
NP10 . . . . .163 E3
Green Lawn Jun Sch
NP4 . . . . .63 B4
Green Lawns CF62 . . .215 A7
Green Mdw
Glyncorrwg SA13 . . . . . .227 C2
Tredegar NP22 . . . . .6 F1
Green Mdws CF3 . . . .179 C5
Green Meadow Terr
CF32 . . . . .130 B4
Green Park St SA12 . .125 A8
Green Pk
Pontyclun CF72 . . . . . .154 F1
Talbot Green CF72 . . . .155 C2
Green Row CF83 . . . . .139 F6
Green St
7 Aberavon SA12 . . . . .124 F8
Bridgend CF31 . . . . . . .168 F5
Cardiff CF11 . . . . .194 F5
Ebbw Vale NP23 . . . . . . .14 E1
Neath SA11 . . . . .71 D7
Swansea SA6 . . . . .69 A8
Green The
Abertsywg NP22 . . . . . .33 C8
Bryn NP12 . . . . .85 D4
Leckwith CF11 . . . . . . .194 B1
Neath SA11 . . . . .71 D7
Pencoed CF35 . . . . . . .170 E8
Radyr CF15 . . . . .176 C5
Sarn CF32 . . . . .150 E3
Trefechan CF48 . . . . . . .10 B6
Green Villas NP13 . . . . .36 B6
Green Way NP4 . . . . . . .37 E5
Green Willows NP44 . .116 F8
Green Wood Dr CF38 156 B7
Greenacre Dr
Bedwas CF83 . . . . .138 D6
Cardiff CF23 . . . . .161 B2
Glais SA7 . . . . .47 A5
Swansea SA6 . . . . .170 C8
Greenacre Gdns
CF83 . . . . .138 F6
Greenacres
Barry CF63 . . . . .215 D7
Pen-clawdd SA4 . . . . . .64 D4
Port Talbot SA13 . . . . .126 A1
South Cornelly CF33 . . .165 F5
Greenbanks Dr CF62 .214 D6
Greenbay Rd CF24 . . .196 A6
Greenclose Rd CF14 .177 C6
Greencourt NP44 . . . . .90 A6
Greencroft Ave CF5 . .193 F6
Greene Cl NP19 . . . . . .144 F5
Greenfield
Caerleon CF18 . . . . . . .117 F3
New Tredegar NP24 . . . .33 D4
Newbridge NP11 . . . . . .87 A7
Greenfield Ave
Cardiff CF11 . . . . .194 C7
Cardiff CF14 . . . . .177 C5
Dinas Powys CF64 . . . .206 B3
2 Margam SA13 . . . . .125 E4
Newbridge NP11 . . . . . .87 A7
Pontypridd CF37 . . . . . .109 C5

Greenfield Cl
Cwmbran NP44 . . . . .89 D6
Swansea SA7 . . . . .69 F7
Greenfield Cotts NP22 . .6 C1
Greenfield Cres
Ebbw Vale NP23 . . . . .7 C4
Swansea SA7 . . . . .69 F7
Greenfield Gdns CF48 .31 A4
Greenfield Pl
Abertridwr CF83 . . . . . .136 E7
Blaenavon NP4 . . . . . . .17 D6
Loughor SA4 . . . . .65 F8
Greenfield Rd
Barry CF62 . . . . .214 D7
Cardiff CF14 . . . . .177 C5
Glanaman SA18 . . . . . .220 B8
Rogerstone NP10 . . . . .142 B4
Greenfield Sch CF48 . .31 A4
Greenfield St
Bargoed CF81 . . . . .58 A4
Pontlottyn CF81 . . . . . . .32 F8
Tonypandy CF40 . . . . . .107 A3
Greenfield Stores
NP10 . . . . .142 C4
Greenfield Terr
Abercynon CF45 . . . . . . .82 E4
Aberdare CF44 . . . . . . .53 F7
Abersychan NP4 . . . . . .37 E7
Argoed NP12 . . . . .58 F4
Blaengarw CF32 . . . . . .103 E7
Bryncethin CF32 . . . . .151 E6
Cwmparc CF42 . . . . .78 A4
Ebbw Vale NP23 . . . . . . .14 E6
Maesteg CF34 . . . . . . .102 B3
Maesteg CF34 . . . . .75 B1
Merthyr Tydfil CF47 . . . .11 A4
Mountain Ash CF45 . . . .54 B6
North Cornelly CF33 . . .165 F8
Ogmore Vale CF32 . . . .104 E1
Pont Rhyd-y-cyff CF34 .128 E6
Swansea SA1 . . . . .68 D4
Swansea SA7 . . . . .69 D8
Tredegar NP22 . . . . .13 F6
Troedyrhiw CF48 . . . . . .31 C2
Ynysddu NP11 . . . . . . .112 F6
Pentrebach CF48 . . . . . .31 A4
Greenfield Way
Llanblethian CF71 . . . .188 D1
Porthcawl CF36 . . . . . .165 F2
Greenfields Ave CF31 168 C4
Greenfields Terr SA2 . .94 C7
Greenforge Way NP44 .89 C4
Greenhaven Rise
CF64 . . . . .206 E6
Greenhill Ct CF14 . . . .177 A8
Greenhill Dr CF44 . . . . .53 C7
Greenhill Pl CF82 . . . . .84 C6
Greenhill Prim Sch
CF82 . . . . .84 C7
Greenhill Rd
Cwmbran NP44 . . . . .89 D4
Pontypool NP4 . . . . .62 E2
Greenhill Specl Sch
CF14 . . . . .177 A8
Greenhill St SA1 . . . . .68 D1
Greenland Cres CF5 . .193 C8
Greenland Rd
Brynmawr NP23 . . . . . . .8 C4
Pontypool NP4 . . . . .62 C8
Greenlands
Blackwood NP11 . . . . . .59 D1
Newbridge NP11 . . . . . .87 A4
Greenlands Rd CF72 . .155 E3
Greenlawns CF23 . . . .178 D2
Greenmeadow
Bettws CF32 . . . . .129 C2
Cefn Cribwr CF32 . . . . .149 B2
Machen CF83 . . . . .139 D5
Greenmeadow Ave
NP19 . . . . .144 C3
Greenmeadow Bglws
NP12 . . . . .85 A7
Greenmeadow Cl
Cwmbran NP44 . . . . .89 D2
5 Dinas Powys CF64 .206 B2
Pontypridd CF37 . . . . . .109 D5
Greenmeadow Community
Farm NP44 . . . . .89 B4
Greenmeadow Cres
NP4 . . . . .39 C3
Greenmeadow Ct
CF72 . . . . .155 E2
Greenmeadow Dr
Cardiff CF15 . . . . .176 D6
Risca NP11 . . . . .114 D4
Greenmeadow Ho
NP44 . . . . .89 D2
Greenmeadow Prim Sch
NP44 . . . . .89 A4
Greenmeadow Rd
Cwmfelinfach NP11 . . . .113 C3
Newport NP19 . . . . . . .144 C3
Greenmeadow Terr
Abertillery NP13 . . . . . . .36 B7
Tonypandy CF40 . . . . . .107 A2
Greenmeadow Way
NP44 . . . . .89 D2
Greenmeadows CF31 168 F5
Greenock Rd CF3 . . . .179 D6
Greenside CF71 . . . . . .188 F1
Greensway NP22 . . . . .33 C8
Greenway CF83 . . . . . .138 C6
Greenway Ave CF3 . . .179 C3
Greenway Cl
Llandough CF64 . . . . . .206 D7
Pontypool NP4 . . . . .62 D2
Greenway Ct CF63 . . .215 D8
Greenway Dr NP4 . . . . .62 D2

Greenway Jun & Inf Sch
CF3 . . . . .179 C4
Greenway Rd
Cardiff CF3 . . . . .179 D5
Neath SA11 . . . . .71 E7
Greenway St SA15 . . . .40 C6
Greenways The CF34 .102 A2
Greenway Wlk NP4 . . .62 D2
Greenway Workshops
CF83 . . . . .138 D6
Greenways
Aberdare CF44 . . . . .29 D3
Ebbw Vale NP23 . . . . . . .14 B8
Porthcawl CF36 . . . . . .183 B8
Waunarlwydd SA5 . . . . . .66 D3
Greenways The CF34 .102 A2
Greenwich Rd
Cardiff CF5 . . . . .194 B7
Newport NP20 . . . . . . .143 B7
Greenwillows NP44 . . .116 F8
Greenwood NP18 . . . .144 A8
Greenwood Ave
Cwmbran NP44 . . . . .89 C5
Maesteg CF34 . . . . . . .102 A1
Tredegar NP22 . . . . .6 C1
Greenwood Cl
Bridgend CF31 . . . . . . .168 F7
Cardiff CF23 . . . . .161 B2
Swansea SA2 . . . . .94 C6
Merthyr Tydfil CF47 . . . .30 F7
Greenwood Ct
Caerphilly CF83 . . . . . .138 C3
New Tredegar NP24 . . . .33 D3
Greenwood Dr
Cimla SA11 . . . . .72 C5
Cwmbran NP44 . . . . . . .115 E8
Hirwaun CF44 . . . . .27 F7
Risca NP11 . . . . .114 F3
Greenwood La CF5 . . . .193 B7
Greenwood Pl SA5 . . . .67 D6
Greenwood Rd
Abersychan NP4 . . . . . . .37 F5
Baglan SA12 . . . . .98 D7
Blackwood NP12 . . . . . . .58 D1
Cardiff CF5 . . . . .176 F2
Neath SA11 . . . . .71 D4
Greenwood St CF63 . .214 F4
Gregory Cl CF35 . . . . .170 B8
Greig Cl SA12 . . . . .98 B3
Greig Ct 7 SA12 . . . . . .98 B3
Grenadier Dr NP18 . . .145 C4
Grenfell Ave SA4 . . . . . .43 A3
Grenfell Park Rd SA1 . .95 F7
Grenfell Town SA1 . . . . .68 F3
Grenig Rd SA18 . . . . . .220 B6
Grenville Rd CF23 . . . .195 B6
Gresford Cl CF3 . . . . .179 D6
Gresham Pl CF46 . . . . .83 A6
Grey Cres CF82 . . . . . . .85 A6
Grey St SA1 . . . . .68 D3
Grey Waters NP4 . . . . .90 A3
Grey's Dr CF61 . . . . . .210 B6
Grey's Pl CF44 . . . . . . .28 F7
Greyfriars CF31 . . . . . .168 F5
Greyfriars Ct CF30 . . .183 D8
Greyfriars Pl 3 CF10 195 A6
Greyfriars Rd CF10 . . .195 A6
Greys Rd NP4 . . . . .62 C5
Greys Terr SA7 . . . . . . .47 B1
Griffin Ave NP4 . . . . . . .17 D6
Griffin Cl CF62 . . . . . . .214 C8
Griffin Ct NP4 . . . . .62 A7
Griffin Park Ct CF36 .183 A4
Griffin St
Abertillery NP13 . . . . . . .36 C3
3 Newport NP20 . . .143 C5
Griffin The NP11 . . . . . .59 D1
Griffith John St SA1 . . .68 D1
Griffith St
1 Aberdare CF44 . . . . .29 A1
Maerdy CF43 . . . . .52 A2
Pentre CF41 . . . . .78 F4
Griffith Terr CF48 . . . . .55 C4
Griffiths Ct NP4 . . . . . . .17 A6
Griffiths Gdns NP22 . . . .6 C1
Griffiths Sq NP22 . . . . . .6 C1
Griffiths St CF82 . . . . . .84 E2
Griffiths Terr CF34 . . . . .75 A2
Griffiths Way NP4 . . . . .37 E5
Griffithstown Inf Sch
NP4 . . . . .62 E2
Griffithstown Jun Sch
NP4 . . . . .62 E2
Grimson Cl CF64 . . . . .216 B5
Grindle Wlk NP10 . . . .142 A6
Gripoly Mills CF11 . . . .194 E3
Grisedale Cl CF23 . . . .178 B2
Groes Cl NP10 . . . . . . .142 A7
Groes Lon CF14 . . . . . .177 B8
Groes Prim Sch CF33 125 F3
Groes Rd
Rogerstone NP10 . . . . . .142 A6
Rogerstone NP10 . . . . . .142 A7
Groes-Faen Terr CF81 .57 D5
Groes-Wen La 1
SA13 . . . . .125 D5
Groeswen CF61 . . . . . .209 F7
Groeswen Dr CF83 . . .137 D4
Groeswen Hospl
SA13 . . . . .125 C6
Groeswen Rd
Caerphilly CF15, CF83 .137 C3
Caerphilly CF83 . . . . . .137 D4
Gron Ffordd CF14 . . . .159 B1
Gron Rd SA18 . . . . . . .220 D6
Grongaer Terr CF37 . . .135 C8
Grosmont Cl NP12 . . . .58 E1
Grosmont Pl NP44 . . . .90 A6
Grosmont Rd NP4 . . . . .63 B5

Grosmont Way NP10 .163 E5
Grosvenor Pl NP4 . . . . .62 E1
Grosvenor Rd
Abertillery NP13 . . . . . . .36 B6
Swansea SA2 . . . . .94 D7
Grosvenor St CF5 . . . .194 B6
Grosvenor Terr CF34 . .75 A1
Grouse St CF24 . . . . . .195 C7
Grove Cres NP4 . . . . . . .38 B1
Grove Est
Bedwas CF83 . . . . .139 A7
Pontypool NP4 . . . . .38 A1
Grove Farm Rd SA4 . . .43 C7
Grove Hill Pk SA14 . . .218 C6
Grove House Ct CF43 .80 C1
Grove La Neath SA10 . . .70 E7
Grove Park Ave NP44 . .89 E6
Grove Park Dr NP20 . .117 B1
Grove Pk
Cwmbran NP44 . . . . .89 E6
Merthyr Tydfil CF47 . . . .10 D3
Grove Pl Cardiff CF14 .177 D5
Penarth CF64 . . . . .207 A4
Pontypool NP4 . . . . .62 E2
Port Talbot SA13 . . . . .125 B8
Swansea SA1 . . . . .95 C7
Grove Place La 4
CF64 . . . . .207 A4
Grove Rd
Bridgend CF31 . . . . . . .168 F3
Clydach SA6 . . . . .22 D1
Llandow CF71 . . . . .199 A2
Pontardawe SA8 . . . . . . .23 F5
Pontypool NP4 . . . . .62 A8
Risca NP11 . . . . .114 F3
Grove St Gorseinon SA4 .43 B3
Llanbradach CF83 . . . . .111 F1
Maesteg CF34 . . . . . . .102 A6
Newbridge NP11 . . . . . .86 F6
Grove Terr
Abercwmboi CF44 . . . . . .53 E5
Bedlinog CF46 . . . . .56 A7
Llanharan CF72 . . . . . .153 F3
Penarth CF64 . . . . .207 A4
10 Pontypool NP4 . . . .38 A1
Senghenydd CF83 . . . . .110 E2
Ynysybwl CF37 . . . . . . .109 A8
Grove The
Aberdare CF44 . . . . .29 A1
Aberfan CF48 . . . . .55 C6
Barry CF62 . . . . .214 C2
Bryn NP12 . . . . .85 C6
Cardiff CF3 . . . . .179 C3
Fochriw CF81 . . . . .32 D7
Merthyr Tydfil CF47 . . . .10 D3
Mumbles SA3 . . . . .123 A5
Pontypridd CF37 . . . . . .109 D6
Swansea SA2 . . . . .94 F6
Grove Way CF3 . . . . . .179 C3
Grove Wlk NP11 . . . . . .59 D1
Grovefield Ho 9
CF40 . . . . .106 F4
Grovefield Terr 8
CF40 . . . . .106 F4
Groveland Rd CF14 . . .177 D5
Grovenor Rd NP10 . . . .141 F3
Grover St CF37 . . . . . .135 E8
Grovers Cl CF37 . . . . .109 D6
Grovers Field CF45 . . .109 D8
Groves Ave SA3 . . . . . .122 F4
Groves Rd Neath SA11 . .71 F5
Newport NP20 . . . . . . .142 D4
Groveside Rd NP12 . . . .86 A8
Groveside Villas 8
NP4 . . . . .38 A1
Gruffyd Dr CF83 . . . . .138 A5
Grwyne Terr NP12 . . . . .58 F4
Guardian Ind Est
CF24 . . . . .195 F7
Guenever Cl CF14 . . . .159 D2
Guest Cotts CF48 . . . . .11 B5
Guest Rd CF24 . . . . . .195 E4
Guest St CF81 . . . . .32 C7
Guildford Cres CF10 . .195 B5
Guildford St 3 CF10 .195 B5
Guildhall Pl CF10 . . . .195 A4
Guildhall Rd N SA1 . . . .95 A5
Guildhall Rd S SA1 . . . .95 A5
Gulf Ind Area CF11 . . .194 E2
Gulliver's Cl SA3 . . . . .123 B8
Gurnos CP Jun Sch
SA9 . . . . .2 D8
Gurnos Est NP23 . . . . . .8 A5
Gurnos Rd
Gowerton SA4 . . . . .66 B5
Merthyr Tydfil CF47 . . . .10 C4
Ystradgynlais SA9 . . . . . .2 C7
Guthrie St CF43 . . . . . .215 A5
Guy's Rd CF63 . . . . . . .215 B6
Gwaelod y Foel CF38 156 D8
Gwaelod-y-Garth Ind Est
CF15 . . . . .158 A2
Gwaelod-y-Garth Rd
CF37 . . . . .136 C2
Gwaelodygarth Cl
CF47 . . . . .10 D3
Gwaelodygarth Rd
CF47 . . . . .10 D3
Gwaelodywaun Villas
CF81 . . . . .58 B3
Gwaila Gr 5 CF37 . . . .135 F6
Gwalch y Penwaig
CF62 . . . . .214 F2
Gwalia Cl
Bridgend CF31 . . . . . . .150 F1
Gorseinon SA4 . . . . .43 D2

Gwalia Cres SA4 . . . . . .43 D2
Gwalia Ct Clydach SA6 .46 D7
Swansea SA1 . . . . .95 B5
Gwalia Rd CF35 . . . . .170 E4
Gwalia Terr
Aberdare CF44 . . . . .53 C8
Blaina NP13 . . . . .15 E6
Gorseinon SA4 . . . . .43 D2
Gwalin y Cwrt CF43 . .137 D1
Gwan-y-garw CF32 . . .103 F3
Gwar-y-Caeau SA13 . .125 C8
Gwaun Bedw CF39 . . .107 E2
Gwaun Cae Gurwen Prim
Sch SA18 . . . . .220 D7
Gwaun Cl CF14 . . . . . .176 E4
Gwaun Coed CF31 . . . .169 A4
Gwaun Cotts CF72 . . .172 A8
Gwaun Delyn Cl NP23 .15 D7
Gwaun Helyg NP23 . . . .14 B8
Gwaun Helyg Rd NP23 . .7 B1
Gwaun Newydd CF83 .138 D4
Gwaun-Bant CF32 . . . .103 E4
Gwaun-Fro CF82 . . . . . .84 D7
Gwaun-Hyfryd CF83 . .138 D4
Gwaun-Ruperra Cl
CF72 . . . . .155 D4
Gwaun-y-groes CF72 .155 F4
Gwauncelyn Jun & Inf Sch
CF38 . . . . .135 F1
Gwaunfarren Cl CF47 . .10 F4
Gwaunfarren Gr CF47 .10 E3
Gwaunfarren Prim Sch
CF47 . . . . .10 F4
Gwaunfarren Rd CF47 .10 F3
Gwaunfelin Wlk 8
NP4 . . . . .17 D7
Gwaunmeisgyn Jun & Inf
Sch CF38 . . . . .156 A6
Gwaunmiskin Rd
CF38 . . . . .156 A6
Gwaunrhydd 2 CF38 156 A6
Gwaunruperra Rd
CF72 . . . . .155 D4
Gwawr St CF44 . . . . . . .53 B8
Gwbert Cl CF3 . . . . . . .179 C5
Gwelfor
Cefn Cribwr CF32 . . . . .149 A3
Dunvant SA2 . . . . .93 E8
Llanelli SA14 . . . . .41 E4
Gwendoline Pl 13
CF24 . . . . .195 D5
Gwendoline Rd NP11 .114 F1
Gwendoline St
4 Aberavon SA12 . . . . .99 A1
Blaengarw CF32 . . . . . .103 E6
12 Cardiff CF24 . . . . .195 D5
Merthyr Tydfil CF47 . . . .10 E3
Nant-y-Moel CF32 . . . .104 F3
Treherbert CF42 . . . . . . .50 E2
Gwendoline Terr
Abercynon CF45 . . . . . . .82 E3
Cwmfelin CF34 . . . . . . .128 B8
Gwendraeth Pl SA1 . . . .69 B2
Gwenfo CH in W Prim Sch
CF5 . . . . .205 A6
Gwenfo Dr CF5 . . . . . .205 A7
Gwenlais Rd SA4 . . . . . .43 E7
Gwenllian St CF43 . . . .215 D6
Gwenllian Terr CF37 . .135 F4
Gwennol y Mor CF62 .214 F2
Gwennyth St CF24 . . . .178 A1
Gwenog Ct CF62 . . . . .214 C5
Gwent CF44 . . . . .207 C5
Gwent Ct
Ebbw Vale NP23 . . . . . . .14 E3
Fleur De Lis NP12 . . . . . .85 E4
Gwent Gdns SA1 . . . . .67 F1
Gwent Gr SA2 . . . . .94 A4
Gwent Ho
4 Cardiff CF23 . . . . . .178 C2
Port Talbot SA12 . . . . .124 D8
Gwent Rd Cardiff CF5 .193 B4
Swansea SA1 . . . . .68 A1
Upper Boat CF37 . . . . .136 D1
Gwent Sh Ctr NP22 . . . .13 D2
Gwent Sq NP44 . . . . . . .89 E3
Gwent St NP4 . . . . .62 B2
Gwent Terr Blaina NP13 15 E6
Nantyglo NP23 . . . . .8 D1
Porth CF39 . . . . .107 E4
Gwent Way NP22 . . . . . .13 D8
Gwern Ave CF83 . . . . .110 F2
Gwern Einon Rd SA2 . . .94 B3
Gwern Fadog Rd SA6 . .46 A3
Gwern Las NP13 . . . . . .36 B6
Gwern Rhuddi Rd
CF23 . . . . .160 D1
Gwern-Berthi Rd
NP13 . . . . .36 B7
Gwern-Rhuddi Rd
CF23 . . . . .178 C2
Gwerna Cres CF82 . . . .85 A1
Gwernant SA9 . . . . . . .221 B2
Gwernifor St CF45 . . . .54 D1
Gwernllwyn Cl CF43 . . .11 A4
Gwernllwyn Jun Sch
CF48 . . . . .11 C4
Gwernllwyn Terr CF43 .80 D4
Gwernllwynchwyth Rd
Llansamlet SA7 . . . . . . .46 F1
Swansea SA7 . . . . .69 F8
Gwernllyn Rd CF48 . . . .11 B4
Gwernos SA4 . . . . .46 A2
Gwerthonor La
Bargoed CF81 . . . . .58 A1
Gilfach CF81 . . . . .85 A1
Gwerthonor Pl CF81 . . .58 A1

Gwerthonor Rd
Bargoed CF81 . . . . .58 A1
Gilfach CF81 . . . . .85 A8
Gwili Ave SA14 . . . .218 C6
Gwili Terr SA1 . . . . . .68 B1
Gwilym Pl 6 CF63 . .215 A8
Gwilym Rd SA9 . . . . .221 B8
Gwilym St CF37 . . . .135 F4
Gwlad Du Gwyrdd
CF14 . . . . .132 B5
Gwlad-y-Gan SA6 . . . .45 D1
Gwladys Pl NP18 . . . .118 A3
Gwladys St
Merthyr Tydfil CF47 . . . . .10 F3
Pant CF48 . . . . .11 B7
Penywaun CF44 . . . . .28 B6
Gwrhyd Rd
Pen-Rhiw-fawr SA9 . . . .221 A4
Pontardawe SA8,SA9 . . .220 F2
Rhydyfro SA8 . . . . .23 D8
Gwyddon Cl NP11 . . . .87 B2
Gwyddon Rd NP11 . . . .87 C3
Gwydr Cres SA2 . . . . .94 F6
Gwydr Mews SA2 . . . .94 F6
Gwydr Pl SA4 . . . . . . .42 D1
Gwydr Sq SA2 . . . . . .94 F6
Gwylfa SA14 . . . . .41 D6
Gwylfa Rd SA1 . . . . . .67 F1
Gwylym SA5 . . . . .68 A2
Gwyn Cres NP4 . . . . . .37 E7
Gwyn Ct 3 SA12 . . . .125 A8
Gwyn Dr CF83 . . . . . .138 A4
Gwyn James Ct CF64 .206 E5
Gwyn Rd CF40 . . . . . .107 A4
Gwyn St
Pontardawe SA8 . . . . . . .23 C3
Pontypridd CF37 . . . . . .135 E5
Gwyn Terr
2 Aberavon SA12 . . . .125 A8
Crynant SA10 . . . . .226 A7
Gwyn's Pl SA8 . . . . . .23 F3
Gwynant Cres CF23 . .178 B5
Gwyndy Rd SA1 . . . . . .69 A2
Gwynedd Ave
Cymmer SA13 . . . . .75 D3
Swansea SA1 . . . . .67 F1
Gwynedd Gdns SA1 . . .48 A4
Gwynedd Ho 5 CF23 .178 C2
Gwynfan Pl CF47 . . . . .30 E7
Gwynfe Rd SA4 . . . . . .42 E3
Gwynfi St
Blaengwynfi SA13 . . . . . .76 B6
Swansea SA5 . . . . .68 C5
Gwynfi Terr CF72 . . . .154 A3
Gwynfor Rd SA4 . . . . .67 E1
Gwynfryn SA18 . . . . .219 B7
Gwynfryn Rd SA4 . . . .19 C3
Gwynfryn Terr CF38 . .156 D7
Gwynllyw 3 NP44 . . . .89 C6
Gwynne Terr SA1 . . . .96 A8
Gwynnes Cl CF47 . . . .10 E2
Gwyrddgoed SA8 . . . . .23 E6
Gwyrosydd Jun & Inf Sch
SA5 . . . . .68 C5
Gwysfa Rd SA6 . . . . . .46 B5
Gwysfryn SA9 . . . . . .221 C6
Gyfeillon Rd CF37 . . .108 C2
Gynol Rd SA9 . . . . . .221 B7
Gynor Ave CF39 . . . . .107 C5
Gynor Pl CF39 . . . . . .107 C6
Gypsy La
Caerphilly CF15 . . . . . .137 C2
Pontypool NP4 . . . . .37 E1
Gyrnosfa SA9 . . . . .2 D8

H

Habershon St CF24 . .195 C6
Hackerford Rd CF23 . .178 C8
Haden St NP4 . . . . . . .62 B6
Hadfield Cl CF11 . . . .194 C2
Hadfield Rd CF11 . . . .194 D2
Hadland Terr SA3 . . . .123 A6
Hadrian Cl NP18 . . . .118 A3
Hadrian's Cl CF82 . . . .84 C7
Hael La SA3 . . . . .121 B4
Hafan Cardiff CF5 . . . .193 E6
4 Llanelli SA15 . . . . .40 D4
Hafan Deg
Aberkenfig CF32 . . . . . .150 C3
Cwmfelin CF34 . . . . . . .128 C8
Pencoed CF35 . . . . .170 D8
Seven Sisters SA10 . . . .222 C3
Hafan Elim CF47 . . . . .10 F3
Hafan Glyd SA6 . . . . . .46 E8
Hafan Heulog CF37 . . .109 D7
Hafan y Don SA2 . . . . .93 E8
Hafan-Werdd CF83 . . .138 D5
Hafandeg CF44 . . . . . .28 F6
Hafnant SA1 . . . . .69 D5
Hafod Bryan SA14 . . . .41 C4
Hafod Cl
Fleur De Lis NP12 . . . . . .85 A6
Ponthir NP18 . . . . .117 F6
Hafod Cotts CF48 . . . .11 B6
Hafod Court Rd NP44 . .89 A5
Hafod Decaf CF33 . . . .148 B2
Hafod Pk SA1 . . . . . . .68 D2
Hafod Prim Sch
Swansea SA1 . . . . .68 D1

Hafod Prim Sch continued
Trehafod CF37 . . . . . . .108 C2
Hafod Rd
Ammanford SA18 . . . . .219 A6
Ponthir NP18 . . . . .117 F6
Tycroes SA18 . . . . .218 F6
Hafod St Cardiff CF11 .194 F4
Pentrebach CF48 . . . . . .31 B3
Swansea SA1 . . . . .68 D1
Hafod The CF48 . . . . .107 F3
Hafod Tudor Terr
NP11 . . . . .113 E3
Hafod Wen
Cwmdare CF44 . . . . .28 C3
Tonyrefail CF39 . . . . . .133 D6
Hafod-Arthen Rd
NP13 . . . . .60 B7
Hafod-Fach Rd NP13 . . .36 C3
Hafod-fan Terr NP13 . . .36 C3
Hafod-y- Bryn NP11 . .115 B1
Hafod-y-Mynydd NP12 . .12 F3
Hafod-Yr-Ynys Rd
NP11 . . . . .60 B7
Hafodyrynys Clos
CF3 . . . . .179 F6
Hafon Mews NP18 . . .117 F6
Haford St SA13 . . . . . .125 C8
Hafordarthen NP13 . . . .60 B7
Hafren Ct CF11 . . . . .194 D7
Hafren Rd Barry CF62 .214 E5
Cwmbran NP44 . . . . .89 A4
Haig Pl Cardiff CF5 . . .193 A3
Swansea SA5 . . . . .67 F4
Hailey Ct CF14 . . . . . .176 F3
Haines Ct CF83 . . . . . .137 E1
Haldane Cl CF83 . . . . .138 D3
Haldane Pl NP20 . . . . .117 A2
Haldens The NP44 . . . .89 B1
Halfway Cty Prim Sch
SA14 . . . . .41 A6
Halifax Cl CF24 . . . . .196 A7
Halifax Terr CF42 . . . . .50 E3
Hall Cl CF33 . . . . .166 A8
Hall Dr CF33 . . . . .166 A8
Hall La SA4 . . . . .64 D4
Hall St Aberdare CF44 . .29 A2
Ammanford SA18 . . . . .219 C7
Blackwood NP12 . . . . . . .85 F7
Brynamman SA18 . . . . .220 E8
Ebbw Vale NP23 . . . . . . .14 E2
Llanelli SA15 . . . . .40 D6
Swansea SA1 . . . . .68 D1
Hall's Rd NP11 . . . . . .114 C5
Hall's Road Terr
NP11 . . . . .114 C5
Hallam Ho SA12 . . . . . .98 A2
Hallbank SA3 . . . . . . .123 B4
Hallbank Terr SA3 . . .123 B4
Halle Cl NP19 . . . . . . .145 A5
Halliard Ct CF10 . . . . .195 C3
Halls Rd NP19 . . . . . . .86 E6
Halsbury Rd CF5 . . . . .194 B7
Halstead St NP19 . . . .143 E4
Halswell St CF45 . . . . .82 B6
Halt Cl CF44 . . . . .224 B1
Halt Rd CF44 . . . . . . .224 B1
Halton Cl CF64 . . . . . .217 A8
Ham La E CF61 . . . . . .210 A5
Ham La S CF61 . . . . . .210 A5
Ham Manor CF61 . . . .210 A5
Ham Manor Caravan Pk
CF61 . . . . .210 A4
Ham Mews CF61 . . . . .210 A4
Hamadryad Rd CF10 . .195 A1
Haman Pl CF82 . . . . . . .84 C6
Hamilton St
Cardiff CF11 . . . . .194 E6
Mountain Ash CF45 . . . . .54 C3
Newport NP19 . . . . .143 F3
Pentrebach CF48 . . . . . .31 A4
Swansea SA1 . . . . .68 D4
Hamilton Terr CF34 . . .29 A2
Hammond Dr NP19 . . .143 F4
Hammond Way CF23 . .178 F1
Hampden Ct NP19 . . . .144 A3
Hampden Rd NP19 . . . .144 A3
Hampshire Ave NP19 . .144 B2
Hampshire Cl NP19 . . .144 B2
Hampshire Cres
NP19 . . . . .144 B2
Hampstead Wlk CF5 . .192 F4
Hampton Court Rd
CF23 . . . . .178 E2
Hampton Cres E
CF23 . . . . .160 D1
Hampton Cres W
CF23 . . . . .160 D1
Hampton Rd CF14 . . . .177 D4
Hampton St CF47 . . . . .30 E8
Hanbury Cl
Caerleon NP18 . . . . . . .118 C1
Cardiff CF14 . . . . .176 E5
Cwmbran NP44 . . . . .89 E4
Hanbury Gdns NP4 . . . .62 A8
Hanbury Rd
Bargoed CF81 . . . . .58 A4
Pontypool NP4 . . . . .62 B6
Pontypool NP4 . . . . .62 C6
Hanbury Sq CF81 . . . . .58 A4
Hanbury St NP12 . . . . .85 A7
Hand Farm Rd NP4 . . . .62 A5
Handel Ave SA12 . . . . .98 B3
Handel Cl
Newport NP19 . . . . .145 A5
Penarth CF64 . . . . .206 F1
Handley Rd CF24 . . . . .196 A7
Handsworth St NP19 . .143 F4

Hanfield Pk NP44 . . . . .90 A4
Hangman's Cross
SA3 . . . . .231 C5
Hankey Pl CF47 . . . . . .30 E7
Hankey Terr CF47 . . . . .30 E7
Hanley Path 8 NP44 . . .89 C2
Hannah Cl CF14 . . . . .177 F6
Hannah St Barry CF63 .215 A6
Cardiff CF10 . . . . .195 B3
Porth CF39 . . . . .107 C7
Hannants The SA10 . . . .71 C8
Hanover Cl SA3 . . . . . .123 A6
Hanover Ct
Barry CF63 . . . . .215 D7
Bridgend CF31 . . . . . . .168 E5
9 Cardiff CF14 . . . . .176 F6
Swansea SA2 . . . . .94 D7
Hanover La SA1 . . . . . .95 A7
Hanover St
2 Barry CF62 . . . . . .214 F5
Cardiff CF5 . . . . .194 A5
Merthyr Tydfil CF47 . . . . .10 D2
Swansea SA1 . . . . .95 B7
Hansom Pl CF11 . . . . .194 B3
Harbour Dr CF10 . . . . .195 C1
Harbour Rd CF62 . . . . .214 D2
Harbour View Rd
Penarth CF64 . . . . .207 A5
Swansea SA1 . . . . .96 A8
Harcombe Rd CF40 . . .107 A8
Harcourt Pl NP22 . . . . .12 D5
Harcourt Rd
Brynmawr NP23 . . . . .8 B5
Mountain Ash CF45 . . . . .54 C3
Harcourt St
Ebbw Vale NP23 . . . . .7 D1
Swansea SA1 . . . . .95 B7
Harcourt Terr
Abertillery NP13 . . . . . . .36 A6
Mountain Ash CF45 . . . . .81 F8
New Tredegar NP24 . . . . .34 A1
Tredegar NP22 . . . . .13 E6
Harddfan SA14 . . . . . . .41 F6
Harding Ave NP20 . . . .117 A3
Harding Cl CF61 . . . . .210 C6
Hardingsdown La
SA3 . . . . .228 E2
Hardwicke Ct CF5 . . . .194 A8
Hardy Cl Barry CF62 . .215 A8
Newport NP20 . . . . .142 E1
Hardy Ct 17 NP4 . . . . .38 A1
Hardy Pl CF24 . . . . . . .195 C7
Harebell Cl SA6 . . . . . .46 B4
Harefield Cl CF23 . . . .161 B1
Harford Cl CF14 . . . . .176 E5
Harford Ct SA2 . . . . . . .94 C5
Harford Gdns NP22 . . . .13 F8
Harford Sq NP23 . . . . . .7 C1
Harford St NP22 . . . . . .13 F8
Hargreaves Dr NP20 . .117 A3
Harle St SA11 . . . . .71 F8
Harlequin Ct
Cardiff CF24 . . . . .195 E8
Newport NP20 . . . . .142 F4
Harlequin Dr NP20 . . . .143 B6
Harlequin Rd SA12 . . . .98 F1
Harlequin Rdbt 3
NP20 . . . . .143 C6
Harleyford Rd SA4 . . . .19 A4
Harlington Rd SA5 . . . . .68 A2
Harold St Cardiff CF24 .195 E7
6 Cwmbran NP44 . . . .89 C5
Llanharan CF72 . . . . . . .153 F2
Harper's Rd NP4 . . . . . .37 F5
Harpur St CF10 . . . . . .195 A2
Harries Ave SA15 . . . . .40 C6
Harries St SA1 . . . . . . .95 B8
Harriet St
Aberdare CF44 . . . . .28 A4
Cardiff CF24 . . . . .195 A8
Penarth CF64 . . . . .206 F5
Harriet Town 2 CF48 . . .31 B1
Harrington Ct CF5 . . . .193 B3
Harrington Pl 3 SA1 . . .68 D1
Harrington St SA1 . . . . .68 D1
Harris Ave CF3 . . . . . .179 D4
Harris Rd SA9 . . . . . . .221 B7
Harris St Hirwaun CF44 . .27 D7
Swansea SA6 . . . . .68 F8
Harris View SA6 . . . . . .81 F7
Harrismith Rd CF23 . . .178 C1
Harrison Dr CF3 . . . . . .180 A5
Harrison St CF47 . . . . . .10 F4
Harrison Way CF11 . . .206 F4
Harrogate Rd 2
NP19 . . . . .143 E8
Harrow Cl NP18 . . . . . .117 B8
Harrow Rd NP19 . . . . .143 D5
Harrowby La CF10 . . . .195 B2

Harrowby Pl CF10 . . . .195 B1
Harrowby St CF10 . . . .195 B1
Harry St SA6 . . . . .45 E1
Hart Gdns 16 NP20 . . .143 C3
Hartfield Cl SA2 . . . . . .94 A7
Hartland Rd CF3 . . . . .179 A5
Hartley Pl CF11 . . . . . .194 E3
Hartridge Farm Rd
NP18,NP19 . . . . .144 E4
Hartridge High Sch
NP18 . . . . .144 E4
Hartshorn Cl CF83 . . . .138 D3
Hartshorn Terr CF34 . . .75 A2
Harvey Cl NP20 . . . . . .117 A2
Harvey Cres SA12 . . . .124 E8
Harvey St Barry CF63 . .215 C6
12 Cardiff CF5 . . . . . .194 C6
Maesteg CF34 . . . . .103 B3
Harvey Wlk NP20 . . . .116 C1
Hassocks Lea 5 NP44 . .89 B1
Hastings Ave CF64 . . . .206 E4
Hastings Cl CF64 . . . . .206 E4
Hastings Cres CF3 . . . .179 D8
Hastings Pl CF64 . . . . .206 E4
Hatfield Cl SA5 . . . . . . .67 C5
Hathaway Ho SA12 . . . .98 F2
Hathaway Rd CF3 . . . . .179 C8
Hathaway St NP19 . . . .143 F4
Hatherleigh NP19 . . . . .144 B6
Hatherleigh Dr SA3 . . .122 C5
Hatherleigh Rd CF3 . . .179 A3
Hatter St 4 NP23 . . . . . .8 B4
Haul Bryn CF32 . . . . . .104 F6
Haul Fron CF40 . . . . . .107 A2
Haul Fryn Cardiff CF14 .176 F2
Pyle CF33 . . . . .148 E3
Haulfryn Birchgrove SA7 . .47 A2
Bryn SA14 . . . . .41 F6
Brynmenyn CF32 . . . . . .150 E6
Clydach NP7 . . . . .9 D6
Penywaun CF44 . . . . .28 B6
Pontardawe SA8 . . . . . . .23 C5
Haulwen SA14 . . . . .28 D3
Haulwen Rd
Penpedairheol CF82 . . . . .84 E8
Swansea SA2 . . . . .67 D1
Haulwen Terr SA15 . . . .40 E7
Havannah St CF10 . . . .195 B1
Havant Cl CF62 . . . . . .213 A1
Havard Rd
Abertridwr CF83 . . . . . .136 F7
Llanelli SA15 . . . . .41 A6
Havard's Row NP22 . . . .12 F3
Havelock Pl CF11 . . . . .194 F3
Havelock St
Cardiff CF10 . . . . .195 A5
Llanelli SA15 . . . . .40 D4
8 Newport NP20 . . . .143 B4
Haven Cl CF48 . . . . . . .31 B1
Haven The
Hirwaun CF44 . . . . .27 D7
Penperlleni NP4 . . . . . . .39 E6
Havenwood Dr CF14 . .159 D3
Haverford Way CF5 . . .193 D4
Havergal Cl SA3 . . . . .122 D4
Hawarden Gn NP44 . . . .90 B2
Hawarden Pl 6 CF48 . . .31 A1
Hawarden Rd NP19 . . .144 A3
Hawfinch Cl CF23 . . . .178 D7
Hawke Cl NP19 . . . . . .144 E7
Hawker Cl CF24 . . . . . .196 A7
Hawkes Ridge NP44 . . . .88 F2
Hawkhurst Ct CF36 . . .165 E1
Hawkins Cres NP11 . . .144 E6
Hawks Moor Cl NP10 . .142 B6
Hawkstone Cl SA3 . . . .122 E7
Hawksworth Gr NP19 . .144 B4
Hawkwood Cl CF5 . . . .176 B1
Hawse La NP10 . . . . . .163 C2
Hawthorn Ave
Baglan SA12 . . . . .98 D6
Gorseinon SA4 . . . . .43 A2
Hengoed CF82 . . . . .84 F3
Merthyr Tydfil CF47 . . . . .10 E4
Neath SA11 . . . . .71 F6
Newport NP19 . . . . .144 C2
Penarth CF64 . . . . .206 E3
Hawthorn Cl
Cwmavon SA12 . . . . .99 E4
Dinas Powys CF64 . . . . .206 B2
Llanmartin NP18 . . . . . .145 E6
Hawthorn Cres CF37 . .136 B4
Hawthorn Ct NP44 . . . .90 A5
Hawthorn Dr
Bridgend CF35 . . . . .169 F3
Bryn NP12 . . . . .85 E3
South Cornelly CF33 . . . .165 F5
Hawthorn High Sch
CF37 . . . . .136 B3
Hawthorn Hill CF48 . . . .10 B7
Hawthorn Inf Sch
CF14 . . . . .176 F3
Hawthorn Jun Sch
CF14 . . . . .176 F3
Hawthorn Pk CF72 . . . .153 D3
Hawthorn Rd CF36 . . . .183 D8
Hawthorn Prim Sch
CF37 . . . . .136 B4
Hawthorn Rd
Barry CF62 . . . . .214 C4
Ebbw Vale NP23 . . . . .7 D4
Llanharry CF72 . . . . . . .172 C5
Pontypool NP4 . . . . .62 D1
Rhydyfelin CF37 . . . . . .136 B4
Hawthorn Rd E CF14 . .176 F3
Hawthorn Rd W CF14 .176 F3
Hawthorn Rise CF3 . . . .28 D3
Hawthorn Terr CF45 . . .81 F8

Hawthorn Villas SA9 . . . .1 F1
Hawthorn Way CF31 . .169 D4
Hawthorne Ave SA2 . . . .94 F7
Hawthorne Fosse
NP19 . . . . .144 B4
Hawthorne Rd CF46 . . .83 F2
Hawthorne Sq 7
NP19 . . . . .144 A4
Hawthorne Terr 12
CF44 . . . . .29 A1
Hawthorns The
Caerleon NP18 . . . . . . .118 B3
Cardiff CF23 . . . . .178 E6
Cwmbran NP44 . . . . .89 B6
Pant CF48 . . . . .11 A7
Hawtin Pk Ind Est
NP12 . . . . .85 C4
Haxby Ct 16 CF10 . . . .195 C4
Hay's Cres SA11 . . . . .223 D1
Haydn Terr CF47 . . . . . .10 F4
Hayes Bridge Rd
CF10 . . . . .195 B5
Hayes La Barry CF64 . .215 D3
Barry CF64 . . . . .215 D4
Hayes Rd CF64 . . . . . .215 E4
Hayes The CF10 . . . . . .195 A5
Hayling Cl NP19 . . . . . .143 F7
Haynes Ct NP20 . . . . . .143 D2
Hayswayn 2 NP44 . . . . .89 B1
Haywain Ct CF31 . . . . .169 A3
Hazel Cl Pontypool NP4 . .63 B5
Porthcawl CF36 . . . . . . .183 D8
Hazel Ct Ebbw Vale NP23 . .7 C5
Swansea SA2 . . . . .94 B6
Tonyrefail CF39 . . . . . . .133 D6
Hazel Dr CF44 . . . . . . .28 D2
Hazel Gr Bedwas CF83 .138 F6
Caerphilly CF83 . . . . . . .138 C5
Dinas Powys CF64 . . . . .206 B2
Hazel Mead CF32 . . . . .150 E6
Hazel Rd
Llanmartin NP18 . . . . . .145 F7
Penarth CF64 . . . . .206 F2
Swansea SA2 . . . . .94 B7
Hazel Terr
Mountain Ash CF45 . . . . .81 F8
Troedyrhiw CF48 . . . . . . .31 B2
Hazel Tree Cl CF15 . . . .176 A6
Hazel Tree Ct SA10 . . . .48 C2
Hazel Tree Ho SA12 . . . .98 E6
Hazel Tree Way CF31 . .169 D5
Hazel Wlk
Caerleon NP18 . . . . . . .117 F2
Croesyceiliog NP44 . . . . .90 A6
Hazeldene CF72 . . . . . .172 B5
Hazeldene Ave
Bridgend CF31 . . . . . . .169 D4
Cardiff CF24 . . . . .178 A4
Hazelhurst Ct CF14 . . .176 F3
Hazelhurst Rd CF14 . . .176 F3
Hazelmere Rd SA12 . . . .99 F5
Hazeltree Copse SA4 . . .64 B2
Hazelwell Rd CF36 . . . .182 F8
Hazelwood CF32 . . . . .184 D2
Hazelwood Dr CF3 . . . .179 E7
Hazelwood Rd
Neath SA11 . . . . .71 F8
Newbridge NP11 . . . . . . .87 B8
Hazelwood Row 3
SA12 . . . . .99 F5
Hazelwood Terr 2
SA12 . . . . .99 F5
Hazledene Cl CF63 . . . .215 A7
Hazlitt Cl Cardiff CF3 . .179 C8
Newport NP20 . . . . .142 E1
Headland Cl SA3 . . . . .122 A5
Headland Rd
Bishopston SA3 . . . . . . .122 A5
Swansea SA1 . . . . .95 F8
Heads Of The Valleys Ind
Est NP22 . . . . .12 D5
Heads Of The Valleys Rd
Aberdare CF44 . . . . .28 A7
Brynmawr NP23 . . . . .8 D5
Clydach NP7 . . . . .9 D6
Dowlais CF48 . . . . .11 E6
Ebbw Vale NP23 . . . . .7 C4
Merthyr Tydfil CF48,
CF48,CF47 . . . . .225 D2
Rhymney NP22 . . . . .12 C7
Tredegar NP22 . . . . .6 D2
Hearte Cl CF62 . . . . . .213 A2
Hearts Of Oak Cotts
CF34 . . . . .102 A7
Heaselands Pl SA2 . . . .93 D7
Heath Ave CF64 . . . . . .206 D5
Heath Cl Aberdare CF44 .29 D1
Mumbles SA3 . . . . .122 F6
Newport NP19 . . . . .144 C2
Heath Cres CF37 . . . . .109 B1
Heath Ct SA3 . . . . .122 F6
Heath Halt Rd CF14,
CF23 . . . . .178 A5
Heath High Level Sta
CF23 . . . . .178 A5
Heath Low Level Sta
CF23 . . . . .178 A4
Heath Mead CF14 . . . .178 A5
Heath Park Ave CF14 . .178 A4
Heath Park Cres
CF14 . . . . .178 A4
Heath Park Ct CF14 . . .178 A5
Heath Park Dr CF14 . . .178 A5
Heath Park La
Cardiff CF14 . . . . .177 D3
Cardiff CF23 . . . . .178 A5

Heath Park Way (Ffordd
Parc y Mynydd Bychan)
CF14 . . . . .177 F3
Heath Rd NP12 . . . . . . .85 D4
Heath St CF11 . . . . . . .194 E5
Heath Terr
4 Pontypridd CF37 . . .109 B1
Porth CF39 . . . . .107 F7
Heathbrook CF23 . . . . .178 A5
Heathcliffe Cl 4 CF3 . .179 D8
Heather Ave CF5 . . . . .193 F6
Heather Cl Sarn CF32 . .150 E3
Tonypandy CF40 . . . . . .106 F6
Tredegar NP22 . . . . .6 F1
Heather Cres SA2 . . . . .94 B6
Heather Ct NP44 . . . . . .88 F5
Heather Rd
Merthyr Tydfil CF47 . . . . .10 C5
Newport NP19 . . . . .143 F7
Heather Way
7 Cardiff CF5 . . . . . . .193 D8
Porth CF39 . . . . .108 A3
Heathers The CF62 . . . .214 D5
Heatherslade Cl
Mumbles SA3 . . . . .123 B4
Southgate SA3 . . . . .121 A3
Heatherslade Rd SA3 . .121 B4
Heatherview Rd CF37 . .109 E2
Heathfield
Gorseinon SA4 . . . . .43 A1
Swansea SA1 . . . . .95 C7
Tredegar NP22 . . . . .14 A3
Heathfield Ave SA11 . .223 D1
Heathfield Cl NP23 . . . . .7 D5
Heathfield Cres CF72 . .153 E2
Heathfield Dr CF62 . . . .214 E7
Heathfield Ind Pk
SA14 . . . . .218 C6
Heathfield Pl CF14 . . . .177 E2
Heathfield Rd
Cardiff CF14 . . . . .177 E2
Pontardawe SA8 . . . . . . .23 F6
Heathfield Villas 4
CF37 . . . . .135 E7
Heathfield Wlk CF31 . . .58 A5
Heathlands CF82 . . . . . .84 E2
Heathlands The CF39 . .132 C6
Heathway CF14 . . . . . .177 E5
Heathwood Ct CF14 . . .177 E5
Heathwood Gr CF14 . . .178 A4
Heathwood Rd
Cardiff CF14 . . . . .177 E5
Mumbles SA3 . . . . .123 A6
Hebbles La CF63 . . . . .215 B7
Hebron Rd SA6 . . . . . . .46 D7
Hebron Villas CF45 . . . .82 C6
Hector Ave NP11 . . . . . .60 B2
Hedd Aberth SA10 . . . .222 D4
Heddfaen N CF23 . . . . .178 F7
Heddfaen S CF23 . . . . .178 F7
Heddfan NP23 . . . . .8 C5
Heddwch Cl CF48 . . . . .11 A6
Hedel Rd CF11 . . . . . . .194 A6
Hedgemoor CF31 . . . . .169 D4
Hedl-y Delyn Du
CF31 . . . . .168 B5
Hedley Terr SA15 . . . . .40 D6
Hedreladus SA9 . . . . . .222 A3
Hefod CF72 . . . . .155 A5
Heilbronn Way SA12 . . .99 A1
Hel Ton CF33 . . . . .165 C2
Helen Pl CF24 . . . . .195 D7
Helen St CF24 . . . . . . .195 D7
Helen's Rd SA11 . . . . . .71 C5
Helford Sq NP20 . . . . .116 D2
Helig Fan CF33 . . . . . . .148 B1
Hellas Dr CF62 . . . . . .214 C8
Helpstone Terr NP4 . . . .62 A7
Helwick Cl SA3 . . . . . .123 A5
Hemingway Rd CF10 . .195 C2
Hen Felin
Pontardawe SA8 . . . . . . .24 B5
Ystradgynlais SA9 . . . . . .2 C7
Hen Parc Ave SA2 . . . . .93 B4
Hen Parc La SA2 . . . . . .93 C4
Henderson Rd NP23 . . . .8 A4
Hendre
Caerphilly CF83 . . . . . . .137 F6
Dunvant SA2 . . . . .93 D8
Dyffryn Cellwen SA10 . . .222 F5
Ebbw Vale NP23 . . . . .7 E1
Hendre Ave CF32 . . . . .104 E4
Hendre Cl Cardiff CF5 . .194 A8
Llangennech SA14 . . . . . .42 A7
Hendre Cres SA14 . . . .115 F8
Hendre Ct
NP19 . . . . .144 F6
Hendre Dr
NP19 . . . . .144 F5
Hendre Farm Ct
NP19 . . . . .144 F6
Hendre Farm Dr
NP19 . . . . .144 F5
Hendre Farm Gdns
NP19 . . . . .144 E5
Hendre Gdns CF5 . . . .194 A8
Hendre Isaf SA14 . . . . .41 D4
Hendre Owain SA2 . . . .94 C8
Hendre Owen Rd SA13 .74 D4
Hendre Pk SA14 . . . . . .42 A7
Hendre Rd
Abertridwr CF83 . . . . . .136 E7
Capel Hendre SA18 . . . .218 E5
Cardiff CF3 . . . . .179 E5
Glanaman SA18 . . . . . . .220 B8
Llanelli SA14 . . . . .41 D4
Llangennech SA14 . . . . . .42 B7

Hendre Rd continued
Pencoed CF35 ....170 B8
Tycroes SA18 ....218 F6
Hendre Selaig CF42 ...50 D3
Hendre Terr 3 CF40 ...107 A4
Hendre-Foilan Rd SA2 94 B8
Hendrecafn Rd CF40 ..106 F4
Hendredenny Dr
CF83 ....137 D4
Hendredenny Inf Sch
CF83 ....137 E4
Hendredenny Jun Sch
CF83 ....137 E4
Hendredenny Park Prim
Sch CF83 ....137 E4
Hendrefadog St CF43 ..80 C4
Hendrefoilan Ave SA2 ..94 B7
Hendrefoilan Cl SA2 ...94 B8
Hendrefoilan Dr SA2 ...94 A7
Hendrefoilan Prim Sch
SA2 ....93 F7
Hendrefoilan Student
Village CF39 ....94 B8
Hendreforgan Cres
CF39 ....132 C5
Hendreforgan Jun & Inf
Schs CF39 ....132 C5
Hendregwilym CF40 ...106 F3
Hendremawr Cl SA2 ...94 C8
Hendrewen Rd CF42 ...50 C2
Hendy Cl SA2 ....94 B4
Hendy Ind Est SA4 .....19 A4
Hendy Prim Sch SA4 ...19 A4
Hendy Rd SA4 ....64 F4
Hendy St CF23 ....178 B1
Heneage Dr SA2 ......94 B1
Henfaes Rd SA11 ......49 C2
Henfaes Terr SA11 ....49 C2
Hengoed Ave CF82 .....85 A4
Hengoed Cl 10 CF5 ...193 C4
Hengoed Cres CF82 ....84 F4
Hengoed Hall Cl CF82 84 F3
Hengoed Hall Dr CF82 84 F3
Hengoed Parc CF82 ....85 A3
Hengoed Prim Sch
CF82 ....84 F3
Hengoed Rd
Hengoed CF82 ....84 F3
Penpedairheol CF82 ...84 D6
Hengoed Sta CF82 ....85 A2
Henke Ct CF10 ......195 C3
Henllys CF3 ....133 E8
Henllys CW Sch NP44 ..88 F1
Henllys La NP44 .....115 F7
Henllys Rd CF23 .....178 C2
Henllys Village Rd
NP44 ....115 F8
Henllys Way
Cwmbran NP44 ....115 F8
Cwmbran NP44 ....89 E1
Henneuadd SA9 ......222 C7
Hennoyadd Rd SA9 ...222 C7
Henrhyd Falls SA10 ..222 C8
Henrietta St SA1 .....95 B6
Henry Morgan Cl
NP10 ....163 F6
Henry Richard St CF48 55 C8
Henry St Aberdare CF44 53 C8
Bargoed CF81 ....57 F4
Barry CF63 ....215 D6
Cardiff CF10 ....195 B3
Mountain Ash CF45 ....54 D3
Neath SA11 ....71 E6
Pontypridd CF37 ....109 A2
Henry Wood Cl NP19 144 C4
Henry Wood Wlk
NP19 ....144 C4
Henshaw St SA12 ....124 F8
Hensol Cl
Llanyravon NP44 ......90 A3
Rogerstone NP10 ....142 B6
Hensol Hospl CF72 ...173 D2
Hensol Rd CF72 .....173 C5
Hensol Villas CF72 ..173 E3
Henson St NP19 .....143 F3
Henwaun Bglws NP13 ..15 E3
Henwaun St NP13 .....15 E3
Henwysg Cl CF37 ....109 A2
Heol Aaron SA9 ....2 D8
Heol Abram SA9 ......2 D8
Heol Adam CF82 ......84 B8
Heol Adare CF32 .....150 D5
Heol Aer CF14 ......177 C8
Heol Alfred CF43 ......79 B8
Heol Amlwch CF14 ...177 B3
Heol Amman SA14 ....219 F8
Heol Aneurin
Caerphilly CF83 .....137 E6
Tonyrefail CF39 .....133 C5
Heol Ansurin Bevan
NP22 ....12 E5
Heol Ap Gethin NP23 ..15 E7
Heol Ap Pryce CF38 ..136 A6
Heol Aradur CF5 .....176 D3
Heol Arfryn CF23 ....129 E2
Heol Argoed SA18 ...219 C5
Heol Arthur Fear NP13 15 E5
Heol Aur CF14 ....41 C5
Heol Awstin SA5 ......67 E5
Heol Barcud SA7 ......70 B8
Heol Barri CF83 .....137 F5
Heol Bedw CF39 .....107 E2
Heol Bedwas SA7 .....47 A1

Heol Berllan
Caerphilly CF83 .....138 B5
Crynant SA10 ....226 A8
Heol Berry CF15 .....158 A3
Heol Beulah CF83 ....137 F8
Heol Billingsley CF15 157 F8
Heol Blakemore CF14 176 F5
Heol Bonymaen CF48 ..11 A6
Heol Booker CF14 ....176 F5
Heol Bradford CF32 ..129 E2
Heol Briallu SA6 .....45 F2
Heol Brithdir SA7 .....70 B8
Heol Briwnant CF14 ..159 B1
Heol Bro Wen CF83 ...138 B5
Heol Broadland CF62 214 E4
Heol Broch SA7 ....70 B8
Heol Brofiscin CF72 ..174 B7
Heol Bronallt SA4 .....19 A5
Heol Bronwen SA12 ....98 E1
Heol Broom CF33 ....165 E7
Heol Brown
Ammanford SA18 .....219 C5
Tycroes SA18 ....218 F5
Heol Brychan
Bargoed CF81 ....57 E3
Merthyr Tydfil CF48 ...10 A3
Heol Bryn CF33 .....165 E8
Heol Bryn Fab CF46 ...83 D3
Heol Bryn Glas CF38 156 D7
Heol Bryn Gwyn CF44 ..28 A6
Heol Bryn Hebog 4
CF38 ....156 D8
Heol Bryn Heulog
CF38 ....156 D8
Heol Bryn Man 1
CF38 ....225 F2
Heol Bryn Padell
CF48 ....225 F2
Heol Bryn Seion
SA10 ....222 F5
Heol Bryn Selu 2
CF48 ....225 F2
Heol Bryn-gwyn
SA13 ....227 C2
Heol Bryn-y-Gwyddyl
CF48 ....10 A3
Heol Brynbrain SA9 ..221 B8
Heol Bryncelyn SA14 ..41 C8
Heol Bryncwils CF32 .150 E3
Heol Bryncwtyn CF35 170 D6
Heol Bryncyn SA7 .....47 A1
Heol Brynglas
Bridgend CF31 ......169 A5
Cardiff CF14 ....177 A8
Gorseinon SA4 ....66 B8
Heol Bryngwili SA14 ..218 A7
Heol Brynhyfryd
CF38 ....156 B7
Heol Brynmor John
CF38 ....135 E1
Heol Brynna SA11 .....72 C5
Heol Brynnau CF44 ....28 C3
Heol Brynteg
Tonyrefail CF39 .....133 B4
Ystrad Mynach CF82 ..111 E8
Heol Brython SA7 .....93 B8
Heol Buckley SA15 ....40 E8
Heol Cadifor SA5 .....68 B6
Heol Cadnawes SA6 ....45 F4
Heol Cadrawd CF34 ...128 D6
Heol Cae Bach CF83 ..138 B5
Heol Cae Celynnen
CF83 ....138 B5
Heol Cae Copyn SA4 ...42 E1
Heol Cae Fan Heulog
CF83 ....138 B5
Heol Cae Glas CF32 ..150 F3
Heol Cae Gwyn CF83 ..137 E1
Heol Cae Maen CF83 ..138 B5
Heol Cae Rhosyn SA7 ..47 A1
Heol Cae Tynewydd
SA4 ....42 F1
Heol Cae-Defaid
CF34 ....102 C3
Heol Cae-Derwen
CF81 ....57 E3
Heol Cae-Glas SA7 ....69 F6
Heol Caeglas CF32 ...150 D5
Heol Caer Bont
Margam SA13 ....146 E7
Port Talbot SA13 ....147 A8
Heol Caerhys CF14 ...177 C7
Heol Caerlan CF38 ...155 F6
Heol Caerllion SA6 ....46 B5
Heol Calfin SA5 ......67 E4
Heol Cambrensis
CF34 ....102 C3
Heol Camddwr CF23 ..161 B1
Heol Camlan SA7 ......47 A1
Heol Camlas SA12 ....99 E6
Heol Canola CF32 ....150 F4
Heol Capel CF39 .....133 C6
Heol Cara Hir SA10 ..226 A8
Heol Caradoc
Bargoed CF81 ....57 E3
Penywaun CF44 ....28 C6
Heol Caredig SA11 ....49 D3
Heol Carnau CF5 .....193 D3
Heol Carne CF14 .....177 C4
Heol Carodog SA13 ...125 D7
Heol Castell CF32 ....149 A2
Heol Castell Coety
CF31 ....169 A8
Heol Cattwg
Cardiff CF14 ....177 B3
Gelligaer CF82 ......84 D6
Heol Catwg SA10 .....48 D2

Heol Cawrdaf CF38 ...156 A6
Heol Cefn On CF14 ...160 A3
Heol Cefn Ydfa
Coytrahen CF32 .....150 B8
Maesteg CF34 ......101 F1
Heol Cefn-yr Hendy
CF72 ....173 C7
Heol Cefni SA6 ....68 E3
Heol Ceiriog CF39 .....80 D1
Heol Celyn
Church Village CF38 ..135 F1
Cimla SA11 ....72 B6
Hengoed CF82 ....85 A3
Heol Celynen CF37 ...109 D6
Heol Cerdin CF34 ....128 D8
Heol Ceri SA5 ....66 D3
Heol Ceulanydd CF34 ..75 A2
Heol Chappell CF14 ..166 A7
Heol Claerwen NP23 ...7 B5
Heol Cleddau SA5 .....66 D3
Heol Cledwyn SA7 .....47 A1
Heol Clwyddau CF38 ..156 A5
Heol Clyd CF83 ......137 D5
Heol Coch CF31 .....169 D5
Heol Coed Cae CF14 ..177 C3
Heol Coed Leyshon
CF32 ....150 B8
Heol Coedcae CF81 ....57 E3
Heol Colforna CF46 ....83 C6
Heol Collen CF5 .....193 A2
Heol Coroniad CF38 ..156 A7
Heol Creigiau CF38,
CF15 ....156 D3
Heol Crochendy CF15,
CF37 ....136 E1
Heol Croes Faen
CF36 ....165 F1
Heol Cronfa CF37 ....109 F4
Heol Cropin SA14 .....41 C8
Heol Crwys SA4 ....43 B4
Heol Cumfferws
SA18 ....218 F6
Heol Cwarrel Clark
CF83 ....137 E7
Heol Cwm Ifor CF38 ..137 D6
Heol Cwm Mawr SA12 99 D6
Heol Cwrdy CF32 ....150 E4
Heol Cynan
Gorseinon SA4 ....43 B4
Pont Rhyd-y-cyff CF34 128 D6
Heol Cynllan CF72 ...154 A2
Heol Cynwyd CF34 ...128 D6
Heol Dafydd CF72 ....173 A7
Heol Dalycopa SA7 ....69 E6
Heol Daniel
Cwmllynfell SA9 ....221 B7
Llanelli SA14, SA15 ...40 F3
Heol Danyrodyn
CF15 ....157 C1
Heol Dderwen
Church Village CF38 ..136 A2
Llanelli SA15 ....40 F4
Heol Ddeusant CF38 ..155 F6
Heol Ddu
Ammanford SA18 .....219 D8
Beddau CF72 ....134 C1
Swansea SA5 ....68 B7
Tycroes SA18 ....218 F5
Heol Ddwr SA4 ....19 E7
Heol Deg CF38 ......136 A1
Heol Degwm CF33 ....165 E8
Heol Deiniol NP4 .....63 A5
Heol Dennant CF5 ...193 E8
Heol Derlwyn CF14 ...177 B8
Heol Derw
Brynmawr NP23 ....8 A5
Hengoed CF82 ....84 F3
Heol Derwen
Cimla SA11 ....72 B5
Pontypool NP4 ....63 A5
Heol Deva CF5 ......193 C3
Heol Dewi
Brynna CF72 ....153 C3
Hengoed CF82 ....85 A2
Heol Dewi Sant
Barry CF62 ....214 E5
Bettws CF32 ....129 D3
Penllergaer SA4 ......44 A2
Heol Dinbych SA15 ....40 F4
Heol Dolfain SA6 .....46 A4
Heol Dolwen CF14 ...177 C4
Heol Don CF14 ......176 F4
Heol Don Ct CF14 ...176 F4
Heol Dowlais CF38 ...156 E5
Heol Dowr SA4 ....19 E6
Heol Draenen Wen
CF5 ....193 A2
Heol Drewi CF33,CF36 165 E4
Heol Dulais SA7 ......47 A1
Heol Dwr SA18 ......219 E7
Heol Dwyrain CF31 ...169 A4
Heol Dyddwr SA11 ....49 D3
Heol Dyfan SA6 ....45 F3
Heol Dyfed
Beddau CF38 ....155 F6
Cardiff CF14 ....177 D5
Gorseinon SA4 ....43 B4
Maesteg CF34 ......102 D2
Penrhys CF43 ....80 A2
Penywaun CF44 ....28 C6
Heol Dyfodwg CF72 ..155 D4
Heol Dyhewydd CF38 156 B7
Heol Dylan
Gorseinon SA4 ....43 B4
North Cornelly CF33 ..165 F8
Heol Dynys SA5 ......67 E5
Heol Dywyll SA6 .....46 C7

Heol Ebwy CF5 ......193 D4
Heol Edward Lewis
CF82 ....84 C6
Heol Edwards CF15 ..158 A8
Heol Eglwys
Cardiff CF5 ....193 E4
Coelbren SA10 .....222 F6
Pen-y-fai CF31 .....150 C1
Ystradgynlais SA9 .....1 F1
Heol Eifion SA4 ......43 C2
Heol Eifion Wyn SA7 ..69 E6
Heol Eirlys SA6 ......45 F2
Heol Eithrim SA6 .....46 D8
Heol Elan NP23 ....7 B5
Heol Elfed
Gorseinon SA4 ....43 B4
Llanelli SA14 ....41 C5
Maesteg CF34 ......102 D2
Swansea SA7 ....69 E6
Heol Elli SA15 ....40 F5
Heol Emrys SA5 ......68 A5
Heol Erw-y-Rhos
CF83 ....138 B5
Heol Erwin CF14 ....159 C1
Heol Esgyn
Cardiff CF23 ....178 A6
Neath SA10 ....48 B1
Rhigos CF44 ....26 C8
Heol Evan Wynne
CF81 ....12 F1
Heol Ewenny CF35 ...170 D6
Heol Fach
Ammanford SA18 .....218 E8
Bargoed CF81 ....57 F2
Caerphilly CF83 .....137 E4
Nantgarw CF15 ......158 A8
North Cornelly CF33 ..165 F8
Pencoed CF35 ......170 D8
Sarn CF32 ....150 F4
Swansea SA5 ....68 C6
Swansea SA5 ....68 C6
Heol Faen CF34 .....102 D2
Heol Faenor CF38 ....155 F5
Heol Fair Sarn CF32 ..150 E3
Wick CF71 ....198 B5
Heol Fair CF5 ......194 A8
Heol Fargoed CF81 ....57 F2
Heol Fawr
Caerphilly CF83 .....137 D6
Nelson CF46 ....83 D2
North Cornelly CF33 ..166 A7
Tredomen CF46 ....84 A1
Heol Fechan CF31 ...168 B6
Heol Fedw
Cwmrhydyceirw SA6 ...46 A3
Swansea SA6 ....45 F3
Heol Felen SA18 ....220 B8
Heol Felyn Fach
CF32 ....150 C5
Heol Fer CF83 ......137 E6
Heol Ffaldau CF31 ...169 B6
Heol Ffion SA4 ......43 C2
Heol Fforest (Fforest
Road) SA4 ....19 B5
Heol Ffranc SA10 .....70 C6
Heol Ffrwd Philip
CF38 ....156 F5
Heol Ffynnon
Llanelli SA15 ....40 F4
Loughor SA4 ....42 E1
Heol Ffynnon Wen
CF14 ....176 F8
Heol Frank SA5 ......68 B5
Heol Gabriel CF14 ...177 C3
Heol Gadlys CF33 ....169 A7
Heol Gaer SA10 .....223 A5
Heol Gam
Bridgend CF31 ......168 E2
Pentyrch CF15 ......157 B1
Heol Ganol
Brynmawr NP23 ....8 B4
Caerphilly CF83 .....137 F3
Nant-y-Moel CF32 ...104 F6
Heol Gelli Lenor
CF34 ....101 F1
Heol Gelynen CF44 ....28 A6
Heol Gelynog 4
CF38 ....156 A6
Heol Ger-y-Felin
CF61 ....210 A7
Heol Gerrig SA5 ......68 C6
Heol Gethin CF82 .....85 A4
Heol Giedd SA9 ....1 F3
Heol Glan Elai CF72 ..173 A6
Heol Glan-Nant SA6 ...46 A4
Heol Glan-Yr-Afon
NP11 ....113 C3
Heol Glandulais CF23 160 F1
Heol Glanllechau SA8 .23 D1
Heol Glannant
Bettws CF32 ....129 D3
Tonypandy CF40 ....107 B1
Heol Glaslyn CF23 ...161 B1
Heol Glasnant SA2 ....93 F7
Heol Gledyr CF83 ....138 A3
Heol Gleien SA9 ......1 A2
Heol Glyn CF23 .....157 F5
Heol Glyn Derwen
SA10 ....48 C1
Heol Glyn-Dyfal SA5 ..20 C1
Heol Glyncoch CF39 ..132 C5
Heol Glyndernwen
SA8 ....23 C1
Heol Glynderwen
SA10 ....48 C1
Heol Glyndwr CF31 ...169 D6
Heol Goch CF15 .....157 E2
Heol Godfrey SA18 ..220 D8

Heol Goedog CF32 ...149 B2
Heol Goffa SA15 ......40 E7
Heol Goronwy CF39 ...80 D1
Heol Graig Wen CF83 137 E6
Heol Graig-Felen SA6 46 D8
Heol Groeswen CF37 136 D3
Heol Gron SA7 ....2 D8
Heol Gruffydd SA5 ....67 F5
Heol Grug SA6 ....45 E2
Heol Gwalia SA14 ....41 C5
Heol Gwanwyn SA7 ...69 F7
Heol Gwaun Rhos
CF83 ....138 B5
Heol Gwell SA5 ......68 D5
Heol Gwenallt SA4 ....43 B4
Heol Gwendoline
CF62 ....214 E4
Heol Gwent CF14 ....177 D5
Heol Gwernen
Cwmrhydyceirw SA6 ...46 A3
Swansea SA6 ....45 F3
Heol Gwili
Gorseinon SA4 ....43 B4
Llanelli SA14 ....41 D5
Swansea SA7 ....69 E6
Heol Gwilym CF5 ....176 D1
Heol Gwrangfryn CF44 26 C8
Heol Gwrgan
Beddau CF38 ....155 F6
Cardiff CF14 ....177 B5
Heol Gwyn Lliw NP23 ..7 F3
Heol Gwyndaf CF14 ..177 F7
Heol Gwynedd CF14 ..177 D5
Heol Gwynno CF72 ...155 D4
Heol Gwyrosydd SA5 ..68 B5
Heol Gwys SA9 ......221 C6
Heol Gyfinia CF62 ...214 F2
Heol Hafdy SA7 ......69 F7
Heol Harlech CF5 ....194 A8
Heol Harri Lewis CF46 83 D3
Heol Haulfryn CF39 ..133 B4
Heol Haydn SA18 ....219 B7
Heol Heddwch
Neath SA10 ....48 A1
Seven Sisters SA10 ..222 D3
Heol Helig NP23 ......8 A4
Seven Sisters SA10 ..222 C3
Heol Hendre
Bryn-côch SA10 ......48 C5
Cardiff CF14 ....177 D8
Heol Hensol CF38 ....156 A6
Heol Herbert SA11 ..226 D5
Heol Hermas SA5 .....68 B6
Heol Heulog CF39 ....132 B7
Heol Hir Cardiff CF14 ..159 F1
Gwaun-Cae-Gurwen
SA18 ....220 E6
Heol Homfray CF5 ...193 A3
Heol Hopcyn John
CF35 ....151 B2
Heol Horeb CF39 ....107 E2
Heol Iago CF81 ......32 D7
Heol Ida CF38 ......156 A7
Heol Iestyn CF14 ....177 B5
Heol Ifor CF14 .....177 C5
Heol Illtyd
Llantrisant CF72 ....155 D4
Neath SA10 ....48 D1
Heol Innes SA15 .....40 E8
Heol Ioan CF43 ......80 A2
Heol Isaf Brynmawr NP23 8 B4
Cardiff CF14 ....159 C1
Cimla SA11 ....72 C5
4 Cwmavon SA12 ....99 D5
Nelson CF46 ....83 F3
Pontypool NP4 ....63 A5
Radyr CF15 ....176 C5
Tonyrefail CF39 ....133 C2
Trelewis CF46 ....83 C8
Heol Isaf Hendy CF72 173 C7
Heol Iscoed
Cardiff CF14 ....177 C8
Efail Isaf CF38 .....156 E5
Heol Iscoed (Iscoed Road)
SA4 ....19 A4
Heol Islwyn
Gorseinon SA4 ....43 B4
Nelson CF46 ....83 D2
Tonyrefail CF39 ....133 C6
Heol Johnson CF72 ..155 C2
Heol Keir Hardie CF44 28 B5
Heol Klockner NP22 ..12 D4
Heol Laethog CF32 ...151 E5
Heol Las
Caerphilly CF83 .....137 E7
Coity CF35 ....169 D8
Cross Hands SA14 ...218 B8
Godrergraig SA8 ....221 A1
Llantrisant CF72 ....155 C4
Marshfield CF3 .....180 D6
North Cornelly CF33 ..165 E8
North Cornelly CF33 ..165 E8
Pencoed CF35 ......170 D8
Pontardawe SA8 ......24 A8
Tredomen CF46 .....111 B8
Wick CF71 ....198 A4
Heol Las Fawr SA10 ..226 A8
Heol Las Villas CF33 .165 E8
Heol Lewis
Caerphilly CF83 .....138 D5
Cardiff CF14 ....159 C1
Heol Llan Coity CF35 ..151 E3
North Cornelly CF33 ..165 E8
Heol Llanbedr CF5 ...191 E6
Heol Llangan CF14 ...177 B6

Heol Llangeinor
CF32 ....130 A3
Heol Llanishen Fach
CF14 ....177 C8
Heol Llansantffraid
CF32 ....150 E4
Heol Llechau CF39 ....80 D1
Heol Llidiard CF35 ...170 F1
Heol Llinos CF14 ....159 E4
Heol Llwyd
Ammanford SA18 .....219 B8
Ebbw Vale NP23 ......7 B5
Heol Llwyn Bedw SA4 .18 F4
Heol Llwyn Brain CF48 10 A3
Heol Llwyn Celyn
SA10 ....48 D2
Heol Llwyn Deri CF48 .10 A3
Heol Llwyn Drysi CF48 10 A3
Heol Llwyn Gollen
CF48 ....10 A3
Heol Llwyn Onnen
CF48 ....10 A3
Heol Llwyndyrus
CF34 ....128 C6
Heol Llwynon SA10 ...48 D2
Heol Llwynyffynnon
CF32 ....130 A3
Heol Llynfi NP23 ......7 B5
Heol Llyswen CF46 ....83 E4
Heol Lotwen SA18 ...218 D6
Heol Mabon
Cardiff CF14 ....177 C8
Cwmavon SA12 ......99 E6
Nelson CF46 ....83 D3
Heol Madoc
Cardiff CF14 ....177 C4
Pontypool NP4 ....63 A5
Heol Maendy
North Cornelly CF33 ..165 E8
Sarn CF32 ....150 F4
Heol Maes Eglwys SA6 45 E4
Heol Maes Eirwg 14
CF3 ....179 F6
Heol Maes Eiwrg
CF3 ....180 A6
Heol Maes y Cerrig
SA4 ....42 E1
Heol Maes-y-Dre SA9 ..1 F1
Heol Maes-y-Gelynen
SA6 ....45 F2
Heol Maes-yr-Haf
CF35 ....170 D6
Heol Maesbryn SA4 ...42 F1
Heol Maespica SA9 ....1 B2
Heol Mair
Bridgend CF31 ......150 F1
Penrhys CF43 ....80 A2
Heol Marlais SA18 ...219 B8
Heol Mathew CF14 ...176 F5
Heol Merioneth CF21 210 C6
Heol Merlin CF14 ....177 F7
Heol Meurig SA9 ......2 D1
Heol Miaren
Barry CF63 ....215 C8
Swansea SA6 ....45 F2
Heol Miles CF72 .....155 B2
Heol Miskin CF72 ...173 B7
Heol Moor CF62 .....214 B4
Heol Morfa
Llanelli SA15 ....40 F3
Pyle CF33 ....166 C8
Heol Morien CF46 .....83 D3
Heol Morlais SA4 .....18 F3
Heol Mostyn CF33 ...148 C1
Heol Muston CF5 ....193 D6
Heol Mwrwg SA14 ....42 B8
Heol Mwyrdy CF38 ...155 F6
Heol Mynydd
Church Village CF38 ..136 A1
Cowbridge CF71 ....189 F5
Pontypridd CF37 ....110 A4
Heol Nant
Church Village CF38 ..135 F1
Clyne SA11 ....226 B3
Cwmdare CF44 ....28 C3
North Cornelly CF33 ..165 E8
Pontypridd CF37 ....109 F4
Heol Nant Bran SA7 ...47 A2
Heol Nant Caiach
CF46 ....83 C6
Heol Nant Castan
CF14 ....177 B8
Heol Nant Gelli SA5 ..68 D5
Heol Nant-y-Felin
SA15 ....40 E2
Heol Nantgau CF48 ...10 A2
Heol Nedd SA11 .....227 B8
Heol Nest CF14 .....177 C5
Heol Neuadd CF33 ...166 A7
Heol Neuadd Domos
CF34 ....128 C8
Heol Newydd
Cardiff CF3 ....179 D4
Cefn Cribwr CF32 ...149 B2
Swansea SA5 ....67 F5
Heol Newydd (New Rd)
SA9 ....221 C7
Heol Norman 5
SA18 ....219 B7
Heol Onen NP23 ......8 A4
Heol Onnen CF33 ....165 E8
Heol Orchwy CF42 ....78 D7
Heol Padarn NP4 .....63 A5
Heol Pal CF62 ......214 F2
Heol Pandy CF32 ....129 F2
Heol Pant Glas SA11 227 B8
Heol Pant Gwyn
CF72 ....172 C5

Heol Pant Ruthin
CF35 ....170 D6
Heol Pant y Dwr SA4 ..42 F2
Heol Pant y Rhyn
CF14 ....176 F7
Heol Pantglas SA10 ...48 C5
Heol Pant-y-Gored
Creigiau CF15 ....175 A7
Pentyrch CF15 ....175 A7
Heol Pant-y-Lliw SA4 ..44 A6
Heol Pant-yr-Awel
CF32 ....130 D4
Heol Pantycelyn
Barry CF62 ....214 D4
Cardiff CF14 ....176 F7
Heol Pantyderi CF5 ..193 D4
Heol Parc Glas 🖪
CF48 ....225 F2
Heol Parc Maen CF48 ..10 A2
Heol Parc Mawr
SA14 ....218 C7
Heol Pardoe CF15 ....136 F1
Heol Pen y Cae SA4 ...42 F2
Heol Pen-Nant SA6 ....46 A4
Heol Pen-Rhiw'r Eglwys
NP12 ....58 E6
Heol Pen-Rhiw'r-Eglwys
NP12 ....58 F6
Heol Pen-Tir-Garw
SA5 ....67 F6
Heol Pen-y-Beili SA4 ..42 F2
Heol Pen-y-Bryn CF43 80 A2
Heol Pen-y-Coed
SA11 ....72 B5
Heol Pen-y-Foel
CF37 ....109 D6
Heol Pen-y-Parc
Llantrisant CF37 ....155 D3
Pontypridd CF37 .....109 D7
Heol Pen-y-Scallen
SA4 ....42 E1
Heol Penallta CF82 ...84 D6
Heol Penar SA5 ....68 B6
Heol Pencarreg
Bargoed CF81 ....57 F3
Cardiff CF14 ....177 B2
Heol Pencastell CF48 148 D2
Heol Pencerdd CF34 ..102 D2
Heol Pendarren CF44 ..26 C8
Heol Penderyn
Bridgend CF31 ....169 D6
Neath SA10 ....48 A1
Heol Pendyrus CF43 ...80 B3
Heol Penhydd SA13 ..100 E5
Heol Penlan
Cardiff CF14 ....176 F7
Neath SA10 ....48 A1
Neath Abbey SA10 .....71 A8
Heol Penllwyn CF15 ..157 B1
Heol Penmaen 🖪
CF72 ....155 D3
Heol Penmar CF5 .....193 D4
Heol Penprys SA14 ....41 E6
Heol Penrhiw
🖪 Merthyr Tydfil CF48 .225 F2
Mountain Ash CF45 ....54 B5
Heol Pentre CF34 ....101 F1
Heol Pentre Bach SA4 .42 F2
Heol Pentre Felin SA6 45 C1
Heol Pentre'r Cwrt
CF61 ....210 A7
Heol Pentre'r Felin
CF61 ....210 B7
Heol Pentwyn
Cardiff CF14 ....176 F7
Neath SA10 ....70 C6
Tonyrefail CF39 .....133 B4
Heol Pentyla
Sarn CF32 ....150 D3
Swansea SA7 ....69 F6
Heol Penyfai CF14 ...177 C4
Heol Peredur CF14 ...159 D2
Heol Persondy
Aberkenfig CF32 .....150 D3
Aberkenfig CF32 .....150 D4
Bettws CF32 ....129 D2
Heol Philip SA9 ......1 D1
Heol Phillip SA8 .....23 E3
Heol Pit-y-Ceiliogod
NP12 ....58 E2
Heol Plas Isaf SA14 ..42 B7
Heol Pont George
CF33 ....148 B2
Heol Pont y Seison
CF46 ....84 C2
Heol Pont-y-Cwcw
NP10 ....164 A5
Heol Pontprennau
CF23 ....160 F1
Heol Powis CF14 .....177 D5
Heol Poyston CF5 ....193 C3
Heol Pwllypant CF37 137 F6
Heol Pwllyplaca 🔢
CF3 ....179 F6
Heol Pymmer CF39 ...133 B4
Heol Rees CF82 ....85 A2
Heol Rhayader CF14 .176 E4
Heol Rheidol NP23 ....7 B5
Heol Rhos CF83 ......137 D3
Heol Rhos Las CF48 ..10 A3
Heol Rhosyn SA6 .....45 F2
Heol Rhuddos SA7 ....70 A7
Heol Rhyd SA6 ....22 B3
Heol Rhyd-Ddu-Fach
SA9 ....221 B8
Heol Rhyd-y-Bedd
CF48 ....11 A6

Heol Rhys CF44 ....53 F8
Heol Richard Price
CF32 ....129 E3
Heol Robart CF72 ....173 B7
Heol S O Davies CF48 .10 C1
Heol Saffrwm SA6 .....45 F2
Heol Sant Bridget
CF32 ....185 C2
Heol Scwrfa CF48 .....10 A3
Heol Seddon CF5 ....176 D2
Heol Seion SA14 ......42 B7
Heol Serth CF83 .....137 D5
Heol Seward CF38 ....155 F6
Heol Shon CF32 ......149 A2
Heol Shwlac CF32 ....198 A7
Heol Siloam NP23 .....7 E4
Heol Siloh SA15 ......40 C4
Heol Silyn CF44 ......28 C6
Heol Simonston
CF35 ....169 D7
Heol Sirhwi CF62 ....214 C6
Heol Solva CF5 ......193 E4
Heol Spencer CF32,
CF35 ....155 E1
Heol St Cattwg CF71 191 A6
Heol St Denys CF14 ..160 A3
Heol Stanllyd SA14 ..218 B7
Heol Sticil-y-Beddau 🔢
CF72 ....155 D3
Heol Stradling CF14 .177 B4
Heol Syr Lewis CF15 .176 B8
Heol Syr William SA13 75 D3
Heol Tabor SA12 .....199 E6
Heol Tai Mawr CF48 ...10 A3
Heol Taliesin SA12 ..199 F6
Heol Tasker CF46 .....83 D5
Heol Tawe SA9 ......222 D7
Heol Tegfryn CF33 ...148 B2
Heol Teifi NP23 ....7 B5
Heol Teifionydd CF43 ..80 A2
Heol Teilo NP4 ....63 A5
Heol Tewgoed SA12 ...99 E6
Heol Tir Coch CF38 ..156 E5
Heol Tir Du
Cwmrhydyceirw SA6 ...46 A3
Swansea SA6 ....45 F3
Heol Tir Gibbon CF43 137 E5
Heol Tir Gwaidd CF43 80 A3
Heol Tir Ton NP11 ...113 B3
Heol Tir-Lan SA11 ...223 C5
Heol Tirbach CF43 ...137 D6
Heol Tircoed SA4 .....44 B5
Heol Ton
North Cornelly CF33 .165 D6
Sarn CF32 ....150 F3
Tonyrefail CF39 .....133 B4
Heol Tonmaen SA11 ..226 E5
Heol Trane CF39 .....133 B4
Heol Tre Dwr CF31 ...169 B2
Heol Trecastell CF38 .142 A2
Heol Tredeg SA9 .....221 C6
Heol Treferig CF38 ..156 A6
Heol Treffynnon SA6 ..46 B5
Heol Trefgarne CF5 ..193 C3
Heol Trefor SA5 ......68 B6
Heol Trefrhiw SA18 ..219 A6
Heol Tregonig SA15 ...40 F2
Heol Treharne
Abergwynfi SA13 .....76 A6
Coytrahen CF32 .....150 B7
Heol Trelai CF5 .....193 C3
Heol Trelales CF32 ..167 F4
Heol Trenewydd CF5 .193 C3
Heol Treth CF33 .....148 C1
Heol Trewilliam CF40 107 B1
Heol Troeon Bach
SA4 ....218 D2
Heol Trostre CF3 ....179 F6
Heol Trubshaw SA15 ..40 E8
Heol Twrch SA9 ....1 B1
Heol Twyn Du CF48 ...10 A3
Heol Ty Aberaman
CF44 ....53 D6
Heol Ty Crwn CF83 ..138 B5
Heol Ty Ffynnon
CF23 ....160 F1
Heol Ty Gwyn
Bryn-côch SA10 ......48 C4
Maesteg CF34 ....101 F4
Heol Ty Gwyn Ind Est
CF34 ....101 F4
Heol Ty Maen CF34 ..136 D2
Heol Ty Mawr CF71 ..190 F6
Heol Ty Merchant
CF83 ....138 B5
Heol Ty Nant CF32 ..130 B4
Heol Ty'n y Coed
CF14 ....177 C8
Heol Ty'n-y-Cae
CF14 ....177 C6
Heol Ty'n-y-Garn
CF31 ....150 D2
Heol Ty-Gwyn CF83 ..112 A3
Heol Tyddyn CF83 ...137 D1
Heol Tydraw CF33 ...166 B8
Heol Tyle-Du CF42 ...78 D7
Heol Tylluan SA7 .....70 B8
Heol Tyllwyd CF39 ..133 D6
Heol Tyn-y-Waun
CF34 ....128 D6
Heol Tynewydd NP12 ..58 B4
Heol Tynygarn CF31 ..150 D2
Heol Tyr Brodya 🔢
CF10 ....195 A6
Heol Tyr-y-Llan CF81 ..58 B4
Heol Tysant CF31 ....169 A2
Heol Tywith CF34 ...102 A6

Heol Uchaf
Cardiff CF14 ....159 B1
Cimla SA11 ....72 C5
Hengoed CF82 ....84 F3
Hirwaun CF44 ....27 D7
Nelson CF46 ....83 F3
🖪 Penywaun CF44 .....28 A6
Heol Undeb
Beddau CF38 ....155 F6
Cwmavon SA12 ....99 F5
Heol Urban CF5 .....176 E2
Heol Valentine SA6 ...46 D8
Heol Waen NP23 ....7 B4
Heol Wallasey SA18 .219 C7
Heol Wastadwaun
CF35 ....170 C8
Heol Waun
Abersychan NP4 ......37 E4
Tonyrefail CF39 .....133 A4
Heol Waun Fawr
CF83 ....137 E1
Heol Waun Waelod
CF83 ....137 F1
Heol Waun Wen SA6 ..45 B1
Heol Waun y Nant
CF14 ....177 B3
Heol Wen CF14 ......177 B7
Heol Wernlas CF14 ..177 C4
Heol West Plas CF31,
CF35 ....169 B7
Heol Westfa SA14 .....40 F8
Heol Wil Hopcyn
CF34 ....128 D6
Heol Will George SA5 .66 E3
Heol William Trigg
CF32 ....103 E6
Heol Wyllt SA4 ....19 E4
Heol y Barcud CF14 .159 E4
Heol y Barna SA4 .....19 E4
Heol y Beddau CF83 .138 A2
Heol y Bedw-Hirion
NP12 ....58 D4
Heol y Berllan CF83 .148 B2
Heol y Bwlch SA12 ...99 C5
Heol y Caeau-Meinion
NP12 ....58 D4
Heol y Carnau CF83 .138 B5
Heol y Cawl CF71 ...187 E1
Heol y Cefn NP12 .....58 C2
Heol y Celyn SA7 .....46 D7
Heol y Clun CF38 ....155 F6
Heol y Cnap SA5 .....68 D5
Heol y Coed
Beddau CF38 ....155 F6
Glyncorrwg SA13 ....227 C2
Heol y Cwm CF15 ....176 A7
Heol y Cyw SA7 ......70 B8
Heol y Dderwen NP12 .85 C7
Heol y Delyn CF14 ..160 A2
Heol y Derw CF39 ...132 B7
Heol y Drudwen SA6 ..45 F5
Heol y Felin
Bettws CF32 ....129 E1
Fforest SA4 ....18 F5
Seven Sisters SA10 ..222 D4
Heol y Ffynon SA11 ..72 C5
Heol y Fran SA6 .....45 F5
Heol y Frenhines
CF64 ....206 A2
Heol y Gamlas CF15,
CF37 ....136 E1
Heol y Garn SA18 ...219 B4
Heol y Garth CF83 ..139 B3
Heol y Glyn
Tonyrefail CF39 .....133 C5
Treharris CF46 ....83 C6
Heol y Gors CF14 ...177 C3
Heol y Gwydde SA9 .222 E7
Heol y Gyfraith CF72 155 C2
Heol y Moch CF34 ...101 C3
Heol y Mynydd
Ammanford SA18 ....219 B3
Bargoed CF81 ....57 E3
Gorseinon SA4 ....43 D3
Heol y Nant
Gorseinon SA4 ....42 F3
Heol-y-Cyw CF35 ....152 B5
Heol y Nantlais SA4 ..43 B4
Heol y Onnen CF72 ..172 D5
Heol y Parc Hendy SA4 .18 F4
Pontardawe SA8 ......23 F3
Heol y Pentre CF15 ..157 C1
Heol y Pia CF83 .....137 E3
Heol y Pwca NP44 ....89 C6
Heol y Pwll CF15 ....157 F8
Heol y Rhosog CF3 ..179 D2
Heol y Twyni CF35 ..186 A4
Heol y Twyn CF39 ....80 D1
Heol y Waun
Pontlliw SA4 ....43 F7
Pontlottyn CF81 ......33 A8
Heol y Waunfach SA14 41 C8
Heol y Wern CF14 ...177 C8
Heol Ynys Ddu CF83 .137 E1
Heol Ynysawdre
CF32 ....150 E4
Heol Yr Afon
Bridgend CF31 ....168 E7
Glyncorrwg SA13 ....227 C2
Heol Yr Eglwys
Bryncethin CF32 ....151 A5
Coity CF35 ....169 C7
Heol Yr Eithen SA6 ...46 A3
Heol Yr Eryr
Cwmrhydyceirw SA6 ...46 A5
Swansea SA6 ....45 F5
Heol Yr Odyn CF15 ..157 F8

Heol yr Orsaf CF72 ..173 A7
Heol Yr Wylan SA6 ...45 F5
Heol yr Ysgol
Bedwas CF83 ....139 A6
Bridgend CF31 ....168 C5
Cefn-bryn-brain SA9 .221 B8
Heol Ysgawen SA2 ....94 C8
Heol Ysgubor CF31 ..158 E8
Heol Ysgyfarnog SA7 ..70 B8
Heol Ystwyth NP23 ....7 B5
Heol-Ael-y-Bryn NP23 ..7 C3
Heol-Cae-Globe SA4 ..65 F8
Heol-Cae-Gwrwen
SA18 ....220 D6
Heol-Croeserw SA13 ..75 D4
Heol-Croesty CF35 ...170 D6
Heol-Crwys SA12 .....99 E6
Heol-Fair CF36 ......183 A7
Heol-Jwbili SA12 .....99 E5
Heol-Las
Ammanford SA18 ....219 B6
Birchgrove SA7 ......46 F2
Heol-Las Cl SA7 .....46 F1
Heol-Pen-y-Bryn
CF83 ....158 E5
Heol-Tewdwr SA13 ...75 D4
Heol-Treventy SA14 .218 A8
Heol-Ty-Cribwr CF31 168 B6
Heol-Ty-Maen CF31 ..168 B6
Heol-Uchaf NP22 .....12 C5
Heol-wenallt SA11 ...227 B8
Heol-y- Bryn CF37 ...136 B6
Heol-y- Coed CF15 ..158 B8
Heol-y- Dail CF31 ...168 B6
Heol-y- Deiliaid
SA13 ....126 A1
Heol-y-Bardd CF31 ..168 C3
Heol-y-Beddau CF38 156 A7
Heol-y-Beiliau 🖪
CF72 ....155 D3
Heol-y-Berllan CF5 ..193 C3
Heol-y-Berth CF83 ..158 E8
Heol-y-Blodau CF31 .168 B5
Heol-y-Bont
Cardiff CF14 ....177 C7
Tondu CF32 ....150 E4
Heol-y-Bryn
Barry CF62 ....214 C2
Cardiff CF14 ....177 A7
Fochriw CF81 ....32 C8
Hendreforgan CF39 ..132 D5
Pentyrch CF15 ......157 B1
Pont Rhyd-y-cyff CF34 128 D6
Pontyclun CF72 .....173 C7
Rhigos CF44 ....26 C8
Sarn CF32 ....150 F3
Heol-y-Bryniau CF48 ..41 A4
Heol-y-Bwlch SA14 ...42 A2
Heol-y-Bwnsi CF15 ..136 F2
Heol-y-Cadno CF14 ..159 E3
Heol-y-Cae
Cefn Coed CF48 .....10 A4
Clydach SA6 ....46 D7
Pontarddulais SA4 ...19 E5
Heol-y-Capel
Bridgend CF35 ......169 F4
Porthcawl CF36 .....165 F1
Heol-y-Carw CF14 ..159 E3
Heol-y-Castell
Cardiff CF5 ....193 C3
Duffryn SA13 ....74 D4
Pant CF48 ....11 A7
Heol-y-Cawl
Corntown CF35 ......186 C4
Dinas Powys CF64 ..206 A3
Heol-y-Coed
Cardiff CF14 ....177 A7
Llantwit Major CF61 .210 A5
Pontarddulais SA4 ...19 E5
Pontyclun CF72 .....173 C8
Wyllie NP12 ....85 F1
Heol-y-Coed Rise
CF31 ....169 A5
Heol-y-Coedcae SA21 B27
Heol-y-Craig SA10 ..226 A7
Heol-y-Cwm CF83 ...137 F1
Heol-y-Cyw Prim Sch
CF35 ....152 B5
Heol-y-Dderwen
CF15 ....158 B8
Heol-y-Ddol CF83 ...138 B5
Heol-y-De CF44 ......26 C8
Heol-y-Deiliaid SA13 121 F1
Heol-y-Delyn CF14 ..160 B3
Heol-y-Deri
Capel Hendre SA14 .218 C5
Cardiff CF14 ....177 B7
Cwmrhydyceirw SA6 ..46 A3
Pontypridd CF37 ....109 D7
Swansea SA6 ....45 F3
Heol-y-Deryn SA13 .227 C2
Heol-y-Dre SA14 ....218 A8
Heol-y-Dreflan CF83 138 B5
Heol-y-Fagwr SA6 ...22 F1
Heol-y-Fedw SA13 ...75 D4
Heol-y-Fedwen
Church Village CF38 .136 A2
Nant-y-Moel CF32 ...104 F6
Heol-y-Felin
Abergwynfi SA13 .....75 F6
Ammanford SA18 ....219 C6
Blaengwrach SA11 ..227 B8
Caerphilly CF83 .....137 F3
Cardiff CF14 ....177 C7
Cardiff CF5 ....193 E6
Cefn Hengoed CF82 ..84 C5
Heol-y-Cyw CF35 ....152 B6

Heol-y-Felin continued
Llantwit Major CF61 .210 A5
Neath SA10 ....48 D2
Penllergaer SA4 .....44 B2
Pontyclun CF72 .....173 A7
Heol-y-Ffin CF31 ....168 C4
Heol-y-Fforest CF14,
CF15, cf83 ....158 E3
Heol-y-Ffowndri
SA18 ....219 C7
Heol-y-Ffynnon CF38 156 F6
Heol-y-Ffynon CF43 ..80 A2
Heol-y-Foel
Cwmavon SA12 ......99 F8
Llantwit Fardre CF38 .156 D8
Heol-y-Foelas CF31 .168 C5
Heol-y-Forlan CF14 .177 A6
Heol-y-Frenhines
CF31 ....168 C5
Heol-y-Fro
Church Village CF38 .135 E1
Llantwit Major CF61 .210 A7
Heol-y-Gadarn SA13 ..74 E4
Heol-y-Gaer
Barry CF62 ....214 B2
Cardiff CF5 ....193 C3
Heol-y-Geifr
Pencoed CF35 ....170 D7
Swansea SA5 ....45 B2
Heol-y-Gelli
Aberdare CF44 ....53 B5
Penllergaer SA4 .....43 F2
Heol-y-Gerddi CF35 .152 D1
Heol-y-Glo Pyle CF33 148 C5
Tonna SA11 ....49 E3
Heol-y-glyn
Cymmer SA13 ....75 C7
Glynneath SA11 .....223 D1
Heol-y-Goedlan SA9 .221 B6
Heol-y-Goedwig
CF36 ....183 A8
Heol-y-Gog SA4 ......66 B5
Heol-y-Gogledd
CF83 ....137 E6
Heol-y-Gors
Caerphilly CF83 .....138 B5
Gwaun-Cae-Gurwen
SA18 ....220 D5
Nantgarw CF15 .....158 B8
Pyle SA13 ....147 C6
Swansea SA1,SA5 ....68 A2
Heol-y-Graig
Blaengwrach SA11 ..227 B8
Clydach SA6 ....46 D7
Llanelli SA14 ....41 E4
Llantrisant CF72 ...155 D3
Penrhys CF43 ....80 A3
Porthcawl CF36 .....183 D8
Rhigos CF44 ....224 B1
Tonna SA11 ....49 D3
Ystrad Mynach CF82 111 E8
Heol-y-Groes
Bridgend CF31 ......150 F1
Pencoed CF35 ....170 D4
Pontarddulais SA4 ...19 E5
Heol-y-Grug CF39 ...132 D5
Heol-y-Gwaudd SA9 .222 A4
Heol-y-Gwrgan SA13 125 E3
Heol-y-Llan SA4 .....65 E8
Heol-y-Llwynan SA8 ..23 B1
Heol-y-Llwyni CF34 .102 C2
Heol-y-Llyfrall CF32 .150 C4
Heol-y-Maes
Llantwit Fardre CF38 .156 D7
Pontardulais SA4 ....19 E5
Heol-y-Mynach CF37 ..81 E3
Heol-y-Mynydd
Aberdare CF44 ....28 F1
Bryn SA4 ....41 F6
Cefn Coed CF48 .....10 A5
Glyncorrwg SA13 ....227 C2
Hendreforgan CF39 ..132 D5
Sarn CF32 ....150 F3
Ystrad CF41 ....79 C3
Heol-y-Nant
Baglan SA12 ....98 E4
Barry CF63 ....215 A7
Blaengwynfi SA13 ...76 B6
Bridgend CF31 ......168 D5
Caerphilly CF83 .....137 F3
Cardiff CF14 ....177 B6
Clydach SA6 ....46 E8
Llandow CF71 ....199 A7
Maesteg CF34 ....102 D2
Neath SA10 ....48 D2
Pontardawe SA8 .....24 B3
Sarn CF32 ....150 F4
Taffs Well CF15 .....157 F3
Heol-y-Parc
Aberdare CF44 ....29 C3
Caerphilly CF83 .....138 A3
Cardiff CF14 ....161 A4
Cefneithin SA14 ....218 A8
Cwmavon SA12 ....99 D5
Efail Isaf CF38 .....156 F6
Evanstown CF39 ....132 D7
North Cornelly CF33 .166 A8
Pentyrch CF15 ......175 B7
Pontlliw SA4 ....44 A7
Heol-y-Pavin CF5 ...177 A1
Heol-y-Plas SA4 .....18 F6
Heol-y-Plwyf CF37 ...81 F2
Heol-y-Rhedyn SA6 ..45 E2
Heol-y-Rhos CF31 ...169 A5
Heol-y-Sarn CF72 ...155 D5
Heol-y-Sheet
North Cornelly CF33 .166 C5
North Cornelly CF33 .166 C6
Heol-y-Slough CF32 .185 B2

Heol-y-Splot CF33 ...166 C5
Heol-y-Twyn
Cwmdare CF44 ....28 C4
Pontlliw SA4 ....43 F7
Rhymney NP22 ....12 E6
Heol-y-Tyla SA13 .....74 E4
Heol-y-Waun
Cardiff CF14 ....177 B3
Gelligaer CF82 ....84 C6
Penrhys CF43 ....80 A3
Pontarddulais SA4 ...19 D5
Seven Sisters SA10 ..222 D4
Heol-y-Wern
Caerphilly CF83 .....138 B5
Loughor SA4 ....65 E8
Neath SA10 ....48 D1
Nelson CF46 ....83 F4
Heol-y-Wyrddol
SA18 ....219 B8
Heol-Yr-Afael SA13 ..74 E4
Heol-Yr-Afon CF32 ..150 D5
Heol-Yr-Efail CF14 ..177 D7
Heol-Yr-Enfys CF31 .168 B6
Heol-Yr-Eos SA4 .....43 F2
Heol-yr-Haul CF72 ..174 C7
Heol-yr-Odyn CF5 ...193 E4
Heol-yr-Onen CF83 .137 F3
Heol-yr-Onnen
Bridgend CF31 ......168 B4
Pencoed CF35 ....170 E7
Heol-Yr-Orsaf CF33 .148 D3
Heol-yr-Orsedd
SA13 ....125 D6
Heol-yr-Ynys CF15 .158 B2
Heol-yr-Ysbyty CF83 137 E1
Heol-yr-Ysgol
Cefneithin SA14 ....218 A8
Ebbw Vale NP23 ......14 B7
Pont Rhyd-y-cyff CF34 128 D6
St Brides Major CF32 .185 C2
Tondu CF32 ....150 D5
Heolaelfryn CF32 ....130 E4
Heoldu Ave CF81 .....57 E4
Heolddu Comp Sch (Ysgol
Gyfun Heol-ddu)
CF81 ....57 E4
Heolddu Cres CF81 ...57 F4
Heolddu Dr CF81 .....57 F4
Heolddu Gn CF81 .....57 F4
Heolddu Gr CF81 .....57 F4
Heolddu Rd
Bargoed CF81 ....57 F4
Gelligross NP12 ......85 F2
Heolganol CF32 .....150 E4
Heolgerrig
Abertillery NP13 ....36 B5
Heolgerrig CF48 .....10 A1
Merthyr Tydfil CF48 ..29 F8
Heolgerrig Sch CF48 ..30 A8
Heoltynton CF32 ....130 A3
Heolyffin SA8 ....23 B1
Herbert Av NP11 ....141 C8
Herbert Cl CF3 .....180 E3
Herbert Dr 🔢 CF83 .137 F5
Herbert March Cl
CF5 ....176 D3
Herbert Rd Neath SA11 71 D5
Newport NP19 ......143 D6
Herbert St
Abercynon CF45 .....82 E2
Aberdare CF44 ....29 A1
Barry CF63 ....215 A2
Blaengarw CF32 .....103 E7
Bridgend CF31 ......169 A5
Cardiff CF10 ....195 B4
Cardiff CF14 ....177 L1
New Tredegar NP24 ..34 A1
Newbridge NP11 .....60 D2
🔢 Newport NP20 ...143 C3
Pontardawe SA8 .....23 E4
Treherbert CF42 ......51 B3
Treorchy CF42 ....78 D6
Herbert Terr
Newbridge NP11 ......60 D2
🖪 Penarth CF64 ....207 A4
Herbert Thompson Jun &
Inf Sch CF5 ....193 C3
Herbert's Cl NP4 .....37 E6
Herbert's Rd NP4 .....37 E6
Hereford Ct NP18 ...118 A3
Hereford Rd NP23 .....7 E3
Hereford St
Cardiff CF11 ....194 E4
Newport NP19 ......143 D6
Heritage Ct CF47 .....10 E2
Heritage Dr CF62 ...214 D5
Heritage Pk CF3 ....179 F8
Hermon Cl CF48 ......11 A4
Hermon Hill CF15 ...158 C1
Hermon Rd CF34 ....102 A8
Hermon St CF42 ......78 E6
Herne St SA11 ....71 B1
Hernston La CF31 ..168 F1
Heron Ave SA15 ......40 B5
Heron Rd CF3 ....179 C3
Heron Way NP10 ....163 F7
Herons Way
Caerphilly CF83 .....137 E1
Neath SA10 ....48 B1
Heronsbridge Sch
CF31 ....168 F2
Herrick Pl CF3 ......139 D7
Hertford Pl NP19 ...143 F6
Heulwen Cl CF48 .....11 A6

Heulwen Clos CF15 . . .**158** A6
Hewell Ct CF11 . . . .**194** F2
Hewell St Cardiff CF11 **194** F2
  Penarth CF64 . . . .**206** F5
Hewson St SA1 . . . .**95** B8
Hibbert Rd SA11 . . . .**71** F8
Hibiscus Ct CF38 . . . . . .**156** C5
Hick St SA15 . . . .**40** D4
Hickman Rd CF44 . . . . . .**207** A4
Hickman St CF48 . . . .**31** A4
Hickory Ct **5** CF24 . . .**195** D5
High Bank CF23 . . . .**161** B2
High Banks NP19 . . . .**143** E5
High Cl Llanyravon NP44 **90** B1
  Nelson CF46 . . . .**83** E3
High Cnr CF15 . . . .**157** C1
High Croft Wlk CF3 . .**179** B4
High Cross Cl NP10 . .**142** C4
High Cross Dr NP10 . .**142** C4
High Cross Jun & Inf Sch
  NP10 . . . .**142** C5
High Cross La NP10 . .**142** C4
High Mdw CF61 . . . .**209** F5
High Row CF45 . . . .**54** C5
High St Abercarn NP11 **114** C4
  Aberdare CF44 . . . .**29** A2
  Abergwynfi SA13 . . . .**76** C5
  Abersychan NP4 . . . .**37** E6
  Abersychan NP4 . . . .**37** F3
  Abertillery NP13 . . . .**36** B5
  Abertillery NP13 . . . .**36** C3
  Abertillery NP13 . . . .**60** C6
  Abertridwr CF83 . . . .**137** A8
  Argoed NP12 . . . .**58** F5
  Bargoed CF81 . . . .**58** A4
  Bedlinog CF46 . . . .**56** A7
  Blackwood NP12 . . . .**58** F1
  Blackwood NP12 . . . .**85** E7
  Blaenavon NP4 . . . .**17** C6
  Blaengwrach SA11 . . . .**227** B8
  Blaina NP13 . . . .**15** D5
  Caerleon NP18 . . . .**118** B2
  Cardiff CF10 . . . .**195** A5
  Cardiff CF5 . . . .**194** A8
  Cefn Coed CF48 . . . .**10** A4
  Clydach SA6 . . . .**46** E7
  Cowbridge CF71 . . . .**188** E2
  Cwmavon SA12 . . . .**99** D5
  Cwmfelinfach NP11 . . . .**113** A5
  Dowlais CF48 . . . .**11** C4
  Ebbw Vale NP23 . . . .**14** D6
  Ferndale CF43 . . . .**79** F6
  Fleur De Lis NP12 . . . .**85** B6
  Gilfach Goch CF39 . . . . .**132** C7
  Glanaman SA18 . . . .**220** A8
  Glynneath SA11 . . . .**223** D1
  Gorseinon SA4 . . . .**43** C2
  Grovesend SA4 . . . .**43** C6
  Heol-y-Cyw CF35 . . . . . .**152** B5
  Hirwaun CF44 . . . .**27** D8
  Laleston CF32 . . . .**167** F4
  Llanbradach CF83 . . . . .**111** F1
  Llanelli SA15 . . . .**40** C4
  1 Llantrisant CF72 . . .**155** D3
  Llantwit Major CF61 . . .**209** F7
  Maesteg CF34 . . . .**102** A5
  Merthyr Tydfil CF47 . . . .**10** D1
  Merthyr Tydfil CF47 . . . .**10** F3
  Mountain Ash CF45 . . . . .**30** F4
  Mountain Ash CF45 . . . . .**54** D3
  Neath SA10 . . . .**70** F7
  Neath SA11 . . . .**71** E8
  Nelson CF46 . . . .**83** C3
  New Tredegar NP24 . . . . .**33** C5
  Newbridge NP11 . . . .**86** C5
  Newbridge NP11 . . . .**86** F6
  Newport NP20 . . . .**143** C5
  Ogmore Vale CF32 . . . . .**104** E1
  Penarth CF64 . . . .**207** A5
  Pengam NP12 . . . .**85** B8
  Penydarren CF47 . . . .**10** E2
  Pontardawe SA8 . . . .**23** E5
  Pontardawe SA8 . . . .**23** F3
  Pontarddulais SA4 . . . . . .**19** C5
  Pontlottyn CF81 . . . .**12** F1
  Pontneddfechan SA11 .**223** F2
  Pontyclun CF72 . . . .**172** F6
  Pontycymer CF32 . . . . . .**103** F3
  Pontypool NP4 . . . .**62** B6
  Pontypool NP4 . . . .**62** E3
  Pontypridd CF37 . . . . . .**135** C8
  Port Talbot SA13 . . . .**99** B1
  Porth CF39 . . . .**107** E2
  Pyle CF32,CF33 . . . .**148** E2
  Rhymney NP22 . . . .**12** E4
  Senghenydd CF83 . . . . .**110** F2
  Seven Sisters SA10 . . . .**222** C3
  Tonypandy CF40 . . . .**106** B6
  Tonyrefail CF39 . . . .**133** C5
  Trelewis CF46 . . . .**83** C7
  Treorchy CF42 . . . .**78** E6
  Ynysddu NP11 . . . .**112** F6
  Ynysybwl CF37 . . . .**81** F1
High Street (Stryd Fawr)
  SA1 . . . .**95** D8
High Street Arc **6**
  CF10 . . . .**195** A5
High Street Jun & Inf Sch
  CF62 . . . .**214** E4
High Street Prim Sch
  CF62 . . . .**214** E4
High Street Sta CF62 . . .**95** D8
High Trees CF48 . . . .**10** B7

High View
  Bridgend CF31 . . . .**168** F5
  Swansea SA1 . . . .**95** C1
High View Gdns SA2 . . . .**94** B2
High View Way CF37 . .**109** D5
High Way The NP4 . . . . . .**63** A4
Highbridge Cl CF64 . .**216** C4
Highbury Cl SA5 . . . .**68** B2
Highbury Cres CF31 . .**168** C6
Highbury Dr NP12 . . . . . .**85** E6
Highbury Pl CF5 . . . .**193** B4
Highbury Rd CF5 . . . . . .**193** C5
Highcliffe Ct SA3 . . . . . .**122** F4
Highcroft Rd NP20 . . . .**143** A6
Highcross Rd NP10 . . .**142** C5
Highdale Cl CF72 . . . . .**155** E2
Highfield Ferndale CF43 **79** D8
  Gorseinon SA4 . . . .**66** A8
  9 Penarth CF64 . . . . . .**207** B4
  Penperlleni NP4 . . . .**39** E7
Highfield Ave
  Bridgend CF31 . . . .**168** F8
  Porthcawl CF36 . . . .**182** F6
Highfield Cl
  Caerleon NP18 . . . .**117** F4
  Church Village CF38 . . . .**136** A1
  Dinas Powys CF64 . . . . .**206** C4
  Neath SA10 . . . .**48** E2
  Pontypool NP4 . . . .**37** F1
  Porthcawl CF36 . . . .**182** F6
  Risca NP11 . . . .**114** F2
  Sarn CF32 . . . .**150** E3
  Tredegar NP22 . . . .**6** C2
Highfield Cres
  Aberbargoed CF81 . . . . .**58** B6
  Bryn NP12 . . . .**85** E3
Highfield Ct
  Bassaleg NP10 . . . .**141** F3
  Porthcawl CF36 . . . .**182** F6
Highfield Gdns NP10 **141** F3
Highfield Ind Est CF43 **79** D7
Highfield La NP10 . . . .**141** F3
Highfield Pl CF32 . . . .**150** E3
Highfield Rd
  Barry CF62 . . . .**214** D7
  Bassaleg NP10 . . . .**142** A3
  Briton Ferry SA11 . . . . . .**71** B2
  Bryn NP12 . . . .**85** E3
  Caerleon NP18 . . . .**117** F4
  Cardiff CF14 CF23 . . . . .**178** A4
  Glanaman SA18 . . . .**220** C8
  Newport NP20 . . . .**142** E3
Highfield Terr
  Llanelli SA15 . . . .**40** E4
  2 Pontypridd CF37 . . .**109** B1
Highfield Way NP18 .**117** F4
Highfields
  Bridgend CF31 . . . .**169** B5
  Cardiff CF5 . . . .**176** F2
Highfields Holiday Pk
  SA3 . . . .**231** A4
Highfields Way NP12 . .**85** D5
Highgrove CF71 . . . .**189** D8
Highland Ave CF32 . . .**151** A6
Highland Cl
  Merthyr Tydfil CF47 . . . .**30** E8
  Neath SA10 . . . .**70** F8
  Sarn CF32 . . . .**150** E3
Highland Cres
  Dyffryn Cellwen SA10 .**223** A5
  Pontllanfraith NP12 . . . . .**86** A4
Highland Ct CF32 . . . .**151** A6
Highland Gdns SA10 . .**48** A1
Highland Gr NP44 . . . . .**89** E6
Highland Pl
  Aberdare CF44 . . . .**28** E1
  Bridgend CF31 . . . .**168** F5
  Ogmore Vale CF32 . . . . .**104** E1
Highland Terr
  Blackwood NP12 . . . .**85** E7
  Pontarddulais SA4 . . . . . .**19** E3
Highland View CF47 . . .**30** E8
Highlands Cardiff CF3 .**179** A2
  Tonyrefail CF39 . . . .**133** D6
Highlands Cl CF39 . . . .**133** C6
Highlands Cres NP23 . . .**7** E4
Highlands Rd NP23 . . . . .**7** E4
Highlands The SA10 . . .**71** A8
Highlight La
  Barry CF62 . . . .**214** C7
  Barry CF62 . . . .**214** C8
Highmead Ave
  Llanelli SA15 . . . .**40** E4
  Mumbles SA3 . . . .**122** E6
Highmead Cl SA3 . . . .**122** E6
Highmead Rd CF5 . . . .**193** D5
Highmoor SA1 . . . .**95** D5
Highpool Cl SA3 . . . . .**122** E5
Highpool La SA3 . . . . .**122** E5
Hightree Rise NP12 . . .**86** A4
Highview Rd CF44 . . . .**206** F5
Highwalls Ave CF64 . .**206** A3
Highwalls End CF64 . .**206** A3
Highwalls Rd CF64 . . .**206** A3
Highway The
  Croesyceiliog NP44 . . . . .**90** B5
  Cwmbran NP44 . . . .**116** D4
Hilary Rd NP11 . . . .**87** B8
Hilary Way CF36 . . . . . .**165** E2
Hilda St Barry CF62 . . .**214** E4
  Pontypridd CF37 . . . . . .**135** E5
Hiles Rd CF5 . . . .**193** C5
Hileys Row NP7 . . . .**9** E7
Hill Cres NP23 . . . .**8** B4
Hill Crest
  Brynmawr NP23 . . . .**8** B4
  Mumbles SA3 . . . .**123** B4

Hill Dr CF38 . . . .**156** D7
Hill Flats NP4 . . . .**62** B6
Hill Head NP4 . . . .**62** B6
Hill Ho **10** CF45 . . . .**54** E1
Hill House Hospl SA12 .**94** D8
Hill Rd
  Abertysswg NP22 . . . .**33** C8
  Neath Abbey SA10 . . . . . .**71** A4
  Pontlottyn CF81 . . . .**12** E1
Hill Side CF45 . . . .**81** B8
Hill Side Rd NP4 . . . .**62** D3
Hill Side St CF41 . . . .**78** F5
Hill St Abercarn NP11 . .**87** B4
  Abercynon CF45 . . . .**82** D1
  Aberdare CF44 . . . .**53** C7
  Abertillery NP13 . . . .**36** B4
  Bargoed CF81 . . . .**57** F5
  Barry CF63 . . . .**215** B5
  Blaenavon NP4 . . . .**17** C6
  Briton Ferry SA11 . . . . . .**71** C1
  Brynmawr NP23 . . . .**8** A1
  Deri CF81 . . . .**57** C8
  Ebbw Vale NP23 . . . .**14** E1
  Gowerton SA4 . . . .**66** B5
  Hendreforgan CF39 . . . .**132** C5
  Maerdy CF43 . . . .**52** A1
  Maesteg CF34 . . . .**102** A6
  Mumbles SA3 . . . .**123** C4
  Nant-y-Moel CF32 . . . . .**104** F5
  Newbridge NP11 . . . .**86** F6
  Newport NP20 . . . .**143** C4
  Ogmore Vale CF32 . . . . .**104** E2
  8 Penarth CF64 . . . . . .**207** B5
  Pontypool NP4 . . . .**62** A8
  Pontypool NP4 . . . .**62** E3
  Resolven SA11 . . . .**226** C4
  Rhymney NP22 . . . .**12** F3
  Risca NP11 . . . .**115** A1
  Swansea SA1 . . . .**95** C8
  Tonypandy CF40 . . . .**106** F4
  Treherbert CF42 . . . .**50** F2
  Treorchy CF42 . . . .**78** B6
  Troedyrhiw CF48 . . . .**31** B1
  Ystrad Mynach CF82 . . . .**84** E2
Hill Terr Aberavon SA12 **99** B2
  Penarth CF64 . . . .**206** F5
  Wenvoe CF5 . . . .**204** F8
Hill Top NP44 . . . .**89** D2
Hill View Beddau SA18 .**156** A6
  Bridgend CF31 . . . .**168** A5
  Bryn NP12 . . . .**85** E4
  Cardiff CF5 . . . .**193** C8
  Cwmfelinfach NP11 . . . .**113** B4
  Hengoed CF82 . . . .**85** A2
  Maesycwmmer CF82 . . . .**85** B1
  Pencoed CF35 . . . .**170** B8
  Pontycymer CF32 . . . . . .**103** E4
  Pyle CF33 . . . .**148** C2
  Swansea SA3 . . . .**97** B8
  Tredegar NP22 . . . .**13** F5
Hill View Cres SA6 . . . .**68** D8
Hill's St CF10 . . . .**195** A5
Hill-Snook Rd CF5 . . .**193** C4
Hilla Rd NP20 . . . .**143** A4
Hilland Dr SA3 . . . .**122** B6
Hillary Cl CF14 . . . .**159** F1
Hillary Ho SA11 . . . .**71** D8
Hillary Mews **13** CF63 **215** B6
Hillary Rise
  Abercarn NP11 . . . .**114** C6
  Barry CF63 . . . .**215** B6
Hillbrook Cl
  Aberdare CF44 . . . .**53** B7
  Waunarlwydd SA5 . . . .**66** D3
Hillcot Cl CF14 . . . . . .**160** A2
Hillcrest
  Abersychan NP4 . . . .**37** E6
  Brynna CF72 . . . .**153** E3
  Caerleon NP18 . . . .**117** F4
  Merthyr Tydfil CF47 . . . . .**10** F4
  Pen-y-fai CF31 . . . .**150** D1
  Pontypool NP4 . . . .**63** B4
Hillcrest Ave CF44 . . . .**53** B7
Hillcrest Cl CF14 . . . . .**159** F1
Hillcrest Dr CF39 . . . .**107** F2
Hillcrest Rd NP4 . . . .**62** F5
Hillcrest View
  Abertillery NP13 . . . .**36** B7
  Maerdy CF43 . . . .**79** C8
Hillcroft Cres SA13 . . .**75** D3
Hillfort Cl CF5 . . . .**193** D3
Hillgrove SA3 . . . .**122** E4
Hillrise Abersychan NP4 **37** F5
  Cardiff CF23 . . . .**178** D5
Hillrise Pk SA6 . . . .**46** C7
Hillsboro CF11 . . . .**168** C5
Hillsboro Pl CF36 . . . .**182** F6
Hillside
  Caerphilly CF83 . . . .**138** B1
  Cwmdare CF44 . . . .**28** D3
  Fochriw CF81 . . . .**32** D8
  Llanelli SA15 . . . .**40** C7
  Loughor SA4 . . . .**42** E1
  Neath SA11 . . . .**71** F6
  Newbridge NP11 . . . .**60** A1
  Pantyrawel NP12 . . . . . .**130** D4
  Pen-y-fai CF31 . . . .**150** D1
  Risca NP11 . . . .**115** A1
Hillside Ave
  Abertridwr CF83 . . . .**136** E7
  Blaenavon NP4 . . . .**17** D7
  Llanharan CF72 . . . .**154** A3
  Markham NP12 . . . .**58** D5
Hillside Cl
  Aberfan CF48 . . . .**55** C5
  Barry CF63 . . . .**215** C6
Hillside Cres
  Rogerstone NP10 . . . . .**142** B4

Hillside Cres continued
  Swansea SA2 . . . .**95** A7
Hillside Ct
  Cardiff CF24 . . . .**178** C1
  Cwmbran NP44 . . . .**89** D5
  Llantwit Fardre CF38 . . .**156** C6
Hillside Day Hospl
  NP22 . . . .**13** E6
Hillside Dr
  Cowbridge CF71 . . . .**188** F1
  Pontypool NP4 . . . .**62** C4
Hillside Gdns CF81 . . .**57** F2
Hillside Gn CF31 . . . . .**150** D1
Hillside Pk CF81 . . . . . .**57** F2
Hillside Prim Sch NP4 **17** D7
Hillside Rd CF39 . . . . .**133** D5
Hillside Terr
  Abertillery NP13 . . . .**60** C6
  Bedwas CF83 . . . .**138** E6
  Blackwood NP12 . . . .**85** E7
  Deri CF81 . . . .**33** A2
  Ebbw Vale NP23 . . . .**14** F2
  Pantyrawel CF32 . . . . . .**130** D4
  Pontypridd CF37 . . . . . .**109** C2
  Ton Pentre CF41 . . . .**79** B2
  Tonypandy CF40 . . . .**106** E7
  Tredomen CF82 . . . .**84** D1
  Wattstown CF39 . . . .**107** D8
Hillside View
  Bargoed CF81 . . . .**57** F2
  Pontypridd CF37 . . . . . .**109** B2
Hilltop Ave CF37 . . . . .**109** F3
Hilltop Cl Baglan SA12 .**98** F6
  Treharris CF46 . . . .**83** A6
Hilltop Cres
  Newbridge NP11 . . . .**87** A7
  Pontypridd CF37 . . . . . .**109** E1
Hilltop Gn NP44 . . . .**89** C5
Hilltop Sh Ctr NP23 . . .**14** C8
Hillview NP20 . . . .**142** F3
Hillview Cres NP19 . . .**144** B3
Hillview Terr **4** SA13 .**125** C8
Hilton Pl CF14 . . . .**176** F3
Hinchsliff Ave CF62 . .**214** E8
Hinter Path NP44 . . . . .**89** B1
Hinton St CF24 . . . .**195** E5
Hirst Cres CF5 . . . .**176** D1
Hirwain Pl CF43 . . . .**80** C4
Hirwain St CF24 . . . . . .**194** F8
Hirwain Terr CF47 . . . . .**10** E3
Hirwaun Ind Est
  CF44 . . . .**224** C1
Hirwaun Prim Sch
  CF44 . . . .**27** D7
Hirwaun Rd
  Aberdare CF44 . . . .**28** F3
  Penywaun CF44 . . . .**28** B5
Hilside Dr CF71 . . . . . .**188** F1
Hobart Cl NP20 . . . . . .**142** E4
Hodges Cres NP12 . . . .**58** B2
Hodges Row CF10 . . . .**195** A3
Hodges Sq CF10 . . . . .**195** B3
Hodges St CF47 . . . .**10** F4
Hodges Terr NP44 . . . . .**89** D3
Hodgson's Rd SA9 . . . . . .**2** A4
Hoel Cwmamman
  SA18 . . . .**220** B8
Hoel Gellilodra CF32 .**130** A3
Hoel Llwchwr SA18 . .**219** B6
Hoel y Mwyn Ct NP23 .**14** D6
Hoel-y-Graig SA12 . . .**99** F7
Hoel-y-Tyla SA13 . . . . .**74** D4
Hogarth Cl
  Cwmbran NP44 . . . .**117** A8
  Newport NP19 . . . .**143** F7
Hogarth Ho SA12 . . . .**124** D8
Hogarth Pl SA12 . . . . .**124** D8
Holbein Rd NP19 . . . .**144** A2
Holbrook Cl CF42 . . . . .**78** D7
Holden Rd CF11 . . . . .**194** D2
Holdings La CF5 . . . . .**175** B5
Holford St
  Aberdare CF44 . . . .**53** C8
  Cefn Coed CF48 . . . .**10** A4
Holford Terr **3** CF44 . .**28** C3
Holgate Cl CF15 . . . . .**176** D4
Holland St
  Ebbw Vale NP23 . . . .**14** F1
  Port Talbot SA13 . . . . . .**125** C8
Holland Way CF63 . . .**215** A7
Hollett Rd SA5 . . . .**68** C4
Hollies Sch The CF23 .**178** F7
Hollies The
  Blackwood NP11 . . . .**59** D1
  Bridgend CF31 . . . .**169** D4
  Heolgerrig CF48 . . . .**10** B1
  Pontyclun CF72 . . . .**173** A6
  Quakers Yard CF46 . . . . .**83** C5
Hollington Dr CF23 . .**161** A1
Hollins The SA11 . . . . . .**72** A5
Holly Cl NP23 . . . .**7** C5
Holly Ct CF62 . . . .**214** C3
Holly Dr CF44 . . . .**28** C3
Holly Gr CF14 . . . .**160** A4
Holly Lodge Gdns
  NP44 . . . .**90** B6
Holly Lodge Gn NP44 .**90** B6
Holly Lodge Rd NP44 .**90** B6
Holly Rd Cardiff CF5 . .**193** D8
  Llanharry CF72 . . . .**172** C5
  Neath SA11 . . . .**72** A5
  Risca NP11 . . . .**115** B2
Holly Row CF45 . . . .**81** E8
Holly St
  Gilfach Goch CF39 . . . . .**132** B5
  Pontardawe SA8 . . . .**23** E5
  Rhydyfelin CF37 . . . .**136** B5

Holly Terr
  Cardiff CF14 . . . .**177** A2
  Newbridge NP11 . . . .**86** F6
  Troedyrhiw CF48 . . . .**31** B2
Holly Way CF47 . . . .**10** D4
Holly Wlk CF36 . . . . . .**183** E8
Hollybush SA4 . . . .**89** D1
Hollybush Ave NP20 .**117** A2
Hollybush Cl
  Church Village CF38 . . . .**136** A1
  Newport NP20 . . . .**117** A2
Hollybush Ct CF23 . . .**178** D6
Hollybush Dr SA2 . . . . .**67** B1
Hollybush Gn CF31 . .**150** D1
Hollybush Hts CF23 . .**178** D7
Hollybush Prim Sch
  NP44 . . . .**89** C1
Hollybush Rd CF23 . . .**178** D6
Hollybush Rise CF23 .**178** D6
Hollybush Terr
  Church Village CF38 . . . .**136** A1
  Pontypool NP4 . . . .**62** A8
Hollybush View NP44 **116** B3
Hollybush Villas CF38 **135** F1
Hollybush Way NP44 **116** D8
Hollybush Wlk NP10 .**141** F3
Hollycroft Cl CF5 . . . .**193** C6
Hollylodge Cl NP44 . . .**90** B6
Hollyoak Cl CF62 . . . .**214** C8
Holm View L Ctr
  CF62 . . . .**214** F8
Holmdale **8** NP44 . . . .**89** B3
Holmes St CF63 . . . . . .**215** B6
Holmesdale Ct CF11 .**194** F1
Holmesdale St CF11 .**194** F2
Holmeside CF14 . . . . . .**160** A3
Holms Ct CF64 . . . .**216** A5
Holmsdale Pl CF64 . . .**207** B3
Holmview Ct CF3 . . . . .**179** C5
Holmwood Cl CF23 . .**178** C4
Holst Cl NP19 . . . .**145** A6
Holton Prim Sch
  CF63 . . . .**215** A5
Holton Rd CF63 . . . . . .**215** A5
Holy Family RC Jun & Inf
  Sch CF5 . . . .**193** B8
Holyhead Ct CF83 . . . .**137** C4
Holyoake Terr
  Abersychan NP4 . . . .**37** F5
  Pontypool NP4 . . . .**62** A8
Holyrood Terr CF40 . .**106** E8
Holywell Rd CF38 . . . .**136** A2
Home Farm Cl NP18 .**117** F2
Home Farm Cres
  NP18 . . . .**117** F2
Home Farm Gn NP18 **117** F2
Home Farm Way SA4 .**44** C2
Home Leigh NP11 . . . . .**86** F7
Homeland Pl SA12 . . . .**85** F6
Homelands Rd CF14 .**177** C5
Homelong Ho CF14 . .**177** F8
Homerton St CF45 . . . .**82** B6
Homeside Ho **8**
  CF64 . . . .**207** B4
Homevalley Ho **4**
  NP20 . . . .**142** F4
Homfray St CF34 . . . .**102** A6
Hondonu PJ SA6 . . . .**45** D1
Honeyfield Rd NP23 . . . .**7** B4
Honeysuckel Cl NP10 **142** B3
Honeysuckle Cl
  Cardiff CF5 . . . .**193** C6
  Ebbw Vale NP23 . . . .**7** C5
  Merthyr Tydfil CF47 . . . . .**10** C5
Honeysuckle Way
  CF31 . . . .**169** D5
Hong Kong Terr
  CF32 . . . .**151** A4
Honiton Rd CF3 . . . . . .**179** C7
Hoo St
  Briton Ferry SA11 . . . . . .**71** C2
  Swansea SA1 . . . .**96** B7
Hood Rd Barry CF62 . .**214** E3
  Newport NP19 . . . .**144** F7
Hookland Rd CF36 . . .**183** C8
Hope Ave CF32 . . . . . .**150** C4
Hope Ho CF10 . . . .**194** E8
Hope St NP13 . . . .**15** E5
Hopefield NP20 . . . . . .**143** B7
Hopefield Ct NP20 . . .**143** B7
Hopkin St
  Aberavon SA12 . . . .**98** F1
  Pontardawe SA8 . . . .**23** E5
  Treherbert CF42 . . . .**78** A8
Hopkins Cl CF48 . . . . . .**30** F4
Hopkins Cl SA5 . . . .**68** C4
Hopkins Terr SA13 . . . .**74** F6
Hopkinstown Rd
  CF37 . . . .**109** A1
Hopyard Mdw CF71 . .**188** D2
Horab Ct NP11 . . . .**59** F5
Horace Terr CF83 . . . .**137** F8
Horeb Cl CF47 . . . .**10** F3
Horeb Rd SA6 . . . .**68** F8
Horeb St
  Merthyr Tydfil CF48 . . . . .**29** F8
  Treorchy CF42 . . . .**78** B6
Horeb Terr CF44 . . . . . .**28** E7
Horizon Pk SA6 . . . .**69** A6
Hornbeam Cl
  Caerleon NP18 . . . .**117** C6
  5 Cardiff CF3 . . . .**180** A7
  Cimla SA12 . . . .**72** C5
  Merthyr Tydfil CF47 . . . . .**10** C6
Hornbeam Wlk NP10 **141** F3
Hornchurch Cl CF5 . .**176** E1
Horner St CF82 . . . .**85** A4

Horrocks Cl NP20 . . . .**117** A4
Horsefair Rd CF31 . . .**169** F2
Horton St **8** SA1 . . . . . .**95** C7
Horton Way CF64 . . . .**215** A6
Horwood CF24 . . . .**195** E7
Hosea Row SA1 . . . .**68** D4
Hosking Ind Est CF10 **195** B2
Hoskins St NP20 . . . . .**143** C6
Hospital Rd
  Gorseinon SA4 . . . .**66** F8
  Nantyglo NP23 . . . .**15** D8
  Penllergaer SA4 . . . .**43** E1
  Penpedairheol CF82 . . . .**84** D8
  Pontypool NP4 . . . .**62** B8
  Pontypridd CF37 . . . . . .**109** E1
  Port Talbot SA12 . . . . . .**124** E8
Hotham Cl CF23 . . . . . .**161** A1
Houlson St CF44 . . . . . .**11** B5
Houlston Ct CF24 . . . .**195** F7
Housman Cl CF3 . . . . .**179** C8
Hove Ave NP19 . . . . . .**144** A6
Howard Cl NP19 . . . . .**144** A6
Howard Dr CF83 . . . . .**138** A5
Howard Gdns CF24 . .**195** C6
Howard Pl **1** CF24 . .**195** C6
Howard St
  Cardiff CF24 . . . .**195** D5
  Tonypandy CF40 . . . .**106** A6
  Treorchy CF42 . . . .**78** D6
Howard Terr CF24 . . . .**195** C6
Howardian Cl **4**
  CF23 . . . .**178** E1
Howards Way
  Ebbw Vale NP23 . . . .**14** E3
  Gorseinon SA4 . . . .**43** C3
Howe Circ NP19 . . . . .**144** F7
Howel Rd SA11 . . . .**71** C4
Howell Cl SA4 . . . .**10** C1
Howell Rd CF5 . . . .**193** C5
Howell St
  Nant-y-Moel CF32 . . . . .**104** E7
  Pontypridd CF37 . . . . . .**109** F5
Howell's Cres CF5 . . . .**194** B8
Howell's Row CF44 . . .**53** C5
Howell's Sch CF5 . . . .**194** B8
Howells Rd SA2 . . . .**93** C8
Howells Row **1** CF44 .**28** C3
Howy Rd NP11 . . . .**87** B5
Hr Hen Dy CF5 . . . .**177** A1
Hubert Dr CF31 . . . . . .**168** F7
Hubert Rd NP19 . . . . .**143** F2
Hubert Rise
  Rogerstone NP10 . . . . .**142** B4
  Rogerstone NP10 . . . . .**142** B5
Hughes Ave NP23 . . . . . .**7** C1
Hughes St
  4 Mountain Ash CF45 . .**54** E1
  Tonypandy CF40 . . . .**106** F4
Hughs Cl CF5 . . . .**176** E3
Hugon Dr **2** CF23 . . .**178** E1
Humber Cl NP20 . . . . .**116** E1
Humber St NP20 . . . . .**116** E1
Humphrey St SA1 . . . . .**95** B7
Humphreys Terr
  CF34 . . . .**102** A8
Hunt Cl CF14 . . . .**159** F1
Hunt Pl **12** CF62 . . . .**215** B6
Hunter Cl NP10 . . . . . .**142** A6
Hunter St Barry CF63 .**215** C6
  Briton Ferry SA11 . . . . . .**71** C1
  Cardiff CF10 . . . .**195** B1
Hunters Ridge
  Bridgend CF31 . . . .**169** C5
  Cardiff CF23 . . . .**178** B4
  Tonna SA11 . . . .**49** B1
Huntingdon Cl NP44 .**89** B3
Huntingdon Ct SA3 . .**123** B8
Huntingdon Dr CF23 .**161** A1
Huntingdon Way SA2 .**94** B8
Huntington Cl SA3 . . .**123** B8
Huntmans Cove SA3 .**122** E7
Huntsmead Cl CF14 . .**159** E2
Hurford Cres CF37 . . .**109** B1
Hurford Pl CF23 . . . . .**178** C8
Hurford St CF37 . . . . .**135** A8
Hurman St CF10 . . . . .**195** B2
Huron Cres CF23 . . . . .**178** B4
Hurst Gr CF44 . . . .**29** B3
Hutchwns Cl CF36 . . .**182** D7
Hutchwns Terr CF36 .**182** F7
Huxley Gn NP20 . . . . .**117** A2
Hyacinth Dr CF31 . . . .**169** D6
Hyde St NP13 . . . .**60** C6
Hydrangea Cl
  Cardiff CF23 . . . .**178** D7
  Rogerstone NP10 . . . . .**142** B3
Hyland Pl NP44 . . . .**27** E8
Hylton Terr CF44 . . . . . .**56** A7
Hynam Pl NP4 . . . .**37** F5
Hyssop Cl CF23 . . . . . .**178** D8
Hywel Cres CF63 . . . . .**215** A6
Hywel Dda Jun & Inf Schs
  CF5 . . . .**193** B4
Hywel Ho **9** CF47 . . . .**30** D8

I

Ian's Wlk SA6 . . . .**46** B4
Idencroft Cl CF23 . . . .**161** A1
Idris Davies Pl NP22 . .**12** F2
Idris Pl CF31 . . . .**168** F7
Idris Terr SA6 . . . .**68** E6
Idwal Pl SA5 . . . .**68** B5
Idwal St SA11 . . . .**72** A8
Iestyn Dr CF35 . . . . . .**152** D1

Iestyn St Aberdare CF44 .. 28 E4
Cardiff CF11 ....194 D7
Iestynian Ave CF11 ....194 D7
Ifor Hael Rd NP10 .....141 F6
Ifor Jones Ct CF23 ...178 C5
Ifor St CF45 ....54 C2
Ifor CF35 ....130 E3
Ifton St NP19 ....144 A3
Ilan Ave CF37 ....135 F6
Ilan Rd CF83 ....137 A7
Ilchester Rd CF3 .....179 C6
Ilex Cl CF47 ....194 E4
Ilfracombe Cres CF3 ..179 C5
Illtyd Ave CF61 ......210 A5
Illtyd Rd CF5 ....193 B6
Illtyd St Neath SA11 ...72 A8
Pontypridd CF37 ......135 B7
Treorchy CF42 ....78 D6
Ilminster Cl CF63 ....215 B6
Ilminster Ct CF63 ....215 B6
Ilston SA15 ....40 F4
Ilston Way SA3 ....123 A4
Ilton Rd CF23 ....178 D1
Imperial Bldgs
Cardiff CF15 ....194 A8
Glan y Nant NP12 ......85 A8
Imperial Ct CF45 ......82 E2
Imperial Ctr SA7 ......69 B7
Imperial Way NP10 ...163 D6
Inchmarnock St 8 .....195 D5
CF24
Incline Rd
Aberdare CF44 ....29 F1
Abersychan NP4 ....37 F4
Incline Row SA13 .....125 D6
Incline Side CF48 .....31 B8
Incline Top CF45 ......82 F4
Industrial Terr 3 .....31 C1
CF48
Inglefield Ave CF14 ..177 F2
Ingles 13 NP44 ....89 B1
Inkerman Row
Blaina NP13 ....15 D5
Port Talbot SA13 .....125 D6
Inkerman St
Llanelli SA15 ....40 D5
Swansea SA1 ....95 E7
Inkerman Terr NP22 ....13 D5
Insole Cl CF5 ....193 F8
Insole Gdns CF5 ......194 A8
Insole Gr E CF5 ......193 F8
Insole Gr W CF5 ......193 F8
Insole Pl CF5 ....194 A8
Inst of Higher Ed
CF24 ....195 C6
Institute Pl CF40 ....106 E7
Institute Rd CF40 ....106 E7
Institute St CF43 .....52 A1
Institution Terr NP23 .14 D1
Instow Pl CF3 ....179 D6
Inter-Valley Rd SA10, ...223 D4
SA11
Intermediate Rd NP23 ..8 C5
Inverleith Terr CF40 .106 E7
Inverness Pl CF24 ....178 B1
Investiture Pl CF39 ..133 D6
Iolo Pl CF63 ....215 B7
Iorwerth St SA5 ....68 C2
Ipswich Rd CF23 ......178 F1
Ireland Cl CF3 ....180 A5
Irene St CF45 ....81 E8
Ireton Ct CF23 ....161 A1
Irfon St CF43 ....79 F6
Iris Cl SA12 ....98 B3
Iron Bridge Rd CF15 ..176 C8
Iron Row NP22 ....13 E6
Iron St Cardiff CF24 .195 D6
Tredegar NP22 ....13 E6
Ironworks Rd CF44 ....27 D8
Irvine Ct SA3 ....123 B4
Irving Ho 1 SA12 .....98 F3
Irving Pl CF24 ....214 E5
Is y Coed CF43 ....79 C8
Is-Fryn NP22 ....12 E6
Is-y-Bryniau SA9 .....221 B8
Is-y-Coed CF5 ....205 A6
Isaac's 9 SA12 ....124 F8
Isaf Rd NP11 ....115 B1
Isca Cl NP44 ....89 F4
Isca Ct NP18 ....118 B3
Isca Mews NP18 ......118 C1
Isca Rd NP18 ....118 C1
Iscoed SA15 ....40 B6
Isfryn Ind Est CF35 ..130 F2
Island Farm Cl CF31 ..168 E1
Island Farm Rd CF31 ..168 E1
Island Mews SA13 .....99 B1
Island Rd CF62 ....214 D4
Islawen Mdws CF35 ...152 E1
Islington CF31 ....168 C6
Islwyn SA14 ....41 E5
Islwyn Cl
Ebbw Vale NP23 ....14 C3
Pengam NP12 ....85 B7
Ynysddu NP11 ....112 F6
Islwyn Ct NP11 ....115 B1
Islwyn Dr CF83 ....138 A4
Islwyn Rd
Cwmfelinfach NP11 ...113 C3
Swansea SA1 ....95 B8
Islwyn St
Abercarn NP11 ....87 A3
Cwmfelinfach NP11 ...113 B4
Islwyn Terr
Pontllanfraith NP12 ...86 A4
Porth CF39 ....107 D4
Tredegar NP22 ....13 E6

Islwyn Way CF63 ......215 A8
Islwyn Workshops
NP11 ....141 A8
Isyrhos SA9 ....222 B6
Itchen Cl NP20 ....116 D3
Itchen Rd NP20 ....116 D3
Itton St NP23 ....35 A7
Ivey Pl SA1 ....95 D8
Ivor John Wlk NP18 ..118 A4
Ivor Pk CF72 ....173 F8
Ivor St Abercarn NP11 .114 C7
Barry CF62 ....214 F2
Blaenavon NP4 ....17 C6
Dowlais CF48 ....11 B4
Fleur De Lis NP12 .....85 B6
Maesteg CF34 ....102 A2
Newport NP20 ....143 C4
Pontycymer CF32 ......103 F3
Trehafod CF37 ....108 D2
Ystrad CF41 ....79 D3
Ivor Terr CF48 ....11 A5
Ivorites Row SA11 ....223 D1
Ivy Ave SA11 ....72 A8
Ivy Bush Ct SA1 ....95 E7
Ivy Cl Ebbw Vale NP23 ...7 A4
Merthyr Tydfil CF47 ...10 E3
Ivy Cottage Ct NP12 ...86 A8
Ivy Dene Cl NP4 ....38 B1
Ivy Row NP24 ....58 A8
Ivy St Cardiff CF5 ...194 B6
Penarth CF64 ....207 A4
Ivy Terr CF37 ....109 A2
Ivydale CF14 ....160 A3

J

Jack-y-Ddu Rd SA11 ...71 B2
Jacks Pill Ind Est
NP20 ....143 D3
Jackson Cl CF62 ......113 D4
Jackson Ct 2 NP19 ...143 E6
Jackson Pl 3 NP19 ...143 E6
Jackson Rd CF5 ......193 B5
Jade Cl CF14 ....160 A4
James Cl
Fleur De Lis NP12 .....85 B6
Sarn CF32 ....150 F4
James Ct Cardiff CF23 .178 B5
Swansea SA1 ....69 D6
James Griffiths Rd
SA18 ....219 D7
James Pl CF37 ....135 E7
James St
Aberbargoed CF81 .....58 B4
Aberdare CF44 ....53 C6
Abertillery NP13 ......36 B5
Barry CF63 ....215 D6
Bedwas CF83 ....139 A7
Blaenavon NP4 ....17 C6
Cardiff CF10 ....195 B2
Cwmdare CF44 ....28 C3
Ebbw Vale NP23 ....14 D8
3 Llanbradach CF83 ..111 F1
Llanelli SA15 ....40 E6
Maerdy CF43 ....52 A2
Markham NP12 ....58 D7
20 Merthyr Tydfil CF47 .10 E8
5 Mountain Ash CF45 ..54 E1
New Tredegar NP24 ....33 E3
New Tredegar NP24 ....34 A1
Newport NP20 ....143 D2
Pontardawe SA8 ....23 D5
Pontarddulais SA4 ....9 D3
Pontypool NP4 ....62 D7
Pontypridd CF37 .....135 C8
1 Port Talbot SA13 ..125 C8
Porthcawl CF36 ......182 F6
Tonypandy CF40 ......107 A4
Tredegar NP22 ....13 F5
Treorchy CF42 ....78 E6
Ystradgynlais SA9 .....2 F8
Ystradgynlais SA9 ...222 A4
James Terr
Cheltenham NP7 ....9 C6
Hengoed CF82 ....85 A3
Porth CF39 ....107 E5
James' Rd CF32 ......103 E6
James's Row NP23 ......7 C4
Jamesville NP11 .....114 B8
Jancell Ho CF33 .....148 D3
Jane Austen Cl NP20 .142 E1
Jane Cl NP10 ....163 F6
Janet St Cardiff CF24 .195 E6
Pontypridd CF37 .....135 E7
Japonica Cl NP20 ....117 B3
Japonica Dr CF48 .....11 C4
Jasmin Cl SA12 ....98 C3
Jasmine Cl
Merthyr Tydfil CF47 ...10 C5
Swansea SA2 ....94 B7
Jasmine Dr CF3 ......180 A7
Jasper Cl CF5 ....176 E2
Jaycroft Cl CF23 ....161 B1
Jeans Cl NP20 ....117 A3
Jeddo Cl NP20 ....143 C2
Jeddo St NP20 ....143 C2
Jeffcott Pl CF64 ....207 A6
Jeffrey St
Mountain Ash CF45 ....54 D3
Newport NP19 ....143 E5
Jeffreys Ct SA5 ....68 B8
Jellicoe Ct NP19 ....144 F7
Jellicoe St 6 CF10 ..195 C4
Jellicoe Gdns CF23 ..178 A5
Jenkin St
Abercwmboi CF44 ......53 F4
4 Aberdare CF44 ......29 A1

Jenkin St continued
2 Barry CF63 ....215 B7
Bridgend CF31 ....168 F3
Maesycwmmer CF82 ....85 B2
Jenkins Pl 18 CF47 ...30 E8
Jenkins Rd Neath SA11 .71 F5
Skewen SA10 ....71 A7
Jenkins Row Deri CF81 .57 B8
Rhymney NP22 ....12 F3
Jenkins St
Abercwmboi CF45 ......82 F3
Newport NP19 ....143 F3
Pontypridd CF37 .....109 A1
Porth CF39 ....107 F3
Jenkins Terr
Abergwynfi SA13 ......76 C5
Cwmfelin CF34 ....128 C8
Port Talbot SA13 ....125 D7
Jenner Rd CF62 ......214 D5
Jenner St CF63 ......215 C6
Jericho Rd SA1 ....95 E8
Jerry's La CF83 ......138 C7
Jersey Rd
Blaengwynfi SA13 .....76 C6
Swansea SA1 ....69 B4
Jersey Row SA12 ......99 E5
Jersey St
Port Talbot SA13 .....99 C1
Swansea SA1 ....68 D1
Jersey Terr
Briton Ferry SA11 ....71 B1
Cwmavon SA12 ....99 E5
Swansea SA1 ....96 A7
Jerusalem Ct NP4 .....63 B3
Jerusalem La NP4 .....63 B3
Jerusalem St NP22 ....12 F3
Jervis Wlk NP19 .....144 F6
Jesmond Dene CF15 ..158 B4
Jessop Cl NP10 ......142 B6
Jessop Rd NP10 ......142 B6
Jestyn Cl Cardiff CF5 .192 F4
Dinas Powys CF64 ....206 B4
Jestyn St CF39 ......107 E4
Jevan Cl CF5 ....176 D3
Jewel St CF63 ....215 B5
Jewell La NP20 ......143 B6
Jim Driscoll Way
CF11 ....195 A1
Jim Harvard Ct 5 SA6 69 A8
Job's La CF44 ....10 A4
Jockey St SA1 ....95 D8
John Baker Cl NP44 ..116 F8
John Batchelor Way
CF64 ....207 A6
John Bull Cl NP19 ...144 D5
John Croft CF62 .....212 F6
John Field Wlk NP19 .144 F4
John Frost Sq 2 .....143 C4
NP20
John Ireland Cl NP19 144 D5
John Morgan Cl CF5 .176 E3
John Penry Cres SA5 ..68 B6
John Pl CF37 ....135 E6
John St Aberavon SA12 .99 A1
Abercarn NP11 ....114 C8
Abercwmboi CF44 .....53 F4
7 Aberdare CF44 ......29 A1
Bargoed CF81 ....57 F3
Barry CF63 ....215 D6
Cardiff CF10 ....195 B4
Cefn Cribwr CF32 ....149 C2
Ebbw Vale NP23 ....7 C1
Hirwaun CF44 ....27 E8
Llanelli SA15 ....40 D5
Maesteg CF34 ....101 F5
Markham NP12 ....58 E7
Merthyr Tydfil CF47 ..10 D1
Mountain Ash CF45 ....54 F2
Mumbles SA3 ....123 A4
Nant-y-Moel CF32 ....104 F5
Newport NP20 ....143 D3
Penarth CF64 ....207 B5
Pentre CF41 ....78 F5
Pontypool NP4 ....62 C6
Pontypridd CF37 .....135 E6
Porth CF39 ....107 F3
Porth CF39 ....107 F6
Porthcawl CF36 ......182 F6
Resolven SA11 ....226 D5
3 Swansea SA1 ....95 B8
Swansea SA2 ....67 D2
Treharris CF46 ....83 B6
Treherbert CF42 ......51 A1
Ynysddu NP11 ....112 F5
Johns La CF14 ....177 A2
John's Dr CF35 ......170 D7
John's Hill CF62 ....211 D5
John's Terr SA12 .....73 C5
John's Villas CF32 ..151 A5
Johnson Pk CF44 ......27 E7
Johnston Cl NP20 ....142 A7
Johnston Rd CF14 ...159 D1
Joiners Rd SA4 ....65 D1
Jolly Rd SA18 ....220 C8
Jonathans Terr CF37 .109 F5
Jones Pl 3 CF37 .....109 A2
Jones St Dowlais CF48 .11 B5
3 Mountain Ash CF45 ..54 E1
New Tredegar NP24 ....33 F3
Newport NP20 ....143 B4
Pontardawe SA8 ....23 D5
Pontypridd CF37 .....109 F6
Tonypandy CF40 ......106 C6
Treherbert CF42 ......78 B8
Jones Terr
Merthyr Tydfil CF47 ..10 F1
Swansea SA1 ....95 C8
Jones' Terr SA18 ....219 F8

Jonquil Cl CF3 ....180 A7
Joseph Davies' Cl 6
SA1 ....68 C2
Joseph Parry Cl CF64 206 E6
Joseph Parry Ct 8 ....30 D8
CF47
Joseph Parry's Cottage
Mus 10 C2
Joseph Row CF33 ....148 D3
Joseph St SA13 ....99 B2
Joslin Rd CF31 ......169 A7
Joslin Terr CF31 ....169 A7
Jowett Ave CF47 ......30 F8
Joyce Cl NP20 ....142 E2
Joyce Ho 2 SA12 .....98 F1
Jubilee Cres
Bridgend CF31 ....169 A3
Neath SA10 ....70 F8
Sarn CF32 ....150 E4
Jubilee Ct CF43 ......80 B2
Jubilee Gdns
Barry CF63 ....215 D8
Porthcawl CF36 ......166 A2
Jubilee Ind Est CF47 .195 D5
Jubilee La
Gorseinon SA4 ....66 A8
Penarth CF64 ....207 B4
Jubilee Pl NP4 ....37 F5
Jubilee Rd
Aberdare CF44 ....53 C6
Abertillery NP13 .....36 C3
Bridgend CF31 ....169 A3
New Tredegar NP22 ...34 A2
Jubilee St
Cardiff CF11 ....194 E4
Llanharan CF72 ......153 F2
Jubilee Terr NP4 .....62 E8
Jule Rd NP4 ....89 B1
Julian Terr SA12 ......98 F1
Julian's Cl CF82 ......84 C7
Julian's Way CF33 ...166 A7
Julius Cl NP18 ......117 F3
Junction Ind Est
CF72 ....173 A7
Junction Lock Rd
CF10 ....195 D2
Junction Rd NP19 ...143 D6
Junction Terr CF15 ..176 C5
Juniper Cl
Porthcawl CF36 ......183 E7
Swansea SA2 ....94 B8
Juniper Cres NP44 ...116 A7
Justin Cl CF23 ......178 C4

K

Kames Pl CF24 ....195 C5
Kamsley Ho 4 CF47 ...30 D8
Kane Cl CF14 ....177 F7
Kathleen St CF62 ....214 F4
Katie St CF32 ....103 E7
Kays & Kears Ind Est
NP4 ....17 A7
Kean Ho 9 SA12 ....98 B3
Kear Cl NP20 ....143 C4
Kear's Row NP4 ....17 F1
Keats Cl
Bridgend CF31 ....168 D6
Cwmbran NP44 ....89 D2
Newport NP20 ....142 E2
Keats Gr SA2 ....93 F7
Keats Way CF62 ......214 E8
Keble Ct CF83 ....139 D7
Keen Rd Cardiff CF24 .195 D4
Cardiff CF24 ....195 D5
Keen's Pl CF32 ......150 F4
Keene Ave NP10 ......142 C3
Keene St NP19 ....143 F4
Keepers Cl SA4 ....44 C2
Keir Hardie Cl NP23 ..7 D6
Keir Hardie Rd
Baglan SA12 ....98 D7
Maesteg CF34 ....101 F4
Keir Hardie Terr NP11 60 A7
Keith St CF43 ....80 B4
Keller Ho 1 SA12 .....98 F1
Kelly Rd NP19 ....144 A7
Kelston Cl CF14 .....176 F5
Kelston Pl CF14 .....176 F5
Kelston Rd CF14 .....176 F5
Kelvedon St NP19 ....143 E4
Kelvin Cl NP20 ......117 A2
Kelvin Rd Cardiff CF24 178 B1
Clydach SA6 ....22 E1
Kember Cl CF3 ....180 A6
Kemble Ho SA12 ......98 A2
Kemble St SA2 ....94 C7
Kemeys Fawr Cl NP4 ..62 D1
Kemeys Fawr Inf Sch
NP4 ....62 D1
Kemeys Rd CF62 .....213 A2
Kemp Ho 2 SA12 ......98 B3
Kemps Covert CF61 ..208 F5
Kemys Fold CF14 ....177 C3
Kemys St NP4 ....62 D1
Kemys Way SA6 ....69 B7
Kemys Wlk NP44 ......89 D1
Kendal Cl CF44 ....29 D1
Kendle Dr SA2 ....94 C8
Kendon Ct CF44 ......27 D8
Kendon Rd NP11 .....159 F2
Kendrick Rd CF62 ...214 F2
Kenfig Ind Est SA13 .147 B4
Kenfig Pl
Llanyravon NP44 ......90 A3
Swansea SA1 ....69 C4
Kenfig Rd CF14 .....177 D3

Kenilworth Ct
Baglan SA12 ....98 E5
Cardiff CF5 ....193 F7
Kenilworth Ho 6 .....194 F5
CF10
Kenilworth Pl
Cwmbran NP44 ....89 C1
Mumbles SA3 ....123 A8
Kenilworth Rd
Barry CF63 ....215 B6
3 Newport NP19 .....144 A5
Kenley Ct CF23 .....176 E1
Kenmare Mews CF23 .161 A2
Kenmuir Rd CF24 ....195 F7
Kennard Cres NP4 ....17 B6
Kennard Ct NP4 ......17 B6
Kennard Pl NP4 ......17 B7
Kennard St CF41 .....78 F2
Kennard Terr NP11 ...59 F1
Kennedy Cl CF38 ....156 A7
Kennedy Dr CF35 ....170 C8
Kennedy Rise CF62 ..214 C5
Kennel Row SA11 .....71 B1
Kennerleigh Rd CF3 .179 A4
Kenneth Treasure Ct 2 ..179 D7
CF3
Kennington Cl
Cardiff CF14 ....159 E2
Killay SA2 ....93 D6
Kenry St
Evanstown CF39 .....132 B8
Tonypandy CF40 .....106 E5
Treorchy CF42 ....78 B8
Kensington Ave CF5 .194 A6
Kensington Dr
Bridgend CF31 ......168 C6
Porth CF39 ....108 A2
Kensington Gdns 6 ..143 F6
NP19
Kensington Gr NP19 .143 F5
Kensington Pl NP19 .143 F5
Kenson Cl CF62 .....212 E1
Kenson Hill CF62 ....212 E2
Kent Cl NP10 ....142 A7
Kent Ct NP18 ....118 A3
Kent Gn CF62 ....214 C6
Kent Rd CF31 ....169 B3
Kent St CF11 ....194 F2
Kenway Ave CF11 .....71 F6
Kenwood Rd CF5 .....193 B5
Kenyon Rd CF24 .....196 A7
Keppoch St CF24 ....195 C8
Keralake Terr 3 .....106 F3
CF40
Kern Cl SA12 ....98 B3
Kerrigan Cl CF5 .....176 C6
Kerrycroy St 10 CF24 195 D5
Kestell Dr CF11 ....207 A8
Kestrel Cl
Bridgend CF31 ......169 D3
Cardiff CF23 ....178 D7
Neath SA10 ....48 E2
Kestrel View CF82 ...84 F3
Kestrel Way
Newport NP10 ....163 E7
Penarth NP10 ....217 A8
Keswick Ave CF23 ...178 A3
Keteringham Cl CF64 216 A5
Kewstoke Ave CF3 ..179 B5
Kewstoke Pl CF3 ....179 B5
Keyes Ave CF23 .....178 A3
Keyes Ct 3 CF10 ....195 C4
Keynsham Ave NP20 .143 C3
Keynsham Rd CF14 ..177 C5
Keys The CF61 ......209 F6
Keyston Rd CF5 .....176 E1
Khartoum Terr SA10 .222 F5
Kidwelly Cl
Blackwood NP12 .....58 E2
Llanyravon NP44 .....90 A2
Kidwelly Ct CF83 ...137 D4
Kidwelly Gr CF48 ...225 F1
Kidwelly Rd NP44 ....90 B2
Kier Hardie Cl NP19 .144 D7
Kier Hardie Cres
NP19 ....144 D7
Kilcatten St 9 CF24 .195 D5
Kildare St SA5 ....68 C3
Kilfield Rd SA3 .....122 B5
Kilgetty Cl CF5 .....193 C4
Killan Rd SA2 ....93 B8
Kiln St CF44 ....53 C8
Kilvey Cl CF44 ....29 D1
Kilvey Rd SA1 ....68 E1
Kilvey Terr SA1 ......95 E8
Kimberley Cl SA2 ...94 D7
Kimberley Ct CF31 ..169 B4
Kimberley Pl CF48 ...31 C2
Kimberley Rd
Abertillery NP13 .....36 C3
Cardiff CF23 ....178 D1
Swansea SA2 ....94 D7
Kimberley Terr
Cardiff CF14 ....177 F8
Tredegar NP22 ....13 F6
Kimberley Way CF37 .107 F2
Kincoed Rd NP12 .....59 B1
Kincraig St CF24 ....195 B8
King Charles Rd NP11 86 D5
King Edward Ave
CF83 ....138 B2
King Edward Rd
Brynmawr NP23 ....8 C5
Gwaun-Cae-Gurwen ..220 F6
SA18
King Edward St
Blaengarw CF32 .....103 E5
8 Merthyr Tydfil CF47 .10 D2

King Edward Terr
NP22 ....12 E5
King Edward VII Ave
CF10 ....195 A7
King Edward's Rd SA1 .95 A7
King George Ave SA15 40 E5
King George Ct SA2 ...94 B3
King George V Dr E
Cardiff CF14 ....177 F3
Cardiff CF14 ....177 F3
King George V Dr N
CF14 ....177 F5
King George V Dr W
CF14 ....177 E4
King La 12 NP20 ....143 C4
King St Abercynon CF45 82 F3
Aberdare CF44 ....53 C8
Abertillery NP13 .....36 B5
Abertridwr CF83 ....137 A7
Blaenavon NP4 ....17 C7
Brynmawr NP23 ....8 B4
Cwm NP23 ....35 B6
Cwmdare CF44 ....28 C3
Cwmfelinfach NP11 ..113 A4
Ebbw Vale NP23 ......7 F4
Ferndale CF43 ....80 A5
Mountain Ash CF45 ..81 E8
Nantyglo NP23 ....8 C1
Neath SA11 ....71 E7
Newport NP20 ......143 C4
Pant CF48 ....11 A4
Penarth CF64 ....207 B5
Pontlottyn CF81 .....12 F1
Pontypool NP4 ....62 B7
Pontypridd CF37 ....135 E6
Port Talbot SA13 ....99 C1
5 Swansea SA1 ....95 D7
Taffs Well CF15 ....158 A3
Ton Pentre CF41 ....79 B2
Tredegar NP22 ....6 F1
King Wood Cl CF23 ..178 E1
King's Ave CF15 ....176 C5
King's Head Rd SA5 ..67 F3
King's Hill
Hengoed CF82 ....85 A3
Porthcawl CF36 .....183 A7
King's Par NP20 ....143 D2
King's Rd Cardiff CF11 194 D6
Radyr CF15 ....176 E5
King's Road (Heol y
Brenin) SA1 ....95 E6
Kingarth St 6 CF24 .195 D5
Kingcraft St CF45 ...54 D2
Kingdon-Owen Rd
SA11 ....71 F5
Kingfisher Cl CF3 ..179 F7
Kingfisher Cl SA15 ..41 A5
Kingfisher Pl NP10 .163 E6
Kingfisher Sq CF62 .210 D6
Kingleys The SA4 ...102 A8
Kingrosia Pk SA6 ...47 A8
Kings Acre NP20 ....142 F5
Kings Ave NP22 .....12 E5
Kings Cl CF83 ......137 A7
Kings Ct 5 CF64 ....206 A2
Kings La SA1 ....95 D7
Kings Monkton Sch
CF24 ....195 B6
Kings Rd Cardiff CF11 194 D7
Mumbles SA3 ....123 A4
Kings Ride CF64 ....205 F3
Kings Terr CF34 ....101 F6
Kingsacre CF38 .....156 C6
Kingsbridge Bsns Pk
SA4 ....66 C8
Kingsbury Ct CF44 ..28 E6
Kingsbury Pl
Aberdare CF44 ....52 F4
Cwmaman CF44 ....53 A4
Llwydcoed CF44 .....28 E6
Kingsdale Ct NP20 ..143 A3
Kingsfield NP23 ......7 E1
Kingshill Ct 9 NP20 148 C4
Kingsland Cres CF63 215 A4
Kingsland Rd
Cardiff CF11 ....176 F4
Cardiff CF5 ....194 B6
Kingsland Terr CF37 .135 E7
Kingsland Wlk NP44 ..89 B2
Kingslea 10 NP44 ....89 B1
Kingsley Cl CF64 ...216 B5
Kingsley Pl CF83 ...110 F2
Kingsley Terr
Aberfan CF48 ....55 C4
Merthyr Tydfil CF47 ..10 F1
Kingsmill Terr 3 ....143 B4
NP20
Kingston Rd
Cardiff CF11 ....194 D5
Newport NP19 ....143 E5
Swansea SA2 ....94 D7
Kingsvale 10 NP20 ..143 C4
Kingsway
Bridgend CF31 ......169 C2
Newport NP20 ......143 C4
Swansea SA5 ....67 C4
Kingsway (Ffordd y
Brenin) The SA1 ....95 C7
Kingsway Bldgs CF31 169 D2
Kingsway Ctr 5 .....143 C4
NP20
Kingsway Ffordd y Brenin
CF10 ....195 A6

Kingswood
(Coed-y-Brenin)
CF37 ....135 A8
Kingswood Cl
Ewenny CF35 ....185 E3
Hengoed CF82 ....85 A3
Kinley St SA1 ....95 F7
Kinnock Ct NP44 ......90 A6
Kinsale Cl CF23 ......161 A2
Kipling Cl Cardiff CF3 .179 B7
Penarth CF64 ....206 F5
Kipling Gdns CF31 ...168 C5
Kipling Hill NP20 ....142 E2
Kirby Daniel Ct 26
NP20 ....143 C3
Kirby La NP20 ......143 C3
Kirkby St 15 CF10 ...195 C4
Kirkhouse St CF37 ...135 B8
Kirkwall Ct CF24 ....195 F7
Kirton Cl CF5 ....176 E1
Kitchener Com Jun & Inf
Sch CF11 ....194 D5
Kitchener Rd CF11 ...194 D5
Kitchener St NP4 ......61 F8
Kittiwake Cl CF36 ...182 D8
Kittle Gn SA3 ....121 E7
Kittle Hill La SA3 ...121 E7
Kitty Hawk Dr NP19 ..144 B3
Knap Car Terr CF62 ..214 B2
Knelston Pl SA5 ......67 F7
Knelston Prim Sch
SA3 ....231 A8
Knight Cl 25 NP20 ....143 C3
Knight St
Aberavon SA12 ....99 A1
8 Mountain Ash CF45 .54 D1
Knighton Cl
Caerleon NP18 ......118 B2
6 Cardiff CF24 .....195 D6
Knights Rd SA13 .....125 E3
Knights Terr CF45 ....82 F3
Knightswell Cl CF5 ..193 A2
Knightswell Rd CF5 ..193 A3
Knole Cl CF23 ....161 A1
Knoll Ave SA2 ....94 E6
Knoll Terr CF40 .....106 D2
Knowbury Ave CF64 ...217 B8
Knox Rd CF24 ....195 B6
Knox St SA13 ....125 E3
Knoyle Dr SA5 ....68 C7
Knoyle St SA5 ....68 C7
Kyfts La SA3 ....228 E3
Kyle Ave CF14 ......177 C5
Kyle Cres CF14 .....177 C5
Kymin Rd CF64 ......207 B4
Kymin Terr CF64 ....207 B4
Kyveilog St CF11 ....194 D7

L

Laburnam Ave NP22 .....6 D1
Laburnam La CF48 ....10 B6
Laburnam Terr CF48 ...31 B2
Laburnam Way CF64 ..206 D3
Laburnham Bush La
NP19 ....144 C3
Laburnham Cl NP10 ...141 E7
Laburnham Pl NP22 ....94 B6
Laburnum Ave
Baglan SA12 ....98 E7
Newport NP19 ......144 B4
Laburnum Cl
Barry CF62 ....214 F7
Ebbw Vale NP23 ....7 C5
Merthyr Tydfil CF47 ...10 D4
Laburnum Ct CF37 ...136 B5
Laburnum Dr
Cwmbran NP44 ......116 A8
Cwmdare CF44 ....28 D3
Pontypool NP4 ....63 B5
Porthcawl CF36 .....183 E8
Laburnum Gr NP12 ....85 E3
Laburnum Pl CF5 ....193 D8
Laburnum Terr
Abercarn NP11 ....87 C4
Rhydyfelin CF37 ....136 B5
Laburnum Way CF64 ..206 B2
Ladies Row NP22 ....6 F1
Lady Abardare Flats
CF45 ....54 D4
Lady Housty Ave SA3 .122 E5
Lady Jane St 4 SA12 .124 F8
Lady Margaret Ct 5
CF23 ....178 E1
Lady Margaret Villas
SA2 ....94 E7
Lady Mary Rd CF23 ..178 B3
Lady Tyler Terr NP22 ..12 F3
Ladybench NP44 ......89 B1
Ladyhill Gn NP19 ....144 C4
Ladyhill Rd NP19 ....144 C4
Ladysmith Terr
Tredegar NP22 ....13 F6
Troedyrhiw CF48 .....31 C2
Ladywell NP44 ....89 C5
Laing St CF33 ......148 C1
Lake Ct SA12 ....124 E7
Lake Hill Dr CF71 ...188 F1
Lake Rd Brynmawr NP23 .8 C4

Lake Rd continued
Newport NP19 ......144 C1
Port Talbot SA12 ...124 E7
Lake Rd E CF23 .....178 B4
Lake Rd N CF23 .....178 A5
Lake Rd W CF23 .....178 A4
Lake St CF43 ....79 F6
Lake View Cl
Cardiff CF23 ....178 B4
Llanelli SA15 ....40 C7
Lake View Ct CF23 ...178 B4
Lakefield Cl 1 SA15 ..40 C4
Lakefield Cty Prim Sch
SA15 ....40 C4
Lakefield Pl SA15 ....40 C4
Lakefield Rd SA15 ....40 C4
Lakeside Barry CF62 .214 C1
Cwmdare CF44 ....28 C2
Lakeside Cl NP22 ......6 B1
Lakeside Cty Jun & Inf Sch
CF23 ....178 B5
Lakeside Dr CF23 ...178 B5
Lakeside Gdns CF48 ...10 B4
Lakeside Tech Pk SA7 .69 B6
Lakeview Cl CF36 ....183 A8
Lakeview Terr SA15 ...40 C7
Lakin Dr CF62 ......214 C8
Laleston Cl
Barry CF63 ....215 A8
8 Cardiff CF5 ......193 C4
Porthcawl CF36 .....165 E2
Laleston Ct CF32 ....167 E5
Lamb & Flag Cotts
SA9 ....222 B7
Lamb Cl NP20 ....142 E1
Lamb La Ponthir NP18 .117 E7
Swansea SA2 ....93 E8
Lamb Rd CF44 ....224 D3
Lamb Row CF33 .....166 A5
Lamb's Sq NP23 ......7 C4
Lambert Cl NP20 ....143 B7
Lambert St NP20 ....143 B7
Lambert Terr CF44 ....28 F2
Lambourne Cres
Bettws NP20 ....116 D2
Cardiff CF14 ....177 E7
Lambourne Dr SA3 ...122 F6
Lambourne Way
NP20 ....116 D2
Lambourne Wlk
NP20 ....116 D1
Lambs Well Cl SA3 ..123 B4
Lamby Ind Pk CF3 ....179 C1
Lamby Way CF3,CF24 .179 B1
Lamby Way Workshops
CF3 ....179 C2
Lan Ave 1 SA6 ....68 F8
Lan Cl CF37 ....109 B2
Lan Coed SA1 ....69 D5
Lan Deri SA1 ....69 C5
Lan Manor SA6 ....68 E8
Lan St SA6 ....45 F1
Lan-y-Parc CF46 .....83 E4
Lancaster Cl SA11 ...223 C1
Lancaster Ct SA5 ....67 D5
Lancaster Dr CF38 ...156 D7
Lancaster Rd NP4 ....63 A2
Lancaster St
Abertillery NP13 ....36 B3
Blaina NP13 ....15 E3
Merthyr Tydfil CF47 ..10 D2
Landeg St SA6 ....68 E5
Landings The CF64 ..206 F5
Landor Ave SA2 ......93 F7
Landor Dr SA4 ....42 D1
Landraw Rd CF37 ....109 A1
Landsdowne Ct SA5 ...67 D3
Landseer Cl NP19 ...144 A7
Landwade Cl CF5 ....193 C7
Landwr Parc SA6 .....69 A6
Lane The CF5 ....192 D2
Lanelay Cl CF72 ....155 A2
Lanelay Cres CF37 ..109 B1
Lanelay Ind Est CF72 .155 B2
Lanelay Pk CF72 ....155 B2
Lanelay Rd CF72 ....155 B2
Lanelay Terr CF37 ..135 B8
Lanes The CF61 .....209 F6
Langcliff Pk SA3 ...123 C3
Langdale Cl CF23 ...178 C2
Langdon Road SA1 ....96 A6
Langdon Road (Heol
Langdon) SA1 ......95 F7
Langer Way SA6 ......22 E1
Langham Way CF11 ..194 E3
Langland Bay Rd SA3 .122 F3
Langland Cl
Hirwaun CF44 ....27 D7
Mumbles SA3 ......123 A4
Langland Court Rd
SA3 ....122 F4
Langland Mews SA15 .40 E3
Langland Rd
Cardiff CF3 ....179 C3
Llanelli SA15 ....40 E3
Mumbles SA3 ......123 A4
Langland Terr SA2 ....94 E5
Langland Villas SA3 .123 A4
Langland Way NP19 ..144 A1
Langlands Rd CF63 ..215 D2
Langport Ave CF3 ...179 D6
Langstone Bsns Vill
NP18 ....145 A8
Langstone Cotts
NP18 ....145 A8

Langstone Court Rd
NP18 ....145 C8
Langstone Ct NP44 ...89 C1
Langstone Jun & Inf Sch
NP18 ....119 E2
Langstone La NP18 ...145 B6
Lanhydrock Cl 11
CF3 ....179 F6
Lanpark Rd CF37 ....109 C2
Lansbury Ave
Cefn Hengoed CF82 ...84 F4
Margam SA13 ....125 E1
Lansbury Cl
Caerphilly CF83 ....137 F5
Maesteg CF34 ......101 F1
Lansbury Cres CF34 .101 F1
Lansbury Park Jun & Inf
Sch CF83 ....138 D4
Lansbury Rd
Brynmawr NP23 ....8 A4
Merthyr Tydfil CF48 ..10 A3
Lansbury Terr NP23 ....7 F4
Lansdale Dr CF38 ...136 A1
Lansdown SA3 ....122 F4
Lansdowne NP4 ....62 E1
Lansdowne Ave CF14 .177 C6
Lansdowne Ave E
CF11 ....194 C5
Lansdowne Ave W
CF11 ....194 B5
Lansdowne Com Jun & Inf
Sch CF5 ....194 B6
Lansdowne Hospl
CF11 ....194 B5
Lansdowne Rd
Caerleon NP18 ......118 B2
Cardiff CF5 ....194 B5
Ebbw Vale NP23 ....7 D5
Newport NP20 ......142 F2
Lanstone Rise NP18 ..119 F2
Lanwern Rd CF37 ....135 B8
Lanwood Rd CF37 ...109 C2
Lapwing Cl
Penarth CF64 ......217 A7
Porthcawl CF36 ....182 D8
Lapwing Ag SA15 .....40 B5
Larch Cl Cimla SA11 ..72 C5
Merthyr Tydfil CF47 ..10 D5
Pontypool NP4 ......63 A4
Porthcawl CF36 ....183 E7
Larch Ct Cardiff CF15 .158 D1
Newport NP20 ......117 A3
Larch Dr CF72 ......155 F3
Larch Gr
Caerphilly CF83 ....138 C5
Cardiff CF14 ......160 B3
Llanmartin NP18 ...145 E6
Newport NP20 ......117 B3
Larch Ho CF14 ......176 E6
Larches The CF71 ...189 C8
Larchwood CF5 .....205 A6
Lark Pl SA5 ....67 E7
Lark Rise CF31 .....169 D5
Larkfield Ave CF44 ...29 D1
Larkfield Cl NP18 ...118 A4
Larkhill SA12 ....98 F7
Larkspur Cl SA10 ....48 E2
Larkspur Dr SA3 ....122 E7
Larkwood Ave CF64 ..207 A2
Lascelles Dr CF23 ...161 B1
Lasgarn La NP4 ......38 B3
Lasgarn Pl NP4 ......38 A3
Lasgarn View NP4 ....37 F7
Latimer Ct SA5 ......67 E5
Latt The SA11 ....71 E8
Lauderdale Rd SA18 .220 E7
Laugharne Ave CF3 ..179 C3
Laugharne Ct
Barry CF62 ....214 F7
Swansea SA2 ....94 A6
Laugharne Rd CF3 ...179 C3
Launcelot Cres CF14 .159 E2
Laundry Rd CF37 ....109 B1
Laura St Barry CF63 .215 D6
Pontypridd CF37 ...135 D8
Laural Wlk NP44 .....89 B6
Laureate Cl CF3 .....179 B7
Laurel Ave Baglan SA12 .98 E6
Rhydyfelin CF37 ....136 B4
Laurel Cl
Cwmdare CF44 ....28 D3
Sarn CF32 ....150 F4
Laurel Cres NP20 ...117 B2
Laurel Ct Barry CF62 .214 C3
Cardiff CF5 ....193 D8
Laurel Dr
Ammanford SA18 ...219 D7
Bassaleg NP10 .....142 B3
Bryn NP12 ....85 E3
Penperlleni NP4 .....39 E7
Waunarlwydd SA5 ...66 D4
Laurel Gn NP44 ......89 B6
Laurel Pl SA2 ....94 B6
Laurel Rd NP10 .....142 A3
Laureldene CF72 ....172 B5
Laurels Bsns Pk The
CF3 ....179 D2
Laurels The NP13 ....15 E5
Lauriston Cl CF5 ....193 C2
Lauriston Pk CF5 ...193 C2
Lavender Ct
Bridgend CF31 .....169 D5
Swansea SA5 ....68 A5
Lavender Gr CF5 ....193 C8
Lavender Rd CF47 ....10 B5
Lavender Way NP10 ..141 D7
Lavernock Rd CF64 ..216 E5

Lavery Cl NP19 .....144 A7
Law St CF32 ....149 D4
Lawn Terr
Newbridge NP11 ......60 A2
Pontypridd CF37 ...135 E7
Rhymney NP22 ....12 E4
Lawns Ind Est The
NP22 ....12 E3
Lawrence Ave
Abertillery NP13 ....35 F7
Markham NP12 ....58 D7
Penywaun CF44 ......28 A6
Lawrence Cl CF31 ...168 E6
Lawrence Hill NP19 ..144 B5
Lawrence Hill Ave
NP19 ....144 B5
Lawrence St CF83 ...138 B3
Lawrence Terr 2
SA15 ....40 E5
Lawrenny Ave CF11 ..194 E4
Laybourne NP44 ......89 C5
Laytonia Ave CF14 ..177 E2
Le Pouliguen Way
CF61 ....210 A6
Le Sor Hill CF5 .....191 E6
Le-Breos SA3 ....93 F1
Le-Breos Ave SA2 ....94 E6
Lea Cl NP20 ....116 C2
Lea Ct NP12 ....86 A3
Leach Rd NP20 .....116 D3
Lead St CF24 ......195 D6
Leadon Ct NP44 .....89 A4
Leamington Rd CF14 .177 B6
Leas The NP44 ......89 C5
Leckwith Ave CF11 ..194 D4
Leckwith Cl CF11 ...194 D4
Leckwith St
Bridgend CF31 .....168 C4
Cardiff CF5 ....193 D4
Leckwith Pl CF11 ...194 D4
Leckwith Rd
Cardiff CF11,CF64 ..194 C2
Leckwith CF11 .....194 B1
Ledbrooke Cl NP44 ...89 C1
Ledbury Dr NP20 ...143 C6
Lee Cl Cardiff CF23 .178 C4
Dinas Powys CF64 ..206 B4
Lee Ct CF14 ....159 C1
Lee H0 CF23 ....178 D4
Lee Rd CF63 ....215 A6
Lee St Pontypridd CF37 .109 B1
Swansea SA1 ....95 F7
Lee Way NP19 ......144 C1
Leeway Ct NP19 ....144 D1
Legion's Way CF82 ...84 B7
Leicester Dr NP44 ...89 A3
Leicester Rd NP19 ..143 E6
Leicester Sq CF82 ...84 F7
Leigh Cl CF61 ......210 C2
Leigh Terr CF46 .....83 C2
Leighton Ct NP44 ....89 C2
Leighton Rees Cl CF37 .84 B5
Leiros Parc Dr SA10 ..48 E2
Lennard St NP19 ....143 E4
Lennox Gn CF63 .....215 D6
Leoline Cl CF71 ....188 D2
Leon Ave CF15 .....158 A3
Leonard St
Fleur De Lis NP12 ....85 B6
Neath SA11 ....71 F8
Leslie Green Ct NP10 .163 E8
Leslie St 14 SA12 ...98 F1
Leslie Terr CF39 .....108 A3
Rogerstone NP10 ...142 B4
Letch Sq 15 NP20 ...143 C3
Letchworth Rd CF37 ...7 C1
Lethbridge Terr NP4 ..37 F3
Letterston Rd CF3 ..179 D5
Letton Rd CF10 .....195 B3
Lettons Way CF64 ...206 A4
Letty St CF24 ......195 A8
Level The NP23 ......14 D7
Leven Cl CF23 .....178 B5
Lewis Ave
Blackwood NP12 .....85 E8
Bridgend CF31 .....168 E5
Cwmllynfell SA9 ...221 B8
Lewis Boys Comp Sch
NP12 ....85 A8
Lewis Boys Lower Comp
Sch CF82 ....111 E8
Lewis Cl
Abersychan NP4 .....37 E6
Newbridge NP11 .....60 B2
Newport NP20 .....143 C3
Lewis Cres
Bargoed CF81 ....58 A1
Gilfach CF81 ....85 A8
Llanelli SA14 ....41 D5
Lewis Dr CF83 ......137 F5
Lewis Girls' Comp Sch
CF82 ....84 F1
Lewis Pl Porth CF39 .107 C2
Porthcawl CF36 ....182 F7
Lewis Rd Cardiff CF24 .195 E5
Crynant SA10 ......226 A7
Llandough CF64 ....206 D7
Maesteg CF34 .....102 B3
Neath SA11 ....71 F6
Lewis Sq CF48 ....30 E5
Lewis St
Aberbargoed CF81 ...58 B6
Aberdare CF44 ......53 C7
Abersychan NP4 .....37 F4
Barry CF62 ....214 C4
Bedlinog CF46 ......56 B7
Blackwood NP12 .....85 E7
Cardiff CF11 ....194 E5

Lewis St continued
Church Village CF38 ..156 F8
Machen CF83 ......140 A7
Mountain Ash CF45 ...54 D4
Newbridge NP11 .....60 B2
Pentre CF41 ....78 F4
Pontyclun CF72 ....173 B8
Pontypridd CF37 ...135 C8
Pontypridd CF37 ...135 E7
Swansea SA1 ....95 F1
Swansea SA2 ....94 C6
Tonypandy CF40 ....107 A3
Trehafod CF37 .....108 C2
Ystrad Mynach CF82 ..84 C1
Lewis Terr
6 Llanbradach CF83 .111 F1
Merthyr Tydfil CF47 ..10 C3
Pontypool NP4 ......62 B8
Pontypridd CF37 ...109 D2
Porth CF39 ....108 B3
Wattstown CF39 ...107 D8
Lewis View NP10 ....142 B5
Lewis Wood NP4 ......37 F1
Lewis's Terr CF48 ....10 B1
Leydene Cl NP11 ....114 F3
Leyshon Wlk SA3 ...122 E8
Leyshon Cl SA10 .....71 A7
Leyshon Rd
Gwaun-Cae-Gurwen
SA18 ....220 D7
Ynysmeudwy SA8 ....23 F6
Leyshon St CF37 ....135 B7
Leyshon Terr CF39 ..108 A2
Lias Rd CF36 ....182 F6
Lias St CF31 ....168 E4
Libanus Jun & Inf Sch
NP12 ....85 E5
Libanus Rd
Ebbw Vale NP23 ......7 D1
Gorseinon SA4 ......43 C1
Pontllanfraith NP12 ..85 E5
Libanus St CF48 .....11 A5
Libby Rd SA3 ....123 C3
Libby Way SA3 .....123 C3
Libeneth Rd NP19 ...144 B4
Library Cl
Rhydyfelin CF37 ....136 A5
Treorchy CF41 ......79 A4
Library La
Merthyr Tydfil CF47 ..10 C1
5 Port Talbot SA13 .125 C6
Library Rd
Maesteg CF34 ....75 B1
Pontypridd CF37 ...109 C1
Tonypandy CF40 ...106 F4
Library St CF5 .....194 D6
Liddel Cl CF23 .....161 B1
Liddicoat Ct CF63 ..215 C6
Lidmore Rd CF62 ...214 C5
Lifeboat Rd CF36 ...182 F6
Lighthouse Pk NP10 .181 F8
Lighthouse Rd
Newport NP10 .....164 A4
St Brides Wentlooge
NP10 ....182 A8
Lilac Cl Cardiff CF5 ..176 C1
Mumbles SA3 ......122 F8
Lilac Dr CF38 ......156 C6
Lilac Gr SA12 ....98 E7
Lilburne Cl CF23 ...161 A1
Lilian Gr NP23 ....7 D2
Lilian Rd NP12 ......85 E6
Lilian St SA12 ....98 F1
Lilleshall St NP19 ..143 E4
Lilliput La SA3 .....123 B8
Lily St CF24 ....195 C2
Limburne Dr NP19 ..143 F4
Lime Cl Newport NP20 .143 C2
Radyr CF15 ....176 C4
Lime Cres NP19 ....144 B4
Lime Ct NP11 ....87 B8
Lime Gr Bryn NP12 ...85 E3
Cardiff CF5 ....176 B1
Cimla SA11 ....72 A5
Killay SA2 ....93 D7
Llanmartin NP18 ...145 F7
St Athan CF62 .....211 B7
Lime Kiln La SA3 ...122 B6
Lime St Ferndale CF43 ..79 F6
Gorseinon SA4 ......43 C2
Rhydyfelin CF37 ...136 A5
Lime Tree Gr 6 SA6 ..69 A8
Lime Tree Wlk CF36 .183 E8
Limebourne Ct CF14 .177 B3
Limekiln Rd
Abersychan NP4 .....33 A3
Mumbles SA3 ......123 A5
Limes Ct CF71 ......188 F2
Limes The CF71 ....188 F2
Limeslade Cl
Cardiff CF5 ....193 F7
Hirwaun CF44 ....27 D7
Limeslade Dr SA3 ...123 C3
Limestone Rd NP23 ...8 C2
Limestone Rd E NP23 ..8 D3
Limewood Cl CF3 ...179 E7
Lincoln Cl NP19 ....143 F6
Lincoln Ct
Caerleon NP18 .....118 A3
Cardiff CF23 ....178 D5
Lincoln St Cardiff CF5 .194 B6
Porth CF39 ....107 E2
Lincoln Terr 22 CF47 ..30 E8
Lindbergh Cl NP19 ..144 A3
Linden Ave
Cardiff CF23 ....178 C1

Linden Ave continued
Mumbles SA3 ......123 A8
Linden Cl SA10 ......48 C5
Linden Cres CF44 ....28 D2
Linden Ct
Cwmbran NP44 ......89 B1
Llanharry CF72 ....172 B5
Newbridge NP11 .....87 C8
Linden Gr
Caerphilly CF83 ...138 C5
Cardiff CF3 ....179 C8
Linden Lea Dr NP12 ..85 D6
Linden Rd NP19 ....144 A5
Linden Way
Porthcawl CF36 ....183 E8
Trefechan CF48 .....10 B7
Lindens The CF64 ...207 A4
Lindsay Cl CF35 ....170 C8
Lindsay Ct CF31 ....169 A3
Lindsay Gdns NP22 ....6 D1
Lindway Ct 4 CF5 ...194 B7
Lingfield Ave
Port Talbot SA12 ....98 D2
Port Talbot SA12 ....98 E1
Lingholm Cl 3 CF3 ..179 F6
Link Rd NP4 ....63 A4
Link The SA2 ....94 A5
Links Ct SA3 ....122 E3
Links The NP4 ....38 C1
Linkside SA3 ....122 E4
Linkside Dr SA3 ....121 A6
Linley Cl NP19 .....145 A6
Linnet Cl CF23 .....178 D7
Linnet Way CF31 ...169 D7
Linton Cl NP4 ....38 A3
Linton St NP20 .....143 D2
Lion Cl CF5 ....176 C6
Lion Ct 1 NP4 ....17 C6
Lion St Blaenavon NP4 .17 C6
Swansea SA1 ....68 C2
Lion Way SA7 ....69 B7
Lionel Rd CF5 .....194 B6
Lionel Terr CF37 ...135 F5
Lisbon Ct CF82 ......84 E1
Lisburn Rd CF82 ....84 E1
Lisburn Rise CF44 ...27 D8
Liscombe St NP19 ..144 A4
Liscum Way CF62 ...214 C7
Lisnagarvey Ct CF14 .176 F8
Lister Ave 6 SA12 ...98 F1
Lister Gn NP20 .....117 A2
Lisvane Ho CF14 ....160 B2
Lisvane Rd CF14 ....160 B2
Lisvane St CF24 ....177 F1
Liswerry Cl 2 NP44 ..90 B2
Liswerry Dr NP44 ....90 B2
Liswerry Inf Sch
NP19 ....144 B3
Liswerry Jun Sch
NP19 ....144 B3
Liswerry Park Dr
NP19 ....144 C4
Liswerry Rd NP19 ..144 C4
Litchard Bglws CF31 .168 F7
Litchard Cross CF31 .168 F8
Litchard Hill CF31 ..168 F7
Litchard Ind Est CF31 .169 A7
Litchard Inf Sch CF31 .168 F8
Litchard Jun Sch
CF31 ....168 F8
Litchard Pk CF31 ...168 F7
Litchard Rise CF31 ..168 F8
Litchard Terr CF31 ..168 F8
Litchfield Ct CF11 ..194 F4
Little Ave CF5 ......191 F5
Little Brynhill La
CF62 ....214 D8
Little Dock St CF64 .206 F5
Little Frederick St 4
CF10 ....195 B5
Little Gam St 3 SA1 ..95 C6
Little La NP23 ....7 F4
Little London SA9 ..222 B7
Little Mill CF14 ....177 A3
Little Moors Hill
CF63 ....215 C6
Little Oaks View
NP10 ....142 A6
Little Orch CF64 ...206 C3
Little Wind St 9 SA44 .29 A1
Littlecroft Ave CF5 .193 F6
Littledene NP44 .....89 B3
Littleton St CF11 ...194 E5
Littlewoods CF45 ....82 D2
Livale Cl NP20 .....116 E2
Livale Ct NP20 .....116 E2
Livale Rd NP20 .....116 E2
Livale Wlk NP20 ....116 E2
Liverpool St 5 NP19 .143 E6
Livingstone Pl NP19 .143 E5
Livingstone Way
CF62 ....211 D7
Livorno Ho CF10 ...195 C3
Llamsamlet Ind Est
SA6 ....68 C5
Llan Rd
Llangynwyd CF34 ...128 B3
Marcross CF61 ....198 E2
Llan-Fach Rd NP11 ...87 B3
Llan-gan Prim Sch
CF35 ....187 F7
Llan-Yr-Avon Sq
NP44 ....90 A2
Llan-Yr-Avon Way
NP44 ....90 A2
Llan-yr-Eos CF46 ....83 E4
Llanarth Cl CF83 ...140 B6
Llanarth Rd
Newbridge NP11 .....86 F8

Llanarth Rd continued
Pontllanfraith NP12 ....86 A4
Llanarth Sq NP11 ....115 A1
Llanarth St
Cwmfelinfach NP11 ...113 E3
Machen CF83 ......140 B7
3 Newport NP20 ....143 C4
Llanbad CF72 ....153 D3
Llanbedr Rd CF5 ......193 E2
Llanberis Cl CF38 ....135 E2
Llanbleddian Ct 2
CF24 ....195 B7
Llanbleddian Gdns
CF24 ....195 A7
Llanbradach St
Cardiff CF11 ....194 F3
3 Pontypridd CF37 ..109 B1
Llanbradach Sta
CF83 ....111 F1
Llanbryn Gdns CF72 ..153 E3
Llancaeach Jun & Inf Schs
CF46 ....83 E3
Llancaiach Ct CF46 ...83 E3
Llancaiach Rd 4
CF14 ....177 B4
Llancaiach View CF46 .83 E5
Llancaiach-fawr CF48 .83 E6
Llancarfan Prim Sch
CF62 ....202 E1
Llancayo Pk CF81 ....57 F5
Llancayo St CF81 ....57 F5
Llandaf Sta CF14 .....176 F4
Llandafen Rd SA14 ...41 B5
Llandaff Arc 8 CF10 ..176 E4
Llandaff Campus (UWIC)
CF14 ....177 B1
Llandaff Chase CF5 ..176 F1
Llandaff Cl CF64 .....207 A2
Llandaff CW Prim Sch
CF5 ....194 A8
Llandaff Gn 3 NP44 ..89 C4
Llandaff Rd
Cardiff CF5 ....194 C6
Ebbw Vale NP23 .....7 E3
Llandaff St NP20 .....143 A3
Llandaff Way CF39 ...133 C8
Llanddewi Ct CF44 ...53 C7
Llanddewi St CF44 ...53 C7
Llandegefedd Way
NP4 ....63 A3
Llandegfedd Cl
Cardiff CF14 ....159 F3
Rogerstone NP10 ...142 B7
Llandegveth Cl NP44 .90 B6
Llandeilo Rd
Cross Hands SA14 ..218 B8
Glanaman SA18 ....220 C8
Llandennis Ave CF23 178 C6
Llandennis Gn CF23 .178 B6
Llandennis Rd CF23 .178 B6
Llandenny Wlk NP44 .89 C3
Llanderfel Ct NP44 ...89 A5
Llandetty Rd CF5 ....193 E7
Llandilo Cl CF64 .....206 C3
Llandinam Cres CF14 177 B1
Llandinam Rd CF62 ..214 E5
Llandogo Rd CF3 ....79 C1
Llandough Hill CF64 .206 D7
Llandough Hospl
CF64 ....206 C6
Llandough Prim Sch
CF64 ....206 D7
Llandough St CF24 ..195 A7
Llandough Trad Est
CF64 ....206 D8
Llandovery Cl 12 CF5 193 C4
Llandovery Villas
NP13 ....15 E2
Llandow Rd CF5 .....193 D5
Llandow Trad Est
CF71 ....199 D4
Llandowlais St NP44 .90 A2
Llandraw Ct CF37 ...109 A1
Llandraw Woods
CF37 ....135 A8
Llandudno Rd CF3 ..179 C4
Llandybie Rd SA18 ..132 B8
Llandyfrig Cl 9 CF64 206 C3
Llanedeyrn Cl CF23 .178 D3
Llanedeyrn Dr CF23 .178 E4
Llanedeyrn High Sch
CF23 ....178 E4
Llanedeyrn Jun & Inf Sch
CF23 ....178 E4
Llanedeyrn Rd CF23 .178 E3
Llanedi Rd
Llanedi SA4 ....218 D1
Pontarddulais SA4 ..19 A7
Llanedy Cty Prim Sch
SA4 ....218 D2
Llanelli Campus of the
Carmarthenshire Coll of
Tech SA15 ....40 C1
Llanelli Ent Workshops
SA15 ....40 F3
Llanelli Sta SA15 ....40 D3
Llanelli Workshops
SA14 ....41 A3
Llanerch Cotts SA15 .40 E7
Llanerch Cres SA4 ...43 B3
Llanerch Goed CF38 .135 D1
Llanerch La NP11 ....59 F4
Llanerch Path NP44 ..89 B2
Llanerch Rd
Abertillery NP11 ....59 E6
Dunvant SA2 ....93 D8
Swansea SA1 ....69 B2
Llanerch Terr SA15 ..40 E7

Llanerch Vineyard
CF72 ....173 E4
Llanerchwrwg Way CF3 179 E7
Llanfabon Ct CF37 ...109 F4
Llanfabon Dr CF83 ...138 F7
Llanfabon Inf Sch
CF46 ....83 E3
Llanfabon Rd CF46 ...83 D2
Llanfaes SA9 ....2 F8
Llanfair Gdns SA3 ...123 A6
Llanfair Hill CF41 ....79 A2
Llanfair Prim Sch
CF71 ....200 F5
Llanfair Rd
Cardiff CF11 ....194 C7
Pontypridd CF37 ...135 B8
Tonypandy CF40 ...107 A4
Llanfedw Cl CF83 ....138 C5
Llanfoist Cres 4 NP4 17 D7
Llanfoist St CF11 ....79 A3
Llanfrechfa Grange Hospl
NP44 ....90 C2
Llanfrechfa Way NP44 90 C1
Llangattock Ct NP44 .90 B5
Llangattock Rd CF5 ..193 E7
Llangattwg Cl NP23 ..7 E1
Llangattwg Comp Sch
SA10 ....49 B3
Llangefni Pl CF14 ...159 E1
Llangeinor Rd CF32 .150 F6
Llangeinor Terr CF32 130 E5
Llangennech Cty Prim Jun
& Inf Schs SA14 ....18 D1
Llangennech Sta SA14 42 C7
Llangewydd Grange
CF32 ....167 E7
Llangewydd Jun Sch
CF31 ....168 C5
Llangewydd Rd
Bridgend CF31 .....168 C5
Laleston CF32 .....167 E6
Llangiwg Prim Sch
SA8 ....23 E6
Llangorse Cotts NP13 36 B8
Llangorse Dr NP10 ...142 A3
Llangorse Path NP44 .90 A2
Llangorse Rd
Aberdare CF44 ......29 E1
Cardiff CF23 ....178 C2
Llanyravon NP44 ....90 A2
Swansea SA5 ....68 B5
Llangranog Pl CF14 .159 E1
Llangranog Rd CF14 .159 E1
Llangwm SA5 ....67 F6
Llangwm Pl CF3 .....179 C4
Llangwm Way CF36 ..182 F7
Llangybi Cl CF5 ......192 F3
Llangyfelach Prim Sch
SA5 ....45 B2
Llangyfelach Rd SA5 .68 C5
Llangyfelach St SA1 ..68 C1
Llangynidr Rd
Cardiff CF5 ....193 E7
Ebbw Vale NP23 .....7 D6
Llangynwyd Prim Sch
CF34 ....128 D6
Llanharan Prim Sch
CF72 ....154 A3
Llanhari Prim Sch
CF72 ....172 A5
Llanharran Terr CF32 104 F5
Llanharry Rd
Llanharry CF72 ....172 A8
Llanharry CF72 ....172 C6
Llanhilleth Ind Est
NP13 ....60 C5
Llanidloes Rd CF14 .177 B2
Llanilltud Faerdref Prim
CF38 ....135 F1
Llanilltud Fawr Prim Sch
CF61 ....210 A1
Llanina Gr CF3 ......179 E5
Llanishen Ct CF14 ...177 F8
Llanishen Fach Inf & Jun
Sch CF14 ....159 C1
Llanishen High sch
CF14 ....159 F1
Llanishen St CF14 ...177 F2
Llanishen Sta CF14 .160 A1
Llanllienwen Cl
Swansea SA6 ....45 F4
Ynysforgan SA6 ....46 A4
Llanllienwen Rd
Swansea SA6 ....45 F3
Ynysforgan SA6 ....46 A3
Llanmaes Rd CF61 ...210 A7
Llanmaes St CF11 ...194 F2
Llanmartin Jun & Inf Sch
NP18 ....145 E6
Llanmead Gdns CF62 212 F1
Llanmihangel Rd
CF71 ....200 D7
Llanmihangel Rise
CF71 ....200 D8
Llanmorlais Cty Prim Sch
SA4 ....64 B1
Llanmorlais Rd CF14 177 C1
Llannant Rd SA4 .....42 F5
Llanofer Rd SA13 ....75 D3
Llanon NP44 ....89 F6
Llanon Rd CF14 .....159 E1
Llanover Ave NP12 ...85 E4
Llanover Cl
Blaenavon NP4 .....17 E6
Newport NP20 .....117 A1
Llanover Rd
Blaenavon NP4 .....17 D6
Cardiff CF5 ....192 F3

Llanover Rd continued
Cwmavon NP4 ......17 F1
Pontypridd CF37 ...109 D2
Llanover St
Abercarn NP11 ......87 A3
2 Barry CF63 ......215 B6
Pontypridd CF37 ...109 D1
Llanquain Rd CF71 ..189 C3
Llanquian Castle
CF71 ....189 D1
Llanquian Cl CF71 ..188 F1
Llanquian Rd CF71 ..189 C2
Llanrhidian Prim Sch
SA3 ....229 D3
Llanrhyd 8 CF48 .....31 B1
Llanrumney Ave CF3 179 B5
Llanrumney High Sch
CF3 ....179 A6
Llansamlet Ind Est
SA7 ....69 B7
Llansamlet Sta SA7 ..69 F8
Llansannor & Llanharry
CW Prim Sch CF71 .172 A3
Llansannor Dr CF10 .195 C4
Llansawel SA11 ......71 C1
Llansawel Cres SA11 .71 B3
Llansawel Prim Sch
SA11 ....71 B1
Llanstephan Rd CF3 .179 C3
Llantarnam Cl NP44 ..89 F2
Llantarnam Hall
Rougemont Sch
NP20 ....116 F4
Llantarnam Ind Pk
NP44 ....116 F7
Llantarnam Park Way
NP44 ....117 A6
Llantarnam Rd
Cardiff CF14 ....177 D2
Cwmbran NP44 ......89 F1
Llantarnam Sch
NP44 ....117 A7
Llanthewy Cl NP44 ..90 B6
Llanthewy Rd NP20 .143 A4
Llantrisant Bsns Pk
CF72 ....155 C6
Llantrisant Ho 8
CF72 ....155 D3
Llantrisant Rd
Beddau CF38 ......155 F7
Cardiff CF5 ....176 D3
Llantrisant CF72 ...155 F3
Pentyrch CF5,CF15 .175 C4
Penycoedcae CF37 .135 B5
Pontyclun CF72 ....173 B8
Tonyrefail CF39 ....133 D6
Llantrisant Rise CF5 .176 F2
Llantrisant St CF24 .194 F8
Llantrithyd Rd CF71 .201 D7
Llantwit Gardens Cl
CF62 ....211 D5
Llantwit Major Rd
Cowbridge CF71 ...188 C4
Llandow CF71 .....199 A4
Llantwit Neath SA11 72 A8
Pontypridd CF37 ...135 B4
St Athan CF62 .....211 C5
Wick CF71 ....198 D5
Llantwit St Barry CF63 215 A5
Cardiff CF24 ....195 B7
Llanvair Rd NP19 ...143 D6
Llanwern Rd
Cardiff CF5 ....193 C5
Newport NP19 .....144 E4
Llanwern St NP19 ...143 E5
Llanwonno Cl CF37 .109 A2
Llanwonno Rd
Cwmaman CF44 .....53 A3
Mountain Ash CF45 .54 D1
Pontypridd CF37 ...109 A2
Porth CF39 ....107 F5
Llanyrafon Farm Mus
NP44 ....90 A2
Llanyrafon Prim Sch
NP44 ....90 A2
Llanyrnewydd SA4 ...64 F3
Lle Canol SA13 .....227 C1
Lle Hyfryd CF44 ......28 E6
Llest Terr CF38 ......156 C6
Lletai Ave CF38 .....170 E8
Lletty Dafydd SA11 .226 C4
Llettyharri SA13 ......99 C2
Llety'r Bugail CF34 ..128 C7
Llewellin St 4 NP19 .144 A5
Llewellyn Ave
Cardiff CF5 ....193 B6
Neath SA10 ....48 D1
Llewellyn Cl SA13 ...125 D7
Llewellyn Ct CF41 ...79 A4
Llewellyn Dr
Caerphilly CF83 ....138 A4
Pen-y-fai CF31 ....150 D1
Llewellyn Rd CF41 ...79 A4
Llewellyn Rd SA4 ....44 A2
Llewellyn St
Aberavon SA12 .....99 A1
Aberdare CF44 ......28 A4
Barry CF63 ....215 A6
Blaencwm CF42 ....50 C2
Glynneath SA11 ...223 D1
Hendreforgan CF39 .132 C5
Llanelli SA15 ......40 D4
Merthyr Tydfil CF47 .10 D2
Neath SA11 ....71 D4
Pentre CF41,CF40 ..78 F5
Tonypandy CF40 ...106 A4
Treorchy CF41 ......79 A4
Llewellyn St continued

Llewellyn St continued
Tylorstown CF40 ....80 B1
Llewellyn Terr
Tonypandy CF40 ...106 E7
Ynysybwl CF37 ......81 F1
Llewellyn's Rd SA13 .125 D5
Llewelyn Ave NP11 ..59 D2
Llewelyn Circ SA1 ....95 B8
Llewelyn Ct CF44 .....28 D4
Llewelyn Park Dr SA6 68 E7
Llewelyn St
Bargoed CF81 ......58 A1
Dowlais CF48 ....11 A5
Nant-y-Moel CF32 ..104 E7
Pontypridd CF37 ...109 A2
Swansea SA2 ....94 C6
Llewitna Terr SA5 ....67 B6
Lliedi Cres SA14 .....40 E6
Lliswerry High Sch
NP19 ....144 C1
Lliw Cotts SA4 ....43 D6
Lliw Valley Cl SA4 ...66 C6
Lloyd Ave Barry CF62 214 B5
Cardiff CF5 ....193 F7
Newbridge NP11 ....65 A4
Lloyd George Ave (Rhodfa
Lloyd George) CF10 .195 B3
Lloyd Pl CF3 ....180 A6
Lloyd Rd SA5 ....68 C5
Lloyd St
11 Ammanford SA18 219 B7
Llanelli SA15 ......40 C5
Maesteg CF34 ......75 B1
Newport NP19 .....144 A3
Pontardawe SA8 ....23 B2
Ton Pentre CF41 ....79 B3
Lloyd's Terr SA13 ....75 C4
Lloyds Terr CF47 .....10 F3
Lluest SA9 ....222 A5
Llwncelyn Cl CF48 ...10 C1
Llwycelyn Cl CF48 ...30 C8
Llwyd Coed CF14 ...158 F1
Llwyd y Berth CF83 .137 E2
Llwydarth Cotts CF34 102 B1
Llwydarth Rd CF34 ..102 C1
Llwydcoed Prim Sch
CF44 ....28 E6
Llwyfen CF47 ....10 D2
Llwyfen St CF47 .....10 D2
Llwyn Afanc SA4 .....45 F5
Llwyn Arian SA13 ...148 A6
Llwyn Arosfa SA2 ....94 C7
Llwyn Bedw
Mountain Ash CF45 .54 B6
Pencoed CF35 .....170 C8
Swansea SA5 ....67 D4
Llwyn Berry CF48 ....10 C1
Llwyn Brwydrau SA7 .70 A6
Llwyn Bryn Melyn
CF15 ....176 A6
Llwyn Celyn
Capel Hendre SA18 218 D6
Cwmbran NP44 ......89 D1
Ebbw Vale NP23 ....14 B8
Swansea SA5 ....67 D4
Llwyn Cl SA15 ....40 F5
Llwyn Coed NP12 ....85 D6
Llwyn Deri Cl NP10 .141 E2
Llwyn Derw
Pontardawe SA8 ....23 E4
Swansea SA5 ....67 D4
Llwyn Derwen 4
Tonypandy CF40 ...106 E7
Llwyn Derwen CF33 .165 F7
Llwyn Dic Penderyn
CF48 ....10 C1
Llwyn Drysgol CF15 .176 A6
Llwyn Eithin
Caerphilly CF83 ....138 D5
Swansea SA5 ....67 D4
Llwyn Glas CF31 ....168 C3
Llwyn Grug CF14 ...177 C8
Llwyn Gwern CF35 ..170 C8
Llwyn Gwyn CF72 ...172 B5
Llwyn Helig CF33 ...148 E1
Llwyn Helyg
Swansea SA5 ....67 D5
Tredegar NP22 ......6 C2
Llwyn Mallt CF15 ...176 B8
Llwyn Mawr Cl SA2 ..94 B8
Llwyn Mawr Rd SA2 .94 C8
Llwyn On
North Cornelly CF33 166 A8
Swansea SA5 ....67 D4
Llwyn Onn
Caerleon NP18 .....118 A6
Cardiff CF14 ....159 A1
Croesyceiliog NP44 ..90 B4
Penderyn CF44 ....224 D2
Penpedairheol CF82 .84 E7
Pontyclun CF72 ....173 A8
Llwyn Passat CF64 ..207 B6
Llwyn Rd SA18 .....220 D5
Llwyn Rhedyn SA2 ..94 B8
Llwyn Rhosyn CF14 .177 C8
Llwyn y Bioden SA6 .45 E5
Llwyn y Gog
Cwmrhydyceirw SA6 46 A5
Swansea SA6 ....46 A5
Llwyn y Golomen SA6 46 A5
Llwyn y Graig SA4 ...43 F1
Llwyn y Groes CF31 .168 B4
Llwyn y Pia Rd CF14 160 B3
Llwyn Ynys SA14 ....41 C4
Llwyn Yr Eos SA14 ...41 B6
Llwyn Yr Hebog SA6 .46 A5
Llwyn Yr Iar SA14 ....46 A5
Llwyn-Bach Terr NP12 34 C2

Llwyn-Crwn Rd SA7 ..69 D7
Llwyn-ifan SA14 .....18 B2
Llwyn-Nant SA18 ...220 D4
Llwyn-On Cl CF83 ...137 F4
Llwyn-on Cres NP12 .59 B1
Llwyn-on La NP12 ...59 B1
Llwyn-On Rd
Abertillery NP13 ....36 C3
Blackwood NP12 ....59 B1
Llwyn-On St CF83 ...137 F4
Llwyn-y-Bryn
Ammanford SA18 ..219 B8
Neath SA10 ....70 C6
Llwyn-y-Gelynen
CF48 ....30 C8
Llwyn-y-Grant Pl
CF23 ....178 D2
Llwyn-y-Grant Rd
CF23 ....178 D2
Llwyn-y-Grant Terr
CF23 ....178 D2
Llwyn-y-Mor SA3 ...122 E4
Llwyn-Yr-Eos
Abercanaid CF48 ....30 F4
Swansea SA6 ....45 E2
Llwynbrain Terr
CF72 ....154 A3
Llwyncarw SA6 ......45 F5
Llwyncelyn
Bettws CF32 ....129 E3
Llanelli SA15 ......40 E4
Llwyncelyn Ave SA14 .19 D4
Llwyncelyn Ct CF39 .108 A3
Llwyncelyn Ind Est
CF39 ....108 A3
Llwyncelyn Inf Sch
CF39 ....108 A3
Llwyncelyn Parc
CF39 ....108 A3
Llwyncelyn Rd
Glanaman SA18 ....219 F8
Gwaun-Cae-Gurwen
SA18 ....220 E6
Porth CF39 ....108 A3
Llwyncelyn Terr
Abertillery NP13 ....59 E6
Coelbren SA10 ....222 F6
Nelson CF46 ....83 D3
Llwyncethin Rd SA5 ..68 A3
Llwyncrwn Cty Prim Sch
CF38 ....155 F6
Llwyncrwn Rd CF38 .155 F6
Llwyncyfarthwch SA15 41 A5
Llwynderi CF44 ......28 E6
Llwynderi Rd NP20 .143 A4
Llwynderw
Gorseinon SA4 ......43 B1
Porthcawl CF36 ....182 F7
Three Crosses SA4 ..65 E1
Llwynderw Ave CF14 102 C3
Llwynderw Cl SA2 ...94 B1
Llwynderw Dr SA3 ..123 B8
Llwynderw Inf Sch
CF34 ....102 C3
Llwynderw Rd CF14 .177 C8
Llwyneryr Unit Hospl
SA6 ....45 E2
Llwynfedw Gdns
CF14 ....177 D5
Llwynfedw Rd CF14 .177 D5
Llwynfen Rd CF72 ...173 B7
Llwynhendy Jun Sch
SA14 ....41 D5
Llwynhendy Rd SA14 41 D4
Llwynmadoc St CF37 109 B1
Llwynmawr La SA4 ..65 C5
Llwynon Clydach SA6 .22 C1
Crynant SA10 ......226 A7
Risca NP11 ....115 A7
Llwynpennau Cotts
CF72 ....174 C6
Llwynwhilwg Terr 3
SA14 ....40 F4
Llwynypia Hospl CF40 79 F1
Llwynypia Prim Sch
CF40 ....106 E7
Llwynypia Rd CF40 ..106 E7
Llwynypia Sta CF40 .106 E8
Llwynypia Terr CF40 .106 E8
Llygad-Yr-Haul
Glynneath SA11 ...223 B1
Neath SA10 ....48 D2
Llyn Berwyn Cl NP10 142 B6
Llyn Castan CF23 ...178 E2
Llyn Celyn Cl NP10 .142 B7
Llyn Cres CF43 ......79 F6
Llyn Cwm Llwydrhew
NP13 ....36 C2
Llyn Tircoed SA4 ....44 C5
Llynfa Rd SA4 ....65 A4
Llynfi Hospl CF34 ...101 F1
Llynfi La
Bridgend CF31 .....168 F4
Maesteg CF34 ......102 A3
Llynfi Rd CF34 ......102 A3
Llynfi St
1 Bridgend CF31 ...168 F4
Tondu CF32 ....150 C5
Llynfi View CF34 ....102 B8
Llys Aaron SA4 ......19 C4
Llys Alys SA15 ......40 E5
Llys Andrew SA10 ...70 F6
Llys Aneirin SA4 .....66 D8
Llys Baldwin SA4 ....66 B6
Llys Bartlett SA11 ...71 F4
Llys Bathania SA11 .226 D5
Llys Bethel SA14 ....41 C5

Llys Briallen CF31 ...169 D6
Llys Bryn Felin CF39 133 C5
Llys Brynteg SA4 ....43 B3
Llys Cambria CF83 ..137 F8
Llys Caradog
Creigiau CF15 .....174 D7
Llanelli SA14 ......41 D5
Llys Castell SA13 ...148 A6
Llys Catwg
Glynneath SA11 ...227 C8
Talbot Green CF72 .155 C2
Llys Celyn CF38 .....136 A1
Llys Cennech SA14 ..18 C1
Llys Cilsaig SA14 ....41 B8
Llys Coed
Bridgend CF31 .....168 C3
Pontypridd CF37 ...109 D6
Llys Coed Derw CF38 156 D8
Llys Coleg 4 CF14 ..177 B3
Llys Corrwg CF37 ...136 C5
Llys Cynffig CF33 ...148 B2
Llys Cynon CF44 .....27 F7
Llys Deri CF72 ......172 B5
Llys Derwen
Llantrisant CF72 ...155 D2
Pontypridd CF37 ...109 D6
Llys Dewi CF61 .....209 F7
Llys Dewi Dinefwr
CF15 ....174 E7
Llys Dewi Sant
Gorseinon SA4 .....43 C2
3 Swansea SA1 ....95 D6
Llys Dol SA6 ....46 A2
Llys Dulais SA10 ...226 A7
Llys Dur SA6 ....46 A2
Llys Dwfnant SA11 .226 C4
Llys Dwrgi SA7 ......70 B8
Llys Dwynwen CF61 209 F8
Llys Dyfodwg
Creigiau CF15 .....174 E6
Talbot Green CF72 .155 C2
Llys Dyfrig CF15 ....174 D6
Llys Ebwy NP23 .....14 D7
Llys Eglwys CF31 ...168 C3
Llys Eithin SA14 ....218 C3
Llys Elba SA4 ....66 B6
Llys Faen CF31 .....168 F5
Llys Felin SA10 .....49 C4
Llys Felin Newydd
SA7 ....69 C6
Llys Fran SA15 ......40 E7
Llys Fredrick Jones
SA9 ....2 C7
Llys Garth CF38 ....135 D1
Llys Ger y Llan SA4 .19 D3
Llys Glan y Mor 2
SA15 ....40 C3
Llys Glanrafon SA8 ..23 E4
Llys Glanrhondda
CF41 ....78 F5
Llys Glowr CF37 .....82 A1
Llys Groeswen SA13 125 D6
Llys Gwalia SA4 .....43 D2
Llys Gwenci SA7 .....70 B8
Llys Gwent CF63 ...215 C8
Llys Gwernen
Cwmrhydyceirw SA6 .46 A2
Swansea SA6 ....45 F2
Llys Gwyn
Bridgend CF31 .....168 F6
Maesteg CF34 .....102 A3
Llys Gwynfaen SA4 ..42 F2
Llys Gwynfryn SA10 .48 C5
Llys Gwynno CF15 ..174 E6
Llys Gwyrdd NP44 ..116 A7
Llys Hafn CF15 .....158 A3
Llys Hebog SA7 .....70 B8
Llys Hebron CF41 ...79 A3
Llys Illtyd CF15 .....174 D7
Llys Iris SA10 ....48 C1
Llys Jernegan 2 SA1 .95 E6
Llys John Davies 5
SA1 ....95 D8
Llys Llywelyn CF38 .156 D8
Llys Mabon NP22 ...12 D5
Llys Maelwg CF72 ..155 C2
Llys Maendy CF41 ...79 A3
Llys Nant Fer SA18 .220 D7
Llys Nant Glas CF45 .82 A7
Llys Nant Pandy
CF83 ....138 A4
Llys Nazereth CF41 ..78 F5
Llys Nedd SA10 .....48 D2
Llys Onnen NP23 ....14 B8
Llys Pat Chown SA8 .23 E4
Llys Penderi SA14 ...41 F5
Llys Penpant SA4 ....45 C2
Llys Pentre SA5 .....68 D4
Llys Pum Cyfair CF14 177 C2
Llys Sant Teilo SA5 ..45 B2
Llys Siloh CF41 ......78 F5
Llys Soar CF42 ......50 E2
Llys Steffan CF61 ...209 F7
Llys Tal-y-Bont Rd
CF14 ....177 E1
Llys Teg CF31 ......168 B3
Llys Teilo
Creigiau CF15 .....174 E6
Llantwit Major CF61 209 F7
Talbot Green CF72 .155 C2
Llys Trerobant CF37 .109 A7
Llys Tripp CF15 .....158 A3
Llys Tudful CF15 ....174 D7
Llys Ty Gwyn 6 CF37 109 E2

Llys Tylcha Fawr
CF39 . . . . .133 C5
Llys Tynewydd CF35 .169 C7
Llys Warner SA15 . . . .40 E7
Llys Wenallt SA11 . . . .49 E3
Llys Wern SA10 . . . . .48 C2
Llys y Brenin SA4 . . . .66 B8
Llys y Coed
Barry CF62 . . . . .214 C4
Ystrad Mynach CF82 .111 E7
Llys y Drindod SA15 . .40 E3
Llys y Felin SA14 . . . . .18 B1
Llys y Fran CF38 . . . .156 E8
Llys y Gof SA15 . . . . .40 C4
Llys y Morwr SA15 . . .40 D4
Llys Yr Ardd
Morriston SA6 . . . . . . .46 A2
Swansea SA6 . . . . . . .45 F2
Llys Yr Efail
Blaina NP13 . . . . .15 D5
Tonyrefail CF39 . . . . .133 C5
Llys Yr Onnen SA14 . .41 A8
Llys Yr Orsaf [7] SA15 .40 C4
Llys Yr Ysgol SA18 . . .218 E6
Llys-Coed SA7 . . . . . . .47 B1
Llys-faen (Lisvane & Thornhill Sta) CF14 .159 F3
Llys-Gwyn Terr SA4 . .19 D5
Llys-Le-Breos SA3 . . . .93 F1
Llys-Teg SA2 . . . . .93 D8
Llys-Uchaf SA7 . . . . . .70 B8
Llys-y- Coed SA4 . . . . .42 D1
Llys-y-Bryn SA7 . . . . . .70 B8
Llys-y-Celyn CF83 . . .138 C5
Llys-y-Coed SA10 . . . .71 D8
Llys-y-Deri SA18 . . . . .219 D7
Llys-y-Fedwen CF83 .138 C4
Llys-y-Felin SA5 . . . . .68 D2
Llys-y-Fran CF31 . . . .168 B6
Llys-y-graig SA10 . . . .70 F8
Llys-y-Nant SA11 . . . .71 C4
Llys-y-Waun SA7 . . . .47 B1
Llys-yr-Eglwys [10]
CF64 . . . . .207 B5
Llysfaen Prim Sch
CF14 . . . . .160 B3
Llysgwyn SA6 . . . . . . .45 C2
Llysnewydd [4] SA15 . .40 C3
Llyswen Bardstn CF83 .139 F7
Penpedairheol CF82 . .84 F7
Penywaun CF44 . . . . . .28 B6
Llyswen Clos CF82 . . . .84 F7
Llyswen Rd CF23 . . . .178 B7
Llyswen Wlk NP44 . . . .90 A1
Llythrid Ave SA2 . . . . .94 E6
Llywelyn Ho NP44 . . . .89 F2
Llywelyn Rd NP44 . . . .89 E3
Llywelyn St CF32 . . . .104 E2
Load Of Hay Rd NP11 .59 F2
Lochaber St CF24 . . . .178 C1
Lock Ct CF37 . . . . . . .109 D1
Lock St CF45 . . . . .82 F3
Lock's Common Rd
CF36 . . . . .182 D7
Lock's Ct CF36 . . . . . .182 E8
Lock's La CF36 . . . . . .182 E8
Lock-Up La NP4 . . . . . .37 F3
Locke Gr [12] CF3 . . . .180 A6
Locke St NP20 . . . . . .143 B5
Locks Rd CF10 . . . . . .207 C8
Lodden Cl NP20 . . . . .116 E2
Lodge Ave NP18 . . . . .118 A3
Lodge Cl CF14 . . . . . .160 A4
Lodge Cl The SA2 . . . . .94 A7
Lodge Ct SA11 . . . . . . .71 C2
Lodge Dr SA12 . . . . . . .98 D6
Lodge Hill
Caerleon NP18 . . . . . .117 F3
Llanwern NP18 . . . . . .145 B5
Lodge Rd
Abersychan NP4 . . . . . .37 E3
Caerleon NP18 . . . . . .118 A3
Lodge Wood NP4 . . . . .62 E5
Lodwick Rise CF3 . . . .180 A5
Loftus St CF5 . . . . . . .194 B6
Login Rd SA5 . . . . .67 A3
Lombard Cl CF36 . . . .165 E1
Lombard St
Barry CF62 . . . . .214 F5
Neath SA11 . . . . .71 D6
Lombardy Villas SA10 .48 E1
Lomond Cres CF23 . . .178 C5
Lon Aber SA15 . . . . . . .40 F4
Lon Alfa SA2 . . . . .93 F8
Lon Bedwen SA2 . . . . .94 D8
Lon Beili Glas SA18 . .220 D6
Lon Brydwen SA4 . . . . .43 B1
Lon Bryn-Mawr [7]
SA18 . . . . .219 B7
Lon Brynawel SA7 . . . .69 F6
Lon Bryngwyn SA2 . . . .94 E8
Lon Brynneuadd
SA18 . . . . .220 D7
Lon Brynteg SA10 . . . .48 C1
Lon Cadog SA2 . . . . . .94 E7
Lon Cae Banc SA2 . . . .94 D7
Lon Camlad SA6 . . . . . .68 E8
Lon Caron SA2 . . . . . . .94 E7
Lon Carreg Bica SA7 . .72 B8
Lon Catwg SA8 . . . . . . .24 B5
Lon Cedwyn SA2 . . . . .94 E7
Lon Cefn Mably CF62 212 F1
Lon Ceiriog SA14 . . . . .41 D5
Lon Claerwen SA6 . . . .68 E8
Lon Coed Bran SA2 . . .94 E8

Lon Coed Parc SA2 . . .94 E8
Lon Cothi SA2 . . . . . . .67 E1
Lon Cwmgwyn SA2 . . . .94 E8
Lon Cwrt Ynyston
CF11 . . . . .194 C2
Lon Cynfor SA2 . . . . . .94 E7
Lon Cynlais SA2 . . . . . .94 D7
Lon Dan-y-Coed SA2 .94 E8
Lon Derw SA2 . . . . .94 D8
Lon Draenen SA2 . . . . .94 C7
Lon Draenog SA6 . . . . .45 F5
Lon Einon SA4 . . . . . . .43 F2
Lon Eithrym SA6 . . . . .46 D8
Lon Elai CF72 . . . . . . .173 B8
Lon Enfys SA7 . . . . . . .69 D6
Lon Fach
Caerphilly CF83 . . . . . .137 C8
Cardiff CF14 . . . . .177 B7
Lon Fawr CF83 . . . . . .137 F2
Lon Fferm Felin CF62 214 B4
Lon Gaer SA4 . . . . .43 F2
Lon Ganol CF14 . . . . .177 B7
Lon Gellideg NP11 . . . .59 C4
Lon Ger-y-Coed
Ammanford SA18 . . . .219 D7
Swansea SA2 . . . . .94 E8
Lon Glynfelin SA10 . . . .48 B1
Lon Gwendraeth SA6 . .68 E8
Lon Gwesyn SA7 . . . . .47 A1
Lon Gwynfryn SA2 . . . .94 E7
Lon Hafren
Caerphilly CF83 . . . . . .137 C1
Swansea SA6 . . . . .68 E8
Lon Heddwch
Craig-Cefn-Parc SA6 . . .22 B2
Swansea SA7 . . . . .69 C6
Lon Helyg NP44 . . . . . .90 B1
Lon Helygen CF37 . . .109 D6
Lon Heulog
Brynmenyn CF32 . . . .150 D6
Hawthorn CF37 . . . . . .136 A4
Lon Hir SA8 . . . . .23 F4
Lon Illtyd SA2 . . . . .94 E7
Lon Iorwg SA2 . . . . . . .94 C7
Lon Irfon SA2 . . . . .67 E1
Lon Isa CF14 . . . . .177 B7
Lon Isaf CF83 . . . . . . .137 F2
Lon Ithon SA6 . . . . . . .68 E8
Lon Killan SA2 . . . . . . .93 C8
Lon Las CF44 . . . . .28 D6
Lon Llwyd SA18 . . . . . .220 B8
Lon Llys Havard
SA18 . . . . .219 C6
Lon Madoc CF14 . . . . .177 C4
Lon Mafon SA2 . . . . . . .94 E7
Lon Masarn SA2 . . . . . .94 C8
Lon Mefus SA2 . . . . . . .94 D8
Lon Menai SA7 . . . . . . .47 A1
Lon Nant NP44 . . . . . . .89 F5
Lon Nedd SA6 . . . . .68 F8
Lon Ogwen SA7 . . . . . .47 A1
Lon Olchfa SA2 . . . . . . .94 A6
Lon Owain CF5 . . . . . .193 B3
Lon Pen-y-Coed SA2 . .67 D1
Lon Penfro SA6 . . . . . .46 A4
Lon Penllyn CF14 . . . .177 B6
Lon Pennant NP12 . . . .58 E1
Lon Pinwydden CF71 189 C8
Lon Robin Goch CF83 137 E3
Lon Sawdde SA6 . . . . .68 E8
Lon Tanyrallt SA8 . . . . .23 E3
Lon Teify SA2 . . . . .67 E1
Lon Tir-y-Dail SA18 . . .219 B7
Lon Towy SA2 . . . . .67 D1
Lon Ty'n-y-Cae CF14 .177 C6
Lon Tyr Haul SA7 . . . . .69 F6
Lon Ucha CF14 . . . . . .177 B7
Lon Uchaf CF83 . . . . . .137 F2
Lon y Bedydd [12]
SA18 . . . . .219 B7
Lon y Dderwen SA4 . .40 E8
Lon y Fran CF83 . . . . .137 E3
Lon y Goch CF5 . . . . .175 C6
Lon y Maes SA14 . . . . .41 B4
Lon y Nant CF14 . . . . .177 C7
Lon y Tresglen CF83 .137 E3
Lon yr Odyn CF83 . . . .138 C4
Lon Yr Ysgol SA14 . . . .42 C7
Lon-Od-Nant CF41 . . .210 A5
Lon-Werdd Cl CF5 . . .193 A5
Lon-y-Barri CF83 . . . .137 F5
Lon-y-Bryn SA11 . . . . .223 D1
Lon-y-Bugail CF31 . . .168 B6
Lon-y-Byrnnau CF44 .28 C3
Lon-y-Cariadon
CF33 . . . . .148 A1
Lon-y-Castell CF5 . . . .193 C3
Lon-y-Celyn
Cardiff CF14 . . . . .176 F6
Nelson CF46 . . . . .83 D4
Lon-y-Coed
Bridgend CF31 . . . . . .168 A4
Pontardawe SA8 . . . . . .23 D6
Lon-y-Dail CF14 . . . .177 B7
Lon-y-Dderwen
Cardiff CF14 . . . . .177 B7
Nelson CF46 . . . . .83 D4
Lon-y-Deri
Caerphilly CF83 . . . . . .137 F2
Lon-y-Felin
Garnswllt SA18 . . . . . .219 B5
Mountain Ash CF45 . . . .54 C6
Lon-y-Ffin CF5 . . . . . .193 A5
Lon-y-Fro CF5 . . . . . . .175 C8
Lon-y-Garwa CF83 . . .137 F1
Lon-y-Gors CF83 . . . .137 D5
Lon-y-Groes CF14 . . .177 D3

Lon-y-Gruglas SA18 . .219 A6
Lon-y-Llwyn CF46 . . . .83 D4
Lon-y-Llyn CF83 . . . . .137 F2
Lon-y-Mynydd CF14 .177 D7
Lon-y-Nant SA11 . . . .223 D1
Lon-y-Odraenen
CF83 . . . . .137 F2
Lon-y-Parc
Cardiff CF14 . . . . .177 B5
Glynneath SA11 . . . . .223 C1
Maesteg CF34 . . . . . . .75 A2
Lon-y-Rhedyn CF83 .177 F2
Lon-y-Rhyd CF14 . . . .177 B8
Lon-y-Twyn CF83 . . . .138 B2
Lon-y-Waun CF83 . . . .137 E2
Lon-y-Wern
Caerphilly CF83 . . . . . .137 F2
Pontardawe SA8 . . . . . .23 F3
Lon-y-Winci CF14 . . . .177 B8
Lon-yr-Afon CF83 . . . .112 A2
Lon-yr-Awel CF27 . . . .173 C8
Lon-yr-Efail CF5 . . . . .193 B3
Lon-yr-Eglwys CF32 .185 C2
Lon-Yr-Ysgol
Llanelli SA14 . . . . .41 A7
Pontardawe SA8 . . . . . .24 A7
Lon-Ysgubor CF14 . . .177 B8
Loncae Porth CF14 . . .159 C1
Londeg SA8 . . . . .23 D6
Londen Cl SA12 . . . . . .99 D4
London Rd SA11 . . . . . .71 E7
London Row CF12 . . . .99 D4
London St
Mountain Ash CF45 . . . .54 D3
Newport NP19 . . . . . . .143 E6
London Terr SA12 . . . . .99 D4
Lone Rd SA6 . . . . .22 D1
Long Acre
Bishopston SA3 . . . . . .122 B6
Cwmbran NP44 . . . . . . .89 B1
North Cornelly CF33 . .165 E7
Long Acre Ct
Bishopston SA3 . . . . . .122 B6
Porthcawl CF36 . . . . . .165 D2
Long Acre Dr CF36 . . .165 E2
Long Cairn SA3 . . . . . .120 D8
Long Hollow [1] NP4 . .89 E4
Long House Barn Est
NP4 . . . . .39 E7
Long House Ct CF14 .160 A2
Long Meadow Ct
NP19 . . . . .144 C3
Long Meadow Dr
CF62 . . . . .215 A4
Long Oaks Ave SA2 . . .94 E6
Long Oaks Ct SA2 . . . .94 E7
Long Oaks Mews SA2 .94 E7
Long Ridge SA1 . . . . . .68 C1
Long Row
Ferndale CF43 . . . . . . .79 F8
Llanelli SA15 . . . . .40 E6
New Tredegar NP24 . . .33 F7
Pontypridd CF37 . . . . .135 E6
Long Shepherds Dr
SA3 . . . . .122 A4
Long St SA9 . . . . .222 A6
Long View Rd
Swansea SA6 . . . . .45 D1
Swansea SA6 . . . . .68 D8
Long Vue Rd SA12 . . . .98 C2
Longacre Cl
Barry CF63 . . . . .215 D8
Llantrisant CF72 . . . . .155 E2
Longbridge NP18 . . . .117 F8
Longcross St CF24 . . .195 C6
Longditch Rd NP19 . . .144 E1
Longfellow Dr CF31 . .168 D6
Longfellow Gdns
CF83 . . . . .139 D7
Longfield Ct CF44 . . . .27 D7
Longford Cres SA1 . . . .96 A7
Longford La SA10 . . . . .48 A1
Longford Rd
Neath SA10 . . . . .48 B2
Neath Abbey SA10 . . . .48 B2
Longhouse Gr NP44 . .115 F8
Longlands CF33 . . . . . .148 B2
Longleat Cl CF14 . . . .160 B2
Longmeadow Dr
CF64 . . . . .206 B2
Longmede Pk CF44 . .224 B1
Longreach Cl CF5 . . . .192 F4
Longships Rd CF10 . . .195 F1
Longspears Ave CF14 177 E3
Longtown Gr NP10 . . .163 E5
Longueil Cl CF10 . . . .195 C3
Longwood Dr CF14 . . .176 C7
Lonlas Ave SA10 . . . . . .70 D8
Lonlas Bsns Pk SA10 .70 D8
Lonlas Village Workshops
SA10 . . . . .70 D7
Lonsdale Rd CF23 . . . .178 E3
Lord Pontypridd Ho [6]
CF5 . . . . .194 B7
Lord St Aberdare CF44 .53 C8
[4] Newport NP19 . . . .143 D6
Penarth CF64 . . . . . . .207 B5
Lorraine Cl SA12 . . . .98 D1
Lothian Cres CF23 . . .178 D3
Loudoun Sq CF10 . . . .195 B3
Lougher Cl CF5 . . . . . .193 C4
Lougher Gdns CF36 . .182 E6
Lougher Pl
North Cornelly CF33 . .165 F7
St Athan CF62 . . . . . .211 C4
Loughor Comm SA4 . . .43 B2
Loughor Rd SA4 . . . . . .66 B8
Loughor Row CF36 . . .165 F1

Louisa Pl CF10 . . . . . .195 B2
Louise Cl SA11 . . . . . .226 C4
Louise Ct [1] CF14 . . .176 F3
Louvain Terr NP23 . . . .14 C3
Lovage Cl CF23 . . . . . .178 E8
Love La Cardiff CF10 .195 B5
Llanbethian CF71 . . . .188 E1
Loveluck Ct CF61 . . . .209 F6
Low Row CF45 . . . . . . .54 C5
Lowdon Terr CF62 . . .214 E5
Lower Acre CF5 . . . . . .193 B3
Lower Adare St CF32 103 E4
Lower Alma Pl CF41 . .79 A4
Lower Alma Terr
CF37 . . . . .135 D8
Lower Bailey St
[4] Brynmawr NP23 . . . . .8 C1
Wattstown CF39 . . . . .107 E8
Lower Bridge St NP4 .62 C6
Lower Brynhyfryd Terr
CF83 . . . . .110 F2
Lower Castle St NP13 .36 B4
Lower Cathedral Rd
CF11 . . . . .194 F5
Lower Church St CF32 .103 F3
Lower Colbren Rd
SA18 . . . . .220 D6
Lower Coronation St
NP22 . . . . .13 E6
Lower Court Terr
NP13 . . . . .60 B6
Lower Cross Rd SA15 .40 F5
Lower Cross St
Hirwaun CF44 . . . . . . .27 D8
New Tredegar NP24 . . .33 D3
Lower Dell The [1]
SA15 . . . . .40 C7
Lower Dock St NP20 .143 D4
Lower Dunraven St
CF40 . . . . .106 F5
Lower Edward St [13]
CF47 . . . . .10 D2
Lower Farm Ct CF62 .213 A2
Lower Forest Level
CF45 . . . . .54 C2
Lower Glantorvaen Terr
NP4 . . . . .17 B6
Lower Glyn-gwyn St
CF83 . . . . .139 A6
Lower Guthrie St
CF63 . . . . .215 A5
Lower Gwastad Terr
NP13 . . . . .36 B8
Lower Harper's Rd
NP4 . . . . .37 F5
Lower Hill St [14] NP4 .17 C6
Lower Holmes St
CF63 . . . . .215 C6
Lower James St NP12 .58 F4
Lower Lancaster St
NP13 . . . . .36 B3
Lower Leigh Rd NP4 . .38 B1
Lower Llansantffraid Rd
CF32 . . . . .150 D4
Lower Morel St CF63 215 A5
Lower Mount Pleasant [9]
CF48 . . . . .31 C1
Lower Pantteg SA9 . . . .2 A4
Lower Park Gdns NP4 .62 C6
Lower Park Terr NP4 . .62 C6
Lower Pyke St CF63 .215 A5
Lower Rd NP24 . . . . . . .34 A1
Lower Rhymney Prim Sch
NP22 . . . . .12 F3
Lower Row
Dowlais CF48 . . . . .11 B5
Rhymney NP22 . . . . . . .12 C7
Lower Royal La NP13 .36 A4
Lower Royal Lane Terr
NP13 . . . . .36 A4
Lower Salisbury St
NP22 . . . . .13 E6
Lower Sq NP23 . . . . .7 C4
Lower St CF44 . . . . . . .53 D7
Lower Station Rd [4]
SA18 . . . . .220 B8
Lower Station St [2]
CF44 . . . . .224 A1
Lower Stoney Rd NP4 .37 F5
Lower Taff View
CF37 . . . . .109 E3
Lower Ten Hos NP13 . .15 C6
Lower Terr
Treorchy CF42 . . . . . . .78 C5
Tylorstown CF43 . . . . . .80 C2
Lower Thomas St
CF47 . . . . .10 E1
Lower Trostre Rd
SA15 . . . . .40 F3
Lower Ty-Gwyn Rd
Abersychan NP4 . . . . . .37 E6
Abersychan NP4 . . . . . .37 E7
Lower Union St CF48 . .11 B4
Lower Vaynor Rd CF48 .10 A5
Lower Waun St NP4 . . .17 C7
Lower Wern Rd SA9 . . . .2 B6
Lower West End [1]
SA13 . . . . .125 C6
Lower Woodland St [11]
NP4 . . . . .17 D7
Lower Wyndham Terr
NP11 . . . . .115 B1
Lowerdale Rd CF72 . . .155 E2
Lowfield Dr CF14 . . . . .159 E2
Lowland Dr CF38 . . . .136 A1
Lowlands Cres NP44 . . .89 E6
Lowlands Ct NP44 . . . .89 E6

Lowlands Rd NP44 . . . .89 E6
Lowndes Cl NP10 . . . .141 F3
Lowther Rd CF24 . . . .195 B7
Lucania Bldgs [1]
SA13 . . . . .125 C7
Lucas Cl CF63 . . . . . . .215 C8
Lucas Rd SA7 . . . . .42 F8
Lucas St Cardiff CF24 .178 A1
Newport NP20 . . . . . . .143 B6
Lucerne Dr CF14 . . . . .159 D3
Lucknow St CF11 . . . .194 E3
Lucy Rd SA10 . . . . .70 D7
Ludlow Cl
Cardiff CF11 . . . . .195 A2
Llanyravon NP44 . . . . . .90 B1
Newport NP19 . . . . . . .143 F4
Ludlow La CF64 . . . . . .207 B4
Ludlow St
Caerphilly CF83 . . . . . .138 A2
Cardiff CF11 . . . . .194 F2
Penarth CF64 . . . . . . .207 A4
Lulworth Rd NP18 . . . .118 C1
Lundy Cl Cardiff CF14 .177 E8
Porthcawl CF36 . . . . . .165 E1
Lundy Dr
Mumbles SA3 . . . . .122 F7
Newport NP19 . . . . . . .143 F7
Lunnon Cl SA3 . . . . . .120 F8
Lupin Cl
Merthyr Tydfil CF47 . . . .10 B5
Merthyr Tydfil CF47 . . . .10 C5
Port Talbot SA12 . . . . . .98 C3
Luther La CF47 . . . . . . .10 F1
Luther St CF47 . . . . . . .30 F8
Luton Ho [5] CF24 . . .195 C6
Luton St CF42 . . . . .78 D6
Luton Terr [4] SA15 . . .40 C7
Lydbrook Cl [2] SA1 . . .68 C2
Lydford Ave SA1 . . . . . .95 E8
Lydford Cl CF14 . . . . .177 B6
Lydstep Cres CF14 . . .177 B2
Lydstep Flats CF14 . . .177 B2
Lydstep Rd CF62 . . . . .214 F7
Lydwood Cl CF83 . . . .140 A7
Lyle St CF45 . . . . .54 E3
Lyn Pac Trad Est NP44 .89 C5
Lynch Blosse Cl CF5 .176 B2
Lyncroft NP44 . . . . .89 B3
Lyncroft Cl CF3 . . . . . .179 D8
Lynden SA9 . . . . .1 D1
Lyndhurst Ave NP20 .143 A2
Lyndhurst St
Cardiff CF11 . . . . .194 D5
Mountain Ash CF45 . . . .54 D4
Lyndon Way NP10 . . . .142 B4
Lyne Rd Newport NP20 143 C7
Risca NP11 . . . . .115 A1
Lynmouth Cres CF3 . .179 A3
Lynmouth Dr CF64 . . .216 A4
Lynn Davies Ave
CF32 . . . . .130 E5
Lynn St SA5 . . . . .68 E2
Lynsdale Rd SA5 . . . . . .68 C4
Lynton Cl Cardiff CF3 .179 B4
Sully CF64 . . . . .216 B5
Lynton Ct SA3 . . . . . . .122 C6
Lynton Pl CF3 . . . . . . .179 B4
Lynton Terr CF3 . . . . .179 A4
Lynwood Ct
[10] Cardiff CF24 . . . .195 C7
Radyr CF15 . . . . .176 B5
Lyon Cl CF11 . . . . .194 D1
Lyon's Pl SA11 . . . . .226 E5
Lyric Ct SA8 . . . . .23 E4
Lyric Way CF14 . . . . . .159 C2
Lysander Ct CF24 . . . .196 A7
Lystep Ho NP44 . . . . . .89 D2
Lytham Gr [1] CF3 . . .180 A8

M

Maberly Ct CF14 . . . . .178 A7
Mabon Cl SA4 . . . . . . .42 F3
Macaulay Ave CF3 . . .179 B2
Macaulay Gdns NP20 142 F1
Macauley Rd CF5 . . .192 F4
Macdonald Ave CF5 . .170 D7
Macdonald Cl CF5 . . .193 A4
Macdonald Pl CF5 . . .193 A4
Macdonald Rd CF5 . . .193 A4
Mace La CF42 . . . . .78 B8
Macgregor Row
CF34 . . . . .102 A4
Machen Cl Cardiff CF3 180 A7
Risca NP11 . . . . .115 B1
Machen Pl CF11 . . . . .194 E5
Machen Prim Sch
CF83 . . . . .139 F7
Machen St
Cardiff CF11 . . . . .194 E3
[3] Penarth CF64 . . . .206 F4
Risca NP11 . . . . .114 F2
Machine Mdw [3] NP4 .38 A1
Machynys Rd
Llanelli SA15 . . . . . . .229 E8
Llanelli SA15 . . . . .40 E1
Mackintosh Pl CF24 . .178 B1
Mackintosh Rd CF37 .109 D1
Mackintosh St CF48 . . .55 C5
Mackintosh Terr CF46 .83 B6
Mackworth Cl CF83 . .158 F8
Mackworth Dr SA11 . .22 D7
Mackworth Rd CF63 . .183 A7
Mackworth St SA1 . . . .95 F7
Mackworth Terr SA1 . .95 F7
Maddox St CF40 . . . . .106 D6
Madeline St
Pentre CF41 . . . . .78 F5

Madeline St continued
Tylorstown CF40 . . . . . .80 B1
Madoc Cl
Bridgend CF31 . . . . . .169 A5
Dinas Powys CF64 . . . .206 C3
Madoc Pl SA1 . . . . .95 C6
Madoc Rd CF24 . . . . . .195 F6
Madoc St
Pontypridd CF37 . . . . .135 C8
Swansea SA1 . . . . .95 C6
Maelfa CF23 . . . . .178 E4
Maelgwyn Terr CF44 . . .28 E2
Maelog Cl CF72 . . . . . .173 B8
Maelog Pl CF14 . . . . . .177 E1
Maelog Rd CF14 . . . . .177 C4
Maen Dy CF48 . . . . .10 A2
Maen Ganol
Trelewis CF46 . . . . .56 D1
Trelewis CF46 . . . . .83 D8
Maen Gilfach
Trelewis CF46 . . . . .56 D1
Trelewis CF46 . . . . .83 D8
Maen Moel NP23 . . . . .14 D6
Maendy Pl NP44 . . . . . .89 C6
Maendy Prim Sch
NP44 . . . . .89 C4
Maendy Rd CF71 . . . .189 B4
Maendy Sq NP44 . . . . .89 C5
Maendy Way NP44 . . . .89 C5
Maendy Wood Rise
NP44 . . . . .89 C5
Maengwyn SA8 . . . . . .221 B1
Maerdy Cl NP20 . . . . .142 F1
Maerdy Cl CF43 . . . . . .52 A1
Maerdy Heol CF83 . . .138 C4
Maerdy Inf Sch CF43 . .52 A1
Maerdy Jun Sch CF43 .79 B8
Maerdy La CF14 . . . . .160 C2
Maerdy Rd
Aberdare CF44 . . . . . . .52 E7
Ammanford SA18 . . . .219 B5
Maerdy CF43 . . . . .52 B1
Maerdy Rd Flats CF43 .52 B1
Maerdy Road Ind Est
CF43 . . . . .79 D8
Maerdy View NP22 . . . .13 A1
Maerdypark CF35 . . . .170 D6
Maes Bedw CF39 . . . .107 E2
Maes Briallu
Caerphilly CF83 . . . . . .138 D4
Swansea SA7 . . . . .69 F7
Maes Bryn CF31 . . . . .168 B6
Maes Brynna CF44 . . . .28 C4
Maes Cadwgan CF15 .174 F2
Maes Collen
Cwmrhydyceirw SA6 . . .46 A3
Swansea SA6 . . . . .45 F3
Maes Dafydd SA4 . . . . .66 B8
Maes Ganol CF37 . . . .136 C4
Maes Gareth Edwards
SA18 . . . . .220 D7
Maes Glas Barry CF62 214 C5
Caerphilly CF83 . . . . . .138 C2
Cardiff CF14 . . . . .177 B4
Cefn Cribwr CF32 . . . .149 B2
Ebbw Vale NP23 . . . . . . .7 B4
Gorseinon SA4 . . . . . . .43 B1
Pontypridd CF37 . . . . .109 D6
Tondu CF32 . . . . .150 E5
Tredegar NP22 . . . . . . .13 E8
Maes Golau SA15 . . . . .40 F8
Maes Gwair CF31 . . . .168 B6
Maes Gwyn CF83 . . . .138 B2
Maes Hir CF83 . . . . . .137 F5
Maes Hyfryd CF46 . . . .53 F7
Maes Illtuds CF61 . . . .210 A4
Maes Lan CF33 . . . . . .148 D2
Maes Llewellyn SA18 .219 F8
Maes Lliedi SA15 . . . . .40 F8
Maes Lloi CF71 . . . . . .189 B3
Maes Llwynonn SA10 .48 E1
Maes Maddock SA4 . . .43 B1
Maes Melyn St [2]
SA13 . . . . .125 C5
Maes Pwll SA11 . . . . .226 B3
Maes Rhedyn SA12 . . .98 D6
Maes Rhosyn SA8 . . . . .24 B3
Maes Road (Heol Maes)
SA14 . . . . .42 C8
Maes Sant Teilo SA5 . .45 B2
Maes SA1 . . . . .95 F7
Maes Talcen CF31 . . . .169 B5
Maes Teg SA4 . . . . .19 D5
Maes Trane CF38 . . . .156 A6
Maes Triasnt CF72 . . .155 C2
Maes Ty Gwyn SA14 . .18 C1
Maes Ty-canol SA12 . .98 F4
Maes Uchaf CF37 . . . .136 C4
Maes Watford CF83 . .158 F8
Maes y Briallu CF15 .176 F4
Maes y Celyn SA4 . . . .65 D1
Maes y Coed NP12 . . .165 D6
Maes y Cornel SA8 . . . .24 A3
Maes y Crofft CF15 . .176 F4
Maes y Deri SA18 . . . .220 E8
Maes y Draenog
CF15 . . . . .158 D2
Maes y Drudwen
SA18 . . . . .137 E2
Maes y Fedwen
Bridgend CF31 . . . . . .168 C2
Swansea SA6 . . . . .45 F3
Maes y Felin SA5 . . . . .45 F3
Maes y Fron [1] SA18 .220 B8
Maes y Gad CF5 . . . . .192 F7
Maes y Gollen SA2 . . . .94 B6
Maes y Gors SA15 . . . .40 D4

Maes y Gruffydd Rd
SA2 ....94 C8
Maes y Grug
Bridgend CF31 ....168 C3
Church Village CF38 ...135 E1
Maes y Gwernen Cl
SA6 ....45 E4
Maes y Gwernen Dr
SA6 ....45 E4
Maes y Hedydd CF23 .160 F2
Maes y Meillion SA7 ..69 F7
Maes y Mynnydd SA10 48 A1
Maes y Odyn CF15 .176 A7
Maes y Pandy CF83 .138 C7
Maes y Parc
Cardiff CF14 ....177 B6
Swansea SA5 ....67 D5
Maes y Rhedyn CF43 ..79 B8
Maes y Siglen CF83 .137 E3
Maes y Wennol CF23 .160 F2
Maes Yr Annedd CF5 .194 B7
Maes yr Awel
Radyr CF15 ....176 B6
Rhydyfelin CF37 .....136 C4
Swansea SA7 ....69 F7
Maes Yr Haf
Cardiff CF14 ....176 F6
Llwydcoed CF44 .....28 F6
Maes Yr Hafod SA10 ..48 E1
Maes Yr Haul Cotts
CF72 ....155 E2
Maes yr Odyn CF15 .176 A7
Maes yr Orchis CF15 .176 A7
Maes-Ar-Ddafen Rd
SA14 ....41 C4
Maes-Cefn-Mabley
CF72 ....155 D4
Maes-Deri SA1 ....69 D5
Maes-Gwyn SA12 ....73 B5
Maes-Gwyn St SA12 .124 E8
Maes-Lan SA7 ....69 F6
Maes-Mawr Rd
Crynant 226 A7
Crynant SA10 ....25 F6
Maes-rhydwen Flats [1]
CF44 ....28 E4
Maes-y-Bedw CF46 ...55 F8
Maes-y-berllan SA18 219 C6
Maes-y-Bettws SA12 100 A8
Maes-y-Bryn
Colwinston CF71 ....187 A4
Radyr CF15 ....176 B7
Swansea SA6 ....45 F2
Tonyrefail CF39 .....133 C6
Maes-y-Bryn Rd
CF14,CF23 ....161 B4
Maes-y-Byrn Prim Sch
CF38 ....156 D7
Maes-y-Celyn NP4 ...62 D4
Maes-y-Cnyw Terr
NP13 ....60 C6
Maes-y-Coed
Barry CF62 ....214 B2
Cwmdare CF44 ....28 C3
Gorseinon SA4 ......66 B8
Llanelli SA15 ......40 B6
Swansea SA6 ....45 F2
Tredomen CF82 ......84 D1
Trelewis CF46 ......83 D6
Maes-y-Coed Cty Prim
Sch CF37 ....135 B8
Maes-y-Coed Rd
CF14 ....177 E6
Maes-y-Crochan CF3 180 B7
Maes-y-Cwm St
CF63 ....215 A5
Maes-y-Cwrt Terr [5]
SA13 ....125 C7
Maes-y-Dail SA18 ...219 A4
Maes-y-darren SA9 ....2 C7
Maes-y-Dderwen
Creigiau CF15 ......174 E6
Maesteg CF34 ......102 A6
Penpedairheol CF82 ..84 D7
Swansea SA6 ....45 B2
Swansea SA7 ....70 A6
Maes-y-Deri
Cardiff CF14 ....177 B7
Cilfrew SA10 ....49 C6
Pontypridd CF37 ....109 A2
Maes-y-Deri Cl CF35 170 C8
Maes-y-Dre SA11 ....227 C8
Maes-y-Felin
Bridgend CF31 .....168 E7
Caerphilly CF83 ....138 B3
Cardiff CF14 ....177 B6
Llandow CF71 ......199 A4
Rhydyfelin CF37 ....136 B4
Maes-y-Ffynnon
Bonvilston CF5 .....191 B1
Dowlais CF48 ....11 B4
Maes-y-Ffynnon Cl
SA11 ....71 E6
Maes-y-Ffynnon La
CF44 ....53 A8
Maes-y-Ffynon SA11 223 C1
Maes-y-Fioled CF15 .174 E7
Maes-y-Garn Rd NP12 59 B1
Maes-y-Garreg
Ebbw Vale NP23 .....7 A4
Merthyr Tydfil CF48 ..225 F2
Maes-y-Glyn SA18 ..220 D8
Maes-y-Gollen CF15 .174 E7
Maes-y-Graig St SA1 58 A2
Maes-y-Gwrnen Rd
SA6 ....45 F4
Maes-y-Meillion SA10 48 C2
Maes-y-Nant CF15 ..174 D7

Maes-y-Parc SA12 ....99 E5
Maes-y-Pergwm
SA11 ....223 C1
Maes-y-Rhedyn
Creigiau CF15 ......174 E6
Neath SA10 ....48 C1
Talbot Green CF72 ..155 B2
Maes-y-Sarn CF15 ..157 B1
Maes-y-Tyra SA11 ..226 E5
Maes-Yr-Wennol
CF72 ....173 D8
Maes-y-Wern CF35 ..170 D8
Maes-Yr Haf SA4 ....64 E4
Maes-yr-Afon
Caerphilly CF83 ....138 D5
Pontyclun CF72 ....173 A6
Maes-Yr-Awel CF34 ..75 A2
Maes-Yr-Efail
Dunvant SA2 ....93 D8
Gorseinon SA4 ......43 B1
Maes-Yr-Eglwys
SA11 ....223 C1
Maes-yr-eirlys CF31 168 C2
Maes-Yr-Eithin SA7 ..47 B1
Maes-yr-Haf
Ammanford SA18 ....219 A7
Merthyr Tydfil CF47 ..10 F1
Rhymney NP22 ......12 F2
Rhymney NP22 ......13 A3
Swansea SA7 ....69 F6
Maes-Yr-Haf Rd
Neath SA11 ....71 E8
North Cornelly CF33 .166 A7
Maes-yr-Hafod CF15 174 E7
Maes-yr-Haul CF32 .150 E6
Maes-yr-Helyg CF44 ..28 E6
Maes-yr-Onen CF46 ..83 D4
Maes-yr-Onnen
Creigiau CF15 ......174 E6
Cwmrhydyceirw SA6 ..46 A3
Maes-yr-Ysgol
Barry CF62 ....214 E5
Pyle CF33 ....148 D1
Maescanner Rd SA14 .41 E7
Maescynog SA9 ....1 F1
Maescynon CF44 .....27 E8
Maesderi SA4 ....18 F4
Maesderwen Cres
NP4 ....62 D5
Maesderwen Rd NP4 ..62 C5
Maesglas Bettws CF32 129 E2
Bridgend CF31 .....168 C5
Cwmavon SA12 .....99 D5
Penygroes SA14 ....218 D7
Pyle CF33 ....148 C2
Maesglas Ave CF23 .142 F1
Maesglas Cl NP20 ..164 A8
Maesglas Cres NP20 163 F8
Maesglas Gr NP20 ..163 F8
Maesglas Ind Est
NP20 ....143 B1
Maesglas Jun & Inf Sch
NP20 ....164 A8
Maesglas Rd
Newport NP20 ......142 F1
Swansea SA5 ....68 B3
Maesglas St NP20 ..164 A8
Maesgrenig SA18 ...219 F8
Maesgwyn
Cwmbran NP44 .....89 D7
Cwmdare CF44 .....28 C4
Maesgwyn Dr SA4 ...19 C4
Maesgwyn Hospl
CF32 ....151 A6
Maesgwyn Rd SA4 ...19 C4
Maesgwyn Specl Sch
CF44 ....28 D4
Maesgwynne CF48 ...10 B3
Maeshafod NP13 .....15 E3
Maeshir SA11 ....223 C1
Maeslan SA8 ....24 B3
Maesllwyn SA18 ....219 B8
Maesmelyn [4] CF44 ..28 C3
Maestaf SA8 ....31 A4
Maesteg Bsns Ctr
CF34 ....101 D4
Maesteg Comp (Lower)
Sch CF34 ....102 C3
Maesteg Comp (upper)
Sch CF34 ....128 D8
Maesteg Cres CF38 .136 A1
Maesteg Gdns CF38 .136 A1
Maesteg Gr CF38 ...136 A1
Maesteg Rd
Bryn SA13 ....100 F5
Cwmfelin CF34 .....128 C7
Cymmer SA13 ......75 C4
Cymmer SA13 ......75 C5
Tondu CF32 ....150 C5
Maesteg Row CF34 ..102 B2
Maesteg St SA1 .....95 E8
Maesteg Terr CF36 .183 A4
Maestir SA15 ....40 F7
Maestref SA15 ......40 F8
Maeswerdd SA15 ....40 F8
Maesybedol SA18 ...220 B8
Maesycoed SA18 ....219 D7
Maesycoed Rd
Godrergraig SA8 ...221 B1
Pontypridd CF37 ...135 B8
Maesycwm SA9 ....1 F1
Maesycwmmer Prim Sch
CF82 ....85 B2
Maesydderwen
Llangennech SA14 ...18 D1
Ystradgynlais SA9 ...2 E7
Maesydderwen Comp Sch
SA9 ....2 E7

Maesyfelin Cres
CF72 ....173 A7
Maesyffynon Gr CF44 .53 B8
Maesyffynon Terr
CF40 ....107 A5
Maesyfron Terr SA9 .222 F7
Maesyglyn SA18 ....219 F8
Maesygors SA14 ....218 C8
Maesyrhaf
Cross Hands SA14 ..218 A1
Llanelli SA15 ......40 F7
Maesyrhaf Pl SA4 ....43 A1
Maesyrhendre SA18 .220 B8
Maesywerin SA18 ...220 D7
Maesywern Rd
Glanaman SA18 ....219 F8
Glanaman SA18 ....219 F8
Mafeking Rd CF23 ..178 E1
Mafeking Terr NP22 ..13 F6
Mafon Rd CF46 ......83 D3
Magazine St CF34 ..102 A8
Magellan Cl CF62 ..215 A8
Magna Porta Gdns
NP44 ....117 B6
Magnolia Cl
Cardiff CF23 ......178 D7
Merthyr Tydfil CF47 ..10 D5
Newport NP20 .....117 B3
Porth CF39 ....108 A3
Magnolia Dr NP12 ...85 E5
Magnolia Way CF38 .156 F4
Magor Rd NP18 .....145 F8
Magor St NP19 .....143 F3
Magpie Rd CF62 ....210 D6
Maiden St CF34 .....128 C8
Maillard's Haven
CF64 ....207 H3
Main Access Rd CF62 211 F1
Main Ave
Bridgend CF31 .....169 B7
Cardiff CF23 ....178 B1
Hirwaun CF44 ......224 C1
Peterston-Super-Ely
CF5 ....191 E5
Upper Boat CF37 ..136 D1
Main Rd
Aberdulais SA10 ....49 C4
Bryn-côch SA10 ....48 C4
Cheltenham NP7 .....9 C6
Church Village CF38 136 A2
Cilfrew SA10 ....49 C5
Crynant SA10 ......226 A8
Dyffryn Cellwen SA10 223 A4
Llantrisant CF72 ...155 F3
Maesycwmmer CF82 ..85 A2
Mountain Ash CF45 ..82 B6
Neath SA10 ....48 E1
Ogmore-By-Sea CF32 184 C1
Pontrhydyfen SA12 ..73 A1
Taffs Well CF15 ....157 F4
Tonna SA10 ....49 A3
Main St Barry CF63 ..215 B3
Newbridge NP11 .....60 A1
Newbridge NP11 .....86 F6
Maindee Jun & Inf Sch
NP19 ....143 D5
Maindee Par NP19 ..143 E6
Maindee Rd NP11 ...113 A3
Maindee Terr NP44 ..89 D5
Maindy Cres CF41 ...78 F4
Maindy Croft CF41 ...78 F4
Maindy Ct CF38 ....135 E1
Maindy Gr CF41 .....78 F3
Maindy Rd
Cardiff CF24 ....194 F8
Penycoedcae CF37 .135 B6
Ton Pentre CF41 ....78 F3
Ton Pentre CF41 ....78 F3
Mainwaring Terr SA1 .68 D2
Maitland Pl CF11 ...194 A4
Maitland St CF14 ...177 E2
Major Cl NP44 ......88 F2
Major Rd CF5 ......194 D5
Major St SA5 ....68 C2
Malcolm Sargent Cl
NP19 ....144 D4
Maldwyn St CF11 ...194 D7
Malefant St CF24 ...178 A1
Maliphant St SA1 ...68 E1
Mall The NP44 ......89 E3
Mallard Cl [8] CF3 ..179 E7
Mallard Way
Newport NP10 ......163 F6
Penarth CF64 ......217 A2
Porthcawl CF36 ....182 D7
Mallards Reach CF3 162 D1
Mallory Cl CF62 ....211 D7
Malmesbury Cl [7]
NP20 ....143 C6
Malmsmead Rd CF3 179 C7
Malpas Church in Wales
Jun & Inf Schs
NP20 ....117 B2
Malpas Cl [1] CF3 ..179 F7
Malpas La NP20 .....117 B3
Malpas Park Jun & Inf Sch
NP20 ....117 A3
Malpas Rd NP20 ....117 A3
Malpas St NP4 ......89 E2
Malpes Court Jun & Inf
Sch NP20 ....116 F3
Malt Hall SA3 ......229 D3
Malthouse Ave CF23 .161 A2
Malthouse La NP4 ...62 B7
Malthouse Rd
Caerleon NP18 .....145 B7
Ponthir NP18,NP44 .117 D6
Maltings The CF23 ..160 F1

Malus Ave CF38 ....156 C5
Malvern Cl
Newport NP19 .....144 A8
Risca NP11 ....115 D1
Malvern Dr CF14 ...177 D7
Malvern Rd NP19 ...143 D7
Malvern Terr
Risca NP11 ....115 A1
Swansea SA2 ......94 F5
Man-Moel Rd
Ebbw Vale NP22,NP23 ..14 C5
Hollybush NP12,NP23 ..34 F6
Manchester Ho NP13 .59 F8
Manchester Pl CF11 ..27 D7
Manchester St NP19 143 D6
Mandeg CF46 ....83 D6
Mandela Ave CF31 ..169 D5
Mandeville Pl [6]
CF11 ....194 E5
Mandeville Rd NP12 .85 C7
Mandeville St [7]
CF11 ....194 E5
Mandinam Pk SA2 ...94 A7
Manest St NP22 .....12 E4
Mangoed CF44 ......28 A6
Manitoba Cl CF23 ..178 C5
Manley Cl CF39 ....133 C5
Manley Rd NP20 ...143 A4
Manmoel Cl NP12 ...59 C1
Manmoel Rd NP11 ...59 C2
Mannesmann Cl SA7 ..69 C7
Manod Rd CF14 ....177 A2
Manor Chase [2]
CF38 ....156 A5
Manor Cl CF14 .....177 B5
Manor Ct
[5] Cardiff CF14 ...177 A6
Church Village CF38 .135 E1
Ewenny CF35 ......185 E7
Swansea SA5 ....68 C3
Manor Ct Flats NP11 115 B2
Manor Dr
Bridgend CF35 ....169 F4
Glynneath SA11 ....223 B1
Manor Gr CF36 .....183 D8
Manor Hill CF72 ....173 D7
Manor Pk
Llantwit Major CF61 .210 A5
Newbridge NP11 ....87 A8
Newport NP10 .....163 F6
Manor Rd
Abersychan NP4 ....37 F4
Pontllanfraith NP12 ..85 F3
Risca NP11 ....115 B1
Swansea SA5 ......68 C3
Manor Rise CF14 ...177 C4
Manor Sq CF61 .....210 A4
Manor St Cardiff CF14 177 F2
Port Talbot SA13 ...125 C8
Manor View CF61 ...210 A4
Manor Way
Abersychan NP4 ....37 F4
Briton Ferry SA11 ...71 D3
Risca NP11 ....115 C1
Manorbier Cl
Blackwood NP12 ....58 D1
Church Village CF38 .135 E1
[2] Dinas Powys CF64 206 C3
Manorbier Cres CF3 179 C4
Manorbier Ct CF62 ..214 F8
Manorbier Dr NP44 ..90 A3
Mansel Cl SA4 ......66 B5
Mansel Dr SA3 .....122 C6
Mansel Rd SA1 .....69 B4
Mansel St
Briton Ferry SA11 ...71 C2
Gowerton SA4 ......66 B5
Llanelli SA15 ......40 E4
Newport NP19 .....144 A5
Port Talbot SA13 ...125 B8
Port Talbot SA13 ...99 B1
Swansea SA1 ....95 C7
Mansfield Rd SA3 ..122 C6
Mansell Ave CF5 ...192 F4
Manselton Prim Sch
SA5 ....68 C3
Manselton Rd SA5 ..68 B3
Mansfield St [1] CF11 194 E5
Mansfield Terr CF47 ..11 A1
Manston Cl [5] CF5 176 E2
Maple Ave Baglan SA12 98 E1
Risca NP11 ....115 B2
Tredegar NP22 ......6 D1
Maple Cl Barry CF62 215 A7
Bryn NP12 ....85 D3
Cimla SA11 ....72 C6
Gorseinon SA4 .....43 A3
Llanharry CF72 ....172 B5
Llanmartin NP18 ...145 E6
Merthyr Tydfil CF47 .10 D4
Maple Cres
Pontypool NP4 .....62 D1
Swansea SA2 ......94 E7
Trefechan CF48 .....10 B6
Maple Ct CF39 .....133 D5
Maple Dr
Aberdare CF44 .....28 D2
Bridgend CF31 .....169 E4
Waunarlwydd SA5 ..66 D4
Maple Gdns NP11 ..141 C8
Maple Gr SA2 ....94 E6
Maple Rd CF64 CF5 ..176 B1
Penarth CF64 ......206 E3
Pontypool NP4 .....62 D2
Maple Rd S NP4 ....62 D1
Maple St CF37 .....136 A5
Maple Terr
Abercarn NP11 .....87 B3

Maple Terr *continued*
Abercwmboi CF44 ...53 F4
Maesteg CF34 ......102 A2
Maple Tree Cl CF15 .176 A6
Maple Way NP22 .....7 C5
Maple Wlk CF36 ....183 E8
Maplewood Ave [3]
CF14 ....176 F3
Maplewood Cl SA10 ..48 C4
Maplewood Flats [2]
CF14 ....176 F3
Marayat Wlk NP20 ..142 E1
Marblehall Rd SA15 ..40 E5
March Hywel
Cilfrew SA10 ....49 C5
Pontardawe SA8 ....24 C3
Marchwood Cl CF3 .179 C5
Marconi Ave CF44 ..206 F6
Marconi Cl NP20 ...116 F2
Marcross Rd CF5 ...193 A4
Mardy CF72 ....155 A5
Mardy Cl
Caerphilly CF83 ....138 C3
Merthyr Tydfil CF47 ..30 F7
Mardy Cres CF83 ...138 C3
Mardy Ct CF11 .....194 F4
Mardy Rd CF3 ......179 C2
Mardy St Cardiff CF11 194 F4
Merthyr Tydfil CF47 ..11 A1
Mardy Terr CF47 ....30 E7
Margam Ave SA6 ...69 A8
Margam Cl CF62 ...211 C7
Margam Ho
SA13 ....126 C3
Margam Pl SA15 ....40 E4
Margam Rd
Cardiff CF14 ......177 D2
Margam SA13 ......125 C4
Port Talbot SA13 ..126 A2
Margam Row CF33 .148 D3
Margam St
Cymmer SA13 ......75 B5
Maesteg CF34 ......102 B8
Margaret Ave
Barry CF62 ....204 F1
Newport NP19 .....143 D7
Margaret St
Abercwmboi CF44 ..53 F4
Abercynon CF45 ...82 E2
Aberdare CF44 .....28 E3
Aberdare CF44 .....53 D6
Bargoed CF81 ......58 A1
Bryn-côch SA10 ....48 C4
Merthyr Tydfil CF47 ..10 C2
Pentre CF41 ....78 F5
Pontypridd CF37 ...108 F2
Port Talbot SA13 ..99 C1
Trehafod CF37 .....108 D2
Treherbert CF42 ...50 E2
Tylorstown CF43,CF39 107 C8
Margaret Terr
Blaengwynfi SA13 ...76 C5
Swansea SA1 ......96 A7
Margaret's Cl SA11 ..71 B1
Marged St SA15 ....40 D3
Marguerites Way
CF5 ....193 A5
Maria Ct CF10 .....195 B3
Maria St CF10 .....195 B3
Marian St
Blaengarw CF32 ...103 F2
Tonypandy CF40 ...106 A7
Llanelli SA15 ......40 D4
Marianwen St NP12 ..85 C8
Marigold Cl
Merthyr Tydfil CF47 ..10 C5
Rogerstone NP10 ..141 D6
Marigold Ct CF31 ..169 D5
Marigold Pl SA10 ..222 D4
Marina Ct [6] NP19 143 E8
Marine Bldgs CF64 .207 B5
Marine Cl SA12 .....98 C1
Marine Dr Barry CF62 214 B2
Ogmore-By-Sea CF32 184 C3
Port Talbot SA13 ...98 C1
Marine Ho SA10 ....97 C8
Marine Ind Est SA1 ..35 B6
Marine Par CF64 ...207 B2
Marine St Cwm NP22 35 B6
Llanelli SA15 ......40 C3
Marine Terr CF36 ...182 F6
Marine Wlk
Ogmore-By-Sea CF32 184 C3
[4] Swansea SA1 ...95 D5
Mariner St [8] SA1 ..95 D8
Mariner Way NP19 ..164 E8
Mariner's Hts CF64 207 B5
Mariners The SA15 ..40 C3
Mariners Way CF62 212 F1
Marion Ct CF14 ....160 A1
Marion Jones Ct NP12 85 F1
Marion Pl NP20 ....143 C4
Marion St Cardiff CF24 195 E6
Newport NP20 .....143 C5
Marionville Gdns CF5 193 E8
Maritime Ind Est
CF37 ....135 C4
Maritime Rd
Cardiff CF10 ....195 C2
Port Talbot SA13 ...125 B7
Maritime St CF37 ...135 C4
Maritime Terr CF37 .135 B8
Marjorie St CF40 ...107 B4
Mark St CF11 ......194 E5
Market Arc [3] NP20 143 C5
Market Mews [4] SA6 .68 F8

Market Pl
Abercarn NP11 .....87 B2
Cardiff CF5 ....194 D6
Market Rd Cardiff CF5 194 C6
Nantyglo NP23 .....8 C2
Market Sq
Brynmawr NP23 .....8 C4
Ebbw Vale NP23 ....14 D8
[5] Merthyr Tydfil CF47 ..10 D1
Pontypool NP4 .....62 C6
Market St
[7] Aberdare CF44 ...29 A2
Abertillery NP13 ....36 B5
Barry CF62 ....214 D3
Blaenavon NP4 .....17 C6
Bridgend CF31 .....168 C4
Caerphilly CF83 ....138 B2
Cardiff CF15 ....158 C1
Dowlais CF48 ......11 B4
Ebbw Vale NP23 ....14 D8
Llanelli SA15 ......40 D5
[2] Newport NP20 ..143 C5
Pontypool NP4 .....62 C6
Pontypridd CF37 ..109 C1
[5] Swansea SA6 ...68 F8
[8] Swansea SA6 ...69 A8
Tredegar NP22 .....13 E6
Markham Cres NP22 .59 B2
Markham Prim Sch
NP12 ....58 D7
Markham Terr NP12 .58 D8
Marl Ct Cardiff CF11 .194 F1
Cwmbran NP44 .....89 B5
Marland Ho
[1] Cardiff CF10 ...195 A4
[14] Cardiff CF10 ..195 A4
Marlas Cl CF33 .....148 B1
Marlas Rd CF33 ....148 A1
Marlborough Cl
Barry CF63 ....215 C7
Llantwit Fardre CF38 .156 D6
Marlborough Com Inf Sch
CF23 ....195 D8
Marlborough Com Jun Sch
CF23 ....195 D8
Marlborough Ho [2]
CF10 ....195 A5
Marlborough Rd
Abertillery NP13 ....36 C3
Cardiff CF23 ....195 D8
Cwmbran NP44 .....89 A3
Gorseinon SA4 .....66 B8
Newport NP19 .....143 D5
Swansea SA2 ......94 F6
Marlborough Terr
CF10 ....194 E8
Marloes Cl CF62 ...214 F7
Marloes Ct SA5 .....67 F6
Marloes Rd CF5 ....193 B5
Marloss Path [1] NP44 89 B5
Marlow Cl NP10 ....142 B6
Marlowe Gdns NP20 142 F1
Marlowe Ho [4] SA12 .98 B3
Marlpit La CF5 .....166 A1
Marne St NP11 .....114 B8
Marquis Cl CF72 ...155 A5
Marsden St [5] SA1 ..68 C2
Marsh St
[9] Aberavon SA12 124 F8
Aberavon SA12 .....98 F1
Llanelli SA15 ......40 D4
Marshall Cl [2] CF5 .176 E2
Marshall Cres CF5 ..10 F5
Marshfield Ave CF33 148 B1
Marshfield
Pontllanfraith NP12 ..85 F2
Tonyrefail CF39 ....133 D5
Marshfield Jun & Inf Sch
CF3 ....162 C2
Marshfield Rd
Abertillery NP11 ....59 F5
Maerdy CF43 ....79 C8
Marshfield CF3 .....162 D1
Neath SA11 ....71 D6
Marshfield St NP19 .144 A4
Marston Ct NP20 ...143 B7
Martell St SA5 ......67 E3
Martin Cl CF48 .....10 F6
Martin Cres CF39 ..133 C5
Martin Rd
Cardiff CF24 ....196 A4
Llanelli SA15 ......40 E4
Martin St Clydach SA6 46 D7
Swansea SA6 ......68 F8
Martin Terr NP4 ....17 C4
Martin's Field NP11 ..86 E6
Martin's La CF45 ...82 E2
Martin's Terr CF45 ..82 E2
Martindale Cl NP22 ..6 D1
Martindale Rd NP4 ..62 E2
Martins Cl CF45 ....82 E2
Martins Row CF81 ..32 C8
Martyn's Ave SA10 .222 C3
Marwyn Gdns CF81 ..57 F2
Mary Ann St CF10 .195 B5
Mary Immaculate High Sch
(Lower) CF5 ....193 B2
Mary Immaculate High Sch
(Upper) CF5 ....193 B2
Mary St
Abercwmboi CF44 ...53 F4
[6] Aberdare CF44 ..29 A1
Bedlinog CF46 .....56 A7
Bedwas CF83 ......139 A6
[13] Blaenavon NP4 ..17 C6

Mary St *continued*
Blaengwynfi SA13 . . . . . .76 C6
Cardiff CF14 . . . . .176 F2
Crynant SA10 . . . . .226 A7
Dowlais CF48 . . . . .11 A4
Merthyr Tydfil CF47 . . . . .30 E8
Mountain Ash CF45 . . . . .54 E2
Neath SA11 . . . . .71 D7
Pontypridd CF37 . . . . . .109 F5
Porth CF39 . . . . .107 F4
Porthcawl CF36 . . . . . . .182 F6
Seven Sisters SA10 . . . . .222 D4
Treharris CF46 . . . . .83 B6
Treherbert CF42 . . . . . . .51 A1
Mary Twill La SA3 . . . . .122 E4
Maryland Rd NP11 . . . . .115 A1
Maryport Rd CF23 . . . . .178 B2
Marysfield Cl CF3 . . . . .162 E1
Masefield Mews
CF31 . . . . .168 D6
Masefield Rd CF64 . . . .206 F4
Masefield Vale NP20 . .142 F2
Masefield Way
Rhydyfelin CF37 . . . . . .136 B6
Swansea SA2 . . . . .94 E6
Mason St CF44 . . . . . . .53 C7
Masonic St
11 Merthyr Tydfil CF47 . .10 D1
13 Merthyr Tydfil CF47 . .30 D8
Matexa St CF41 . . . . . . .78 F3
Mathew Wlk CF5 . . . . .176 E2
Mathews Terr CF37 . . . .135 A4
Mathias Cl 1 CF23 . . . .178 E1
Matthew Cl CF62 . . . . .212 E2
Matthew St SA1 . . . . . .95 D8
Matthew Terr
Dinas Powys CF64 . . . . .206 C4
Pontypool NP4 . . . . . . .61 F8
Matthews' St SA13 . . . .227 C2
Matthewson Cl CF14 . . .177 C2
Matthysens Way CF3 . .179 F5
Mattie Collins Way The
CF42 . . . . .78 D5
Mattysens Way CF3 . . . .180 A5
Maugham Cl NP20 . . . . .142 F1
Maughan La 6 CF64 . . .207 B5
Maughan Terr 5
CF64 . . . . .207 B5
Maun Rhydd CF82 . . . . .84 D6
Maureen Ave CF5 . . . . .193 E6
Mavis Gr CF14 . . . . . . .177 C6
Mawsons Mead CF5 . . .192 A1
Maximin Rd SA13 . . . . .125 E3
Maxton Ct CF83 . . . . . .138 C3
Maxwell Rd CF3 . . . . . .179 C4
Maxwell St CF43 . . . . . .79 F6
Maxworthy Rd 1 NP4 . .17 C7
May St Cardiff CF24 . . . .178 A1
Newport NP19 . . . . . . .143 E5
May's Ct SA11 . . . . .71 F7
Mayals Ave SA2 . . . . . . .94 A1
Mayals Gn SA3 . . . . .93 F1
Mayals Prim Sch SA3 . .123 A8
Mayals Rd SA2 . . . . .94 A1
Mayberry Rd SA12 . . . . .98 D7
Maybury Ho 9 NP44 . . . .89 B3
Mayfair CF5 . . . . .193 A2
Mayfair Dr CF14 . . . . . .159 E3
Mayfield Ave
Cardiff CF5 . . . . .194 A6
Laleston CF32 . . . . .167 F4
Porthcawl CF36 . . . . . . .183 D7
Mayfield Pl CF72 . . . . . .155 E2
Mayfield Rd CF37 . . . . .109 B2
Mayfield St 2 SA13 . . . .125 C7
Mayfield Terr
Ebbw Vale NP23 . . . . . . .7 D4
Swansea SA5 . . . . .68 B3
Mayflower Ave CF14 . . . .159 D1
Mayflower Cl SA2 . . . . . .94 B6
Mayflower Way CF62 . . .213 A2
Mayhill Cl CF14 . . . . . . .159 F3
Mayhill Gdns SA1 . . . . .68 B1
Mayhill Inf Sch SA1 . . . .95 C8
Mayhill Jun Sch SA1 . . .95 C8
Mayhill Rd SA1 . . . . . . .68 B1
Maynard Ct CF5 . . . . . .194 A8
Maynes 4 NP4 . . . . . . .89 B1
Maytree Ave SA3 . . . . . .122 F7
Maytree Cl Loughor SA4 .42 D7
Swansea SA6 . . . . .68 D8
Maywood CF72 . . . . . . .153 D3
McCale Ave CF5 . . . . . . .193 E7
McDonnel Rd CF81 . . . . .57 F4
McLaren Cotts
Abertysswg NP22 . . . . . .33 C8
Abertysswg NP22 . . . . . .33 D8
McQuade Pl CF62 . . . . .214 E2
McRitchie Pl SA5 . . . . . .67 F3
Mead La SA4 . . . . .89 E4
Mead The SA2 . . . . .93 D8
Meadow Ave CF33 . . . . .148 C1
Meadow Bank NP4 . . . . .39 E6
Meadow Cl
Bridgend CF35 . . . . .169 F4
Cardiff CF23 . . . . .178 D8
Hirwaun CF44 . . . . .27 F4
Llanharan CF72 . . . . . . .153 F3
Mountain Ash CF45 . . . . .54 B3
Pengam NP12 . . . . .85 B6
Pontypool NP4 . . . . .89 E8
Risca NP11 . . . . .114 D3
Meadow Cres
Caerphilly CF83 . . . . . . .138 B2
Church Village CF38 . . . .136 A1

Meadow Cres *continued*
Risca NP11 . . . . .141 B1
Tredegar NP22 . . . . .6 D2
Meadow Croft CF62 . . .213 B2
Meadow Croft Cl SA5 . .66 E4
Meadow Ct
Llanelli SA14 . . . . .C8
St Brides Major CF32 . . .185 D3
Meadow Dr SA4 . . . . . . .42 F2
Meadow La
Croesyceiliog NP44 . . . . . .90 B5
Gilfach Goch CF39 . . . . .132 B6
Hirwaun CF44 . . . . .27 C8
Penarth CF64 . . . . .206 F1
Porthcawl CF36 . . . . . . .183 B8
Meadow Rd
Neath SA11 . . . . .41 D4
Pontllanfraith NP12 . . . . .86 A4
Meadow Rise
Brynna CF72 . . . . .153 E4
Sarn CF32 . . . . .150 F4
Swansea SA2 . . . . .94 C4
Meadow St
Aberkenfig CF32 . . . . . .150 C4
Abertillery NP13 . . . . . . .60 B6
Bridgend CF31 . . . . .168 F5
Cardiff CF11 . . . . .194 C7
Cwmavon SA12 . . . . .99 F6
Gilfach Goch CF39 . . . . .132 B6
Maesteg CF34 . . . . .102 A3
North Cornelly CF33 . . . .165 F8
Ogmore Vale NP20 . . . . .104 F1
Pontycymer CF32 . . . . . .103 E3
Pontypridd CF37 . . . . . .135 E5
Swansea SA1 . . . . .67 F2
Meadow Sweet Dr
CF3 . . . . .180 B6
Meadow Terr NP24 . . . . .33 F4
Meadow The CF71 . . . . .189 C8
Meadow Vale CF63 . . . .215 C8
Meadow View
Barry CF63 . . . . .215 D8
Bedwas CF83 . . . . .138 C7
Blackmill CF35 . . . . .130 E2
Dunvant SA2 . . . . .93 C8
Peterstone Wentlooge
CF3 . . . . .180 F5
Swansea SA7 . . . . .70 A6
Meadow View Ct
CF64 . . . . .216 A5
Meadow Way
Caerphilly CF83 . . . . . . .137 D1
Penperlleni NP4 . . . . .39 E7
Meadow Wlk
Blackwood NP11 . . . . . . .59 D1
Bridgend CF31 . . . . .169 A5
Ton Pentre CF41 . . . . . . .79 B3
Meadowbank Cl CF44 . .29 D1
Meadowbank Ct CF5 . .176 D2
Meadowbank Res Sch
CF14 . . . . .177 B2
Meadowbrook Ave
NP44 . . . . .89 D6
Meadowcroft SA3 . . . . .121 A5
Meadowgate Cl CF14 . .176 F7
Meadowlane Prim Sch
CF3 . . . . .179 F5
Meadowlark Cl 6
CF3 . . . . .179 C7
Meadows Rd
Cross Hands SA14 . . . . .218 B7
Cross Hands SA14 . . . . .218 C6
Newport NP19 . . . . . . .144 D1
Meadows The
Cimla SA11 . . . . .72 C6
Corntown CF35 . . . . . . .186 B7
Marshfield CF3 . . . . .162 D1
Pennline CF71 . . . . .188 A5
Porthcawl CF36 . . . . . . .183 C7
Risca NP11 . . . . .141 B1
Meadowside CF64 . . . . .206 D3
Meads CF NP19 . . . . . . .144 C2
Meadvale Rd CF3 . . . . . .179 D6
Mechanic's Sq NP22 . . . . .6 E1
Medart Pl NP11 . . . . . . .114 D4
Medart St NP11 . . . . . . .114 D4
Medlock Cl NP20 . . . . . .116 E2
Medlock Cres NP20 . . . .116 E3
Medlock Wlk NP20 . . . .116 E2
Medway Cl NP20 . . . . . .116 D2
Medway Ct NP20 . . . . . .116 D2
Medway Rd NP20 . . . . . .116 C2
Megan Cl SA4 . . . . .43 C3
Megan St SA5 . . . . .68 A2
Meggitt Rd CF62 . . . . . .214 E8
Meini Tirion CF31 . . . . .168 B6
Meirion Cl CF63 . . . . . .215 B8
Meirion Pl CF24 . . . . . .196 A6
Meirion St CF44 . . . . . . .28 F4
Meirwen Dr CF5 . . . . . .193 A2
Melbourne Ct
Caerphilly NP12 . . . . .85 C6
Cardiff CF14 . . . . .177 B6
Cwmbran NP44 . . . . .89 D2
Melbourne Rd
Abertillery NP13 . . . . . . .36 B5
Cardiff CF14 . . . . .177 B6
Melbourne Terr CF72 . .153 D3
Melbourne Way
NP20 . . . . .142 D3
Melcorn Dr SA3 . . . . . . .122 E5
Melfort Gdns NP20 . . . .142 F2
Melfort Rd NP20 . . . . . .142 F2
Meliden La CF64 . . . . . .206 F3
Meliden Rd CF64 . . . . . .206 F3
Melin Court Waterfall
SA11 . . . . .226 D4
Melin Gwlan CF83 . . . . .137 F4

Melin Inf Sch SA11 . . . . .71 D5
Melin Jun Sch SA11 . . . .71 D5
Melin St NP11 . . . . .113 B4
Melingriffith Dr CF14 . .176 E5
Mellon St NP20 . . . . . . .143 C4
Mellte Ave SA11 . . . . . .223 E2
Mellte Villas CF44 . . . . .28 E6
Melrose Ave CF23 . . . . .178 D1
Melrose Cl Cardiff CF23 .179 F8
Swansea SA6 . . . . .69 B7
Melrose Ct
Cardiff CF11 . . . . .194 C7
6 Cardiff CF23 . . . . . .178 C2
Melrose Gdns CF23 . . . .178 D1
Melrose St CF63 . . . . . .215 B6
Melton Dr CF31 . . . . . . .168 E2
Melville Ave CF14 . . . . .179 F8
Melville Cl CF62 . . . . . .204 E1
Melville Terr CF83 . . . . .138 B4
Melyn Bach Ave NP4 . . .39 E3
Melyn Cl SA11 . . . . .71 C5
Melyn St SA13 . . . . .227 C2
Menai Ave SA13 . . . . . . .75 C3
Menai Cl CF38 . . . . .135 E2
Menai Way CF3 . . . . . . .179 D6
Mendalgief Rd NP20 . . .143 C2
Mendip Cl
Newport NP19 . . . . . . .144 D6
Risca NP11 . . . . .115 D1
Swansea SA5 . . . . .67 C3
Mendip Rd CF3 . . . . . . .179 A5
Mendip View CF63 . . . .215 C6
Menelaus Sq CF48 . . . . .11 B4
Meon Cl NP20 . . . . .116 F2
Merchant St
15 Aberdare CF44 . . . . .29 A1
Pontlottyn CF81 . . . . .12 F1
Pontlottyn CF81 . . . . .32 F8
Merchant's Hill NP4 . . .62 B8
Merchant's Hill Cl NP4 .62 A8
Merches Gdns CF11 . . . .194 F4
Merches Pl CF11 . . . . . .194 F4
Mercia Rd CF24 . . . . . . .195 E6
Mercies The CF36 . . . . .183 B7
Mere Path NP4 . . . . .89 B3
Meredith Cl NP20 . . . . .142 F2
Meredith Rd CF24 . . . . .195 F6
Meredith Terr NP11 . . . .86 F6
Merevale CF64 . . . . .205 F3
Merfield Cl CF32 . . . . . .150 E4
Merfield Ho CF32 . . . . . .150 E4
Merganser Cl CF36 . . . .182 E8
Merganser St CF63 . . . .214 F5
Meridian Ct 1 CF14 . . .177 E2
Meridian The CF64 . . . .207 A5
Merion St CF40 . . . . . . .107 A3
Merioneth Ho 5
CF64 . . . . .206 F2
Merioneth Pl CF62 . . . .214 F7
Merlin Cl Cardiff CF14 . .159 E2
Penarth CF64 . . . . .217 A8
8 Pontypridd CF37 . . . .109 B1
Porthcawl CF36 . . . . . . .182 E8
Merlin Cres
Bridgend CF31 . . . . .168 C6
Newport NP19 . . . . . . .143 F7
Swansea SA1 . . . . .94 F8
Merlin Pl CF63 . . . . . . .215 A4
Merret Ct CF24 . . . . . . .196 A7
Merrick Cotts CF5 . . . . .191 F1
Merriots Pl NP19 . . . . . .143 E5
Mersey Cl NP12 . . . . . . .85 D3
Merthyr Dyfan Rd
CF62 . . . . .204 F1
Merthyr Rd
Abercanaid CF48 . . . . . . .30 C5
Aberdare CF44 . . . . .29 A8
Cardiff CF14 . . . . .177 B4
Cardiff CF14 . . . . .177 D3
Cardiff CF15 . . . . .158 C1
Hirwaun CF44 . . . . .27 D7
Llwydcoed CF44 . . . . . . .28 E7
Merthyr Tydfil CF44 . . . .225 D1
Merthyr Tydfil CF47 . . . .10 F4
Pontwalby SA11 . . . . . . .223 E1
Pontypridd CF37 . . . . . .109 D2
Tredegar NP22 . . . . .5 F1
Tredegar NP22 . . . . .6 B1
Troedyrhiw CF48 . . . . . . .31 C2
Merthyr St Barry CF62 . .214 F5
Cardiff CF24 . . . . .194 F8
Pontyclun CF72 . . . . . . .173 B8
Merthyr Tydfil Coll 10
CF48 . . . . .10 D1
Merthyr Tydfil Ind Pk
CF48 . . . . .31 A4
Merthyr Tydfil Sta
CF47 . . . . .10 E1
Merthyr Vale Sta CF48 . .55 D3
Merthyrmawr Rd
Bridgend CF31 . . . . .168 E2
Bridgend CF32 . . . . .185 B8
Merthyr Mawr CF32 . . . .168 D1
Mervinian Rd 13 CF10 . .195 C4
Mervyn Rd
Cardiff CF14 . . . . .177 B4
Cardiff CF24 . . . . .177 B4
Mervyn St Aberfan CF48 .55 C5
Pontypridd CF37 . . . . . .135 F5
Mervyn Terr
Cwmavon SA12 . . . . .99 C5
Pontypool NP4 . . . . .62 B7
Mervyn Way CF35 . . . . .170 B8
Mescoed Rd NP10 . . . . .142 B8
Metal St CF24 . . . . .195 D6
Metcalfe St CF34 . . . . . .102 B8
Meteor St CF24 . . . . . . .195 C6
Methodist La CF61 . . . . .209 F6

Methuen Rd NP19 . . . . .143 E5
Metro Mon Ind Est
NP44 . . . . .89 F7
Metz Cotts SA9 . . . . . . .222 A6
Mews The
Abercarn NP11 . . . . .114 C7
7 Barry CF63 . . . . .214 F5
Newport NP20 . . . . . . .143 A5
Mewslade Ave SA5 . . . . .67 E6
Meyler St CF39 . . . . . . .133 B2
Meyrick Rd CF15 . . . . . .193 A4
Meyrick Villas CF47 . . . .10 D3
Meyricks NP44 . . . . .116 B8
Michael Way NP4 . . . . . .62 B7
Michael's Field SA3 . . . .123 C3
Michael's Rd CF42 . . . . .50 B2
Michaelston Cl CF63 . . .215 B8
Michaelston Ct CF5 . . . .192 F4
Michaelstone Ct SA12 . .99 D4
Michelston Ct 3 CF5 . .192 F4
Michna St SA13 . . . . .98 F1
Mid Glamorgan Centre for
Art, Design & Technology
CF37 . . . . .135 F8
Middle Coedcae Rd
NP4 . . . . .17 D6
Middle Rd SA5 . . . . .67 F4
Middle Row
Ferndale CF43 . . . . .79 F8
Mountain Ash CF45 . . . . .54 C5
Rhymney NP22 . . . . .12 C7
Middle St
Pontypridd CF37 . . . . . .109 D2
4 Tonypandy CF40 . . . .106 F4
Middle Terr CF43 . . . . . .80 C2
Middlecroft La SA3 . . . . .121 F7
Middlegate CF71 . . . . . .188 E2
Middlegate Wlk CF71 . . .188 F2
Middleton St
Blaengwynfi SA13 . . . . . .76 C6
Briton Ferry SA11 . . . . . .71 C2
Swansea SA1 . . . . .95 F7
Midfield NP4 . . . . .39 E6
Midland Cl SA1 . . . . .95 E7
Midland Pl SA7 . . . . .69 D7
Midland Rd SA7 . . . . . . .69 D7
Midland Terr SA9 . . . . . . .2 D8
Midway NP4 . . . . .39 B2
Miers St SA1 . . . . .95 E7
Mikado St CF40 . . . . . . .106 F4
Milborough Ct SA3 . . . . .2 B7
Milborough Rd SA9 . . . . .2 B7
Milbourne Cl CF47 . . . . .30 F7
Milbourne St
Mountain Ash CF45 . . . . .82 B6
Tonypandy CF40 . . . . . . .107 A4
Milbourne Terr CF47 . . . .30 F7
Milburn Cl CF62 . . . . . .212 F1
Mildred Cl CF38 . . . . . . .156 A4
Mildred St CF38 . . . . . . .156 A4
Mile End Cl SA5 . . . . . . .67 F3
Mile End Row SA11 . . . . .71 D5
Miles Ct CF15 . . . . .158 A3
Miles La SA3 . . . . .122 C6
Miles Rd SA5 . . . . .68 C4
Miles St Llanelli SA15 . . .40 C1
Maerdy CF43 . . . . .52 A1
Merthyr Tydfil CF47 . . . .10 C2
Milford Cl CF38 . . . . . . .135 F2
Milford Ho NP44 . . . . . . .89 D2
Milford Way SA5 . . . . . . .67 F6
Milfraen Ave NP23 . . . . .8 D1
Military Mus CF10 . . . . .195 A6
Mill Brook SA12 . . . . . . .98 E5
Mill Cl Caerphilly CF83 . .137 F4
Cardiff CF14 . . . . .160 A1
Dinas Powys CF64 . . . . .206 A3
Mill Heath NP20 . . . . . . .116 E3
Mill La Bridgend CF31 . . .168 E5
Cardiff CF10 . . . . .195 A5
Cardiff CF5 . . . . .179 C8
Cardiff CF5 . . . . .179 D8
Cardiff CF5 . . . . .194 B8
Castleton CF3 . . . . .162 C4
Llanelli SA15 . . . . .40 D6
Llanrhidian SA3 . . . . . . .229 D3
Llanyravon NP44 . . . . . . .90 B2
Mumbles SA3 . . . . .94 B2
Ystrad Mynach CF82 . . . .111 E6
Mill Lay La CF61 . . . . . .209 F4
Mill Par NP20 . . . . .143 D1
Mill Pk CF71 . . . . .188 E1
Mill Pl Cardiff CF14 . . . .160 B1
Cardiff CF5 . . . . .193 E6
Mill Race CF72 . . . . . . .173 D6
Mill Race Cafn y Felin
SA10 . . . . .71 B8
Mill Rd Caerphilly CF83 . .138 A3
Cardiff CF14 . . . . .160 A2
Cardiff CF15 . . . . .158 C1
Cardiff CF5 . . . . .193 E6
Deri CF81 . . . . .57 B8
Dinas Powys CF64 . . . . .206 A3
Mountain Ash CF45 . . . . .54 C5
Neath SA10 . . . . .48 D2
Pontllanfraith NP12 . . . . .86 A3
Pontypool NP4 . . . . .62 B8
Pyle CF33 . . . . .148 A1
Ynysybwl CF37 . . . . .81 E3
Mill St Aberdare CF44 . . .28 E4
Aberdare CF44 . . . . .28 F4
Blaina NP13 . . . . .15 E4
Caerleon NP18 . . . . .118 C2
Cwmfelin CF34 . . . . .128 C8
Cwmfelinfach NP11 . . . . .113 A4
Gorseinon SA4 . . . . .43 C2

Mill St *continued*
Gowerton SA4 . . . . .66 B5
Llanelli SA15 . . . . .40 D4
Newport NP20 . . . . .143 B5
Pen-clawdd SA4 . . . . . . .65 E4
Pontypridd CF37 . . . . . .109 B1
Risca NP11 . . . . .115 B1
Tonyrefail CF39 . . . . . . .133 B4
Treharris CF46 . . . . .83 C6
Ystrad CF41 . . . . .79 D2
Mill Terr
Ammanford SA18 . . . . . .219 A5
Cwm NP23 . . . . .35 A7
Glynneath SA11 . . . . . . .223 C1
Risca NP11 . . . . .115 B1
Mill View CF34 . . . . .102 D1
Mill's Ho 2 SA12 . . . . . .98 B2
Milland Rd SA11 . . . . . . .71 D7
Milland Road Ind Est
SA11 . . . . .71 D6
Millands Cl SA3 . . . . . . .122 C5
Millbank Jun & Inf Sch
CF5 . . . . .193 F6
Millbrook Cl CF64 . . . . .206 B4
Millbrook Ct NP44 . . . . .39 E3
Millbrook Hts CF64 . . . .206 B4
Millbrook Jun & Inf Schs
NP20 . . . . .116 F2
Millbrook Pk CF14 . . . . .160 A3
Millbrook Rd NP44 . . . . .39 E2
Millbrook Rd
Dinas Powys CF64 . . . . .206 B4
Pontllanfraith NP12 . . . . .86 A4
Millcroft CF71 . . . . .201 A4
Millennium Coastal Pk
SA14, SA15 . . . . .41 B1
Millennium Stad
CF10 . . . . .194 F5
Miller Cl NP18 . . . . .119 F1
Miller's Ct SA5 . . . . .67 F6
Millers Ave CF32 . . . . . .150 F5
Millers Ride NP44 . . . . . .90 A3
Millfield
Bridgend CF31 . . . . .168 E5
Cardiff CF14 . . . . .160 A3
Pontyclun CF72 . . . . . . .173 A7
Quakers Yard CF46 . . . . .83 C6
Millfield Cl
Cardiff CF3 . . . . .179 E6
Swansea SA2 . . . . .94 B5
Millfield Dr CF71 . . . . . .188 F2
Millgate CF71 . . . . .160 A1
Millheath Dr CF14 . . . . .160 A2
Millicent St CF10 . . . . . .195 B5
Millrace Cl CF14 . . . . . . .160 A2
Millwood CF14 . . . . .160 A3
Millwood Cl 3 SA1 . . . . .68 C2
Millwood Rise CF62 . . . .214 C4
Millwood St SA5 . . . . . . .68 C3
Milman St NP20 . . . . . . .143 C1
Milner St NP19 . . . . . . .143 F3
Milton Cl
Aberbargoed CF81 . . . . . .58 B4
Beddau CF38 . . . . .156 A5
Cwmbran NP44 . . . . .89 D2
Ebbw Vale NP23 . . . . . . .14 B8
Llantwit Major CF61 . . . .210 B5
Milton Ct NP19 . . . . . . .144 F6
Milton Dr CF31 . . . . . . .168 C5
Milton Hill NP18 . . . . . .145 B5
Milton Inf Sch NP19 . . . .144 F6
Milton Jun Sch NP19 . . .144 F6
Milton Pl Cardiff CF5 . . .193 E8
Machen CF83 . . . . .139 C7
Milton Rd Barry CF62 . . .214 E8
Newport NP19 . . . . . . .144 A5
Penarth CF64 . . . . .206 F4
Milton St Cardiff CF24 . .195 C7
Cwmaman CF44 . . . . . . .53 A4
Milton Terr
New Tredegar NP24 . . . . .33 F1
Swansea SA1 . . . . .95 C8
Milverton Rd CF3 . . . . . .179 C7
Milward Rd CF63 . . . . . .215 B6
Min y Coed Cimla SA11 . .72 B6
Lewistown CF32 . . . . . . .130 E5
Min y Mor SA15 . . . . . . .40 C5
Min yr Afon CF83 . . . . . .140 A7
Min-y-Coed
Bridgend CF31 . . . . .169 C5
Glynneath SA11 . . . . . . .223 C1
Pontrhydyfen SA12 . . . . .73 B5
Pyle SA13 . . . . .148 A6
Radyr CF15 . . . . .176 B7
Min-y-Don SA13 . . . . . .125 C3
Min-y-Mor CF62 . . . . . .214 B2
Min-y-Nant
Cardiff CF14 . . . . .177 B7
Pencoed CF35 . . . . .170 D8
Min-y-Rhos SA9 . . . . . . .222 A6
Min-yr-Allt SA10 . . . . . . .48 E2
Min-yr-awel CF31 . . . . . .168 D8
Minafon CF14 . . . . .159 B1
Minavon 1 CF14 . . . . . . .177 B5
Mincing La SA1 . . . . .68 B2
Minehead Ave CF64 . . . .216 A5
Minehead Rd CF3 . . . . . .179 C6
Minerva St CF31 . . . . . . .168 F5
Minffrwd Cl CF35 . . . . . .152 E1
Minffrwd Rd
Pencoed CF35 . . . . .152 E1
Pencoed CF35 . . . . .152 F2
Mining School Hill
NP11 . . . . .60 A1
Minister St CF24 . . . . . .195 A8

Minny St CF24 . . . . .195 A8
Minori Ho CF10 . . . . . . .195 C2
Minories 15 NP44 . . . . . .89 B1
Minsmere Cl CF3 . . . . . .180 B7
Minster Cl Barry CF63 . .215 B8
Swansea SA6 . . . . .69 B7
Minster Cl SA6 . . . . .69 B7
Minster Rd CF23 . . . . . .195 E8
Minyrafon SA9 . . . . .2 B5
Minyrafon Rd SA6 . . . . . .22 D1
Mirador Cres SA2 . . . . . .95 A6
Miskin Cres CF72 . . . . . .173 D7
Miskin Gn NP44 . . . . .90 A3
Miskin Ho NP44 . . . . .90 A3
Miskin Prim Sch CF45 . .54 D1
Miskin Rd
Mountain Ash CF45 . . . . .54 E1
Mountain Ash CF45 . . . . .54 E2
Tonypandy CF40 . . . . . . .106 F5
Miskin St Barry CF62 . . .214 D3
Cardiff CF24 . . . . .195 A7
Treherbert CF42 . . . . . . .50 E2
Miskin Terr CF45 . . . . . . .54 E2
Mission Rd CF34 . . . . . .102 C1
Misty Hills Cl SA4 . . . . . .65 C1
Mitchell Cl
Cardiff CF38 . . . . .180 A5
Llanyravon NP44 . . . . . . .90 B1
Mitchell Cres CF47 . . . . .10 F8
Mitchell Ct 2 CF40 . . . .106 E6
Mitchell Terr
4 Pontypridd NP4 . . . . .38 A1
Pontypridd CF37 . . . . . .135 D8
Miterdale Cl CF23 . . . . . .178 B3
Mithras Way NP18 . . . . .118 A4
Mitre Cl CF5 . . . . .177 A1
Mitre Pl CF5 . . . . .177 A1
Mitre St NP13 . . . . .36 B5
Mixen Cl SA3 . . . . .122 F5
Model Cotts CF47 . . . . . .10 F2
Moel Fryn CF83 . . . . . . .137 D6
Moel Gilau CF32,CF34 . .129 D5
Moir Ct CF83 . . . . .137 F5
Moira Pl CF24 . . . . .195 C6
Moira St CF24 . . . . .195 C6
Moira Terr
Cardiff CF24 . . . . .195 C6
Ogmore Vale CF32 . . . . .104 C3
Mole Cl NP20 . . . . .116 C2
Molescombe 6 NP44 . . . .89 B1
Mona Cwmbran NP44 . . .89 F5
Swansea SA6 . . . . .69 A6
Mona Pl Cardiff CF24 . . .195 F7
Maerdy CF43 . . . . .52 A2
Monastery Rd
SA10 . . . . .71 B8
Monastery Bsns Ctr
SA10 . . . . .71 B8
Monet Cres NP44 . . . . . .144 A7
Monger St 1 SA1 . . . . . .68 C3
Monica St CF34 . . . . . . .102 B2
Monk St CF44 . . . . .29 A1
Monk's Cl CF33 . . . . . . .148 B2
Monks Cl SA10 . . . . .71 C8
Monksland SA3 . . . . .231 A6
Monkstone Cl CF64 . . . .206 E1
Monkstone Rise CF3 . . . .179 C5
Monkton Cl CF5 . . . . . . .193 C7
Monmouth Cl
Church Village CF38 . . . .135 F2
Pontypool NP4 . . . . .63 A2
Monmouth Ct CF83 . . . .137 D4
Monmouth Dr
Merthyr Tydfil CF48 . . . .225 F1
Newport NP19 . . . . . . .144 A8
Monmouth Ho
Cwmbran NP44 . . . . .89 A2
8 Penarth CF64 . . . . . .206 E4
7 Swansea SA1 . . . . . . .95 E6
Monmouth Pl CF3 . . . . .162 C4
Monmouth St
Cardiff CF11 . . . . .194 A4
Mountain Ash CF45 . . . . .81 F7
Monmouth View
CF83 . . . . .112 A1
Monmouth Way
Barry CF62 . . . . .214 F6
Boverton CF61 . . . . .210 B7
Monmouth Wlk
Cwmbran NP44 . . . . .89 E3
Markham NP12 . . . . .58 D7
Monnow Ct NP44 . . . . . .89 A4
Monnow Inf Sch
NP20 . . . . .116 D2
Monnow Jun Sch
NP20 . . . . .116 D2
Monnow Way NP20 . . . .116 D2
Monnow Wlk NP20 . . . .116 D2
Montague St NP13 . . . . . .36 B6
Montana Pk CF44 . . . . . .27 D2
Montana Pl SA1 . . . . . . .67 E6
Montclaire Ave NP12 . . .85 E6
Monterey St SA5 . . . . . . .68 C3
Montgomery Rd
Barry CF62 . . . . .214 E4
Newport NP20 . . . . . . .117 A4
Montgomery St CF24 . . .178 A1
Monthermer Rd CF24 . . .178 A1
Monton Terr SA1 . . . . . . .96 A7
Montpellier Terr SA1 . . .95 B7
Montreal Cl NP20 . . . . . .142 C1
Montrose Ct NP44 . . . . .117 A7
Monumental Terr
CF48 . . . . .10 A4
Moor King Cl CF3 . . . . .180 B6
Moor La
Llangennith SA3 . . . . . . .228 C2
Porthcawl CF36 . . . . . . .165 F3
Moor Rd Baglan SA12 . . .98 D3

Moor Rd continued
Bridgend CF31 ......**169** F2
Moor View
Bishton NP18 ......**145** A1
Ebbw Vale NP23 ....**14** C8
Ebbw Vale NP23 ......**7** A4
Moorby St CF10 ...**195** C4
Moordale Rd CF11 .**195** A4
Moore Cl CF5 .....**193** C5
Moore Cres NP19 ..**145** A6
Moore Rd CF5 .....**193** B5
Moore's Row CF81 ...**32** D7
Moorings The
Newport NP19 ....**143** F8
Newport NP19 ....**144** A8
Penarth CF64 ....**207** A5
Moorland Ave
Mumbles SA3 ....**122** C6
Newport NP19 ....**144** C3
Moorland Cl CF44 ...**27** F7
Moorland Com Jun & Inf
Sch CF24 ....**195** C5
Moorland Cres CF38 .**156** A7
Moorland Hts CF37 .**135** E8
Moorland Pk NP19 ..**144** C3
Moorland Rd
Bargoed CF81 ....**57** E4
Cardiff CF24 ....**195** C6
Cardiff CF24 ....**195** F5
Ebbw Vale NP23 ....**14** C1
Neath SA11 ....**71** F5
Port Talbot SA12 ...**124** D8
8 Port Talbot SA12 ..**98** E1
Moorlands SA10 ...**223** A5
Moorlands Rd CF31 .**168** F2
Moorings The NP4 ..**62** E5
Moors La CF24 .....**195** D5
Moorside Rd SA3 ...**122** F7
Moorside Villas SA10 .**222** F6
Moorview CF1 SA5 ...**67** F4
Moorview Rd SA5 ....**67** F4
Mor-Awel SA14 ....**41** C5
Morawel SA1 ....**69** D5
Morden La NP19 ...**143** E7
Morden Rd NP19 ...**143** E6
Morel Ct CF11 .....**206** F8
Morel St CF63 .....**215** A5
Morfa Ave SA13 ...**125** E5
Morfa CP Jun Sch
SA15 ....**40** F3
Morfa Cres CF3 ....**179** E5
Morfa Glas SA11 ...**223** C1
Morfa Inf Sch SA15 .**40** E2
Morfa La
Llantwit Major CF61 ..**199** D1
Wenvoe CF5 ....**205** A6
Morfa Rd
Margam SA13 ....**125** C4
Swansea SA1 ....**68** C1
Swansea SA1 ....**95** D8
Morfa St CF31 ....**168** F5
Morfa Stadium (Regional
Sports Ctr) SA1 ....**68** E4
Morfydd St
Swansea SA6 ....**68** F8
3 Swansea SA6 ....**69** A8
Morgan Arc 17 CF10 .**195** A5
Morgan Ct CF40 ....**79** F1
Morgan Jones Flats
CF83 ....**138** A3
Morgan Jones Sq 4
CF48 ....**31** C1
Morgan Rise 7 NP4 ..**17** D7
Morgan St
Abercraf SA9 ....**222** D7
Aberdare CF44 ....**28** F2
Abertillery NP13 ....**36** B6
Barry CF63 ....**215** B5
Blaenavon NP4 ......**17** C6
Caerphilly CF83 ....**138** A4
Cardiff CF24 ....**195** B5
Dowlais CF48 ....**11** A4
Llanbradach CF83 ...**111** F2
4 Merthyr Tydfil CF47 ..**10** D2
9 Mountain Ash CF45 ..**54** E1
New Tredegar NP24 ...**33** E3
Newport NP19 ......**143** D6
Pontardawe SA8 .....**23** C2
Pontypridd CF37 ...**109** C2
Porth CF39 ....**107** F3
Swansea SA1 ....**68** D2
Tredegar NP22 ......**13** E6
Morgan Terr
Porth CF39 ....**107** F2
Tredegar NP22 ......**13** D5
Treorchy CF42 ......**78** B4
Morgan Way NP10 ..**163** F6
Morgan's Rd SA11 ...**71** C5
Morgan's Terr
Briton Ferry SA11 ....**71** C3
Pontrhydyfen SA12 ...**73** A2
Morgannwg Ho SA12 **124** D8
Morgannwg St CF37 .**108** D2
Morgraig Ave NP10 .**163** E5
Moriah Hill NP11 ...**115** A2
Moriah Pl
Llwydcoed CF44 .....**28** E6
Pyle CF33 ....**148** D2
Moriah Rd SA5 .....**66** D6
Moriah St
Bedlinog CF46 ....**56** A7
15 Merthyr Tydfil CF47 ..**10** E1
Rhymney NP22 ....**12** F2
Morien Cres CF37 ...**135** F6
Morlais Bldgs 1 CF47 .**10** E1
Morlais Cl CF48 ...**225** F2
Morlais Ct
Caerphilly CF83 .....**137** D4

Morlais Ct continued
11 Merthyr Tydfil CF47 ...**30** D8
Morlais Rd
Llangennech SA14 ....**42** B7
Margam SA13 ....**125** E4
Swansea SA5 ....**68** B5
Morlais St Barry CF63 .**215** C6
Cardiff CF23 ....**178** B1
Dowlais CF48 ....**11** A5
Pentrebach CF48 .....**31** A4
Morley Cl NP19 ....**144** E5
Morley Rd NP13 ....**36** A6
Morningside Wlk
CF62 ....**204** F1
Mornington Ct CF3 ..**179** A3
Morrell St 18 CF47 ...**30** E8
Morris Ave
Cardiff CF14 ....**195** F5
Mountain Ash CF45 ...**81** F7
Morris Finer Cl CF45 .**213** E5
Morris La Swansea SA1 **95** E7
Swansea SA5 ....**95** F8
Morris Rise 6 NP4 ...**17** D7
Morris St
Cwmaman CF44 ......**53** A4
Maesteg CF34 ......**102** A3
Newport NP19 ......**143** E4
7 Swansea SA6 ......**69** A8
3 Treherbert CF42 ....**51** A1
Morris Terr
Ferndale CF43 ....**79** E7
Swansea SA5 ....**67** B6
Morrison Cres SA12 ..**98** D1
Morrison Ct SA12 ....**98** D1
Morrison Ho 5 SA12 .**98** D1
Morrison Rd SA12 ...**98** B1
Morrison St NP12 ...**85** E7
Morrison Comp Sch
SA6 ....**45** F4
Morrison Hospl SA6 ..**45** F4
Morriston North Ind Est
Swansea SA6 ....**69** C8
Swansea SA6 ....**46** B1
Morriston Pl SA18 ..**220** E6
Morriston Prim Sch
SA6 ....**69** A8
Morriston South Ind Est
SA6 ....**69** A7
Morrisville NP11 ...**113** D3
Morse Row CF32 ....**150** F4
Mortimer Rd CF11 ...**194** D7
Morton Ct CF14 ....**178** A4
Morton Terr CF40 ...**106** A4
Morton Way NP20 ...**142** F1
Morton's Farm NP23 ...**8** A4
Moseley Terr NP44 ...**89** E7
Moses Row SA11 ....**226** D5
Moss Rd Aberdare CF44 **29** B4
Cwmbran NP44 ......**89** B3
Mostyn Cl CF72 ....**153** D3
Mostyn Mews CF72 ..**153** D3
Mostyn Rd CF5 .....**193** A4
Mostyn St CF44 ....**53** F4
Mostyn Thomas Cl
NP13 ....**15** D5
Mound Rd CF37 ....**135** B8
Mount Cres
Penllergaer SA4 .....**43** F2
Swansea SA6 ....**45** D2
Mount Earl CF31 ...**168** E2
Mount Earl Cl CF31 ..**168** E2
Mount Hill St CF44 ...**53** C7
Mount Libanus St
CF42 ....**51** A1
Mount Pleasant
Aberkenfig CF32 ....**150** C3
Abersychan NP4 .....**37** F4
Bargoed CF81 ....**57** F5
Barry CF63 ....**215** B6
Bedlinog CF46 ....**56** A7
Blaengarw CF32 ....**103** E7
Blaina NP13 ....**15** D5
Bridgend CF31 .....**168** B5
Cwmfelinfach NP11 ...**11** A4
Gowerton SA4 ....**66** B4
Heolgerrig CF48 .....**10** A1
Llanelly Hill NP7 ....**9** C5
Maesycwmmer CF82 ...**85** B2
Newport NP20 ......**117** A3
Pen-y-fai CF31 .....**150** C1
Penpedairheol CF82 ...**84** E8
Pontycymer CF32 ...**103** E3
Swansea SA1 ....**95** C7
Tonna SA11 ....**49** C2
Trehafod CF37 .....**108** C2
Merthyr Vale CF48 ...**55** D2
Mount Pleasant Ave
CF3 ....**179** C6
Mount Pleasant Bldgs 2
SA15 ....**40** D6
Mount Pleasant Cl
NP44 ....**89** D5
Mount Pleasant Cotts
Abertillery NP13 .....**36** B5
Llangeinor CF32 ....**130** B5
1 Mountain Ash CF45 ..**54** E1
Mount Pleasant Ct
Abertillery NP13 ....**60** A7
Neath SA11 ....**70** E7
Pontypool NP4 ......**62** C6
Mount Pleasant Dr 3
SA1 ....**95** C7
Mount Pleasant Est
NP13 ....**60** B7
Mount Pleasant Jun & Inf
Sch NP10 ....**142** A6
Mount Pleasant La
CF3 ....**179** C6

Mount Pleasant Pl 6
CF45 ....**54** E1
Mount Pleasant Prim Sch
CF48 ....**55** D2
Mount Pleasant Rd
Cwmbran NP44 ......**89** D5
Ebbw Vale NP23 ......**7** C1
Pontypool NP4 ......**62** A8
Porth CF39 ....**107** E4
Porthcawl CF33 ....**166** C4
Risca NP11 ....**115** A2
Mount Pleasant Row
NP13 ....**36** B7
Mount Pleasant Sq
NP23 ....**7** C1
Mount Pleasant St
Aberbargoed CF81 ...**58** A5
Aberdare CF44 ....**28** F3
Dowlais CF48 ....**11** A5
Mount Pleasant Terr
Abercarn NP11 .....**114** C5
Mountain Ash CF45 ...**54** E1
Mount Rd
Dinas Powys CF64 ..**206** A3
Pontypool NP4 ....**38** D1
Rhigos CF44 ....**224** A1
Risca NP11 ....**115** A2
Mount St
Aberdare CF44 ....**53** C7
Ebbw Vale NP23 .....**14** D6
Gowerton SA4 ....**66** B5
1 Merthyr Tydfil CF47 ..**10** D2
Pontlottyn CF81 ....**12** F1
Swansea SA6 ....**45** E1
Tredegar NP22 ......**13** E7
Mount St Denys CF14 .**160** B4
Mount Stuart Sq
CF10 ....**195** B2
Mount Terr 3 CF47 ...**10** D7
Mount The
Cardiff CF3 ....**194** C7
Dinas Powys CF64 ..**206** A3
Gowerton SA4 ....**66** B5
Mount View
Merthyr Tydfil CF47 ...**11** A1
Merthyr Vale CF48 ...**55** D2
Mount View Terr 2
SA12 ....**99** A1
Mountain Ash Comp Sch
CF45 ....**54** C4
Mountain Ash General
Hospl CF45 ....**54** D4
Mountain Ash Rd
CF45 ....**82** D2
Mountain Ash Sta
CF45 ....**54** D3
Mountain La NP4 ...**62** D3
Mountain Rd
Aberavon SA12 ......**99** A2
Bedwas CF83 ......**138** D8
Caerphilly CF83 ....**159** B8
Craig-Cefn-Parc SA6 ...**22** C1
Cwmaman CF44 ......**53** A4
Cwmbran NP44 ......**89** B7
Pentyrch CF15 .....**157** C1
Risca NP11 ....**115** C2
Rogerstone NP10 ...**142** A8
Tonypandy CF40 ...**107** A2
Mountain Row CF43 ..**79** F8
Mountain Stream
SA10 ....**48** C1
Mountain View
Briton Ferry SA11 ....**71** B3
5 Brynmawr NP23 ....**8** B4
Educationllypant CF83 **138** A6
Machen CF83 ....**139** F7
Markham NP12 ....**58** D7
North Cornelly CF33 .**166** A4
Pontypool NP4 ......**61** F8
4 Pontypridd CF37 ...**135** F6
Tonypandy CF40 ....**106** F8
Tonyrefail CF39 ....**132** E5
Treherbert CF42 .....**50** E2
Mountain View Rd
NP4 ....**61** F8
Mountain Way NP46 ..**83** F2
Mountbatten NP22 ...**12** F3
Mountbatten Cl
Cardiff CF23 ....**178** A5
Newport NP19 ......**144** F7
Mountbatten Ct SA5 ..**67** E5
Mountbatten Rd
CF62 ....**205** A1
Mountford Cl NP10 ..**142** A7
Mountjoy Ave CF64 .**206** F4
Mountjoy Cl 1 CF64 ..**206** F4
Mountjoy Cres 1
CF64 ....**206** F4
Mountjoy La 2 CF64 .**206** F3
Mountjoy Pl
4 Newport NP20 ....**143** C2
Penarth CF64 ......**206** F4
Mountjoy Rd 5 NP20 **143** C2
Mountjoy St 6 NP20 .**143** C2
Mountside NP11 ...**115** D1
Mountstuart Com Jun &
Inf Sch CF10 ......**195** B1
Moxon Rd NP20 ....**117** A1
Moxon St CF63 ....**215** C6
Moy Rd Aberfan CF48 ...**55** B5
Cardiff CF24 ....**195** B8
Taffs Well CF15 ....**158** A4
Moyle Gr NP18 ....**117** C7
Mozart Dr SA12 ....**98** B3
Mozart Mews 5 SA12 ..**98** B3
Mr Speakers Way (Ffordd
Mr Llefarydd) CF40 .**107** A4

Muirfield Dr SA3 ....**93** F1
Muirton Rd CF24 ...**195** F6
Mulberry Ave SA3 ..**122** F8
Mulberry Cl
Llantwit Fardre CF38 .**156** C5
Rogerstone NP10 ...**141** E7
Mulberry Ct CF62 ...**213** C3
Mulcaster Ave NP19 **144** C2
Mulgrave Way SA2 ...**94** A1
Mullins Ave CF3 ....**179** D5
Multi Trad Ctr CF15 .**157** F8
Mumbles Bay Ct SA2 ..**94** B1
Mumbles Pier SA3 ..**123** E3
Mumbles Rd
Mumbles SA3 ....**123** A7
Swansea SA2 ....**94** D3
Mundy Pl CF24 .....**195** A8
Munnings Dr NP19 .**144** A7
Munro Pl CF62 ....**214** E6
Mur Gwyn CF14 ...**177** C8
Murch Cres CF64 ...**206** C3
Murch Jun Sch CF64 .**206** B3
Murch Rd CF64 ....**206** C3
Muriel Terr
Bedlinog CF46 ....**56** B7
Dowlais CF48 ....**11** C5
Murlande Way CF62 .**213** C2
Murray St SA15 ....**40** D5
Murray Wlk 18 CF14 .**194** D5
Murrayfield Cl SA5 ...**67** D3
Murrayfield Rd CF14 .**177** C5
Murrells Cl CF38 ...**156** B6
Murrys Wlk CF32 ...**167** F4
Murton La SA3 .....**122** D5
Museum Ave CF10 ..**195** A7
Museum Pl CF10 ...**195** A7
Museum St NP18 ...**118** B1
Musselwhite Ct NP12 .**86** A4
Mwyndy Cross Industries
CF72 ....**173** F8
Mwyndy Terr CF72 .**173** F8
Mydam La SA4 .....**43** A2
Myddynfych SA18 ...**219** B8
Mydriam Pl NP22 ....**6** E1
Mylo-Griffiths Cl CF5 **176** A3
Mynachdy Rd
Cardiff CF14 ....**177** D2
Ynysybwl CF37 ....**110** E4
Mynachlog Nedd Jun Sch
SA10 ....**71** A7
Mynydd Cynffig Inf Sch
CF33 ....**148** D2
Mynydd Cynffig Jun Sch
CF33 ....**148** D2
Mynydd Garnllwyd Rd
SA6 ....**68** D8
Mynydd Gelli Wastad Rd
Clydach SA6 ....**46** B6
Swansea SA6 ....**45** C5
Mynydd Islwyn Cl
NP12 ....**85** E9
Mynydd Maen Rd
NP44 ....**89** C6
Mynydd View
Pontypool NP4 ......**62** B4
Pontypool NP4 ......**62** B4
Pontypool NP4 ......**62** C4
Mynydd y Seren
CF39 ....**133** A3
Mynydd-Newydd Rd
SA5 ....**68** A2
Mynydd-Yr-Eos CF40 **107** A4
Mynyddbach SA18 ..**218** F5
Mynyddbach Comp Sch for
Girls SA5 ....**68** C7
Myra Hess Cl NP19 .**144** F6
Myrddin Gdns SA1 ...**69** B3
Myrddin Rd SA1 ....**69** B3
Myrtle SA4 ....**64** C3
Myrtle Cl
Penarth CF64 ......**206** E3
Rogerstone NP10 ...**142** B3
Myrtle Cotts NP18 ..**118** C2
Myrtle Dr NP10 ....**142** B3
Myrtle Gr Barry CF63 .**215** C7
Hengoed CF82 ....**84** F3
Newport NP19 ......**144** B5
Swansea SA2 ....**94** E7
Myrtle Hill SA4 .....**19** C5
Myrtle Rd
Gorseinon SA4 ......**66** B8
Neath SA11 ....**72** A6
Myrtle Row CF42 ...**78** F6
Myrtle Terr
Llanelli SA15 ....**40** E5
Mumbles SA3 ......**123** B4
Mysydd Rd SA1 .....**68** D3
Mysydd Terr SA1 ...**68** D3

N

Naddocks Pl CF31 ..**168** F3
Nailsea Ct CF64 ...**216** C5
Nant Arw SA18 ....**218** D6
Nant Cadle SA5 ....**67** E6
Nant Canna CF3 ...**170** A1
Nant Celyn CF38 ...**156** F5
Nant Celyn Cl NP44 ...**89** C6
Nant Coch Dr NP20 .**142** E4
Nant Coch House
Rougemont Sch
NP20 ....**142** E4
Nant Ddu CF83 ....**138** A2
Nant Dyfed CF72 ...**155** F5
Nant Eirin CF39 ...**133** A4

Nant Ffornwg CF31 .**168** B6
Nant Glas SA4 .....**44** C5
Nant Gwineu Rd
SA18 ....**220** C8
Nant Gwyn
Porth CF39 ....**107** D1
Trelewis CF46 ....**83** D6
Nant Hir SA11 ....**223** B1
Nant Isaf CF5 .....**205** A7
Nant Lais CF31 ....**168** D5
Nant Melyn NP23 ....**7** A4
Nant Melyn Terr
CF39 ....**133** D2
Nant Morlais CF48 ...**11** B6
Nant Row 16 NP44 ...**29** A1
Nant Talwg Way
CF62 ....**214** B5
Nant The CF81 .....**32** D7
Nant Walla CF14 ...**177** C8
Nant y Coed CF37 ..**108** F2
Nant y Dowlais CF5 .**192** E4
Nant y Felin
Efail Isaf CF38 .....**156** C5
Machen NP10 ....**140** C3
Nant y Garth CF15 .**157** F3
Nant y Hwyad CF83 .**137** C3
Nant y parc Prim Sch
CF83 ....**110** E3
Nant y Pepra CF5 ...**192** F4
Nant y Plac CF5 ...**192** F4
Nant y Rhos CF5 ...**192** F4
Nant y Wedal CF14 .**178** A2
Nant yr Wennol CF31 **168** C3
Nant yr Arthur CF5 .**192** F4
Nant-cae'r-efael
SA9 ....**222** E8
Nant-Fawr Cl CF23 .**178** B6
Nant-Fawr Cres CF23 **178** B6
Nant-Fawr Rd CF23 .**178** B6
Nant-gau NP12 .....**59** B2
Nant-y-Ci Rd SA18 .**218** F7
Nant-y-coed
Thomastown CF39 ...**133** A3
3 Troedyrhiw CF48 ...**31** B1
Nant-y-croft NP22 ...**6** C4
Nant-y-Cwm NP13 ...**60** C9
Nant-y-Dall Ave
CF37 ....**136** A4
Nant-y-Dderwen
SA18 ....**218** F8
Nant-y-Drope CF5 ..**192** F4
Nant-y-Fedw CF45 ...**82** C5
Nant-y-Fedw Rd SA13 **75** D3
Nant-y-Ffyddlon CF82 **84** D7
Nant-y-Ffynnon
CF31 ....**169** B5
Nant-y-Gleisiad
SA11 ....**226** D5
Nant-y-glo Round Twrs
NP23 ....**8** B1
Nant-y-Gro
Llanelli SA14 ....**41** C6
Llangennech SA14 ...**18** B1
Nant-y-Gwyddon Rd
CF40, CF41 ....**79** D2
Nant-y-Milwr Cl
NP44 ....**115** F7
Nant-y-moel Row
CF39 ....**104** E7
Nant-y-Mynydd
Pontypridd CF37 ...**109** D7
Seven Sisters SA10 .**222** E4
Nant-yr-Adar
Bridgend CF31 .....**168** B6
Llantwit Major CF61 .**210** A5
Nant-yr-Ely CF5 ...**192** E4
Nantcarn Rd NP11 .**114** C8
Nantddu Terr CF46 ...**82** F6
Nantlais
Ammanford SA18 ...**219** B8
Corntown CF35 ....**186** B7
Nantong Way SA1 ...**68** F4
Nantwen SA14 .....**41** F4
Nantyboda SA13 ...**100** E4
Nantybryn SA14 ....**41** A7
Nantydd Terr SA14 ..**41** C5
Nantyffin N SA7 ....**69** D7
Nantyffin Rd
Pontarddulais SA4 ...**19** D3
Swansea SA7 ....**69** C7
Nantyffin S SA7 ....**69** C6
Nantyffyllon Prim Sch
CF34 ....**101** F5
Nantyffyllon Terr
CF34 ....**101** F6
Nantyglo Comp Sch
NP23 ....**8** B2
Nantyglyn Rd SA18 .**219** F8
Nantygwenith St CF48 **10** C1
Nantygwenith St CF48 **10** C1
Nantymoel Prim Sch
CF32 ....**104** E5
Nantyrychain Terr
CF32 ....**103** F2
Napier Cl CF31 ....**169** A4

Napier St
Machen CF83 ....**140** A7
Mountain Ash CF45 ...**54** D2
Narberth Cres NP44 ...**90** B3
Narberth Ct CF83 ..**137** C4
Narberth Rd CF5 ...**193** D5
Narberth Ct CF62 ..**214** F7
Naseby Cl CF23 ....**160** F1
Nash Cl NP10 .....**142** B6
Nash Dr NP19 .....**144** B2
Nash Gr NP19 .....**144** B3
Nash Rd NP19 ....**144** B2
Nash St CF5 ....**82** D2
Nash View CF71 ...**187** F4
Nasturtium Way
CF23 ....**160** D1
Nat Assembly for Wales
CF10 ....**195** C2
Nat Cricket Ctr (Canolfan
Criced Genedlaethol)
CF11 ....**194** E7
Nat Mus of Wales
CF10 ....**195** A7
Nathan Ho CF23 .....**12** C4
Nathan St SA15 ....**40** C3
National Bldgs 13
NP20 ....**143** C4
Navigation Cl CF44 ...**83** C7
Navigation Rd NP11 **114** F3
Navigation St
Bedwas CF83 ....**139** A7
1 Mountain Ash CF45 .**54** D3
Navigation Terr CF34 **73** A1
Navigation Villas 2
CF45 ....**54** E1
Navigation Yd CF45 ..**54** E1
Neale St CF62 ....**214** E6
Neath Abbey SA10 ...**71** B7
Neath Abbey Bsns Pk
SA10 ....**71** A7
Neath Abbey Inf Sch
SA10 ....**71** B8
Neath Abbey Rd SA10 **71** C8
Neath Coll SA10 ....**48** D1
Neath Ct NP44 .....**89** A4
Neath General Hospl
SA11 ....**71** C4
Neath General Sta
SA11 ....**71** E7
Neath Mus & Art Gallery
SA11 ....**71** E8
Neath Rd
Briton Ferry SA11 ....**71** C1
Bryn-côch SA10 .....**48** C7
Crynant SA10 .....**226** A7
Maesteg CF34 .....**101** E4
Morriston SA6 ......**46** A2
Pontrhydyfen SA12,
SA13 ....**100** C7
Resolven SA11 ....**226** C5
Resolven SA11 ....**226** D5
Swansea SA6 ....**68** E5
Swansea SA6 ....**69** A8
Tonna SA11 ....**49** B1
Ystradgynlais SA9 ....**2** F6
Ystradgynlais SA9 ..**222** A4
Neath St CF24 ....**195** E5
Neath Villas NP4 ...**37** E3
Nebo Ct CF41 .....**79** C3
Neerings NP44 .....**89** A1
Neilson Cl 1 CF10 .**195** C4
Nelson Dr NP19 ...**144** E6
Nelson Rd CF62 ...**215** A8
Nelson St
Aberdare CF44 ......**53** B5
Ebbw Vale NP23 .....**7** D4
Swansea SA1 ....**95** C6
Nelson Terr
Llanelli SA15 ....**40** C4
New Tredegar NP24 ...**33** F1
Neol St CF44 ......**53** B4
Nesta Rd CF5 .....**194** B6
Neston Rd NP19 ...**144** D6
Nethercourt NP44 ...**89** B3
Nettlefold Rd CF24 .**195** D4
Neuadd Rd SA18 ...**220** C8
Neuadd St NP13 ....**36** A6
Neuadda Cl NP10 ..**141** D2
Neuaddwen St CF81 ..**58** B5
Nevern Wlk 8 NP44 ...**90** B2
Nevill St SA15 .....**40** C4
Nevill Terr 2 NP4 ...**17** D7
Neville Pk NP10 ...**163** E1
Neville Pl 18 CF11 .**194** E5
Neville Rd
Bridgend CF31 .....**168** E2
Porthcawl CF36 ....**183** A7
Neville St
Abersychan NP4 .....**37** E6
Cardiff CF11 ....**194** E5
Neville Terr CF44 ...**28** F2
Nevills Cl SA4 .....**66** C6
Nevin Cres CF3 ...**179** C4
New Barn CF62 ....**201** B1
New Bldgs The NP10 .**163** C6
New Bryn Terr CF39 .**107** D8
New Bryngwyn Rd
NP11 ....**86** E6
New Bryngwyn St
NP12 ....**85** B6
New Castle St 3 CF47 .**10** E1
New Ceidrim Rd
SA18 ....**220** B8
New Century St CF40 **107** B5

New Chapel Ct NP44 . . . .89 D1
New Chapel St CF42 . . . .78 D6
New Church St CF48 . . . .10 A5
New Coll CF10 . . . . .195 B5
New College Prim Sch
CF10 . . . . .195 B4
New Cross Bldgs 3
SA6 . . . . .46 A1
New Cut Rd SA1 . . . . . . .95 D8
New Cwm Terr NP23 . . .35 B7
New Dock Rd SA15 . . . .40 D3
New Dock St SA15 . . . . .40 D2
New Forest View
CF71 . . . . .189 A1
New George St CF10 . . .195 C2
New Gladstone St
NP13 . . . . .15 E5
New Henry St SA11 . . . .71 D6
New High St SA1 . . . . . .36 C2
New Hos Pant CF48 . . . .11 B6
Pontypool NP4 . . . . .61 C4
New House Ct 4
CF63 . . . . .215 B7
New Inn Inf Sch NP4 . .63 A4
New Inn Pl SA11 . . . . . .226 D5
New Inn Rd CF31,
CF32 . . . . .168 C1
New James St 2 NP4 .17 D6
New King St CF41 . . . . .79 B2
New Mill Cnr CF72 . . . .173 D6
New Mill Rd SA2 . . . . . .94 A6
New Orchard St SA1 . . .95 D8
New Park Cres 2
CF37 . . . . .135 E7
New Park Holiday Pk
SA3 . . . . .231 A4
New Park Rd NP11 . . . .114 D3
New Park Terr CF37 . . .135 E6
New Pastures NP20 . . .143 A2
New Quarr Rd SA5 . . . . .68 C5
New Quay Rd NP19 . . .164 E8
New Rank NP7 . . . . .9 C5
New Rd
Abersychan NP4 . . . . . . .37 D5
Abersychan NP4 . . . . . . .37 E6
Ammanford SA18 . . . . .219 B6
Argoed NP12 . . . . .58 F4
Caerleon NP18 . . . . . . .118 C1
Cardiff CF3 . . . . .179 B2
Cilfrew SA10 . . . . .49 C5
Crofty SA4 . . . . .64 B3
Cwmfelinfach NP11 . . .113 B4
Deri CF81 . . . . .57 C8
Dowlais CF48 . . . . .11 A4
Grovesend SA4 . . . . . . .43 C6
Gwaun-Cae-Gurwen
SA18 . . . . .220 E7
Hengoed CF82, NP12 . . .85 A3
Llanelli SA14 . . . . .41 B6
Llanelli SA15 . . . . .40 C6
Llansamlet SA7 . . . . . . .46 F1
Mountain Ash CF45 . . . .54 D3
Mountain Ash CF45 . . . .82 A7
Mountain Ash CF45 . . . .82 C6
Nantyglo NP23 . . . . .8 C2
Neath SA10 . . . . .70 C1
Neath SA10 . . . . .70 F7
Neath Abbey SA10 . . . . .71 B8
Pencoed CF72 . . . . .153 C1
Pontardawe SA8 . . . . . .23 B2
Pontardawe SA8 . . . . . .24 A7
Pontardawe SA8 . . . . . .24 B4
Pontarddulais SA4 . . . . .19 B4
Pontypool NP4 . . . . .62 F3
Porthcawl CF36 . . . . . .183 B7
Pyle CF33 . . . . .148 B3
Skewen SA10 . . . . .71 A7
Swansea SA2 . . . . .67 D1
Swansea SA5 . . . . .68 C6
Tondu CF32 . . . . .150 B5
Ynysmeudwy SA8 . . . . .23 F6
Ynysybwl CF37 . . . . . . .109 A7
New Terr NP4 . . . . .62 A8
New Tynybedw St
CF42 . . . . .78 E6
New Villas
Cwmaman CF44 . . . . . . .53 A3
Mumbles SA3 . . . . .123 B4
New Well La SA3 . . . . .122 F5
New William St 16
NP4 . . . . .17 C6

New Zealand Rd
CF14 . . . . .177 E2
New Zealand St SA15 . .40 C6
Newall St NP13 . . . . . . .36 B5
Newborough Ave
CF14 . . . . .177 E8
Newbridge Comp Sch
NP11 . . . . .87 A6
Newbridge Ct 7
CF37 . . . . .109 D2
Newbridge Gdns
CF31 . . . . .168 E3
Newbridge Rd
Llantrisant CF72 . . . . . .155 E4
Pontllanfraith NP12 . . . .86 A4
Port Talbot SA13 . . . . .124 E8
Newby Ct 5 CF10 . . . .195 B4
Newcastle Hill CF31 . .168 E4
Newchurch Ct NP44 . . .89 C3
Newchurch Rd NP23 . . .7 D2
Newell Rd SA10 . . . . . . .70 E8
Newent Rd CF3 . . . . . .179 F6
Newfoundland Rd
CF14 . . . . .177 E2
Newfoundland Way
NP12 . . . . .85 D6
Newgale Cl
Barry CF62 . . . . .214 F8
Swansea SA5 . . . . .67 F7
Newgale Ho NP44 . . . . .89 C3
Newgale Pl CF5 . . . . . .193 D4
Newgale Row NP44 . . . .89 F3
Newlands SA12 . . . . .98 F5
Newlands Ave CF31 . . .169 B7
Newlands Cl CF33 . . . .148 C2
Newlands Ct
Cardiff CF14 . . . . .160 A1
12 Pontypool NP4 . . . . .38 A1
Newlands Rd CF3 . . . . .179 F3
Newlands St CF62 . . . .214 F5
Newlyn Rd NP11 . . . . . .87 B7
Newman Cl NP19 . . . . .144 F5
Newman Rd NP4 . . . . . .38 B1
Newmarket Wlk 9
CF47 . . . . .10 D1
Newmill Gdns CF72 . . .173 D8
Newminster Rd CF23 . .195 E8
Newnham Cres SA2 . . . .94 E7
Newnham Pl NP44 . . . . .89 C3
Newpark District Shopping
Ctr CF72 . . . . .155 C2
Newport (Casnewydd) Sta
NP20 . . . . .143 B5
Newport Arc 3 NP20 .143 B5
Newport Castle NP20 143 C5
Newport Ctr(L Ctr)
NP20 . . . . .143 C4
Newport Mkt NP20 . . .143 C5
Newport Mus & Art Gal
NP20 . . . . .143 C4
Newport Nash Campus
NP19 . . . . .144 C2
Newport Rd
Abercarn NP11 . . . . . . .114 B8
Bedwas CF83 . . . . .138 E6
Cardiff CF3 . . . . .179 C5
Croesyceiliog NP44 . . . .90 B6
Cwmbran NP44 . . . . . .117 A6
Hollybush NP22,NP12 . .34 C4
Machen CF83 . . . . .139 C6
Pontllanfraith NP12 . . . .85 F3
Pontypool NP4 . . . . .63 A2
Risca NP11 . . . . .141 C8
Newport Retail Pk
NP19 . . . . .144 D2
Newport Road La
CF24 . . . . .195 C6
Newport St CF11 . . . . .195 A2
Newton Ave SA12 . . . . .98 F1
Newton Cl CF82 . . . . . . .84 E7
Newton Nottage Rd
CF36 . . . . .183 B8
Newton Prim Sch
Mountain Ash CF45 . . . .54 E2
Mumbles SA3 . . . . .122 E5
Porthcawl CF36 . . . . . .183 A7
Newton Rd
Cardiff CF11 . . . . .194 D4
Clydach SA6 . . . . .22 D1
Mumbles SA3 . . . . .123 A5
Rumney CF3 . . . . .179 F2
Newton St
Abercanaid CF48 . . . . . .30 F3
Barry CF63 . . . . .215 B6
Swansea SA1 . . . . .95 C6
Newton Terr 9 CF47 . .30 E8
Newton Way NP20 . . . .116 F2
Newton Wynd NP44 . . .89 B1
Newtown SA18 . . . . .219 A4
Newtown Cl SA18 . . . . .219 A7
Newtown Ct 2 CF24 . .195 C5
Newtown Ind Est
Abercarn NP11 . . . . . . .114 B4
Llantwit Fardre CF38 . . .156 D7
Newydd Rd
Ammanford SA18 . . . . .219 A7
Penperlleni NP4 . . . . . . .39 F6
Newydd Ct CF15 . . . . . .176 C3
Newydd The CF33 . . . .148 D2
Neyland Cl CF38 . . . . . .135 F2
Neyland Ct CF62 . . . . .214 F8
Neyland Dr SA5 . . . . . . .67 F7
Neyland Path NP44 . . . .89 F2
Neyland Pl CF5 . . . . . .193 D4
Niagara St CF37 . . . . . .135 D8
Nibloe Terr 2 CF47 . . .10 F4
Nicander Par SA1 . . . . .95 B8
Nicander Pl SA1 . . . . . .95 B8

Nicholas Rd SA7 . . . . . .47 A6
Nicholas St NP4 . . . . . . .62 C6
Nicholes Ct CF41 . . . . . .78 F3
Nicholl Ct
Boverton CF61 . . . . . . .210 B6
Mumbles SA3 . . . . .123 C3
Nicholl St SA1 . . . . .95 B6
Nicholls Ave CF36 . . . .183 A5
Nicholls Rd CF32 . . . . .150 C8
Nicholson Webb Cl
CF5 . . . . .176 D3
Nidd Cl NP20 . . . . .116 C1
Nidd Wlk NP20 . . . . . .116 C1
Nidum Cl SA10 . . . . . . .71 C8
Nightingale Ct
Llanelli SA15 . . . . .41 A5
Newport NP10 . . . . . . .163 E7
Nightingale Ho
3 Aberavon SA12 . . . . .98 F1
Cwmbran NP44 . . . . . . .89 D5
Nightingale Pk SA11 . . .72 A5
Nightingale Pl CF48 . . .206 C3
Nightingale St CF48 . . . .30 F4
Nightingale Terr NP4 . .62 A8
Nightingale's Bush
CF37 . . . . .135 E8
Nile Rd CF40 . . . . .107 B5
Nile St CF37 . . . . .135 D8
Nine Mile Point Ct
NP11 . . . . .113 B4
Nine Mile Point Ind Est
NP11 . . . . .113 C3
Nine Mile Point Rd
NP11 . . . . .113 E3
Ninian Park (Cardiff City
AFC) CF11 . . . . .194 E3
Ninian Park Jun & Inf Sch
CF11 . . . . .194 E3
Ninian Park Rd CF11 . .194 E5
Ninian Park Sta CF11 194 D4
Ninian Rd CF23 . . . . . .178 B1
Ninian St
Treherbert CF42 . . . . . . .51 A1
Treorchy CF42 . . . . .78 D7
Ninth Ave
Hirwaun CF44 . . . . .224 D1
Merthyr Tydfil CF47 . . . .10 E5
Swansea SA6 . . . . .45 D2
Nixon Terr SA6 . . . . . . .46 A1
Nixonville CF48 . . . . . . .55 C4
Nobel Ave SA12 . . . . . . .98 F1
Nobel Square Ind Est
NP23 . . . . .8 D4
Noel Terr CF48 . . . . . . .55 C4
Nolan Arc 6 CF31 . . . .168 E4
Nolton Arc CF31 . . . . . .67 F6
Nolton Pl NP44 . . . . . . .89 C1
Nolton St CF31 . . . . . . .168 E4
Nora St CF24 . . . . .195 D6
Norbury Ave CF5 . . . . .193 B4
Norbury Ct CF5 . . . . . .193 E7
Norbury Ho 10 NP44 . .89 C2
Norbury Rd CF5 . . . . . .193 E7
Nordale Ct CF14 . . . . . .178 A8
Nordale Rd CF61 . . . . .210 B6
Nordale Rise CF63 . . . .215 C6
Norfolk Cl NP44 . . . . . . .89 A3
Norfolk Ct CF5 . . . . . . .175 B6
Norfolk Ho 2 SA12 . . . .98 C3
Norfolk Rd NP19 . . . . .143 F6
Norfolk St Cardiff CF5 .194 B4
Swansea SA1 . . . . .95 B7
Norman Cotts CF64 . . .206 A4
Norman Rd CF14 . . . . .177 B4
Norman St
Aberavon SA12 . . . . . . .99 A1
Abertillery NP13 . . . . . . .36 B6
Caerleon NP18 . . . . . . .118 B2
1 Cardiff CF24 . . . . . .195 B8
Norman Terr
Merthyr Tydfil CF47 . . . .10 D2
Pentrebach CF48 . . . . . .31 B4
Normands Ho NP44 . . .116 C8
Normandy Rd SA1 . . . . .68 A3
Norris Cl CF64 . . . . . . .206 D5
Norseman Cl CF62 . . . .212 E2
North Ave
Aberdare CF44 . . . . .28 F2
Maesycwmmer CF82 . . .85 B2
Pyle CF33 . . . . .148 C2
Tredegar NP22 . . . . .6 C1
North Blackvein Ind Est
NP11 . . . . .114 A4
North Church St
CF10 . . . . .195 B4
North Clive St CF11 . . .194 E3
North Ct CF31 . . . . . . .169 E3
North Dock Bsns
Workshops SA15 . . . . .40 B4
North Edward St
CF10 . . . . .195 B6
North Hill Rd SA1 . . . . .95 C8
North Hills La SA3 . . . .120 C6
North Lake Dr NP10 . . .163 C6
North Luton Pl CF24 . .195 C5
North Mead CF32 . . . . .150 B3
North Morgan St 1
CF11 . . . . .194 E5
North Park Rd CF24 . . .195 E6
North Rd
Abercarn NP11 . . . . . . .114 C6
Abersychan NP4 . . . . . . .37 F3
Bargoed CF81 . . . . .57 F4
Barry CF64 . . . . .215 E6
Bridgend CF31 . . . . . . .169 C3
Cardiff CF10 . . . . .194 F2
Cefn Hengoed CF82 . . . .84 E5

North Rd continued
Cowbridge CF71 . . . . . .188 E2
Croesyceiliog NP44 . . . .90 A5
Ferndale CF43 . . . . .79 F7
Ferndale CF43 . . . . .79 F7
Gileston CF62 . . . . .211 E1
Loughor SA4 . . . . .42 F1
Newport NP11 . . . . .60 A1
Newbridge NP11 . . . . . . .87 A7
Ogmore Vale CF32 . . . .104 E2
Pontypool NP4 . . . . .62 B6
Porth CF39 . . . . .107 F3
North Rise CF14 . . . . . .160 A1
North St
Abercynon CF45 . . . . . . .82 E3
Blaenavon NP4 . . . . .17 B7
Cardiff CF11 . . . . .194 F3
Dowlais CF48 . . . . .11 A4
Ebbw Vale NP23 . . . . . . .7 E4
Maesteg CF34 . . . . .75 B2
Newport NP20 . . . . .143 B4
Penydarren CF47 . . . . . .10 F4
Pontypridd CF37 . . . . . .109 D2
Port Talbot SA13 . . . . .125 D7
North Terr Llanelli SA14 .41 D1
Maerdy CF43 . . . . .52 A2
Tonypandy CF40 . . . . . .106 C6
North Vale View
CF32 . . . . .104 E7
North View CF15 . . . . .158 B4
North View Terr
Aberdare CF44 . . . . .53 C5
Caerphilly CF83 . . . . . .138 B3
North Wall Rd CF62 . . .211 E1
North Wlk Barry CF62 . .214 E1
Cwmbran NP44 . . . . . . .89 E4
Northam Ave CF3 . . . . .179 A5
Northampton La SA1 . . .95 C7
Northcliffe Dr CF36 . . .207 B5
Northcote La CF24 . . . .195 B7
Northcote St CF24 . . . .195 B8
Northcote Terr CF63 . . .215 C6
Northern Ave
Cardiff CF14 . . . . .176 E8
Northern Avenue Ash Gr
CF14 . . . . .177 A6
Northern Avenue Manor
Way CF14 . . . . .177 C5
Northeron SA3 . . . . . . .122 F8
Northfield Cl NP18 . . . .118 A4
Northfield Rd NP18 . . .118 A4
Northlands CF3 . . . . . . .179 B2
Northlands Pk SA3 . . .122 A7
Northumberland Rd 2
NP19 . . . . .143 F6
Northumberland St
CF5 . . . . .194 C5
Northway
Bishopston SA3 . . . . . . .122 B7
Pontypool NP4 . . . . .39 B2
Northways CF36 . . . . . .183 A7
Norton Ave
Cardiff CF14 . . . . .177 D4
Mumbles SA3 . . . . .123 A6
Norton Dr SA3 . . . . . . .121 A6
Norton La SA3 . . . . . . .121 B7
Norton Rd
Glyncorrwg SA13 . . . . .227 D2
Mumbles SA3 . . . . .123 A6
Penygroes SA14 . . . . . .218 D8
Norton Terr SA13 . . . . .227 C2
Norwich Rd CF23 . . . . .178 F1
Norwood CF14 . . . . . . .159 F2
Norwood Cres CF63 . . .215 C7
Norwood Ct 1 CF24 . .195 D7
Nottage Ct CF36 . . . . .166 A1
Nottage Mdws CF36 . . .165 E2
Nottage Mead CF36 . . .165 E2
Nottage Mews SA3 . . .122 E4
Nottage Prim Sch
CF36 . . . . .182 F7
Nottage Rd
Cardiff CF5 . . . . .193 C4
Mumbles SA3 . . . . .122 E4
Nottingham St CF5 . . . .194 B6
Notts Gdns SA2 . . . . . . .94 F7
Novello Ho SA12 . . . . . .98 A2
Nuns Cres CF37 . . . . . .109 B2
Nurseries The NP18 . . .145 D8
Nursery Cres NP22 . . . .13 A2
Nursery Gdns CF31 . . .168 F8
Nursery Rd SA13 . . . . .227 C1
Nursery Rise CF83 . . . .138 C7
Nursery Terr NP22 . . . .13 E8
Nurses Cnr SA4 . . . . . . .64 F4
Nurston Cl CF62 . . . . . .212 E2
Nut Wlk CF61 . . . . .210 A4
Nydfa Rd NP22 . . . . . . .85 A7
Nythbran Terr CF39 . . .108 B3
Nythfa SA4 . . . . .44 C5

O

O'Donnell Rd CF63 . . .215 A4
Oak Cl CF72 . . . . .155 C2
Oak Ct Caerphilly NP12 .85 F6
Cardiff CF15 . . . . .158 D2
14 Cardiff CF24 . . . . . .195 C7
Penarth CF64 . . . . .206 E2
11 Pontypool NP4 . . . .38 A1
Oak Dr SA5 . . . . .66 D4
Oak Gr Cimla SA11 . . . .72 B5
St Athan CF62 . . . . .211 B7
Oak Hill Pk SA10 . . . . . .70 D4
Oak Ho CF14 . . . . .176 A1

Oak La CF83 . . . . .140 B6
Oak Pl CF81 . . . . .57 E2
Oak Rd Llanharry CF72 172 B5
Merthyr Tydfil CF47 . . . .10 D3
Rogerstone NP10 . . . . .141 F6
Oak Ridge
Blackmill CF35 . . . . . . .130 E2
Swansea SA2 . . . . .94 A6
Oak St Abercarn NP11 . .87 B4
Aberdare CF44 . . . . .29 A1
Aberkenfig CF32 . . . . . .150 C4
Abertillery NP13 . . . . . . .36 A5
Blackwood NP12 . . . . . .85 E7
Cwm NP23 . . . . .35 A7
Cwmbran NP44 . . . . . . .89 E2
Ferndale CF43 . . . . .79 F7
Gorseinon SA4 . . . . .66 D8
Hendreforgan CF39 . . .132 C5
Newport NP19 . . . . . . .143 E8
Rhydyfelin CF37 . . . . . .136 B5
Ton Pentre CF41 . . . . . .79 A2
Tonypandy CF40 . . . . . .106 B7
Treherbert CF42 . . . . . . .78 A8
Treorchy CF42 . . . . .78 E6
Oak Terr
Abercarn NP11 . . . . . . .114 C5
Abercwmboi CF44 . . . . .53 E4
Coytrahen CF32 . . . . . .150 C8
Fleur De Lis NP12 . . . . .85 B6
5 Llanbradach CF83 . .111 F1
Mountain Ash CF45 . . . .81 F8
Ogmore Vale CF32 . . . .104 E1
Oak Tree Ave SA2 . . . . .94 C6
Oak Tree Cl
Pontypool NP4 . . . . .63 A5
Radyr CF15 . . . . .176 A6
Oak Tree Ct
Bridgend CF31 . . . . . . .169 D5
Newbridge NP11 . . . . . . .60 C1
Newport NP19 . . . . . . .144 B5
Oak Tree Dr
Cefn Hengoed CF82 . . . .84 E5
Porthcawl CF36 . . . . . .183 E7
Rogerstone NP10 . . . . .141 D7
Rogerstone NP10 . . . . .141 E7
Oak View
Blaenavon NP4 . . . . .17 E6
Cilfrew SA10 . . . . .49 C6
Oak Way CF32 . . . . . . .150 F4
Oak Wood Ave CF23 . . .178 E3
Oakdale Cl NP18 . . . . . .117 F2
Oakdale Comp Sch
NP12 . . . . .86 A8
Oakdale Hospl NP12 . . .59 A1
Oakdale Inf Sch NP12 . .59 B2
Oakdale Path 5 NP44 .89 C2
Oakdale Pl NP44 . . . . . .62 A8
Oakdale Rd CF40 . . . . .107 A1
Oakdale Terr
Blackwood NP12 . . . . . .86 A8
Tonypandy CF40 . . . . . .107 A2
Oakdene CF14 . . . . . . .160 A1
Oakdene Cl
Baglan SA12 . . . . .98 E5
Cardiff CF23 . . . . .178 C4
Oakengates CF36 . . . . .183 D8
Oakfield
Caerleon NP18 . . . . . . .117 F3
Pontllanfraith NP12 . . . .86 B4
Oakfield Cres CF38 . . .136 E1
Oakfield Gdns
Machen CF83 . . . . .140 B6
Newport NP20 . . . . . . .143 A4
Oakfield Jun & Inf Sch
CF3 . . . . .179 E7
Oakfield Prim Sch
NP44 . . . . .116 F8
Oakfield Rd
Barry CF62 . . . . .214 D7
Cwmbran NP44 . . . . . . .89 F1
Glanaman SA18 . . . . . .220 B8
Newport NP20 . . . . . . .143 A4
Pontardawe SA8 . . . . . .23 E5
Tredegar NP22 . . . . .13 F5
Oakfield St
Aberfan CF48 . . . . .55 C6
Cardiff CF24 . . . . .195 D7
Llanbradach CF83 . . . . .112 A3
Pontarddulais SA4 . . . . .19 C4
Ystrad Mynach CF82 . . .84 F1
Oakford Cl CF23 . . . . . .160 E1
Oakford Pl SA5 . . . . . . .66 D4
Oakland Cl SA7 . . . . . . .47 A5
Oakland Cres CF37 . . .109 F4
Oakland Dr SA10 . . . . . .48 C3
Oakland Gdns CF81 . . . .57 F3
Oakland Rd SA3 . . . . . .123 A4
Oakland St
Bedlinog CF46 . . . . .56 B6
Mountain Ash CF45 . . . .54 E1
Oakland Terr
Cwmbran NP44 . . . . . . .116 E8
Ferndale CF43 . . . . .80 A5
Newbridge NP11 . . . . . . .60 C1
Pontypridd CF37 . . . . . .109 F4
Rhymney NP22 . . . . .12 F5
Treharris CF46 . . . . .83 B7
Oaklands Bargoed CF81 .57 F2
Merthyr Vale CF48 . . . . .55 D3
Miskin CF72 . . . . .173 D8
Mumbles SA3 . . . . .122 F6
Ponthir NP18 . . . . .117 E6

Oaklands continued
Port Talbot SA13 . . . . . .99 C2
Oaklands Ave CF31 . . .168 C4
Oaklands Bsns Pk
CF43 . . . . .80 A4
Oaklands Cl
Bridgend CF31 . . . . . . .168 D4
Cardiff CF3 . . . . .179 E7
Oaklands Ct SA2 . . . . . .94 A1
Oaklands Dr
Bridgend CF31 . . . . . . .168 D4
Ton Pentre CF41 . . . . . .79 B3
Oaklands Park Dr
NP10 . . . . .141 E2
Oaklands Prim Sch
CF44 . . . . .53 D6
Oaklands Rd
Bridgend CF31 . . . . . . .168 C4
Newport NP19 . . . . . . .143 F5
Pontlliw SA4 . . . . .44 A6
Pontypool NP4 . . . . .62 D1
Pontypool NP4 . . . . .89 D8
Oaklands Rise CF31 . . .168 C4
Oaklands Terr SA1 . . . . .95 B7
Oaklands View NP4 . . . .89 A3
Oakleafe Dr CF23 . . . . .178 E3
Oakleigh Ct NP44 . . . .115 F8
Oakleigh House Sch
SA2 . . . . .94 F7
Oakleigh Rd SA4 . . . . . .42 F7
Oakley Pl CF11 . . . . . . .194 F2
Oakley St NP19 . . . . . .143 F5
Oakley Terr CF40 . . . . .107 A2
Oakmead Cl CF23 . . . . .160 F1
Oakmeadow Ct 3
CF3 . . . . .179 F7
Oakmeadow Dr CF3 . .179 F6
Oakridge CF14 . . . . . . .159 F2
Oakridge E CF14 . . . . .159 F2
Oakridge W CF14 . . . .159 F2
Oaks Cl NP4 . . . . .37 F3
Oaks Ct NP4 . . . . .37 F3
Oaks End Ct CF82 . . . . .84 E7
Oaks Rd NP4 . . . . .37 F3
Oaks The
Blackwood NP12 . . . . . .59 C1
Cardiff CF14 . . . . .160 B2
Croesyceiliog NP44 . . . .90 B7
Llanmartin NP18 . . . . . .145 E7
Llantwit Fardre CF38 . . .156 D6
Machen CF83 . . . . .140 B6
Quakers Yard CF46 . . . .83 C5
Oaksford NP44 . . . . . . .89 A2
Oaktree Ct
Cwmbran NP44 . . . . . . .89 E1
Llangennech SA14 . . . . .42 B7
Oakway CF5 . . . . .193 C8
Oakwood CF34 . . . . . . .102 C1
Oakwood Ave SA12 . . . .73 A6
Oakwood Cl
Blackwood NP11 . . . . . .59 D4
Clydach SA8 . . . . .23 A1
Llandough CF64 . . . . . .206 E6
Oakwood Ct CF44 . . . . .28 D2
Oakwood Dr
Clydach SA8 . . . . .23 A1
Gowerton SA4 . . . . .66 D4
Maesteg CF34 . . . . .102 C2
Thomastown CF37 . . . .133 B3
Oakwood Ho SA12 . . . .100 A8
Oakwood Pl 1 SA13 . .99 C1
Oakwood Rd
Neath SA11 . . . . .71 F8
Port Talbot SA13 . . . . .125 B8
Swansea SA2 . . . . .94 A6
Oakwood St
Pontypridd CF37 . . . . . .135 C4
Port Talbot SA13 . . . . .125 B8
6 Port Talbot SA13 . . . .99 B8
Oban St CF63 . . . . .215 B6
Ocean Cres 6 SA1 . . . .95 D5
Ocean House Rd
CF62 . . . . .211 B5
Ocean St CF42 . . . . .78 B4
Ocean View (Golwg y Mor)
SA10 . . . . .97 C8
Ocean View Cl SA2 . . . .94 B3
Ocean Way
Cardiff CF24 . . . . .195 A4
Port Talbot SA12 . . . . . .98 C1
Ochr-y-Waun Rd
SA9 . . . . .221 B2
Octavius Cl NP10 . . . . .163 E5
Oddfellows St SA11 . . .223 D1
Oddfellows' St
2 Bridgend CF31 . . . . .168 F4
Ystradgynlais SA9 . . . . . .1 F2
Odessa St CF48 . . . . . . .11 A5
Odet Ct CF14 . . . . .176 E7
Odette Ho 4 SA12 . . . .98 F1
Odo St SA1 . . . . .68 D2
Odyn's Fee CF62 . . . . . .212 E2
Office St CF39 . . . . .107 F3
Offway NP44 . . . . .116 C3
Ogilvie Terr Deri CF81 . .33 A2
Fochriw CF81 . . . . .32 D1
Ogmore Castle CF32 . .185 A6
Ogmore Comp Sch
CF32 . . . . .151 A6
Ogmore Cres
Bettws NP20 . . . . .116 C1
Bridgend CF31 . . . . . . .169 A3
Ogmore Ct
Bridgend CF31 . . . . . . .168 D2
Caerphilly CF83 . . . . . .137 C4
Ogmore Vale CF32 . . . .104 E2
Ogmore Dr CF36 . . . . .165 E2
Ogmore Pl Barry CF63 215 A8

Ogmore Pl continued
8 Llanyravon NP44 . . . .90 B2
Ogmore Rd
Cardiff CF5 . . . . .193 C4
Ewenny CF32, CF35 . .185 D7
Swansea SA1 . . . . .69 A2
Ogmore Terr
Bridgend CF31 . . . . . .168 F4
Bryncethin CF32 . . . . .151 A5
Nant-y-Moel CF32 . . . .104 F6
Ogwen Dr CF23 . . . . .178 C5
Ogwen Ho NP44 . . . . .89 C2
Ogwr Ent Ctr CF32 . .150 C5
Ogwy St CF32 . . . . . .104 F5
Okehampton Ave
CF3 . . . . .179 C8
Olchfa Cl SA2 . . . . . . .94 A6
Olchfa La SA2 . . . . . . .94 A7
Olchfa Sch SA2 . . . . . .94 A6
Old Abergavenny Rd
NP4 . . . . .39 B5
Old Bakery Ct CF15 . .157 C1
Old Bakery The NP13 . .36 A6
Old Barn 4 NP19 . . .143 F8
Old Barn Way NP13 . . .36 C4
Old Barry Rd CF64 . . .206 E6
Old Blaen-Afon Rd
7 Brynmawr NP23 . . . . .8 C4
Brynmawr NP23 . . . . . .8 D4
Old Blaina Rd NP13 . . .35 F6
Old Brewery La NP22 . .12 D4
Old Bridge CF31 . . . .168 E4
Old Brithweunydd Rd
CF40 . . . . .107 A3
Old Cardiff Rd NP20 . .142 F1
Old Castle Rd
Llanelli SA15 . . . . .40 B4
Llanelli SA15 . . . . .40 C5
Old Chapel Rd CF48 . . .10 A4
Old Chepstow Rd
NP18 . . . . .145 D8
Old Church La CF82,
NP12 . . . . .85 B3
Old Church St CF15 . .177 B5
Old Church St CF48 . . .10 A4
Old Clipper Rd CF10 . .195 F3
Old Duke Rd NP22 . . . . .6 C2
Old Estate Yd NP4 . . . .62 E5
Old Farm La CF15 . . .174 E7
Old Farm Mews CF64 .206 A3
Old Forge The CF5 . . .191 B1
Old Furnace SA10 . . . .48 C5
Old Furnace Ho SA11 . .71 C5
Old Garden Ct 7
CF15 . . . . .176 B6
Old Green Intc NP20 . .143 C5
Old Hill Cardiff CF5 . .179 D6
Newport NP18 . . . . . .144 C8
Old Hill Cres NP18 . .144 D7
Old James St 10 NP4 . .17 C6
Old Kittle Rd SA3 . . .121 F7
Old La NP4 . . . . .37 F4
Old Langstone Court Rd
NP18 . . . . .145 B8
Old Library Flats
CF34 . . . . .102 A5
Old Llanharan Rd
CF72 . . . . .153 C1
Old Lodge SA15 . . . . . .40 D4
Old Malt Ho CF64 . . .206 A3
Old Market CF5 . . . . .205 A6
Old Market Pl SA12 . . .99 D5
Old Market St SA11 . . .71 E4
Old Mill La CF47 . . . . .10 D1
Old Mill Rd CF14 . . . .160 A2
Old Nantgarw Rd
CF15 . . . . .137 B1
Old Newport Rd CF3 . .179 F8
Old Pant Rd
Newbridge NP11 . . . . . .60 C1
Newbridge NP11 . . . . . .87 B7
Old Parish Rd
Blackmill CF35 . . . . . .130 F2
Hengoed CF82 . . . . . . .85 A3
Ynysybwl CF37 . . . . . .109 A7
Old Parish Road Ind Est
CF37 . . . . .109 A7
Old Park Rd SA13 . . .147 D4
Old Park Terr CF37 . .135 E4
Old Pen-Rhys Rd CF41 .79 E2
Old Pol Sta CF33 . . . .148 D2
Old Police Sta The
CF3 . . . . .179 B4
Old Port Rd CF5 . . . .205 A6
Old Queen St 2 NP4 . .17 C6
Old Rd Abersychan NP4 .37 F3
Ammanford SA18 . . . .219 B8
Baglan SA12 . . . . .98 C7
Llanelli SA15 . . . . .40 D6
Neath SA10 . . . . .70 F7
Neath SA11 . . . . .71 D4
Pontardawe SA8 . . . . . .24 A7
Skewen SA10 . . . . .71 A7
Old Rectory 4 CF5 . .194 C6
Old Road Cty Prim Sch
SA15 . . . . .40 D6
Old Row NP44 . . . . . . .88 E1
Old School Cl CF48 . . .10 C2
Old School Ct
Abercarn NP11 . . . . . .114 C5
Cardiff CF15 . . . . .158 C1
Old School Grange
CF82 . . . . .84 F2
Old School Pl NP4 . . . .61 F8
Old School Rd CF36 . .182 F6
Old St CF40 . . . . .106 D6
Old Stables CF32 . . . .104 F5
Old Station Rd CF36 . .182 F7
Old Station Yd 2
CF46 . . . . .83 B6
Old Stone Row SA13 .227 C2
Old Tavern CF32 . . . .130 B4
Old Vicarage Cl
Cardiff CF14 . . . . .177 F8
Glan y Nant NP12 . . . . .85 A7
Old Village La CF36 . .165 F1
Old Village Rd CF62 . .214 C3
Old Wern Rd SA9 . . . . .2 B6
Old William St 12 NP4 .17 C6
Old Winch Fawr Rd
CF48 . . . . .225 F1
Old Ynysbwl Rd CF37 .109 A8
Oldbridge Ct NP44 . . . .89 A5
Oldbury Bsns Ctr NP44 89 E2
Oldbury Rd NP44 . . . . .89 E2
Oldcastle Cty Jun & Inf
Schs CF31 . . . . .168 F3
Oldmill Rd CF63 . . . . .215 C7
Oldway SA3 . . . . .122 A6
Oldwell Ct 9 CF23 . . .178 C2
Oliphant Circ NP20 . .116 F3
Olive Branch Cres
SA11 . . . . .71 B3
Olive Rd SA3 . . . . . . .122 F6
Olive St Aberavon SA12 99 A1
Llanelli SA15 . . . . .40 F3
Olive Terr CF39 . . . . .107 D1
Oliver Jones Cres
NP22 . . . . .13 D7
Oliver Rd NP19 . . . . .144 A3
Oliver St CF37 . . . . . .109 A1
Oliver Terr CF37 . . . .135 E6
Ollivant Cl CF5 . . . . .176 D3
Olway Cl NP44 . . . . . . .90 A1
Ombersley La NP20 . .142 F4
Ombersley Rd NP20 . .142 F4
Onllwyn Rd
Coelbren SA10 . . . . . .222 F6
Dyffryn Cellwen SA10 . .222 E5
Onslow Terr CF32 . . . .150 D6
Ontario Way CF24 . . .178 C5
Open Hearth Cl NP4 . . .62 D4
Orange Gr CF5 . . . . . .176 C1
Orbit St CF24 . . . . . . .195 C6
Orchard Castle CF14 .159 E2
Orchard Cl
Aberfan CF48 . . . . .55 C6
Bassaleg NP10 . . . . . .141 F3
Boverton CF61 . . . . . .210 D5
Marshfield CF3 . . . . . .180 D8
Pencoed CF35 . . . . . .152 E1
Pontypool NP4 . . . . . . .38 B1
Porteynon SA3 . . . . . .231 A4
Porth CF39 . . . . .108 A3
Sigingstone CF71 . . . .200 A4
Wenvoe CF5 . . . . .220 D4
Orchard Cres CF64 . .206 B3
Orchard Ct
Cardiff CF14 . . . . .159 F4
Newport NP19 . . . . . .143 D7
Pontllanfraith NP12 . . .86 B4
10 Swansea SA1 . . . . . .95 D8
Orchard Dr
Barry CF62 . . . . .214 F6
Cardiff CF14 . . . . .177 A5
Llantwit Major CF61 . .210 A4
Pontypridd CF37 . . . . .109 C5
Porthcawl CF36 . . . . .183 E8
Three Crosses SA4 . . . .65 D1
Orchard Farm Est NP4 38 C1
Orchard Gr
Morganstown CF15 . . .176 B8
Penllergaer SA4 . . . . . .44 A2
Orchard La
Blackwood NP12 . . . . . .58 B2
Cwmbran NP44 . . . . . .89 F4
Newport NP19 . . . . . .143 E7
Orchard Lodge CF61 .210 C5
Orchard Mews NP19 .143 D7
Orchard Park Cl CF3 .179 E7
Orchard Pk CF3 . . . . .179 E7
Orchard Pl
Cardiff CF11 . . . . .194 D6
Cwmbran NP44 . . . . . .89 D7
Orchard Rd NP18 . . . .118 A4
Orchard Rise CF64 . . .206 E4
Orchard St
Brynmawr NP23 . . . . . . .8 B4
Neath SA11 . . . . .71 E7
New Tredegar NP24 . . . .33 E4
Newport NP19 . . . . . .143 D7
Pontardawe SA8 . . . . . .23 E5
Swansea SA1 . . . . .95 D7
Orchard Terr SA4 . . . .229 F4
Orchard The
Aberthin CF71 . . . . . .189 B3
Cardiff CF5 . . . . .193 A5
Mumbles SA3 . . . . . . .122 F5
Ponthir NP18 . . . . . . .117 F6
Orchard Way CF62 . . .211 D3
Orchid Cl Cardiff CF3 .180 A6
Port Talbot SA12 . . . . .98 C2
Tir-y-Berth CF82 . . . . . .84 F6
Orchid Ct NP44 . . . . . .89 A1
Ordell St CF24 . . . . . .195 D5
Oregano Cl 15 CF3 . . .180 A8
Oriel Rd NP19 . . . . . .143 E5
Oriel Rheifford Railway
Gallery CF10 . . . . . .195 C2
Orion Ct 6 CF24 . . . .195 C6
Orion Suite The
NP20 . . . . .143 D3
Ormes Rd SA10 . . . . . .70 D3
Ormond St SA11 . . . . .71 C3
Ormonde Cl CF23 . . . .178 E3
Ormsby Terr SA1 . . . . .96 A7
Orpheus Rd SA6 . . . . .46 B4
Osborne Cl
Bridgend CF31 . . . . . .150 F1
Newport NP19 . . . . . .143 E5
Osborne Pl CF32 . . . .150 E6
Osborne Rd
Abertillery NP11 . . . . . .59 F5
Brynmawr NP23 . . . . . . .8 A4
Pontypool NP4 . . . . . . .62 A8
Pontypool NP4 . . . . . . .62 B7
Pontypool NP4 . . . . . . .62 B8
Osborne Sq CF11 . . . .194 E3
Osborne St SA11 . . . . .71 E7
Osborne Terr
Nant-y-Moel CF32 . . . .104 F6
Swansea SA2 . . . . .94 C5
Osprey Cl Cardiff CF3 .179 F8
Mumbles SA3 . . . . . . .122 E7
Neath SA10 . . . . .48 E2
Penarth CF64 . . . . . . .217 A7
Osprey Ct CF63 . . . . .214 F4
Osprey Dr SA11 . . . . . .72 B5
Osterley St
Briton Ferry SA11 . . . . .71 C4
Swansea SA1 . . . . .95 F7
Swansea SA1 . . . . .96 A7
Oswald Rd NP20 . . . .143 C2
Oswestry Cl CF3 . . . .179 C3
Other St CF37 . . . . . . .81 F2
Othery Pl CF3 . . . . . .179 C8
Otter Cl NP20 . . . . . .116 C2
Our Lady of the Angels Rc
Prim Sch NP44 . . . . .89 E2
Our Lady's RC Prim Sch
CF45 . . . . .54 E2
Outfall La NP10 . . . . .181 E7
Oval The CF47 . . . . . . .10 F1
Overdale Wlk NP11 . . .59 D1
Overdene NP12 . . . . . .85 F3
Overland Cl SA3 . . . . .123 A4
Overland Rd SA3 . . . . .123 A4
Overton Cl CF36 . . . . .182 F8
Overton St CF48 . . . . .11 A5
Ovington Terr CF5 . . .194 B7
Owain Cl Cardiff CF23 .178 C4
Penarth CF64 . . . . . . .206 E3
Owen Cl CF62 . . . . . . .211 D4
Owen Cl NP18 . . . . . . .118 A4
Owen St CF37 . . . . . . .136 A4
Owen's La SA9 . . . . . .221 C2
Owen's Pl SA12 . . . . . .98 C1
Owendale Terr NP4 . . .37 F2
Owens Cl CF62 . . . . . .214 E5
Owls Lodge La SA3 . . .93 F1
Oxford Arc 10 CF10 . .117 F4
Oxford Cl NP18 . . . . . .117 F4
Oxford Cl CF32 . . . . . .104 E2
Oxford La CF24 . . . . . .195 C6
Oxford Pl NP13 . . . . . .60 C6
Oxford St
Aberdare CF44 . . . . . . .28 F2
Abertillery NP13 . . . . . .36 B6
Barry CF62 . . . . .214 C3
Cardiff CF24 . . . . .195 C7
Gelligaer CF82 . . . . . . .84 D7
Maerdy CF43 . . . . .52 B1
Mountain Ash CF45 . . . .54 B3
Newport NP19 . . . . . .143 E5
Pontycymer CF32 . . . .103 A3
Pontypool NP4 . . . . . . .62 E2
Pontypridd CF37 . . . . .135 E6
Upper Boat CF15 . . . . .157 F8
Oxford Terr NP4 . . . . .17 A5
Oxtens NP44 . . . . .116 B8
Oxwich Castle SA3 . . .231 D5
Oxwich Cl Cardiff CF5 .193 F7
Cefn Hengoed CF82 . . . .84 F5
Oxwich Ct SA6 . . . . . . .69 A7
Oxwich Leisure Pk
SA3 . . . . .231 D5
Oxwich Rd NP19 . . . .144 A1
Oyster Bend CF64 . . .216 B4
Oystermouth Castle
SA3 . . . . .123 A5
Oystermouth Ct SA3 .123 A6
Oystermouth Prim Sch
SA3 . . . . .123 A5
Oystermouth Rd SA1 . .95 C5
Ozanam Ct SA5 . . . . . .67 F6

P

Pace Cl CF5 . . . . .176 D2
Pace Rd NP44 . . . . . . .89 B1
Packers Rd CF39 . . . .107 E4
Padarn Cl CF23 . . . . .178 B5
Padarn Pl 8 CF23 . . .178 B5
Paddock Cl NP44 . . . . .89 D5
Paddock Pl 1 CF63 . .215 B7
Paddock Rise NP44 . . .90 B1
Paddock St SA15 . . . . .40 D4
Paddock The
Cardiff CF14 . . . . .160 A3
Cardiff CF23 . . . . .178 C2
Cowbridge CF71 . . . . .189 A1
Mumbles SA3 . . . . . . .123 A8
Paddocks Cres CF72 . .172 F6
Paddocks The
Aberdare CF44 . . . . . . .53 C8
Blackwood NP12 . . . . . .58 E1
Caerleon NP18 . . . . . .117 F3
Church Village CF38 . . .135 D1
Groesfaen CF72 . . . . . .174 C6
Llanyravon NP44 . . . . . .90 B1
Penarth CF64 . . . . . . .217 A8
Tonna SA11 . . . . .49 B2
Tonyrefail CF39 . . . . . .133 D6
Padley's Cl CF34 . . . .102 D2
Page La SA1 . . . . .95 B6
Page St SA1 . . . . .95 B7
Paget La CF11 . . . . . .194 F3
Paget Pl CF64 . . . . . .207 B5
Paget Rd Barry CF62 . .214 E2
Penarth CF64 . . . . . . .207 B5
Paget St Cardiff CF11 .194 F2
Ynysybwl CF37 . . . . . . .81 F1
Paget Terr CF64 . . . . .207 B5
Painter's Row CF42 . . .78 B8
Palace Ave
Cardiff CF5 . . . . .194 B8
Llanelli SA15 . . . . .40 E5
Palace Ct CF23 . . . . . .178 C6
Palace Rd CF5 . . . . . .194 B8
Palace Row NP13 . . . . .16 B1
Palalwyf Ave CF72 . . .173 B7
Pale Rd SA10 . . . . .70 F6
Palleg Rd SA9 . . . . .1 C2
Palm Cl NP4 . . . . .63 B5
Palm Rd CF47 . . . . . . .10 D5
Palm Sq NP19 . . . . . .144 A4
Palmer Pl NP12 . . . . . .85 D7
Palmer St CF63 . . . . .215 D7
Palmers Dr CF5 . . . . .193 E5
Palmers Vale Bsns Ctr
CF63 . . . . .215 D7
Palmerston Prim Sch
CF63 . . . . .215 D6
Palmerston Rd CF63 . .215 D6
Palmerston Workshops
CF63 . . . . .215 D7
Palmerstown Ho
CF63 . . . . .215 D6
Palmyra Ct SA3 . . . . .123 A6
Palmyra Pl 11 NP20 . .143 C4
Pamela St CF45 . . . . . .54 C2
Pandy NP44 . . . . .89 C3
Pandy Cl CF47 . . . . . . .10 B3
Pandy Cres CF33 . . . .148 A1
Pandy Inf Sch CF32 . .150 D4
Pandy La CF83 . . . . . .140 A7
Pandy Pk CF32 . . . . . .150 D4
Pandy Rd
Aberkenfig CF32 . . . . .150 D4
Bedwas CF83 . . . . . . .138 C7
Blackwood NP11 . . . . . .59 D2
Pandy The CF44 . . . . . .27 D8
Pandy View
Abercarn NP11 . . . . . .114 C5
Neath SA11 . . . . .72 A4
Trelewis CF46 . . . . .83 D6
Pandy-Mawr Rd
CF83 . . . . .138 C8
Pangbourne Cl CF36 . .165 E1
Pant Bach CF33 . . . . .148 A2
Pant Celydd SA13 . . . .125 E4
Pant Cl Pant CF48 . . . .11 B4
St Brides Major CF32 . .185 D3
Pant Cotts CF48 . . . . . .11 A7
Pant Farm CF11 . . . . . .87 A6
Pant Glas Cardiff CF23 179 A7
Llanbradach CF83 . . . .112 A3
Pencoed CF35 . . . . . .170 D8
Pant Glas Ct NP10 . . .141 F2
Pant Glas Ind Est
CF83 . . . . .138 C5
Pant Gwyn
Bridgend CF31 . . . . . .168 B3
Swansea SA2 . . . . .94 C6
Pant Gwyn Cl NP44 . .115 F7
Pant Hirgoed CF35 . . .152 C1
Pant Hirwaun CF32,
CF35 . . . . .151 F4
Pant Howel Ddu CF47 . .71 E2
Pant Howellddu SA11 . .71 D3
Pant La NP20 . . . . . . .143 B8
Pant Lasau Rd SA5,SA6 45 C4
Pant Llygodfa CF83 . . .137 D1
Pant Mawr CF31 . . . . .168 B3
Pant Morfa CF36 . . . .183 B8
Pant Pl CF15 . . . . . . .157 F5
Pant Poeth CF31 . . . .168 B3
Pant Rd
Newbridge NP11 . . . . . .87 A6
Newport NP20 . . . . . .143 B8
Pant CF48 . . . . .11 B4
Pant St
Aberbargoed CF81 . . . . .58 B5
Pontycymer CF32 . . . .103 F2
Swansea SA1 . . . . .96 A7
Pant Sta CF48 . . . . . . .10 F8
Pant Tawel La CF15 . .175 F6
Pant View
Nantyglo NP23 . . . . . . .15 E7
Newbridge NP11 . . . . . .87 A7
Pant y Brwyn SA9 . . . .221 C2
Pant y Celyn SA14 . . . .41 C5
Pant y Dderwen CF72 .155 B1
Pant y Dwr SA4 . . . . . .65 D1
Pant y Fedwen
Bridgend CF31 . . . . . .168 C2
Gwaun-Cae-Gurwen
SA18 . . . . .220 D6
Pant Yr Hebog CF31 . .168 C2
Pant Yr Helys SA5 . . . .67 B6
Pant-Bach Rd CF14 . .177 C5
Pant-Du Rd CF37 . . . .110 A6
Pant-glas NP4 . . . . . . .37 D3
Pant-Teg SA15 . . . . . . .40 F8
Pant-y-Blawd Rd
Morriston SA6 . . . . .46 B1
Morriston SA7 . . . . .46 C1

Pant-y-Blawd Rd continued
Swansea SA6 . . . . .69 A8
Swansea SA7 . . . . .69 B8
Pant-y-Blodau SA6 . . .45 B2
Pant-y-Celyn Pl
CF62 . . . . .211 D4
Pant-y-Celyn Rd SA1 . .94 F8
Pant-y-Cerdin CF44 . . .53 C5
Pant-y-Coed CF62 . . . .212 B8
Pant-y-Deri Cl 6
CF5 . . . . .193 C4
Pant-y-Dwr NP22 . . . . .6 C2
Pant-y-Fedwen CF44 . .53 C5
Pant-y-Felin Rd SA4 . . .19 D6
Pant-y-Fforest CF35 . .152 F1
Pant-y-Ffynnon CF35 .152 F1
Pant-y-Glan NP23 . . . .7 F4
Pant-y-Gog CF32 . . . .103 F2
Pant-y-Mynydd NP23 . . .7 F4
Pant-y-Pistyll SA8 . . . .23 C3
Pant-y-Pwdyn Rd
NP13 . . . . .36 C4
Pant-y-Resk Rd NP11 . .86 F4
Pant-y-Rheol Cl
NP44 . . . . .115 F7
Pant-y-Sais SA10 . . . . .70 C1
Pant-y-Seren CF39 . . .133 B2
Pant-Yr-Arian La
SA12 . . . . .98 F5
Pant-Yr-Eos
Aberdare CF44 . . . . . . .29 C4
Cwmbran NP44 . . . . . .89 E4
Pant-yr-Odyn
Swansea SA2 . . . . .67 C1
Swansea SA2 . . . . .94 C1
Pantanas CF46 . . . . . . .83 B6
Pantquesta Cotts
CF72 . . . . .173 C5
Pantbach Rd CF15 . . .175 C8
Pantbach Ave CF14 . .177 D4
Pantbach Pl CF14 . . . .177 D4
Pantddu Rd NP13 . . . . .59 F8
Panteg Ebbw Vale NP23 .7 D2
Pentyrch CF15 . . . . . .175 C8
Panteg Cl CF5 . . . . . .192 F3
Panteg Inf Sch NP4 . . . .61 F6
Panteg Mews 3 CF5 .194 B7
Panteg Terr NP11 . . . .86 F6
Panteg Way NP4 . . . . .62 F4
Pantglas Gorseinon SA4 43 B1
Pentyrch CF15 . . . . . .175 C8
Pantglas Fawr CF48 . . .55 C6
Pantglas Rd CF48 . . . .55 C6
Pantglas View CF83 . .138 F6
Pantgwynlais CF15 . . .158 D1
Pantiago Rd SA4 . . . . . .19 D4
Pantile Row SA13 . . . .227 C2
Pantmawr Ct CF14 . . .176 F7
Pantmawr Rd CF14 . . .176 F7
Pantside Prim Sch
NP11 . . . . .87 B7
Pantsygallog Terr
CF48 . . . . .11 B6
Pantyblodau Rd SA18 .218 F8
Pantycefn Rd CF15 . . .58 D7
Pantycelyn SA4 . . . . . .43 B1
Pantycelyn Dr 3
CF83 . . . . .137 F5
Pantycelyn Rd CF64 . .206 D6
Pantycelyn St CF82 . . .84 E2
Pantyceulwen CF44 . . .10 B1
Pantyffyn Rd CF47 . . .10 F1
Pantyffynnon Rd
SA18 . . . . .219 B6
Pantyffynnon Sta
SA18 . . . . .219 B5
Pantyffynnon Terr SA9 . .2 A4
Pantyffynnon Rd SA9 . . .2 F8
Pantyfid Rd CF81 . . . . .58 B6
Pantygasseg Rd NP4 . .61 D5
Pantygraigwen Rd
CF37 . . . . .109 A2
Pantygwydr Rd SA2 . . .94 F6
Pantyrheol SA11 . . . . .71 C4
Pantysgallog SA11 . . .11 A7
Pantysgallog Prim Sch
CF48 . . . . .11 A6
Paper Mill Rd CF5,
CF11 . . . . .194 A6
Parade The
Barry CF62 . . . . .214 C2
Cardiff CF14 . . . . .176 F4
Cardiff CF24 . . . . .195 C6
Cwmbran NP44 . . . . . .89 E4
7 Dinas Powys CF64 .206 C3
Ferndale CF43 . . . . . . .79 E7
Llantwit Fardre CF38 . .156 A4
Merthyr Tydfil CF47 . . .10 E1
Neath SA11 . . . . .71 E8
Porth CF39 . . . . .107 F3
Ton Pentre CF41 . . . . . .78 F3
Paradise Cotts SA14 . .41 D4
Paradise View SA1 . . . .95 A8
Parc Afon CF40 . . . . . .107 C4
Parc Andrew SA10 . . . .70 F6
Parc Ave
Caerphilly CF83 . . . . . .138 C5
Cwmbran NP44 . . . . . .89 D6
Swansea SA6 . . . . .68 F6
Swansea SA6 . . . . .68 F7
Parc Berwig SA14 . . . .41 F2
Parc Bryn Bryn NP12 . .58 F1
Neath SA10 . . . . .70 E5
Parc Bryn Derwen
CF72 . . . . .153 F1

Parc Bwtrimawr
SA18 . . . . .219 C6
Parc Bychan NP23 . . . .7 E1
Parc Castell-y-Mynach
Creigiau CF15 . . . . . . .174 E7
Creigiau CF15 . . . . . . .174 E8
Parc Cefn Onn Ctry Pk
CF14 . . . . .159 F5
Parc Clwyd 2 CF63 .215 C8
Parc Cotts
Bridgend CF35 . . . . . .151 E8
Senghenydd CF83 . . . .110 F2
Parc Cres CF31 . . . . . .169 F1
Parc Cwm Darran
CF81 . . . . .32 F3
Parc Ddiwydiannol Betws
SA18 . . . . .219 C7
Parc Derwen CF82 . . . .84 F5
Parc Gitto SA14 . . . . . .41 D4
Parc Glanffrwd 2
SA18 . . . . .220 B8
Parc Glas
Cwmdare CF44 . . . . . . .28 D3
Neath SA10 . . . . .70 F6
Parc Hafod CF14 . . . . .176 F6
Parc Hendy Cres SA4 . .64 F3
Parc Howard Ave
SA15 . . . . .40 D7
Parc Howard Mus
SA15 . . . . .40 D7
Parc Mawr Cl SA4 . . . .44 B2
Parc Menter SA14 . . . .218 C7
Parc Morlais SA14 . . . .18 C5
Parc Nant Celyn
CF38 . . . . .157 A6
Parc Nantgarw CF15 . .157 F8
Parc Newydd
Briton Ferry SA11 . . . . .71 B3
Talbot Green CF72 . . . .155 C2
Parc Onen SA18 . . . . .219 C5
Parc Penrhiw SA18 . . .219 C5
Parc Plas NP12 . . . . . .85 D6
Parc Pontypandy
CF83 . . . . .138 C5
Parc Prim Sch CF42 . .78 C5
Parc Rd SA6 . . . . .68 F6
Parc Richard SA14 . . . .41 E4
Parc St Catwg CF15 . .175 C8
Parc St Joseff SA12 . . .98 C1
Parc Terr
Senghenydd CF83 . . . .110 E2
Swansea SA6 . . . . .68 F7
Parc The CF31 . . . . . .168 F1
Parc Trostre SA14 . . . .41 A4
Parc Ty Glas CF14 . . . .177 E7
Parc Ty Glas Ind Est
CF14 . . . . .177 E7
Parc Wenallt CF46 . . . .83 B7
Parc Wern SA10 . . . . . .70 F6
Parc Wern Rd SA2 . . . .94 C4
Parc Wood CF61 . . . . .208 F5
Parc-Henry La SA18 . .219 B8
Parc-Tyn-y-Waun
CF34 . . . . .128 D6
Parc-y-Bont CF32 . . . .150 F4
Parc-y-Brain Rd
NP10 . . . . .142 B8
Parc-y-Bryn
Creigiau CF15 . . . . . . .174 D8
Goytre SA13 . . . . .125 E8
Llantwit Fardre CF38 . .156 D6
Parc-y-Coed CF15 . . . .174 E7
Parc-y-Delyn SA6 . . . . .45 C4
Parc-y-Deri SA10 . . . . .70 E6
Parc-y-Felin CF15 . . . .174 D7
Parc-y-Felin St CF83 .138 B4
Parc-y-Fro CF15 . . . . .174 E8
Parc-y-Nant CF15 . . . .158 D2
Parc-y-Rhos CF35 . . . .170 D8
Parc-Yr-Helyg Rd
Birchgrove SA7 . . . . . . .47 B1
Swansea SA7 . . . . .70 B8
Parcau Ave CF31 . . . . .168 C4
Parcau Rd CF31 . . . . .168 C4
Parclewis Cty Prim Sch
CF37 . . . . .135 E7
Parcyrhun SA18 . . . . .219 B6
Parcyrhun Cty Prim Sch
SA18 . . . . .219 B6
Pardoe Cres CF62 . . . .214 E6
Pardoe-Thomas Cl 17
NP20 . . . . .143 C3
Parfitt Cl CF43 . . . . . . .80 B4
Parfitt Pl NP12 . . . . . . .85 D7
Parfitt St NP19 . . . . . .144 B3
Parfitt Terr
Cwmbran NP44 . . . . . .89 D5
2 Merthyr Tydfil CF47 . .30 F8
Parish Rd
Beddau CF38 . . . . .156 A7
Blaengwrach SA11 . . . .227 C8
Park Ave Barry CF62 . .214 D3
Bedwas CF83 . . . . . . .138 E6
Capel Hendre SA18 . . .218 C6
Cardiff CF14 . . . . .176 F6
Cardiff CF5 . . . . .193 A2
Glynneath SA11 . . . . . .223 C1
Mumbles SA3 . . . . . . .123 B4
Neath SA10 . . . . .70 C7
Newport NP20 . . . . . .142 E1
Ogmore Vale CF32 . . . .130 D8
Porthcawl CF36 . . . . . .182 E7
Rogerstone NP10 . . . . .141 F6
Park Cl Cwmbran NP44 115 F8
Gorseinon SA4 . . . . . . .43 B2

Park Cl continued
Newport NP20 . . . .**142** E1
Pontarddulais SA4 . . . . . .**19** C3
Pontypridd CF37 . . . . .**135** D6
Swansea SA1 . . . .**69** B3
Swansea SA6 . . . .**45** E1
Treherbert CF42 . . . .**50** F1
Park Court Rd CF31 .**168** D4
Park Cres Bargoed CF81 **57** F3
Barry CF62 . . . .**214** C4
Brynmawr NP23 . . . .**8** B4
Cardiff CF14 . . . .**176** F6
Clydach NP7 . . . .**9** D7
Llanelli SA15 . . . .**40** C5
9 Merthyr Tydfil CF47 . .**10** E1
Neath SA10 . . . .**70** C7
Pontyclun CF72 . . . . . .**173** A7
Pontypool NP4 . . . .**62** D7
Porth CF39 . . . .**107** E3
Treharris CF46 . . . .**83** B7
Treorchy CF42 . . . .**78** D5
Park Ct Barry CF62 . . . .**214** C3
Bridgend CF31 . . . .**168** D4
Park Dr Bargoed CF81 . .**57** F3
Neath SA10 . . . .**70** C7
Newport NP20 . . . .**142** F1
Swansea SA2 . . . .**94** F7
Park End NP18 . . . . . .**145** C8
Park End Ct CF23 . . . .**178** A6
Park End La CF23 . . . .**178** A6
Park Eynon 6 SA15 . . .**40** D5
Park Field SA11 . . . . . .**49** D3
Park Gdns
Blaenavon NP4 . . . .**17** C6
Newport NP20 . . . .**142** E1
Pontypool NP4 . . . .**62** C7
Park Gr Aberdare CF44 .**28** F3
Cardiff CF10 . . . .**195** B7
Park Hill
Mountain Ash CF45 . . . .**54** D3
11 Mountain Ash CF45 . .**54** D3
Tredegar NP22 . . . .**13** D5
Park Ho 3 SA13 . . . .**125** C7
Park House Flats NP4 .**62** C7
Park La Aberdare CF44 . .**28** E4
Blaengwynfi SA13 . . . . . .**76** C5
Blaengwynfi SA13 . . . . . .**76** C6
Brynamman SA18 . . . . .**220** D8
Caerphilly CF83 . . . . . .**138** A2
Cardiff CF14 . . . .**176** F6
Cardiff CF24 . . . .**195** B6
Groesfaen CF72 . . . . . .**174** B7
Llangennech SA14 . . . . . .**42** C8
Taffs Well CF15 . . . . . .**157** F4
Tredomen CF82 . . . .**84** D1
Treharris CF46 . . . .**83** A6
Park Lane Specl Sch
CF44 . . . .**28** E3
Park Mill Rd SA11 . .**219** A7
Park Pl Abercarn NP11 **114** C5
Abertillery NP13 . . . .**36** B5
Bargoed CF81 . . . .**58** A4
Ebbw Vale NP23 . . . .**14** F2
Maerdy CF43 . . . .**52** A2
Newbridge NP11 . . . .**86** F7
Pontypridd CF37 . . . . . .**109** F6
Risca NP11 . . . .**115** A1
Sarn CF32 . . . .**150** F4
Swansea SA2 . . . .**94** E5
Tonypandy CF40 . . . . . .**106** G6
Tredegar NP22 . . . .**13** F5
Treherbert CF42 . . . .**50** F2
Troedyrhiw CF48 . . . . . .**55** C8
Park Pl (Plas y Parc)
CF10 . . . .**195** A7
Park Prospect CF37 . .**109** B2
Park Rd Abercynon CF45 **82** E3
Aberdare CF44 . . . .**53** C7
Aberkenfig CF32 . . . . . .**150** C3
Bargoed CF81 . . . .**57** F4
Barry CF62 . . . .**214** C3
Cardiff CF14 . . . .**176** F6
Clydach SA6 . . . .**46** E8
Dinas Powys CF64 . . . .**206** A4
Ebbw Vale NP23 . . . .**14** D4
Ebbw Vale NP23 . . . .**14** E3
Ferndale CF43 . . . .**80** A5
Gorseinon SA4 . . . .**43** B2
Gowerton SA4 . . . .**66** C4
Hengoed CF82 . . . .**85** A2
Maerdy CF43 . . . .**52** A2
Maesycwmmer CF82 . . .**85** A1
Newbridge NP11 . . . .**86** F7
Pen-clawdd SA4 . . . .**64** E4
Penarth CF64 . . . .**207** B3
Pontypool NP4 . . . .**62** C7
Radyr CF15 . . . .**176** B6
Risca NP11 . . . .**115** A1
Southgate SA3 . . . .**121** A5
Tonypandy CF40 . . . . . .**107** A4
Treorchy CF42 . . . .**78** B4
Ynystawe SA6 . . . .**46** C4
Park Road Ind Est
NP11 . . . .**115** A1
Park Row
Cwmaman SA12 . . . .**99** E6
Tredegar NP22 . . . .**13** E6
Park Row Gdns CF47 .**10** D3
Park Side CF37 . . . . . .**109** C1
Park Slip Nature Pk
CF32 . . . .**149** F5
Park Sq NP20 . . . .**142** F1
Park St Abercarn NP11 **114** B5
Abercarn NP11 . . . .**114** C8
Abercynon CF45 . . . .**82** D1

Park St continued
Blaenavon NP4 . . . .**17** C6
Bridgend CF31 . . . .**168** D4
Brynamman SA18 . . . . .**220** D8
Cardiff CF10 . . . .**195** A5
Glyncorrwg SA13 . . . . .**227** C1
Llanelli SA15 . . . .**40** D5
Maesteg CF34 . . . .**102** B2
13 Mountain Ash CF45 . .**54** E1
Mountain Ash CF45 . . . .**81** E8
Mumbles SA3 . . . .**123** B5
Nant-y-Moel CF32 . . . .**104** F5
Neath SA11 . . . .**71** F8
Pontycymer CF32 . . . . .**103** F4
Pontypool NP4 . . . .**62** E2
Pontypridd CF37 . . . . . .**135** E7
Port Talbot SA13 . . . . .**125** C7
Porth CF39 . . . .**107** D4
Pyle CF33 . . . .**148** C2
Skewen SA10 . . . .**71** A7
Swansea SA1 . . . .**95** C7
Tonna SA11 . . . .**49** D3
Tonypandy CF40 . . . . . .**106** B6
Tylorstown CF43 . . . . . .**80** B4
Park Terr
Caerphilly NP12 . . . .**85** F6
Llanharan CF72 . . . . . .**153** F3
Merthyr Tydfil CF47 . . . .**10** D2
Pontarddulais SA4 . . . . .**19** D2
6 Pontypool NP4 . . . . . .**38** A1
Swansea SA1 . . . .**68** C1
Tondu CF32 . . . .**150** B5
Trelewis CF46 . . . .**83** D6
Treorchy CF42 . . . .**78** B5
Park Terrace Prim Sch
NP4 . . . .**62** C6
Park The
Blaenavon NP4 . . . .**17** C7
Swansea SA2 . . . .**94** A7
Treharris CF46 . . . .**83** B7
Park View
Abercarn NP11 . . . .**114** B5
Abercynon CF45 . . . .**82** E4
Bargoed CF81 . . . .**57** E3
Bassaleg NP10 . . . .**142** B3
Bridgend CF31 . . . .**168** B5
Bridgend CF35 . . . .**169** F4
Brynmawr NP23 . . . .**8** B4
Ebbw Vale NP23 . . . .**7** D4
2 Llanbradach CF83 . .**111** F1
Llanharan CF72 . . . .**154** A2
Llantrisant CF72 . . . . . .**155** D3
Loughor SA4 . . . .**65** D8
Maesteg CF34 . . . .**102** C1
Nantyglo NP13 . . . .**15** E7
1 Pontypool NP4 . . . . . .**38** A1
Port Talbot SA13 . . . . .**125** C7
Ton Pentre CF41 . . . .**79** A3
Tondu CF32 . . . .**150** A5
Tredegar NP22 . . . .**13** D6
Tylorstown CF43 . . . . . .**80** C3
Wattstown CF39 . . . . . .**107** E8
Park View Bglws NP12 **85** F7
Park View Ct SA11 . . .**71** C1
Park View Ct
2 Cardiff CF11 . . . . . .**194** F5
11 Cardiff CF14 . . . . . .**177** A6
Park View Gdns
NP10 . . . .**142** B3
Park View St NP23 . . .**14** F2
Park View Terr
Abercwmboi CF44 . . . . . .**53** E5
Aberdare CF44 . . . .**29** B3
Swansea SA2 . . . .**94** D6
Park Way SA2 . . . .**94** B6
Park Wood Cl NP18 .**117** E3
Park y Brain La NP4 . .**39** D7
Parkdale View CF72 . .**155** E2
Parker Pl CF5 . . . .**193** B4
Parker Rd CF5 . . . . . .**193** B4
Parkfield Pl
Cardiff CF11 . . . .**177** E1
Newport NP20 . . . .**143** A5
Parkfield Rd CF44 . . . .**29** D1
Parkfields CF31 . . . . .**168** D8
Parkfields Rd CF31 . .**168** D4
Parkhill Cres NP23 . . . . .**7** E3
Parkhill Rd SA5 . . . . . .**68** C5
Parkhill Terr SA5 . . . . .**68** C5
Parkland Cres CF39 . .**133** C5
Parkland Rd CF39 . . . .**133** C5
Parkland Sch SA2 . . . . . .**94** B6
Parkland Wlk CF62 . .**214** C4
Parklands
Blaenavon NP12 . . . .**85** E8
Cardiff CF24 . . . .**195** C5
Corntown CF35 . . . .**186** B7
Penperlleni NP4 . . . .**39** F7
Parklands Cl
Cwmbran NP44 . . . .**89** E6
Rogerstone NP10 . . . . .**142** C3
Parklands Ct
Ammanford SA18 . . . . .**219** A6
Swansea SA2 . . . .**94** B6
Parklands Rd SA18 . .**219** A6
Parklands View SA2 . .**94** B5
Parklawn Cl NP44 . . . .**89** C6
Parkside NP44 . . . .**89** D2
Parkside Ct
2 Cardiff CF5 . . . . . .**194** C6
18 Pontypool NP4 . . . . . .**38** A1
Parkside Gdns CF23 .**178** B2
Parkstone Ave CF3 . . .**179** E8
Parkview Ct CF64 . . . .**206** E5
Parkview Terr SA15 . . .**40** C6

Parkville NP22 . . . .**13** E5
Parkwall Rd CF14,
CF23 . . . .**161** A3
Parkway
Blackwood NP11 . . . .**59** D5
Cardiff CF3 . . . .**179** D2
Parkway Sta SA13 . . .**125** B8
Parkwood CF5 . . . .**66** C4
Parkwood Dr NP10 . .**141** E2
Parr Ave SA11 . . . .**71** F8
Parracombe Cl CF3 . .**179** C7
Parracombe Cres
CF3 . . . .**179** C7
Parret Cl NP20 . . . . . .**116** F2
Parret Rd NP20 . . . . . .**116** F2
Parret Wlk NP20 . . . . .**116** F2
Parrish Pl CF83 . . . . . .**110** F2
Parrot Row NP3 . . . . . .**15** D7
Parry Cl SA10 . . . .**71** B8
Parry Dr NP19 . . . .**144** B8
Parry Jones Cl NP13 . .**15** D5
Parry Rd
Port Talbot SA12 . . . . . .**98** B3
Swansea SA6 . . . .**45** E1
Parry St
5 Cardiff CF5 . . . . . .**194** C6
Ton Pentre CF41 . . . .**78** F3
Ton Pentre CF41 . . . .**79** A3
Treorchy CF43 . . . .**80** B2
Parry Terr NP11 . . . . . .**59** F1
Parrys Dr CF45 . . . .**82** C5
Parson's Row NP13 . . .**15** D5
Parsons La SA11 . . . . . .**49** C2
Part St NP13 . . . .**15** E3
Partridge Ave CF44 .**106** F8
Partridge La CF24 . . . .**195** D7
Partridge Rd
Abertillery NP13 . . . .**60** A6
Cardiff CF24 . . . .**195** C7
St Athan CF62 . . . .**210** E6
Tonypandy CF40 . . . .**79** F1
Partridge Row NP23 . . .**7** F4
Partridge Sq CF41 . . . .**79** A3
Partridge Way NP10 .**163** F7
Pascal Cl CF3 . . . .**180** B8
Pascall Ct CF14 . . . . .**195** C7
Pascoes Ave CF31 . . . .**168** C5
Pastoral Way SA2 . . . .**94** B8
Pastures The
Barry CF62 . . . .**214** E7
Llanyravon NP44 . . . .**89** C6
Patagonia Wlk 5 SA1 .**95** D5
Patch The CF72 . . . . . .**172** B6
Patchway Cres CF3 . .**179** A4
Patmore Cl CF45 . . . . .**157** F4
Patreane Way CF5 . . .**192** F3
Patterdale Cl CF23 . .**178** B2
Patti Cl NP19 . . . .**144** F6
Patti Ho 8 SA12 . . . . . .**98** F1
Pavaland Cl 5 CF3 . . .**179** F6
Pavia Ct CF37 . . . .**109** C1
Paviland Pl SA5 . . . .**67** F5
Pavilion Ct CF36 . . . . .**182** F6
Pavilion Est NP4 . . . .**62** A8
Pavillion Bldgs CF40 . .**106** C6
Pavin Ct CF5 . . . .**177** A1
Paxton Cl CF82 . . . .**84** E7
Paxton Dr SA1 . . . .**95** C5
Paxton St SA1 . . . .**95** C6
Paxton Wlk NP10 . . . .**142** A7
Payne St SA11 . . . .**71** D6
Peacehaven NP22 . . . .**14** A3
Peacehaven Ct NP22 . .**14** A3
Peach Pl 2 CF5 . . . . .**193** D8
Pear Tree Ct NP18 . . .**117** E2
Pearce Cl CF3 . . . .**180** A5
Pearce Ct CF63 . . . . . .**215** A8
Pearce's Ct CF48 . . . . . .**10** A5
Pearl Pl CF24 . . . .**195** D6
Pearl St Cardiff CF24 . .**195** D6
Cardiff CF24 . . . .**195** E7
Pearson Cres CF37 . . .**109** D5
Pearson St CF24 . . . . .**195** C7
Pease La CF47 . . . .**30** E7
Peckham Cl CF5 . . . . .**176** D3
Pedair Erw Rd CF14 .**177** D5
Pedrog Terr SA1 . . . . . .**68** B1
Pegler St SA5 . . . .**68** C3
Pelican St SA9 . . . .**1** F2
Pell St SA1 . . . .**95** C7
Pellau Rd SA13 . . . . . .**125** E5
Pellett St CF10 . . . . . .**195** B5
Pemberton Pk SA14 . . .**41** C6
Pemberton Rd SA14 . . .**41** C5
Pemberton St SA15 . . .**40** D4
Pembrey Gdns NP11 . . .**86** A4
Pembrey Rd SA15 . . . . .**40** C6
Pembroke Cl
Blackwood NP12 . . . .**58** D1
Church Village CF38 . . .**135** F2
4 Dinas Powys CF64 . .**206** C3
Merthyr Tydfil CF48 . . .**225** F1
Ystrad CF41 . . . .**79** D3
Pembroke Cres CF72 .**155** A5
Pembroke Ct
Caerphilly CF83 . . . . . .**137** D4
6 Cardiff CF14 . . . . . .**177** A6
Pembroke Gr NP19 . .**144** A2
Pembroke Ho SA12 . .**124** D8
Pembroke Pl
Barry CF63 . . . .**214** F6
Boverton CF61 . . . .**210** B6
Llanyravon NP44 . . . .**90** B3
Merthyr Tydfil CF47 . . . .**10** D4
4 Swansea SA1 . . . . . .**95** C6
Pembroke Rd CF5 . . .**194** C6

Pembroke St
Aberdare CF44 . . . .**29** A2
Swansea SA5 . . . .**68** B3
Tredegar NP22 . . . .**6** C1
Troedyrhiw CF48 . . . . . .**31** C2
Pembroke Terr
10 Aberavon SA12 . . . .**124** F8
Nant-y-Moel CF32 . . . .**104** F6
Penarth CF64 . . . .**207** B5
Varteg NP4 . . . .**17** E1
Pembroke Mews CF5 .**194** B6
Pembrook St CF39 . . .**133** B2
Pen Bryn Hendy
CF72 . . . .**173** C7
Pen Coed Isaf Rd SA14 **42** B4
Pen Darren CF39 . . . .**107** C1
Pen Dinas CF40 . . . . . .**107** C4
Pen Gurnos CF47 . . . . .**10** C5
Pen Gwern CF35 . . . . .**152** D1
Pen Hendy CF72 . . . . .**173** C7
Pen Heol-Shenkyn
NP12 . . . .**58** D5
Pen Isa Coed SA1 . . . .**95** F7
Pen Llew Ct CF44 . . . .**28** D3
Pen Locks CF46 . . . . . .**83** A5
Pen Onnen CF31 . . . .**169** C5
Pen Parcau CF32 . . . .**129** D3
Pen Pentre SA10 . . . .**226** A7
Pen Tyntyla CF43 . . . . .**80** A2
Pen y Cwm SA2 . . . . . .**67** D2
Pen y Dre CF39 . . . . . .**133** D8
Pen y Groes CF72 . . . .**174** B7
Pen y Groes Gr NP10 **141** E2
Pen y Maes SA6 . . . . . .**45** C2
Pen y Morfa SA4 . . . . .**65** A4
Pen y Mynydd CF32 . .**129** D3
Pen y Parc NP23 . . . . .**14** B8
Pen Yr Alltwen SA8 . . .**24** A3
Pen-Cae-Crwn Rd
SA4 . . . .**43** A3
Pen-Cefn-Arda-Rd
SA4 . . . .**43** B4
Pen-clawdd Prim Sch
SA4 . . . .**64** E4
Pen-Deri Cl NP12 . . . .**59** C1
Pen-Hill Rd CF11 . . . .**194** C7
Pen-Hydd St SA12 . . . .**73** A1
Pen-Llwyn Ave NP12 .**85** F4
Pen-Llwyn-March Rd
SA5 . . . .**68** A3
Pen-Mynydd NP4 . . . . .**17** E1
Pen-Pych Cl CF42 . . . .**50** D3
Pen-Rhiw Ave NP12 . . .**59** B1
Pen-Rhiw Bengi La
NP12 . . . .**59** B1
Pen-Rhiw Est NP13 . . .**60** A8
Pen-Rhiw Terr
Abercarn NP11 . . . .**87** C3
Blackwood NP12 . . . .**59** A2
Pen-Rhiw-Garreg Rd
NP13 . . . .**36** C5
Pen-Twyn La NP20 . .**116** E3
Pen-Twyn Rd CF41,
CF42 . . . .**78** E4
Pen-y-Banc
Bridgend CF31 . . . .**169** A4
Cwmavon SA12 . . . .**100** A7
Porth CF39 . . . .**107** D1
Seven Sisters SA10 . . . .**222** C3
Pen-y-Banc Rd SA18 **219** A6
Pen-y-Bigyn SA15 . . . .**40** E4
Pen-y-bont
Crynant SA10 . . . .**222** A1
Penpedairheol CF82 . . . .**84** D8
Tredegar NP22 . . . .**6** C2
Pen-y-Bont Rd NP13 . .**36** D7
Pen-y-Bryn
Barry CF62 . . . .**214** B2
Bridgend CF31 . . . .**168** C5
Caerphilly CF83 . . . . . .**137** E6
Cwmllynfell SA9 . . . . . .**221** B7
Cymmer SA13 . . . .**75** C3
Maesteg CF34 . . . .**102** B8
Neath SA10 . . . .**70** E6
Neath SA11 . . . .**71** F5
Pontypridd CF37 . . . . . .**109** D5
Seven Sisters SA10 . . . .**222** D3
Tonna SA11 . . . .**49** D3
Ystradgynlais SA9 . . . . .**222** A5
Pen-y-Bryn Cl
Bettws NP20 . . . .**116** E2
Penllergaer SA4 . . . .**44** B2
Pen-y-Bryn Ct NP11 . .**59** D2
Pen-y-Bryn Pl CF14 .**177** E2
Pen-y-Bryn Rd
Cardiff CF14 . . . .**177** E2
Cardiff CF23 . . . .**178** C2
Pen-y-bryn Terr
Bryn NP12 . . . .**85** D3
Ebbw Vale NP23 . . . .**14** D6
Pen-y-Bryn View
CF32 . . . .**150** F4
Pen-y-Bryn Way 2
CF14 . . . .**177** E2
Pen-y-byrn Jun & Inf Sch
CF3 . . . .**179** D7
Pen-y-Cae
Caerphilly CF83 . . . . . .**138** D5
Ystrad Mynach CF82 . . .**111** E8
Pen-y-Cae Cl NP11 . . .**59** D1
Pen-y-Cae La SA4 . . . .**42** E2
Pen-y-cae Prim Sch
SA9 . . . .**222** F8
Pen-y-Cae Rd SA13 . .**125** C8
Pen-y-caeau Ct NP11 **.60** C1
Pen-y-Cefn CF14 . . . .**159** D2
Pen-y-Craig CF82 . . . . .**84** E7
Pen-y-Crug NP23 . . . . . .**7** B5

Pen-y-Cwarel Rd
NP12 . . . .**112** F8
Pen-y-cwm
Pentyrch CF15 . . . .**157** C1
Rhymney NP22 . . . .**13** A1
Pen-y-cwm Specl Sch
NP23 . . . .**7** F4
Pen-y-Darren Cl
CF37 . . . .**109** C2
Pen-y-Dre
Caerphilly CF83 . . . . . .**137** E7
Cardiff CF14 . . . .**177** B6
Ebbw Vale NP23 . . . .**7** C3
Gowerton SA4 . . . .**66** B4
Merthyr Tydfil CF47 . . . .**10** C5
Neath SA11 . . . .**71** A7
Rhymney NP22 . . . .**12** E6
Pen-y-dre High Comp Sch
CF47 . . . .**10** D6
Pen-y-Fai La SA15 . . . .**40** B8
Pen-y-Fan SA7 . . . .**69** F6
Pen-y-Fon Cl NP11 . . .**59** F6
Pen-y-fan Ind Est
NP11 . . . .**59** D4
Pen-y-fan Pond Ctry Pk
NP11,NP13 . . . .**59** D6
Pen-y-Fan Way NP12 .**59** C1
Pen-y-Ffordd CF33 . .**166** A7
Pen-y-Fro St SA15 . . . .**40** E3
Pen-y-Fro
Cwmdare CF44 . . . .**28** C3
Dunvant SA2 . . . .**66** B1
Pencoed CF35 . . . .**152** C1
Pen-y-Fro Cl SA2 . . . . .**66** B1
Pen-y-fro Prim Sch
SA2 . . . .**93** B8
Pen-y-gaer Cotts
SA14 . . . .**41** A8
Pen-y-garn
Pontsticill CF48 . . . .**3** F2
Swansea SA1 . . . .**69** A3
Pen-y-Graig Rd
Pontardawe SA8 . . . .**23** F3
Swansea SA1 . . . .**95** B8
Ystradowen SA9 . . . . . .**221** C2
Pen-y-Graig Terr
Abertillery NP13 . . . .**60** A4
Pontypool NP4 . . . .**62** D5
Pen-y-Groes
Blackwood NP11 . . . .**59** C2
Caerphilly CF83 . . . . . .**137** E6
Pen-y-Groes Ave
CF14 . . . .**177** D7
Pen-y-Groes Rd
CF14 . . . .**177** D7
Pen-y-Heol SA10 . . . . .**70** C4
Pen-y-Lan
Ebbw Vale NP23 . . . .**7** C3
Pen-clawdd SA4 . . . .**64** D7
Pen-y-Ian Ct CF23 . . .**178** C3
Pen-y-Lan Pl CF23 . . .**178** C1
Pen-y-Lan Rd
Aberthin CF71 . . . .**189** B3
6 Cardiff CF23 . . . . . .**178** C1
Cardiff CF24 . . . .**195** C8
Pen-y-Lan Terr
Cardiff CF23 . . . .**178** C2
Newbridge NP11 . . . .**86** F7
Pen-y-Llan La NP4 . . . .**63** B8
Pen-y-Mead NP12 . . . .**85** D4
Pen-y-Mor Rd SA5 . . . .**68** C5
Pen-y-Morfa SA15 . . . .**40** E3
Pen-y-Mynydd
Cymmer SA13 . . . .**75** D3
Pontypridd CF37 . . . . . .**109** D6
Pen-y-Parc CF38 . . . . .**156** A7
Pen-y-Peel Rd CF5 . . .**194** C6
Pen-y-pych Prim Sch
CF42 . . . .**50** D3
Pen-y-Rhiw
Pen-Rhiw-fawr SA9 . . . .**221** B5
Ystrad CF41 . . . .**79** D3
Pen-y-Turnpike Rd
CF64 . . . .**206** B6
Pen-y-Wain La CF24 .**178** A4
Pen-y-Wain Pl CF24 .**178** A4
Pen-y-Wain Rd CF24 .**178** A4
Pen-y-Waun
Dinas Powys CF64 . . . .**206** A3
Pentyrch CF15 . . . .**157** C1
Pen-y-Waun Cl NP44 . .**89** D2
Pen-y-Waun Rd
Abertillery NP11 . . . .**59** F5
Cwmbran NP44 . . . .**89** D2
Pen-y-Werlod Rd
NP12 . . . .**58** D8
Pen-y-werlod Terr
NP12 . . . .**58** D8
Pen-y-Wern SA13 . . . . .**75** C3
Pen-y-Wern Rd SA6 . . .**46** E8
Pen-y-Wern Terr SA1 . .**68** C4
Pen-Yr-Alley Ave
SA10 . . . .**70** C6
Pen-yr-Allt
Caerphilly CF83 . . . . . .**158** F8
Ystalyfera SA9 . . . .**2** D8
Pen-Yr-Eglwys CF38 **135** D1
Pen-Yr-Grug SA9 . . . . . .**2** A8
Pen-Yr-Heol
Neath SA10 . . . .**70** C5
North Cornelly CF33 . . .**166** A7
Pen-y-fai CF31 . . . .**150** C1
Penywaun CF44 . . . .**28** C3
Pen-Yr-Heol Dr SA2 . .**94** B7
Pen-Yr-Heol Rd
Abertillery NP11 . . . .**60** D5
Pontypool NP4 . . . .**61** A4
Pen-Yr-Yrfa SA6 . . . . . .**45** D1

Pen-Yr-Ysgol CF34 .**102** A2
Penallt Dunvant SA2 . . . .**93** E8
Llanelly Hill NP7 . . . .**9** D5
Penallt Rd SA15 . . . . . .**40** F6
Penallt Terr SA15 . . . . .**40** F6
Penallta Ind Est CF82 .**84** D5
Penallta Rd CF82 . . . . .**84** E3
Penallta Villas CF82 . .**84** E3
Penally Rd CF5 . . . . . .**193** E4
Penarth Ct NP44 . . . . .**90** B1
Penarth CW Prim Sch
CF64 . . . .**207** A5
Penarth Head La
CF64 . . . .**207** B4
Penarth Portway
CF64 . . . .**207** B5
Penarth Rd
Cardiff CF10 . . . .**195** A3
Cardiff CF10 . . . .**195** A4
Cardiff CF11 . . . .**194** D1
Cardiff CF11 . . . .**194** E2
Cardiff CF11 . . . .**194** F3
Llandough CF11 . . . . . .**206** A2
Penarth Sta CF11 . . . . .**207** A3
Penbedw NP44 . . . .**90** B4
Penbryn CF32 . . . .**103** E3
Penbryn Rd SA10 . . . . .**70** F7
Penbryn Terr SA2 . . . . .**94** F5
Pencader Rd CF5 . . . .**193** E6
Pencae Terr SA15 . . . . .**40** F5
Pencaerfenni La SA4 . .**64** B3
Pencaerfenni Pk SA4 . .**64** B3
Pencai Terr CF42 . . . . . .**78** D5
Pencarn Ave NP10 . . .**163** C6
Pencarn La
Newport NP10 . . . .**163** D6
Newport NP10 . . . .**163** E5
Pencarn Way NP10 . . .**163** D6
Pencerrig St
Llanbradach CF83 . . . .**111** F1
Pontypridd CF37 . . . . . .**109** B1
Pencisely Cres CF5 . .**194** A7
Pencisely Rd CF5 . . . .**194** B7
Pencisely Rise CF5 . . .**194** B7
Pencisley Ave CF5 . . .**194** A7
Penclawdd CF83 . . . . .**138** D5
Penclawdd Rd SA4 . . . .**65** C5
Pencoed Dunvant SA2 . .**93** E8
Tredegar NP22 . . . .**13** D6
Pencoed Ave
Blackwood NP12 . . . .**85** C8
Pontypridd CF37 . . . . . .**109** E1
Pencoed Comp Sch
CF35 . . . .**170** E7
Pencoed Jun Sch
CF35 . . . .**152** E1
Pencoed Pl NP44 . . . . .**90** B4
Pencoed Sta CF35 . . . .**170** D8
Pencoedtre Rd
Barry CF63 . . . .**205** A1
Barry CF63 . . . .**215** B8
Pencwmdu SA8 . . . . . .**221** A1
Pendarren St
Aberdare CF44 . . . .**28** F1
Penpedairheol CF82 . . . .**84** E8
Pendarvis St SA12 . . . .**98** E1
Pendarvis Terr 6
SA12 . . . .**124** F8
Pendderi Rd
Bynea SA14 . . . .**42** A4
Llanelli SA14 . . . .**41** F5
Penderry Rd SA5 . . . . . .**68** B4
Penderyn Ave SA13 . .**125** C5
Penderyn Cty Prim Sch
CF44 . . . .**224** E3
Penderyn Pl CF44 . . . . .**53** B8
Penderyn Rd SA13 . . . .**75** D3
Pendinas Ave NP11 . . .**59** D2
Pendine Cl CF62 . . . . .**214** F4
Pendine Rd CF5 . . . . .**193** E6
Pendine Wlk NP44 . . . .**89** B2
Pendoylan Cl CF63 . .**215** B8
Pendoylan Ct
11 Cardiff CF5 . . . . . .**193** C4
Cardiff CF5 . . . .**193** C4
Pendoylan CW Prim Sch
CF71 . . . .**190** F6
Pendoylan Wlk NP44 . .**89** C1
Pendragon Cl CF14 . .**159** D2
Pendraw Pl CF23 . . . .**178** B6
Pendre CF31 . . . .**168** B7
Pendre Cres CF72 . . . .**153** F3
Pendrill St SA11 . . . . . .**71** D6
Pendwyallt Rd CF14 .**176** F2
Pendyris Ct CF43 . . . . .**80** C4
Penedre CF5 . . . .**177** A1
Penfelyn Heol SA6 . . . .**45** F5
Penfforld CF15 . . . . . .**175** C8
Penfilia Rd SA5 . . . .**68** C4
Penfilia Terr 3 SA5 . . .**68** C4
Penford Ct 5 CF24 . .**195** B7
Pengam Prim Sch
NP12 . . . .**85** B7
Pengam Rd
Blackwood NP12 . . . .**58** B2
Cardiff CF24 . . . .**195** F8
Pengam NP12 . . . .**85** B8
Penpedairheol CF82,
NP12 . . . .**84** F8
Ystrad Mynach CF82 . . . .**84** F2
Pengam St NP12 . . . . . .**85** A7
Pengelli Prim Sch SA4 **43** C6
Pengeulan Prim Sch
CF45 . . . .**54** E1
Pengham Sta NP12 . . . .**85** A8
Pengorof Ct SA9 . . . .**1** E1

Pengors Rd SA5 . . . . . .45 B2
Pengry Rd SA4 . . . . . .42 F1
Pengwern Rd
 Cardiff CF5 . . . . . . .193 E6
 Swansea SA6 . . . . . . .68 C8
Penheol Ely Rd CF37 .109 F2
Penheolferthyr CF47 . . .11 A1
Penhevad St CF11 . . . .194 F2
Penhill Cl CF5 . . . . . .194 C7
Penhiwfer Prim Sch
 CF40 . . . . .133 A8
Penhydd Ho SA12 . . . .100 A8
Penhydd Rd SA13 . . . . .75 D3
Penhydd-waelod Cotts
 SA13 . . . . .100 C4
Peniel Green Rd SA7 . .70 A8
Peniel Rd SA5 . . . . . . .68 D5
Penkin Cl NP19 . . . . .144 D4
Penkin Hill NP19 . . . .144 D4
Penlan SA13 . . . . .4 A8
Penlan Comp Sch (Boys)
 SA5 . . . . .68 A6
Penlan Cres SA2 . . . . .94 F7
Penlan Fach SA5 . . . . .68 C4
Penlan Gr SA5 . . . . . . .68 B5
Penlan Rd
 Llandough CF64 . . . . .206 D6
 Loughor SA4 . . . . . . .42 F1
 Neath SA10 . . . . .70 D8
 Swansea SA5 . . . . . . .68 C6
Penlan Rise CF64 . . . .206 D6
Penlan Terr SA5 . . . . .68 C6
Penlan View CF48 . . . .30 C8
Penlas NP23 . . . . .14 B8
Penllergaer Bsns Pk
 SA5 . . . . .44 D3
Penllergaer Forest Walks
 SA4 . . . . .44 D4
Penllergaer Prim Sch
 SA4 . . . . .44 A2
Penlline Ct CF14 . . . .177 A5
Penlline Rd CF14 . . . .177 A5
Penlline St CF24 . . . .195 B7
Penllwyn Inf Sch NP12 85 E4
Penllwyn La
 Machen CF83 . . . . . . .139 D7
 Pontllanfraith NP12 . . .85 F4
Penllwyn St NP11 . . . .113 A4
Penllwyn Wlk CF83 . . .139 C7
Penllwyngwent Ind Est
 CF32 . . . . .104 E3
Penllwyngwyn Farm Dr
 SA14 . . . . .41 F6
Penllwyngwyn Rd
 SA14 . . . . .42 A6
Penllwynrhodyn Rd
 SA14 . . . . .41 E4
Penllyn SA12 . . . . .99 E5
Penllyn Ave
 Cwmbran NP44 . . . . . .89 E6
 Newport NP20 . . . . . .142 F4
Penllyn La NP20 . . . . .142 F4
Penllyn Rd CF5 . . . . . .194 D5
Penmachno SA6 . . . . . .45 D1
Penmaen Ave NP12 . . .59 B2
Penmaen Bsns Ctr
 NP12 . . . . .86 A5
Penmaen Cl CF82 . . . . .84 F5
Penmaen Cnr NP12 . . . .86 A8
Penmaen Est NP12 . . . .86 A8
Penmaen Ind Est NP12 86 F5
Penmaen Rd NP12 . . . .86 A5
Penmaen Terr SA1 . . . .95 B7
Penmaen Villas NP12 . .86 A8
Penmaen Wlk CF5 . . . .192 F3
Penmaes CF15 . . . . . .157 C1
Penmaes Rd NP44 . . . . .88 F3
Penmaesglas Terr ☑
 CF40 . . . . .106 A4
Penmain St CF39 . . . .107 E4
Penmark Rd CF5 . . . . .193 A4
Penmark Rd CF5 . . . . .193 A4
Penmark Row CF44 . . . .27 C4
Penmynydd SA4 . . . . . .43 B1
Penmynydd Rd SA5 . . . .68 B5
Penn St CF46 . . . . .83 B7
Pennant Cres CF23 . . .178 C6
Pennant St NP23 . . . . .14 D8
Pennar Cl NP11 . . . . . .86 E6
Pennar La NP11 . . . . . .86 D6
Pennar St NP11 . . . . . .86 F6
Pennard Dr SA3 . . . . .121 A6
Pennard Pl CF14 . . . . .177 D3
Pennard Prim Sch
 SA3 . . . . .121 A5
Pennard Rd
 Bishopston SA3 . . . . .121 E7
 Southgate SA3 . . . . . .121 B5
Pennard St SA5 . . . . . .68 C3
Pennine Cl
 Cardiff CF14 . . . . . . .177 E7
 Risca NP11 . . . . .115 D1
 Swansea SA5 . . . . . . .67 E3
Pennsylvania CF23 . . .178 D5
Penny Cres NP20 . . . .116 F3
Pennyfields ☑ NP44 . . .89 B3
Pennyroyal Cl CF3 . . . .180 A8
Penpisgah Rd CF40 . . .106 F4
Penplas Rd
 Swansea SA5 . . . . . . .67 E4
 Swansea SA5 . . . . . . .67 F8
Penpound La SA18 . . . .219 E6
Penprys Rd SA14 . . . . .41 E2
Penprysg Rd CF35 . . . .152 E1
Penrhiw La CF83 . . . . .140 A8

Penrhiw Rd
 Pontypridd CF37 . . . .135 B7
 Risca NP11 . . . . .115 A2
 Swansea SA6 . . . . . . .45 D2
 Ton Pentre SA18 . . . . .79 A2
Penrhiw St SA13 . . . . .100 E5
Penrhiw-ceibr Inf Sch
 CF45 . . . . .81 F8
Penrhiw-ceibr Jun Sch
 CF45 . . . . .81 F8
Penrhiw-Fer Rd
 CF40 . . . . .133 B7
Penrhiwceiber Rd
 CF45 . . . . .54 E1
Penrhiwceiber Sta
 CF45 . . . . .82 A8
Penrhiwgarreg NP13 . . .36 C4
Penrhiwgoch SA12 . . . .98 C8
Penrhiwgwynt Rd
 CF39 . . . . .107 F3
Penrhiwiau SA8 . . . . . .23 E4
Penrhiwtyn St SA11 . . .71 C4
Penrhos Gorseinon SA4 .43 A1
 Radyr CF15 . . . . .176 A7
Penrhos Cres CF5 . . . .179 C4
Penrhos Cty Prim Sch
 SA9 . . . . .222 A6
Penrhos Pl SA5 . . . . . .67 F4
Penrhyn Ave SA5 . . . . .68 A4
Penrhyn Cl CF3 . . . . . .179 E5
Penrhyn Ct SA6 . . . . . .46 A3
Penrhyn St SA13 . . . . .125 D6
Penrhyn Terr NP24 . . . .33 F3
Penrhys Ave CF43 . . . . .80 B2
Penrhys Inf & Jun Schs
 CF43 . . . . .80 A2
Penrhys Rd
 Treorchy CF43 . . . . . .80 B2
 Ystrad CF41 . . . . .79 F2
Penrhys Uchaf CF43 . . .80 B2
Penrice Ct SA6 . . . . . . .69 A6
Penrice Gn ☑ NP44 . . . .90 B2
Penrice St SA6 . . . . . . .45 F1
Penri Pl SA15 . . . . .40 E5
Penry St CF48 . . . . . . .10 D1
Penryce Ct ☑ SA1 . . . . .95 D6
Pensalem Rd SA5 . . . . .68 B5
Pensarn Rd CF3 . . . . . .179 C5
Pensarn Way
 Cwmbran NP44 . . . . .115 F8
 Cwmbran NP44 . . . . .116 A8
Penscynor SA10 . . . . . .49 B3
Penshannel Neath SA10 70 F8
 Neath Abbey SA10 . . . .47 F1
Pensidan View NP10 . .141 F2
Pent Lee CF23 . . . . . .178 E7
Pentewan Cl SA6 . . . . .46 A4
Pentip Church in Wales
 Prim Sch SA15 . . . . . .40 C6
Pentland Cl
 Cardiff CF14 . . . . . . .177 D7
 Risca NP11 . . . . .115 D1
 Swansea SA5 . . . . . . .67 D4
Pentonville NP20 . . . .143 B5
Pentre CF72 . . . . .155 A5
Pentre Afan SA12 . . . . .98 E3
Pentre Banadl SA2 . . . .93 E7
Pentre Cl NP44 . . . . . .116 B8
Pentre Ct CF41 . . . . . . .79 F4
Pentre Fedwen SA11 . . .72 B5
Pentre Gdns CF11 . . . .194 F3
Pentre Howell CF35 . . .170 E8
Pentre La
 Llantarnam NP44 . . . .116 E5
 Penperlleni NP4 . . . . . .39 C4
Pentre Mawr Rd SA1 . . .68 D2
Pentre Pl Cardiff CF11 .194 F3
 Pyle CF33 . . . . .148 C2
Pentre Prim Sch CF41 .78 F5
 Pentre CF41 . . . . .78 F5
 Pontarddulais SA4 . . . .19 C2
 Treorchy CF41 . . . . . . .79 A5
Pentre St Cardiff CF11 .194 F3
 Glynneath SA11 . . . . .223 C1
 Glynneath SA11 . . . . .227 C8
Pentre Tai Rd NP10 . . .141 D5
Pentre Wern SA13 . . . .125 D5
Pentre-Chwyth Rd
 SA1 . . . . .68 F2
Pentre-Dwr Rd SA7 . . .69 E5
Pentre-Poeth Cl
 NP10 . . . . .141 E2
Pentre-Poeth Rd
 NP10 . . . . .141 E2
Pentre-Treharne Hill
 SA1 . . . . .68 D4
Pentre-Treharne Rd
 SA1 . . . . .68 D3
Pentrebach Ind Est
 CF48 . . . . .31 A5
Pentrebach Rd
 Merthyr Tydfil CF48 . . .30 F6
 Pontypridd CF37 . . . .135 B8
Pentrebach Sch CF48 . .31 A4
Pentrebach Sta CF48 . . .30 F4
Pentrebane Prim Sch
 CF5 . . . . .193 C8
Pentrebane Rd CF5 . . .176 E1
Pentrebane St
 Caerphilly CF83 . . . . .138 A2
 Cardiff CF11 . . . . . . .194 F2
Pentrebeili Pl CF32 . . .130 E5
Pentrebeili Terr
 CF32 . . . . .130 E5
Pentrechwyth Prim Sch
 SA1 . . . . .69 A3
Pentregethin Rd SA5 . .67 E5

Pentreguinea Rd SA1 . .95 E8
Pentrehafod Comp Sch
 SA1 . . . . .68 D3
Pentremalwed Rd SA6 68 F7
Pentrepiod Rd NP4 . . . .37 F1
Pentrepoeth Jun & Inf Sch
 NP10 . . . . .141 F9
Pentrepoeth Prim Sch
 NP10 . . . . .141 F9
Pentrepoeth Rd
 Llanelli SA15 . . . . . . .40 D8
 Swansea SA6 . . . . . . .45 F2
Pentrepoeth School Rd
 Morriston SA6 . . . . . .46 A1
 Swansea SA6 . . . . . . .45 F1
Pentwyn
 Bryn-côch SA10 . . . . . .48 B4
 Caerphilly CF83 . . . . .137 E6
 Ebbw Vale NP23 . . . . .14 C7
 Heolgerrig CF48 . . . . .10 A1
 Neath SA11 . . . . .71 E5
 Radyr CF15 . . . . .176 A6
 Three Crosses SA4 . . . .65 E1
Pentwyn Ave
 Blackwood NP12 . . . . .85 E8
 Mountain Ash CF45 . . .82 A6
Pentwyn Baglan Rd
 SA12 . . . . .98 E5
Pentwyn Cl CF44 . . . . .28 A6
Pentwyn Ct
 Blackwood NP12 . . . . .85 E8
 Cardiff CF14 . . . . . . .177 A7
Pentwyn Deintyr CF46 83 A4
Pentwyn Dr
 Baglan SA12 . . . . .98 E5
 Cardiff CF23 . . . . . . .178 F7
Pentwyn Hts NP4 . . . . .37 F3
Pentwyn Isaf
 Blaina NP13 . . . . .15 E4
 Caerphilly CF83 . . . . .137 F6
Pentwyn La NP4 . . . . . .37 F3
Pentwyn Link Rd CF3,
 CF23 . . . . .161 B2
Pentwyn Prim Sch
 NP4 . . . . .37 E3
Pentwyn Rd
 Abersychan NP4 . . . . . .37 F2
 Abertillery NP11 . . . . .59 F5
 Blackwood NP12 . . . . .85 E7
 Cardiff CF23 . . . . . . .178 E8
 Cynonville SA13 . . . . .74 B3
 Pencoed CF35 . . . . . .152 E1
 Quakers Yard CF46 . . . .83 C4
 Resolven SA11 . . . . . .226 E5
 Ystalyfera SA9 . . . . . . .2 B7
Pentwyn Terr
 Abersychan NP4 . . . . . .37 F3
 Abertillery NP11 . . . . .59 F6
 Marshfield CF3 . . . . . .180 E8
Pentwyn Villas CF47 . . .10 D3
Pentwynmawr Jun & Sch
 CF83 . . . . .139 B4
Pentyla Maesteg CF34 .101 F4
 Neath SA10 . . . . .70 F7
Pentyla Rd SA2 . . . . . . .94 E8
Pentyla-Baglan Rd
 SA12 . . . . .99 A2
Pentyrch Prim Sch
 CF15 . . . . .175 B8
Pentyrch St CF24 . . . .177 F1
Penuel Cl SA4 . . . . . . .43 A1
Penuel La CF37 . . . . . .109 C1
Penuel Rd CF15 . . . . . .175 B8
Penuel St ☑ CF47 . . . . .30 F8
Penyard Rd
 Hirwaun CF44 . . . . . . .27 D8
 Merthyr Tydfil CF47 . . .10 E2
 Neath Abbey SA10 . . . .71 B8
Penybanc La SA4 . . . . .43 A4
Penybont Prim Sch
 CF31 . . . . .168 F5
Penybont Rd CF35 . . . .152 F1
Penybryn Llanelli SA14 .41 E6
 Merthyr Tydfil CF47 . . .10 F4
Penybryn Ave NP12 . . .85 C8
Penybryn Rd
 Brynmenyn CF32 . . . .150 E6
 Gorseinon SA4 . . . . . .43 B2
 Mountain Ash CF45 . . .81 F7
Penybryn Senior Specl Sch
 SA6 . . . . .68 D7
Penybryn St
 Aberdare CF44 . . . . . .28 F2
 Hendreforgan CF39 . . .132 C5
Penybryn Terr
 Brynmenyn CF32 . . . .150 E6
 Mountain Ash CF45 . . .81 F8
 Penybryn CF82 . . . . . .84 D5
Penybryn Villas ☑
 CF47 . . . . .10 F4
Penycoedcae Rd
 CF37,CF38 . . . . .134 F2
Penydarren Dr CF14 . .176 E5
Penydarren Gdns CF47 10 E2
Penydarren Pk CF47 . . .10 E2
Penydarren Rd CF47 . . .10 E2
Penyfai Prim Sch
 CF31 . . . . .150 C1
Penyfai CW Prim Sch
 CF31 . . . . .150 C1
Penyfan Rd SA15 . . . . .40 F4
Penyfan View CF47 . . . .10 C5
Penyffordd CF83 . . . . .137 F4
Penygaer Prim Sch
 SA14 . . . . .40 F7

Penygaer Rd SA14,
 SA15 . . . . .40 F6
Penygarn Inf Sch NP4 62 D8
Penygarn Jun Sch
 NP4 . . . . .62 D8
Penygarn Rd
 Cardiff CF5 . . . . .193 D6
 Pontypool NP4 . . . . . .62 D8
 Tycroes SA18 . . . . . . .218 F5
Penygarn Terr CF34 . . .102 B2
Penygarreg Rd CF39 . .133 C2
Penygawsi Prim Sch
 CF72 . . . . .155 D2
Penygraig CF14 . . . . . .159 B1
Penygraig Ind Est
 CF40 . . . . .106 F4
Penygraig Inf Sch
 CF40 . . . . .106 F4
Penygraig Jun Sch
 CF40 . . . . .106 F4
Penygraig Rd
 Llanelli SA14 . . . . . . .41 E4
 Tonypandy CF40 . . . .106 F3
Penygraig Terr CF37 . . .81 F1
Penygroes Cty Prim Sch
 SA14 . . . . .218 D8
Penygroes Rd
 Ammanford SA18 . . . .218 F8
 Gorslas SA14 . . . . . . .218 C8
Penylan CF31 . . . . . . .168 F8
Penylan Ave CF36 . . . .182 E7
Penylan Cl
 Bassaleg NP10 . . . . . .142 A3
 Pontypool NP4 . . . . . .63 B4
 Porthcawl CF36 . . . . .182 E7
Penylan Ct
 ☑ Cardiff CF24 . . . . .178 C1
 Cwmbran NP44 . . . . .116 B8
Penylan Oval CF23 . . .178 C3
Penylan Rd
 Abersychan NP4 . . . . . .37 E2
 Argoed NP12 . . . . . . .58 F6
 Newport NP19 . . . . . .144 A5
 Pencoed CF35 . . . . . .152 E1
 Pontypridd CF37 . . . .135 B8
 St Brides Major CF32 . .185 D2
Penylan Way NP44 . . .116 B8
Penyparc NP44 . . . . . .89 D6
Penyrallt SA18 . . . . . . .220 C7
Penyrallt Ave CF31 . . .168 F8
Penyralltwen Pk SA8 . .24 A3
Penyrenglyn Inf Sch
 CF42 . . . . .78 B8
Penyrenglyn Jun Sch
 CF42 . . . . .78 B8
Penyrheol Com Sch
 SA4 . . . . .43 B3
Penyrheol Dr SA15 . . . .40 E8
Penyrheol Prim Sch
 SA4 . . . . .43 B3
Penyrheol Rd
 Gorseinon SA4 . . . . . .43 A4
 Pontypool NP4 . . . . . .62 C3
Penyrheol Terr CF71 . .199 F8
Penyturnpike View
 CF64 . . . . .206 D4
Penywain La NP4 . . . . .62 B6
Penywain Rd NP4 . . . . .62 A7
Penywain St NP4 . . . . .62 B7
Penywain Terr NP4 . . . .62 B7
Penywarc Rd SA15 . . . .40 F5
Penywaun CF38 . . . . . .156 F5
Penywern Inf Sch
 CF44 . . . . .28 B6
Penywern Llanelli SA15 40 A7
 Ystalyfera SA9 . . . . . . .2 A7
Penywern Rd
 Neath SA11 . . . . .48 E2
 Ystalyfera SA9 . . . . . . .2 A6
Penywrlod CF82 . . . . . .84 C7
Peppermint Dr CF3 . . .160 D1
Pepys Cres CF3 . . . . . .179 B6
Pepys Gr NP20 . . . . . .142 E2
Percival Cl CF14 . . . . .159 D2
Perclose CF64 . . . . . . .206 D3
Percoed La NP10 . . . . .163 C4
Percy Rd SA13 . . . . . . .74 B3
Percy St CF10 . . . . . . .195 A4
Percy Smith Rd CF61 . .210 C6
Percy St CF10 . . . . . . .195 A4
Pergoed La NP4 . . . . . .63 F7
Pergwm St CF40 . . . . .107 B5
Peris Rd SA5 . . . . .68 A5
Perrington Villas
 CF32 . . . . .151 E4
Perrots Cl CF5 . . . . . . .193 E8
Perrott Pl CF46 . . . . . .83 B6
Perrott St CF46 . . . . . .83 B6
Perry Cl SA11 . . . . . . .71 C1
Perry Ct NP44 . . . . . . .89 A4
Persondy La CF5 . . . . .192 F6
Persondy Terr NP11 . . .87 C3
Perth Ct NP12 . . . . . . .85 A8
Perthcelyn Com Primary
 Sch CF45 . . . . .81 F7
Perthlwyd CF44 . . . . . .28 A6
Perthy Cl NP44 . . . . . .116 B8
Perthgleision CF48 . . . .55 C3
Peter Cash No SA1 . . . .95 A5
Peter Lea Prim Sch
 CF5 . . . . .176 D1
Peter St SA1 . . . . .68 C1
Peter Terr SA1 . . . . . . .68 C1
Peterston Castle CF5 191 E5
Peterston-Super-Ely Sch
 CF5 . . . . .191 E6
Peterswell Rd CF62 . . .214 C5
Petherton Pl ☑ CF5 . . .179 C6
Pethybridge Rd CF5 . .193 C6

Petrel Cl CF64 . . . . . . .217 A7
Pettingale Rd NP44 . . . .90 B5
Petunia Wlk NP10 . . . .141 D7
Pheasant Rd SA8 . . . . .23 B2
Phelps Ho ☑ SA2 . . . . .98 B3
Philadelphia Ct CF63 215 D7
Philadelphia Ct ☑
 SA6 . . . . .69 A8
Philadelphia La SA1 . . .68 D2
Philadelphia Rd CF36 182 F7
Philip Ave CF31 . . . . . .168 C5
Philip Cl CF14 . . . . . . .177 D6
Philip St
 Abertillery NP11 . . . . .59 F6
 Cardiff CF11 . . . . . . .194 D5
Philip's Wlk NP22 . . . . .12 E5
Philippa Freeth Ct
 CF63 . . . . .215 A4
Phillip Row CF44 . . . . .53 F8
Phillip St
 Aberdare CF44 . . . . . .29 A3
 Mountain Ash CF45 . . .54 D3
 Newport NP19 . . . . . .143 E5
 Risca NP11 . . . . .114 F2
 Swansea SA5 . . . . . . .68 C2
Phillips Terr
 Senghenydd CF83 . . . .110 F3
 Trehafod CF37 . . . . . .108 C3
Phillipstown Prim Sch
 NP24 . . . . .33 E4
Philog Ct CF14 . . . . . .177 C4
Philog The CF14 . . . . .177 C4
Philsay Ho NP44 . . . . .116 C8
Phoenix Ave SA13 . . . .125 D5
Phoenix Bsns Pk SA7 . .69 B7
Phoenix Ctr SA7 . . . . . .69 C7
Phoenix Ho ☑ CF24 . . .195 D6
Phoenix Way
 Garngoch Ind Est SA4 . .43 F1
 Swansea SA7 . . . . . . .69 B6
Phyllis Ave CF31 . . . . .168 C3
Phyllis St Barry CF62 . .214 F3
 Swansea SA5 . . . . . . .68 A2
 Troedyrhiw CF48 . . . . .31 C2
Piccadilly CF71 . . . . . .200 D8
Piccadilly Sq CF83 . . . .138 B3
Picket Mead Rd SA3 . .122 E5
Picketston Cl CF62 . . .211 A7
Pickwick Cl CF14 . . . . .159 F2
Picton Arc ☑ SA1 . . . . .95 C6
Picton Ave
 Bridgend CF31 . . . . . .168 E2
 Porthcawl CF36 . . . . .182 F6
Picton Cl CF33 . . . . . .169 A2
Picton Cl CF61 . . . . . .210 A7
Picton Gdns CF3 . . . . .169 A2
Picton La SA1 . . . . .95 C6
Picton Pl Cardiff CF11 194 D5
 Maesteg CF34 . . . . . .102 A6
Picton St
 Maesteg CF34 . . . . . .102 A6
 Pontlottyn CF81 . . . . .12 F1
 Pontypool NP4 . . . . . .62 E3
 Pyle CF33 . . . . .148 D3
Picton Terr
 Llanharan CF72 . . . . .154 A3
 Swansea SA1 . . . . . . .95 C8
Picton Wlk
 ☑ Cardiff CF11 . . . . .194 D5
 Cwmbran NP44 . . . . . .89 B2
Picwic Gn NP44 . . . . . .89 B2
Pier Cl SA12 . . . . .98 C1
Pier St SA1 . . . . .95 E6
Pier Way SA12 . . . . . . .98 C1
Piercefield Pl CF24 . . .195 D6
Pierhead St
 Cardiff CF10 . . . . . . .195 C2
 Cardiff CF10 . . . . . . .195 D2
Pil Prim Sch CF33 . . . .148 B2
Pil-y-Cynffig CF33 . . . .166 A8
Pilgrims Cl SA10 . . . . .71 C8
Pill St CF64 . . . . .206 F5
Pill Terr SA11 . . . . . . .71 B2
Pillgwenlly Jun & Inf Sch
 NP20 . . . . .143 C2
Pillmawr Circ NP20 . . .117 B2
Pillmawr Rd
 Caerleon NP18 . . . . . .118 A3
 Newport NP18,NP20 . .117 D2
Pilton Pl CF14 . . . . . . .177 D2
Pilton Vale NP20 . . . . .117 B3
Pine
 Merthyr Tydfil CF47 . . .10 F4
 Porthcawl CF36 . . . . .183 D7
 Risca NP11 . . . . .115 A2
Pine Cres SA6 . . . . . . .45 E2
Pine Ct Cardiff CF15 . .158 D1
 Llantrisant CF72 . . . . .159 F3
 Llantwit Fardre CF38 . .156 F5
Pine Gdns NP4 . . . . . . .62 A6
Pine Gr Cimla SA11 . . . .72 B5
 Newport NP10 . . . . . .163 D4
 Ystrad Mynach CF82 . .84 E1
Pine St CF43 . . . . .79 F7
Pine Tree Cl CF15 . . . .176 A7
Pine Tree Ho SA12 . . . .98 E6

Pine Tree Rd NP4 . . . . .63 B4
Pine Tree Way CF46 . . . .83 F2
Pine Valley SA12 . . . . . .99 C5
Pine Walk Dr CF39 . . . .108 A2
Pine Wood Cres
 CF23 . . . . .178 E3
Pineacre Cl SA2 . . . . . .94 C6
Pinecrest Dr CF14 . . . .159 F3
Pinecroft Ave CF44 . . . .29 D1
Pinehurst Rd CF5 . . . .193 C8
Pines The
 Abertillery NP13 . . . . .36 C6
 Cardiff CF14 . . . . . . .177 A5
 Cilfrew SA10 . . . . .49 B4
 Hirwaun CF44 . . . . . . .27 F7
 Machen CF83 . . . . . . .139 D5
Pinetree Ct SA2 . . . . . .94 C6
Pineway SA5 . . . . .68 C2
Pinewood Ave CF37 . . .136 C5
Pinewood Cl
 Llandough CF64 . . . . .206 E6
 Newport NP20 . . . . . .117 B2
Pinewood Ct
 Bryn NP12 . . . . .85 E5
 Llanelli SA14 . . . . . . .41 D6
Pinewood Dr CF40 . . . .107 A5
Pinewood Hill CF72 . . .155 A2
Pinewood Rd
 Ammanford SA18 . . . .219 D7
 Swansea SA2 . . . . . . .94 C6
Pinewood Sq CF62 . . . .211 B7
Pinewood Terr SA12 . . .98 D6
Pinewood View CF37 . .109 C6
Pinkney St SA1 . . . . . . .95 E7
Pinnell Pl ☑ NP20 . . . .143 C3
Pintail Cl CF3 . . . . . . .165 D1
Piper Cl Cardiff CF5 . . .176 D2
 Newport NP19 . . . . . .144 A8
Pisgah Cl NP4 . . . . . . .37 E5
Pisgah Rd NP4 . . . . . . .37 E5
Pisgah St CF33 . . . . . .148 C2
Pit junction Sta SA7 . . .69 C6
Pit Pl ☑ CF44 . . . . .53 E8
Pit St CF34 . . . . .102 B1
Pitman La CF11 . . . . . .194 E6
Pitman St CF11 . . . . . .194 E6
Pitmedden Cl ☑ CF3 . . .179 F7
Pittsburgh St SA5 . . . . .67 F7
Plane Gr CF47 . . . . . . .10 D5
Plane St CF37 . . . . . . .136 A5
Plane Tree Cl NP18 . . . .117 F6
Planet St CF24 . . . . . . .195 C6
Plantagenet St CF11 . .194 F5
Plantasia SA1 . . . . .95 D7
Plantation Cl CF47 . . . .10 E3
Plantation Dr NP44 . . . .90 B4
Plantation Gdns CF45 . .82 E3
Plantation Rd CF45 . . . .82 E3
Plantation Row NP23 . .14 D6
Plantation Sq ☑ CF48 . .31 B1
Plantation Terr
 Fochriw CF81 . . . . . . .32 C7
 Rhymney NP22 . . . . . .12 F2
Plas Bryn Gomer NP44 90 A6
Plas Cadwgan SA4 . . . .44 C2
Plas Cae Llwyd ☑
 CF83 . . . . .111 F1
Plas Cleddau CF62 . . .214 C5
Plas Craig SA4 . . . . . . .89 F4
Plas Croeso SA4 . . . . . .43 B1
Plas Cwm Parc CF83 . .110 F3
Plas Dafydd CF44 . . . . .28 E3
Plas Derwen
 Croesyceiliog NP44 . . .90 A4
 Troedyrhiw CF48 . . . . .31 B2
Plas Ebbw NP44 . . . . . .89 F4
Plas Essyllt CF64 . . . . .206 B3
Plas Glen Rosa CF64 . .207 A5
Plas Grug CF83 . . . . . .137 F1
Plas Gwernfadog Dr
 SA6 . . . . .46 A3
Plas Heddwch CF33 . . .166 A8
Plas Horab CF42 . . . . . .50 F2
Plas Islwyn NP44 . . . . .89 E4
Plas Kenfig CF33 . . . . .165 F1
Plas Melin CF14 . . . . . .176 F4
Plas Melyn SA5 . . . . . .67 F6
Plas Morlais CF33 . . . .166 A8
Plas Nant CF83 . . . . . .137 A7
Plas Newydd
 Cardiff CF14 . . . . . . .177 A4
 Dunvant SA2 . . . . . . .93 B8
 Ebbw Vale NP23 . . . . .14 D6
 Grovesend SA4 . . . . . .43 C6
Plas Pamir CF64 . . . . .207 B6
Plas Phillips CF83 . . . .137 F3
Plas Rd
 Fleur De Lis NP12 . . . .85 B6
 Grovesend SA4 . . . . . .43 C6
 Pontardawe SA8 . . . . .24 C4
Plas St Andresse
 CF64 . . . . .207 B6
Plas St Pol De Leon ☑
 CF64 . . . . .207 B5
Plas Taliesin CF64 . . . .207 B6
Plas Terr NP12 . . . . . . .85 B6
Plas Thomas CF83 . . . .137 F3
Plas Treoda CF14 . . . . .176 F4
Plas Twyn NP44 . . . . . .89 F5
Plas Ty-Coch NP44 . . .116 F4
Plas Tymawr CF31 . . . .168 D7
Plas View NP12 . . . . . .85 E6
Plas y Biswail CF3 . . . .179 C6
Plas y Coed Ave SA6 . . .68 F8

Plas y Coed Rd SA6 ....**68** F8
Plas y Delyn CF14 ...**160** B3
Plas y Felin Inf & Jun Schs
CF83 ....**138** A4
Plas y Wan NP23 ....**14** B8
Plas Yr Eglwys 🔟
CF37 ....**109** D2
Plas-Cadwgan Rd SA4 **46** C5
Plas-Gwyn Rd SA14 .**218** D8
Plas-Mawr Rd CF5 ..**193** D8
Plas-y-Coed
Cardiff CF23 ....**178** B3
Glynneath SA11 .....**223** C1
Plas-y-Fedwen CF37 **109** D6
Plas-y-Fforest
Fforest SA4 ....**18** F6
Penllergaer SA4 .....**44** C2
Plas-y-Llan CF14 ...**177** A5
Plasbach 🔟 CF5 ....**193** D8
Plascoed SA9 ....**1** F2
Plasdraw Ave CF44 ....**29** B2
Plasdraw Pl CF44 .....**29** B2
Plasdraw Rd CF44 ....**29** B2
Plasgwyn SA14 ....**9** D4
Plasgwyn Terr NP12 ..**85** B6
Plasmarl CF44 ....**29** B2
Plasmarl Ind Est SA6 .**68** F6
Plasmarl Prim Sch
SA6 ....**68** E5
Plasmarl Terr SA6 ....**68** E5
Plasnewydd Pl 🔟
CF24 ....**195** C8
Plasnewydd Prim Sch
CF34 ....**102** A3
Plasnewydd Rd
Cardiff CF24 ....**195** B8
Cardiff CF24 ....**195** C7
Plasnewydd Sq CF24 **195** C8
Plasnewydd St CF34 ..**102** A3
Plassey Ho 🔟 CF64 ..**207** A5
Plassey Sq CF64 .....**207** A5
Plassey St CF64 ......**207** A4
Plasturton Ave CF11 .**194** D7
Plasturton Gdns
CF11 ....**194** E6
Plasturton Pl CF11 ...**194** E6
Plasturtwyn CF83 ....**112** A3
Plasycoed Rd NP4 ....**61** E7
Players Ave SA6 ....**46** D8
Playford Cres NP19 ..**144** F5
Plaza Ct 🔟 NP12 .....**85** F4
Pleasant Cl SA4 ....**42** F3
Pleasant Ct NP44 .....**38** A3
Pleasant Hill
Cilfrew SA11 ....**49** C5
Ferndale CF43 ....**80** A6
Pleasant Hts CF39 ...**107** E8
Pleasant Pl CF83 ....**137** E5
Pleasant Rd
Gorseinon SA4 ....**43** E2
🔟 Tonypandy CF40 .**106** F3
Pleasant Row
🔟 Llanelli SA15 .....**40** E5
Swansea SA5 ....**68** C3
Pleasant St
Pentre CF41 ....**78** F4
🔟 Swansea SA1 ....**95** D7
Swansea SA6 ....**45** F1
Pleasant Terr
Tonypandy CF40 ...**106** B7
Ystrad CF41 ....**79** D7
Pleasant View
Aberfan CF48 ....**55** C3
Aberkenfig CF32 ...**150** C3
Abersychan NP4 .....**37** F4
Barry CF62 ....**214** D8
Beddau CF38 ....**156** A6
Bedlinog CF46 ....**56** B8
Blackwood NP11 .....**59** D2
Blackwood NP12 .....**85** D2
Brynmawr NP23 ......**8** B5
Brynmenyn CF32 ...**150** F4
Cefn Cribwr CF32 ...**149** B2
Cymmer SA13 ....**75** C5
Ebbw Vale NP23 .....**14** D8
Fochriw CF81 ....**32** D7
Llanelli SA15 ....**40** E8
Maesteg CF34 ....**75** B2
New Tredegar NP24 ..**13** E2
Pontypool NP4 ....**61** F8
Pontypridd CF37 ...**109** D2
Tonypandy CF40 ...**133** A8
Trehafod CF37 .....**108** C2
Treharris CF46 ....**83** A6
Treorchy CF41 ....**79** A4
Treorchy CF43 ....**80** B2
🔟 Troedyrhiw CF48 .**31** C1
Wattstown CF39 ....**107** D8
Ynysybwl CF37 ......**81** E4
Pleasant View St CF44 .**53** C6
Pleasant View Terr
Swansea SA1 ....**95** C8
🔟 Swansea SA5 ....**68** C4
Pleasantview St CF47 .**10** C2
Plough Cnr NP12 ......**86** A4
Plough Rd
Penperlleni NP4 ......**39** F5
Swansea SA1 ....**68** D3
Plover Cl
Newport NP19 ......**144** E1
Swansea SA6 ....**68** C7
Plover Way CF64 ....**217** A8
Plumley Cl CF33 ....**165** F8
Plunch La SA3 ......**123** C3

Plunch Rd SA3 ......**123** B3
Plym Wlk NP20 ......**116** E2
Plymouth Dr CF15 ..**176** C5
Plymouth Rd
Barry CF62 ....**214** F2
Penarth CF64 ....**207** B2
Pontypridd CF37 ...**109** A1
Plymouth St
Merthyr Tydfil CF47 ...**30** E7
Swansea SA1 ....**95** C6
Plymouth Wood Cl
CF5 ....**193** D6
Plymouth Wood Cres
CF5 ....**193** C6
Plymouth Wood Rd
CF5 ....**193** D6
Plynlimon Ave NP11 ..**59** E2
Plynlimon Cl NP11 ....**59** E2
Pobbles Cl SA3 ......**121** A4
Pochin Cres NP22 .....**14** A4
Pochin Hos NP22 ......**34** C6
Pocketts Wharf 🔟
SA1 ....**95** E6
Poets Cl CF37 ....**136** A6
Police Row NP22 ....**6** D2
Pollard NP18 ....**117** E2
Polo Ground Ind Est
NP4 ....**62** F4
Pomeroy St CF10 ....**195** B1
Pommergelli Rd
CF14 ....**176** F4
Pond Mawr CF34 ....**102** D1
Pond Pl CF44 ....**53** F8
Pond Rd NP23 ....**8** B3
Pond Row
Abercanaid CF48 .....**30** E5
Abercarn NP11 .....**114** C7
Pont Aur SA3 ....**2** E7
Pont Faen Rd NP19 ..**144** C3
Pont George Rd CF23 **148** B3
Pont Newydd CF35 ..**170** D6
Pont St SA13 ....**125** C8
Pont Yr Ochain CF44 **224** C1
Pont-Sion-Norton Prim
Sch CF37 ....**109** E3
Pont-y-clun Prim Sch
CF72 ....**173** A7
Pont-y-Cob Rd SA4 ...**65** F6
Pont-y-Felin Ave NP4 .**62** F2
Pont-y-Felin La NP4 ..**63** A2
Pont-y-Felin Rd NP4 ..**63** A2
Pont-y-Garreg Jun & Inf
Sch NP23 ....**7** B4
Pont-y-Glasdwr 🔟
SA1 ....**68** D1
Pont-y-Gof NP23 ....**7** D1
Pont-y-Shoot SA6 ....**68** D5
Pontalun Cl CF63 ....**215** A8
Pontamman Rd SA18 **219** D7
Pontardawe Ind Est
SA8 ....**23** F5
Pontardawe Rd
Clydach SA6 ....**47** A8
Pontardawe SA8 ...**220** D3
Pontardulais Cty Prim
Sch SA4 ....**19** D3
Pontardulais Comp Sch
SA4 ....**19** D5
Pontardulais Ind Est
SA4 ....**19** C6
Pontardulais Junc
SA4 ....**19** B5
Pontardulais Rd
Cross Hands SA14 ...**218** B6
Gorseinon SA4 ....**43** C3
Llangennech SA14 ...**18** E2
Swansea SA5 ....**67** C6
Tycroes SA18 ....**218** B3
Pontardulais Workshops
SA4 ....**19** C6
Pontcanna Ct CF5 ...**194** C2
Pontcanna Pl CF11 ..**194** D7
Pontcanna St CF11 ..**194** D7
Pontcynon Terr CF45 ..**82** D4
Pontfaen CF23 ....**178** D8
Pontgam Terr NP11 ..**112** F8
Pontnir Rd NP18 ....**118** B4
Pontllanfraith Comp Sch
NP12 ....**85** F4
Pontllanfraith Prim Sch
NP12 ....**86** A5
Pontlliw Prim Sch
SA4 ....**44** A4
Pontlottyn Inf Sch
CF81 ....**32** F8
Pontlottyn Jun Sch
CF81 ....**32** F8
Pontlottyn Rd CF81 ...**32** D8
Pontlottyn Sta CF81 ...**12** F1
Pontmorlais CF47 .....**10** D1
Pontmorlais W CF47 ...**10** D2
Pontneathvaughan Rd
SA11 ....**223** E2
Pontnewydd Prim Sch
NP44 ....**89** D3
Pontnewydd Wlk NP44 **89** E4
Pontnewydd Ind Est
NP4 ....**62** A8
Pontnewynydd Prim Sch
NP4 ....**38** A2
Pontnewynydd Small Bsns
Ctr NP4 ....**61** F8
Pontpren
Penderyn CF44 .....**224** D2
Penderyn CF44 .....**224** E2
Pontrhondda Ave
CF40 ....**79** E1

Pontrhondda Prim Sch
CF40 ....**79** F1
Pontrhondda Rd CF40 .**79** F1
Pontrhydyfen Prim Sch
SA12 ....**73** A1
Pontrhydyrun Ho
NP44 ....**90** A7
Pontrhydyrun Rd NP44 **89** F7
Pontrilas Cl CF5 ....**192** F3
Pontsarn Cl CF48 .....**10** D7
Pontsarn Flats CF48 ..**10** D7
Pontshonnorton Rd
CF37 ....**109** C3
Pontsticill Sta CF48 ....**4** A5
Pontybrenin Cty Prim Sch
SA4 ....**43** B1
Pontycapel Rd CF48 ..**10** A4
Pontyclun Prim Sch (Ysgol
Gynradd Pontyclun)
CF72 ....**173** B7
Pontyclun Sta CF72 ..**173** B7
Pontyfelin Ind Est NP4 **63** A3
Pontygof NP23 ....**8** D5
Pontygof Jun & Inf Sch
NP23 ....**7** D1
Pontygwaith Prim Sch
CF40 ....**80** B1
Pontygwindy Ind Est
Caerphilly CF83 ....**137** F6
Caerphilly CF83 ....**138** A6
Pontygwindy Rd
CF83 ....**138** A5
Pontymason Cl NP10 .**141** F7
Pontymason Rd NP10 **141** F7
Pontymason La NP1 .**141** E8
Pontymister Ind Est
NP11 ....**141** A8
Pontymoel Prim Sch
NP4 ....**62** D5
Pontypandy La CF83 .**138** A5
Pontypool & Blaenavon Rly
NP4 ....**16** E8
Pontypool & New Inn Sta
NP4 ....**63** A5
Pontypool Campus
NP4 ....**62** B5
Pontypool North Ind Est
NP4 ....**62** A8
Pontypool Street Mus
NP4 ....**38** A2
Pontypridd & District
Hospl CF37 ....**109** E1
Pontypridd Coll
Rhydyfelin CF37 ...**136** A3
Tonypandy CF40 .....**79** E1
Pontypridd Historical &
Cultural Ctr (Mus)
CF37 ....**109** C1
Pontypridd Rd
Barry CF62 ....**214** C5
Porth CF39 ....**107** F3
Pontypridd St CF63 ..**215** B6
Pontypridd Sta CF37 ..**135** C8
Pool La NP19 ....**143** E7
Poplar Ave
Pontypool NP4 ....**63** B5
Porthcawl CF36 ....**183** A7
Poplar Cl Cardiff CF5 .**176** C1
Swansea SA2 ....**94** B8
Poplar Cres CF36 ...**183** A7
Poplar Ct Barry CF63 .**215** A7
Barry CF63 ....**215** A7
Poplar Ho CF14 .....**176** E6
Poplar Mews
Porthcawl CF36 ....**183** A7
🔟 Troedyrhiw CF48 ..**31** C1
Poplar Pl CF48 ....**10** B7
Poplar Rd
Caerphilly CF83 ....**138** C2
Cardiff CF5 ....**176** C1
Cardiff CF5 ....**193** D8
Croesyceiliog NP44 ..**90** A4
Newport NP19 .....**144** B5
Porthcawl CF36 ....**183** A7
Rhydyfelin CF37 ...**136** A5
Tredegar NP22 ......**13** F5
Poplar St CF48 ....**31** C1
Poplar Terr
Pentrebach CF48 ....**31** A4
Pontypool NP4 ....**62** A8
Poplar Way CF47 .....**10** D5
Poplars SA12 ....98** E1
Poplars Ave SA11 .....**72** A6
Poplars Ct NP18 ....**117** F3
Poplars The
Llanharry CF72 .....**172** C5
🔟 Mountain Ash CF45 .**54** D3
Mountain Ash CF45 ..**54** E3
Risca NP11 ....**114** D3
Poppy Cl SA12 ....**98** C3
Poppy Court (Llys Pabi)
SA11 ....**71** E6
Poppyfield Cl CF3 ...**179** E6
Porcher Ave CF37 ...**109** D5
Porlock Dr CF64 ....**216** B4
Porlock Rd CF3 .....**179** D7
Porset Cl CF83 ......**138** C3
Porset Dr CF83 .....**138** C2
Porset Row CF83 ...**138** D5
Port Madoc Rd CF3 ..**179** E8
Port Mews CF62 ....**204** F1
Port Rd Barry CF62 ..**214** E8
Cardiff CF5 ....**192** F2
East Aberthaw CF62 **212** D3
Newport NP20 .....**143** B1
Rhoose CF62 ....**213** D4
Rhoose CF62 ....**213** F5

Port Rd *continued*
Wenvoe CF5 ....**205** A5
Bridgend CF31 .....**168** E7
Church Village CF38 **136** A4
Llantwit Major CF61 **209** F6
Porthcawl CF36 ....**165** E1
Port Rd E CF62 .....**204** E1
Port Rd W Barry CF62 **214** C4
Barry CF62 ....**214** D7
Port Talbot General Hospl
SA12 ....**128** E8
Port Talbot Ind Est
SA13 ....**125** A8
Port Talbot Pl SA5 ...**67** E5
Port Talbot Workshops
SA12 ....**124** E8
Port Talbot Wrkshps 🔟
SA12 ....**98** E1
Port Tennant Rd SA1 ..**96** A7
Port Terr CF47 ......**102** A3
Portal Ho 🔟 CF47 ...**30** D8
Porters Rd NP23 ....**8** C2
Portfield Cres CF14 .**177** F7
Porth Cty Com Sch
CF39 ....**107** D4
Porth Inf Sch CF39 ..**107** D4
Porth Jun Sch CF39 .**107** D4
Porth Mawr Rd NP44 .**89** E4
Porth Pl CF39 ....**107** F3
Porth St CF39 ......**107** F3
Porth Sta CF39 .....**107** F3
Porth y Waun SA4 ....**66** A6
Porth-y-Castell CF62 **214** B2
Porth-y-Green Cl
CF71 ....**188** C1
Porthamal Gdns
CF14 ....**177** C6
Porthamal Rd CF14 .**177** C6
Porthcawl Comp Sch
CF36 ....**182** E7
Porthcawl Prim Sch
CF36 ....**183** B8
Porthcawl Rd
Cardiff CF5 ....**193** C4
South Cornelly CF33 **165** F6
Porthkerry Ctry Pk
CF62 ....**214** A3
Porthkerry Pl CF14 .**177** D2
Porthkerry Rd
Barry CF62 ....**214** D4
Rhoose CF62 ....**213** D2
Portia Terr SA1 ......**95** C8
Portland Cl CF64 ....**207** B2
Portland Pl
Caerphilly CF12 .....**85** D6
Cardiff CF14 ....**160** D2
Portland St
Abertillery NP13 .....**36** B6
Newport NP20 .....**143** D2
Swansea SA1 ....**95** C7
Portmanmoor Rd
Cardiff CF24 ....**195** E4
Cardiff CF24 ....**195** E5
Portmanmoor Road Ind Est
CF24 ....**195** E5
Portmanmoor Road La
CF24 ....**195** E5
Portmead Ave SA5 ....**67** E7
Portmead Pl SA5 .....**67** E7
Portmead Prim Sch
SA5 ....**67** F5
Portreeve Cl CF72 ..**155** D2
Portskewett St NP19 **143** F3
Portway
Bishopston SA3 ....**121** F7
Bishopston SA3 ....**122** A7
Portway The CF64 ..**182** F6
Post Office La 🔟 CF47 **10** D1
Post Office Row 🔟
CF40 ....**106** E6
Postern 🔟 NP44 .....**89** B1
Potter St NP20 .....**143** D2
Potters Field CF44 ...**28** E4
Potters Gn CF32 ....**150** F4
Pottery Pl SA15 ......**40** D5
Pottery Rd
Cefn Hengoed CF82 ..**84** E5
Newport NP20 .....**143** D2
Pottery St 🔟 SA15 ...**40** D5
Pottery Terr NP20 ..**143** C2
Pound Field
Llantwit Major CF61 **209** F6
Llantwit Major CF61 **210** A6
Pound Hill NP10 ....**162** E5
Pound La CF5 ....**204** F6
Pound Rd NP23 ....**8** C5
Powderham Dr CF11 .**194** C4
Powell Duffryn Way
CF62 ....**214** E3
Powell St
Abertillery NP13 .....**36** B5
Bedlinog CF46 ....**56** A7
Swansea SA1 ....**95** D8
Tir-y-Berth CF82 .....**85** A6
Powell's Pl NP20 ....**143** A4
Powell's Terr NP24 ...**33** E4
Power St NP20 ......**143** B7
Powis Cl NP12 ....**58** D1
Powis View CF63 ....**215** C7
Powys Ave SA1 ....**95** A8
Powys Cl CF64 ......**206** B4
Powys Dr CF64 .....**206** B4
Powys Gdns
Dinas Powys CF64 ..**206** C4
Swansea SA1 ....**94** F8
Powys Ho 🔟 CF23 ..**178** C2
Powys Pl
Dinas Powys CF64 ..**206** C4
Pontypridd CF37 ...**135** D2
Powys Rd
🔟 Penarth CF64 ...**206** F2
Upper Boat CF37 ...**136** D1

Precinct The
Bridgend CF31 .....**168** E7
Precipitation Rd
CF62 ....**211** E1
Prendergast Pl CF5 .**193** D3
Prendergast St SA15 ..**40** E4
Presceli Cl NP11 ....**115** C2
Prescelli Rd SA5 ......**68** A5
Prescelly Rd SA13 ....**75** D3
Prescilla Terr CF44 ...**83** C8
Prescoch La NP4 .....**62** D5
Presswylfa Rd SA15 ..**40** D3
Prestatyn Rd CF3 ...**179** D5
Presteigne Ave CF38 .**135** F2
Presteigne Wlk NP44 .**89** C1
Preston Ave NP20 ...**142** F4
Preston St NP23 ......**13** B6
Preswylfa Ct CF31 ..**168** E2
Preswylfa Row 🔟
SA15 ....**40** D3
Preswylfa St CF5 ...**194** B7
Pretoria Rd
Abertillery NP13 .....**36** C3
Tonyrefail CF39 ...**133** D5
Pretoria St CF32 ...**103** E6
Pretoria Terr NP22 ...**13** F6
Prettyman Dr SA10 ...**70** D3
Price Ave CF62 .....**215** B7
Price Cl Newport NP20 **143** C2
Pontypool NP4 ......**38** C1
Price St
🔟 Aberdare CF44 ...**29** A1
Cefn Coed CF48 .....**10** A4
Pentre CF41 ....**78** F5
Rhymney NP22 ......**12** E5
Price's Pl CF44 ......**28** F2
Price's Row SA13 ...**222** F6
Prichard St CF39 ...**133** C5
Priest Rd CF24 .....**195** D7
Priestley Cl NP20 ..**142** F1
Primitive Pl NP23 .....**7** D4
Primrose Bank SA10 ..**48** B5
Primrose Cl
Bridgend CF31 .....**169** C6
Cardiff CF3 ....**179** B2
Cowbridge CF71 ...**189** A1
Nelson CF46 ....**83** E4
Pant CF48 ....**11** A6
Primrose Ct
Cwmbran NP44 ......**88** F1
Swansea SA5 ....**68** A5
Tonyrefail CF39 ...**133** D6
Primrose Hill
Aberdare CF44 ......**28** E4
Cowbridge CF71 ...**189** B1
Merthyr Tydfil CF47 ..**30** D4
Swansea SA1 ....**95** B7
Primrose La
Pontardawe SA8 .....**23** D5
Pontardawe SA8 .....**24** B2
Primrose Rd SA11 ....**71** D4
Primrose St
Swansea SA1 ....**95** B7
Tonypandy CF40 ...**106** F5
Primrose Terr
Aberdare CF44 ......**53** C8
Porth CF39 ....**107** F4
Porth CF39 ....**108** A3
Primrose Way NP10 .**141** D7
Prince Andrew Rd
NP11 ....**59** E5
Prince Charles Ct
CF64 ....**207** A6
Prince Charles Hospl
CF47 ....**10** C5
Prince Edward Cres
NP23 ....**14** D4
Prince Edward Ho 🔟
CF64 ....**207** A5
Prince Leopold St 🔟
CF24 ....**195** D7
Prince Llewellyn Ho 🔟
CF64 ....**207** A5
Prince Of Wales Dr
SA11 ....**71** E8
Prince of Wales Ind Est
NP11 ....**87** A2
Prince Of Wales Rd 🔟
SA1 ....**95** D8
Prince Philip Hospl The
SA14 ....**41** B7
Prince Rd CF33 .....**148** D3
Prince Rhodry Ho 🔟
CF64 ....**207** A5
Prince St
Blaenavon NP4 ......**17** C6
Margam SA13 .....**125** D5
Nantyglo NP23 ....**8** C1
Newport NP19 .....**143** D6
Pontypool NP4 ......**62** B7
Prince's St
🔟 Treherbert CF42 ..**51** A1
Treorchy CF42 ......**78** E6
Prince's Wlk NP4 .....**63** B4
Princes Ave
Caerphilly CF83 ....**138** C1
Cardiff CF24 ....**195** D7
Princes Ct
🔟 Cardiff CF24 ....**195** B6
Ebbw Vale NP23 .....**7** C1
Princes Rise CF83 ...**138** B1
Princes St Barry CF62 **214** D4
Cardiff CF24 ....**195** D7
Princes Way CF31 ..**169** B3

Princess Cres NP13 ...**59** E6
Princess Ct
Llanelli SA15 ....**40** C5
Tredegar NP22 ......**13** E8
Princess Dr SA10 .....**48** C2
Princess Louise Rd
CF40 ....**106** F8
Princess Margaret Way
The SA12 ....**98** B1
Princess of Wales Ct
SA1 ....**69** C5
Princess of Wales Hospl
CF31 ....**169** A6
Princess St
Abertillery NP13 .....**36** B4
Ferndale CF43 ....**79** B1
Gorseinon SA4 ......**43** B2
Llanelli SA15 ....**40** C5
Maesteg CF34 .....**102** B2
Pontypridd CF37 ...**135** E7
Ton Pentre CF41 .....**79** C3
Princess Way
Bridgend CF31 .....**169** A4
Swansea SA1 ....**95** C6
Prior St SA13 ....**99** B1
Priority Bsns Pk
CF10 ....**195** A3
Priority Ent Pk CF63 .**215** E7
Priority Workshops
CF63 ....**215** E7
Priors Cres SA2 ......**93** B8
Priors Way SA2 ......**93** B8
Priorsgate NP12 .....**59** C2
Priory Ave CF31 ....**168** F1
Priory Cl
Bridgend CF31 .....**168** F1
Caerleon NP18 ....**117** E3
Pontypridd CF37 ...**109** B3
Priory Ct
Abercarn NP11 ....**114** B8
Neath SA10 ....**48** C2
Priory Dr NP18 .....**145** B8
Priory Gdns
Barry CF63 ....**215** B8
Bridgend CF31 .....**168** F2
Priory Oak CF31 ....**169** A4
Priory Rd CF31 .....**168** F2
Priory St NP11 .....**115** A1
Priory Terr CF34 ...**101** F3
Priory Way NP18 ...**145** B8
Pritchard Cl 🔟 CF5 .**176** E2
Pritchard St CF46 ....**83** B8
Pritchard Terr NP24 ..**33** E4
Pritchards Terr NP12 .**85** B4
Probert Pl NP19 ....**143** E5
Proctor Cl CF62 ....**214** C5
Promenade
Barry CF62 ....**214** C1
Barry CF62 ....**214** E1
Swansea SA1 ....**95** B7
Promenade D'orvault The
NP22 ....**13** E6
Promenade Terr SA3 .**123** B4
Promenade The
Abersychan NP4 .....**37** E3
Mumbles SA3 ......**123** B8
Pen-clawdd SA4 ....**64** C4
Swansea SA2 ....**94** E4
Promenade View SA12 **98** C1
Prospect Dr CF5 ....**193** F8
Prospect Pl
Abertysswg NP22 ...**33** B8
Cwmaman CF44 .....**53** A4
Cwmbran NP44 .....**89** E2
Cwmllynfell SA9 ...**221** B7
Llanelli SA15 ....**40** D6
Ogmore Vale CF32 .**103** E3
Pont Rhyd-y-cyff CF34 **128** D6
Pontycymer CF32 ..**103** E3
Pontypool NP4 ......**37** F1
Pontypool NP4 ......**63** A4
Swansea SA2 ....**94** C7
Tredegar NP22 ......**13** F6
Treorchy CF43 ......**78** E6
Tylorstown CF43 ....**80** C4
Ystalyfera SA9 ......**90** A6
Prospect St NP20 ..**143** B7
Prosser La 🔟 NP20 .**142** F4
Prosser St
🔟 Mountain Ash CF45 .**54** E1
🔟 Treharris CF46 ...**83** B8
Protheroe Ave CF31 .**168** C8
Protheroe St
Ferndale CF43 ......**80** A5
Maesteg CF34 ......**75** B2
Provident Cotts CF82 .**85** B2
Pryce St Llanelli SA15 .**40** C6
Mountain Ash CF45 ..**54** D3
Treorchy CF41 ....**79** P2
Pryderi Foopath SA1 ..**95** B8
Prydwen Rd SA5 .....**67** B8
Pugsley Gdns CF32 .**150** F4
Pugsley St NP20 ....**143** C6
Pum Erw Rd CF14 ...**177** D5
Pump House Rd CF62 **211** E1
Pump St 🔟 NP20 ...**143** B5
Punch House Flats
NP22 ....**13** E6
Purbeck St CF5 .....**194** C6
Purcell Ave SA12 .....**98** D3
Purcell Rd Cardiff CF3 **179** D7
Penarth CF64 ....**206** F1
Purcell Sq NP19 ....**144** C5
Purdey Cl CF62 .....**214** C7
Purple Cl SA12 ......**98** B3
Pwll Mawr Ave CF3 .**179** C3
Pwll Melyn CF35 ...**152** C1

Pwll St SA1 ......68 D4
Pwll y Min Cres CF5 .191 E5
Pwll-Evan-Ddu CF35 .169 C8
Pwll-y-Domen Rd SA5 68 D3
Pwll-y-Glaw SA12 ....100 A7
Pwll-y-Waun CF36 ..183 B8
Pwll-yr-Hwyaid SA5 ..67 E6
Pwllcarn Terr SA12 ..103 E8
Pwlldu La SA3 ....121 F4
Pwllfa Rd CF44 ....53 A4
Pwllglas Rd CF37 .....85 C7
Pwllgwaun Rd CF37 .109 B1
Pwllheli Ct CF3 .....179 C4
Pwllhelyg CF15 ......176 D8
Pwllmelin La CF5 ....193 F8
Pwllmelin Rd CF5 ...176 E1
Pwllygath St CF33 ...148 D2
Pye Cnr NP10 ....142 C3
Pyke St CF63 ....215 A5
Pyle Cross CF33 .....148 B1
Pyle Ct SA3 ....122 A5
Pyle Inn Way CF33 ..148 B2
Pyle Sta CF33 ....148 A1
Pyle Rd
  Bishopston SA3 .....122 A6
  Cardiff CF5 ....193 C4
  Porthcawl CF36 .....166 A2
  Pyle CF33 ....148 B2
Pyntws Terr **2** SA15 ..40 F4
Pyra Ct CF62 ....214 C3
Pytchley Cl CF72 ....155 E2

Q

Quadrangle The
  Pyle CF33 ....148 A1
  Sarn CF32 ....150 E4
Quadrant Ctr SA1 ....95 C6
Quadrant The SA2 ....94 E6
Quail Ct CF24 ....195 C7
Quakers View CF46 ..82 F6
Quakers Yard Sta
  CF46 ....82 F6
Quantock Cl NP11 ...115 C1
Quantock Dr NP19 ..144 C6
Quar Rd SA11 ....71 E6
Quarella CF31 ....168 E6
Quarella Cres CF31 .168 E6
Quarella Rd CF31 ...168 E6
Quarella St CF63 ....215 B6
Quarr Dr SA6 ....46 D7
Quarr Rd Clydach SA6 ..46 D7
  Pontardawe SA8 ......23 E5
Quarry Cl CF5 ....193 C8
Quarry Cotts **11** CF45 ..54 D3
Quarry Cres CF5 ....193 C7
Quarry Dale CF72 ...179 B2
Quarry Hill CF37 ....109 A1
Quarry Pl SA18 .....220 D7
Quarry Rd
  10 Mountain Ash CF45 ..54 D3
  Pontypridd CF37 ....109 A1
  Swansea SA5 ....68 D5
  Tonna SA11 ....49 C2
Quarry Row
  Blaina NP13 ....15 F6
  Merthyr Tydfil CF47 ..10 D2
Quarry St
  Nantgarw CF15 .....157 F8
  11 Swansea SA1 ....95 D8
  Tylorstown CF43 .....80 B4
Quay Par SA1 ....95 E7
Quay Rd SA11 ....71 E8
Quay Row CF48 ......30 E5
Quay St
  Ammanford SA18 ...219 C2
  Cardiff CF10 ....195 A6
Quay W SA1 ....95 C5
Quebec Cl NP20 ....142 D3
Queen Anne Sq CF10 .194 F7
Queen Charlotte Dr
  CF15 ....174 F6
Queen Mary's Wlk
  SA15 ....40 E4
Queen Sq **6** NP23 .....8 A4
Queen St
  Aberdare CF44 ....53 C7
  Abertillery NP13 .....36 B4
  Barry CF62 ....214 D4
  Blaenavon NP4 ....17 D6
  Blaengarw CF32 ....103 E4
  Blaina NP13 ....15 E5
  Bridgend CF31 .....168 F4
  Brynmawr NP23 ......8 C5
  Brynmenyn CF32 ...150 E6
  Cardiff CF15 ....158 C1
  Cwmdare CF44 ....28 C3
  Ebbw Vale NP23 .....14 E2
  Glyncorrwg SA13 ..227 C2
  Maesteg CF34 ......102 A3
  Nantyglo NP23 ......15 D8
  Neath SA11 ....71 E7
  Newport NP20 ......143 C3
  Pant CF48 ....11 B6
  Pentre CF41 ....78 F5
  Pontllotyn CF81 .....12 E1
  Pontrhydyfen SA12 ..73 A1
  Pontypool NP4 ....62 B7
  Pontypridd CF37 ...135 E6
  Ton Pentre CF41 .....78 F3
  Treorchy CF41 ....79 A3
Queen St (Heol y
  Frenhines) CF10 ...195 A6
Queen Street Back Rd
  SA11 ....71 E7

Queen Street Prim Sch
  NP13 ....36 C4
Queen Victoria Meml
  Almshouses **11**
  NP20 ....143 B4
Queen Victoria Rd
  SA15 ....40 C4
Queen Victoria St
  NP22 ....13 D6
Queen Wood Cl CF23 178 C3
Queen's Ave
  Gorseinon SA4 ....43 B1
  Porthcawl CF36 ....183 B7
  Sarn CF32 ....150 E4
Queen's Chambers **11**
  NP20 ....143 B5
Queen's Cl NP20 ....143 B6
Queen's Cres NP22 ..12 E5
Queen's Croft NP20 .143 B6
Queen's Hill NP20 ..143 B6
Queen's Hill Cres
  NP20 ....143 B6
Queen's Rd
  Merthyr Tydfil CF47 ..10 E1
  Mumbles SA3 ....123 A5
  Neath SA10 ....70 F7
  New Tredegar NP24 ..34 A2
  Penarth CF64 ....207 B5
Queen's Sq CF11 .....14 D8
Queen's Way NP18,
  NP26 ....145 D1
Queens Arc **8** CF10 ..195 A5
Queens Ct CF31 .....169 C3
Queens Ct The SA12 124 D7
Queens Dr Cardiff CF5 193 C4
  Llantwit Fardre CF38 156 D6
Queens Rd
  Bridgend CF31 .....169 C2
  Bridgend CF31 .....169 C2
  Cymmer SA13 ....75 D3
  Newbridge NP11 .....87 A7
  Swansea SA2 ....94 D6
Queens Rd S CF10 ..207 D8
Queens Villas NP23 ...7 D2
Queens W CF10 .....195 A6
Queens Way CF63 ..215 A5
Queensbury Rd CF23 178 C3
Queensway
  Ebbw Vale NP23 ......7 D5
  Nantgarw CF15 .....158 A7
  Newport NP20 ......143 B5
  Newport NP20 ......143 C5
  Swansea SA5 ....67 D4
Queensway Mdws
  NP19 ....144 D2
Queensway Meadows Ind
  Est NP19 ....144 A2
Queenwood CF23 ...178 E3
Quentin St CF14 ....177 E2
Quilter Cl NP19 ....144 A4

R

Raby St SA15 ....40 C6
Rachebites Hall CF48 .55 D4
Rachel Cl CF5 ......176 D3
Rachel Sq NP10 ....163 E6
Rachel St **3** CF44 ...29 A1
Radcliff Wlk CF71 ..189 C8
Radford Terr NP23 ....7 D4
Radnor Com Jun & Inf Sch
  CF5 ....194 C6
Radnor Dr
  Church Village CF38 135 F2
  Morriston SA6 ....46 B4
Radnor Gn CF62 ....214 F7
Radnor Ho
  6 Penarth CF64 ...206 F2
  Port Talbot SA12 ...124 D8
  8 Swansea SA1 .....95 E6
Radnor Rd
  Boverton CF61 .....210 C6
  Cardiff CF5 ....194 C6
  Newport NP19 .....143 F6
Radnor Way
  Cwmbran NP44 ......89 C3
  Porth CF39 ....133 D8
Radyr Ave SA3 ....93 F2
Radyr Comp Sch
  CF15 ....176 D4
Radyr Court Cl CF5 .176 E3
Radyr Court Rd
  Cardiff CF5 ....176 E3
  Cardiff CF5 ....176 F2
Radyr Court Rise CF5 176 E2
Radyr Court Sh Prec
  CF5 ....176 E2
Radyr Farm Rd CF15 176 C4
Radyr Pl CF14 ......177 C2
Radyr Rd CF14 .....176 F3
Radyr Sta CF15 .....176 C5
Raglan Cl
  Abersychan NP4 .....37 E4
  Blackwood NP12 .....58 D1
  Cardiff CF3 ....180 A7
  Dinas Powys CF64 ..206 C4
Raglan Ct
  Caerphilly CF83 ....137 D4
  Croesyceiliog NP44 ..89 F6
  Newport NP20 ......143 C2
Raglan Gr CF48 .....225 F1
Raglan Ho **4** CF10 .194 F5
Raglan Mews NP10 .163 E5
Raglan Rd
  Hengoed CF82 ....85 A3
  Swansea SA2 ....94 C7
Raglan St NP11 .....114 E3

Raglan Terr NP23 .....7 D3
Raglande Ct CF61 ..210 A5
Railmill La SA12 .....99 F5
Railway Cotts SA6 ...45 F3
Railway Cres
  8 Cardiff CF24 ....195 D5
  Cymmer SA13 ....75 B5
Railway Heritage Mus
  CF62 ....214 F2
Railway Hos
  East Aberthaw CF62 212 C1
  Tredegar NP22 ....34 B8
Railway Pl SA15 .....40 C4
Railway Row CF32 ..129 C2
Railway St
  Aberdare CF44 ....28 F3
  Abertillery NP13 .....60 B6
  Cardiff CF14 ....177 E1
  Cardiff CF24 ....195 B6
  Newport NP20 ......143 B5
  Risca NP11 ....114 F2
  Trelewis CF46 ....83 C7
Railway Terr
  Abercarn NP11 ....87 A3
  Abertillery NP13 .....59 F8
  Bargoed CF81 ....58 A2
  Blaenavon NP4 ....17 B6
  Blaengarw CF32 ...103 D7
  Blaina NP13 ....15 D5
  Briton Ferry SA11 ...71 C1
  Bryncethin CF32 ...151 E6
  Caerphilly CF83 ....138 E2
  Cardiff CF11 ....194 D5
  Cardiff CF15 ....158 C1
  Cwm NP23 ....35 B7
  Cwmllynfell SA9 ...221 B7
  Cymmer SA13 ....75 D5
  Dinas Powys CF64 ..206 C4
  Fochriw CF81 ....32 C8
  Gorseinon SA4 ....43 C1
  Hirwaun CF44 ......224 E1
  Hollybush NP12 ......34 D3
  Llanelli SA15 ....40 C4
  Maesteg CF34 ....75 B1
  Merthyr Tydfil CF47 ..30 E7
  Mountain Ash CF45 ..82 A8
  New Tredegar NP24 ..33 D3
  Ogmore Vale CF32 ..104 E1
  Penarth CF64 ....207 A4
  Pontrhydyfen SA12 ..73 D5
  Pontycymer CF32 ..103 E4
  Pontypool NP4 ....62 E1
  Porth CF39 ....107 E6
  Resolven SA11 .....226 D5
  South Cornelly CF33 166 A5
  Swansea SA5 ....67 E3
  Ton Pentre CF41 .....79 B3
  Tonypandy CF40 ...106 C6
  Tonypandy CF40 ...106 F4
  Tredegar NP22 ....6 A4
  Treharris CF46 ....83 C7
  Treorchy CF41 ....78 B4
  Ystradgynlais SA9 ..222 A4
Railway View
  Ebbw Vale NP23 .....14 D6
  Ebbw Vale NP23 ......7 D5
  Fleur De Lis NP12 ...85 B4
  Tonypandy CF40 ...107 A2
  Tonypandy CF40 .....79 F1
  Tredegar NP22 ....13 E8
Rainbow Bsns Ctr SA7 62 F6
Raisdale Gdns CF64 207 B2
Raisdale Rd CF64 ..207 A2
Raldan Cl CF63 .....215 B8
Raleigh Cl SA2 ......94 C6
Raleigh Wlk **2** CF10 195 B4
  Pontypridd CF37 ...109 D2
Ralph St Llanelli SA15 40 D5
Ralph Terr SA15 ....40 C4
Ramah St SA12 ......78 C7
Rambler Cl CF14 ...159 F3
Ramping Rd NP11 ..114 C8
Ramsay Rd SA6 .....22 C1
Ramsden Cl SA12 ...98 F1
Ramsden St NP22 ..12 F3
Ramsey Cl CF36 ....165 D1
Ramsey Dr SA6 .....45 D1
Ramsey Pl SA5 ......67 E7
Ramsey Rd CF62 ...214 F8
Ramsey Wlk
  Cwmbran NP44 ......89 C5
  Newport NP19 .....143 F7
Ramson Cl CF82 .....84 E6
Ramsons Way CF5 ..193 A5
Rankine Cl NP20 ...116 F2
Rannoch Dr CF23 ..178 C5
Rannoch Ho **1** NP44 .89 C2
Raphael Ave CF31 ..169 D6
Raphael Cl NP19 ...144 A7
Raphael Ho **3** SA12 ..98 D1
Rassau Ind Est NP23 ..7 A6
Rassau Jun & Inf Sch
  NP23 ....7 B4
Rassau Rd **7** NP23 ...7 B4
Rathbone Terr CF34 ..75 A2
Raven Cl CF31 ......169 B3
Raven Way CF64 ...217 A4
Ravenhill Rd SA5 ....67 F4
Ravenhill St CF41 ...79 B2
Ravens Court Cl CF23 178 E2
Ravens Ct SA11 .....72 B5
Ravens Wlk SA3 ....122 F6
Ravensbrook CF15 ..176 B8
Ravenscourt
  1 Cardiff CF24 ....195 B7
  Cwmbran NP44 ......89 B3
Ravensfield SA4 ......66 D3

Ravenshoe CF63 ....215 D7
Ravenswood Cl SA10 ..48 E2
Ravenswood Ct CF11 194 E5
Rawden Mews CF11 .194 E5
Rawden PI CF11 ....194 E5
Rawlinson Terr NP22 .13 F5
Raymond Terr CF37 ..13 F6
Readers La CF62 ....213 A4
Readers Way
  Rhoose CF62 ....212 F2
  Rhoose CF62 ....213 A2
Recorder St **7** SA1 ..95 C6
Rectory Cl
  Caerphilly CF83 ....138 A1
  Dowlais CF48 ....11 B5
  Loughor SA4 ....42 F1
  Sarn CF32 ....150 E4
  Wenvoe CF5 ....205 A6
Rectory Ct CF61 ....210 B8
Rectory Dr CF62 ...211 D5
Rectory Gdns CF83 .140 A7
Rectory Rd
  8 Barry CF63 .....215 B6
  Bedwas CF83 ....138 E7
  Caerphilly CF83 ....138 A2
  Cardiff CF5 ....194 C6
  Gelligaer CF82 ......84 C7
  Neath SA11 ....71 E7
  Newbridge NP11 .....60 C2
  Penarth CF64 ......207 B4
  St Athan CF62 .....211 D5
Rectory Road La
  CF64 ....207 B4
Red Brink St CF5 ...193 C6
Red House Cl CF5 .193 D6
Red House Pl CF5 .193 D6
Red House Rd CF5 .193 D6
Red Lion Cotts CF5 .191 B1
Redberth Cl CF62 ..214 F7
Redbrink Cres CF62 215 A2
Redbrook Ave CF83 139 A6
Redbrook Ct CF83 ..138 A5
Redbrook Ho NP44 ..89 F3
Redbrook Rd NP20 .142 E4
Redbrook Way NP44 ..89 F3
Redcliffe Ave CF5 ..194 A6
Rede Rd NP44 ....89 B1
Redfield St CF11 .....79 D2
Redgate Terr CF72 ..174 C7
Redhill Cl NP44 ......27 C8
Redland St NP20 ...143 D7
Redlands Ave CF64 .206 E4
Redlands Cl CF35 ..170 D7
Redlands Rd CF64 .206 E4
Redlands The NP19 .144 C4
Redlaver St CF11 ...194 F3
Redrose Hill CF41 ...79 B3
Redshank Cl CF36 ..182 D8
Redvers St NP19 ...143 F4
Redway Rd CF5 ....190 F1
Redwell Ct **8** CF23 ..178 C2
Redwick Ho NP44 ...89 F2
Redwood Cl
  Boverton CF61 .....210 C5
  Bryn-côch SA10 .....48 C5
  Caerleon NP18 .....117 C2
  2 Cardiff CF3 .....179 E2
Redwood Ct
  Cardiff CF14 ....177 F8
  Swansea SA5 ....68 A5
Redwood Dr
  Cwmdare CF44 ......28 D3
  Llantwit Fardre CF38 156 C4
Redwood Meml Hospl
  NP22 ....12 E4
Redwood Pl NP23 ...14 D6
Redwood Rd SA3 ...122 F7
Reece's Terr NP11 ..114 D8
Reene Ct NP19 .....144 A3
Rees Cl CF61 ....210 B6
Rees PI Neath SA11 ..71 E7
  Pentre CF41 ....78 F5
Rees Rd NP44 ....89 E3
Rees Row CF32 ....104 E1
Rees St Aberavon SA12 98 F1
  Dowlais CF48 ....11 B5
  Ebbw Vale NP23 .....14 D8
  Merthyr Tydfil CF47 ..30 E8
  Ton Pentre CF41 .....79 B2
  Tonypandy CF40 ...107 A1
  Treorchy CF42 ....78 E6
Rees Terr
  Llanbradach CF83 ..111 F1
  Pontypridd CF37 ...135 E6
Reevesland Ind Est
  NP19 ....144 A4
Reform St CF11 ......32 F8
Regalia Terr SA15 ...40 C6
Regency Cl CF61 ...210 A7
Regency Ho **6** SA1 ..95 C7
Regent Ave CF5 ....193 A2
Regent St
  Aberdare CF44 ....53 C7
  Abertillery NP13 .....60 C6
  Barry CF62 ....214 F5
  Dowlais CF48 ....11 A5
  Ferndale CF43 ....79 D6
  Treorchy CF42 ....78 E6
Regent St E SA11 ....71 C1
Regent St W SA11 ...71 B1
Regina Terr CF5 ....194 B7
Reginald St
  Port Talbot SA13 ....99 C1
  Swansea SA1 ....96 A1
Reginald Terr NP10 .142 B4

Reigate Cl CF14 ....159 E3
Reigit La SA3 ....122 C6
Relf Rd CF3 ....179 C4
Rembrandt Ho **2**
  SA12 ....98 E1
Rembrandt PI **1** SA12 .98 E1
Rembrandt Way
  NP19 ....143 F7
Rennie St CF11 .....194 E5
Renoir Ho **10** SA12 ...98 D1
Renoir Rd NP19 ....144 A7
Reservoir Cl NP20 ..142 B4
Reservoir Rd NP23 ...7 C5
Rest Bay Cl CF36 ..182 D8
Restway Ct CF5 ....176 E3
Restway Gdns CF31 .168 E5
Restways CF36 .....182 E7
Restways Cl CF5 ...176 D2
Retford Ct CF14 ...177 C4
Retreat The
  Bridgend CF31 .....168 E2
  Cardiff CF23 ....178 D2
  Porthcawl CF36 ....165 E2
  Sarn CF32 ....150 E4
Reynallt PI CF36 ...182 F7
Reynolds Cl
  Newport NP19 .....143 F7
  North Cornelly CF33 165 E8
Rhanallt St **3** SA13 .125 C5
Rhandir CF14 ....41 E4
Rhandir Terr SA14 ...18 B1
Rheidol Ave SA6 .....68 C8
Rheidol Cl
  Aberdare CF44 ......29 C1
  Cardiff CF14 ....178 A8
  Treherbert CF42 .....78 B8
Rheidol Ct SA6 ......68 C8
Rheidol Dr CF62 ...214 C5
Rheola Ave SA11 ...226 D5
Rheola Ind Est CF39 .107 E4
Rheola St CF45 ......82 A7
Rheolau Terr CF37 .108 C2
Rhes Gwaith Tyn SA15 .40 F2
Rhestr Fawr SA9 ......1 F2
Rhianfa Gdns SA1 ..95 A7
Rhianfa La SA1 .....95 A7
Rhiannon Cl CF14 ..159 D2
Rhigos Gdns CF24 .177 F1
Rhigos Prim Sch CF44 26 C8
Rhigos Rd
  Blaenrhondda CF42 ..50 E5
  Hirwaun CF44 ......224 B1
  Hirwaun CF44 ....27 A8
  Hirwaun CF44 ....27 C8
Rhiw Cae Mawr CF31 169 E5
Rhiw Ceris CF44 .....53 E8
Rhiw Ctr The **5** CF31 168 F4
Rhiw Fach CF83 ....137 E5
Rhiw Farm Cres NP11 .59 F2
Rhiw Felin CF37 ....136 A6
Rhiw Las CF31 .....169 C5
Rhiw Llech View SA13 .75 E3
Rhiw Melin NP44 ....89 B6
Rhiw Park Rd NP13 ..36 B5
Rhiw Park Terr NP13 ..36 B5
Rhiw Rd SA9 ....221 C5
Rhiw Syr Dafydd Hill
  NP12 ....59 A2
Rhiw Syr Dafydd Jun Sch
  NP12 ....59 B2
Rhiw The
  Bridgend CF31 .....168 F4
  Graig Penllyn CF71 .188 B8
Rhiw Tremaen CF31 .169 B5
Rhiw Wen NP23 ......7 C2
Rhiw'r Ddar CF15 ..158 A5
Rhiwamoth St CF81 ..58 B5
Rhiwbina Hill CF14,
  CF83 ....158 E3
Rhiwbina Jun & Inf Schs
  CF14 ....177 E5
Rhiwbina Sta CF14 .177 E5
Rhiwddar Ho CF15 .158 A4
Rhiwderyn SA7 ......70 B8
Rhiwderyn Cl CF5 ..192 F3
Rhiwfawr Rd SA9 .....1 A1
Rhiwfer CF44 ....83 D3
Rhiwgarn Porth CF39 .107 D1
  Porth CF39 ....133 D8
Rhiwgarn Inf Sch
  CF39 ....133 D8
Rhiwglyn Rd
  Ogmore Vale CF32 ..104 C1
  Ogmore Vale CF32 ..130 F7
Rhiwlas Cardiff CF14 .159 C3
  Dunvant SA2 ....93 E8
  Neath SA10 ....48 B2
Rhiwsaeson Rd CF72 .156 A2
Rhodes Ave CF14 ....98 F1
Rhodfa Bryn Rhos
  SA18 ....220 A8
Rhodfa Bryn-Mawr
  SA18 ....219 B7
Rhodfa Fadog
  Cwmrhydyceirw SA6 ..46 A4
  Swansea SA6 ....45 F4
Rhodfa Felin CF24 ..214 C4
Rhodfa Frank SA18 .219 B7
Rhodfa Ganol CF81 ..32 D7
Rhodfa Glascoed
  NP12 ....85 D6
Rhodfa Llwyneithin
  SA15 ....40 D7
Rhodfa Newydd CF44 .53 E8
Rhodfa Sweldon
  CF62 ....214 C4
Rhodfa Terr CF48 ...31 C2
Rhodfa'r CF48 ....11 A7

Rhodfa'r Brain SA5 ..67 E5
Rhodfa'r Coed CF34 .128 C8
Rhodfa'r Dryw
  Cwmrhydyceirw SA6 ..46 A5
  Swansea SA6 ....45 F5
Rhodfa'r Eos
  Cwmrhydyceirw SA6 ..46 A5
  Swansea SA6 ....45 F5
Rhodfa'r Wennol SA6 ..46 A5
Rhododendron Cl
  CF23 ....178 D7
Rhodri PI **5** NP44 ....90 B2
Rhondda CF NP23 .....7 B4
Rhondda Fechan Farm
  CF43 ....79 F7
Rhondda Heritage Ctr
  CF37 ....108 C3
Rhondda Rd
  Ferndale CF43 ....79 F7
  Pontypridd CF37 ...109 B1
Rhondda Specl Sch
  CF40 ....107 C4
Rhondda St SA1 .....95 B7
Rhondda Terr
  Ferndale CF43 ....79 F6
  Tonypandy CF40 ...106 F8
Rhonos Rd NP7 ......9 D7
Rhoose Rd CF62 ...213 B2
Rhos Ave CF82 ......84 E8
Rhos Cotts SA10 .....2 F3
Rhos Dyfed CF44 ....53 B7
Rhos Helyg
  Caerphilly CF83 ....138 C4
  Cwmfelin CF34 ....128 C8
Rhos Llan CF14 ....177 C6
Rhos Nathan Wyn
  CF44 ....53 B8
Rhos Prim Sch SA8 ..24 B3
Rhos Rd SA5 ....67 F4
Rhos St CF83 ....138 A5
Rhos y Dderwen NP12 85 D6
Rhos-y-Bettws CF82 ..84 D7
Rhoshyfryd CF44 ...224 D3
Rhosili Rd CF82 ......84 F5
Rhoslan NP22 ....6 F1
Rhossilli Ct CF44 ....27 D7
Rhossilli Ave CF3 ...179 C4
Rhossilly Rd CF3 ...179 C4
Rhosyn Gwyn NP24 ..33 F2
Rhuddlan Cl NP10 ..141 E3
Rhuddlan Ct CF83 ..137 D4
Rhuddlan Way CF64 .206 C4
Rhws Prim Sch CF62 .213 A1
Rhych Ave CF36 ...183 B6
Rhyd Clydach NP23 ...8 B5
Rhyd Terr NP22 ......14 A4
Rhyd The NP22 ......14 A4
Rhyd y Fenni SA4 ....64 B3
Rhyd y Gwern Isaf
  CF83 ....140 A7
Rhyd y Nant CF72 ..173 B7
Rhyd y Polan SA4 ...43 B1
Rhyd-Hir SA10 ....48 A1
Rhyd-y-Cae NP23 .....7 B4
Rhyd-y-Coed SA7 ...70 A8
Rhyd-y-Defaid Dr SA2 94 B5
Rhyd-y-Felin CF37 ...69 F5
Rhyd-y-fro Prim Sch
  SA8 ....23 B8
Rhyd-y-Glyn SA7 ....69 F6
Rhyd-y-Gwern Cl
  CF83 ....138 E5
Rhyd-y-Nant CF35 ..152 C1
Rhyd-y-Pandy Rd SA6 45 E7
Rhyd-y-Penau Cl
  Cardiff CF14 ....178 A6
  Cardiff CF14 ....178 A7
Rhyd-y-Penau Jun & Inf
  Sch CF14 ....178 A7
Rhyd-y-Penau Rd
  CF23 ....178 B7
Rhyd-y-Pennau SA10 ..48 C2
Rhyd-Yr-Helyg
  Swansea SA2 ....94 C5
  Upper Boat CF15 ...157 F8
Rhyddings Park Rd
  SA2 ....94 F6
Rhyddings Terr SA2 ..94 F6
Rhydwen PI SA6 .....22 B1
Rhyddwen Rd
  Craig-Cefn-Parc SA6 ..22 B1
  Swansea SA6 ....21 F1
Rhydfach CF48 ......31 B3
Rhydhelig Ave CF14 .177 E4
Rhydri Prim Sch
  CF83 ....139 C3
Rhydwen SA9 ....2 E6
Rhydynos St NP4 ...17 C6
Rhydyrafon SA15 ....40 F7
Rhygoes St CF24 ...177 F1
Rhyl Rd CF3 ....179 C4
Rhymney CI Bryn NP12 58 D8
  Ebbw Vale NP23 ......7 C4
Rhymney Comp Sch
  NP22 ....33 A8
Rhymney Ct
  Cardiff CF24 ....195 B8
  Cwmbran NP44 ......89 A5
Rhymney River Bridge Rd
  CF23 ....179 A1
Rhymney Row NP22 ...6 B7
Rhymney St
  Cardiff CF24 ....195 B8
  Cardiff CF24 ....195 B8
Rhymney Sta NP22 ..12 E3

Rhymney Terr
Caerphilly CF83 ......**138** A2
Cardiff CF24 ....**195** A8
Rhys Rd NP12 ....**85** C6
Rhys St
Tonypandy CF40 ......**106** F5
Tonypandy CF40 ......**106** F6
Tylorstown CF43 ......**107** C8
Rhyswg Rd NP11 .....**87** B2
Rialto Ct CF14 ......**177** B5
Ribble Sq NP20 .....**116** E2
Ribble Wlk NP20 ....**116** E2
Rice St Bridgend CF31 .**168** E4
Llanelli SA15 ....**40** E4
Port Talbot SA13 ......**125** C7
Rice Street SA18 ....**219** C6
Richard Burton Ho ❶
SA12 ....**98** B2
Richard Lewis Cl CF5 **176** E2
Richard St
Abercwmboi CF44 .....**53** E4
Barry CF62 ....**214** F5
❿ Llanelli SA15 ....**40** D5
Maerdy CF43 ....**79** B8
Pontycymer CF32 .....**103** F3
Pontypridd CF37 ......**109** F5
Swansea SA5 ....**68** C2
Richard's Pl ❸ SA1 ...**95** D7
Richard's Terr CF44 ..**53** F7
Richards Pl CF24 ....**195** D7
Richards Row CF44 ...**53** F7
Richards St CF24 ....**195** A8
Richards Terr
Cardiff CF24 ....**195** D7
Tonypandy CF40 ......**106** E6
Trelewis CF46 ....**83** C7
Richardson Rd SA1 ...**95** B6
Richardson St
Pontardawe SA8 ......**23** C3
Swansea SA1 ....**95** B6
Richley Cl SA12 ......**98** C5
Richmond Cl
Cwmbran NP44 ....**89** E5
❽ Llanbradach CF83 .**111** F1
Richmond Cres CF24 .**195** B7
Richmond Ct
❻ Cardiff CF24 .....**195** B7
Swansea SA1 ....**95** A7
Richmond Dr CF44 ...**224** E1
Richmond Mews ❶
SA1 ....**95** A6
Richmond Pk
Loughor SA4 ....**42** F1
Ystradgynlais SA9 ....**222** A5
Richmond Pl
Cwmbran NP44 ....**89** E5
Port Talbot SA13 .....**125** D6
Richmond Rd
Abertillery NP13 ......**36** C3
Cardiff CF24 ....**195** B4
Cwmbran NP44 ....**89** E5
Loughor SA4 ....**42** F1
Mountain Ash CF45 ....**54** D4
Newport NP19 ....**143** E6
Pontypool NP4 ....**62** E1
Swansea SA2 ....**95** A7
Richmond St
❶ Cwmbran NP44 ....**89** E5
Neath SA11 ....**71** E7
Richmond Terr
Aberdare CF44 ....**29** B3
Llanelli SA15 ....**40** C4
Swansea SA2 ....**94** F7
Tredegar NP22 ....**13** C1
Richmond Villas SA1 .**95** A7
Richmond Way SA5 ...**67** C4
Richs Rd CF14 ....**177** D4
Rickards St
Pontypridd CF37 .....**135** C8
Porth CF39 ....**107** F5
Rickards Terr CF37 ..**135** C8
Rickyard The SA10 ...**48** D3
Ridge Acre SA2 ......**94** C4
Ridge The SA2 ....**94** C4
Ridgeway Cardiff CF14 **159** F3
Killay SA2 ....**93** D6
Machen CF83 ....**139** B6
Newport NP20 ....**142** E4
Pontypool NP4 ....**38** D1
Ridgeway Ave NP20 ..**142** E5
Ridgeway Cl
Newport NP20 ....**142** F5
Pontypridd CF37 .....**135** A1
Ridgeway Cres NP20 .**142** E4
Ridgeway Ct NP20 ...**142** E5
Ridgeway Dr NP20 ...**142** F4
Ridgeway Gr NP20 ...**142** E4
Ridgeway Hill NP20 ..**142** F5
Ridgeway Park Rd
NP20 ....**142** E5
Ridgeway Pl CF38 ....**136** A1
Ridgeway Rd
Barry CF62 ....**214** D8
Cardiff CF3 ....**179** A4
Ridgewood Gdns SA11 **72** C5
Ridgewood Pk SA15 ..**41** A5
Ridings The
Aberdare CF44 ....**28** D2
Church Village CF38 ..**136** A1
Ridley Way SA3 .....**122** A6
Rifle Gn ❷ NP4 ......**17** C7
Rifle St NP4 ....**17** C7
Rifleman St ❹ CF14 .**114** F3
Rifleman's Row SA1 ..**68** C7
Rimini Ho CF10 ......**195** C3

Rinastone Ct CF5 ....**193** F8
Ringland Circ NP19 ..**144** E5
Ringland Ctr NP19 ...**144** F6
Ringland Inf Sch
NP19 ....**144** E5
Ringland Jun Sch
NP19 ....**144** E5
Ringland Way NP18,
NP19 ....**145** A6
Ringside Bsns Ctr
CF3 ....**179** D2
Ringwood Ave NP19 ..**144** D6
Ringwood Cres CF62 .**211** D8
Ringwood Hill NP19 ..**144** C5
Ringwood Pl NP19 ...**144** D5
Rink The CF47 ....**10** E2
Risca Cl CF3 ....**179** F7
Risca Com Comp Sch
NP11 ....**115** D1
Risca Prim Sch NP11 .**114** F1
Risca Rd
Abercarn NP11 ....**114** C4
Newport NP20 ....**142** E4
Newport NP20 ....**143** A4
Rogerstone NP10 .....**141** E7
Rise The Barry CF62 .**214** F6
Cardiff CF14 ....**160** A1
Church Village CF38 ..**135** F2
Cwmbran NP44 ....**89** C5
Cwmdare CF44 ....**28** C3
Nantyglo NP23 ....**15** D7
Pant CF48 ....**11** B7
Pengam NP12 ....**85** B7
Porth CF39 ....**107** E5
Ton Pentre CF41 ......**79** B2
Upper Boat CF37 .....**136** C3
Rising Sun Cl NP12 ..**59** A2
Rising Sun Ind Est
NP13 ....**15** D6
Ritson St SA11 ....**71** C1
River Bank Specl Sch
CF5 ....**193** E5
River Dale CF5 ......**193** D6
River Glade CF15 ....**158** A3
River Rd Cwm NP23 ...**35** A7
Pontlottyn CF81 ......**12** F1
River Row
Abercanaid CF48 ......**30** F4
Abercynon CF45 ......**82** E3
Blaina NP13 ....**15** E4
Pontypool NP4 ....**38** A1
River St Maesteg CF32 **102** B3
Ogmore Vale CF32 ....**104** E1
Pontypridd CF37 ......**135** E7
Ystrad CF41 ....**79** D3
River Terr
Glan y Nant NP12 .....**85** A7
Hendy SA4 ....**19** A4
❼ Porth CF39 ......**107** F3
Treorchy CF42 ....**78** C6
River View
Cardiff CF14 ....**177** A2
Cardiff CF14 ....**177** C1
Tonypandy CF40 ......**106** E4
River View Ct CF5 ...**176** F2
River Wlk
Cowbridge CF71 ......**188** E1
❽ Merthyr Tydfil CF47 **10** D1
River's Edge CF72 ...**173** A4
Rivermead Way
NP10 ....**141** D7
Riversdale CF5 ......**176** F2
Riversdale Rd SA3 ...**122** F6
Riverside
Aberkenfig CF32 .....**150** D3
Blaina NP13 ....**15** E5
Ebbw Vale NP23 ....**7** C4
Hirwaun CF44 ....**27** F7
Llanmorlais SA4 ....**64** B2
Newport NP19 ....**143** C6
Pontypool NP4 ....**62** C7
Tonna SA10 ....**49** C3
Riverside Cl CF48 ....**55** C5
Riverside Cotts CF32 .**150** C7
Riverside Ct
Blackwood NP12 ......**85** F7
Pontypool NP4 ....**62** C7
Senghenydd CF83 ....**110** F2
Riverside Dr
Blaenavon NP4 ....**17** C5
Neath SA11 ....**71** E4
Riverside Flats CF32 .**130** E8
Riverside Gdns
Abercraf SA9 ....**222** E8
Glynneath SA11 .....**223** D1
Riverside Ho SA12 ...**99** E4
Riverside Ind Est
CF37 ....**136** D1
Riverside Pk
Bedwas CF83 ....**138** C7
Merthyr Tydfil CF47 ...**10** C2
Riverside Pl CF63 ...**215** D6
Riverside St CF15 ...**157** F5
Riverside Terr
Cardiff CF5 ....**193** F6
Machen CF83 ....**139** F6
Riverside View SA11 .**226** C5
Riversmead NP44 .....**90** A2
Riverview SA4 ....**19** A5
Road No 1 SA12 ......**98** B4
Road No 2 SA12 ......**98** C5
Road No 3 SA12 ......**98** B6
Roath Court Pl CF24 .**195** D8
Roath Court Rd CF24 .**195** D8
Roath Ct NP44 ....**90** A3
Roath Dock Rd CF10 .**195** E3

Roath Park Jun & Inf Sch
CF24 ....**178** B1
Robbin's La ❿ NP20 .**143** C4
Robert Cl NP20 ......**143** C2
Robert Davies Ct SA4 .**19** C4
Robert Owen Gdns
SA1 ....**96** B8
Robert St Barry CF63 .**215** B5
Cardiff CF24 ....**178** A1
Cardiff CF5 ....**193** F6
Glynneath SA11 .....**223** C1
Llanharan CF72 ......**153** F2
Pentre CF41 ....**78** F4
Swansea SA5 ....**68** C3
Ynysybwl CF37 ....**109** A8
Robert's Row NP13 ...**16** B1
Roberts Ave CF47 ....**10** F5
Roberts Cl
Glynneath SA11 .....**223** C1
Rogerstone NP10 .....**142** A7
St Athan CF62 ....**211** D5
Roberts La ❷ CF47 ...**10** D1
Roberts Road (Heol
Roberts) SA1 ....**95** F5
Roberts Terr NP22 ...**13** F6
Roberts Villas CF14 ..**176** F4
Robertson Ho ❿ SA12 **98** B3
Robertson Way NP20 .**117** A4
Robin Cl CF23 ....**178** D7
Robin Hill CF64 .....**206** B2
Robin Hood La NP18 .**119** E2
Robin Rd SA5 ....**67** E7
Robins Hill CF31 ....**169** C4
Robins La Barry CF63 .**215** B7
Reynoldston SA3 .....**229** C1
Robinson St SA15 ....**40** D5
Robinswood Cl CF64 .**207** A2
Robinswood Cres
CF64 ....**207** A2
Roch St SA15 ....**36** C6
Rochdale Terr ❺ NP4 .**38** C4
Roche Cres CF5 .....**176** C1
Rochester Mans ❹
CF14 ....**176** F6
Rochester Rd NP19 ..**143** F5
Rock SA12 ....**100** A7
Rock Chwyth Rd SA8 ..**23** F3
Rock Cotts
Pen-y-fai CF31 ......**150** C1
Pontypridd CF37 .....**109** A2
Rock Dr CF41 ....**79** A2
Rock Hos CF46 ....**83** A5
Rock La Cefn Coed CF48 .**10** A4
Horton SA3 ....**231** B4
Rock St
Aberkenfig CF32 .....**150** C4
Glynneath SA11 .....**223** C1
Mountain Ash CF45 ....**54** D2
Rock Terr SA6 ....**45** F1
Rock View CF46 ......**82** F6
Rock Villa Cl NP4 .....**37** E7
Rock Villas NP12 .....**59** A3
Rockfield Ho NP4 .....**62** B8
Rockfield St NP19 ...**143** D7
Rockfield Terr SA11 ..**71** D5
Rockfields CF36 .....**165** E1
Rockfields Cl CF36 ..**165** F1
Rockfields Cres CF36 .**165** F1
Rockhill SA3 ....**123** B4
Rockhill Rd NP4 ......**62** D5
Rockingham Terr
SA11 ....**71** C2
Rockland Terr SA1 ...**68** C1
Rockleigh Ave CF81 ..**58** B5
Rockrose Way CF64 ..**206** E5
Rockwood Rd CF15 ..**158** B4
Rocky Rd CF47 ....**10** F5
Roden Ct ❽ CF24 ...**195** C7
Roderick Hill Ct NP22 ..**6** C2
Roderick Pl NP23 .....**14** D6
Rodericks Terr CF46 ..**83** B6
Roding Cl NP20 .....**116** D1
Rodney Par NP19 ....**143** C5
Rodney Rd NP19 ....**143** C5
Rodney St SA1 ......**95** B5
Roehampton Ct CF3 .**179** A3
Rofton Bglws SA12 ...**99** E6
Rogart Terr CF37 ....**109** D4
Roger Beck Way SA2 ..**94** E6
Roger Cl SA3 ....**124** D6
Roger's La CF32 .....**167** E4
Roger's St SA5 ....**68** B7
Rogersmoor Cl NP4 .**207** A4
Roland Ave SA15 .....**40** C7
Roland St CF10 .....**195** B4
Rolls Ave CF82 ....**84** E7
Rolls Cl NP44 ....**89** A2
Rolls St CF11 ....**194** D5
Rolls Wlk NP10 .....**142** A6
Roman Baths Mus
NP18 ....**118** C2
Roman Bridge Cl SA3 .**94** B2
Roman Cl CF5 ....**193** D3
Roman Ct SA3 ....**94** B2
Roman Gates NP18 ..**118** C2
Roman Legionary Mus
NP18 ....**118** B2
Roman Rd SA10 .....**223** A4
Roman Reach NP18 ..**117** F2
Roman Ridge CF82 ...**84** B7
Roman Way
Caerleon NP18 ....**117** F3
Caerleon NP18 ....**118** A3
Neath SA11 ....**71** D8
Romilly Ave CF62 ...**214** C3

Romilly Bldgs
Barry CF62 ....**214** D3
Barry CF63 ....**215** B4
Romilly Cres CF11 ..**194** D6
Romilly Ct CF62 ....**214** D4
Romilly Inf & Nursery Sch
CF62 ....**214** D4
Romilly Jun Sch
CF62 ....**214** C2
Romilly Pl ❸ CF5 ...**194** C6
Romilly Park Rd
CF62 ....**214** C2
Romilly Rd
Barry CF62 ....**214** D3
Cardiff CF5 ....**194** C6
Rhoose CF62 ....**213** A1
Romilly Rd W CF5 ...**194** B7
Romney Cl NP19 ....**144** B7
Romney Ho SA12 ....**124** D8
Romney Rd SA12 ....**124** D8
Romney Wlk ❺ CF64 .**206** F5
Romsley Ct ❾ NP44 ..**89** C2
Ronald Rd NP19 ....**143** E6
Ronald St CF47 ......**10** D5
Rook Cl CF62 ....**210** D5
Rookery Cl CF64 ....**216** A5
Rookery Wood CF64 .**216** A5
Rookwood Ave CF5 ..**176** F1
Rookwood Cl
Cardiff CF5 ....**176** F1
Merthyr Tydfil CF47 ...**10** D3
Neath SA11 ....**71** F7
Rookwood Hospl
CF5 ....**177** A1
Rookwood St CF11 ..**194** E3
Roper Cl CF5 ....**176** C1
Roperwright Cl SA4 ..**66** B5
Ropewalk Rd SA15 ...**40** F2
Ropewalk The SA11 ..**71** E7
Rosamund Cl NP10 ..**163** F5
Rose Cotts
Abersychan NP4 ......**37** F8
Llangeinor CF32 .....**130** B4
Llanrhidian SA4 .....**229** F5
❺ Pontypridd CF37 ..**109** B1
Rose Ct Cwmbran NP44 .**88** F2
Newbridge NP11 ......**87** B8
Rose Farm Bglws NP22 ..**6** B1
Rose Gdns NP44 .....**90** B4
Rose Heyworth Bsns Pk
NP13 ....**35** E8
Rose Heyworth Rd
NP13 ....**35** F7
Rose Hill SA1 ....**95** A7
Rose Row CF44 ......**53** F7
Rose St Cardiff CF24 ..**195** C7
Newport NP20 ....**143** B6
Rose Terr
Bettws CF32 ....**129** D2
Llanharan CF72 ......**153** F2
Pontypool NP4 ....**61** F8
Rose Wlk NP10 .....**141** D7
Roseberry Terr SA6 ..**68** E5
Rosebery Pl ❺ CF64 .**207** A3
Rosebery St
Abertillery NP13 ......**36** A5
Pontypool NP4 ....**62** E3
Rosecroft Dr NP18 ..**145** C8
Rosedale Cl CF5 ....**193** D8
Rosedale Terr CF40 .**106** E4
Rosegarden The
NP20 ....**142** F5
Rosehill Terr
Gilfach Goch CF39 ...**106** C1
Swansea SA1 ....**95** B7
Roseland Rd SA5 .....**66** F4
Roseland Terr SA1 ...**95** F7
Rosemary Cl SA2 .....**67** B1
Rosemary Ct SA6 .....**45** F1
Rosemary La NP4 ....**62** C6
Rosemary St CF10 ..**195** B5
Rosemead NP44 ......**88** F3
Rosemont Ave NP11 .**115** A3
Rosemont Pl CF14 ..**177** D3
Rosendale Ct ❺
NP19 ....**143** F5
Rosewarne Cl SA5 ...**66** F4
Rosewood Ave SA12 ..**98** E6
Rosewood Cl
Bryn-côch SA10 ......**48** C4
Cardiff CF14 ....**160** A3
Rosewood Way SA5 ..**67** F5
Ross Cl CF37 ....**135** B6
Ross Ho NP44 ....**89** F2
Ross La NP20 ....**143** B7
Ross Rise CF42 ......**51** A1
Ross St NP20 ....**143** B8
Rosser St
Ferndale CF43 ....**80** A5
Neath SA11 ....**71** F8
Pontypool NP4 ....**62** A7
Pontypridd CF37 .....**135** B8
Rosser Terr SA10 ....**49** C4
Rosser's Field SA3 ..**123** C3
Rosset Cl CF3 ......**179** E6
Rossetti Cl CF5 .....**176** C3
Rosslyn Rd NP19 ...**143** F5
Rother Cl NP20 .....**116** D3
Rotherslade Rd SA3 .**122** F4
Rothesay Rd NP19 ..**143** F5
Round Wood CF23 ..**178** E5
Round Wood Cl CF23 .**178** E5
Roundel Cl CF14 ....**159** F4
Roundhouse Cl NP23 ..**8** C1
Routs View NP18 ....**145** B5
Rover Way
Cardiff CF24 ....**196** A8
Cardiff CF24 ....**196** B6

Row The NP10 ......**140** C3
Rowan Ave SA2 ......**94** B8
Rowan Cl
Gorseinon SA4 ....**43** A4
Killay SA2 ....**93** D5
Mountain Ash CF45 ....**54** E3
Nelson CF46 ....**83** E4
Penarth CF64 ....**207** A1
Rowan Cres NP4 .....**62** D2
Rowan Ct
Aberdare CF44 ....**28** D2
Barry CF62 ....**214** C3
Cardiff CF5 ....**194** C4
Llanharry CF72 ......**172** B5
Rowan Dr CF36 .....**183** E8
Rowan Gr CF62 .....**211** B7
Rowan Ho
❶ Cwmbran NP44 ....**89** B1
❸ Penarth CF64 ....**206** F5
Rowan Rd NP11 ....**115** B2
Rowan Rise CF48 ....**10** B6
Rowan Tree Cl SA10 ..**48** D3
Rowan Tree La CF72 .**173** D8
Rowan Way
Cardiff CF14 ....**160** B3
Ebbw Vale NP23 ....**7** C5
Merthyr Tydfil CF47 ...**10** D4
Newport NP20 ....**117** B3
Rowan's La CF32 ....**151** A5
Rowena Ct CF5 .....**193** C8
Rowland Ho SA11 ....**72** B5
Rowland Terr CF32 ..**104** F6
Rowlands Cotts SA13 .**100** F5
Rowley Terr CF43 ....**52** B1
Rowling St CF40 ....**107** A3
Roxburgh Garden Ct
CF64 ....**207** A3
Roxby Ct CF10 ......**195** B4
Royal Arc ❷ CF10 ...**195** A4
Royal Bldgs
❻ Cardiff CF10 .....**195** B6
Penarth CF64 ....**207** A4
Royal Cl Abercarn NP11 .**87** A3
Penarth CF64 ....**207** A5
Royal Cotts CF43 ....**79** B8
Royal Cres
Merthyr Tydfil CF47 ...**10** F3
Newbridge NP11 ......**59** F1
Royal Glamorgan Hospl
CF72 ....**155** B6
Royal Gwent General
Hospl NP20 ....**143** B3
Royal Hamadryad Hospl
CF10 ....**195** B1
Royal La NP13 ....**36** A6
Royal London Pk The
CF31 ....**169** E4
Royal Mint CF83 ....**155** B6
Royal Oak CF83 .....**140** B6
Royal Oak CF83 .....140** B6
Royal Oak Dr NP18 ..**144** D4
Royal Oak Gn NP44 ..**90** B4
Royal Oak Hill NP18 .**144** E7
Royal Oak Ho NP11 ..**60** C4
Royal Oak Rd SA2 ...**94** B3
Royal Stuart La CF10 .**195** B2
Royal Terr CF40 ....**107** A5
Royce Cl CF82 ....**84** E7
Royce Wlk NP10 ....**142** A6
Royde Cl CF5 ....**192** E4
Royston Cres NP19 ..**144** B4
Rubens Cl NP19 ....**143** F7
Ruby Cl CF83 ....**138** E5
Rudry Cl CF83 ......**138** E5
Rudry Rd
Caerphilly CF83 ......**138** C5
Cardiff CF14 ....**160** C5
Rudry St Cardiff CF11 .**194** E3
Newport NP19 ....**143** C6
Penarth CF64 ....**206** F4
Rufus Lewis Ave SA4 ..**43** A4
Rugby Ave SA11 ......**71** E7
Rugby Rd
Newport NP19 ....**143** D5
Resolven SA11 ....**226** D5
Ruggles Terr SA6 ....**45** D1
Rumney High Sch
CF3 ....**179** C5
Rumney Jun Sch CF3 **179** B3
Rumney Pottery CF3 .**179** A2
Rumney Prim Sch
CF3 ....**179** B3
Rumney Wlk NP44 ...**90** B3
Runcorn Cl
Barry CF62 ....**215** D7
Cardiff CF3 ....**179** D8
Runnymede SA2 ......**94** B3
Runway Rd CF24 ....**196** A7
Ruperra Cl
Bassaleg NP10 ....**142** B3
Cardiff CF3 ....**179** D8
Ruperra La NP20 ....**143** C3
Ruperra St
Llantrisant CF72 .....**155** D4
New Tredegar NP24 ...**33** E3
Newport NP20 ....**143** D3
Rupert Brooke Dr
NP20 ....**142** F2
Rural Way SA2 ....**94** B8
Rush Dr NP11 ....**59** D5
Rushbrook Cl CF14 ..**176** E4
Rushfield Gdns CF83 .**169** A6
Rushmere Rd NP12 ..**85** E3
Rushwind Cl SA3 ...**122** E6
Rushwind Mews SA3 .**122** E6

Ruskin Ave
Port Talbot SA12 .....**124** E8
Rogerstone NP10 .....**142** A7
Ruskin Cl Cardiff CF3 .**179** B7
Cwmbran NP44 ....**89** A2
Ruskin Rise NP20 ...**142** E2
Ruskin St SA11 ......**71** B3
Russel Cl NP4 ....**63** B4
Russell Cl NP10 ....**141** F3
Russell Dr NP20 ....**117** A2
Russell Drive Gdns
NP20 ....**117** A2
Russell St Cardiff CF24 **195** B7
❹ Cwmbran NP44 ....**89** E5
Dowlais CF48 ....**11** A4
Llanelli SA15 ....**40** D3
New Tredegar NP24 ...**34** A1
Swansea SA1 ....**95** B7
Russell Terr ❿ CF47 ..**30** E8
Russet Cl
Langstone NP18 .....**145** C8
Port Talbot SA12 .....**98** B3
Rustic Cl SA2 ....**94** B8
Ruth Rd NP4 ....**62** F5
Ruth St CF81 ....**57** F3
Ruthen Terr CF62 ...**214** D5
Rutherford Hill NP20 .**117** A2
Ruthin Ct CF35 .....**169** F4
Ruthin Gdns CF24 ..**195** A2
Ruthin Way CF38 ...**136** A2
Rutland Cl CF62 ....**214** C8
Rutland Pl ❿ NP20 ..**143** C3
Rutland St CF11 ....**194** E4
Ryans Cl SA10 ....**71** C8
Ryder St CF11 ......**194** E6
Ryw Blodyn SA7 .....**69** D6**

S

Sable Ave SA12 ......**98** B2
Sable Cl Cardiff CF14 .**160** A4
Port Talbot SA12 .....**98** B2
Sachville Ave CF14 ..**177** E3
Saddler St SA1 ....**68** C4
Saffron Dr NP44 .....**88** F1
Saffron Dr CF3 .....**180** A8
St Aarons Dr CF72 ..**153** F4
St Agatha Rd CF14 ..**177** E4
St Agnes Rd CF14 ...**177** D4
St Aidan Cres CF14 .**177** E4
St Aidan's Rise CF63 .**215** C6
St Aiden Dr SA2 ......**93** D6
St Alban Ave CF14 ..**177** D4
St Alban's RC High Sch
CF24 ....**62** C6
St Alban's RC Prim Sch
NP4 ....**62** B7
St Alban's Rd
Swansea SA2 ....**94** F5
Treherbert CF42 ......**50** D3
St Alban's Terr
❻ Port Talbot SA13 .**125** C6
Treherbert CF42 ......**50** E3
St Albans RC Prim Sch
CF24 ....**195** F7
St Aloysius RC Prim Sch
CF47 ....**10** D4
St Ambrose Cl ❸
CF64 ....**206** A2
St Ambrose Rd CF14 .**177** E4
St Andrew's Cl CF37 .**135** B6
St Andrew's Cres ❷
CF10 ....**195** B6
St Andrew's Inf Sch
NP19 ....**143** F3
St Andrew's Jun Sch
NP19 ....**143** F3
St Andrew's La ❸
CF10 ....**195** B6
St Andrew's Pl CF10 .**195** B6
St Andrew's Rd
Barry CF62 ....**214** E6
Bridgend CF31 ....**168** E7
Dinas Powys CF5 .....**205** D3
St Andrews Cl
Cwmbran NP44 ....**89** E7
Llantwit Fardre CF38 .**156** D6
Mumbles SA3 ....**93** E1
St Andrews Ct ❺
CF40 ....**106** E5
St Andrews Dr NP12 ..**85** E3
St Andrews Major CW
Prim Sch CF5 ....**205** F3
St Angela Rd CF14 ..**177** E3
St Ann St CF81 ......**57** F2
St Anne's Ave CF64 .**206** F2
St Anne's Cl
Cwmbran NP44 ....**89** E5
Mumbles SA3 ....**123** A3
Newbridge NP11 ......**86** D5
Rogerstone NP10 ....**142** B4
St Anne's Cres
Bargoed CF81 ....**58** A2
Newport NP19 ....**143** F7
Porthcawl CF36 .....**183** C7
St Anne's CW Inf Sch
CF24 ....**195** C7
St Anne's Dr SA11 ...**49** C2
St Anne's Gdns CF82 ..**85** B2
St Anne's Terr SA11 ..**49** C2
St Annes Ct CF72 ...**172** E5
St Annes Dr CF38 ...**156** D6
St Annes Gdns CF83 .**137** A7
St Annes Rd NP12 ...**85** C7
St Anthony Rd CF14 ..**177** E3
St Anthony's Cl NP4 ..**62** D2
St Arvan's Terr NP13 ..**15** E5

St Arvans Cres CF3 ..179 F7
St Arvans Rd NP44 ....89 F3
St Asaph Cl CF14 ....177 E6
St Asaph Dr SA12 ....98 C2
St Asaph's Way CF83 .138 A1
St Asaphs Ct SA12 ....98 C2
St Athan Prim Sch
 CF62 ....211 D4
St Athan Rd CF71 ...200 F4
St Athan's Ct CF83 ..137 F2
St Augustine Rd
 Cardiff CF14 ....177 E4
 Pontypool NP4 ......62 D2
St Augustine's Cres 11
 CF64 ....207 B5
St Augustine's Path 9
 CF64 ....207 B5
St Augustine's Pl 12
 CF64 ....207 B5
St Augustine's Rd
 CF64 ....207 B5
St Baruch Cl 4 CF64 206 A2
St Baruchs Ct CF62 ..214 F2
St Basil's Cres NP10 .142 A3
St Basil's Stores
 NP10 ....142 A3
St Benedict Cl NP4 ..62 D2
St Benedict Cres
 CF14 ....177 E4
St Benedette Rd NP10 142 A2
St Bernadettes RC Jun &
 Inf Sch CF23 ....178 F8
St Bleddian Cl CF71 .188 D2
St Brannocks Cl
 CF62 ....214 C5
St Briavels Mews
 NP10 ....163 E5
St Bride's Cl CF36 ..165 F1
St Bride's Rd
 Aberkenfig CF32 ....150 C4
 Ewenny CF35 ....185 E7
 St Fagans CF5 ....175 D1
St Bride's Way CF63 215 A8
St Brides Cl
 Llanyravon NP44 ....90 A2
 Pontarddulais SA4 ...19 D4
St Brides Cres NP20 .163 F8
St Brides Ct 5 CF5 .193 C4
St Brides Gdns
 Newport NP20 ......142 E1
 Newport NP20 ......163 F8
St Brides Major Church in
 Wales Prim Sch
 CF32 ....185 C2
St Brides Pl CF5 ....192 B8
St Brides Rd CF71 ..198 C5
St Brigid Rd CF14 ...177 E6
St Brioc Rd CF14 ...177 E6
St Cadoc Rd CF14 ..177 E5
St Cadoc's Ave CF64 206 A2
St Cadoc's Cl NP18 .118 A3
St Cadoc's Hosp
 NP18 ....118 A2
St Cadoc's Hospl
 NP18 ....117 F2
St Cadoc's Rd NP4 ..38 D1
St Cadoc's Rise CF63 215 D5
St Catherine's Cl
 CF83 ....138 D6
St Catherine's Ct
 Abercarn NP11 .....114 B4
 Barry CF62 ....214 F8
St Catherine's Rd
 SA12 ....98 E5
St Catherines Cl SA11 .71 D5
St Cattwg's Ave CF82 .84 C6
St Catwg Wlk SA2 ...94 A2
St Cenydd Cl
 Bryn NP12 ....85 E5
 Caerphilly CF83 .....137 E4
St Cenydd Rd
 Caerphilly CF83 .....137 E3
 Cardiff CF14 ....177 F6
 Swansea SA5 ....67 F6
St Cenydd Sch CF83 .137 D4
St Christopher Dr SA2 93 D6
St Christopher's Dr
 CF83 ....137 F2
St Christopher's Rd
 Bridgend CF31 ......168 E8
 Porthcawl CF36 .....183 C7
St Christophers Ct
 CF35 ....169 B8
St Clair Ct CF10 ....195 C4
St Clare's Convent Sch
 CF36 ....183 D8
St Clare's Jun Sch
 CF36 ....183 D8
St Clares NP22 ......12 F2
St Clears Cl CF83 ...138 A4
St Clears Pl SA5 .....68 B7
St Curig's Cl CF62 ...213 A1
St Cuthbert's RC Sch
 CF10 ....195 B5
St Cynons Ct CF40 ..106 F8
St Cynwyd's Ave
 CF34 ....102 A1
St Cyres Cl CF64 ....206 E4
St Cyres Rd CF64 ...206 E4
St Cyres Sch
 Dinas Powys CF64 ..206 C2
 Penarth CF64 ....206 E4
St David Ave CF64 ..206 B4
St David Dr SA2 .....93 D6
St David Lewis RC Jun &
 Inf Sch NP20 ....116 F2
St David St
 Pontycymer CF32 ....103 E4

St David St continued
 Ton Pentre CF41 .....79 A3
St David''s Est SA6 ..69 B8
St David's Ave
 Blackwood NP12 .....85 F7
 Llantwit Major CF61 .210 A5
St David's Cl
 Bridgend CF31 ......168 E6
 Ebbw Vale NP23 .....14 C8
 Hendy SA4 ....19 E6
 Llanelli SA15 ....40 C3
 Loughor SA4 ....42 F1
 Merthyr Tydfil CF48 .225 F1
 Penpedairheol CF82 ..84 C7
 Pontypool NP4 ......62 C7
 Ton Pentre CF41 .....78 F3
 Upper Boat CF15 ...157 E8
St David's Cres CF63 206 D3
St David's Ct CF3 ...162 E1
St David's Ctr CF10 .195 A5
St David's CW Prim Sch
 CF71 ....187 A4
St David's Dr CF83 ..139 C6
St David's Metropolitan
 Cathedral Church
 CF10 ....195 B5
St David's Mkt 2
 CF10 ....195 B5
St David's Pl
 Llantrisant CF72 ....155 E4
 Maesteg CF34 ......102 A1
 2 Swansea SA1 ....95 D6
St David's RC Jun & Inf
 Sch NP20 ....142 E1
St David's Rd
 Bridgend CF31 ......168 D6
 Cardiff CF14 ....177 B4
 Cwmbran NP44 .....89 F3
 Maesycwmmer CF82 ..85 B2
 Pengam NP12 ....85 B7
 Port Talbot SA12 ...124 E8
 Swansea SA6 ....69 B8
 Ystalyfera SA9 ......2 C6
St David's Sq SA1 ...95 D6
St David's St SA11 ...71 E7
St David's Way
 Caerphilly CF83 .....137 F1
 Cardiff CF10 ....195 A5
 Porthcawl CF36 .....183 B8
St David's Well
 CF36 ....166 A2
St Davids Cl
 Bridgend CF31 ......169 C6
 Bryn NP12 ....85 E5
 Penllergaer SA4 .....44 B2
 Porth CF39 ....133 D8
 Rhymney NP22 .....12 E4
St Davids Cres
 Cardiff CF5 ....193 D5
 Newport NP20 ......142 F1
 St Athan CF62 ......211 D5
St Davids Ho 15 CF10 195 A5
St Davids Ind Est NP12 85 B8
St Davids Pk SA13 ..147 C6
St Davids RC Prim Sch
 Cwmbran NP44 .....89 F5
 Mumbles SA3 ....123 A6
St Davids RC Sixth Form
 Coll CF23 ....178 C2
St Davids Rd
 Gwaun-Cae-Gurwen
 SA18 ....220 E7
 Miskin CF72 ....173 D6
St Deinols Cl NP12 ..85 B6
St Denis Rd CF14 ...177 F5
St Dials Cl NP44 ....89 C2
St Dials Rd NP44 ....89 D3
St Dogmael's Ave
 CF14 ....177 F7
St Dominics Retreat
 NP4 ....62 B6
St Donat's Ave SA2 ..94 B7
St Donat's Cl
 Caerphilly CF83 .....137 F2
 Llantwit Major CF61 .210 A5
St Donats Cl
 Dinas Powys CF64 ..206 C3
 Merthyr Tydfil CF48 .225 F1
St Donats Ct 7 CF5 .193 C4
St Donats Pl 7 NP44 .90 B2
St Donats Rd CF11 ..194 D4
St Dyfrig Cl 1 CF64 206 B2
St Dyfrig Rd CF64 ...206 E2
St Dyfrig's Ct 4 CF3 .179 C6
St Edeyrn's Rd CF23 178 C6
St Edeyrns Cl CF23 ..178 D6
St Edward St NP20 ..143 B4
St Edwen Gdns CF14 177 E5
St Elmo Ave SA1 ....95 E8
St Fagan's Ho CF83 ..138 A2
St Fagan's St CF11 ..194 F2
St Fagans Ave CF62 .214 E6
St Fagans Cl CF5 ...193 E2
St Fagans Ct CF5 ...192 F4
St Fagans CW Jun & Inf
 Sch CF5 ....192 F4
St Fagans Dr CF5 ...193 A7
St Fagans Gr CF48 ..225 F2
St Fagans Rd CF5 ...193 D7
St Fagans Rise CF5 .193 C8
St Fagans St CF83 ..138 A2
St Francis Ct
 Cardiff CF14 ....177 A5
 Cardiff CF24 ....195 F5
St Francis Inf Sch
 CF5 ....193 B5
St Francis Jun Sch
 CF5 ....193 B5

St Francis RC Prim Sch
 NP4 ....37 F4
St Francis Rd
 Bridgend CF31 ......168 E7
 Cardiff CF14 ....177 A5
St Gabriel & St Raphael RC
 Prim Sch CF44 .....106 F5
St Gabriel's RC Jun & Inf
 Sch NP19 ....144 E6
St Garmon Rd CF64 .206 E2
St George SA15 .....41 A4
St George's Ave CF31 168 E8
St George's Cres
 NP19 ....143 F7
St George's Ct NP22 .13 E7
St George's Terr
 SA3 ....229 C1
St Georges Rd CF74 .177 D3
St Germans Mews 4
 CF24 ....195 D6
St Gildas Rd CF14 ..177 D5
St Govan's Cl CF62 ..216 F8
St Govans Pl SA5 ...66 D3
St Gowan Ave CF14 .177 C6
St Gwladys Ave CF81 .57 F5
St Gwladys Ct CF81 ..57 F4
St Gwynnos Cl CF64 206 B3
St Helen's Ave SA1 ..95 A5
St Helen's Cres SA1 ..95 A6
St Helen's Ct CF83 ..137 F2
St Helen's Rc Prim Sch
 CF83 ....138 D4
St Helen's Rd
 Cardiff CF14 ....177 D4
 Swansea SA1 ....95 B6
St Helens Jun RC Sch
 CF62 ....214 F6
St Helens Prim Sch
 SA1 ....95 B6
St Helens RC Inf Sch
 CF63 ....215 A5
St Helens Rugby & Cricket
 Gd SA1 ....94 F5
St Helier Dr SA1 .....98 B3
St Hilary Cl CF5 ....193 D4
St Hilary Dr SA2 .....93 D7
St Hilda's Rd NP4 ...142 C2
St Ilan Comp Sch
 CF83 ....138 A4
St Ilan's Way CF83 ..138 A1
St Illtyd Cl 2 CF64 ..206 B2
St Illtyd Rd CF38 ....135 E1
St Illtyd's Cl SA12 ...98 E5
St Illtyd's Cres SA1 ..96 A7
St Illtyd's Dr SA12 ..98 F5
St Illtyd's Jun & Inf Sch
 CF61 ....209 F6
St Illtyd's RC Comp Sch
 CF48 ....11 A4
St Illtyd's RC Prim Sch
 SA1 ....69 A3
St Illtyd's Rd CF11 ..168 D5
St Illtyds Cl CF31 ...169 C6
St Illtyyd's RC High Sch
 CF3 ....179 D5
St Ina Rd CF14 .....177 E6
St Isan Rd CF14 ....177 E5
St James Cl
 Caerphilly CF83 .....138 E5
 Maesycwmmer CF82 ..85 B1
St James Cres 3 SA1 .95 A6
St James Ct 3 SA1 ..95 A6
St James Gdns SA1 ..95 A7
St James Pk
 Bridgend CF31 ......169 D4
 Tredegar NP22 ......14 A5
St James Way NP22 ..13 F7
St James' Cl CF48 ...31 A5
St James' Cres CF33 .148 B2
St James' Field NP4 ..62 C6
St James' Rise CF31 .169 A3
St James's Cres SA1 ..95 A6
St Joeseph's Prim Sch
 CF14 ....177 E2
St John Baptist CW Comp
 Sch CF44 ....28 E2
St John Lloyd RC Comp
 Sch SA14 ....41 B6
St John Lloyd RC Jun & Inf
 Sch CF3 ....179 E5
St John St
 2 Aberdare CF44 ...28 E4
 Cardiff CF10 ....195 A5
 Ogmore Vale CF32 ..130 E8
St John's Cl
 Cefn Coed CF48 ....10 A5
 Cowbridge CF71 ....188 F1
 Maesteg CF34 ......102 D2
St John's Coll CF3 ..179 E8
St John's Cres
 Cardiff CF14 ....177 A6
 Cardiff CF5 ....194 D5
St John's Cres NP4 ..62 A7
St John's Cres NP10 .141 F6
St John's Ct
 2 Cardiff CF11 .....194 D5
 Rogerstone NP10 ...141 F6
St John's Dr
 Pencoed CF35 ......170 D7
 Porthcawl CF36 .....183 C7
St John's Gdns 21
 CF47 ....30 E8
St John's Gr CF47 ...10 F3
St John's La CF46 ...83 D3
St John's Pl
 2 Cardiff CF14 .....177 A6
 Rhoose CF62 ....212 E2

St John's Prep Sch
 CF36 ....183 D8
St John's Priory CF31 168 F3
St John's Rd
 Bridgend CF31 ......168 D5
 Clydach SA6 ....46 E7
 Swansea SA5 ....68 B3
 Tonyrefail CF39 .....133 C5
St John's St CF39 ...107 F2
St John's Terr SA10 ..71 A7
St John's View CF62 .211 C5
St Johns Cl NP4 .....62 A7
St Johns Ct SA6 ....46 B1
St Johns Dr Bryn NP12 85 E5
St Johns Rd NP19 ...143 F5
St Joseph Pl NP44 ..117 B6
St Joseph's Ct 6
 SA15 ....40 E5
St Joseph's Prim Sch
 SA11 ....71 F6
St Joseph's Private Hospl
 NP20 ....117 B4
St Joseph's RC Comp Sch
 SA12 ....98 F2
St Joseph's RC Comp Sch
 NP10 ....163 F7
St Joseph's RC Inf Sch
 Aberavon SA12 .....99 A1
 Swansea SA1 ....68 D1
St Joseph's RC Ju & Inf
 Sch NP19 ....143 E6
St Joseph's RC Jun & Inf
 Sch NP22 ....13 D7
St Joseph's RC Jun Sch
 Aberavon SA12 .....98 F2
 Swansea SA1 ....68 D1
St Joseph's Rc Primry Sch
 CF44 ....206 E4
St Joseph's School Ho 5
 CF64 ....207 A5
St Joseph's Terr CF44 .53 A3
St Josephs Pk SA12 ..98 E2
St Judes Cl SA5 .....68 C7
St Julian Cl CF63 ...215 C7
St Julian St NP20 ...143 B4
St Julian's Ave NP19 143 F7
St Julian's Comp Sch
 NP19 ....143 E8
St Julian's Ct SA1 ...137 F1
St Julian's Inf Sch
 NP19 ....144 A7
St Julian's Jun Sch
 NP19 ....144 A7
St Julian's Rd NP19 .143 F7
St Julians Hts CF82 ..85 A4
St Julians Lo 5
 NP19 ....143 E8
St Julius Cres CF72 .153 F3
St Katherines Ct SA1 .69 D6
St Kitts Pl SA12 .....98 C2
St Lawrence Ct SA5 ..68 B7
St Leger Cres SA1 ...95 F7
St Leonard's Rd CF31 168 D4
St Leonards SA3 ....122 F3
St Luke's Ave
 Hawthorn CF37 .....136 A4
 Penarth CF64 ....206 E2
St Luke's Cl
 Llanharan CF72 .....153 F4
 Pant CF48 ....11 A6
St Luke's Rd
 Pontypool NP4 .....38 A1
 Porth CF39 ....108 A3
 Tredegar NP22 .....6 D2
St Lukes Ct SA1 ....69 D6
St Lythan Cl 2 CF64 206 A4
St Lythan Ct 9 CF5 .193 C4
St Lythan's Ct CF62 .214 C5
St Lythans Burial Chamber
 CF5 ....204 C3
St Maddock's Cl
 CF31 ....169 C6
St Madoc Cl NP12 ..85 E5
St Maelog Cl NP12 ..85 E5
St Malo Rd CF14 ...177 E6
St Margaret's Ave
 Blackwood NP12 .....85 C7
 Neath SA10 ....97 C8
St Margaret's Cl 10
 CF14 ....177 A6
St Margaret's Cres 3
 CF23 ....195 D8
St Margaret's Dr SA6 .40 B7
St Margaret's Pk CF5 193 E6
St Margaret's Pl 9
 CF14 ....177 A6
St Margaret's RC Sch
 CF44 ....28 F1
St Margaret's Rd
 Caerphilly CF83 .....137 F2
 Cardiff CF14 ....177 F6
St Margarets Cl CF83 138 F6
St Marie St CF31 ....168 F3
St Mark's Ave CF14 .177 F2
St Mark's Cl CF72 ..153 F4
St Mark's Cres NP20 143 B5
St Mark's Gdns CF14 177 E5
St Mark's Rd CF64 ..206 F2
St Mark's Villas CF37 109 A1
St Martin's Cl CF24 ..177 F1
St Martin's Comp Sch
 CF83 ....138 B1
St Martin's Cres CF83 138 A1
St Martin's Rd CF83 .138 A1

St Martins Cres
 Cardiff CF14 ....177 F7
 Tredegar NP81 ......6 C1
St Martins Ct NP20 .142 F3
St Martins Row CF24 195 B8
St Mary Pl 6 SA12 ...99 A1
St Mary St
 Aberavon SA12 .....99 A1
 Bargoed CF81 ......58 A2
 Newport NP20 ......143 B4
 Pontypool NP4 ......62 D3
 Risca NP11 ....114 F3
 1 Swansea SA1 .....95 D6
 Trelewis CF46 ......83 C7
St Mary St (Heol Eglwys
 Fair) CF10 ....195 A5
St Mary the Virgin Jun &
 Inf Sch CF10 ....195 B4
St Mary's (Brynmawr)
 Church in Wales Jun &
 Inf Sch NP23 ....8 C5
St Mary's Ave CF63 .215 A5
 Blaengwrach SA11 ..227 C8
 Briton Ferry SA11 ...71 B1
 Merthyr Tydfil CF47 ..10 D3
 Pontypool NP4 ......62 D3
St Mary's Cl CF42 ...51 A2
St Mary's Cres CF34 102 D1
St Mary's Ct
 7 Newport NP20 ...143 B4
 Porthcawl CF36 .....183 C8
St Mary's Day Hospl
 CF64 ....206 C6
St Mary's Prim RC Sch
 CF31 ....168 E5
St Mary's RC Prim Sch
 CF47 ....30 D8
St Mary's RC Sch
 CF11 ....194 D6
St Mary's Rd Bryn NP12 85 E4
 Cardiff CF11 ....177 A6
 Croesyceiliog NP44 ..90 A5
 Pontardawe SA8 ....24 B8
St Mary's Sq CF5 ...95 D6
St Mary's View CF35 .170 A4
St Mary's Well Bay Rd
 CF64 ....216 C6
St Marys & St Patricks RC
 Sch CF34 ....102 B3
St Marys Cl CF5 ....193 D3
St Marys Ct CF14 ...177 A5
St Marys RC Sch SA14 41 B6
St Matthew's Rd NP4 .62 D5
St Matthews Ct 6
 SA1 ....95 B4
St Mellons Ct CF83 .137 F6
St Mellons Rd
 Cardiff CF14 ....160 E2
 Marshfield CF3 .....180 D8
St Melons Bsns Pk
 CF3 ....180 B8
St Melons Rd
 CF3 ....180 B8
St Michael Gr NP44 .117 B7
St Michael St NP20 .143 D2
St Michael's Ave
 Pontarddulais SA4 ...19 B4
 Pontypridd CF37 ....135 D7
St Michael's Cl
 Cardiff CF15 ....158 C1
 St Athan CF62 ......211 D5
St Michael's RC Prim Sch
 CF37 ....135 E6
St Michael's Rd
 Cardiff CF5 ....194 A7
 Cardiff CF5 ....194 B8
 Maesteg CF34 ......102 A3
 Porthcawl CF36 .....183 C8
St Michael's Sch
 SA14 ....41 E6
St Michael's Way
 CF31 ....169 C6
St Michaels Cl CF38 .155 F6
St Michaels Coll CF5 .194 A8
St Michaels Ct
 Cardiff CF24 ....177 F1
 Cardiff CF5 ....194 B8
St Michaels Gdns
 CF62 ....214 E8
St Michaels Mews
 NP20 ....143 D2
St Michaels RC Jun & Inf
 Sch NP20 ....143 C2
St Monica's Sch (Jun &
 Inf) CF24 ....194 F8
St Nicholas Cl
 1 Dinas Powys CF64 206 A4
 Waunarlwydd SA5 ...66 E3
St Nicholas Cl
 Barry CF62 ....214 C3
 Caerphilly CF83 .....137 F2
 4 Cardiff CF5 ......193 C4
 Swansea SA2 ....93 F6
St Nicholas Rd CF31 .168 E8
St Nicholas Rd CF5 ..191 F1
St Nicholas Sq 12 SA1 95 E6
St Nicholas' Rd CF62 214 C3
St Nicolas Ct CF23 ..178 E8
St Non's Cl CF31 ....169 C6
St Oswald's Rd CF63 215 C1
St Oswalds Cl NP4 ..62 E1
St Osyth Cl CF62 ....214 C2
St Owains Cres CF71 189 C8
St Patrick's Dr CF31 .168 E7
St Patrick's RC Jun & Inf
 Sch
 Cardiff CF11 ....194 F3
 Newport NP19 ......144 A4

St Paul's Ave
 Barry CF62 ....214 E4
 Penarth CF64 ....206 F2
St Paul's CW Jun & Inf Sch
 CF11 ....194 F2
St Paul's Rd SA12 ...124 E4
St Paul's Terr SA4 ...66 D8
St Peter's Ave SA5 ..67 D3
St Peter's Cl NP11 ..87 B7
St Peter's Ct CF41 ..78 F5
St Peter's Prim Sch
 NP4 ....17 C6
St Peter's RC Prim Sch
 CF24 ....195 C7
St Peter's Rd
 Mumbles SA3 ....122 C5
 Penarth CF64 ....206 E2
St Peter's St CF24 ...195 B7
St Peter's Terr SA2 ..67 C2
St Peters Cl
 Abercwmboi CF44 ...53 E4
 Llanharan CF72 .....153 F4
St Peters Dr NP12 ...85 E5
 1 Swansea SA1 .....95 D6
St Peters Terr 1 SA15 40 C4
St Philip Evens' RC Prim
 Sch CF23 ....178 E5
St Philips NP19 .....143 F4
St Pierre Cl 2 CF3 ..180 A4
St Quentins Cl CF71 .188 E1
St Quentins Hill CF71 188 D1
St Rhidan Cl NP12 ..85 E5
St Rhidian Dr SA2 ...93 D7
St Rhidian Rd SA5 ...67 F6
St Richard Gwyn RC High
 Sch CF63 ....215 D8
St Roberts RC Prim Sch
 CF32 ....150 C3
St Sannan Rd NP12 ..85 D4
St Siors Meade CF62 .212 F2
St Stephen's Ave CF41 .78 F5
St Stephen's Rd
 NP20 ....143 D2
St Stephens Dr CF35 152 C1
St Tanwg Rd CF14 ..177 E5
St Teilo Ave CF62 ...214 E6
St Teilo Cl 3 CF64 ..206 B2
St Teilo St SA4 .....19 C4
St TeilO's Cl Bryn NP12 85 E5
 Ebbw Vale NP23 .....14 C8
St Teilo's Ct SA3 ...121 F6
St Teilo's CW High Sch
 CF23 ....178 D3
St TeilO's Rd CF31 ..168 D5
St Teilo's Way CF83 .137 F1
St Telio's Ct 2 CF23 .195 D8
St Theodore's Way
 CF32 ....150 F5
St Therese's Prim Sch
 SA12 ....98 C1
St Thomas Cl CF31 ..169 C6
St Thomas Ct NP4 ...37 E5
St Thomas Prim Sch
 SA1 ....95 E8
St Thomas' Ct CF63 .215 C6
St Tudor's View NP12 .85 E6
St Tydfil's Ave CF47 ..10 E1
St Tydfil's Ct 10 CF47 .30 D8
St Tydfils Hospl CF47 .10 E1
St Vincent Cres 3
 SA1 ....95 D5
St Vincent Rd NP19 .143 C5
St Winifred's Rd
 CF31 ....168 D6
St Winifreds Cl 5
 CF64 ....206 A2
St Woolos Ct 10
 NP20 ....143 B4
St Woolos Gn 2 NP20 89 E4
St Woolos Hospl (General)
 NP20 ....143 B3
St Woolos Jun & Inf Sch
 NP20 ....143 B4
St Woolos Pl NP20 ..143 B4
St Woolos Rd NP20 .143 B4
St Woolos' Cath
 NP20 ....143 B4
Salem Cotts NP22 ...13 E8
Salem La CF38 .....135 F1
Salem Rd
 Cwmavon SA12 .....99 F6
 Llanelli SA15 ....40 F8
 Swansea SA6 ....68 D5
Salem Row CF15 ...157 F5
Salem Terr CF40 ...106 F8
Salisbury Ave CF64 .206 F3
Salisbury Cl
 Merthyr Tydfil CF48 .225 F1
 2 Newport NP20 ...143 C6
 3 Penarth CF64 ....206 F2
 Scurlage SA3 ....231 A6
Salisbury Ct
 Cwmbran NP44 .....89 C3
 Penarth CF64 ....206 F3
Salisbury Rd
 Abercynon CF45 ....82 D2
 Barry CF62 ....214 C4
 Cardiff CF24 ....195 B7
 Maesteg CF34 ......101 F3
Salisbury St NP11 ...114 C4
Salisbury Terr
 New Tredegar NP24 .34 A1
 Varteg NP4 ....17 E1
Salmon Cl CF23 ....178 E1
Salmons Wood CF71 188 B8

Salop Ho 8 CF64 ....207 A5
Salop Pl CF64 ......207 B5
Salop St
  Caerphilly CF83 ......138 B2
  Penarth CF64 ......207 A4
Salthouse Cl SA4 ....64 A3
Saltmead Ct CF11 ....194 B4
Saltoun St SA13 ....125 E3
Salubrious Pl SA1 ...95 D6
Salvia Cl CF3 ....180 A7
Salway Ave CF1 ......58 B2
Sambucus Ave CF71 .199 C4
Samlet Rd SA7 ......69 C8
Samlet Sh Ctr SA7 ...69 C8
Samson St CF61 .....209 F7
Samson's Ave NP4 ....37 E7
Samuel Cres SA5 ....68 A3
Samuels Rd SA9 .....221 B7
Sanatorium Rd CF11 .194 B5
Sanctuary Ct CF5 ....193 A2
Sanctuary The CF5 ...193 A2
Sand La SA11 ....98 C8
Sand St 12 CF47 .....10 D2
Sandbrook Rd CF3 ...180 B6
Sanderling Cl CF36 ..182 D8
Sanderling Dr CF3 ...179 F8
Sandfields Comp Sch
  SA12 ....98 C3
Sandfields Prim Sch
  SA12 ....98 F1
Sandfields Rd
  Aberavon SA12 ......98 F1
  Aberkenfig CF32 ....150 D4
Sandon St CF24 .....195 B5
Sandown Ct CF5 ....193 E5
Sandown Ho 7 SA12 ..98 D1
Sandown Rd SA12 ...124 E8
Sandpiper Cl CF3 ...179 F8
Sandpiper Ct SA12 ...98 C1
Sandpiper Rd
  Llanelli SA15 ....40 B6
  Porthcawl CF36 .....165 D1
Sandpiper Way NP10 .163 E6
Sandringham Cl
  Barry CF62 ....214 C4
  Gorseinon SA4 ......66 B8
Sandringham Rd
  CF23 ....178 C1
Sandwick Ct CF23 ...178 C7
Sandy Cl SA12 ....98 C1
Sandy La
  Newport NP10 ......163 B7
  Porthcawl CF36 .....183 A7
  Southgate SA3 ......121 A4
Sandy Rd SA15 ....40 A6
Sandy Ridge SA12 ....98 C1
Sandybank Rd CF41 ...79 C3
Sandybrook Cl NP44 ..89 C1
Sandymeers CF36 ...183 A7
Sannan St CF81 ......58 B5
Sanquahar St CF24 ..195 D5
Sansom St NP11 .....114 C3
Sapele Dr CF24 .....195 D5
Sapphire St CF24 ....195 D7
Sarah St CF48 ....55 D5
Sardis Cl SA5 ....66 E3
Sardis Rd
  Pontypridd CF37 ....135 B8
  Pontypridd CF37 ....135 C8
Sarlou Cl SA3 ....123 C3
Sarn Helen SA11 ....223 E6
Sarn Hill CF32 ......150 E3
Sarn Pl 7 NP11 .....114 F3
Sarn Sta CF32 ......150 D3
Sarn Villas CF32 ....150 E3
Sarnfan Baglan Rd
  SA12 ....98 E4
Saron Cl SA4 ....42 F3
Saron Cotts 4 SA13 .99 C1
Saron Cty Prim Sch
  SA18 ....218 E6
Saron Pl NP23 ......14 D6
Saron Rd
  Ammanford SA18 ....218 F8
  Bynea SA14 ....41 F4
  Capel Hendre SA18 ..218 E6
  Penperlleni NP4 .....39 C8
Saron St CF37 ......135 E7
Saunders Rd CF10 ...195 A4
Saunders Way SA2 ...94 B5
Saundersfoot Cl CF5 193 D3
Saville Rd CF32 ....104 E3
Savine NP4 ....89 C1
Sawel Ct SA4 ....19 A4
Sawel Terr SA4 .....19 A4
Sawtells Terr NP4 ...61 F8
Saxon St CF47 ......10 D2
Saxons Hos NP4 .....37 F4
Scales Hos CF44 ....28 E6
Scarborough Rd
  1 Newport NP19 ...143 E8
  2 Pontypridd CF37 ..109 E2
Scard St 5 NP20 ....143 B4
Scarlet Ave SA12 ....98 A2
Sch of Nursing &
  Midwifery Studies
  NP18 ....118 A2
School Ave NP23 ....8 D1
School Cl NP4 ......62 B6
School Cres NP4 ....62 E1
School Ct
  Cwmbran NP44 ......89 E2
  Neath SA11 ....71 D1
School La
  Abersychan NP4 ....37 F4

School La continued
  Ebbw Vale NP23 .....7 B4
  Newport NP20 ......143 C4
  Penperlleni NP4 .....39 E6
  Pontardawe SA8 ....23 E5
  Pontypool NP4 ......62 B7
  Rhydyfelin CF37 ....136 B4
  Taffs Well CF15 ....157 F4
School Rd
  Abercraf SA9 ....222 C7
  Crynant SA10 ......226 A8
  Cwmavon SA12 .....75 C5
  Dyffryn Cellwen SA10 223 A4
  Glais SA7 ....47 A5
  Llanelli SA15 ....40 F2
  Maesteg CF34 ......102 A3
  Miskin CF72 ....173 D7
  Miskin CF72 ....173 D7
  Neath SA10 ....70 C1
  Neath SA11 ....71 D5
  Ogmore Vale CF32 ..104 E1
  Pyle CF33 ....148 D3
  Tonna SA11 ....49 C2
  Troedyrhiw CF48 ...31 C1
  Ystalyfera SA9 .....2 B6
  Ystradgynlais SA9 ..2 D8
School St
  Aberbargoed CF81 ..58 A5
  Abercwmboi CF44 ..53 E5
  Blaencwm CF42 .....50 B2
  Blaengwrach SA11 ..227 B8
  Brynamman SA18 ...220 D8
  Caerphilly CF83 .....137 F8
  Cardiff CF10 ....195 B4
  Deri CF81 ....57 B8
  Ferndale CF43 ......79 B4
  Fleur De Lis NP12 ..85 B5
  Llantrisant CF72 ....155 D3
  Maerdy CF43 ....52 A1
  New Tredegar NP24 ..33 D3
  New Tredegar NP24 ..33 F2
  New Tredegar NP24 ..34 A1
  Pontlottyn CF81 ....12 F1
  Pontrhydyfen SA12 ..73 A1
  Pontyclun CF72 ....173 B8
  Porth CF39 ....107 F2
  Porth CF39 ....107 F4
  Senghenydd CF83 ..110 F3
  Ton Pentre CF41 ....79 A3
  Tonypandy CF40 ...107 A2
  Tonyrefail CF39 ....133 C5
  Tylorstown CF40 ...80 B1
School Terr
  Blaengarw CF32 ....103 E5
  Cwm NP23 ....35 A8
  Cwmavon SA12 .....99 E5
  Llanharan CF72 ....153 F3
  North Cornelly CF33 .165 F7
  Pontycymer CF32 ..103 F3
  Pontypool NP4 ......61 F8
  Rogerstone NP10 ...141 F5
  Tonypandy CF40 ...106 E7
  Wattstown CF39 ....107 D8
School View
  Nantyglo NP23 .....8 B2
  Pontypool NP4 ......62 D5
Schooner Way
  Cardiff CF10 ....195 C3
  Cardiff CF10 ....195 C4
Scotch St SA13 .....76 C5
Scotney Way CF23 ...161 A1
Scott Cl
  Bridgend CF31 .....168 D6
  Newport NP20 .....142 E1
  St Athan CF62 .....211 D7
Scott Ct CF23 ......178 E3
Scott Rd CF10 .....195 A5
Scott St CF42 ......50 E2
Scott Wlk NP10 ....142 A6
Scutari Row SA13 ...125 C6
Scwd-yr-Afon SA10 ..49 C4
Scwrfa Rd NP22 ....6 E1
Sea Breeze SA12 ....98 C1
Sea View SA4 ......64 E4
Sea View Terr
  Aberavon SA12 .....99 A2
  Barry CF63 ....215 C7
  Swansea SA1 ....68 D1
Seabank Ct CF36 ...182 E6
Seabrook Pl SA12 ...124 E8
Seaforth Cl SA12 ...98 B3
Seager Dr CF11 ....206 F8
Seagull Cl CF36 ....165 E1
Sealands Dr SA3 ...123 C3
Sealawns CF62 .....214 C1
Seaside Cres 4 SA15 40 C4
Seaton St CF37 ....109 B1
Seaton's Pl CF37 ...109 B1
Seaview
  Cefn Cribwr CF32 ..148 F2
  Swansea SA1 ....69 C2
Seaview Ct 6 CF64 .207 B4
Seaview Dr CF23 ...184 C3
Seaview Ind Est CF24 195 E5
Seaview Pl CF61 ...209 F6
Seawall Rd CF24 ...196 A6
Seaward Ave SA12 ..98 C1
Seaward Cl SA12 ...98 C1
Seawatch Ctr CF61 .210 E1
Seaway Par SA12 ...98 C4
Seaway Parade Ind Est
  SA12 ....98 C5
Sebastopol St SA1 ..95 F7
Second Ave
  Caerphilly CF83 ....137 F3
  Cardiff CF23 ....178 E1

Second Ave continued
  Merthyr Tydfil CF47 ..10 E5
  Swansea SA6 ....68 C8
Sedd Goch CF31 ....169 B4
Sedgemoor Ct NP20 .143 A6
Sedgemoor Rd CF3 ..179 C7
Sefton Ct 8 CF15 ...176 B6
Selby Cl NP44 ......90 B2
Selina Rd CF45 .....82 C5
Selwyn Morris Ct
  CF24 ....195 E5
Senghennydd Pl 3
  CF24 ....195 B7
Senghenydd St CF24 .78 D6
Senlan Ind Est CF23 .179 A1
Senni Cl CF62 ......214 C6
Sepia Cl SA12 ......98 B2
Serecold Ave SA10 ..70 B6
Serpentine Rd NP20 .143 B5
Seven Sisters Mus & Saw
  Mill SA10 ....222 C3
Seven Stiles Ave
  NP19 ....144 D2
Sevenoaks Rd CF5 ..193 B5
Sevenoaks St CF11 ..194 F2
Seventeenth Ave
  CF44 ....224 B1
Seventh Ave
  Merthyr Tydfil CF47 ..10 E5
  Swansea SA6 ....45 D1
Severn Ave
  Barry CF62 ....214 C6
  Barry CF62 ....214 D5
Severn Cl NP11 .....115 B1
Severn Cres SA12 ...98 D1
Severn Ct CF11 .....194 D6
Severn Gr CF11 .....194 D7
Severn Rd Bryn NP12 .85 D4
  Cardiff CF11 ....194 D6
  Porthcawl CF36 ....182 E7
  Swansea SA6 ....68 D8
  Upper Boat CF37 ...136 C2
Severn Road Inf Sch
  CF11 ....194 D6
Severn Road Jun Sch
  CF11 ....194 D6
Severn Terr 12 NP20 143 B4
Severn View
  Abersychan NP4 ....37 F6
  Cwmbran NP44 ....89 A6
Severn View Terr NP4 37 F3
Seward St CF47 ....10 F3
Seymour Ave CF72 ..154 A4
Seymour St
  Aberdare CF44 .....29 A2
  Cardiff CF24 ....195 E6
  Mountain Ash CF45 ..54 D3
Seys Cl CF71 ....188 C2
Seys Ct CF61 ....210 B7
Sgubor Goch CF72 ..172 D5
Shackleton Cl CF62 .211 D7
Shady Rd CF41 .....79 B2
Shaftesbury Cl CF14 .159 E3
Shaftesbury St
  Newport NP20 .....143 B7
  Newport NP20 .....143 C6
Shaftesbury Wlk 5
  NP20 ....143 C6
Shakespeare Ave
  Bridgend CF31 .....168 C5
  Penarth CF64 ......206 E4
Shakespeare Cres
  Ebbw Vale NP23 ....14 C8
  Newport NP20 .....142 E2
Shakespeare Ct 3
  CF24 ....195 C7
Shakespeare Dr CF61 210 B5
Shakespeare Rd
  Barry CF62 ....214 F8
  Cwmbran NP44 ....89 C2
Shakespeare Rise
  CF37 ....136 A6
Shakespeare St 2
  CF24 ....195 C7
Shamrock Rd CF5 ..193 C8
Shannon Cl NP12 ...85 D4
Shannon Rd NP20 ..116 F2
Shap Row NP22 ....6 A6
Sharpe Cl 3 CF23 ..178 E1
Sharpsburgh Pl SA1 .68 D3
Shaw Cl Cardiff CF3 .179 B7
  Ebbw Vale NP23 ....14 A8
Shaw Gr NP20 ......142 E2
Shaw St SA4 ....66 B5
Shawley Ct 7 NP44 .89 C2
Shea Gdns 24 NP20 .143 C3
Sheaf La NP19 .....144 C6
Shearman Pl CF11 ..207 A8
Shears Rd CF5 .....193 F7
Shearwater Cl
  Mumbles SA3 ......122 F6
  Penarth CF36 ......217 A7
  Porthcawl CF36 ....182 D8
Sheen Ct 2 CF62 ...84 F2
Sheerwater Cl 3
  CF3 ....179 E7
Shelburn Cl CF11 ...194 E4
Shelley Cl
  Aberbargoed CF81 ..58 B4
  Blackwood NP11 ...59 D1
Shelley Cres
  Barry CF62 ....214 E8
  Penarth CF64 ......206 F4
Shelley Ct CF83 ....139 C7
Shelley Dr CF31 ....168 C6
Shelley Gn NP44 ...89 C2
Shelley Rd NP19 ...143 F5

Shelley Wlk
  5 Cardiff CF24 ....195 C7
  Rhydyfelin CF37 ...136 A6
Shelone Rd SA11 ...71 B2
Shelone Terr SA11 ..71 C3
Shepherd Dr NP18 ..119 E1
Shepherd's Rd SA4 .43 A3
Shepherd's Terr SA4 .43 A3
Shepherds Cl NP22 ..6 E1
Sheppard St CF37 ..109 B1
Sherborne Ave CF23 .94 A1
Sherborne Cl CF62 .214 B8
Sherborne Wlk SA2 .94 A1
Sherbourne Cl CF14 .177 A4
Sherbourne Ct NP4 ..62 C1
Sherbourne Rd NP4 ..62 C1
Sheridan Cl
  Cardiff CF3 ....179 B7
  Newport NP20 .....142 E4
Sherringham Dr SA3 .122 F5
Sherwood Ct CF5 ...176 D1
Sherwood St CF40 ..79 F1
Shetland Cl NP19 ...143 F7
Shetland Wlk NP19 .143 F7
Shields Cl CF23 ....161 B1
Shiloh La CF47 .....10 E1
Shingrig Rd CF46 ...83 E4
Ship La CF10 ......195 C2
Shirdale Cl CF82 ...85 B2
Shire Ct CF46 ......83 C6
Shires The CF3 ....162 D1
Shirley Cl CF63 ....215 D7
Shirley Dr CF48 ....10 A1
Shirley Rd CF23 ...178 A2
Shoemakers' Row
  CF34 ....102 B3
Shop Hos CF44 ....28 F5
Shop Rd NP4 ....17 F1
Shop Row Blaina NP13 15 D5
  Tredegar NP22 .....13 C6
Shopper's Wlk 1
  SA1 ....95 C6
Shopping Ctr 1 CF44 28 A6
Short St
  Briton Ferry SA11 ...71 C3
  Clydach SA6 ....22 D1
  Swansea SA1 ......95 C8
Showle Acre CF62 ..212 F2
Shrewsbury Ave
  CF39 ....133 D8
Shrewsbury Cl 8
  NP20 ....143 C6
Sibrwd y Dail CF31 .168 D8
Sickert Cl NP19 ....144 A6
Siding Terr SA10 ...70 D7
Sidney Ames Ct 9
  CF24 ....195 D6
Sidney St NP20 ....143 B4
Siemens Way SA7 ..69 A5
Sierra Pines CF45 ..54 A3
Siloam Hill CF83 ...139 F7
Siloan Ct CF41 .....79 A2
Siloh Cres SA1 .....68 D4
Siloh Rd SA1 ......68 D4
Silurian Way CF33 ..148 D2
Silver Ave SA12 ....98 B2
Silver Birch Cl
  Caerleon NP18 ....117 E2
  Cardiff CF14 ......177 C3
Silver Cl Mumbles SA3 122 F7
  Port Talbot SA12 ...98 B3
Silver Ct 8 SA12 ...98 B3
Silver Fir Sq NP10 .142 B3
Silver Jubilee Cotts
  CF5 ....193 D5
Silver St
  Abercarn NP11 ....114 C6
  Cardiff CF24 ......195 D6
Silverhill Cl CF37 ..109 F4
Silverstone Cl 5 CF3 179 D8
Silverton Dr CF72 ..155 E2
Simon Cl CF40 .....107 B2
Simpson Cl NP20 ...117 A4
Simpson's Way CF3 .148 B2
Sims Sq NP19 .....144 D5
Sinclair Dr CF23 ...178 E1
Sindercombe Cl CF23 160 F1
Singleton Hospl SA2 .94 D4
Singleton Rd CF24 ..195 E5
Singleton St SA1 ...95 C6
Sinnatts The SA10 ..71 C8
Sion Pl CF44 ....53 E8
Sion St CF37 ......109 C2
Sion Terr CF44 ....53 E8
Sir Alfred Owen Way
  CF83 ....138 A6
Sir Charles Cres
  NP10 ....163 C5
Sir Charles Sq NP10 163 F6
Sir David's Ct CF5 ..194 B7
Sir Ivor Pl CF64 ...206 C2
Sir Ivor's Rd NP12 ..85 F4
Sir Stafford Cl CF83 .138 C5
Sirhowy Ct
  Cwmbran NP44 ....89 B4
  Tredegar NP22 .....6 F1
Sirhowy Hill Ind Est
  NP22 ....13 F7
Sirhowy Inf Sch NP22 .6 F1
Sirhowy Valley Ctry Pk
  NP11 ....113 F2
Sirhowy View NP12 ..86 A3
Sitwell Way SA12 ...124 E7
Six Bells Est CF48 ..10 B1
Six Bells Rd NP44 ..36 A2
Sixteenth Ave CF44 .224 B1
Sixth Ave
  Merthyr Tydfil CF47 ..10 E5
  Swansea SA6 ......45 D1

Skaithmuir Rd CF24 .195 F7
Skelmuir Rd CF24 ..195 F7
Skenfrith CF12 ....58 E1
Sker Ct CF36 ....165 E1
Sker House (rems of)
  CF36 ....165 A4
Sker Wlk CF36 .....165 E1
Sketty Ave SA2 ....94 D7
Sketty Cl SA2 .....94 D6
Sketty La SA2 .....94 D4
Sketty Park Cl SA2 ..94 C6
Sketty Park Dr SA2 ..94 B6
Sketty Park Rd SA2 ..94 C6
Sketty Prim Sch SA2 .94 C7
Sketty Rd SA2 .....94 E6
Skewen Sta SA10 ...70 E7
Skibereen Cl CF23 .161 A1
Skinner La 4 NP20 .143 C5
Skinner St
  Newport NP20 .....143 C5
  Swansea SA1 ......68 C1
Skokholm Cl CF36 ..165 E1
Skomer Cl CF36 ....165 E1
Skomer Ct 2 CF11 .194 F3
Skomer Pl SA5 .....67 D7
Skomer Rd CF62 ...215 A8
Slade Cl
  Cowbridge CF71 ...188 F2
  Sully CF64 ....216 B5
Slade Gdns SA3 ....122 F6
Slade Rd Barry CF62 214 F7
  Mumbles SA3 ......122 F5
Slade St NP19 .....143 F3
Slade Wood Ho CF62 214 F8
Slate St SA6 ......68 F8
Slipway The CF64 ...207 A5
Slocombe Trust Cotts 1
  CF5 ....194 B7
Slon La CF32 ......184 D2
Sloper Rd
  Cardiff CF11 ......194 D3
  Cardiff CF11 ......194 D4
Sluvad Rd NP4 .....63 C3
Smallbrook Cl NP44 .89 F3
Smallwood Rd SA12 .98 E5
Smeaton Cl CF62 ...212 E1
Smeaton St CF11 ...194 E6
Smith Rd NP13 .....36 A6
Smith Row
  St Nicholas CF5 ...191 F1
  Tonypandy CF40 ...133 B8
Smith St
  Maesteg CF34 .....101 F3
  Ton Pentre CF41 ...79 F2
Smith's Ave CF44 ..224 A1
Smith's Rd SA12 ...47 A2
Smithfield Rd SA8 ..23 E5
Smithies Ave CF64 .216 B4
Smiths Ct CF48 ....11 D5
Smiths Terr NP12 ..86 A6
Smyrna Cotts SA13 .125 C6
Smyrna St SA6 ....68 E5
Snatchwood Cl NP4 .37 F1
Snatchwood Rd NP4 .37 F1
Snatchwood Terr NP4 37 F2
Sneyd St CF11 .....194 D7
Snipe St CF24 .....195 C7
Snow Terr SA9 ....2 E6
Snowden Ct CF83 ...138 C3
Snowden Rd CF5 ...193 B5
Snowdon Cl NP11 ..115 B2
Snowdon Ct NP44 ..90 A5
Snowdon Dr SA5 ...67 D7
Soane St NP10 .....142 A7
Soar Cl
  Croesyceiliog NP44 .90 B6
  Loughor SA4 ......42 F1
Soar Rd SA14 .....41 E4
Soar Terr SA6 .....46 A1
Soberton Ave CF14 .177 F2
Sofrydd Prim Sch
  NP11 ....60 B2
Sofrydd Rd NP11 ...60 B2
Soho St Newport NP19 143 E5
  Newport NP19 .....143 F5
Solent Cl NP12 ....85 D4
Solent Rd CF63 ....215 C8
Solva Ave CF14 ....178 A8
Solva Cl CF62 .....214 F7
Solva Rd SA6 ......68 C8
Somerset Cl CF48 ..10 A5
Somerset Ho 4 SA12 98 B3
Somerset La
  Cefn Coed CF48 ...10 A5
  Port Talbot SA13 ..125 D6
Somerset Pl
  Cwmavon SA12 ....99 E5
  7 Merthyr Tydfil CF47 10 A5
  Swansea SA1 ......95 E6
Somerset Rd
  Barry CF62 ....214 F6
  Cwmbran NP44 ....89 F4
  Mumbles SA3 ......123 A4
  Newport NP19 .....143 E7
Somerset Rd E CF63 214 F6
Somerset St
  Abertillery NP13 ...36 B4
  Cardiff CF11 ......194 E4
  Port Talbot SA13 ..125 D6
Somerset View
  Ogmore-By-Sea CF32 184 D2
  Sully CF64 ....216 E4
Somerton Cres NP19 144 B5
Somerton Ct 1 NP19 144 B3

Somerton Jun & Inf Sch
  NP19 ....144 B6
Somerton La NP19 .144 A4
Somerton Pk NP19 .144 A4
Somerton Pl NP19 ..144 B5
Somerton Rd NP19 .144 A4
Somerville St SA2 ..94 E7
Sophia Cl CF11 ....194 E6
Sophia Wlk CF11 ...194 E6
Sor Brook Picnic Site
  NP44 ....90 E8
Sorrel Dr
  Newport NP20 .....143 A6
  Penpedairheol CF82 .84 E6
South Ave
  Aberdare CF44 .....28 F2
  Cymmer SA13 .....75 D3
  Pontypool NP4 .....62 D1
South Bank NP23 ..7 F4
South Bargod Inf Sch
  CF81 ....57 F3
South Blackvein Ind Est
  NP11 ....114 B4
South Cl
  Bishopston SA3 ...122 A6
  Llanyravon NP44 ..90 B1
  Pencoed CF35 .....170 D8
  Porthcawl CF36 ...182 F7
South Clive St CF11 .194 F1
South Cornelly Ind Est
  CF33 ....166 A5
South Cross Way 5
  SA12 ....98 C2
South Ct NP44 ....62 A8
South Dr CF72 .....155 E3
South Griffin Terr
  NP13 ....15 E2
South Lake Dr NP10 .163 D5
South Loudoun Pl
  CF10 ....195 B3
South Luton Pl CF24 195 C5
South Market St
  NP20 ....143 D3
South Morgan Pl 5
  CF11 ....194 E5
South Pandy Rd
  CF83 ....138 C3
South Par
  Maesteg CF34 .....102 B3
  3 Port Talbot SA13 .99 B3
South Park Rd
  Cardiff CF24 ......195 E5
  Cardiff CF24 ......195 F5
South Pl
  Bridgend CF31 .....168 F3
  Porthcawl CF36 ...182 F7
South Pontypool Ind Pk
  NP4 ....62 F4
South Prospect SA1 .95 D7
South Rd
  Bridgend CF31 .....169 D2
  Cwmbran NP44 ....116 F8
  Gileston CF62 .....211 E1
  Penybryn CF82 ....84 D5
  Porthcawl CF36 ...182 F8
  Sully CF64 ....216 D5
South Rise CF14 ...178 A8
South St
  Abercynon CF45 ...82 C4
  Bargoed CF81 .....57 F4
  Bridgend CF31 .....168 F3
  Dowlais CF48 .....11 F4
  Ebbw Vale NP23 ...7 E4
  Pontypool NP4 .....62 D1
  Pontypridd CF37 ..109 D1
  Port Talbot SA13 ..125 C2
  Porth CF39 ....107 C4
South Terr
  Cefn Coed CF48 ...10 A4
  Southerndown CF32 185 A1
South View
  Bryncae CF72 .....153 E2
  Gorseinon SA4 ....43 D2
  Merthyr Vale CF48 .55 D2
  Pencoed CF35 .....170 D8
  Pontypool NP4 .....62 B2
  Pyle CF33 ....148 D1
  Rhoose CF62 ......213 A4
  Taffs Well CF15 ...158 B4
  Troedyrhiw CF48 ..31 C2
South View Dr CF3 .179 C5
South View Rd NP12 .85 D3
South View Terr NP24 33 E2
South Wlk Barry CF62 214 E6
  Cwmbran NP44 ....89 A3
Southall Ave SA10 ..70 E6
Southall St CF72 ...153 D3
Southbourne Cl CF62 214 F2
Southcourt Rd CF23 178 D1
Southcross Rd SA12 .98 C2
Southdown Rd SA12 .98 C2
Southdown View SA12 98 C1
Southend
  Mumbles SA3 .....123 C4
  Tredegar NP22 ....14 A4
Southend Terr CF81 .32 F3
Southern St CF83 ..138 B2
Southern Way CF23 .178 C2
Southerndown Ave
  SA3 ....93 F1
Southerndown Rd
  CF32 ....185 C2
Southesk Pl CF62 ..214 C2
Southey St Barry CF62 214 F5
  9 Cardiff CF11 ....195 C2
Southgate Ave CF72 155 E3
Southgate Rd SA3 ..121 A4
Southgate St SA11 ..71 E6

Southlands NP13 .....15 E5
Southlands Dr SA3 ...122 F6
Southminster Rd
CF23 ....195 E8
Southra CF64 ......206 A2
Southview Terr 15
NP4 ....17 C6
Southville Rd
8 Newport NP20 ..142 F4
Port Talbot SA12 ...98 C2
Southward La SA3 ..122 F4
Southway NP4 ......39 B1
Sovereign Arc 4
NP20 ....143 C4
Spartan Cl NP18 ...145 C8
Speedwell Dr CF62 .212 F2
Speke St NP19 .....143 E5
Spelter Site CF34 ..102 A7
Spencer Dr CF64 ...206 D7
Spencer La CF37 ...136 A4
Spencer Pl CF37 ...136 A4
Spencer Rd NP20 ..143 A4
Spencer St
6 Barry CF62 ....214 F5
Cwmaman CF44 ....53 A4
Ebbw Vale NP23 ...14 D6
Swansea SA5 ......68 C4
Spencer Terr SA9 ...2 D8
Spencer's Row CF5 .177 A1
Spien Rd SA14 ....218 D7
Spillers & Bakers 12
CF10 ....195 C4
Spinney Cl CF5 ....193 C6
Spinney The
Bridgend CF31 ....169 D4
Bryn NP12 ....85 D3
Cardiff CF14 .....160 B2
Newport NP20 ....117 B2
Swansea SA2 ......94 A6
Spionkop Rd SA6 ...46 C6
Spires Wlk CF63 ..215 B8
Spitzkop CF61 ....209 F6
Splott Ind Est CF24 .195 E5
Splott Rd CF24 ...195 E6
Spoonbill Cl CF36 .165 E1
Spowart Ave SA15 ..40 A6
Spring Bank NP13 ..36 A6
Spring Gardens Pl
CF24 ....195 E7
Spring Gardens Terr
CF24 ....195 E7
Spring Gdns
Gorseinon SA4 .....43 D1
Newport NP20 ....143 C2
Spring Gdns N SA10 .70 F7
Spring Gdns S SA10 .70 F7
Spring Gr Cardiff CF14 159 F2
Cwmbran NP44 .....89 A3
Spring La
Croesyceiliog NP44 ..90 A5
Newport NP20 ....143 A4
Spring Meadow Bsns Pk
CF3 ....179 C2
Spring Meadow Rd
CF3 ....179 D2
Spring Meadow Trad Est
CF3 ....179 D2
Spring St Barry CF63 215 D6
Dowlais CF48 ......11 A5
Newport NP20 ....143 B7
Spring Terr SA1 ....95 B6
Springbourne Cl SA4 .66 D3
Springfield
Horton SA3 ......231 B4
Maesycwmmer CF82 .85 A1
Porth CF39 ......107 F7
Springfield Ave
Porthcawl CF36 ...182 D7
Upper Killay SA2 ...93 B5
Springfield Cl
Aberdare CF44 .....53 F8
Bassaleg NP10 ....141 D3
Bridgend CF31 ....168 F6
Croesyceiliog NP44 .90 A6
Gowerton SA4 .....66 B5
Wenvoe CF5 ......205 A6
Springfield Ct
Church Village CF38 .135 E1
Pontllanfraith NP12 .86 A3
Springfield Dr
Abercynon CF45 ....82 F3
Newport NP20 ....144 D6
Springfield Gdns
Bridgend CF31 ....169 A6
Hirwaun CF44 ......27 F8
Morganstown CF15 .176 B8
Springfield La
Bassaleg NP10 ....141 D3
Bridgend CF31 ....169 A6
Springfield Pl CF11 .194 D6
Springfield Rd
Bassaleg NP10 ....141 D3
Maerdy CF43 ......52 A2
Neath SA10 ....70 F7
Pontypool NP4 .....62 D1
Risca NP11 ....141 B8
Tonyrefail CF39 ...133 D5
Springfield Rise
CF63 ....215 A7
Springfield St SA6 ..45 F1
Springfield Terr
Aberavon SA12 .....99 A2
Abertillery NP13 ....60 B6
Hollybush NP12 ....34 C2
Nelson CF46 ......83 F3
Pontllanfraith NP11 .86 C5

Springfield Terr continued
Pontypool NP4 .....61 E7
Pontypool NP4 .....63 A3
2 Pontypridd CF37 .135 F6
Springfields
Blackwood NP11 ...59 D1
Castleton CF3 .....162 D2
Llanelli SA15 ......40 F2
Springhurst Cl CF14 .176 F7
Springvale NP44 ...89 C4
Springvale Ind Est
NP44 ....89 C4
Springvale Way NP44 89 C4
Springwood CF23 ..178 D5
Springwood Jun & Inf Sch
CF23 ....178 D5
Spruce Cl CF24 ....195 D5
Spruce Tree Gr CF47 .10 D4
Spruce Way SA4 ...44 C2
Spytty Rd NP19 ...144 C2
Square The
Abertridwr CF83 ...136 F7
Beddau CF38 .....155 F6
Bridgend CF31 ....168 E5
Bryncethin CF32 ...151 E3
Crynant SA10 .....226 A7
Cwmbran NP44 .....89 A6
Dinas Powys CF64 .206 A3
Glan y Nant NP12 ...85 A8
Laleston CF32 .....167 E5
Llanharan CF72 ...154 A3
Neath SA11 ....71 E8
Nelson CF46 ......83 E4
New Tredegar NP24 .33 D3
Pencoed CF35 .....170 D8
2 Porth CF39 .....107 F3
Porthcawl CF36 ...182 F6
Treharris CF46 ....83 B7
Squire Cl 7 SA1 ...95 D6
Squire Dr SA2 ....150 F5
Squire St CF71 ...187 E1
Squires Cl NP10 ..142 B6
Squires Ct CF38 ..156 A5
Squires Gate
Rogerstone NP10 ..142 A6
Rogerstone NP10 ..142 A6
Squirrel Walk (Rhodfa'r
Wiwer) SA2 ....19 A5
Stable La NP22 ....13 E5
Stable Row NP4 ...17 C7
Stables Ct CF48 ...11 B4
Stacey Com Jun & Inf Sch
CF24 ....195 D8
Stacey Ct 6 CF24 .195 D8
Stacey Rd
Cardiff CF24 .....195 D7
Dinas Powys CF64 .206 A3
Stack Sq 6 NP4 ...17 C7
Stadium Cl CF11 ..194 E1
Stadwen Rd SA7 ...69 E7
Stafford Comm SA4 .66 D7
Stafford Rd
Cardiff CF11 .....194 F4
Newport NP19 ....143 A4
Pontypool NP4 .....62 E4
Stafford St SA15 ..40 D3
Stag La CF61 .....209 F6
Stag St CF44 .....28 E4
Staines St CF5 ...194 B7
Stair St 8 SA12 ...98 E1
Stallcourt Ave
Cardiff CF23 .....195 D8
Llantwit Major CF61 209 F6
Stallcourt Cl
Cardiff CF23 .....178 E1
Llanblethian CF71 .188 D1
Stallcourt Rd SA13 .125 E4
Stamford St NP20 .143 A6
Standard Signs Est
NP19 ....143 D7
Standard St CF83 ..139 A6
Standard Terr CF39 .107 F7
Standard View CF39 .107 F7
Standard Villas CF83 139 A6
Standert Terr SA10 .222 D3
Stanfield Cl CF48 ..30 E4
Stanfield St NP23 ..35 B6
Stanford Rd NP19 .144 D5
Stangate Ho 1 CF64 207 B4
Stanier Ct 7 CF24 .195 D6
Stanley Ct
2 Newport NP20 ..143 B5
Treorchy CF42 ....78 B5
Stanley Dr 2 CF83 137 F5
Stanley Pl
7 Cwmbran NP44 ..89 E5
Neath SA10 ....48 F2
Swansea SA1 .....95 C7
Stanley St
Abersychan NP4 ...37 E6
4 Llanelli SA15 ...40 D3
Neath SA10 ....70 F7
Newport NP20 ....143 B5
Ton Pentre CF41 ...79 A2
Stanley Sq CF43 ...80 C2
Stanley Terr SA1 ...95 C7
Stanton Way CF64 .127 B8
Stanway Rd CF5 ..193 B6
Stanway Rd CF5 ..193 C5

Stanwell Comp Sch
CF64 ....206 F3
Stanwell Cres CF64 206 B5
Stanwell Rd
Penarth CF64 .....206 F3
Penarth CF64 .....207 B4
Stapleton Pl 2 SA6 .68 F8
Star La Pentyrch CF15 175 C5
Pontypool NP4 .....62 B8
Star Rd NP4 ......39 F6
Star St Cardiff CF24 195 D6
Cwmbran NP44 .....89 E2
Tredegar NP22 .....6 D2
Star Trad Est NP18 118 A5
Star Villas NP18 ..118 A5
Starbuck St CF83 .139 B3
Starling Rd CF62 .210 D6
Station App
Bassaleg NP10 ....142 B3
Ebbw Vale NP23 ....7 D1
Penarth CF64 .....207 A3
Pontyclun CF72 ...173 B7
Tondu CF32 ......150 C5
Station Approach Rd
CF62 ....214 E2
Station Ave NP11 ..112 F6
Station Bldgs 3 NP20 143 A2
Station Farm NP44 .89 F5
Station Hill
Bridgend CF31 ....168 F4
Maesteg CF34 ....102 A3
Station Ho CF15 ..174 E7
Station Pl NP11 ...114 F2
Station Rd
Abercraf SA9 .....222 D7
Abercynon CF45 ...82 E2
Abergwynfi SA13 ...76 C5
Abertysswg SA13 ...14 F3
Abertysswg NP23 ..33 C8
Bargoed CF81 ....58 A5
Blaina NP13 ......15 D5
Briton Ferry SA11 ..71 C3
11 Brynmawr NP23 ..8 C4
Bynea SA14 ......42 A3
Caerleon NP18 ...118 B3
Cardiff CF14 .....160 A1
Cardiff CF14 .....176 F3
Cardiff CF14 .....177 E8
Cefn Coed CF48 ...10 A4
Clydach NP7 ....9 E7
Coedely CF72 ....174 A1
Creigiau CF15 ....174 A7
Crynant SA10 ....226 A7
Cwmbran NP44 .....89 C5
Cymmer SA13 .....75 C5
Dinas Powys CF64 .206 A3
Dowlais CF48 .....11 B5
Ebbw Vale NP23 ...14 D8
Ferndale CF43 ....80 A7
Glais SA7 ....47 A6
Glan y Nant NP12 ..85 A8
Glanaman SA18 ...220 A8
Gowerton SA4 ....66 C5
Grovesend SA4 ....43 D6
Hirwaun CF44 .....27 D8
Llanbradach CF83 .111 F1
Llanelli SA15 .....40 D4
Llangennech SA14 .42 C8
Llanmorlais SA4 ...64 C2
Llantwit Fardre CF38 156 F7
Llantwit Major CF61 209 F6
Llanwern NP18 ...145 B4
Loughor SA4 ......65 C8
Maerdy CF43 ......52 A1
Nant-y-Moel CF32 .104 C7
Neath SA10 ....70 F7
New Tredegar NP24 .34 A1
Newbridge NP11 ...60 A1
Pen-clawdd SA4 ...64 F4
Penarth CF64 .....207 A3
Pont Rhyd-y-cyff CF34 128 E6
Pontarddulais SA4 .19 B5
Ponthir NP18 ....117 F6
Pontrhydyfen SA12 .73 B1
Pontypool NP4 .....62 E2
Port Talbot SA13 ..125 B8
Porth CF39 ......107 F6
Pyle CF33 ....148 D3
Radyr CF15 ......176 C5
Rhoose CF62 .....213 A1
Risca NP11 ......114 F1
Seven Sisters SA10 222 D3
Swansea SA1 .....68 D4
Swansea SA5 .....67 E3
Swansea SA7 .....69 C7
Tonna SA10 ......49 C3
Tonypandy CF40 ..107 A5
Tonyrefail CF39 ...133 B5
Tredegar NP22 .....6 C2
Treorchy CF42 ....78 D5
Tylorstown CF43 ..80 C1
Ystrad Mynach CF82 84 E2
Ystradgynlais SA9 ..2 F8
Station Rd E CF5 ..205 B7
Station Rd W CF5 .205 A6
Station Row
New Tredegar NP24 .33 E3
Pontyrhyl CF32 ...129 F7
Station Sq CF48 ...55 D4
Station St
8 Aberdare CF44 ..29 A2
Abersychan NP4 ...38 A4
Barry CF63 ......215 A4
Blaengarw CF32 ..103 E6
Machen CF83 ....140 A7
Maesteg CF34 ....102 A2
Newbridge NP11 ...86 C5
Pontllottyn CF81 ...12 F1

Station St continued
CF64 ....206 F3
3 Porth CF39 .....107 F3
Tonypandy CF40 ..106 F4
Tonypandy CF40 ..106 F4
Treherbert CF42 ...50 F1
Station Terr
Aberdare CF44 .....53 B5
Bedlinog CF46 ....56 A7
Bryn SA13 ....100 F4
Caerphilly CF83 ...137 E4
Caerphilly CF83 ...138 B2
Cardiff CF10 .....195 B6
Cardiff CF5 ......193 F6
Cwm NP23 ....35 B7
3 Cwmbran NP44 ..89 C5
Dowlais CF48 .....11 C5
East Aberthaw CF62 212 B2
Fochriw CF81 .....32 C7
Llanharry CF72 ...172 D6
Llantwit Fardre CF38 156 D7
Maerdy CF43 ......52 A1
Merthyr Vale CF48 .55 D3
Mountain Ash CF45 .81 F8
Nelson CF46 ......83 E4
Pen-clawdd SA4 ...64 F4
Penarth CF64 .....207 A3
Peterston-Super-Ely
CF5 ....191 D5
Pontyclun CF72 ...173 A7
2 Port Talbot SA12 124 F8
Senghenydd CF83 .110 E2
Tonypandy CF40 ..106 E8
Tredegar NP22 .....6 B2
Treherbert CF42 ...50 F1
Station Yd CF83 ...138 D7
StCadoc's RC Sch
CF3 ....179 B7
Stebonheath Cty Prim Sch
SA15 ....40 F5
Stebonheath Terr
SA15 ....40 F5
Steel Works Rd NP23 14 E6
Steep St 7 CF64 ..207 A5
Steepfield NP44 ...90 A6
Steepholm Cl CF36 165 E1
Steer Cres NP19 ..144 A7
Stella Cl CF14 ...159 F3
Stelvio Park Ave
NP20 ....142 F3
Stelvio Park Cres
NP20 ....142 F3
Stelvio Park Ct NP20 142 F3
Stelvio Park Dr NP20 142 F3
Stembridge Ave SA5 67 E5
Stenhousemuir Pl
CF24 ....195 F7
Stephen's Terr CF14 82 F3
Stephenson Ct 8
CF24 ....195 C6
Stephenson Rd SA2 93 F6
Stephenson St
Cardiff CF11 .....194 E5
Newport NP19 ....143 E1
Stepney La SA2 ...67 C2
Stepney Pl SA15 ..40 D5
Stepney Prec 4 SA15 40 D5
Stepney Rd
Glanaman SA18 ...220 C8
Swansea SA2 .....67 D1
Waunarlwydd SA5 .66 E3
Stepney St
3 Llanelli SA15 ...40 D5
Swansea SA18 ....68 B2
Stepping Stones The
NP4 ....39 E7
Sterndale Bennett Rd
NP19 ....144 F5
Sterry Rd SA4 ....66 B5
Stevelee NP44 ....89 C1
Stevenson Cl
Rogerstone NP10 ..142 A6
Rogerstone NP10 ..142 B6
Stevenson Ct NP10 142 A6
Stevenson Street Ind Est
NP19 ....164 F8
Stewart Rd NP20 ..213 A1
Stewart St Cwm NP23 35 B6
Llanelli SA15 .....40 C6
Steynton Path NP44 89 C2
Stiels NP44 ......89 C2
Stirling Rd Barry CF62 214 C7
Cardiff CF5 ......193 A4
Stockland St
Caerphilly CF83 ...138 A2
Cardiff CF24 .....194 F3
Stockton Cl 9 NP19 143 E8
Stockton Rd NP19 .143 D8
Stockton Way NP22 13 E8
Stocktonville NP22 13 D8
Stokes Cotts NP18 117 F6
Stokes Ct NP18 ...117 F6
Stokes Dr NP18 ...118 A6
Stone's Hos NP13 ..15 D6
Stonebridge Rd NP23 7 A4
Stonechat Cl
2 Cardiff CF23 ...180 A6
Porthcawl CF36 ...165 D1
Stonerwood View
NP11 ....87 B8
Stones Mus SA13 .126 C5
Stonewell St 7 CF23 178 C2
Stony La CF35 ....186 A6
Stony Rd NP4 .....37 F5
Stormy La
Nant-y-Moel CF32 .104 F8
North Cornelly CF33 165 E7

Storrar Pl CF24 ...196 A8
Storrar Rd CF24 ..196 A8
Stour Ct NP44 ....89 A4
Stow Hill
Newport NP20 ....143 A4
Newport NP20 ....143 B4
Pontypridd CF37 ..135 D7
Stow Park Ave NP20 143 A3
Stow Park Circ NP20 143 A3
Stow Park Cres NP20 143 A4
Stow Park Dr NP20 143 A3
Stow Park Gdns
NP20 ....143 A3
Stowe Path 4 NP44 90 B2
Stradey Ct 3 SA15 40 C7
Stradey Park Ave
SA15 ....40 C6
Stradey Rd SA15 ..40 C7
Stradling Cl
Barry CF62 ......214 B6
Cowbridge CF71 ..188 D2
Sarn CF32 ....150 F4
Sully CF64 ......216 B5
Stradling Pl CF61 .210 A5
Stradmore Cl CF15 157 F5
Strand Ferndale CF43 79 F6
Swansea SA1 .....95 D7
Strand Row SA1 ...95 D7
Strand St CF45 ....54 F2
Strand The
Blaengarw CF32 ..103 E7
Cwmbran NP44 .....89 E4
Llantwit Major CF61 209 F6
Stratford Dr CF36 .182 E8
Stratford Gn 5 CF63 215 C8
Stratford Ho NP20 142 E3
Strathnairn St CF24 195 B8
Strathview NP11 ...86 C5
Strathy Rd CF3 ...180 A7
Stratton Way SA10 71 C8
Strauss Rd SA12 ..98 A2
Strawberry Pl SA6 41 F1
Stream St CF45 ....54 D2
Street No 17 SA12 98 B4
Street No 19 SA12 98 B5
Street No 21 SA12 98 B5
Stryd Arthur SA18 219 B7
Stryd Fawr SA18 ..219 C7
Stryd Harold 6 SA18 219 B7
Stryd Hywel Harris
CF82 ....111 E7
Stryd Marged SA18 219 C7
Stryd y Parc SA18 219 C6
Stryd-y-Coleg SA18 219 B7
Stryd-y-Gwynt SA18 219 B7
Stryd-yr-Eglwys 8
SA18 ....219 B7
Stuart Cl Cardiff CF11 194 D1
Stuart Pl CF10 ....195 C1
Stuart St Aberdare CF44 29 A1
Cardiff CF10 .....195 B1
Merthyr Tydfil CF47 10 D2
Pontlottyn CF81 ...12 F1
Pontyclun CF72 ...173 B7
Treherbert CF42 ...50 F2
Treorchy CF42 ....78 D7
Stuart Terr CF72 ..155 B2
Sturmi Way CF33 .148 C1
Sturminster Rd CF23 195 E8
Stuttgarter Strasse
CF10 ....195 B6
Subway Rd CF63 ..215 A4
Sudbury Wlk 1 NP10 143 C6
Sudcroft St CF11 ..194 C4
Suffolk Cl CF36 ...182 F4
Suffolk Ho 1 SA12 98 C3
Suffolk Pl
Ogmore Vale CF32 104 C4
Porthcawl CF36 ...182 F7
Suffolk St CF31 ...168 A3
Sullivan Circ NP10 144 D4
Sullivan Cl Cardiff CF3 179 D7
Penarth CF64 .....206 F1
Sully Cty Prim Sch
CF64 ....216 A4
Sully Moors Rd
Barry CF64 ......215 F5
Barry CF64 ......215 F6
Sully Pl CF64 ....207 B4
Sully Rd CF64 ....206 D1
Sully Terr CF64 ...207 A4
Sully Terrace La
CF64 ....207 A2
Sully View CF63 ..215 C4
Summer Pl SA7 ...69 F7
Summerau Ct CF5 194 C7
Summercliffe Chalet Pk
SA3 ....122 D4
Summerdale Cl CF38 135 F1
Summerfield Ave
CF14 ....177 F2
Summerfield Ct CF40 107 A5
Summerfield Dr
Llantrisant CF72 ..155 E2
Porthcawl CF36 ...165 E1
Summerfield Hall La
CF82 ....85 B3
Summerfield La
CF83 ....139 C6
Summerfield Pl
Cardiff CF14 .....177 D5
Neath SA11 ......71 E2
Summerfield Rd NP23 7 D5
Summerfield Terr
Fleur De Lis NP12 .85 B5
3 Merthyr Tydfil CF47 10 F4

Summerhill CF47 ...10 F1
Summerhill Ave
NP19 ....143 E6
Summerhill Cl CF3 180 A7
Summerhill Ct NP4 37 E7
Summerhill Ho 9
NP19 ....143 E6
Summerhill Pl CF47 10 F1
Summerland Cl CF62 206 D6
Summerland Cres
CF64 ....206 D6
Summerland La SA3 122 E5
Summerland Pk SA2 93 B5
Summerwood Cl CF5 193 B8
Sumner Cl CF5 ...176 E2
Sun St CF24 .....195 D6
Sundew Cl Cardiff CF5 176 D2
Penarth CF64 .....206 E5
Sunlea Cres NP4 ..62 F6
Sunningdale CF83 .137 E2
Sunningdale Ave SA3 93 F1
Sunningdale Cl CF23 178 B4
Sunningdale Cl NP19 144 D6
Sunningdale Dr SA4 43 B4
Sunningdale Rd SA12 98 E5
Sunninghill Terr SA15 40 E6
Sunny Bank
Glyncorrwg SA13 .227 C2
Llantrisant CF72 ..155 D3
Ogmore Vale CF32 104 E2
Porth CF39 ......107 E5
Tonypandy CF40 ..106 D7
Tonypandy CF40 ..107 A3
Treharris CF46 ....83 A5
Sunny Bank Terr
CF83 ....139 F7
Sunny Cres SA13 ..75 D3
Sunny Crest NP11 .87 A7
Sunny Hill Llanelli SA15 40 E6
Maerdy CF43 ......52 A1
Rhymney NP22 ....13 A2
Sunny Rd Llanelli SA15 40 D6
Port Talbot SA12 ..124 D8
Sunny Side CF37 ..109 B2
Sunny View CF81 ..32 F8
Sunny View Terr NP12 58 F4
Sunny-Mount SA12 98 D5
Sunnybank
Bassaleg NP10 ....141 E4
Cwmbran NP44 ....115 F8
Dinas Powys CF64 206 C4
Merthyr Tydfil CF47 10 D2
Neath SA10 ....48 C1
New Tredegar NP24 33 E3
Pyle CF33 ....148 B2
Sunnybank Cl
Cardiff CF14 .....177 C3
Mumbles SA3 ....122 F8
Sunnybank Ct
Bridgend CF31 ....169 C5
Pontypool NP4 .....62 E3
Sunnybank Pl SA12 124 D8
Sunnybank Rd
Blackwood NP12 ..85 E8
Pontypool NP4 .....62 D3
Port Talbot SA12 ..124 D8
Sunnybank St SA44 53 B8
Sunnybank Terr
Abertillery NP13 ...59 F7
Treorchy CF42 ....78 C5
Sunnybank Way NP13 59 F7
Sunnybrook Ct CF5 176 D1
Sunnycroft Cl CF64 206 B3
Sunnycroft La CF64 206 B2
Sunnycroft Rise 4
CF64 ....206 B2
Sunnyland Cres SA10 70 F8
Sunnyside
Llanelli Hill NP7 ...9 C4
Ogmore Vale CF32 130 E8
Sunnyside Rd CF31 168 E4
Sunnyside Terr SA13 75 C6
Sunnyview NP22 ...13 D7
Surgery Rd NP13 ..15 E6
Surgery Road Bglws
NP13 ....15 E6
Surrey Pl NP19 ...143 E7
Surrey St CF5 ....194 B6
Susannah Pl CF46 83 A6
Sussex Cl NP19 ...144 A2
Sussex St CF11 ...194 F4
Sutherland Cres
NP19 ....144 A7
Sutherland Mans 8
CF14 ....176 F6
Sutton Gr CF23 ...160 C3
Sutton La CF32 ...184 C4
Sutton Rd
Llandow CF71 ....199 C5
Newport NP19 ....143 D8
Ogmore-By-Sea CF32 184 D3
Sutton Rise CF32 .184 D4
Sutton Spring Rd
CF71 ....199 C4
Swallow Tree Cl SA10 48 E2
Swallow Way NP10 163 E8
Swallowhurst Cl CF5 192 F4
Swan Cres NP23 ...7 F4
Swan Ct SA2 .....93 E6
Swan La SA9 .....2 C7
Swan Rd SA12 ....98 C7
Swan Sq NP4 ....37 F3
Swan St Baglan SA12 98 C7
Llantrisant CF72 ..155 D3

Swan St continued
Merthyr Tydfil CF47 ....30 D8
Swansea SA1 ....95 D8
Swan Terr 7 CF40 ...106 F4
Swan Wlk SA15 ....40 B5
Swanage Cl CF3 .....180 A7
Swanbridge Farm
CF64 ....216 D3
Swanbridge Gr CF64 ..216 C5
Swanbridge Rd CF64 .216 C5
Swanfield CF3 ....180 A7
Swanfield Pl 3 SA15 .40 D6
Swansea Castle SA1 ....95 D7
Swansea Coll SA2 ......94 D7
Swansea Coll of Art
SA1 ....95 D7
**Swansea Inst of Higher Ed
(Townhill Campus)**
SA1 ....94 F8
**Swansea Inst of Higher
Educ (Mount Pleasant
Campus)** SA1 ....95 C8
**Swansea Maritime &
Industrial Mus** SA1 ..95 D5
Swansea Mus SA1 .....95 D5
Swansea Rd
Gorseinon SA4 ....66 E7
Hirwaun CF44 ....27 E8
Llanelli SA15 ....40 E6
Merthyr Tydfil CF48 ...10 A2
Penllergaer SA4 ....44 B2
Pontardawe SA8 ....23 C2
Pontlliw SA4 ....44 A4
Swansea SA5 ....45 B2
Waunarlwydd SA5 ......66 E4
Swansea St CF24 .....195 E6
Swansea Vale Rly SA7 .69 B5
Swansea West Ind Pk
SA5 ....67 C4
Sward Cl NP10 ....142 A7
Sway Rd SA6 ....46 A1
Sweet Briar La SA3 ..123 A8
Sweetwater Pk CF48 ..10 B7
Sweetwells Cotts
CF32 ....129 F7
Sweldon Cl CF5 ......193 B3
Swift Bsns Ctr The
CF24 ....195 D5
Swift Cl CF3 ....179 B7
Swilym Terr CF47 .....30 E7
Swinburne Cl NP19 ..144 A5
Swinton St CF24 .....195 E6
Swn y Mor CF32 ......185 A1
Swn Yr Adar CF31 ....168 D8
Swn Yr Aderyn CF33 ..148 D2
Swn Yr Afon CF42 .....78 E5
Swn yr Eos SA9 ....2 E7
Swn-y-gwent Day Hosp
SA18 ....219 B7
Swn-y-Mor
Barry CF62 ....214 A3
Port Talbot SA12 ......98 D1
Swn-y-Nant
Abergwynfi SA13 ......76 B6
Church Village CF38 ..135 E1
Crynant SA10 ....226 A8
Cwm-twrch Isaf SA9 ....1 B2
Pencoed CF35 ....152 C1
Swn-yr Afon CF48 .....10 B4
Swn-yr-Afon
Aberdulais SA10 ....49 C4
Gilfach Goch CF39 ....132 B7
Pyle CF33 ....148 E3
Ton Pentre CF41 ....79 B3
Swn-yr-Nant CF82 .....84 D7
Sybil St SA6 ....46 E7
Sycamore Ave
Neath SA11 ....72 A6
Newport NP19 ....144 B4
Porthcawl CF36 ......183 D8
Pyle CF33 ....148 C2
St Athan CF62 ....211 B7
Tredegar NP22 ....6 D1
Sycamore Cl
Aberdare CF44 ....28 C3
Bridgend CF31 ....168 F8
Dinas Powys CF64 ....206 B2
Llandough CF64 ......206 E6
Swansea SA2 ....94 A7
Sycamore Cres
Baglan SA12 ....98 D7
Barry CF62 ....215 A4
Risca NP11 ....115 B1
Trefechan CF48 ....10 B6
Sycamore Cross CF5 .191 D1
Sycamore Ct
Baglan SA12 ....98 D7
Bargoed CF81 ....57 E2
Caerphilly NP12 ......85 F6
Cwmbran NP44 ....115 F8
Sycamore Dr CF40 ....107 A5
Sycamore Ho CF14 ...176 E6
Sycamore Pl
1 Cardiff CF5 ......193 D8
Cwmbran NP44 ....89 B6
Sycamore Rd
Llanharry CF72 ......172 C5
Merthyr Tydfil CF47 ...10 E4
Mumbles SA3 ....123 A8
Pontypool NP4 ....62 D2
Sycamore Rd S NP4 ..62 D1
Sycamore St
Rhydyfelin CF37 .....136 A5
Taffs Well CF15 .....158 A4
Sycamore Terr NP11 ..87 B4

Sycamore Tree Cl
CF15 ....176 A6
Sychbant Ave CF34 ..102 A1
Sydney Ct NP12 ....85 C6
Sydney St SA5 ....68 B4
Sylvan Cl Cardiff CF5 .176 E1
Newport NP20 ....117 B3
Sylvan Way SA2 ....94 C7
Sylvia Terr SA5 ....68 C4
Symmons St SA1 ......68 C4
Syon Park Cl CF3 ....180 A7
Syr' David's Ave CF24 ..195 D6
Syon Park Cl CF3 ....180 A7
Syphon St CF39 ......107 F3
Syr' David's Ave CF24 .195 D6
Syr-Dafydd Ave NP12 .59 B2
System CF24 ....195 D6

T

Tabernacle Ct NP23 ...14 F2
Tabernacle Rd
Glanaman SA18 ......219 F8
Glanaman SA18 ......220 A8
Tabernacle St
Neath SA10 ....70 F7
Swansea SA1 ....68 D3
Tabernacle Terr 5
SA12 ....99 D5
Tabor Pl CF34 ....102 B3
Tabor Rd CF82 ....85 B2
Tabor St CF15 ....158 A4
Tabor Terr SA14 ......41 E6
Tacoma Sq CF10 .....195 C1
Taf Cl CF62 ....214 C6
Taf Fachan Ho CF48 ...3 F4
Taf Olwg CF46 ....83 D3
Tafarnaubach Ind Est
NP22 ....6 A2
Taff Bargoed Ctr CF46 .56 C4
Taff Bsns Ctr CF37 ...136 C3
Taff Cl NP23 ....7 C4
Taff Cotts
Llantrisant CF72 ....155 E2
Tonypandy CF40 .....106 E8
Taff Ct NP44 ....89 A5
Taff Emb Cardiff CF11 .194 F3
Cardiff CF11 ....195 A4
Taff Fawr Ho CF48 ....10 A3
Taff Fechan Ho CF48 ..10 A3
Taff Glen View CF47 ..30 F8
Taff Gorge Countryside Ctr
CF15 ....158 D2
Taff St 5 Cardiff CF10 .195 B5
Ferndale CF43 ....79 F7
Merthyr Vale CF48 ....55 D3
Pontypridd CF37 .....109 C1
Treherbert CF42 ......50 F1
Taff Terr
Abercynon CF45 ......82 D1
Cardiff CF11 ....195 A2
Radyr CF15 ....176 C5
Tonypandy CF40 .....106 C7
Treorchy CF42 ....78 D6
Taff Vale CF46 ....82 F6
Taff Vale Ct CF47 .....10 E2
Taff Vale Flats CF37 .135 C8
Taff Vale Prec 1
CF37 ....109 C1
Taff Workshops 5
CF10 ....195 A4
Taffs Fall Rd CF37 ...136 D2
Taffs Mead Emb
CF11 ....194 F4
Taffs Mead Rd CF37 ..136 D2
Tafwys Wlk CF83 .....118 A3
Tai Ann CF37 ....109 F5
Tai Arfryn CF31 ......168 C3
Tai Cwm CF39 ....107 F3
Tai Duffryn CF15 ....158 A7
Tai Gwalia SA9 ......221 C5
Tai Llanbedr CF5 ....191 E6
Tai Mawr Rd CF48 ....10 A3
Tai Mesen NP23 ....14 E3
Tai Newydd
Rhydyfelin CF37 .....136 B4
Ynysybwl CF37 ....81 F2
Tai Penyard CF47 .....10 E2
Tai Siriol CF34 ....83 D3
Tai Ysgol Fach CF48 ..29 F8
Tai'r Felin SA10 ......49 C4
Tai'r Heol CF37 ......109 B6
Tai'r Twynau CF48 .....11 B7
Tai'r Ynys Fawr SA12 .73 C1
Tai'r-Heol CF82 ....84 D8
Tai-Canol CF48 ....10 B3
Tai-Yr-Efail CF5 ......11 A7
Taicanol SA12 ....99 E6
Taillwyd Rd Neath SA10 .48 B1
Neath Abbey SA10 .....71 B8
Tair Erw Rd CF14 ....177 D5
Tair Grawen 6 CF47 ..10 D2
Tair Waun Rd CF34 ..101 E4
Tairfelin CF31 ......168 E7
Tairgwaith Prim Sch
SA18 ....220 E6
Tal y Coed SA14 ......18 F3
Tal-y-Wern SA13 .....125 D5
Talana Terr CF34 ......75 A1
Talbot Cl CF72 ......155 D3
Talbot Gn SA4 ....66 C5
Talbot La NP20 ......143 C4
Talbot Rd
Llantrisant CF72 ....155 D3

Talbot Rd continued
Neath SA10 ....70 F6
Neath SA11 ....71 F5
Penllergaer SA4 ......43 F4
Port Talbot SA13 ....125 C2
Pyle CF33 ....148 D3
Talbot Green CF72 ...155 C2
Talbot Sq
Merthyr Tydfil CF47 ...10 F3
Talbot Green CF72 ...155 B2
Talbot St Cardiff CF11 .194 E6
Gowerton SA4 ....66 B5
Llanelli SA15 ....40 D4
Maesteg CF34 ....102 A3
Talbot Terr
Maesteg CF34 ....102 A4
St Mary Church CF71 .201 A4
Talcennau Rd SA13 ..125 C7
Taldwyn Terr CF48 ....31 C2
Talfaen Cl NP4 ....38 C1
Talfan Rd SA1 ....69 B3
Talgarth Cl NP44 ......89 C2
Talgarth St CF34 .....102 C2
Taliesin NP44 ....89 C4
Taliesin Cl
Pencoed CF35 ....152 B1
Rogerstone NP10 ....142 B6
Taliesin Dr NP10 ....142 B6
Taliesin Pl SA4 ....42 C1
Taliesyn Rd SA1 ......95 A8
Talley Rd SA5 ....68 B5
Tallis Cl NP19 ....144 E5
Tallis St CF42 ....78 B5
Talworth St CF24 ....195 C7
Talybont CF62 ....211 D7
Talybont Rd CF5 .....193 D5
Talyclun SA14 ....18 E2
Talycopa Prim Sch
SA7 ....69 F7
Talyfan CF72 ....154 A3
Talyfan CF71 ....188 F1
Talygarn Cl CF72 ....172 F5
Talygarn Dr CF72 ....172 F6
Talygarn St CF14 ....177 F2
Talywain Ho NP4 ......37 E5
Talywern SA14 ....42 B7
Tamar Cl Bettws NP20 .116 E2
Bryn NP12 ....85 D3
Tan House Dr NP18 ..118 C2
Tan y Bryn CF43 ......79 B8
Tan y Marian CF43 ....79 B8
Tan y Marian Rd SA1 ..95 B8
Tan-y-Bryn
Beddau CF38 ....156 A7
Brynna CF72 ....153 D4
Pencoed CF35 ....152 F1
Porth CF39 ....107 D2
Rhymney NP22 ....13 A2
Senghenydd CF83 ....110 F1
Senghenydd CF83 ....111 A1
Tan-y-Bryn St CF44 ...29 A1
Tan-y-bryn Terr SA4 ..64 F4
Tan-y-Coed NP44 ......37 F1
Tan-y-Farteg SA9 ......2 C7
Tan-y-Fron
Barry CF62 ....214 B3
Treorchy CF42 ....78 D5
Tan-y-Gelli SA18 ....220 B8
Tan-y-graig SA9 .....222 B7
Tan-y-Groes Pl SA13 .125 D8
Tan-y-Groes St SA13 .125 C8
Tan-y-Lan Terr SA6 ...68 F8
Tan-y-Llan Terr NP22 .12 E4
Tan-y-Lon SA6 ....22 D1
Tan-y-Pych CF42 ......50 D4
Tan-y-Rhiw SA10 ....222 D3
Tan-Yr-Allt CF72 .....155 E2
Tanglewood Cl CF14 ..160 A2
Tangmere Dr CF5 ....176 D2
Tank Farm Rd SA10 ...70 C3
Tank Farm Way CF64 .215 D6
Tanlan Sq NP24 ....33 F2
Tansy Cl Cardiff CF14 .159 D3
Penpedairheol CF82 ...84 E6
Tanyard Pl CF44 ....53 B8
Tanybryn
Mountain Ash CF45 ...81 F8
Risca NP11 ....141 C8
Tanybryn Pl CF41 .....10 F4
Tanybryn Terr CF43 ..107 C8
Tanycoed Rd SA6 ......22 F1
Tanycoed St SA15 .....81 F8
Tanycoed Terr CF44 ...53 F4
Tanydarren SA8 ....221 B1
Tanyfan SA18 ....218 E6
Tanygarth SA9 ....222 C7
Tanygraig Rd SA14 ....41 E4
Tanyrallt Abercraf SA9 .222 C7
Clydach SA6 ....22 D1
Tanyrallt Ave CF31 ..168 F7
Tanyrhiw Rd SA11 ....226 E5
Tanywaun SA9 ....222 B6
Tanywern La SA9 ....2 B7
Tanyryallt Ave CF31 ..168 F7
Tapley Cl CF5 ....193 C3
Taplow Terr SA1 ....68 F2
Tarragon Way CF23 ..160 E1
Tarran Workshops
CF31 ....168 F3
Tarren Terr SA12 ....100 A3
Tarrws Cl CF5 ....205 A4
Tarwick Dr CF3 ......179 E6
Tatem Dr CF5 ....193 C7
Tathan Cres CF62 ....211 D5
Talbot La NP20 ......143 C4
Taunton Ave CF3 .....179 C5
Taunton Cres CF3 ....179 C5
Tavistock Cl SA2 ......94 A7
Tavistock St SA2 ......94 D7

Tavistock St CF24 ....195 B7
Tawe Bsns Village
SA6 ....69 A5
Tawe Pk SA9 ....46 E7
Tawe Pl SA6 ....46 E7
Tawe Rd SA7 ....69 E7
Tawe St SA6 ....69 A8
Tawe Terr SA8 ....23 E4
Tawe View Cres SA6 ..45 F1
Tawel Fan SA14 ....41 A6
Tawelfan Nelson CF46 .83 E4
Ystradgynlais SA9 ......1 F4
Tawelfryn CF48 ......225 F3
Taylor Rd CF31 ......168 F7
Taylor St NP11 ......114 F3
Taylor's Row SA11 ....71 D6
Taymuir Green Ind Pk
CF24 ....195 F8
Taymuir Rd CF24 .....195 F8
Teal Cl CF36 ....182 E8
Teal St CF24 ....195 C7
Tealham Dr CF3 .....180 B7
Teamans Row CF15 ..176 B8
Teasel Ave CF64 .....206 E5
Techniquest CF10 ...195 B1
Technology Dr CF31 ..168 C2
Ted Davies Cl CF33 ..166 E5
Tedder Cl CF14 ......177 F7
Tees Cl NP20 ....116 F2
Teg Fan SA10 ....70 E6
Tegfan Caerphilly CF83 .137 E3
Cardiff CF11 ....194 D6
Ferndale CF43 ....79 D7
Pontlliw SA4 ....44 C5
Tegfan Cl CF14 ......177 F8
Tegfan Ct NP44 ......115 F8
Tegid Rd SA1 ....68 B1
Teglan Pk SA18 .....218 F5
Teifi Dr CF62 ....214 C5
Teifi Pl CF5 ....193 D5
Teify Cres CF32 .....104 E7
Teilo Cres SA1 ....95 B8
Teilo St CF11 ....194 D7
Teilos Dr CF31 ......169 A5
Telekebir Rd CF37 ..109 A2
Telford Cl
Penpedairheol CF82 ...84 E7
Rogerstone NP10 ....142 B6
Telford St
Cardiff CF11 ....194 E5
Newport NP19 ......143 E4
Telor-y-Coed CF83 ..112 A5
Telyn Aur SA6 ....45 E2
Temperance Ct CF15 .157 B1
Temperance Hill
NP11 ....114 F3
Temperance La SA9 ....1 F1
Temperance Pl CF37 .109 C1
Templar Parc 4 CF24 .195 C4
Temple St Llanelli SA15 .40 E5
Maesteg CF34 ....102 B3
Newport NP20 ......143 D2
Swansea SA1 ....95 D7
Templeton Ave CF14 .159 E5
Templeton Cl CF14 ..159 E5
Templeton Way SA5 ...67 F7
Ten Acre Wood SA13 .126 B1
Tenby Cl
Dinas Powys CF64 ...206 C3
Llanyravon NP44 ......90 A3
Tenby Ct CF83 ......137 D4
Tenison Rd NP4 ....38 D1
Tennyson Ave NP18 ..145 A4
Tennyson Cl CF37 ...136 A6
Tennyson Dr CF31 ...168 D6
Tennyson Rd
Barry CF62 ....214 E8
Newport NP19 ......144 A5
Penarth CF64 ....206 F4
Tennyson Terr NP24 ..33 F1
Tennyson Way
Llantwit Major CF61 .210 B5
Swansea SA2 ....93 F8
Tensing Cl CF14 .....159 F1
Tensing Terr 11 CF63 .215 B6
Tenth Ave
Merthyr Tydfil CF47 ...10 F5
Swansea SA6 ....45 D2
Teras Brynteg 1
SA18 ....219 B7
Terfyn Ynysawdre
CF32 ....150 E4
Tern Cl CF3 ....179 F8
Tern Ct NP44 ....89 A5
Tern Rd CF36 ....182 D8
Terra Nova Way CF64 .206 F5
Terrace Rd SA1 ....95 B7
Terrace Road Prim Sch
SA1 ....95 B7
Terrace The
Creigiau CF15 ....174 E8
Rhymney NP22 ....12 E4
Tetbury Cl NP20 ....143 C7
Tewdric Ct NP44 ......90 B5
Tewdrig Cl CF61 ....209 F5
Tewends 12 NP44 ......89 B1
Tewkesbury Pl CF24 .178 A1
Tewkesbury St CF24 .178 A1
Tewkesbury Wlk 6
NP20 ....143 C6
Teynes NP44 ....89 B1
Thackeray Cres CF3 ..179 B7
Thames Cl
Bettws NP20 ....116 E1
Bryn NP12 ....85 D4
Thaw Cl CF62 ....212 E1

Theobald Rd CF5 .....194 C5
Theodora St CF24 ...195 E7
Theodore Rd CF24 ...125 C7
Thesiger Ct 7 CF24 ..195 A8
Thesiger St CF24 ....195 A8
Third Ave
Caerphilly CF83 ......137 E3
Merthyr Tydfil CF47 ...10 E5
Swansea SA6 ....45 D1
Thirlamere Terr 1
CF44 ....53 E8
Thirlmere Pl 5 NP19 .143 F8
Thirteenth Ave CF44 .224 C1
Thistle Cl CF62 .....214 D6
Thistle Ct NP44 ......88 F2
Thistle Terr 1 CF40 .106 E6
Thistle Way
Cardiff CF5 ....194 A8
Risca NP11 ....115 B2
Thistleboon Dr SA3 ..123 C4
Thistleboon Gdns
SA3 ....123 B3
Thistleboon Rd SA3 ..123 B4
Thomas Cres CF33 ..166 A7
Thomas Davies Ct 3
CF3 ....179 B3
Thomas Ellis Way
NP22 ....13 F7
Thomas Evans Ho SA1 .67 F1
Thomas Fields NP22 ..12 F3
Thomas Jones Sq 6
CF48 ....31 C1
Thomas Row SA1 .....95 D8
Thomas St
Aberavon SA12 ....98 F1
Aberbargoed CF81 ....58 B5
Aberdare CF44 ....29 A3
Aberfan CF48 ....55 C4
Abertridwr CF83 .....137 A7
Bargoed CF81 ....58 A2
Bedwas CF83 ....139 A6
Briton Ferry SA11 ....71 C1
Cardiff CF11 ....194 F3
Hendreforgan CF39 ..132 C5
Llanbradach CF83 ...111 F1
Llanelli SA15 ....40 D6
Maerdy CF43 ....52 A1
Maesycwmmer CF82 ...85 B2
Mountain Ash CF45 ...54 C1
Nelson CF46 ....83 E4
New Tredegar NP24 ...33 E3
Pontardawe SA8 ......23 E5
Pontypridd CF37 .....109 B1
Pontypridd CF37 .....109 C1
Swansea SA1 ....95 E7
Tonypandy CF40 .....106 D6
Tonyrefail CF40 .....106 E4
Treharris CF46 ....83 B6
Treorchy CF41 ....79 A5
Thomas Terr
Dowlais CF48 ....11 A5
Resolven SA11 ......226 D5
Swansea SA6 ....68 E6
Thomas' Pl CF39 ....107 F2
Thomas's Pl CF39 ...107 E7
Thomasville CF83 ...137 E5
Thompson Ave
Cardiff CF5 ....194 A7
Newport NP19 ......144 B3
Thompson Cl NP19 ..144 C3
Thompson Ct
1 Cardiff CF5 ......194 C6
Gorseinon SA4 ....66 D8
Thompson Pl CF5 ....194 A7
Thompson St
Barry CF63 ....214 F4
Pontypridd CF37 .....109 A1
Ynysybwl CF37 ....109 A8
Thompson Villas
CF37 ....109 A8
Thorburn Cl SA11 .....71 F8
Thorley Cl CF23 .....178 E4
Thorn Gr CF64 ....217 A8
Thornaby Ct CF10 ...195 B4
Thornbury Cl
Baglan SA12 ....98 E4
Cardiff CF14 ....177 C5
Merthyr Tydfil CF48 ..225 F1
Thornbury Park Sh Ctr
NP10 ....142 B4
Thornbury Pk NP10 ..142 B4
Thorncliff Ct 11 NP44 .89 C2
Thorncombe Rd NP22 .85 F6
Thorne Ave NP11 ......86 F7
Thorney Rd SA12 ......98 D7
Thornfield Mews
CF31 ....150 C1
Thornhill Cl
Brynmawr NP22 ....8 C5
Cwmbran NP44 ....89 B6
Thornhill Ct CF14 ...177 D8
Thornhill Gdns NP10 .141 E7
Thornhill Prim sch
CF14 ....159 E3
Thornhill Rd
Capel Hendre SA14 ..218 C6
Cardiff CF14 ....159 C3
Cwmbran NP44 ....89 B5
Thornhill St 8 CF5 ..194 C6
Thornhill Way NP10 ..141 E6
Thornleigh Rd NP11 ..59 F5
Thornton Cres CF32 .103 F2
Thornwood Cl CF46 ...83 B6
Thornwood Cl CF14 ..159 E3
Thornwood Pl CF46 ...83 B6
Three Arches Ave
CF14 ....178 A6
Three Cliffs Dr SA3 ..121 A6

Three Elms Cl CF82 ..84 F4
Three Oaks Cl CF83 .138 C4
Three Salmon St CF47 .30 D8
Three Ships Ct SA3 ..123 C3
Thrush Cl 1 CF3 .....180 A6
Thurston Rd CF37 ...109 D2
Thurston St
Abercynon CF45 ......82 C1
6 Cardiff CF5 ....194 D5
Tibdeunaw Cl SA5 .....68 C7
Tichbourne St SA3 ...123 B4
Tide Fields Rd CF24 .196 A5
Tidenham Ct CF5 ....193 D5
Tidenham Rd CF5 ....193 D4
Till Gr NP18 ....117 F3
Tillery Rd NP13 ....36 B7
Tillery St NP13 ....36 B6
Tillsland NP44 ......116 C8
Timber Yd The CF24 .195 D8
Timbers Sq CF24 ....195 D8
Timbre Pl 3 SA12 ....98 C2
Timothy Pl CF44 ......53 D8
Timothy Rees Cl CF5 .176 D3
Tin St CF24 ....195 D6
Tingle La CF35 ......186 A7
**Tinkinswood Burial
Chamber** CF5 ....204 A7
Tintagel Cl CF14 ....159 D2
Tintern Cl
Cwmbran NP44 ....89 F2
St Athan CF62 ......211 C7
Tintern St CF5 ......194 C6
Tippett Cl NP19 .....144 E5
Tir Bach Rd NP12 .....85 F1
Tir Capel SA14 ....41 A6
Tir Einon SA14 ....41 C4
Tir John North Rd SA1 .96 C8
Tir Meibion La CF72 .155 D3
Tir Morfa Prim Sch
SA12 ....98 B1
Tir Morfa Rd SA12 ....98 B1
Tir Newydd
Llanelli SA14 ....41 D4
North Cornelly CF33 .166 A8
Tir y Waun SA9 ......222 A5
Tir-Afon Ct CF72 ....173 B7
Tir-Berllan NP12 .....59 B2
Tir-Philkins NP12 ....86 B6
Tir-y-Berth CF82 ......7 C3
Tir-y-berth Prim Sch
CF82 ....85 A6
Tir-y-Berth St CF82 ..85 A6
Tir-y-Cwm La NP11 ..114 F1
Tir-y-Cwm Rd NP11 ..114 F1
Tirbach Rd SA9 ....2 C7
Tirforgan SA14 ....41 A7
Tirfounder Rd CF44 ...53 E7
Tirgof SA14 ....42 B8
Tirmynydd SA4 ....43 B1
Tirmynydd Rd SA2,SA4 .92 D8
Tirpenry St SA6 ....46 A1
Tirphil Prim Sch NP24 .33 D3
Tirphil Sta NP24 ......33 E3
Tirprys SA18 ....219 A5
Tirwaun SA14 ....218 E6
Tirycoed Rd SA18 ....220 A8
Tirynys SA15 ....40 F1
Titan Rd CF24 ....195 D4
Tiverton Dr CF3 .....179 A4
Toft Pl SA15 ....40 E6
Toftingall Ave CF14 ..177 D5
Toghill Dr CF15 .....158 B3
Tollgate Cl
Caerphilly CF83 ......138 C5
Cardiff CF11 ....194 D1
Tollgate Rd SA13 ....125 C4
Tolpath NP44 ....89 A1
Tom Mann Cl NP19 ..144 F4
Tom Williams Ct 2
SA1 ....95 D8
Ton Glas
Bridgend CF31 ......168 B5
Pyle CF33 ....148 A2
Ton Hywel CF79 .....107 D1
Ton Inf Sch CF41 .....79 A3
Ton Jun Mix Sch CF41 .78 F3
Ton Pentre Ind Est
CF41 ....107 A6
Ton Rd Cwmbran NP44 .89 B2
Cwmbran NP44 ....89 C1
Ton Rhosyn CF31 ....169 B5
Ton Row CF41 ....79 A4
Ton Teg CF35 ....170 D7
Ton The CF3 ....179 D7
Ton View CF33 ......148 D2
Ton y Felin CF37 ....136 A6
Ton-Bach St NP4 ......17 D6
Ton-coch Terr CF45 ...54 B6
Ton-Mawr Ave NP4 ....17 D7
Ton-Mawr Rd
Blaenavon NP4 ....17 D6
Pontrhydyfen SA12 ...73 B5
Ton-Mawr St 17 NP4 ..17 C6
Ton-y-Felin Rd CF83 .138 B3
Ton-y-Groes CF35 ...170 D7
Ton-y-Pistyll Rd NP11 .86 D5
Ton-Yr-Ywen Ave
CF14 ....177 E5
Ton-yr-ywen Sch
CF14 ....177 E6
Tonclwyda SA11 .....226 B3
Tondu Prim Sch
CF32 ....150 C4
Tondu Rd CF31 ......168 C4
Tondu Sta CF32 .....150 D5
Tone Cl NP20 ....116 D2
Tone Rd NP20 ....116 D2

Tone Sq NP20 ....116 D2
Tongwynlais Prim Sch
  Cardiff CF15 ....158 C1
  Tongwynlais CF15 ....176 C8
Tonmawr Bsns Pk
  SA12 ....73 B5
Tonna Hospl SA11 ....49 E3
Tonna Rd CF34 ......102 A7
Tonna Uchaf SA11 ....49 D3
Tonnau Prim Sch
  SA11 ....49 C2
Tonteg Cl CF38 ......136 A2
Tonteg Hospl CF38 ...136 F2
Tonteg Rd CF37 ......136 B3
Tontine St SA1 ....95 D8
Tonypandy Comp Sch
  CF40 ....106 E4
Tonypandy Ent Ctr
  CF40 ....106 E7
Tonypandy Prim Sch
  CF40 ....106 E5
Tonypandy Sta CF40 ..106 F5
Tonyrefail Comp Sch
  CF39 ....133 A4
Tonyrefail Prim Sch
  CF39 ....133 C5
Tonyrefail Rd CF37 ...134 E5
Tonysguboriau Cty Prim
  Sch CF72 ....155 B2
Top Rd NP4 ....37 F6
Topaz St CF24 ....195 D6
Tor Ho SA3 ....123 A3
Tor View
  Bedwas CF83 ......138 C7
  Penmaen SA3 ......120 B5
Tor-y-Crug NP23 ....7 B5
Torbay Terr CF62 ....213 A1
Tordoff Way CF62 ...214 E6
Torfaen Terr [2] NP4 ..38 A1
Torlais St NP11 ......73 B5
Toronto Ave SA13 ...125 E4
Toronto Cl
  Blackwood NP12 ....85 F8
  Newport NP20 .....142 D3
Torrdge Rd NP20 ....116 C3
Torrens Dr CF23 .....178 B4
Torrington Rd
  Cardiff CF3 ....179 C7
  Swansea SA5 ....68 A3
Tothill St NP23 ......7 C1
Tower Cl CF31 ....169 A4
Tower Ct Swansea SA1 .67 F1
  Swansea SA6 ......69 B8
Tower Gdns SA1 .....67 F1
Tower Hill CF64 .....207 B3
Tower Hill Ave CF64 .207 B3
Tower Rd
  Gileston CF62 ......211 E1
  Hirwaun CF44 ......27 C7
Tower St CF37 ......135 D7
Tower Way CF64 ....215 E6
Towers The
  Cwmbran NP44 .....89 F3
  Hirwaun CF44 ......27 D7
Town Bridge Bldgs
  NP4 ....62 C7
Town Hall Sq CF71 ..188 E2
Town Mill Rd CF71 ...188 E1
Town Reach NP20 ...143 C5
Towngate Bsns Ctr
  SA13 ....125 B8
Townhill Comm Sch
  SA1 ....95 A8
Townhill Gdns SA2 ..94 F8
Townhill Rd SA1,SA2 .95 A8
Towy Rd CF14 ......178 A7
Towyn Rd CF3 ......179 C4
Towyn Way CF38 ...136 A2
Trade La CF10 ......195 A3
Trade St CF10 ......195 A4
Traeth Ffordd
  Llanelli SA15 ....40 B4
  Llanelli SA15 ....40 C4
Traethmelyn SA12 ...98 A3
Trafalgar Cl [3] NP23 ..8 C4
Trafalgar Ct [1] CF24 .178 C1
Trafalgar Pl SA2 .....94 F5
Trafalgar Rd CF23 ...195 D8
Trafalgar St NP11 ...115 A1
Trafalgar Terr CF41 ..79 D2
Trahearne La SA10 ..71 C8
Traherne Dr CF5 ....192 F4
Trallwm Rd SA14 ....41 D5
Trallwn Pl SA7 ......69 E6
Trallwn Prim Sch SA7 .69 E7
Trallwn Rd SA7 .....69 E6
Trallwng Inf Sch
  CF37 ....109 D2
Tram La NP44 ......117 D7
Tram Rd
  Caerleon NP18 .....118 C4
  Cwmbran NP44 .....89 B6
  Pontllanfraith NP12 ..85 F4
Tram Road Side
  Quakers Yard CF46 ..83 A4
  Treharris CF46 ......83 A6
Tramore Way CF23 ..161 A1
Tramroad La CF47 ...10 E8
Tramroad Side CF48 ..10 E1
Tramroad Side N CF47 10 E1
Tramroad Side S CF47 .30 E8
Tramroad Terr [4]
  CF47 ....10 E1
Tramroadside
  Ebbw Vale NP23 ....7 A4
  Newbridge NP11 ....86 F6
Tramway CF44 ......27 E7
Tramway Cl NP44 ...89 A1

Tramway Rd SA8 ....24 B5
Tranch Rd NP4 .....62 A6
Trannon Ct NP44 ...89 A4
Tranquil Pl NP19 ...89 E1
Trap Well CF83 .....138 D5
Traston Ave NP19 ..144 B1
Traston Cl NP19 ....144 B1
Traston La NP19 ....144 B1
Traston Rd
  Newport NP19 .....144 B1
  Newport NP19 .....164 F8
Traverner Trad Est
  NP18 ....118 B3
Travis Way CF36 ...165 E2
Trawler Rd SA1 .....95 D5
Traws Fynydd CF31 ..169 B4
Trawsffordd SA9 ....2 E8
Trawsmawr La NP20,
  NP44 ....116 E4
Tre Gwilym CF44 ...53 E8
Tre Newydd CF23 ...7 E1
Tre Telynog CF44 ...53 E8
Tre Uchaf Prim Sch
  SA4 ....42 F1
Tre-banog Terr CF44 .224 D4
Tre-Beferad CF61 ...210 C5
Tre-Edwards NP22 ...12 C5
Tre-Herbert Rd NP44 .90 D6
Tre-Ifor CF44 ......28 E8
Tre-Lyn La NP12 ....85 A6
Tre-Pit Rd CF11 ....198 B5
Tre-York St NP22 ...12 E4
Trealaw Prim Sch
  CF40 ....106 F5
Trealaw Rd
  Tonypandy CF40 ...106 F5
  Tonypandy CF40 ...106 F6
Treasure St CF42 ...78 D7
Trebannws Prim Sch
  SA6 ....46 E8
Trebanog Cl CF3 ...179 E6
Trebanog Cres CF3 .179 E5
Trebanog Rd CF39 ..133 D8
Treberth Est NP19 ..144 E6
Treberth Rd CF3 ...179 E5
Trecastle Ave CF14 ..159 E1
Trecenydd Ind Est
  CF83 ....137 F3
Trecinon Rd CF3 ...179 F5
Tredegar Ave
  Ebbw Vale NP23 ...14 C7
  Llanharan CF72 ....153 F3
Tredegar Cl CF72 ...153 F4
Tredegar Comp sch
  NP22 ....13 E5
Tredegar Ct
  Abercarn NP11 ....114 B3
  Cardiff CF14 ......176 F5
  Newport NP20 .....143 C2
Tredegar Gap NP23 ..14 D8
Tredegar House Ctry Pk
  NP10 ....163 D7
Tredegar House Dr
  NP10 ....163 E6
Tredegar Park View
  NP10 ....142 C4
Tredegar Rd
  Ebbw Vale NP23 ...14 C7
  Gorseinon SA4 ....43 C1
  New Tredegar NP24 .33 E3
Tredegar St
  Abercarn NP11 ....114 B4
  Bassaleg NP10 .....141 E4
  Cardiff CF10 ......195 B5
  Newport NP20 .....143 C3
  Risca NP11 ....114 F2
Tredegar Terr
  Aberbargoed CF81 ..58 A4
  Abercarn NP11 ....114 B4
  Risca NP11 ....114 F1
Tredegarville CW Jun & Inf
  Sch CF24 ....195 C6
Tredelerch Rd CF3 ..179 A2
Trederwen NP23 ....14 B8
Tredogan Rd
  Rhoose CF62 ......213 A6
  Rhoose CF62 ......213 B4
  Rhoose CF62 ......213 C3
Tredomen Ind Pk
  CF82 ....84 D2
Tredomen Terr
  Tredomen CF82 ....84 D1
  Tredomen CF82 ....84 D2
Tree Tops Ave NP12 .85 E8
Treetops Cl CF5 ....176 B1
Tref-y-Rhyg Prim Sch
  CF39 ....133 D5
Trefaser Cres CF3 ..179 E6
Trefelin CF44 ......28 E4
Trefelin Cres SA13 ..99 C2
Trefelin St SA13 ....99 C2
Trefforest Cty Prim Sch
  CF37 ....135 E7
Trefforest Sta CF37 .135 E6
Trefil Rd NP22 .....6 A4
Treforest Ct CF37 ...135 E6
Treforest Estate Halt
  CF38 ....136 D1
Treforest Ind Est
  Upper Boat CF15 ..157 E8
  Upper Boat CF15 ..136 C2
Treforgan Rd
  Crynant SA10 .....222 A1
  Crynant SA10 .....226 A8
Treforis SA18 ......219 C6
Tregare St NP19 ...143 D6
Tregarn Cl NP18 ...119 E2
Tregarn Ct NP18 ...119 F2

Tregarn Rd NP18 ...119 F2
Tregarne Cl SA6 ....45 F4
Tregaron Ho SA13 ..125 E3
Tregaron Rd CF5 ...193 B5
Tregarth Cl CF15 ...174 D8
Tregarth St CF15 ...174 D8
Tregelles Ct
  Cwmrhydyceirw SA6 .46 A4
  Swansea SA6 ......45 F3
Tregelles Rd SA10 ..48 B1
Tregroes (College of
  Agriculture & Hort)
  CF35 ....170 F8
Tregwilym Cl NP10 .142 B4
Tregwilym Ind Est
  NP10 ....142 A4
Tregwilym Rd
  Rogerstone NP10 ..141 F5
  Rogerstone NP10 ..142 A4
Tregwilym Wlk NP10 .142 B4
Tregwyr Jun Sch SA4 .66 B5
Tregwyr Inf Sch SA4 .66 B5
Trehafod Rd CF37 ..108 D2
Trehafod Sta CF37 ..108 C3
Treharne Dr CF31 ..150 D1
Treharne Flats CF37 .136 B5
Treharne Rd
  Barry CF63 ....215 A7
  Maesteg CF34 .....75 B1
  Swansea SA6 ......45 F1
  Treharris CF46 .....82 F6
Treharne Row
  Maesteg CF34 .....102 A4
  Pontyrhyl CF32 ....129 E8
Treharne St
  Merthyr Vale CF48 ..55 D5
  Pentre CF41 ......78 F4
  Treorchy CF42 ....78 B4
Treharne Terr CF46 ..82 F6
Treharris St CF24 ..195 C7
Treherbert Hospl CF42 50 F1
Treherbert Ind Est
  CF42 ....78 A4
Treherbert Inf Sch
  CF42 ....50 F2
Treherbert St CF24 ..194 B3
Treherbert Sta CF42 .50 F1
Trehopcyn Prim Sch
  CF37 ....109 A2
Trelai Ct CF5 ......193 C3
Trelai Jun & Inf Sch
  CF5 ....193 C5
Trelales Prim Sch
  CF32 ....167 E4
Trelawney Ave [1]
  CF3 ....179 B3
Trelawney Cres [2]
  CF3 ....179 B3
Trelech Cl NP44 ....89 F2
Trelewis Prim Sch
  CF46 ....83 D7
Trelys Cl NP12 .....85 A5
Trem Powys CF63 ..215 C8
Trem Twynbarlwm
  NP44 ....89 D1
Trem y Bryn CF31 ..168 E2
Trem y Castell CF83 .137 D1
Trem y Coed CF63 ..205 B1
Trem y Mor SA4 ....64 B2
Trem-y- Dyffryn
  SA11 ....226 C4
Trem-y-Cwm [3]
  CF38 ....156 A6
Trem-y-Don CF62 ..214 B2
Trem-y-duffryn CF31 .168 C3
Trem-y-Garth CF72 .172 D5
Trem-y-Glyn CF39 ..107 D1
Trem-y-Mor CF31 ..169 B4
Trem-y-Mynydd
  Blaenavon NP4 ....17 D6
  Treherbert CF42 ...50 F1
Tremadoc Wlk CF3 ..179 E5
Tremains Ct CF31 ..169 B4
Tremains Inf Sch
  CF31 ....169 C5
Tremains Jun Sch
  CF31 ....169 C5
Tremains Rd CF31 ..168 F4
Tremgarth CF31 ....168 E6
Tremorfa Ind Est
  CF24 ....195 F4
Tremorpha Ind Est
  CF24 ....196 A4
Trenant
  Ebbw Vale NP23 ...14 C8
  Hirwaun CF44 .....27 D7
Trenchard Dr CF14 ..177 F6
Treneol CF44 ......53 B5
Trenewydd Rd CF3 ..179 E5
Trenewydd Rise SA11 .71 F6
Trenos Gdns CF72 ..153 C2
Trenos Pl CF72 ....153 E2
Trent Rd NP20 .....116 C3
Treochy Sta CF42 ..78 D5
Treoda Ct [3] CF14 ..177 B5
Treoes Rd CF35 ....169 F3
Treorchy Comp Sch
  CF42 ....78 B4
Treorchy Ind Est CF42 .78 E5
Treorchy Prim Sch
  CF42 ....78 D6
Treorky St [4] CF24 ..195 A8
Treowen Ave NP12 ..85 E4
Treowen Rd NP11 ...59 F1
Trerobart Prim Sch
  CF37 ....109 A8
Treseder Way CF5 ..193 E5
Tresigin Rd CF3 ....179 E6

Tresilian Cl CF61 ...209 F5
Tresilian Terr [4]
  CF10 ....195 A4
Tresillian Way
  Cardiff CF10 ......195 A4
  Cardiff CF10 ......195 B4
Tressilian Pl CF45 ..82 D2
Tretower Ct NP44 ..90 B3
Trevallen Ave SA11 .72 A5
Trevelyan Ct
  Caerphilly CF83 ...138 C3
  Llantwit Major CF61 .210 B7
Trevethick Ho [6] CF47 30 D8
Trevethick St
  Cardiff CF11 ......194 E5
  Merthyr Tydfil CF47 .10 E2
Trevethin Com Sch
  NP4 ....62 C7
Trevine Path NP44 ..89 C2
Trevithick Cl NP20 ..116 F3
Trevithick Gdns CF47 .30 E8
Trevor Cl CF48 .....11 B7
Trevor St
  Aberdare CF44 .....29 A1
  Treorchy CF42 ....78 D7
Trewaun CF44 .....27 F2
Trewen Rd
  Birchgrove SA7 ....47 A1
  Swansea SA7 .....70 A8
Trews Field Ind Site
  CF31 ....168 E6
Trewartha Ct [7] CF14 177 B5
Trewyddfa Comm SA6 .68 F6
Trewyddfa Gdns SA6 .68 F6
Trewyddfa Rd SA6 ..68 E6
Trewyddfa Terr SA6 ..68 E6
Triangle CF62 ......214 F2
Triangle Bsns Pk CF48 .30 F5
Triangle The
  Bridgend CF31 .....169 B4
  Mountain Ash CF45 ..54 D4
Tribute Ave NP11 ...114 C8
Trident Ct CF24 ....195 C4
Tridwr Rd CF83 ....136 F7
Trigfan Dawi CF63 ..99 D6
Trinant Inf Sch NP11 .59 F5
Trinant Jun Sch NP11 .59 F5
Trinant Terr NP11 ...59 F6
Trinity Cl
  Mumbles SA3 .....123 A5
  Pontarddulais SA4 ..19 C3
  Ystrad Mynach CF82 .84 E1
Trinity Ct
  Newport NP20 .....143 D2
  Port Talbot SA12 ..98 D2
  Risca NP11 ....114 F2
  [10] Swansea SA1 ...95 C7
Trinity Fields Specl Sch
  CF82 ....84 E1
Trinity Hill NP11 ...114 C6
Trinity La
  Caerleon NP18 ....117 F3
  Pen-clawdd SA4 ...64 D4
Trinity Pl
  Newport NP20 .....143 D2
  Pontarddulais SA4 ..19 C3
  [9] Swansea SA1 ...95 C7
Trinity Rd
  Cwmbran NP44 ....89 D5
  Llanelli SA15 ......40 E3
  Tonypandy CF40 ...106 F5
Trinity St Barry CF62 .214 D4
  Cardiff CF10 ......195 A5
  Gorseinon SA4 ....43 C1
Trinity Terr SA15 ...40 D3
Trinity View NP18 ..117 F3
Trip Terr CF41 .....79 A5
Triscombe Dr CF5 ..176 E1
Tristram Cl CF14 ...159 D2
Troed y Rhiw CF14 ..159 A1
Troed-y-Bryn
  Blaina NP13 ....15 E6
  Caerphilly CF83 ...137 E5
Troed-y-Garth CF15 .157 B1
Troed-y-Rhiw
  Abercarn NP11 ....87 A3
  Abercraf SA9 ......222 B7
  Swansea SA7 .....69 F6
Troed-y-Rhiw Rd
  Cwmfelinfach NP11 ..113 E4
  Mountain Ash CF45 ..54 E3
Troed-y-rhiw Sta
  CF48 ....31 C1
Troedpennar Terr
  CF45 ....82 E3
Troedrhiw-gwair
  NP22 ....14 B2
Troedrhiw-trwyn
  CF37 ....108 F2
Troedyrhiw CF82 ...111 D8
Troedyrhiw Jun Sch
  CF48 ....31 C1
Troedyrhiw Rd CF39 .107 C4
Troedyrhiw Terr CF42 .78 E6
Tros- Maen SA14 ...40 F3
Troserch Rd SA14 ..18 B2
Trosnant Cres CF82 .84 D5
Trosnant St NP4 ...62 C6
Trosnant Villa NP4 ..62 C5
Trostre Ind Pk SA14 .41 A3
Trostre Rd
  Llanelli SA14, SA15 ..40 F3
  Llanelli SA15 ......40 F4
Trostrey NP44 .....116 C8
Trostrey Cl NP4 ....63 B4
Trostrey St NP19 ...143 B4
Trotman Dickinson Pl
  CF14 ....177 E1

Trowbridge Gn CF3 .179 E6
Trowbridge Inf Sch
  CF3 ....179 E6
Trowbridge Jun Sch
  CF3 ....179 E6
Trowbridge Rd CF3 .179 D4
Troweyrhiw Inf Sch
  CF48 ....31 C1
Troy Rd NP13 .....60 B7
Trussel Rd NP44 ...89 E4
Tucker St SA11 ....71 C3
Tuckers Villas NP12 .85 E7
Tudno Pl SA5 ......68 A5
Tudor Ave CF44 ...27 D8
Tudor Cl Cardiff CF5 .193 D7
  Ebbw Vale NP23 ...7 B5
  Merthyr Vale CF48 ..55 D5
  Penarth CF64 .....207 A1
Tudor Cres [7]
  Brynmawr NP23 ...8 B8
  Rogerstone NP10 ..142 B4
  Rogerstone NP10 ..142 C4
Tudor Ct
  Aberbargoed CF81 ..58 B4
  Bishopston SA3 ...122 A6
  Cardiff CF14 ......177 D5
  Llanelli SA4 ......218 D1
Tudor Dr CF32 .....129 E1
Tudor Est CF34 ....75 A1
Tudor Gdns
  Machen CF83 .....139 E6
  Neath SA10 ......48 C1
Tudor La CF11 .....194 F4
Tudor Mews CF72 ..173 D7
Tudor Pl CF61 .....210 C5
Tudor Rd
  Cwmbran NP44 ....89 E3
  Newport NP19 .....143 E8
  Swansea SA5 .....68 C5
  Ton Pentre CF41 ...79 A2
Tudor St Cardiff CF11 .194 E4
  Ferndale CF43 ....79 F6
  Hawthorn CF37 ...136 A4
  [1] Port Talbot SA13 ..99 B1
  Ystradgynlais SA9 .2 E7
Tudor Terr
  Aberdare CF44 .....28 F3
  Merthyr Tydfil CF47 .10 E2
Tudor Way
  Bishopston SA3 ...122 B7
  Llantwit Fardre CF38 .156 D6
Tudor Woods NP44 ..90 B2
Tudors The CF23 ...178 D1
Tulloch St [4] CF24 ..178 C1
Tummel Cl CF23 ...178 C5
Tumulus Way CF71 .199 D4
Tunnel Rd SA15 ...40 E5
Tunnel Row NP11 ..86 E6
Tunnel Terr NP20 ..143 B4
Turberville Cres
  CF31 ....150 F1
Turberville Pl CF11 .194 D6
Turberville Rd
  Cwmbran NP44 ....89 E4
  Porth CF39 ....107 C5
Turberville St
  Maesteg CF34 ....102 C2
  Tonypandy CF40 ...79 F1
Turberville Terr [5]
  CF40 ....106 F4
Turbine Annexe Rd
  CF62 ....211 E1
Turkey St CF61 ....207 B3
Turner House Gallery
  CF64 ....207 B3
Turner Rd CF5 .....194 B6
Turner St NP19 ....143 D6
Turners End NP44 ..89 B1
Turnham Gn CF23 ..178 E2
Turnpike Cl
  Dinas Powys CF64 .206 B4
  Pontypool NP4 ....62 F6
Turnpike Rd NP44 ..90 B1
Turnstiles The NP20 .143 C2
Turnstone Cl SA12 ..98 C1
Turnstone Rd CF36 ..165 E1
Tuscan Cl CF64 ....206 D2
Twchwyn Garth CF35 .187 E8
Tweedsmuir Rd CF24 .195 F2
Tweedy La NP19 ...143 F5
Twelfth Ave CF7 ...10 F5
Twinings The [6] NP44 .89 B3
Twissell's Rd NP44 ..62 A6
Twll-Yn-y-Wal Rd [4]
  SA13 ....125 E4
Twm Barlwm Cl
  NP11 ....115 C2
Twm Barlwm View
  NP44 ....90 B2
Twmbarlwm Rise
  NP44 ....88 E1
Twmpath Gdns NP4 ..62 B6
Two Locks Rd NP44 ..89 D1
Two Stones Cres
  CF33 ....148 D2
Twympath Rd NP4 ..62 B6
Twyn NP12 ....85 A5
Twyn Bedw CF39 ...107 E1
Twyn Bedw Rd SA6 ..46 D7
Twyn Carn Terr NP11 .114 C7
Twyn Carno NP22 ..12 E5
Twyn Cty Prim Sch
  SA18 ....220 B8
Twyn Gdns NP12 ..85 C7
Twyn Gwyn Rd
  Cwmfelinfach NP11 ..113 A5
  Tonypandy CF40 ...107 B4
Twyn Inf Sch CF83 ..138 B2

Twyn Jun Sch CF83 .138 B2
Twyn Oaks NP18 ...118 D3
Twyn Pl NP11 ......87 C3
Twyn Rd Abercarn NP11 87 B3
  Ystrad Mynach CF82 .111 F8
Twyn Star NP22 ....6 D1
Twyn Teg SA10 ....48 D1
Twyn The CF83 ....138 B2
Twyn-gwyn Terr NP11 .86 E6
Twyn-y-Fedwen
  CF14 ....177 D3
Twyn-y-Gored SA12 .100 A7
Twyn-Yr-Eos CF42 ..51 A1
Twyn-Yr-Ynys SA12 .100 A7
Twyn-Yr-Ysgol SA9 ..2 B7
Twyncarmel CF48 ..225 C5
Twyncarn Rd NP11 ..114 B6
Twyncyn CF64 .....205 F3
Twyncynghordy NP23 .8 A4
Twyncynghordy Pl
  NP23 ....8 A4
Twyncynghordy Rd
  Brynmawr NP23 ...8 A4
  Ebbw Vale NP23 ...7 F4
Twynderwen Flats
  NP23 ....8 D2
Twyni Teg SA2 .....93 D8
Twyniago SA4 .....19 D4
Twynrefail Pl SA18 ..220 D6
Twynyffald Rd NP12 .85 D8
Twynygarreg CF46 ..83 B7
Twynyrodyn Inf Sch
  CF47 ....10 F1
Twynyrodyn Jun Sch
  CF47 ....30 F8
Twynyrodyn Rd [10]
  CF47 ....30 E8
Ty Alban CF40 .....106 E7
Ty Box Cl NP44 ....89 D5
Ty Box Rd NP44 ...89 D5
Ty Bruce Rd CF44 ..27 E8
Ty Brunel SA1 .....71 C1
Ty Bryn
  Aberbargoed CF81 ..58 A5
  Tredegar NP22 ....13 E7
Ty Bryn Rd NP13 ...36 A6
Ty Bryncoch CF15 ..158 A4
Ty Canol CF36 .....165 F1
Ty Canol La CF83 ..139 F7
Ty Canol Way NP44 ..88 F2
Ty Capel Zion CF43 ..80 B2
Ty Cerrig
  [5] Barry CF63 .....215 B7
  Cardiff CF23 ......178 E8
Ty Coch NP22 .....12 E8
Ty Coch Distribution Ctr
  NP44 ....116 E8
Ty Coch Way NP44 ..116 E8
Ty Cornel CF81 ....58 A5
Ty Crwyn CF38 ....156 C6
Ty Cydwel [10] SA15 ..40 D4
Ty Dawel CF39 ....133 C5
Ty Ddewi CF41 ....79 A2
Ty Dewi Sant SA10 ..48 A1
Ty Draw
  Church Village CF38 .135 E1
  Llantrisant CF72 ...155 A5
Ty Draw La
  Penperlleni NP4 ...39 E3
  South Cornelly CF33 .165 F6
Ty Ebenezer CF43 ..80 C3
Ty Einon Day Hospl
  SA4 ....43 A3
Ty Elizabeth [6] SA15 .40 D4
Ty Ffynnon CF62 ...214 F8
Ty Florence Asher
  SA6 ....22 E1
Ty Fry CF44 ....28 E1
Ty Fry Cl NP44 ....17 D7
Ty Fry Rd
  Aberbargoed CF81 ..58 B4
  Cefn Cribwr CF32 ..149 A2
Ty Glas Sta CF14 ..177 E6
Ty Gnoll Newydd SA11 .71 F7
Ty Gwenfo CF63 ...215 C6
Ty Gwyn SA4 ......66 C5
Ty Gwyn Cl CF35 ...152 B5
Ty Gwyn Dr CF31 ..169 D4
Ty Gwyn Rd
  Cwmbran NP44 ....89 B3
  Penperlleni NP4 ...39 E3
Ty Gwyn Sch CF23 ..178 C3
Ty Gwyn Way NP44 ..89 B4
Ty Hedd-wyn [1] SA12 .99 D5
Ty Howard [7] SA15 ..40 D4
Ty Isaf CF72 ......172 B5
Ty Llunfan CF39 ...132 C7
Ty Llwyd Parc CF46 ..83 C5
Ty Mawr Parc CF37 ..108 F2
Ty Mawr Uchaf CF37 .108 F2
Ty Merchant CF35 ..152 F1
Ty Meriel [8] SA15 ..40 D4
Ty Mynydd
  Blaenavon NP4 ....17 D6
  Cwmbran NP44 ....89 E5
Ty Nant Bridgend CF31 168 C5
  Caerphilly CF83 ...137 E4
Ty Nant Ct CF15 ...158 B1
Ty Newydd
  Cardiff CF11 ......177 A4
  Machen CF83 .....139 D5
  Seven Sisters SA10 .222 D4
Ty Newydd Terr SA14 .218 B8
Ty Parc Cl CF5 ....176 D3

Ty Penry Thomas
NP23 . . . . .14 D7
Ty Pontrhun CF48 . . . .31 B2
Ty Pucca Cl CF83 . . . .140 A6
Ty Pwca Pl NP44 . . . . .89 C6
Ty Pwca Rd NP44 . . . .89 C6
Ty Rhiw CF15 . . . . . .158 B4
Ty Seion 6 CF45 . . . . .54 D3
Ty Sign Inf Sch NP11 . .115 A2
Ty Sign Jun Sch
NP11 . . . . .115 A2
Ty Sivertsen SA1 . . . . .95 B6
Ty Stafford 9 SA15 . . .40 D4
Ty Trappa NP44 . . . . . .89 C6
Ty Trappa Pl 1 NP44 . .89 C6
Ty Tudor NP44 . . . . . .89 E3
Ty Twyn CF38 . . . . . .135 D1
Ty Twyn Tag SA10 . . . .48 D1
Ty Ysgol Ynyshir
CF39 . . . . .107 E6
Ty'n y Wern CF39 . . . .133 C2
Ty'n Yr Haul CF32 . . .150 E6
Tyn-y-Bonau Rd SA4 . . .19 C5
Tyn-y-Cae Gr CF14 . . .177 C6
Tyn-y-coed NP44 . . . . .89 C6
Tyn-y-Coed La CF24 . .178 B1
Tyn-y-Coed Pl CF24 . .178 B1
Tyn-y-Coed Terr
CF32 . . . . .150 E4
Tyn-y-Graig Rd CF83 .111 F1
Tyn-y-Pant Rd SA8 . . .23 C5
Tyn-y-Parc Rd CF14 . .177 B6
Tyn-y-Pwll Rd CF14 . .177 A5
Tyn-yr-Heol Rd SA10 . .48 C3
Ty'r Felin SA5 . . . . . . .67 F6
Ty'r Fran SA7 . . . . . . .47 A2
Ty'r Graig Cty Prim Sch
NP13 . . . . .60 A7
Ty'r Holl St 7 CF24 . .195 C5
Ty'r Maes SA5 . . . . . . .67 F6
Ty'r Person CF38 . . . .135 E1
Ty'r Pobydd SA11 . . . . .71 E6
Ty'r Waun CF15 . . . . .158 B8
Ty'r Ysgol 6 CF24 . . .195 C5
Ty'r Ysgol CF15 . . . . .189 C3
Ty'r-Groes Dr SA13 . .125 F3
Ty'r-owen SA12 . . . . . .99 E4
Ty'r-Owen Row SA12 . .99 D5
Ty'r-Owen Terr 6
SA12 . . . . .99 D5
Ty'rfelin St CF45 . . . . .81 E8
Ty'rfran Ave SA15 . . . .40 E7
Ty-brachty Terr NP12 . .59 D2
Ty-Bwmpyn Rd NP4 . . .61 D7
Ty-canol Ct NP44 . . . . .89 A1
Ty-Canol La CF83 . . . .139 A8
Ty-Canol Row NP44 . . .89 A1
Ty-capel CF15 . . . . . .158 A3
Ty-Cefn Rd CF5 . . . . .193 D6
Ty-Coch Cl NP10 . . . .141 F2
Ty-Coch La
Cwmbran NP44 . . . . . .116 B8
Cwmbran NP44 . . . . . .116 F6
Ty-coch Maisonettes
SA2 . . . . .94 C7
Ty-Coch Rd
Cardiff CF5 . . . . .193 C5
Swansea SA2 . . . . .94 D7
Ty-Coch Terr NP44 . . .116 B8
Ty-Coed NP44 . . . . . . .89 B5
Ty-Dan-y-Wal NP13 . . .16 B1
Ty-Dan-y-Wal Rd
Abertillery NP13 . . . . . . .36 A7
Abertillery NP13 . . . . . . .36 B8
Ty-Draw
Llandow CF71 . . . . .199 A7
Penperlleni NP4 . . . . . . .39 E3
Ty-Draw Cres SA1 . . . .69 B2
Ty-Draw Hill SA13 . . . .99 C1
Ty-Draw Pl
Cardiff CF23 . . . . .178 C1
Port Talbot SA13 . . . . . .125 B8
Swansea SA1 . . . . .69 B2
Ty-Draw Rd
Aberdare CF44 . . . . .29 C2
Cardiff CF23 . . . . .160 E1
Cardiff CF23 . . . . .178 B2
Swansea SA1 . . . . .69 C2
Ty-Draw St SA13 . . . .125 B8
Ty-Fry Ave CF3 . . . . .179 B3
Ty-Fry Cl
Brynmenyn CF32 . . . . . .150 F2
Cardiff CF3 . . . . .179 C4
Ty-Fry Gdns CF3 . . . .179 C4
Ty-Fry Rd Cardiff CF3 .179 B4
Margam SA13 . . . . .125 E4
Ty-Glas Ave CF14 . . .177 F8
Ty-Glas Rd
Cardiff CF14 . . . . .177 D7
Cardiff CF14 . . . . .177 E8
Ty-Gwyn NP44 . . . . . . .89 C4
Ty-Gwyn Ave CF23 . . .178 C2
Ty-Gwyn Cres CF23 . .178 C3
Ty-Gwyn Rd
Abersychan NP4 . . . . . . .37 E2
Cardiff CF14 . . . . .177 C7
Cardiff CF23 . . . . .178 C2
Ty-Haulwen NP23 . . . . .8 C2
Ty-Isaf CF83 . . . . .137 D5
Ty-Isaf Complex
NP11 . . . . .141 B8
Ty-Isaf Cres NP11 . . .141 B8
Ty-Isaf Inf Sch NP11 .115 B1
Ty-Isaf Park Ave
NP11 . . . . .141 C8

Ty-Isaf Park Circ
NP11 . . . . .141 C8
Ty-Isaf Park Cres
NP11 . . . . .141 B8
Ty-Isaf Park Rd
NP11 . . . . .141 C8
Ty-Isaf Park Villas
NP11 . . . . .141 B8
Ty-Isaf Rd CF32 . . . . .149 B1
Ty-Isha Terr NP12 . . . .85 D8
Ty-Llwyd Wlk CF81 . . .58 B5
Ty-Llwydd Pl NP11 . . .86 F6
Ty-Mawr SA8 . . . . .23 E4
Ty-Mawr Ave CF3 . . . .179 A2
Ty-Mawr Rd
Cardiff CF14 . . . . .176 E4
Cardiff CF3 . . . . .179 A2
Ty-myrtwydd SA4 . . . . .65 E8
Ty-Nant CF82 . . . . .84 D8
Ty-Nant Rd CF15 . . . .176 B7
Ty-Nant St CF11 . . . .194 A3
Ty-Newydd Ct NP44 . . .89 E5
Ty-Newydd Rd
Barry CF62 . . . . .214 F6
Cwmbran NP44 . . . . . . .89 E5
Ty-Pica Dr CF5 . . . . . .205 A7
Ty-Rosser-Gwyn NP4 . .37 E7
Ty-to-Maen Cl CF3 . . .202 E2
Ty-To-Maen Cl CF3 . .179 E8
Ty-Verlon Ind Est
CF63 . . . . .215 E7
Ty-Wern Ave CF14 . . .177 C6
Ty-Wern Rd CF14 . . . .177 C6
Tybryn Terr CF35 . . . .170 B8
Tycribwr Hill CF32 . . .150 A3
Tycroes Cty Prim Sch
SA18 . . . . .218 F5
Tycroes Rd
Ammanford SA18 . . . . .219 A5
Tycroes SA18 . . . . .218 F5
Tyddyn Gwaun CF32 . .167 E4
Tydeg Anerys NP12 . . .85 E7
Tyderwen CF34 . . . . . .102 A7
Tydfil Ho CF41 . . . . . . .78 F5
Tydfil Pl CF23 . . . . . . .178 B2
Tydfil Rd CF83 . . . . . .138 D7
Tydfil St CF63 . . . . . . .215 B6
Tydfil Terr CF48 . . . . . .31 C2
Tydfil Villas CF48 . . . . .11 A7
Tydfil's Terr 2 CF47 . .10 D2
Tydies NP44 . . . . .116 B8
Tydraw Cres CF33 . . .166 B8
Tydraw Terr CF42 . . . . .50 D3
Tydu View NP10 . . . . .142 B4
Tydvil Cl CF46 . . . . . . .83 E6
Tyfica Cres CF37 . . . .109 C1
Tyfica Rd CF37 . . . . . .109 C1
Tygwyn Rd
Church Village CF38 . . .135 F1
Clydach SA6 . . . . .46 E2
Morriston SA6 . . . . .46 C2
Pontypridd CF37 . . . . . .109 E1
Tygwyn St CF47 . . . . . .10 F3
Tyisaf Rd CF41 . . . . . . .79 B3
Tyisha Rd SA15 . . . . . .40 E4
Tyla Glas CF83 . . . . . .158 E8
Tyla Gwyn CF15 . . . . .157 F7
Tyla La CF3 . . . . .162 A3
Tyla Rd SA11 . . . . .71 C3
Tyla Rhosyr CF71 . . . .188 D2
Tyla Teg CF14 . . . . . . .176 F8
Tyla-Gwyn CF82 . . . . . .84 D8
Tylacelyn Rd CF40 . . .106 F4
Tylacoch CF72 . . . . . . .172 B5
Tylacoch Pl CF42 . . . . .78 C6
Tylcha Fach CF39 . . . .133 D2
Tylcha Fach Cl CF39 .133 D2
Tylcha Fach Terr
CF39 . . . . .133 D2
Tylcha Ganol CF39 . . .133 C2
Tylcha Isaf CF39 . . . . .133 D2
Tylcha Wen Cl CF39 . .133 B3
Tylcha Wen Terr
CF39 . . . . .133 B3
Tyle Garw CF42 . . . . .172 F8
Tyle Glas
Glanaman SA18 . . . . . .220 C7
North Cornelly CF33 . . .166 A8
Tyle House Cl CF61 . . .210 B8
Tyle Mali CF71 . . . . . .187 E1
Tyle Teg SA6 . . . . .46 C7
Tyle'r Hendy CF72 . . .173 C7
Tyle-Fforest CF42 . . . . .51 A1
Tylegarw Terr CF72 . .172 F8
Tyler St CF24 . . . . . . .195 E7
Tyleri Gdns NP13 . . . . .36 B6
Tyllwyd
Bryn-côch SA10 . . . . . . .48 B6
Pontardawe SA8 . . . . . . .23 C2
Tyllwyd Rd NP20 . . . . .142 F4
Tyllwyd St CF47 . . . . . .10 F3
Tylors Ct CF43 . . . . . . .80 C4
Tylorstown Prim Sch
CF43 . . . . .80 C3
Tymaen Cres SA12 . . . .99 F6
Tymaen Terr 3 SA12 . .99 F6
Tymawr Cl Cardiff CF3 .179 A2
Ystradowen CF71 . . . . .189 C3
Tymawr Rd CF37 . . . . .108 F2
Tymawr St SA1 . . . . . . .96 B7
Tymawr Terr CF37 . . . .109 A2
Tymeinwr Ave CF32 . . .103 E5
Tymynydd Cl CF15 . . .176 B7
Tyn y Waun Rd CF83 .140 A7
Tyn y Wern Inf Annexe
CF83 . . . . .138 F6
Tyn-y-Banwen Rd
CF46 . . . . .82 F6

Tyn-y-Bettws Cl
CF32 . . . . .129 E1
Tyn-y-Cae SA8 . . . . . . .23 F3
Tyn-y-Cae Rd SA7 . . . .69 D7
Tyn-y-Caeau La
CF36 . . . . .166 C1
Tyn-y-Coed CF82 . . . . .84 E1
Tyn-y-Coed Ffordd
SA6 . . . . .47 A8
Tyn-y-Coed Rd CF15 .157 B1
Tyn-y-Coedcae CF42 . .51 A1
Tyn-y-Cwm Rd NP11 .141 C8
Tyn-y-twr SA12 . . . . . .98 F6
Tyn-y-Waun CF32 . . . .129 E3
Tyn-y-Waun Rd SA7 . . .69 E6
Tyn-y-Wern Ct CF83 . .139 A6
Tyn-y-Wern Inf Sch
CF83 . . . . .139 A6
Tyn-y-Wern Jun Sch
CF83 . . . . .139 A6
Tynant CF14 . . . . .177 B4
Tynant Rd
Beddau CF38 . . . . .156 A7
Creigiau CF15 . . . . .174 D7
Tyndall St CF10 . . . . .195 C4
Tyndall Street Ind Est 1
CF10 . . . . .195 B4
Tyne Cl NP20 . . . . . . .116 D3
Tyneside Rd CF10 . . . .195 D2
Tynewydd
Cardiff CF14 . . . . .177 D6
Tredegar NP22 . . . . .6 B3
Tynewydd Ave NP44 . . .89 E6
Tynewydd Dr CF3 . . . .162 C3
Tynewydd Farm Cl
NP44 . . . . .89 E6
Tynewydd Gn NP44 . . .89 E6
Tynewydd North Cl
NP44 . . . . .89 E6
Tynewydd Prim Sch
NP11 . . . . .86 F6
Tynewydd Row CF32 . .104 E2
Tynewydd South Cl
NP44 . . . . .89 E6
Tynewydd Sq CF29 . . .107 E4
Tynewydd St CF81 . . . .32 F4
Tynewydd Terr NP11 . . .86 F6
Tyntaldwyn Rd 2
CF48 . . . . .31 C1
Tynton Rd CF31 . . . . . .168 E5
Tyntyla Ave CF40 . . . . .79 F1
Tyntyla Pk CF40 . . . . . .79 F1
Tyntyla Rd CF40 . . . . . .79 E2
Tyntyla Terr CF41 . . . . .79 D3
Tynybedw Cl CF42 . . . .78 E6
Tynybedw St CF42 . . . .78 E6
Tynybedw Terr CF42 . . .78 E6
Tynybryn Rd CF39 . . . .133 B4
Tynycai Pl CF40 . . . . . .106 F3
Tynycoed Cres NP12 . .85 C8
Tynycoed Terr CF47 . . .10 F3
Tynycymmer Cl CF39 .107 E3
Tyngraig Terr 1
CF83 . . . . .111 F1
Tynyrheol Flats SA11 . .72 A5
Tynyrheol Prim Sch
CF32 . . . . .130 B4
Tynywaun CF41 . . . . . . .79 D3
Tynywern Terr CF83 . .139 A7
Typica Cotts CF37 . . . .108 F2
Tyr Halen Row SA12 . . .98 D6
Tyr Onen SA12 . . . . . . .98 D6
Tyr Waun CF81 . . . . . . .32 D7
Tyr Winch Rd
Cardiff CF3 . . . . .161 D1
Cardiff CF3 . . . . .179 D8
Tyr-Meddyg NP23 . . . . . .7 C2
Tyr-y-Sarn Rd CF3 . . .179 B2
Tyrisha Ave SA4 . . . . . .43 C6
Tyrisha Ct SA4 . . . . . . .43 C6
Tyrisha Rd SA4 . . . . . . .43 C6
Tyrwhitt Cres CF23 . . .178 A5
Tytalwyn Ave CF33 . . .148 C2
Tythegston Cl CF36 . .165 F2
Tywith Cotts CF34 . . .102 A7
Tywyn Cl SA12 . . . . . .124 C8
Tywyn Cres SA12 . . . .124 D8
Tywyn Prim Sch
SA12 . . . . .124 D7

U

Ullswater Ave CF23 . . .178 A3
Ullswater Cres SA6 . . .68 A7
Ullswater St NP44 . . . . .89 C3
Under Cardiff Rd CF81 .58 A3
Underhill Dr CF38 . . . .136 A1
Underhill La SA3 . . . . .231 B4
Underhill Mans 3
CF14 . . . . .176 F6
Underhill Villas CF44 . .53 B8
Underwood CF83 . . . . .138 D6
Underwood Ave CF82 . .85 A1
Underwood Rd
Blackwood NP12 . . . . . . .86 A8
Tonna SA11 . . . . .49 A3
Underwood Terr
Abertridwr CF83 . . . . . .137 B7
Pontypridd CF37 . . . . . .109 A2
Union Bldgs SA15 . . . . .40 D7
Union Pl
Merthyr Tydfil CF47 . . . . .10 E1
Tylorstown CF43 . . . . . . .80 B4
Union St Aberdare CF44 .28 F4
Abersychan NP4 . . . . . . .37 F3

Union St continued
Ammanford SA18 . . . . .219 C7
Ferndale CF43 . . . . .79 F6
Maesteg CF34 . . . . .101 F5
Merthyr Tydfil CF47 . . . . .10 E1
5 Mountain Ash CF45 . .54 D3
Pontlottyn CF81 . . . . . . .12 F1
Pontypridd CF37 . . . . . .135 C5
Swansea SA1 . . . . .95 C6
Ton Pentre CF41 . . . . . . .79 B3
Tredegar NP22 . . . . .13 D6
Union Terr 6 CF47 . . . .10 E1
United World Coll of the
Atlantic CF61 . . . . .208 F5
Unity St CF44 . . . . .28 F1
Univ Coll (Dept of Music)
CF10 . . . . .194 F7
Univ Coll Cardiff CF5 .177 A1
Univ Coll Cardiff Llys
Tal-y-Bont CF14 . . . . . .177 D1
Univ Coll Humanities Bldg
CF10 . . . . .194 F8
Univ Coll Law Bldg
CF10 . . . . .195 A7
Univ Coll of Swansea
SA2 . . . . .94 D4
Univ Coll of Swansea
(Dept of Bot &
Microbiology) SA2 . . .94 A8
Univ Coll of Wales
NP18 . . . . .118 A3
Univ Coll Redwood Bldg
CF10 . . . . .194 F7
Univ Coll Sch of Home
Economics CF10 . . . . .195 A7
Univ Hall CF23 . . . . . .178 C3
Univ of Glamorgan
CF37 . . . . .135 E6
Univ of Wales CF10 . . .195 A7
Univ of Wales Coll
Newport
Newport NP19 . . . . . . .143 D6
Newport NP20 . . . . . . .142 F5
Univ of Wales Inst Cardiff
Cardiff CF23 . . . . .178 D4
Cardiff CF23 . . . . .178 E1
Cardiff CF24 . . . . .195 C6
Univ of Wales Inst of
Science & Tech
Cardiff CF10 . . . . .194 F7
Cardiff CF10 . . . . .194 F8
Univ of Wales, Coll of
Cardiff CF24 . . . . .195 B6
Universal St CF11 . . . .194 F3
University Hospl of Wales
CF14 . . . . .177 F3
University Pl CF24 . . . .195 E6
Uphill Cl CF64 . . . . . . .216 B6
Uphill Rd CF3 . . . . . . .179 B5
Upland Dr NP4 . . . . . . .38 B1
Upland Rd Neath SA11 . .71 F6
Pontllanfraith NP12 . . . . .86 B4
Uplands Gowerton SA4 . .66 B5
Gwaun-Cae-Gurwen
SA18 . . . . .220 D5
Newbridge NP11 . . . . . . .86 F7
Ton Pentre CF41 . . . . . . .79 B3
Uplands Cres
Llandough CF64 . . . . . .206 E6
Swansea SA2 . . . . .94 F6
Uplands Ct
3 Newport NP19 . . . . .143 F6
Rogerstone NP10 . . . . .141 F6
Uplands Dr CF34 . . . . .101 F5
Uplands Rd
Cardiff CF5 . . . . .179 A2
Pontardawe SA8 . . . . . . .23 D4
Uplands Terr
Cwmbran NP44 . . . . . . .89 C3
Swansea SA2 . . . . .94 F6
Swansea SA6 . . . . .68 F8
Uplands The
Newbridge NP11 . . . . . . .86 F7
Pontrhydyfen SA12 . . . . .73 A1
Port Talbot SA12 . . . . . . .99 C1
Radyr CF15 . . . . .176 C6
Rogerstone NP10 . . . . .141 F6
Upper Adare St CF32 . .103 E4
Upper Alma Pl CF41 . . .78 F5
Upper Alma Terr
CF37 . . . . .135 D8
Upper Arail St NP13 . . .36 B3
Upper Banks Sta SA1 . .69 A4
Upper Boat Ind Pk
CF37 . . . . .136 C3
Upper Bridge St NP4 . .62 C6
Upper Brynhyfryd Terr
CF83 . . . . .110 F3
Upper Canning St
CF41 . . . . .78 F3
Upper Capel St CF81 . .57 F4
Upper Church Pk
SA3 . . . . .123 B4
Upper Church St
Bargoed CF81 . . . . .57 F4
3 Pontypridd CF37 . . . .109 C1
Upper Clifton St 3
CF24 . . . . .195 D7
Upper Coedcae Rd
NP4 . . . . .17 D7
Upper Colbren Rd
SA18 . . . . .220 D6
Upper Colliers' Row
Heolgerrig CF48 . . . . . . .10 B1
Porth CF39 . . . . .107 E4
Upper Cosmeston Farm
CF64 . . . . .217 A2

Upper Court Terr
NP13 . . . . .60 B6
Upper Cross Rd SA15 . .40 F5
Upper Cross St NP24 . .33 D3
Upper Cwmbran Inf Sch
NP44 . . . . .89 C6
Upper Cwmbran Rd
NP44 . . . . .89 B6
Upper Dock St NP20 . .143 C5
Upper Edward St 17
CF47 . . . . .10 D2
Upper Elizabeth St
CF48 . . . . .11 A4
Upper Fforest Way
Swansea SA6 . . . . .46 B1
Swansea SA6 . . . . .69 B8
Upper Forest Level
CF45 . . . . .54 E2
Upper Francis St
CF83 . . . . .136 F7
Upper Garn Terr NP4 . .16 F8
Upper Gendros Cres
SA5 . . . . .68 A3
Upper Gertrude St
CF45 . . . . .82 E2
Upper Glyn Gwyn St
Bedwas CF83 . . . . .139 A7
Bedwas CF83 . . . . .139 A7
Bedwas CF83 . . . . .139 A7
Upper Gwastad Terr
NP13 . . . . .36 C8
Upper Gwyddon Rd
NP11 . . . . .87 B2
Upper Gynor Pl CF39 .107 E5
Upper Heathfield Rd
SA8 . . . . .23 E6
Upper High St
Bargoed CF81 . . . . .58 A4
Bedlinog CF46 . . . . .56 A7
Rhymney NP22 . . . . .12 E6
Upper Hill St NP4 . . . . .17 D6
Upper Inkerman St
SA15 . . . . .40 D5
Upper James St NP12 . .58 F4
Upper Kincraig St
CF24 . . . . .195 C8
Upper King's Head Rd
SA5 . . . . .67 F4
Upper Mdw CF5 . . . . . .193 B3
Upper Mill SA15 . . . . . .40 E6
Upper Mill Rd SA4 . . . . .19 D4
Upper Mount Pleasant 7
CF48 . . . . .31 C1
Upper North Rd CF81 . .57 F5
Upper Park St 5 SA15 .40 D5
Upper Park Terr NP4 . .62 C6
Upper Power St
NP20 . . . . .143 B7
Upper Rd NP24 . . . . . . .34 A1
Upper Regent St 10
SA15 . . . . .29 A1
Upper Rhymney Prim & Inf
Schs NP22 . . . . .12 E5
Upper Robinson St 11
SA15 . . . . .40 D5
Upper Row CF48 . . . . . .11 B5
Upper Royal La NP13 . .36 A6
Upper Salisbury St
NP22 . . . . .13 E6
Upper St CF34 . . . . . . .101 F3
Upper St Alban's Rd
CF42 . . . . .50 D3
Upper Stanley Terr
NP24 . . . . .33 F2
Upper Station Rd 5
SA18 . . . . .220 B8
Upper Strand SA1 . . . . .68 D1
Upper Taff St CF32 . . . .50 F1
Upper Tennyson Rd
NP19 . . . . .144 A5
Upper Terr CF43 . . . . . .80 C2
Upper Thomas St 2
CF47 . . . . .10 E1
Upper Trelyn Rd NP12 .85 D4
Upper Tribute Ave
NP11 . . . . .114 C8
Upper Trosnant St
NP4 . . . . .62 C6
Upper Ty' n-y-parc Terr
CF37 . . . . .177 B6
Upper Union St CF48 . .11 B4
Upper Vaughan St 7
CF37 . . . . .109 B1
Upper Viaduct Terr
NP11 . . . . .60 A2
Upper Waun St NP4 . . .17 C7
Upper West End 2
SA13 . . . . .125 C6
Upper William St 1
SA15 . . . . .40 E5
Upper Wood St CF81 . .57 F3
Upper Woodland St
NP4 . . . . .17 D7
Uppercliff Cl CF64 . . . .207 C5
Uppercliff Dr CF64 . . . .207 C5
Uppingham Ct CF5 . . .193 E6
Upton La NP20 . . . . . . .142 F4
Upton Pl CF38 . . . . . . .156 A6
Upton Rd NP20 . . . . . .142 F4
Upton St
Blaengwynfi SA13 . . . . . .76 C6
Porth CF39 . . . . .107 E4
Upton Terr
Swansea SA1 . . . . .96 A7
Tonypandy CF40 . . . . . .106 E4
Urban St CF47 . . . . .10 F4

Usk Ct Cwmbran NP44 . .89 B4
8 Cardiff CF14 . . . . . .177 A6
Usk Pl
Cwmrhydyceirw SA6 . . . .46 A5
Ebbw Vale NP23 . . . . . . .7 C5
Usk Rd Bargoed CF81 . .57 F5
Caerleon NP18 . . . . . . .118 C3
Cardiff CF14 . . . . .178 A8
Pontypool NP4 . . . . .39 D3
Pontypool NP4 . . . . .62 F6
Usk St NP19 . . . . .143 D6
Usk Vale Cl NP18 . . . .118 B3
Usk Vale Ct NP4 . . . . . .62 F6
Usk Vale Dr NP18 . . . .118 B3
Usk Vale Mews NP18 .118 B3
Usk View NP19 . . . . . .144 A8
Usk Way Barry CF62 . .214 C6
Newport NP20 . . . . . . .143 D1
Newport NP20 . . . . . . .143 D4
Uskley Ct CF3 . . . . . . .179 E6
Uxilla Terr CF31 . . . . . .169 A3

V

Vachell Ct CF61 . . . . . .210 B6
Vachell Rd CF5 . . . . . .193 D5
Vaendre Cl CF3 . . . . . .162 A1
Vaindre Cl 5 CF3 . . . .180 A8
Vaindre Dr 6 CF3 . . . .180 A8
Vaindre La Cardiff CF3 .179 F8
Cardiff CF3 . . . . .180 A8
Valarian Cl CF3 . . . . . .180 B3
Vale Ct
Cowbridge CF71 . . . . . .189 A1
Dinas Powys CF64 . . . . .206 B3
Vale Ent Ctr CF64 . . . .215 F5
Vale Gdns CF37 . . . . . .109 B2
Vale Of Neath Bsns Pk
SA10 . . . . .48 E1
Vale Of Wern Terr
SA1 . . . . .96 B7
Vale Rd CF24 . . . . .195 E7
Vale Reach CF35 . . . . .152 E2
Vale St CF62 . . . . .214 C3
Vale Terr NP22 . . . . . . .13 F5
Vale Veiw NP19 . . . . . .144 A8
Vale View Bargoed CF81 .58 F2
Barry CF62 . . . . .214 C6
Bridgend CF31 . . . . . . .169 C6
Ebbw Vale NP23 . . . . . . .7 E4
Llanharan CF72 . . . . . . .153 F3
Maesycwmmer CF82 . . .85 A1
Ogmore Vale CF32 . . . .130 B8
Pontneddfechan SA11 . .223 F2
Risca CF32 . . . . .115 A2
Sarn CF32 . . . . .150 E3
Tonypandy CF40 . . . . . .107 A3
Tredegar NP22 . . . . .14 A4
Vale View Cl CF64 . . . .206 D6
Vale View Cres CF64 . .206 D6
Vale View Rd SA44 . . . .53 C6
Vale View Terr CF45 . . .81 E8
Valegate Ret Pk CF5 . .192 F2
Valentine St NP44 . . . . .38 A3
Valeview Terr CF32 . . .104 F2
Valley Inheritance Mus
The NP4 . . . . .62 C7
Valley Rd NP23 . . . . . . .7 D1
Valley View
Abertillery NP11 . . . . . . .59 F6
Bryn NP12 . . . . .85 E3
Cardiff CF3 . . . . .179 E4
Cefn Hengoed CF82 . . . .84 F5
Neath SA11 . . . . .72 A5
Swansea SA2 . . . . .94 B6
Valley View Rd NP13 . . .36 B7
Valley View Terr SA44 . .53 B7
Valley Way SA6 . . . . . . .69 A6
Van Cres CF83 . . . . . . .138 D2
Van Dyke Cl NP19 . . . .143 F7
Van Rd Caerphilly CF83 .138 B2
Caerphilly CF83 . . . . . .138 D2
Van St CF11 . . . . .194 E3
Vanbrugh Cl NP10 . . . .142 B4
Vanbrugh Gdns NP20 .142 B1
Vancouver Dr
Blackwood NP12 . . . . . . .85 F8
Newport NP20 . . . . . . .142 D3
Vanewood Ct SA3 . . . .123 C3
Vanfield Cl CF83 . . . . .138 C2
Varna Terr SA13 . . . . .125 D7
Vardre Rd SA6 . . . . . . .46 B3
Varteg Pl NP22 . . . . .6 C1
Varteg Rd
Abersychan NP4 . . . . . . .37 E8
Blaenavon NP4 . . . . .17 E3
Ystalyfera SA9 . . . . .2 B5
Vaughan Ave
Cardiff CF5 . . . . .194 A8
Resolven SA11 . . . . . . .226 D5
Vaughan Cl 1 SA12 . . .99 A1
Vaughan Pl SA4 . . . . . .42 C1
Vaughan St
Dowlais CF48 . . . . .11 A4
Llanelli SA15 . . . . .40 D5
6 Pontypridd CF37 . . . .109 B1
Vaughan Terr CF45 . . . .82 A7
Vaughan Williams Dr
NP19 . . . . .144 C5
Vauxhall Cl SA15 . . . . . .40 D5
Vaynor & Penderyn High
Comp Sch CF48 . . . . . .10 A4
Vaynor La CF48 . . . . . . .10 A5
Vaynor Rd CF48 . . . . . .10 A5
Vaynor St CF39 . . . . . .107 E3
Velindre Ct CF14 . . . . .176 F5

Velindre Hospl CF14 .176 F5
Velindre Pl CF14 ....176 F5
Velindre Rd CF14 ...176 F5
Velindre St SA13 ......99 B2
Venables Cl SA5 .....67 D2
Vennaway La SA3 ..121 D7
Venosa Trad Est
　CF83 ....138 C4
Vensland SA3 ....122 A6
Ventnor Pl CF14 ....177 D2
Ventnor Rd NP44 .....89 E2
Venwood Cl CF5 ....205 A6
Vera Rd SA6 ....46 E8
Verandah St **5** SA1 ...95 C7
Verbena Cl CF3 ....180 A8
Verdi Rd SA12 ......98 B2
Vere Pl CF81 ....58 A1
Vere St Bargoed CF81 ..58 A1
　Barry CF63 ....215 C6
　Cardiff CF24 ......195 C7
Verig St SA5 ....68 C3
Verland Cl CF5 .....194 A8
Verland Ct CF35 ....170 C8
Verland Way CF35 ..170 C8
Verlands The CF71 ..188 D2
Verlon Cl CF63 ....215 E7
Vermeer Cres NP19 .144 A7
Vernon Cl
　Merthyr Tydfil CF47 ....10 F2
　Pontlliw SA4 ....44 A5
Vernon Ho CF31 ....169 A5
Vernon Pl
　Blackwood NP11 ......59 D1
　Briton Ferry SA11 ....71 B1
Vernon Rd CF36 ....183 A7
Vernon St
　Bridgend CF31 .....169 A5
　Briton Ferry SA11 ...71 C2
　Swansea SA1 ....68 D1
Verona Pl CF63 ....215 C7
Veronica Cl NP10 ..142 B3
Versil Terr SA4 .....65 F8
Vervain Cl CF5 .....193 A5
Verwey Rd NP23 .....15 D8
Vetch Field (Swansea City
　Fball Gd SA1 ......95 C6
Viaduct Ct NP4 ......62 D5
Viaduct Rd
　Abersychan NP4 .....37 E5
　Barry CF63 ....215 B4
Viaduct Terr NP11 ....60 A2
Vibernum Rise CF38 .156 C5
Vicarage Cl
　Bargoed CF81 ....57 F4
　Bassaleg NP10 .....142 B2
　1 Tonypandy CF40 ..107 A4
　Ystrad CF41 ....79 D3
Vicarage Ct CF38 ...135 F2
Vicarage Dr SA8 .....23 F6
Vicarage Gdns
　Marshfield CF3 ....162 D1
　Rogerstone NP10 ..141 F6
Vicarage Hill NP20 .143 B4
Vicarage La
　Abersychan NP4 .....37 F5
　Bargoed CF81 ....57 F4
　Pontllotyn CF81 .....32 F8
　Swansea SA5 ....68 A2
Vicarage Rd
　Glanaman SA18 ....220 B8
　Porth CF39 ....107 E5
　Swansea SA6 ....45 F2
　Tonypandy CF40 ...107 A4
　Tonypandy CF40 ...107 B4
　Tredegar NP22 ....6 E1
Vicarage Terr
　Abersychan NP4 .....38 A5
　Maesteg CF34 ......101 F3
　Swansea SA1 ....95 E7
　Treorchy CF42 ....78 B5
Vickery Ho **10** SA12 ..98 F1
Victor Rd NP13 ......36 B6
Victor St CF45 ......54 C2
Victoria Ave
　Cardiff CF5 ....194 B6
　Mumbles SA3 ....123 A6
　Newport NP19 .....143 F6
　Penarth CF64 ......207 A3
　Porthcawl CF36 ....182 E6
　Swansea SA1 ....95 A5
Victoria Bldgs
　Abercarn NP11 ......87 A2
　Coytrahen CF32 ....150 C8
　1 Troedyrhiw CF48 ..31 C1
Victoria Cl **7** NP20 .143 C4
Victoria Cres NP20 .143 B4
Victoria Ct
　Mumbles SA3 ....122 D4
　Newport NP19 .....143 E5
Victoria Gdns SA11 ..71 E7
Victoria La NP19 ...143 F6
Victoria Mews
　3 Cardiff CF14 ....177 E2
　Pontyclun CF72 ....173 B8
Victoria Park Rd
　CF63 ....215 C6
Victoria Park Rd E
　CF5 ....194 B6
Victoria Park Rd W
　CF5 ....194 A6
Victoria Pl
　Abersychan NP4 .....37 F5
　Bargoed CF81 ....58 A2
　6 Newport NP20 ...143 C4
Victoria Prim Sch
　Abersychan NP4 .....37 F4
　Penarth CF64 ......206 F4
Victoria Quay SA1 ...95 D6

Victoria Rd
　Abersychan NP4 .....37 F5
　Abertillery NP13 .....36 B1
　Barry CF62 ....214 C3
　Cardiff CF14 ......177 A5
　Fleur De Lis NP12 ...85 B4
　Gowerton SA4 ....66 B7
　8 Newport NP20 ...143 C4
　Pen-clawdd SA4 .....64 E3
　Penarth CF64 ......207 A3
　Pontypool NP4 ......62 D5
　Port Talbot SA12 ...124 E8
　Pyle CF33 ....148 D3
　Rhymney NP22 ......12 E4
　Swansea SA1 ....95 D6
　Waunarlwydd SA5 ...66 E3
Victoria Row SA4 ....64 E4
Victoria Sq
　Aberdare CF44 ......29 A2
　Penarth CF64 ......207 A3
Victoria St
　Abertillery NP13 .....36 A6
　Blaina NP13 ....15 D4
　Briton Ferry SA11 ...71 B1
　Cwmbran NP44 ......89 E2
　Dowlais CF48 ....11 A4
　Llanbradach CF83 ..112 A3
　Maesteg CF34 ....75 B2
　Merthyr Tydfil CF47 ..10 D1
　Merthyr Vale CF48 ...55 D5
　Mountain Ash CF45 ..54 E1
　Pontycymer CF32 ..103 E4
　Pontypool NP4 ......62 D5
　Swansea SA2 ....94 F7
　Ton Pentre CF41 ....79 A3
　Tonypandy CF40 ...107 A5
　3 Treharris CF46 ....83 B6
　Treherbert CF42 .....50 F2
　Wattstown CF39 ...107 D8
　Ystrad CF41 ....79 D3
Victoria Terr
　Abertillery NP13 .....60 B6
　3 Cwmavon SA12 ...99 D5
　Newbridge NP11 .....86 F6
　Pyle CF33 ....148 B1
　Quakers Yard CF46 ..83 B5
　Swansea SA1 ....95 A5
　Tredegar NP22 ......13 F6
Victory Ave CF39 ...107 E4
View Rd SA6 ....46 D7
Viking Pl CF10 .....195 F2
Viking Way SA1 ......69 D6
Villa Terr SA5 ....68 C5
Village Cl SA10 ......48 D3
Village Ct
　Blackwood NP12 .....59 B1
　Pyle CF33 ....148 C1
Village Farm
　Bonvilston CF5 ....191 B1
　North Cornelly CF33 .166 C8
Village Farm Ind Est
　North Cornelly CF33 .166 C8
　Pyle CF33 ....148 C1
Village Farm Rd
　CF33 ....166 C8
Village Farm Starter Units
　CF33 ....148 C1
Village Gdns SA12 ...98 C4
Village La
　Ebbw Vale NP23 ....14 E2
　Mumbles SA3 ....123 B4
Villas The
　Markham NP12 ......58 D7
　Newbridge NP11 ....86 E6
Villiers Ct
　Briton Ferry SA11 ...71 B1
　9 Port Talbot SA13 ..99 B1
Villiers Rd
　Ammanford SA18 ...219 B6
　Blaengwynfi SA13 ...76 C6
　Skewen SA10 ....71 A7
Villiers St
　Briton Ferry SA11 ...71 C1
　Port Talbot SA13 ....99 C1
　Swansea SA1 ....68 D1
Vincent Ave NP23 ....8 D1
Vincent Cl CF63 ....215 C7
Vincent Ct CF5 .....193 E5
Vincent Pl CF47 .....10 D1
Vincent Rd CF5 ....193 E5
Vincent St
　7 Blaenavon NP4 ....17 C7
　Swansea SA1 ....95 B6
Vine Pl **7** NP19 .....143 E6
Vine Row SA9 ....2 A6
Vine St NP11 ....87 B3
Vintin La CF36 .....183 A4
Vintin Terr CF36 ....183 A4
Viola Rd SA12 ....98 C2
Violet Pl CF14 .....177 D4
Violet Row CF24 ...195 B8
Violet St SA44 ......53 B8
Violet Wlk NP10 ....141 D7
Virgil St CF11 .....194 E3
Virginia Cl CF83 ...138 B4
Virginia View CF83 .138 B4
Viriamu Jones Jun & Inf
　Sch CF14 ....177 C3
Vishwell Rd
　Cardiff CF5 ....194 B7
　Wenvoe CF5 ....205 A5
Vista Ct **3** CF64 ....207 B5
Vista Rise CF5 .....176 D2
Vivian Cotts NP13 ...36 C3
Vivian Ct
　Aberavon SA12 ....124 D1
　Swansea SA2 ....94 D7

Vivian Mans SA2 .....94 D7
Vivian Park Dr SA12 .98 D2
Vivian Rd
　Newport NP19 .....143 E4
　Swansea SA2 ....94 D7
Vivian St
　Abertillery NP13 .....36 B4
　Swansea SA1 ....68 D2
　Tylorstown CF43 .....80 B3
Vivian Terr SA12 ....98 F1
Volunteer St CF14 ...78 F5
Voss Park Cl CF61 .210 A6
Voss Park Dr CF61 .210 B6
Voylart Cl SA2 ......93 C8
Voylart Rd SA2 ......93 C8
Voysey Pl CF5 .....193 C7
Vulcan Rd CF47 .....10 C1

W

Wade Ave SA9 ....2 B6
Wades The **14** NP44 ..89 B1
Waen-Fawr NP23 .....8 B2
Waengron NP13 ......15 E5
Wagner Rd SA12 .....98 B3
Wagtail Rd CF62 ...210 E6
Wain Cl CF23 ......161 B1
Wainfelin Ave NP4 ..62 B7
Wainfelin Rd NP4 ...62 B7
Wakehurst Pl CF3 ..179 F7
Walden Grange Cl
　NP19 ....144 B5
Waldhof Ct SA5 .....67 E7
Walford Davies Dr
　NP19 ....144 C5
Walford Pl CF11 ...194 D5
Walford St NP20 ....142 B3
Walk Farm Dr CF3 ..162 C4
Walk The
　Aberdare CF44 ......29 B3
　Cardiff CF24 ......195 B6
　Cardiff CF3 ....179 A4
　Ebbw Vale NP23 ....14 D7
　Merthyr Tydfil CF47 ..10 D2
　Nantyglo NP23 ......15 D8
　Pontypool NP4 ......63 A4
　Ystrad Mynach CF82 ..84 F2
Walkdens **3** NP44 ....89 E3
Walker Rd Barry CF62 .214 E5
　Cardiff CF24 ......195 C5
Wall St NP23 ....14 D8
Wallace Rd Neath SA11 71 E6
　Swansea SA1 ....95 F7
Wallhead Rd CF47 ...30 F8
Wallis Dr CF82 ......84 E7
Wallis St NP20 .....143 D2
Walmer Rd NP19 ...143 F5
Walnut Cl Miskin CF72 173 D8
　Mumbles SA3 ....122 E7
Walnut Dr NP18 ....117 E2
Walnut Gr CF62 ....211 B7
Walnut Tree Cl CF15 .176 A4
Walnut Way CF47 ....10 E4
Walpole Cl CF3 ....179 C8
Walsall St NP19 ...143 E4
Walsh Cl CF45 ......82 B6
Walston Cl CF5 ....205 A7
Walston Rd CF5 ....205 A6
Walter Conway Ave
　NP22 ....13 D5
Walter Rd SA1 ......95 B6
Walters Ave
　Abercynon CF45 .....82 E2
　Abertillery NP13 .....36 B6
　Abertysswg NP22 ....33 B8
　Dowlais CF48 ....11 A5
　Ferndale CF43 ......79 F7
　Tredegar NP22 ......13 F4
Walter's Rd
　Llanelli SA15 ....40 E4
　Neath SA11 ....71 D5
Walter's Terr
　Aberfan CF48 ....55 C4
　Merthyr Tydfil CF47 ..30 F8
Walters Row SA2 ....93 C8
Walters St SA5 ......68 C3
Waltham Cl SA6 .....68 D7
Walton Cl NP44 ....144 C4
Walton Pl CF11 ....194 D3
Waltwood Park Dr
　NP18 ....145 F7
Walwyn Pl CF3 ....180 A5
Wanderers Cres 5 .193 A4
Warborough Cl SA15 .40 C7
Warborough Rd SA15 40 C7
Ward Cl NP3 ....179 A4
Ware Rd CF83 ......137 E1
Warlock Cl NP19 ...144 A4
Warlow Cl CF62 ....211 D4
Warmington Pl NP22 .12 E5
Warn's Terr NP22 ....33 B8
Warne St NP2 ....85 B6
Warner Pl SA15 .....40 E7
Warren Cl
　Bridgend CF31 .....169 C4
　Pontypridd CF37 ..136 A5

Warren Ct NP12 .....86 A3
Warren Dr CF83 ....138 B1
Warren Evans Ct **1**
　CF14 ....177 B4
Warren Hill SA11 ....71 B1
Warren Mill Farm Pk
　CF71 ....190 E4
Warren Terr CF46 ...83 D6
Warrendale NP44 ....89 B1
Warwick Cl
　Cwmbran NP44 ......89 A3
　Pontypool NP4 ......63 A2
Warwick Cres CF36 .182 E8
Warwick Ho **7** CF10 194 E5
Warwick La **2** NP18 .144 A5
Warwick Pl
　1 Cardiff CF11 ....194 E3
　Mumbles SA3 ....123 A8
Warwick Rd
　Brynmawr NP23 ......8 B3
　Newport NP19 .....144 A5
　Swansea SA2 ....94 B4
Warwick St CF11 ...194 E3
Warwick Way CF62 .214 F6
Wasdale Cl CF23 ...178 B2
Washford Ave CF3 .179 C7
Washington Bldgs **8**
　CF64 ....207 A4
Washington Flats **7**
　CF64 ....207 A4
Washington Shops
　CF64 ....207 A4
Washington St SA1 ..68 D3
Watch House Par
　Newport NP20 .....143 A1
　Newport NP20 .....143 B1
Watchet Cl CF3 ....179 A6
Water Avens Cl CF3 .180 B6
Water La SA6 ....69 A7
Water St
　Aberavon SA12 ....125 A4
　Bridgend CF31 .....168 E4
　Gwaun-Cae-Gurwen
　　SA18 ....220 D6
　Llanelli SA15 ....40 D6
　Margam SA13 ......147 C4
　Monknash CF71 ....198 C2
　Neath SA11 ....71 E8
　Ogmore Vale CF32 .130 E8
　Pontarddulais SA4 ...19 A4
　Pontarddulais SA4 ...19 C4
Waterfall Cotts SA13 .125 D6
Waterfall Mews CF41 210 A4
Waterfall Rd SA11 ..226 D4
Waterfall Terr SA11 .226 D4
Waterfalls Wlk SA11 .223 E2
Waterford Cl CF11 ..194 E4
Waterhall Rd
　Cardiff CF5 ....176 D2
　Pyle CF33 ....148 C3
Waterhouse Dr CF11 .194 E3
Waterloo Cl NP12 ...59 B2
Waterloo Cl **6** CF23 .178 E1
Waterloo Ct NP44 ...89 E8
Waterloo Gdns CF23 195 D8
Waterloo Pl
　Aberdare CF44 ......28 F4
　Abersychan NP4 .....37 F4
　Machen CF83 ......139 D5
　Swansea SA2 ....94 F4
Waterloo Rd
　Abersychan NP4 .....37 F4
　Cardiff CF24 ......178 D1
　Newport NP20 .....143 A4
　Penygroes SA14,SA18 .218 D7
Waterloo St
　Aberdare CF44 ......29 F1
　Llanelli SA15 ....40 D4
Waterloo Terr
　Capel Hendre SA18 .218 D6
　Pontllotyn CF81 .....32 F8
Waterloo Terrace Rd
　CF83 ....139 C5
Waters La NP20 ....143 C5
Waterside Cl NP10 .142 A7
Waterside Ct
　Cwmbran NP44 ......89 E2
　Newport NP20 .....143 C8
Waterside Wlk W
　NP10 ....142 A6
Waterston Rd CF14 .177 B2
Waterton Cross CF31 169 B2
Waterton Ind Est
　CF31 ....169 C2
Waterton La CF31 ..169 E2
Waterton Rd
　Bridgend CF31 .....169 D2
　Bridgend CF35 .....169 F3
Waterworks La NP4 ..38 A5
Watery La CF71 ....189 D5
Watford Cl CF83 ...137 F1
Watford Rd
　Caerphilly CF83 ...158 F8
　Cardiff CF24 ......195 F8
Watford Rise CF83 .138 A1
Watkin St SA1 ....95 C8
Watkins La **2** NP20 .142 F4
Watkins Terr SA9 ..222 B6
Watson Rd CF14 ....177 A2
Watson Row CF81 ...57 B8
Watson St CF63 ....215 A5
Watson Terr CF81 ...57 B8
Watton Cl CF14 ....177 E8
Watts Cl NP10 .....142 B6
Waun Ave SA13 ....227 C1
Waun Bant Rd CF38 .148 D2
Waun Borfa Rd NP12 .85 C8
Waun Cl SA4 ....65 F8

Waun Daniel SA8 ....24 B2
Waun Dew NP23 .....7 F4
Waun Erw CF83 ....138 B5
Waun Fach CF23 ...178 E7
Waun Fach Terr CF32 104 F5
Waun Fawr NP23 .....7 B4
Waun Ganol St CF83 .138 B4
Waun Goch CF82 ....84 E5
Waun Goch District
　NP23 ....7 D4
Waun Goch Terr
　Ebbw Vale NP23 ....7 D7
　Nant-y-Moel CF32 .104 F5
Waun Gyrlais SA9 ..222 A6
Waun Hir CF38 .....156 F5
Waun Hywel Rd NP44 .89 C6
Waun Illtuds CF61 .210 A7
Waun Las SA10 ......48 C1
Waun Lee CF23 ....178 E8
Waun Lwyd Terr
　CF32 ....104 F5
Waun Newydd CF35 .152 B5
Waun Penlan SA8 ...23 D7
Waun Rd
　Cwmbran NP44 ......89 C1
　Llanelli SA15 ....40 E7
　Loughor SA4 ....65 F8
　Morriston SA6 ......46 A2
　Swansea SA6 ....45 F2
　Tonypandy CF40 ...106 D6
Waun St SA13 ....76 C5
Waun The SA12 ......99 F5
Waun Wen
　Cwmavon SA12 ......99 F6
　Porth CF39 ....133 D8
Waun Wen Prim Sch
　SA1 ....68 C2
Waun Wen Terr CF32 104 F5
Waun y Felin SA4 ...65 A4
Waun-Ebbw Bglws
　NP23 ....8 B2
Waun-Ebbw Rd NP23 ..8 B2
Waun-Fawr Rd CF14 .177 D6
Waun-Gron Cl SA5 ..68 C6
Waun-Gron Park Halt
　CF5 ....193 F7
Waun-Gron Rd
　Cardiff CF5 ....193 F7
　Cardiff CF5 ....194 A7
　Swansea SA5 ....68 C6
　Ammanford SA18 ...219 D6
Waun-Wen Rd SA1 ..68 C1
Waun-Wen Terr SA1 ..68 C1
Waun-y-Groes Ave
　CF14 ....177 D7
Waun-y-Groes Rd
　CF14 ....177 D7
Waun-y-Pistyll SA5 ..68 C5
Waun-y-Pound Ind Est
　NP23 ....7 A2
Waun-y-Pound Rd
　NP23 ....7 B2
Waunarlwydd Prim Sch
　SA5 ....66 D3
Waunarlwydd Rd SA2,
　SA5 ....67 B2
Waunbant Ct CF48 .225 F2
Waunceirch Prim Sch
　SA10 ....48 C2
Waunddu NP4 ....61 F8
Waunfach CF32 ....129 E3
Waunfach Flats CF83 138 B4
Waunfach St CF83 .138 B4
Waunfain CF83 .....137 F6
Waunfarlais Rd SA18 219 A8
Waunfawr SA18 ....219 A7
Waunfawr Gdns
　NP11 ....114 C4
Waunfawr Jun Sch
　NP11 ....114 C4
Waunfawr Park Rd
　NP11 ....114 C4
Waunfawr Rd NP11 .114 C4
Waunfawr Terr NP11 114 C4
Waungoch Rd NP12 ..59 C1
Waungron
　Bettws CF32 ....129 C3
　Glynneath SA11 ...223 D1
Waungron Rd SA6 ...46 D8
Waunhafod Rd SA18 219 A8
Waunheulog NP23 ...8 A3
Waunlanyrafon SA15 ..40 D5
Waunleision SA18 ..220 D7
Waunllapria NP7 .....9 D5
Waunllwyd **2** CF44 ..28 A6
Waunllwyn Cres NP12 .85 D7
Waunlon CF36 .....183 C8
Waunlwyd Jun & Inf Sch
　NP23 ....14 F3
Waunrhydd Rd CF39 .133 B7
Waunscil Ave CF31 .169 A4
Wauntreoda Rd CF14 177 C5
Wavell Cl CF14 .....177 F6
Wavell Dr NP20 ....117 A3
Waveney Cl NP20 ..116 C2
Waverley Cl CF64 ..206 E6
Waverley Ct CF63 ..215 A4
Waverley Dr SA3 ...123 A5
Waverley Sq CF10 .195 B1
Waverly Cl SA6 .....46 D7
Waverly Pk SA6 .....46 D7
Waycock Cross CF62 214 B6
Waycock Rd CF62 ..214 A6

Wayfield Cres NP44 ..89 E5
Wayne Cotts CF44 ...53 C7
Wayne St
　Aberdare CF44 ......28 F3
　Porth CF39 ....107 E4
　Trehafod CF37 .....108 C2
Weare Cl NP20 .....116 C2
Weatheral St **4** CF44 .29 A2
Weavers Ho **6** SA1 ..95 E6
Webb Pl SA12 ......124 E7
Webbons Way SA1 ...67 F2
Webley Cl NP18 ....118 A4
Webley Gdns NP18 .118 A4
Webster St CF46 ....83 B7
Wedal Rd CF14 ....178 A2
Wedgewood CF83 ..138 D3
Wedmore Rd CF11 .194 E4
Wednesbury St NP19 143 F4
Weekes Cl CF3 ....179 D7
Weig Fach La SA5 ...67 D3
Weig Gdns SA5 ......68 A4
Weig La SA5 ....67 F3
Weig Rd SA5 ....67 F3
Weir View NP20 .....6 D2
Welby Rd **4** CF5 ...194 D5
Welcome La SA1 ....95 D7
Weldon Cl NP44 .....90 B5
Welfare Ave SA13 ..100 E5
Welford St CF62 ...214 C3
Well Field SA2 ......93 E8
Well La CF5 ....191 F2
Well Pl CF44 ....29 D1
Well Rd CF62 ......212 A2
Well St Abercynon CF45 .82 D2
　Brynmawr NP23 ......8 A4
　Cefn Coed CF48 ....10 B4
　Laleston CF32 .....167 F4
　Merthyr Tydfil CF47 ..10 D6
　Porthcawl CF36 ....182 F6
Well The CF32 .....167 E4
Well Wlk CF62 ....214 C2
Well Wood Cl CF23 .178 E2
Welland Circ NP20 .116 C2
Welland Cres NP20 .116 C2
Wellfield Beddau CF38 156 A8
　Bishopston SA3 ....121 F6
　Resolven SA11 ....226 D4
Wellfield Ave
　Neath SA11 ....71 E6
　Porthcawl CF36 ....183 A7
Wellfield Cl SA4 .....43 B1
Wellfield Cres CF36 .183 A7
Wellfield Ct
　Barry CF63 ....205 B1
　Church Village CF38 135 E1
　Marshfield CF3 ....180 E8
Wellfield La SA4 .....62 D1
Wellfield Mews CF38 156 A8
Wellfield Pl **2** CF24 195 C8
Wellfield Rd
　Aberavon SA12 .....99 A2
　Cardiff CF24 ......178 C1
　Marshfield CF3 ....180 E8
Wellfield Sq SA11 ...71 E6
Wellington Ct **2**
　CF11 ....194 E5
Wellington Dr NP44 ..89 A3
Wellington Mews **3**
　CF11 ....194 E5
Wellington Pl **11**
　SA12 ....124 F8
Wellington Rd
　Abersychan NP4 .....37 F4
　Newport NP20 .....142 D3
Wellington St
　Aberdare CF44 ......29 A3
　Cardiff CF11 ......194 E5
　Cardiff CF15 ......158 C1
　Swansea SA1 ....95 C6
Wellington Terr NP24 .33 F1
Wellington Way NP22 .12 F2
Wellingtonia Cl CF47 .10 D6
Wellpark SA3 ......228 C2
Wellright Rd CF5 ..193 D7
Wells Cl Baglan SA12 ..98 E5
　Newport NP20 .....142 E1
Wells Rd SA12 ......98 E5
Wells St CF11 .....194 E5
Wellspring Terr
　NP11 ....115 A1
Wellwood CF23 ....178 E5
Wellwood Dr CF64 .206 A2
Welsh Coll of Music &
　Drama (Coleg Cerdd a
　Drama Cymru) CF10 194 F6
Welsh Folk Mus CF5 .192 F7
Welsh Hawking Ctr
　CF62 ....214 A7
Welsh Ind & Maritime Mus
　CF10 ....195 C4
Welsh Inst of Sport
　(Athrofa Chwaraeon
　Cymru) CF11 ......194 E7
Welsh Miners Mus
　SA13 ....74 A3
Welsh National Tennis Ctr
　CF24 ....195 D4
Welsh Office CF10 ..194 F7
Welwyn Rd CF14 ...177 D5
Wembley SA11 ......71 D4
Wembley Ave SA10 222 F5
Wembley Rd
　Cardiff CF5 ....194 C5
　Ystalyfera SA9 ......2 A6

Wenallt Ct
Aberdare CF44 . . . . . . .29 B3
Cardiff CF14 . . . . . . .177 B8

Wenallt Rd
Aberdare CF44 . . . . . . .29 B3
Cardiff CF14, CF83 . . .159 A3
Tonna SA11 . . . . .49 D2

Wengraig Rd CF40 .106 F5
Wenham Pl SA11 . . . .71 F7

Wentloog Rd
Cardiff CF3 . . . . .179 B3
Cardiff CF3 . . . . .179 D3
Peterstone Wentlooge
CF3 . . . . .180 C1

Wentloog Ave
Cardiff CF3 . . . . .179 C2
Cardiff CF3 . . . . .179 E2

Wentloog Cl
Cardiff CF3 . . . . .179 B3
Cwmbran NP44 . . . . . . .89 C3

Wentloog Corporate Ind
Pk CF3 . . . . .179 F4
Wentloog Ct CF3 . . .179 B3
Wentsland Cres NP4 .62 A6
Wentsland Rd NP4 . . .62 A6
Wentwood Cl NP44 . . .89 C2
Wentwood Rd NP18 .117 C2

Wentworth
Bassaleg NP10 . . . . . .141 F3
4 Cardiff CF3 . . . . . .180 A8

Wentworth Cres SA3 . .93 E1
Wentworth La CF3 . . .180 A8
Wenvoe Cl CF5 . . . . .205 A6
Wenvoe Ct 13 CF5 . .193 C4
Wenvoe Terr CF62 . . .214 D4
Weobley Castle SA3 .229 B3
Weobley Ct SA5 . . . . . .67 F6
Werfa Cl CF44 . . . . . . .29 D3
Werfa La CF44 . . . . . . .29 D3
Werfa St CF23 . . . . . .178 B1

Wern Cres Neath SA10 .70 E5
Nelson CF46 . . . . .83 F4

Wern Ddu CF32 . . . . .150 D3
Wern Deg CF35 . . . . .170 D8
Wern Fach Ct NP44 . .115 F8
Wern Fawr La CF3 . . .179 E8

Wern Fawr Rd
Pencoed CF35 . . . . . .152 E5
Swansea SA1 . . . . .96 C7

Wern Fraith SA10 . . . .48 C1
Wern Gethin La CF3 .179 F6

Wern Goch E
Cardiff CF23 . . . . . . .178 D5
Cardiff CF23 . . . . . . .178 E6

Wern Goch W CF23 .178 D6
Wern Hill NP4 . . . . . . .62 B6

Wern Ind Est
Rogerstone NP10 . . . .141 F5
Rogerstone NP10 . . . .142 A3

Wern Isaf CF48 . . . . . .11 C5
Wern La CF48 . . . . . . .30 C8
Wern Olau SA10 . . . . .49 B6

Wern Rd
Cefn Coed CF48 . . . . . .10 A4
Glanaman SA18 . . . . .220 B8
Llanelli SA15 . . . . .40 E5
Llanmorlais SA4 . . . . . .64 C1
Margam SA13 . . . . . . .125 E4
Neath SA10 . . . . .70 E7
Pontypool NP4 . . . . . . .62 E1
Swansea SA1 . . . . .68 D4
Tonypandy CF40 . . . .106 E5
Ystalyfera SA9 . . . . .2 B6

Wern School Cl NP4 . .62 E1
Wern St CF40 . . . . . .106 B7

Wern Terr
Ammanford SA18 . . . .219 D6
Cymmer SA13 . . . . . . .75 D4
Pontypool NP4 . . . . . . .62 B6
Rogerstone NP10 . . . .141 F6
Swansea SA1 . . . . .96 C7

Wern View SA12 . . . . .73 A2
Wern-Ddu SA13 . . . . .219 D4
Wern-Ddu Rd SA18 . .219 D8
Wern-Ddu Row CF83 .138 E1
Wernddu Ct CF83 . . .138 D1
Werngoch Rd CF23 . .178 C6
Wernlys Rd CF31 . . . .150 D1
Wernoleu Rd SA18 . . .219 D7
Wernwood Rd SA9 . . . .2 B6
Wesley Ave CF62 . . . .212 F1
Wesley Bldgs NP23 . . .8 C2

Wesley Cl
Cwmbran NP44 . . . . . . .89 D2
Dowlais CF48 . . . . .11 A4

Wesley Ct Cardiff CF3 .179 C5
Dinas Powys CF64 . . . .206 A3

Wesley Hill CF83 . . . .139 F7
Wesley Ho 6 NP23 . . . .8 E4
Wesley La CF10 . . . . .195 B5

Wesley Pl
Merthyr Vale CF48 . . . . .55 D4
Risca NP11 . . . . .114 F1
Treorchy CF42 . . . . . . .79 A4

Wesley Rd
Blackwood NP12 . . . . . .85 E7
Caerphilly CF83 . . . . .137 D1

Wesley St
Abercynon CF45 . . . . . .82 D2
Cwmbran NP44 . . . . . . .89 D2
Llantwit Major CF61 . . .209 A6
Maesteg CF34 . . . . . . .75 B1

Wesley Terr
Abertillery NP11 . . . . . .59 F4
Pontypool NP4 . . . . . . .61 D7

Wesleyan Flats CF39 .107 F4
Wesleyan Pl NP23 . . . .7 D4
Wesleyan Row NP23 . . .7 D1
Wessex Pl CF62 . . . . .214 C2
Wessex St CF5 . . . . . .194 B6
West Acre CF61 . . . . .210 B8

West Ave
Caerphilly CF83 . . . . .137 E3
Cefn Cribwr CF32 . . . .149 B2
Maesycwmmer CF82 . . .85 B2
Pontypool NP4 . . . . . . .62 D1

West Bank
Abertillery NP13 . . . . . .36 A4
Llanyravon NP44 . . . . . .90 B2

West Bank Ct 16 NP4 . .38 A1
West Bute St CF10 . . .195 C2

West Canal Wharf 6
CF10 . . . . .195 A4

West Cl CF10 . . . . . . .195 B2
West Cliff SA3 . . . . . .121 A3
West Crossways SA8 . .23 D6
West Ct 2 CF64 . . . . .207 A4

West Dr
Porthcawl CF36 . . . . . .182 E6
St Donat's CF61 . . . . .208 F5

West End Llanelli SA15 . .40 C6
Pen-clawdd SA4 . . . . . .64 D4
Port Talbot SA13 . . . . .125 C6

West End Ave
Pontypool NP4 . . . . . . .37 F2
Porthcawl CF36 . . . . . .165 F1

West End Terr
Ebbw Vale NP23 . . . . . .14 D8
Llantwit Major CF61 . . .209 A6

West Farm Cl CF62 . . .184 D2
West Farm Rd CF32 . .184 E2
West Gr Cardiff CF24 . .195 B6
Merthyr Tydfil CF47 . . . .10 D3

West Grove Ct 5
CF24 . . . . .195 B6

West Hill NP22 . . . . . . .13 D7
West Hill Rd NP4 . . . . .38 B1
West House Rd CF31 .168 D4
West Lee CF11 . . . . . .194 E6

West Luton Pl 4
CF24 . . . . .195 C5

West Market St
9 Newport NP20 . . . . .143 C3
Newport NP20 . . . . . . .143 D3

West Monmouth Sch
NP4 . . . . .62 C5

West Mount Cres
CF38 . . . . .136 A1

West Orchard Cres
CF5 . . . . .194 A7

West Park Dr CF36 . . .165 E1

West Park La 1
NP20 . . . . .142 F4

West Park Prim Sch
CF36 . . . . .165 F1

West Park Rd NP20 . .142 F4

West Point Ind Est
CF64 . . . . .206 D8

West Rd
Bridgend CF31 . . . . . .168 D4
Cardiff CF14 . . . . .176 F3
Penybryn CF82 . . . . . . .84 D5
Porthcawl CF36 . . . . . .165 E2

West Rhondda CF32 . .129 F7
West Rise CF14 . . . . .178 A8
West Roedin NP44 . . .116 C8

West St Abercynon CF45 .82 E3
Aberkenfig CF32 . . . . .150 C4
Bargoed CF81 . . . . . . .57 F4
Gorseinon SA4 . . . . . . .43 B1
Llantwit Major CF61 . . .209 A6
Maesteg CF34 . . . . . . .102 A2
Monknash CF71 . . . . . .198 C3
Newport NP20 . . . . . . .143 B4
Pontypridd CF37 . . . . .109 D2

West Taff St CF39 . . . .107 F3
West Terr CF64 . . . . . .207 A4

West View
Bettws CF32 . . . . .129 E1
Newbridge NP11 . . . . . .86 F4
Taffs Well CF15 . . . . . .158 B4

West View Cres
Blackwood NP12 . . . . . .59 A1
Trelewis CF46 . . . . .83 D6

West View Terr
Blaenavon NP4 . . . . . . .17 B7
Ebbw Vale NP23 . . . . . .14 E6

West View Villas CF81 . .58 A4

**West Way (Ffordd y
Gorllewin)** SA1 . . . . . .95 C6
West Way Rd NP20 . . .143 B1
West Wlk CF62 . . . . . .214 D6

Westbourne Cres
CF14 . . . . .176 F4

Westbourne Ct
Cardiff CF5 . . . . .179 C2
Penarth CF64 . . . . . . .207 A1
Porthcawl CF36 . . . . . .182 E4

Westbourne Gr SA2 . . .94 C7

Westbourne Pl
Merthyr Tydfil CF47 . . . .30 E7
Mumbles SA3 . . . . . . .123 B4
Porthcawl CF36 . . . . . .182 F7

Westbourne Rd
Cardiff CF14 . . . . .176 F4
Penarth CF64 . . . . . . .207 A2
Penrhiwtyn SA11 . . . . . .71 C4
Swansea SA2 . . . . .94 C7

Westbourne Sch
Penarth CF64 . . . . . . .207 A3
Penarth CF64 . . . . . . .207 A4

Westbourne Terr
CF72 . . . . .153 E2
Westbury Bglws SA15 .40 E3
Westbury Cl CF63 . . . .215 B7

Westbury St
Llanelli SA15 . . . . .40 E3
Swansea SA1 . . . . .95 A6

Westbury Terr CF5 . . .194 B7
Westcliff SA3 . . . . . . .123 C3
Westcliff Mews SA3 . .123 C3
Westcross Ave SA3 . . .123 A6
Westcross La SA3 . . . .122 F7
Westdale Rd SA5 . . . . .67 D7
Western Arc CF62 . . . .214 E1

Western Ave
Bridgend CF31 . . . . . .169 C3
Brynmawr NP23 . . . . . . .8 A4
Cardiff CF14,CF5 . . . . .194 B8
Newport NP20 . . . . . . .142 C3
Port Talbot SA13 . . . . . .98 C2

Western Ave N CF14 .177 C2

Western Bsns Ctr
CF5 . . . . .193 F6

Western Cl SA3 . . . . . .123 B4
Western Cres NP22 . . .13 D7

Western Ct
10 Barry CF63 . . . . . .215 B6
Bridgend CF31 . . . . . .168 D4

Western Dr
Bargoed CF81 . . . . . . .57 E2
Cardiff CF14 . . . . .177 C2

Western Ind Est
Caerleon NP18 . . . . . .118 B4
Caerphilly CF83 . . . . .137 E2

Western La SA3 . . . . . .123 B4

Western Rd
Clydach SA6 . . . . .46 C6
Pontardawe SA8 . . . . . .23 D4

Western St
Swansea SA1 . . . . .95 B6
Trehafod CF37 . . . . . .108 D3

Western Terr
Abercarn NP11 . . . . . .114 B5
Blaengwynfi SA13 . . . . .76 D5
Cwmfelinfach NP11 . . .113 A4
Ebbw Vale NP23 . . . . . . .7 D1
Swansea SA1 . . . . .68 D3

Western Valley Rd
NP10 . . . . .142 C3
Westernmoor Rd SA11 .71 F6
Westfa Rd SA2 . . . . . . .94 F7

Westfield Ave
Bridgend CF31 . . . . . .168 C5
Cardiff CF14 . . . . .177 C5
Newport NP20 . . . . . . .117 A2

Westfield Cl NP18 . . . .117 F4
Westfield Cres CF36 .165 F2
Westfield Ct CF72 . . . .155 E2

Westfield Dr
Newport NP20 . . . . . . .117 A2
Penarth CF64 . . . . . . .206 E2

Westfield Lower Specl Sch
NP20 . . . . .117 A2

Westfield Rd
Caerleon NP18 . . . . . .117 F3
Cardiff CF14 . . . . .177 C4
Newport NP20 . . . . . . .143 A5
Pontypridd CF37 . . . . .109 C5
Waunarlwydd SA5 . . . . .66 D4

Westfield Specl Upper Sch
NP20 . . . . .163 F8

Westfield Way NP20 . .117 A2
Westgate CF71 . . . . . .188 E2
Westgate Cl CF36 . . . .165 F1
Westgate St NP18 . . . .117 A2

Westgate St (Heol y Porth)
CF10 . . . . .195 A5

Westgil Pen Fforedd
NP12 . . . . .85 D6

Westgrove Ct SA4 . . . . .43 B4
Westhill Dr CF72 . . . . .155 E2
Westhill St CF61 . . . . .209 F6
Westland Ave SA3 . . . .122 F7

Westland Cl
Cardiff CF5 . . . . .196 A7
Loughor SA4 . . . . .42 E1

Westlands SA12 . . . . . .98 D4

Westminster Cres
CF23 . . . . .178 C7

Westminster Dr
Cardiff CF23 . . . . .178 C8
Sully CF64 . . . . .216 B5

Westminster Way
CF31 . . . . .168 C6
Westmoor Cl NP19 . . .144 C3

Westmoreland St
CF5 . . . . .194 C5
Weston Ave CF64 . . . .216 B4
Weston Rd Cardiff CF3 .179 B5
Tonypandy CF40 . . . . .107 B1
Weston Sq CF63 . . . . .215 C6
Weston St 7 CF63 . . .215 B6

Weston Terr
Porth CF39 . . . . .107 E6
Treorchy CF42 . . . . . . .78 B4

Westonbirt Ct CF3 . . . .179 F6
Westport Ave SA2 . . . .94 A7
Westra CF64 . . . . .205 E2
Westra Ct 2 CF5 . . . .194 B7
Westray NP19 . . . . . . .143 F7
Westside Rd CF83 . . . .110 E3

Westview Terr
Abertillery NP13 . . . . . .36 C2
Caerphilly CF83 . . . . .138 D5
Westville NP22 . . . . . . .33 B7

Westville Rd
Cardiff CF23 . . . . .178 D1
9 Newport NP20 . . . . .142 F4

Westville Wlk CF23 . . .178 C1

Westward Cl
Bridgend CF31 . . . . . .168 B6
Mumbles SA3 . . . . .94 A1

Westward Pl CF31 . . . .168 B6
Westward Rise CF62 . .214 B3
Westwinds SA3 . . . . . .122 E3
Westwinds Cl SA5 . . . . .66 E3

Westwood Ct 9
CF64 . . . . .207 A4

Westwood Dr CF46 . . . .83 A6
Wexford Cl CF23 . . . . .161 A2
Wharf La NP19 . . . . . .143 E5
Wharf Rd NP19 . . . . . .143 E5
Wharfedale Rd CF23 .178 F8
Wharton Cl CF62 . . . . .212 E1
Wharton St CF10 . . . . .195 A5
Wheate Cl The CF62 . .213 A2
Wheatfield Terr SA1 . . .68 C1
Wheatley Ave SA12 . . .124 E8

Wheatley Pl
Blackwood NP12 . . . . . .85 D8
Merthyr Tydfil CF47 . . . .30 F7

Wheatley Rd
Cardiff CF5 . . . . .193 C5
Neath SA11 . . . . .95 A6

Wheatsheaf Dr SA6 . . .46 A4
Wheatsheaf La CF47 . .10 D2
Wheeler St NP20 . . . . .143 C6
Whimbrels The CF36 .182 D3
Whinberry Way CF5 . .193 A5
Whinchat Cl 8 CF3 . .180 A7
Whistle Rd CF3 . . . . . . .9 D1
Whistler Cl NP19 . . . . .143 F7
Whitaker Rd CF24 . . . .196 A8
Whitby Pl NP19 . . . . . .143 D6

Whitchurch High Sch
(Lower) CF14 . . . . . .177 B5

Whitchurch High Sch
(Upper) CF14 . . . . . .177 A5

Whitchurch Pl 1
CF24 . . . . .178 A1

Whitchurch Psychiatric
Hospl CF14 . . . . .176 F5

Whitchurch Rd CF14 .177 A6
Whitchurch Sta CF14 177 A6
Whitcliffe Dr CF64 . . .217 B8
Whitcombe St 3 CF44 .29 A2

White Ash Glade
NP18 . . . . .117 F2
White Ave NP10 . . . . .163 E5
White Barn Rd CF14 . . .85 A8
White City Rd SA5 . . . . .67 D4
White Cl SA12 . . . . .98 B3
White Gates SA10 . . . .123 A7
White Gr SA3 . . . . . . .122 E7
White Hall La NP44 . . . .90 B1

White Hart Cotts
CF34 . . . . .128 B6
White Hart Dr CF83 . .139 E7
White Ho CF62 . . . . . .214 C1
White Horse NP13 . . . .36 B7
White House Cl CF3 . . .9 D5
White House Rd NP44 . .90 A5
White Lion Cotts NP22 .6 C2
White Oaks Dr CF3 . . .179 E8
White Rose Way NP24 .33 E2

White St
Caerphilly CF83 . . . . .138 B2
Dowlais CF48 . . . . .11 A5
Swansea SA1 . . . . .95 B7

Whiteacre Cl CF14 . . .159 F2
Whitebeam Cl CF47 . . .10 D6
Whitebrook Way NP44 .89 F2
Whitefield Cl SA11 . . .223 C1
Whitefield Rd CF14 . .177 A2
Whitefield St CF41 . . . .78 F3
Whiteford Rd SA5 . . . . .67 F6
Whitegates SA2 . . . . . .94 A1
Whitehall Ave CF3 . . .179 B3
Whitehall Cl CF5 . . . . .204 F7
Whitehall Par CF3 . . . .179 B3
Whitehall Pl CF3 . . . . .179 A3
Whitehall Rd CF5 . . . .176 F1
Whitehart La NP18 . . .118 C1
Whiterock Ave CF37 . .109 B2
Whiterock Cl CF37 . . .109 B2
Whiterock Dr CF37 . . .109 B2
Whitesands Rd CF14 .159 D1
Whiteshell Dr SA3 . . . .122 E4
Whitestone Ave SA3 . .122 A5
Whitestone Cl SA3 . . .122 F4

Whitestone Cty Prim Sch
SA3 . . . . .122 A5

Whitestone La SA3 . . .122 E5
Whitestone Rd SA3 . . .122 A5
Whitethorn Cl SA5 . . . .67 F5
Whitethorn Dr CF31 . .169 B4
Whitethorn Pl SA2 . . . .94 B6
Whitethorn Way CF37 .180 E8
Whitethorne St NP11 . .60 A1
Whiteways CF14 . . . . .210 B7
Whitewell Dr CF61 . . .210 A5
Whitewell Rd CF62 . . .214 E2

Whitland Cl
Cardiff CF5 . . . . .176 D1
Swansea SA5 . . . . .67 F6

Whitland Cres CF5 . . .176 E1
Whitley Rd SA4 . . . . . . .42 F1
Whitmore Park Dr
CF62 . . . . .214 C2
Whitmuir Rd CF24 . . . .195 F7
Whitstone Rd NP19 . . .144 B6
Whittan Cl CF62 . . . . .212 E1
Whitting St SA11 . . . . .223 D1
Whitting Terr CF39 . . .107 E5

Whittington St
Neath SA11 . . . . .71 E6
Tonna SA11 . . . . .49 D3

Whittington Terr SA11 .43 D2
Whittle Ct NP20 . . . . .117 A3
Whittle Dr NP20 . . . . .117 A3
Whittle Rd CF11 . . . . .194 D3
Whitworth Ct CF11 . . .194 F4
Whitworth Terr NP22 . .13 F1

Wick & Warcross Prim Sch
CF71 . . . . .198 D5

Wick Rd
Castle-upon-Alun CF35 .186 B4
Ewenny CF35 . . . . . . .185 F2
Llantwit Major CF61 . . .199 B2
Llantwit Major CF61 . . .209 A7
Llantwit Major CF61 . . .209 A7
St Brides Major CF32 . .185 D1

Wicken Cl CF3 . . . . . .180 A7
Wicklow Cl CF3 . . . . . .161 A1
Widecombe Dr CF3 . . .179 A3
Widgeon Cl CF36 . . . .165 E1
Wigan Terr CF32 . . . . .151 A5
Wigmore Cl CF14 . . . .159 E2

Wild Gardens Rd
CF23 . . . . .178 B5
Wild Mill La CF31 . . . .168 E2
Wildbrook SA13 . . . . . .125 D8
Wilden Ave SA13 . . . . .125 D5

Wildfowl & Wetlands Ctr
SA14 . . . . .41 C2

Wilfred Brook Ho
CF11 . . . . .194 F2
Wilfred St CF63 . . . . . .215 B5

Wilkins Terr
Caerphilly CF83 . . . . .137 F6
Caerphilly CF83 . . . . .138 A6

Wilkinson Cl CF24 . . . .195 D5

Willet Cl
Caerphilly CF83 . . . . .137 F6
Caerphilly CF83 . . . . .138 A6

Wilks Row 3 SA1 . . . . .95 C8
Willenhall St NP19 . . .143 E6
Willesden Rd CF31 . . .168 C6
Willet Cl SA11 . . . . . . .71 EF

William Adams Ct
NP23 . . . . .14 D8
William Belcher Dr
CF3 . . . . .180 A5
William Bowen Cl SA4 .66 A5

William Brown Cl
NP44 . . . . .117 A7
William Ct
5 Swansea SA1 . . . . . .95 C6
Ystrad CF41 . . . . .79 C3
William Dennis Ave
SA4 . . . . .66 A8
William Forbes Bnglws
CF81 . . . . .58 A6
William Harris Bglws
CF83 . . . . .137 A7
William Lovett Gdns 1
NP20 . . . . .143 B4
William Morris Dr 1
NP19 . . . . .144 D6
William Morris Gdns
SA1 . . . . .96 B7
William Nicholls Dr
CF3 . . . . .179 E8
William Pl CF39 . . . . .107 E2

William St
Aberbargoed CF81 . . . . .58 B4
Abercwmboi CF44 . . . . .53 E4
Abercynon CF45 . . . . . .82 E2
Abertridwr CF83 . . . . .137 A7
Bargoed CF81 . . . . . . .58 A2
Bedwas CF83 . . . . . . .139 A6
Cardiff CF11 . . . . .194 D7
Cwm NP23 . . . . .35 A7
Cwmfelinfach NP11 . . .113 B3
Fleur De Lis NP12 . . . . .85 B5
11 Merthyr Tydfil CF47 .10 D8
16 Merthyr Tydfil CF47 .30 E8
Mumbles SA3 . . . . . . .123 A5
Newbridge NP11 . . . . . .59 F1
Pontardawe SA8 . . . . . .23 B1
Pontypridd CF37 . . . . .109 F6
Porth CF39 . . . . .107 F6
Swansea SA1 . . . . .95 C6
Tir-y-Berth CF82 . . . . . .85 A6
Treherbert CF42 . . . . . .50 F2
Ystrad CF41 . . . . .79 C3
Ystradgynlais SA9 . . . . . .2 E7

William Thomas Meml
Chapel NP11 . . . . . . .113 B3
Williams Ave SA11 . . .226 D5
Williams Church Terr
CF32 . . . . .150 E6
Williams Cl 28 NP20 .143 C3

Williams Cres
Barry CF62 . . . . .214 E5
Sarn CF32 . . . . .150 F5

Williams Pl
Merthyr Tydfil CF47 . . . .10 E5
Upper Boat CF37 . . . . .136 C3

Williams St
Blackwood NP12 . . . . . .85 E7
Brynna CF72 . . . . .153 C3
Hollybush NP12 . . . . . .34 D4
Pontardulais SA4 . . . . .19 C4
Tonypandy CF40 . . . . .106 C3

Williams Terr
Treharris CF46 . . . . . . .83 B7
5 Merthyr Tydfil CF47 . .30 F4
Williams Way CF10 . . .195 A3
Williamstown Prim Sch
CF40 . . . . .107 A2
Willie Seager Cotts
CF23 . . . . .178 D1

Willins NP44 . . . . .116 A3
Williton Rd SA13 . . . . .179 C7
Willow Bank SA4 . . . . .66 D3

Willow Cl
Beddau CF38 . . . . . . .155 F6
Bridgend CF35 . . . . . .169 F3
Ebbw Vale NP23 . . . . . .7 C1
Newport NP19 . . . . . . .144 B2
Penarth CF64 . . . . . . .206 E3
Porthcawl CF36 . . . . . .183 E8
Rogerstone NP10 . . . .141 D7

Willow Ct
13 Cardiff CF24 . . . . .195 C7
Newbridge NP11 . . . . . .87 C8
Tredegar NP22 . . . . . . .6 C2

Willow Dr
Caerphilly CF12 . . . . . .85 F6
Llanmartin NP18 . . . . .145 E4
Willow Gn NP18 . . . . .117 F3

Willow Gr
Aberdare CF44 . . . . . . .28 E2
Baglan SA12 . . . . .98 E6
Cardiff CF23 . . . . .180 A8
Willow Herb Cl CF3 . .180 B6
Willow Parc NP11 . . . . .59 D1

Willow Rd
Blackwood NP11 . . . . . .59 D3
Llanharry CF72 . . . . . .172 C5
Merthyr Tydfil CF47 . . . .10 D5
Willow Rise CF82 . . . . .84 D7
Willow St CF37 . . . . . .136 A5
Willow Terr CF45 . . . . .81 F8
Willow Tree Cl CF15 . .175 F6
Willow Way SA12 . . . . .98 D6
Willow Wlk Cimla SA11 .72 C6
Cowbridge CF71 . . . . .188 F2
Willowbrook Dr CF3 . .179 E6

Willowbrook Gdns
SA3 . . . . .93 F1

Willowbrook Jun & Inf Sch
CF3 . . . . .180 A6

Willowbrook Laboratory
Units CF3 . . . . .179 F7
Willowdale Cl CF5 . . . .193 C8

Willowdale Rd
Cardiff CF5 . . . . .193 B8
Cardiff CF5 . . . . .193 C8
Willowdene Way CF3 .180 A8
Willowfield CF15 . . . . .157 E8
Willowford CF15 . . . . .157 C3
Willowmere CF64 . . . .206 D7

Willows Com High Sch
CF24 . . . . .196 A6
Willows Cres CF63 . . .215 A2
Willows Pl SA1 . . . . . . .95 C7

Willows The
Abertillery NP13 . . . . . .36 C4
Bedwas CF83 . . . . . . .138 E2
Bridgend CF31 . . . . . .169 A4
Croesyceiliog NP44 . . . .90 A5
Laleston CF32 . . . . . . .167 E4
Llanelli SA15 . . . . .40 C7
St Athan CF62 . . . . . . .211 D4

Willowtown Jun & Inf Sch
NP23 . . . . .14 C8
Willowturf Ct CF32 . . .150 E4
Wills Ct CF62 . . . . . . .213 A1
Wills Row NP10 . . . . . .142 B4
Wilmot St SA11 . . . . . .71 E6
Wilson Ct 2 CF47 . . . . .30 D8
Wilson Pl Cardiff CF5 . .193 C4
Maerdy CF43 . . . . .52 A1
Wilson Rd Cardiff CF5 .193 B5
Newport NP19 . . . . . . .144 A7
Wilson St Cardiff CF5 . .194 E7
Wilton Terr 7 CF47 . . . .30 E8
Wimble Wood Cl SA3 .123 A5
Wimborne Cres CF64 .216 B5
Wimborne Rd CF35 . . .152 E1
Wimborne Rise NP44 . .89 C5
Wimborne St CF48 . . . .11 A3

Wimbourne Bldgs
CF63 . . . . .215 C4
Wimbourne Cl CF61 . .209 C5

Wimbourne Cres
CF35 . . . . .152 E1
Wimbourne Rd CF63 . .215 C5
Wimbourne Terr CF82 . .57 A1
Wimmerfield Ave SA2 .93 E7
Wimmerfield Cl SA2 . . .93 E7
Wimmerfield Cres SA2 .93 E7
Winch Fawr Ho CF48 . .10 A3
Winch Fawr Pk CF48 . .225 F1

Winch Fawr Rd
Heolgerrig CF48 . . . . . .10 A1
Merthyr Tydfil CF48 . . .225 F1
Merthyr Tydfil CF48 . . . .29 F8

Winch Wen Ind Est
SA6 . . . . .69 C6
Winchester Ave CF23 178 D2

Winchester Cl
Barry CF62 . . . . .214 D5
Newport NP20 . . . . . . .143 A1
Wind Rd SA9 . . . . .2 D7
Wind St Aberdare CF44 . .29 A1
Ferndale CF43 . . . . . . .80 A7
Laleston CF32 . . . . . . .167 E5
Neath SA11 . . . . .71 E8
Porth CF39 . . . . .107 E6
Swansea SA1 . . . . .95 D6
Windermere Ave
CF23 . . . . .178 A3
Windermere Cl CF44 . .29 D1
Windermere Ct NP44 . .89 C3
Windermere Rd SA6 . . .68 C7

Windermere Sq 4
NP19 . . . . .143 E8

Windflower Cl 7
CF3 . . . . .180 A7

Windhover Cl 3 CF3 .180 A6

Windlass Ct CF10 . . .195 C3

Windmill Cl
Cardiff CF14 . . . . . . .159 E2
Llantwit Major CF61 . .210 A4
Wick CF71 . . . . .198 D5

Windmill Ind Area
CF64 . . . . .215 D4

Windmill La
Llanblethian CF71 . . . .188 E1
Llantwit Major CF61 . .210 A4

Windmill Sq 7 NP20 .143 C3

Windmill Terr SA1 . . .95 E8

Windrush Cl NP20 . . .116 E2

Windrush Pl 6 CF5 . . .193 D8

Windsor Arc 3 CF64 .207 B4

Windsor Ave
Newbridge NP11 . . . . . .86 F6
Radyr CF15 . . . . .176 B6

Windsor Cl
Boverton CF61 . . . . . .210 B6
Radyr CF15 . . . . .176 B6

Windsor Clive Inf Sch
CF5 . . . . .193 C5

Windsor Clive Jun Sch
CF5 . . . . .193 C5

Windsor Cres CF15 . .176 C5

Windsor Ct
4 Cardiff CF24 . . . .195 C6
Penarth CF64 . . . . . . .207 B3
Pontyclun CF72 . . . . . .173 B8
2 Radyr CF15 . . . . .176 B6
4 Swansea SA1 . . . . .95 C7
Ynysybwl CF37 . . . . . . .81 F1

Windsor Dr CF72 . . .173 D7

Windsor Espl CF10 . .195 B1

Windsor Gdns
Beddau CF38 . . . . . . .156 A8
Cardiff CF5 . . . . .193 E6

Windsor Gn CF5 . . . .193 E6

Windsor Gr CF15 . . .176 B6

Windsor Ho 8 CF10 .194 F5

Windsor La
7 Cardiff CF10 . . . .195 B6
Penarth CF64 . . . . . . .207 A5

Windsor Mews 5
CF24 . . . . .195 C5

Windsor Pl
Abertridwr CF83 . . . . .136 F7
Cardiff CF10 . . . . . . .195 B6
Merthyr Vale CF48 . . . . .55 D4
Mumbles SA3 . . . . . . .123 B5
Pant CF48 . . . . .11 B6
1 Penarth CF64 . . . .207 A4
Pentre CF41 . . . . .78 F4
Rogerstone NP10 . . . .142 B4
Senghenydd CF83 . . . .110 B2
Ynysybwl CF37 . . . . . . .81 F1

Windsor Rd
Abertillery NP13 . . . . . .36 C5
Barry CF62 . . . . .214 D3
Brynmawr NP23 . . . . . . .8 A4
Cardiff CF24 . . . . . . .195 C5
Cwmbran NP44 . . . . . . .89 C2
Mountain Ash CF45 . . . .54 D1
Neath SA11 . . . . .71 E7
Newport NP19 . . . . . . .143 F5
Penarth CF64 . . . . . . .206 F5
Pontypool NP4 . . . . . . .62 B2
Pontypridd CF37 . . . . .135 E7
Porthcawl CF36 . . . . . .182 E7
Radyr CF15 . . . . .176 C5
Treharris CF46 . . . . . . .82 F6

Windsor St
Aberdare CF44 . . . . . . .28 C4
Caerphilly CF83 . . . . .138 B2
Pentre CF41 . . . . .78 F5
Swansea SA2 . . . . .94 F7
Treherbert CF42 . . . . . .50 F2
Treorchy CF42 . . . . . . .78 C4
Troedyrhiw CF48 . . . . . .31 B1

Windsor Terr
Aberdare CF44 . . . . . . .29 C3
Abertillery NP13 . . . . . .59 F7
Gorseinon SA4 . . . . . . .43 D2
6 Merthyr Tydfil CF47 . .30 E8
2 Newport NP20 . . . .143 B4
Penarth CF64 . . . . . . .207 A4

Windsor Terrace La
CF64 . . . . .207 B4

Windsor Village SA12 . .98 D3

Windway Ave CF5 . . .194 A7

Windway Rd CF5 . . . .194 A7

Windyridge CF64 . . . .206 C2

Wine St
Llantwit Major CF61 . .209 F6
Pontlottyn CF81 . . . . . .12 F1

Wingate Dr CF14 . . . .177 F6

Wingate St NP20 . . . .143 C1

Wingfield Ave CF38 . .155 F7

Wingfield Cl CF37 . . .109 E1

Wingfield Cres CF83 . .112 A3

Wingfield Rd CF14 . . .177 A4

Wingfield Rise CF46 . . .83 B5

Wingfield St CF48 . . . .55 C5

Wingfield Terr CF46 . . .83 B5

Winifred Ave CF24 . . .214 E8

Winifred Rd SA10 . . . .70 E7

Winifred St
Dowlais CF48 . . . . .11 A5
Mountain Ash CF45 . . . .81 F8

Winifred Terr NP13 . . .36 B8

Winnipeg Dr CF23 . . .178 C5

Winsford Rd CF64 . . .216 C4

Winslade Ave CF39 . .133 C6

Winston Ave CF5 . . . .193 A2

Winston Rd CF62 . . . .214 E8

Winston St SA1 . . . . .95 C8

Winstone Cotts NP4 . . .37 F5

Winstone Rd NP4 . . . .38 B1

Wistaria Cl NP44 . . . .117 B3

Wiston Path NP44 . . . .89 B2

Witham St NP19 . . . .143 E4

Witherdene Rd CF43 . . .80 C2

Withy Pk SA3 . . . . . .122 A6

Withycombe Rd CF3 . .179 C7

Witla Court Rd CF3 . .179 C5

Wolfe Cl CF63 . . . . . .215 C7

Wolffe Cl CF71 . . . . .188 D2

Wolfs Castle Ave
CF14 . . . . .159 E1

Wolseley St
Newport NP20 . . . . . . .143 C1
Newport NP20 . . . . . . .143 C1

Womanby St CF10 . . .195 A5

Wood Cl Cardiff CF14 .160 B1
Llanyravon NP44 . . . . . .90 B1
Neath SA11 . . . . .71 D4

Wood Cres NP10 . . . .142 A7

Wood Path NP44 . . . . .90 A6

Wood Rd
Abercynon CF45 . . . . . .82 E2
Pontypridd CF37 . . . . .135 D7

Wood St
Abercarn NP11 . . . . . .114 B8
Bargoed CF81 . . . . .58 A4
Cardiff CF10 . . . . .195 A4
Ferndale CF43 . . . . .79 F7
Gilfach Goch CF39 . . . .132 B5
Maerdy CF43 . . . . .52 A2
Maesteg CF34 . . . . . . .102 B2
Penarth CF64 . . . . .207 A4
Pontycymer CF32 . . . . .103 F3
Pontypridd CF37 . . . . .109 F5
Port Talbot SA13 . . . . .125 D6

Wood View SA11 . . . . .72 B6

Wood View Cl SA11 . . .71 C1

Wood View Cres
NP11 . . . . .115 A1

Wood View Rd NP11 . .115 A2

Woodbine Cotts
SA11 . . . . .226 C4

Woodbine Rd NP12 . . . .85 E7

Woodburn Dr SA3 . . .123 A6

Woodcock St CF24 . . .195 C7

Woodcote SA2 . . . . . . .93 D6

Woodcote Gn SA4 . . . .43 C7

Woodend Rd SA15 . . . .40 E6

Woodfield Ave
Pontlliw SA4 . . . . .44 A5
Radyr CF15 . . . . .176 C4

Woodfield Bldgs
CF39 . . . . .107 F4

Woodfield Cross NP22 . .13 F4

Woodfield Park Cres
NP12 . . . . .85 F6

Woodfield Rd
Cwm NP4 . . . . .35 B8
Pontypool NP4 . . . . . . .63 A4
Talbot Green CF72 . . . .155 A2
Tredegar NP22 . . . . . . .13 F5

Woodfield St
Bryncae CF72 . . . . . . .153 E2
1 Morriston SA6 . . . . .46 A1
Pontllanfraith NP12 . . . .86 A4
7 Port Talbot SA13 . . .125 C6
Swansea SA6 . . . . .68 F8

Woodfield Terr
Mountain Ash CF45 . . . .81 F8
Pontllanfraith NP12 . . . .86 A4
Porth CF39 . . . . .107 F4
Tir-y-Berth CF82 . . . . . .84 F6
Trehafod CF37 . . . . . .108 C2

Woodfieldside Bsns Pk
NP12 . . . . .86 A5

Woodford Cl CF5 . . . .176 E1

Woodford Rd SA5 . . . .67 E7

Woodham Cl CF62 . . .214 D6

Woodham Pk CF62 . . .214 D6

Woodham Rd CF63 . . .215 A4

Woodland Ave
1 Margam SA13 . . . .125 E4
Mumbles SA3 . . . . . . .122 F7
Pencoed CF35 . . . . . . .170 D8
Porthcawl CF36 . . . . . .183 B8

Woodland Cl
Bettws CF72 . . . . .129 E1
Briton Ferry SA11 . . . . .71 B3
Neath SA10 . . . . .70 E8

Woodland Cotts CF46 . .56 A7

Woodland Cres
Abercynon CF45 . . . . . .82 F3
Cardiff CF23 . . . . .178 C4
Creigiau CF15 . . . . . . .174 E8

Woodland Ct NP44 . . . .90 A4

Woodland Dr
Abertillery NP11 . . . . . .59 F5
Bassaleg NP10 . . . . . . .141 F3
Newbridge NP11 . . . . . .87 A6
Penarth CF64 . . . . . . .207 A4
Rogerstone NP10 . . . . .141 E7

Woodland Flats 4
CF83 . . . . .111 F1

Woodland Park Rd
NP19 . . . . .163 E7

Woodland Park View 5
NP19 . . . . .143 F6

Woodland Pk
Glynneath SA11 . . . . . .223 D1
Penderyn CF44 . . . . . .224 D2

Woodland Pk continued
Ynystawe SA6 . . . . .46 B5

Woodland Pl
Bargoed CF81 . . . . .58 A1
Bedlinog CF46 . . . . . . .56 B7
Cefn Hengoed CF82 . . . .84 F4
North Cornelly CF33 . . .166 A7
Penarth CF64 . . . . .207 A4
Pengam NP12 . . . . .85 B7

Woodland Rd
Beddau CF38 . . . . .156 B6
Cardiff CF14 . . . . .176 F4
Croesyceiliog NP44 . . . .90 A4
Crynant SA10 . . . . . . .226 A7
Glyncorrwg SA13 . . . . .227 C2
Llanmartin NP18 . . . . .145 E6
Mountain Ash CF45 . . . .54 C3
Neath SA10 . . . . .70 E8
Neath SA11 . . . . .71 F7
Newport NP19 . . . . . . .143 F6
Pontllanfraith NP12 . . . .86 A4
Treorchy CF42 . . . . . . .80 B2
Ystradowen SA9 . . . . . .221 C7

Woodland Rise CF31 . .150 D1

Woodland Row SA12 . . .99 D6

Woodland St
Blaenavon NP4 . . . . . . .17 D7
Cwmbran NP44 . . . . . . .89 D4
Mountain Ash CF45 . . . .54 C3
Pontardawe SA8 . . . . . .23 F5

Woodland Terr
Abercarn NP11 . . . . . . .87 A3
Aberdare CF44 . . . . . . .53 C6
Abertillery NP13 . . . . . .36 A1
Abertillery NP13 . . . . . .36 B8
Abertridwr CF83 . . . . .136 F7
Argoed NP12 . . . . .58 F4
Merthyr Tydfil CF47 . . . .10 E1
Mountain Ash CF45 . . . .54 C3
Nantyglo NP23 . . . . .8 C1
Neath SA10 . . . . .48 A2
New Tredegar NP24 . . . .33 D5
Pantyrawel CF32 . . . . .130 D4
Pontyclun CF72 . . . . . .172 F8
Pontypool NP4 . . . . . . .61 F8
Senghenydd CF83 . . . . .110 F3
Treorchy CF42 . . . . . . .78 B4
Treorchy CF42 . . . . . . .78 C7

Woodland Vale CF42 . . .78 D7

Woodland View
Abersychan NP4 . . . . . .37 E7
Cwmfelinfach NP11 . . . .113 F3
Pontypool NP4 . . . . . . .62 B8

Woodland Way
Merthyr Tydfil CF48 . . . .30 A8
Sarn CF32 . . . . .150 E3

Woodland Wlk NP18 . .145 C4

Woodlands
Beddau CF38 . . . . .156 B7
Gowerton SA4 . . . . . . .66 C5
Tredegar NP22 . . . . .6 C1

Woodlands Ave
Clydach SA6 . . . . .46 F8
Treharris CF46 . . . . . . .83 B6

Woodlands Bsns Pk
SA9 . . . . .2 D7

Woodlands Cl CF71 . . .188 D2

Woodlands Cres CF83 . .83 B5

Woodlands Ct 4
CF62 . . . . .214 F5

Woodlands Dr NP20 . . .117 A4

Woodlands Gr CF23 . . .178 C4

Woodlands Jun & Inf Sch
NP44 . . . . .89 B5

Woodlands Park Dr
Cardiff CF5 . . . . .193 C3
Neath SA10 . . . . .48 E1

Woodlands Pk
Ammanford SA18 . . . . .219 C6
Pencoed CF35 . . . . . . .170 C8
Pyle CF33 . . . . .148 D1

Woodlands Rd
Barry CF63 . . . . .214 F5
Loughor SA4 . . . . .42 F1

Woodlands Rise
CF31 . . . . .168 C4

Woodlands Specl High Sch
CF5 . . . . .191 E5

Woodlands St CF32 . . .104 E3

Woodlands Terr
Cross Hands SA14 . . . .218 B7
Maesteg CF34 . . . . .75 A1
Resolven SA11 . . . . . . .226 E6
Swansea SA1 . . . . .95 B7

Woodlands The
Abersychan NP4 . . . . . .37 E5
Bridgend CF31 . . . . . .169 C5
Cardiff CF14 . . . . .160 B2
Pontypool NP4 . . . . . . .62 B8

Woodlands Workshop Ctr
CF72 . . . . .155 A1

Woodlawn Way CF14 . .159 E2

Woodmans Terr SA9 . . . .2 B6

Woodpecker Sq CF62 . .210 E6

Woodridge Ct SA3 . . . .122 F4

Woods Gelliwion
CF37 . . . . .135 A8

Woodside
Newport NP10 . . . . . . .163 E7
Tonna SA11 . . . . .49 A4

Woodside Ave
Bridgend CF31 . . . . . .168 F8
Neath SA11 . . . . .71 F5
Swansea SA2 . . . . .93 E6

Woodside Cl
Bishopston SA3 . . . . . .122 A5
Swansea SA2 . . . . .93 E6

Woodside Cres
Clydach SA6 . . . . .46 C8
Ebbw Vale NP23 . . . . . .14 D6
7 Cardiff CF24 . . . .195 C7
10 Merthyr Tydfil CF47 . .10 E1

Woodside Ct CF14 . . . .160 A1

Woodside Rd
Cwmbran NP44 . . . . . . .89 D4
Pontypool NP4 . . . . . . .38 B2

Woodside Terr
Abertillery NP13 . . . . . .60 B6
Newbridge NP11 . . . . . .60 B2

Woodside Way NP44 . . .89 D4

Woodstock Cl CF62 . . .214 D5

Woodstock Gdns
CF35 . . . . .152 D1

Woodstock Mews
CF71 . . . . .188 E2

Woodvale Ave CF23 . . .178 D7

Woodview SA4 . . . . . . .66 D4

Woodview Cl NP4 . . . . .62 B6

Woodview Pl SA5 . . . . .67 E6

Woodview Terr
Bryn-côch SA10 . . . . . .48 C4
Newbridge NP11 . . . . . .59 F2
Pontypool NP4 . . . . . . .62 B6

Woodville Ct 6 CF24 195 A8

Woodville Pl
Ebbw Vale NP23 . . . . . .14 D6
Cardiff CF24 . . . . .79 F7

Woodville Rd
3 Cardiff CF24 . . . .178 A1
Cardiff CF24 . . . . .195 A4
Mumbles SA3 . . . . . . .123 A7
Newport NP20 . . . . . . .142 F4

Woodville St SA4 . . . . .19 C5

Woodville Terr NP12 . . .58 F5

Woodward Ave NP11 . .114 B4

Woodward Rd NP11 . . .114 C4

Woolacombe Ave
CF3 . . . . .179 C6

Woolaston Ave CF23 . .178 C5

Woolacott Dr SA3 . . . .122 D5

Woollacott Mews
SA3 . . . . .122 D5

Wooller Ho 9 SA12 . . .98 F1

Woolmer Cl CF5 . . . . .176 D2

Woolpitch NP44 . . . . . .89 B3

Woosnam Cl CF23 . . . .178 E1

Worcester Cl
Heolgerrig CF48 . . . . . .10 A1
Llanyravon NP44 . . . . . .90 A3

Worcester Ct
Cardiff CF11 . . . . .194 F1
Swansea SA7 . . . . .69 C7

Worcester Cres NP19 144 A8

Worcester Path NP44 . . .90 A3

Worcester Pl SA1 . . . . .95 D7

Worcester Rd SA13 . . .123 B4

Worcester St
Brynmawr NP23 . . . . . . .8 C4
Cardiff CF11 . . . . .194 F2

Wordsworth Ave
Bridgend CF31 . . . . . .168 C6
Cardiff CF24 . . . . .195 C7
Penarth CF64 . . . . . . .206 F4

Wordsworth Cl
Cwmbran NP44 . . . . . . .89 D2
Ebbw Vale NP23 . . . . . .14 B8
Llantwit Major CF61 . .210 B4

Wordsworth Gdns
CF37 . . . . .136 B6

Wordsworth Rd NP19 144 A5

Wordsworth St
Cwmaman CF44 . . . . . .53 A4
1 Swansea SA1 . . . . .95 C6

Working St CF10 . . . . .195 A5

Works Rd SA8 . . . . . . .23 E4

Worle Ave CF3 . . . . . .179 B5

Worle Pl CF3 . . . . .179 B5

Wren Ave SA11 . . . . . . .72 B5

Wren Bank SA11 . . . . . .71 B2

Wren Cl
Bridgend CF31 . . . . . .169 C4
Cardiff CF3 . . . . .180 A6

Wren Rd CF62 . . . . . .210 E6

Wrexham Ct CF3 . . . . .179 E5

Wrgant Pl CF43 . . . . . .52 A2

Wright Cl NP19 . . . . .144 B3

Wroughton Pl CF5 . . . .193 E6

Wychtree St SA6 . . . . .69 A7

Wychwood Cl SA3 . . . .123 A4

Wye Cl Barry CF62 . . . .214 C6
Swansea SA3 . . . . .69 B3

Wye Cres NP20 . . . . . .116 C2

Wye Ct NP44 . . . . .89 B4

Wyeverne Rd
Cardiff CF24 . . . . .195 A8
1 Newport NP19 . . . .144 A5

Wyfan Pl CF14 . . . . . .177 D2

Wyncliffe Rd CF23 . . . .179 A8

Wynd St CF63 . . . . . . .215 B6

Wyndham Arc 13
CF10 . . . . .195 A5

Wyndham Cl
Bridgend CF31 . . . . . .169 C6
Pontarddulais SA4 . . . . .19 C3

Wyndham Cres
7 Aberdare CF44 . . . .53 D7
Bridgend CF31 . . . . . .168 F2
Cardiff CF11 . . . . .194 D6

Wyndham Park Way
CF5 . . . . .191 E5

Wyndham Pl NP11 . . . .194 E5

Wyndham Rd CF11 . . .194 D6

Wyndham St
Barry CF63 . . . . .215 A5
Bridgend CF31 . . . . . .168 F4
Cardiff CF11 . . . . .194 E5
Cardiff CF11 . . . . .194 E5
Cardiff CF15 . . . . .158 C5
Dowlais CF48 . . . . .11 A4
Evanstown CF39 . . . . . .132 B8
Machen CF83 . . . . . . .140 A7
Newport NP20 . . . . . . .143 C6
Ogmore Vale CF32 . . . .104 E4
6 Port Talbot SA13 . .125 C7
Porth CF39 . . . . .107 F2
Swansea SA1 . . . . .95 B6
Ton Pentre CF41 . . . . . .79 A2
Tonypandy CF40 . . . . .106 F4
Treherbert CF42 . . . . . .50 E2
Troedyrhiw CF48 . . . . . .31 C1

Wyndham Terr
Cardiff CF14 . . . . .178 A8
Risca NP11 . . . . .115 B1

Wyngarth SA1 . . . . . . .69 D5

Wynnstay Cl CF11 . . . .194 E3

Wynter Ct SA5 . . . . . . .68 C6

Wyon Cl CF5 . . . . .176 D3

Wyvern Ave SA12 . . . . .98 C2

Wyvern Ho 1 SA12 . . . .98 C2

Y

Y Berllan Cimla SA11 . .72 B6
Dunvant SA2 . . . . .93 D7
Swansea SA2 . . . . .45 C2
Ystradgynlais SA9 . . . . . .2 D7

Y Bont Faen Prim Sch
CF71 . . . . .188 E1

Y Bwthyn SA15 . . . . . .40 E4

Y Cedrwydden NP12 . . .85 D5

Y Cilgant CF83 . . . . . .137 E6

Y Clos Cwmllynfell SA9 221 B7
Llanelli SA15 . . . . .41 A5

Y Cyswllt SA4 . . . . . . .44 B8

Y Dderwen CF34 . . . . .128 D7

Y Deri CF38 . . . . .156 C6

Y Dolau SA6 . . . . .45 C2

Y Dolydd CF83 . . . . . .137 F1

Y Felin Ffrwd CF83 . . .137 F4

Y Fron SA14 . . . . .218 A8

Y Ganolfan CF48 . . . . . .11 A4

Y Garn SA4 . . . . .44 A2

Y Garth SA4 . . . . .28 C4

Y Gefnen SA7 . . . . .69 F6

Y Gilfach SA9 . . . . .2 B6

Y Glyn Cefneithin SA14 218 A8
Dunvant SA2 . . . . .93 D7
Maesycwmmer CF82 . . . .85 A1

Y Goedlan
Cwm-twrch Uchaf SA9 . .222 D7
Cwmfelin CF34 . . . . . .128 C8

Y Goedwig CF14 . . . . .177 A8

Y Gorlan SA2 . . . . .93 D7

Y Graig CF48 . . . . .11 A7

Y Groes Cardiff CF14 . .177 B7
Sarn CF32 . . . . .150 F3

Y Gwernydd SA7 . . . . . .46 F6

Y Lan CF35 . . . . .152 F1

Y Llest CF31 . . . . .150 C1

Y Llwyn SA15 . . . . .41 A5

Y Llwyni SA6 . . . . .45 C2

Y Pant Comp Sch
CF72 . . . . .155 C1

Y Parc CF72 . . . . .174 B7

Y Rhodfa CF62,CF63 . .214 F4

Y Rhos SA15 . . . . .40 F7

Y Waun Llanelli SA14 . . .41 C6
Ynysybwl CF37 . . . . . . .81 F2

Y Waun Fach SA6 . . . . .45 B2

Y Wern CF32 . . . . .129 E3

Y-fan SA14 . . . . .41 A8

Y-Gaer SA14 . . . . .41 A8

Y-Wern SA6 . . . . .45 B2

Yalton SA3 . . . . .122 F7

Yard Coal Rise NP11 . . .59 C3

Yard Row NP23 . . . . .7 D3

Yarrow Cl CF5 . . . . . . .193 A5

Yellow Row NP22 . . . . . .6 E2

Yeo Cl NP20 . . . . .116 E1

Yeo Rd NP20 . . . . .116 E1

Yeo St SA11 . . . . .226 D5

Yew Cl CF47 . . . . .10 D5

Yew Gr Caerphilly NP12 .85 F6
Pontllanfraith NP12 . . . .86 A6

Yew St
Aberbargoed CF81 . . . . .58 B5
Merthyr Tydfil CF47 . . . .30 E8
Taffs Well CF15 . . . . . .158 A5
Troedyrhiw CF48 . . . . . .31 C1

Yew Tree Cl CF71 . . . . .187 B4

Yew Tree Ct
Barry CF62 . . . . .214 C3
Cardiff CF23 . . . . .178 C2

Yew Tree La NP18 . . . .113 B7

Yew Tree Terr
Croesyceiliog NP44 . . . .90 A5
Cwmbran NP44 . . . . . . .89 D4

Yewberry Cl NP20 . . . .117 B2

Yewberry La NP20 . . . .117 B2

Yewtree Cl
Cardiff CF5 . . . . .193 C8
Mumbles SA3 . . . . . . .122 F5

Yewtree Gr CF62 . . . . .211 B2

Yewtree Rd NP11 . . . . .87 A7

Ymyl-yr-Afon SA10 . . . .49 C4

Yniscedwyn Rd SA9 . . . .2 E8

Ynisderw Rd SA8 . . . . .23 E4

Ynisisaf Cotts SA9 . . . .222 A6

Ynisydarren Rd SA9 . . . .2 B6

Ynys Cadwyn SA11 . . .227 C8

Ynys Cl CF37 . . . . . . .135 F6

Ynys Ct
Glyncorrwg SA13 . . . . .227 C1
Swansea SA6 . . . . .45 B7

Ynys Fach Ave SA11 . .226 E5

Ynys Fawr Ave SA11 . .226 E5

Ynys Glyd St CF82 . . . .111 F7

Ynys Hir CF37 . . . . . . .109 D7

Ynys Hywel Visitor Ctr
NP11 . . . . .113 B3

Ynys La NP44 . . . . .90 A1

Ynys Las CF46 . . . . . . .83 D4

Ynys Nedd SA11 . . . . .226 E5

Ynys Newydd Rd SA2 . .94 B4

Ynys Park Cotts CF41 . .79 A3

Ynys St
Port Talbot SA13 . . . . . .99 C1
Porth CF39 . . . . .107 F7

Ynys Terr CF37 . . . . . .135 F5

Ynys y Coed CF5 . . . . .194 A8

Ynys-bydafau SA9 . . . .222 B7

Ynys-Cedwyn Lodge
SA9 . . . . .2 D7

Ynys-Gyfeillon Rd
CF37 . . . . .109 C2

Ynys-Las SA14 . . . . . . .41 C5

Ynys-Lee SA12 . . . . . . .99 E4

Ynys-Lwyd Rd CF44 . . .53 C8

Ynys-Lwyd St CF44 . . . .29 A1

Ynys-Meudwy Rd SA8 . .24 B8

Ynys-Penllwch Rd
SA6,SA7 . . . . .46 F7

Ynys-y-Coed NP12 . . . .86 B8

Ynys-y-Cwm Rd SA15 . .40 C7

Ynys-y-gwial SA9 . . . . . .1 F5

Ynys-y-Mond Rd
Glais SA7 . . . . .47 B1
Pontardawe SA8 . . . . . .23 E2

Ynys-yr-Nos Ave
SA11 . . . . .223 E1

Ynys-yr-Afon SA11 . . . .49 A4

Ynysallan Rd SA6,SA7 . .46 D3

Ynysangharad Rd
CF37 . . . . .109 D1

Ynysawdre Comp Sch
CF32 . . . . .150 E5

Ynysboeth Inf Sch
CF45 . . . . .82 C6

Ynysboeth Jun Sch
CF45 . . . . .82 C5

Ynysbryn Cl CF72 . . . .155 C3

Ynyscedwyn Ind Est
SA9 . . . . .2 E8

Ynyscorrwg Rd CF37 . .136 B4

Ynyscynon Rd CF40 . . .106 F7

Ynyscynon St CF44 . . . .29 D1

Ynyscynon Terr CF44 . . .29 D1

Ynysddu
Pontyclun CF72 . . . . . .173 A8
Talbot Green CF72 . . . .155 A1

Ynysddu Farm CF72 . . .173 A8

Ynysddu Jun & Prim Sch
NP11 . . . . .113 A5

Ynysfach Iron Heritage
Mus CF48 . . . . .10 D1

Ynysfach Jun & Inf Sch
SA11 . . . . .226 E5

Ynysfeio Ave CF41 . . . .51 B1

Ynysgau St CF41 . . . . . .79 C4

Ynyshir Inf Sch CF39 . .107 F5

Ynyshir Jun Sch
CF39 . . . . .107 F6

Ynyshir Rd CF39 . . . . .107 F7

Ynyslas CF36 . . . . . . .183 B8

Ynyslas Cres SA11 . . . .223 D1

Ynyslyn Rd CF37 . . . . .136 B4

Ynysmaerdy Prim Sch
SA11 . . . . .71 C2

Ynysmaerdy Terr
CF72 . . . . .155 A6

Ynysmeurig Rd CF45 . . .82 E2

Ynysowen Inf & Jun Sch
CF48 . . . . .55 C4

Ynystawe Prim Sch
SA6 . . . . .46 C5

Ynysteg CF32 . . . . . . .150 E5

Ynyswan NP12 . . . . . . .86 A3

Ynyswen Abercraf SA9 222 E8
Llanelli SA14 . . . . .41 A8

Ynyswen Ind Est CF42 .78 B8

Ynyswen Inf Sch CF42 . .78 B7

Ynyswen Rd CF42 . . . . .78 C7

Ynyswen Sta CF42 . . . . .78 B7

Ynysybwl Rd SA4 . . . . .44 B2

Ynysybwl Rd CF37 . . . .109 D6

Ynysygerwn Ave SA10 . .49 D4

Ynysygerwn Cres
SA10 . . . . .49 D4

Ynysygored Rd CF48 . . .55 C6

Ynysygwas Hill SA12 . . .99 E4

Ynysygwas Way SA12 . . .99 E4

Ynysymaerdy Rd SA11 . 71 D3

Yorath Rd CF14 . . . . . .177 B5

York Ave
Blackwood NP12 . . . . . .59 B1
Ebbw Vale NP23 . . . . . .14 C6

York Cl Cwmbran NP44 . .89 A3
Heolgerrig CF48 . . . . . .10 A1

York Ct
10 Cardiff CF10 . . . .195 C4

York Ct *continued*
🖪 Radyr CF15 ....**176** B6
🖻 Swansea SA1 .....**95** D6
York Dr CF38 ......**156** D6
York Mans 🖬 CF14 ..**176** F6
York Pl Barry CF62 ...**214** D3
  Newport NP20 .....**143** B4
  Port Talbot SA13 ....**125** C8
🖪 Risca NP11 ......**114** F3
York Rd Bridgend CF31 **169** B2
  Newport NP19 .....**143** B4
York St Aberdare CF44 ..**53** C6
  Abertillery NP13 .....**36** A5
  Cardiff CF5 ....**194** C5
  Cardiff CF5 ....**194** C6
  Mountain Ash CF45 ...**54** D1
  Porth CF39 ....**107** F3
  Swansea SA1 ....**95** D6
York Terr Cwm NP23 ..**35** B7
  Tredegar NP22 ......**13** F6
Youldon Ho CF64 ....**206** B3
Yr Allt
  Llangennech SA14 .....**18** B1
  Llantrisant CF72 .....**155** D3
Yr Aran SA2 ....**93** D8
Yr Efail CF35 ....**170** B1
Yr Elain SA2 ....**93** D8
Yr Hafan CF32 ......**103** E1
Yr Hafod Llanelli SA15 ..**40** E7
  Swansea SA6 ....**45** C2
Yr Hendre
  Nantgarw CF15 .....**158** A8
  Pyle CF33 ....**148** D3
Yr Ysfa CF34 ....**102** A2
Yr-Hen-Lawnt CF40 ..**106** F3
Yryswen Terr SA10 ..**222** A1
Ysbryd-y-coed
  Pen-y-Fai CF31 ......**168** D8
  Pen-y-Fai CF31 ......**168** D8
Ysbyty Gymuned
  Ystradgynlais SA9 ...**2** E7

Ysbyty'r Tri Chwm
  NP23 ....**7** C3
Ysgol Bro Eirwg CF3 .**179** A4
Ysgol Bryn Castell Sch
  CF31 ....**168** D5
Ysgol Bryn Onnen y Farteg
  NP4 ....**37** F8
Ysgol Crug Glas SA1 .**95** D8
Ysgol Cwmgors SA18 **220** D5
Ysgol Cymraeg Ystrad
  Mynach CF82 ....**84** E1
Ysgol Erw'r Delyn
  CF64 ....**206** D3
Ysgol Gyfun Bryntirion
  CF31 ....**168** C7
Ysgol Gyfun Cwm Rhymni
  CF81 ....**57** F3
Ysgol Gyfun Cwm Rhymni
  (Ysgol Isaf) CF81 ...**58** B4
Ysgol Gyfun Cymer
  Rhondda CF39 .....**107** E2
Ysgol Gyfun Gwynllyw
  NP4 ....**38** C1
Ysgol Gyfun Gwyr SA4 **66** C5
Ysgol Gyfun Gymraeg
  Glantaf CF14 ......**177** A2
Ysgol Gyfun Gymraeg
  Glantaff CF5 .....**176** F2
Ysgol Gyfun Gymraeg
  Plasmawr CF5 ....**176** D1
Ysgol Gyfun Llanhari
  CF72 ....**172** A5
Ysgol Gyfun Maes Yr Yrfa
  SA14 ....**218** A8
Ysgol Gyfun Rhydfelen
  CF37 ....**135** F5
Ysgol Gyfun Rhydyfelin
  CF37 ....**79** D3
Ysgol Gyfun Rhydywaun
  CF44 ....**27** F7
Ysgol Gyfun y Strade
  SA15 ....**40** A6
Ysgol Gyfun Ystalyfere
  SA9 ....**2** C6

Ysgol Gymraeg Bro Ogwr
  CF31 ....**169** A6
Ysgol Gymraeg
  Bryn-y-mor SA2 ....**94** F5
Ysgol Gymraeg Brynmawr
  Jun & Inf Schs NP23 ..**8** B4
Ysgol Gymraeg Casnewydd
  NP18 ....**144** E4
Ysgol Gymraeg Cwm
  Gwyddon NP11 .....**87** B2
Ysgol Gymraeg Cwmbran
  Jun & Inf Sch NP44 ..**89** D2
Ysgol Gymraeg Cwmtwrch
  SA9 ....**1** B1
Ysgol Gymraeg Dewi Sant
  SA14 ....**40** F7
Ysgol Gymraeg Melin
  Prim Sch CF14 ....**177** A4
Ysgol Gymraeg Pwll Coch
  CF11 ....**194** C4
Ysgol Gymraeg
  Ynysgedwyn SA9 ....**2** F8
Ysgol Gynradd Brynnau
  CF72 ....**153** D3
Ysgol Gynradd Cymraeg
  Cwm Ned SA11 ....**223** D1
Ysgol Gynradd
  Gwaelod-y-garth
  CF15 ....**157** F4
Ysgol Gynradd Gymraeg
  Caerphilly CF83 ...**138** B4
  Tonyrefail CF39 ...**133** C5
  Treorchy CF42 ......**78** B7
Ysgol Gynradd Gymraeg
  Bargod CF81 ......**58** A1
Ysgol Gynradd Gymraeg
  Bodringallt CF41 ...**79** D3
Ysgol Gynradd Gymraeg
  Bronllwyn CF41 ....**79** A2
Ysgol Gynradd Gymraeg
  Bryniago SA4 ....**19** D4
Ysgol Gynradd Gymraeg
  Castell Nedd SA11 ..**71** F7

Ysgol Gynradd Gymraeg
  Castellau CF38 ....**155** F7
Ysgol Gynradd Gymraeg
  Cwm Garw CF32 ...**103** E4
Ysgol Gynradd Gymraeg
  Cynwyd Sant CF34 .**102** A2
Ysgol Gynradd Gymraeg
  Evan James CF37 ...**109** B1
Ysgol Gynradd Gymraeg
  Felindre SA5 ....**20** F2
Ysgol Gynradd Gymraeg
  Garth Olwg CF38 ..**135** C4
Ysgol Gynradd Gymraeg
  Llantrisant CF72 ...**155** D3
Ysgol Gynradd Gymraeg
  Llwyncelyn CF39 ...**108** A3
Ysgol Gynradd Gymraeg
  Lon Las SA7 ....**69** D8
Ysgol Gynradd Gymraeg
  Pont-Sion-Norton
  CF37 ....**109** E3
Ysgol Gynradd Gymraeg
  Pontardawe SA8 ....**23** E6
Ysgol Gynradd Gymraeg
  Pontybrenin SA4 ...**66** B8
Ysgol Gynradd Gymraeg
  Tyle'R Ynn SA11 .....**71** B4
Ysgol Gynradd Gymraeg y
  Login Fach SA5 ....**66** F3
Ysgol Gynradd Trebannws
  Prim Sch SA8 ......**23** C2
Ysgol Hendre Specl Sch
  SA10 ....**48** C5
Ysgol Heol Goffa SA15 **40** E7
Ysgol Heol-y-Celyn
  CF37 ....**136** A5
Ysgol Ifor Bach CF83 .**110** F3
Ysgol Iolo Morganwg
  CF71 ....**188** F1
Ysgol Llanilltud Fawr
  CF61 ....**210** A5
Ysgol Llyn-y-forwyn
  CF43 ....**79** F6
Ysgol Maes Dyfan
  CF63 ....**215** A7

Ysgol Mynydd Bychan
  CF14 ....**177** F2
Ysgol Pen-y-garth
  CF64 ....**206** D5
Ysgol Pencae CF5 ...**176** F2
Ysgol Pl NP44 ......**89** C6
Ysgol Rhiwfawr Sch
  SA9 ....**221** B5
Ysgol Sant Curig
  CF62 ....**214** E5
Ysgol St SA1 ....**96** B7
Ysgol Synradd Cymraeg
  Aberdar CF44 ......**29** B1
Ysgol Thomas Stephens
  CP Sch SA11 ......**223** F3
Ysgol Ty Coch CF38 .**136** B1
Ysgol y Babanod SA14 **41** A8
Ysgol y Castell CF83 .**138** A2
Ysgol y Ferch Sger Corneli
  CF33 ....**165** F8
Ysgol y Glyn SA18 ..**220** D8
Ysgol y Lawnt NP22 ..**12** E3
Ysgol Yr Ynys SA14 ..**41** C4
Ysgol-y-Graig Prim Sch
  CF48 ....**10** A5
Ysgubor Fach CF83 .**139** F7
Ysgubor Fach St SA1 .**68** C2
Ysguborwen NP22 ....**6** F1
Yspitty Rd SA14 .....**42** B1
Ystad Celyn CF34 ...**102** A1
Ystad Deri NP22 ......**6** E2
Ysticl-Garu CF71 ....**199** F8
Ysticlau Rd SA10 ...**222** D4
Ystrad Bldgs CF83 ..**139** A6
Ystrad Cl CF3 ......**180** A7
Ystrad Einon SA4 ....**43** B1
Ystrad Fawr CF31 ...**168** D5
Ystrad Mynach Coll
  CF82 ....**111** E8
Ystrad Mynach Hospl
  CF82 ....**111** E8
Ystrad Mynach Inf Sch
  CF82 ....**84** E1

Ystrad Mynach Jun Sch
  CF82 ....**84** E1
Ystrad Mynach Sta
  CF82 ....**84** E1
Ystrad Rd Swansea SA5 **67** B4
  Ton Pentre CF41 .....**79** B3
Ystrad Rhondda Sta
  CF41 ....**79** D2
Ystrad Sta CF41 .....**79** A3
Ystrad Terr
  Abercarn NP11 ......**87** C4
  Ton Pentre CF41 .....**79** B3
Ystrad-Fawr Villas
  SA9 ....**222** A5
Ystradbarwig Terr
  CF38 ....**156** C6
Ystradgynlais Workshops
  SA9 ....**2** E8
Ystradowen CP Sch
  SA9 ....**221** C7
Ystwyth Pl SA6 ......**45** D1

Z

Zammit Cres SA15 ....**41** A5
Zephaniah Way NP13 .**15** D5
Zig-Zag La CF36 ....**166** B2
Zinc St CF24 ....**195** D6
Zion Ct CF38 ....**156** A2
Zion Pl NP23 ....**14** D6
Zion Row SA15 ......**40** E6
Zion St NP23 ....**14** D6
Zion Terr CF40 .....**106** E6
Zoar Ave CF34 .....**102** A4
Zoar Pl CF34 ....**102** A4
Zoar Rd Neath SA11 ...**71** D3
  Ystalyfera SA9 ....**2** B6
Zoar Terr CF46 ......**83** A5
Zouch St SA5 ....**68** C3